NINTH
EDITION

WORLD HISTORY

VOLUME I: TO 1800

William J. Duiker
The Pennsylvania State University

Jackson J. Spielvogel
The Pennsylvania State University

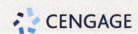

Australia • Brazil • Canada • Mexico • Singapore • United Kingdom • United States

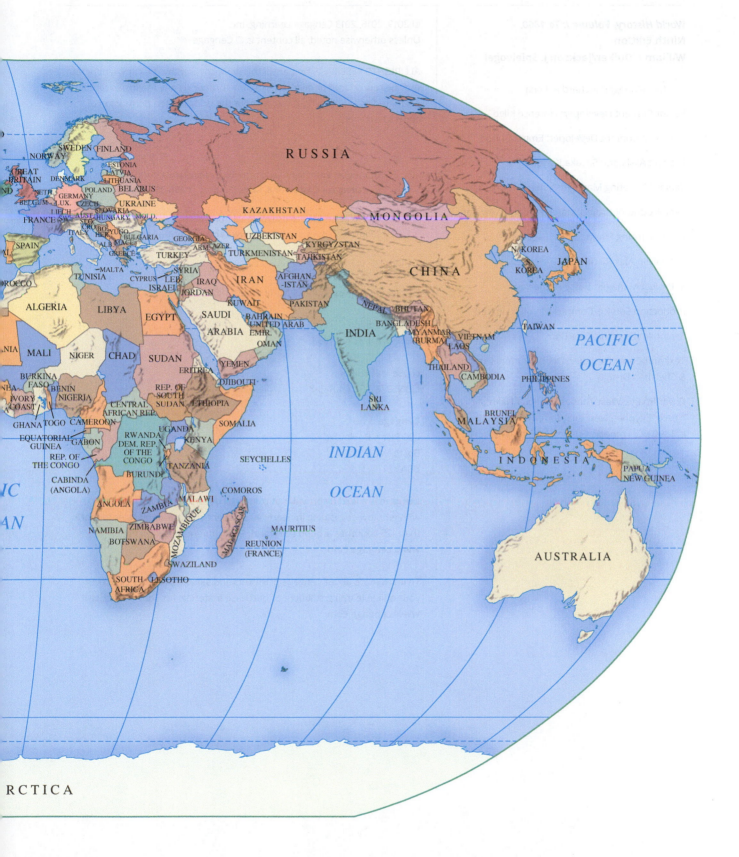

World History, Volume I: To 1800,
Ninth Edition
William J. Duiker/Jackson J. Spielvogel

Product Manager: Richard A. Lena

Senior Content Developer: Florence Kilgo

Associate Content Developer: Emma Guiton

Product Assistant: Sayaka Kawano

Senior Marketing Manager: Valerie Hartman

Senior Content Project Manager: Carol Newman

Manufacturing Planner: Julio Esperas

IP Analyst: Alex Ricciardi

IP Project Manager: Betsy Hathaway

Production Service/Compositor: MPS Limited

Senior Art Director: Cate Barr

Text and Cover Designer: Debby Dutton, Dutton & Sherman Design

Cover Image: West Thebes, Tomb of Nakht, fresco. Egyptian New Kingdom, 18th dynasty, c. 1390 BC. François Guénet/AKG Images

For product information and technology assistance, contact us at
Cengage Customer & Sales Support, 1-800-354-9706

For permission to use material from this text or product,
submit all requests online at **www.cengage.com/permissions.**

Library of Congress Control Number: 2017955521

Student Edition:
ISBN: 978-1-337-40105-0

Loose-leaf Edition:
ISBN: 978-1-337-40125-8

Cengage
200 Pier 4 Boulevard
Boston, MA 02210
USA

Cengage is a leading provider of customized learning solutions with employees residing in nearly 40 different countries and sales in more than 125 countries around the world. Find your local representative at: **www.cengage.com**.

To learn more about Cengage platforms and services, register or access your online learning solution, or purchase materials for your course, visit **www.cengage.com**.

Printed at CLDPC, USA, 10-21

ABOUT THE AUTHORS

WILLIAM J. DUIKER is liberal arts professor emeritus of East Asian studies at The Pennsylvania State University. A former U.S. diplomat with service in Taiwan, South Vietnam, and Washington, D.C., he received his doctorate in Far Eastern history from Georgetown University in 1968, where his dissertation dealt with the Chinese educator and reformer Cai Yuanpei. At Penn State, he has written widely on the history of Vietnam and modern China, including the widely acclaimed *Communist Road to Power in Vietnam* (revised edition, Westview Press, 1996), which was selected for a Choice Outstanding Academic Book Award in 1982–1983 and 1996–1997. Other recent books are *China and Vietnam: The Roots of Conflict* (Berkeley, 1987), *U.S. Containment Policy and the Conflict in Indochina* (Stanford, 1995), *Sacred War: Nationalism and Revolution in a Divided Vietnam* (McGraw-Hill, 1995), and *Ho Chi Minh* (Hyperion, 2000), which was nominated for a Pulitzer Prize in 2001. Although his research specialization is in the field of nationalism and Asian revolutions, his intellectual interests are considerably more diverse. He has traveled widely and has taught courses on the history of communism and non-Western civilizations at Penn State, where he was awarded a Faculty Scholar Medal for Outstanding Achievement in the spring of 1996. In 2002 the College of Liberal Arts honored him with an Emeritus Distinction Award.

TO YVONNE,
FOR ADDING SPARKLE TO THIS BOOK AND TO MY LIFE
W.J.D.

JACKSON J. SPIELVOGEL is associate professor emeritus of history at The Pennsylvania State University. He received his Ph.D. from The Ohio State University, where he specialized in Reformation history under Harold J. Grimm. His articles and reviews have appeared in such journals as *Moreana, Journal of General Education, Catholic Historical Review, Archiv für Reformationsgeschichte*, and *American Historical Review*. He has also contributed chapters or articles to *The Social History of the Reformation, The Holy Roman Empire: A Dictionary Handbook, Simon Wiesenthal Center Annual of Holocaust Studies*, and *Utopian Studies*. His work has been supported by fellowships from the Fulbright Foundation and the Foundation for Reformation Research. At Penn State, he helped inaugurate the Western civilization course as well as a popular course on Nazi Germany. His book *Hitler and Nazi Germany* was published in 1987 (seventh edition, 2014). He is the author of *Western Civilization*, published in 1991 (tenth edition, 2018). Professor Spielvogel has won five major university-wide teaching awards. During the year 1988–1989, he held the Penn State Teaching Fellowship, the university's most prestigious teaching award. In 1996, he won the Dean Arthur Ray Warnock Award for Outstanding Faculty Member and in 2000 received the Schreyer Honors College Excellence in Teaching Award.

TO DIANE,
WHOSE LOVE AND SUPPORT MADE IT ALL POSSIBLE
J.J.S.

BRIEF CONTENTS

CONTENTS

MAPS

CHRONOLOGIES

FEATURES

DOCUMENTS

(Continued on page 546)

For several million years after primates first appeared on the surface of the earth, human beings lived in small communities, seeking to survive by hunting, fishing, and foraging in a frequently hostile environment. Then suddenly, in the space of a few thousand years, there was an abrupt change of direction as humans in a few widely scattered areas of the globe began to congregate in larger communities. A key reason for this development was their new mastery of the art of cultivating food crops. As food production increased, the population in those areas rose correspondingly, and settled communities began to proliferate in arable parts of the world. Governments arose to provide protection and other needed services to the local population. Cities appeared and became the focal point of cultural and religious development. Historians refer to this process as the beginnings of civilization.

For generations, historians in Europe and the United States pointed to the rise of such civilizations as marking the origins of the modern world. Courses on Western civilization conventionally began with a chapter or two on the emergence of advanced societies in Egypt and Mesopotamia and then proceeded to ancient Greece and the Roman Empire. From Greece and Rome, the road led directly to the rise of modern civilization in the West.

There is nothing inherently wrong with this approach. Important aspects of our world today can indeed be traced back to these early civilizations, and all human beings the world over owe a considerable debt to their achievements. But all too often this interpretation has been used to imply that the course of civilization has been linear, leading directly from the emergence of agricultural societies in ancient Mesopotamia to the rise of advanced industrial societies in Europe and North America. Until recently, most courses on world history taught in the United States routinely focused almost exclusively on the rise of the West, with only a passing glance at other parts of the world, such as Africa, India, and East Asia. The contributions made by those societies to the culture and technology of our own time were often passed over in silence.

Two major reasons have been advanced to justify this approach. Some people have argued that it is more important that young minds understand the roots of their own heritage than that of peoples elsewhere in the world. In many cases, however, the motivation for this Eurocentric approach has been the belief that since the time of Socrates and Aristotle, Western civilization has been the main driving force in the evolution of human society.

Such an interpretation, however, represents a serious distortion of the process. During most of the course of human history, the most advanced civilizations have flourished in East Asia or the Middle East, not in the West. A relatively brief period of European dominance culminated with the era of imperialism in the late nineteenth century, when the political, military, and economic power of the advanced nations of the West spanned the globe. During recent decades, however, that dominance has gradually eroded, partly as a result of changes taking place in Western societies and partly because new centers of development are emerging elsewhere on the globe—notably in Asia, especially with the growing economic strength of China and India.

World history, then, has been a complex process in which many branches of the human community have played an active part, and the dominance of any one area of the world has been a temporary rather than a permanent phenomenon. It will be our purpose in this book to present a balanced picture of this story, with all respect for the richness and diversity of the tapestry of the human experience. Due attention must be paid to the rise of the West, of course, since that has been the most dominant aspect of world history in recent centuries. But the contributions made by other peoples must be given adequate consideration as well, not only in the period prior to 1500, when the major centers of civilization were located in Asia, but also in our own day, where a multipolar picture of development is clearly beginning to emerge.

Anyone who wishes to teach or write about world history must decide whether to present the topic as an integrated whole or as a collection of different cultures. The world that we live in today, of course, is in many respects an increasingly interdependent one in terms of economics as well as culture and communications, a reality that is often expressed by the phrase "global village." The convergence of peoples across the surface of the earth into an integrated world system began in early times and intensified after the rise of capitalism in the early modern era. In recognition of this trend, historians trained in global history, as well as instructors in the growing number of world history courses, have now begun to speak and write of a "global approach" that gives less attention to the study of individual civilizations and focuses instead on the "big picture" or, as the world historian Fernand Braudel termed it, interpreting world history as a river with no banks.

On the whole, this development is to be welcomed as a means of bringing the common elements of the evolution of human society to our attention. But this approach also involves two problems. For the vast majority of their time on earth, human beings have lived in partial or virtually total isolation from each other. Differences in climate, location, and geographic features have created human societies very different from each other in culture and historical experience. Only in relatively recent times (the commonly accepted date has long been the beginning of the age of European exploration at the end of the fifteenth century, but some would now push it back to the era of the Mongol Empire or even earlier) have cultural interchanges begun to create a common "world system," in which events taking place in one part of the world are rapidly transmitted throughout the globe, often with momentous consequences. In recent generations, of course, the process of global interdependence has been proceeding even more rapidly. Nevertheless, even now the process is by no means complete, as ethnic and regional differences continue to exist and to shape the course of world history. The tenacity of these differences and sensitivities is reflected not only in the rise of internecine conflicts in such divergent areas as Africa, India, the Middle East, and eastern Europe but also in the emergence in recent years of such regional organizations as the African Union, the Association for the Southeast Asian Nations, and the European Union. To look at the forest does not mean we should ignore the individual trees living therein.

The second problem is a practical one. College students today often are not well informed about the distinctive character of civilizations such as China and India and, without sufficient exposure to the historical evolution of such societies, will assume all too readily that the peoples in these countries have had historical experiences similar to ours and will respond to various stimuli in a similar fashion to those living in western Europe or the United States. If it is a mistake to ignore those forces that link us together, it is equally a mistake to underestimate those factors that continue to divide us and to differentiate us into a world of diverse peoples.

Our response to this challenge has been to adopt a global approach to world history while at the same time attempting to do justice to the distinctive character and development of individual civilizations and regions of the world. The presentation of individual cultures is especially important in Parts I and II, which cover a time when it is generally agreed that the process of global integration was not yet far advanced. Later chapters adopt a more comparative and thematic approach, in deference to the greater number of connections that have been established among the world's peoples since the fifteenth and sixteenth centuries. Part V consists of a series of chapters that center on individual regions of the world while at the same time focusing on common problems related to the Cold War and the rise of global problems such as overproduction and environmental pollution.

We have sought balance in another way as well. Many textbooks tend to simplify the content of history courses by emphasizing an intellectual or political perspective or, most recently, a social perspective, often at the expense of sufficient details in a chronological framework. This approach is confusing to students whose high school social studies programs have often neglected a systematic study of world history. We have attempted to write a well-balanced work in which political, economic, social, religious, intellectual, cultural, and military history are integrated into a chronologically ordered synthesis.

FEATURES OF THE TEXT

Primary Sources   To enliven the past and let readers see for themselves the materials that historians use to create their pictures of the past, we have included **primary sources** (boxed documents) in each chapter that are keyed to the seven major themes of world history and relate to the surrounding discussion in the text. The documents include examples of the religious, artistic, intellectual, social, economic, and political aspects of life in different societies and reveal in a vivid fashion what civilization meant to the individual men and women who shaped it by their actions. A question at the end of each box helps to guide students in analyzing the documents. The Opposing Viewpoints feature (see full description later in the Preface) provides additional primary source materials.

Introduction and Conclusion   Each chapter includes a lengthy **introduction and conclusion** to help maintain the continuity of the narrative and to provide a synthesis of important themes. Anecdotes in the chapter introductions dramatically convey the major theme or themes of each chapter.

Timeline and Chronology Features   A **timeline** at the end of each chapter enables students to see the major developments of an era at a glance and within cross-cultural categories, while the more **detailed chronologies** interspersed within the narrative reinforce the events discussed in the text.

Maps and Illustrations   **Updated maps and extensive illustrations** serve to deepen the reader's understanding of the text. **Map captions** are designed to enrich students' awareness of the importance of geography to history, and numerous **spot maps** enable students to see at a glance the region or subject being discussed in the text. Map captions also include a question to guide students' reading of the map. To facilitate understanding of cultural movements, illustrations of artistic works discussed in the text are placed near the discussions.

Chapter Opener Materials   **Chapter outlines and focus questions, including Critical Thinking and new Connections to Today questions**, at the beginning of each chapter give students a useful overview and guide them to the main subjects of each chapter. The focus questions are then repeated at the beginning of each major section in the chapter.

Glossary and Guide to Pronunciation   A **glossary of important terms** (boldfaced in the text when they are introduced and defined) is provided at the back of the book to maximize reader comprehension. A **guide to pronunciation** is now provided in parentheses in the text, following the first mention of a complex name or term.

Comparative Essays and Comparative Illustrations   Keyed to the seven major themes of world history (see p. xxxiii), **Comparative Essays** enable us to draw more concrete comparisons and contrasts across geographic, cultural, and chronological lines. **Comparative Illustrations**, also keyed to the seven major themes, continue to be a feature in each chapter. Both the Comparative Essays and the Comparative Illustrations conclude with focus questions to help students develop their analytical skills. We hope that the Comparative Essays and the Comparative Illustrations will assist instructors who wish to encourage their students to adopt a comparative approach to their understanding of the human experience.

Film & History   The **Film & History** feature, which appears in many chapters, is now presented in a new, brief format that outlines the major ideas of the film. New features have been added on films such as *Luther, Suffragette, A Passage to India,* and *Bridge of Spies.*

Opposing Viewpoints   This feature presents a comparison of two or three primary sources to facilitate student analysis of historical documents. It has been expanded and now appears in almost every chapter. Focus questions are included to help students evaluate the documents.

End-of-Chapter Tools   These elements provide study aids for class discussion, individual review, and/or further research. The **Chapter Summary** is illustrated with thumbnail images of chapter illustrations and combined with a **Chapter Timeline**. A **Chapter Review**, which includes **Upon Reflection** essay questions and a list of **Key Terms**, assists students in studying the chapter.

NEW TO THIS EDITION

After reexamining the entire book and analyzing the comments and reviews of many colleagues who have found the book to be a useful instrument for introducing their students to world history, we have also made a number of other changes for the ninth edition.

We have continued to strengthen the global framework of the book, but not at the expense of reducing the attention assigned to individual regions of the world. New material has been added to most chapters to help students be aware of similar developments globally, including new comparative sections.

The enthusiastic response to the primary sources (boxed documents) led us to evaluate the content of each document carefully and add new documents throughout the text, including new comparative documents in the **Opposing Viewpoints** feature.

New illustrations were added to every chapter. **Chapter Notes** have now been placed at the end of each chapter.

New **historiographical subsections** (now marked by the heading **Historians Debate**, often in question format), which examine how and why historians differ in their interpretation of specific topics, have also been added. To keep up with the ever-growing body of historical scholarship, new or revised material has been added throughout the book on many topics (see specific notes below).

CHAPTER-BY-CHAPTER CONTENT REVISIONS

Chapter 1   New and revised material on possible discovery of new hominids in Indonesia; Neanderthals and modern humans; Lascaux cave; the Hebrew Bible, including the Documentary Hypothesis; the Ten Commandments; Assyrian

society; Assyrian women; new Historians Debate: "Why Did Early Civilizations Develop?"; new document, "The Code of the Assura."

Chapter 2   New opening vignette on Mohenjo-Daro; revised discussion of the Indus Valley civilization; revised section on Indian religion; revised Comparative Essay on writing and civilization.

Chapter 3   Revised Comparative Essay on metals; new document, "Love Spurned in Ancient China."

Chapter 4   New and revised material on Minoan Crete; Mycenaean Greece; the so-called Dark Age in Greece; the *polis*; Greek cultural identity; Greek settlements abroad; role of Persian threat for a growing sense of Greek cultural identity; growing sense of Greek cultural identity due to athletic games; Hellenistic political institutions; new map, "Greece and Its Colonies in the Archaic Age."

Chapter 5   New material on Aeneas and Romulus and Remus and the legendary founding of Rome; citizenship policy and the Roman army; the Punic Wars; Roman imperialism; comparison of Augustus and Julius Caesar; revolts against Roman rule during the *Pax Romana*; contacts with Han China; Roman women; revolts against Roman rule in Judaea; new Historians Debate: "What Was Romanization?"; new document, "The Daily Life of an Upper-Class Roman."

Chapter 6   Revised section on stateless societies now under Section 6-3, "Peoples and Societies in Early North America"; added material on Inka civilization; new document, "The Legend of the Feathery Serpent"; revised Comparative Essay on the environment.

Chapter 7   Revised opening vignette on Mecca and Muhammad; new documents, "Passions of a Sufi Mystic" and "Ibn Khaldun: Islam's Greatest Historian"; new historical interpretation question on the reasons for Islamic expansion.

Chapter 8   Two new documents, "Fault Line in the Desert" and "The Gold Rush, African Style."

Chapter 9   Revised section on Hinduism and popular religion; revised section on Southeast Asia; new document, "The Islamic Conquest of India."

Chapter 10   Added information on China's only female ruler, Empress Wu; revised section on traditional society in China; two new documents, "The Good Life in the High Tang" and "The Saintly Miss Wu."

Chapter 11   New document, " Life in the Land of Wa"; added information on maritime trade.

Chapter 12   New material on the Ostrogothic Kingdom of Italy; Arianism; monks as missionaries, particularly St. Patrick; Charlemagne as emperor; peasant women; role of agriculture in the development of trade in the High Middle Ages; Bernard of Clairvaux; Hildegard of Bingen, a female mystic of the twelfth century; the Fourth Crusade; new Historians Debate: "What Was Feudalism?"; new document, "The Miraculous Power of the Sacraments"; new Historians Debate: "What Motivated the Crusaders?"; new material in Historians Debate: "What Were the Effects of the Crusades?"

Chapter 13   New material on the English use of the longbow; the Great Schism; the Renaissance artist Masaccio; new Historians Debate: "Why Did the Eastern Roman Empire

(Byzantine Empire) Last a Thousand Years Longer Than the Western Roman Empire?"; new C-section, "The Artist and Social Status," new document, "The Genius of Michelangelo."

Part III opener revised.

Chapter 14 New document, "For God, Gold, and Glory in the Age of Exploration"; added information on the role of Southeast Asia in maritime trade; more information on the nature of slave trade on the island of Gorée; revised section on the motives for European exploration.

Chapter 15 New material on the Jesuits; women and witch-craft; the Thirty Years' War; Peter the Great's reforms; new Film & History on *Luther*; new document, "The Destruction of Magdeburg in the Thirty Year's War."

Chapter 16 Revised and expanded section on Safavid Persia; new documents, "Suleyman the Magnificent" and "A Religion Fit for a King"; revised Comparative Essay on war; new Historical Interpretation question: "The Ottoman Empire: A Civilization in Decline?"

Chapter 17 New documents, "The Debate over Christianity" and "Last Will and Testament"; New Historical Interpretation question: "The Qing Economy: Ready for Takeoff?"

Chapter 18 New material on Rococo art; global trade; the consumer revolution; Jamestown; early American religious culture; the Seven Years' War; the American Revolution; Frederick II of Prussia; the Three Estates; French finances; the French clergy; the flight to Varennes; the Reign of Terror; new document, "Frederick the Great and His Father."

INSTRUCTOR RESOURCES

MindTap

MindTap Instant Access Code: ISBN 9781337401074
MindTap Printed Access Card: ISBN 9781337401081

MindTap for *World History*, Ninth Edition, is a flexible online learning platform that provides students with an immersive learning experience to build and foster critical thinking skills. Through a carefully designed chapter-based learning path, MindTap allows students to easily identify learning objectives; draw connections and improve writing skills by completing unit-level essay assignments; read short, manageable sections from the e-book; and test their content knowledge with map- and timeline-based critical thinking questions.

MindTap allows instructors to customize their content, providing tools that seamlessly integrate YouTube clips, outside websites, and personal content directly into the learning path. Instructors can assign additional primary source content through the Instructor Resource Center and Questia primary- and secondary-source databases that house thousands of peer-reviewed journals, newspapers, magazines, and full-length books.

The additional content available in MindTap mirrors and complements the authors' narrative, but also includes primary-source content and assessments not found in the printed text. To learn more, ask your Cengage Learning sales representative to demo it for you—or go to www.Cengage.com/MindTap.

The following quick overview lists some of the MindTap for World History offerings:

- **Setting the Scene:** A short video familiarizes the student with some of the chapter content and is followed by a short-answer essay prompt to start reflecting on what you will learn.

- **Primary Sources Checklist:** This list links out all of the primary sources featured in the chapter.

- **Section Reading** with a **Check Your Understanding Aplia-based interactive quiz.**

- **Chapter Test:** A short Aplia-based end-of-chapter test helps prepare for the exam.

- **Chapter Reflection Activity:** This essay activity provides a critical thinking and writing opportunity.

- **Part Suggested Reading:** Additional readings, found in the Questia database, for each chapter are provided.

- **Part Interactive Timeline:** The timeline provides an interactive exploration of the main events within a time period and a way to learn how to evaluate history like historians do by responding to an essay prompt related to the timeline content.

- **Part Essay Activity:** This career-building activity allows students to evaluate primary sources and build historical and critical thinking skills by writing an essay related to the sources, within an environment that provides outcomes and a rubric.

- **Part Primary Sources Activities:** This Aplia-based activity affords further opportunity for analysis of primary sources.

Instructor Companion Website

This website is an all-in-one resource for class preparation, presentation, and testing for instructors. Accessible through Cengage.com/login with your faculty account, you will find an Instructor's Manual, PowerPoint presentations (descriptions below), and test bank files.

Instructor's Manual

For each chapter, this manual contains chapter outlines, lecture suggestions, primary source discussion questions, student research topics, and web and video resources.

PowerPoint® Lecture Tools

These presentations—ready-to-use, visual outlines of each chapter—are easily customized for your lectures. There are presentations of only lectures or only images, as well as combined lecture and image presentations. Also available is a per-chapter JPEG library of images and maps.

Test Bank

It is accessible through MindTap's Aplia and the Instructor Companion Website—where it is available as LMS-integrated files. This test bank contains multiple-choice and essay questions for each chapter and may be delivered through your LMS from your classroom, or wherever you may be, with no special installs or downloads required.

The following format types are available for download from the Instructor Companion Website: Blackboard, Angel, Moodle, Canvas, and Desire2Learn. You can import these files directly into your LMS to edit, manage questions, and create tests.

CourseReader

CourseReader is an online collection of primary and secondary sources that lets you create a customized electronic reader in minutes. With an easy-to-use interface and assessment tool, you can choose exactly what your students will be assigned—simply search or browse Cengage Learning's extensive document database to preview and select your customized collection of readings. In addition to print sources of all types (letters, diary entries, speeches, newspaper accounts, etc.), their collection includes a growing number of images and video and audio clips. Each primary source document includes a descriptive headnote that puts the reading into context and is further supported by both critical thinking and multiple-choice questions designed to reinforce key points. For more information, visit www.cengage.com/coursereader.

Reader Program

Cengage Learning publishes a number of readers, some containing exclusively primary sources, others containing a combination of primary and secondary sources, and some designed to guide students through the process of historical inquiry. Visit Cengage.com/history for a complete list of readers.

Cengagebrain.com

Save your students time and money. Direct them to www.cengagebrain.com for choice in formats and savings and a better chance to succeed in your class. Cengagebrain.com, Cengage Learning's online store, is a single destination for more than 10,000 new textbooks, eTextbooks, eChapters, study tools, and audio supplements. Students have the freedom to purchase à la carte exactly what they need when they need it. Students can save 50 percent on the electronic textbook and can pay as little as $1.99 for an individual eChapter.

Custom Options

Nobody knows your students like you, so why not give them a text that is tailored to their needs? Cengage Learning offers custom solutions for your course—whether it's making a small modification to *World History* to match your syllabus or combining multiple sources to create something truly unique. You can pick and choose chapters, include your own material, and add additional map exercises along with the Rand McNally Atlas to create a text that fits the way you teach. Ensure that your students get the most out of their textbook dollar by giving them exactly what they need. Contact your Cengage Learning representative to explore custom solutions for your course.

STUDENT RESOURCES

MindTap Reader

MindTap Reader is an eBook specifically designed to address the ways students assimilate content and media assets. MindTap Reader combines thoughtful navigation ergonomics, advanced student annotation, note-taking, search tools, and embedded media assets such as video and MP3 chapter summaries, primary source documents with critical thinking questions, and interactive (zoomable) maps. Students can use the eBook as their primary text or as a multimedia companion to their printed book. The MindTap Reader eBook is available within the MindTap found at www.cengagebrain.com.

Reader Program

Cengage Learning publishes a number of readers, some containing exclusively primary sources, others containing a combination of primary and secondary sources, and some designed to guide students through the process of historical inquiry. Visit Cengage.com/history for a complete list of readers.

Cengagebrain.com

Save time and money! Go to www.cengagebrain.com for choice in formats and savings and a better chance to succeed in your class. Cengagebrain.com, Cengage Learning's online store, is a single destination for more than 10,000 new textbooks, eTextbooks, eChapters, study tools, and audio supplements. Students have the freedom to purchase à la carte exactly what they need when they need it. Students can save 50 percent on the electronic textbook and can pay as little as $1.99 for an individual eChapter.

Writing for College History, 1e

[ISBN: 9780618306039] Prepared by Robert M. Frakes, Clarion University. This brief handbook for survey courses in American history, Western Civilization/European history, and world civilization guides students through the various types of writing assignments they encounter in a history class. Providing examples of student writing and candid assessments of student work, this text focuses on the rules and conventions of writing for the college history course.

The History Handbook, 2e

[ISBN: 9780495906766] Prepared by Carol Berkin of Baruch College, City University of New York, and Betty Anderson of Boston University. This book teaches students both basic and history-specific study skills such as how to read primary sources, research historical topics, and correctly cite sources. Substantially less expensive than comparable skill-building texts, *The History Handbook* also offers tips for Internet research and evaluating online sources.

Doing History: Research and Writing in the Digital Age, 2e

[ISBN: 9781133587880] Prepared by Michael J. Galgano, J. Chris Arndt, and Raymond M. Hyser of James Madison University. Whether you're starting down the path as a history major or simply looking for a straightforward and systematic guide to writing a successful paper, you'll find this text to be an indispensable handbook to historical research. This text's "soup to nuts" approach to researching and writing about history addresses every step of the process, from locating your sources and gathering information, to writing clearly and making proper use of various citation styles to avoid plagiarism. You'll also learn how to make the most of every tool available to you—especially the technology that helps you conduct the process efficiently and effectively.

The Modern Researcher, 6e

[ISBN: 9780495318705] Prepared by Jacques Barzun and Henry F. Graff of Columbia University. This classic introduction to the techniques of research and the art of expression is used widely in history courses, but is also appropriate for writing and research methods courses in other departments. Barzun and Graff thoroughly cover every aspect of research, from the selection of a topic through the gathering, analysis, writing, revision, and publication of findings, presenting the process not as a set of rules but through actual cases that put the subtleties of research in a useful context. Part One covers the principles and methods of research; Part Two covers writing, speaking, and getting one's work published.

Rand McNally Historical Atlas of the World, 2e

[ISBN: 9780618841912] This valuable resource features over seventy maps that portray the rich panoply of the world's history from preliterate times to the present. They show how cultures and civilization were linked and how they interacted. The maps make it clear that history is not static. Rather, it is about change and movement across time. The maps show change by presenting the dynamics of expansion, cooperation, and conflict. This atlas includes maps that display the world from the beginning of civilization; the political development of all major areas of the world; expanded coverage of Africa, Latin America, and the Middle East; the current Islamic world; and the world population change in 1900 and 2000.

ACKNOWLEDGMENTS

BOTH AUTHORS GRATEFULLY ACKNOWLEDGE that without the generosity of many others, this project could not have been completed.

William Duiker would like to thank Kumkum Chatterjee and On-cho Ng for their helpful comments about issues related to the history of India and premodern China. His longtime colleague Cyril Griffith, now deceased, was a cherished friend and a constant source of information about modern Africa. Art Goldschmidt has been of invaluable assistance in reading several chapters of the manuscript, as well as in unraveling many of the mysteries of Middle Eastern civilization. He has benefited from comments by Charles Ingrao on Spanish policies in Latin America, and from Tony Hopkins and Dan Baugh on British imperial policy. Dale Peterson has been an unending source of useful news items. He would like to thank Ian Bell, Carol C. Coffin, his daughter Claire L. Duiker, and Ruth Petzold for permission to use their photographs in the book. Finally, he remains profoundly grateful to his wife, Yvonne V. Duiker, Ph.D. She has not only given her usual measure of love and support when this appeared to be an insuperable task, but she has also contributed her own time and expertise to enrich the sections on art and literature, thereby adding life and sparkle to this edition, as well as the earlier editions, of the book. To her, and to his daughters Laura and Claire, he will be forever thankful for bringing joy to his life.

Jackson Spielvogel would like to thank Art Goldschmidt, David Redles, and Christine Colin for their time and ideas. Daniel Haxall of Kutztown University provided valuable assistance with materials on postwar art, popular culture, Postmodern art and thought, and the digital age. He is especially grateful to Kathryn Spielvogel for her work as editorial associate. Above all, he thanks his family for their support. The gifts of love, laughter, and patience from his daughters, Jennifer and Kathryn; his sons, Eric and Christian; his daughters-in-law, Liz and Laurie; and his sons-in-law, Daniel and Eddie, were especially valuable. He also wishes to acknowledge his grandchildren, Devyn, Bryn, Drew, Elena, Sean, Emma, and Jackson, who bring great joy to his life. Diane, his wife and best friend, provided him with editorial assistance, wise counsel, and the loving support that made a project of this magnitude possible.

Thanks to Cengage's comprehensive review process, many historians were asked to evaluate our manuscript. We are grateful to the following for the innumerable suggestions that have greatly improved our work:

Najia Aarim, SUNY College at Fredonia; Jacob Abadi, U.S. Air Force Academy; Henry Maurice Abramson, Florida Atlantic University; Wayne Ackerson, Salisbury University; Charles F. Ames Jr., Salem State College; Nancy Anderson, Loyola University; J. Lee Annis, Montgomery College; Monty Armstrong, Cerritos High School; Gloria M. Aronson, Normandale College; Heather Barry, St. Joseph's College; Charlotte Beahan, Murray State University; Doris Bergen, University of Vermont; Martin Berger, Youngstown State University; Deborah Biffton, University of Wisconsin—La Crosse; Charmarie Blaisdell, Northeastern University; Brian Bonhomme, Youngstown State University; Patricia J. Bradley, Auburn University at Montgomery; Matt Brent, Rappahannock Community College; Dewey Browder, Austin Peay State University; Steve Bsharah, Bakersfield College; Nancy Cade, Pikeville College; Antonio Calabria, University of Texas at San Antonio; Alice-Catherine Carls, University of Tennessee—Martin; Harry Carpenter, Western Piedmont Community College; Yuan Ling Chao, Middle Tennessee State University; Mark W. Chavalas, University of Wisconsin; Hugh Clark, Ursinus College; Robert Cliver, Humboldt State University; Joan Coffey, Sam Houston State University; Eleanor A. Congdon, Youngstown State University; Jason P. Coy, College of Charleston; Edward R. Crowther, Adams State College; John Davis, Radford University; Ross Dunn, San Diego State University; Lane Earn, University of Wisconsin—Oshkosh; Roxanne Easley, Central Washington University; C. T. Evans, Northern Virginia Community

College; Edward L. Farmer, University of Minnesota; William W. Farris, University of Tennessee; Nancy Fitch, California State University, Fullerton; Kristine Frederickson, Utah Valley University; Ronald Fritze, Lamar University; Joe Fuhrmann, Murray State University; Robert Gerlich, Loyola University; Marc J. Gilbert, North Georgia College; William J. Gilmore-Lehne, Richard Stockton College of New Jersey; Richard M. Golden, University of North Texas; Candice Goucher, Washington State University—Vancouver; Joseph M. Gowaskie, Rider College; Jonathan Grant, Florida State University; Don Gustafson, Augsburg College; Deanna Haney, Lansing Community College; Jason Hardgrave, University of Southern Indiana; Jay Harmon, Catholic High School; Ed Haynes, Winthrop College; Robert Henry, Grossmont College; Marilynn Jo Hitchens University of Colorado Denver; Tamara L. Hunt, University of Southern Indiana; Charles Keller, Southern Arkansas University; Linda Kerr, University of Alberta at Edmonton; David Koeller, North Park University; Zoltan Kramar, Central Washington University; Douglas Lea, Kutztown University; David Leinweber, Emory University; Thomas T. Lewis, Mount Senario College; Craig A. Lockard, University of Wisconsin—Green Bay; George Longenecker, Norwich University; Norman D. Love, El Paso Community College; Andrew Lowder, Lord Fairfax Community College; Robert Luczak, Vincennes University; Yuxin Ma, University of Louisville; Aran MacKinnon, State University of West Georgia Matthew Maher, Metropolitan State College of Denver; Patrick Manning, Northeastern University; Maxim Matusevich, Seton Hall University; Eric Mayer, Victor Valley College; Dolores Nason McBroome, Humboldt State University; John McDonald, Northern Essex Community College; Andrea McElderry, University of Louisville; Jeff McEwen, Chattanooga State Technical Community College; Margaret McKee, Castilleja High School; Nancy McKnight, Stockton High School; Robert McMichael, Wayland Baptist University; David L. McMullen, University of North Carolina at Charlotte; John A. Mears, Southern Methodist University; Cristina Mehrtens, University of Massachusetts, Dartmouth; David A. Meier, Dickinson State University; Marc A. Meyer, Berry College; Stephen S. Michot, Mississippi County Community College; John Ashby Morton, Benedict College; William H. Mulligan, Murray State University; Henry A. Myers, James Madison University; Marian P. Nelson, University of Nebraska at Omaha; Sandy Norman Florida Atlantic University; Patrick M. O'Neill, Broome Community College; Roger Pauly, University of Central Arkansas; Norman G. Raiford, Greenville Technical College; Jane Rausch, University of Massachusetts—Amherst; Michael Redman, University of Louisville Dianna K. Rhyan, Columbus State Community College; Merle Rife, Indiana University of Pennsylvania; Patrice C. Ross, Columbus State Community College; John Rossi, LaSalle University; Eric C. Rust, Baylor University; Maura M. Ryan, Springbrook High School; Jane Samson, University of Alberta; Keith Sandiford University of Manitoba; Anthony R. Santoro, Christopher Newport University; Elizabeth Sarkinnen, Mount Hood Community College; Pamela Sayre, Henry Ford College; Bill Schell, Murray State University; Linda Scherr, Mercer County Community College; Robert M. Seltzer, Hunter College; Patrick Shan, Grand Valley State University; David Shriver, Cuyahoga Community College; Brett Shufelt, Copiah-Lincoln Community College; David Simonelli, Youngstown State University; Amos E. Simpson, University of Southwestern Louisiana; Wendy Singer, Kenyon College; Christopher Sleeper, MiraCosta College; Marvin Slind, Washington State University; Paul Smith, Washington State University; Matthew Sneider, University of Massachusetts, Dartmouth; John Snetsinger, California Polytechnic State University; George Stow, LaSalle University; John C. Swanson, Utica College of Syracuse; Patrick Tabor, Chemeketa Community College; Anara Tabyshalieva, Marshall University; Tom Taylor, Seattle University; John G. Tuthill, University of Guam; Salli Vaegis, Georgia Perimeter College; Joanne Van Horn, Fairmont State College; Gilmar Visoni, Queensborough Community College; Peter von Sivers, University of Utah; Michael Walker, Utah Valley University; Christopher J. Ward, Clayton College and State University; Walter Ward, Georgia State University; Pat Weber, University of Texas—El Paso; Lucius Wedge, Walsh University; Douglas L. Wheeler, University of New Hampshire; David L. White, Appalachian State University; Elmira B. Wicker, Southern University—Baton Rouge; Glee Wilson, Kent State University; Jason Wolfe, Cleveland State Community College; Laura Matysek Wood, Tarrant County College; Joseph Yick, Texas State University—San Marcos; Harry Zee, Cumberland County College; and Colleen Shaughnessy Zeena, Salem State University

The authors are truly grateful to the people who have helped us to produce this book. We especially want to thank Clark Baxter, whose faith in our ability to do this project was inspiring. Tonya Lobato and Florence Kilgo thoughtfully, wisely, efficiently, and cheerfully guided the overall development of the ninth edition. We also thank Scott Greenan for his suggestions and valuable insights. Carol Newman and Mary Stone were as cooperative and cheerful as they were competent in matters of production management.

A NOTE TO STUDENTS ABOUT LANGUAGE AND THE DATING OF TIME

One of the most difficult challenges in studying world history is coming to grips with the multitude of names, words, and phrases in unfamiliar languages. Unfortunately, this problem has no easy solution. We have tried to alleviate the difficulty, where possible, by providing an English-language translation of foreign words or phrases, a glossary, and a pronunciation guide. The issue is especially complicated in the case of Chinese because two separate systems are commonly used to transliterate the spoken Chinese language into the Roman alphabet. The Wade-Giles system, invented in the nineteenth century, was the more frequently used until recent years, when the pinyin system was adopted by the People's Republic of China as its own official form of transliteration. We have opted to use the latter, as it appears to be gaining acceptance in the United States.

In our examination of world history, we also need to be aware of the dating of time. In recording the past, historians try to determine the exact time when events occurred. World War II in Europe, for example, began on September 1, 1939, when Adolf Hitler sent German troops into Poland, and ended on May 7, 1945, when Germany surrendered. By using dates, historians can place events in order and try to determine the development of patterns over periods of time.

If someone asked you when you were born, you would reply with a number, such as 1999. In the United States, we would all accept that number without question because it is part of the dating system followed in the Western world (Europe and the Western Hemisphere). In this system, events are dated by counting backward or forward from the birth of Jesus Christ (assumed to be the year 1). An event that took place 400 years before the birth of Christ would most commonly be dated 400 BC (before Christ). Dates after the birth of Christ are labeled as AD. These letters stand for the Latin words *anno Domini,* which mean "in the year of the Lord" (the year since the birth of Christ). Thus, an event that took place 250 years after the birth of Christ is written AD 250. It can also be written as 250, just as you would not give your birth year as "AD 1999" but simply as "1999."

Many historians now prefer to use the abbreviations BCE ("before the common era") and CE ("common era") instead of BC and AD. This is especially true of world historians who prefer to use symbols that are not so Western or Christian oriented. The dates, of course, remain the same. Thus, 1950 BCE and 1950 BC refer to the same year, as do AD 40 and 40 CE. In keeping with the current usage by world historians, this book uses the terms BCE and CE.

Historians also make use of other terms to refer to time. A decade is 10 years, a century is 100 years, and a millennium is 1,000 years. The phrase "fourth century BCE" refers to the fourth period of 100 years counting backward from 1, the assumed date of the birth of Christ. Since the first century BCE would be the years 100 BCE to 1 BCE, the fourth century BCE would be the years 400 BCE to 301 BCE. We could say, then, that an event in 350 BCE took place in the fourth century BCE.

The phrase "fourth century CE" refers to the fourth period of 100 years after the birth of Christ. Since the first period of 100 years would be the years 1 to 100, the fourth period or fourth century would be the years 301 to 400. We could say, then, for example, that an event in 350 took place in the fourth century. Likewise, the first millennium BCE refers to the years 1000 BCE to 1 BCE, and the second millennium CE refers to the years 1001 to 2000.

The dating of events can also vary from people to people. Most people in the Western world use the Western calendar, also known as the Gregorian calendar after Pope Gregory XIII, who refined it in 1582. The Hebrew calendar uses a different system in which the year 1 is the equivalent of the Western year 3760 BCE, once calculated to be the date of the creation of the world, according to the Old Testament. Thus, the Western year 2013 corresponds to the year 5777 on the Jewish calendar. The Islamic calendar begins year 1 on the day Muhammad fled from Mecca, which is the year 622 on the Western calendar.

THEMES FOR UNDERSTANDING WORLD HISTORY

As they pursue their craft, historians often organize their material on the basis of themes that enable them to ask and try to answer basic questions about the past. Such is our intention here. In preparing the ninth edition of this book, we have selected several major themes that we believe are especially important in understanding the course of world history. These themes transcend the boundaries of time and space and have relevance to all cultures since the beginning of the human experience.

In the chapters that follow, we will refer to these themes frequently as we advance from the prehistoric era to the present. Where appropriate, we shall make comparisons across cultural boundaries or across different time periods. To facilitate this process, we have included a Comparative Essay in each chapter that focuses on a particular theme within the specific time period discussed in that section of the book. For example, the Comparative Essays in Chapters 1 and 6 deal with the human impact on the natural environment during the premodern era, while those in Chapters 22 and 30 discuss the issue during the age of imperialism and in the contemporary world. Each Comparative Essay is identified with a particular theme, although it should be noted that many essays deal with several themes at the same time.

We have also sought to illustrate these themes through the use of Comparative Illustrations in each chapter. These illustrations are comparative in nature and seek to encourage the reader to think about thematic issues in cross-cultural terms, while not losing sight of the unique characteristics of individual societies. Our seven themes, each divided into two subtopics, are listed below.

Politics & Government   *1. Politics and Government*   The study of politics seeks to answer certain basic questions that historians have about the structure of a society: How were people governed? What was the relationship between the ruler and the ruled? What people or groups of people (the political elites) held political power? What actions did people take to guarantee their security or change their form of government?

Art & Ideas   *2. Art and Ideas*   We cannot understand a society without looking at its culture, or the common ideas, beliefs, and patterns of behavior that are passed on from one generation to the next. Culture includes both high culture and popular culture. High culture consists of the writings of a society's thinkers and the works of its artists. A society's popular culture is the world of ideas and experiences of ordinary people. Today, the media have embraced the term *popular culture* to describe the current trends and fashionable styles.

Religion & Philosophy   *3. Religion and Philosophy*   Throughout history, people have sought to find a deeper meaning in human life. How have the world's great religions, such as Hinduism, Buddhism, Judaism, Christianity, and Islam, influenced people's lives? How have they spread to create new patterns of culture in other parts of the world?

Family & Society   *4. Family and Society*   The most basic social unit in human society has always been the family. From a study of family and social patterns, we learn about the different social classes that make up a society and their relationships with one another. We also learn about the role of gender in individual societies. What different roles did men and women play in their societies? How and why were those roles different?

Science & Technology   *5. Science and Technology*   For thousands of years, people around the world have made scientific discoveries and technological innovations that have changed our world. From the creation of stone tools that made farming easier to advanced computers that guide our airplanes, science and technology have altered how humans have related to their world.

Earth & Environment   *6. Earth and the Environment*   Throughout history, peoples and societies have been affected by the physical world in which they live. Climatic changes alone have been an important factor in human history. Through their economic activities, peoples and societies, in turn, have also made an impact on their world. Human activities have affected the physical environment and even endangered the very existence of entire societies and species.

Interaction & Exchange   *7. Interaction and Exchange*   Many world historians believe that the exchange of ideas and innovations is the driving force behind the evolution of human societies. Knowledge of agriculture, writing and printing, metalworking, and navigational techniques, for example, spread gradually from one part of the world to other regions and eventually changed the face of the entire globe. The process of cultural and technological exchange took place in various ways, including trade, conquest, and the migration of peoples.

PART I

THE FIRST CIVILIZATIONS AND THE RISE OF EMPIRES (PREHISTORY TO 500 CE)

1 **Early Humans and the First Civilizations**

2 **Ancient India**

3 **China in Antiquity**

4 **The Civilization of the Greeks**

5 **The Roman World Empire**

FOR HUNDREDS OF THOUSANDS of years, human beings lived in small groups or villages, seeking to survive by hunting, fishing, and foraging in an often hostile environment. Then, in the space of a few thousand years, an abrupt change occurred as people in a few areas of the globe began to master the art of cultivating food crops. As food production increased, the population in these areas grew, and people began to live in larger communities. Cities appeared and became centers of cultural and religious development. Historians refer to these changes as the beginnings of civilization.

How and why did the first civilizations arise? What role did cross-cultural contacts play in their development? What was the nature of the relationship between these permanent settlements and nonagricultural peoples living elsewhere in the world? Finally, what brought about the demise of these early civilizations, and what legacy did they leave for their successors in the region? The first civilizations that emerged in Mesopotamia, Egypt, India, and China in the fourth and third millennia BCE all shared a number of basic characteristics. Perhaps most important was that each developed in a river valley that was able to provide the agricultural resources needed to maintain a large population.

The emergence of these sedentary societies had a major impact on the social organizations, religious beliefs, and ways of life of the peoples living in them. As population increased and cities sprang up, centralized authority became a necessity. And in the cities, new forms of livelihood arose to satisfy the growing demand for social services and consumer goods. Some people became artisans or merchants, while others became warriors, scholars, or priests. In some cases, the early cities reflected the hierarchical character of the society as a whole, with a central royal palace surrounded by an imposing wall to separate the rulers from the remainder of the urban population.

Although the emergence of the first civilizations led to the formation of cities governed by elites, the vast majority of the population consisted of peasants or slaves working on the lands of the wealthy. In general, the changes affected rural peoples less than their urban counterparts. Farmers continued to live in simple mud-and-thatch huts, and many continued to face legal restrictions on their freedom of action and movement. Slavery was common in virtually all ancient societies.

Within these civilizations, the nature of social organization and relationships also began to change. As the concept of private property spread, people were less likely to live in large kinship groups, and the nuclear family became increasingly prevalent. Gender roles came to be differentiated, with men working in the fields or at various specialized occupations and women remaining in the home. Wives were less likely to be viewed as partners than as possessions under the control of their husbands.

These new civilizations were also the sites of significant religious and cultural developments. All of them gave birth to new religions that sought to explain and even influence the forces of nature. Winning the approval of the gods was deemed crucial to a community's success, and a

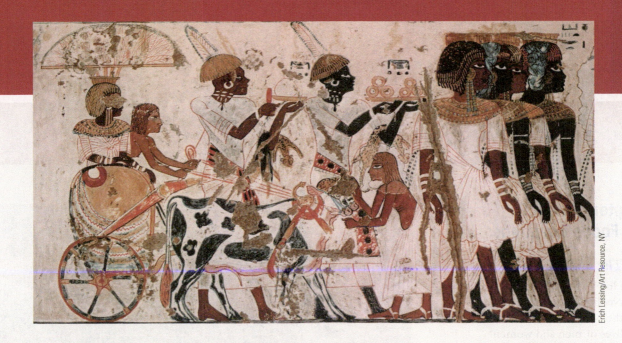

professional class of priests emerged to handle relations with the divine world.

Writing was an important development in the evolution of these new civilizations. Eventually, all of them used writing as both a means of communication and an avenue of creative expression.

From the beginnings of the first civilizations around 3000 BCE, the trend was toward the creation of larger territorial states with more sophisticated systems of control. This process reached a high point in the first millennium BCE. Between 1000 and 500 BCE, the Assyrians and Persians amassed empires that encompassed large areas of the Middle East. The conquests of Alexander the Great in the fourth century BCE created an even larger, if short-lived, empire that soon divided into four kingdoms. Later, the western portion of these kingdoms, along with the Mediterranean world and much of western Europe, fell subject to the mighty empire of the Romans. At the same time, much of India became part of the Mauryan Empire. Finally, in the last few centuries BCE, the Qin and Han dynasties of China governed a unified Chinese empire.

At first, these new civilizations had relatively little contact with peoples in the surrounding regions. But regional trade had started to take hold in the Middle East, and probably in southern and eastern Asia as well, at a very early date. As the population increased, the volume of trade rose with it, and the new civilizations moved outward to acquire new lands and access needed resources. As they expanded, they began to encounter peoples along the periphery of their empires.

Little evidence has survived to know the nature of these first encounters, but it is likely that the results varied according to time and place. In some cases, the growing civilizations found it relatively easy to absorb isolated communities of agricultural or food-gathering peoples that they encountered. Such was the case in southern China and southern India. But in other instances, notably among the nomadic or seminomadic peoples in the central and northeastern parts of Asia, the problem was more complicated and often resulted in bitter and extended conflict.

Over a long period of time, contacts between these nomadic or seminomadic peoples and settled civilizations gradually developed. Often the relationship, at least at the outset, was mutually beneficial, as each needed goods produced by the other. Nomadic peoples in Central Asia also served as an important link for goods and ideas transported over long distances between sedentary civilizations as early as 3000 BCE. Overland trade throughout southwestern Asia was already well established by the third millennium BCE.

Eventually, the relationship between the settled peoples and the nomadic peoples became increasingly tense. Where conflict occurred, the governments of the sedentary civilizations used a variety of techniques to resolve the problem, including negotiations, conquest, or alliance with other pastoral peoples to isolate their primary tormentors.

In the end, these early civilizations collapsed not only as a result of nomadic invasions but also because of their own weaknesses, which made them increasingly vulnerable to attacks along the frontier. Some of their problems were political, and others were related to climatic change or environmental problems.

The fall of the ancient empires did not mark the end of civilization, of course, but rather served as a transition to a new stage of increasing complexity in the evolution of human society.

EARLY HUMANS AND THE FIRST CIVILIZATIONS

Chapter Outline and Focus Questions

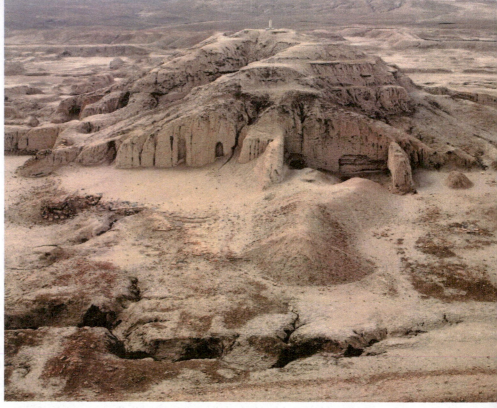

Excavation of Warka showing the ruins of Uruk. Nik Wheeler/CORBIS

Critical Thinking

Q *In what ways were the civilizations of Mesopotamia and Egypt alike? In what ways were they different? What accounts for the similarities and differences?*

Connections to Today

Q *What lessons can you learn from the decline and fall of early civilizations in Mesopotamia, Egypt, Assyria, and Persia, and how do those lessons apply to today's civilizations?*

IN 1849, A DARING YOUNG ENGLISHMAN made a hazardous journey into the deserts and swamps of southern Iraq. Braving high winds and temperatures that reached 120 degrees Fahrenheit, William Loftus led a small expedition southward along the banks of the Euphrates River in search of the roots of civilization. He said, "From our childhood we have been led to regard this place as the cradle of the human race."

Guided by native Arabs into the southernmost reaches of Iraq, Loftus and his small band of explorers were soon overwhelmed by what they saw. He wrote, "I know of nothing more exciting or impressive than the first sight of one of these great piles, looming in solitary grandeur from the surrounding plains and marshes." One of these piles, known to the natives as the mound of Warka, contained the ruins of Uruk, one of the first cities in the world and part of the world's first civilization.

Southern Iraq, known to the ancient Greeks as Mesopotamia, was one of the areas in the world where civilization began. In the fertile valleys of large rivers—the Tigris and Euphrates in Mesopotamia, the Nile in Egypt, the Indus in India, and the Yellow River in China—intensive agriculture became capable of supporting large groups of people. In these regions, civilization was born. The first civilizations emerged in western Asia (now known as the Middle East) and Egypt, where people developed organized societies and created the ideas and institutions that we associate with civilization.

Before considering the early civilizations of western Asia and Egypt, however, we must briefly examine our prehistory and observe how human beings made the shift from hunting and gathering to agricultural communities and ultimately to cities and civilization.

1–1 THE FIRST HUMANS

 Focus Question: How did the Paleolithic and Neolithic Ages differ, and how did the Neolithic Revolution affect the lives of men and women?

Historians rely mostly on documents to create their pictures of the past, but no written records exist for the prehistory of humankind. In their absence, the story of early humanity depends on archaeological and, more recently, biological information, which anthropologists and archaeologists use to formulate theories about our early past. Although modern science has given us more precise methods for examining prehistory, much of our understanding of early humans still relies on considerable conjecture.

The earliest humanlike creatures—known as **hominids**—lived in Africa some 3 to 4 million years ago. Called Australopithecines (aw-stray-loh-PITH-uh-synz), or "southern apemen," by their discoverers, they flourished in eastern and southern Africa and were the first hominids to make simple stone tools. Australopithecines may also have been bipedal—that is, they may have walked upright on two legs, a trait that would have

enabled them to move over long distances and make use of their arms and legs for different purposes.

In 1959, Louis and Mary Leakey discovered a new form of hominid in Africa that they labeled *Homo habilis* ("skillful human"). The Leakeys believed that *Homo habilis*, which had a brain almost 50 percent larger than that of the Australopithecines, was the earliest toolmaking hominid. Their larger brains and ability to walk upright allowed these hominids to become more sophisticated in searching for meat, seeds, and nuts for nourishment.

New hominids continue to be found, although considerable controversy can surround them. The belief that a 2003 discovery in Indonesia of a distinct hominid species, known as the "hobbit" because of its small body, is a distinct hominid species has been challenged by other scientists.

A new phase in early human development occurred around 1.5 million years ago with the emergence of *Homo erectus* ("upright human"). A more advanced human form, *Homo erectus* made use of larger and more varied tools and was the first hominid to leave Africa and move into Europe and Asia.

1–1a The Emergence of *Homo sapiens*

Around 250,000 years ago, a crucial stage in human development began with the emergence of *Homo sapiens* (HOH-moh SAY-pee-unz) ("wise human being"). The first anatomically modern humans, known as *Homo sapiens sapiens* ("wise, wise human being"), appeared in Africa between 200,000 and 150,000 years ago. Recent evidence indicates that they began to spread outside Africa around 70,000 years ago. Map 1.1 shows probable dates for different movements, although many of these are still controversial.

These modern humans, who were our direct ancestors, soon encountered other hominids, such as the Neanderthals, whose remains were first found in the Neander Valley in Germany. Neanderthal remains have since been found in both Europe and western Asia and have been dated to between 200,000 and 30,000 BCE. New genetic evidence has indicated that European, and even more so, East Asian humans interbred with Neanderthals. Neanderthals relied on a variety of stone tools and were the first early people to bury their dead. By 30,000 BCE, *Homo sapiens sapiens* had replaced the Neanderthals, who had largely become extinct.

HISTORIANS DEBATE **The Spread of Humans: Out of Africa or Multiregional?** The movements of the first modern humans were rarely sudden or rapid. Groups of people advanced beyond their old hunting grounds at a rate of only 2 to 3 miles per generation. This was enough, however, to populate the world in some tens of thousands of years. Some scholars, who advocate a multiregional theory, have suggested that advanced human creatures may have emerged independently in different parts of the world, rather than in Africa alone. But the latest genetic, archaeological, and climatic evidence strongly supports the out-of-Africa theory as the most likely explanation of human origin. In any case, by 10,000 BCE, members of the *Homo sapiens sapiens* species could be found throughout the

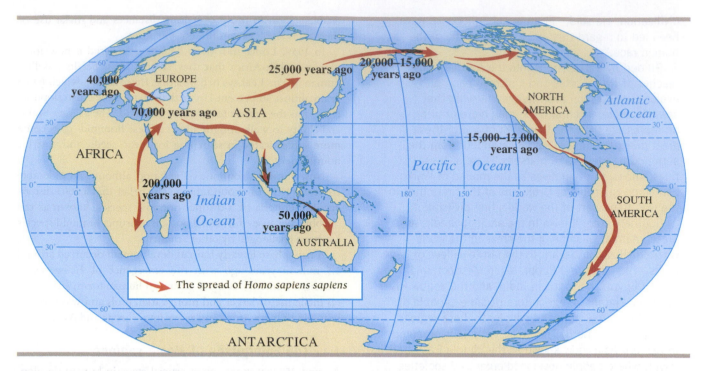

Map 1.1 The Spread of *Homo sapiens sapiens*. *Homo sapiens sapiens* spread from Africa beginning about 70,000 years ago. Living and traveling in small groups, these anatomically modern humans were hunter-gatherers.

Q *Given that some diffusion of humans occurred during ice ages, how would such climate change affect humans and their movements, especially from Asia to Australia and Asia to North America?*

world. By that time, it was the only human species left. All humans today, be they Europeans, Australian Aborigines, or Africans, belong to the same subspecies of human being.

1–1b The Hunter-Gatherers of the Paleolithic Age

One of the basic distinguishing features of the human species is the ability to make tools. The earliest tools were made of stone, and so this early period of human history (c. 2,500,000–10,000 BCE) has been designated the **Paleolithic Age** (*paleolithic* is Greek for "old stone").

For hundreds of thousands of years, humans relied on gathering and hunting for their daily food. Paleolithic peoples had a close relationship with the world around them, and over a period of time, they came to know which plants to eat and which animals to hunt. They did not know how to grow crops or raise animals, however. They gathered wild nuts, berries, fruits, and a variety of wild grains and green plants. Around the world, they captured and consumed various animals, including buffalo, horses, bison, wild goats, reindeer, and fish.

The gathering of wild plants and the hunting of animals no doubt led to certain patterns of living. Archaeologists and anthropologists have speculated that Paleolithic people lived in small bands of twenty to thirty individuals. They were nomadic, moving from place to place to follow animal migrations and vegetation cycles. Hunting depended on careful observation of animal behavior patterns and required a group effort for success. Over the years, tools became more refined and more useful. The invention of the spear and later the bow and arrow

made hunting considerably easier. Harpoons and fishhooks made of bone increased the catch of fish.

Both men and women were responsible for finding food—the chief work of Paleolithic people. Since women bore and raised the children, they generally stayed close to the camps, but they played an important role in acquiring food by gathering berries, nuts, and grains. Men hunted for wild animals, an activity that often took them far from camp. Because both men and women played important roles in providing for the band's survival, many scientists believe that a rough equality existed between men and women. Indeed, some speculate that both men and women made the decisions that affected the activities of the Paleolithic band.

Some groups of Paleolithic peoples found shelter in caves, but over time, they also created new types of shelter. Perhaps the most common was a simple structure of wood poles or sticks covered with animal hides. Where wood was scarce, Paleolithic hunter-gatherers might use the bones of mammoths for the framework and cover it with animal hides. The systematic use of fire, which archaeologists believe began around 500,000 years ago, made it possible for the caves and human-made structures to have a source of light and heat. Fire also enabled early humans to cook their food, making it taste better, last longer, and in the case of some plants, such as wild grains, easier to chew and digest.

The making of tools and the use of fire—two important technological innovations of Paleolithic peoples—remind us how crucial the ability to adapt was to human survival. Changing physical conditions during periodic ice ages posed a considerable threat to human existence. Paleolithic peoples used their technological innovations to change their physical environment. By working together, they found a way to survive.

But Paleolithic peoples did more than just survive. The cave paintings of large animals found in southwestern France and northern Spain bear witness to the cultural activity of Paleolithic peoples. A cave discovered in southern France in 1994—known as the Chauvet (shoh-VAY) cave after the leader of the expedition that found it—contains more than three hundred paintings of lions, oxen, owls, bears, and other animals. Most of these are animals that Paleolithic people did not hunt, which suggests to some scholars that the paintings were made for religious or even decorative purposes. The discoverers were overwhelmed by what they saw: "There was a moment of ecstasy. . . . They overflowed with joy and emotion in their turn. . . . These were moments of indescribable madness."[1]

1–1c The Neolithic Revolution, c. 10,000–4000 BCE

The end of the last ice age around 10,000 BCE was followed by what is called the **Neolithic Revolution**, a significant change in living patterns that occurred in the New Stone Age (*neolithic* is Greek for "new stone"). The name "New Stone Age" is misleading, however. Although Neolithic peoples made a new type of polished stone axes, this was not the most significant change they introduced.

An Agricultural Revolution The biggest change was the shift from gathering plants and hunting animals for sustenance

Pictures from History/Bridgeman Images

Paleolithic Cave Painting: The Lascaux Cave. Cave paintings of large animals reveal the cultural creativity of Paleolithic peoples. This scene is part of a large underground chamber found accidentally in 1940 at Lascaux, France, by some boys looking for their dog. This work is dated around 15,000 BCE. To make their paintings, Paleolithic artists used stone lamps that burned animal fat to illuminate the cave walls and mixed powdered mineral ores with animal fat to create red, yellow, and black pigments. Some artists even made brushes out of animal hairs with which to apply the paints.

(food gathering) to producing food by systematic agriculture (food production; see Map 1.2). The planting of grains and vegetables provided a regular supply of food, while the

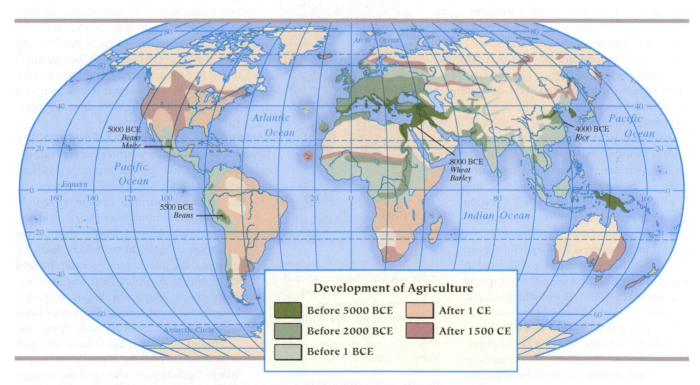

Development of Agriculture

- Before 5000 BCE
- Before 2000 BCE
- Before 1 BCE
- After 1 CE
- After 1500 CE

Map 1.2 The Development of Agriculture. Agriculture first began between 8000 and 5000 BCE in four different parts of the world. It allowed the establishment of permanent settlements where crops could be grown and domesticated animals that produced meat and milk could be easily tended.

Q *What geographic and human factors might explain relationships between latitude and the beginning of agriculture?*

domestication of animals, such as sheep, goats, cattle, and pigs, added a steady source of meat, milk, and fibers such as wool for clothing. Larger animals could also be used as beasts of burden. The growing of crops and the taming of food-producing animals created a new relationship between humans and nature. Historians like to speak of this as an agricultural revolution. Revolutionary change is dramatic and requires great effort, but the ability to acquire food on a regular basis gave humans greater control over their environment. It enabled them to give up their nomadic ways of life and begin to live in settled communities. The increase in food supplies also led to a noticeable expansion of the population.

The shift from hunting and gathering to food producing was not as sudden as was once believed, however. The **Mesolithic Age** ("Middle Stone Age," c. 10,000–7000 BCE) saw a gradual transition from a food-gathering and hunting economy to a food-producing one and witnessed a gradual domestication of animals as well. Likewise, the movement toward the use of plants and their seeds as an important source of nourishment was not sudden. Moreover, throughout the Neolithic period, hunting and gathering as well as nomadic herding remained ways of life for many people around the world.

Systematic agriculture developed independently in different areas of the world between 8000 and 5000 BCE. Inhabitants of the Middle East began cultivating wheat and barley and domesticating pigs, cattle, goats, and sheep by 8000 BCE. From the Middle East, farming spread into southeastern Europe and, by 4000 BCE, was well established in central Europe and the coastal regions of the Mediterranean. The cultivation of wheat and barley also spread from western Asia into the Nile Valley of Egypt by 6000 BCE and soon moved up the Nile to other areas of Africa, especially Ethiopia. In the woodlands and tropical forests of West Africa, a separate agricultural system emerged, based on the cultivation of tubers or root crops such as yams. The cultivation of wheat and barley also moved eastward into the highlands of northwestern and central India between 7000 and 5000 BCE. By 5000 BCE, rice was being cultivated in southeastern Asia, and from there it spread into southern China. In northern China, the cultivation of millet and the domestication of pigs and dogs seem well established by 6000 BCE. In the Western Hemisphere, Mesoamericans (inhabitants of present-day Mexico and Central America) domesticated beans, squash, and maize (corn) as well as dogs and fowl between 7000 and 5000 BCE (see Comparative Essay "From Hunter-Gatherers and Herders to Farmers").

Statue from Ain Ghazal. This life-size statue made of plaster, sand, and crushed chalk was discovered in 1984 at Ain Ghazal, an archaeological site near Amman, Jordan. Dating from around 6500 BCE, it is among the oldest known statues of the human figure. Although it appears lifelike, its features are too generic to be a portrait of a particular individual. The purpose of this sculpture and the reason for its creation may never be known. Erich Lessing/Art Resource, NY

Neolithic Farming Villages The growing of crops on a regular basis gave rise to more permanent settlements, which historians refer to as Neolithic farming villages or towns. Although Neolithic villages appeared in Europe, India, Egypt, China, and Mesoamerica, the oldest and most extensive ones were located in the Middle East. Jericho, in Canaan near the Dead Sea, was in existence by 8000 BCE and covered several acres by 7000 BCE. It had a wall several feet thick that enclosed houses made of sun-dried mudbricks. Çatal Hüyük (chaht-ul hoo-YOOK), located in modern Turkey, was an even larger community. Its walls enclosed 32 acres, and its population probably reached six thousand inhabitants during its high point from 6700 to 5700 BCE. People lived in simple mudbrick houses that were built so close to one another that there were few streets. To get to their homes, people would walk along the rooftops and enter the house through a hole in the roof.

Archaeologists have discovered twelve cultivated products in Çatal Hüyük, including fruits, nuts, and three kinds of wheat. People grew their own food and stored it in storerooms in their homes. Domesticated animals, especially cattle, yielded meat, milk, and hides. Food surpluses also made it possible for people to engage in activities other than farming. Some people became artisans and made weapons and jewelry that were traded with neighboring peoples.

Religious shrines housing figures of gods and goddesses have been found at Çatal Hüyük, as have a number of female statuettes. Molded with noticeably large breasts and buttocks, these "earth mothers" perhaps symbolically represented the fertility of both "our mother" earth and human mothers. The shrines and the statues point to the important role of religious practices in the lives of these Neolithic peoples.

Consequences of the Neolithic Revolution The Neolithic agricultural revolution had far-reaching consequences. Once people settled in villages or towns, they built houses for protection and other structures for the storage of goods. As organized communities stored food and accumulated material goods, they began to engage in trade. In the Middle East, for example, the new communities exchanged such objects as shells, flint, and semiprecious stones. People also began to specialize in certain crafts, and a division of labor developed. Pottery was made from clay and baked in fire to make it hard. The pots were used for cooking and to store grains. Woven baskets were also used for storage. Stone tools became refined as flint blades were used to make sickles and hoes for use in the fields. Obsidian—a volcanic glass that was easily flaked—was also used to create

From Hunter-Gatherers and Herders to Farmers

Earth & Environment

ABOUT TEN THOUSAND YEARS AGO, human beings began to practice the cultivation of crops and the domestication of animals. The exact time and place that crops were first cultivated successfully is uncertain. The first farmers undoubtedly used simple techniques and still relied primarily on other forms of food production, such as hunting, foraging, and pastoralism (herding). The real breakthrough came when farmers began to cultivate crops along the floodplains of river systems. The advantage was that crops grown in such areas were not as dependent on rainfall and therefore produced a more reliable harvest. An additional benefit was that the sediment carried by the river waters deposited nutrients in the soil, enabling the farmer to cultivate a single plot of land for many years without moving to a new location. Thus, the first truly sedentary societies were born.

The spread of river valley agriculture in various parts of Asia and Africa was the decisive factor in the rise of the first civilizations. The increase in food production in these regions led to a significant growth in population, while efforts to control the flow of water to maximize the irrigation of cultivated areas and to protect the local inhabitants from hostile forces outside the community provoked the first steps toward cooperative activities on a large scale. The need to oversee the entire process brought about the emergence of an elite that was eventually transformed into a government.

We shall investigate this process in the next several chapters as we explore the rise of civilizations in the Middle East, the Mediterranean, South Asia, China, and the Americas. We shall also raise a number of important questions: Why did human communities in some areas that had the capacity to support agriculture not take the leap to farming? Why did other groups that had managed to master the cultivation of crops not take the next step and create large and advanced societies? Finally, what happened to the existing communities of hunter-gatherers who were overrun or driven out as the agricultural revolution spread throughout the world?

Over the years, a number of possible explanations, some of them biological, others cultural or environmental, have been advanced to answer such questions. According to Jared Diamond, in *Guns, Germs, and Steel: The Fates of Human Societies*, the ultimate causes of such differences lie not within the character or cultural values of the resident population but in the nature of the local climate and topography. These influence the degree to which local crops and animals can be put to human use and then be transmitted to adjoining regions. In Mesopotamia, for example, the widespread availability of edible crops, such as wheat and barley, helped promote the transition to agriculture in the region. At the same time, the absence of land barriers between Mesopotamia and its neighbors to the east and west facilitated the rapid spread of agricultural techniques and crops to climatically similar regions in the Indus River Valley and Egypt.

 What role did the development of agriculture play in the emergence of civilization?

Women's Work. This rock painting from a cave in modern-day Algeria, dating from around the fourth millennium BCE, shows women harvesting grain.

Erich Lessing/Art Resource, NY

very sharp tools. In the course of the Neolithic Age, many of the food plants still in use today began to be cultivated. Moreover, vegetable fibers from such plants as flax and cotton were used to make thread that was woven into cloth.

The change to systematic agriculture in the Neolithic Age also had consequences for the relationship between men and women. Men assumed the primary responsibility for working in the fields and herding animals, jobs that kept them away from the home. Women remained behind, grinding grain into flour, caring for the children, weaving cloth, making cheese from milk, and performing other household tasks that required considerable labor. In time, as work outside the home was increasingly perceived as more important than work done in the home, men came to play the more dominant role in human society, which gave rise to the practice of **patriarchy** (PAY-tree-ark-ee), or a society dominated by men, a basic pattern that has persisted to our own times.

Other patterns set in the Neolithic Age also proved to be enduring elements of human history. Fixed dwellings, domesticated animals, regular farming, a division of labor, men holding power—all of these are part of the human story. For all of our scientific and technological progress, human survival still depends on the growing and storing of food, an accomplishment of people in the Neolithic Age. The Neolithic Revolution was truly a turning point in human history.

Between 4000 and 3000 BCE, significant technical developments began to transform the Neolithic towns. The invention of writing enabled records to be kept, and the use of metals marked a new level of human control over the environment and its resources. Already before 4000 BCE, artisans had discovered that metal-bearing rocks could be heated to liquefy the metal, which could then be cast in molds to produce tools and weapons that were more useful than stone instruments. Although copper was the first metal to be used for producing tools, after 4000 BCE, metalworkers in western Asia discovered that a combination of copper and tin produced bronze, a much harder and more durable metal than copper. Its widespread use has led historians to call the period from around 3000 to 1200 BCE the Bronze Age; thereafter, bronze was increasingly replaced by iron.

At first, Neolithic settlements were hardly more than villages. But as their inhabitants mastered the art of farming, more complex human societies gradually emerged. As wealth increased, these societies sought to protect it from being plundered by outsiders and so began to develop armies and to build walled cities. By the beginning of the Bronze Age, the concentration of larger numbers of people in river valleys was leading to a whole new pattern for human life.

1–2 THE EMERGENCE OF CIVILIZATION

Focus Question: What are the characteristics of civilization, and what are some explanations for why early civilizations emerged?

As we have seen, early human beings formed small groups that developed a simple culture that enabled them to survive. As human societies grew and developed greater complexity, civilization came into being. A **civilization** is a complex culture in which large numbers of people share a variety of common elements. Historians have identified a number of basic characteristics of civilization, including the following:

1. *An urban focus.* Cities became the centers for political, economic, social, cultural, and religious development. The cities that emerged were much larger than the Neolithic towns that preceded them.
2. *New political and military structures.* An organized government bureaucracy arose to meet the administrative demands of the growing population, and armies were organized to gain land and power and for defense.

3. *A new social structure based on economic power.* While kings and an upper class of priests, political leaders, and warriors dominated, there also existed large groups of free common people (farmers, artisans, craftspeople) and, at the very bottom of the social hierarchy, a class of slaves.
4. *The development of more complexity in a material sense.* Surpluses of agricultural crops freed some people to work in occupations other than farming. Demand among ruling elites for luxury items encouraged the creation of new products. And as urban populations exported finished goods in exchange for raw materials from neighboring populations, organized trade grew substantially.
5. *A distinct religious structure.* The gods were deemed crucial to the community's success, and a professional priestly class, serving as stewards of the gods' property, regulated relations with the gods.
6. *The development of writing.* Kings, priests, merchants, and artisans used writing to keep records.
7. *New forms of significant artistic and intellectual activity.* For example, monumental architectural structures, usually religious, occupied a prominent place in urban environments.

1–2a Early Civilizations Around the World

The first civilizations that developed in Mesopotamia and Egypt will be examined in detail in this chapter. But civilizations also developed independently in other parts of the world. Between 3000 and 1500 BCE, the valleys of the Indus River in India supported a flourishing civilization that extended hundreds of miles from the Himalayas to the coast of the Arabian Sea (see Chapter 2). Two major cities—Harappa and Mohenjo-Daro—were at the heart of this advanced civilization, which flourished for hundreds of years. As in the city-states that arose in Mesopotamia and along the Nile, the Harappan economy was based primarily on farming, but Harappan civilization also carried on extensive trade with Mesopotamia. Textiles and food were imported from the Mesopotamian city-states in exchange for copper, lumber, precious stones, cotton, and various types of luxury goods.

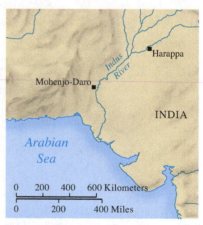

Harappa and Mohenjo-Daro

Another river valley civilization emerged along the Yellow River in northern China about four thousand years ago (see Chapter 3). Under the Shang dynasty of kings, which ruled from 1570 to 1045 BCE, this civilization contained impressive cities with huge city walls, royal palaces, and large royal tombs. A system of irrigation enabled early Chinese civilization to

The Yellow River, China

Central Asia Civilization

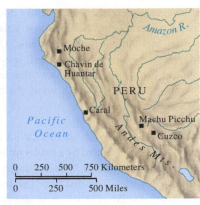

Caral, Peru

CHRONOLOGY	The Birth of Early Civilizations
Egypt	c. 3100 BCE
Mesopotamia	c. 3000 BCE
India	c. 3000 BCE
Peru	c. 2600 BCE
China	c. 2000 BCE
Central Asia	c. 2000 BCE

maintain a prosperous farming society ruled by an aristocratic class whose major concern was war.

Scholars long believed that civilization emerged only in four areas—the fertile river valleys of the Tigris and Euphrates, the Nile, the Indus, and the Yellow River—that is, in Southwest Asia, Egypt, India, and China. Recently, however, archaeologists have discovered other early civilizations. One of these flourished in Central Asia (in what are now the republics of Turkmenistan and Uzbekistan) around four thousand years ago. People in this civilization built mudbrick buildings, raised sheep and goats, had bronze tools, used a system of irrigation to grow wheat and barley, and developed a writing system.

Another early civilization emerged in the Supe River Valley of Peru. At the center of this civilization was the city of Caral, which flourished around 2600 BCE. It contained buildings for officials, apartment buildings, and grand residences, all built of stone. The inhabitants of Caral also developed a system of irrigation by diverting a river more than a mile upstream into their fields. This Peruvian culture reached its height during the first millennium BCE (see Chapter 6).

 HISTORIANS DEBATE 1–2b **Why Did Early Civilizations Develop?**

Since civilizations developed independently in different parts of the world, can general causes be identified that would explain why all of these civilizations emerged? A number of possible explanations of the beginning of civilization have been suggested. One theory maintains that challenges forced human beings to make efforts that resulted in the rise of civilization. Some scholars have adhered to a material explanation and have argued that material forces, such as the accumulation of food surpluses, made possible the specialization of labor and development of large communities with bureaucratic organization. But some areas, such as that of the Fertile Crescent, in which civilization emerged in Southwest Asia, were not naturally conducive to agriculture. Abundant food could be produced only through a massive human effort to manage the water, an undertaking that required organization and bureaucratic control and led to civilized cities. Other historians have argued that nonmaterial forces, primarily religious, provided the sense of unity and purpose that made such organized activities possible. Finally, some scholars doubt that we will ever discover the actual causes of early civilization.

1–3 CIVILIZATION IN MESOPOTAMIA

Q Focus Question: How are the chief characteristics of civilization evident in ancient Mesopotamia?

The Greeks spoke of the valley between the Tigris and Euphrates Rivers as Mesopotamia (mess-uh-puh-TAY-mee-uh), the land "between the rivers." The region receives little rain, but the soil of the plain of southern Mesopotamia was enlarged and enriched over the years by layers of silt deposited by the two rivers. In late spring, the Tigris and Euphrates overflow their banks and deposit their fertile silt, but since this flooding depends on the melting of snows in the upland mountains where the rivers begin, it is irregular and sometimes catastrophic. In such circumstances, farming could be accomplished only with human intervention in the form of irrigation and drainage ditches. A complex system was required to control the flow of the rivers and produce the crops. Large-scale irrigation made possible the expansion of agriculture in this region, and the abundant food provided the material base for the emergence of civilization in Mesopotamia.

1–3a The City-States of Ancient Mesopotamia

The creators of the first Mesopotamian civilization were the Sumerians (soo-MER-ee-unz *or* soo-MEER-ee-unz), a people whose origins remain unclear. By 3000 BCE, they had established a number of independent cities in southern Mesopotamia, including Eridu, Ur, Uruk, Umma, and Lagash (see Map 1.3). As the cities expanded, they came to exercise political and economic control over the surrounding countryside, forming city-states, which were the basic units of Sumerian civilization.

Sumerian Cities Walls surrounded Sumerian cities. Uruk, for example, was encircled by a wall 6 miles long with defense towers located every 30 to 35 feet along it. City dwellings, built of sun-dried bricks, included both the small flats of peasants and the larger dwellings of the civic and priestly officials. Although Mesopotamia had little stone or wood for building purposes, it did have plenty of mud. Mudbricks, easily shaped by hand, were left to bake in the hot sun until they were hard enough to use for building. People in Mesopotamia were remarkably innovative with mudbricks, inventing the arch and the dome and constructing some of the largest brick buildings in the world.

The most prominent building in a Sumerian city was the temple, which was dedicated to the chief god or goddess of the city and often built atop a massive stepped tower called a **ziggurat** (ZIG-uh-rat). The Sumerians believed that gods and goddesses owned the cities, and much wealth was used to build temples as well as elaborate houses for the priests and priestesses who served the deities. Priests and priestesses, who supervised the temples and their property, had great power. In fact, historians believe that in the early stages of certain city-states, priests and priestesses may have had an important role in governance. The Sumerians believed that the gods ruled the cities, making the state a **theocracy** (government by a divine authority). Ruling power, however, was primarily in the hands of worldly figures known as kings.

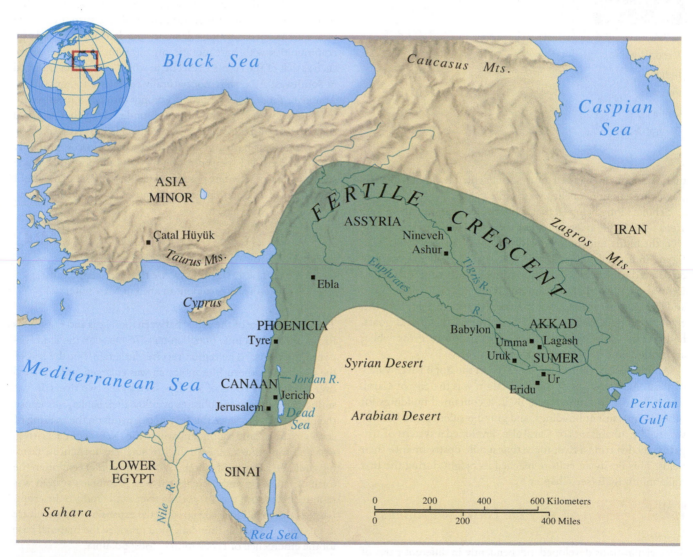

Map 1.3 The Ancient Near East. The Fertile Crescent encompassed land with access to water. Employing flood management and irrigation systems, the peoples of the region established civilizations based on agriculture. These civilizations developed writing, law codes, and economic specialization.

Q *What geographic aspects of the Mesopotamian city-states made conflict between them likely?*

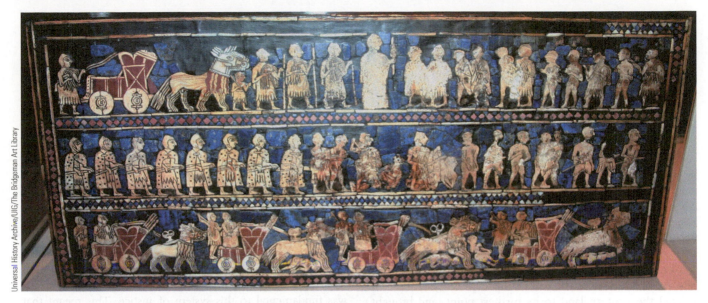

The "Royal Standard" of Ur. This detail is from the "Royal Standard" of Ur, a box dating from around 2700 BCE that was discovered in a stone tomb from the royal cemetery of the Sumerian city-state of Ur. The scenes on one side of the box depict the activities of the king and his military forces. Shown in the bottom panel are four Sumerian battle chariots. Each chariot held two men, one who held the reins and the other armed with a spear for combat. A special compartment in the chariot held a number of spears. The charging chariots are seen defeating the enemy. In the middle band, the Sumerian soldiers round up the captured enemies. In the top band, the captives are presented to the king, who has alighted from his chariot and is shown standing above all the others in the center of the panel.

Kingship Sumerians viewed kingship as divine in origin—kings, they believed, derived their power from the gods and were the agents of the gods. As one person said in a petition to his king, "You in your judgment, you are the son of Anu [god of the sky]; your commands, like the word of a god, cannot be reversed; your words, like rain pouring down from heaven, are without number."[2] Regardless of their origins, kings had power—they led armies and organized workers for the irrigation projects on which Mesopotamian farming depended. The army, the government bureaucracy, and the priests and priestesses all aided the kings in their rule. Befitting their power, Sumerian kings lived in large palaces with their wives and children.

Economy and Society The economy of the Sumerian city-states was primarily agricultural, but commerce and industry became important as well. The people of Mesopotamia produced woolen textiles, pottery, and metalwork. The Sumerians imported copper, tin, and timber in exchange for dried fish, wool, barley, wheat, and metal goods. Traders traveled by land to the eastern Mediterranean in the west and by sea to India in the east. The introduction of the wheel, which had been invented around 3000 BCE by nomadic people living in the region north of the Black Sea, led to carts with wheels that made the transport of goods easier.

Sumerian city-states probably contained four major social groups: elites, dependent commoners, free commoners, and slaves. Elites included royal and priestly officials and their families. Dependent commoners included the elites' clients, who worked for the palace and temple estates. Free commoners worked as farmers, merchants, fishers, scribes, and craftspeople. Probably 90 percent or more of the population were farmers. Slaves belonged to palace officials, who used them in building projects; to temple officials, who used mostly female slaves to weave cloth and grind grain; and to rich landowners, who used them for agricultural and domestic work.

1-3b Empires in Ancient Mesopotamia

As the number of Sumerian city-states grew and the states expanded, new conflicts arose as city-state fought city-state for control of land and water. The fortunes of various city-states rose and fell over the centuries. The constant wars, with their burning and sacking of cities, left many Sumerians in deep despair, as is evident in the words of this Sumerian poem from the city of Ur:

> Ur is destroyed, bitter is its lament.
> The country's blood now fills its holes like hot bronze in a mold.
> Bodies dissolve like fat in the sun.
> Our temple is destroyed, the gods have abandoned us, like
>   migrating birds.
> Smoke lies on our city like a shroud.[3]

The Akkadian Empire Located in the flat land of Mesopotamia, the Sumerian city-states were also open to invasion. To the north of the Sumerian city-states were the Akkadians (uh-KAY-dee-unz). We call them a Semitic people because of the type of language they spoke (see Table 1.1). Around 2340 BCE, Sargon, leader of the Akkadians, overran the Sumerian city-states and established a dynastic empire. Sargon

TABLE 1.1	Some Semitic Languages	
Akkadian	*Assyrian*	Hebrew
Arabic	*Babylonian*	*Phoenician*
Aramaic	*Canaanitic*	*Syriac*

Note: Languages in italic type are no longer spoken.

used the former rulers of the conquered city-states as his governors. His power was based on the military, namely, his standing army of 5,400 men. Sargon's empire, including all of Mesopotamia as well as lands westward to the Mediterranean, inspired generations of Near Eastern leaders to emulate his accomplishment. Even in the first millennium BCE, Sargon was still remembered in chronicles as a king of Akkad who "had no rival or equal, spread his splendor over all the lands, and crossed the sea in the east. In his eleventh year, he conquered the western land to its furthest point, and brought it under his sole authority."[4] Attacks from neighboring hill peoples eventually caused the Akkadian empire to fall, and its end by 2100 BCE brought a return to independent city-states and the conflicts between them. It was not until 1792 BCE that a new empire came to control much of Mesopotamia under Hammurabi (ham-uh-RAH-bee), who ruled over the Amorites or Old Babylonians, a large group of Semitic-speaking seminomads.

Hammurabi's Empire Hammurabi (1792–1750 BCE) employed a well-disciplined army of foot soldiers who carried axes, spears, and copper or bronze daggers. He learned to divide his opponents and subdue them one by one. Using such methods, he gained control of Sumer and Akkad, creating a new Mesopotamian kingdom. After his conquests, he called himself "the sun of Babylon, the king who has made the four quarters of the world subservient," and established a new capital at Babylon.

Hammurabi's Empire

- Hammurabi's empire
- Sumerian civilization

Hammurabi, the man of war, was also a man of peace. A collection of his letters, found by archaeologists, reveals that he took a strong interest in state affairs. He built temples, defensive walls, and irrigation canals; encouraged trade; and brought about an economic revival. Indeed, Hammurabi saw himself as a shepherd to his people: "I am indeed the shepherd who brings peace, whose scepter is just. My benevolent shade was spread over my city. I held the people of the lands of Sumer and Akkad safely on my lap."[5] After his death, however, a series of weak kings were unable to keep Hammurabi's empire united, and it finally fell to new invaders.

The Code of Hammurabi: Society in Mesopotamia Hammurabi is best remembered for his law code, a collection of 282 laws. Although many scholars today view Hammurabi's collection less as a code of laws and more as an attempt by Hammurabi to portray himself as the source of justice to his people, the code still gives us a glimpse of the Mesopotamian society of his time (see "The Code of Hammurabi").

The Code of Hammurabi reveals a society with a system of strict justice. Penalties for criminal offenses were severe and varied according to the social class of the victim. A crime against a member of the upper class (a noble) by a member of the lower class (a commoner) was punished more severely than the same offense against a member of the lower class. Moreover, the principle of "an eye for an eye, a tooth for a tooth" was fundamental to this system of justice. This meant that punishments should fit the crime: "If a freeman has destroyed the eye of a member of the aristocracy, they shall destroy his eye" (Code of Hammurabi, No. 196). Hammurabi's code also had an impact on legal ideas in Southwest Asia for hundreds of years, as the following verse from the Hebrew Bible (Leviticus 24:19–20) demonstrates: "If anyone injures his neighbor, whatever he has done must be done to him: fracture for fracture, eye for eye, tooth for tooth. As he has injured the other, so he is to be injured."

The largest category of laws in the Code of Hammurabi focused on marriage and the family. Parents arranged marriages for their children. After marriage, the parties involved signed a marriage contract; without it, no one was considered legally married. While the husband provided a bridal payment to the bride's parents, the woman's parents were responsible for a dowry to the new husband.

As in many patriarchal societies, women possessed far fewer privileges and rights in the married relationship than men. A woman's place was in the home, and failure to fulfill her expected duties was grounds for divorce. If she was not able to bear children, her husband could divorce her. Furthermore, a wife who was a "gadabout, . . . neglecting her house [and] humiliating her husband, shall be prosecuted" (No. 143). We do know that in practice not all women remained at home. Some worked in the fields and others in business, where they were especially prominent in running taverns.

Women had some rights, however. If a woman was divorced without good reason, she received the dowry back. A woman could seek a divorce and get her dowry back if her husband was unable to show that she had done anything wrong. In theory, a wife was guaranteed the use of her husband's legal property in the event of his death. A mother could also decide which of her sons would receive an inheritance.

Sexual relations were strictly regulated as well. Husbands, but not wives, were permitted sexual activity outside marriage. A wife and her lover caught committing adultery were pitched into the river, although if the husband pardoned his wife, the king could pardon the guilty man. Incest was strictly forbidden.

THE CODE OF HAMMURABI

ALTHOUGH IT IS NOT THE EARLIEST MESOPOTAMIAN LAW CODE, Hammurabi's is the most complete. The code emphasizes the principle of retribution ("an eye for an eye") and punishments that vary according to social status. Punishments could be severe. The following selections illustrate these concerns.

The Code of Hammurabi

25. If a fire break out in a man's house and a man who goes to extinguish it cast his eye on the furniture of the owner of the house and take the furniture of the owner of the house, that free man shall be thrown into that fire.

129. If the wife of a man be taken in lying with another man, they shall bind them and throw them into the water. If the husband of the woman would save his wife, or if the king would save his male servant (he may).

131. If a man accuse his wife and she has not been taken in lying with another man, she shall take an oath in the name of god and she shall return to her house.

196. If a man destroy the eye of another man, they shall destroy his eye.

198. If one destroy the eye of a freeman or break the bone of a freeman, he shall pay one mina of silver.

199. If one destroy the eye of a man's slave or break a bone of a man's slave, he shall pay one-half his price.

209. If a man strike a man's daughter and bring about a miscarriage, he shall pay ten shekels of silver for her miscarriage.

210. If that woman die, they shall put his daughter to death.

211. If, through a stroke, he bring about a miscarriage to the daughter of a freeman, he shall pay five shekels of silver.

212. If that woman die, he shall pay one-half mina of silver.

213. If he strike the female slave of a man and bring about a miscarriage, he shall pay two shekels of silver.

214. If that female slave die, he shall pay one-third mina of silver.

 What do these points of law from the Code of Hammurabi reveal to you about Mesopotamian society?

Source: Pritchard, James B., ed., *Ancient Near Eastern Texts Relating to the Old Testament*, 3rd Edition with Supplement. Copyright 1950, 1955, 1969, renewed 1978 by Princeton University Press.

If a father had incestuous relations with his daughter, he would be banished. Incest between a son and his mother resulted in both being burned.

Fathers ruled their children as well as their wives. Obedience was duly expected: "If a son has struck his father, they shall cut off his hand" (No. 195). If a son committed a serious enough offense, his father could disinherit him, although fathers were not permitted to disinherit their sons arbitrarily.

1–3c The Culture of Mesopotamia

A spiritual worldview was of fundamental importance to Mesopotamian culture. To the peoples of Mesopotamia, the gods were living realities who affected all aspects of life. It was crucial, therefore, that the correct hierarchies be observed. Leaders could prepare armies for war, but success really depended on a favorable relationship with the gods. This helps explain the importance of the priestly class and is the reason why even the kings took great care to dedicate offerings and monuments to the gods.

The Importance of Religion The physical environment had an obvious impact on the Mesopotamian view of the universe. Ferocious floods, heavy downpours, scorching winds, and oppressive humidity were all part of the Mesopotamian climate. These conditions and the resulting famines easily convinced Mesopotamians that this world was controlled by supernatural forces and that the days of human beings "are numbered; whatever he may do, he is but wind," as *The Epic of Gilgamesh*

put it. In the presence of nature, Mesopotamians could easily feel helpless, as this poem relates:

> *The rampant flood which no man can oppose,*
> *Which shakes the heavens and causes earth to tremble,*
> *In an appalling blanket folds mother and child,*
> *Beats down the canebrake's full luxuriant greenery,*
> *And drowns the harvest in its time of ripeness.*[6]

The Mesopotamians discerned cosmic rhythms in the universe and accepted its order but perceived that it was not completely safe because of the presence of willful, powerful cosmic powers that they identified with gods and goddesses.

With its numerous gods and goddesses animating all aspects of the universe, Mesopotamian religion was a form of **polytheism**. The four most important deities were An, god of the sky and hence the most important force in the universe; Enlil (EN-lil), god of wind; Enki (EN-kee), god of the earth, rivers, wells, and canals as well as inventions and crafts; and Ninhursaga (nin-HUR-sah-guh), a goddess associated with soil, mountains, and vegetation, who came to be worshiped as a mother goddess, a "mother of all children," who manifested her power by giving birth to kings and conferring the royal insignia on them.

Human relationships with the gods were based on subservience since, according to Sumerian myth, human beings were created to do the manual labor the gods were unwilling to do for themselves. Moreover, humans were insecure because they could never predict the gods' actions. But humans did attempt to relieve their anxiety by discovering the intentions of the gods through **divination**.

Divination took a variety of forms. A common form, at least for kings and priests who could afford it, involved killing animals, such as sheep or goats, and examining their livers or other organs. Supposedly, features seen in the organs of the sacrificed animals foretold events to come. Thus, one handbook states that if the animal organ has shape *x*, the outcome of the military campaign will be *y*. The Mesopotamian arts of divination arose out of the desire to discover the purposes of the gods. If people could decipher the signs that foretold events, the events would be predictable and humans could act wisely.

The Cultivation of Writing and Sciences The realization of writing's great potential was another aspect of Mesopotamian culture. The oldest Mesopotamian texts date to around 3000 BCE and were written by the Sumerians, who used a **cuneiform** ("wedge-shaped") system of writing. Using a reed stylus, they made wedge-shaped impressions on clay tablets, which were then baked or dried in the sun. Once dried, these tablets were virtually indestructible, and the several hundred thousand that have been found so far have been a valuable source of information for modern scholars. Sumerian writing evolved from pictures of concrete objects to simplified and stylized signs, leading eventually to a phonetic system that made possible the written expression of abstract ideas.

Mesopotamian peoples used writing primarily for record keeping, but cuneiform texts were also used in schools set up to teach the cuneiform system of writing. The primary goal of scribal education was to produce professionally trained scribes for careers in the temples and palaces, the military, and government service. Pupils were male and primarily from wealthy families.

Writing was important because it enabled a society to keep records and maintain knowledge of previous practices and events (see Comparative Illustration "Early Writing" on p. 17). Writing also made it possible for people to communicate ideas in new ways, which is especially evident in the most famous piece of Mesopotamian literature, *The Epic of Gilgamesh*, an epic poem that records the exploits of a legendary king of Uruk. Gilgamesh (GILL-guh-mesh), wise, strong, and perfect in body, part man and part god, befriends a hairy beast named Enkidu. Together they set off in pursuit of heroic deeds. When Enkidu dies, Gilgamesh experiences the pain of mortality and begins a search for the secret of immortality. He finds Utnapishtim, who was granted immortality by the gods after he survived the Great Flood sent by the gods to destroy humankind (see Opposing Viewpoints "The Great Flood: Two Versions" p. 18). Utnapishtim tries to help Gilgamesh gain immortality, but his efforts fail, and Gilgamesh remains mortal. The desire for immortality, one of humankind's great searches, ends in complete frustration. "Everlasting life," as this Mesopotamian epic makes clear, is only for the gods.

Mesopotamians also made outstanding achievements in mathematics and astronomy. In math, the Sumerians devised a number system based on 60, using combinations of 6 and 10 for practical solutions. Geometry was used to measure fields and erect buildings. In astronomy, the Sumerians made use of units of 60 and charted the heavenly constellations. Their calendar was based on twelve lunar months and was brought into harmony with the solar year by adding an extra month from time to time.

Pictographic sign, c. 3100 BCE									
Interpretation	star	?sun over horizon	?stream	ear of barley	bull's head	bowl	head + bowl	lower leg	?shrouded body
Cuneiform sign, c. 2400 BCE									
Cuneiform sign c. 700 BCE (turned through 90°)									
Phonetic value*	dingir, an	u₄, ud	a	še	gu₄	nig₂, ninda	ku₂	du, gin, gub	lu₂
Meaning	god, sky	day, sun	water, seed, son	barley	ox	food, bread	to eat	to walk, to stand	man

*Some signs have more than one phonetic value and some sounds are represented by more than one sign; for example, u_4 means the fourth sign with the phonetic value *u*.

The Development of Cuneiform Writing. This chart shows the evolution of writing from pictographic signs around 3100 BCE to cuneiform signs by about 700 BCE. Note that the sign for *star* came to mean "god" or "sky." Pictographic signs for *head* and *bowl* came eventually to mean "to eat" in their simplified cuneiform version.

© Sandro Vannini/CORBIS

Early Writing. Pictured in A is the upper part of the cone of Uruinimgina, covered in cuneiform script from an early Sumerian dynasty. The first Egyptian writing was also pictographic, as shown in the hieroglyphs in the detail from the mural in the tomb of Ramesses I in B. In Central America, the Mayan civilization had a well-developed writing system, also based on hieroglyphs, as seen in C in the text carved on a stone platform in front of the Palace of the Large Masks in Kabah, Mexico.

Q *What common feature is evident in these early writing systems? How might you explain that?*

A

RMN-Grand Palais/Art Resource, NY

C

Erich Lessing/Art Resource, NY

1–4 EGYPTIAN CIVILIZATION: "THE GIFT OF THE NILE"

Q **Focus Questions:** What are the basic features of the three major periods of Egyptian history? What elements of continuity are evident in the three periods? What are their major differences?

"The Egyptian Nile," wrote one Arab traveler, "surpasses all the rivers of the world in sweetness of taste, in length of course and usefulness. No other river in the world can show such a continuous series of towns and villages along its banks." The Nile River was crucial to the development of Egyptian civilization (see "The Significance of the Nile River and the Pharaoh" on p. 19). Egypt, like Mesopotamia, was a river valley civilization.

1–4a The Impact of Geography

The Nile is a unique river, beginning in the heart of Africa and coursing northward for thousands of miles. It is the longest river in the world. The Nile was responsible for creating an area several miles wide on both banks of the river that was fertile and capable of producing abundant harvests. The "miracle" of the Nile was its annual flooding. The river rose in the summer from rains in Central Africa, crested in Egypt in September and October, and left a deposit of silt that enriched the soil. The Egyptians called this fertile land the "Black Land" because it was dark in color from the silt and the crops that grew on it so densely. Beyond these narrow strips of fertile fields lay the deserts (the "Red Land"). About 100 miles before it empties into the Mediterranean, the river splits into two major branches, forming the delta, a triangular-shaped territory called Lower Egypt to distinguish it from Upper Egypt, the land upstream

The Great Flood: Two Versions

BOTH THE MESOPOTAMIAN POEM, *THE EPIC OF GILGAMESH*, AND THE HEBREW BIBLE (OLD TESTAMENT) include accounts of a great flood. In the first selection, taken from the *The Epic of Gilgamesh*, Utnapishtim tells Gilgamesh the story of how he survived the flood unleashed by the gods to destroy humankind. Utnapishtim recounts how the god Ea advised him to build a boat and how he came to land the boat at the end of the flood. The second selection is the account of the great flood that appears in the book of Genesis in the Hebrew Bible. The biblical Noah appears to be a later version of the Mesopotamian Utnapishtim.

The Epic of Gilgamesh

In those days the world teemed, the people multiplied, the world bellowed like a wild bull, and the great god was aroused by the clamor. Enlil heard the clamor and he said to the gods in council, "The uproar of mankind is intolerable and sleep is no longer possible by reason of the babel." So the gods agreed to exterminate mankind. Enlil did this, but Ea [Sumerian Enki, god of the waters] because of his oath warned me in a dream . . . "tear down your house and build a boat, abandon possessions and look for life, despise worldly goods and save your soul alive. Tear down your house, I say, and build a boat. . . . Then take up into the boat the seed of all living creatures. . . ." [Utnapishtim did as he was told, and then the destruction came.]

 For six days and six nights the winds blew, torrent and tempest and flood overwhelmed the world, tempest and flood raged together like warring hosts. When the seventh day dawned the storm from the south subsided, the sea grew calm, the flood was stilled; I looked at the face of the world and there was silence, all mankind was turned to clay. The surface of the sea stretched as flat as a rooftop; I opened a hatch and the light fell on my face. Then I bowed low, I sat down and I wept, the tears streamed down my face, for on every side was the waste of water. I looked for land in vain, but fourteen leagues distant there appeared a mountain, and there the boat grounded; on the mountain of Nisir the boat held fast, she held fast and did not budge.

 . . . When the seventh day dawned I loosed a dove and let her go. She flew away, but finding no resting-place she returned. Then I loosed a swallow, and she flew away but finding no resting-place she returned. I loosed a raven, she saw that the waters had retreated, she ate, she flew around, she

cawed, and she did not come back. Then I threw everything open to the four winds, I made a sacrifice and poured out a libation on the mountain top.

Genesis 6:11–15, 17–19; 7:24; 8:3, 13–21

Now the earth was corrupted in God's sight and was full of violence. God saw how corrupt the earth had become, for all the people on earth had corrupted their ways. So God said to Noah, "I am going to put an end to all people, for the earth is filled with violence because of them. I am surely going to destroy both them and the earth. So make yourself an ark of cypress wood: make rooms in it and coat it with pitch inside and out. . . . I am going to bring flood waters on the earth to destroy all life under the heavens, every creature that has the breath of life in it. Everything on earth will perish. But I will establish my covenant with you, and you will enter the ark—you and your sons and your wife and your sons' wives with you. You are to bring into the ark two of all living creatures, male and female, to keep them alive with you. . . ."

 The waters flooded the earth for a hundred and fifty days. . . . By the first day of the first month of Noah's six hundred and first year, the water had dried up from the earth. Noah then removed the covering from the ark and saw that the surface of the ground was dry. . . . Then God said to Noah, "Come out of the ark, you and your wife and your sons and their wives. Bring out every kind of living creature that is with you—the birds, the animals, and all the creatures that move along the ground—so they can multiply on the earth and be fruitful and increase in number upon it." So Noah came out, together with his sons and his wife and his sons' wives . . . [and all the animals]. Then Noah built an altar to the Lord and, taking some of all the clean animals and clean birds, he sacrificed burnt offerings on it. The Lord smelled the pleasing aroma and said in his heart, "Never again will I curse the ground because of man, even though every inclination of his heart is evil from childhood. And never again will I destroy all living creatures, as I have done."

 What does the selection from The Epic of Gilgamesh *tell you about the relationship between the Mesopotamians and their gods? How might you explain the similarities and differences between this account and the biblical flood story in Genesis?*

Sources: From *The Epic of Gilgamesh* translated with an introduction by N. K. Sandars (Penguin Classics 1960). *The Holy Bible, New International Version* (Colorado Springs, CO: Biblica, 1973).

THE SIGNIFICANCE OF THE NILE RIVER AND THE PHARAOH

Religion & Philosophy TWO OF THE MOST IMPORTANT SOURCES OF LIFE for the ancient Egyptians were the Nile River and the pharaoh. Egyptians perceived that the Nile made possible the abundant food that was a major source of their well-being. This *Hymn to the Nile*, probably from the nineteenth and twentieth dynasties in the New Kingdom, expresses the gratitude Egyptians felt for the great river.

Hymn to the Nile

Hail to you, O Nile, that issues from the earth and comes to keep
Egypt alive! . . .
He that waters the meadows which Re created, in order to keep
every kid alive.
He that makes to drink the desert and the place distant from
water: that is his dew coming down from heaven. . . .
The lord of fishes, he who makes the marsh-birds to go
upstream. . . .
He who makes barley and brings emmer [wheat] into being,
that he may make the temples festive.
If he is sluggish, then nostrils are stopped up, and everybody
is poor. . . .
When he rises, then the land is in jubilation, then every belly
is in joy, every backbone takes on laughter, and every tooth
is exposed.
The bringer of good, rich in provisions, creator of all good, lord
of majesty, sweet of fragrance. . . .
He who makes every beloved tree to grow, without lack of them.

The Egyptian king, or pharaoh, was viewed as a god and the absolute ruler of Egypt. His significance and the gratitude of the Egyptian people for his existence are evident in this hymn from the reign of Sesotris III (c. 1880–1840 BCE).

Hymn to the Pharaoh

He has come to us, he has taken the land of the well,
the double crown [crown of Upper and Lower Egypt] is placed
on his head.
He has come, he has united the two lands,
he has joined the kingdom of the upper land with the lower.
He has come, he has ruled Egypt,
he has placed the desert in his power.
He has come, he has protected the two lands,
he has given peace in the two regions.
He has come, he has made Egypt to live,
he has destroyed its afflictions.
He has come, he has made the aged to live,
he has opened the breath of the people.
He has come, he has trampled on the nations,
he has smitten the [enemies], who knew not his terror.
He has come, he has protected his frontier,
he has rescued the robbed.

 How do these two hymns underscore the importance of the Nile River and the institution of the pharaoh to Egyptian civilization?

Sources: Pritchard, James B., ed., *Ancient Near Eastern Texts Relating to the Old Testament*, 3rd Edition with Supplement. Copyright © 1950, 1955, 1969, renewed 1978 by Princeton University Press. W. M. Flinders-Petrie, *A History of Egypt*, Fifth Edition (Methuen & Co.: London, 1903), Vol. 1, p. 183.

to the south (see Map 1.4). Egypt's important cities developed at the tip of the delta. Even today, most of Egypt's people are crowded along the banks of the Nile River.

Unlike Mesopotamia's rivers, the flooding of the Nile was gradual and usually predictable, and the river itself was seen as life-enhancing, not life-threatening. Although a system of organized irrigation was still necessary, the small villages along the Nile could create such systems without the massive state intervention that was required in Mesopotamia. Egyptian civilization consequently tended to remain more rural, with many small population centers congregated along a narrow band on both sides of the Nile.

The surpluses of food that Egyptian farmers grew in the fertile Nile Valley made Egypt prosperous. But the Nile also served as a unifying factor in Egyptian history. In ancient times, the Nile was the fastest way to travel through the land, making both transportation and communication easier. Winds from the north pushed sailboats south, and the current of the Nile carried them north.

Unlike Mesopotamia, which was subject to constant invasion, Egypt had natural barriers that fostered isolation,

protected it from invasion, and gave it a sense of security. These barriers included deserts to the west and east; cataracts (rapids) on the southern part of the river, which made defense relatively easy; and the Mediterranean Sea to the north. These barriers, however, were effective only when combined with Egyptian fortifications at strategic locations. Nor did these barriers prevent the development of trade. Indeed, there is evidence of very early trade between Egypt and Mesopotamia.

The regularity of the Nile floods and the relative isolation of the Egyptians created a sense of security and a feeling of changelessness. To the ancient Egyptians, when the Nile flooded each year, "the fields laugh, and people's faces light up." Unlike people in Mesopotamia, Egyptians faced life with a spirit of confidence in the stability of things. Ancient Egyptian civilization was characterized by a remarkable degree of continuity for thousands of years.

1–4b The Old and Middle Kingdoms

Modern historians have divided Egyptian history into three major periods, known as the Old Kingdom, the Middle Kingdom, and the New Kingdom. These were periods of long-term

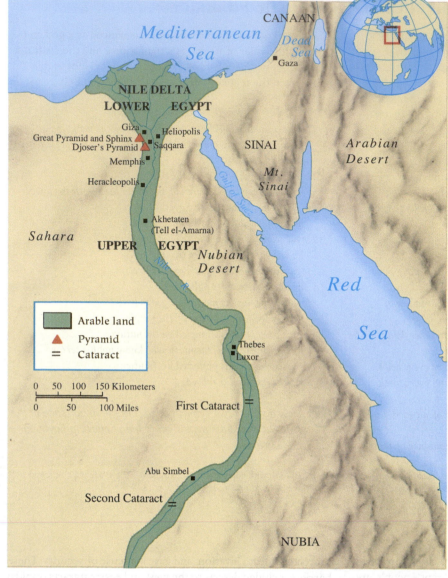

Map 1.4 Ancient Egypt. Egyptian civilization centered on the life-giving water and flood silts of the Nile River, with most of the population living in Lower Egypt, where the river splits to form the Nile delta. Most of the pyramids, built during the Old Kingdom, are clustered south and west of Cairo.

Q *How did the lands to the east and west of the river help to protect Egypt from invasion?*

and Lower Egypt into a single kingdom. Henceforth, the king would be called "king of Upper and Lower Egypt," and a royal crown, the Double Crown, was created, combining the White Crown of Upper Egypt and the Red Crown of Lower Egypt. Just as the Nile served to unite Upper and Lower Egypt physically, the king served to unite the two areas politically.

The Old Kingdom encompassed the fourth through eighth dynasties of Egyptian kings, lasting from around 2575 to 2125 BCE. It was an age of prosperity and splendor, made visible in the construction of the greatest and largest pyramids in Egypt's history. The capital of the Old Kingdom was located at Memphis, south of the delta.

Kingship was a divine institution in ancient Egypt and formed part of a universal cosmic scheme (see "The Significance of the Nile River and the Pharaoh" on p. 19): "What is the king of Upper and Lower Egypt? He is a god by whose dealings one lives, the father and mother of all men, alone by himself, without an equal."[7] In obeying their king, subjects helped maintain the cosmic order. A breakdown in royal power could only mean that citizens were offending divinity and weakening the universal structure. Among the various titles of Egyptian kings, that of **pharaoh** (originally meaning "great house" or "palace") eventually came to be the most common.

Although they possessed absolute power, Egyptian kings were supposed to rule not arbitrarily but according to set principles. The chief principle was called *Ma'at* (MAH-ut), a spiritual precept that conveyed the ideas of truth and justice and especially right order and harmony. To ancient Egyptians, this fundamental order and harmony had existed throughout the universe since the beginning of time. Pharaohs were the divine instruments who maintained it and were themselves subject to it.

Although theoretically absolute in their power, in practice Egyptian kings did not rule alone. Initially, members of the king's family performed administrative tasks, but by the fourth dynasty, a bureaucracy with regular procedures had developed. Especially important was the office of vizier, "steward of the whole land." Directly responsible to the king, the vizier was in charge of the bureaucracy. For administrative purposes, Egypt was divided into provinces, or *nomes* as they were later called by the Greeks—twenty-two in Upper Egypt and twenty

stability characterized by strong monarchical authority, competent bureaucracy, freedom from invasion, much construction of temples and pyramids, and considerable intellectual and cultural activity. But between the periods of stability were intervals known as the Intermediate Periods, characterized by weak political structures and rivalry for leadership, invasions, a decline in building activity, and a restructuring of society.

The Old Kingdom According to the Egyptians' own tradition, their land consisted initially of numerous populated areas ruled by tribal chieftains. Around 3100 BCE, the first Egyptian royal dynasty, under a king called Menes, united Upper in Lower Egypt. A governor, called by the Greeks a *nomarch*, was head of each nome and was responsible to the king and vizier. Nomarchs, however, tended to build up large holdings of land and power within their nomes, creating a potential rivalry with the pharaohs.

The Middle Kingdom Despite the theory of divine order, the Old Kingdom eventually collapsed, ushering in a period of disarray. Finally, a new royal dynasty managed to pacify all Egypt and inaugurated the Middle Kingdom, a period of stability lasting from around 2010 to 1630 BCE. Egyptians later portrayed the Middle Kingdom as a golden age, a clear indication of its stability. Several factors contributed to its vitality. The nome structure was reorganized. The boundaries of each nome were now settled precisely, and the obligations of the nomes to the state were clearly delineated. Nomarchs were confirmed as hereditary officeholders but with the understanding that their duties must be performed faithfully. These included the collection of taxes for the state and the recruitment of labor forces for royal projects, such as stone quarrying.

The Middle Kingdom was characterized by a new concern of the pharaohs for the people. In the Old Kingdom, the pharaoh had been viewed as an inaccessible god-king. Now he was portrayed as the shepherd of his people with the responsibility to build public works and provide for the public welfare. As one pharaoh expressed it, "He [a particular god] created me as one who should do that which he had done, and to carry out that which he commanded should be done. He appointed me herdsman of this land, for he knew who would keep it in order for him."[8]

1–4c Society and Economy in Ancient Egypt

Egyptian society had a simple structure in the Old and Middle Kingdoms; basically, it was organized along hierarchical lines with the god-king at the top. An upper class of nobles and priests aided the king and participated in the elaborate rituals of life that surrounded the pharaoh. This ruling class ran the government and managed its own landed estates, which provided much of its wealth.

Below the upper classes were merchants and artisans. Merchants engaged in an active trade up and down the Nile as well as in town and village markets. Some merchants also engaged in international trade; the king sent them to Crete and Syria, where they obtained wood and other products. Expeditions traveled into Nubia for ivory and down the Red Sea to Punt for incense and spices. Eventually, trade links were established between ports in the Red Sea and countries as far away as the Indonesian archipelago. Egyptian artisans made an incredible variety of well-built and beautiful goods: stone dishes; painted boxes made of clay; wooden furniture; gold, silver, and copper tools and containers; paper and rope made of papyrus; and linen clothes.

By far the largest number of people in Egypt simply worked the land. In theory, the king owned all the land but granted

The Making of Jewelry. In ancient Egypt, people used jewelry for self-adornment as well as a mark of social status. This photo of a wall fragment from a tomb in Thebes around 1400 BCE shows jewelers and metal craftspeople at work. At the top, jewelers are seen drilling holes in hard-stone beads with three or four bow drills. The beads were then polished and strung in collars, as seen in the lower panel. The Trustees of the British Museum/Art Resource, NY

portions of it to his subjects. Large sections were in the possession of nobles and the temple complexes. Most of the lower classes were serfs, or common people bound to the land, who cultivated the estates. They paid taxes in the form of crops to the king, nobles, and priests; lived in small villages or towns; and provided military service and forced labor for building projects.

1–4d The Culture of Egypt

Egypt produced a culture that dazzled and awed its later conquerors. The Egyptians' technical achievements, especially visible in the construction of the pyramids, demonstrated a measure of skill unequaled in the world at that time. To the Egyptians, all of these achievements were part of a cosmic order suffused with the presence of the divine.

Spiritual Life in Egyptian Society The Egyptians had no word for religion because it was an inseparable element of the entire world order to which Egyptian society belonged. Egypt was part of the universal cosmic scheme, and the pharaoh was the divine being whose function was to maintain Egypt's stability within the cosmic order.

This perspective helps explain the importance of ritual in ancient Egypt. Through their rituals, Egyptians worked to maintain the cosmic order by appeasing the gods and goddesses who controlled the universe. Egyptian ritual ceremonies focused on an image of a deity, providing it with food and sustenance and thereby performing an act of ritual worship to appease the god. The pharaoh was at the heart of Egypt's ritual life. He supervised the sacred ceremonies that were performed in the temples, although it was the pharaoh's religious deputies—the priests—who executed the daily ceremonies.

The Egyptians had a remarkable number of gods associated with heavenly bodies and natural forces, hardly unusual in view of the importance to Egypt's well-being of the sun, the river, and the fertile land along its banks. The sun was the source of life and hence worthy of worship. A sun cult developed, and the sun god took on different forms and names, depending on his specific role. He was worshiped as Atum in human form and also as Re, who had a human body but the head of a falcon. The pharaoh took the title of "Son of Re" because he was regarded as the earthly embodiment of Re.

River and land deities included Osiris (oh-SY-russ) and Isis (Y-sis) with their child Horus, who was related to the Nile and to the sun as well. Osiris became especially important as a symbol of resurrection or rebirth. A famous Egyptian myth told of the struggle between Osiris, who brought civilization to Egypt, and his evil brother Seth, who killed him, cut his body into fourteen parts, and tossed them into the Nile River. Isis, the faithful wife of Osiris, found the pieces and, with help from other gods, restored Osiris to life. As a symbol of resurrection and as judge of the dead, Osiris took on an important role for the Egyptians. By identifying with Osiris, one could hope to gain new life just as Osiris had done. The dead, embalmed and mummified, were placed in tombs (in the case of kings, in pyramidal tombs), given the name of Osiris, and by a process of magical identification became Osiris. Like Osiris, they could then be reborn. The flood of the Nile and the new life it brought to Egypt were symbolized by Isis gathering all of the parts of Osiris together and were celebrated each spring in the Festival of the New Land.

Later Egyptian spiritual practice began to emphasize morality by stressing the role of Osiris as judge of the dead. The dead were asked to give an account of their earthly deeds so that Osiris could determine whether they deserved a reward. At first, the Osiris cult was reserved for the very wealthy, who could afford to take expensive measures to preserve the body after death. During the Middle Kingdom, however, the cult became "democratized" and was extended to all Egyptians who aspired to an afterlife.

The Pyramids One of the great achievements of Egyptian civilization, the building of pyramids, occurred in the time of the Old Kingdom. Pyramids were built as part of a larger complex of buildings dedicated to the dead—in effect, a city of the dead. The area included a large pyramid for the king's burial, smaller pyramids for his family, and *mastabas*, rectangular structures with flat roofs, as tombs for the pharaoh's noble officials.

The tombs were well prepared for their residents, their rooms furnished and stocked with numerous supplies, including chairs, boats, chests, weapons, games, dishes, and a variety of foods. The Egyptians believed that human beings had two bodies, a physical one and a spiritual one they called the *ka*. If the physical body was properly preserved (by mummification) and the tomb was furnished with all the objects of regular life, the *ka* could return, surrounded by earthly comforts, and continue its life despite the death of the physical body.

To preserve the physical body after death, the Egyptians practiced mummification, a process of slowly drying a dead body to prevent it from decomposing. Special workshops, run by priests, performed this procedure, primarily for the wealthy families who could afford it. According to an ancient Greek historian who visited Egypt around 450 BCE, "The most refined method is as follows: first of all they draw out the brain through the nostrils with an iron hook. . . . Then they make an incision in the flank with a sharp Ethiopian stone through which they extract all the internal organs."[9] The liver, lungs, stomach, and intestines were placed in four special jars that were put in the tomb with the mummy. The priests then covered the corpse with a natural salt that absorbed the body's water. Later, they filled the body with spices and wrapped it with layers of linen soaked in resin. At the end of the process, which took about seventy days, a lifelike mask was placed over the head and shoulders of the mummy, which was then sealed in a case and placed in its tomb.

Pyramids were tombs for the mummified bodies of the pharaohs. The largest and most magnificent of all the pyramids was built under King Khufu. Constructed at Giza around 2540 BCE, this famous Great Pyramid covers 13 acres, measures 756 feet at each side of its base, and stands 481 feet high (see Comparative Illustration "The Pyramid," in Section 6-2c, p. 165). Its four sides are almost precisely oriented to the four points of the compass. The interior included a grand gallery to the burial chamber, which was built of granite with a lidless sarcophagus for the pharaoh's body. The Great Pyramid still stands as a visible symbol of the power of Egyptian kings and the spiritual conviction that underlay Egyptian society. No pyramid built later ever matched its size or splendor. The pyramid was not only the king's tomb; it was also an important symbol of royal power. It could be seen from miles away, a visible reminder of the glory and might of the ruler who was a living god on earth.

Art and Writing Commissioned by kings or nobles for use in temples and tombs, Egyptian art was largely functional. Wall paintings and statues of gods and kings in temples served a strictly spiritual purpose. They were an integral part of the performance of ritual, which was thought necessary to preserve the cosmic order and hence the well-being of Egypt. Likewise, the mural scenes and sculptured figures found in the tombs had a specific function: they were supposed to assist the journey of the deceased into the afterworld.

Egyptian art was also formulaic. Artists and sculptors observed a strict canon of proportions that determined both form and presentation. This canon gave Egyptian art a distinctive appearance for thousands of years. Especially characteristic was the convention of combining the profile, semiprofile, and frontal views of the human body in relief work and painting in order to represent each part of the body accurately. The result was an art that was highly stylized yet still allowed distinctive features to be displayed.

Writing emerged in Egypt during the first two dynasties. The Greeks later called Egyptian writing **hieroglyphics** (HY-uh-roh-glif-iks), meaning "priest-carvings" or "sacred writings." Hieroglyphs were signs that depicted objects and had a sacred value at the same time. Although hieroglyphs were later simplified into two scripts for writing purposes, they never developed into an alphabet. Egyptian hieroglyphs were initially carved in stone, but later the two simplified scripts were written on papyrus, a paper made from the reeds that grew along the Nile. Most of the ancient Egyptian literature that has come down to us was written on papyrus rolls and wooden tablets.

1-4e Disorder and a New Order: The New Kingdom

The Middle Kingdom came to an end around 1650 BCE with the invasion of Egypt by a people from western Asia known to the Egyptians as the Hyksos. The Hyksos used horse-drawn war chariots and overwhelmed the Egyptian soldiers, who fought from donkey carts. For almost a hundred years, the Hyksos ruled much of Egypt, but the conquered took much from their conquerors. From the Hyksos, the Egyptians learned to use bronze in making new farming tools and weapons. They also mastered the military skills of the Hyksos, especially the use of horse-drawn war chariots.

The Egyptian Empire Eventually, a new line of pharaohs—the eighteenth dynasty—made use of the new weapons to throw off Hyksos domination, reunite Egypt, establish the New Kingdom (c. 1539–1069 BCE), and launch the Egyptians along a new militaristic and imperialistic path, characterized by the development of a more professional army. During the period of the New Kingdom, Egypt assembled an empire and became the most powerful state in the Middle East.

Massive wealth aided the power of the New Kingdom pharaohs. The Egyptian rulers showed their wealth by building new temples. Queen Hatshepsut (hat-SHEP-soot) (c. 1503–1480 BCE), in particular, one of the first women to become pharaoh in her own right, built a great temple at Deir el Bahri (dayr ahl BAH-ree) near Thebes. As pharaoh, Hatshepsut sent out military expeditions, encouraged mining, fostered agriculture, and sent a trading expedition up the Nile. Hatshepsut's official statues sometimes show her clothed and bearded like a king. She was referred to as "His Majesty." Hatshepsut was succeeded by her nephew, Thutmosis (thoot-MOH-suss) III (c. 1480–1450 BCE), who led seventeen military campaigns into Syria and Canaan and even reached the Euphrates River. Egyptian forces occupied Canaan and Syria and also moved westward into Libya.

Akhenaten and Religious Change The eighteenth dynasty was not without its troubles, however. Amenhotep (ah-mun-HOH-tep) IV (c. 1353–1336 BCE) introduced the worship of Aten, god of the sun disk, as the supreme god and, later in his reign, as the only god. In the pharaoh's eyes, he and Aten had become co-rulers of Egypt. Changing his own name to Akhenaten (ah-kuh-NAH-tun) ("servant of Aten"), the pharaoh closed the temples of other gods and especially endeavored to lessen the power of the priesthood dedicated to the god Amon-Re at Thebes. Akhenaten strove to reduce the priests' influence by replacing Thebes as the capital of Egypt with Akhetaten (ah-kuh-TAH-tun) ("horizon of Aten"), a new city located at modern Tell el-Amarna, 200 miles north of Thebes. The pharaoh decreed that Akhetaten, not Thebes, would be his final resting place.

Akhenaten's attempt at religious change failed. It was too much to ask Egyptians to give up their traditional ways and beliefs, especially since they saw the destruction of the old gods as subversive of the very cosmic order on which Egypt's survival and continuing prosperity depended. Moreover, the priests at Thebes were unalterably opposed to the changes, which had diminished their influence and power. At the same time, Akhenaten's preoccupation with religion caused him to ignore foreign affairs and led to the loss of both Syria and Canaan. Akhenaten's changes were soon undone after his death by those who influenced his successor, the boy-pharaoh Tutankhamun (too-tang-KAH-mun) (c. 1332–1322 BCE). Tutankhamun returned the government to Thebes and restored the old gods. The Aten experiment had failed to take hold, and the eighteenth dynasty itself soon came to an end.

Decline of the Egyptian Empire The nineteenth dynasty managed to restore Egyptian power one more time. Under Ramesses (RAM-uh-seez) II (c. 1279–1213 BCE), the Egyptians went on the offensive, regained control of Canaan, and restored Egypt as an imperial power. During his long sixty-seven year reign, Ramesses II provided visible demonstrations of his power by constructing mammoth new temple buildings, many of which were characterized by colossal statues of himself.

Bildarchiv Steffens/The Bridgeman Art Library

Statues of Ramesses II at Abu Simbel. After being driven out of Canaan and Syria by the Hittites, the Egyptian empire grew to power one final time under Ramesses II. He succeeded in reconquering Canaan but was unable to restore the boundaries of the previous empire. The massive Temple of Ramesses II, located at Abu Simbel, was carved out of a cliff of Nubian sandstone. The giant statues represent Ramesses II.

Early Dynastic Period (Dynasties 1–3)	c. 3100–2575 BCE
Old Kingdom (Dynasties 4–8)	c. 2575–2125 BCE
First Intermediate Period (Dynasties 9–11)	c. 2125–2010 BCE
Middle Kingdom (Dynasties 12–13)	c. 2010–1630 BCE
Second Intermediate Period (Dynasties 14–17)	c. 1630–1539 BCE
New Kingdom (Dynasties 18–20)	c. 1539–1069 BCE
Post-Empire (Dynasties 21–31)	c. 1069–30 BCE

After the death of Ramesses II, struggles for the throne weakened the government, and new invasions in the thirteenth century by the "Sea Peoples," as the Egyptians called them, destroyed Egyptian power in Canaan and drove the Egyptians back within their old frontiers. The days of Egyptian empire were ended, and the New Kingdom itself expired with the end of the twentieth dynasty in 1069 BCE. For the next thousand years, despite periodical revivals of strength, Egypt was dominated by Libyans, Nubians, Assyrians, Persians, and finally Macedonians, after the conquest of Alexander the Great (see Chapter 4). In the first century BCE, Egypt became a province in Rome's mighty empire.

1–4f Daily Life in Ancient Egypt: Family and Marriage

Ancient Egyptians had a very positive attitude toward daily life on earth and followed the advice of the wisdom literature, which suggested that people marry young and establish a home and family. Monogamy was the general rule, although a husband was allowed to keep additional wives if his first wife was childless. Pharaohs were entitled to harems; the queen, however, was acknowledged as the "great wife," with a status higher than that of the other wives. The husband was master in the house, but wives were very much respected and in charge of the household and the education of the children. From a book of wise sayings (which the Egyptians called "instructions") came this advice:

> If you are a man of standing, you should found your household and love your wife at home as is fitting. Fill her belly; clothe her back. Ointment is the prescription for her body. Make her heart glad as long as you live. She is a profitable field for her lord. You should not contend with her at law, and keep her far from gaining control. . . . Let her heart be soothed through what may accrue to you; it means keeping her long in your house.[10]

Women's property and inheritance remained in their hands, even in marriage. Although most careers and public offices were closed to women, some women did operate businesses. Peasant women worked long hours in the fields and at numerous domestic tasks. Upper-class women could function as priestesses,

and a few queens, such as Hatshepsut, even became pharaohs in their own right.

Parents arranged marriages. The primary concerns were family and property, and the chief purpose of marriage was to produce children, especially sons. From the New Kingdom came this piece of wisdom: "Take to yourself a wife while you are [still] a youth, that she may produce a son for you."[11] Daughters were not slighted, however. Numerous tomb paintings show the close and affectionate relationship parents had with both sons and daughters. Marriages could and did end in divorce, which was allowed, apparently with compensation for the wife. Adultery, however, was strictly prohibited, with stiff punishments—especially for women, who could have their noses cut off or be burned at the stake.

1–4g The Spread of Egyptian Influence: Nubia

The civilization of Egypt had an impact on other peoples in the lands of the eastern Mediterranean. Egyptian products have been found in Crete and Cretan products in Egypt (see Chapter 4). Egyptian influence is also evident in early Greek statues. The Egyptians also had an impact to the south in Nubia (the northern part of modern Sudan). In fact, some archaeologists have recently suggested that the African kingdom of Nubia may have arisen even before the kingdoms of Egypt.

It is clear that contacts between the upper and lower Nile had been established by the late third millennium BCE, when Egyptian merchants traveled to Nubia to obtain ivory, ebony, frankincense, and leopard skins. A few centuries later, Nubia had become an Egyptian tributary. At the end of the second millennium BCE, Nubia profited from the disintegration of the Egyptian New Kingdom to become the independent state of Kush. Egyptian influence continued, however, as Kushite culture borrowed extensively from Egypt, including religious beliefs, the practice of interring kings in pyramids, and hieroglyphs.

But in the first millennium BCE, Kush also had a direct impact on Egypt. During the second half of the eighth century BCE, Kushite monarchs took control of Egypt and formed the twenty-fifth dynasty of Egyptian rulers. It was not until 663 BCE that the last Kushite ruler was expelled from Egypt. During this period, the Kushite rulers of Egypt even aided the Israelites in their struggle with the Assyrians (see "The Hebrews: The 'Children of Israel'" on p. 27).

Although its economy was probably founded primarily on agriculture and animal husbandry, Kush developed into a major trading state in Africa that endured for hundreds of years. Its commercial activities were stimulated by the discovery of iron ore in a floodplain near the river at Meroë. Strategically located at the point where a land route across the desert to the south intersected the Nile River, Meroë eventually became the capital of a new state. In addition to iron products, Kush and Meroë supplied goods from Central and East Africa, notably ivory, gold, ebony, and slaves, to the Romans, Arabia, and India. At first, goods were transported by donkey caravans to the point where the river north was navigable. By the last centuries of the first millennium BCE, however, the donkeys were being replaced by camels, newly introduced from the Arabian peninsula.

Nubians in Egypt. During the New Kingdom, Egypt expanded to include Canaan and Syria to the north and the kingdom of Nubia to the south. Nubia had emerged as an African kingdom around 2300 BCE. Shown in a fourteenth-century BCE painting from an Egyptian official's tomb in Nubia are Nubians arriving in Egypt with bags and rings of gold. Nubia was a major source of gold for the Egyptians.

1–5 NEW CENTERS OF CIVILIZATION

 Focus Questions: What was the significance of the Indo-Europeans? How did Judaism differ from the religions of Mesopotamia and Egypt?

Mesopotamia and Egypt have dominated our story of civilization so far, but significant developments were also taking place on the fringes of these civilizations. Farming had spread into the Balkan peninsula of Europe by 6500 BCE, and by 4000 BCE,

it was well established in southern France, central Europe, and the coastal regions of the Mediterranean. Although migrating farmers from the Anatolian peninsula may have brought some farming techniques into Europe, some historians believe that the Neolithic peoples of Europe domesticated animals and began to farm largely on their own.

One outstanding feature of late Neolithic Europe was the erection of **megaliths** (*megalith* is Greek for "large stone"). Radiocarbon dating, a technique that allows scientists to determine the age of objects, shows that the first megalithic structures were constructed around 4000 BCE, more than a thousand years before the great pyramids were built in Egypt. Between 3200 and 1500 BCE, standing stones, placed in circles or lined up in rows, were erected throughout the British Isles and northwestern France. Other megalithic constructions have been found as far north as Scandinavia and as far south as the islands of Corsica, Sardinia, and Malta. Archaeologists have demonstrated that the stone circles were used as observatories to detect not only such simple astronomical phenomena as the midwinter and midsummer sunrises but also such sophisticated phenomena as the major and minor standstills of the moon.

Stonehenge. The Bronze Age in northwestern Europe is known for its megaliths, large standing stones. Between 3200 and 1500 BCE, standing stones, placed in circles or lined up in rows, were erected throughout the British Isles and northwestern France. The most famous of these megalithic constructions is Stonehenge in England.

1–5a Nomadic Peoples: Impact of the Indo-Europeans

On the fringes of civilization lived nomadic peoples who depended on hunting and gathering, herding, and sometimes a bit of farming for their survival. Most important were the pastoral nomads who on occasion overran civilized communities and forged their own empires. Pastoral nomads domesticated animals for both food and clothing and moved along regular migratory routes to provide steady sources of nourishment for their animals.

The Indo-Europeans were among the most important nomadic peoples. These groups spoke languages derived from a single parent tongue. Indo-European languages include Greek, Latin, Persian, Sanskrit, and the Germanic and Slavic tongues (see Table 1.2). The original Indo-European-speaking peoples were probably based in the steppe region north of the Black Sea or in southwestern Asia, in modern Iran or Afghanistan, but around 2000 BCE, they began to move into Europe, India, and western Asia. The domestication of horses and the importation of the wheel and wagon from Mesopotamia facilitated the Indo-European migrations to other lands (see Map 1.5).

The Hittites One group of Indo-Europeans who moved into Asia Minor and Anatolia (modern Turkey) around 1750 BCE

TABLE 1.2	Some Indo-European Languages
Subfamily	**Languages**
Indo-Iranian	*Sanskrit*, Persian
Balto-Slavic	Russian, Serbo-Croatian, Czech, Polish, Lithuanian
Hellenic	Greek
Italic	*Latin*, Romance languages (French, Italian, Spanish, Portuguese, Romanian)
Celtic	Irish, Gaelic
Germanic	Swedish, Danish, Norwegian, German, Dutch, English

Note: Languages in italic type are no longer spoken.

coalesced with the native peoples to form the Hittite kingdom, with its capital at Hattusha (Bogazköy in modern Turkey). Between 1600 and 1200 BCE, the Hittites formed their own empire in western Asia and even threatened the power of the Egyptians.

The Hittites were the first of the Indo-European peoples to make use of iron, enabling them to construct weapons that

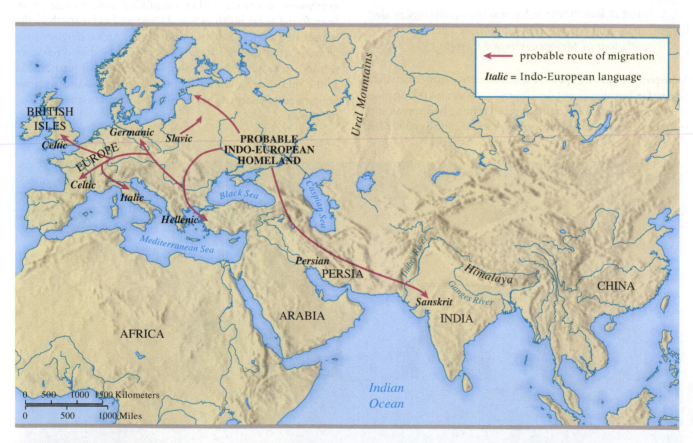

Map 1.5 The Spread of the Indo-Europeans. From their probable homeland in the steppe region north of the Black Sea, Indo-European-speaking peoples moved eventually into Europe, India, and western Asia. The languages shown on the map are all Indo-European languages (see Table 1.2).

Q *How do you explain the movements of the Indo-European-speaking peoples?*

were stronger and cheaper to make because of the widespread availability of iron ore. During its height, the Hittite Empire also demonstrated an interesting ability to assimilate other cultures into its own. In language, literature, art, law, and religion, the Hittites borrowed much from Mesopotamia as well as from the native peoples they had subdued. Recent scholarship has stressed the important role of the Hittites in transmitting Mesopotamian culture, as they transformed it, to later civilizations in the Mediterranean area, especially to the Mycenaean Greeks (see Chapter 4).

1-5b Territorial States in Western Asia: The Phoenicians

During its heyday, the Hittite Empire was one of the great powers in western Asia. Constant squabbling over succession to the throne, however, tended to weaken royal authority at times. Especially devastating, were attacks by the Sea Peoples from the west and aggressive neighboring tribes. By 1190 BCE, Hittite power had come to an end. The destruction of the Hittite kingdom and the weakening of Egypt around 1200 BCE left no dominant powers in western Asia, allowing a patchwork of petty kingdoms and city-states to emerge, especially in the area of Syria and Canaan. The Phoenicians (fuh-NEE-shunz) were one of these peoples.

A Semitic-speaking people (see Table 1.1 on p. 14), the Phoenicians lived in the area of Canaan along the Mediterranean coast on a narrow band of land 120 miles long. Their newfound political independence after the demise of Hittite and Egyptian power helped the Phoenicians expand the trade that was already the foundation of their prosperity. The chief cities of Phoenicia—Byblos, Tyre, and Sidon—were ports on the eastern Mediterranean, but they also served as distribution centers for the lands to the east in Mesopotamia. The Phoenicians themselves produced a number of goods for foreign markets, including purple dye, glass, wine, and lumber from the famous cedars of Lebanon. In addition, the Phoenicians improved

their ships and became great international sea traders. They charted new routes, not only in the Mediterranean but also in the Atlantic Ocean, where they reached Britain and sailed south along the west coast of Africa. The Phoenicians established a number of colonies in the western Mediterranean, including settlements in southern Spain, Sicily, and Sardinia. Carthage, the Phoenicians' most famous colony, was located on the north coast of Africa.

Culturally, the Phoenicians are best known as transmitters. Instead of using pictographs or signs to represent whole words and syllables as the Mesopotamians and Egyptians did, the Phoenicians simplified their writing by using twenty-two different signs to represent the sounds of their speech. These twenty-two characters or letters could be used to spell out all the words in the Phoenician language. Although the Phoenicians were not the only people to invent an alphabet, theirs would have special significance because it was eventually passed on to the Greeks. From the Greek alphabet was derived the Roman alphabet that we still use today (Table 1.3 shows the derivation of the letters A to F). The Phoenicians achieved much while independent, but they ultimately fell subject to the Assyrians and Persians.

1-5c The Hebrews: The "Children of Israel"

To the south of the Phoenicians lived another group of Semitic-speaking people known as the Hebrews. Although they were a minor factor in the politics of the region, their monotheism—belief in but one God—later influenced both Christianity and Islam and flourished as a world religion in its own right. The Hebrews had a tradition concerning their origins and history that was eventually written down as part of the Hebrew Bible, known to Christians as the Old Testament. Describing themselves as a nomadic people, the Hebrews' own tradition states that they were descendants of the patriarch Abraham, who had migrated from Mesopotamia to the land of Canaan, where the Hebrews became identified as the "Children of Israel." Moreover, according to tradition, a drought in Canaan caused many

TABLE 1.3	The Phoenician, Greek, and Roman Alphabets						
Phoenician			**Greek**			**Roman**	
Phoenician	Phoenician Name	Modern Symbol	Early Greek	Classical Greek	Greek Name	Early Latin	Classical Latin
K	'aleph	'	Λ	A	alpha	A	A
ʯ	beth	B	প	B	beta		B
ʌ	gimel	G	ʔ	Γ	gamma		C
◿	daleth	D	△	Δ	delta	◖	D
F	he	H	ʭ	E	epsilon	∃	E
ʏ	waw	W	ʮ		digamma	ʮ	F

Source: Andrew Robinson, *The Story of Writing* (London, 1995), 170.

Hebrews to migrate to Egypt, where they lived peacefully until they were enslaved by pharaohs who used them as laborers on building projects. The Hebrews remained in bondage until Moses supposedly led his people out of Egypt in the Exodus in the first half of the thirteenth century BCE. According to the biblical account, the Hebrews then wandered for many years in the desert until they entered Canaan. Organized into twelve tribes, the Hebrews became embroiled in conflict with the Philistines, who had settled along the coast of Canaan but were beginning to move inland.

Many scholars today doubt that the biblical account reflects the true history of the early Israelites. The Hebrew Bible is a collection of twenty-four books written over hundreds of years. Dating of the biblical books is problematic, although scholars have advanced a Documentary Hypothesis, which maintains that a series of authors wrote different books of the Bible over a period of hundreds of years until the books were finally consolidated around 250 BCE. They argue that the early books of the Bible, written centuries after the events described, preserve only the cultural memory of what the Israelites came to believe about themselves and that recent archaeological evidence often contradicts the details of the biblical account. There is, for example, no archaeological or other evidence for the Exodus from Egypt. These scholars also argue that the Israelites were not nomadic invaders but indigenous peoples in the Canaanite hill country. What is generally agreed, however, is that between 1200 and 1000 BCE, the Israelites emerged as a distinct group of people, possibly organized into tribes or a league of tribes.

HISTORIANS DEBATE **Was There a United Kingdom of Israel?** According to the Hebrew Bible, the Israelites established a united kingdom of Israel beginning with Saul (c. 1020–1000 BCE), who supposedly achieved some success in the ongoing struggle with the Philistines. But after his death, a brief period of anarchy ensued until one of Saul's lieutenants, David (c. 1000–970 BCE), reunited the Israelites, defeated the Philistines, and established control over all of Canaan. Among David's conquests was the city of Jerusalem, which he supposedly made into the capital of a united kingdom.

According to the biblical account, David's son Solomon (c. 970–930 BCE) did even more to strengthen royal power. He expanded the political and military establishments and extended the trading activities of the Israelites. Solomon is portrayed as a great builder who was responsible for the Temple in the city of Jerusalem. The Israelites viewed the Temple as the symbolic center of their religion and hence of the kingdom of Israel itself. Under Solomon, ancient Israel supposedly reached the height of its power.

The accuracy of this biblical account of the united kingdom of Israel under Saul, David, and Solomon has recently been challenged by a new generation of archaeologists and historians. Although they mostly accept Saul, David, and Solomon as historical figures, they view them more as chief warlords than as kings. If a kingdom of Israel did exist during these years, it was not as powerful or as well organized as the Hebrew Bible says. Furthermore, they argue, there is no definitive archaeological evidence that Solomon built the Temple in Jerusalem.

The Kingdoms of Israel and Judah There may or may not have been a united kingdom of Israel, but after the death of Solomon, tensions between northern and southern tribes in Israel led to the establishment of two separate kingdoms—the kingdom of Israel, composed of the ten northern tribes, with its capital eventually at Samaria, and the southern kingdom of Judah, consisting of two tribes, with its capital at Jerusalem (see Map 1.6). In 722 or 721 BCE, the Assyrians (uh-SEER-ee-unz) destroyed Samaria, overran the kingdom of Israel, and deported many Hebrews to other parts of the Assyrian Empire. These dispersed Hebrews (the "ten lost tribes") merged with neighboring peoples and gradually lost their identity.

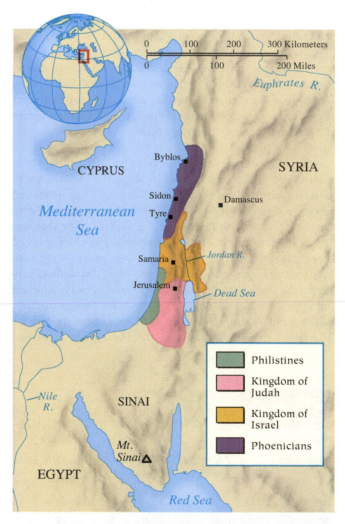

Map 1.6 The Israelites and Their Neighbors in the First Millennium BCE. After the death of Solomon, tensions between the tribes in Israel led to the creation of two kingdoms—a northern kingdom of Israel and a southern kingdom of Judah. With power divided, the Israelites could not resist invasions that dispersed many of them from Canaan. Some, such as the "ten lost tribes," never returned. Others were sent to Babylon but were later allowed to return under the rule of the Persians.

 Why was Israel more vulnerable to the Assyrian Empire than Judah was?

The southern kingdom of Judah was also forced to pay tribute to Assyria but managed to retain its independence as Assyrian power declined. A new enemy, however, appeared on the horizon. The Chaldeans (kal-DEE-unz) defeated Assyria, conquered the kingdom of Judah, and completely destroyed Jerusalem in 586 BCE. Many upper-class people from Judah were deported to Babylonia; the memory of their exile is still evoked in the stirring words of Psalm 137:

> By the rivers of Babylon, we sat and wept when we remembered Zion. . . .
> How can we sing the songs of the Lord while in a foreign land?
> If I forget you, O Jerusalem, may my right hand forget its skill.
> May my tongue cling to the roof of my mouth if I do not remember you,
> If I do not consider Jerusalem my highest joy.[12]

But the Babylonian captivity of the people of Judah did not last. A new set of conquerors, the Persians, destroyed the Chaldean kingdom and allowed the people of Judah to return to Jerusalem and rebuild their city and Temple. The revived kingdom of Judah remained under Persian control until the conquests of Alexander the Great in the fourth century BCE. The people of Judah survived, eventually becoming known as the Jews and giving their name to Judaism, the religion of Yahweh (YAH-way), the Israelite God.

The Spiritual Dimensions of Israel

The spiritual perspective of the Israelites evolved over time. Early Israelites probably worshiped many gods, including nature spirits dwelling in trees and rocks. For some Israelites, Yahweh was the chief god of Israel, but many, including kings of Israel and Judah, worshiped other gods as well. It was among the Babylonian exiles in the sixth century BCE that Yahweh—the God of Israel—came to be seen as the only God. After these exiles returned to Judah, their point of view eventually became dominant, and pure monotheism came to be the major tenet of Judaism.

According to the Hebrew conception, there is but one God, called Yahweh, who created the world and everything in it. Yahweh ruled the world and was subject to nothing. This omnipotent creator was not removed from the life he had created, however, but was a just and good God who expected goodness from his people. If they did not obey his will, they would be punished. But he was primarily a God of mercy and love: "The Lord is gracious and compassionate, slow to anger and rich in love. The Lord is good to all; he has compassion on all he has made."[13] Each individual could have a personal relationship with this being.

Three aspects of the Hebrew religious tradition had special significance: the covenant, the law, and the prophets. The Israelites believed that during the exodus from Egypt, when Moses, according to biblical tradition, led his people out of bondage and into the Promised Land, God made a covenant or contract with the tribes of Israel, who believed that Yahweh had spoken to them through Moses (see "The Covenant and the Law: The Book of Exodus" on p. 30). The Israelites promised to obey Yahweh and follow his law. In return, Yahweh promised to take special care of his chosen people, "a peculiar treasure unto me above all people."

This covenant between Yahweh and his chosen people could be fulfilled, however, only by obedience to the law of God. Most important were the ethical concerns that stood at the center of the law. Sometimes these took the form of specific standards of moral behavior: "You shall not murder. You shall not commit adultery. You shall not steal."[14] True freedom consisted of following God's moral standards voluntarily. If people chose to ignore the good, suffering and evil would follow.

The Israelites believed that certain religious teachers, called prophets, were sent by God to serve as his voice to his people. The golden age of prophecy began in the mid-eighth century BCE and continued during the time when the people of Israel and Judah were threatened by Assyrian and Chaldean conquerors. The "men of God" went through the land warning the

Alfredo Dagli Orti/Art Resource, NY

Moses and the Ten Commandments. As we have seen, according to the Hebrew Bible, God gave to Moses a set of commandments for the Israelites to obey. Although these commandments are interpreted and numbered differently by religious groups, the early Christian church came to consider the Ten Commandments given to Moses by God as a summary of God's law and a standard for ethical behavior. This is evident in this sixth-century detail of Moses and the Ten Commandments in the Eastern Roman (later known as Byzantine) church of San Vitale in Italy. The Israelites shown in the photo are, of course, garbed in the clothing styles of the sixth century.

THE COVENANT AND THE LAW: THE BOOK OF EXODUS

Religion & Philosophy **ACCORDING TO THE BIBLICAL ACCOUNT**, it was during the exodus from Egypt that the Israelites supposedly made their covenant with Yahweh. They agreed to obey their God and follow his law. In return, Yahweh promised to take special care of his chosen people. This selection from the biblical book of Exodus describes the making of the covenant and God's commandments to the Israelites.

Exodus 19:1–8

In the third month after the Israelites left Egypt—on the very day—they came to the Desert of Sinai. After they set out from Rephidim, they entered the desert of Sinai, and Israel camped there in the desert in front of the mountain. Then Moses went up to God, and the Lord called to him from the mountain, and said, "This is what you are to say to the house of Jacob and what you are to tell the people of Israel: 'You yourselves have seen what I did to Egypt, and how I carried you on eagles' wings and brought you to myself. Now if you obey me fully and keep my covenant, then out of all nations you will be my treasured possession. Although the whole earth is mine, you will be for me a kingdom of priests and a holy nation.' These are the words you are to speak to the Israelites." So Moses went back and summoned the elders of the people and set before them all the words the Lord had commanded him to speak. The people all responded together, "We will do everything the Lord has said." So Moses brought their answer back to the Lord.

Source: The Holy Bible, New International Version (Colorado Springs, CO, Biblica, 1973).

Exodus 20:1–3, 7–17

And God spoke all these words, "I am the Lord your God, who brought you out of Egypt, out of the land of slavery. You shall have no other gods before me. . . . You shall not misuse the name of the Lord your God, for the Lord will not hold anyone guiltless who misuses his name. Remember the Sabbath day by keeping it holy. Six days you shall labor and do all your work, but the seventh day is a Sabbath to the Lord your God. On it you shall not do any work, neither you, nor your son or daughter, nor your manservant or maidservant, nor your animals, nor the alien within your gates. For in six days the Lord made the heavens and the earth, the sea, and all that is in them, but he rested on the seventh day. Therefore the Lord blessed the Sabbath day and made it holy. Honor your father and your mother, so that you may live long in the land the Lord your God is giving you. You shall not murder. You shall not commit adultery. You shall not steal. You shall not give false testimony against your neighbor. You shall not covet your neighbor's house. You shall not covet your neighbor's wife, or his manservant or maidservant, his ox or donkey, or anything that belongs to your neighbor."

 What was the nature of the covenant between Yahweh and the Israelites? What was its moral significance for the Israelites? How does it differ from Hammurabi's code, and how might you explain those differences?

Israelites that they had failed to keep God's commandments and would be punished for breaking the covenant: "I will punish you for all your iniquities."

Out of the words of the prophets came new concepts that enriched the Jewish tradition. The prophets embraced a concern for all humanity. All nations would someday come to the God of Israel: "All the earth shall worship thee." This vision encompassed the elimination of war and the establishment of peace for all nations. In the words of the prophet Isaiah, "He will judge between the nations and will settle disputes for many people. They will beat their swords into plowshares and their spears into pruning hooks. Nation will not take up sword against nation, nor will they train for war anymore."[15]

Although the prophets developed a sense of universalism, the demands of the Jewish religion (the need to obey God) eventually encouraged a separation between the Jews and their non-Jewish neighbors. Unlike most other peoples of the Middle East, Jews could not simply be amalgamated into a community by accepting the gods of their conquerors and their neighbors. To remain faithful to the demands of their God, they might even have to refuse loyalty to political leaders.

1–6 THE RISE OF NEW EMPIRES

 Focus Question: What methods and institutions did the Assyrians and Persians use to amass and maintain their respective empires?

Small and independent states could exist only as long as no larger state dominated western Asia. New empires soon arose, however, and conquered vast stretches of the ancient world.

1–6a The Assyrian Empire

The first of these empires emerged in Assyria, located on the upper Tigris River, an area that brought it into both cultural and political contact with southern Mesopotamia. The Assyrians were a Semitic-speaking people who exploited the use of iron weapons, first developed by the Hittites, to establish an empire that by 700 BCE included Mesopotamia, parts of the Iranian Plateau, sections of Asia Minor, Syria, Canaan, and Egypt down to Thebes (see Map 1.7). Ashurbanipal (ah-shur-BAH-nuh-pahl) (669–627 BCE) was one of the strongest Assyrian rulers, but during his

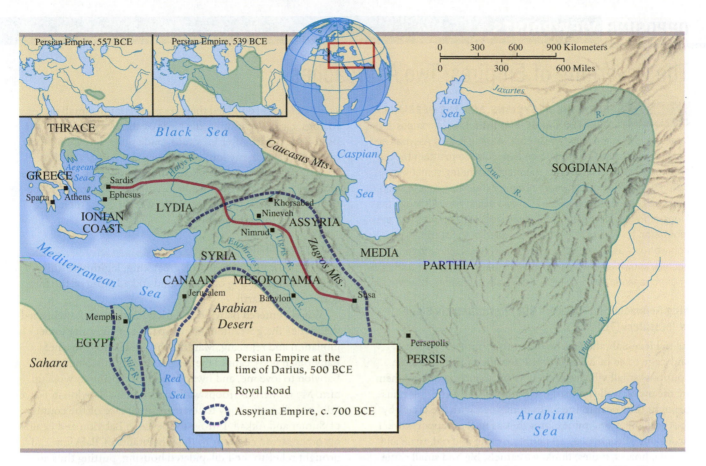

Map 1.7 The Assyrian and Persian Empires. Cyrus the Great united the Persians and led them in a successful conquest of much of the Near East, including most of the lands of the Assyrian Empire. By the time of Darius, the Persian Empire was the largest the world had yet seen.

 Based on your examination of this map of the Assyrian and Persian Empires, what do you think would be the challenges of governing a large empire?

reign it was already becoming apparent that the Assyrian Empire was greatly overextended. Moreover, subject peoples, such as the Babylonians, greatly resented Assyrian rule and rebelled against it. Soon after Ashurbanipal's reign, the Assyrian Empire began to disintegrate. The capital city of Nineveh fell to a coalition of Chaldeans and Medes in 612 BCE, and in 605 BCE, the rest of the empire was finally divided between the two powers.

At its height, kings whose power was considered absolute ruled the Assyrian Empire. Under their leadership, the empire came to be well organized. Local officials were directly responsible to the king. The Assyrians also developed an efficient system of communication to administer their empire more effectively. A network of staging posts was established throughout the empire that used relays of horses (mules or donkeys in mountainous terrain) to carry messages. The system was so effective that a provincial governor anywhere in the empire (except Egypt) could send a question and receive an answer from the king in his palace within a week.

The Assyrians' ability to conquer and maintain an empire was due to a combination of factors. Over many years of practice, the Assyrians developed effective military leaders and fighters. They were able to enlist and deploy troops numbering

in the hundreds of thousands, although most campaigns were not on such a large scale. Size alone was not decisive, however. The Assyrian army was well organized and disciplined. It included a standing army of infantry as its core, accompanied by cavalry and horse-drawn war chariots that were used as mobile platforms for shooting arrows. In addition to fighting set battles on open ground, the Assyrian army was also capable of waging guerrilla warfare in the mountains and laying siege to cities.

Another factor in the effectiveness of the Assyrian military machine was its use of terror as an instrument of warfare. As a matter of regular policy, the Assyrians laid waste to the land in which they were fighting, smashing dams, looting and destroying towns, setting crops on fire, and cutting down trees, particularly fruit trees. They were especially known for committing atrocities on their captives. King Ashurnasirpal (ah-shur-NAH-zur-pahl) recorded this account of his treatment of prisoners:

3000 of their combat troops I felled with weapons. . . . Many of the captives taken from them I burned in a fire. Many I took alive; from some of these I cut off their hands to the wrist, from others I cut off their noses, ears and fingers; I put out the eyes of many of the soldiers. . . . I burned their young men and women to death.[16]

The Governing of Empires: Two Approaches

Politics & Government | **BOTH THE ASSYRIANS AND THE PERSIANS CREATED LARGE EMPIRES** that encompassed large areas of the ancient Near East. Although both Assyrian and Persian rulers used military force and violence to attain their empires, their approaches to conquest and ruling sometimes differed. Assyrian rulers were known for their terror tactics and atrocities, as described in the first two selections. Although the kings of Persia also used terror when needed, they also had a reputation for less cruelty and more tolerance. Especially noteworthy was Cyrus, as is evident in this selection from a decree (known as the Cyrus Cylinder) that he issued in 538 BCE. The propaganda value of his words is also apparent, however.

King Sennacherib (704–681 BCE) Describes His Siege of Jerusalem (701 BCE)

As to Hezekiah, the Jew, he did not submit to my yoke, I laid siege to 46 of his strong cities, walled forts and to the countless small villages in their vicinity, and conquered them by means of well-stamped earth-ramps, and battering-rams brought thus near to the walls combined with the attack by foot soldiers, using mines, breaches as well as sapper work. I drove out of them 200,150 people, young and old, male and female, horses, mules, donkeys, camels, big and small cattle beyond counting, and considered them booty. Himself I made a prisoner in Jerusalem, his royal residence, like a bird in a cage. I surrounded him with earthwork in order to molest those who were leaving his city's gate.

King Ashurbanipal (669–627 BCE) Describes His Treatment of Conquered Babylon

I tore out the tongues of those whose slanderous mouths had uttered blasphemies against my god Ashur and had plotted against me, his god-fearing prince; I defeated them completely. The others, I smashed alive with the very same statues of protective deities with which they had smashed my own grandfather Sennacherib—now finally as a belated burial sacrifice for his soul. I fed their corpses, cut into small pieces, to dogs, pigs, . . . vultures, the birds of the sky and also to the fish of the ocean. After I . . . thus made quiet again the hearts of the great gods, my lords, I removed the corpses of those whom the pestilence had felled, whose leftovers after the dogs and pigs had fed on them were obstructing the streets, filling the places of Babylon, and of those who had lost their lives through the terrible famine.

The Cyrus Cylinder

I am Cyrus, king of the world, great king, legitimate king, king of Babylon, king of Sumer and Akkad, king of the four corners of the earth. . . .

When I entered Babylon as a friend and when I established the seat of the government in the palace of the ruler under jubilation and rejoicing, Marduk, the great lord [the chief Babylonian god], caused the magnanimous inhabitants of Babylon to love me, and I was daily endeavoring to worship him. My numerous troops walked around in Babylon in peace. I did not allow anybody to terrorize any place of the country of Sumer and Akkad. I strove for peace in Babylon and in all his other sacred cities. As to the inhabitants of Babylon . . . I brought relief to their dilapidated housing, putting thus an end to their main complaints. . . .

As to the region from as far as Ashur and Susa . . . I returned to these sacred cities on the other side of the Tigris, the sanctuaries of which have been ruins for a long time, the images which used to live therein and established for them permanent sanctuaries. I also gathered all their former inhabitants and returned to them their dwellings.

 Both Ashurbanipal and Cyrus entered Babylon as conquerors. How did their treatment of the conquered city differ? How do you explain the differences? Which method do you think was more effective? Why?

Sources: Pritchard, James B., ed., *Ancient Near Eastern Texts Relating to the Old Testament*, Third Edition with Supplement. © 1950, 1955, 1969, renewed 1978 by Princeton University Press. Reprinted by permission of Princeton University Press.

After conquering another city, the same king wrote, "I fixed up a pile of corpses in front of the city's gate. I flayed the nobles, as many as had rebelled, and spread their skins out on the piles. . . . I flayed many within my land and spread their skins out on the walls."[17] It should be noted that this policy of extreme cruelty to prisoners was not used against all enemies but was primarily reserved for those who were already part of the empire and then rebelled against Assyrian rule (see Opposing Viewpoints "The Governing of Empires: Two Approaches").

Assyrian Society Unlike the Hebrews, the Assyrians were not fearful of mixing with other people. In fact, the Assyrian policy of deporting many prisoners of newly conquered territories to Assyria created a polyglot society in which ethnic differences were not very important. What gave identity to the Assyrians themselves was their language, although even that was akin to the language of their southern neighbors in Babylonia, who also spoke a Semitic tongue. Religion was also a cohesive force. Assyria was literally "the land of Ashur," a reference to

THE CODE OF THE ASSURA

Assyrian law was similar to Sumerian and Babylonian law, but it could be considerably harsher, especially in regard to women. The excerpts below are taken from one compilation of Assyrian laws known as the Code of the Assura, which is dated around 1075 BCE.

The Code of the Assura

I.7. If a woman bring her hand against a man, they shall prosecute her; 30 manas of lead shall she pay, 20 blows shall they inflict on her.

I.8. If a woman in a quarrel injure the testicle of a man, one of her fingers they shall cut off. And if a physician bind it up and the other testicle which is beside it be infected thereby, or take harm; or in a quarrel she injure the other testicle, they shall destroy both of her eyes.

I.9. If a man bring his hand against the wife of a man, treating her like a little child, and they prove it against him, and convict him, one of his fingers they shall cut off. If he kiss her, his lower lip with the blade of an axe they shall draw down and they shall cut off.

I.13. If the wife of a man go out from her house and visit a man where he lives, and he have intercourse with her, knowing that she is a man's wife, the man and also the woman they shall put to death.

I.15. If a man catch a man with his wife, both of them shall they put to death. If the husband of the woman put his wife to death, he shall also put the man to death. If he cut off the nose of his wife, he shall turn the man into a eunuch, and they shall disfigure the whole of his face.

I.16. If a man have relations with the wife of a man at her wish, there is no penalty for that man. The man shall lay upon the woman, his wife, the penalty he wishes.

I.40. If the wives of a man, or the daughters of a man go out into the street, their heads are to be veiled. The prostitute is not to be veiled. Maidservants are not to veil themselves. Veiled harlots and maidservants shall have their garments seized and 50 blows inflicted on them and bitumen poured on their heads.

I.50. If a man strike the wife of a man, in her first stage of pregnancy, and cause her to drop that which is in her, it is a crime; two talents of lead he shall pay.

I.52. If a woman of her own accord drop that which is in her, they shall prosecute her, they shall convict her, they shall crucify her, they shall not bury her. . . .

I.57. In the case of every crime for which there is the penalty of the cutting-off of ear or nose or ruining or reputation or condition, as it is written it shall be carried out.

I.58. Unless it is forbidden in the tablets, a man may strike his wife, pull her hair, her ear he may bruise or pierce. He commits no misdeed thereby.

Q *Compare these excerpts from the Code of the Assura with the Code of Hammurabi in Chapter 1. How are they similar? How are they different? What do the differences reveal about Assyrian society?*

Source: Internet Ancient History Sourcebook.

---

its chief god. The king, as Ashur's representative on earth, provided a final unifying focus.

Assyrian society was hierarchical. There was a noticeable gap between kings, royal officials, and warriors at the top and the merchants, peasants, and slaves below them. As in other ancient Near East societies, the Assyrian family was patriarchal.

The father held authority over his wife and children; women were expected to take care of the household and bear children. Although women were not equal to men, legal documents indicate that some Assyrian women could purchase and sell property, take part in business for themselves, and assist their husbands in legal matters. There were also enormous differences between high and low class women. The former included the wives and daughters of rulers and royal officials; the latter included lower-class wives and slaves who worked in households and temples. Their lives were regulated by harsh laws (see "The Code of the Assura").

Agriculture formed the principal basis of Assyrian life. Assyria was a land of farming villages with relatively few significant cities, especially in comparison to southern Mesopotamia. Unlike the river valleys, where farming required the minute organization of large numbers of people to control irrigation, Assyrian farms received sufficient moisture from regular rainfall.

Trade was second to agriculture in economic importance. For internal trade, metals—including gold, silver, copper, and bronze—were used as a medium of exchange. Various agricultural products also served as a form of payment or exchange. Because of their geographic location, the Assyrians served as intermediaries and participated in an international trade, importing timber, wine, and precious metals and stones while exporting textiles produced in palaces, temples, and private workshops.

Assyrian Culture The Assyrians assimilated much of Mesopotamian civilization and saw themselves as guardians of Sumerian and Babylonian culture. Assyrian kings also tried to maintain old traditions when they rebuilt damaged temples by constructing the new buildings on the original foundations rather than in new locations.

King Ashurbanipal's Lion Hunt. This relief, sculpted on alabaster as a decoration for the Assyrian northern palace in Nineveh, depicts King Ashurbanipal engaged in a lion hunt. Lion hunts were not conducted in the wild but were held under controlled circumstances: the king and his retainers faced lions released from cages in an arena. The scene was intended to glorify the king as the conqueror of the king of beasts. Relief sculpture, one of the best-known forms of Assyrian art, reached its zenith under Ashurbanipal just before the Assyrian Empire began its rapid disintegration.

Among the best-known objects of Assyrian art are the relief sculptures found in the royal palaces in three of the Assyrian capital cities, Nimrud, Nineveh, and Khorsabad. These reliefs, which were begun in the ninth century BCE and reached their high point in the reign of Ashurbanipal in the seventh, depicted two different kinds of subject matter: ritual or ceremonial scenes revolving around the king and scenes of hunting and war. The latter show realistic action scenes of the king and his warriors engaged in battle or hunting animals, especially lions. These images depict a strongly masculine world where discipline, brute force, and toughness are the enduring values—indeed, the very values of the Assyrian military monarchy.

1–6b The Persian Empire

After the collapse of the Assyrian Empire, the Chaldeans, under their king Nebuchadnezzar (neb-uh-kud-NEZZ-ur) II (605–562 BCE), made Babylonia the leading state in western Asia. Nebuchadnezzar rebuilt Babylon as the center of his empire, giving it a reputation as one of the great cities of the ancient world. But the splendor of Chaldean Babylonia proved to be short-lived when Babylon fell to the Persians in 539 BCE.

The Persians were an Indo-European-speaking people who lived in southwestern Iran. Primarily nomadic, the Persians were organized into tribes until the Achaemenid (ah-KEE-muh-nud) dynasty managed to unify them. One of the dynasty's members, Cyrus (559–530 BCE), created a powerful Persian state that rearranged the political map of western Asia.

Cyrus the Great In 550 BCE, Cyrus extended Persian control over the Medes, making Media the first Persian **satrapy** (SAY-truh-pee), or province. Three years later, Cyrus defeated the prosperous Lydian kingdom in western Asia Minor, and Lydia became another Persian satrapy. Cyrus's forces then went on to conquer the Greek city-states that had been established on the Ionian coast. Cyrus then turned eastward, subduing the eastern part of the Iranian Plateau, Sogdia, and even western India. His eastern frontiers secured, Cyrus entered Mesopotamia in 539 and captured Babylon (see Map 1.7 on p. 31). His treatment of Babylonia showed remarkable restraint and wisdom. Babylonia was made into a Persian province under a Persian **satrap** (SAY-trap), or governor, but many government officials were kept in their positions. Cyrus took the title "King of All, Great King, Mighty King, King of Babylon, King of the Land of Sumer and Akkad, King of the Four Rims [of the earth], the Son of Cambyses the Great King, King of Anshan"[18] and insisted that he stood in the ancient, unbroken line of Babylonian kings. By appealing to the vanity of the Babylonians, he won their loyalty. Cyrus also issued an edict permitting the Jews, who had been brought to Babylon in the sixth century BCE, to return to Jerusalem with their sacred objects and to rebuild their Temple as well.

To his contemporaries, Cyrus deserved to be called Cyrus the Great. The Greek historian Herodotus recounted that the Persians viewed him as a "father," a ruler who was "gentle, and procured them all manner of goods."[19] Cyrus must have been an unusual ruler for his time, a man who demonstrated considerable wisdom and compassion in the conquest and organization of his empire (see Opposing Viewpoints "The Governing of Empires: Two Approaches" on p. 32). He won approval by using not only Persians but also native peoples as government officials in their own states. Unlike the Assyrian rulers of an earlier empire, he had a reputation for mercy. Medes, Babylonians, and Jews all accepted him as their legitimate ruler. Indeed, the Jews regarded him as the anointed one of God: "I am the Lord who says of Cyrus, 'He is my shepherd and will accomplish all that I please'; he will say of Jerusalem, 'Let it be rebuilt'; and of the Temple, 'Let its foundations be laid.' This is what the Lord says to his anointed, to Cyrus, whose right hand I take hold of to subdue nations before him."[20]

Expanding the Empire Cyrus's successors extended the territory of the Persian Empire. His son Cambyses (kam-BY-seez) (530–522 BCE) undertook a successful invasion of Egypt. Darius (duh-RY-uss) (521–486 BCE) added a new Persian province in western India that extended to the Indus River and moved into Europe proper, conquering Thrace and making the Macedonian king a vassal. A revolt of the Ionian Greek cities in 499 BCE resulted in temporary freedom for these communities in western Asia Minor. Aid from the Greek mainland, most notably from Athens, encouraged the Ionians to invade Lydia and burn Sardis, center of the Lydian satrapy. This event led to Darius's involvement with the mainland Greeks. After reestablishing control of the Ionian Greek cities, Darius undertook an invasion of the Greek mainland, which culminated in the Athenian victory in the Battle of Marathon, in 490 BCE (see Chapter 4).

Governing the Empire By the reign of Darius, the Persians had assembled the largest empire the world had yet seen. It not only included all the old centers of power in Egypt and western Asia but also extended into Thrace and Asia Minor in the west and into India in the east. For administrative purposes, the empire had been divided into approximately twenty satrapies. Each province was ruled by a satrap, literally a "protector of the kingdom." Satraps collected tributes, were responsible for justice and security, raised military levies for the royal army, and normally commanded the military forces within their satrapies. In terms of real power, the satraps were miniature kings who created courts imitative of the Great King's.

An efficient system of communication was crucial to sustaining the Persian Empire. Well-maintained roads facilitated the rapid transit of military and government personnel. One in particular, the so-called Royal Road, stretched from Sardis, the center of Lydia in Asia Minor, to Susa, the chief capital of the Persian Empire. Like the Assyrians, the Persians established staging posts equipped with fresh horses for the king's messengers.

The Great King In this vast administrative system, the Persian king occupied an exalted position. Although not considered a god in the manner of an Egyptian pharaoh, he was nevertheless the elect one or regent of the Persian god Ahuramazda (uh-HOOR-uh-MAHZ-duh) (see next section, "Persian Religion"). All subjects were the king's servants, and he was the source of all justice, possessing the power of life and death over everyone. Persian kings were largely secluded and not easily accessible. They resided in a series of splendid palaces. Darius in particular was a palace builder on a grand scale.

The policies of Darius also tended to widen the gap between the king and his subjects. As the Great King himself said of all his subjects, "What was said to them by me, night and

Gianni Dagli Orti/The Art Archive/Picture Desk

Darius, the Great King. Darius ruled the Persian Empire from 521 to 486 BCE. He is shown on his throne in Persepolis, the new capital city he built. In his right hand, Darius holds the royal staff; with his left, he grasps a lotus blossom with two buds, a symbol of royalty.

day it was done."[21] Over a period of time, the Great Kings in their greed came to hoard immense quantities of gold and silver in treasuries located in the capital cities. Both their hoarding of wealth and their later over-taxation of their subjects were crucial factors in the ultimate weakening of the Persian Empire.

In its heyday, however, the empire stood supreme, and much of its power depended on the military. By the time of Darius, the Persian monarchs had created a standing army of professional soldiers. This army was truly international, composed of contingents from the various peoples who made up the empire. At its core was a cavalry force of ten thousand and an elite infantry force of ten thousand Medes and Persians known as the Immortals because they were never allowed to fall below ten thousand in number. When one was killed, he was immediately replaced.

Persian Religion Of all the Persians' cultural contributions, the most original was their religion, **Zoroastrianism**. According to Persian tradition, Zoroaster (ZOR-oh-ass-tur) was born in 660 BCE. After a period of wandering and solitude, he experienced revelations that caused him to be revered as a prophet of the "true religion." His teachings were eventually written down in the third century BCE in the *Zend Avesta*, the sacred book of Zoroastrianism.

CHRONOLOGY	Early Empires	
The Assyrians		
Height of power	700 BCE	
Ashurbanipal	669–627 BCE	
Fall of Nineveh	612 BCE	
Assyrian Empire destroyed	605 BCE	
The Persians		
Unification under Achaemenid dynasty	600s BCE	
Persian control over Medes	550 BCE	
Conquests of Cyrus the Great	559–530 BCE	
Cambyses and conquest of Egypt	530–522 BCE	
Reign of Darius	521–486 BCE	

According to Zoroaster, Ahuramazda also possessed qualities that all humans should aspire to, such as good thought, right action, and piety. Although Ahuramazda was supreme, he was not unopposed; this gave a dualistic element to Zoroastrianism. At the beginning of the world, the good spirit of Ahuramazda was opposed by the evil spirit, later identified as Ahriman.

Humans also played a role in this cosmic struggle between good and evil. Ahuramazda, the creator, gave all humans free will and the power to choose between right and wrong. The good person chooses the right way of Ahuramazda. Zoroaster taught that there would be an end to the struggle between good and evil. Ahuramazda would eventually triumph, and at the last judgment at the end of the world, the final separation of good and evil would occur. Individuals, too, would be judged. Each soul faced a final evaluation of its actions. The soul of a person who had performed good deeds would achieve paradise; but if deeds had been evil, the person would be thrown into an abyss of torment. Some historians believe that Zoroastrianism, with its emphasis on good and evil, heaven and hell, and a last judgment, had an impact on Christianity, a religion that eventually surpassed it in significance.

Zoroaster's spiritual message was basically monotheistic. To Zoroaster, the religion he preached was the only perfect one, and Ahuramazda was the only god. Ahuramazda ("Wise Lord") was the supreme deity, "creator of all things."

CHAPTER SUMMARY

Humanlike creatures first emerged in Africa around 3 to 4 million years ago. Over a period of time, Paleolithic people learned to create sophisticated tools, to use fire, and to adapt to and even change their physical world. They were primarily nomads, who hunted animals and gathered wild plants for survival. The agricultural revolution of the Neolithic Age, which began around 10,000 BCE, dramatically changed human patterns of living. The growing of food on a regular basis and the taming of animals enabled humans to stop their nomadic ways and settle in permanent settlements, which gave rise to more complex human societies.

These more complex human societies, which we call the first civilizations, emerged around 3000 BCE in the river valleys of Mesopotamia, Egypt, India, and China. An increase in food production in these regions led to a significant growth in human population and the rise of cities. The peoples of Southwest Asia and Egypt developed cities and struggled with the problems of organized states as they moved from individual communities to larger territorial units and eventually to empires. They invented writing to keep records and created literature. They constructed monumental buildings to please their

gods, give witness to their power, and preserve their culture. They developed new political, military, social, and religious structures to deal with the basic problems of human existence and organization. These first civilizations left detailed records that allow us to view how they grappled with three of the fundamental problems that humans have pondered: the nature of human relationships, the nature of the universe, and the role of divine forces in that cosmos.

By the middle of the second millennium BCE, much of the creative impulse of the Mesopotamian and Egyptian civilizations was beginning to wane. Around 1200 BCE, a number of small states emerged, but all of them were eventually overshadowed by the rise of the great empires of the Assyrians and Persians. The Assyrian Empire was the first to unite almost all of the ancient Middle East. Even larger, however, was the empire of the Great Kings of Persia. The many years of peace that the Persian Empire brought to the Middle East facilitated trade and the general well-being of its peoples. It is no wonder that many peoples expressed their gratitude for being subjects of the Great Kings of Persia. Among these peoples were the Hebrews, who created no empire but nevertheless left an important spiritual legacy. The embrace of monotheism created in Judaism one of the world's greatest religions, one that went on to influence the development of both Christianity and Islam.

CHAPTER TIMELINE

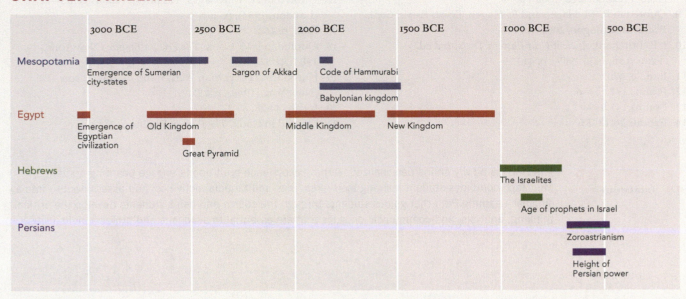

	3000 BCE	2500 BCE	2000 BCE	1500 BCE	1000 BCE	500 BCE

Mesopotamia
Emergence of Sumerian city-states
Sargon of Akkad
Code of Hammurabi
Babylonian kingdom

Egypt
Emergence of Egyptian civilization
Old Kingdom
Great Pyramid
Middle Kingdom
New Kingdom

Hebrews
The Israelites
Age of prophets in Israel

Persians
Zoroastrianism
Height of Persian power

CHAPTER REVIEW

Upon Reflection

Q What achievements did early humans make during the Paleolithic and Neolithic Ages, and how did those achievements eventually make possible the emergence of civilization?

Q What roles did geography, environmental conditions, religion, politics, economics, and women and families play in the civilizations of Southwest Asia and Egypt?

Q Compare and contrast the administrative and military structures and the attitudes toward subject peoples of the Assyrian and Persian Empires.

Key Terms

hominids (p. 5)
Paleolithic Age (p. 6)
Neolithic Revolution (p. 7)
Mesolithic Age (p. 8)
patriarchy (p. 10)
civilization (p. 10)
ziggurat (p. 12)
theocracy (p. 12)
polytheism (p. 15)

divination (p. 16)
cuneiform (p. 16)
pharaoh (p. 20)
hieroglyphics (p. 22)
megaliths (p. 25)
monotheism (p. 27)
satrapy (p. 34)
satrap (p. 34)
Zoroastrianism (p. 35)

Chapter Notes

1. J. M. Chauvet et al., *Dawn of Art: The Chauvet Cave* (New York, 1996), pp. 49–50.
2. Quoted in A. Kuhrt, *The Ancient Near East, c. 3000–330 BC* (London, 1995), vol. 1, p. 68.
3. Quoted in M. Wood, *Legacy: The Search for Ancient Cultures* (New York, 1995), p. 34.
4. Quoted in M. Van de Mieroop, *A History of the Ancient Near East, ca. 3000–323 BC* (Oxford, 2004), p. 69.
5. Quoted in ibid., p. 106.
6. Quoted in T. Jacobsen, "Mesopotamia," in H. Frankfort et al., *Before Philosophy* (Baltimore, 1949), p. 139.
7. Quoted in M. Covensky, *The Ancient Near Eastern Tradition* (New York, 1966), p. 51.

8. Quoted in B. G. Trigger et al., *Ancient Egypt: A Social History* (Cambridge, 1983), p. 74.

9. Quoted in R.-M. Hagen and R. Hagen, *Egypt: People, Gods, Pharaohs* (Cologne, 2002), p. 148.

10. J. B. Pritchard, *Ancient Near Eastern Texts*, 3rd ed. (Princeton, N.J., 1969), p. 413.

11. Ibid., p. 420.

12. Psalms 137:1, 4–6.

13. Psalms 145:8–9.

14. Exodus 20:13–15.

15. Isaiah 2:4.

16. Quoted in H. W. F. Saggs, *The Might That Was Assyria* (London, 1984), p. 261.

17. Ibid., p. 262.

18. Quoted in J. M. Cook, *The Persian Empire* (New York, 1983), p. 32.

19. Herodotus, *The Persian Wars*, trans. G. Rawlinson (New York, 1942), p. 257.

20. Isaiah, 44:28, 45:1.

21. Quoted in Cook, *The Persian Empire*, p. 76.

MindTap® is a fully online personalized learning experience built upon Cengage Learning content. MindTap® combines student learning tools—readings, multimedia, activities, and assessments—into a singular Learning Path that guides students through the course and helps students develop the critical thinking, analysis, and communication skills that are essential to academic and professional success.

Chapter Outline and Focus Questions

Mohenjo-Daro: Ancient city on the Indus. William J. Duiker

Critical Thinking

Q *What role did geography and the local environment play in affecting the nature of the first civilization that developed in the South Asian subcontinent? In what ways were these factors different from those that affected the civilizations discussed in Chapter 1?*

Connections to Today

Q *How would you compare the class system in ancient India as described in the* Law of Manu *with that of the United States at the present time? What do you think accounts for the differences?*

IN THE EARLY 1920S, an archaeological team led by the British colonial official John Marshall uncovered the remains of an ancient city that had been buried under the silt of the Indus River for over three thousand years. Suddenly, the fabled civilizations in Mesopotamia and the Nile River Valley (see Chapter 1) had a contemporary equivalent far to the east on the edge of the Indian subcontinent. As excavations continued, diggers at the site discovered the skeletal remains of several human beings caught in positions of sudden flight, provoking the assumption that the ancient city—now dubbed Mohenjo-Daro, or "City of the Dead"—had come to an abrupt end as the result of an invasion by nomadic peoples who began arriving in the regions about 1500 BCE. Over the next several hundred years, these immigrants, who called themselves the Aryans, set out to create the civilization that we know today as India.

Today, nearly a century after the Marshall team began its labors, much about the Indus Valley civilization—as this ancient culture is now commonly labeled by specialists—still remains a mystery, mainly because its writing system, inscribed on clay seals and tablets found at various sites in the region, remains undeciphered, and the connections between it and the later culture that developed in the Indian subcontinent under the Aryans remain in dispute among historians (see Historians Debate "Who Were the Aryans?" on p. 42). Nevertheless, many scholars today agree with John Marshall's conclusion at the time that many aspects of this long dead civilization still persist among the peoples, cultures, and values of the Indian people today.

2–1 THE EMERGENCE OF CIVILIZATION IN INDIA: THE INDUS VALLEY SOCIETY

 Focus Question: What were the chief features of Indus Valley civilization, and in what ways was it similar to the civilizations that arose in Egypt and Mesopotamia?

Like the civilizations of Mesopotamia and Egypt, the earliest civilizations in India arose in river valleys and were shaped, in part, by their environment. Thus, from its beginnings, Indian civilization has been intimately associated with the geography of the subcontinent.

2–1a A Land of Diversity

India was and still is a land of diversity. This diversity is evident in its languages and cultures as well as in its physical characteristics. India possesses an incredible array of languages. It has a deserved reputation, along with the Middle East, as a cradle of religion. Two of the world's major religions, Hinduism and Buddhism, originated in India, and a number of others,

including Sikhism and Islam (the latter of which entered the South Asian subcontinent in the ninth or tenth century CE), continue to flourish there.

In its size and geographical complexity, India seems more like a continent than a nation. That complexity begins with the physical environment. The Indian subcontinent, shaped like a spade hanging from the southern ridge of Asia, is composed of a number of core regions. In the far north are the Himalayan and Karakoram mountain ranges, home of the highest peaks in the world. Directly to the south of the Himalayas and the Karakoram range is the rich valley of the Ganges, India's "holy river" and one of the core regions of Indian culture. To the west is the Indus River valley. Today, the latter is a relatively arid plateau that forms the backbone of the modern state of Pakistan, but in ancient times it enjoyed a more temperate climate and served as the cradle of Indian civilization.

South of India's two major river valleys lies the Deccan, a region of hills and an upland plateau that extends from the Ganges Valley to the southern tip of the Indian subcontinent. The interior of the plateau is relatively hilly and dry, but the eastern and western coasts are occupied by lush plains, which have historically been among the most densely populated regions of India. Off the southeastern coast is the island known today as Sri Lanka. Although Sri Lanka is now a separate country quite distinct politically and culturally from India, the island's history is intimately linked with that of its larger neighbor.

In this vast region live a rich mixture of peoples: people speaking one of the languages in the Dravidian family, who may have descended from the Indus River culture that flourished at the dawn of Indian civilization more than four thousand years ago; Aryans, descended from the pastoral peoples who flooded southward from Central Asia in the second millennium BCE; and hill peoples, who may be the descendants of the first migrants passing through the area and hence may have been the earliest inhabitants of all. Although today this beautiful mosaic of peoples and cultures has been broken up into a number of separate independent states, the region still possesses a coherent history that is recognizably Indian.

2–1b The Indus Valley Civilization: A Fascinating Enigma

The first signs that an ancient civilization had emerged in the Indus River Valley appeared in the early nineteenth century, when archaeologists discovered the remains of an urban settlement at Harappa, a town located several hundred miles north of the site at Mohenjo-Daro. Today over one thousand small agricultural settlements have been unearthed in the region, many of them dating back to over nine thousand years ago. Those small mudbrick villages eventually gave rise to the sophisticated human communities that historians call Indus Valley civilization. Although today the area is relatively arid, during the third and fourth millennia BCE, it evidently received much more abundant rainfall, and the valleys of the Indus River and its tributaries supported a thriving civilization that may have covered a total area of more

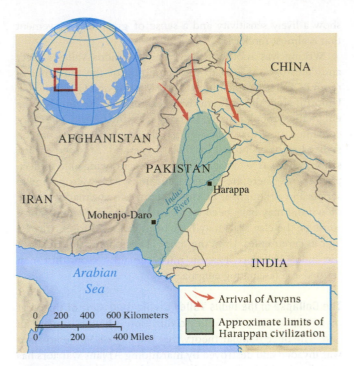

Map 2.1 **Ancient Indus Valley Civilization.** This map shows the location of the first civilization that arose in the Indus River valley, which today is located in Pakistan.

 Based on this map, why do you think the Indus Valley civilization resembled the civilizations of Mesopotamia and Egypt?

than 700,000 square miles, from the Himalayas to the Indian Ocean. More than seventy sites have been unearthed since the area was discovered in the 1850s, but the main sites are at the two major cities, Harappa, in the Punjab, and Mohenjo-Daro, nearly 400 miles to the south near the mouth of the Indus River (see Map 2.1).

Political and Social Structures In several respects, the Indus Valley civilization closely resembled the cultures of Mesopotamia and the Nile Valley. Like them, it probably began in tiny farming villages scattered throughout the river valley, some dating back to as early as 6500 or 7000 BCE. These villages thrived and grew until by the middle of the third millennium BCE they could support a privileged ruling elite living in walled cities of considerable magnitude and affluence. The center of power was the city of Harappa, which was surrounded by a brick wall over 40 feet thick at its base and more than 3.5 miles in circumference. The city was laid out on an essentially rectangular grid, with some streets as wide as 30 feet. Most buildings were constructed of kiln-dried mudbricks and were square in shape, reflecting the grid pattern. At its height, the city may have had as many as 80,000 inhabitants, making it as large as some of the most populous Sumerian urban centers.

Both Harappa and Mohenjo-Daro were divided into large walled neighborhoods, with narrow lanes separating the rows of houses. Houses varied in size, with some as high as three stories, but all followed the same general plan based on a square courtyard surrounded by rooms. Bathrooms featured an advanced drainage system, which carried wastewater out to drains located under the streets and thence to sewage pits beyond the city walls. But the cities also had the equivalent of the modern slum. At Harappa, tiny dwellings for workers have been found near metal furnaces and the open areas used for pounding grain.

Unfortunately, the Indus Valley writing system has not yet been deciphered, so historians know relatively little about the organization of Indus society, nor even the name that it called itself (Sumerian sources referred to it as Meluhha). Recent archaeological evidence suggests, however, that unlike its contemporaries in Egypt and Sumer, the Indus Valley society was not a centralized monarchy with a theocratic base but a collection of more than 1,500 towns and cities loosely connected by ties of trade and alliance and ruled by a coalition of landlords and rich merchants. There were no royal precincts or imposing burial monuments, and there are few surviving stone or terracotta images that might represent kings, priests, or military commanders. It is possible that religion had advanced beyond the stage of spirit worship to belief in a single god or goddess of fertility. Drawings of animals on many of the clay seals suggest the possibility of animal sacrifice at ceremonies undertaken to maintain the fertility of the soil and guarantee the annual harvest.

As in Mesopotamia and Egypt, the Indus Valley economy was based primarily on agriculture, and there is evidence that grain crops like wheat, barley, and rice, as well as peas, were cultured as early as seven thousand years ago. The presence of cotton seeds at various sites suggests that the Indus Valley peoples may have been the first to master the cultivation of this useful crop and possibly introduced it, along with rice, to other societies in the region. But they also developed an extensive trading network that extended to Sumer and other

A Mother Goddess. During its period of florescence, from 2600 and 1900 BCE, the craftsmen of the Indus Valley civilization created a variety of terracotta objects, including whimsical toy animals, whistles, and tops, as well as dice, for children. Most enigmatic, however, are the numerous female figurines, such as the one shown here, with elaborate headdress and numerous strands of necklaces. Their meaning and purpose, however, remain elusive. Were they representatives of an earth goddess, reminiscent of a number of other female deities throughout the ancient world? Although the evidence is inconclusive, it is likely that the concept of a fertility goddess was worshiped in the Indus Valley, as it was in other river valleys throughout the region. © DeA Picture Library/Art Resource, NY

civilizations to the west. Textiles and foodstuffs were apparently imported from Sumer in exchange for metals such as copper, lumber, precious stones, and various types of luxury goods. Much of this trade was conducted by ship via the Persian Gulf, although some undoubtedly went by land.

Indus Valley Culture Archaeological remains indicate that the Indus Valley peoples possessed a culture as sophisticated in some ways as that of the Sumerians to the west. Although the architecture was purely functional and shows little artistic sensitivity, the aesthetic quality of some of the pottery and sculpture is superb. Painted pottery, wheel-turned and kiln-fired, rivals equivalent work produced elsewhere. Sculpture, however, was the Indus peoples' highest artistic achievement. Some artifacts possess a wonderful vitality of expression. Fired clay seals show a deft touch in carving animals such as elephants, tigers, rhinoceroses, and antelope, and figures made of copper or terra-cotta

show a lively sensitivity and a sense of grace and movement that is almost modern.

Writing was another achievement of Indus Valley society and dates back at least to the beginning of the third millennium BCE (see Comparative Essay "Writing and Civilization"). Unfortunately, the only surviving examples of writing are the enigmatic symbols inscribed on clay seals and tablets. The script contained more than four hundred characters, but most are too stylized to be identified by their shape and, as noted earlier, scholars have as yet made little progress in being able to decipher them. There are no apparent links with Mesopotamian scripts and although, as in Mesopotamia, the primary purpose of writing may have been to record commercial transactions, some of the clay seals may have been intended to portray religious ceremonies. Until the script is deciphered, much about the Indus Valley civilization must remain, as one historian termed it, a fascinating enigma.

The Collapse of the Indus Valley Civilization One of the great mysteries of the Indus Valley civilization is how it came to an end. The once popular theory that the city of Mohenjo-Daro was invaded and destroyed by marauding Aryans warriors has now been widely dismissed, since the Aryan peoples apparently did not begin to arrive in northwest India until about 1500 BCE, at least four centuries after the apparent abandonment of Mohenjo-Daro. More likely, the Indus Valley civilization had already fallen on hard times, probably as a result of natural causes. Archaeologists have found clear signs of social decay, including evidence of trash in the streets, neglect of public services, and overcrowding in urban neighborhoods. Mohenjo-Daro itself may have been destroyed by an epidemic or by natural phenomena such as floods, an earthquake, or a shift in the course of the Indus River. Some climatologists speculate that the monsoon rains that regularly water the region had weakened at the outset of the second millennium BCE. If that was the case, any migrating peoples arrived in the area after the greatness of Indus Valley civilization had already passed.

The Dancing Girl. Relatively few objects reflecting the creative talents of the Indus Valley peoples have survived. This bronze figure of a young dancer in repose, 5 inches tall, is a rare metal sculpture from Mohenjo-Daro. The detail and grace of her stance reflect the skill of the artist who molded her some four thousand years ago.

Harappan/National Museum of India, New Delhi, India/Bridgeman Images

HISTORIANS DEBATE **Who Were the Aryans?** Historians know relatively little about the origins and culture of the Aryans. The traditional view is that they were Indo-European-speaking peoples who once inhabited vast areas in the steppes north and east of the Black and Caspian Seas. The Indo-Europeans were primarily pastoral peoples who migrated from season to season in search of fodder for their herds, although they may have begun to cultivate grain crops in parts of Central Asia by the fifth millennium BCE. Historians have credited the Aryans with a number of technological achievements, including the invention of horse-drawn chariots and the stirrup, both of which were eventually introduced throughout much of the Eurasian supercontinent.

Whereas many other Indo-European-speaking peoples moved westward and eventually settled throughout Europe, the Aryans began to settle in an area around the Oxus River in Central Asia and then moved south across the Hindu Kush

Writing and Civilization

Art & Ideas

When evidence of the complexity and sophistication of the Indus Valley civilization began to emerge in the early twentieth century, among the most tantalizing objects to appear were the clay seals and tablets that contained mysterious inscription in a written language that has not yet been deciphered. Without a greater understanding of the meaning of these enigmatic signs, our knowledge of the Indus Valley civilization must remain rudimentary. This challenge is a testament to the importance of the presence of a written language to enable historians to uncover the secrets of ancient cultures.

According to prehistorians, human beings invented the first spoken language about 50,000 years ago. As human beings spread from Africa to other continents, that initial language gradually fragmented and evolved into innumerable separate tongues. By the time the agricultural revolution began about 10,000 BCE, there were perhaps nearly twenty distinct language families in existence around the world.

During the later stages of the agricultural revolution, the first writing systems also began to emerge in various places around the world (see Map 2.2). The first successful efforts were apparently achieved in Mesopotamia and Egypt, but knowledge of writing soon spread to peoples along the shores of the Mediterranean and in the Indus River Valley in South Asia. Wholly independent systems were also invented in China and Mesoamerica. Writing was used for a variety of purposes. One reason was to enable a ruler to communicate with his subjects on matters of official concern, as when the Egyptian king Scorpion in about 3250 BCE ordered that a decree announcing that his forces had achieved a major victory over rivals in the region be inscribed on a limestone cliff in the Nile River Valley. In other cases, the purpose was to enable human beings to communicate with supernatural forces. In China and Egypt, for example, priests used writing to communicate with the gods. In Mesopotamia and in the Indus River Valley, merchants apparently used writing to mark official events or to record commercial and other legal transactions. Finally, writing was also used to present ideas in new ways, giving rise to such early Mesopotamian literature as *The Epic of Gilgamesh*.

How did these early written languages evolve into the complex systems in use today? In almost all cases, the first systems consisted of pictographs, pictorial images of various concrete objects such as trees, water, cattle, body parts, and the heavenly bodies. Eventually, the pictographs became more stylized to facilitate transcription—much as we often use a cursive script instead of block printing today. Finally, and most important for their future development, these pictorial images began to take on specific phonetic meanings so that they could represent sounds in the written language. Most sophisticated written systems eventually evolved to a phonetic script, based on an alphabet of symbols to represent all sounds in the spoken language, but others went only part of the way by adding phonetic signs to the individual character to suggest pronunciation while keeping the essence of the original pictograph to indicate meaning. Most of the latter systems, such as hieroglyphics in Egypt and cuneiform in Mesopotamia, eventually became extinct, but the ancient Chinese writing system survives today, in greatly altered form.

 What are the various purposes for which writing systems were developed in the ancient world? What appears to have been the initial purpose for the development of the Indus Valley script?

Scala/Art Resource, NY

Indus Valley Seals. The Indus Valley peoples, like their contemporaries in Mesopotamia, developed a writing system to record their spoken language. Unfortunately, it has not yet been deciphered. Most extant examples of early writing from the area are found on fired clay seals depicting human figures and animals. These seals have been found in houses and were probably used to identify the owners of goods for sale. Other seals may have been used as amulets or have had other religious significance. Several depict religious figures or ritualistic scenes of sacrifice.

into the plains of northern India. Between 1500 and 1000 BCE, they gradually advanced eastward from the Indus Valley, across the fertile plain of the Ganges River, and some migrated southward into the Deccan Plateau. Eventually, they extended their political mastery over the entire subcontinent and its mainly Dravidian-speaking inhabitants, although the indigenous culture undoubtedly survived to remain a prominent element in the evolution of traditional Indian civilization.

In recent years, a new theory has been proposed by some historians in India, who contend that the Aryan peoples did not migrate into the Indian subcontinent from Central Asia, but were in fact descendants of the indigenous population that

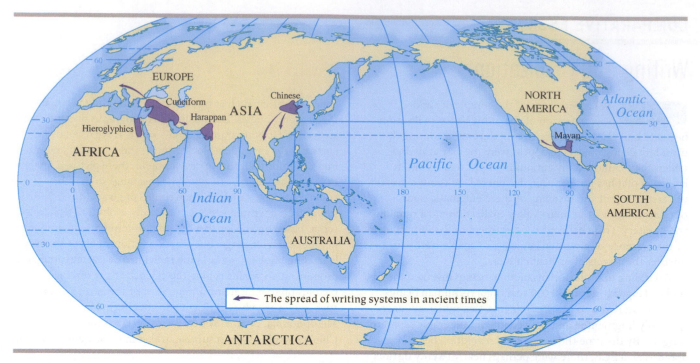

Map 2.2 Writing Systems in the Ancient World. One of the chief characteristics of the first civilizations was the development of a system of written communication.

 Based on the Comparative Essay, "Writing and Civilization," in what ways were these first writing systems similar, and how were they different?

had originally created the Indus Valley civilization. Most scholars, however, continue to support the migration hypothesis, although the evidence is not conclusive. They point out that the spoken language of the Aryan people, known as Sanskrit, is widely recognized as a branch of the Indo-European family of languages. Moreover, the earliest account produced by the Aryan people themselves, known as the Rig Veda (RIK VAY-duh) (see next section), describes a culture based primarily on pastoralism, a pursuit not particularly suited to the Indus River valley. Significantly, the tradition of buffalo sacrifice, inscribed on innumerable seals throughout the Indus River Valley, is not mentioned in the Rig Veda. A definitive solution to the debate will have to await further evidence.

2–2 THE ARYANS IN INDIA

 Focus Question: What were some of the distinctive features of the class system introduced by the Aryan peoples, and what effects did it have on Indian civilization?

After they settled in India, the Aryans gradually adapted to the geographic realities of their new homeland and abandoned the pastoral life for agricultural pursuits. They were assisted by the invention of iron, which was probably introduced from the Middle East, where it had been introduced by the Hittites (see Chapter 1) about 1500 BCE. The invention of the iron plow, along with the development of irrigation, enabled the Aryans

and their indigenous subjects to clear the dense jungle growth along the Ganges River and transform the Ganges Valley into one of the richest agricultural regions in South Asia. The Aryans also developed their own writing system, based on the Aramaic script of the Middle East, and were thus able to transcribe the legends that previously had been passed down from generation to generation by memory (see "Writing and Civilization" on p. 43). Most of what is known about the early Aryans is based on oral traditions passed on in the Rig Veda, an ancient work that was written down after the Aryans arrived in India (it is one of several Vedas, or collections of sacred instructions and rituals, see "In the Beginning").

2–2a From Chieftains to Kings

As in other Indo-European societies, each of the various Aryan tribes was led by a chieftain, called a **raja** (RAH-juh), who was assisted by a council of elders composed of other leading members of the community; like them, he was normally a member of the warrior class, called the *kshatriya* (kshuh-TREE-yuh). The chief derived his power from his ability to protect his people from rival groups, a skill that was crucial in the warring kingdoms and shifting alliances that were typical of early Aryan society. Though the rajas claimed to be representatives of the gods, they were not viewed as gods themselves.

As Aryan society grew in size and complexity, the chieftains began to be transformed into kings, usually called **maharajas** (mah-huh-RAH-juhs) ("great rajas"). Nevertheless, the tradition that the ruler did not possess absolute authority

IN THE BEGINNING

Religion & Philosophy

AS THE INDIANS BEGAN TO SPECULATE about the nature of the cosmic order, they came to believe in the existence of a single monistic force in the universe, a form of ultimate reality called *Brahman*. Today the early form of Hinduism is sometimes called Brahmanism. In the Upanishads (oo-PAHN-ih-shahds), the concept began to emerge as an important element of Indian religious belief. It was the duty of the individual self—called the *Atman*—to achieve an understanding of this ultimate reality so that after death the self would merge in spiritual form with *Brahman*. Sometimes *Brahman* was described in more concrete terms as a creator god—eventually known as Vishnu—but more often in terms of a shadowy ultimate reality. In the following passage from the Upanishads, the author speculates on the nature of ultimate reality.

The Upanishads

In the beginning . . ., this world was just being, one only, without a second. Some people, no doubt, say: "In the beginning . . ., this world was just nonbeing, one only, without

a second; from that nonbeing, being was produced." But how indeed . . . could it be so? How could being be produced from nonbeing? . . .

In the beginning this world was being alone, one only, without a second. Being thought to itself: "May I be many, may I procreate." It produced fire. That fire thought to itself: "May I be many, may I procreate." It produced water. Therefore, whenever a person grieves or perspires, then it is from fire [heat] alone that water is produced. That water thought to itself: "May I be many, may I procreate." It produced food; it is from water alone that food for eating is produced. . . . That divinity (Being) thought to itself: "Well, having entered into these three divinities [fire, water, and food] by means of this living self, let me develop names and forms."

 How would you compare this passage from the Upanishads with the accounts about the origins of life from Egyptian and Hebrew sources as cited in Chapter 1?

Source: From *The Upanishads*, tr. Juan Mascaro. Viking Press, 1965.

---

remained strong. Like all human beings, the ruler was required to follow the *dharma* (DAR-muh), a set of laws that set behavioral standards for all individuals and classes in Indian society.

The Impact of the Greeks While competing groups squabbled for precedence in India, powerful new empires were rising to the west. First came the Persian Empire of Cyrus and Darius. Then came the Greeks. After two centuries of sporadic rivalry and warfare, the Greeks achieved a brief period of regional dominance in the late fourth century BCE with the rise of Macedonia under Alexander the Great. Alexander had heard of the riches of India, and in 330 BCE, after conquering Persia, he launched an invasion of the east (see Chapter 4). In 326 BCE, his armies arrived in the plains of northwestern India and the Indus River Valley. They departed almost as suddenly as they had come, leaving in their wake Greek administrators

Alexander the Great's Movements in Asia

and a veneer of cultural influence that would affect the area for generations to come.

2–2b The Mauryan Empire

The Alexandrian conquest was a brief interlude in the history of the Indian subcontinent, but it played a formative role, for on the heels of Alexander's departure came the rise of the first dynasty to control much of the region. The founder of the new state, who took the royal title Chandragupta Maurya (chun-druh-GOOP-tuh MOWR-yuh) (324–301 BCE), drove out the Greek administrators that Alexander had left behind and solidified his control over the northern Indian plain. He established the capital of his new Mauryan Empire at Pataliputra (pah-tah-lee-POO-truh) (modern Patna) in the Ganges Valley (see Map 2.3). Little is known of his origins, although some sources say he had originally fought on the side of the invading Greek forces but then angered Alexander with his outspoken advice.

Little, too, is known of Chandragupta Maurya's empire. Most accounts of his reign rely on the scattered remnants of a lost work written by Megasthenes (muh-GAS-thuh-neez), a Greek ambassador to the Mauryan court, in about 302 BCE. Chandragupta Maurya was apparently advised by a brilliant court official named Kautilya (kow-TIL-yuh), whose name has been attached to a treatise on politics called the *Arthasastra*. The work actually dates from a later time, but it may well reflect Kautilya's ideas.

Although the author of the *Arthasastra* follows Aryan tradition in stating that the happiness of the king lies in the happiness of his subjects, the treatise also asserts that when the sacred law of the *dharma* and practical politics collide, the latter must take precedence: "Whenever there is disagreement between history and sacred law or between evidence and sacred law, then the matter should be settled in accordance with sacred law. But whenever sacred law is in conflict with rational law, then reason shall be held authoritative."[1] The *Arthasastra* also emphasizes ends rather than means, achieved results rather than the methods employed. For this reason, it has often been compared to Machiavelli's famous political treatise of the Italian Renaissance, *The Prince*, written more than a thousand years later.

As described in the *Arthasastra*, Chandragupta Maurya's government was highly centralized and even despotic: "It is power and power alone which, only when exercised by the king with impartiality, and in proportion to guilt, over his son or his enemy, maintains both this world and the next."[2] The king possessed a large army and a secret police responsible to his orders (according to the Greek ambassador Megasthenes, Chandragupta Maurya was chronically fearful of assassination, a not unrealistic concern for someone who had allegedly come to power by violence). Reportedly, all food was tasted in his presence, and he made a practice of never sleeping twice in the same bed in his sumptuous palace. To guard against corruption, a board of censors was empowered to investigate cases of possible malfeasance and incompetence within the bureaucracy.

The ruler's authority beyond the confines of the capital may often have been limited, however. The empire was divided into provinces that were ruled by governors. At first, most of these governors were appointed by and reported to the ruler, but later the position became hereditary. The provinces themselves were divided into districts, each under a chief magistrate appointed by the governor. At the base of the government pyramid was the village, where the vast majority of the Indian people lived. The village was governed by a council of elders; membership in the council was normally hereditary and was shared by the wealthiest families in the village.

2–2c Caste and Class: Social Structures in Ancient India

When the Aryans arrived in India, they already possessed a social system based on a ruling warrior class and other groupings characteristic of a pastoral society. In the subcontinent, they encountered peoples living by farming or, in some cases, by other pursuits such as fishing, hunting, or food gathering. Although the immediate consequences of this mixture of cultures are still unclear, the ultimate result was the emergence of a complex set of social institutions that continues to have relevance down to the present day.

The Class System At the crux of the social system that emerged from the clash of cultures was the concept of a hierarchical division of society that placed each individual within a ritual framework that defined the person's occupation and status within the broader community. In part, this division may have been an outgrowth of attitudes held by the Aryan peoples with regard to the indigenous population. The Aryans, who followed primarily pastoral pursuits, tended to look askance at their new neighbors, who lived by tilling the soil. Further, the Aryans, a mostly light-skinned people, were contemptuous of the indigenous peoples, who were darker. Light skin came to imply high status, whereas dark skin suggested the opposite.

The concept of color, however, was only the physical manifestation of a division that took place in Indian society on the basis of economic functions. Indian classes (called **varna**, literally, "color," and commonly but mistakenly translated as "castes" in English) did not simply reflect an informal division of labor. Instead, at least in theory, they were a set of rigid social classifications that determined not only one's occupation but also one's status in society and one's hope for ultimate salvation (see Section 2-3, "Escaping the Wheel of Life" on p. 51). There were five major *varna* in Indian society in ancient times (see "Social Classes in Ancient India"). At the top were two classes, collectively viewed as the aristocracy, which represented the ruling elites in Aryan society prior to their arrival in India: the priests and the warriors.

The priestly class, known as the **brahmins**, was usually considered to be at the top of the social scale. Descended from seers who had advised the ruler on religious matters in Aryan tribal society—*brahmin* meant "one possessed of **Brahman**" (BRAH-mun), a term for the supreme god—they were eventually transformed into an official class after their religious role declined in importance. Megasthenes described this class as follows:

> From the time of their conception in the womb they are under the care and guardianship of learned men who go to the mother and . . . give her prudent hints and counsels, and the women who listen to them most willingly are thought to be the most fortunate in their offspring. After their birth the children are in the care of one person after another, and as they advance in years their masters are men of superior accomplishments. The philosophers reside in a grove in front of the city within a moderate-sized enclosure. They live in a simple style and lie on pallets of straw and [deer] skins. They abstain from animal food and sexual pleasures, and occupy their time in listening to serious discourse and in imparting knowledge to willing ears.[3]

The second class was the *kshatriya*, the warriors. Although often listed below the *brahmins* in social status, many *kshatriyas* were probably descended from the ruling warrior class in Aryan society prior to the conquest of India and thus may have originally ranked socially above the *brahmins*, although they were ranked lower in religious terms. Like the *brahmins*, the *kshatriyas* were originally identified with a single occupation—fighting—but as the character of Aryan society changed, they often switched to other forms of employment. At the same time, new families from other classes were sometimes tacitly accepted into the ranks of the warriors.

SOCIAL CLASSES IN ANCIENT INDIA

Family & Society

THE *LAW OF MANU* IS A SET OF BEHAVIORAL NORMS that, according to tradition, were prescribed by India's mythical founding ruler, Manu. The treatise was probably written in the first or second century BCE. The following excerpt describes the various social classes in India and their prescribed duties. Many scholars doubt that the social system in India was ever as rigid as it was portrayed here, and some suggest that upper-class Indians may have used the idea of *varna* to enhance their own status in society.

The *Law of Manu*

For the sake of the preservation of this entire creation, the Exceedingly Resplendent One [the Creator of the Universe] assigned separate duties to the classes which had sprung from his mouth, arms, thighs, and feet.

Teaching, studying, performing sacrificial rites, so too making others perform sacrificial rites, and giving away and receiving gifts—these he assigned to the [brahmins].

Protection of the people, giving away of wealth, performance of sacrificial rites, study, and nonattachment to sensual pleasures—these are, in short, the duties of a *kshatriya*.

Tending of cattle, giving away of wealth, performance of sacrificial rites, study, trade and commerce, usury, and agriculture—these are the occupations of a *vaisya*.

The Lord has prescribed only one occupation [*karma*] for a *sudra*, namely, service without malice of even these other three classes.

Of created beings, those which are animate are the best; of the animate, those which subsist by means of their intellect; of the intelligent, men are the best; and of men, the [brahmins] are traditionally declared to be the best.

The code of conduct—prescribed by scriptures and ordained by sacred tradition—constitutes the highest *dharma*; hence a twice-born person, conscious of his own Self [seeking spiritual salvation], should be always scrupulous in respect of it.

 Based on this description, how does the class system in ancient India compare with social class divisions in other societies in Asia? Why do you think the class system, as described here, developed in India? What is the difference between the class system (varna) and the jati (discussed later in this chapter)?

Source: Manu Smrti 3.55–57: Ed. J. Jolly. London: Trubner, 1887 (Trubner Oriental Series).

The third-ranked class in Indian society was the ***vaisya*** (VISH-yuh) (literally, "commoner"). The *vaisyas* were usually viewed in economic terms as the merchant class. Some historians have speculated that the *vaisyas* were originally guardians of the tribal herds but that after settling in India, many moved into commercial pursuits. Megasthenes noted that members of this class "alone are permitted to hunt and keep cattle and to sell beasts of burden or to let them out on hire. In return for clearing the land of wild beasts and birds which infest sown fields, they receive an allowance of corn from the king. They lead a wandering life and dwell in tents."[4] Although this class was ranked below the first two in social status, it shared with them the privilege of being considered "**twice-born**," a term referring to a ceremony at puberty whereby young males were initiated into adulthood and introduced into Indian society. After the ceremony, male members of the top three classes were allowed to wear the "sacred thread" for the remainder of their lives.

Below the three "twice-born" classes were the ***sudras*** (SOO-druhs or SHOO-druhs), who represented the great bulk of the Indian population. The *sudras* were not considered fully Aryan, and the term probably originally referred to the indigenous population. Most *sudras* were peasants or artisans or worked at other forms of manual labor. They had only limited rights in society. In recent years, DNA samples have revealed that most upper-class South Indians today share more genetic characteristics with modern Europeans than their lower-class counterparts do,

CHRONOLOGY	Ancient India
Indus Valley civilization	c. 2600–1900 BCE
Arrival of the Aryans	c. 1500 BCE
Life of Gautama Buddha	c. 560–480 BCE
Invasion of India by Alexander the Great	326 BCE
Mauryan dynasty founded	324 BCE
Reign of Chandragupta Maurya	324–301 BCE
Reign of Ashoka	269–232 BCE
Collapse of Mauryan dynasty	183 BCE
Rise of Kushan kingdom	c. first century CE

a finding that supports the hypothesis that the Aryans established their political and social dominance over the indigenous population.

At the lowest level of Indian society, and in fact not even considered a legitimate part of the class system, were the untouchables (also known as outcastes or **pariahs**). The untouchables probably originated as a slave class consisting of prisoners of war, criminals, ethnic minorities, and other groups considered outside Indian society. Even after slavery was outlawed, the untouchables were given menial and degrading tasks that other Indians would not accept, such as collecting trash, handling dead bodies, or serving as butchers or tanners. One historian estimates that they may have accounted for a little more than 5 percent of the total population of India in antiquity.

The lives of the untouchables were extremely demeaning. They were regarded as being not fully human, and their very presence was considered polluting to members of the other *varna*. No Indian would touch or eat food handled or prepared by an untouchable. Untouchables lived in ghettos and, according to a foreign observer, were required to tap two sticks together to announce their approach when they traveled outside their quarters so that others could avoid them.

Technically, these class divisions were absolute. Individuals supposedly were born, lived, and died in the same class. In practice, upward or downward mobility probably took place, and there was undoubtedly some flexibility in economic functions. But throughout most of Indian history, class taboos remained strict. Members generally were not permitted to marry outside their class (although in practice, men were occasionally allowed to marry below their class but not above it). At first, attitudes toward the handling of food were relatively loose, but eventually that taboo grew stronger, and social mores dictated that sharing meals and marrying outside one's class were unacceptable.

The *Jati* The people of ancient India did not belong to a particular class as individuals but as part of a larger kin group commonly referred to as the *jati* (JAH-tee) (in Portuguese, *casta*, which evolved into the English term *caste*), a system of extended families that originated in ancient India and still exists in somewhat changed form today. Although the origins of the *jati* system are unknown (there are no indications of strict class distinctions in Harappan society), the *jati* eventually became identified with a specific kinship group living in a specific area and carrying out a specific function in society. Each *jati* was identified with a particular *varna*, and each had its own separate economic function.

Jatis were thus the basic social organization into which traditional Indian society was divided. Each *jati* was composed of hundreds or thousands of individual nuclear families and was governed by its own council of elders. Membership in this ruling council was usually hereditary and was based on the wealth or social status of particular families within the community.

In theory, each *jati* was assigned a particular form of economic activity. Obviously, though, not all families in a given *jati* could take part in the same vocation, and as time went on, members of a single *jati* commonly engaged in several different lines of work. Sometimes an entire *jati* would have to move its location in order to continue a particular form of activity. In other cases, a *jati* would adopt an entirely new occupation in order to remain in a certain area. Such changes in habitat or occupation introduced the possibility of movement up or down the social scale. In this way, an entire *jati* could sometimes engage in upward mobility, even though that normally was not possible for individuals, who were tied to their class identity for life.

The class system in ancient India may sound highly constricting, but there were persuasive social and economic reasons why it survived for so many centuries. In the first place, it provided an identity for individuals in a highly hierarchical society. Although an individual might rank lower on the social scale than members of other classes, it was always possible to find others ranked even lower. Class was also a means for new groups, such as mountain tribal people, to achieve a recognizable place in the broader community. Perhaps equally important, the *jati* was a primitive form of welfare system. Each *jati* was obliged to provide for any of its members who were poor or destitute. It also provided an element of stability in a society that all too often was in a state of political turmoil.

2–2d Daily Life in Ancient India

Beyond these rigid social stratifications was the Indian family. Not only was life centered around the family, but the family, not the individual, was the most basic unit in society.

The Family The ideal social unit was an extended family, with three generations living under the same roof. It was essentially patriarchal, except along the Malabar coast, near the southwestern tip of the subcontinent, where a matriarchal form of social organization prevailed down to modern times. In the rest of India, the oldest male traditionally possessed legal authority over the entire family unit.

The family was linked together in a religious sense to its ancestral members by a series of commemorative rites. Family ceremonies were conducted to honor the departed and to link the living and the dead. The male family head was responsible for leading the ritual. At his death, his eldest son had the duty of conducting the funeral rites.

The importance of the father and the son in family ritual underlined the importance of males in Indian society. Male superiority was expressed in a variety of ways. Women could not serve as priests (although some were accepted as seers), nor were they normally permitted to study the Vedas. In general, males had a monopoly on education, since the primary goal of learning to read was to conduct family rituals. In high-class families, young men, after having been initiated into the sacred thread, began Vedic studies with a ***guru*** (teacher). Some then went on to higher studies in one of the major cities. The goal of such an education might be either professional or religious. Such young men were not supposed to marry until after twelve years of study.

The Role of Women In general, only males could inherit property, except in a few cases when there were no sons. According to law, a woman was always considered a minor. Divorce was prohibited, although it sometimes took place. According to the *Arthasastra*, a wife who had been deserted by her husband could seek a divorce. Polygamy was fairly rare and apparently occurred mainly among the higher classes, but husbands were permitted to take a second wife if the first was barren. Producing children was an important aspect of marriage, both because children provided security for their parents in old age and because they were a physical proof of male potency. Child marriage was common for young girls, whether because of the desire for children or because daughters represented an economic liability to their parents. But perhaps the most graphic symbol of women's subjection to men was the ritual of *sati* (suh-TEE) (often written *suttee*), which encouraged the wife to throw herself on her dead husband's funeral pyre. The Greek visitor Megasthenes reported "that he had heard from some persons of wives burning themselves along with their deceased husbands and doing so gladly; and that those women who refused to burn themselves were held in disgrace."[5] All in all, it was undoubtedly a difficult existence. According to the *Law of Manu*, an early treatise on social organization and behavior in ancient India, probably written in the first or second century BCE, a woman was subordinated to men throughout her life—first to her father, then to her husband, and finally to her sons:

> She should do nothing independently
> 	even in her own house.
> In childhood subject to her father,
> 	in youth to her husband,
> and when her husband is dead to her sons,
> 	she should never enjoy independence. . . .
> Though he be uncouth and prone to pleasure,
> 	though he have no good points at all,
> the virtuous wife should ever
> 	worship her lord as a god.[6]

At the root of female subordination to the male was the practical fact that as in most agricultural societies, men did most of the work in the fields. Females were viewed as having little utility outside the home and indeed were considered an economic burden, since parents were obliged to provide a dowry to acquire a husband for a daughter. Female children also appeared to offer little advantage in maintaining the family unit, since they joined the families of their husbands after the wedding ceremony.

Despite all of these indications of female subjection to the male, there are numerous signs that in some ways women often played an influential role in Indian society, and the code of behavior set out in the *Law of Manu* stressed that they should be treated with respect (see "The Position of Women in Ancient India" on p. 50). Indians appeared to be fascinated by female sexuality, and tradition held that women often used their sexual powers to achieve domination over men. The author of the Mahabharata, a vast epic of early Indian society, complained that "the fire has never too many logs, the ocean never too many rivers, death never too many living souls, and fair-eyed woman never too many men." Despite the legal and social constraints, women often played an important role within the family unit, and many were admired and honored for their talents. It is probably significant that paintings and sculpture from ancient and medieval India frequently show women in a role equal to that of men, and the tradition of the henpecked husband is as prevalent in India as in many Western societies today.

2–2e The Economy

The arrival of the Aryans did not drastically change the economic character of Indian society. Not only did most Aryans eventually take up farming, but it is likely that agriculture expanded rapidly under Aryan rule with the invention of the iron plow and the spread of northern Indian culture into the Deccan Plateau. One

Female Earth Spirit. This earth spirit, carved on a gatepost of the Buddhist stupa at Sanchi 2,200 years ago, illustrates how earlier representations of the fertility goddess were incorporated into Buddhist art. Women were revered as powerful fertility symbols and considered dangerous when menstruating or immediately after giving birth. Voluptuous and idealized, the earth spirit was believed to be able to cause a tree to blossom by wrapping her leg around its trunk or even merely touching a branch with her arm. Belief in the sacred quality of the banyan and the pipal tree, two of the most majestic trees found throughout South Asia, has been a characteristic of religious belief in the subcontinent since the Indus Valley civilization.

consequence of this process was to shift the focus of Indian culture from the Indus Valley farther eastward to the Ganges River Valley, which even today is one of the most densely populated regions on earth. The flatter areas in the Deccan Plateau and in the coastal plains were also turned into cropland.

Indian Farmers For most Indian farmers, life was harsh. Among the most fortunate were those who owned their own land, although they were required to pay taxes to the state. Many others were sharecroppers or landless laborers. They were subject to the vicissitudes of the market and often paid exorbitant rents to their landlord. Concentration of land in large holdings was limited by the tradition of dividing property among all the sons, but large estates worked by hired laborers or rented out to sharecroppers were not uncommon, particularly in areas where local rajas derived much of their wealth from their property.

THE POSITION OF WOMEN IN ANCIENT INDIA

Family & Society

THE AMBIVALENT ATTITUDE TOWARD WOMEN IN ANCIENT INDIA is evident in this passage from the *Law of Manu*, which states that respect for women is the responsibility of men. At the same time, it also makes clear that a woman's place is in the home.

The *Law of Manu*

Women must be honored and adorned by their father, brothers, husbands, and brother-in-law who desire great good fortune.

Where women, verily, are honored, there the gods rejoice, where, however they are not honored, there all sacred rites prove fruitless.

Where the female relations live in grief—that family soon perishes completely; where, however, they do not suffer from any grievance—that family always prospers. . . .

The father who does not give away his daughter in marriage at the proper time is censurable; censurable is the husband who does not approach his wife in due season; and after the husband is dead, the son, verily is censurable, who does not protect his mother.

Source: Manu Smrti 3.55–57: Ed. J. Jolly. London: Trubner, 1887 (Trubner Oriental Series).

Even against the slightest provocations should women be particularly guarded; for unguarded they would bring grief to both the families.

Regarding this as the highest *dharma* of all four classes, husbands though weak, must strive to protect their wives.

His own offspring, character, family, self, and *dharma* does one protect when he protects his wife scrupulously. . . .

The husband should engage his wife in the collections and expenditure of his wealth, in cleanliness, in *dharma*, in cooking food for the family, and in looking after the necessities of the household. . . .

Women destined to bear children, enjoying great good fortune, deserving of worship, the resplendent lights of homes on the one hand and divinities of good luck who reside in the houses on the other—between these there is no difference whatsoever.

 How do these attitudes toward women compare with those we have encountered in the Middle East and North Africa?

Another problem for Indian farmers was the unpredictability of the climate. India is in the monsoon zone. The monsoon is a seasonal wind pattern in southern Asia that blows from the southwest during the summer months and from the northeast during the winter. The southwest monsoon, originating in the Indian Ocean, is commonly marked by heavy rains. When the rains were late, thousands starved, particularly in the drier areas, which were especially dependent on rainfall. Strong governments attempted to deal with such problems by building state-operated granaries and maintaining the irrigation works, but strong governments were rare, and famine was probably all too common. As noted above, a lengthy interruption in the seasonal monsoon pattern may have contributed to the collapse of the Indus Valley civilization. The staple crops in the north were wheat, barley, and millet, while wet rice was common in the fertile river valleys. In the south, grain and vegetables were supplemented by various tropical products, cotton, and spices such as pepper, ginger, cinnamon, and saffron.

Trade and Manufacturing By no means were all Indians farmers. As time passed, India became one of the most advanced trading and manufacturing civilizations in the ancient world. After the rise of the Mauryas, India's role in regional trade began to expand, and the subcontinent became a major transit point in a vast commercial network that extended from the rim of the Pacific Ocean to the Middle East and the Mediterranean Sea. This regional trade went both by sea and by camel caravan. Overland trade via what is now known as the

Silk Road was under way by at least the millennium BCE (see Chapters 9 and 10). Maritime commerce across the Indian Ocean may have begun as early as the fifth century BCE. It extended eastward as far as Southeast Asia and China and southward as far as the straits between Africa and the island of Madagascar. Westward to Egypt went spices, teakwood, perfumes, jewels, textiles, precious stones and ivory, and wild animals. In return, India received gold, tin, lead, and wine. The subcontinent had become a major crossroads of trade in the ancient world.

India's expanding role as a manufacturing and commercial hub was undoubtedly a spur to the growth of the state. Under Chandragupta Maurya, the central government became actively involved in commercial and manufacturing activities. It owned mines and land and undoubtedly earned massive profits from its role in regional commerce. Separate government departments were established for trade, agriculture, mining, and the manufacture of weapons, and the movement of private goods was vigorously taxed. Nevertheless, a significant private sector also flourished; it was dominated by great caste guilds, which monopolized key sectors of the economy. A money economy probably came into operation during the second century BCE, when copper and gold coins were introduced from the Middle East. This in turn led to the development of banking. But village trade continued to be conducted by means of cowry shells (highly polished shells used as a medium of exchange throughout much of Africa and Asia) or barter throughout the ancient period.

COMPARATIVE ILLUSTRATION

The First Money. Before the invention of metal coins, many societies used items from nature like beads or shells as an early form of currency. Cowry shells (in A) have been found in coastal areas throughout the Indian Ocean; their use later spread to China and as far as Africa, where they continued to be used until the early modern era. In this illustration, a string of cowrie shells adorns a small fishing vessel in the Persian Gulf, presumably in the expectation that it will provide its owner with good fortune. The first metal coins appeared around 500 BCE, when Greek communities along the Turkish coast began to mint silver coins decorated with portraits of rulers or deities. The practice spread to Central and South Asia in the fourth century BCE with the armies of Alexander the Great. After his departure, Hellenistic kingdoms founded in the region minted beautiful silver and gold coins in the Greek style and carried them southward with the Greco-Bactrian invasion of northwest India (symbolized by the elephant headdress on King Demetrius I in image B) in 180 BCE. From that time on, metal coins were used for most important transactions in South Asian societies, with cowry shells used for items of lesser value.

Q *How does the monetary system used in ancient India compare with that practiced in ancient societies in the Mediterranean and the Middle East?*

A

B

2–3 ESCAPING THE WHEEL OF LIFE: THE RELIGIOUS WORLD OF ANCIENT INDIA

 Focus Questions: What are the main tenets of Brahmanism and Buddhism? How did they differ, and how did each religion influence Indian civilization?

As with Indian politics and society, Indian religion is a blend of Aryan and Dravidian culture. The intermingling of those two civilizations gave rise to an extraordinarily complex set of religious beliefs and practices, filled with diversity and contrast. Out of this cultural mix came two of the world's great religions, Buddhism and Hinduism, and several smaller ones, including Jainism and Sikhism. Early Aryan religious beliefs, however, are known to historians as **Brahmanism**. In time, Brahmanical beliefs and practices would give rise to Hinduism, as will be discussed in Chapter 9. Here we will focus on the earliest religious traditions and on the origins of Buddhism.

2–3a Brahmanism

While little is known about the form of religion practiced in the Indus Valley civilization, evidence about the earliest religious beliefs of the Aryan peoples is better documented, and comes primarily from sacred texts such as the Vedas, four collections of hymns and religious ceremonies originally transmitted by memory by Aryan priests, and systematized in form by about 1000 BCE. Many of these religious ideas were probably common to all of the Indo-European peoples before their separation into different groups at least four thousand years ago. Early Aryan beliefs were based on the common concept of a pantheon of gods and goddesses representing great forces of nature similar to the immortals of Greek mythology. The Aryan ancestor of the Greek father-god Zeus, for example, may have been the deity known in early Aryan tradition as Dyaus (see Chapter 4).

The parent god Dyaus was a somewhat distant figure, however, who was eventually overshadowed by other, more functional gods possessing more familiar human traits. For a while, the primary Aryan god was the great warrior god Indra. Indra summoned the Aryan tribal peoples to war and was represented in nature by thunder. Later, Indra declined in importance and was replaced by Varuna, lord of justice. Other gods and goddesses represented various forces of nature or the needs of human beings, such as fire, fertility, and wealth. During Vedic times, the concept of sacrifice was a key means of communicating with celestial forces. As in many other ancient cultures, the practice may have begun as human sacrifice, but later animals were used as substitutes. The priestly class, the *brahmins*, played a key role in these ceremonies.

Another element of Indian religious belief in ancient times was the ideal of *asceticism*. Although there is no reference to such practices in the Vedas, by the sixth century BCE, self-discipline or subjecting oneself to painful stimuli had begun to replace sacrifice as a means of placating or communicating with the gods. Apparently, the original motive for asceticism was to achieve magical powers, but later, in the Upanishads—a set of commentaries on the Vedas compiled in the sixth century BCE—it was seen as a means of spiritual meditation that would enable the practitioner to reach beyond material reality to a world of truth and bliss beyond earthly joy and sorrow. It is possible that another motive was to permit those with strong religious convictions to communicate directly with metaphysical reality without having to rely on the priestly class at court.

Asceticism, of course, has been practiced in other religions, including Christianity and Islam, but it seems particularly identified with Hinduism, the religion that emerged from the early Indian religious tradition. Eventually, asceticism evolved into the modern practice of body training that we know as *yoga* ("union"), which is accepted today as a meaningful element of Hindu religious practice.

The Searcher. In their search for truth and the ultimate reality, some early followers of Brahmanism embarked on a lifelong retreat from the material world. The holy scripture for such early ascetics was the Upanishads, a collection of writings dating from the middle of the first millennium BCE extolling a life of privation and self-denial. The practice continues today, as this photograph of an Indian mendicant wandering in the mountains of the Deccan Plateau attests.

William J. Duiker

Reincarnation Another new concept that probably began to appear around the time the Upanishads were written was **reincarnation**. This is the idea that the individual soul is reborn in a different form after death and progresses through several existences on the wheel of life until it reaches its final destination in a union with the Great World Soul, *Brahman*. Because life is harsh, this final release is the objective of all living souls. From this concept comes the term *Brahmanism*, referring to the early Aryan religious tradition.

A key element in this process is the idea of *karma*—that one's rebirth in a next life is determined by one's actions (*karma*) in this life (see Opposing Viewpoints "The Search for Truth" on p. 54). Hinduism, as it emerged from Brahmanism, placed all living species on a vast scale of existence, including the four classes and the untouchables in human society. The current status of an individual soul, then, is not simply a cosmic accident but the inevitable result of actions that that soul has committed in its past existence.

At the top of the scale are the *brahmins*, who by definition are closest to ultimate release from the law of reincarnation. The *brahmins* are followed in descending order by the other classes in human society and the world of the beasts. Within the animal kingdom, an especially high position is reserved for the cow, which even today is revered by Hindus as a sacred beast. Some scholars have speculated that the unique role played by the cow in Hinduism derives from the value of cattle in Aryan pastoral society. But others have pointed out that cattle were a source of both money and food and suggest that the cow's sacred position may have descended from the concept of the sacred bull in Harappan culture.

The concept of *karma* is governed by the *dharma*, or the law. A law regulating human behavior, the *dharma* imposes different requirements on different individuals depending on their status in society. Those high on the social scale, such as *brahmins* and *kshatriyas*, are held to a stricter form of behavior than *sudras* are. The *brahmin*, for example, is expected to abstain from eating meat, because that would entail the killing of another living being, thus interrupting its *karma*.

How the concept of reincarnation originated is not known, although it was apparently not unusual for early peoples to believe that the individual soul would be reborn in a different form in a later life. In any case, in India the concept may have had practical causes as well as consequences. In the first place, it tended to provide religious sanction for the rigid class divisions that had begun to emerge in Indian society after the arrival of the Aryans, while at the same time providing certain compensations for those lower on the ladder of life. For example, it gave hope to the poor that if they behaved properly in this life, they might improve their condition in the next. It also provided a means for unassimilated groups such as ethnic minorities to find a place in Indian society while at the same time permitting them to maintain their distinctive way of life. The ultimate goal of achieving "good" *karma*, for all believers, was to escape the cycle of existence. To the sophisticated, the nature of that release was a spiritual union of the individual soul with the Great World Soul, *Brahman*, described in the

Upanishads as a form of dreamless sleep, free from earthly desires.

What about the religious beliefs of the vast majority of the Indian people during this formative stage in South Asian society? In all likelihood, popular religion during the first millennium BCE broadly resembled that of peoples elsewhere throughout the world at the time. Belief in the existence of spirits related to natural events, such as thunder or rainfall, or to natural objects such as mountains or trees, was probably commonplace. By the end of the first millennium BCE, a number of primary dieties had begun to appear, including the so-called trinity of gods: Brahman the Creator, Vishnu the Preserver, and Shiva (SHIV-uh) (originally the Vedic god Rudra) the Destroyer. Although Brahman (sometimes in his concrete form called Brahma) was considered to be the highest god, Vishnu and Shiva eventually began to take precedence in the devotional exercises of many Indians, who could be roughly divided into Vishnuites and Shaivites.

Over the centuries, religious practices among Aryan elites changed radically from its origins in Aryan pastoral society. The early belief in deities representing forces of nature gradually gave way to a more formalized system as described above, with a priestly class at court performing sacrifices in order to obtain heavenly favors. But during the first millennium BCE, for some people religious belief began to evolve into a more personal experience (see Opposing Viewpoints "The Search for Truth"), with an emphasis on ethics as a means of obtaining a union between the individual soul (**Atman**) and the ultimate reality (**Brahman**).

Such a concept, however, was probably too ethereal for the average Indian, who looked for a more concrete form of heavenly salvation, a place of beauty and bliss after a life of disease and privation. In later centuries, the Brahmanical beliefs and practices of early Aryan society would gradually be replaced by a more popular faith that would henceforth become known as Hinduism. We will discuss that transformation in Chapter 9.

2–3b Buddhism: The Middle Path

In the sixth century BCE, a new doctrine appeared in northern India that would eventually begin to rival the popularity of Brahmanical beliefs throughout the subcontinent. This new doctrine was called **Buddhism**.

The Three Faces of Shiva. In the first centuries CE, Hindus began to adopt Buddhist rock art. One outstanding example is at the Elephanta Caves, near the modern city of Mumbai (Bombay). Dominating the cave is this 18-foot-high triple-headed statue of Shiva, representing the Hindu deity in all his various aspects. The central figure shows him in total serenity, enveloped in absolute knowledge. The angry profile on the left portrays him as the destroyer, struggling against time, death, and other negative forces. The right-hand profile shows his loving and feminine side in the guise of his beautiful wife, Parvati. William J. Duiker

The Life of Siddhartha Gautama The historical founder of Buddhism, Siddhartha Gautama (si-DAR-tuh GAW-tuh-muh) (c. 560–480 BCE), was a native of a small kingdom in the foothills of the Himalaya Mountains in what is today southern Nepal. He was born in the mid-sixth century BCE, the son of a ruling *kshatriya* family (see Comparative Illustration "The Buddha and Jesus" on p. 62). According to tradition, the young Siddhartha was raised in affluent surroundings and trained, like many other members of his class, in the martial arts. On reaching maturity, he married and began to raise a family. At the age of twenty-nine, however, he suddenly discovered the pain of illness, the sorrow of death, and the degradation caused by old age in the lives of ordinary people and exclaimed, "Would that sickness, age, and death might be forever bound!" From that time on, he decided to dedicate his life to determining the cause and seeking the cure for human suffering.

To find the answers to these questions, Siddhartha abandoned his home and family and traveled widely. At first he tried to follow the model of the ascetics, but he eventually decided that self-mortification did not lead to a greater understanding of life and abandoned the practice. Then one day after a lengthy period of meditation under a tree, he achieved enlightenment as to the meaning of life and spent the remainder of his life preaching it. His conclusions, as embodied in his teachings, became the philosophy (or as some would have it, the religion) of Buddhism. According to legend, the Devil (the Indian term is *Mara*) attempted desperately to tempt him with political power and the company of beautiful girls. But Siddhartha Gautama resisted:

Pleasure is brief as a flash of lightning
Or like an autumn shower, only for a moment. . . .
Why should I then covet the pleasures you speak of?
I see your bodies are full of all impurity:
Birth and death, sickness and age are yours.
I seek the highest prize, hard to attain by men—
The true and constant wisdom of the wise.[7]

Buddhism and Brahmanism How much the modern doctrine of Buddhism resembles the original teachings of Siddhartha Gautama is open to debate, for much time has elapsed since his death and original texts relating his ideas are lacking. Nor is it certain that Siddhartha even intended to found a new religion or doctrine. In some respects, his ideas could be viewed as a reformist form of Brahmanism, designed to transfer

The Search for Truth

Opposing Viewpoints **AT THE TIME THE RIG VEDA WAS ORIGINALLY COMPOSED IN THE SECOND MILLENNIUM BCE,** *brahmins* at court believed that the best way to communicate with the gods was through sacrifice, a procedure that was carried out through the intermediation of the fire god Agni. The first selection is an incantation uttered by priests at the sacrificial ceremony.

By the middle of the first millennium BCE, however, the tradition of offering sacrifices had come under attack by opponents, who argued that the best way to seek truth and tranquility was by renouncing material existence and adopting the life of a wandering mendicant. In the second selection, from the Mundaka Upanishad, an advocate of this position forcefully presents his views. The similarity with the fervent believers of early Christianity, who renounced the corrupting forces of everyday life by seeking refuge in isolated monasteries in the desert, is striking.

The Rig Veda

When the gods made a sacrifice
 With the Man as their victim,
 Spring was the melted butter, Summer the fuel,
 And Autumn the oblation.

When they divided the Man,
 Into how many parts did they divide him?
 What was his mouth, what were his arms,
 What were his thighs and his feet called?

The Brahman was his mouth,
 Of his arms was made the warrior,
 his thighs became the vaisya,
 Of his feet the sudra was born.

The moon arose from his mind,
 From his eye was born the sun,
 from his mouth Indra and Agni,
 from his breath the wind was born

With Sacrifice the gods sacrificed to Sacrifice -
 These were the first of the sacred laws.
 These mighty beings reached the sky,
 Where are the eternal spirits, the gods.

The Mundaka Upanishad

Finite and transient are the fruits of sacrificial rites.
 The deluded, who regard them as the highest good, remain subject to birth and death.

Living in the abyss of ignorance, the deluded think themselves blest. Attached to works, they know not God. Works lead them only to heaven, whence, to their sorrow, their rewards quickly exhausted, they are flung back to earth.

Considering religion to be observance of rituals, and performance of acts of charity, the deluded remain ignorant of the highest good. Having enjoyed in heaven the reward of their good works, they enter again into the world of mortals.

But wise, self-controlled, and tranquil souls, who are contented in spirit, and who practice austerity and mediation in solitude and silence, are freed from all impurities and attain by the path of liberation to the immortal, the truly existing, the changeless Self.

Let a man devoted to spiritual life examine carefully the ephemeral nature of such enjoyment, whether here or hereafter, as may be won by good works, and so realize that it is not by works that one gains the Eternal. Let him give no thought to transient things, but, absorbed in meditation, let him renounce the world. If he would know the Eternal, let him humbly approach a Guru devoted to Brahman and well versed in the scriptures. . . .

 In which passages in these two documents do you find a reference to the idea of karma? Which document makes use of the concept, and how? What role does asceticism play in these documents

Sources: (1): *Rig Veda*, x, 90, cited in A.L. Basham, *The Wonder that was India* (London: Sidgwick and Jackson, 1954), pp. 240–241. (2) *The Upanishads: Breath of the Eternal,* translated by S. Prabhavananda and Frederick Manchester (Hollywood, CA: The Vedanta Society of California, 1948). Published by The New American Library, Mentor, 1964, pp. 44–45.

responsibility from the priests to the individual, much as the sixteenth-century German monk Martin Luther saw his ideas as a reformation of Christianity (see Chapter 15). Siddhartha accepted much of the belief system of Brahmanism, if not all of its practices. For example, he accepted the concept of reincarnation and the role of *karma* as a means of influencing the movement of individual souls up and down the scale of life. He praised nonviolence and borrowed the idea of living a life of simplicity and chastity from the ascetics. Moreover, his vision of metaphysical reality—commonly known as **Nirvana**—is closer to the Aryan concept of *Brahman* than it is to the Christian concept of heavenly salvation. Nirvana, which involves an extinction of selfhood and a final reunion with the Great World Soul, is sometimes likened to a dreamless sleep or to

HOW TO ACHIEVE ENLIGHTENMENT

Religion &
Philosophy **ONE OF THE MOST FAMOUS PASSAGES** in Buddhist literature is the sermon at Sarnath, which Siddhartha Gautama delivered to his followers in a deer park outside the holy city of Varanasi (Benares), in the Ganges River Valley. Here he set forth the key ideas that would define Buddhist beliefs for centuries to come. During an official visit to Sarnath nearly three centuries later, Emperor Ashoka ordered the construction of a stupa (reliquary) in honor of the Buddha's message.

The Sermon at Benares

Thus have I heard. Once the Lord was at Varanasi, at the deer park called Isipatana. There he addressed the five monks:

"There are two ends not to be served by a wanderer. What are these two? The pursuit of desires and the pleasure which springs from desire, which is base, common, leading to rebirth, ignoble, and unprofitable; and the pursuit of pain and hardship, which is grievous, ignoble, and unprofitable. The Middle Way of the Tathagata [the Buddha] avoids both these ends. It is enlightened, it brings clear vision, it makes for wisdom and leads to peace, insight, enlightenment, and Nirvana. What is the Middle Way? . . . It is the Noble Eightfold Path—Right Views, Right Resolve, Right Speech, Right Conduct, Right Livelihood, Right Effort, Right Mindfulness, and Right Concentration. This is the Middle Way. . . .

"And this is the Noble Truth of Sorrow. Birth is sorrow, age is sorrow, disease is sorrow, death is sorrow; contact with the unpleasant is sorrow, separation from the pleasant is sorrow, every wish unfulfilled is sorrow—in short all the five components of individuality are sorrow.

"And this is the Noble Truth of the Arising of Sorrow. It arises from craving, which leads to rebirth, which brings delight and passion and seeks pleasure now here, now there— the craving for sensual pleasure, the craving for continued life, the craving for power.

"And this is the Noble Truth of the Stopping of Sorrow. It is the complete stopping of that craving, so that no passion remains, leaving it, being emancipated from it, being released from it, giving no place to it.

"And this is the Noble Truth of the Way which Leads to the Stopping of Sorrow. It is the Noble Eightfold Path— Right Views, Right Resolve, Right Speech, Right Conduct, Right Livelihood, Right Effort, Right Mindfulness, and Right Concentration."

 How did Siddhartha Gautama reach the conclusion that the "four noble truths" were the proper course in living a moral life? How do his ideas compare with the commandments that God gave to the Israelites (see Chapter 1)?

Source: Samyutta Nikaya (ed. Leon Feer and C. A. F. Rhys Davids), 6 vols. London: Oxford, 1884–1904 (Pali Text Society), p. 5.421 ff.

---

a kind of "blowing out" (as of a candle). Buddhists occasionally remark that someone who asks for a description does not understand the concept.

At the same time, however, the new doctrine differed from existing practices in a number of key ways. In the first place, Siddhartha denied the existence of an individual soul. To him, the concept of *Atman*—the individual soul—meant that the soul was subject to rebirth and thus did not achieve a complete liberation from the cares of this world. In fact, Siddhartha denied the ultimate reality of the material world in its entirety and taught that it was an illusion that had to be transcended. Siddhartha's idea of achieving Nirvana was based on his conviction that the pain, poverty, and sorrow that afflict human beings are caused essentially by their attachment to the things of this world. Once worldly cares are abandoned, pain and sorrow can be overcome. With this knowledge comes *bodhi*, or wisdom (source of the term *Buddhism* and the familiar name for Gautama the Wise: Gautama Buddha).

Achieving this understanding is a key step on the road to Nirvana, which, as in Brahmanism, is a form of release from the wheel of life. According to tradition, Siddhartha transmitted this message in a sermon to his disciples in a deer park at Sarnath, not far from the modern city of Varanasi (Benares). Like so many messages, it is deceptively simple and is enclosed in four noble truths: life is suffering, suffering is caused by desire, the way to end suffering is to end desire, and the way to end desire is to avoid the extremes of a life of vulgar materialism and a life of self-torture and to follow the **Middle Path**. Also known as the Eightfold Way, the Middle Path calls for right knowledge, right purpose, right speech, right conduct, right occupation, right effort, right awareness, and right meditation (see "How to Achieve Enlightenment").

Another characteristic of Buddhism was its relative egalitarianism. Although Siddhartha accepted the idea of reincarnation (and hence the idea that human beings differ as a result of *karma* accumulated in a previous existence), he rejected the division of humanity into rigidly defined classes based on previous reincarnations and taught that all human beings could aspire to Nirvana as a result of their behavior in this life—a message that likely helped Buddhism win support among people at the lower end of the social scale.

In addition, Buddhism was much simpler than existing beliefs. Siddhartha rejected the panoply of gods that had become identified with Brahmanism and forbade his followers to worship his person or his image after his death. In fact, even today many Buddhists view Buddhism as a philosophy rather than a religion.

After Siddhartha Gautama's death in about 480 BCE, dedicated disciples carried his message the length and breadth of India. Buddhist monasteries were established throughout the subcontinent, including the adjoining island of Sri Lanka, and temples and **stupas** (STOO-puhs) (stone towers intended to

Symbols of the Buddha. Early Buddhist sculptures depicted the Buddha only through visual symbols that represented his life on the path to enlightenment. In this relief from the stupa at Bharhut, carved in the second century BCE, we see four devotees paying homage to the Buddha, who is portrayed as a giant wheel dispensing his "wheel of the law." The riderless horse on the left represents Siddhartha Gautama's departure from his father's home as he set out on his search for the meaning of life.

of the reality of the material world, Jainism was more extreme in practice. Where Siddhartha Gautama called for the "middle way" between passion and luxury on one extreme and pain and self-torture on the other, Mahavira preached a doctrine of extreme simplicity to his followers, who kept no possessions and relied on begging for a living. Some even rejected clothing and wandered through the world naked. Perhaps because of its insistence on a life of poverty, Jainism failed to attract enough adherents to become a major doctrine and never received official support. According to tradition, however, Chandragupta Maurya accepted Mahavira's doctrine after abdicating the throne and fasted to death in a Jain monastery.

Ashoka, a Buddhist Monarch

Buddhism received an important boost when Ashoka (uh-SHOH-kuh), the grandson of Chandragupta Maurya, converted to Buddhism in the third century BCE. Ashoka

house relics of the Buddha) sprang up throughout the countryside.

Women were permitted to join the monastic order but only in an inferior position. As Siddhartha had explained, women are "soon angered," "full of passion," and "stupid": "That is the reason . . . why women have no place in public assemblies . . . and do not earn their living by any profession." Still, the position of women tended to be better in Buddhist societies than it was elsewhere in ancient India.

Jainism

During the next centuries, Buddhism began to compete actively with the existing Aryan beliefs, as well as with another new faith known as Jainism. **Jainism** (JY-ni-zuhm) was founded by Mahavira (mah-hah-VEE-ruh), a contemporary of Siddhartha Gautama. Resembling Buddhism in its rejection

The Stupa at Sarnath. After Emperor Ashoka became converted to Buddhism, he ordered the erection of a stupa at Sarnath in honor of the location of Siddhartha's famous sermon on how to achieve enlightenment to his followers. Simple in its design, the stupa at Sarnath is considered a prototype of many other such structures located throughout the world.

(r. 269–232 BCE) is widely considered the greatest ruler in the history of India. By his own admission, as noted in rock edicts placed around his kingdom, Ashoka began his reign conquering, pillaging, and killing, but after his conversion to Buddhism, he began to regret his bloodthirsty past and attempted to rule benevolently.

Ashoka directed that banyan trees and shelters be placed along the road to provide shade and rest for weary travelers. He sent Buddhist missionaries throughout India and ordered the erection of stone pillars with official edicts and Buddhist inscriptions to instruct people in the proper way (see Map 2.3 and the illustration "The Lions of Sarnath"). In time, much of the population living under Mauryan rule may have converted to Buddhism (see "A Singular Debate" on p. 58). According to tradition, his son converted the island of Sri Lanka to Buddhism, and the peoples there accepted a tributary relationship with the Mauryan Empire.

After Ashoka: The Rule of the Fishes After Ashoka's death in 232 BCE, the Mauryan Empire began to decline. In 183 BCE, the last Mauryan ruler was overthrown by one of his military commanders, and India began to fragment into separate states. A number of new kingdoms, some of them perhaps influenced by the memory of the Alexandrian conquests, arose along the fringes of the subcontinent in Bactria, known today as Afghanistan. In the first century CE, Indo-European-speaking peoples fleeing from the nomadic Xiongnu (SHYAHNG-noo) warriors in Central Asia seized power in the area and proclaimed the new Kushan (koo-SHAHN) kingdom (see Chapter 9). For the next two centuries, the Kushans extended their political sway over northern India as far as the central Ganges Valley, while other kingdoms scuffled for predominance elsewhere on the subcontinent. India would not see unity again for another five hundred years.

Detail from an Ashoka Pillar (photo), Indian school (3rd century BC)/Sarnath, Uttar Pradesh, India/Bridgeman Images

Map 2.3 The Empire of Ashoka. Ashoka, the greatest Indian monarch, ruled over much of the subcontinent in the third century BCE. This map shows the extent of his empire and the locations of the pillar edicts that were erected along major trade routes.

Q *Why do you think the pillars and rocks were placed where they were?*

The Lions of Sarnath. Their beauty and Buddhist symbolism make the Lions of Sarnath the most famous of the capitals topping Ashoka's pillars. Sarnath was the holy site where the Buddha first preached, and these roaring lions echo the proclamation of Buddhist teachings to the four corners of the world. The wheel not only represents the Buddha's laws but also proclaims Ashoka's imperial legitimacy as the enlightened Indian ruler.

A SINGULAR DEBATE

Religion & Philosophy **ONE OF THE KEY POINTS OF CONTENTION** between advocates of Brahmanism and Buddhism was the belief on the part of the former that members of the highest social class—the Brahmins—were purer than those lower on the social scale, based on their past actions (*karma*). Siddhartha Gautama, however, had argued that all humans were inherently equal at birth and could obtain Nirvana—the state of release from earthly cares—as a consequence of their behavior in this life.

In this passage from the *Tripitaka* (Three Baskets), a collection of Buddhist writings collated by Theravada Buddhists on the island of Sri Lanka, Siddhartha Gautama confronts a devotee of Brahmanism and demonstrates the superiority of Buddhist teachings. Whether the debate actually took place is unlikely, and the date of the passage is uncertain, but it effectively singles out one of the key points of difference between the two teachings.

The Tripitaka

Once when the Lord was staying at Savatthi there were five hundred brahmans from various countries in the city . . . and they thought: "This ascetic Gautama preaches that all four classes are pure. Who can refute him?"

At that time there was a young brahman named Assalayana in the city, . . . a youth of sixteen, thoroughly versed in the Vedas . . . and in all brahmanic learning. "He can do it!," thought the brahmans, and so they asked him to try; . . . he agreed, and so, surrounded by a crowd of brahmans, he went to the Lord, and, after greeting him, sat down and said:

"Brahmans maintain that only they are the highest class, and the others are below them. They are white, the others black; only they are pure, and not the others. Only they are the true sons of Brahma, born from his mouth, born of Brahma, creations of Brahma, heirs of Brahma. Now what does the worthy Gautama say to that?"

"Do the brahmans really maintain this, Assalayana, when they're born of women just like anyone else, of brahman women who have their periods and conceive, give birth and nurse their children, just like any other women?"

"For all you say, this is what they think. . . ."

. . .

"Again if a man is a murderer, a thief, or an adulterer, or commits other grave sins, when his body breaks up on death does he pass on to purgatory if he's a kshatriya, vaishya, or shudra, but not if he's a brahman?"

"No, Gautama. In such a case, the same fate is in store for all men, whatever their class."

. . .

"And is a brahman capable of developing a mind of love without hate or ill will, but not a man of the other classes?"

"No, Gautama. All four classes are capable of doing so."

"Can only a brahman go down to a river and wash away dust and dirt, and not men of the other classes?"

"No, Gautama. All four classes can."

. . .

"Suppose there are two young brahman brothers, one a scholar and the other uneducated. Which of them would be served first at memorial feasts, festivals, and sacrifices, or when entertained as guests?"

"The scholar, of course; for what great benefit would accrue from entertaining the uneducated one?"

"But suppose the scholar is ill-behaved and wicked, while the uneducated one is well-behaved and virtuous?"

"Then the uneducated one would be served first, for what great benefit would accrue from entertaining an ill-behaved and wicked man?"

"First, Assalayana, you based your claim on birth, then you gave up birth for learning, and finally you have come round to my way of thinking, that all four classes are equally pure!"

At this Assalayana sat silent . . . his shoulders hunched, his eyes cast down, thoughtful in mind, and with no answer at hand.

 What arguments does the Brahmanic scholar present to Siddhartha Gautama? How does the latter respond?

Source: Ainslee T. Embree (ed.), *Sources of Indian Tradition*, vol. I (New York: Columbia University Press, 1988), pp. 140–141.

Several reasons for India's failure to maintain a unified empire have been proposed. Some historians suggest that a decline in regional trade during the first millennium CE may have contributed to the growth of small land-based kingdoms, which drew their primary income from agriculture. The tenacity of the Aryan tradition, with its emphasis on tribal rivalries, may also have contributed. Although the Mauryan rulers tried to impose a more centralized organization, clan loyalties once again came to the fore after the collapse of the

Mauryan dynasty. Furthermore, the behavior of the ruling class was characterized by what Indians call the "rule of the fishes," which glorified warfare as the natural activity of the king and the aristocracy. The *Arthasastra*, which set forth a model of a centralized Indian state, assumed that war was the "sport of kings." Still, this was not an uneventful period in the history of India, as Indo-Aryan ideas continued to spread southward and both Brahmanism and Buddhism evolved in new directions.

2–4 THE EXUBERANT WORLD OF INDIAN CULTURE

 Focus Question: In what ways did the culture of ancient India resemble and differ from the cultural experience of ancient Mesopotamia and Egypt?

Few cultures in the world are as rich and varied as that of India. Most societies excel in some forms of artistic and literary achievement and not in others, but India has produced great works in almost all fields of cultural endeavor—art and sculpture, science, architecture, literature, and music.

2–4a Literature

The earliest known Indian literature consists of the four Vedas, which were passed down orally from generation to generation until they were finally written down after the Aryans arrived in India. The Rig Veda dates from the second millennium BCE and consists of more than a thousand hymns that were used at religious ceremonies. The other three Vedas were written considerably later and contain instructions for performing ritual sacrifices and other ceremonies. The Brahmanas and the Upanishads served as commentaries on the Vedas.

The language of the Vedas was **Sanskrit** (SAN-skrit), a member of the Indo-European family of languages. After the arrival of the Aryans in India, Sanskrit gradually declined as a spoken language and was replaced in northern India by a simpler tongue known as **Prakrit** (PRAH-krit). Nevertheless, Sanskrit continued to be used as the language of the bureaucracy and of literary expression for many centuries after that. Like Latin in medieval Europe, it also served as a common language of communication between various regions of India. In the south, a variety of Dravidian languages continued to be spoken.

As early as the fifth century BCE, Indian grammarians had codified Sanskrit to preserve the authenticity of the Vedas for the spiritual edification of future generations. A famous grammar written by the scholar Panini in the fourth century BCE set forth four thousand grammatical rules prescribing the correct usage of the spoken and written language. This achievement is particularly impressive in that Europe did not have a science of linguistics until the nineteenth century, when it was developed partly as a result of the discovery of the works of Panini and later Indian linguists.

After the development of a writing system in the first millennium BCE, India's holy literature was probably inscribed on palm leaves stitched together into a book somewhat similar to the first books produced on papyrus or parchment in the Mediterranean region. Also written for the first time were India's great historical epics, the Mahabharata and the Ramayana (rah-mah-YAH-nah). Both of these epics may have originally been recited at religious ceremonies, but they are essentially histories that recount the martial exploits of great Aryan rulers and warriors.

The Mahabharata, consisting of more than 90,000 stanzas, was probably written about 100 BCE and describes in great detail a war between cousins for control of the kingdom nine hundred years earlier. Interwoven in the narrative are many fantastic legends of the gods. Above all, the Mahabharata is a tale of moral confrontations and an elucidation of the ethical precepts of the *dharma*. The most famous section of the book is the so-called Bhagavad Gita, a sermon by the legendary Indian figure Krishna on the eve of a major battle. In this sermon, given in the form of advice to a colleague, Krishna sets forth one of the key ethical maxims of Indian society: in taking action, one must be indifferent to success or failure and consider only the moral rightness of the act itself.

The Ramayana, written at about the same time, is much shorter than the Mahabharata. It is an account of a semilegendary ruler named Rama (RAH-mah) who, as a result of a palace intrigue, is banished from the kingdom and forced to live as a hermit in the forest. Later he fights the demon-king of Sri Lanka, who has kidnapped his beloved wife, Sita (SEE-tuh). Like the Mahabharata, the Ramayana is strongly imbued with religious and moral significance. Rama is portrayed as the ideal Aryan hero, a perfect ruler and an ideal son, while Sita projects the supreme duty of female chastity and wifely loyalty to her husband. The Ramayana is a story of the triumph of good over evil, duty over self-indulgence, and generosity over selfishness. It combines filial and erotic love, conflicts of human passion, character analysis, and poetic descriptions of nature (see "Rama and Sita" on p. 60).

The Ramayana also has all the ingredients of an enthralling adventure: giants, wondrous flying chariots, invincible arrows and swords, and magic potions and mantras. One of the real heroes of the story is the monkey-king Hanuman, who flies from India to Sri Lanka to set the great battle in motion. It is no wonder that for millennia the Ramayana has remained a favorite among Indians of all age groups, often performed at festivals today and inspiring a hugely popular TV version produced in recent years.

2–4b Architecture and Sculpture

After literature, the greatest achievements of early Indian civilization were in architecture and sculpture. Some of the earliest examples of Indian architecture stem from the time of Emperor Ashoka, when Buddhism became the religion of the state. Until the time of the Mauryas, Aryan buildings had been constructed of wood. With the rise of the empire, stone began to be used, as artisans arrived in India seeking employment after the destruction of the Persian Empire by Alexander. Many of these stone carvers accepted the patronage of Emperor Ashoka, who used them to spread Buddhist ideas throughout the subcontinent.

There were three main types of religious structures: the pillar, the stupa, and the rock chamber. As noted earlier, during Ashoka's reign, many stone columns were erected alongside roads to commemorate the events in the Buddha's life and mark

RAMA AND SITA

OVER THE AGES, THE CONCLUSION OF THE INDIAN EPIC known as the Ramayana has been the focus of considerable debate. After a long period of captivity at the hands of the demon Ravana, Sita is finally liberated by her husband, King Rama. Although the two have a joyful reunion, the people of Rama's kingdom voice suspicions that she has been defiled by her captor, and Rama is forced to banish her to a forest, where she gives birth to twin sons. The account reflects the belief, expressed in the *Arthasastra*, that a king must place the needs of his subjects over his personal desires. Here we read of Rama's anguished decision as he consults with his brother, Lakshmana.

By accepting banishment, Sita bows to the authority of her husband and the established moral order. Subservient and long-suffering, she has been lauded as the ideal heroine and feminine role model, imitated by generations of Indian women. At the close of the Ramayana, Rama decides to take Sita back "before all my people." She continues to feel humiliated, however, and begs Mother Earth to open up and swallow her.

The Ramayana

"A king must be blameless."

"Such words pierce my heart," said Lakshmana. "Fire himself proved her innocent. She is fired gold, poured into golden fire!"

Rama said, "Lakshmana, consider what is a king. Kings cannot afford blame. Ill fame is evil to kings; they above all men must be beyond reproach. . . . See into what a chasm of sorrow a King may fall. . . ."

Lakshmana said, "Gradually everything seems to change again, and even an Emperor must pay his way through life."

Rama faced his brother. "It must be! It's all the same, can't you see? Where there is growth there is decay; where there is prosperity there is ruin; and where there is birth there is death."

Lakshmana sighed hopelessly. "Well, what will you do?"

"Sita expects to go to the forests tomorrow. Let Sumantra the Charioteer drive you both there, and when you arrive by the river Ganga abandon her."

"She will die. Your child will die!"

"No," said Rama. "I command you! Not a word to anyone."

Source: From *The Ramayana* by R. K. Narayan. Viking Books, 1972.

Lakshmana said, "Surely a king is remote and lonely, and very far from reason. We cannot speak to you. . . ."

Rama said, "Each person can be told what he will understand of the nature of the world, and no more than that—for the rest, take my word. . . ."

Sita was forever beautiful. Wearing her ornaments she turned slowly around and looked at every person there. "Rama, let me prove my innocence, here before everyone."

"I give my permission," said Rama.

Then Sita stepped a little away from him and said, "Mother Earth, if I have been faithful to Rama take me home, hide me!"

Earth rolled and moved beneath our feet. With a great rumbling noise the ground broke apart near Sita and a deep chasm opened, lighted from below with bright lights like lightning flashes, from the castles of the Naga serpent kings. . . .

On that throne sat Mother Earth. Earth was not old, she was fair to look on, she was not sad but smiling. She wore flowers and a girdle of seas. Earth supports all life, but she feels no burden in all that. She is patient. She was patient then, under the Sun and Moon and through the rainfalls of countless years. She was patient with seasons and with kings and farmers; she endured all things and bore no line of care from it.

But this was the end of her long patience with Rama. Earth looked at her husband Janaka and smiled. Then she stretched out her arms and took her only child Sita on her lap. She folded her beautiful arms around her daughter and laid Sita's head softly against her shoulder as a mother would. Earth stroked her hair with her fair hands, and Sita closed her eyes like a little girl.

The throne sank back underground and they all were gone; the Nagas dove beneath the ground and the crevice closed gently over them, forever.

 How does this story reflect some of the basic values of traditional Indian civilization? Why do you think it was necessary for the story to have an unhappy ending, unlike Homer's epic The Odyssey, which ends with the return of the hero Odysseus to his wife, Penelope, after many arduous travels?

---

pilgrim routes to holy places. Weighing up to 50 tons each and rising as high as 32 feet, these polished sandstone pillars were topped with a carved capital, usually depicting lions uttering the Buddha's message. Ten remain standing today (a photograph of one of these pillars appears in the Comparative Illustration "The Stele," Section 8-5c, p. 236).

A stupa was originally meant to house a relic of the Buddha, such as a lock of his hair or a branch of the famous Bodhi tree (the tree beneath which Siddhartha Gautama had first achieved enlightenment), and was constructed in the form of a burial mound (the pyramids in Egypt also derived from burial mounds). Eventually, the stupa became a place for devotion and

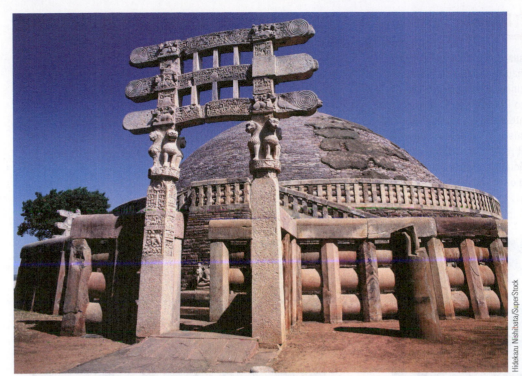

Sanchi Gate and Stupa. Constructed during the reign of Emperor Ashoka in the third century BCE, the stupa at Sanchi was enlarged over time, eventually becoming the greatest Buddhist monument on the Indian subcontinent. Originally intended to house a relic of the Buddha, the stupa became a holy place for devotion and a familiar form of Buddhist architecture. Sanchi's four elaborately carved stone gates, each more than 40 feet high, tell stories of the Buddha set in joyful scenes of everyday life. Christian churches would later similarly portray events in the life of Jesus to instruct the faithful.

the most familiar form of Buddhist architecture. Stupas rose to considerable heights and were surmounted with a spire, possibly representing the stages of existence en route to Nirvana. According to legend, Ashoka ordered the construction of 84,000 stupas throughout India to promote the Buddha's message. A few survive today, including the one at Sarnath (see the illustration "The Stupa at Sarnath" on p. 56) and its more elaborate prototype at Sanchi, begun under Ashoka and completed two centuries later.

The final form of early Indian architecture is the rock chamber carved out of a cliff on the side of a mountain. Ashoka began the construction of these chambers to provide rooms to house monks or wandering ascetics and to serve as halls for religious ceremonies. The chambers were rectangular, with pillars, an altar, and a vault, reminiscent of Roman basilicas in the West. The three most famous chambers of this period are at Bhaja, Karli, and Ajanta (uh-JUHN-tuh); the last one contains twenty-nine rooms.

A Carved Chapel. Carved out of solid rock cliffs during the Mauryan dynasty, rock chambers served as meditation halls for traveling Buddhist monks. Initially, they resembled freestanding shrines of wood and thatch from the Vedic period but evolved into magnificent chapels carved deep into the mountainside, such as the chapel at Ajanta shown here. The first caves were dug out at Ajanta during the reign of Ashoka, and a monastery for Buddhist monks was established there by about 200 BCE. Working downward from the top, stonecutters removed tons of rock, and sculptors embellished and polished the interior. Notice the rounded vault and multicolumned sides reminiscent of Roman basilicas in the West.

All three forms of architecture were embellished with detailed reliefs and freestanding statues of deities, other human figures, and animals that are permeated with a sense of nature and the vitality of life. Many reflect an amalgamation of popular and sacred themes, of Buddhist, Vedic, and pre-Aryan religious motifs, such as male and female earth spirits. Until the second century CE, Siddhartha Gautama was represented only through symbols, such as the wheel of life, the Bodhi tree, and the footprint, perhaps because artists deemed it improper to portray him in human form, since he had escaped his corporeal confines into enlightenment. After the spread of Mahayana Buddhism in the second century, when the Buddha was no longer portrayed as a teacher but rather as a god, his image began to appear in stone as an object for divine worship (see Comparative Illustration "The Buddha and Jesus" on p. 62).

COMPARATIVE ILLUSTRATION

Religion &
Philosophy **The Buddha and Jesus.** As Buddhism evolved, transforming Siddhartha Gautama, known as the Buddha, from mortal to god, Buddhist art changed as well. Statuary and relief panels began to illustrate the story of his life. In A, a frieze from the second century CE, the infant Siddhartha is seen emerging from the hip of his mother, Queen Maya. Although dressed in draperies that reflect Greek influences from Alexander the Great's brief incursion into northwestern India, her sensuous stance and the touching of the tree evoke the female earth spirit of traditional Indian art. In B is a Byzantine painting depicting the infant Jesus with his mother, the Virgin Mary, dating from the sixth century CE. Notice that a halo surrounds the head of both the Buddha and Jesus. The halo—a circle of light—is an ancient symbol of divinity. In Hindu, Greek, and Roman art, the heads of gods were depicted emitting sunlike divine radiances. Early kings adopted crowns made of gold and precious gems to symbolize their own divine authority.

Q *What similarities and differences do you see in these depictions of the mothers of key religious figures?*

A

William J. Duiker

B

Erich Lessing/Art Resource, NY

By this time, India had established its own unique religious art. The art is permeated by sensuousness and exuberance and is often overtly sexual. These scenes are meant to express otherworldly delights, not the pleasures of this world. The sensuous paradise that adorned the religious art of ancient India represented salvation and fulfillment for the ordinary Indian.

2–4c Science

Our knowledge of Indian science is limited by the paucity of written sources, but it is evident that ancient Indians had amassed an impressive amount of scientific knowledge in a number of areas. Especially notable was their work in mathematics, where they devised the numerical system that we know as Arabic numbers and use today, and in astronomy, where they charted the movements of the heavenly bodies and recognized the spherical nature of the earth at an early date. Their ideas of physics were similar to those of the Greeks; matter was divided into the five elements of earth, air, fire, water, and ether. Many of their technological achievements are impressive, notably the quality of their textiles and the massive stone pillars erected during the reign of Ashoka. As noted, the pillars weighed up to 50 tons each and were transported many miles to their final destination.

While the peoples of North Africa and the Middle East were actively building the first civilizations, a similar process was getting under way in the Indus River Valley. Much has been learned about the nature of the Indus Valley civilization in recent years, but the lack of written records limits our understanding. How did the Indus Valley people deal with the fundamental human problems mentioned at the close of Chapter 1? The answers remain tantalizingly elusive.

As often happened elsewhere, however, the collapse of Indus Valley civilization did not lead to the total disappearance of its culture. The new society that eventually emerged throughout the subcontinent after the coming of the Aryans was an amalgam of two highly distinctive cultures, each of which made a significant contribution to the politics, social institutions, and creative impulse of ancient Indian civilization.

With the rise of the Mauryan dynasty in the fourth century BCE, the distinctive features of a great civilization begin to be clearly visible. It was extensive in its scope, embracing the entire Indian subcontinent and eventually, in the form of Buddhism and Hinduism, spreading to China and Southeast Asia. But the underlying ethnic, linguistic, and cultural diversity of the Indian people posed a constant challenge to the unity of the state. After the collapse of the Mauryas, the subcontinent would not come under a single authority again for several hundred years.

In the meantime, another great experiment was taking place far to the northeast, across the Himalaya Mountains. Like many other civilizations of antiquity, the first Chinese state was concentrated on a major river system. And like them, too, its political and cultural achievements eventually spread far beyond their original habitat. In the next chapter, we turn to the civilization of ancient China.

CHAPTER TIMELINE

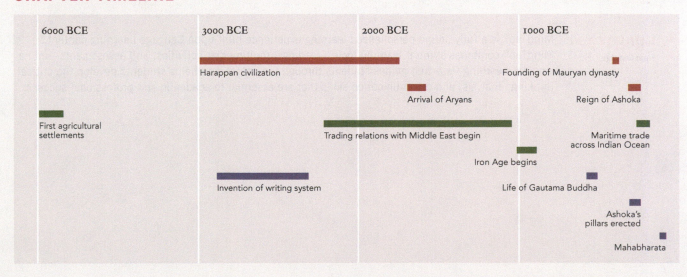

6000 BCE	3000 BCE	2000 BCE	1000 BCE
	Harappan civilization		Founding of Mauryan dynasty
		Arrival of Aryans	Reign of Ashoka
First agricultural settlements		Trading relations with Middle East begin	Maritime trade across Indian Ocean
			Iron Age begins
	Invention of writing system		Life of Gautama Buddha
			Ashoka's pillars erected
			Mahabharata

CHAPTER REVIEW

Upon Reflection

Q What is the debate over the origins of the Aryan peoples, and why do many historians of India consider it to be such an important question?

Q Why was Buddhism able to make such inroads among the Indian people at a time when Brahmanical beliefs had long been dominant in the subcontinent?

Q What were some of the main characteristics of Indian politics and government during the first millennium BCE, and how can they be compared and contrasted with those of ancient Egypt and Mesopotamia?

Key Terms

raja (p. 44)
kshatriya (p. 44)
maharajas (p. 44)
dharma (p. 45)
varna (p. 46)
brahmins (p. 46)
Brahman (p. 46)
vaisya (p. 47)
twice-born (p. 47)
sudras (p. 47)
pariahs (p. 47)
jati (p. 48)
guru (p. 48)

sati (p. 48)
Brahmanism (p. 51)
reincarnation (p. 52)
karma (p. 52)
Atman (p. 53)
Buddhism (p. 53)
Nirvana (p. 54)
bodhi (p. 55)
Middle Path (p. 55)
stupas (p. 55)
Jainism (p. 56)
Sanskrit (p. 59)
Prakrit (p. 59)

Chapter Notes

1. Quoted in R. Lannoy, *The Speaking Tree: A Study of Indian Culture and Society* (London, 1971), p. 318.
2. The quotation is from ibid., p. 319. Note also that the *Law of Manu* says that "punishment alone governs all created beings. . . . The whole world is kept in order by punishment, for a guiltless man is hard to find."
3. Strabo's *Geography*, bk. 15, quoted in M. Edwardes, *A History of India: From the Earliest Times to the Present Day* (London, 1961), p. 55.
4. Ibid., p. 54.
5. Ibid., p. 57.
6. From the *Law of Manu*, quoted in A. L. Basham, *The Wonder That Was India* (London, 1961), pp. 180–181. © 1961 Pan Macmillan, London.
7. Quoted in A. K. Coomaraswamy, *Buddha and the Gospel of Buddhism* (New York, 1964), p. 34.

CHAPTER 3

CHINA IN ANTIQUITY

Chapter Outline and Focus Questions

3-1 The Dawn of Chinese Civilization

Q How did geography influence the civilization that arose in China? To what degree do geographical realities explain the unique characteristics that differentiate China from other civilizations in the ancient world?

3-2 The Zhou Dynasty

Q What were the major tenets of Confucianism, Legalism, and Daoism, and to what degree do they compare with philosophical and intellectual trends elsewhere in the ancient world?

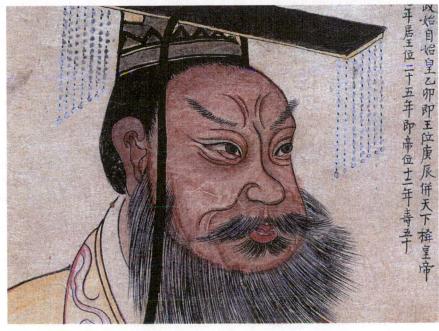

The first emperor of Qin. World History Archive/Alamy

3-3 The First Chinese Empire: The Qin Dynasty

Q How did the first emperor of the Qin dynasty transform the political, social, and economic institutions of early China?

3-4 The Glorious Han Dynasty (202 BCE–221 CE)

Q Why and to what degree did the Han dynasty turn to Confucianism as an ideology of the state? How in turn did Han rulers adjust Confucian ideas to serve their own needs?

3-5 Daily Life in Ancient China

Q What were the key aspects of social and economic life in early China, and how did they compare with conditions elsewhere in the ancient world?

3-6 Chinese Culture

Q What were the chief characteristics of the Chinese arts and writing system? How did they differ from those in Egypt and Mesopotamia?

Critical Thinking

Q *The civilization of ancient China resembled those of its contemporaries in Mesopotamia and North Africa in several respects, but the contrasts were equally significant. What were some of these differences, and how might geography and the environment have contributed to them?*

Connections to Today

Q *Which aspects of Confucian thought as depicted in the* Analects *appear to have particular relevance in today's world? What lessons can we learn today from the teachings of Master Kung?*

HIS AMBITION WAS limitless. After mounting the throne of his native state of Qin at the age of thirteen, he immediately set out to conquer all the neighboring states in the region and unite all of China under his rule. Having achieved that objective in the year 221 BCE, he then sought to create a highly regimented society according to his own plan. Potential rivals were executed, and their writings

65

were destroyed. Peasants and workers were organized to serve the interests of the state, and thousands of laborers were mobilized to build a gigantic mausoleum, guarded by thousands of molded terra-cotta warriors, to provide for his afterlife. But the vaulting ambitions of the ruler known as Qin Shi Huangdi (chin shee hwang-DEE), or the First Emperor of Qin—as he styled himself—were ultimately destined to be thwarted. After he died at the age of forty-nine in 210 BCE, Qin Shi Huangdi's dynasty rapidly fell apart. But although the Qin dynasty was broadly reviled by later generations of historians as an unfortunate aberration in the long course of Chinese history, his legacy lived on in the form of a strong and centralized empire that survived over two millennia and has traditionally been viewed as one of the greatest civilizations in the course of human history.

3–1 THE DAWN OF CHINESE CIVILIZATION

 Focus Questions: How did geography influence the civilization that arose in China? To what degree do geographical realities explain the unique characteristics that differentiate China from other civilizations in the ancient world?

According to a familiar legend, Chinese society was founded by a series of rulers who brought the first rudiments of civilization to the region nearly five thousand years ago. The first was Fu Xi (foo SHEE), the ox-tamer, who "knotted cords for hunting and fishing," domesticated animals, and introduced the beginnings of family life (for translation of the Chinese written language, we use the pinyin system adopted by the People's Republic of China, see "A Note to Students About Language and the Dating of Time" in the front matter). The second was Shen Nong (shun NOONG), the divine farmer, who "bent wood for plows and hewed wood for plowshares." He taught the people the techniques of agriculture. Last came Huang Di (hwahng DEE), the Yellow Emperor, who "strung a piece of wood for the bow, and whittled little sticks of wood for the arrows." Legend credits Huang Di with creating the Chinese system of writing, as well as with inventing the bow and arrow.[1] Modern historians, of course, do not accept the literal accuracy of such legends but view them instead as part of the process whereby early peoples attempt to make sense of the world and their role in it. Nevertheless, such re-creations of a mythical past often contain an element of truth. Although there is no clear evidence that the "three sovereigns" actually existed, their achievements do symbolize some of the defining characteristics of Chinese civilization: the interaction between nomadic and agricultural peoples, the importance of the family as the basic unit of Chinese life, and the development of a unique system of writing.

3–1a The Land and People of China

Although human communities have existed in China for several hundred thousand years, the first *Homo sapiens* arrived in the area sometime after 80,000 BCE as part of the great migration out of Africa. At least as early as the eighth millennium BCE, the early peoples living on the hillsides and along the riverbanks of northern and central China began to master the cultivation of crops, especially dry crops such as millet and sorghum, which required little water and had a short growing season. A number of these early agricultural settlements were in the neighborhood of the Yellow River, where they gave birth to two Neolithic societies known to archaeologists as the **Yangshao** (yahng-SHOW ["ow" as in "how"]) and the **Longshan** (loong-SHAHN) cultures (sometimes identified in terms of their pottery as the painted and black pottery cultures, respectively). Similar communities began to appear in the Yangzi Valley in central China and along the coast to the south. The southern settlements were based on the cultivation of rice, which had been domesticated in China as early as the sixth millennium BCE. Thus, agriculture, and perhaps other elements of early civilization, may have developed spontaneously in several areas of China rather than radiating outward from one central region.

At first, these simple Neolithic communities were hardly more than villages, but as the inhabitants mastered the rudiments of agriculture, they gradually gave rise to more sophisticated and complex societies. In a pattern that we have already seen elsewhere, civilization gradually spread from these nuclear settlements in the valleys of the Yellow and Yangzi Rivers to other lowland areas of eastern and central China. The two great river valleys, then, can be considered the core regions in the development of Chinese civilization (see Map 3.1).

Although these densely cultivated valleys eventually became two of the great food-producing areas of the ancient world, China is more than a land of fertile fields. In fact, only 12 percent of the total land area is arable, compared with 23 percent in the United States. Much of the remainder consists of mountains and deserts that ring the country on its northern and western frontiers.

This often arid and forbidding landscape is a dominant feature of Chinese life and has played a significant role in Chinese history. The geographic barriers served to isolate the Chinese people from advanced agrarian societies in other parts of Asia. The frontier regions in the Gobi (GOH-bee) Desert, Central Asia, and the Tibetan plateau were sparsely inhabited by peoples of Mongolian, Indo-European, or Turkic extraction. Most were primarily pastoral societies, and relations between the Chinese and the steppe peoples, like the contacts between other ancient river valley civilizations and their neighbors, were intermittent and frequently unstable. Sometimes the two sides engaged in productive trade relations, swapping grain and manufactured goods for hides and other animal products. On other occasions, however, mutual suspicion and contrasting interests led to conflict. Although less numerous than the Chinese, many of the peoples along the frontiers possessed impressive skills in war and were sometimes aggressive in

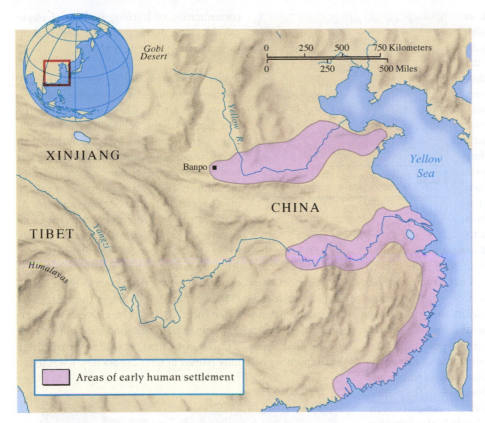

 Areas of early human settlement

Map 3.1 Neolithic China. Like the ancient civilizations that arose in North Africa and western Asia, early Chinese society emerged along the banks of two major river systems, the Yellow and the Yangzi. China was separated from the other civilizations by snow-capped mountains and forbidding deserts, however, and thus was compelled to develop essentially on its own, without contacts from other societies going through a similar process.

Q *Based on the discussions in the preceding chapters, what are the advantages and disadvantages of close contact with other human societies?*

Historians of China have traditionally dated the beginning of Chinese civilization to the founding of the Xia (shee-AH) dynasty more than four thousand years ago. Although the precise date for the rise of the Xia is in dispute, recent archaeological evidence from various sites in north-central China provides credence for its existence. Legend maintains that the founder of the Xia was a ruler named Yu, who is also credited with introducing irrigation and draining the floodwaters that periodically threatened to inundate the North China plain. The Xia dynasty was eventually replaced by a second dynasty, the Shang (SHAHNG), around the sixteenth century BCE. The late Shang capital at Anyang (ahn-YAHNG), just north of the Yellow River in north-central China, has been excavated by archaeologists. Among the finds were thousands of so-called oracle bones, ox and chicken bones or turtle shells that were used by Shang rulers for divination and to communicate with the gods. The inscriptions on these oracle bones—a form of pictographic writing similar to those we have encountered in Egypt and Mesopotamia—are the earliest known form of Chinese writing and provide much of our information about the beginnings of civilization in China. They describe a culture gradually emerging from the Neolithic to the early Bronze Age.

Political Organization China under the Shang dynasty was a predominantly agricultural society ruled by an aristocratic class whose major occupation was war and control over key resources such as metals and salt. One ancient chronicler complained that "the big affairs of state consist of sacrifice and soldiery."[2] Combat was carried on by means of two-horse chariots. The appearance of chariots in China in the mid-second millennium BCE coincides roughly with similar developments elsewhere, leading some historians to suggest that the Shang ruling class may originally have invaded China from far to the west. But items found in Shang burial mounds are similar to Longshan pottery, implying that the Shang ruling elites were linear descendants of the indigenous Neolithic peoples in the area. If that was the case, the Shang may have acquired their knowledge of horse-drawn chariots through contact with the peoples of neighboring regions.

Some recent support for that assumption has come from evidence unearthed in the sandy wastes of Xinjiang (SHIN-jyahng), China's far-northwestern province. There archaeologists have

seeking wealth or territory in the settled regions south of the Gobi Desert. Over the next two thousand years, the northern and western frontier regions became one of the great fault lines of conflict in Asia as Chinese forces attempted to protect precious farmlands from marauding peoples from beyond the frontier. In turn, nomadic peoples often took offense at Chinese efforts to encroach on their own grazing lands. When China was unified and blessed with capable rulers, it could usually keep the nomadic intruders at bay and even bring them under a loose form of Chinese administration. But in times of internal weakness, China was vulnerable to attack from the north, and on several occasions, nomadic armies succeeded in overthrowing native Chinese rulers and setting up their own dynastic regimes.

From other directions, China normally had little to fear. To the east lay the China Sea, a lair for pirates and the source of powerful typhoons that occasionally ravaged the Chinese coast but otherwise rarely a source of concern. South of the Yangzi River was a hilly region inhabited by a mixture of peoples of varied linguistic and ethnic stock who lived by farming, fishing, or food gathering. They were gradually absorbed in the inexorable expansion of Chinese civilization.

discovered human remains dating back as early as the second millennium BCE with physical characteristics resembling those of Europeans (one famous example is the so-called Beauty of Xiaohe, whose remains, unearthed in the Taklamakan desert, have pronounced Caucasian characteristics). They are also clothed in textiles similar to those worn at the time in central Asia and eastern Europe, suggesting that they may have been members of a migration by Indo-European-speaking peoples from areas much farther to the west. If that is the case, they were probably familiar with advances in chariot making that occurred a few hundred years earlier in southern Russia and Kazakhstan (ka-zak-STAN *or* kuh-zahk-STAHN). By about 2000 BCE, spoked wheels were being deposited at grave sites in Ukraine and also in the Gobi Desert, just north of the great bend of the Yellow River. According to some Western scholars, it seems likely that the new technology became available to the founders of the Shang dynasty and may have aided their rise to power in northern China. Chinese scholars are more reluctant to challenge the official view in Beijing that Chinese civilization is *sui generis*, and thus unaffected by events taking place elsewhere in the world.

The Shang king ruled with the assistance of a central bureaucracy in the capital city. His realm was divided into a number of territories governed by aristocratic chieftains, but the king appointed these chieftains and could apparently depose them at will. He was also responsible for the defense of the realm and controlled large armies that often fought on the fringes of the kingdom. The transcendent importance of the ruler was graphically displayed in the ritual sacrifices undertaken at his death, when hundreds of his retainers were buried with him in the royal tomb.

As the inscriptions on the oracle bones make clear, the Shang ruling elite believed in the existence of supernatural forces and thought that they could communicate with those forces to obtain divine intervention on matters of this world. In fact, the main purpose of the oracle bones seems to have been to communicate with the gods. Supreme among the heavenly forces was the sky god, known as Di. Evidence from the oracle bones also suggests that the king was already being viewed as an intermediary between heaven and earth. An early Shang character for king (王) consists of three horizontal lines connected by a single vertical line; the middle horizontal line represents the king's place between human society and the divine forces in nature.

The early Chinese also had a clear sense of life in the hereafter. Though some of the human sacrifices discovered in the royal tombs were presumably intended to propitiate the gods, others were meant to accompany the king or members of his family on the journey to the next world (see Comparative Illustration "The Afterlife and Prized Possessions"). From this conviction would come the concept of **veneration of ancestors** (mistakenly known in the West as "ancestor worship") and the practice, which continues to the present day in many Chinese

Shang China

communities, of burning replicas of physical objects to accompany the departed on their journey to the next world.

Social Structures In the Neolithic period, the farming village was apparently the basic social unit of China, at least in the core region of the Yellow River valley. Villages were organized by clans rather than by nuclear family units, and all residents probably took the common clan name of the entire village. In some cases, a village may have included more than one clan. At Banpo, an archaeological site near the modern city of Xian (shih-AHN) that dates back at least seven thousand years, the houses in the village are separated by a ditch, which some scholars think may have served as a divider between two clans. The individual dwellings at Banpo housed nuclear families, but a larger building in the village was apparently used as a clan meeting hall. The clan-based origins of Chinese society may help explain the continued importance of the joint family in traditional China, as well as the relatively small number of family names in Chinese society. Even today

Shell and Bone Writing. The earliest known form of true writing in China dates back to the Shang dynasty and was inscribed on shells or animal bones. Questions for the gods were scratched on bones, which cracked after being exposed to fire. The cracks were then interpreted by sorcerers. The questions often expressed practical concerns: Will it rain? Will the king be victorious in battle? Will he recover from his illness? Originally composed of pictographs and ideographs four thousand years ago, Chinese writing has evolved into an elaborate set of symbols that combine meaning and pronunciation in a single character. RMN-Grand Palais/Art Resource, NY

COMPARATIVE ILLUSTRATION

Religion & Philosophy

The Afterlife and Prized Possessions. Like the pharaohs in Egypt, Chinese rulers filled their tombs with prized possessions from daily life. It was believed that if a tomb was furnished and stocked with supplies, including chairs, boats, chests, weapons, games, and dishes, the spiritual body could continue its life despite the death of the physical body. In A, we see the remains of a chariot and horses in a burial pit in China's Hebei province that dates from the early Zhou dynasty. As image B shows, the tradition of providing items of daily use for the departed continues today in many Chinese communities throughout Asia. In this Buddhist temple located in an overseas Chinese community in Singapore, a paper automobile is about to be burned for the use of a departed family member. Image C shows a small boat from the tomb of Tutankhamun in the Valley of the Kings in Egypt.

Q *How did ancient Chinese tombs compare with the tombs of Egyptian pharaohs? What do the differences tell you about these two societies? What do all of the items shown here have in common?*

B

William J. Duiker

A

Keren Su/Getty Images

C

Model of one of the pharaoh's boats, from the tomb of Tutankhamun (c.1370–52 BC) New Kingdom (wood)/ Egyptian 18th Dynasty (c.1567–1320 BC)/Egyptian National Museum, Cairo, Egypt/Bridgeman Images

---

there are only about four hundred commonly used family names in a society of more than one billion people, and a colloquial expression for the common people in China today is "the old hundred names."

By Shang times, the classes were becoming increasingly differentiated. It is likely that some poorer peasants did not own their farms but were obliged to work the land of the chieftain and other elite families in the village. The aristocrats not only made war and served as officials (indeed, the first Chinese character for *official* originally meant "warrior"), but they were also the primary landowners. In addition to the aristocratic elite and the peasants, there were a small number of merchants and artisans, as well as slaves, probably consisting primarily of criminals or prisoners taken in battle.

The Shang are perhaps best known for their mastery of the art of casting bronze. Utensils, weapons, and ritual objects made of bronze (see Comparative Essay "The Use of Metals," p. 70) have been found in royal tombs in urban centers

throughout the area known to be under Shang influence. It is also clear that the Shang had achieved a fairly sophisticated writing system that would eventually spread throughout East Asia and evolve into the written language that is still used in China today.

HISTORIANS DEBATE

The Shang Dynasty: China's "Mother Culture"?

Until recently, the prevailing wisdom among historians—both Chinese and non-Chinese—was that the Yellow River Valley was the ancient heartland of Chinese civilization and that technological and cultural achievements gradually radiated from there to other areas in East Asia. Here, it was thought, occurred the first technological breakthroughs, including the development of a writing system, advanced farming techniques, and the ability to make bronze ritual vessels. Supporting this idea was the fact that the first significant archaeological finds in China, including the last Shang capital at Anyang, were made in that region.

The Use of Metals

Science & Technology Around 6000 BCE, people in western Asia discovered how to use metals. They soon realized the advantage of using metal instead of stone to make both tools and weapons. Metal could be shaped more precisely, allowing artisans to make more refined tools and weapons with sharper edges and more regular shapes. Copper, silver, and gold, which were commonly found in their elemental form, were the first metals to be used. These were relatively soft and could be easily pounded into different shapes. But an important step was taken when people discovered that a rock that contained metal could be heated to liquefy the metal (a process called smelting). The liquid metal could then be poured into molds of clay or stone to make precisely shaped tools and weapons.

Copper was the first metal to be used in making tools. The first known copper smelting furnace, dated to 3800 BCE, was found in the Sinai. Within the next centuries, artisans in western Asia discovered that tin could be added to copper to make bronze. Bronze has a lower melting point that makes it easier to cast, but it is also a harder metal than copper and corrodes less. The widespread use of bronze that ensued has led historians to speak of the period from around 3000 to 1200 BCE as the Bronze Age, although this is somewhat misleading in that many peoples continued to use stone tools and weapons even after bronze became available.

But there were limitations to the use of bronze. Tin was not as readily available as copper, so bronze tools and weapons were expensive. After 1200 BCE, bronze was increasingly replaced by iron, which was probably first used around 1500 BCE in western Asia, where the Hittites made weapons from it. Between 1500 and 600 BCE, ironmaking spread across Europe, North Africa, and Asia. Bronze continued to be used, but mostly for jewelry and other domestic purposes. Iron was used to make tools and weapons with sharp edges. Because iron weapons were cheaper than bronze ones, more warriors could be armed, and wars could be fought on a larger scale.

The Chinese were slower to master the use of metals than some of their counterparts in the ancient world—entering the Bronze Age only at the end of the third millennium BCE. But they were quick to excel in bronze technology, and by 1400 BCE, Chinese metalworkers were making beautiful bronze ritual objects with a high degree of technological expertise. Eventually, they also took the lead in iron technology as well. Iron was handled differently from bronze: it was heated until it could be beaten into a desired shape. Each hammering made the metal stronger. This wrought iron, as it was called, was typical of iron manufacturing in the West until the late Middle Ages. In China, however, the use of heat-resistant clay in the walls of blast furnaces raised temperatures to 1,537 degrees Celsius, enabling artisans to liquefy iron as early as the fourth century BCE so that it too could be cast in molds to produce high quality weapons and farming tools. Europeans would not develop such blast furnaces until the fifteenth century CE.

Photograph by William J. Duiker/Ceremonial Jade Daggers, Freer Gallery, Washington, D.C.

Shang Dynasty Ceremonial Jade and Bronze Daggers. These ceremonial weapons found in a tomb dating back to the Shang dynasty are among the earliest examples of metalwork in ancient China.

 What were the advantages of making objects out of bronze versus iron in the ancient world? Which metal ultimately triumphed in China?

Today, this **diffusion hypothesis**, as it is sometimes called, is no longer so widely accepted. The remains of early agricultural communities have now been unearthed in the Yangzi River Valley and along the southern coast, and a rich trove of bronze vessels has been discovered in grave sites in central Sichuan (suh-CHWAHN) province. Such finds suggest that although the Yellow River civilization may have taken the lead in some areas, such as complex political organization and the development of writing, similar advances were already occurring in other parts of China, suggesting that communication between regions was already well under way.

3-2 THE ZHOU DYNASTY

 Focus Question: What were the major tenets of Confucianism, Legalism, and Daoism, and to what degree do they compare with philosophical and intellectual trends elsewhere in the ancient world?

Around the mid-eleventh century BCE, the Shang dynasty was overthrown by an aggressive young state located to the west of Anyang, the Shang capital, and near the great bend of the Yellow River as it begins to flow directly eastward to the sea. The new dynasty, which called itself the Zhou, survived for about eight hundred years, making it the longest-lived dynasty in the history of China. According to tradition, the last of the Shang rulers was a tyrant who oppressed the people (Chinese sources assert that he was a degenerate who built "ponds of wine" and ordered the composing of lustful music that "ruined the morale of the nation"),[3] leading the ruler of the principality of Zhou to revolt and establish a new dynasty.

The Zhou located their capital in their home territory, near the present-day city of Xian. Later they established a second capital city at modern Luoyang (LWOH-yahng), farther to the east, to administer new territories captured from the Shang. This established a pattern of eastern and western capitals—based on defensive needs or climatic conditions—that would endure off and on in China for nearly two thousand years.

3-2a Political Structures

The Zhou dynasty (1040–221 BCE) adopted the political system of its predecessors, with some changes. The Shang practice of dividing the kingdom into a number of territories governed by officials appointed by the king was continued under the Zhou. At the apex of the government hierarchy was the Zhou king, who was served by a bureaucracy of growing size and complexity. It now included several ministries responsible for rites, education, law, and public works. Beyond the capital, the Zhou kingdom was divided into a number of principalities, governed by members of the hereditary aristocracy, who were appointed by the king and were at least theoretically subordinated to his authority.

The Mandate of Heaven But the Zhou kings also introduced some innovations. According to the *Rites of Zhou*, one of the oldest surviving documents on statecraft, the Zhou dynasty ruled China because it possessed the **mandate of Heaven**. According to this concept, Heaven (now viewed as an impersonal law of nature rather than as an anthropomorphic deity) maintained order in the universe through the Zhou king, who thus ruled as a representative of Heaven but not as a divine being. The king, who was selected to rule because of his talent and virtue, was then responsible for governing the people with compassion and efficiency (see "The Mandate of Heaven," p. 72). It was his duty to appease the gods in order to protect the people from natural calamities or bad harvests. But if the king failed to rule effectively, he could, theoretically at least, be overthrown and replaced by a new ruler. As noted earlier, this idea was used to justify the Zhou conquest of the Shang. Eventually, the concept of the heavenly mandate would become a cardinal principle of Chinese statecraft.[4] Each founder of a new dynasty would routinely assert that he had earned the mandate of Heaven, and who could disprove it except by overthrowing the king? As a pragmatic Chinese proverb put it, "He who wins is the king; he who loses is the rebel."

In asserting that the ruler had a direct connection with the divine forces presiding over the universe, Chinese tradition reflected a belief that was prevalent in all ancient civilizations. But whereas in some societies, notably in Mesopotamia and Greece (see Chapter 4), the gods were seen as capricious and not subject to human understanding, in China, Heaven was viewed as an essentially benevolent force devoted to universal harmony and order that could be influenced by positive human action. Perhaps this attitude reflected the fact that China, though subject to some of the same climatic vicissitudes that plagued other parts of the world, experienced a somewhat more predictable and beneficial environment than regions like the Middle East.

Later Chinese would regard the period of the early Zhou dynasty, as portrayed in the *Rites of Zhou*, as a golden age when there was harmony in the world and all was right under Heaven. Whether the system functioned in such an ideal manner, of course, is open to question, since the *Rites of Zhou* is no more a reliable source of accurate information than any official document. In any case, the golden age did not last, whether because it never existed in practice or because of the increasing complexity of Chinese civilization. Perhaps, too, its disappearance was a consequence of the intellectual and moral weakness of the rulers of the Zhou royal house.

By the sixth century BCE, the power of the Zhou ruling class began to disintegrate, and bitter internal rivalries arose among the various principalities, where the governing officials had succeeded in making their positions hereditary at the expense of the Zhou king. As the power of these officials grew, they began to regulate the local economy and seek reliable sources of revenue for their expanding armies, such as a uniform tax system and government monopolies on key commodities such as salt and iron. A century later, the Zhou rulers had lost all pretense of authority, and China was divided into a cauldron of squabbling states, an era known to Chinese historians as the "Period of the Warring States" (see Section 3-3 "The First Chinese Empire: The Qin Dynasty," p. 79).

3-2b Economy and Society

During the Zhou dynasty, the essential characteristics of Chinese economic and social institutions began to take shape. The pattern of land ownership that had existed under the Shang remained in operation: the peasants worked on lands owned by their lord but also had land that they cultivated for their own use. The practice was called the **well-field system** because the Chinese character for "well" (井) calls to mind the division of land into nine separate segments. Each peasant family tilled an outer plot for its own use and joined with other families to work the inner one for the hereditary lord. How widely this system was used is unclear, but it represented an ideal described by

THE MANDATE OF HEAVEN

Politics & Government

WHEN THE RULERS of the rising state of Zhou overthrew the last king of the Shang (described in the document below as the Yin) dynasty in the middle of the eleventh century BCE, they declared the founding of a new dynasty with its capital located near the Yellow River in central China. To justify their action, they issued an official decree asserting that the mandate of Heaven—according to which each ruling family was anointed by Heaven provisional on its ability to govern by virtue and wisdom—had been passed from one dynastic family to another, as the Shang had previously replaced their predecessors, the Xia.

Such, at any rate, is the historical account presented in the ancient Chinese classic known as the *Book of History* (*Shujing*), a collection of sayings and documents compiled sometime during the Zhou dynasty (1045–221 BCE). The concept of the mandate of Heaven gradually evolved into an essential element in Chinese political culture over the next two millennia.

The *Book of History*

Oh! God dwelling in the great heavens has changed his decree respecting his great son and the great dynasty of Yin [Shang]. Our king has received that decree. Unbounded is the happiness connected with it, and unbounded is the anxiety. Oh! How can he be other than reverent?

When Heaven rejected and made an end of the decree in favor of the great dynasty of Yin, there were many of its former wise kings in Heaven. The king, however, who had succeeded to them, the last of his race, from the time of his entering into their appointment, proceeded in such a way as to keep the wise in obscurity and the vicious in office. The poor people in such a case, carrying their children and leading their wives, made their moan to Heaven. They even fled, but were apprehended again. Oh! Heaven had compassion on the people of the four quarters; its favoring decree lighted on our

earnest founders. Let the king sedulously cultivate the virtue of reverence.

Examining the men of antiquity, there was Yu, founder of the Hsia [Xia] dynasty. Heaven guided his mind, allowed his descendants to succeed him, and protected them. He acquainted himself with Heaven, and was obedient to it. But in process of time the decree in his favor fell to the ground. So also is it now when we examine the case of Yin. There was the same guiding of its founder T'ang, who corrected the errors of Hsia, and whose descendants enjoyed the protection of Heaven. He also acquainted himself with Heaven, and was obedient to it. But now the decree in favor of him has fallen to the ground. Our king has now come to the throne in his youth. Let him not slight the aged and experienced, for it may be said of them that they have studied the virtuous conduct of the ancients and have matured their counsels in the sight of Heaven.

Oh! Although the king is young, yet he is the eldest son of Heaven. Let him effect a great harmony with the lower people and that will be the blessing of the present time. Let not the king presume to be remiss in this but continually regard and stand in awe of the perilous uncertainty of the people's attachment.

Let the king come here as the vice-regent of God and undertake the duties of government in this center of the land. Tan said, "Now that this great city has been built, from henceforth he may be the mate of great Heaven, and reverently sacrifice to the spirits above and below; henceforth he may from this central spot administer successful government" Thus shall the king enjoy the favoring regard of Heaven all complete, and the government of the people will now be prosperous.

 How would you compare the advice in this statement with that provided by the author of the Arthasastra *in Chapter 2 (see Section 2-2b)? Are there any key differences?*

Source: Clae Waltham, *Shu Ching: Book of History: A Modernized Edition of the Translation of James Legge* (Chicago: Henry Regnery Co. 1971), pp. 162–164.

Confucian scholars of a later day. As the following passage from *The Book of Songs* indicates, the life of the average farmer was a difficult one. The "big rat" is probably the government or a lord who has imposed high taxes on the peasants.

> Big rat, big rat,
> Do not eat my millet!
> Three years I have served you,
> But you will not care for me.
> I am going to leave you
> And go to that happy land;
> Happy land, happy land,
> Where I will find my place.[5]

Trade and manufacturing were carried out by merchants and artisans, who lived in walled towns under the direct

control of the local lord. Merchants did not operate independently but were considered the property of the local lord and on occasion could even be bought and sold like chattels. A class of slaves performed a variety of menial tasks and perhaps worked on local irrigation projects. Most of them were probably prisoners of war captured during conflicts with the neighboring principalities. Scholars do not know how extensive slavery was in ancient times, but slaves probably did not constitute a large portion of the total population.

The period of the later Zhou, from the sixth to the third century BCE, was an era of significant economic growth and technological innovation, especially in agriculture (see Comparative Illustration "Early Agricultural Technology," p. 73). During that time, large-scale water control projects

A

William J. Duiker

William J. Duiker

COMPARATIVE ILLUSTRATION

Science & Technology **Early Agricultural Technology.** For centuries, farmers across the globe have adopted various techniques to guarantee the flow of adequate amounts of water for their crops. One of the most effective ways to irrigate fields in hilly regions is to construct terraces to channel the flow of water from higher elevations. Shown in A is a hillside terrace near the Yellow River in northern China, an area where dry crops such as oats and millet have been cultivated since the sixth millennium BCE. Image B shows a terraced hillside in the southwestern corner of the Arabian Peninsula. Excavations show that despite dry conditions through much of the peninsula, terraced agriculture has been practiced in mountainous parts of the region for as long as five thousand years.

Q *In what other areas of the Middle East is irrigated agriculture practiced?*

were undertaken to regulate the flow of rivers and distribute water evenly to the fields, as well as to construct canals to facilitate the transport of goods from one region to another. Perhaps the most impressive technological achievement of the period was the construction of a massive water control project on the Min River, a tributary of the Yangzi. This system of canals and spillways, put into operation by the state of Qin a few years prior to the end of the Zhou dynasty, diverted excess water from the river into the local irrigation network and watered an area populated by as many as 5 million people. The system is still in use today, more than two thousand years later.

Food production was also stimulated by a number of advances in farm technology. By the mid-sixth century BCE, the introduction of iron had led to the development of iron plowshares, which permitted deep plowing for the first time. Other innovations dating from the later Zhou were the use of natural fertilizer, the collar harness, and the technique of leaving land fallow to preserve or replenish nutrients in the soil. By the late Zhou dynasty, the cultivation of wet rice had become one of the prime sources of food in China. Although rice was difficult and time-consuming to produce, it replaced other grain crops in areas with a warm climate because of its good taste, relative ease of preparation, and high nutritional value.

The advances in agriculture, which enabled the population of China to rise as high as 20 million people during the late Zhou era, were also undoubtedly a major factor in the growth of commerce and manufacturing. During the late Zhou,

economic wealth began to replace noble birth as the prime source of power and influence. Tools made of iron became more common, and trade developed in a variety of useful commodities, including cloth, salt, and manufactured goods.

One of the most important items of trade in ancient China was silk. There is evidence of silkworms being raised as early as the Neolithic period. Remains of silk material have been found on Shang bronzes, and a large number of fragments have been recovered in tombs dating from the mid-Zhou era. Silk cloth was used not only for clothing and quilts but also to wrap the bodies of the dead prior to burial. Fragments dating back to pre-Christian times have been found throughout Central Asia and as far away as Greece, suggesting that trade between China and countries in the Middle East and the region of the Mediterranean Sea was in operation as early as the fifth century BCE.

Initially, however, jade was probably a more important item of trade carried along the Silk Road. Blocks of the precious stone were mined in the mountains of northern Tibet as early as the sixth millennium BCE, and jade items were interred in the tombs of the elite in China as early as the Shang dynasty. Later, jade was praised by the sixth century BCE philosopher Confucius as a symbol of purity and virtue, suggesting that jade had assumed an almost sacred quality among Chinese during the Zhou dynasty.

With the development of trade and manufacturing, China began to move toward a money economy. The first form of money, as in much of the rest of the world, may have been cowries or other seashells (the Chinese character for goods

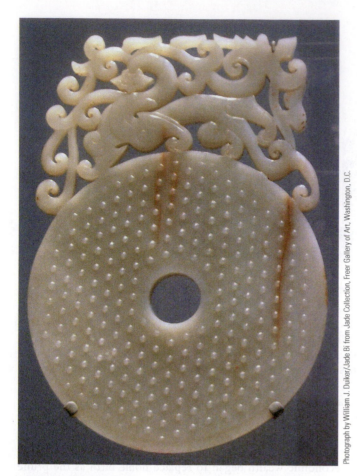

A Ritual Jade Object. Jade has been prized, in the words of a Han dynasty writer, as "the fairest of stones" since the dawn of Chinese civilization. Noted for its hardness and purity of color, it is considered symbolic of many of the finest human virtues and has been found in royal tombs dating back to the period before the rise of the Shang dynasty. Whereas early examples were of relatively simple design, such as ceremonial axes and stone circles, eventually jade appeared in increasingly intricate forms. Shown here is a Zhou dynasty stone circle with a hole in the center—symbolizing Heaven—and surmounted by an elaborately carved dragon.

or property contains the ideographic symbol for "shell" 貝), but by the Zhou dynasty, pieces of iron shaped like a knife or round coins with a hole in the middle so they could be carried in strings of a thousand were being used. Most ordinary Chinese, however, simply used a system of barter. Taxes, rents, and even the salaries of government officials were normally paid in grain.

3–2c The Hundred Schools of Ancient Philosophy

In China, as in other great river valley societies, the birth of civilization was accompanied by the emergence of an organized effort to comprehend the nature of the cosmos and the role of human beings within it. Speculation over such questions began in the very early stages of civilization and culminated at the end of the Zhou era in the "hundred schools" of ancient philosophy, a wide-ranging debate over the nature of human beings, society, and the universe.

Early Beliefs The first hint of religious belief in ancient China comes from relics found in royal tombs of Neolithic times. By then, the Chinese had already developed a religious sense beyond the primitive belief in the existence of spirits in nature. The Shang had begun to believe in the existence of one transcendent god, known as Shang Di, who presided over all the forces of nature. As time went on, the Chinese concept of religion evolved from a vaguely anthropomorphic god to a somewhat more impersonal symbol of universal order known as Heaven (*Tian*). There was also much speculation among Chinese intellectuals about the nature of the cosmic order. One of the earliest ideas was that the universe was divided into two primary forces of good and evil, light and dark, male and female, represented symbolically by the sun (*yang*) and the moon (*yin*). According to this theory, life was a dynamic process of interaction between the forces of *yang* and *yin*, and one led inexorably to the other, and back again. Early Chinese could only attempt to understand the process and perhaps to have some minimal effect on its operation. They could not hope to reverse it. It is sometimes asserted that this belief has contributed to the heavy element of fatalism in Chinese popular wisdom. The Chinese have traditionally believed that bad times will be followed by good times and vice versa.

The belief that there was some mysterious "law of nature" that could be interpreted by human beings led to various attempts to predict the future, such as the Shang oracle bones and other methods of divination. Philosophers invented ways to interpret the will of nature, while shamans, playing a role similar to the *brahmins* in India, were employed at court to assist the emperor in his policy deliberations until at least the fifth century CE. One of the most famous manuals used for this purpose was the *Yi Jing*, known in English as the *Book of Changes*.

Confucianism Efforts to divine the mysterious purposes of Heaven notwithstanding, Chinese thinking about metaphysical reality also contained a strain of pragmatism, readily apparent in the ideas of the great philosopher Confucius. Confucius (*Kung fuci*, or "Master Kung") was born in the state of Lu, in the modern province of Shandong (shahn-DOONG), in 551 BCE. After reaching maturity, he apparently hoped to find employment as a political adviser in one of the principalities into which China was divided at that time, but he had little success in finding a patron. Nevertheless, he won over a number of followers, and his ideas, as drawn together by them in the *Analects* and other works attributed to him, made an indelible mark on Chinese history and culture (see "The Wit and Wisdom of Confucious," p. 75).

In conversations with his disciples contained in the *Analects*, Confucius often adopted a detached and almost skeptical view of Heaven. He believed it was useless to speculate too much about metaphysical questions. It was better by far to assume

THE WIT AND WISDOM OF CONFUCIUS

Religion & Philosophy

THE *ANALECTS* (*LUN YU*), a collection of sayings supposedly uttered by the ancient Chinese philosopher Confucius and drawn up after his death by his disciples, is considered to be a primary source for the Master's ideas and thought. The degree to which the collection provides an accurate account of his remarks on various subjects has long been a matter of debate among specialists. Some scholars argue that the sayings in the *Analects* reflect the views of his followers two centuries after his death in the fifth century BCE more than they do those of Confucius himself.

Whatever the truth of this contention, the sayings in the *Analects* are generally accepted to be representative of Confucius's own views and have provided moral and philosophical guidance to countless generations of Chinese over the centuries. As such, they have played a major role in shaping the lives and culture of the Chinese people. Presented here are a number of familiar passages from the *Analects* on a variety of subjects.

The Confucian *Analects*

On Human Nature

17.2. By their nature, men are quite similar; in practice, they become far apart.

17.3. Only the wisest and the most ignorant of men cannot be changed.

16.9. Those born with innate knowledge are the highest of men; those who become learned are next in line; those who study but fail to learn follow; those who are ignorant yet do not study are the lowest of men.

On Morality

4.5. All men desire wealth and honor. But unless they can be achieved by virtuous means, they should not be sought after.

4.16. The moral man seeks righteousness; the immoral man seeks profit.

6.28. The virtuous man thinks of the needs of others before those of his own; he seeks to benefit others before himself.

15.23. Tzu Kung [one of the Master's disciples] asked if there was one word that could be applied as a standard for virtuous behavior. Confucius replied: It is reciprocity; do not do unto others what you would not wish done to yourself.

On Filial Piety

2.6. What is filial piety? Confucius said: Parents are concerned when their children become ill.

2.5. [Asked about filial piety] Confucius replied: It consists in not being disobedient; when they are alive, parents should be served according to the rules of propriety; after their death, they should be buried correctly and sacrifices should be carried out in a proper manner.

4.18. Confucius said: When serving one's parents, it is permissible to remonstrate with them, but in a respectful manner; if they do not agree, one should not oppose their wishes and even accept punishment without complaint.

On Education

2.15. Study without thought is a waste of time; thought without study is dangerous.

8.12. It is rare to find a man who has studied for three years without making progress.

On Government

2.3. If the government seeks to rule by decrees and the threat of punishment, the people will have no sense of shame; but if they are governed by virtue and a sense of propriety, they will feel shame and seek to behave correctly.

13.6. If its conduct is correct, a government can succeed without issuing directives; if not, directives will not be obeyed.

12.7. Confucius said: Without the confidence of the people, government cannot succeed.

On Religion

13.3. With regard to what he does not know, the superior man reserves judgment.

7.20. The Master did not comment on the supernatural, on feats of strength, on disorder, and on the spirits.

6.20. To meet one's human obligations, to respect the spirits but maintain distance from them, such indeed may be called wisdom.

11.11. [Asked about serving the spirits of the departed], Confucius replied: If you are unable to serve men, how can you serve the spirits? If you don't understand life, how can you understand death?

Q *Confucius is viewed by some observers as a reformer, and by others as a conservative. Based on the information available to you in this chapter, how would you classify his ideas, as expressed in the* Analects?

Source: *The Four Books: Confucian Analects*, by James Legge (Hong Kong: The International Publication Society, n.d.). Translation by William J. Duiker and © 2011 William J. Duiker.

that there was a rational order to the universe and then concentrate on ordering the affairs of this world.

Confucius's interest in philosophy, then, was essentially political and ethical. The universe was constructed in such a way that if human beings could act harmoniously in accordance with its purposes, their own affairs would prosper. Much of his concern was with human behavior. The key to proper behavior was to behave in accordance with the **Dao** (DOW) (Way). Confucius assumed that all human beings had their own *Dao*, depending on their individual role in life, and it was their duty to follow it. Even the ruler had his own *Dao*, and he ignored it at his peril, for to do so could mean the loss of the mandate of Heaven. The idea of the *Dao* is reminiscent of the concept of *dharma* in ancient India and played a similar role in governing the affairs of society.

Two elements in the Confucian interpretation of the *Dao* are particularly worthy of mention. The first is the concept of duty. It was the responsibility of all individuals to subordinate their own interests and aspirations to the broader needs of the family and the community. Confucius assumed that if each individual worked hard to fulfill his or her assigned destiny, the affairs of society as a whole would prosper as well. In this respect, it was important for the ruler to set a good example. If he followed his "kingly way," the beneficial effects would radiate throughout society.

The second key element is the idea of humanity, sometimes translated as "human-heartedness." This concept involves a sense of compassion and empathy for others. It is similar in some ways to Christian concepts, but with a subtle twist. Where Christian teachings call on human beings to "behave toward others as you would have them behave toward you," the Confucian maxim is put in a different way: "Do not do unto others what you would not wish done to yourself." To many Chinese, this attitude symbolizes an element of tolerance in the Chinese character that has not always been practiced in other societies.

Confucius may have considered himself a failure because he never attained the position he wanted, but many of his contemporaries found his ideas appealing, and in the generations after his death, his message spread widely throughout China. Confucius was an outspoken critic of his times and lamented the disappearance of what he regarded as the golden age of the early Zhou.

Yet Confucius was not just another disgruntled Chinese conservative mourning the passing of the good old days; rather, he was a revolutionary thinker, many of whose key ideas looked forward rather than backward. Perhaps his most striking political idea was that the government should be open to all men of superior quality, not limited to those of noble birth. Confucius undoubtedly had himself in mind as one of those "superior" men, but the rapacity of the hereditary lords must have added strength to his convictions.

The concept of rule by merit was, of course, not an unfamiliar idea in the China of his day; the *Rites of Zhou* had clearly stated that the king deserved to rule because of his talent and virtue, not as the result of noble birth. In practice, however, aristocratic privilege must often have opened the doors to political influence, and many of Confucius's contemporaries must have regarded his appeal for government by talent as both exciting and dangerous. Although his ideas did not have much effect in his lifetime, they introduced a new concept that was later implemented in the form of a bureaucracy selected through a civil service examination (see Chapter 10).

Confucius's ideas, passed on to later generations through the *Analects* as well as through other writings attributed to him, had a strong impact on Chinese political thinkers of the late Zhou period, a time when the existing system was in disarray and open to serious question. But as with most great thinkers, Confucius's ideas were sufficiently ambiguous to be interpreted in contradictory ways. Some, like the philosopher Mencius (MEN-shuss) (370–290 BCE), stressed the humanistic side of Confucian ideas, arguing that human beings were by nature good and hence could be taught their civic responsibilities by example. He also stressed that the ruler had a duty to govern with compassion:

> Here is the way to win the empire: win the people and you win the empire. Here is the way to win the people: win their hearts and you win the people. Here is the way to win their hearts: give them and share with them what they like, and do not do to them what they do not like. The people turn to a humane ruler as water flows downward or beasts take to wilderness.[6]

Here is a prescription for political behavior that could win wide support in our own day. Other thinkers, however, rejected Mencius's rosy view of human nature and argued for a different approach (see Opposing Viewpoints "A Debate over Good and Evil," p. 77). The ambiguity over this issue would resonate through the Chinese political debate for centuries.

Legalism One school of thought that became quite popular during the "hundred schools" era in ancient China was the philosophy of **Legalism**. Taking issue with the view of Mencius and other disciples of Confucius that human nature was essentially good, the Legalists argued that human beings were by nature evil and would follow the correct path only if coerced by harsh laws and stiff punishments. These thinkers were referred to as the School of Law because they rejected the Confucian view that government by "superior men" could solve society's problems and argued instead for a system of impersonal laws that would achieve the same purpose.

The Legalists also disagreed with the Confucian belief that the universe has a moral core. They therefore argued that only firm action by the state could bring about social order. Fear of harsh punishment, more than the promise of material reward, could best motivate the common people to serve the interests of the ruler. Because human nature was essentially corrupt, officials could not be trusted to carry out their duties in a fair and evenhanded manner, and only a strong ruler could create an orderly society. All human actions should be directed to the effort to create a strong and prosperous state subject to his will.

A Debate over Good and Evil

Religion & Philosophy **DURING THE LATTER PART OF THE ZHOU DYNASTY**, one of the major preoccupations of Chinese philosophers was to determine the essential qualities of human nature. In the *Analects*, Confucius was cited as asserting that humans' moral instincts were essentially neutral at birth; their minds must be cultivated to bring out the potential goodness therein. In later years, the Master's disciples elaborated on this issue. The great humanitarian philosopher Mencius maintained that human nature was essentially good. But his rival Xunzi (SHYOON-zuh) took the opposite tack, arguing that evil is inherent in human nature and could be eradicated only by rigorous training at the hands of an instructor. Later, Xunzi's views would be adopted by the Legalist philosophers of the Qin dynasty, although his belief in the efficacy of education earned him a place in the community of Confucian scholars.

The Book of Mencius

1. Mencius said, "All men have a mind which cannot bear to see the sufferings of others.

"2. The ancient kings had this commiserating mind, and they, as a matter of course, had likewise a commiserating government. When with a commiserating mind was practiced a commiserating government, the government of the empire was as easy a matter as the making anything go around the palm.

"3. When I say that all men have a mind which cannot bear to see the sufferings of others, my meaning may be illustrated thus: - even nowadays, if men suddenly see a child about to fall into a well, they will without exception experience a feeling of alarm and distress. They will feel so, not as a ground on which they may gain the favor of the child's parents, nor as a ground on which they may seek the praise of their neighbors and friends, nor from a dislike to the reputations of having been unmoved by such a thing.

"4. From this case we may perceive that the feeling of commiseration is essential to man, that the feeling of shame and dislike is essential to man, that the feeling of modesty and complaisance is essential to man, and that the feeling of approving and disapproving is essential to man.

"5. The feeling of commiseration is the principle of benevolence. The feeling of shame and dislike is the principle of righteousness.

The Book of Xunzi

The nature of man is evil; his goodness is only acquired training. The original nature of man today is to seek for gain. If this desire is followed, strife and rapacity results, and courtesy dies. Man originally is envious and naturally hates others. If these tendencies are followed, injury and destruction follows; loyalty and faithfulness are destroyed. Man originally possesses the desires of the ear and eye; he likes praise and is lustful. If these are followed impurity and disorder results, and the rules of proper conduct and justice and etiquette are destroyed. Therefore to give rein to man's original nature, to follow man's feelings, inevitably results in strife and rapacity, together with violation of etiquette and confusion in the proper way of doing things, and reverts to a state of violence. Therefore the civilizing influence of teachers and laws, the guidance of the rules of proper conduct and justice are absolutely necessary. Thereupon courtesy results; public and private etiquette is observed; and good government is the consequence. By this line of reasoning it is evident that the nature of man is evil and his goodness is acquired.

 What arguments do these two Confucian thinkers advance to support their point of view about the essential elements of human nature? In your view, which argument is more persuasive?

Source: *The Works of Mencius*, 2A.6, from J. Legge [tr.], *The Four Books* (Wen Yuan Publishing House, no date.)

Source: *The Hsun Tzu*, translated in Sebastian de Grazia (ed.), *Masters of Chinese Political Thought: From the Beginnings to the Han Dynasty* (New York: Viking, 1973), p. 176.

Daoism One of the most popular alternatives to **Confucianism** was the philosophy of **Daoism** (DOW-iz-uhm) (frequently spelled Taoism). According to Chinese tradition, the Daoist school was founded by a contemporary of Confucius popularly known as Lao Zi (LOW ["ow" as in "how"] dzuh), or the Old Master. Many modern scholars, however, are skeptical that Lao Zi actually existed or believe that he lived several generations after the lifetime of Confucius.

Obtaining a clear understanding of the original concepts of Daoism is difficult because its primary document, a short treatise known as the *Dao De Jing* (DOW deh JING) (sometimes translated as *The Way of the Tao*), is an enigmatic

Lao Zi and Confucius. Little is known about the life of Lao Zi (shown on the left in the illustration), and it is unlikely that he and Confucius ever met. According to tradition, though, the two held a face-to-face meeting. The discussion must have been interesting, for their views about the nature of reality were diametrically opposed. Nevertheless, the Chinese have managed to preserve both traditions, perhaps a reflection of the dualities represented in the Chinese approach to life. A similar duality existed among Platonists and Aristotelians in ancient Greece (see Chapter 4).

book whose interpretation has baffled scholars for centuries. The opening line, for example, explains less what the *Dao* is than what it is not: "The Tao [Way] that can be told of is not the eternal Tao. The name that can be named is not the eternal name."[7]

Nevertheless, the basic concepts of Daoism are not especially difficult to understand. Like Confucianism, Daoism does not anguish over the underlying meaning of the cosmos. Rather, it attempts to set forth proper forms of behavior for human beings here on earth. In most other respects, however, Daoism presents a view of life and its ultimate meaning that is almost diametrically opposed to that of Confucianism. Whereas Confucian doctrine asserts that it is the duty of human beings to work hard to improve life here on earth, Daoists contend that the true way to interpret the will of Heaven is not action but inaction (*wu wei*). The best way to act in harmony with the universal order is to act spontaneously and let nature take its course (see "The Daoist Answer to Confucianism," p. 79).

Such a message could be very appealing to people who were uncomfortable with the somewhat rigid flavor of the Confucian work ethic and preferred a more individualistic approach. This image would eventually find graphic expression in Chinese landscape painting, which in its classic form would depict naturalistic scenes of mountains, water, and clouds and underscore the fragility and smallness of individual human beings.

Daoism achieved considerable popularity in the waning years of the Zhou dynasty. It was especially popular among intellectuals, who may have found it appealing as an escapist antidote in a world characterized by growing disorder.

Popular Beliefs Daoism also played a second role as a framework for popular spiritualistic and animistic beliefs among the common people. Popular Daoism was less a philosophy than a religion; it comprised a variety of rituals and behaviors that were regarded as a means of achieving heavenly salvation or even a state of immortality on earth. Daoist sorcerers practiced various types of exercises for training the mind and body in the hope of achieving power, sexual prowess, and long life. It was primarily this form of Daoism that survived into a later age.

The philosophical forms of Confucianism and Daoism did not provide much in the way of concrete significance to the mass of the population, for whom philosophical debate over the ultimate meaning of life was less important than the daily struggle for survival. Even among the elites, interest in the occult and in astrology was high, and many royal courts included a hereditary astrologer to help predict the intentions of the heavenly forces. Throughout the ancient period, magico-religious ideas coexisted with interest in natural science and humanistic philosophy.

For most Chinese, Heaven was not a vague, impersonal law of nature, as it was for many Confucian and Daoist intellectuals. Instead, it was a terrain peopled with innumerable gods and spirits of nature, both good and evil, who existed in trees, mountains, and streams as well as in heavenly bodies. As human beings mastered the techniques of farming, they called on divine intervention to guarantee a good harvest. Other gods were responsible for the safety of fishermen, transportation workers, or prospective mothers.

Another aspect of popular religion was the belief that the spirits of deceased human beings lived in the atmosphere for a time before ascending to heaven or descending to hell. During that period, surviving family members had to care for the spirits through proper ritual, or they would become evil spirits and haunt the survivors.

Thus, in ancient China, human beings were offered a variety of interpretations regarding the nature of the universe. Confucianism satisfied the need for a rational doctrine of nation building and social organization at a time when the existing political and social structure was beginning to disintegrate. Philosophical Daoism provided a more sensitive approach to the vicissitudes of fate and nature and a framework for a set of diverse animistic beliefs at the popular level. But neither could satisfy the deeper emotional needs that sometimes inspire the human spirit. Neither could effectively provide solace in a time of sorrow or the hope of a better life in the hereafter. Something else would be needed to fill the gap.

THE DAOIST ANSWER TO CONFUCIANISM

Religion & Philosophy

THE *DAO DE JING* (*The Way of the Tao*) is the great classic of philosophical Daoism (Taoism). Traditionally attributed to the legendary Chinese philosopher Lao Zi (Old Master), it was probably written during the era of Confucius. This opening passage illustrates two of the key ideas that characterize Daoist belief: it is impossible to define the nature of the universe, and inaction (not Confucian action) is the key to ordering the affairs of human beings.

The Way of the Tao

The Tao that can be told of is not the eternal Tao;
The name that can be named is not the eternal name.
The Nameless is the origin of Heaven and Earth;
The Named is the mother of all things.

Therefore let there always be nonbeing, so we may see their subtlety.
And let there always be being, so we may see their outcome.
The two are the same,
But after they are produced, they have different names.
They both may be called deep and profound.
Deeper and more profound,
The door of all subtleties!
When the people of the world all know beauty as beauty,
There arises the recognition of ugliness.

When they all know the good as good,
There arises the recognition of evil.
Therefore:
Being and nonbeing produce each other;
Difficult and easy complete each other;
Long and short contrast each other;
High and low distinguish each other;
Sound and voice harmonize each other;
Front and behind accompany each other.

Therefore the sage manages affairs without action
And spreads doctrines without words.
All things arise, and he does not turn away from them.
He produces them but does not take possession of them.
He acts but does not rely on his own ability.
He accomplishes his task but does not claim credit for it.
It is precisely because he does not claim credit that his accomplishment remains with him.

 What is Lao Zi, the presumed author of this document, trying to express about the basic nature of the universe? Based on the Confucian Analects *and* The Way of the Tao, *how do you think the Chinese attempted to understand the order of nature through their philosophies?*

Source: From *The Way of Lao Tzu* (Tao-te Ching), by Wing-Tsit Chan, trans. Copyright © 1963 by Macmillan College Publishing Company, Inc.

3–3 THE FIRST CHINESE EMPIRE: THE QIN DYNASTY

Focus Question: How did the first emperor of the Qin dynasty transform the political, social, and economic institutions of early China?

During the last two centuries of the Zhou dynasty (the fourth and third centuries BCE), the authority of the king became increasingly nominal, and several of the small principalities into which the Zhou kingdom had been divided began to evolve into powerful states that presented a potential challenge to the Zhou ruler himself. Chief among these were Qu (CHOO) in the central Yangzi Valley, Wu (WOO) in the Yangzi delta, and Yue (yoo-EH) along the southeastern coast. At first, their mutual rivalries were held in check, but by the late fifth century BCE, competition intensified into civil war, giving birth to the so-called Period of the Warring States (see "The Art of War," p. 80). Powerful principalities vied with each other for preeminence and largely ignored the now purely titular authority of the Zhou court (see Map 3.2). New forms of warfare also emerged with the invention of iron weapons and the introduction of the foot soldier. Cavalry, too, made its first appearance, armed with the powerful crossbow. Cities were now threatened by larger and more competent armies. When they sought to protect themselves by erecting high walls, their opponents countered by developing new techniques in siege warfare.

Eventually, the relatively young state of Qin (CHIN), located in the original homeland of the Zhou, emerged as a key player in these conflicts. By the mid-fourth century BCE, it had become a major force in the contest for hegemony in late-Zhou China by adopting a number of reforms in agriculture, government administration, military organization, and fiscal policy. As a result of policies put into effect by the adviser Shang Yang (SHAHNG yahng) in the mid-fourth century BCE, Qin society was ruled with ruthless efficiency. In the words of Sima Qian (SUH-mah chee-AHN), a famous historian of the Han dynasty:

> He commanded that the people be divided into tens and fives and that they supervise each other and be mutually liable. Anyone who failed to report criminal activity would be chopped in two at the waist, while those who reported it would receive the same reward as that for obtaining the head of an enemy.[8]

Benefiting from a strong defensive position in the mountains to the west of the great bend of the Yellow River, as well as from their control of the rich Sichuan plains, the Qin gradually subdued their main rivals through conquest or diplomatic maneuvering. In 221 BCE, the Qin ruler declared the establishment of a new dynasty, the first truly unified government in Chinese history.

THE ART OF WAR

Politics & Government

WITH THE POSSIBLE EXCEPTION of the nineteenth-century German military strategist Carl von Clausewitz, there is probably no more famous or respected writer on the art of war than the ancient Chinese thinker Sun Tzu (SOON dzuh). Yet surprisingly little is known about him. Recently discovered evidence suggests that he lived in the fifth century BCE, during the chronic conflict of the Period of Warring States, and that he was an early member of an illustrious family of military strategists who advised Zhou rulers for more than two hundred years. But despite the mystery surrounding his life, there is no doubt of his influence on later generations of military planners. Among his most avid followers in our day have been the revolutionary leaders Mao Zedong and Ho Chi Minh, as well as the Japanese military strategists who planned the attacks on Port Arthur and Pearl Harbor.

The following brief excerpt from his classic, *The Art of War*, provides a glimmer into the nature of his advice, still so timely today.

Selections from Sun Tzu

Sun Tzu said:

"In general, the method for employing the military is this: . . . Attaining one hundred victories in one hundred battles is not the pinnacle of excellence. Subjugating the enemy's army without fighting is the true pinnacle of excellence. . . .

"Thus the highest realization of warfare is to attack the enemy's plans; next is to attack their alliances; next to attack their army; and the lowest is to attack their fortified cities.

"This tactic of attacking fortified cities is adopted only when unavoidable. Preparing large movable protective shields, armored assault wagons, and other equipment and devices will require three months. Building earthworks will require another three months to complete. If the general cannot overcome his impatience but instead launches an assault wherein his men swarm over the walls like ants, he will kill one-third of his officers and troops, and the city will still

not be taken. This is the disaster that results from attacking [fortified cities].

"Thus, one who excels at employing the military subjugates other people's armies without engaging in battle, captures other people's fortified cities without attacking them, and destroys others people's states without prolonged fighting. He must fight under Heaven with the paramount aim of 'preservation.' . . .

"In general, the strategy of employing the military is this: If your strength is ten times theirs, surround them; if five, then attack them; if double, then divide your forces. If you are equal in strength to the enemy, you can engage him. If fewer, you can circumvent him. If outmatched, you can avoid him. . . .

"Thus, there are five factors from which victory can be known:

"*One who knows when he can fight, and when he cannot fight, will be victorious.*

"*One who recognizes how to employ large and small numbers will be victorious.*

"*One whose upper and lower ranks have the same desires will be victorious.*

"*One who, fully prepared, awaits the unprepared will be victorious.*

"*One whose general is capable and not interfered with by the ruler will be victorious.*

"These five are the Way (Tao) to know victory. . . .

"Thus it is said that one who knows the enemy and knows himself will not be endangered in a hundred engagements. One who does not know the enemy but knows himself will sometimes be victorious, sometimes meet with defeat. One who knows neither the enemy nor himself will invariably be defeated in every engagement."

 Why are the ideas of Sun Tzu about the art of war still so popular among military strategists after 2,500 years? How might he advise U.S. and other statesmen to deal with the problem of international terrorism today?

Source: From *Sun Tzu: The Art of War*, Ralph D. Sawyer (Boulder: Westview Press, 1994), pp. 177–179.

3–3a The Qin Dynasty (221–206 BCE)

One of the primary reasons for the triumph of the Qin was probably the character of the Qin ruler, known to history as Qin Shi Huangdi, or the First Emperor of Qin. A man of forceful personality and immense ambition, Qin Shi Huangdi had ascended to the throne of Qin in 246 BCE at the age of thirteen. Described by the Han dynasty historian Sima Qian as having "the chest of a bird of prey, the voice of a jackal, and the heart of a tiger," the new king found the Legalist views of his adviser

Li Su (lee SUH) all too appealing. In 221 BCE, Qin Shi Huangdi defeated the last of his rivals and founded a new dynasty with himself as emperor.

Political Structures The Qin dynasty transformed Chinese politics. Philosophical doctrines that had proliferated during the late Zhou period were prohibited, and Legalism was adopted as the official ideology. Those who opposed the policies of the new regime were punished and sometimes executed,

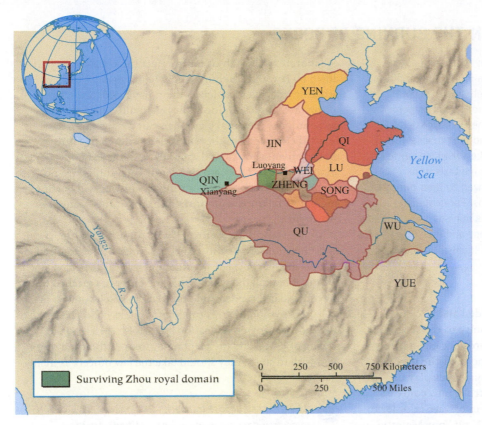

the court and were subject to dismissal at the emperor's whim. A penal code provided for harsh punishments for all wrongdoers. Officials were watched by the censors, who reported directly to the throne. Those guilty of malfeasance in office were executed.

Society and the Economy Qin Shi Huangdi, who had a passion for centralization, also unified the system of weights and measures, standardized the monetary system and the written forms of Chinese characters, and ordered the construction of a system of roads extending throughout the empire. He also attempted to eliminate the remaining powers of the landed aristocrats and divided their estates among the peasants, who were now taxed directly by the state. He thus eliminated potential rivals and secured tax revenues for the central government. Members of the aristocratic clans were required to live in the capital city at Xianyang (shi-AHN-yahng), just north of modern Xian, so that the court could monitor their activities. Such a system may not necessarily have been advantageous to the peasants, however, since the central government could now collect taxes more effec-

Map 3.2 China During the Period of the Warring States. From the fifth to the third centuries BCE, China was locked in a time of civil strife known as the Period of the Warring States. This map shows the Zhou dynasty capital at Luoyang, along with the major states that were squabbling for precedence in the region.

Q *Why did most of the early states emerge in areas adjacent to China's two major river systems, the Yellow and the Yangzi?*

while books presenting ideas contrary to the official orthodoxy were publicly put to the torch, perhaps the first example of book burning in history (see "Memorandum on the Burning of Books," p. 81).

Legalistic theory gave birth to a number of fundamental administrative and political developments, some of which would survive the Qin and serve as a model for future dynasties. In the first place, unlike the Zhou, the Qin was a highly centralized state. The central bureaucracy was divided into three primary ministries: a civil authority, a military authority, and a censorate, whose inspectors surveyed the efficiency of officials throughout the system. This would later become standard administrative procedure for future Chinese dynasties.

Below the central government were two levels of administration: provinces and counties. Unlike the Zhou system, officials at these levels did not inherit their positions but were appointed by

tively and mobilize the peasants for military service and for various public works projects.

The Qin dynasty was equally unsympathetic to the merchants, whom it viewed as parasites. Private commercial activities were severely restricted and heavily taxed, and many vital forms of commerce and manufacturing, including mining, wine making, and the distribution of salt, were placed under a government monopoly.

Qin Shi Huangdi was equally aggressive in foreign affairs. His armies continued the gradual advance to the south that had taken place during the final years of the Zhou dynasty, extending the border of China to the edge of the Red River in modern Vietnam. To supply the Qin armies operating in the area, a canal was dug that provided direct inland navigation from the Yangzi River in central China to what is now the modern city of Guangzhou (gwahng-JOE) (Canton) in the south.

The Qin Empire, 221–206 BCE

MEMORANDUM ON THE BURNING OF BOOKS

Politics & Government

LI SU, who is quoted in the following passage, was a chief minister of the First Emperor of Qin. An exponent of Legalism, Li Su hoped to eliminate all rival theories of government. His recommendation to the emperor on how to accomplish this was recorded by the Han dynasty historian Sima Qian. The emperor approved the proposal and ordered all books contrary to the spirit of Legalist ideology to be destroyed on pain of death. Fortunately, some texts were preserved by being hidden or even memorized by their owners and were thus available to later generations. For centuries afterward, the First Emperor of Qin and his minister were singled out for criticism because of their intolerance and their effort to control the minds of their subjects. Totalitarianism, it seems, is not a modern concept.

Sima Qian, *Historical Records*

In antiquity all under Heaven was divided and in chaos, and nobody was capable of bringing unity to the rest, and it was for this reason that the feudal lords became active together. In their utterances they all spoke of the past in order to injure the present, and they made a display of empty verbiage in order to throw the truth into confusion. People approved what they had learnt in private in order to reject what their superiors laid down. Now Your Majesty has unified and taken possession of all under Heaven. You have distinguish white from black and fixed a single focus of adulation. But those who have studied privately in fact collaborate with each other to reject the regulations laid down by law and teaching; and when they hear orders promulgated, each criticizes them in accordance with his private studies. Indoors they mentally reject them, and outdoors they make criticisms in the byways. To reject their sovereign they consider a source of fame, disagreement they regard as noble, and they encourage all the orders to fabricate slander. If such things are not prohibited then above the sovereign's power will decline, and below factions will form. To prohibit this would be expedient.

Your servant requests that all who possess literature such as *the Songs*, *the Documents*, and the sayings of the hundred schools should get rid of it without penalty. If they have not got rid of it a full thirty days after the order has reached them, they should be branded and sent to do forced labour on the walls. There should be exemption for books concerned with medicine, pharmacy, divination by tortoise-shell . . . , the sowing of crops, and the planting of trees. If there are those who wish to study, they should take the law officers as their teachers.

 Why did the Legalist thinker Li Su believe that his proposal to destroy dangerous ideas was justified? Are there examples of similar thinking in our own time? Are there occasions when it might be permissible to outlaw unpopular ideas?

Source: R. Dawson (tr.), *Sima Qian: Historical Records* (Oxford: Oxford University Press, 1994), pp. 30–31.

Beyond the Frontier: The Nomadic Peoples and the Great Wall

The main area of concern for the Qin emperor, however, was in the north, where a nomadic people, known to the Chinese as the Xiongnu (SHYOHNG-noo) and possibly related to the Huns (see Chapter 5) or to Indo-European-speaking people in the area, had become increasingly active in the area of the Gobi Desert. The area north of the Yellow River had been sparsely inhabited since prehistoric times. During the Qin period, the climate of northern China was somewhat milder and moister than it is today, and parts of the region were heavily forested. The local population probably lived by hunting and fishing, practicing limited forms of agriculture, or herding animals such as cattle or sheep.

As the climate gradually became drier, people were forced to rely increasingly on animal husbandry as a means of livelihood. Their response was to master the art of riding on horseback and to adopt the nomadic life. Organized loosely into communities consisting of a number of kinship groups, they ranged far and wide in search of pasture for their herds of cattle, goats, or sheep. As they moved seasonally from one pasture to another, they often traveled several hundred miles carrying their goods and their circular felt tents, called *yurts*.

But the new way of life presented its own challenges. Increased food production led to a growing population, which in times of drought outstripped the available resources. Rival groups then competed for the best pastures. After they mastered the art of fighting on horseback in the middle of the first millennium BCE, territorial warfare became commonplace throughout the entire frontier region, from the Pacific Ocean to Central Asia.

By the end of the third century BCE, the nomadic Xiongnu had unified many of the groups operating in the region and began to pose a serious threat to the security of China's northern frontier. A number of Chinese principalities in the area began to build walls of tamped earth or stones to keep them out, but warriors on horseback possessed significant advantages over the infantry of the Chinese. Qin Shi Huangdi's answer to the problem was to introduce archers, mounted on sturdy horses imported from Central Asia, into his military units stationed in the north to counter nomad attacks. He also strengthened the system of walls that had already been erected under the Zhou, while adding fortifications at strategic points to keep the marauders out. In the historian Sima Qian's words:

> First Emperor of the [Qin] . . . seized control of all the lands south of the Yellow River and established border defenses along the river, constructing forty-four walled district cities overlooking the river and manning them with convict laborers transported to the border for garrison duty. Thus, he utilized the natural mountain barriers to establish the border defenses, scooping out the valleys and constructing ramparts and building installations at other points where they were needed. The whole line of defenses stretched over ten thousand *li* [a *li* is one-third of a mile]. . . .[9]

Today, of course, we know Qin Shi Huangdi's project as the Great Wall, which extends nearly 5,000 miles from the sandy wastes of Central Asia to the sea. Some of it is constructed of massive granite blocks, and its top is wide enough to serve as a roadway for horse-drawn chariots (see Chapter 10). Although the wall that appears in most photographs today was built during the Ming dynasty, 1,500 years after the Qin, some of the walls built by the Qin remain standing. Their construction was a massive project that required the efforts of thousands of laborers, many of whom met their deaths there and, according to legend, are buried within the wall (see illustration "The Great Walls of China" in Chapter 10 in Section 10-3).

The Fall of the Qin The Legalist system put in place by the First Emperor of Qin was designed to achieve maximum efficiency as well as total security for the state. It did neither. Qin Shi Huangdi was apparently aware of the dangers of factions within the imperial family and established a class of **eunuchs** (castrated males) who served as personal attendants for himself and female members of the royal family. The original idea may have been to restrict the influence of male courtiers, and the eunuch system later became a standard feature of the Chinese imperial system. But as confidential advisers to the royal family, eunuchs were in a position of influence. The rivalry between the "inner" imperial court and the "outer" court of bureaucratic officials led to tensions that persisted until the end of the imperial system.

By ruthlessly gathering control over the empire into his own hands, Qin Shi Huangdi had hoped to establish a rule that, in the words of Sima Qian, "would be enjoyed by his sons for ten thousand generations." In fact, his centralizing zeal alienated many key groups. Landed aristocrats and Confucian intellectuals, as well as the common people, groaned under the censorship of thought and speech, harsh taxes, and forced labor projects. "He killed men," recounted the historian, "as though he thought he could never finish, he punished men as though he were afraid he would never get around to them all, and the whole world revolted against him."[10] Shortly after the emperor died in 210 BCE, the dynasty descended into factional rivalry, and four years later it was overthrown.

3–4 THE GLORIOUS HAN DYNASTY (202 BCE–221 CE)

 Focus Questions: Why and to what degree did the Han dynasty turn to Confucianism as an ideology of the state? How in turn did Han rulers adjust Confucian ideas to serve their own needs?

The fall of the Qin dynasty in 206 BCE was followed by a brief period of civil strife as aspiring successors competed for hegemony. Out of this conflict emerged one of the greatest and most durable dynasties in Chinese history—the Han (HAHN). The Han dynasty would later become so closely identified with the advance of Chinese civilization that even today the Chinese sometimes refer to themselves as "people of Han" and to their language as the "language of Han."

The founder of the Han dynasty was Liu Bang (lyoo BAHNG), a commoner of peasant origin who would be known historically by his imperial title of Han Gaozu (HAHN gow-DZOO), or Exalted Emperor of Han. Under his strong rule and that of his successors, the new dynasty quickly moved to consolidate its control over the empire and promote the welfare of its subjects. Efficient and benevolent, at least by the standards of the time, Gaozu maintained the centralized political institutions of the Qin but abandoned its harsh Legalistic approach to law enforcement. Han rulers discovered in Confucian principles a useful foundation for the creation of a new state philosophy. Under the Han, Confucianism, supplemented by elements from the surviving classics of the "hundred schools" period, began to take on the character of an official ideology.

3–4a Confucianism and the State

The integration of Confucian doctrine with Legalist institutions, creating a system generally known as **State Confucianism**, took a while to accomplish. At first, Emperor Han Gaozu departed from the Qin policy of centralized rule by rewarding some of his key allies with vast fiefdoms, restricting his own territory to lands around the new capital of Chang'an (CHENG-AHN). But chronic unrest throughout the countryside eventually forced a change in policy. By the mid-second century BCE, the influence of unruly aristocratic forces had been curbed, and once again power was concentrated at the imperial court.

Once this was accomplished, the Han rulers sought to restore key components of the Qin system of centralized government. For example, they borrowed the tripartite division of the central government into civilian and military authorities and a censorate. The government was headed by a "grand council" including representatives from all three segments of government. The Han also retained the system of local government, dividing the empire into provinces and districts.

Finally, the Han sought to apply the Qin system of selecting government officials on the basis of merit rather than birth. Shortly after founding the new dynasty, Emperor Gaozu decreed that local officials would be asked to recommend promising candidates for public service. Thirty years later, in 165 BCE, the first known **civil service examination** was administered to candidates for positions in the bureaucracy. Shortly after that, an academy was established to train candidates. The first candidates were almost all from aristocratic or other wealthy families, and the Han bureaucracy itself was still dominated by the traditional hereditary elite. Still, the principle of selecting officials on the basis of talent had been established and would eventually become standard practice. By the end of the first century BCE, as many as 30,000 students were enrolled at the academy.

Driven by government policies that used tax incentives to promote large families, the population of the empire increased rapidly—by some estimates rising from about 20 million to more than 60 million at the height of the dynasty—creating a growing need for a large and efficient bureaucracy to maintain the state in proper working order. Unfortunately, the Han were unable to resolve all of the problems left over from the past. Factionalism at court remained a serious problem and undermined the efficiency of the central government. Equally important, despite their efforts, the Han rulers were never able to restrain the great aristocratic families, who continued to play a dominant role in political and economic affairs. The failure to curb the power of the wealthy clans eventually became a major factor in the collapse of the dynasty.

3–4b The Economy

Han rulers unwittingly contributed to their own problems by adopting fiscal policies that led eventually to greater concentration of land in the hands of the wealthy. They were aware that a free peasantry paying taxes directly to the state would both limit the wealth and power of the great noble families and increase the state's revenues. They had difficulty, however, in preventing the recurrence of the economic inequities that had characterized the last years of the Zhou. Land taxes were not especially high but had to be paid in cash rather than in grain to make collection easier. In years of bad harvests, poor farmers were unable to pay their taxes and were forced to sell their land and become tenant farmers, paying rents of up to half the annual harvest. Although food production increased steadily due to the application of natural fertilizer and the use of iron tools that brought new lands under the plow, the trebling of the population under the early Han eventually reduced the average size of a family's farm plot to about one acre per person, barely enough for survival.

Farm families also faced a number of other exactions, including compulsory military service for adult males and forced labor of up to one month annually. As rural protests escalated during the first decades of Han rule, the imperial government finally ended military conscription and began to rely on professional armies, recruited primarily among non-Chinese minorities living along the periphery of the

empire. That strategy, however, would eventually lead to its own problems (see Section 3-4d "The Decline and Fall of the Han," p. 86).

Manufacturing and Trade Although such economic problems contributed to the eventual downfall of the dynasty, in general the period of the early Han was one of unparalleled productivity and prosperity, marked by a major expansion of trade, both domestic and foreign. This was not necessarily due to official encouragement. In fact, the Han were as suspicious of private merchants as their predecessors had been and levied stiff taxes on trade in an effort to limit commercial activities. Merchants were also subject to severe social constraints. They were disqualified from seeking office, restricted in their place of residence, and generally viewed as parasites providing little true value to Chinese society.

The state itself directed much trade and manufacturing; it produced weapons, for example, and operated shipyards, granaries, and mines. The system of roads was expanded and modernized, and new bridges, rest houses, and post stations for changing horses were added. Unlike the Romans, however (see Chapter 5), the Han rulers relied on waterways for the bulk of their transportation needs. To supplement the numerous major rivers crisscrossing the densely populated heartland of China, new canals were dug to facilitate the moving of goods from one end of the vast empire to the other.

The Han dynasty also began to move cautiously into foreign trade, mostly with neighboring areas in Central and Southeast Asia, although trade relations were established with countries as far away as India and the Mediterranean, where active contacts were maintained with the Roman Empire. Some of this long-distance trade was carried by sea through southern ports like Guangzhou (gwahng-JOH), but more was transported by overland caravans on the Silk Road (see next section and Chapter 10) and other routes that led westward into Central Asia.

New technology contributed to the economic prosperity of the Han era. Following the initiatives adopted under the Qin, the currency was further standardized for use throughout the empire, while significant progress was achieved in such areas as textile manufacturing, water mills (chain pumps with wooden pellets appeared in the first century BCE), and iron casting; skill at ironworking led to the production of steel a few centuries later. Paper was invented during the first century CE, and the development of the rudder and fore-and-aft rigging permitted ships to sail into the wind for the first time. Thus equipped, Chinese merchant ships carrying heavy cargoes could sail throughout the islands of Southeast Asia and into the Indian Ocean.

3–4c Imperial Expansion and the Origins of the Silk Road

The Han emperors continued the process of territorial expansion and consolidation that had begun under the Zhou and the Qin. Han rulers, notably Han Wudi (HAHN woo-DEE), or "Martial

Making Paper. One of China's most important contributions to the world was the invention of paper during the Han dynasty. Although the first known use of paper for writing dates back to the first century BCE, paper was also used for clothing, wrapping materials, military armor, and toilet tissue. It was even suggested to a prince in 93 BCE that he use a paper handkerchief. Paper was made by pounding fibers of hemp and linen. Then the crushed fibers were placed on a flat meshed surface and soaked in a large vat. After the residue dried, it was peeled away as a sheet of paper, seen piled at the right in this eighteenth-century painting.

Emperor of Han," who ruled from 141 to 87 BCE, successfully completed the assimilation into the empire of the regions south of the Yangzi River, including the Red River delta in what is today northern Vietnam. Han armies also marched westward as far as the Caspian Sea, pacifying nomadic tribal peoples and extending China's boundary far into Central Asia (see Map 3.3).

The latter project apparently was originally planned as a means to fend off pressure from the nomadic Xiongnu peoples, who periodically threatened Chinese lands from their base area north of the Great Wall. In 138 BCE, Emperor Wudi dispatched the courtier Zhang Qian (JANG chee-AHN) on a mission westward into Central Asia to seek alliances with peoples living in the area against the common menace. Although he failed in his assigned task, Zhang Qian returned home with ample information about political and economic conditions in Central Asia. The new knowledge permitted the Han court to establish the first Chinese military presence in the area of the Taklimakan (tah-kluh-muh-KAHN) Desert and the Tian Shan (TEE-en SHAHN) (Heavenly Mountains). Eventually, this area would become known to the Chinese people as Xinjiang, or "new region."

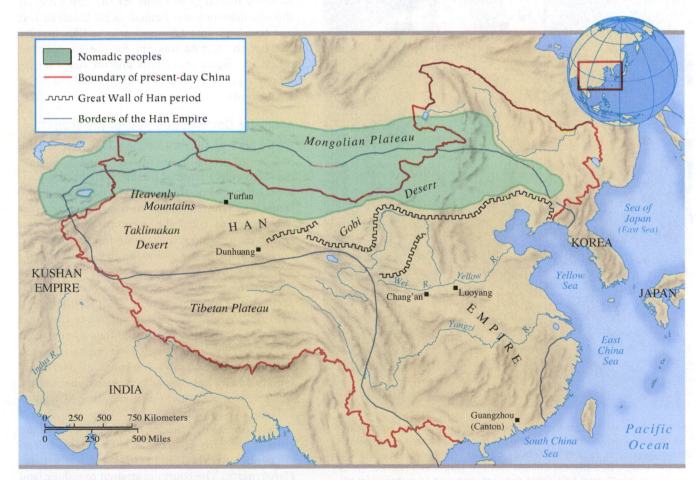

Map 3.3 The Han Empire. This map shows the territory under the control of the Han Empire at its greatest extent during the first century BCE. Note the Great Wall's placement relative to nomadic peoples.

Q *How did the expansion of Han rule to the west parallel the Silk Road?*

Chinese commercial exchanges with peoples in Central Asia now began to expand dramatically. Eastward into China came grapes, precious metals, glass objects, and horses from Persia and Central Asia. Horses were of particular significance because Chinese military strategists had learned of the importance of cavalry in their battles against the Xiongnu and sought the sturdy Ferghana horses of Bactria to increase their own military effectiveness. In return, China exported goods, especially silk, to countries to the west.

Silk, a filament recovered from the cocoons of silkworms, had been produced in China since the fourth millennium BCE. Eventually, knowledge of the wonder product reached the outside world, and Chinese silk exports began to rise dramatically. By the second century BCE, the first items made from silk reached the Mediterranean Sea, stimulating the first significant contacts between China and Rome, its great counterpart in the west (see Chapter 5). The bulk of the trade went overland through Central Asia (thus earning this route its modern name, the Silk Road), although significant exchanges also took place via the maritime route (see Chapter 9). Silk became a

craze among Roman elites, leading to a vast outflow of silver from Rome to China and provoking complaints that silk clothing worn by upper-class women was far too revealing. There were economic factors as well: the Roman emperor Tiberius grumbled that "the ladies and their baubles are transferring our money to foreigners."

The silk trade also stimulated an increase in mutual curiosity between China and other civilizations farther to the west. Roman authors such as Pliny the Elder and the geographer Strabo (who speculated that silk was produced from the leaves of a "silk tree") wrote of a strange land called "Seres" far to the east, while Chinese sources mentioned the empire of "Great Qin" at the far end of the Silk Road to the west. Of more immediate consequence was the increased communication that took place with societies in the South Asian subcontinent. One of the most important consequences was the introduction of Buddhism from India. The Han dynasty's adoption of State Confucianism did not have much direct impact on the religious beliefs of the Chinese people, most of whom continued to worship the pantheon of local deities and spirits of nature connected with popular Daoism. But in the first century CE, a new salvationist faith appeared on the horizon as merchants from Central Asia brought Buddhist teachings to China for the first time. At first, its influence was limited, as no Buddhist text was translated into Chinese until the fifth century CE. But the terrain was ripe for the introduction of a new religion into China, and the first Chinese monks departed for India shortly after the end of the Han dynasty.

3–4d The Decline and Fall of the Han

By the end of the first century BCE, the empire had been crumbling for decades. As frivolous or depraved rulers amused themselves with the pleasures of court life, the power and influence of the central government began to wane, and the great noble families filled the vacuum, amassing vast landed estates and transforming free farmers into tenants. In 9 CE, the reformist official Wang Mang (wahng MAHNG), who was troubled by the plight of the peasants, seized power from the Han court and declared the foundation of the Xin (SHIN) (New) dynasty. Wang Mang tried to confiscate the great estates, restore the ancient well-field system, and abolish slavery. In so doing, however, he alienated powerful interests, who conspired to overthrow him. In 23 CE, beset by administrative chaos and a collapse of the frontier defenses, Wang Mang was killed in a coup d'état.

For a time, strong leadership revived some of the glory of the early Han. (Chinese historians refer to the period after the Wang Mang revolt as the Later Han dynasty.) The court did attempt to reduce land taxes and carry out land resettlement programs. The growing popularity of nutritious crops like rice, wheat, and soybeans, along with the introduction

Han Dynasty Horse. This terra-cotta horse and rider is a striking example of Han dynasty artistry. Although the Chinese had domesticated the smaller Mongolian pony as early as 2000 BCE, it was not until toward the end of the first millennium BCE that the Chinese acquired horses as a result of military expeditions into Central Asia. Often they were acquired in exchange for silk, an item much prized by peoples living throughout the region. Admired for their power and grace, horses made of terra-cotta or bronze were often placed in Qin or Han tombs.

DEA Picture Library/Getty Images

of new crops such as alfalfa and grapes, helped boost food production. But the great landed families' firm grip on land and power continued. Weak rulers were isolated within their imperial chambers and dominated by eunuchs and other powerful court insiders. Official corruption and the concentration of land in the hands of the wealthy led to widespread peasant unrest.

The Han also continued to have problems with the Xiongnu beyond the Great Wall to the north. In part, the conflict focused on control over the area between the grazing lands and farming areas in North China. But trade disputes were also involved, as silk and other commodities from China were in great demand by pastoral communities, and conflict over availability and price often led to conflict. After their attempts to pacify the Xiongnu leaders through negotiations failed to resolve the situation, Han rulers—tired of paying tribute to maintain peace—turned once again to military force. When military operations became too expensive, they returned to the negotiating table. The threat from the north did not abate until the end of the first century CE, when the alliance among the various nomadic groups fractured into disunity. The respite proved to be short-lived, however, as raids on Chinese territory continued intermittently up to the end of the dynasty, sometimes reaching almost to the gates of the capital city. The Han responded by seeking to strengthen its presence in the far western province of Xinjiang, opening up a number of forts and stationing garrisons in the scattered oases in the desert.

Buffeted by insurmountable problems within and without, in the late second century CE the dynasty entered a period of inexorable decline. The population, which had been estimated at about 60 million in China's first census in the year 2 CE, had shrunk to less than one-third that number two hundred years later. In the early third century CE, the dynasty was finally brought to an end when power was seized by Cao Cao (TSOW tsow), a general known to later generations as one of the main characters in the famous Chinese epic *The Romance of the Three Kingdoms*. But Cao Cao was unable to consolidate his power, and China entered a period of almost constant anarchy and internal divisions, compounded by invasions of northern nomadic peoples. The next great dynasty did not arise until the beginning of the seventh century, four hundred years later.

3–5 DAILY LIFE IN ANCIENT CHINA

Q **Focus Question:** What were the key aspects of social and economic life in early China, and how did they compare with conditions elsewhere in the ancient world?

Few social institutions have been as closely identified with China as the family. As in most agricultural civilizations, the family served as the basic economic and social unit in society. In traditional China, however, it took on an almost sacred quality as a microcosm of the entire social order.

3–5a The Role of the Family

In Neolithic times, the farm village, organized around the clan, was the basic social unit in China, at least in the core region of the Yellow River Valley. Even then, however, the smaller family unit was becoming more important. At the Banpo archaeological site in central China, the remains of a Neolithic village dating back several thousand years contain the foundations of what appear to be several small nuclear family dwellings, in addition to a communal longhouse, all built as early as the end of the second millennium BCE. The concept of family was especially important to the nobility, who attached considerable significance to the veneration of their ancestors.

During the Zhou dynasty, the family took on increasing importance, in part because of the need for cooperation

The First Villages in Ancient China. Because of the climatic conditions that prevail in much of East Asia, very few structures from the ancient period of China have survived into the present day. At the Banpo archaeological site, located not far from the city of Xian in Shaanxi province, however, researchers have unearthed the remains of an entire village that dates back to the Neolithic era at least 7,000 years ago. In addition to the foundation of a communal longhouse, evidence also points to the existence of several smaller dwellings, suggesting that the nuclear family system was in operation in the area at least by the end of the second millennium BCE. The model house shown here was constructed on the basis of evidence at the site, and was built of mud and thatch, as was appropriate for a temperate climate.

in agriculture. Rice had become the primary crop along the Yangzi River and in the provinces to the south because of its taste, its productivity, and its high nutrient value. But the cultivation of rice is highly labor-intensive. The seedlings must be planted in several inches of water in a nursery bed and then transferred individually to the paddy beds, which must be irrigated constantly (see illustration "Rice Culture in Southeast Asia," Section 9-5a, p. 260). During the harvest, the stalks must be cut and the kernels carefully separated from the stalks and husks. As a result, children—and the labor they supplied—were considered essential to the survival of the family unit, not only during their youthful years but also later, when sons were expected to provide for their parents. Loyalty to family members came to be considered even more important than loyalty to the broader community or the state. Confucius himself commented that it was the hallmark of a civilized society that a son should protect his father even if the latter has committed a crime against the community.

At the crux of the concept of family was the idea of **filial piety**, which called on all members of the family to subordinate their personal needs and desires to the patriarchal head of the family. More broadly, it created a hierarchical system in which every family member had a place. All Chinese learned the **five relationships** that were the key to a proper social order. The son was subordinate to his father, the wife to her husband, the younger brother to his older brother, and all were subject to their ruler. The final relationship was the proper one between friend and friend. Only if all members of the family and the community as a whole behaved in a properly filial manner would society function effectively.

A stable family system based on obedient and hardworking members can serve as a bulwark for an efficient government, but putting loyalty to the family and the clan over loyalty to the state can also present a threat to a centralizing monarch. For that reason, the Qin dynasty attempted to destroy the clan system in China and assert the primacy of the state. Legalists even imposed heavy taxes on any family with more than two adult sons in order to break down the family concept. The Qin reportedly also originated the practice of organizing several family units into larger groups of five and ten families that would exercise mutual control and surveillance. Later dynasties continued the practice under the name of the *Bao-jia* (BOW-jah ["ow" as in "how"]) **system**.

But the efforts of the Qin to eradicate or at least reduce the importance of the family system ran against tradition and the dynamics of the Chinese economy, and under the Han dynasty, which followed the Qin, the family system revived and increased in importance. With official encouragement, the family began to take on the character that it would possess until our own day. The family was not only the basic economic unit; it was also the primary social unit for education, religious observances, and training in ethical principles.

3–5b Lifestyles

We know much more about the lifestyle of the elites than that of the common people in ancient China. The first houses for

the former were probably constructed of wooden planks, but later Chinese mastered the art of building in tile and brick. By the first millennium BCE, most public buildings and the houses of the wealthy were probably constructed in this manner. The latter often had several wings surrounding a central courtyard to provide space for several generations under one roof, a style that has continued down to modern times. By the second century BCE, most Chinese, however, probably lived in simple houses of mud, wooden planks, or brick with thatch or occasionally tile roofs. But in some areas, especially in the loess (LESS) (a type of soil common in North China) regions of northern China, cave dwelling remained common down to modern times. The most famous cave dweller of modern times was the revolutionary leader Mao Zedong, who lived in a cave in Yan'an (yuh-NAHN) during his long struggle against Chiang Kai-shek (see Chapter 24).

Chinese houses in ancient times usually had little furniture; most people squatted or sat with their legs spread out on the packed-mud floor. Chairs were apparently not introduced until the sixth or seventh century CE. Clothing was simple, consisting of cotton trousers and shirts in the summer and wool or burlap in the winter.

The staple foods in the north were dry grain crops like millet, barley, and wheat, while wet rice predominated in the south. Other common foods were soybeans, mustard greens, and bamboo shoots. Archaeologists have discovered the remains of millet noodles dating back to 2000 BCE. In early times, most foods were often consumed in a porridge, but by the Zhou dynasty, stir-frying in a wok was becoming common. When possible, the Chinese family would vary its diet of grain foods with vegetables, fruit (including pears, peaches, apricots, and plums), and fish or meat; but for most, such additions to the daily plate of rice, millet, or soybeans were a rare luxury.

Alcohol in the form of ale was drunk at least by the higher classes and by the early Zhou era had already begun to inspire official concern. According to the *Book of History*, "King Wen admonished . . . the young nobles . . . that they should not ordinarily use spirits; and throughout all the states he required that they should be drunk only on occasion of sacrifices, and that then virtue should preside so that there might be no drunkenness."[11] For the poorer classes, alcohol in any form was probably a rare luxury. Chinese legend hints that tea—a plant originally found in upland regions in southern China and Southeast Asia—was introduced by the mythical emperor Shen Nong. In fact, however, tea drinking did not become widespread in China until around 500 CE. By then tea was lauded for its medicinal qualities and its capacity to soothe the spirit.

3–5c Cities

With the rise to power of the Qin, cities began to take on the central importance they would hold through later Chinese history. Urban centers were divided into neighborhoods—perhaps a forerunner of the grid pattern assumed by imperial cities under later dynasties—as a means of facilitating control over the population. As mentioned earlier, landed aristocrats, many of them former opponents of the Qin, were forcibly resettled in the new capital of Xianyang—a pattern that we shall see repeated, notably in France and Japan, in later centuries. Their villas and gardens aped the splendor of the imperial palace, which formed the centerpiece of the urban landscape.

Under the Qin and the Han, as never before, cities became the cultural hub of Chinese society, although their residents made up only a tiny proportion of the total population. In the crowded streets, haughty nobles sought to avoid rubbing shoulders with commoners, while merchants, workers, wandering gangs, and prostitutes relentlessly imitated the mannerisms of the elite. As a poem of the time satirically noted:

> In the city, if they love to have their hair dressed up high,
> Then everywhere else they dress their hair an inch higher.
> In the city, if they love to enlarge their eyebrows,
> Then everywhere else they will make their eyebrows cover half
>   their foreheads.
> In the city, if they love large sleeves,
> Then everywhere else they will use up whole bolts of silk.[12]

It sounds like things haven't changed much in the last two thousand years.

3–5d The Humble Estate: Women in Ancient China

Male dominance was a key element in the social system of ancient China. As in many traditional societies, the male was considered of transcendent importance because of his role as food procurer or, in the case of farming communities, food producer. In ancient China, men worked in the fields, while women raised children and served in the home. This differential in gender roles goes back to prehistoric times and is embedded in Chinese creation myths. According to legend, Fu Xi's wife Nu Wa (noo WAH) assisted her husband in organizing society by establishing the institution of marriage and the family. Yet Nu Wa was not just a household drudge. After Fu Xi's death, she became China's first female sovereign.

During ancient times, women apparently did not normally occupy formal positions of authority, but they often became a force in politics, especially at court, where wives of the ruler or other female members of the royal family were often influential in palace intrigues. Such activities were frowned on, however, as the following passage from *The Book of Songs* attests:

> A clever man builds a city,
> A clever woman lays one low;
> With all her qualifications, that clever woman
> Is but an ill-omened bird.
> A woman with a long tongue
> Is a flight of steps leading to calamity;
> For disorder does not come from heaven,
> But is brought about by women.
> Among those who cannot be trained or taught
> Are women and eunuchs.[13]

The nature of gender relationships was also graphically demonstrated in the Chinese written language. The character for man (男) combines the symbols for strength and rice field, while the character for woman (女) represents a person in a posture of deference and respect. The character for peace (安) is a woman under a roof. A wife is symbolized by a woman with a broom. Male chauvinism has deep linguistic roots in China.

Confucian thought, while not denigrating the importance of women as mothers and homemakers, accepted the dual roles of men and women in Chinese society. Men governed society. They carried on family ritual through the veneration of ancestors. They were the warriors, scholars, and ministers. Their dominant role was firmly enshrined in the legal system. Men were permitted to have more than one wife and to divorce a spouse who did not produce a male child. Women were denied the right to own property, and there was no dowry system in ancient China that would have provided the wife with a degree of financial security from her husband and his family. However, there were exceptions, including Ban Zhao (bahn ZHOW), who, although a woman, was one of the most prominent historians of the Han dynasty. But even she conceded that a woman's role in China was to be "humble, yielding, respectful and reverential" in her dealings with others. As the third-century CE poet Fu Xuan (foo SHWAHN), a woman, lamented:

> How sad it is to be a woman
> Nothing on earth is held so cheap.
> No one is glad when a girl is born.
> By her the family sets no store.
> No one cries when she leaves her home
> Sudden as clouds when the rain stops.[14]

3–6 CHINESE CULTURE

 Focus Questions: What were the chief characteristics of the Chinese arts and writing system? How did they differ from those in Egypt and Mesopotamia?

Modern knowledge about artistic achievements in ancient civilizations is limited because often little has survived the ravages of time. Fortunately, many ancient civilizations, such as Egypt and Mesopotamia, were located in relatively arid areas where many artifacts were preserved, even over thousands of years. In more humid regions, such as China and South Asia, the cultural residue left by the civilizations of antiquity has been adversely affected by climate.

As a result, relatively little remains of the cultural achievements of the prehistoric Chinese aside from Neolithic pottery and the relics found in tombs dating from the Shang dynasty. In recent years, a rich trove from the time of the Qin Empire has been unearthed near the tomb of Qin Shi Huangdi near Xian and at Han tombs nearby. But little remains of the literature of ancient China and almost none of the painting, architecture, and music.

3–6a Metalwork and Sculpture

Discoveries at archaeological sites indicate that ancient China was a society rich in cultural achievement. Handmade pottery dates back at least to the sixth millennium BCE, and pottery found at Neolithic sites such as Longshan and Yangshao exhibits a freshness and vitality of form and design, while the ornaments, such as rings and beads, show a strong aesthetic sense.

Bronze Casting The pace of Chinese cultural development began to quicken during the Shang dynasty, which ruled in northern China from the sixteenth to the eleventh century BCE. By that time, objects cast in bronze with an astonishing degree of delicacy began to appear. Various bronze vessels were produced for use in preparing and serving food and drink in the royal ancestral rites. Eventually such vessels were probably used for decoration or for dining at court.

The method of casting used was one reason for the extraordinary quality of Shang bronze work. Bronze workers in most ancient civilizations used the lost-wax method, in which a model was first made in wax. After a clay mold had been formed around it, the model was heated so that the wax would melt away, and the empty space was filled with molten metal. In China, clay molds composed of several sections were tightly fitted together prior to the introduction of the liquid bronze. This technique, which had evolved from ceramic techniques used during the Neolithic period, enabled the artisans to apply the design directly to the mold and thus contributed to the clarity of line and rich surface decoration of the Shang bronzes.

Bronze casting became a large-scale business, and more than ten thousand vessels of an incredible variety of form and design survive today. Factories were located not only in the Yellow River Valley but also in Sichuan province, in southern China. The art of bronze working continued into the Zhou dynasty, but the quality and originality declined. The Shang bronzes remain the pinnacle of creative art in ancient China.

One reason for the decline of bronze casting in China was the rise in popularity of iron. Ironmaking developed in China around the ninth or eighth century BCE, much later than in the Middle East, where it had been mastered almost a thousand years earlier. Once familiar with the process, however, the Chinese quickly moved to the forefront. Ironworkers in Europe and the Middle East, lacking the technology to achieve the high temperatures necessary to melt iron ore for casting, were forced to work with wrought iron, a cumbersome and expensive process. By the fourth century BCE, the Chinese had invented the technique of the blast furnace, powered by a worker operating a bellows. They were therefore able to manufacture cast iron ritual vessels and agricultural tools centuries before an equivalent technology appeared in the West.

Another reason for the deterioration of the bronze-casting tradition was the development of cheaper materials such as lacquerware and ceramics. Lacquer, made from resins obtained

William J. Duiker

A Shang Wine Vessel. Used initially as food containers in royal ceremonial rites during the Shang dynasty, Chinese bronzes were the product of an advanced technology unmatched by any contemporary civilization. This wine vessel displays a deep green patina as well as a monster motif, complete with large globular eyes, nostrils, and fangs, typical of many Shang bronzes. Known as the *taotie* (TOW-tee-YUH ["ow" as in "how"]), this fanciful beast is normally presented in silhouette as two dragons face to face so that each side forms half of the mask. Although the *taotie* presumably served as a guardian force against evil spirits, scholars are still not aware of its exact significance for early Chinese peoples.

from the juices of sumac trees native to the region, had been produced since Neolithic times, and by the second century BCE it had become a popular method of applying a hard coating to objects made of wood or fabric. Pottery, too, had existed since early times, but technological advances led in Han times to the production of a high-fired form of pottery covered with a brown or gray-green glaze, the latter known popularly as celadon. By the end of the first millennium BCE, both lacquerware and pottery had replaced bronze in popularity, much as plastic goods have replaced more expensive materials in our own time. This trend continued into the Han dynasty, as bronze was increasingly replaced by iron as the medium of choice. Less expensive to produce, iron was better able to satisfy the growing popular demand during a time of increasing economic affluence. Also during the Han, painting—often in the form of wall

William J. Duiker

Martin Puddy/Asia Images/Getty Images

The Tomb of Qin Shi Huangdi. The First Emperor of Qin ordered the construction of an elaborate mausoleum, an underground palace complex protected by an army of terra-cotta soldiers and horses to accompany him on his journey to the afterlife. This massive formation of six thousand life-size armed soldiers, discovered accidentally by farmers in 1974, reflects Qin Shi Huangdi's grandeur and power.

frescoes—became increasingly popular in the homes and tombs of the wealthy, although little has survived the ravages of time.

The First Emperor's Tomb In 1974, in a remarkable discovery, farmers digging a well about 35 miles east of Xian unearthed a number of terra-cotta figures in an underground pit about one mile east of the burial mound of the First Emperor of Qin. Chinese archaeologists sent to work at the site discovered a vast terra-cotta army that they believed was a recreation of Qin Shi Huangdi's imperial guard, which was to accompany the emperor on his journey to the next world.

One of the astounding features of the terra-cotta army is its size. The army is enclosed in four pits that were originally encased in a wooden framework, which has disintegrated. More than a thousand figures have been unearthed in the first pit, along with horses, wooden chariots, and seven thousand bronze weapons. Archaeologists estimate that there are more than eight thousand figures in that pit alone.

Equally impressive is the quality of the work. Slightly larger than life size, the figures were molded of finely textured clay and then fired and painted. The detail on the uniforms is realistic and sophisticated, but the most striking feature is the individuality of the facial features of the soldiers. Apparently, ten different head shapes were used and were then modeled further by hand to reflect the variety of ethnic groups and personality types in the army.

The discovery of the terra-cotta army also shows that the Chinese had come a long way from the human sacrifices that

had taken place at the death of Shang sovereigns more than a thousand years earlier. But the project must have been ruinously expensive and is additional evidence of the burden the Qin ruler imposed on his subjects. One historian has estimated that one-third of the national income in Qin times may have been spent on preparations for the ruler's afterlife. The emperor's mausoleum has not yet been unearthed, but it is enclosed in a mound nearly 250 feet high surrounded by a rectangular wall extending for nearly 4 miles. According to the Han historian Sima Qian, the ceiling was a replica of the heavens, while the floor contained a relief model of the entire Qin kingdom, with rivers flowing in mercury. According to tradition, traps were set within the mausoleum to prevent intruders, and the workers applying the final touches were buried alive in the tomb with its secrets.

3–6b Language and Literature

Precisely when writing developed in China cannot be determined, but certainly by Shang times, as the oracle bones demonstrate, the Chinese had developed a simple but functional script. Like many other languages of antiquity, it was primarily ideographic and pictographic in form. Symbols, usually called characters, were created to represent an idea or to form a picture of the object to be represented. For example, the Chinese characters for mountain (山), the sun (日), and the moon (月) were meant to represent the objects themselves. Other characters, such as "big" (大) (a man with his arms outstretched), represent an idea. The character for "east" (東) symbolizes the sun coming up behind the trees.

Each character, of course, would be given a sound by the speaker when pronounced. In other cultures, this process led to the abandonment of the system of ideographs and the adoption of a written language based on phonetic symbols. The Chinese language, however, has never entirely abandoned its original ideographic format, although the phonetic element has developed into a significant part of the individual character. In that sense, the Chinese written language is virtually unique in the world today.

One reason the language retained its ideographic quality may have been the aesthetics of the written characters. By the time of the Qin dynasty, if not earlier, the written language came to be seen as an art form as well as a means of communication, and calligraphy became one of the most prized forms of painting in China.

Even more important, if the written language had developed in the direction of a phonetic alphabet, it could no longer have served as the written system for all the peoples of the expanding Chinese civilization. Although most spoke a tongue derived from a parent Sinitic language (a system distinguished by variations in pitch, a characteristic that gives Chinese its lilting quality even today), the languages spoken in various regions of the country differed from each other in pronunciation and to a lesser degree in vocabulary and syntax; for the most part, they were (and are today) mutually unintelligible.

The Chinese answer to this problem was to give all the spoken languages the same writing system. Although any character might be pronounced differently in different regions of China, that character would be written the same way (after the standardization undertaken under the Qin). Written characters could therefore be read by educated Chinese from one end of the country to the other. This became the language of the bureaucracy and the vehicle for the transmission of Chinese culture from the Great Wall to the southern border and beyond. The written language was not identical to the spoken form, however; it eventually evolved its own vocabulary and grammatical structure, and as a result, users of written Chinese required special training.

The earliest extant form of Chinese literature dates from the Zhou dynasty. It was written on silk or strips of bamboo and consisted primarily of historical records such as the *Rites of Zhou*, philosophical treatises such as the *Analects* and *The Way of the Tao*, and poetry, as recorded in *The Book of Songs* and the *Song of the South* (see "Love Spurned in Ancient China"). In later years, when Confucian principles had been elevated to a state ideology, the key works identified with the Confucian school were integrated into a set of so-called Confucian Classics. These works became required reading for generations of Chinese schoolchildren and introduced them to the forms of behavior that would be required of them as adults.

By the Han dynasty, there was considerable experimentation with new forms of expression in literature. Poetry and philosophical essays continued to be popular, but historical writing became the primary form of literary creativity. Historians such as Sima Qian and Ban Gu (the dynasty's official historian and the older brother of the female historian Ban Zhao) wrote works that became models for later dynastic histories. These historical works combined political and social history with biographies of key figures. Like so much literary work in China, their primary purpose was moral and political—to explain the underlying reasons for the rise and fall of individual human beings and dynasties.

3–6c Music

From early times in China, music was viewed not just as an aesthetic pleasure but also as a means of achieving political order and refining the human character. In fact, music may have originated as an accompaniment to sacred rituals at the royal court. According to the *Historical Records*, written during the Han dynasty, "When our sage-kings of the past instituted rites and music, their objective was far from making people indulge in the . . . amusements of singing and dancing. . . . Music is produced to purify the heart, and rites introduced to rectify the behavior."[15] Eventually, however, music began to be appreciated for its own sake as well as to accompany singing and dancing.

Photograph by William J. Duiker/Freer Gallery of Art, Washington, D.C.

Ancient Chinese Writing. Although the origins of the Chinese character remain shrouded in mystery, the first extant texts that can be clearly deciphered date from the late Shang dynasty and were inscribed on tortoise shells and chicken bones. Eventually, however, characters became increasingly stylized and began to be engraved on metal objects. The text shown here was engraved on a bronze vessel that was commonly used for ritual purposes and dates back to the early Zhou era. The text itself describes the results of an administrative meeting that took place at the royal court in the city of Chengzhou.

LOVE SPURNED IN ANCIENT CHINA

Art & Ideas *The Book of Songs* is an anthology of about three hundred poems written during the early Zhou dynasty. According to tradition, they were selected by Confucius from a much larger collection. In later years, many were given political interpretations. The poem presented here, however, expresses a very human cry of love spurned.

The Book of Songs: The Odes

You seemed a guileless youth enough,
Offering for silk your woven stuff;
But silk was not required by you;
I was the silk you had in view.
With you I crossed the ford, and while
We wandered on for many a mile
I said, "I do not wish delay,
But friends must fix our wedding-day....
Oh, do not let my words give pain,
But with the autumn come again."

And then I used to watch and wait
To see you passing through the gate;
And sometimes, when I watched in vain,
My tears would flow like falling rain;
But when I saw my darling boy,
I laughed and cried aloud for joy.
The fortune-tellers, you declared,
Had all pronounced us duly paired;
"Then bring a carriage," I replied,
"And I'll away to be your bride."

The mulberry tree upon the ground,
Now sheds its yellow leaves around.
Three years have slipped away from me
Since first I shared your poverty;

And now again, alas the day!
Back through the ford I take my way.

My heart is still unchanged, but you
Have uttered words now proved untrue;
And you have left me to deplore
A love that can be mine no more.

For three long years I was your wife,
And led in truth a toilsome life;
Early to rise and late to bed,
Each day alike passed o'er my head.
I honestly fulfilled my part,
And you—well, you have broke my heart.
The truth my brothers will not know,
So all the more their gibes will flow.
I grieve in silence and repine
That such a wretched fate is mine.

Ah, hand in hand to face old age!—
Instead, I turn a bitter page.
O for the riverbanks of yore;
O for the much-loved marshy shore;
The hours of girlhood, with my hair
Ungathered, as we lingered there.
The words we spoke, that seemed so true,
I little thought that I should rue;
I little thought the vows we swore
Would some day bind us two no more.

 It has been said that traditional Chinese thought lacked a sense of tragedy similar to the great dramatic tragedies of ancient Greece. Does this passage qualify as tragedy? If not, why not?

Source: From *A History of Chinese Literature*, by Herbert A. Giles (New York: Grove Press 1923), pp. 15–16.

A wide variety of musical instruments were used, including flutes, various stringed instruments, bells and chimes, drums, and gourds. Bells cast in bronze were first used as musical instruments in the Shang period; they were hung in rows and struck with a wooden mallet. The finest bells have been found in tombs dating from the mid-Zhou era and are considered among the best examples of early bronze work in China. Some weighed more than two tons and, in combination, covered a range of several octaves. Bronze bells have not been found in any other contemporary civilization and are considered one of the great cultural achievements of ancient China. The largest known bell dating from the Roman Empire, for example, is less than 3 inches high.

By the late Zhou era, bells had begun to give way as the instrument of choice to strings and wind instruments, and the purpose of music shifted from ceremony to entertainment. This led conservative critics to rail against the onset of an age of debauchery.

Ancient historians stressed the relationship between music and court life, but it is highly probable that music, singing, and dancing were equally popular among the common people. The *Book of History*, purporting to describe conditions in the late third millennium BCE, suggests that ballads emanating from the popular culture were welcomed at court. Nevertheless, court music and popular music differed in several respects. Among other things, popular music was more likely to be motivated by the desire for pleasure than for the purpose of law and order and moral uplift. Those differences continued to be reflected in the evolution of music in China down to modern times.

CHAPTER SUMMARY

Of the great classical civilizations discussed in Part I of this book, China was the last to come into full flower. By the time the Shang began to emerge as an organized state, the societies in Mesopotamia and the Nile Valley had already reached an advanced level of civilization. Unfortunately, not enough is known about the early stages of these civilizations to allow us to determine why some developed earlier than others, but one likely reason for China's comparatively late arrival was that it was virtually isolated from other emerging centers of culture elsewhere in the world and thus was compelled to develop essentially on its own. Only at the end of the first millennium BCE did China come into regular contact with other civilizations in South Asia, the Middle East, and the Mediterranean.

the Gobi Desert in the north to the subtropical regions near the borders of modern Vietnam in the south. Chinese philosophers had engaged in debate over intricate questions relating to human nature and the state of the universe, and China's artistic and technological achievements—especially in terms of bronze casting and the terra-cotta figures entombed in Qin Shi Huangdi's mausoleum—were unsurpassed throughout the world.

Meanwhile, another great civilization was beginning to take form on the northern shores of the Mediterranean Sea. Unlike China and the other ancient societies discussed thus far, this new civilization in Europe was based as much on trade as on agriculture. Yet the political and cultural achievements of ancient Greece were the equal of any of the great human experiments that had preceded it and soon began to exert a significant impact on the rest of the ancient world.

Once embarked on its own path toward the creation of a complex society, however, China achieved results that were in all respects the equal of its counterparts elsewhere. By the rise of the first unified empire in the late third century BCE, the state extended from the edge of

CHAPTER TIMELINE

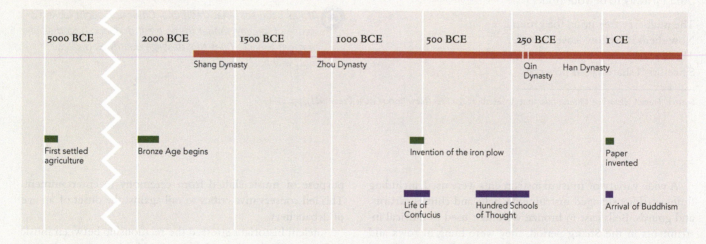

5000 BCE	2000 BCE	1500 BCE	1000 BCE	500 BCE	250 BCE	1 CE
		Shang Dynasty	Zhou Dynasty		Qin Dynasty Han Dynasty	
First settled agriculture	Bronze Age begins		Invention of the iron plow			Paper invented
			Life of Confucius	Hundred Schools of Thought		Arrival of Buddhism

CHAPTER REVIEW

Upon Reflection

Q What were some of the key contributions in political structures, social organization, and culture that the Shang dynasty bequeathed to its successor, the Zhou dynasty? Does the Shang deserve to be called the "mother culture" of China?

Q What kinds of relationships did the Chinese people have with the pastoral peoples living along the frontier? How

did these relationships compare with those experienced by advanced societies in North Africa and Western Asia?

Q What contributions did the ancient Chinese people make in the field of metallurgy? How do their achievements compare with developments in ancient Egypt and the Middle East?

Key Terms

Yangshao (p. 66)
Longshan (p. 66)
veneration of ancestors (p. 68)
diffusion hypothesis (p. 70)
mandate of Heaven (p. 71)
well-field system (p. 71)
Dao (p. 76)
Legalism (p. 76)

Confucianism (p. 77)
Daoism (p. 77)
eunuchs (p. 83)
State Confucianism (p. 83)
civil service examination (p. 84)
filial piety (p. 88)
five relationships (p. 88)
Bao-jia system (p. 88)

Chapter Notes

1. *Book of Changes*, quoted in Chang Chi-yun, *Chinese History of Fifty Centuries*, vol. 1, *Ancient Times* (Taipei, 1962), pp. 15, 31, and 65.
2. Ibid., p. 381.
3. Quoted in E. N. Anderson, *The Food of China* (New Haven, Conn., 1988), p. 21.
4. According to Chinese tradition, the *Rites of Zhou* was written by the duke of Zhou himself near the time of the founding of the Zhou dynasty. However, modern historians believe that it was written much later, perhaps as late as the fourth century BCE.
5. From *The Book of Songs*, quoted in S. de Grazia, ed., *Masters of Chinese Political Thought: From the Beginnings to the Han Dynasty* (New York, 1973), pp. 40–41.
6. *Book of Mencius* (Meng Zi), 4A:9, quoted in de Bary, *Sources of Chinese Tradition*, p. 93.
7. Quoted in ibid., p. 51.
8. M. Lewis, *The Early Chinese Empires: Qin and Han* (Cambridge, Mass., 2007), p. 31, citing *Shiji* 68, pp. 2230, 2232.
9. B. Watson, *Records of the Grand Historian of China* (New York, 1961), vol. 2, pp. 155, 160.
10. Ibid., pp. 32, 53.
11. C. Waltham, *Shu Ching: Book of History* (Chicago, 1971), p. 154.
12. Lewis, *Early Chinese Empires*, p. 85.
13. Quoted in H. A. Giles, *A History of Chinese Literature* (New York, 1923), p. 19.
14. Waley, ed., *Chinese Poems* (London, 1983), p. xx.
15. Chang Chi-yun, *Chinese History*, vol. 1, p. 187.

Chapter Outline and Focus Questions

A bust of Pericles. British Museum, London, UK/The Bridgeman Art Library

Critical Thinking

Q *In what ways did the culture of the Hellenistic period differ from that of the Classical period, and what do those differences suggest about society in the two periods?*

Connections to Today

Q *What are the similarities and differences between ancient Athenian democracy and modern democracy in the United States?*

DURING THE ERA OF CIVIL WAR in China known as the Period of the Warring States, a civil war also erupted on the northern shores of the Mediterranean Sea. In 431 BCE, two dramatically different Greek city-states—Athens and Sparta—fought for domination of the Greek world. The people of Athens felt secure behind their walls and, in the first winter of the war, held a public funeral to honor those who had died in battle. On the day of the ceremony, the citizens of Athens joined in a procession, with the relatives of the dead wailing for their loved ones. As was the custom in Athens, one leading citizen was asked to address the crowd, and on this day it was Pericles who spoke to the people. He talked about the greatness of Athens and reminded the Athenians of the strength of their political system: "Our constitution," he said, "is called a democracy because power is in the hands not of a minority but of the whole people. When it is a question of settling private disputes, everyone is equal before the law. . . . Just as our political life is free and open, so is our day-to-day life in our relations with each other. . . . Here each individual is interested not only in his own affairs but in the affairs of the state as well."

In this famous Funeral Oration, Pericles gave voice to the ideals of democracy and the importance of the individual, ideals that were quite different from those of some other ancient societies, in which the individual was subordinated to a larger order based on obedience to an exalted emperor. The Greeks asked some basic questions about human life: What is the nature of the universe? What is the purpose of human existence? What is our relationship to divine forces? What constitutes a community? What constitutes a state? What is true education? What are the true sources of law? What is truth itself, and how do we realize it? Not only did the Greeks provide answers to these questions, but they also created a system of logical, analytical thought to examine them. Their answers and their system of rational thought laid the intellectual foundation for Western civilization's understanding of the human condition.

The remarkable story of ancient Greek civilization begins with the arrival of the Greeks around 1900 BCE. By the eighth century BCE, the characteristic institution of ancient Greek life, the *polis*, or city-state, had emerged. Greek civilization flourished and reached its height in the Classical era of the fifth century BCE, but the inability of the Greek city-states to end their fratricidal warfare eventually left them vulnerable to the Macedonian king Philip II and helped bring an end to the era of independent Greek city-states.

Although the city-states were never the same after their defeat by the Macedonian monarch, this defeat did not end the influence of the Greeks. Philip's son Alexander led the Macedonians and Greeks on a spectacular conquest of the Persian Empire and opened the door to the spread of Greek culture throughout the Middle East.

4–1 EARLY GREECE

 Focus Questions: How did the geography of Greece affect Greek history in terms of politics, military developments, and the economy? Who was Homer, and why was his work used as the basis for Greek education?

Geography played an important role in Greek history. Compared to Mesopotamia and Egypt, Greece occupied a small area, a mountainous peninsula that encompassed only 45,000 square miles of territory, about the size of the state of Louisiana. The mountains and the sea were especially significant. Much of Greece consists of small plains and river valleys surrounded by mountain ranges 8,000 to 10,000 feet high. The mountains isolated Greeks from one another, causing Greek communities to follow their own separate paths and develop their own ways of life. Over a period of time, these communities became so fiercely attached to their independence that they were willing to fight one another to gain advantage. No doubt the small size of these independent Greek communities fostered participation in political affairs and unique cultural expressions, but the rivalry among them also led to the bitter warfare that ultimately devastated Greek society.

The sea also influenced Greek society. Greece had a long seacoast, dotted by bays and inlets that provided numerous harbors. The Greeks also inhabited a number of islands to the west, south, and east of the Greek mainland. It is no accident that the Greeks became seafarers who sailed out into the Aegean and Mediterranean Seas to make contact with the outside world and later to establish colonies that would spread Greek civilization throughout the Mediterranean region.

Topography helped determine the major territories into which Greece was ultimately divided (see Map 4.1). South of the Gulf of Corinth was the Peloponnesus (pell-uh-puh-NEE-suss), virtually an island attached by a tiny isthmus to the mainland. Consisting mostly of hills, mountains, and small valleys, the Peloponnesus was the location of Sparta, as well as the site of Olympia, where athletic games were held. Northeast of the Peloponnesus was the Attic peninsula (or Attica), the home of Athens, hemmed in by mountains to the north and west and surrounded by the sea to the south and east. Northwest of Attica was Boeotia (bee-OH-shuh) in central Greece, with its chief city of Thebes (THEEBZ). To the north of Boeotia was Thessaly, which contained the largest plains and became a great producer of grain and horses. To the north of Thessaly lay Macedonia, which was not of much importance in Greek history until 338 BCE, when a Macedonian king Philip II conquered the Greeks.

4–1a Minoan Crete

The earliest civilization in the Aegean region emerged on the large island of Crete, southeast of the Greek mainland. A Bronze Age civilization that used metals, especially bronze, in making weapons had been established there by 2800 BCE. This civilization was discovered at the turn of the twentieth

Map 4.1 Ancient Greece (c. 750–338 BCE). Between 750 and 500 BCE, Greek civilization witnessed the emergence of the city-state as the central institution in Greek life and the Greeks' colonization of the Mediterranean and Black Seas. Classical Greece lasted from about 500 to 338 BCE and encompassed the high points of Greek civilization in arts, science, philosophy, and politics, as well as the Persian Wars and the Peloponnesian War.

 How does the geography of Greece help explain the rise and development of the Greek city-state?

century by the English archaeologist Arthur Evans, who named it "Minoan" (mih-NOH-uhn) after Minos (MY-nuss), a legendary king of Crete. In language and religion, the Minoans were not Greek, although they did have some influence on the peoples of the Greek mainland.

Evans's excavations on Crete unearthed an enormous palace complex at Knossus (NOSS-suss), near modern Iràklion (Heracleion), that was most likely the center of a far-ranging "sea empire," probably largely commercial. We know from the archaeological remains that the people of Minoan Crete were accustomed to sea travel and had made contact with the more advanced civilization of Egypt. Egyptian products have been found in Crete and Cretan products in Egypt. Minoan Cretans also had contacts with and exerted influence on the Greek-speaking inhabitants of the Greek mainland.

The Minoan civilization reached its height between 2000 and 1450 BCE. The palace at Knossus, the royal seat of the kings, was an elaborate structure that included numerous private living rooms for the royal family and workshops for making decorated vases, ivory figurines, and jewelry. Even bathrooms with elaborate drains, like those found at Mohenjo-Daro in India, were part of the complex. The rooms were decorated with brightly colored frescoes showing sporting events and nature scenes. Storerooms in the palace held enormous jars of oil, wine, and grain, presumably paid as taxes in kind to the king.

The centers of Minoan civilization on Crete eventually suffered a collapse. Some historians once believed that a tsunami triggered by a powerful volcanic eruption on the island of Thera was responsible for destroying towns and ships on the north coast of Crete, but the latest dating of that eruption places it in the seventeenth century BCE. There is evidence that mainland Greeks, known as the Mycenaeans, invaded and pillaged many centers, including Knossus, which was destroyed around 1400 BCE. However, Knossus was soon rebuilt and made the chief administrative center on Crete for the Mycenaeans.

4–1b The First Greek State: Mycenae

The term *Mycenaean* (my-suh-NEE-un) is derived from Mycenae (my-SEE-nee), a remarkable fortified site excavated by the amateur German archaeologist Heinrich Schliemann (HYN-rikh SHLEE-mahn) starting in 1870. Mycenae was one center in a Mycenaean Greek civilization that flourished between 1600 and 1100 BCE. The Mycenaean Greeks were part of the Indo-European family of peoples (see Chapter 1) who spread from their original location into southern and western Europe, India, and Persia. One group entered the territory of Greece from the north around 1900 BCE and eventually managed to gain control of the Greek mainland and develop a civilization.

Mycenaean civilization, which reached its high point between 1400 and 1200 BCE, consisted of a number of powerful monarchies centered in fortified palace complexes. Like Mycenae itself, the palaces were built on hills and surrounded by gigantic stone walls. These various centers of power probably formed a loose confederacy of independent states, with Mycenae the strongest.

The Mycenaeans were above all a warrior people who prided themselves on their heroic deeds in battle. Archaeological evidence indicates that the Mycenaean monarchies also developed an extensive commercial network. Mycenaean pottery has been found throughout the Mediterranean basin, in Syria and Egypt to the east and Sicily and southern Italy to the west. But some scholars also believe that the Mycenaeans, led by Mycenae itself, spread outward militarily, conquering Crete and making it part of the Mycenaean world. The most famous of all their supposed military adventures has come down to us in the epic poetry of Homer (discussed later in chapter). Did the Mycenaean Greeks, led by Agamemnon, king of Mycenae, sack the city of Troy on the northwestern coast of Asia Minor around 1250 BCE? Scholars have debated this question ever since Schliemann began his excavations in 1870. Some believe that Homer's account does have a basis in fact, although there is little archaeological evidence to support it.

By the late thirteenth century, Mycenaean Greece was showing signs of serious trouble due to two causes. For one, earthquakes caused widespread damage. Then, too, there is evidence of attacks from without. Mycenae itself was torched around 1190 BCE, and other Mycenaean centers show similar patterns of destruction as new waves of Greek-speaking invaders moved into Greece from the north. By 1100 BCE, the Mycenaean culture was coming to an end, and the Greek world was entering a new period of considerable insecurity.

4–1c The Greeks in a "Dark Age" (c. 1100–c. 750 BCE)

After the collapse of Mycenaean civilization, Greece entered a difficult period in which population declined and food production dropped. Because of the difficult conditions and our lack of knowledge about the period, historians refer to it as the "Dark Age," but many historians now view it more as a period of transition from the Bronze Age to the Iron Age in Greece. Iron replaced bronze in the construction of weapons, making them affordable for more people. And farming tools made of iron helped reverse the decline in food production and led to a revival of farming by 850 BCE. At the same time, other new developments were forming the basis for a revived Greece.

During this transitional period, large numbers of Greeks left the mainland and migrated across the Aegean Sea to various islands and especially to the southwestern shore of Asia Minor, a strip of territory that came to be called Ionia (y-OH-nee-uh). Two other major groups of Greeks settled in established parts of Greece. The Aeolian (ee-OH-lee-un) Greeks of northern and central Greece colonized the large island of Lesbos and the adjacent territory of the mainland. The Dorians (DOR-ee-unz) established themselves in southwestern Greece, especially in the Peloponnesus, as well as on some of the south Aegean islands, including Crete.

Other important activities occurred in this period as well. Greece saw a revival of some trade and some economic activity besides agriculture. At some point in the eighth century BCE, the Greeks adopted the Phoenician alphabet to give themselves a new system of writing. And near the very end of the Dark Age appeared the work of Homer, who has come to be viewed as one of the greatest poets of all time.

Lion Gate, Mycenae. The photo shows the Lion Gate to the citadel at Mycenae. The Lion Gate was the chief entryway into the citadel and was a rare piece of monumental sculpture in Mycenaean Greece. It was formed by two standing monoliths supporting a huge lintel topped by two lion sculptures facing a column.

Vanni Archive/Art Resource, NY

HOMER'S IDEAL OF EXCELLENCE

Family & Society

THE *ILIAD* AND THE *ODYSSEY*, which the Greeks believed were written by Homer, were used as basic texts for the education of Greeks for hundreds of years during antiquity. This passage from the *Iliad*, describing a conversation between Hector, prince of Troy, and his wife, Andromache, illustrates the Greek ideal of gaining honor through combat. At the end of the passage, Homer also reveals what became the Greek attitude toward women: they are supposed to spin and weave and take care of their households and children.

Homer, *Iliad*

Hector looked at his son and smiled, but said nothing. Andromache, bursting into tears, went up to him and put her hand in his. "Hector," she said, "you are possessed. This bravery of yours will be your end. You do not think of your little boy or your unhappy wife, whom you will make a widow soon. Some day the Achaeans [Greeks] are bound to kill you in a massed attack. And when I lose you I might as well be dead. . . . I have no father, no mother, now. . . . I had seven brothers too at home. In one day all of them went down to Hades' House. The great Achilles of the swift feet killed them all. . . .

"So you, Hector, are father and mother and brother to me, as well as my beloved husband. Have pity on me now; stay here on the tower; and do not make your boy an orphan and your wife a widow. . . ."

"All that, my dear," said the great Hector of the glittering helmet, "is surely my concern. But if I hid myself like a coward and refused to fight, I could never face the Trojans. . . . Besides, it would go against the grain, for I have trained myself always, like a good soldier, to take my place in the front line and win glory for my father and myself. . . ."

As he finished, glorious Hector held out his arms to take his boy. But the child shrank back with a cry to the bosom of his girdled nurse, alarmed by his father's appearance. He was frightened by the bronze of the helmet and the horsehair plume that he saw nodding grimly down at him. His father and his lady mother had to laugh. But noble Hector quickly took his helmet off and put the dazzling thing on the ground. Then he kissed his son, . . . and prayed to Zeus and the other gods: "Zeus, and you other gods, grant that this boy of mine may be, like me, preeminent in Troy; as strong and brave as I; a mighty king of Ilium. May people say, when he comes back from battle, 'Here is a better man than his father.' Let him bring home the bloodstained armor of the enemy he has killed, and make his mother happy."

Hector handed the boy to his wife. . . . She was smiling through her tears, and when her husband saw this he was moved. He stroked her with his hand and said, "My dear, I beg you not to be too much distressed. No one is going to send me down to Hades before my proper time. But Fate is a thing that no man born of woman, coward, or hero can escape. Go home now, and attend to your own work, the loom and the spindle, and see that the maidservants get on with theirs. War is men's business; and this war is the business of every man in Ilium, myself above all."

 What important ideals for Greek men and women are revealed in this passage from the Iliad? How do the women's ideals compare with those for ancient Indian and Chinese women?

Source: From *The Iliad* by Homer, translated by E. V. Rieu (Penguin Classics, Copyright 1950 the Estate of E. V. Rieu).

Homer and Homeric Greece The *Iliad* and the *Odyssey*, the first great epic poems of early Greece, were based on stories that had been passed down from generation to generation. It is generally assumed that Homer made use of these oral traditions to compose the *Iliad*, his epic poem of the Trojan War. The war was sparked by Paris, a prince of Troy, who kidnapped Helen, wife of the king of the Greek state of Sparta, outraging all the Greeks. Under the leadership of the Spartan king's brother, Agamemnon of Mycenae, the Greeks attacked Troy. After ten years of combat, the Greeks finally sacked the city. The *Iliad* is not so much the story of the war itself, however, as it is the tale of the Greek hero Achilles (uh-KIL-eez) and how the "wrath of Achilles" led to disaster. The *Odyssey*, Homer's other masterpiece, is an epic romance that recounts the journeys of one of the Greek heroes, Odysseus, from the fall of Troy until his eventual return to his wife, Penelope, twenty years later.

Although the *Iliad* and the *Odyssey* supposedly deal with the heroes of the Mycenaean age of the thirteenth century BCE, many scholars believe that they really describe the social conditions of the transitional period from the Bronze to the Iron Age. According to the Homeric view, Greece was a society based on agriculture in which a landed warrior-aristocracy controlled much wealth and exercised considerable power. Homer's world reflects the values of aristocratic heroes.

Homer's Enduring Importance This, of course, explains the importance of Homer to later generations of Greeks. Homer did not so much record history as make it. The Greeks regarded the *Iliad* and the *Odyssey* as authentic history. They gave the Greeks an idealized past, somewhat like the concept of the golden age in ancient China, with a legendary age of heroes, and the poems came to be used as standard texts for the education of generations of Greek males. As one Athenian stated, "my father was anxious to see me develop into a good man . . . and as a means to this end he compelled me to memorize all of Homer."[1] The values Homer inculcated were essentially the aristocratic values of courage and honor (see "Homer's Ideal of Excellence"). It was important to strive for the excellence befitting a hero, which the Greeks called *arete*. In the warrior-aristocratic world of Homer, *arete* is won in a struggle or contest. Through his willingness to fight, the hero protects his family and friends, preserves his own honor and his family's, and earns his reputation.

In the Homeric world, aristocratic women, too, were expected to pursue excellence. Penelope, for example, the wife of Odysseus (oh-DISS-ee-uss), the hero of the *Odyssey*, remains faithful to her husband and displays great courage and intelligence in preserving their household during her husband's long absence. Upon his return, Odysseus praises her for her excellence: "Madame, there is not a man in the wide world who could find fault with you. For your fame has reached heaven itself, like that of some perfect king, ruling a populous and mighty state with the fear of god in his heart, and upholding the right."[2]

To later generations of Greeks, these heroic values formed the core of aristocratic virtue, a fact that explains the tremendous popularity of Homer as an educational tool. Homer gave to the Greeks a single universally accepted model of heroism, honor, and nobility. But in time, as a new world of city-states emerged and Greece became the first urban culture to emerge on the continent of Europe, new values of cooperation and community also transformed what the Greeks learned from Homer.

4–2 THE WORLD OF THE GREEK CITY-STATES (C. 750–C. 500 BCE)

 Focus Question: What were the chief features of the *polis*, or city-state, and how did the city-states of Athens and Sparta differ?

In the eighth century BCE, Greek civilization burst forth with new energies, beginning the period that historians have called the Archaic Age of Greece. Two major developments stand out in this era: the evolution of the city-state, or what the Greeks called a **polis** (plural, *poleis*), as the central institution in Greek life and the movement of people from the Greek states into lands bordering the Mediterranean and Black Seas.

4–2a The *Polis*

The Greek *polis* (plural, *poleis*) developed slowly but by the eighth century BCE had emerged as a unique and fundamental institution in Greek society. In a physical sense, the *polis* encompassed a town or city or even a village and its surrounding countryside. But each had a central place where the citizens of the *polis* could assemble for political, social, and religious activities. In some *poleis*, this central meeting point was a hill, like the Acropolis in Athens, which could serve as a place of refuge during an attack and later at some sites came to be the religious center on which temples and public monuments were erected. Below the acropolis would be an *agora*, an open space that served both as a market and as a place where citizens could assemble.

Poleis varied greatly in size, from a few square miles to a few hundred square miles. They also varied in population. Athens had a population of about 250,000 by the fifth century BCE. But most *poleis* were much smaller, consisting of only a few hundred to several thousand people.

Although our word *politics* is derived from the Greek term *polis*, the *polis* itself was much more than a political institution. It was a community of citizens in which all political, economic, social, cultural, and religious activities were focused. As a community, the *polis* consisted of citizens with political rights (adult males), citizens with no political rights (women and children), and noncitizens (slaves and resident aliens). All citizens of a *polis* possessed rights, but these rights were coupled with responsibilities. The Greek philosopher Aristotle argued that the citizen did not just belong to himself: "We must rather regard every citizen as belonging to the state." The unity of citizens was important and often meant that states would take an active role in directing the patterns of life. This idea of citizenship created a Greek society that was quite different from the societies of the despotic states we have examined and was an important element in the Greeks' contribution to Western civilization.

Nevertheless, the loyalty that citizens had to their city-states also had a negative side. City-states distrusted one another, and the division of Greece into fiercely patriotic independent units helped bring about its ruin. Greece was not a united country but a geographic location. The cultural unity of the Greeks did not mean much politically. And, as we shall see, it took until the sixth century BCE for the Greeks to even begin establishing a common Greek identity.

A New Military System: The Greek Way of War As the *polis* developed, so did a new military system. In earlier times, wars in Greece had been fought by aristocratic cavalry soldiers—nobles on horseback. These aristocrats, who were large landowners, also dominated the political life of their *poleis*. But by the end of the eighth century BCE, a new military order came into being that was based on **hoplites** (HAHP-lyts), heavily armed infantrymen who wore bronze or leather helmets, breastplates, and greaves (shin guards). Each carried a round shield, a short sword, and a thrusting spear about 9 feet long. Hoplites advanced into battle as a unit, shoulder to shoulder, forming a **phalanx** (a rectangular formation) in tight order, usually eight ranks deep. As long as the hoplites kept their order, were not outflanked, and did not break, they either secured victory or, at the very least, suffered no harm. The phalanx was easily routed, however, if it broke its order. Thus, the safety of the phalanx depended above all on the solidarity and discipline of its members. As one seventh-century BCE poet noted, a good hoplite was "a short man firmly placed upon his legs, with a courageous heart, not to be uprooted from the spot where he plants his legs."[3]

The hoplite force had political as well as military repercussions. The aristocratic cavalry was now outdated. Since each hoplite provided his own armor, men of property, both aristocrats and small farmers, made up the new phalanx. Those who could become hoplites and fight for the state could also challenge aristocratic control. Thus, the development of the

The Hoplite Forces. The Greek hoplites were infantrymen equipped with large round shields and long thrusting spears. In battle, they advanced in tight phalanx formation and were dangerous opponents as long as this formation remained unbroken. This vase painting from the seventh century BCE shows two groups of hoplite warriors engaged in battle. The piper on the left is leading another line of soldiers preparing to enter the fray.

hoplite and phalanx became an important factor in the rise of democracy in Greece.

In the world of the Greek city-states, war became an integral part of the Greek way of life. The Greek philosopher Plato described war as "always existing by nature between every Greek city-state."[4] The Greeks created a tradition of warfare that became a prominent element of Western civilization. For example, the Greeks devised excellent weapons and body armor, making effective use of technological improvements. Greek armies included a wide number of citizen-soldiers, who gladly accepted the need for training and discipline, giving them an edge over their opponents' often far-larger armies of mercenaries. Moreover, the Greeks displayed a willingness to engage the enemy head-on, thus deciding a battle quickly and with as few casualties as possible. Finally, the Greeks demonstrated the effectiveness of heavy infantry in determining the outcome of a battle. All these features of Greek warfare remained part of Western warfare for centuries.

4-2b Greek Expansion and the Growth of Trade

Between 750 and 550 BCE, large numbers of Greeks from different city-states left their homeland to settle in distant lands. The growing gulf between rich and poor, overpopulation, and the development of trade were all factors that spurred the establishment of colonies. Each colony was founded as a *polis* and was usually independent of the mother *polis* (the *metropolis*) that had established it.

In the western Mediterranean, new Greek settlements were established along the coastline of southern Italy, including the cities of Tarentum (Taranto) and Neapolis (Naples) (see Map 4.2). So many Greek communities were established in southern Italy that the Romans later called it *Magna Graecia* (MAG-nuh GREE-shuh) ("Great Greece"). Greek settlements were also established in southern France at Massilia—modern Marseilles (mar-SAY)—in eastern Spain, and in northern Africa west of Egypt. To the north, some Greek states set up colonies in Thrace, where they sought good agricultural lands to grow grains. Others also settled along the shores of the Black Sea and secured the approaches to it with cities on the Hellespont and Bosporus, most notably Byzantium, site of the later Constantinople (Istanbul).

In establishing these settlements, the Greeks spread aspects of their culture throughout the Mediterranean basin. Moreover, colonization helped the Greeks foster a greater sense of Greek identity. Before the eighth century, Greek communities were mostly isolated from one another, and many neighboring states were on unfriendly terms. Once Greeks from different communities went abroad and found peoples with unfamiliar

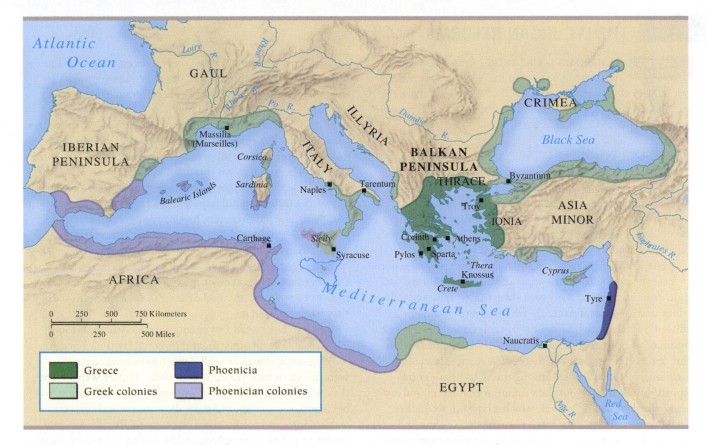

Map 4.2 Greece and Its Colonies in the Archaic Age. Impelled by a variety of factors, Greeks spread out from their homelands during the Archaic Age, establishing colonies in many parts of the Mediterranean. The colonies were independent city-states that traded with the older Greek city-states.

 What aspects of the colonies' locations facilitated trade between them and city-states in Greece?

languages and customs, they became more aware of their own linguistic and cultural similarities, thus aiding in the development of a common Greek identity.

Expansion abroad also led to increased trade and industry. The Greeks on the mainland sent their pottery, wine, and olive oil to these areas; in return, they received grains and metals from the west and fish, timber, wheat, metals, and slaves from the Black Sea region. In many *poleis*, the expansion of trade and industry created a new group of rich men who perceived that the decisions of the *polis* could affect their businesses. They now desired new political privileges but found them impossible to gain because of the power of the ruling aristocrats. This desire for change soon led to political crisis in many Greek states.

4–2c Tyranny in the Greek *Polis*

The aspirations of the new industrial and commercial groups laid the groundwork for the rise of **tyrants** in the seventh and sixth centuries BCE. They were not necessarily oppressive or wicked, as the modern English word *tyrant* connotes. Greek tyrants were rulers who came to power in an unconstitutional way; a tyrant was not subject to the law. Many tyrants were actually aristocrats who opposed the control of the ruling aristocratic faction in their cities. The support for the tyrants, however, came from the new rich who made their money in trade and industry, as well as from poor peasants who were becoming increasingly indebted to landholding aristocrats. Both groups were opposed to the domination of political power by aristocratic **oligarchies** (*oligarchy* means "rule by the few").

Once in power, the tyrants built new marketplaces, temples, and walls that not only glorified the city but also enhanced their own popularity. Tyrants also favored the interests of merchants and traders. Despite these achievements, however, **tyranny** was largely extinguished by the end of the sixth century BCE. Greeks believed in the rule of law, and tyranny made a mockery of that ideal.

Although tyranny did not last, it played a significant role in the evolution of Greek history by ending the rule of narrow aristocratic oligarchies. Once the tyrants were eliminated, the door was opened to the participation of new and more people in governing the affairs of the community. Although this trend culminated in the development of democracy in some communities, in other states expanded oligarchies of one kind or another managed to remain in power. Greek states exhibited considerable variety in their governmental structures; this can perhaps best be seen by examining the two most famous and most powerful Greek city-states, Sparta and Athens.

THE LYCURGAN REFORMS

Family & Society

TO MAINTAIN THEIR CONTROL OVER THE HELOTS, the Spartans instituted the reforms that created their military state. In this account of the lawgiver Lycurgus, the Greek historian Plutarch discusses the effect of these reforms on the treatment and education of boys.

Plutarch, *Lycurgus*

Lycurgus was of another mind; he would not have masters bought out of the market for his young Spartans, . . . nor was it lawful, indeed, for the father himself to breed up the children after his own fancy; but as soon as they were seven years old they were to be enrolled in certain companies and classes, where they all lived under the same order and discipline, doing their exercises and taking their play together. Of these, he who showed the most conduct and courage was made captain; they had their eyes always upon him, obeyed his orders, and underwent patiently whatsoever punishment he inflicted; so that the whole course of their education was one continued exercise of a ready and perfect obedience. The old men, too, were spectators of their performances, and often raised quarrels and disputes among them, to have a good opportunity of finding out their different characters, and of seeing which would be valiant, which a coward, when they should come to more dangerous encounters. Reading and writing they gave them, just enough to serve their turn; their chief care was to make them good subjects, and to teach them to endure pain and conquer in battle. To this end, as they grew in years, their discipline was proportionately increased; their heads were close-clipped, they were accustomed to go barefoot, and for the most part to play naked.

After they were twelve years old, they were no longer allowed to wear any undergarments; they had one coat to serve them a year; their bodies were hard and dry, with but little acquaintance of baths and unguents; these human indulgences they were allowed only on some few particular days in the year. They lodged together in little bands upon beds made of the rushes which grew by the banks of the river Eurotas, which they were to break off with their hands with a knife; if it were winter, they mingled some thistledown with their rushes, which it was thought had the property of giving warmth. By the time they were come to this age there was not any of the more hopeful boys who had not a lover to bear him company. The old men, too, had an eye upon them, coming often to the grounds to hear and see them contend either in wit or strength with one another, and this as seriously . . . as if they were their fathers, their tutors, or their magistrates; so that there scarcely was any time or place without someone present to put them in mind of their duty, and punish them if they had neglected it.

[Spartan boys were also encouraged to steal their food.] They stole, too, all other meat they could lay their hands on, looking out and watching all opportunities, when people were asleep or more careless than usual. If they were caught, they were not only punished with whipping, but hunger, too, being reduced to their ordinary allowance, which was but very slender, and so contrived on purpose, that they might set about to help themselves, and be forced to exercise their energy and address. This was the principal design of their hard fare.

 What does this passage from Plutarch's account of Lycurgus reveal about the nature of the Spartan state? Why would the entire program have been distasteful to the Athenians?

Source: From Plutarch, *The Lives of the Noble Grecians and Romans*, translated by John Dryden, and revised by Arthur Hugh Clough (New York: Modern Library, 1979).

4–2d Sparta

Located in the southeastern Peloponnesus, Sparta, like other Greek states, faced the need for more land. Instead of sending its people out to found new colonies, the Spartans conquered the neighboring Laconians and later, beginning around 730 BCE, undertook the conquest of neighboring Messenia despite its larger size and population. Messenia possessed a large, fertile plain ideal for growing grain. After its conquest in the seventh century BCE, the Messenians, like the Laconians earlier, were reduced to serfdom—they were known as **helots** (HEL-uts), a name derived from a Greek word for "capture"— and forced to work for the Spartans. But the helots drastically outnumbered the Spartan citizens (some estimates are ten to one) and constantly threatened to revolt. To ensure control over them, the Spartans made a conscious decision to create a military state.

The New Sparta Between 800 and 600 BCE, the Spartans instituted a series of reforms that are associated with the name of the lawgiver Lycurgus (ly-KUR-guss) (see "The Lycurgan Reforms"). Although historians are not sure that Lycurgus ever existed, there is no doubt about the result of the reforms that were made: the lives of Spartans were now rigidly organized and tightly controlled (to this day, the word *spartan* means "highly self-disciplined"). Boys were taken from their mothers at the age of seven and put under control of the state. They lived in military-style barracks, where they were subjected to harsh discipline to make them tough and given an education that stressed military training and obedience to authority. At twenty, Spartan males were enrolled in the army for regular military service. Although allowed to marry, they continued to live in the barracks and ate all their meals in public dining halls with their fellow soldiers. Meals were simple; the famous Spartan black broth consisted of a piece of pork boiled in blood, salt, and vinegar, causing a visitor who ate in a public mess to remark that he now understood why Spartans were not afraid to die. At thirty, Spartan males were recognized as mature and allowed to vote in the assembly and live at home, but they remained in military service until the age of sixty.

While their husbands remained in military barracks until age thirty, Spartan women lived at home. Because of this separation, Spartan women had greater freedom of movement. Permitted to own and inherit land, Spartan women had greater power in the household than was common for women elsewhere in Greece and could even supervise large estates. They were encouraged to exercise and remain fit to bear and raise healthy children. Like the men, Spartan women engaged in athletic exercises in the nude. Many Spartan women upheld the strict Spartan values, expecting their husbands and sons to be brave in war. The story is told that as a Spartan mother was burying her son, an old woman came up to her and said, "You poor woman, what a misfortune." "No," replied the mother, "because I bore him so that he might die for Sparta, and that is what has happened, as I wished."[5]

The Spartan State The so-called Lycurgan reforms also reorganized the Spartan government, creating an oligarchy. Two kings from different families were primarily responsible for military affairs and served as the leaders of the Spartan army on its campaigns. A group of five men, known as the *ephors* (EFF-urz), were elected each year and were responsible for the education of youth and the conduct of all citizens. A council of elders, composed of the two kings and twenty-eight male citizens over the age of sixty, decided on the issues that would be presented to an assembly. This assembly of all male citizens did not debate but only voted on the proposals put before it by the council of elders. The assembly also elected the council of elders and the ephors.

To make their new military state secure, the Spartans deliberately turned their backs on the outside world. Foreigners, who might bring in new ideas, were discouraged from visiting Sparta. Nor were Spartans, except for military reasons, allowed to travel abroad, where they might pick up new ideas dangerous to the stability of the state. Likewise, Spartan citizens were discouraged from studying philosophy, literature, or the arts—subjects that might encourage new thoughts. The art of war was the Spartan ideal, and all other arts were frowned on.

In the sixth century, Sparta used its military might and the fear it inspired to gain greater control of the Peloponnesus by organizing an alliance of almost all the Peloponnesian states. Sparta's strength enabled it to dominate this Peloponnesian League and determine its policies. By 500 BCE, the Spartans had organized a powerful military state that maintained order and stability in the Peloponnesus. Raised from early childhood to believe that total loyalty to the Spartan state was the basic reason for existence, the Spartans viewed their strength as justification for their militaristic ideals and regimented society.

4–2e Athens

By 700 BCE, Athens had established a unified *polis* on the peninsula of Attica. Although early Athens had been ruled by a monarchy, by the seventh century BCE it had fallen under the control of its aristocrats. They possessed the best land and controlled political and religious life by means of a council of nobles, assisted by a board of nine officials called archons. Although there was an assembly of full citizens, it possessed few powers.

Near the end of the seventh century BCE, Athens faced political turmoil because of serious economic problems. Increasing numbers of Athenian farmers found themselves sold into slavery when they were unable to repay loans they had obtained from their aristocratic neighbors, pledging themselves as collateral. Repeatedly, there were cries to cancel the debts and give land to the poor.

The Reforms of Solon The ruling Athenian aristocrats responded to this crisis by choosing Solon (SOH-lun), a reform-minded aristocrat, as sole archon in 594 BCE and giving him full power to make changes. Solon canceled all land debts, outlawed new loans based on humans as collateral, and freed people who had fallen into slavery for debts. He refused, however, to carry out land redistribution and hence failed to deal with the basic cause of the economic crisis.

Like his economic reforms, Solon's political measures were also a compromise. Though by no means eliminating the power of the aristocracy, they opened the door to the participation of new people, especially the nonaristocratic wealthy, in the government. But Solon's reforms, though popular, did not solve Athens's problems. Aristocratic factions continued to vie for power, and the poorer peasants resented Solon's failure to institute land redistribution. Internal strife finally led to the very institution Solon had hoped to avoid—tyranny. Pisistratus (puh-SIS-truh-tuss), an aristocrat, seized power in 560 BCE. Pursuing a foreign policy that aided Athenian trade, Pisistratus remained popular with the mercantile and industrial classes. But the Athenians rebelled against his son and ended the tyranny in 510 BCE. Although the aristocrats attempted to reestablish an aristocratic oligarchy, Cleisthenes (KLYSS-thuh-neez), another aristocratic reformer, opposed this plan and, with the backing of the Athenian people, gained the upper hand in 508 BCE.

The Reforms of Cleisthenes Cleisthenes created the Council of Five Hundred, chosen by lot by the ten tribes in which all citizens had been enrolled. The council was responsible for the administration of both foreign and financial affairs and prepared the business that would be handled by the assembly. This assembly of all male citizens had final authority in the passing of laws after free and open debate; thus, Cleisthenes's reforms had reinforced the central role of the assembly of citizens in the Athenian political system.

The reforms of Cleisthenes created the foundations for Athenian democracy. More changes would come in the fifth century, when the Athenians themselves would begin to use the word *democracy* to describe their system (from the Greek words *demos*, "people," and *kratia*, "power"). By 500 BCE, Athens was more united than it had been and was on the verge of playing a more important role in Greek affairs.

4-2f Foreign Influence on Early Greek Culture

As the Greeks moved out into the eastern Mediterranean, they came into increased contact with the older civilizations of the Near East and Egypt, which had a strong impact on early Greek culture. The Greeks adopted new gods and goddesses as well as new myths—such as the story of the flood—from Mesopotamian traditions. Greek pottery in the eighth and seventh centuries began to use new motifs—such as floral designs—borrowed from the Near East. Greek sculpture, particularly that of the Ionian Greek settlements in southwestern Asia Minor, demonstrates the impact of the considerably older Egyptian civilization. There we first see the life-size stone statues of young male nudes known as *kouros* (KOO-rohss) figures. The *kouros* bears a strong resemblance to Egyptian statues of the New Kingdom. The figures are not realistic but stiff, the face bearing the hint of a smile; one leg is advanced ahead of the other, and the arms are held rigidly at the sides of the body.

Greek literature was also the beneficiary of a Greek alphabet that owed much to the Phoenicians (see Chapter 1). The Greeks adopted some of the twenty-two Phoenician consonants as

Kouros. On the left is a statue of a young male nude from around 600 BCE, making it an early example of Greek *kouros* sculpture. Such statues, which were placed in temples along with companion figures of clothed young women, known as *korai*, were meant to be representations of the faithful dedicated to the gods. At the right is an early-seventh-century BCE statue of an Egyptian nobleman. Clearly, Egyptian sculpture had a strong influence on Greek art. Unlike the Egyptians, however, Greek sculptors preferred depicting male figures in the nude.

The Metropolitan Museum of Art. Image source: Art Resource, NY

Greek consonants and used other symbols to represent vowel sounds, which the Phoenicians did not have. In the process, the Greeks created a truly phonetic alphabet, probably between 800 and 750 BCE, thus making the Greek language easier to read and write than Egyptian hieroglyphics and Mesopotamian cuneiform. Greek could be used to record laws and commercial transactions and to write the poetry, philosophical treatises, and other literary works that distinguish Greek culture.

4-3 THE HIGH POINT OF GREEK CIVILIZATION: CLASSICAL GREECE

 Focus Questions: What did the Greeks mean by *democracy*, and in what ways was the Athenian political system a democracy? What effect did the two great conflicts of the fifth century—the Persian Wars and the Peloponnesian War—have on Greek civilization?

Classical Greece is the name given to the period of Greek history from around 500 BCE to the conquest of Greece by the Macedonian king Philip II in 338 BCE. Many of the cultural contributions of the Greeks occurred during this period. The age began with a mighty confrontation between the Greek states and the mammoth Persian Empire.

4-3a The Challenge of Persia

As the Greeks spread throughout the Mediterranean, they came into contact with the Persian Empire to the east (see Chapter 1). In his play *The Persians*, the Greek playwright Aeschylus reflected what some Greeks perceived to be the essential difference between themselves and the Persians. The Persian queen, curious to find out more about the Athenians, asks, "Who commands them? Who is shepherd of their host?" The chorus responds: "They are slaves to none, nor are they subject."[6] Thus, at least, some Greeks saw the struggle with the Persians as a contest between freedom and slavery. To the Greeks, a person was a citizen of the state, not a subject. And for the Greeks, who were still divided into independent city-states, the growing Persian threat would serve to deepen an increased sense of Greek cultural identity.

The Ionian Greek cities in western Asia Minor had already fallen subject to the Persian Empire by the mid-sixth century BCE. An unsuccessful revolt by the Ionian cities in 499 BCE—assisted by the Athenian navy—led the Persian ruler Darius (duh-RY-uss) to seek revenge by attacking the mainland Greeks. In 490 BCE, the Persians landed an army on the plain of Marathon, only 26 miles from Athens (see Map 4.3). The Athenians and their allies were clearly outnumbered, but led by Miltiades (mil-TY-uh-deez), one of the Athenian leaders who insisted on attacking, the Greek hoplites charged across the plain of Marathon and crushed the Persian forces. The Persians did not mount another attack against mainland Greece for ten years. A Persian victory might well have cut short the Athenian experiment with democracy.

Xerxes (ZURK-seez), the new Persian monarch after the death of Darius in 486 BCE, vowed revenge and planned to invade. In

	Persian War battles
	Invasion route of Xerxes's army
	Invasion route of Xerxes's navy

Map 4.3 The Persian Wars. The Athenians defeated Persia in 490 BCE at Marathon. Athens later led a coalition of Greek city-states that decisively defeated Xerxes's navy at the Battle of Salamis in 480 BCE, causing Xerxes to withdraw most of his troops back to Asia.

Q *How far did the Persian army have to walk to get to Athens, and through what types of terrain?*

preparation for the attack, some of the Greek states formed a defensive league under Spartan leadership. The Athenians, in the meantime, had acquired a new leader, Themistocles (thuh-MISS-tuh-kleez), who persuaded his fellow citizens to pursue a new military policy, namely, the development of a navy. By the time of the Persian invasion in 480 BCE, the Athenians had produced a fleet of about two hundred vessels, primarily triremes (TRY-reemz) (ships with three banks of oars).

Xerxes led a massive invasion force into Greece: close to 150,000 troops, almost seven hundred naval ships, and hundreds of supply ships to keep the large army fed. The Greeks tried to delay the Persians at the pass of Thermopylae (thur-MAHP-uh-lee), along the main road into central Greece. A Greek force numbering close to nine thousand, under the leadership of the Spartan king, Leonidas, and his contingent of three hundred Spartans, held off the Persian army for two days. The Spartan troops were especially brave. When told that Persian arrows would darken the sky in battle, one Spartan warrior supposedly

responded, "That is good news. We will fight in the shade!" Unfortunately for the Greeks, a traitor told the Persians how to use a mountain path to outflank the Greek force. The Spartans fought to the last man.

The Athenians, now threatened by the onslaught of the Persian forces, abandoned their city. While the Persians sacked and burned Athens, the Greek fleet remained offshore near the island of Salamis (SAH-luh-miss) and challenged the Persian navy to fight. Although the Greeks were outnumbered, they managed to outmaneuver the Persian fleet and utterly defeated it. A few months later, early in 479 BCE, the Greeks formed the largest Greek army seen up to that time and decisively defeated the Persian army at Plataea (pluh-TEE-uh), northwest of Attica. The remnants of the Persian forces retreated to Asia. At the same time, the Greeks destroyed much of the Persian fleet in a naval battle at Mycale (MIH-kuh-lee) in Ionia. The Greeks were overjoyed at their victory but remained cautious. Would the Persians try again?

Rebellion of Greek cities in Asia Minor	499–494 BCE
Battle of Marathon	490 BCE
Xerxes invades Greece	480–479 BCE
Battles of Thermopylae and Salamis	480 BCE
Battles of Plataea and Mycale	479 BCE

4–3b The Growth of an Athenian Empire in the Age of Pericles

After the defeat of the Persians, Athens took over the leadership of the Greek world by forming a defensive alliance against the Persians called the Delian League in the winter of 478–477 BCE. Its main headquarters was on the island of Delos, but its chief officials, including the treasurers and commanders of the fleet, were Athenian. Under the leadership of the Athenians, the Delian League pursued the attack against the Persian Empire. Virtually all of the Greek states in the Aegean were liberated from Persian control. Arguing that the Persian threat was now over, some members of the Delian League wished to withdraw. But the Athenians forced them to remain in the league and to pay tribute. In 454 BCE, the Athenians moved the treasury of the league from Delos to Athens. By controlling the Delian League, Athens had created an empire.

At home, Athenians favored the new imperial policy, especially after 461 BCE, when politics came to be dominated by a political faction led by a young aristocrat named Pericles (PER-i-kleez). Under Pericles, who remained a leading figure in Athenian politics for more than three decades, Athens embarked on a policy of expanding democracy at home and its new empire abroad. This period of Athenian and Greek history, which historians have subsequently labeled the Age of Pericles, witnessed the height of Athenian power and the culmination of its brilliance as a civilization.

During the Age of Pericles, the Athenians became deeply attached to their democratic system. The sovereignty of the people was embodied in the assembly, which consisted of all male citizens over eighteen years of age. In the 440s, that was probably a group of about 43,000. Not all attended, however, and the number present at the meetings, which were held every ten days on a hillside east of the Acropolis, seldom reached 6,000. The assembly passed all laws and made final decisions on war and foreign policy.

Routine administration of public affairs was handled by a large body of city magistrates, usually chosen by lot without regard to class and usually serving only one-year terms. This meant that many male citizens held public office at some time in their lives. A board of ten officials known as generals (strategoi [strah-tay-GOH-ee]) was elected by public vote to guide affairs of state, although their power depended on the respect they had earned. Generals were usually wealthy aristocrats, even though the people were free to select otherwise. The generals could be reelected, enabling individual leaders to play an important political role. Pericles's frequent reelection (fifteen times) as one of the ten generals made him one of the leading politicians between 461 and 429 BCE.

Pericles expanded the Athenians' involvement in democracy, which is what by now the Athenians had come to call their form of government (see "Athenian Democracy: The Funeral Oration of Pericles"). Power was in the hands of the people; male citizens voted in the assemblies and served as jurors in the courts. Lower-class citizens were now eligible for public offices formerly closed to them. Pericles also introduced state pay for officeholders, including the widely held jury duty. This meant that even poor citizens could afford to participate in public affairs and hold public office. Nevertheless, although the Athenians developed a system of government that was unique in its time in which citizens had equal rights and the people were the government, aristocrats continued to hold the most important offices, and many people, including women, slaves, and foreigners residing in Athens, were not given the same political rights.

Under Pericles, Athens became the leading center of Greek culture. The Persians had destroyed much of the city during the Persian Wars, but Pericles used the treasury money of the Delian League to set in motion a massive rebuilding program. New temples and statues soon made the greatness of Athens more visible. Art, architecture, and philosophy flourished, and Pericles broadly boasted that Athens had become the "school of Greece." But the achievements of Athens alarmed the other Greek states, especially Sparta, and soon all of Greece was confronting a new war.

4–3c The Great Peloponnesian War and the Decline of the Greek States

During the forty years after the defeat of the Persians, the Greek world came to be divided into two major camps: Sparta and its supporters and the Athenian maritime empire. Sparta and its allies feared the growing Athenian Empire. Then, too, Athens and Sparta had created two very different kinds of societies, and neither state was able to tolerate the other's system. A series of disputes finally led to the outbreak of war in 431 BCE.

At the beginning of the war, both sides believed they had winning strategies. The Athenians planned to remain behind the protective walls of Athens while the overseas empire and the navy would keep them supplied. Pericles knew that the Spartans and their allies could beat the Athenians in open battles, which was the chief aim of the Spartan strategy. The Spartans and their allies invaded Attica and ravaged the fields and orchards, hoping that the Athenians would send out their army to fight beyond the walls. But Pericles was convinced that Athens was secure behind its walls and stayed put.

In the second year of the war, however, plague devastated the crowded city of Athens and wiped out possibly one-third of the population. Pericles himself died the following year (429 BCE), a severe loss to Athens. Despite the losses from the plague, the Athenians fought on in a struggle that dragged on for another twenty-seven years. A final crushing blow came in 405 BCE, when the Athenian fleet was destroyed at Aegospotami (ee-guh-SPOT-uh-my) on the Hellespont. Athens was besieged and surrendered in 404. Its walls were torn down, the navy was disbanded, and the Athenian Empire was no more. The great war was finally over.

The Great Peloponnesian War weakened the major Greek states and destroyed any possibility of cooperation among the states. The

ATHENIAN DEMOCRACY: THE FUNERAL ORATION OF PERICLES

Politics & Government

IN HIS *HISTORY OF THE PELOPONNESIAN WAR*, the Greek historian Thucydides presented his reconstruction of the eulogy given by Pericles in the winter of 431–430 BCE to honor the Athenians killed in the first campaigns of the Great Peloponnesian War. It is a magnificent, idealized description of Athenian democracy at its height.

Thucydides, *History of the Peloponnesian War*

Our constitution is called a democracy because power is in the hands not of a minority but of the whole people. When it is a question of settling private disputes, everyone is equal before the law; when it is a question of putting one person before another in positions of public responsibility, what counts is not membership of a particular class, but the actual ability which the man possesses. No one, so long as he has it in him to be of service to the state, is kept in political obscurity because of poverty. And, just as our political life is free and open, so is our day-to-day life in our relations with each other. We do not get into a state with our next-door neighbor if he enjoys himself in his own way, nor do we give him the kind of black looks which, though they do no real harm, still do hurt people's feelings. We are free and tolerant in our private lives; but in public affairs we keep to the law. This is because it commands our deep respect.

We give our obedience to those whom we put in positions of authority, and we obey the laws themselves, especially those which are for the protection of the oppressed, and those unwritten laws which it is an acknowledged shame to break. . . . Here each individual is interested not only in his own affairs but in the affairs of the state as well: even those who are mostly occupied with their own business are extremely well-informed on general politics—this is a peculiarity of ours: we do not say that a man who takes no interest in politics is a man who minds his own business; we say that he has no business here at all. We Athenians, in our own persons, take our decisions on policy or submit them to proper discussions: for we do not think that there is an incompatibility between words and deeds; the worst thing is to rush into action before the consequences have been properly debated. . . . Taking everything together then, I declare that our city is an education to Greece, and I declare that in my opinion each single one of our citizens, in all the manifold aspects of life, is able to show himself the rightful lord and owner of his own person, and do this, moreover, with exceptional grace and exceptional versatility. And to show that this is no empty boasting for the present occasion, but real tangible fact, you have only to consider the power which our city possesses and which has been won by those very qualities which I have mentioned.

 In the eyes of Pericles, what are the ideals of Athenian democracy? In what ways does Pericles exaggerate his claims? Why would the Athenian passion for debate described by Pericles have been distasteful to the Spartans? On the other hand, how does eagerness for discussion perfectly suit democracy?

Source: From *The History of the Peloponnesian War* by Thucydides, translated by Rex Warner. Copyright © Rex Warner 1954.

---

next seventy years of Greek history are a sorry tale of efforts by Sparta, Athens, and Thebes, a new Greek power, to dominate Greek affairs. Focused on their petty wars, the Greek states remained oblivious to the growing power of Macedonia to their north.

4–3d The Culture of Classical Greece

Classical Greece was a period of remarkable intellectual and cultural growth throughout the Greek world, and Periclean Athens was the most important center of Classical Greek culture.

The Writing of History History as we know it, as the systematic analysis of past events, was introduced to the Western world by the Greeks. Herodotus (huh-ROD-uh-tuss) (c. 484–c. 425 BCE) wrote *History of the Persian Wars*, which is commonly regarded as the first real history in Western civilization. The central theme of Herodotus's work was the conflict between the Greeks and the Persians, which he viewed as a struggle between freedom and despotism. Herodotus traveled extensively and questioned many people to obtain his information. He was a master storyteller and sometimes included considerable fanciful material, but he was also capable of exhibiting a critical attitude toward the materials he used.

Thucydides (thoo-SID-uh-deez) (c. 460–c. 400 BCE) was a better historian by far; indeed, he is considered the greatest historian of the ancient world. Thucydides was an Athenian and a participant in the Peloponnesian War. He had been elected a general, but a defeat in battle led the fickle Athenian assembly to send him into exile, which gave him the opportunity to write his *History of the Peloponnesian War*.

Unlike Herodotus, Thucydides was not concerned with underlying divine forces or gods as explanatory causal factors in history. He saw war and politics in purely rational terms, as the activities of human beings. He examined the causes of the Peloponnesian War in a clear, methodical, objective fashion, placing much emphasis on accuracy and the precision of his facts. As he stated:

> With regard to my factual reporting of the events of the war I have made it a principle not to write down the first story that came my way, and not even to be guided by my own general impressions; either I was present myself at the events which I have described or else I heard of them from eyewitnesses whose reports I have checked with as much thoroughness as possible.[7]

Thucydides also provided remarkable insight into the human condition. He believed that political situations recur in similar fashion and that the study of history is therefore of great value in understanding the present.

Greek Drama Drama as we know it in Western culture was originated by the Greeks. Plays were presented in outdoor theaters as part of religious festivals. The plays followed a fairly stable form. Three male actors who wore masks acted all the parts. A chorus, also male, spoke lines that explained what was going on. Action was very limited because the emphasis was on the story and its meaning.

The first Greek dramas were tragedies, plays based on the suffering of a hero and usually ending in disaster. Aeschylus (ESS-kuh-luss) (525–456 BCE) is the first tragedian whose plays are known to us. As was customary in Greek tragedy, his plots are simple, and the entire drama focuses on a single tragic event and its meaning. Greek tragedies were sometimes presented in a trilogy (a set of three plays) built around a common theme. The only complete trilogy we possess, called the *Oresteia* (uh-res-TY-uh), was written by Aeschylus. The theme of this trilogy is derived from Homer. Agamemnon, the king of Mycenae, returns a hero from the defeat of Troy. His wife, Clytemnestra, avenges the sacrificial death of her daughter Iphigenia by murdering Agamemnon, who had been responsible for Iphigenia's death. In the second play of the trilogy, Agamemnon's son Orestes avenges his father by killing his mother. Orestes is then pursued by the avenging Furies, who torment him for killing his mother. Evil acts breed evil acts, and suffering is one's lot, suggests Aeschylus. But Orestes is put on trial and acquitted by Athena, the patron goddess of Athens. Personal vendetta has been eliminated, and law has prevailed.

The most successful writer of Greek tragedies was the Athenian playwright Sophocles (SAHF-uh-kleez) (c. 496–406 BCE), whose most famous work was *Oedipus the King*. In this play, the oracle of Apollo foretells that a man (Oedipus) will kill his own father and marry his mother. Despite all attempts at prevention, the tragic events occur. Although it appears that Oedipus suffered the fate determined by the gods, Oedipus also accepts that he himself as a free man must bear responsibility for his actions: "It was Apollo, friends, Apollo, that brought this bitter bitterness, my sorrows to completion. But the hand that struck me was none but my own."[8]

In *Antigone* (an-TIG-oh-nee), the daughter of Oedipus is caught in the dilemma of following her religious obligations to bury the body of her brother Polynices (pol-ee-NICE-eez), who has died in an attempt to seize the throne of Thebes. Antigone's uncle, Cleon, the king of Thebes, however, has forbidden his burial as a traitor to the state. Should Antigone adhere to her principles and fulfill her obligation to the gods by burying her brother or face death by defying the authority of the state? In this confrontation between Cleon and Antigone, Sophocles bears witness to the complexity of human existence (see "Sophocles: 'The Miracle of Man'").

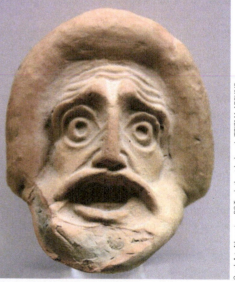

Greek Art. 4th century BC Tragic theatrical mask,/PRISMA ARCHIVO FOTOGRAFICO (Tarker)/Bridgeman Images

Latitude Stock-Ron Badkin/Getty Images

The Amphitheater at Epidaurus. The photo shows the ancient Greek amphitheater at Epidaurus in the eastern Peloponnesus. It held eighteen thousand onlookers for the theatrical presentations and athletic games that were part of the religious festivals dedicated to Asclepius, the god of healing. The inset photo shows an example of a tragic theatrical mask worn by actors. Since Greek dramas used three male actors who might play several roles, masks were necessary to distinguish the characters.

SOPHOCLES: "THE MIRACLE OF MAN"

Religion & Philosophy

IN *ANTIGONE*, Sophocles presents a thoughtful analysis of the painful dilemmas in human existence. In one outstanding passage, the chorus expresses an exalted message on human resourcefulness and the achievements of human beings.

Sophocles, *Antigone*

Is there anything more wonderful on earth,
Our marvelous planet,
Than the miracle of man!
With what arrogant ease
He rides the dangerous seas,
From the waves' towering summit
To the yawning trough beneath.
The earth mother herself, before time began,
The oldest of the ageless gods,
Learned to endure his driving plough,
Turning the earth and breaking the clods
Till by the sweat of his brow
She yielded up her fruitfulness. . . .

He has mastered the mysteries of language:
And thought, which moves faster than the wind,
He has tamed, and made rational.
Political wisdom too, all the knowledge
Of people and States, all the practical

Arts of government he has studied and refined,
Built cities to shelter his head
Against rain and anger and cold
And ordered all things in his mind.
There is no problem he cannot resolve
By the exercise of his brains or his breath,
And the only disease he cannot salve
Or cure, is death.

In action he is subtle beyond imagination,
Limitless is his skill, and these gifts
Are both enemies and friends,
As he applies them, with equal determination,
To good or evil ends.
All men honor, and the State uplifts
That man to the heights of glory, whose powers
Uphold the constitution, and the gods, and their laws.
His city prospers. But if he shifts
His ground, and takes the wrong path,
Despising morality, and blown up with pride,
Indulges himself and his power, at my hearth
May he never warm himself, or sit at my side.

 What is Sophocles's view of humans and their accomplishments? What are the limitations to these human accomplishments?

Source: From Sophocles, *Antigone,* trans. Don Taylor (London: Methuen, 2006), pp. 17–18.

Another outstanding Athenian tragedian, Euripides (yoo-RIP-uh-deez) (c. 485–406 BCE), moved beyond his predecessors by creating more realistic characters. His plots also became more complex, with a greater interest in real-life situations. Euripides was controversial because he questioned traditional moral and religious values. For example, he was critical of the traditional view that war was glorious. Instead, he portrayed war as brutal and barbaric.

Greek tragedies dealt with universal themes still relevant to our day. They probed such problems as the nature of good and evil, the rights of the individual, the nature of divine forces, and the nature of human beings. Over and over, the tragic lesson was repeated: humans were free and yet could operate only within limitations imposed by the gods. Striving to do the best may not always gain a person success in human terms but is nevertheless worthy of the endeavor. Greek pride in human accomplishment and independence was real. As the chorus chants in Sophocles's *Antigone*: "Is there anything more wonderful on earth, our marvelous planet, than the miracle of man?"[9]

Greek comedy developed later than tragedy. The plays of Aristophanes (ar-is-STAH-fuh-neez) (c. 450–c. 385 BCE), who used both grotesque masks and obscene jokes to entertain the Athenian audience, are examples of Old Comedy. But comedy in Athens was also more clearly political than tragedy. It was used to attack or savagely satirize both politicians and intellectuals. Of special importance to Aristophanes was his opposition to the Peloponnesian War.

The Arts: The Classical Ideal The artistic standards established by the Greeks of the Classical period largely dominated the arts of the Western world until the nineteenth and twentieth centuries. Classical Greek art was concerned with expressing eternally true ideals. Its subject matter was basically the human being, expressed harmoniously as an object of great beauty. The Classical style, based on the ideals of reason, moderation, symmetry, balance, and harmony in all things, was meant to civilize the emotions.

In architecture, the most important form was the temple dedicated to a god or goddess. At the center of Greek temples were walled rooms that housed the statues of deities and treasuries in which gifts to the gods and goddesses were safeguarded. These central rooms were surrounded by a screen of columns that made Greek temples open structures rather than closed ones. The columns were originally made of wood but were changed to marble in the fifth century BCE.

IONIC.　　　DORIC.　　　CORINTHIAN.

duncan 1890/Getty Images

Doric, Ionic, and Corinthian Orders. The size and shape of a column constituted one of the most important aspects of Greek temple architecture. The Doric order, with plain capitals and no base, developed first in the Dorian Peloponnesus and was rather simple in comparison to the slender Ionic column, which had an elaborate base and spiral-shaped capitals, and the Corinthian column, which featured leaf-shaped capitals.

Some of the finest examples of Greek Classical architecture were built in fifth-century Athens. The most famous building, regarded as the finest example of the Classical Greek temple, was the Parthenon, built between 447 and 432 BCE. Consecrated to Athena, the patron goddess of Athens, the Parthenon was also dedicated to the glory of the city-state and its inhabitants. The Parthenon typifies the principles of Classical architecture: calmness, clarity, and the avoidance of superfluous detail.

Greek sculpture developed a Classical style that differed significantly from the artificial stiffness of the figures of earlier times, which had been influenced by Egyptian sculpture. Statues of the male nude, the favorite subject of Greek sculptors, now exhibited more relaxed attitudes; their faces were self-assured, their bodies flexible and smooth-muscled. Although the figures possessed natural features that made them lifelike, Greek sculptors sought to achieve not realism but a standard of ideal beauty. Polyclitus (pahl-ee-KLY-tuss), a fifth-century sculptor, wrote a treatise (now lost) on a canon of proportions that he illustrated in a work known as the *Doryphoros* (doh-RIF-uh-rohss). His theory maintained that the use of ideal proportions, based on mathematical ratios found in nature, could produce an ideal human form, beautiful in its perfected and refined features. This search for ideal beauty was the dominant feature of the Classical standard in sculpture.

The Greek Love of Wisdom *Philosophy* is a Greek word that originally meant "love of wisdom." Early Greek philosophers were concerned with the development of critical or rational thought about the nature of the universe and the place of divine forces and souls in it.

Much of early Greek philosophy focused on the attempt to explain the universe on the basis of unifying

The Parthenon. The arts in Classical Greece were designed to express the eternal ideals of reason, moderation, symmetry, balance, and harmony. In architecture, the most important form was the temple, and the classic example of this kind of architecture is the Parthenon, built between 447 and 432 BCE. Located on the Acropolis in Athens, the Parthenon was dedicated to Athena, the patron goddess of the city, but it also served as a shining example of the power and wealth of the Athenian empire.

Adam Crowley/Getty Images

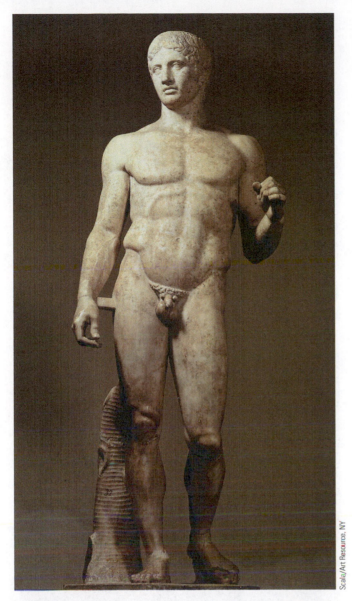

Doryphoros. This statue, known as the *Doryphoros*, or spear carrier, is a Roman copy of the original work by the fifth-century BCE sculptor Polyclitus, who believed it illustrated the ideal proportions of the human figure. Classical Greek sculpture moved away from the stiffness of the *kouros* figure but retained the young male nude as the favorite subject matter. The statues became more lifelike, with relaxed poses and flexible, smooth-muscled bodies. The aim of sculpture, however, was not simply realism but rather the expression of ideal beauty.

principles. Many Greeks, however, were simply not interested in such speculations. The **Sophists** were a group of philosophical teachers in the fifth century BCE who rejected such speculation as foolish. Like their near contemporary Confucius in China (see Chapter 3), they argued that understanding the universe was beyond the reach of the human mind (see Comparative Essay "The Axial Age," p. 114). It was more important for individuals to improve themselves, so the only worthwhile object of study was human behavior. The Sophists were wandering scholars who sold their services as professional teachers to the young men of Greece, especially those of Athens. The Sophists stressed the importance of **rhetoric** (the art of persuasive oratory) in winning debates and swaying an audience, a skill that was especially valuable in democratic Athens. Unlike Confucius, however, the Sophists tended to be skeptics who questioned the traditional values of their societies. To the Sophists, there was no absolute right or wrong. True wisdom consisted of being able to perceive and pursue one's own good. Many people, however, viewed the Sophists as harmful to society and considered their ideas especially dangerous to the values of young people.

In Classical Greece, Athens became the foremost intellectual and artistic center. Its reputation is perhaps strongest of all in philosophy. Socrates, Plato, and Aristotle raised basic questions that have been debated for two thousand years, for the most part the very same philosophical questions we wrestle with today.

Socrates (SAHK-ruh-teez) (469–399 BCE) left no writings, but we know about him from his pupils. Socrates was a stonemason whose true love was philosophy. He taught a number of pupils, but not for pay, because he believed that the goal of education was to improve the individual. His approach, still known as the **Socratic method**, employs a question-and-answer technique to lead pupils to see things for themselves using their own reason. Socrates believed that all knowledge is within each person; only critical examination was needed to call it forth. This was the real task of philosophy, since "the unexamined life is not worth living."

Socrates questioned authority and criticized some traditional Athenian values, and this soon led him into trouble. Athens had had a tradition of free thought and inquiry, but its defeat in the Peloponnesian War had created an environment intolerant of open debate and soul-searching. Socrates was accused of corrupting the youth of Athens by his teaching. An Athenian jury convicted him and sentenced him to death.

One of Socrates's disciples was Plato (PLAY-toh) (c. 429–347 BCE), considered by many the greatest philosopher of Western civilization. Unlike his master Socrates, who wrote nothing, Plato wrote a great deal. He was fascinated with the question of reality: How do we know what is real? According to Plato, a higher world of eternal, unchanging Ideas or Forms has always existed. To know these Forms is to know truth. These ideal Forms constitute reality and can be apprehended only by a trained mind—which, of course, is the goal of philosophy. The objects that we perceive with our senses are simply reflections of the ideal Forms. They are shadows; reality is in the Forms themselves.

Plato's ideas of government were set out in his dialogue titled *The Republic*. Based on his experience in Athens, Plato had come to distrust the workings of democracy. It was obvious to him that individuals could not attain an ethical life unless they lived in a just and rational state. In *The Republic*, he constructed such an ideal state, in which the population was divided into three basic groups. At the top was an upper class, a ruling elite, the philosopher-kings: "Unless . . . political power and philosophy meet together . . ., there can be no rest from troubles . . . for states, nor yet, as I believe, for all mankind."[10] The second

The Axial Age

 Religion & Philosophy By the fourth century BCE, important regional civilizations existed in China, India, Southwest Asia, and the Mediterranean. During their formative periods between 700 and 300 BCE, all were characterized by the emergence of religious and philosophical thinkers who established ideas—or "axes"—that remained the basis for religions and philosophical thought in those societies for hundreds of years. Hence, some historians have referred to the period when these ideas developed as "the Axial Age."

During the fifth and fourth centuries in Greece, the philosophers Socrates, Plato, and Aristotle not only proposed philosophical and political ideas crucial to the Greek world and later to Roman and Western civilization but also conceived of a rational method of inquiry that became important to modern science. By the seventh century BCE, concepts of monotheism had developed in Persia through the teachings of Zoroaster and in Canaan through the Hebrew prophets. In Judaism, the Hebrews developed a world religion that influenced the later religions of Christianity and Islam.

During the sixth century, two major schools of thought—Confucianism and Daoism—emerged in China. Both sought to spell out the principles that would create a stable order in society. And although their views of reality were diametrically opposed, both came to have an impact on Chinese civilization that lasted into the twentieth century.

Two of the world's greatest religions, Hinduism and Buddhism, began in India during the Axial Age. Hinduism was an outgrowth of the religious beliefs of the Aryan peoples who settled in India. These ideas were expressed in the sacred texts known as the Vedas and in the Upanishads, which were commentaries on the Vedas compiled in the sixth century BCE. With its belief in reincarnation, Hinduism provided justification for India's rigid class system. Buddhism was the product of one man, Siddhartha Gautama, known as the Buddha, who lived in the sixth century BCE. The Buddha's simple message of achieving wisdom created a new spiritual philosophy that would rival Hinduism. Although a product of India, Buddhism also spread to other parts of the world.

Although these philosophies and religions developed in different areas of the world, they had some features in common. Like the Chinese philosophers Confucius and Lao Tzu, the Greek philosophers Plato and Aristotle had different ideas about the nature of reality. Thinkers in India and China also developed rational methods of inquiry similar to those of Plato and Aristotle. And regardless of their origins, when we speak of Judaism, Hinduism, Buddhism, Confucianism, Daoism, or Greek philosophical thought, we realize that the ideas of the Axial Age not only spread around the world at different times but are also still an integral part of our world today.

Q *What do historians mean when they speak of the Axial Age? What do you think could explain the emergence of similar ideas in different parts of the world during this period?*

Erich Lessing/Art Resource, NY

Philosophers in the Axial Age. This mosaic from Pompeii re-creates a gathering of Greek philosophers at the school of Plato.

group consisted of the courageous; they would be the warriors who protected the society. All the rest made up the masses, essentially people driven not by wisdom or courage but by desire. They would be the producers—the artisans, tradespeople, and farmers. Contrary to common Greek custom, Plato also believed that men and women should have the same education and equal access to all positions.

Plato established a school at Athens known as the Academy. One of his pupils, who studied there for twenty years, was Aristotle (AR-iss-tot-ul) (384–322 BCE), who later became a tutor to Alexander the Great. Aristotle did not accept Plato's theory of ideal Forms. Instead, he believed that by examining individual objects, we can perceive their form and arrive at universal principles, but these principles do not exist as a separate higher world of reality beyond material things; rather they are a part of things themselves. Aristotle's interests, then, lay in analyzing and classifying things based on thorough research and investigation. His interests were wide-ranging, and he wrote treatises on an enormous number of subjects: ethics, logic, politics, poetry, astronomy, geology, biology, and physics.

Like Plato, Aristotle wished for an effective form of government that would rationally direct human affairs. Unlike Plato, he did not seek an ideal state based on the embodiment of an ideal Form of justice but tried to find the best form of government by a rational examination of existing governments. For his *Politics*, Aristotle examined the constitutions of 158 states and arrived at general categories for organizing governments. He identified three good forms of government: monarchy, aristocracy, and constitutional government. But based on his examination, he warned that monarchy can easily turn into tyranny, aristocracy into oligarchy, and constitutional government into radical democracy or anarchy. He favored constitutional government as the best form for most people.

Aristotle's philosophical and political ideas played an enormous role in the development of Western thought during the Middle Ages (see Chapter 12). So did his ideas on women. Aristotle maintained that women were biologically inferior to men: "A woman is, as it were, an infertile male. She is female in fact on account of a kind of inadequacy." Therefore, according to Aristotle, women must be subordinated to men, not only in the community but also in marriage: "The association between husband and wife is clearly an aristocracy. The man rules by virtue of merit, and in the sphere that is his by right; but he hands over to his wife such matters as are suitable for her."[11]

4–3e Greek Religion

As was the case throughout the ancient world, religion played an important role in Greek society and was intricately connected to every aspect of daily life; it was both social and practical. Public festivals, which originated from religious practices, served specific functions: boys were prepared to be warriors, girls to be mothers. Because religion was related to every aspect of life, citizens had to have a proper attitude toward the gods. Religion was a civic cult necessary for the well-being of the state. Temples dedicated to a god or goddess were the major buildings in Greek cities.

The poetry of Homer gave an account of the gods that provided Greek religion with a definite structure. Over a period of time, all Greeks came to accept a basic polytheistic religion with twelve chief gods who supposedly lived on Mount Olympus, the highest mountain in Greece. Among the twelve were Zeus (ZOOSS), the chief deity and father of the gods; Athena, goddess of wisdom and crafts; Apollo, god of the sun and poetry; Aphrodite, goddess of love; and Poseidon, brother of Zeus and god of the seas and earthquakes. Although the twelve Olympian gods were common to all Greeks, each *polis* usually singled out one of the twelve as a guardian deity for the community. Athena was the patron goddess of Athens, for example.

Because the Greeks wanted the gods to look favorably on their activities, ritual assumed enormous proportions in Greek religion. Prayers were often combined with gifts to the gods based on the principle "I give so that you, the gods, will give in return." Ritual meant sacrifices, whether of animals or agricultural products. Animal sacrifices were burned on an altar in front of a temple or on a small altar in front of a home.

As another practical side of Greek religion, Greeks wanted to know the will of the gods. To do so, they made use of the *oracle*, a sacred shrine dedicated to a god or goddess who revealed the future. The most famous was the oracle of Apollo at Delphi, located on the side of Mount Parnassus, overlooking the Gulf of Corinth. At Delphi, a priestess listened to questions while in a state of ecstasy that was believed to be induced by Apollo. Her responses were interpreted by the priests and given in verse form to the person asking questions. Representatives of states and individuals traveled to Delphi to consult the oracle of Apollo. States might inquire whether they should undertake a military expedition; individuals might raise such questions as "Heracleidas asks whether he will have offspring from the wife he has now." Responses were often enigmatic and at times even politically motivated. Croesus (KREE-suss), the king of Lydia in Asia Minor who was known for his incredible wealth, sent messengers to the oracle at Delphi, asking whether he should go to war with the Persians. The oracle replied that if Croesus attacked the Persians, he would destroy a mighty empire. Overjoyed to hear these words, Croesus made war on the Persians but was crushed. A mighty empire was indeed destroyed—his own.

Festivals also developed as a way to honor the gods and goddesses. Some of these (the Panhellenic celebrations) came to have international significance and were held at special locations, such as those dedicated to the worship of Zeus at Olympia or to Apollo at Delphi. The great festivals incorporated numerous events in honor of the gods, including athletic competitions to which all Greeks were invited.

According to tradition, such athletic games were first held at the Olympic festival in 776 BCE and then held every four years thereafter to honor Zeus. Initially, the Olympic contests consisted of foot races and wrestling, but later boxing, javelin throwing, and various other contests were added. Competitions were always between individuals, not groups. The Greeks looked upon winning athletes as great heroes and often rewarded them with parades, as well as money and free rents for life.

Olympic games were not without danger to the participants. Athletes competed in the nude, and rules were rather relaxed. Wrestlers, for example, were allowed to gouge eyes and even pick up their competitors and bring them down head first onto a hard surface. Boxers wrapped their hands and forearms with heavy leather thongs, making their blows damaging. Some athletes were killed during the games. Given the hatred that often existed between city-states in ancient Greece, their deaths were not always accidental.

The Olympic games, combined with other all-Greek athletic games, served a valuable role. The system of Greek *poleis* had led to separation and individual goals. But participation in these games also caused Greeks to become more aware of a wider sense of community as Greeks. By the sixth century, this led to an emerging sense of Greekness. And as we have seen, the later threat from the Persians would serve to solidify this growing cultural identity.

The Greek Olympic games came to an end in 393 CE, when a Christian Roman emperor banned them as pagan exercises.

Women in Athens and Sparta

Family & Society

IN CLASSICAL ATHENS, A WOMAN'S PLACE was in the home. She had two major responsibilities as a wife—bearing and raising children and managing the household. In the first selection, from a dialogue on estate management, Xenophon (ZEN-uh-fuhn) relates the instructions of an Athenian to his new wife. Although women in Sparta had the same responsibilities as women in Athens, they assumed somewhat different roles as a result of the Spartan lifestyle. The second, third, and fourth selections demonstrate these differences as seen in the accounts of three ancient Greek writers.

Xenophon, *Oeconomicus*

[Ischomachus addresses his new wife:] For it seems to me, dear, that the gods with great discernment have coupled together male and female, as they are called, chiefly in order that they may form a perfect partnership in mutual service. For, in the first place that the various species of living creatures may not fail, they are joined in wedlock for the production of children. Secondly, offspring to support them in old age is provided by this union, to human beings, at any rate. Thirdly, human beings live not in the open air, like beasts, but obviously need shelter. Nevertheless, those who mean to win stores to fill the covered place, have need of someone to work at the open-air occupations; since plowing, sowing, planting and grazing are all such open-air employments; and

these supply the needful food. . . . For he made the man's body and mind more capable of enduring cold and heat, and journeys and campaigns; and therefore imposed on him the outdoor tasks. To the woman, since he had made her body less capable of such endurance, I take it that God has assigned the indoor tasks. And knowing that he had created in the woman and had imposed on her the nourishment of the infants, he meted out to her a larger portion of affection for newborn babes than to the man. . . .

Your duty will be to remain indoors and send out those servants whose work is outside, and superintend those who are to work indoors, and to receive the incomings, and distribute so much of them as must be spent, and watch over so much as is to be kept in store, and take care that the sum laid by for a year be not spent in a month. And when wool is brought to you, you must see that cloaks are made for those that want them. You must see too that the dry corn is in good condition for making food. One of the duties that fall to you, however, will perhaps seem rather thankless: you will have to see that any servant who is ill is cared for.

Xenophon, *Constitution of the Spartans*

First, to begin at the beginning, I will start with the begetting of children. Elsewhere those girls who are going to have children and are considered to have been well brought up are

---

Fifteen hundred years later, the games were revived through the efforts of a French baron, Pierre de Coubertin (PYAYR duh koo-ber-TANH). In 1896, the first modern Olympic games were held in Athens, Greece.

4–3f Life in Classical Athens

The *polis* was above all a male community: only adult male citizens took part in public life. In Athens, this meant the exclusion of women, slaves, and foreign residents, or roughly 85 percent of the total population in Attica. There were probably 150,000 citizens in Athens, of whom about 43,000 were adult males who exercised political power. Resident foreigners, who numbered about 35,000, received the protection of the laws but were also subject to some of the responsibilities of citizens, namely, military service and the funding of festivals. The remaining social group, the slaves, numbered around 100,000. Most slaves in Athens worked in the home as cooks and maids or toiled in the fields. Some were owned by the state and worked on public construction projects.

Economy and Lifestyle The Athenian economy was based largely on agriculture and trade. Athenians grew grains, vegetables, and

fruit for local consumption. Grapes and olives were cultivated for wine and olive oil, which were used locally and also exported. The Athenians raised sheep and goats for wool and dairy products. Because of the size of the population in Attica and the lack of abundant fertile land, Athens had to import 50 to 80 percent of its grain, a staple in the Athenian diet. Trade was thus very important to the Athenian economy. Perhaps that is one reason why the Greeks were among the first to mint silver coins.

The Athenian lifestyle was basically simple. Athenian houses were furnished with necessities bought from artisans, such as beds, couches, tables, chests, pottery, stools, baskets, and cooking utensils. Wives and slaves made clothes and blankets at home. The Athenian diet was rather plain and relied on such basic foods as barley, wheat, millet, lentils, grapes, figs, olives, almonds, bread made at home, vegetables, eggs, fish, cheese, and chicken. Olive oil was widely used, not only for eating but also for burning in lamps and rubbing on the body after washing and exercise. Although country houses kept animals, they were used for reasons other than their flesh: oxen for plowing, sheep for wool, and goats for milk and cheese.

nourished with the plainest diet which is practicable and the smallest amount of luxury good possible; wine is certainly not allowed them at all, or only if well diluted. Just as the majority of craftsmen are sedentary, the other Greeks expect their girls to sit quietly and work wool. But how can one expect girls brought up like this to give birth to healthy babies? Lycurgus (see Section 4-2d, p. 104) considered slave girls quite adequate to produce clothing, and thought that for free women the most important job was to bear children. In the first place, therefore, he prescribed physical training for the female sex no less than for the male; and next, just as for men, he arranged competitions of racing and strength for women also, thinking that if both parents were strong their children would be more robust.

Aristotle, *Politics*

Now, this license of the [Spartan] women, from the earliest times, was to be expected. For the men were absent from home for long periods of time on military expeditions. . . . And nearly two-fifths of the whole country is in the hands of women, both because there have been numerous heiresses, and because large dowries are customary. And yet it would have been better to have regulated them, and given none at all or small or even moderate ones. But at present it is possible for a man to give an inheritance to whomever he chooses.

Plutarch, *Lycurgus*

Since Lycurgus regarded education as the most important and finest duty of the legislator, he began at the earliest stage by looking at matters relating to marriages and births. . . . For he exercised the girls' bodies with races and wrestling and discus and javelin throwing, so that the embryos formed in them would have a strong start in strong bodies and develop better, and they would undergo their pregnancies with vigor and would cope well and easily with childbirth. He got rid of daintiness and sheltered upbringing and effeminacy of all kinds, by accustoming the girls no less than the young men to walking naked in processions and dancing and singing at certain festivals, when young men were present and watching. . . . The nudity of the girls had nothing disgraceful in it for modesty was present and immorality absent, but rather it made them accustomed to simplicity and enthusiastic as to physical fitness, and gave the female sex a taste of noble spirit, in as much as they too had a share in valor and ambition.

 In what ways were the lifestyles of Athenian and Spartan women the same? In what ways were they different? How did the Athenian and Spartan views of the world shape their conceptions of gender and gender roles, and why were those conceptions different?

Sources: From Xenophon: *Oeconomicus*, in *Xenophon, Memorabilia and Oeconomicus*, Volume IV, Loeb Classical Library 168, translated by E. C. Marchant (Cambridge, Mass.: Harvard University Press, 1923) The Loeb Classical Library is a registered trademark of the President and Fellows of Harvard College; Xenophon, *Constitution of the Spartans*, From *Ancient Greece: Social and Historical Documents from Archaic Times to the Death of Socrates*, edited by Matthew Dillon and Lynda Garland (London: Routledge, 1994) pp. 393–95. Copyright 1994 Matthew and Lynda Garland; From Aristotle, *A Treatise on Government*, trans. William Ellis (J. M. Dent & Sons Ltd.: London, 1912), p. 1270a; From *Ideal Commonwealths: Plutarch's Lycurgus*, 5th ed., edited by Henry Morley (George Rutledge and Sons, Limited, London, 1890).

Family and Relationships The family was a central institution in ancient Athens. It was composed of husband, wife, and children (a nuclear family), although other dependent relatives and slaves were regarded as part of the family economic unit. The family's primary social function was to produce new citizens. Strict laws enacted in the fifth century stipulated that a citizen must be the offspring of a legally acknowledged marriage between two Athenian citizens whose parents were also citizens.

Adult female citizens could participate in most religious cults and festivals but were otherwise excluded from public life. They could not own property beyond personal items and always had a male guardian. An Athenian woman was expected to be a good wife. Her foremost obligation was to bear children, especially male children who would preserve the family line. A wife was also to take care of her family and her house, either doing the household work herself or supervising the slaves who did the actual work (see Opposing Viewpoints "Women in Athens and Sparta").

Women were kept under strict control. Because they were married at fourteen or fifteen, they were taught about their responsibilities at an early age. Although many managed to learn to read and play musical instruments, they were not given any formal education. And women were expected to remain at home out of sight unless attending funerals or festivals. If they left the house, they were to be accompanied. A woman working alone in public was either poverty-stricken or not a citizen.

Male homosexuality was also a prominent feature of Athenian life. The Greek homosexual ideal was a relationship between a mature man and a young male. It is most likely that this was an aristocratic ideal and not one practiced by the common people. While the relationship was frequently physical, the Greeks also viewed it as educational. The older male (the "lover") won the love of his "beloved" through his value as a teacher and the devotion he demonstrated in training his charge. In a sense, this love relationship was seen as a way of initiating young males into the male world of political and military dominance. The Greeks did not feel that the coexistence of homosexual and heterosexual predilections created any special problems for individuals or their society.

Women in the Loom Room. In Athens, women were citizens and could participate in religious cults and festivals, but they had no rights and were barred from political activity. Women were thought to belong in the house, caring for the children and the needs of the household. A principal activity of Greek women was the making of clothes. This vase shows two women working on a warp-weighted loom.

 4–4 THE RISE OF MACEDONIA AND THE CONQUESTS OF ALEXANDER

Focus Question: How was Alexander the Great able to amass his empire, and what was his legacy?

While the Greek city-states were continuing to fight each other, to their north a new and ultimately powerful kingdom was emerging in its own right. Its people, the Macedonians, were mostly rural folk, organized in tribes, not city-states, and were viewed as barbarians by their southern neighbors, the Greeks. Not until the end of the fifth century BCE did Macedonia emerge as an important kingdom. But when Philip II (359–336 BCE) came to the throne, he built an efficient army and turned Macedonia into the strongest power of the Greek world—one that was soon drawn into the conflicts among the Greeks.

The Athenians at last took notice of the new contender. Fear of Philip led them to ally with a number of other Greek

states and confront the Macedonians at the Battle of Chaeronea (ker-uh-NEE-uh), near Thebes, in 338 BCE. The Macedonian army crushed the Greeks, and Philip was now free to consolidate his control over the Greek peninsula. The Greek states were joined together in an alliance that we call the Corinthian League because they met at Corinth. All members took an oath of loyalty: "I swear by Zeus, Earth, Sun, Poseidon, Athena, Ares, and all the gods and goddesses. I will abide by the peace, and I will not break the agreements with Philip the Macedonian, nor will I take up arms with hostile intent against any one of those who abide by the oaths either by land or by sea."[12] Philip insisted that the Greek states end their bitter rivalries and cooperate with him in a war against Persia. Before Philip could undertake his invasion of Asia, however, he was assassinated, leaving the task to his son Alexander.

4–4a Alexander the Great

Alexander was only twenty when he became king of Macedonia. He had in many ways been prepared to rule by his father, who had taken Alexander along on military campaigns and had given him control of the cavalry at the important battle of

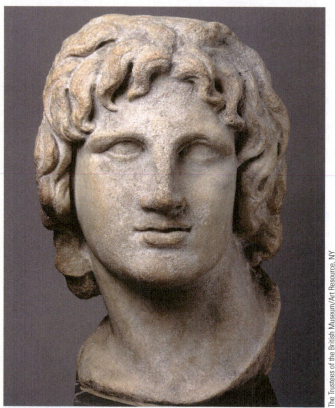

Alexander the Great. This marble head of Alexander the Great was made in the second or first century BCE. The long hair and tilt of his head reflect the description of Alexander in the literary sources of the time. Alexander claimed to be descended from Heracles, a Greek hero worshiped as a god, and when he proclaimed himself pharaoh of Egypt, he gained recognition as a living deity. It is reported that one statue, now lost, showed Alexander gazing at Zeus. At the base of the statue were the words "I place the earth under my sway; you, O Zeus, keep Olympus."

Chaeronea. After his father's assassination, Alexander moved quickly to assert his authority, securing the Macedonian frontiers and smothering a rebellion in Greece. He then turned to his father's dream, the invasion of the Persian Empire.

Alexander's Conquests There is no doubt that Alexander was taking a chance in attacking the Persian Empire, which was still a strong state. In the spring of 334 BCE, Alexander entered Asia Minor with an army of 37,000 men. About half were Macedonians, the rest Greeks and other allies. The cavalry, which would play an important role as a strike force, numbered about 5,000.

Alexander's first confrontation with the Persians, at a battle at the Granicus River in 334 BCE, almost cost him his life but resulted in a major victory. By the following spring, the entire western half of Asia Minor was in Alexander's hands (see Map 4.4). Meanwhile, the Persian king, Darius III, mobilized his forces to stop Alexander's army. Although the Persian troops outnumbered Alexander's, the Battle of Issus (ISS-uss) was fought on a narrow field that canceled the advantage of superior numbers and resulted in another Macedonian success.

After his victory at Issus in 333 BCE, Alexander turned south, and by the winter of 332, Syria, Palestine, and Egypt were under his domination. He took the traditional title of pharaoh of Egypt and founded the first of a series of cities named after him (Alexandria) as the Greek administrative capital of Egypt. It became (and remains today) one of the most important cities in Egypt and in the Mediterranean world.

In 331 BCE, Alexander renewed his offensive, moved into the territory of the ancient Mesopotamian kingdoms, and fought a decisive battle with the Persians at Gaugamela (gaw-guh-MEE-luh), northwest of Babylon. After his victory, Alexander entered Babylon and then proceeded to the Persian capitals at Susa and Persepolis, where he acquired the Persian treasuries and took possession of vast quantities of gold and silver. By 330, Alexander was again on the march, pursuing Darius. After Darius was killed by one of his own men, Alexander took the title and office of Great King of the Persians.

But Alexander was not content to rest with the spoils of the Persian Empire. Over the next three years, he moved east and northeast, as far as modern Pakistan. By the summer of 327 BCE, he had entered India, which at that time was divided

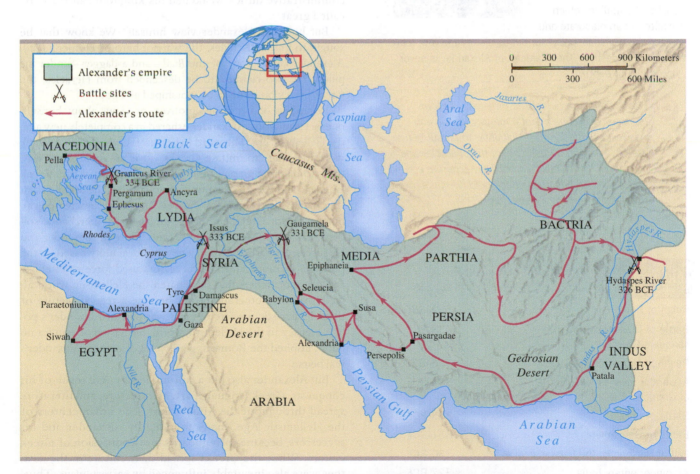

Map 4.4 The Conquests of Alexander the Great. In just twelve years, Alexander the Great conquered vast territories. Dominating lands from west of the Nile to east of the Indus, he brought the Persian Empire, Egypt, and much of the Middle East under his control.

Q *Approximately how far did Alexander and his troops travel during those twelve years?*

into a number of warring states. In 326 BCE, Alexander and his armies arrived in the plains of northwestern India. At the Battle of the Hydaspes River, Alexander won a brutally fought battle. When Alexander made clear his determination to march east to conquer more of India, his soldiers, weary of campaigning year after year, mutinied and refused to go on. Reluctantly, Alexander turned back, leading his men across the arid lands of southern Persia. Conditions in the desert were appalling; the blazing sun and lack of water led to thousands of deaths before Alexander and his remaining troops reached Babylon. Alexander planned still more campaigns, but in June 323 BCE, weakened from wounds, fever, and probably excessive alcohol consumption, he died at the age of thirty-two (see Film & History).

⊘ FILM & HISTORY

Watch *Alexander* (2004), a product of director Oliver Stone's lifelong fascination with Alexander. His epic film cost $150 million, which resulted in an elaborate and a stunningly visual spectacle, but as history the film leaves much to be desired. The character of Alexander is never developed in depth.

Q *Was Alexander an idealistic dreamer, as Stone believes, or was he a brutal military leader who was responsible for mass slaughter in pursuing his dream? What do we learn about the character and sexual practices of Alexander? How accurate are the battle scenes? What objection could be made about the depiction of the Persian forces?*

CHRONOLOGY	The Rise of Macedonia and the Conquests of Alexander
Reign of Philip II	359–336 BCE
Battle of Chaeronea; Philip II conquers Greece	338 BCE
Reign of Alexander the Great	336–323 BCE
Alexander invades Asia; Battle of Granicus River	334 BCE
Battle of Issus	333 BCE
Battle of Gaugamela	331 BCE
Fall of Persepolis, the Persian capital	330 BCE
Alexander enters India	327 BCE
Battle of Hydaspes River	326 BCE
Death of Alexander	323 BCE

The Legacy: Was Alexander Great? Alexander is one of the most puzzling significant figures in history (see "The Character of Alexander"). Historians relying on the same sources draw vastly different pictures of him. For some, his military ability, extensive conquests, and creation of a new empire alone justify calling him Alexander the Great. Other historians also praise Alexander's love of Greek culture and his intellectual brilliance, especially in matters of warfare. In the lands that he conquered, Alexander attempted to fuse the Macedonians, Greeks, and Persians into a new ruling class. Did he do this because he was an idealistic visionary who believed in a concept of universal humanity, as some suggest? Or was he merely trying to bolster his power and create an autocratic monarchy?

Those historians who see Alexander as aspiring to autocratic monarchy present a very different portrait of him as a ruthless Machiavellian. One has titled his biography *Alexander the Great Failure*. These critics ask whether a man who slaughtered indigenous peoples, who risked the lives of his soldiers for his own selfish reasons, whose fierce temper led him to kill his friends, and whose neglect of administrative duties weakened his kingdom can really be called great.

But how did Alexander view himself? We know that he sought to imitate Achilles, the warrior-hero of Homer's *Iliad*. Alexander kept a copy of the *Iliad*—and a dagger—under his pillow. He also claimed to be descended from Heracles, the Greek hero who came to be worshiped as a god.

Regardless of his ideals, motives, or views about himself, one fact stands out: Alexander ushered in a completely new age, the Hellenistic era. The word *Hellenistic* is derived from a Greek word meaning "to imitate Greeks." It is an appropriate way, then, to describe an age that saw the extension of the Greek language and ideas to the non-Greek world of the Middle East. Alexander's destruction of the Persian monarchy created opportunities for Greek engineers, intellectuals, merchants, soldiers, and administrators. Those who followed Alexander and his successors participated in a new political unity based on the principle of monarchy. His successors used force to establish military monarchies that dominated the Hellenistic world after his death. Autocratic power became a regular feature of those Hellenistic monarchies and was part of Alexander's political legacy to the Hellenistic world. His vision of empire no doubt inspired the Romans, who were, of course, Alexander's real heirs.

But Alexander also left a cultural legacy. As a result of his conquests, Greek language, art, architecture, and literature spread throughout the Middle East. The urban centers of the Hellenistic Age, many founded by Alexander and his successors, became springboards for the diffusion of Greek culture. While the Greeks spread their culture in the east, they were also inevitably influenced by eastern ways. Thus, Alexander's legacy included one of the basic characteristics of the Hellenistic world: the clash and fusion of different cultures.

THE CHARACTER OF ALEXANDER

Politics & Government Arrian (c. 86–c. 160) was a Greek historian and Roman citizen in Bithynia. He wrote the *Anabasis of Alexander*, a historical account of Alexander's military campaigns. In this excerpt from the work, he discusses the character of Alexander. He was obviously an admirer of the great conqueror.

Arrian, *The Anabasis of Alexander*

Alexander . . . lived thirty-two years, and had reached the eighth month of his thirty-third year. He had reigned twelve years and these eight months. He was very handsome in person, and much devoted to exertion. He was very active in mind, very heroic in courage, very tenacious of honor, exceedingly fond of incurring danger, and strictly observant of his duty to the gods. In regard to the pleasures of the body, he had perfect self-control; and of those of the mind, praise was the only one of which he was insatiable. . . . In marshaling, equipping, and ruling an army, he was exceedingly skillful. He was very renowned for rousing the courage of his soldiers, filling them with hopes of success, and dispelling their fear in the midst of danger by his own freedom from fear. Therefore, even what he had to in uncertainty of the result, he did with greatest boldness. . . .

That Alexander should have committed errors in conduct from impetuosity or from wrath, and that he should have been induced to act like the Persian monarchs to an immoderate degree, I do not think remarkable, if we fairly consider both his youth and his uninterrupted career of good fortune. . . . However, I am certain that Alexander was the only one of the ancient kings who, from nobility of character, repented of the errors which he had committed . . . I do not think that even Alexander's tracing his origin to a god was a great error on his part, if it was not perhaps merely a device to induce his subjects to show him reverence. . . . His adoption of the Persian mode of dressing also seems to me to have been a political device in regard to the foreigners, that the king might not appear altogether alien to them; and in regard to the Macedonians, to show them that he had a refuge from their rashness of temper and insolence. . . . Aristobulus also asserts that Alexander used to have long drinking parties, not for the purpose of enjoying the wine, as he was not a great wine-drinker, but in order to exhibit his sociability and friendly feeling to his companions.

Whoever, therefore, reproaches Alexander as a bad man, let him do so; but let him first not only bring before his mind all his actions deserving reproach, but also gather into one view all his deeds of every kind. Then, indeed, let him reflect. . .who that man was whom he reproaches as bad, and to what a height of human success he attained, becoming without any dispute a king of both continents and reaching every place by his fame. . . . For my own part, I think there was at that time no race of men, no city, or even a single individual to whom Alexander's name and fame had not penetrated. For this reason it seems to me that a hero, totally unlike any other human being, could not have been born without the agency of the gods. . . .

 What is Arrian's opinion of Alexander? Why do you think he was so praiseworthy of Alexander's character?

Source: From *The Campaigns of Alexander* by Arrian, translated by Aubrey de Selincourt. Viking Press, 1976.

4–5 THE WORLD OF THE HELLENISTIC KINGDOMS

 Focus Question: How did the political, economic, and social institutions of the Hellenistic world differ from those of Classical Greece?

The united empire that Alexander created by his conquests disintegrated after his death. All too soon, Macedonian military leaders were engaged in a struggle for power, and by 301 BCE, all hope of unity was dead.

4–5a Hellenistic Monarchies

Eventually, four major Hellenistic kingdoms emerged as the successors to Alexander (see Map 4.5). In Macedonia, the struggle for power led to the extermination of Alexander the Great's dynasty. Not until 276 BCE did Antigonus Gonatus (an-TIG-oh-nuss guh-NAH-tuss), the grandson of one of Alexander's generals, succeed in establishing the Antigonid (an-TIG-uh-nid) dynasty as rulers of Macedonia and Greece. Another Hellenistic kingdom emerged in Egypt, where a Macedonian general named Ptolemy (TAHL-uh-mee) established himself as king in 305 BCE, initiating the Ptolemaic (tahl-uh-MAY-ik) dynasty of pharaohs. A third Hellenistic kingdom came into being in 230 BCE when Attalus I declared himself king of Pergamum (PURR-guh-mum) in Asia Minor and established the Attalid (AT-uh-lid) dynasty.

The Seleucid Kingdom and India By far the largest of the Hellenistic kingdoms was founded by the general Seleucus (suh-LOO-kuss), who established the Seleucid dynasty of Syria, which controlled much of the old Persian Empire from Turkey in the west to India in the east. The Seleucids, however, found it increasingly difficult to maintain control of the eastern territories. In fact, the Indian ruler Chandragupta Maurya (chun-druh-GOOP-tuh MOWR-yuh) created a new Indian state, the

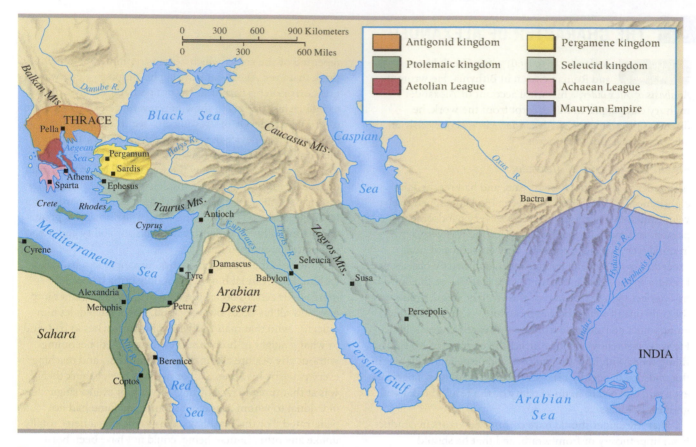

Map 4.5 The World of the Hellenistic Kingdoms. Alexander died unexpectedly at the age of thirty-two and did not designate a successor. After his death, his generals struggled for power, eventually establishing monarchies that spread Hellenistic culture and fostered trade and economic development.

 Which Hellenistic kingdom encompassed most of the old Persian Empire?

Mauryan Empire, in 324 BCE (see Chapter 2) and drove out the Seleucid forces. His grandson Ashoka (uh-SHOH-kuh) extended the empire to include most of India. A pious Buddhist, Ashoka sought to convert the remaining Greek communities in northwestern India to his religion and even sent Buddhist missionaries to Greek rulers.

The Seleucid rulers maintained relations with the Mauryan Empire. Trade was fostered, especially in such luxuries as spices and jewels. Seleucus also sent Greek and Macedonian ambassadors to the Mauryan court. Best known of these was Megasthenes (muh-GAS-thuh-neez), whose report on the people of India remained one of the West's best sources of information until the Middle Ages.

4–5b Political Institutions

The Hellenistic monarchies created a semblance of stability for several centuries, even though Hellenistic kings refused to accept the status quo and periodically engaged in wars to alter it. At the same time, an underlying strain always existed between the new Greco-Macedonian ruling class and the native populations. Together these factors created a certain degree of tension that was never truly ended until the Roman state to the west stepped in and imposed a new order.

Although Alexander the Great had apparently planned to fuse Greeks and easterners—he used Persians as administrators, encouraged his soldiers to marry easterners, and did so himself—Hellenistic monarchs who succeeded him relied primarily on Greeks and Macedonians to form the new ruling class. Even those easterners who did advance to important administrative posts had learned Greek (all government business was transacted in Greek). This often required alienation from one's own culture. Some were willing to do so, since Greekness meant power, giving incentive to local people to become Hellenized in a cultural sense. The policy of excluding non-Greeks from leadership positions was due not to the incompetence of the natives but to the determination of the Greek ruling class to maintain its privileged position. It was the Greco-Macedonian ruling class that provided the only unity in the Hellenistic world.

4–5c Hellenistic Cities

Cities played an especially important role in the Hellenistic kingdoms. Throughout his conquests, Alexander had founded new cities and military settlements, and Hellenistic kings did likewise. The new population centers varied considerably in size and importance. Military settlements were meant to maintain

RELATIONS BETWEEN GREEKS AND NON-GREEKS

Politics & Government

THE RELATIONSHIP BETWEEN THE GREEK CONQUERORS and the native peoples of the Near East was often a difficult one. Although a number of native people learned Greek to advance their economic and political careers, they were often not treated as equals by the dominant Greek minority. The following documents reveal two facets of the problem. The first one is by a native complaining about his treatment by the Greeks. The second document reveals the dangers Greeks sometimes experienced from local peoples.

Letter to Zenon

To Zenon, greeting. You do well if you are healthy. I too am well. You know that you left me in Syria with Krotos and I did everything that was ordered with respect to the camels and was blameless towards you. When you sent an order to give me pay, he gave nothing of what you ordered. When I asked repeatedly that he give me what you ordered and Krotos gave me nothing, but kept telling me to remove myself. . . . So I wrote to you that you might know that Krotos was the cause of it. When you sent me again to Philadelphia to Jason, although I do everything that is ordered, for nine months now he gives me nothing of what you ordered me to have, neither oil nor grain. . . . And I am toiling away both summer and winter. And he orders me to accept sour wine for my ration. Well, they have treated me with scorn because I am a "barbarian." I beg you therefore, if it seems good to you, to give them orders that I am to obtain what is owing and that in future they pay me in full, in order that I may not perish of hunger because I do not know how to speak Greek.

Letter to Dionysios

To Dionysios from Ptolemaios. . . . Being outrageously wronged and often put in danger of my life by the below-listed cleaners from the sanctuary, I am seeking refuge with you thinking that I shall thus particularly receive justice. For in the 21st year, they came to the sanctuary, in which I have been for the aforesaid years, some of them holding stones in their hands, others sticks, and tried to force their way in, so that with this opportunity they might plunder the temple and kill me because I am a Greek, attacking me in concerted fashion. And when I made it to the door of the temple before them and shut it with a great crash, and ordered them to go away quietly, they did not depart; but they struck Diphilos, one of the servants, who showed his indignation at the way they were behaving in the sanctuary, robbing him outrageously and attacking him violently and beating him, so that their illegal violence was made obvious to everybody.

 What do these documents reveal about the problems that arise in the relationship between conquerors and the conquered?

Source: From Roger S. Bagnall and Peter Derow, editors, *The Hellenistic Period* (Oxford: Blackwell Publishing, 2004), pp. 230–231, 232.

---

order and might consist of only a few hundred men strongly dependent on the king. But there were also new independent cities with thousands of inhabitants. Alexandria in Egypt was the largest city in the Mediterranean region by the first century BCE. Seleucus was especially active in founding new cities, according to one ancient writer:

> The other kings have exulted in destroying existing cities; he, on the other hand, arranged to build cities which did not yet exist. He established so many . . . that they were enough to carry the names of towns in Macedonia as well as the names of those in his family. . . . One can go to Phoenicia to see his cities; one can go to Syria and see even more.[13]

Hellenistic rulers encouraged a massive spread of Greek colonists to the Middle East because of their intrinsic value to the new monarchies. Greeks (and Macedonians) provided not only recruits for the army but also a pool of civilian administrators and workers who contributed to economic development. Even architects, engineers, dramatists, and actors were in demand in the new Greek cities. Many Greeks and Macedonians were quick to see the advantages of moving to the new urban centers and gladly sought their fortunes in the Middle East. The Greek cities of the Hellenistic era were the chief agents in the spread of Greek culture in the Middle East—as far, in fact, as modern Afghanistan and India.

The Greeks' belief in their own cultural superiority provided an easy rationalization for their political dominance of the eastern cities (see "Relations Between Greeks and Non-Greeks"). But Greek control of the new cities was also necessary because the kings frequently used the cities as instruments of government, enabling them to rule considerable territory without an extensive bureaucracy. At the same time, for security reasons, the Greeks needed the support of the kings. After all, the Hellenistic cities were islands of Greek culture in a sea of non-Greeks.

4–5d The Importance of Trade

Agriculture was still of primary importance to both the native populations and the new Greek cities of the Hellenistic world. The Greek cities continued their old agrarian patterns. A well defined citizen body owned land and worked it with the assistance of slaves. But these farms were isolated units in a vast area of land ultimately owned by the king or assigned to large estate owners and worked by native peasants dwelling in villages.

Commerce expanded considerably in the Hellenistic era. Indeed, trading contacts linked much of the Hellenistic world.

The decline in the number of political barriers encouraged more commercial traffic. Although Hellenistic monarchs still fought wars, the conquests of Alexander and the policies of his successors made possible greater trade between east and west. Two major trade routes connected the east with the Mediterranean. The major route proceeded by sea from India to the Persian Gulf and then up the Tigris River to Seleucia on the Tigris. Overland routes from Seleucia then led to Antioch and Ephesus. A southern route also began by sea from India but went around Arabia and up the Red Sea to Petra and later Berenice. Caravan routes then led overland to Coptos on the Nile, thence to Alexandria and the Mediterranean.

An incredible variety of products were traded: gold and silver from Spain; salt from Asia Minor; timber from Macedonia; ebony, gems, ivory, and spices from India; frankincense (used on altars) from Arabia; slaves from Thrace, Syria, and Asia Minor; fine wines from Syria and western Asia Minor; olive oil from Athens; and numerous exquisite foodstuffs, such as the famous prunes of Damascus. The greatest trade, however, was in the basic staple of life—grain.

4–5e Social Life: New Opportunities for Women

The development of the kingdom as the focus of political life in the Hellenistic era resulted in fewer restrictions on the role of women. In many cities, for example, women of all classes had a new freedom of movement. However, the most notable gains, especially for upper-class women, came in the economic realm. Documents show increasing numbers of women involved in managing slaves, selling property, and making loans. Even then, legal contracts made by women had to include their official male guardians. Only in Sparta were women free to control their own economic affairs. Many Spartan women were noticeably wealthy; females owned 40 percent of Spartan land.

Spartan women, however, were an exception, especially on the Greek mainland. Women in Athens, for example, still remained highly restricted and supervised. Although a few philosophers welcomed female participation in men's affairs, many philosophers rejected equality between men and women and asserted that the traditional roles of wives and mothers were most satisfying for women. And although they were now less restricted, peasant women experienced no real benefit from this freedom because they were still subject to a lifetime of hard work. The large group of women who were condemned to the practice of prostitution faced an even harsher reality.

But the opinions of philosophers did not prevent upper-class women from making gains in areas other than the economic sphere. New possibilities for females arose when women in some areas of the Hellenistic world were allowed to pursue education in the traditional fields of literature, music, and even athletics. Education, then, provided new opportunities for women: female poets appeared in the third century BCE, and there are instances of women involved in both scholarly and artistic activities.

The creation of the Hellenistic monarchies, which represented a considerable departure from the world of the city-state, also gave new scope to the role played by the monarchs' wives, the Hellenistic queens. In Macedonia, a pattern of alliances between mothers and sons provided openings for women to take an active role in politics, especially in political intrigue. In Egypt, opportunities for royal women were even greater because the Ptolemaic rulers reverted to an Egyptian custom of kings marrying their own sisters. Of the first eight Ptolemaic rulers, four wed their sisters. Ptolemy II and his sister-wife Arsinoë (ahr-SIN-oh-ee) II were both worshiped as gods in their lifetimes. Arsinoë played an energetic role in government and was involved in the expansion of the Egyptian navy. She was also the first Egyptian queen whose portrait appeared on coins with that of her husband.

4–5f Culture in the Hellenistic World

Although the Hellenistic kingdoms encompassed vast territories and many diverse peoples, the diffusion of Greek culture throughout the Hellenistic world provided a sense of unity. The Hellenistic era was a period of considerable accomplishment in many areas—literature, art, science, and philosophy. Although these achievements occurred throughout the Hellenistic world, certain centers, especially the great cities of Alexandria and Pergamum, stood out. In both cities, the rulers themselves encouraged cultural developments. Rich Hellenistic monarchs had considerable resources with which to patronize culture.

New Directions in Literature and Art The Hellenistic Age produced an enormous quantity of literature, most of which has not survived. Hellenistic monarchs, who held literary talent in high esteem, subsidized writers on a grand scale. The Ptolemaic rulers of Egypt were particularly lavish. The combination of their largesse and a famous library with more than 500,000 scrolls drew a host of scholars and authors to Alexandria, including a circle of poets. Theocritus (thee-AHK-ruh-tuss) (c. 315–250 BCE), originally a native of the island of Sicily, wrote "little poems" known as *idylls* dealing with erotic subjects, lovers' complaints, and pastoral themes expressing love of nature and appreciation of nature's beauties.

In the Hellenistic era, Athens remained the theatrical center of the Greek world. Tragedy had fallen by the wayside, but a new style of comedy came to the fore. New Comedy completely rejected political themes and sought only to entertain and amuse. The Athenian playwright Menander (muh-NAN-dur) (c. 342–291 BCE) was perhaps the best representative of New Comedy. Plots were simple: typically, a hero falls in love with a not-really-so-bad prostitute, who turns out eventually to be the long-lost daughter of a rich neighbor. The hero marries her, and they live happily ever after.

In addition to being patrons of literary talent, the Hellenistic monarchs were eager to spend their money to beautify and adorn the cities within their states. The founding of new cities and the rebuilding of old ones provided numerous opportunities for Greek architects and sculptors. The buildings of the Greek homeland—gymnasia, baths, theaters, and, of course, temples—lined the streets of these cities.

Both Hellenistic monarchs and rich citizens patronized sculptors. Thousands of statues, many paid for by the people honored, were erected in towns and cities all over the Hellenistic world. Sculptors traveled throughout this world, attracted

COMPARATIVE ILLUSTRATION

Art & Ideas

Hellenistic Sculpture and a Greek-Style Buddha. Greek architects and sculptors were highly valued throughout the Hellenistic world. Shown in A is a terra-cotta statuette of a draped young woman, made as a tomb offering near Thebes, probably around 300 BCE. The incursion of Alexander into western India resulted in some Greek cultural influences there, especially during the Hellenistic era. During the first century BCE, Indian sculptors in Gandhara, which today is part of Pakistan, began to make statues of the Buddha in a style that combined Indian and Hellenistic artistic traditions, as in the stone sculpture of the Buddha in B. Note the wavy hair topped by a bun tied with a ribbon, also a feature of earlier statues of Greek deities. This Buddha is also seen wearing a Greek-style toga.

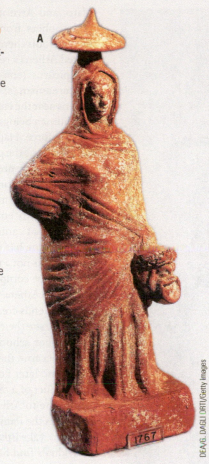

A

B

DEA/G. DAGLI ORTI/Getty Images

Borromeo/Art Resource, NY

Q *How do you explain the influence of Hellenistic styles in India? What can you conclude from this example about the influence of conquerors on conquered people?*

---

by the material rewards offered by wealthy patrons. As a result, Hellenistic sculpture was characterized by a considerable degree of uniformity. Hellenistic artistic styles even affected artists in India (see Comparative Illustration "Hellenistic Sculpture and a Greek-Style Buddha"). While maintaining the technical skill of the Classical period, Hellenistic sculptors moved away from the idealism of fifth-century classicism to a more emotional and realistic art, seen in numerous statues of old women, drunkards, and little children at play.

A Golden Age of Science The Hellenistic era witnessed a more conscious separation of science from philosophy. In Classical Greece, what we would call the physical and life sciences had been divisions of philosophical inquiry. Nevertheless, by the time of Aristotle, the Greeks had already established an important principle of scientific investigation: empirical research, or systematic observation as the basis for generalization. In the Hellenistic Age, the sciences tended to be studied in their own right.

One of the traditional areas of Greek science was astronomy, and two Alexandrian scholars continued this exploration. Aristarchus (ar-iss-TAR-kus) of Samos (c. 310–230 BCE) developed a *heliocentric* view of the universe, contending that the sun and

the fixed stars remain stationary while the earth rotates around the sun in a circular orbit. He also argued that the earth rotates around its own axis. This view was not widely accepted, and most scholars clung to the earlier *geocentric* view of the Greeks, which held that the earth was at the center of the universe. Another astronomer, Eratosthenes (er-uh-TAHSS-thuh-neez) (c. 275–194 BCE), determined that the earth was round and calculated its circumference at 24,675 miles—within 200 miles of the actual figure.

A third Alexandrian scholar was Euclid (YOO-klid), who lived around 300 BCE. He established a school in Alexandria but is primarily known for his work titled *Elements*. This was a systematic organization of the fundamental elements of geometry as they had already been worked out; it became the standard textbook of plane geometry and was used up to modern times.

By far the most famous scientist of the period was Archimedes (ahr-kuh-MEE-deez) (287–212 BCE) of Syracuse. Archimedes was especially important for his work on the geometry of spheres and cylinders and for establishing the value of the mathematical constant pi. Archimedes was also a practical inventor. He may have devised the so-called Archimedean screw, used to pump water out of mines and to lift irrigation water. During the Roman siege of Syracuse, he constructed a number

Vanni Archive/Art Resource, NY

Drunken Old Woman. Unlike the Greek sculptors of the Classical era, Hellenistic sculptors no longer tried to capture ideal beauty in their sculptures but moved toward a more emotional and realistic art. This statue of a drunken old woman is typical of this new trend in art. Old and haggard, mired in poverty, she struggles just to go on living.

of devices to thwart the attackers. According to Plutarch's account, the Romans became so frightened "that if they did but see a little rope or a piece of wood from the wall, instantly crying out, that there it was again, Archimedes was about to let fly some engine at them, they turned their backs and fled."[14] Archimedes's accomplishments inspired a wealth of semi-legendary stories. Supposedly, he discovered specific gravity by observing the water he displaced in his bath and became so excited by his realization that he jumped out of the water and ran home naked, shouting, "Eureka!" ("I have found it!"). He is said to have emphasized the importance of levers by proclaiming to the king of Syracuse, "Give me a lever and a place to stand, and I will move the earth." The king was so impressed that he encouraged Archimedes to lower his sights and build defensive weapons instead.

Philosophy: New Schools of Thought While Alexandria and Pergamum became the renowned cultural centers of the Hellenistic world, Athens remained the prime center for philosophy. After Alexander the Great, the home of Socrates,

Plato, and Aristotle continued to attract the most illustrious philosophers from the Greek world, who chose to establish their schools there. New schools of philosophical thought reinforced Athens's reputation as a philosophical center.

Epicurus (ep-i-KYOOR-uss) (341–270 BCE), the founder of **Epicureanism** (ep-i-kyoo-REE-uh-ni-zum), established a school in Athens near the end of the fourth century BCE. Epicurus believed that human beings were free to follow self-interest as a basic motivating force. Happiness was the goal of life, and the means to achieve it was the pursuit of pleasure, the only true good. But the pursuit of pleasure was not meant in a physical, hedonistic sense (as our word *epicurean* has come to mean). Pleasure was not satisfying one's desire in an active, gluttonous fashion but rather freedom from emotional turmoil, freedom from worry—the freedom that came from a mind at rest. To achieve this kind of pleasure, one had to free oneself from public affairs and politics. But this was not a renunciation of all social life, for to Epicurus, a life could be complete only when it was based on friendship. His own life in Athens was an embodiment of his teachings. Epicurus and his friends created their own private community where they could pursue their ideal of true happiness.

Another school of thought was **Stoicism** (STOH-i-siz-um), which became the most popular philosophy of the Hellenistic world and later flourished in the Roman Empire as well. It was the product of a teacher named Zeno (ZEE-noh) (335–263 BCE), who came to Athens and began to teach in a public colonnade known as the Painted Portico (the *Stoa Poikile*—hence the name *Stoicism*). Like Epicureanism, Stoicism was concerned with how individuals find happiness. But Stoics took a radically different approach to the problem. To them, happiness, the supreme good, could be found only by living in harmony with the divine will, by which people gained inner peace. Life's problems could not disturb these people, and they could bear whatever life offered (hence our word *stoic*). Unlike Epicureans, Stoics did not believe in the need to separate oneself from the world and politics. Public service was regarded as noble, and the real Stoic was a good citizen and could even be a good government official.

Both Epicureanism and Stoicism focused primarily on human happiness, and their popularity would suggest a fundamental change in the Greek lifestyle. In the Classical Greek world, the happiness of individuals and the meaning of life were closely associated with the life of the *polis*. One found fulfillment in the community. In the Hellenistic kingdoms, the sense that one could find satisfaction and fulfillment through life in the *polis* had weakened. People sought new philosophies that offered personal happiness, and in the cosmopolitan world of the Hellenistic states, with their mixture of peoples, a new openness to thoughts of universality could also emerge. For some people, Stoicism embodied this larger sense of community. The appeal of new philosophies in the Hellenistic era can also be explained by the apparent decline in certain aspects of traditional religion.

Religion in the Hellenistic World When the Greeks spread throughout the Hellenistic kingdoms, they took their gods with them. But over a period of time, there was a noticeable decline in the vitality of the traditional Greek religion, which left Greeks receptive to the numerous religious cults of the eastern world. The eastern religions that appealed most to Greeks, however, were the **mystery religions**. What was the source of their attraction?

Mystery cults, with their secret initiations and promises of individual salvation, were not new to the Greek world. But the Greeks of the Hellenistic era were also strongly influenced by eastern mystery cults, such as those of Egypt, which offered a distinct advantage over the Greek mystery religions. The latter had usually been connected to specific locations (such as Eleusis), which meant that a would-be initiate had to undertake a pilgrimage in order to participate in the rites. In contrast, the eastern mystery religions were readily available since temples to their gods and goddesses were located throughout the Greek cities of the east. All of the mystery religions were based on the same fundamental premises. Individuals could pursue a path to salvation and achieve eternal life by being initiated into a union with a savior god or goddess who had died and risen again.

The Egyptian cult of Isis (Y-sis) was one of the most popular mystery religions. Isis was the goddess of women, marriage, and children; as one of her hymns states, "I am she whom women call goddess. I ordained that women should be loved by men: I brought wife and husband together, and invented the marriage contract. I ordained that women should bear children."[15] Isis was also portrayed as the giver of civilization, who had brought laws and letters to all humankind. The cult of Isis offered a precious commodity to its initiates—the promise of eternal life. After the Roman conquest of the Hellenistic world (see Chapter 5), mystery cults would find acceptance in the wider Roman world. And in many ways, the cult of Isis and the other mystery religions of the Hellenistic era helped pave the way for Christianity.

CHAPTER SUMMARY

Unlike the great centralized empires of the Persians and the Chinese, ancient Greece consisted of a large number of small, independent city-states, of which the most famous were Sparta, a militaristic *polis* ruled by an oligarchy, and Athens, which became known for its democratic institutions despite the fact that many slaves and women had no political rights. Despite the small size of their city-states, these ancient Greeks created a civilization that was the fountainhead of Western culture. Socrates, Plato, and Aristotle established the foundations of Western philosophy. Western literary forms are largely derived from Greek poetry and drama. Greek notions of harmony, proportion, and beauty have remained the touchstones for all subsequent Western art. A rational method of inquiry, so important to modern science, was conceived in ancient Greece. Many political terms are Greek in origin, and so too are concepts of the rights and duties of citizenship, especially as they were conceived in Athens, the first great democracy the world had seen. Especially during the Classical era of the fifth century BCE, a century that began with the Persian Wars, the Greeks raised and debated the fundamental questions about the purpose of human existence, the structure of human society, and the nature of the universe that have concerned thinkers ever since.

But the growth of an Athenian Empire in that same century led to a mighty conflict with Sparta—the Great Peloponnesian War—that resulted in the weakening of the Greek city-states and opened the door to an invasion by Philip II of Macedonia that put an end to their freedom in 338 BCE. But Greek culture did not die, and a new age, known as the Hellenistic era, eventually came into being.

That era began with the conquest of the Persian Empire by Alexander the Great, the young successor to his father, Philip II. Though a great military leader, Alexander was not a good political administrator. He failed to establish any definite structure for the empire he had conquered, and four Hellenistic kingdoms eventually emerged as his successors. The society that emerged within those kingdoms is known as *Hellenistic*, meaning Greek-like or in imitation of the Greeks. The Greek language became the dominant one as Greek ideas became influential. Greek merchants, artists, philosophers, and soldiers found opportunities and rewards throughout the Near East, now a world of kingdoms rather than independent city-states.

The Hellenistic period was, in its own way, a vibrant one. New cities arose and flourished. New philosophical doctrines—such as Epicureanism and Stoicism—captured the minds of many. Significant achievements occurred in literature and science, and Greek culture spread throughout the Near East, making an impact wherever it was carried. Although the Hellenistic era achieved a degree of political stability, by the late third century BCE, signs of decline were beginning to multiply, and the growing power of Rome eventually endangered the Hellenistic world.

CHAPTER TIMELINE

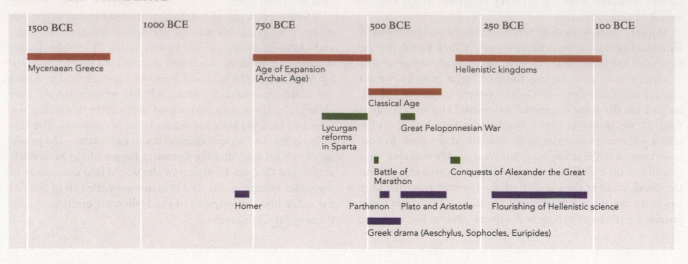

	1500 BCE	1000 BCE	750 BCE	500 BCE	250 BCE	100 BCE

Mycenaean Greece

Age of Expansion (Archaic Age)

Hellenistic kingdoms

Classical Age

Lycurgan reforms in Sparta

Great Peloponnesian War

Battle of Marathon

Conquests of Alexander the Great

Homer

Parthenon

Plato and Aristotle

Flourishing of Hellenistic science

Greek drama (Aeschylus, Sophocles, Euripides)

CHAPTER REVIEW

Upon Reflection

Q Compare Greek civilization with the early civilizations developed in India and China. What are the differences and similarities, and how do you explain them?

Q The Classical Age in Greece is known for its literary, artistic, and intellectual achievements. What basic characteristics of Greek culture are reflected in the major achievements of the Greeks in the writing of history, drama, the arts, and philosophy? What universal human concerns did these same achievements reflect?

Q What were the main achievements of the Hellenistic kingdoms, and why did they fail to bring any lasting order to the lands of the Near East?

Key Terms

polis (p. 101)
hoplites (p. 101)
phalanx (p. 101)
tyrants (p. 103)
oligarchies (p. 103)
tyranny (p. 103)
helots (p. 104)

Sophists (p. 113)
rhetoric (p. 113)
Socratic method (p. 113)
Epicureanism (p. 126)
Stoicism (p. 126)
mystery religions (p. 127)

Chapter Notes

1. Xenophon, *Symposium*, trans. O. J. Todd (New York, 1946), III, 5.
2. Homer, *Odyssey*, pp. 290–291.
3. Quoted in T. R. Martin, *Ancient Greece* (New Haven, Conn., 1996), p. 62.
4. Quoted in V. D. Hanson, *The Wars of the Ancient Greeks*, rev. ed. (London, 2006), p. 14.
5. These words from Plutarch are quoted in E. Fantham et al., *Women in the Classical World* (New York, 1994), p. 64.
6. Aeschylus, *The Persians*, in *The Complete Greek Tragedies*, vol. 1, ed. David Grene and Richard Lattimore (Chicago, 1959), p. 229.
7. Thucydides, *The Peloponnesian War*, trans. R. Warner (New York, 1954), p. 24.
8. Sophocles, *Oedipus the King*, trans. D. Grene (Chicago, 1959), pp. 68–69.
9. Sophocles, *Antigone*, trans. D. Taylor (London, 1986), p. 146.

10. Plato, *The Republic*, trans. F. M. Cornford (New York, 1945), pp. 178–179.

11. Quotations from Aristotle are in S. Blundell, *Women in Ancient Greece* (Cambridge, Mass., 1995), pp. 106, 186.

12. Quoted in S. B. Pomeroy et al., *Ancient Greece: A Political, Social, and Cultural History* (Oxford, 1999), p. 390.

13. Quoted in G. Shipley, *The Greek World After Alexander, 323–30 BC* (London, 2000), p. 304.

14. Plutarch, *Life of Marcellus*, trans. J. Dryden (New York, n.d.), p. 378.

15. Quoted in W. W. Tarn, *Hellenistic Civilization* (London, 1930), p. 324.

 **MINDTAP** From Cengage

MindTap® is a fully online personalized learning experience built upon Cengage Learning content. MindTap® combines student learning tools—readings, multimedia, activities, and assessments—into a singular Learning Path that guides students through the course and helps students develop the critical thinking, analysis, and communication skills that are essential to academic and professional success.

Chapter Outline and Focus Questions

Horatius defending the bridge, as envisioned by Tommaso Laureti, a sixteenth-century Italian painter.
Musei Capitolini, Rome, Italy/Giraudon/The Bridgeman Art Library

Critical Thinking

Q *Compare and contrast the Roman Empire and Han Chinese Empire in regard to dynastic rule, bureaucratic government, trade, the military, and imperial expansion.*

Connections to Today

Q *What lessons does the fall of the Roman Republic offer to the United States today?*

AT THE BEGINNING of the first millennium CE, almost 50 percent of the world's population lived in one of two mighty world empires—the Han and Roman Empires. They were the largest political entities the world had yet seen. The Han Empire (see Chapter 3) extended from Central Asia to the Pacific Ocean;

the Roman Empire encompassed the lands around the Mediterranean, parts of the Middle East, and western and central Europe. Although there were no diplomatic contacts between the two civilizations, the two great empires were linked commercially.

Roman history is the remarkable story of how a group of Latin-speaking people, who established a small community on a plain called Latium in central Italy, went on to conquer all of Italy and then the entire Mediterranean world. Why were the Romans able to do this? Scholars do not really know all the answers, but the Romans had their own explanation. Early Roman history is filled with legendary tales of the heroes who made Rome great. One of the best known is the story of Horatius at the bridge.

Threatened by attack from the neighboring Etruscans, Roman farmers abandoned their fields and moved into the city, where they would be protected by the walls. One weak point in the Roman defenses, however, was a wooden bridge over the Tiber River. Horatius was on guard at the bridge when a sudden assault by the Etruscans caused many Roman troops to throw down their weapons and flee. Horatius urged them to make a stand at the bridge; when they hesitated, he told them to destroy the bridge behind him while he held the Etruscans back. Astonished at the sight of a single defender, the confused Etruscans threw their spears at Horatius, who caught them on his shield and barred the way. By the time the Etruscans were about to overwhelm the lone defender, the Roman soldiers had brought down the bridge. Horatius then dived fully armed into the water and swam safely to the other side through a hail of arrows. Rome had been saved by the courageous act of a Roman who knew his duty and was determined to carry it out. Courage, duty, determination—these qualities would serve the many Romans who believed that it was their divine mission to rule nations and peoples. As one orator proclaimed, "By heaven's will my Rome shall be capital of the world."[1]

Map 5.1 Ancient Italy. Ancient Italy was home to several groups. Both the Etruscans in the north and the Greeks in the south had a major influence on the development of Rome.

 Once Rome conquered the Etruscans and other local groups, what aspects of the Italian peninsula helped make it defensible against outside enemies?

5–1 EARLY ROME AND THE REPUBLIC

 Focus Questions: What policies and institutions help explain the Romans' success in conquering Italy? How did Rome achieve its empire from 264 to 133 BCE, and what problems did Rome face as a result of its growing empire?

Italy is a peninsula extending about 750 miles from north to south (see Map 5.1). It is not very wide, however, averaging about 120 miles across. The Apennines form a ridge down the middle of Italy that divides west from east. Nevertheless, Italy has some fairly large fertile plains that are ideal for farming. Most important are the Po River Valley in the north; the plain

of Latium (LAY-shee-um), on which Rome was located; and Campania to the south of Latium. To the east of the Italian peninsula is the Adriatic Sea and to the west the Tyrrhenian Sea, bounded by the large islands of Corsica and Sardinia. Sicily lies just west of the "toe" of the boot-shaped Italian peninsula.

Geography had an impact on Roman history. Although the Apennines bisected Italy, they were less rugged than the mountain ranges of Greece and did not divide the peninsula into small isolated communities. Italy also possessed considerably more productive agricultural land than Greece, enabling it to support a large population. Rome's location was favorable from a geographic perspective. Located 18 miles inland on the Tiber River, Rome had access to the sea and yet was far enough inland to be safe from pirates. Built on seven hills, it was easily defended. Because the Tiber could be readily forded, Rome became a natural crossing point for north-south traffic in western Italy. All in all, Rome had a good central location in Italy from which to expand.

Moreover, the Italian peninsula juts into the Mediterranean, making Italy an important crossroads between the western and eastern ends of the sea. Once Rome had unified Italy, involvement in Mediterranean affairs was natural. And after the Romans had conquered their Mediterranean empire, governing it was made easier by Italy's central location.

5-1a Early Rome

In order to provide a noble ancestry for their city, the Romans created two significant legends. One was the story of Aeneas, the son of the goddess Venus and a mortal man. He was a Trojan hero fighting the Greeks, who escaped from the sacking of Troy and eventually made his way to Italy. According to one version of the legend, he founded the city of Rome, which he named after a Trojan woman. The legend reflects the desire of the Romans to connect Roman history to Greek history, and especially Greece's heroic age, an indication of the strong impact Greek culture made on the Romans.

The other legend is the story of Romulus and Remus, the twin sons of the god Mars, whose mother was punished for losing her virginity by Amulius, who had become king of Alba Longa by overthrowing her father. Her boys were set adrift on the Tiber River in a reed basket. They were found by a she-wolf, who suckled them, and were then raised by a shepherd's family. When the boys were grown men, they were told of their origins and avenged their mother and grandfather by killing Amulius and then founding the city of Rome. According to the legend, Romulus founded a new city on the Palatine Hill in 753 BCE, killed his brother in an argument, and then became the first king of Rome.

Of course, the Romans invented these stories to provide a noble ancestry for their city. Archaeologists have found, however, that by the eighth century, a village of huts had been built on the tops of Rome's hills. The early Romans, basically a pastoral people, spoke Latin, which, like Greek, belongs to the Indo-European family of languages (see Table 1.2, Section 1-5a, p. 26). The Roman historical tradition also maintained that early Rome (753–509 BCE) had been under the control of seven kings and that two of the last three had been Etruscans (i-TRUSS-kunz), people who lived north of Rome in Etruria. Historians believe that the king list may have some historical accuracy. What is certain is that Rome did fall under the influence of the Etruscans for about a hundred years during the period of the kings and that by the beginning of the sixth century, under Etruscan influence, Rome began to emerge as a city. The Etruscans were responsible for an outstanding building program. They constructed the first roadbed of the chief street through Rome, the Sacred Way, before 575 BCE and oversaw the development of temples, markets, shops, streets, and houses. By 509 BCE, supposedly when the monarchy was overthrown and a republican form of government was established, a new Rome had emerged, essentially a result of the fusion of Etruscan and native Roman elements.

5-1b The Roman Republic

The transition from monarchy to a republican government was not easy. Rome felt threatened by enemies from every direction and, in the process of meeting these threats, embarked on a military course that led to the conquest of the entire Italian peninsula.

The Roman Conquest of Italy At the beginning of the Republic, Rome was surrounded by enemies, including the Latin communities on the plain of Latium. If we are to believe Livy (LIV-ee), one of the chief ancient sources for the history of the early Roman Republic, Rome was engaged in almost continuous warfare with these enemies for the next hundred years. In his account, Livy provided a detailed narrative of Roman efforts. Many of his stories were legendary in character; writing in the first century BCE, he used his stories to teach Romans the moral values and virtues that had made Rome great. As seen in the story of Cincinnatus, these included tenacity, duty, courage, and especially discipline (see "Cincinnatus Saves Rome: A Roman Morality Tale").

By 338 BCE, Rome had crushed the Latin states in Latium. During the next fifty years, the Romans waged a successful struggle with hill peoples from central Italy and then came into direct contact with the Greek communities. The Greeks had arrived on the Italian peninsula in large numbers during the age of Greek colonization (750–550 BCE) (see Section 4-2b, pp. 102–103). Initially, the Greeks settled in southern Italy and then crept around the coast and up the peninsula. They also occupied the eastern two-thirds of Sicily.

The Greeks had much influence on Rome. They cultivated olives and grapes, passed on their alphabet, and provided artistic and cultural models through their sculpture, architecture, and literature. By 267 BCE, the Romans had completed the conquest of southern Italy by defeating the Greek cities. After crushing the remaining Etruscan states to the north in 264 BCE, Rome had conquered most of Italy.

To rule Italy, the Romans devised the Roman Confederation in 338 BCE. Under this system, Rome allowed some peoples—especially the Latins—to have full Roman citizenship. Most of the remaining communities were made allies. They were free to run their own local affairs but were required to provide soldiers for Rome. Moreover, the Romans made it clear that loyal allies could improve their status and even aspire to become Roman citizens. The Romans had found a way to give conquered peoples a stake in Rome's success.

In the course of their expansion throughout Italy, the Romans had pursued consistent policies that help explain their success. The Romans were superb diplomats who excelled in making the correct diplomatic decisions. While firm and even cruel when necessary—rebellions were crushed without mercy—they were also shrewd in extending their citizenship and allowing autonomy in domestic affairs. In addition, the Romans were not only good soldiers but also persistent ones. The loss of an army or a fleet did not cause them to quit but spurred them on to raise new armies and build new fleets. And by granting citizenship to conquered peoples, Rome had achieved the ability to raise new armies following defeats. Finally, the Romans had a practical sense of strategy. As they conquered, the Romans established colonies—fortified towns—at strategic locations throughout Italy. By building roads to these settlements and connecting them, the Romans created an impressive communications and military network that enabled them to rule effectively and efficiently (see Comparative Illustration "Roman and Chinese Roads," p. 134). By insisting on military service from new citizens and the allies in the Roman

CINCINNATUS SAVES ROME: A ROMAN MORALITY TALE

Politics & Government

THERE IS PERHAPS NO BETTER ACCOUNT of how the virtues of duty and simplicity enabled good Roman citizens to prevail during the travails of the fifth century BCE than Livy's account of Cincinnatus (sin-suh-NAT-uss). He was chosen dictator, supposedly in 457 BCE, to defend Rome against the attacks of the Aequi (EYE-kwee or EE-kwy). The position of dictator was a temporary expedient used only in emergencies; the consuls would resign, and a leader with unlimited power would be appointed for a specified period (usually six months). In this account, Cincinnatus did his duty, defeated the Aequi, and returned to his simple farm in just fifteen days.

Livy, *The Early History of Rome*

The city was thrown into a state of turmoil, and the general alarm was as great as if Rome herself were surrounded. Nautius was sent for, but it was quickly decided that he was not the man to inspire full confidence; the situation evidently called for a dictator, and, with no dissentient voice, Lucius Quinctius Cincinnatus was named for the post.

Now I would solicit the particular attention of those numerous people who imagine that money is everything in this world, and that rank and ability are inseparable from wealth: let them observe that Cincinnatus, the one man in whom Rome reposed all her hope of survival, was at that moment working a little three-acre farm . . . west of the Tiber, just opposite the spot where the shipyards are today. A mission from the city found him at work on his land—digging a ditch, maybe, or plowing. Greetings were exchanged, and he was asked—with a prayer for divine blessing on himself and his country—to put on his toga and hear the Senate's instructions.

This naturally surprised him, and, asking if all were well, he told his wife Racilia to run to their cottage and fetch his toga. The toga was brought, and wiping the grimy sweat from his hands and face he put it on; at once the envoys from the city saluted him, with congratulations, as Dictator, invited him to enter Rome, and informed him of the terrible danger of Municius's army. A state vessel was waiting for him on the river, and on the city bank he was welcomed by his three sons who had come to meet him, then by other kinsmen and friends, and finally by nearly the whole body of senators. Closely attended by all these people and preceded by his lictors he was then escorted to his residence through streets lined with great crowds of common folk who, be it said, were by no means so pleased to see the new Dictator, as they thought his power excessive and dreaded the way in which he was likely to use it....

[Cincinnatus proceeds to raise an army, march out, and defeat the Aequi.]

In Rome the Senate was convened by Quintus Fabius the City Prefect, and a decree was passed inviting Cincinnatus to enter in triumph with his troops. The chariot he rode in was preceded by the enemy commanders and the military standards, and followed by his army loaded with its spoils.... Cincinnatus finally resigned after holding office for fifteen days, having originally accepted it for a period of six months.

 What values did Livy emphasize in his account of Cincinnatus? How important were those values to Rome's success? Why did Livy say he wrote his history?

Source: From *The Early History of Rome* by Livy, translated by Aubrey de Selincourt (Penguin Classics, 1960).

Confederation, Rome essentially mobilized the entire military manpower of all Italy for its wars.

The Roman State After the overthrow of the monarchy, Roman nobles, eager to maintain their position of power, established a republican form of government. The chief executive officers of the Roman Republic were the **consuls** (KAHN-sulls) and **praetors** (PREE-turs). Two consuls, chosen annually, administered the government and led the Roman army into battle. The office of praetor was created in 366 BCE. The praetor was in charge of civil law (law as it applied to Roman citizens), but he could also lead armies and govern Rome when the consuls were away from the city. As the Romans' territory expanded, they added another praetor to judge cases in which one or both people were noncitizens. The Roman state also had a number of administrative officials who handled specialized duties, such as the

administration of financial affairs and supervision of the public games of Rome.

The Roman **senate** came to hold an especially important position in the Roman Republic. The senate or council of elders was a select group of about three hundred men who served for life. The senate could only advise the magistrates, but this advice was not taken lightly and by the third century BCE had virtually the force of law.

The Roman Republic had a number of popular assemblies. By far the most important was the **centuriate assembly**. Organized by classes based on wealth, it was structured in such a way that the wealthiest citizens always had a majority. This assembly elected the chief magistrates and passed laws. Another assembly, the **council of the plebs**, came into being in 471 BCE.

The Roman Republic, then, witnessed the interplay of three major elements. Two consuls and later other elected officials served as magistrates and ran the state. An assembly of adult

COMPARATIVE ILLUSTRATION

Interaction & Exchange

Roman and Chinese Roads. The Romans constructed a remarkable system of roads. After laying a foundation of gravel, which allowed for drainage, the Roman builders topped it with flagstones, closely fitted together. Unlike other peoples who built similar kinds of roads, the Romans did not follow the contours of the land but made their roads as straight as possible to facilitate communications and transportation, especially for military purposes. Seen here (A) is a view of the Via Appia (Appian Way), built in 312 BCE to make it easy for Roman armies to march from Rome to the newly conquered city of Capua, a distance of 152 miles (shown on the map). By the beginning of the fourth century CE, the Roman Empire contained 372 major roads covering 50,000 miles.

Like the Roman Empire, the Han Empire relied on roads constructed with stone slabs for the movement of military forces (B). The First Emperor of Qin was responsible for the construction of 4,350 miles of roads, and by the end of the second century CE, China had almost 22,000 miles of roads. Although roads in both the Roman and Chinese Empires were originally constructed for military purposes, they came to be used for communications and commercial traffic as well; however, unlike the Romans, the Han emperors used waterways for most of their transportation needs.

 What was the importance of roads to the Roman and Han Empires?

males (the centuriate assembly), controlled by the wealthiest citizens, elected these officials, while the senate, a small group of large landowners, advised them. Thus, the Roman state was an aristocratic republic controlled by a relatively small group of privileged people.

The Struggle of the Orders: Social Divisions in the Roman Republic The most noticeable element in the social organization of early Rome was the division between two groups—the patricians and the plebeians. The **patricians** were descendants of the original senators appointed during the period of the kings and were great landowners, who constituted an aristocratic governing class. Only they could be consuls, magistrates, and senators. Through their patronage of large numbers of dependent clients, they controlled the centuriate assembly and many other facets of Roman life. The **plebeians** constituted the considerably larger group of non-patrician large landowners, less wealthy landholders, artisans, merchants, and small farmers. Although they, too, were citizens, they did not have the same rights as the patricians.

Both patricians and plebeians could vote, but only the patricians could be elected to governmental offices. Both had the right to make legal contracts and marriages, but intermarriage between patricians and plebeians was forbidden. At the beginning of the fifth century BCE, the plebeians began to seek both political and social equality with the patricians.

The struggle between the patricians and plebeians dragged on for hundreds of years, but the plebeians ultimately were successful. The council of the plebs, a popular assembly for plebeians only, was created in 471 BCE, and new officials, known as **tribunes of the plebs**, were given the power to protect plebeians against arrest by patrician magistrates. A new law allowed marriages between patricians and plebeians, and in the fourth century BCE, plebeians were permitted to become consuls. Finally, in 287 BCE, the council of the plebs received the right to pass laws for all Romans.

The struggle between the patricians and plebeians, then, had a significant impact on the development of the Roman state. Plebeians could now hold the highest offices of state, they could intermarry with the patricians, and they could pass laws binding on the entire Roman community. Theoretically, by 287 BCE, all Roman citizens were equal under the law, and all could strive for political office. But in reality, as a result of the right of intermarriage,

a select number of patrician and plebeian families formed a new senatorial aristocracy that came to dominate the political offices. The Roman Republic had not become a democracy.

5–1c The Roman Conquest of the Mediterranean (264–133 BCE)

After their conquest of the Italian peninsula, the Romans found themselves face to face with a formidable Mediterranean power—Carthage (KAHR-thij). Founded around 800 BCE on the coast of North Africa by Phoenicians, Carthage had flourished and assembled an enormous empire in the western Mediterranean. By the third century BCE, the Carthaginian Empire included the coast of northern Africa, southern Spain, Sardinia, Corsica, and western Sicily. The presence of Carthaginians in Sicily, so close to the Italian coast, made the Romans apprehensive. In 264 BCE, the two powers began a lengthy struggle for control of the western Mediterranean (see Map 5.2).

The Punic Wars The First Punic (PYOO-nik) War (264–241 BCE)—the Latin word for Phoenician was *Punicus*—began when the Romans decided to intervene in a struggle between two Sicilian cities and sent an army to Sicily. The Carthaginians, who considered Sicily within their own sphere of influence,

Map 5.2 Roman Conquests in the Mediterranean, 264–133 BCE. Beginning with the Punic Wars, Rome expanded its holdings, first in the western Mediterranean at the expense of Carthage and later in Greece and western Asia Minor.

Q *What aspects of Mediterranean geography, combined with the territorial holdings and aspirations of Rome and the Carthaginians, made the Punic Wars more likely?*

regarded this as a just cause for war. In going to war, both sides determined on the conquest of Sicily. The Romans realized that the war would be long and drawn out if they could not supplement their land operations with a navy and promptly developed a substantial fleet. After a long struggle, a Roman fleet defeated the Carthaginian navy off Sicily, and the war quickly came to an end. In 241 BCE, Carthage gave up all rights to Sicily and had to pay an indemnity. Sicily became the first Roman province.

Carthage vowed revenge and extended its domains in Spain to compensate for the territory lost to Rome. When the Romans encouraged one of Carthage's Spanish allies to revolt against Carthage, Hannibal (HAN-uh-bul), the greatest of the Carthaginian generals, struck back, beginning the Second Punic War (218–201 BCE).

This time, the Carthaginian strategy aimed at bringing the war home to the Romans and defeating them in their own backyard. Hannibal crossed the Alps with an army of 30,000 to 40,000 men and inflicted a series of defeats on the Romans. At Cannae (KAH-nee) in 216 BCE, the Romans lost an army of almost 40,000 men. The Romans seemed on the brink of disaster but refused to give up, raised yet another army, and began to reconquer some of the Italian cities that had gone over to Hannibal's side. More important, the Romans pursued a strategy aimed at undermining the Carthaginian Empire in Spain. Publius Cornelius Scipio, later known as Scipio Africanus (SIP-ee-oh af-ree-KAY-nuss) the Elder, was given command of the Roman forces in Spain. A brilliant general who learned from Hannibal's tactics, he had pushed the Carthaginians out of Spain by 206 BCE.

The Romans then took the war directly to Carthage, forcing the Carthaginians to recall Hannibal from Italy. At the Battle of Zama (ZAH-muh) in 202 BCE, the Romans crushed Hannibal's forces, and the war was over. By the peace treaty signed in 201 BCE, Carthage lost Spain, which became another Roman province. As a result of the Second Punic War, Rome had become the dominant power in the western Mediterranean.

Fifty years later, the Romans fought their third and final struggle with Carthage. A technical breach in the peace treaty gave the Romans the opportunity to carry out a policy advocated by a number of Romans, especially the conservative politician Cato, who ended every speech he made to the senate with the words, "And I think Carthage must be destroyed." In 146 BCE, Carthage was destroyed. For ten days, Roman soldiers burned and pulled down all of the city's buildings (see "The Destruction of Carthage"). The inhabitants—50,000 men, women, and children—were sold into slavery. The territory of Carthage became a Roman province called Africa.

The Eastern Mediterranean During its struggle with Carthage, Rome also had problems with the Hellenistic states in the eastern Mediterranean, and after the defeat of Carthage, Rome turned its attention there. In 148 BCE, Macedonia was made a Roman province, and two years later, Greece was placed under the control of the Roman governor of Macedonia. In 133 BCE, the king of Pergamum deeded his kingdom to Rome, giving Rome its first province in Asia. Rome was now master of the Mediterranean Sea.

CHRONOLOGY	The Roman Conquest of Italy and the Mediterranean
Conquest of Latins completed	340 BCE
Creation of the Roman Confederation	338 BCE
First Punic War	264–241 BCE
Second Punic War	218–201 BCE
Battle of Cannae	216 BCE
Roman seizure of Spain	206 BCE
Battle of Zama	202 BCE
Third Punic War	149–146 BCE
Macedonia made a Roman province	148 BCE
Destruction of Carthage	146 BCE
Kingdom of Pergamum to Rome	133 BCE

The Nature of Roman Imperialism Rome's empire was built in three stages: the conquest of Italy, the conflict with Carthage and expansion into the western Mediterranean, and the involvement with and domination of the Hellenistic kingdoms in the eastern Mediterranean. The Romans did not possess a master plan for the creation of an empire. Much of their expansion was opportunistic; once involved in a situation that threatened their security, the Romans did not hesitate to act. And the more they expanded, the more threats to their security appeared on the horizon, involving them in yet more conflicts. Indeed, the Romans liked to portray themselves as declaring war only for defensive reasons or to protect allies. That is only part of the story, however. It is likely, as some historians have suggested, that at some point a group of Roman aristocratic leaders emerged who favored expansion both for the glory it offered and for the economic benefits it provided. Certainly, by the second century BCE, aristocratic senators perceived new opportunities for lucrative foreign commands, enormous spoils of war, and an abundant supply of slave labor for their growing landed estates.

At the same time, the Roman political system encouraged an imperialistic policy. There was an intense competition between families for the consulship (as we have seen, there were only two per year). Moreover, many Romans believed in outdoing the deeds of their ancestors. The combination of these factors helped lead upper-class Romans to seek glory and power by winning wars abroad.

By second century BCE, as the destruction of Carthage indicates, Roman imperialism had become more arrogant and brutal as well. Rome's foreign success also had enormous repercussions for the internal development of the Roman Republic.

The Roman Army By the fourth century BCE, the Roman army consisted of four legions, each made up of four thousand to five thousand men; each legion had about three hundred cavalry and the rest infantry. In the early Republic, the army was recruited from citizens between the ages of eighteen and

THE DESTRUCTION OF CARTHAGE

Politics & Government

THE ROMANS USED A TECHNICAL BREACH of Carthage's peace treaty with Rome to undertake a third and final war with Carthage (149–146 BCE). Although Carthage posed no real threat to Rome's security, the Romans still remembered the traumatic experiences of the Second Punic War, when Hannibal had ravaged much of their homeland. The city was razed, the survivors sold into slavery, and the land turned into a province. In this passage, the historian Appian of Alexandria describes the final destruction of Carthage by the Romans under the command of Scipio Aemilianus (SEE-pee-oh ee-mil-YAY-nuss).

Appian, *Roman History*

Then came new scenes of horror. The fire spread and carried everything down, and the soldiers did not wait to destroy the buildings little by little, but pulled them all down together. So the crashing grew louder, and many fell with the stones into the midst dead. Others were seen still living, especially old men, women, and young children who had hidden in the inmost nooks of the houses, some of them wounded, some more or less burned, and uttering horrible cries. Still others, thrust out and falling from such a height with the stones, timbers, and fire, were torn asunder into all kinds of horrible shapes, crushed and mangled. Nor was this the end of their miseries, for the street cleaners, who were removing the rubbish with axes, mattocks, and boat hooks, and making the roads passable, tossed with these instruments the dead and the living together into holes in the ground, sweeping them along like sticks and stones or turning them over with their iron tools, and man was used for filling up a ditch. Some were thrown in head foremost, while their legs, sticking out of the ground, writhed a long time. Others fell with their feet downward and their heads above ground. Horses ran over them, crushing their faces and skulls, not purposely on the part of the riders, but in their headlong haste. Nor did the street cleaners either do these things on purpose; but the press of

war, the glory of approaching victory, the rush of the soldiery, the confused noise of heralds and trumpeters all round, the tribunes and centurions changing guard and marching the cohorts hither and thither—all together made everybody frantic and heedless of the spectacle before their eyes.

Six days and nights were consumed in this kind of turmoil, the soldiers being changed so that they might not be worn out with toil, slaughter, want of sleep, and these horrid sights....

Scipio, beholding this city, which had flourished 700 years from its foundation and had ruled over so many lands, islands, and seas, as rich in arms and fleets, elephants, and money as the mightiest empires, but far surpassing them in hardihood and high spirit … now come to its end in total destruction— Scipio, beholding this spectacle, is said to have shed tears and publicly lamented the fortune of the enemy. After meditating by himself a long time and reflecting on the inevitable fall of cities, nations, and empires, as well as of individuals, upon the fate of Troy, that once proud city, upon the fate of the Assyrian, the Median, and afterwards of the great Persian empire, and, most recently of all, of the splendid empire of Macedon, either voluntarily or otherwise the words of the poet [Homer, *Iliad*] escaped his lips:

> The day shall come in which our sacred Troy
> And Priam, and the people over whom
> Spear-bearing Priam rules, shall perish all.

Being asked by Polybius in familiar conversation (for Polybius had been his tutor) what he meant by using these words, Polybius says that he did not hesitate frankly to name his own country, for whose fate he feared when he considered the mutability of human affairs. And Polybius wrote this down just as he heard it.

 Q What does the description of Rome's destruction of Carthage reveal about the nature of Roman imperialism? What features seem more rhetorical than realistic? Why?

Source: From *Appian: Roman History*, Vol. 1, trans. by Horace White, Cambridge, Mass.: Harvard University Press, 1912.

forty-six who had the resources to equip themselves for battle. Since most of them were farmers, they enrolled only for a year, campaigned during the summer months, and returned home in time for the fall harvest. Later, during the Punic Wars of the third century BCE, the period of service had to be extended, although this was resisted by farmers whose livelihoods could be severely harmed by a long absence. Nevertheless, after the disastrous Battle of Cannae in 216 BCE, the Romans were forced to recruit larger armies, and the number of legions rose to twenty-five. Major changes in recruitment would not come until the first century BCE with the military reforms of Marius (see sections titled "Growing Inequality and Unrest" and "A New Role for the Roman Army").

5–1d The Decline and Fall of the Roman Republic (133–31 BCE)

By the middle of the second century BCE, Roman domination of the Mediterranean Sea was complete. Yet the process of creating an empire had weakened the internal stability of Rome, leading to a series of crises that plagued the Republic for the next hundred years.

Growing Inequality and Unrest By the second century BCE, the senate had become the effective governing body of the Roman state. It comprised three hundred men, drawn primarily from the landed aristocracy; they remained senators for life and held the chief magistracies of the Republic. The

Roman Legionaries. The Roman legionaries, famed for their courage and tenacity, made possible Roman domination of the Mediterranean Sea. At the time of the Punic Wars, a Roman legionary wore chain-mail armor and a plumed helmet and carried an oval shield, as in the bronze statue from the second or first century BCE shown at the left. Heavy javelins and swords were their major weapons. This equipment remained standard until the time of Julius Caesar. The illustration on the right shows a Roman legion on the march from Trajan's column, erected in the second century CE. Left image: DEA/A. Dagli Orti/Getty Images; right image: Roger-Viollet/The Image Works

senate directed the wars of the third and second centuries and took control of both foreign and domestic policy, including financial affairs.

Of course, these aristocrats formed only a tiny minority of the Roman people. The backbone of the Roman state and army had traditionally been the small farmers. But over time, many small farmers had found themselves unable to compete with large, wealthy landowners and had lost their lands. By taking over state-owned land and by buying out small peasant owners, these landed aristocrats had amassed large estates, called *latifundia* (lat-i-FOON-dee-uh), that used slave labor. Thus, the rise of the *latifundia* contributed to a decline in the number of small farmers. Since the latter group traditionally provided the foundation of the Roman army, the number of men available for military service declined. Moreover, many of these small farmers drifted to the cities, especially Rome, forming a large class of landless poor.

Some aristocrats tried to remedy this growing economic and social crisis. Two brothers, Tiberius and Gaius Gracchus (ty-BEER-ee-uss and GY-uss GRAK-us), came to believe that the underlying cause of Rome's problems was the decline of the small farmer. To help the landless poor, they bypassed the senate by having the council of the plebs pass land reform bills that called for the government to reclaim public land held by large landowners and to distribute it to landless Romans. Many senators, themselves large landowners whose estates included broad tracts of public land, were furious. A group of senators took the law into their own hands and murdered Tiberius in 133 BCE. Twelve years later, Gaius suffered the same fate. The attempts of the Gracchus brothers to bring reforms had opened the door to further violence. Changes in the Roman army soon brought even worse problems.

A New Role for the Roman Army In the closing years of the second century BCE, a Roman general named Marius (MAR-ee-uss) began to recruit his armies in a new way. The Roman army had traditionally been a conscript army of small farmers who were landholders. Marius, who held the consulship from 104 to 100 BCE, recruited volunteers from both the urban and rural poor who possessed no property. These volunteers swore an oath of loyalty to the general, not the senate, and thus constituted a professional-type army that might no longer be subject to the state. Moreover, to recruit these men, the generals would promise them land, forcing the generals to play politics in order to get laws passed that would provide the land promised to their veterans. Marius had created a new system of military recruitment that placed much power in the hands of the individual generals.

Lucius Cornelius Sulla was the next general to take advantage of the new military system. The senate had given him command of a war in Asia Minor, but when the council of the plebs tried to transfer command of this war to Marius, a civil war broke out. Sulla won and seized Rome itself in 82 BCE, conducting a reign of terror to wipe out all opposition. Then Sulla restored power to the hands of the senate and eliminated most of the powers of the popular assemblies. Sulla hoped that he had created a firm foundation for the traditional Republic governed by a powerful senate, but his real legacy was quite different from what he had intended. His example of using an army to seize power would prove most attractive to ambitious men.

The Collapse of the Republic For the next fifty years, Roman history was characterized by two important features: the jostling for dominance of a number of powerful individuals and the civil wars generated by their conflicts. Three individuals came to hold enormous military and political power—Crassus (KRASS-uss), Pompey (PAHM-pee), and Julius Caesar. Crassus was known as the richest man in Rome and led a successful military command against a major slave rebellion. Pompey had returned from a successful military command in Spain in 71 BCE and had been hailed as a military hero. Julius Caesar also had a military command in Spain. In 60 BCE, Caesar joined with Crassus and Pompey to form a coalition that historians call the First Triumvirate (*triumvirate* means "three-man rule").

The combined wealth and influence of these three men was enormous, enabling them to dominate the political scene and achieve their basic aims: Pompey received a command in Spain, Crassus a command in Syria, and Caesar a special military command in Gaul (modern France). When Crassus was killed in battle in 53 BCE, his death left two powerful men with armies in direct competition. Caesar had conquered all of Gaul and gained fame, wealth, and military experience as well as an army of seasoned veterans who were loyal to him. When leading senators endorsed Pompey as the less harmful to their cause and voted for Caesar to lay down his command and return as a private citizen to Rome, Caesar refused. He chose to keep his army and moved into Italy illegally by crossing the Rubicon, the river that formed the southern boundary of his province. Caesar marched on Rome and defeated the forces of Pompey and his allies, leaving Caesar in complete control of the Roman government.

Caesar was officially made **dictator** in 47 BCE and three years later was named dictator for life. Realizing the need for reforms, he gave land to the poor and increased the senate to nine hundred members. By filling it with many of his supporters and increasing the membership, he effectively weakened the power of the senate. He also reformed the calendar by introducing the Egyptian solar year of 365 days (with later changes in 1582, it became the basis of our own calendar). Caesar planned much more in the way of building projects and military adventures in the east, but in 44 BCE, a group of leading senators assassinated him (see "The Assassination of Julius Caesar," p. 140).

Within a few years after Caesar's death, two men had divided the Roman world between them—Octavian (ahk-TAY-vee-un), Caesar's grandnephew and adopted son, took the western portion and Antony, Caesar's ally and assistant, the eastern half. But the empire of the Romans, large as it was, was still too small for two masters, and Octavian and Antony eventually came into conflict. Antony allied himself closely with the Egyptian queen, Cleopatra VII. At the Battle of Actium in Greece in 31 BCE, Octavian's forces smashed the army and navy of Antony and Cleopatra, who both fled to Egypt, where they committed suicide a year later. Octavian, at the age of thirty-two, stood supreme over the Roman world. The civil wars had ended. And so had the Republic.

5–2 THE ROMAN EMPIRE AT ITS HEIGHT

 Focus Question: What were the chief features of the Roman Empire at its height in the second century CE?

With the victories of Octavian, peace finally settled on the Roman world. Although civil conflict still erupted occasionally, the new imperial state constructed by Octavian experienced remarkable stability for the next two hundred years. The Romans imposed their peace on the largest empire established in antiquity.

5–2a The Age of Augustus (31 BCE–14 CE)

In 27 BCE, Octavian proclaimed the "restoration of the Republic." He understood that only traditional republican forms would satisfy the senatorial aristocracy. At the same time, Octavian was aware that the Republic could not be fully restored. Although he gave some power to the senate, in fact, Octavian became the first Roman emperor. The senate awarded him the title of Augustus, "the revered one"—a fitting title, in view of his power, that had previously been reserved for gods. Augustus proved highly popular, but the chief source of his power was his continuing control of the army. The senate also gave Augustus the title of *imperator* (im-puh-RAH-tur), or commander in chief. *Imperator* is Latin for our word *emperor*.

Why had Augustus succeeded in establishing a new order while Julius Caesar, his adoptive father, had failed? Caesar had defined himself as a dictator for life, thus raising suspicion among the Romans that he planned to become a king, a position that they strongly disliked. Many Romans believed that Caesar had been justly killed as a tyrant. Augustus was careful to present himself as an ordinary citizen and to exercise power by holding the traditional offices of the Roman Republic.

THE ASSASSINATION OF JULIUS CAESAR

Politics & Government

WHEN IT BECAME APPARENT THAT JULIUS CAESAR had no intention of restoring the Republic as they conceived it, about sixty senators, many of them his friends or pardoned enemies, formed a conspiracy to assassinate the dictator. Gaius Cassius and Marcus Brutus, who led the plot, naively imagined that this act would restore the traditional Republic. The conspirators set the Ides of March (March 15) of 44 BCE as the date for the assassination. Caesar was in the midst of preparations for a campaign in the eastern part of the empire. Although warned about a plot against his life, he chose to disregard it. This account of Caesar's death is taken from his biography by the Greek writer Plutarch.

Plutarch, *Life of Caesar*

Fate, however, is to all appearance more unavoidable than unexpected. For many strange prodigies and apparitions are said to have been observed shortly before this event. . . . One finds it also related by many that a soothsayer bade him [Caesar] prepare for some great danger on the Ides of March. When this day was come, Caesar, as he went to the senate, met this soothsayer, and said to him mockingly, "The Ides of March are come," who answered him calmly, "Yes, they are come, but they are not past. . . ."

All these things might happen by chance. But the place which was destined for the scene of this murder, in which the senate met that day, was the same in which Pompey's statue stood, and was one of the edifices which Pompey had raised and dedicated with his theater to the use of the public, plainly showing that there was something of a supernatural influence which guided the action and ordered it to that particular place. Cassius, just before the act, is said to have looked toward Pompey's statue, and silently implored his assistance. . . . When Caesar entered, the senate stood up to show their respect to him, and of Brutus's confederates, some came about his chair and stood behind it, others met him, pretending to add their petitions to those of Tillius Cimber, in behalf of his brother, who was in exile; and they followed him with their joint applications till he came to his seat. When he sat down, he refused to comply with their requests, and upon their urging him further began to reproach them severely for their demand, when Tillius, laying hold of his robe with both his hands, pulled it down from his neck, which was the signal for the assault. Casca gave him the first cut in the neck, which was not mortal nor dangerous, as coming from one who at the beginning of such a bold action was probably very much disturbed; Caesar immediately turned about, and laid his hand upon the dagger and kept hold of it. And both of them at the same time cried out, he that received the blow, in Latin, "Vile Casca, what does this mean?" and he that gave it, in Greek to his brother, "Brother, help!" Upon this first onset, those who were not privy to the design were astonished, and their horror and amazement at what they saw were so great that they dared not fly nor assist Caesar, nor so much as speak a word. But those who came prepared for the business enclosed him on every side, with their naked daggers in their hands. Which way soever he turned he met with blows, and saw their swords leveled at his face and eyes, and was encompassed like a wild beast in the toils on every side. For it had been agreed they should each of them make a thrust at him, and flesh themselves with his blood: for which reason Brutus also gave him one stab in the groin. Some say that he fought and resisted all the rest, shifting his body to avoid the blows, and calling out for help, but that when he saw Brutus's sword drawn, he covered his face with his robe and submitted, letting himself fall, whether it were by chance or that he was pushed in that direction by his murderers, at the foot of the pedestal on which Pompey's statue stood, and which was thus wetted with his blood. So that Pompey himself seemed to have presided, as it were, over the revenge done upon his adversary, who lay here at his feet, and breathed out his soul through his multitude of wounds, for they say he received three-and-twenty. And the conspirators themselves were many of them wounded by each other while they all leveled their blows at the same person.

 What does this account of Caesar's assassination reveal about the character of Julius Caesar? Based on this selection, what lessons did Classical historians intend their readers to take from their accounts of great and dramatic political events?

Source: From *The Lives of the Noble Grecians and Romans* by Plutarch, translated by John Dryden and edited by Arthur H. Clough.

Augustus maintained a standing army of twenty-eight legions, or about 150,000 men (a legion was a military unit of about 5,000 troops). Only Roman citizens could be legionaries, while subject peoples could serve as auxiliary forces, which numbered around 130,000 under Augustus. Augustus was also responsible for setting up a **praetorian guard** of roughly 9,000 men who had the important task of guarding the emperor. Eventually, the praetorian guard would play a weighty role in making and deposing emperors.

While claiming to have restored the Republic, Augustus inaugurated a new system for governing the provinces. Under the Republic, the senate had appointed the governors of the provinces. Now certain provinces were given to the emperor, who assigned deputies known as legates to govern them. The senate continued to name the governors of the remaining provinces, but the authority of Augustus enabled him to overrule the senatorial governors and establish a uniform imperial policy (see "The Achievements of Augustus," p. 142).

Augustus. Octavian, Caesar's adopted son, emerged victorious from the civil conflict that rocked the Republic after Caesar's assassination. The senate awarded him the title Augustus. This marble statue from Prima Porta, an idealized portrait, is based on Greek rather than Roman models. The statue was meant to be a propaganda piece, depicting a youthful general addressing his troops. At the bottom stands Cupid, the son of Venus, goddess of love, meant to be a reminder that the Julians, Caesar's family, claimed descent from Venus, thus emphasizing the ruler's divine background.

Augustus also stabilized the frontiers of the Roman Empire. He conquered the central and maritime Alps and then expanded Roman control of the Balkan peninsula up to the Danube River. His attempt to conquer Germany failed when three Roman legions, led by a general named Varus, were massacred in 9 CE by a coalition of German tribes. His defeats in Germany taught Augustus that Rome's power was not unlimited and also devastated him; for months, he would beat his head on a door, shouting, "Varus, give me back my legions!"

Augustus died in 14 CE after dominating the Roman world for forty-five years. He had created a new order while placating the old by restoring traditional values, a fitting combination for a leader whose favorite maxim was "make haste slowly." By the time of his death, his new order was so well established that

few agitated for an alternative. Indeed, as the Roman historian Tacitus (TASS-i-tuss) pointed out, "Practically no one had ever seen truly Republican government. . . . Political equality was a thing of the past; all eyes watched for imperial commands."[2] The Republic was now only a memory—and given its last century of warfare, an unpleasant one at that. The new order was here to stay.

5–2b The Early Empire (14–180)

There was no serious opposition to Augustus's choice of his stepson Tiberius (ty-BEER-ee-uss) as his successor. By his actions, Augustus established the Julio-Claudian dynasty; the next four successors of Augustus were related either to his own family or that of his wife, Livia.

Several major tendencies emerged during the reigns of the Julio-Claudians (14–68 CE). In general, more and more of the responsibilities that Augustus had given to the senate tended to be taken over by the emperors, who also instituted an imperial bureaucracy, staffed by talented freedmen, to run the government on a daily basis. As the Julio-Claudian successors of Augustus acted more openly as real rulers rather than "first citizens of the state," the opportunity for arbitrary and corrupt acts also increased. Nero (NEE-roh) (54–68), for example, freely eliminated people he wanted out of the way, including his own mother, whose murder he arranged. Without troops, the senators proved unable to oppose these excesses, but the Roman legions finally revolted. Abandoned by his guards, Nero chose to commit suicide by stabbing himself in the throat after uttering his final words, "What an artist the world is losing in me!"

The Five Good Emperors (96–180) Many historians regard the *Pax Romana* (PAKS *or* PAHKS ro-MAH-nuh) (the "Roman peace") and the prosperity it engendered as the chief benefits of Roman rule during the first and second centuries CE. These benefits were especially noticeable during the reigns of the five so-called **good emperors**. These rulers treated the ruling classes with respect, maintained peace in the empire, and supported generally beneficial domestic policies. Though absolute monarchs, they were known for their tolerance and diplomacy. By adopting capable men as their sons and successors, the first four of these emperors reduced the chances of succession problems.

Under the five good emperors, the powers of the emperor continued to expand at the expense of the senate. Increasingly, imperial officials appointed and directed by the emperor took over the running of the government. The good emperors also extended the scope of imperial administration to areas previously untouched by the imperial government. Trajan (TRAY-jun) (98–117) implemented an alimentary program that provided state funds to assist poor parents in raising and educating their children.

The good emperors were widely praised for their extensive building programs. Trajan and Hadrian (HAY-dree-un) (117–138) were especially active in constructing public works—aqueducts, bridges, roads, and harbor facilities—throughout the provinces and in Rome. Trajan built a new forum in Rome to provide a setting for his celebrated victory column. Hadrian's Pantheon, a temple of "all the gods," is one of the grandest ancient buildings surviving in Rome (see illustrations for the Pantheon, p. 146).

THE ACHIEVEMENTS OF AUGUSTUS

Politics & Government

THIS EXCERPT IS TAKEN FROM A TEXT WRITTEN BY AUGUSTUS and inscribed on a bronze tablet at Rome. Copies of the text in stone were displayed in many provincial capitals. Called "the most famous ancient inscription," the *Res Gestae* of Augustus summarizes his accomplishments in three major areas: his offices, his private expenditures on behalf of the state, and his exploits in war and peace. Though factual in approach, it is a highly subjective account.

Augustus, *Res Gestae*

Below is a copy of the accomplishments of the deified Augustus by which he brought the whole world under the empire of the Roman people, and of the moneys expended by him on the state and the Roman people, as inscribed on two bronze pillars set up in Rome.

1. At the age of nineteen, on my own initiative and at my own expense, I raised an army by means of which I liberated the Republic, which was oppressed by the tyranny of a faction [Mark Antony and his supporters]. . . .

2. Those who assassinated my father [Julius Caesar, his adoptive father] I drove into exile, avenging their crime by due process of law; and afterwards when they waged war against the state, I conquered them twice on the battlefield.

3. I waged many wars throughout the whole world by land and by sea, both civil and foreign, and when victorious I spared all citizens who sought pardon. . . .

5. The dictatorship offered to me . . . by the people and the senate, both in my absence and in my presence, I refused to accept. . . .

17. Four times I came to the assistance of the treasury with my own money, transferring to those in charge of the treasury 150,000,000 sesterces. And in the consulship of Marcus Lepidus and Lucius Arruntius I transferred out of my own patrimony 170,000,000 sesterces to the soldiers' bonus fund, which was established on my advice for the purpose of providing bonuses for soldiers who had completed twenty or more years of service. . . .

22. I gave a gladiatorial show three times in my own name, and five times in the names of my sons or grandsons; at these shows about 10,000 fought. . . .

25. I brought peace to the sea by suppressing the pirates. In that war I turned over to their masters for punishment nearly 30,000 slaves who had run away from their owners and taken up arms against the state. . . .

26. I extended the frontiers of all the provinces of the Roman people on whose boundaries were peoples not subject to our empire. . . .

27. I added Egypt to the empire of the Roman people. . . .

35. When I held my thirteenth consulship, the senate, the equestrian order, and the entire Roman people gave me the title of "father of the country" and decreed that this title should be inscribed in the vestibule of my house, in the Julian senate house, and in the Augustan Forum. . . . At the time I wrote this document I was in my seventy-sixth year.

 What were the achievements of Augustus? To what extent did these accomplishments create the "job" of being emperor? In what sense could this document be called a piece of propaganda?

Source: From *Roman Civilization*, Vol. I, by Naphtali Lewis and Meyer Renhold. Copyright © 1955 Columbia University Press. Reprinted by permission of the publisher.

Although we think of the *Pax Romana* as a time of peace and orderly government, there were rebellions against Roman rule. Revolts of Jews in Egypt and north Africa during the reign of Trajan in 115 were crushed. An Egyptian revolt in 172–173 was also suppressed but not without much damage to the economy. In 60 or 61 CE, there occurred the revolt of Boudica, the British queen of the Iceni tribe. She led an attack against Roman rule that burned and destroyed several cities before Roman forces won out. Rebellions against Roman rule were crushed without mercy, leading one Scottish chieftain to say (according to the Roman author Tacitus), when he was rousing his troops to fight the Romans: "To robbery, slaughter, plunder, they give the lying name of empire; they make a desert and call it peace." Obviously, Roman imperialism had a negative as well as positive side.

Frontiers and the Provinces Although Trajan extended Roman rule into Dacia (modern Romania), Mesopotamia, and the Sinai peninsula (see Map 5.3), his successors recognized that the empire was overextended and returned to Augustus's policy of defensive imperialism. Hadrian withdrew Roman forces from much of Mesopotamia. Although he retained Dacia and Arabia, he went on the defensive in his frontier policy by reinforcing the fortifications along a line connecting the Rhine and Danube Rivers and building a defensive wall 80 miles long across northern Britain to keep the Scots out of Roman Britain. By the end of the second century, the Roman forces were established in permanent bases behind the frontiers. But when one frontier was attacked, troops had to be drawn from other frontiers, leaving them vulnerable to attack.

At its height in the second century CE, the Roman Empire was one of the greatest states the world had seen. It covered about 3.5 million square miles and had a population, like that of Han China, estimated at more than 50 million. While the emperors and the imperial administration provided a degree of unity, considerable leeway was given to local customs, and the privileges of Roman citizenship were extended to many people throughout the empire. In 212, the emperor Caracalla (kar-uh-KAL-uh) completed the process by giving Roman citizenship to

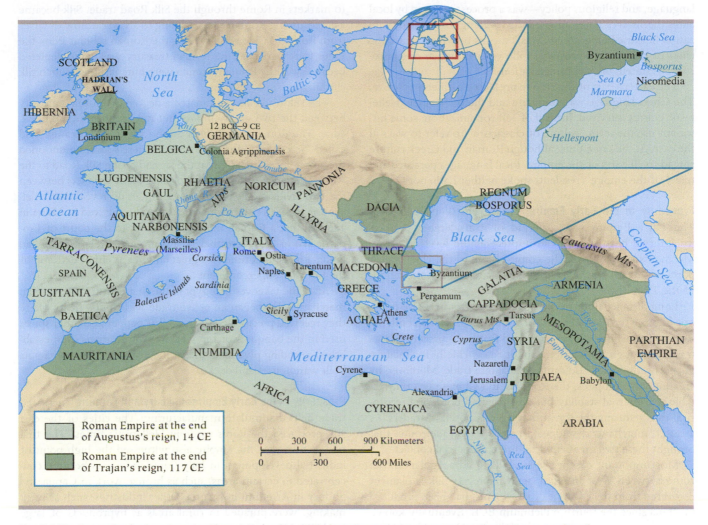

Map 5.3 The Roman Empire from Augustus Through Trajan (14–117). Augustus and later emperors continued the expansion of the Roman Empire, adding more resources but also increasing the tasks of administration and keeping the peace. Compare this map with Map 5.2, Section 5-1c, p. 135.

Q *Which of Trajan's acquisitions were relinquished during Hadrian's reign?*

every free inhabitant of the empire. Latin was the language of the western part of the empire, while Greek was used in the east. Roman culture spread to all parts of the empire and freely mixed with Greek culture, creating what has been called Greco-Roman civilization.

The administration and cultural life of the Roman Empire depended greatly on cities and towns. A provincial governor's staff was not large, so it was left to local city officials to act as Roman agents in carrying out many government functions, especially those related to taxes. Most towns and cities were not large by modern standards. The largest was Rome, but there were also some large cities in the east: Alexandria in Egypt numbered more than 300,000 inhabitants. In the west, cities were usually small, with only a few thousand inhabitants. Cities were important in the spread of Roman culture, law, and the Latin language, and they resembled one another with their temples, markets, amphitheaters, and other public buildings.

The process of Romanization (see next section) in the provinces was reflected in significant changes in the governing classes of the empire. In the course of the first century, there was a noticeable decline in the number of senators from Italian families. By the end of the second century, Italian senators made up less than 50 percent of the total. Increasingly, the Roman senate was being recruited from wealthy provincial families. The provinces also provided many of the legionaries for the Roman army and, beginning with Trajan, supplied many of the emperors.

HISTORIANS DEBATE **What Was Romanization?** Romanization is a controversial term. An earlier generation of historians used the term to describe a process of transformation in which the Roman governors of provinces imposed the Romans' "civilized" ways on conquered peoples. Many historians today reject that model and argue that becoming Roman—in adopting Roman architecture, food, clothing, language, and religious policy—was a process initiated by local elites themselves. They adopted the trappings of Roman civilization because being Roman was a means to power. Thus, the elites of the western provinces followed a policy, as one historian has stated, of "self-romanization."

The eastern part of the empire presented a different picture. The Greek language was dominant and the pre-Roman, Hellenistic culture survived. Instead of self-romanization, some historians use the term "culture of classicism" to refer to ways in the east. At the same time, although Roman and Greek culture spread to all parts of the empire, local languages persisted and many of the empire's residents spoke neither Latin nor Greek.

Prosperity in the Early Empire: Trade with China and India

The Early Empire was a period of considerable prosperity. Internal peace resulted in unprecedented levels of trade. Merchants from all over the empire came to the chief Italian ports of Puteoli on the Bay of Naples and Ostia at the mouth of the Tiber River.

Long-distance trade beyond the Roman frontiers also developed during the Early Empire. Economic expansion in both the Roman and Chinese Empires helped foster the growth of this trade. Although both empires built roads chiefly for military purposes, the roads also came to facilitate trade. Moreover, by creating large empires, the Romans and Chinese not only established internal stability but also pacified bordering territories, thus reducing the threat that bandits posed to traders. As a result, merchants developed a network of trade routes that brought these two great empires into commercial contact.

Most important was the overland Silk Road, a regular caravan route between West and East (see Chapter 3). Silk, a filament recovered from the cocoons of silkworms, had been produced in China since the fourth millennium BCE. Eventually, knowledge of this special product reached the outside world, and Chinese silk exports began to rise. By the second century BCE, the first clothing made from silk reached the Mediterranean Sea, stimulating the contacts between China and the Roman Empire. The bulk of the trade went overland through Central Asia (thus earning this route its modern name, the Silk Road). By the first century CE, large quantities of silk were being delivered to markets in Rome through the Silk Road trade. Silk became a craze among Roman elites, leading to a vast outflow of silver from Rome to China and causing the Roman scholar Pliny the Elder to remark that the Roman treasury was being depleted because wealthy Roman women were purchasing so much silk clothing.

The silk trade also stimulated a degree of mutual curiosity between the two great empires but not much mutual knowledge. The Roman geographer Strabo wrote of a strange land called "Seres" far to the east, while Chinese sources mentioned the empire of "Great Qin" at the far end of the Silk Road to the west. There was little personal or diplomatic contacts between the two civilizations, but Chinese sources do reveal that a delegation from the emperor Marcus Aurelius arrived in China in 166 and that a Roman merchant made it to the court of Emperor Wu in 226. Nevertheless, a commercial relationship had linked for the first time two great empires at either extreme of the Eurasian supercontinent.

After the takeover of Egypt in the first century CE, Roman merchants also began an active trade with India, from where they received precious pearls as well as pepper and other spices used in the banquets of the wealthy. The Romans even established a trading post in southern India where their merchants built warehouses and docks.

Prosperity in the Early Empire: Industry and Farming

Increased trade helped stimulate manufacturing. The cities of the east still produced the items made in Hellenistic times. The first two centuries of the empire also witnessed the high point of industrial development in Italy. Some industries became concentrated in certain areas, such as bronze work in Capua and pottery in Arretium in Etruria. Other industries, such as brick making, were pursued in rural areas as byproducts of large landed estates.

Despite the profits from trade and commerce, agriculture remained the chief pursuit of most people and the underlying basis of Roman prosperity. Although the large *latifundia* still dominated agriculture, especially in southern and central Italy, small peasant farms continued to flourish, particularly in Etruria and the Po Valley. Although large estates depended on slaves

Trade in the Roman Empire. Trade was an important ingredient in the prosperity of the Early Roman Empire. Although Roman roads were excellent, most goods traveled by boat throughout the Mediterranean and beyond. This third-century CE Roman mosaic from Sousse, Tunisia, shows workers unloading a cargo of iron ore from a ship. DEA Picture Library/Getty Images

THE DAILY LIFE OF AN UPPER-CLASS ROMAN

Family & Society There was an enormous gulf between rich and poor in Roman society. The upper classes lived lives of great leisure and luxury in their villas and on their vast estates. Pliny the Younger (c. 62–c. 113) was an upper-class Roman who rose to the position of governor of Bithynia in Asia Minor. In this excerpt from one of his letters, Pliny describes a typical day vacationing at one of his Italian villas. Although Pliny owned four villas in Italy, he did not belong to the ranks of the really rich in Roman society.

Pliny, Letter to Fuscus Salinator

You want to know how I plan the summer days I spend in Tuscany. I wake when I like, usually about sunrise, often earlier but rarely later. My shutters stay closed, for in the stillness and darkness I feel myself surprisingly detached from any distractions and left to myself in freedom. . . . If I have anything on hand I work it out in my head, choosing and correcting the wording, and the amount I achieve depends on the ease or difficulty with which my thoughts can be marshaled and kept in my head. Then I call my secretary, the shutters are opened, and I dictate what I have put into shape; he goes out, is recalled, and again dismissed. Three or four hours after I first wake (but I don't keep to fixed times) I betake myself according to the weather either to the terrace or the covered arcade, work out the rest of my subject, and dictate it.

I go for a drive, and spend the time in the same way as when walking or lying down; my powers of concentration do not flag and are in fact refreshed by the change. After a short sleep and another walk I read a Greek or Latin speech aloud and with emphasis, not so much for the sake of my voice as my digestion, though of course both are strengthened by this. Then I have another walk, am oiled, take exercise, and have a bath. If I am dining alone with my wife or with a few friends, a book is read aloud during the meal and afterward we listen to a comedy or some music; then I walk again with the members of my household, some of whom are educated. Thus, the evening is prolonged with varied conversations, and even when the days are at their longest, comes to a satisfying end.

Part of the day is given up to friends who visit me from neighboring towns and sometimes come to my aid with a welcome interruption when I am tired. Occasionally I go hunting, but not without my notebooks so that I shall have something to bring home even if I catch nothing. I also give some time to my tenants (they think it should be more) and the boorishness of their complaints gives fresh zest to our literary interests and the more civilized pursuits of town.

 What does Pliny's letter tell you about the lifestyle of upper-class Romans? Could this lifestyle be related to the decline of the Roman Empire? Why or why not?

Source: From *The Letters of the Younger Pliny*, translated with an introduction by Betty Radice (Penguin Classics 1963, Reprinted 1969).

---

for the raising of sheep and cattle, the lands of some *latifundia* were also worked by free tenant farmers who paid rent in labor, produce, or sometimes cash.

Despite the prosperity of the Roman world, an enormous gulf existed between rich and poor (see "The Daily Life of an Upper-Class Roman"). The development of towns and cities, so important to the creation of any civilization, is based largely on the agricultural surpluses of the countryside. In ancient times, the margin of surplus produced by each farmer was relatively small. Therefore, the upper classes and urban populations had to be supported by the labor of a large number of agricultural producers, who never found it easy to produce much more than they needed for themselves. In lean years, when there were no surpluses, the townspeople often took what they wanted, leaving little for the peasants.

5-2c Culture and Society in the Roman World

One of the notable characteristics of Roman culture and society is the impact of the Greeks. Greek ambassadors, merchants, and artists traveled to Rome and spread Greek thought and practices. After their conquest of the Hellenistic kingdoms, Roman generals shipped Greek manuscripts and artworks back to Rome. Multitudes of educated Greek slaves labored in Roman households. Rich Romans hired Greek tutors and sent their sons to Athens to study. As the Roman poet Horace (HOR-uss) said, "Captive Greece took captive her rude conqueror." Greek thought captivated Roman minds, and the Romans became willing transmitters of Greek culture.

Roman Literature The high point of Latin literature was reached in the Age of Augustus, often called the golden age of Latin literature. The most distinguished poet of the Augustan Age was Virgil (VUR-jul) (70–19 BCE). The son of a small landholder in northern Italy, he welcomed the rule of Augustus and wrote his greatest work in the emperor's honor. Virgil's masterpiece was the *Aeneid*, an epic poem clearly intended to rival the work of Homer. The connection between Troy and Rome is made in the poem when Aeneas, a hero of Troy, survives the destruction of that city and eventually settles in Latium—establishing a link between Roman civilization and Greek history. Aeneas is portrayed as the ideal Roman—his virtues are duty, piety, and faithfulness. Virgil's overall purpose was to show that Aeneas had fulfilled his mission to establish the Romans in Italy and thereby start Rome on its divine mission to rule the world.

Let others fashion from bronze more lifelike,
*   breathing images—*
For so they shall—and evoke living faces from marble;

*Others excel as orators, others track with their
    instruments
The planets circling in heaven and predict when
    stars will appear.
But, Romans, never forget that government is your
    medium!
Be this your art:—to practice men in the habit of peace,
Generosity to the conquered, and firmness against
    aggressors.*[3]

As Virgil expressed it, ruling was Rome's gift.

Roman Art The Romans were also dependent on the Greeks for artistic inspiration. The Romans developed a taste for Greek statues, which they placed not only in public buildings but also in their private houses. The Romans' own portrait sculpture was characterized by an intense realism that included even unpleasant physical details. Wall paintings and frescoes in the homes of the rich realistically depicted landscapes, portraits, and scenes from mythological stories.

The Romans excelled in architecture, a highly practical art. Although they continued to adapt Greek styles and made use of colonnades and rectangular structures, the Romans were also innovative. They made considerable use of curvilinear forms: the arch, vault, and dome. The Romans were also the first people in antiquity to use concrete on a massive scale. By combining concrete and curvilinear forms, they were able to construct huge buildings—public baths, such as those of Caracalla, and amphitheaters capable of seating 50,000 spectators. These large buildings were made possible by Roman engineering skills.

These same skills were put to use in constructing roads, aqueducts, and bridges: a network of 50,000 miles of roads linked all parts of the empire, and in Rome, almost a dozen aqueducts kept the population of one million supplied with water.

Roman Law One of Rome's chief gifts to the Mediterranean world of its day and to later generations was its system of law. Rome's first code of laws was the Twelve Tables of 450 BCE, but that was designed for a simple farming society and proved inadequate for later needs. So, from the Twelve Tables, the Romans developed a system of civil law that applied to all Roman citizens. As Rome expanded, problems arose between citizens and noncitizens and also among noncitizen residents of the empire. Although some of the rules of civil law could be used in these cases, special rules were often needed. These rules gave rise to a body of law known as the *law of nations*, defined as the part of the law that applied to both Romans and foreigners. Under the influence of Stoicism, the Romans came to identify their law of nations with **natural law**, a set of universal laws based on reason. This enabled them to establish standards of justice that applied to all people.

These standards of justice included principles that we would immediately recognize. A person was regarded as innocent until proved otherwise. People accused of wrongdoing

The Pantheon. Shown here is the Pantheon, one of Rome's greatest buildings. Constructed of brick, six kinds of concrete, and marble, it was a stunning example of the Romans' engineering skills. The outside porch of the Pantheon contained eighteen Corinthian granite columns, but it was the inside of the temple that amazed onlookers. The interior is a large circular space topped by a huge dome. A hole in the center of the roof was the only source of light. The dome, built up by layer after layer of concrete, weighs 5,000 tons. The walls holding the dome are almost 20 feet thick.

were allowed to defend themselves before a judge. A judge, in turn, was expected to weigh evidence carefully before arriving at a decision. These principles lived on long after the fall of the Roman Empire.

The Roman Family At the heart of the Roman social structure stood the family, headed by the *paterfamilias* (pay-tur-fuh-MEE-lee-uss)—the dominant male. The household also included the wife, sons with their wives and children, unmarried daughters, and slaves. Like the Greeks, Roman males believed that females needed male guardians. The *paterfamilias* exercised that authority; on his death, sons or nearest male relatives assumed the role of guardians.

Fathers arranged the marriages of daughters. In the Republic, women married "with legal control" passing from father to husband. By the mid-first century BCE, the dominant practice had changed to "without legal control," which meant that married daughters officially remained within the father's legal power. Since the fathers of most married women died sooner or later, not being in the "legal control" of a husband made possible independent property rights that forceful women could translate into considerable power within the household and outside it.

Like the Greeks, the Romans did not always raise all the children born into their families. Not only were deformed children abandoned to die of exposure, but infant mortality rates were high—as many as half of all infants did not survive into childhood. Nevertheless, upper-class families did take good care of their surviving children. The father was largely responsible for providing for the education of his children. Roman boys learned reading and writing, moral principles and family values, law, and physical training to prepare them to be soldiers. Girls learned at home what they needed to know to be good wives and mothers.

The end of childhood for Roman males came at the age of sixteen, when a young man exchanged his purple-edged toga for a plain white toga—the toga of manhood—and soon after began his career. For Roman girls, childhood ended at age fourteen, the common age of marriage. Although some Roman doctors warned that early pregnancies could be dangerous for young girls, early marriages persisted because

women died at a relatively young age. A good example is Tullia, Cicero's beloved daughter. She was married at sixteen, widowed at twenty-two, remarried one year later, divorced at twenty-eight, remarried at twenty-nine, and divorced at thirty-three. She died at thirty-four, which was not unusually young for women in Roman society.

By the second century CE, significant changes were occurring in the Roman family. The *paterfamilias* no longer had absolute authority over his children; he could no longer sell his children into slavery or have them put to death. Moreover, the husband's absolute authority over his wife had also disappeared, and by the late second century, women were no longer required to have guardians.

Upper-class Roman women in the Early Empire had considerable freedom and independence (see "Women in the Roman Empire," p. 148). They had acquired the right to own, inherit, and dispose of property. Upper-class women could attend races, the theater, and events in the amphitheater, although in the latter two places they were forced to sit in separate female sections. Women still could not participate in politics, but the Early Empire saw a number of important women who influenced politics through their husbands or sons, including Livia, the wife of Augustus, and Plotina, the wife of Trajan. It is important to remember, however, that the advantages of upper-class women were not necessarily true of women's experiences overall. Like the Greeks, the Romans adhered to the belief that a woman's place was in the home, and her role was to perform the domestic tasks crucial to the home. In other words, a Roman woman should be a "good wife" and a "good mother."

Slaves and Their Masters Although slavery was a common institution throughout the ancient world, no people possessed more slaves or relied so much on slave labor as the Romans eventually did. Slaves were used in many ways in Roman society. The rich owned the most and the best. In the late Roman Republic, it became a badge of prestige to be attended by many slaves. Greek slaves were in much demand as tutors, musicians, doctors, and artists. Roman businessmen would employ them as shop assistants or craftspeople. Slaves were also used as farm laborers; in fact, huge gangs of slaves worked

Roman/Getty Images

Childhood in the Roman World. This illustration, a scene from a third-century sarcophagus, shows an idealized version of an upper-class child's life: he is depicted being breast-fed by his mother, being held by his father, playing in a small chariot pulled by a goat, and reciting to his father.

WOMEN IN THE ROMAN EMPIRE

Family & Society

THE EXCERPT BELOW IS TAKEN FROM THE WORK OF A PHILOSOPHER LIVING IN THE ROMAN EMPIRE.
Gaius Musonius Rufus was a philosopher who taught Stoicism in Rome in the first century CE. His students wrote down some of his philosophical opinions. The excerpt here is taken from his thoughts on whether women should study philosophy.

Gaius Musonius Rufus, "That Women Too Should Study Philosophy"

When he was asked whether women ought to study philosophy, he began to answer. . . . Women have received from the gods the same ability to reason that men have. . . . Likewise women have the same senses as men, sight, hearing, smell, and the rest. . . . Since that is so, why is it appropriate for men to seek out and examine how they might live well, that is, to practice philosophy, but not women? . . .

Let us consider in detail the qualities that a woman who seeks to be good must possess, for it will be apparent that she could acquire each of these qualities from the practice of philosophy.

In the first place a woman must run her household and pick out what is beneficial for her home and take charge of the household slaves. . . . Next a woman must be chaste, and capable of keeping herself free from illegal love affairs, . . . and not enjoy quarrels, not be extravagant or occupied with her appearance. . . . There are still other requirements: she must control anger, and not be overcome by grief, and be stronger than every kind of emotion. . . .

[When asked if sons and daughters should be given the same education, he replied,] There are not different sets of virtues for men and women. First, men and women both need to be sensible. . . . Second, both need to live just lives. . . . Third, a wife ought to be chaste, and so should a husband. . . .

Well, then, suppose someone says, "Do you think that men ought to learn spinning like women and that women ought to practice gymnastics like men?" No, that is not what I suggest. I say that because in the case of the human race, the males are naturally stronger, and the women weaker, appropriate work ought to be assigned to each, and the heavier task be given to the stronger, and the lighter to the weaker. For this reason, spinning is more appropriate work for women than for men, and household management. Gymnastics are more appropriate for men than for women, and outdoor work likewise. . . . Some tasks are more appropriate for one nature, others for the other. For that reason some jobs are called men's work, and others women's. . . .

Without philosophy no man and no woman either can be well educated. I do not mean to say that women need to have clarity with or facility in argument, because they will use philosophy as women use it. . . . My point is that women ought to be good and noble in their characters, and that philosophy is no other than the training for that nobility.

 What are the views of Gaius Musonius Rufus on the responsibilities of a woman?

Sources: Lefkowitz, Mary R. and Maureen B. Fant, eds. *Women's Life in Greece and Rome: A Source Book in Translation*, 2nd ed. pp. 50–54 © 1992 M. B. Fant and M. R. Lefkowitz. Reprinted with permission of Johns Hopkins University Press and Bloomsbury Academic; From *Sources of Chinese Tradition*, 2nd edition, Vol. 1, by Wm. T. DeBary and Irene Bloom. Copyright © 1999 Columbia University Press. Reprinted with permission of the publisher.

the large landed estates under pitiful conditions. Many slaves of all nationalities were used as menial household workers, such as cooks, waiters, cleaners, and gardeners. Contractors used slave labor to build roads, aqueducts, and other public structures.

The treatment of Roman slaves varied. There are numerous instances of humane treatment by masters and even reports of slaves who protected their owners from danger out of gratitude and esteem. But slaves were also subject to severe punishments, torture, abuse, and hard labor that drove some to run away, despite stringent laws against aiding a runaway slave. Some slaves revolted against their owners and even murdered them, causing some Romans to live in unspoken fear of their slaves (see "The Roman Fear of Slaves").

Near the end of the second century BCE, large-scale slave revolts occurred in Sicily, where enormous gangs of slaves were subjected to horrible working conditions on large landed estates. The most famous uprising on the Italian peninsula occurred in 73 BCE. Led by a gladiator named Spartacus (SPAR-tuh-kuss), the revolt broke out in southern Italy and involved 70,000 slaves. Spartacus managed to defeat several Roman armies before being trapped and killed in southern Italy in 71 BCE. Six thousand of his followers were crucified, the traditional form of execution for slaves.

Imperial Rome At the center of the colossal Roman Empire was the ancient city of Rome. A true capital city, Rome had the largest population of any city in the empire, close to one million by the time of Augustus. Only Chang'an (CHENG-AHN), the imperial capital of the Han Empire in China, had a comparable population during this time.

An enormous gulf existed between rich and poor in the city of Rome. While the rich had comfortable villas, the poor lived in apartment blocks called *insulae*, which might be six stories high. Constructed of concrete, they were often poorly built and prone to collapse. The use of wooden beams in the floors and movable stoves, torches, candles, and lamps for heat and light created a constant danger of fire. Once started, fires were extremely difficult to put out. The famous conflagration of 64, which Nero was unjustly accused of starting, devastated a good

THE ROMAN FEAR OF SLAVES

Family & Society

THE LOWEST STRATUM OF THE ROMAN POPULATION consisted of slaves. They were used extensively in households, at the court, as artisans in industrial enterprises, as business managers, and in numerous other ways. Although some historians have argued that slaves were treated more humanely during the Early Empire, these selections by the Roman historian Tacitus and the Roman statesman Pliny indicate that slaves still rebelled against their masters because of mistreatment. Many masters continued to live in fear of their slaves, as witnessed by the saying "As many enemies as you have slaves."

Tacitus, *The Annals of Imperial Rome*

Soon afterwards the City Prefect, Lucius Pedanius Secundus, was murdered by one of his slaves [in 61 CE]. Either Pedanius had refused to free the murderer after agreeing to a price, or the slave, in a homosexual infatuation, found competition from his master intolerable. After the murder, ancient custom required that every slave residing under the same roof must be executed. But a crowd gathered, eager to save so many innocent lives; and rioting began. The senate house was besieged. Inside, there was feeling against excessive severity, but the majority opposed any change. Among the latter was Gaius Cassius Longinus, who when his turn came spoke as follows. . . .

"An ex-consul has been deliberately murdered by a slave in his own home. None of his fellow-slaves prevented or betrayed the murderer, though the senatorial decree threatening the whole household with execution still stands. Exempt them from the penalty if you like. But then, if the City Prefect was not important enough to be immune; who will be? Who will have enough slaves to protect him if Pedanius's four hundred were too few? Who can rely on his household's help if even fear for their own lives does not make them shield us?"

[The sentence of death was carried out.]

Pliny the Younger to Acilius

A shocking affair, worthy of more publicity than a letter can bestow, has befallen Larcius Macedo, a man of praetorian rank, at the hands of his own slaves. He was known to be an over-bearing and cruel master, and one who forgot—or rather remembered too keenly—that his own father had been a slave. He was bathing at his villa near Formiae, when he was suddenly surrounded by his slaves. One seized him by the throat, another struck him on the forehead, and others smote him in the chest. . . . When they thought the breath had left his body they flung him on to the hot tiled floor to see if he was still alive. Whether he was insensible, or merely pretended to be so, he certainly did not move, and lying there at full length, he made them think that he was actually dead. At length they carried him out, as though he had been overcome by the heat, and handed him over to his more trusty servants, while his women ran shrieking and wailing to his side. Aroused by their cries and restored by the coolness of the room where he lay, he opened his eyes and moved his limbs, betraying thereby that he was still alive, as it was then safe to do so. His slaves took to flight; most of them have been captured, but some are still being hunted for. Thanks to the attentions he received, Macedo was kept alive for a few days and had the satisfaction of full vengeance before he died, for he exacted the same punishment while he still lived as is usually taken when the victim of a murder dies. You see the dangers, the affronts and insults we are exposed to, and no one can feel at all secure because he is an easy and mild-tempered master. . . .

 What do these texts reveal about the practice of slavery in the Roman Empire? What were Roman attitudes toward the events discussed in these documents?

Sources: From *The Annals of Imperial Rome* by Tacitus, translated by Michael Grant (Penguin Classics, 1956, Sixth revised edition 1989). From *Readings in Ancient History*, Hutton Webster (D.C. Health and Co.: Boston 1919), p. 245.

---

part of the city. Besides the hazards of collapse and fire, living conditions were miserable. High rents forced entire families into one room. In the absence of plumbing and central heating, conditions were so uncomfortable that poorer Romans spent most of their time outdoors in the streets.

Though the center of a great empire, Rome was also a great parasite. Beginning with Augustus, the emperors accepted responsibility for providing food for the urban populace, with about 200,000 people receiving free grain. But even the free grain did not relieve the grim condition of the poor. Early in the second century CE, a Roman doctor claimed that rickets was common among the city's children.

In addition to food, entertainment was also provided on a grand scale for the inhabitants of Rome. The poet Juvenal (JOO-vuh-nul) said of the Roman masses, "But nowadays, with no vote to sell, their motto is 'Couldn't care less.' Time was when their plebiscite elected generals, heads of state, commanders of legions: but now they've pulled in their horns, there's only two things that concern them: Bread and Circuses."[4] The emperor and other state officials provided public spectacles as part of the great festivals—most of them religious in origin—celebrated by the state. The festivals included three major types of entertainment. At the Circus Maximus, horse and chariot races attracted hundreds of thousands, while dramatic and other performances were held in theaters. But the most famous of all the public spectacles were the gladiatorial shows.

The Gladiatorial Shows The gladiatorial shows were an integral part of Roman society. They took place in amphitheaters. Perhaps the most famous was the amphitheater known as the Colosseum, constructed in Rome to seat 50,000 spectators. In most cities and towns, amphitheaters were the biggest buildings, rivaled only by the circuses (arenas) for races and the public baths.

Gladiatorial games were held from dawn to dusk (see Film & History). Contests to the death between trained fighters formed the central focus of these games, but the games included other forms of entertainment as well. Criminals of all ages and both genders were sent into the arena without weapons to face certain death from wild animals who would tear them to pieces. Numerous types of animal contests were also held: wild beasts against each other, such as bears against buffaloes; staged hunts with men shooting safely from behind iron bars; and gladiators in the arena with bulls, tigers, and lions. It is recorded that five thousand beasts were killed in one day of games when Emperor Titus inaugurated the Colosseum in 80 CE.

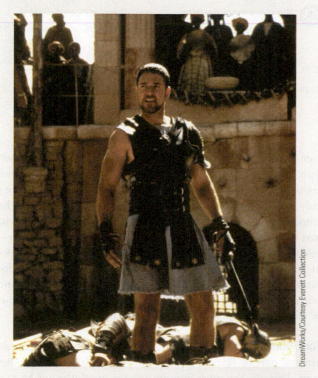
These bloodthirsty spectacles were extremely popular with the Roman people. But the gladiatorial games served a purpose beyond mere entertainment. Like the other forms of public entertainment, the games fulfilled both a political and a social function. Certainly, the games served to divert the idle masses from political unrest. It was said of the emperor Trajan that he understood that although the distribution of grain and money satisfied the individual, spectacles were necessary for the "contentment of the masses."

Disaster in Southern Italy Gladiatorial spectacles were contrived by humans, but the Roman Empire also experienced some spectacular natural disasters. One of the greatest was the eruption of Mount Vesuvius (vuh-SOO-vee-uss) on August 24, 79 CE. Although known to be a volcano, Vesuvius was thought to be extinct, its hillsides green with flourishing vineyards. Its eruption threw up thousands of tons of lava and ash. Toxic fumes killed many people, and the nearby city of Pompeii (pahm-PAY) was quickly buried under volcanic ash. To the west, Herculaneum (hur-kyuh-LAY-nee-um) and other communities around the Bay of Naples were submerged beneath a mud flow. Not for another 1,700 years were systematic excavations begun on the buried towns. Through examination of their preserved remains, archaeologists have been able to reconstruct the everyday life and art of these Roman towns. Their discovery in the eighteenth century was an important force in stimulating both scholarly and public interest in Classical antiquity and helped give rise to the Neoclassical style of that century.

5–3 CRISIS AND THE LATE EMPIRE

 Focus Questions: What reforms did Diocletian and Constantine institute, and to what extent were the reforms successful? What role did the Germanic tribes play in the Late Roman Empire?

During the reign of Marcus Aurelius, the last of the five good emperors, a number of natural catastrophes struck Rome. To many Romans, these natural disasters seemed to portend an ominous future for Rome. New problems arose soon after the death of Marcus Aurelius in 180.

5–3a Crises in the Third Century

In the course of the third century, the Roman Empire came near to collapse. Military monarchy under the Severan rulers (193–235), which restored order after a series of civil wars, was followed by military anarchy. For the next fifty years (235–284), the empire was mired in the chaos of continual civil war. Contenders for the imperial throne found that bribing soldiers was an effective way to become emperor. In these five decades, there were twenty-seven emperors, only four of whom did not meet a violent end. At the same time, the empire was beset by a series of invasions, no doubt exacerbated by the civil wars. In the east, the Sassanid (suh-SAN-id) Persians made inroads into Roman territory. Germanic tribes also poured into the empire. Not until the end of the third century were most of the boundaries restored.

Invasions, civil wars, and plague created new problems for the Roman Empire in the third century. There was a noticeable decline in trade and small industry, and the labor shortage caused by the plague affected both military recruiting and the economy. Farm production deteriorated significantly as fields were ravaged by invaders or, even more often, by the defending Roman armies. The monetary system began to collapse as a result of debased coinage and inflation. Armies were needed more than ever, but financial strains made it difficult to pay and enlist more soldiers. By the mid-third century, the state had to hire Germans to fight under Roman commanders.

5-3b The Late Roman Empire

At the end of the third and beginning of the fourth centuries, the Roman Empire gained a new lease on life through the efforts of two strong emperors, Diocletian (dy-uh-KLEE-shun) and Constantine (KAHN-stun-teen). Their rule transformed the empire into a new state, the so-called Late Empire, distinguished by a new governmental structure, a rigid economic and social system, and a new state religion—Christianity (see "Transformation of the Roman World: The Development of Christianity," p. 153).

The Reforms of Diocletian and Constantine Both Diocletian (284–305) and Constantine (306–337) extended imperial control by strengthening and expanding the administrative bureaucracies of the Roman Empire. A hierarchy of officials exercised control at the various levels of government. The army was enlarged, and mobile units were set up that could be quickly moved to support frontier troops when the borders were threatened.

Constantine's biggest project was the construction of a new capital city in the east, on the site of the Greek city of Byzantium on the shores of the Bosporus. Eventually renamed Constantinople (modern Istanbul), the city was developed for defensive reasons and had an excellent strategic location. Calling it his "New Rome," Constantine endowed the city with a forum, large palaces, and a vast amphitheater.

Location of Constantinople, the "New Rome"

The political and military reforms of Diocletian and Constantine also greatly increased two institutions—the army and the civil service—that drained most of the public funds. Though more revenues were needed to pay for the army and the bureaucracy, the population was not growing, so the tax base could not be expanded. To ensure the tax base and keep the empire going despite the shortage of labor, the emperors issued edicts that forced people to remain in their designated vocations. Basic jobs, such as baker or shipper, became hereditary. The fortunes of free tenant farmers also declined. Soon they found themselves bound to the land by large landowners who took advantage of depressed agricultural conditions to enlarge their landed estates.

In general, the economic and social policies of Diocletian and Constantine were based on an unprecedented degree of control and coercion. Though temporarily successful, such authoritarian policies in the long run stifled the very vitality the Late Empire needed to revive its sagging fortunes.

The End of the Western Empire Constantine had reunited the Roman Empire and restored a semblance of order. After his death, however, the empire continued to divide into western and eastern parts, which had become two virtually independent states by 395. In the course of the fifth century, while the empire in the east remained intact under the Roman emperor in Constantinople, the administrative structure of the empire in the west collapsed and was replaced by an assortment of Germanic kingdoms. The process was a gradual one, beginning with the movement of Germans into the empire.

Although the Romans had established a series of political frontiers along the Rhine and Danube Rivers, Romans and Germans often came into contact across these boundaries. Until the fourth century, the empire had proved capable of absorbing these people without harm to its political structure. In the late fourth century, however, the Germanic tribes came under new pressure when the Huns, a fierce tribe of nomads from the steppes of Asia who may have been related to the Xiongnu (SHYAHNG-noo), the invaders of the Han Empire in China, moved into the Black Sea region, possibly attracted by the riches of the empire to its south. One of the groups displaced by the Huns was the Visigoths (VIZ-uh-gahthz), who moved south and west, crossed the Danube into Roman territory, and settled down as Roman allies. But the Visigoths soon revolted, and the Roman attempt to stop them at Adrianople in 378 led to a crushing defeat for Rome.

Increasing numbers of Germans now crossed the frontiers. In 410, the Visigoths sacked Rome. Vandals poured into southern Spain and Africa, Visigoths into Spain and Gaul. The Vandals crossed into Italy from North Africa and ravaged Rome again in 455. By the middle of the fifth century, the western provinces of the Roman Empire had been taken over by Germanic peoples who set up their own independent kingdoms. At the same time, a semblance of imperial authority remained in Rome, although the real power behind the throne tended to rest in the hands of important military officials known as masters of the soldiers. These military commanders controlled the government and dominated the imperial court. In 476, Odoacer (oh-doh-AY-sur), a new master of the soldiers, himself of German origin, deposed the Roman emperor, the boy Romulus Augustulus (RAHM-yuh-lus ow-GOOS-chuh-luss). To many historians, the deposition of Romulus signaled the end of the Roman Empire in the west. Of course, this is only a symbolic date, as much of direct imperial rule had already been lost in the course of the fifth century.

What Caused the Fall of the Western Roman Empire? The end of the Roman Empire in the west has given rise to numerous theories that attempt to provide a single, all-encompassing reason for the "decline and fall of the Roman Empire." These include the following: Christianity's emphasis on a spiritual kingdom undermined Roman military virtues and patriotism; traditional Roman values declined as non-Italians gained prominence in the empire; lead poisoning caused by water pipes and cups made of lead resulted in a mental decline; plague decimated the population; Rome failed to advance technologically because of slavery; and Rome was unable to achieve a workable political system. There may be an element of truth in each of these theories, but all of them have also been challenged. History is an intricate web of relationships, causes, and effects. No single explanation will ever suffice to explain historical events. One thing is clear, however. Weakened by a shortage of manpower, the Roman army in the west was simply not able to fend off the hordes of people invading Italy and Gaul. In contrast, the Eastern Roman Empire, which would survive for another thousand years, remained largely free from invasion.

5–4 TRANSFORMATION OF THE ROMAN WORLD: THE DEVELOPMENT OF CHRISTIANITY

 Focus Question: What characteristics of Christianity enabled it to grow and ultimately to triumph as the official religion of the Roman Empire?

The rise of Christianity marked a fundamental break with the dominant values of the Greco-Roman world. To understand the rise of Christianity, we must first examine both the religious environment of the Roman world and the Jewish background from which Christianity emerged.

5–4a The Religious World of the Roman Empire

The Roman state religion focused on the worship of a pantheon of Greco-Roman gods and goddesses, including Juno, the patron goddess of women; Minerva, the goddess of craftspeople; Mars, the god of war; and Jupiter Optimus Maximus (JOO-puh-tur AHP-tuh-muss MAK-suh-muss) ("best and greatest"), who became the patron deity of Rome and assumed a central place in the religious life of the city. The Romans believed that the observance of proper ritual by state priests brought them into a right relationship with the gods, thereby guaranteeing security, peace, and prosperity, and that their success in creating an empire confirmed that they enjoyed the favor of the gods. As the first-century BCE politician Cicero claimed, "We have overcome all the nations of the world because we have realized that the world is directed and governed by the gods."[5]

The polytheistic Romans were extremely tolerant of other religions. They allowed the worship of native gods and goddesses throughout their provinces and even adopted some of the local deities. In addition, beginning with Augustus, emperors were often officially made gods by the Roman senate, thus bolstering support for the emperors (see Comparative Essay "Rulers and Gods").

The desire for a more emotional spiritual experience led many people to the mystery religions of the Hellenistic east, which flooded into the western Roman world during the Early Empire. The mystery religions offered their followers entry into a higher world of reality and the promise of a future life superior to the present one.

5–4b The Jewish Background

In addition to the mystery religions, the Romans' expansion into the eastern Mediterranean also brought them into contact with the Jews. Roman involvement with the Jews began in 63 BCE, and by 6 CE, Judaea (which embraced the old Jewish kingdom of Judah) had been made a province and placed under the direction of a Roman procurator. But unrest continued, augmented by divisions among the Jews themselves. One group, the Essenes, awaited a Messiah who would save Israel from oppression, usher in the kingdom of God, and establish paradise on earth. Another group, the Zealots, were militant extremists who advocated the violent overthrow of Roman rule.

Despite their differences, discontent with Roman rule led many Jews in Judaea to rise in revolt in 66 CE. Jewish forces massacred the Roman garrison in Jerusalem, defeated a Roman force sent from Syria, and set up a new government. It was not until 70 CE that Roman forces recaptured the city of Jerusalem, killing many of its inhabitants, and destroying the Jewish Temple. Roman power once more stood supreme in Judaea.

Another Jewish revolt against Roman rule occurred in 132 CE when the emperor Hadrian attempted to set up a new Roman colony on the site of Jerusalem. Although Jewish forces under the leadership of Simon bar Kokhba, who was viewed by many Jews as a Messiah, were initially successful, the Roman legions gradually wore down the Jewish forces and captured Jerusalem in 135. Judaea, now renamed Syria-Palestina, was a wasteland, and Jews were forbidden to enter Jerusalem. The Jews, driven by their religious uniqueness, had tried and failed to maintain an independent state. Another Jewish state would not arise until after World War II with the creation of modern Israel.

5–4c The Rise of Christianity

Jesus of Nazareth (c. 6 BCE–c. 29 CE) was a Palestinian Jew who grew up in Galilee, an important center of the militant Zealots. Jesus's message was simple. He reassured his fellow Jews that he did not plan to undermine their traditional religion. What was important was not strict adherence to the letter of the law but the transformation of the inner person: "So in everything, do to others what you would have them do to you, for this sums up the Law and the Prophets."[6] God's command was simply to love God and one another: "Love the Lord your God with all your heart and with all your soul and with all your mind and with all your strength. The second is this: Love your neighbor as yourself."[7] In his teachings, Jesus

Rulers and Gods

Religion & Philosophy All of the world's earliest civilizations believed that there was a close relationship between rulers and gods. In Egypt, pharaohs were considered gods whose role was to maintain the order and harmony of the universe in their own kingdom. In the words of an Egyptian hymn, "What is the king of Upper and Lower Egypt? He is a god by whose dealings one lives, the father and mother of all men, alone by himself, without an equal." In Mesopotamia, India, and China, rulers were thought to rule with divine assistance. Kings were often seen as rulers who derived their power from the gods and acted as the agents or representatives of the gods. In ancient India, rulers claimed to be representatives of the gods because they were descended from Manu, the first man who had been made a king by Brahman, the chief god. Many Romans believed that their success in creating an empire was a visible sign of divine favor.

Their supposed connection to the gods also caused rulers to seek divine aid in the affairs of the world. This led to the art of divination, an organized method to discover the intentions of the gods. In Mesopotamian and Roman society, one form of divination involved the examination of the livers of sacrificed animals; features seen in the livers were interpreted to foretell events to come. The Chinese used oracle bones to receive advice from supernatural forces that were beyond the power of human beings. Questions for the gods were scratched on turtle shells or animal bones, which were then exposed to fire. Shamans examined the resulting cracks on the surface of the shells or bones and interpreted their meaning as messages from supernatural forces. The Greeks divined the will of the gods by use of the oracle, a sacred shrine dedicated to a god or goddess who revealed the future in response to a question.

Underlying all of these divinatory practices was a belief in a supernatural universe, that is, a world in which divine forces were in charge and on which humans were dependent for their own well-being. It was not until the Scientific Revolution of the modern world that many people began to believe in a natural world that was not governed by spiritual forces.

Q *What role did spiritual forces play in early civilizations?*

Vishnu. Brahman the Creator, Shiva the Destroyer, and Vishnu the Preserver are the three chief Hindu gods of India. Vishnu is known as the Preserver because he mediates between Brahman and Shiva and thus maintains the stability of the universe. Fitzwilliam Museum, University of Cambridge, UK/Bridgeman Images

---

presented the ethical concepts—humility, charity, and brotherly love—that would form the basis of the value system of medieval Western civilization.

To the Roman authorities of Palestine, however, Jesus was a potential revolutionary who might transform Jewish expectations of a messianic kingdom into a revolt against Rome. Therefore, Jesus found himself denounced on many sides, and the procurator Pontius Pilate ordered his crucifixion. But that did not solve the problem. A few loyal followers of Jesus spread the story that Jesus had overcome death, had been resurrected, and had then ascended into heaven. The belief in Jesus's resurrection became an important tenet of Christian doctrine. Jesus was now hailed as "the anointed one" (*Christus* in Greek), the Messiah who would return and usher in the kingdom of God on earth.

Christianity began, then, as a religious movement within Judaism and was viewed that way by Roman authorities for many decades. One of the prominent figures in early Christianity, however, Paul of Tarsus (c. 5–c. 67), believed that the message of Jesus should be preached not only to Jews but to Gentiles (non-Jews) as well. Paul taught that Jesus was the savior, the son of God, who had come to earth to save all humans, who were all sinners as a result of Adam's sin of disobedience against God. By his death, Jesus had atoned for the sins of all humans and made possible their reconciliation with God and hence their salvation. By accepting Jesus as their savior, they too could be saved.

5–4d The Spread of Christianity

Christianity spread slowly at first. Although the teachings of early Christianity were mostly disseminated by preaching, written materials also appeared. Among them were a series of epistles (letters) written by Paul outlining Christian beliefs for different Christian communities. Some of Jesus's disciples may also have preserved some of the sayings of the master in writing and would have passed on personal memories that became the basis of the written *gospels*—the "good news" concerning Jesus—of Matthew, Mark, Luke, and John, which by the end of the first century CE had become the authoritative record of Jesus's life and teachings and formed the core of the New Testament. Recently, some scholars have argued that other gospels, such as that of Thomas, were rejected because they deviated from the beliefs about Jesus held by the emerging church leaders.

Jesus and His Apostles. Pictured is a fourth-century CE fresco from a Roman catacomb depicting Jesus and his apostles. Catacombs were underground cemeteries where early Christians buried their dead. Christian tradition holds that in times of imperial repression, Christians withdrew to the catacombs to pray and hide.

Although Jerusalem was the first center of Christianity, its destruction by the Romans in 70 CE dispersed the Christians and left individual Christian churches with considerable independence. By 100, Christian churches had been established in most of the major cities of the east and in some places in the western part of the empire. Many early Christians came from the ranks of Hellenized Jews and the Greek-speaking populations of the east. But in the second and third centuries, an increasing number of followers came from Latin-speaking peoples.

Initially, the Romans did not pay much attention to the Christians, whom they regarded as simply another Jewish sect. As time passed, however, the Roman attitude toward Christianity began to change. The Romans tolerated other religions as long as they did not threaten public order or public morals. Many Romans came to view Christians as harmful to the Roman state because they refused to worship the state gods and emperors. Nevertheless, Roman persecution of Christians in the first and second centuries was only sporadic and local, never systematic. In the second century, Christians were largely ignored as harmless (see "Roman Authorities and a Christian on Christianity"). By the end of the reigns of the five good emperors, Christians still represented a small minority within the empire, but one of considerable strength.

The Triumph of Christianity Christianity grew slowly in the first century, took root in the second, and by the third had spread widely. Why was the new faith able to attract so many followers? First, the Christian message had much to offer the Roman world. The promise of salvation, made possible by Jesus's death and resurrection, made a resounding impact on a world full of suffering and injustice. Christianity seemed to imbue life with a meaning and purpose beyond the simple material things of everyday reality. Second, Christianity seemed familiar. It was regarded as simply another mystery religion, offering immortality as the result of the sacrificial death of a savior-god. At the same time, it offered more than the other mystery religions did. Jesus had been a human figure, not a mythological one, and people could relate to him. Finally, Christianity fulfilled the human need to belong. Christians formed communities bound to one another in which people could express their love by helping each other and offering assistance to the poor, sick, widowed, and orphaned. Christianity satisfied the need to belong in a way that the huge, impersonal, and remote Roman Empire never could.

Christianity proved attractive to all classes. The promise of eternal life was for all—rich, poor, aristocrats, slaves, men, and women. Christianity emphasized a sense of spiritual equality for all people. Many women, in fact, found that Christianity offered them new roles and new forms of companionship with other women. Christian women fostered the new religion in their homes and preached their convictions to other people in their towns and villages. Many also died for their faith. Perpetua was an aristocratic woman who converted to Christianity. Her pagan family begged her to renounce her new faith, but she refused. Arrested by the Roman authorities, she chose instead to die for her faith and was one of a group of Christians who were slaughtered by wild beasts in the arena at Carthage on March 7, 203.

Moreover, the sporadic persecution of Christians by the Romans in the first and second centuries not only did little to stop the growth of Christianity, but in fact served to strengthen it as an institution in the second and third centuries by causing it to become more organized. Crucial to this change was the emerging role of the bishops, who began to assume more control over church communities. The Christian church was creating a well-defined hierarchical structure in which the bishops and clergy were salaried officers separate from the laity or regular church members.

As the Christian church became more organized, some emperors in the third century responded with more systematic persecutions, but their schemes failed. The last great persecution was at the beginning of the fourth century, but by that time, Christianity had become too strong to be eradicated by force. After Constantine became the first Christian emperor, Christianity flourished. Although Constantine was not baptized until the end of his life, in 313 he issued the Edict of Milan officially tolerating Christianity. Under Theodosius (thee-uh-DOH-shuss) the Great (378–395), it was made the official religion of the Roman Empire. In less than four centuries, Christianity had triumphed.

Roman Authorities and a Christian on Christianity

Religion & Philosophy **AT FIRST, ROMAN AUTHORITIES WERE UNCERTAIN HOW TO DEAL WITH THE CHRISTIANS.** In the second century, Christians were often viewed as harmless and yet were subject to persecution if they persisted in their beliefs. Pliny was governor of the province of Bithynia in northwestern Asia Minor (present-day Turkey). He wrote to the emperor for advice about how to handle people accused of being Christians. Trajan's response reflects the general approach toward Christians by the emperors of the second century. The final selection is taken from *Against Celsus*, written about 246 by Origen of Alexandria. In it, Origen defended the value of Christianity against Celsus, a philosopher who had launched an attack on Christians and their teachings.

An Exchange Between Pliny and Trajan

Pliny to Trajan

It is my custom. Sir, to refer to you in all cases where I do not feel sure, for who can better direct my doubts or inform my ignorance? I have never been present at any legal examination of the Christians, and I do not know, therefore, what are the usual penalties passed upon them or the limits of those penalties, or how searching an inquiry should be made. . . . In the meantime, this is the plan which I have adopted in the case of those Christians who have been brought before me. I ask them if they are Christians. If they say they are, then I repeat the question a second and a third time, warning them of the penalties it entails, and if they still persist, I order them to be taken away to prison. For I do not doubt that, whatever the character of the crime may be which they confess, their pertinacity and inflexible obstinacy certainly ought to be punished.

As is usually the way, the very fact of my taking up this question led subsequently to a great increase of accusations, and a variety of cases were brought before me. . . . So I postponed my examination, and immediately consulted you.

The matter seems to me worthy of your consideration, especially as there are so many people involved in the danger. Many persons of all ages, and of both sexes alike, are being brought into peril of their lives by their accusers, and the process will go on. For the contagion of this superstition has spread, not only through the free cities, but into the villages and the rural districts.

Trajan to Pliny

You have adopted the proper course, my dear Pliny, in examining into the cases of those who have been denounced to you as Christians, for no hard and fast rule can be laid down to meet a question of such wide extent. The Christians are not to be hunted out. If they are brought before you and the offense is proved, they are to be punished, but with this reservation—that if anyone denies that he is a Christian and makes it clear that he is not, by offering prayers to our deities, then he is to be pardoned because of his recantation, however suspicious his past conduct may have been. But pamphlets published anonymously must not carry any weight whatever, no matter what the charge may be, for they are not only a precedent of the very worst type but they are not in consonance with the spirit of our age.

Origen, *Against Celsus*

[Celsus] says that Christians perform their rites and teach their doctrines in secret, and they do this with good reason to escape the death penalty that hangs over them. He compares the danger to the risks encountered for the sake of philosophy as by Socrates. . . . I reply to this that in Socrates's cases the Athenians at once regretted what they had done, and cherished no grievance against him. . . . But in the case of the Christians the Roman Senate, the contemporary emperors, the army, . . . and the relatives of believers fought against the gospel and would have hindered it; and it would have been defeated by the combined force of so many unless it had overcome and risen above the opposition by divine power, so that it has conquered the whole world that was conspiring against it. . . .

He [also] ridicules our teachers of the gospel who try to elevate the soul in every way to the Creator of the universe. . . . He compares them [Christians] to . . . the most obtuse yokels, as if they called children quite in infancy and women to evil practices, telling them to leave their father and teachers and to follow them. But let Celsus . . . tell us how we make women and children leave noble and sound teaching, and call them to wicked practices. But he will not be able to prove anything of any kind against us. On the contrary, we deliver women from licentiousness and from perversion caused by their associates, . . . while we make boys self-controlled when they come to the age of puberty and burn with desires for sexual pleasure, showing them not only the disgrace of their sins, but also what a state these pleasures produce in the souls of bad men, and what penalties they will suffer and how they will be punished.

 What were Pliny's personal opinions of Christians? Why was he willing to execute them? What was Trajan's response, and what were its consequences for the Christians? What major points did Origen make about the benefits of the Christian religion? Why did the Roman authorities consider these ideas dangerous to the Roman state?

Source: From *Readings in Ancient History*, Hutton Webster (D.C. Health and Co.: Boston 1919), p. 250. From Origen, *Contra Celsum*. Trans. Henry Chadwick. Copyright © 1953 Cambridge University Press.

A COMPARISON OF THE ROMAN AND HAN EMPIRES

Q **Focus Question:** In what ways were the Roman Empire and the Han Chinese Empire similar, and in what ways were they different?

At the beginning of the first millennium CE, two great empires—the Roman Empire in the West and the Han Empire in the East—dominated large areas of the world. Although there was little contact between them, the two empires exhibited some remarkable similarities. Both lasted for centuries, and both were extremely successful in establishing centralized control (see Comparative Illustration "Emperors, West and East"). Both built elaborate systems of roads in order to rule efficiently and relied on provincial officials, and especially on towns and cities, for local administration. Architectural features found in the capital cities of Rome and Chang'an were also transferred on a smaller scale to provincial towns and cities. In both empires, settled conditions led to a high level of agricultural production that sustained large populations, estimated at between 50 and 60 million in each empire. Although both empires expanded into areas with different languages, ethnic groups, and ways of life, they managed to extend their legal and political institutions, their technical skills, and their languages throughout their empires. In this way, they integrated local communities into a common political and cultural framework.

COMPARATIVE ILLUSTRATION

Politics & Government **Emperors, West and East.** Two great empires with strong central governments dominated much of the ancient world—the Roman Empire in the West and the Han Empire in the East. Shown here are two emperors from these empires. The Roman emperor Hadrian (A), who ruled from 117 to 138, was the third of the five good emperors. He had been adopted by the emperor Trajan to serve as his successor. Hadrian was a strong and intelligent ruler who took his responsibilities seriously. Between 121 and 132, he visited all of the provinces in the empire. Liu Bang (lyoo BAHNG) (B) came from the peasant class, but through his military prowess, he defeated all

B

Art Archive, The/SuperStock

A

Werner Forman Archive/The Bridgeman Images

rivals in the civil wars that followed the death of the First Emperor of Qin. Liu Bang, who is known historically by his title of Han Gaozu (HAHN gow-DZOO), was the first emperor of the Han dynasty, which ruled China for four hundred years. He won the support of his subjects by reducing their tax burden. He was also responsible for bringing China back under central control but was killed in a frontier battle in 195 BCE.

Q *What similarities do you see in the lives of these two rulers?*

The Roman and Han Empires also had similar social and economic structures. The family stood at the heart of the social structure, and the male head of the family was all-powerful. The family also inculcated the values that helped make the empires strong—duty, courage, obedience, and discipline. The wealth of both societies also depended on agriculture. Although a free peasantry provided a backbone of strength and stability in each empire, wealthy landowners were able to gradually convert the free peasants into tenant farmers and thereby ultimately to undermine the power of the imperial governments.

Of course, there were also significant differences. The empires came into existence in different ways. Han China inherited an ideal of imperial culture on which to build. The Romans, on the other hand, began with a small city-state ruled collectively by its prominent citizens. As the Romans expanded throughout Italy and the Mediterranean, they eventually created a single imperial state.

There were also economic and social differences. Merchants were more highly regarded and allowed more freedom in Rome than they were in China. One key reason for this difference is that whereas many inhabitants of the Roman Empire depended to a considerable degree on commerce to obtain such staples as wheat, olives, wine, cloth, and timber, the vast majority of Chinese were subsistence farmers whose needs—when they were supplied—could normally be met by the local environment. As a result, there was undoubtedly less social mobility in China than in Rome, and many Chinese peasants spent their entire lives without venturing far beyond the village gate.

Another difference is that over the four hundred years of the empires' existence, Chinese imperial authority was far more stable. With a more cohesive territory and a strong dynastic tradition, Chinese rulers could easily pass on their authority to other family members. In contrast in the Roman Empire, political instability was a chronic problem, at least in some periods. Although Roman emperors were accorded divine status by the Roman senate after death, accession to the Roman imperial throne depended less on solid dynastic principles and more on pure military force.

Despite the differences, one major inescapable similarity remains: both empires eventually faced overwhelming problems. Both suffered from overexpansion, and both fortified their long borders with walls, forts, and military garrisons to guard against invasions of nomadic people. Both empires were periodically beset by invasions of nomadic peoples: the Han dynasty was weakened by the incursions of the Xiongnu, and the Western Roman Empire eventually collapsed in the face of incursions by the Germanic peoples.

Nevertheless, one inescapable difference between these two contemporary empires also remains. Although the Han dynasty collapsed, the Chinese imperial tradition, along with the class structure and set of values that sustained that tradition, survived, and the Chinese Empire, under new dynasties, continued well into the twentieth century as a single political entity. In stark contrast, the Roman Empire in the west collapsed and lived on only as an idea.

CHAPTER SUMMARY

Sometime in the eighth century BCE, a group of Latin-speaking people built a small community called Rome on the Tiber River in Italy. Between 509 and 264 BCE, this city expanded and brought almost all of Italy under its control. During this time of conquest, Rome also developed the political institutions of a republic ruled by an aristocratic oligarchy. Between 264 and 133 BCE, Rome expanded to the west and east and became master of the Mediterranean Sea and its surrounding territories, creating one of the largest empires in antiquity. In the second century BCE, the conservative, traditional values of Rome declined as affluence and individualism increased. After 133 BCE, Rome's republican institutions proved inadequate for the task of ruling an empire, and after a series of bloody civil wars, Augustus created a new order that established a Roman imperial state.

The Roman Empire experienced a lengthy period of peace and prosperity between 14 and 180. During this *Pax Romana*, trade flourished and the provinces were governed efficiently. In the course of the third century, however, the empire came near to collapse due to invasions, civil wars, and economic decline. At the same time, a new religion—Christianity—was spreading throughout the empire and slowly gained acceptance. The response to the crises of the third century and the rise of Christianity gradually brought a transformation of the Roman Empire in the fourth and fifth centuries. Although the emperors Diocletian and Constantine brought new life to the so-called Late Empire, their efforts only shored up the empire temporarily. Beginning in 395, the empire divided into western and eastern parts, and in 476, the Roman Empire in the west came to an end.

Although the Roman Empire in the west collapsed and lived on only as an idea, Roman achievements were bequeathed to

the future. The Romance languages of today (French, Italian, Spanish, Portuguese, and Romanian) are based on Latin. Western practices of impartial justice and trial by jury owe much to Roman law. As great builders, the Romans left monuments to their skills throughout Europe, some of which, such as aqueducts and roads, are still in use today. Aspects of Roman administrative practices survived in the Western world for centuries. The Romans also preserved the intellectual heritage of the Greco-Roman world

of antiquity. Nevertheless, although many aspects of the Roman world would continue, the heirs of Rome went on to create new civilizations—European, Islamic, and Byzantine—that would mark yet another stage in the development of human society.

The Han dynasty also created one of the greatest empires in antiquity. Like the Roman Empire, the Han Empire left a rich legacy to its successors. The Confucian institutions and principles enshrined during the long years of Han rule survived several centuries of internal division and eventually reemerged as the governing doctrine of later Chinese empires down to the twentieth century.

CHAPTER TIMELINE

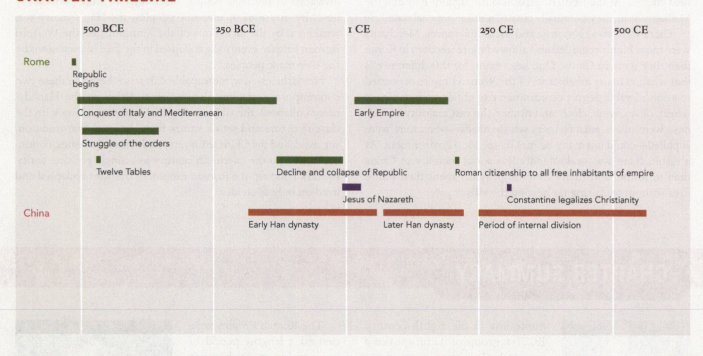

CHAPTER REVIEW

Upon Reflection

Q Was the fall of the Roman Republic due to systemic institutional weaknesses or the personal ambitions of generals and politicians? Explain your answer.

Q In what ways was the rule of the Roman emperors in the first and second centuries CE an improvement over

the Republic of the first century BCE? In what ways was their rule not an improvement over the last century of the Republic?

Q In what ways were the Roman and Han imperial systems of government alike? In what ways were they different?

Key Terms

consuls (p. 133)
praetors (p. 133)
senate (p. 133)
centuriate assembly (p. 133)
council of the plebs (p. 133)

patricians (p. 134)
plebeians (p. 134)
tribunes of the plebs (p. 135)
latifundia (p. 138)
dictator (p. 139)

praetorian guard (p. 140)
Pax Romana (p. 141)
good emperors (p. 141)

natural law (p. 146)
paterfamilias (p. 147)

Chapter Notes

1. Livy, *The Early History of Rome*, trans. A. de Selincourt, 1:16. The words were spoken by Julius Proculus, reportedly relaying to the Roman assembly a message from Romulus, one of Rome's founders, who appeared to him in a dream.
2. Tacitus, *The Annals of Imperial Rome*, trans. M. Grant (Harmondsworth, England, 1964), p. 31.
3. Virgil, *The Aeneid*, trans. C. Day Lewis (Garden City, N.Y., 1952), p. 154.

4. Juvenal, *The Sixteen Satires*, trans. P. Green (New York, 1967), p. 207.
5. Quoted in C. Starr, *Past and Future in Ancient History* (Lanham, Md., 1987), pp. 38–39.
6. Matthew 7:12.
7. Mark 12:30–31.

MindTap® is a fully online personalized learning experience built upon Cengage Learning content. MindTap® combines student learning tools—readings, multimedia, activities, and assessments—into a singular Learning Path that guides students through the course and helps students develop the critical thinking, analysis, and communication skills that are essential to academic and professional success.

NEW PATTERNS OF CIVILIZATION (500–1500 CE)

BY THE BEGINNING of the first millennium CE, many of the great states of the ancient world were in decline; some were even at the point of collapse. On the ruins of these ancient empires, new patterns of civilization began to take shape between 400 and 1500 CE. In some cases, these new societies were built on the political and cultural foundations laid down by their predecessors. The Tang Dynasty in China and the Guptas in India both looked back to the ancient period to provide an ideological model for their own time. The Byzantine Empire carried on parts of the Classical Greek tradition while also adopting the powerful creed of Christianity from the Roman Empire. In other cases, new states incorporated some elements of the former classical civilizations while heading in markedly different directions, as was the case with the Arabic states in the Middle East and the new European civilization of the Middle Ages. In Europe, however, the Renaissance, which began in the fifteenth century, sought to bring about a revival of parts of the old Greco-Roman culture.

During this period, a number of significant forces were at work in human society. The accoutrements of a more technologically advanced society gradually spread from the heartland regions of the Middle East, the Mediterranean basin, the South Asian subcontinent, and China into new areas of the world—sub-Saharan Africa, central and western Europe, Southeast Asia, and even the islands of Japan, off the eastern edge of the Eurasian landmass. Across the oceans, unique but advanced civilizations continued to take shape in isolation in the Americas. In the meantime, the vast migrations of peoples continued, leading not only to bitter conflicts but also to increased interchanges of technology and ideas. The result was the transformation of separate and distinct cultures and civilizations into an increasingly complex and vast world system embracing not only technology and trade but also ideas and religious beliefs.

As had been the case during antiquity, the Middle East was at the heart of this activity. The Arab empire, which took shape after the death of the Prophet Muhammad in the early seventh century, brought a measure of renewed stability to the region and provided the key link in the revived trade routes that threaded their way throughout Africa and much of the Eurasian supercontinent. The new religion of Islam became the cement that held the disparate peoples of the region together. Muslim traders—both Arab and Berber—opened contacts with West African societies south of the Sahara, while ships manned by Arab and South Asian sailors followed the monsoon winds eastward as far as the Spice Islands in Southeast Asia. Traders from Central Asia, some of them Muslim, carried goods back and forth along the Silk Road between the Middle East and China. For the next several hundred years, the great cities of the Middle East—Mecca, Damascus, and Baghdad—became among the wealthiest in the known world.

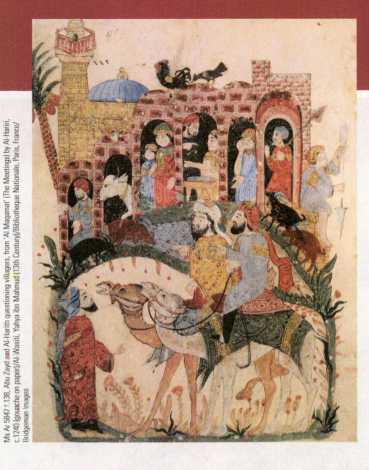

Islam's contributions to the human experience during this period were cultural and technological as well as economic. Muslim philosophers preserved the works of the ancient Greeks for posterity, Muslim scientists and mathematicians made new discoveries about the nature of the universe and the human body, and Muslim cartographers and historians mapped the known world and speculated about the fundamental forces in human society.

But the Middle East was not the only or necessarily even the primary contributor to world trade and civilization during this period. While the Arab empire became the linchpin of trade between the Mediterranean and eastern and southern Asia, another center of primary importance in world trade was emerging in East Asia, focused on China. China had been a major participant in regional trade during the Han dynasty, when its silks were already being transported to Rome via Central Asia, but its role had declined after the fall of the Han. Now, with the rise of the great Tang and Song Dynasties, China re-emerged as a major commercial power in East Asia, trading by sea with Southeast Asia and Japan and by land with the nomadic peoples of Central Asia.

Like the Middle East, China was also a prime source of new technology. From China came paper, printing, the compass, and gunpowder. The double-hulled Chinese junks that entered the Indian Ocean during the Ming Dynasty were slow and cumbersome but extremely seaworthy and capable of carrying substantial quantities of goods over long distances. Many inventions arrived in Europe by way of India

or the Middle East, and their Chinese origins were therefore unknown in the West.

Increasing trade on a regional or global basis also led to the exchange of ideas. Buddhism was brought to China by merchants, and Islam first arrived in sub-Saharan Africa and Southeast Asia in the same manner. Merchants were not the only means by which religious and cultural ideas spread, however. Sometimes migration, conquest, or relatively peaceful processes played a part. The case of the Bantu-speaking peoples in Central Africa is apparently an example of peaceful expansion; and while Islam sometimes followed the path of Arab warriors, they did not always impose their religion by force on the local population. In some instances, as with the Mongols, the conquerors made no effort to convert others to their own religions. By contrast, Christian monks, motivated by missionary fervor, sought to convert many of the peoples of central and eastern Europe. Roman Catholic missionaries brought Latin Christianity to the Germanic and western Slavic peoples, while monks from the Byzantine Empire introduced the southern and eastern Slavic populations to Eastern Orthodox Christianity.

Another characteristic of the period between 500 and 1500 CE was the almost constant migration of nomadic and seminomadic peoples. Dynamic forces in the Gobi Desert, Central Asia, the Arabian Peninsula, and Central Africa provoked vast numbers of peoples to abandon their homelands and seek their livelihood elsewhere. Sometimes the migration was peaceful and had few disruptive consequences. Often, however, migration produced political instability and sometimes invasion and subjugation. As had been the case during antiquity, the most active source of migrants was Central Asia. The region later gave birth to the fearsome Mongols, whose armies advanced to the gates of central Europe and conquered China in the thirteenth century. Wherever they went, they left a trail of enormous destruction and loss of life. Inadvertently, the Mongols were also the source of a new wave of epidemics that swept through much of Europe and the Middle East in the fourteenth century. The spread of the plague—known at the time as the Black Death—took much of the population of Europe to an early grave.

But there was another side to this era of widespread human migration. Even the invasions of the Mongols (the "scourge of God," as Europeans of the thirteenth and fourteenth centuries called them) eventually had constructive as well as destructive consequences. After their initial conquests, the Mongols provided an avenue for the peaceful exchange of goods and ideas throughout the most extensive empire (known as the *Pax Mongolica*) the world had yet seen. The world would never be the same again.

Chapter Outline and Focus Questions

Warriors raiding a village to capture prisoners for the ritual of sacrifice. Sef/Art Resource, NY

Critical Thinking

Q *In what ways were the early civilizations in the Americas similar to the civilizations discussed in Part I, and in what ways were they unique?*

Connections to Today

Q *Do the environmental problems encountered by pre-Columbian societies in the Americas have relevance today? Why or why not?*

IN THE SUMMER OF 2001, a powerful hurricane swept through Central America, destroying houses and flooding villages all along the Caribbean coast of Belize and Guatemala. Farther inland, at the archaeological site of Dos Pilas (dohs PEE-las), it uncovered new evidence concerning a series of dramatic events that had taken place nearly 1,500 years earlier. Beneath a tree uprooted by the storm, archaeologists discovered a block of stones containing hieroglyphics that described a brutal war between two powerful city-states of the area, a conflict that ultimately contributed to the decline and fall of Mayan civilization, perhaps the most advanced society then in existence throughout Central America.

Mayan civilization, the origins of which can be traced back to about 500 BCE, was not as old as some of its counterparts that we have discussed in Part I of this book. But it was the most recent version of a whole series of human societies that had emerged throughout the Western Hemisphere as early as the third millennium BCE. Although these early societies are not yet as well known as those of ancient Egypt, Mesopotamia, and India, evidence is accumulating that advanced civilizations had existed in the Americas thousands of years before the arrival of Hernando Cortés and the Spanish conquistadors in 1519. Because the arrival of the Spanish led to the rapid decline of the traditional cultures in the Western Hemisphere, and because it marked an early stage in the dramatic expansion of European power throughout the world, those events that were initiated by the arrival of the conquistadors will be treated in a later chapter (see Chapter 14).

6-1 THE PEOPLING OF THE AMERICAS

 Focus Question: Who were the first Americans, and when and how did they come?

The Maya (MY-uh) were only the latest in a series of sophisticated societies that had sprung up at various locations in North and South America since human beings first crossed the Bering Strait several millennia earlier. Most of these early peoples, today often referred to as **Amerindians**, lived by hunting and fishing or by food gathering. But eventually organized societies, based on the cultivation of agriculture, began to take root in Central and South America. One key area of development was on the plateau of central Mexico. Another was in the lowland regions along the Gulf of Mexico and extending into modern Guatemala. A third was in the central Andes Mountains, adjacent to the Pacific coast of South America. Others were just beginning to emerge in the vast Amazon River basin and in the river valleys and Great Plains of North America.

For thousands of years, these societies developed in isolation from their counterparts elsewhere in the world. This lack of contact with other human populations deprived them of access to technological and cultural developments taking place in Africa, Asia, and Europe. They did not make use of the wheel, for example, and their written languages were rudimentary compared to those in complex civilizations elsewhere around the globe. They did not benefit from the presence of the horse (which had died out in the Americas thousands of years previously) and of other draft animals such as the ox and the water buffalo. Still, in many respects, their cultural achievements were the equal of those realized elsewhere. When the first European explorers arrived in the region at the turn of the sixteenth century, they described much that they observed in glowing terms.

6-1a The First Americans

When the first human beings arrived in the Western Hemisphere has long been a matter of conjecture. In the centuries following the voyages of Christopher Columbus (1492–1504), speculation centered on the possibility that the first settlers to reach the American continents had crossed the Atlantic Ocean. Were they the lost tribes of Israel? Were they Phoenician seafarers from Carthage? Were they refugees from the legendary lost continent of Atlantis? In all cases, the assumption was that they were relatively recent arrivals.

By the mid-nineteenth century, under the influence of the Darwinian concept of evolution, a new theory developed. It proposed that the peopling of America had taken place much earlier as a result of the migration of small groups across the Bering Strait, at a time when the area was a land bridge uniting the continents of Asia and North America. Recent evidence, including numerous physical similarities between most early Americans and contemporary peoples living in northeastern Asia, has confirmed this hypothesis. The debate on when the migrations began continues, however. The archaeologist Louis Leakey, one of the pioneers in the search for the origins of humankind in Africa, suggested that the first hominids may have arrived in America as long as 100,000 years ago. Most scholars today, however, estimate that the first Americans were *Homo sapiens sapiens* who crossed from Asia via the Bering Strait sometime between 15,000 and 10,000 years ago. Some of them were probably hunters in pursuit of herds of bison and caribou that moved into the area in search of grazing land at the end of the last ice age. Others may have followed a maritime route (sometimes dubbed as "the kelp highway") down the western coast of the Americas, supporting themselves by fishing and feeding on other organisms floating in the sea.

In recent years, a number of fascinating new possibilities have opened up. A number of sites discovered at such disparate locations as Cactus Hill in Virginia, Buttermilk Creek in Texas, and northwestern Brazil show signs of human habitation as long as 20,000 years ago. Other recent discoveries raise the possibility that some early settlers may have originally come from Africa or from the South Pacific rather than from Asia. The question has not yet been answered definitively.

Nevertheless, it is now generally accepted that human beings were living in the Americas at least 15,000 years ago. They gradually spread southward and had penetrated almost to the southern tip of South America by about 11,000 BCE. These first Americans were hunters and food gatherers who lived in small nomadic communities close to the sources of their food supply. Although it is not known when agriculture was first practiced, beans and squash seeds have been found at sites that date back at least 10,000 years, implying that farming arose in America almost as early as in the Middle East. The cultivation of maize (corn), and perhaps other crops as well, appears to have been under way as early as 5000 BCE in the Tehuacán (teh-hwah-KAHN) Valley in central Mexico. Archaeologists have traced the ancestry of corn back at least 9,000 years to a wild Mexican grass called teosinte (tay-oh-SIN-tee). Through a lengthy process of experimentation, local farmers transformed it into a highly productive food crop that enabled the rise of the first civilizations in the Americas. A similar process may have occurred in the lowland regions near the modern city of Veracruz and in the Yucatán (yoo-kuh-TAHN) peninsula farther to the east. There, in the region that archaeologists call Mesoamerica, one of the first civilizations in the Americas began to appear.

6–2 EARLY CIVILIZATIONS IN MESOAMERICA

 Focus Question: What were the main characteristics of religious belief in early Mesoamerica, and how did they compare with belief systems in the ancient empires discussed in Part I of this book?

The first signs of civilization in Mesoamerica appeared at the end of the second millennium BCE, with the emergence of what is called Olmec (AHL-mek *or* OHL-mek) culture in the hot and swampy lowlands along the coast of the Gulf of Mexico south of Veracruz (see Map 6.1).

6–2a The Olmecs: In the Land of Rubber

Olmec civilization was characterized by intensive agriculture along the muddy riverbanks in the area and by the carving of stone ornaments, tools, and monuments at sites such as San

Lorenzo and La Venta. The site at La Venta contains a ceremonial precinct with a 30-foot-high earthen pyramid, the largest of its date in all Mesoamerica. The Olmec peoples organized a widespread trading network, carried on religious rituals, and devised an as yet undeciphered system of hieroglyphics that is similar in some respects to later Mayan writing and may be the ancestor of the first true writing systems in the Americas.

Olmec society apparently consisted of several classes, including a class of skilled artisans who produced a number of massive stone heads, some of which are more than 10 feet high. The Olmec peoples supported themselves primarily by cultivating crops, such as corn and beans, but also engaged in fishing and hunting. The Olmecs apparently played a ceremonial game on a stone ball court, a ritual that would later be widely practiced throughout the region (see "The Maya," Section 6-2e, p. 166). The ball was made from the sap of a local rubber tree, thus providing the name *Olmec:* "people of the land of rubber."

Trade between the Olmecs and their neighbors was apparently quite extensive, and rubber was one of the products most desired by peoples in nearby regions. It was used not only for the manufacture of balls, but also for rubber bands and footwear, as the Olmec learned how to mix the raw latex (the sap of the rubber tree) with other ingredients to make it more supple.

Eventually, Olmec civilization began to decline, and it apparently collapsed around the fourth century BCE. During its heyday, however, it extended from Mexico City to El Salvador and perhaps to the shores of the Pacific Ocean.

6–2b The Zapotecs

Parallel developments were occurring at Monte Albán (MON-tee ahl-BAHN), on a hillside overlooking the modern city of Oaxaca (wah-HAH-kuh), in central Mexico. Around the middle of the first millennium BCE, the Zapotec (zah-puh-TEK) peoples created an extensive civilization that flourished for several hundred years in the highlands. Like the Olmec sites, Monte Albán contains a number of temples and pyramids, but they are located in much more awesome surroundings on a massive stone terrace atop a 1,200-foot-high mountain overlooking the Oaxaca Valley (see illustration "A Ball Court," Section 6-2e, p. 167). The majority of the population, estimated at about 20,000, dwelled on terraces cut into the sides of the mountain known to local residents as Danibaan, or "sacred mountain."

The government at Monte Albán was apparently theocratic, with an elite class of nobles and priests ruling over a population composed primarily of farmers and artisans. Like the Olmecs, the Zapotecs devised a written language that has not been deciphered. Zapotec society survived for several centuries following the collapse of the Olmecs, but Monte Albán was abandoned for unknown reasons in the late eighth century CE.

6–2c Teotihuacán: America's First Metropolis

The first major metropolis in Mesoamerica was the city of Teotihuacán (tay-oh-tee-hwah-KAHN), capital of an early state about 30 miles northeast of Mexico City that arose around the third

Map 6.1 Early Mesoamerica. Mesoamerica was home to some of the first civilizations in the Western Hemisphere. This map shows the major urban settlements in the region.

 What types of ecological areas were most associated with Olmec, Mayan, and Aztec culture?

COMPARATIVE ILLUSTRATION

The Pyramid. The building of monumental structures known as pyramids was characteristic of a number of civilizations that arose in antiquity. The pyramid symbolized the link between the world of human beings and the realm of deities and was often used to house the tomb of a deceased ruler. Shown here are two prominent examples. Image A shows the pyramids of Giza, Egypt, built in the third millennium BCE and located near the modern city of Cairo. Image B photo shows the Pyramid of the Sun at Teotihuacán, erected in central Mexico in the fifth century CE. Similar structures of various sizes were built throughout the Western Hemisphere. The concept of the pyramid was also widely applied in parts of Asia. Scholars still debate the technical aspects of constructing such pyramids.

Q *How do the pyramids erected in the Western Hemisphere compare with similar structures in other parts of the world? What were their symbolic meanings to the builders?*

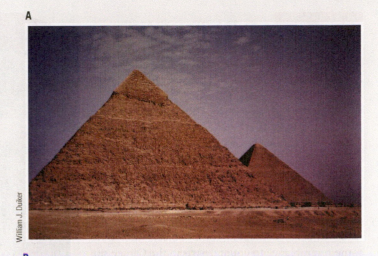

A

William J. Duiker

B

William J. Duiker

---

century BCE and flourished for nearly a millennium until it collapsed under mysterious circumstances about 800 CE. Along the main thoroughfare were temples and palaces, all dominated by the massive Pyramid of the Sun (see Comparative Illustration "The Pyramid"), under which archaeologists have discovered the remains of sacrificial victims, probably put to death during the dedication of the structure. In the vicinity are the remains of a large market where goods from distant regions as well as agricultural produce grown by farmers in the vicinity were exchanged. The products traded included cacao, rubber, feathers, and various types of vegetables and meat. Pulque (POOL-kay), a liquor extracted from the agave (uh-GAH-vee) plant, was used in religious ceremonies. An obsidian mine nearby may explain the location of the city; obsidian is a volcanic glass that was prized in Mesoamerica for use in tools, mirrors, and the blades of sacrificial knives.

Most of the city consisted of one-story stucco apartment compounds; some were as large as 35,000 square feet, sufficient to house more than a hundred people. Each apartment was divided into several rooms, and the compounds were covered by flat roofs made of wooden beams, poles, and stucco. The compounds were separated by wide streets laid out on a rectangular grid and were entered through narrow alleys.

Living in the fertile Valley of Mexico, an upland plateau surrounded by magnificent snowcapped mountains, the inhabitants of Teotihuacán probably obtained the bulk of their wealth from agriculture. At that time, the valley floor was filled with swampy lakes containing the water runoff from the surrounding mountains. The combination of fertile soil and adequate water made the valley one of the richest farming areas in Mesoamerica.

Sometime during the eighth century CE, perhaps because of drought or the overcultivation of the land, the wealth and power of the city began to decline, and eventually its ruling class departed, with the priests carrying stone images of local deities on their backs. The next two centuries were a time of troubles throughout the region as principalities fought over limited farmland. The problem was later compounded when peoples from surrounding areas, attracted by the rich farmlands, migrated into the Valley of Mexico and began to compete for territory with small city-states already established there. As the local population expanded, farmers began to engage in more intensive agriculture. They drained the lakes to build *chinampas* (chee-NAM-pahs), swampy islands crisscrossed by canals that provided water for their crops and easy transportation to local markets for their excess produce.

6–2d The Olmecs: Mother Culture or First Among Equals?

What were the relations among these early societies in Mesoamerica? Trade contacts were apparently quite active, as the Olmecs exported rubber to their neighbors in exchange for salt and obsidian. During its heyday, Olmec influence extended throughout the region, leading some historians to surmise that it was a "mother culture," much as the Shang Dynasty was once thought to be in ancient China (see Chapter 3).

A seventh-century BCE pyramid recently unearthed in the southern Mexican state of Chiapas (chee-AH-pahs) contained tomb objects that bore some resemblance to counterparts in the Olmec site of La Venta, but also displayed characteristics unique to the Zoque (ZOH-kay) culture that was prevalent in that region at the time. Some scholars point to such indigenous elements to suggest that perhaps the Olmec were merely first among equals. This issue has not yet been resolved.

6–2e The Maya

Far to the east of the Valley of Mexico, another major civilization had arisen in what is now the state of Guatemala and the Yucatán peninsula. This was the civilization of the Maya ("those who grow maize" in the Mayan language), which was older, and just as sophisticated as the society at Teotihuacán.

Origins It is not known when human beings first inhabited the Yucatán peninsula, but peoples contemporaneous with the Olmecs were already cultivating such crops as corn, yams, and manioc in the area during the first millennium BCE. As the population increased, an early civilization began to emerge along the Pacific coast directly to the south of the peninsula and in the highlands of modern Guatemala. Contacts were already established with the Olmecs to the west.

Since the area was a source for cacao trees and obsidian, the inhabitants soon developed relations with other early civilizations in the region. Cacao trees (whose name derives from the Mayan word *kakaw*) were the source of chocolate, which had since as early as the second millennium BCE been drunk as a beverage by the upper classes, while cocoa beans, the fruit of the cacao tree, were used as currency in markets throughout the region. A fermented beer was produced from the pulp of the fruit. The chocolate consumed in ancient Mesoamerican cultures was roasted and had a bitter taste. The flavor survives today in a classic sauce—mole (moh-LAY)—that includes unsweetened chocolate and chili peppers among its ingredients and is served with poultry and other meats. Chocolate did not develop its familiar sweet taste until the seventeenth century when cocoa beans were brought to Europe and sugar and milk were added.

Chocolate: Sacred Drink of Mesoamerica. The Maya recorded religious rites, as well as scenes of daily life, on polychrome clay vessels. Used in ritual ceremonies dedicated to their deities, these vessels contained a foamy chocolate beverage called *kakaw*, from which we derive the word *cacao*, the tree that produces the cocoa beans from which chocolate is made. After the Mayan civilization declined, chocolate (*xocoatl*, or "bitter water," in the Aztec language) continued to be used as a sacred beverage by other Mesoamerican peoples. In this image, a Mayan palace servant is apparently preparing cups of the heavenly nectar to use in a religious ceremony in one of the Mayan city-states.

As the population in the area increased, the inhabitants began to migrate into the central Yucatán peninsula and farther to the north. The overcrowding forced farmers in the lowland areas to shift from slash-and-burn cultivation to swamp agriculture of the type practiced in the lake region of the Valley of Mexico. By the middle of the first millennium CE, the entire area was honeycombed with a patchwork of small city-states competing for land and resources. The largest urban centers such as Tikal (tee-KAHL) may have had 100,000 inhabitants at their height and displayed a level of technological and cultural achievement that was unsurpassed in the region. By the end of the third century CE, Mayan civilization had begun to enter its classical phase.

William J. Duiker

Pacal's Palace at Palenque. King Pacal and his eldest son helped create the golden age of Mayan civilization with their innovative architecture and the detailed carvings of glyphs on the many limestone monuments at Palenque. Shown here is the royal palace, which is located adjacent to the Temple of Inscriptions. Pacal was apparently obsessed with the need to legitimize his royal status, since his claim to the throne descended not from his father's line but from that of his mother and grandmother. Some of the temple's glyphs (see illustration "Mayan Writing System," p. 169) portray the former as the first "mother goddess" of Palenque and thus confirm his own divine provenance as her offspring.

Political Structures The power of Mayan rulers was impressive. One of the monarchs at Copán (koh-PAHN)—known to scholars as "18 Rabbit" from the hieroglyphs composing his name—ordered the construction of a grand palace requiring more than 30,000 person-days of labor. Around the ruler gathered a class of aristocrats whose wealth was probably based on the ownership of land farmed by their poorer relatives. Eventually, many of the nobles became priests or scribes at the royal court or adopted honored professions as sculptors or painters. As the society's wealth grew, so did the role of artisans and traders, who began to form a small middle class.

The majority of the population on the peninsula, however (estimated at roughly 3 million at the height of Mayan prosperity), were farmers. They lived on their *chinampa* plots or on terraced hills in the highlands. Houses were built of adobe and thatch and probably resembled the houses of the majority of the population in the area today. There was a fairly clear-cut division of labor along gender lines. The men were responsible for fighting and hunting, the women for homemaking and the preparation of cornmeal, the staple food of much of the population.

Some noblewomen, however, seem to have played important roles in both political and religious life. In the seventh century CE, for example, Pacal (pa-KAL) became king of Palenque (pah-LEN-kay), one of the most powerful of the Mayan city-states, through the royal line of

his mother and grandmother, thereby breaking the patrilineal descent twice. His mother ruled Palenque for three years and was the power behind the throne for her son's first twenty-five years of rule. Pacal sought to legitimize his kingship by transforming his mother into a divine representation of the "first mother" goddess (for a picture of Pacal's death mask, see illustration "Jade and Gold Funeral Masks," Section 6-4b, p. 180).

Mayan Religion Like some of the early religious beliefs in Asia and the Mediterranean, Mayan religion was polytheistic. Although the names were different, Mayan gods shared many of the characteristics of deities of nearby cultures. The supreme god was named Itzamna (eet-SAHM-nuh) ("Lizard House"). Viewed as the creator of all things, he was credited with bringing the knowledge of maize, cacao, medicine, and writing to the Mayan people.

Deities were ranked in order of importance and had human characteristics, as in ancient Greece and India. Some, like the jaguar god of night, were evil rather than good. Many of the nature deities may have been viewed as manifestations of one supreme godhead (see "The Creation of the World: A Mayan View," p. 168). As at Teotihuacán, human sacrifice (normally by decapitation) was practiced to propitiate the heavenly forces.

Mayan cities were built around a ceremonial core dominated by a central pyramid surmounted by a shrine to the gods. Nearby were other temples, palaces, and a sacred ball court. Like many

Claire L. Duiker

A Ball Court. Throughout Mesoamerica, a dangerous game was played on ball courts such as this one. A large ball of solid rubber was propelled from the hip at such tremendous speed that players had to wear extensive padding. The game had religious significance and was not just an athletic contest. The court is thought to have represented the cosmos and the ball the sun, and the losers were sacrificed to the gods in postgame ceremonies. The game apparently originated in prehistoric times and is still played today in parts of Mexico (without the sacrifice, of course). The ball court shown here is located on Monte Alban and was built by the Oaxaca peoples.

THE CREATION OF THE WORLD: A MAYAN VIEW

Religion & Philosophy **POPUL VUH** (puh-PUL VOO), a sacred work of the ancient Maya, is an account of Mayan history and religious beliefs. No written version in the original Mayan script is extant, but shortly after the Spanish conquest, it was written down in Quiché (kee-CHAY) (the spoken language of the Maya), using the Latin script, apparently from memory. This version was later translated into Spanish. The following excerpt from the opening lines of Popul Vuh recounts the Mayan myth of the creation.

Popul Vuh: The Sacred Book of the Maya

This is the account of how all was in suspense, all calm, in silence; all motionless, still, and the expanse of the sky was empty.

This is the first account, the first narrative. There was neither man, nor animal, birds, fishes, crabs, trees, stones, caves, ravines, grasses, nor forests; there was only the sky.

The surface of the earth had not appeared. There was only the calm sea and the great expanse of the sky.

There was nothing brought together, nothing which could make a noise, nor anything which might move, or tremble, or could make noise in the sky.

There was nothing standing; only the calm water, the placid sea, alone and tranquil. Nothing existed.

There was only immobility and silence in the darkness, in the night. Only the Creator, the Maker, Tepeu, Gucumatz, the Forefathers, were in the water surrounded with light. They were hidden under green and blue feathers, and were therefore called Gucumatz. By nature they were great sages and great thinkers. In this manner the sky existed and also the Heart of Heaven, which is the name of God and thus He is called.

Then came the word. Tepeu and Gucumatz came together in the darkness, in the night, and Tepeu and Gucumatz talked together. They talked then, discussing and deliberating; they agreed, they united their words and their thoughts.

Then while they meditated, it became clear to them that when dawn would break, man must appear. Then they planned the creation, and the growth of the trees and the thickets and the birth of life and the creation of man. Thus it was arranged in the darkness and in the night by the Heart of Heaven who is called Huracan.

The first is called Caculha Huracan. The second is Chipi-Caculha. The third is Raxa-Caculha. And these three are the Heart of Heaven.

So it was that they made perfect the work, when they did it after thinking and meditating upon it.

 What similarities and differences do you see between this account of the beginning of the world and those of other ancient civilizations?

Source: From Popul-Vuh, *The Sacred Book of the Ancient Quiche Maya*, translated by Adrian Recinos. Copyright © 1950 by the University of Oklahoma Press.

of their modern counterparts, Mayan cities suffered from urban sprawl, with separate suburbs for the poor and the middle class, and even strip malls stretched along transportation routes, where merchants hawked their wares to pedestrians passing by.

The ball court was a rectangular space surrounded by vertical walls with metal rings through which the contestants attempted to drive a hard rubber ball. Although the rules of the game are only imperfectly understood, it apparently had religious significance, and the vanquished players were sacrificed in ceremonies held after the close of the game. Most of the players were men, although there may have been some women's teams. Similar courts have been found at sites throughout Central and South America, with the earliest, located near Veracruz, dating back to around 1500 BCE.

Hieroglyphs and Calendars The Mayan writing system, developed during the mid-first millennium BCE, was based on hieroglyphs that remained undeciphered until scholars recognized that symbols appearing in many passages represented dates in the Mayan calendar. This elaborate calendar, which measures time back to a particular date in August 3114 BCE, required a sophisticated understanding of astronomical events and mathematics to compile. Starting with these known symbols as a foundation, modern scholars have gradually deciphered the script. Like the scripts of the Sumerians and ancient Egyptians, the Mayan hieroglyphs were both ideographic and phonetic and were becoming more phonetic as time passed.

Responsibility for compiling official records in the Mayan city-states was given to a class of scribes, who wrote on deerskin or strips of tree bark. Unfortunately, virtually all such records have fallen victim to the ravages of a humid climate or were deliberately destroyed by Spanish missionaries after their arrival in the sixteenth century. As one Spanish bishop remarked at the time, "We found a large number of books in these characters and, as they contained nothing in which there were not to be seen superstition and lies of the devil, we burned them all, which they regretted to an amazing degree, and which caused them much affliction."[1]

As a result, almost the only surviving written records dating from the classical Mayan era are those that were carved in stone. One of the most important repositories of Mayan hieroglyphs is at Palenque, an archaeological site deep in the jungles in the neck of the Mexican peninsula, considerably to the west of the Yucatán (see Map 6.2). In a chamber located under the Temple of Inscriptions, archaeologists discovered a royal tomb and a massive limestone slab covered with hieroglyphs. By deciphering the message on the slab, archaeologists for the first time identified a historical figure in Mayan history. He was the ruler named Pacal, known from his glyph as "The Shield"; Pacal ordered the construction of the Temple of Inscriptions in the

Map 6.2 The Maya Heartland. During the classical era, Mayan civilization was centered on modern-day Guatemala and the lower Yucatán peninsula. After the ninth century, new centers of power like Chichén Itzá and Uxmal began to emerge farther north.

Q *What factors appear to have brought an end to classical Mayan civilization?*

Mayan Writing System. The Maya were the only Mesoamerican peoples to devise a complete written language. Although the origins of the Mayan system are unknown, many specialists believe that it may have emerged from scripts invented earlier by the neighboring Zapotecs or Olmecs and that the Maya learned of these experiments through contacts in the first millennium BCE. During the classical era from 300 to 900 CE, the Maya used the script to record dynastic statistics with deliberate precision. The symbols were carved on stone panels, stelae, or were painted with a brush on foldling-screen books made of bark paper.

mid-seventh century, and it was his body that was buried in the tomb at the foot of the staircase leading down into the crypt.

As befits their intense interest in the passage of time, the Maya also had a sophisticated knowledge of astronomy and kept voluminous records of the movements of the heavenly bodies (according to some knowledgeable observers, Mayan pyramids, known today throughout Latin America as *huacas*, were situated to observe the stars). There were practical reasons for their concern. The arrival of the planet Venus in the evening sky, for example, was a traditional time to prepare for war. The Maya also devised the so-called Long Count, a system of calculating time based on a lunar calendar that called for the end of the current cycle of 5,200 years in the year 2012 of the Western solar-based Gregorian calendar.

Scholars once believed that the Maya were a peaceful people who rarely engaged in violence. Now, however, most believe that rivalry among Mayan city-states was endemic and often involved bloody clashes. Scenes from paintings and rock carvings depict a society preoccupied with war and the seizure of captives for sacrifice. The conflict mentioned at the beginning of this chapter is but a recent example. During the seventh century CE, two powerful city-states, Tikal and Calakmul (kah-lahk-MOOL), competed for dominance throughout the region, setting up puppet regimes and waging bloody wars that wavered back and forth for years but ultimately resulted in the total destruction of Calakmul at the end of the century.

HISTORIANS DEBATE **Why Did the Maya Decline?** Sometime in the eighth or ninth century, the classical Mayan civilization in the central Yucatán peninsula began to decline. At Copán, for example, it ended abruptly in 822 CE, when work on various stone sculptures ordered by the ruler suddenly ceased. The end of Palenque soon followed, and the city of Tikal was abandoned by 870 CE. Whether the decline was caused by overuse of the land, incessant warfare, internal revolt, or a natural disaster such as a volcanic eruption is a question that has puzzled archaeologists for decades. Recent evidence supports the theory that overcultivation of the land due to a growing population gradually reduced crop yields. A long drought, which began in the seventh century and lasted throughout most of the ninth and tenth centuries CE, may have played a major role, although it is likely that overuse of the land because of growing population density may also have been a factor. In general, though, as arable land and water became increasingly scarce, conflict among the various mini-states in the region may have intensified, accelerating the process leading to a final collapse.

Whatever the case, cities such as Tikal and Palenque were abandoned to the jungles. In their place, newer urban centers in the northern part of the peninsula, such as Uxmal (oosh-MAHL) and Chichén Itzá (chee-CHEN eet-SAH), continued to prosper, although the level of

A Mayan Bloodletting Ceremony. The Mayan elite drew blood at various ritual ceremonies. Here we see Lady Xok, the wife of a king of Yaxchilian, passing a rope pierced with thorns along her tongue in a bloodletting ritual. Above her, the king holds a flaming torch. This vivid scene from an eighth-century CE palace lintel demonstrates the excellence of Mayan stone sculpture as well as the sophisticated weaving techniques shown in the queen's elegant gown.

Mayan Temple at Tikal. This eighth-century temple, peering over the treetops of a jungle at Tikal, represents the zenith of the engineering and artistry of the Mayan peoples. Erected to house the body of a ruler, such pyramidal tombs contained elaborate works of jade jewelry, polychrome ceramics, and intricate bone carvings depicting the ruler's life and various deities. This temple dominates a great plaza that is surrounded by a royal palace and various religious structures.

cultural achievement in this postclassical era did not match that of previous years. According to local history, this latter area was taken over by peoples known as the Toltecs (TOHL-teks), led by a man known as Kukulcan (koo-kul-KAHN), who migrated to the peninsula from Teotihuacán in central Mexico sometime in the tenth century. Some scholars believe this flight was associated with the legend of the departure from that city of Quetzalcoatl (KWET-sul-koh-AHT-ul), a half-human, half-deity in the form of a feathered serpent who promised that he would someday return to reclaim his homeland (see "The Legend of the Feathered Serpent").

The Toltecs apparently controlled the upper peninsula from their capital at Chichén Itzá for several centuries, but this area was less fertile and more susceptible to drought than the earlier regions of Mayan settlement, and eventually they too declined. By the early sixteenth century, the area was divided into a number of small principalities, and the cities, including Uxmal and Chichén Itzá, had been abandoned.

6–2f The Aztecs

Among the groups moving into the Valley of Mexico after the fall of Teotihuacán were the Mexica (meh-SHEE-kuh). No one knows their origins, although folk legend held that their original homeland was an island in a lake called Aztlán. From that legendary homeland comes the name *Aztec*, by which they are known to the modern world. Sometime during the early twelfth century, the Aztecs left their original habitat and, carrying an image of their patron deity, Huitzilopochtli (WEET-see-loh-POHSHT-lee), began a lengthy migration that climaxed with their arrival in the Valley of Mexico more than one hundred years later.

THE LEGEND OF THE FEATHERED SERPENT

Religion & Philosophy The mythical figure known as Quetzalcoatl permeates the religious belief of Mesoamerican peoples from the first century CE city of Teotihuacan to the Aztecs. Half human, half deity, he is usually portrayed as a feathered serpent, and is identified variously as the god of the Wind, of the Dawn, and of Learning and the Arts. In Mayan and Aztec literature, as a youth he took on his familiar mask to hide his ugliness. Later, his exploits run through the narrative of Mesoamerican history, from the abandonment of Teotihuacan in the eighth century CE to the Toltec conquest of the northern Yucatan many years later. Becoming ashamed after misbehaving in a drunken stupor, he immolated himself on the coast of Yucatan and merged his identity with Venus, the Dawn Star. The excerpts here are from the Codex Chimalpopoca, originally recited verbally by Aztec priests and then written down in Spanish in 1570. The first segment describes his adornment by a feather wizard, and the second portrays his self-immolation and transformation into the Dawn Star.

From the Codex Chimalpopoca

And so then Coyotlinahual the feather-artist fashioned them; first he made Quetzalcoatl's plumed headdress, then his turquoise inlay mask. He took red with which to paint his mouth; he took yellow with which to stripe his face. Next he prepared his serpent teeth, then his beard of cotinga and roseate spoonbill feathers across his lower face.

And so he arrayed him in his attire and he was Quetzalcoatl. Then he handed him the mirror, and when he looked on himself he was very pleased with what he saw. Then Quetzalcoatl abandoned forthwith the place where he was guarded. . . .

And it was again on the day 1 Reed, it is recounted, it is said, when he arrived at Teoapan Illhuicaatenco, "Along the divine water, At the shore of heavenly water." Then he halted and stood; he wept, took up his vestments and adorned himself in his insignia, his turquoise mask, etc.

And when he was fully adorned then with his own hand he set himself on fire, he offered himself up in flame.

So the place where Quetzalcoatl went to immolate himself came to be called Tlatlayan, "Place of the Burning."

And it is said that even as he burned, his ashes emerged and arose: and there appeared, before the sight of everyone, all the birds of great value when emerged and rose into the sky. They saw the roseate spoonbill, the cotinga, the trogon, the heron, the yellow parrot, the scarlet macaw, the white-bellied parrot, and every other bird of precious plumage.

And when the ashes were extinguished, then arose his heart, the quetzal bird itself; they saw it. And so they knew he had entered the sky within the sky.

The old ones used to say he was transformed to the dawn start; thus it is said that when Quetzalcoatl died this star appeared, and so he is named Tlahuizcalpanteuctli, "Lord of the Dawn House."

Source: Roberta H. and Peter T. Markman, *The Flayed God* (San Francisco: Harper Colllins, 1992), pp. 369–377, translated by Willard Gingerich as reproduced in Miguel Léon-Portilla and Earl Shorris, *In the Language of Kings: An Anthology of Mesoamerican Literature* (New York, W.W. Norton, 2001), pp. 188–191.

Less sophisticated than many of their neighbors, the Aztecs were at first forced to seek alliances with stronger city-states. They were excellent warriors, however, and (like Sparta in ancient Greece and the state of Qin in Zhou dynasty China) theirs had become the dominant city-state in the lake region by the early fifteenth century. Establishing their capital at Tenochtitlán (teh-nahch-teet-LAHN), on an island in the middle of Lake Texcoco (tess-KOH-koh), they set out to bring the entire region under their domination (see Map 6.3).

For the remainder of the fifteenth century, the Aztecs consolidated their control over much of what is modern Mexico, from the Atlantic to the Pacific Ocean and as far south as the Guatemalan border. The new kingdom was not a centralized state but a collection of semiautonomous territories. To provide a unifying focus for the kingdom, the Aztecs promoted their patron god, Huitzilopochtli, as the guiding deity of the entire population, which now numbered several million.

Politics Like all great empires in ancient times, the Aztec state was authoritarian. Power was vested in the monarch, whose authority had both a divine and a secular character. The Aztec ruler claimed descent from the gods and served as an intermediary between the material and the metaphysical worlds. Unlike many of his counterparts in other ancient civilizations,

however, the monarch did not obtain his position by a rigid law of succession. On the death of the ruler, his successor was selected from within the royal family by a small group of senior officials, who were also members of the family and were therefore eligible for the position. Once placed on the throne, the Aztec ruler was advised by a small council of lords, headed by a prime minister who served as the chief executive of the government, and a bureaucracy. Beyond the capital, the power of the central government was limited. Rulers of territories subject to the Aztecs were allowed considerable autonomy in return for paying tribute, in the form of goods or captives, to the central government. The most important government officials in the provinces were the tax collectors, who collected the tribute. They used the threat of military action against those who failed to carry out their tribute obligations and therefore, understandably, were not popular with the taxpayers. According to Bernal Díaz, a Spaniard who recorded his impressions of Aztec society during a visit in the early sixteenth century:

> All these towns complained about Montezuma [Moctezuma, the Aztec ruler] and his tax collectors, speaking in private so that the Mexican ambassadors should not hear them, however. They said these officials robbed them of all they possessed, and that if their wives and daughters were pretty they would

violate them in front of their fathers and husbands and carry them away. They also said that the Mexicans [that is, the representatives from the capital] made the men work like slaves, compelling them to carry pine trunks and stone and firewood and maize overland and in canoes, and to perform other tasks, such as planting maize fields, and that they took away the people's lands as well for the service of their idols.[2]

Social Structures Positions in the government bureaucracy were the exclusive privilege of the hereditary nobility, all of whom traced their lineage to the founding family of the Aztec clan. Male children in noble families were sent to temple schools, where they were exposed to a harsh regimen of manual labor, military training, and memorization of information about Aztec society and religion. On reaching adulthood, they would select a career in the military service, the government bureaucracy, or the priesthood. As a reward for their services, senior officials received large estates from the government, and they alone had the right to hire communal labor.

The remainder of the population consisted of commoners, indentured workers, and slaves. Most indentured workers were landless laborers who contracted to work on the nobles' estates, while slaves served in the households of the wealthy. Slavery

was not an inherited status, and the children of slaves were considered free citizens. Commoners might sell themselves into slavery when in debt and then later purchase their freedom.

The vast majority of the population consisted of commoners. All commoners were members of large kinship groups called *calpullis* (kal-PUL-eez). Each *calpulli*, often consisting of as many as a thousand members, was headed by an elected chief, who ran its day-to-day affairs and served as an intermediary with the central government. Each *calpulli* was responsible for providing taxes (usually in the form of goods) and conscript labor to the state.

Each *calpulli* maintained its own temples and schools and administered the land held by the community. Farmland within the *calpulli* was held in common and could not be sold, although it could be passed down within the family. In the cities, each *calpulli* occupied a separate neighborhood, where its members often performed a particular function, such as metalworking, stonecutting, weaving, carpentry, or commerce. Apparently, a large proportion of the population engaged in some form of trade, at least in the densely populated Valley of Mexico, where an estimated half of the people lived in an urban environment. Many farmers, who cultivated their crops in *chinampas* as their predecessors had for centuries, brought their goods to the markets via the canals and sold them directly to retailers (see "Markets and Merchandise in Aztec Mexico").

The *calpulli* compounds themselves were divided into smaller family units. Individual families lived in small flat-roofed dwellings containing one or two rooms. Each house was separate from its neighbors and had direct access to the surrounding streets and canals. The houses of farmers living on the *chinampas* were set on raised dirt platforms built above the surrounding fields to prevent flooding.

Gender roles within the family were rigidly stratified. Male children were trained for war and were expected to serve in the army on reaching adulthood. Women were expected to work in the home, weave textiles, and raise children, although, like their brothers, they were permitted to enter the priesthood. According to Bernal Díaz, a female deity presided over the rites of marriage. As in most traditional societies, chastity and obedience were desirable female characteristics. Although women in Aztec

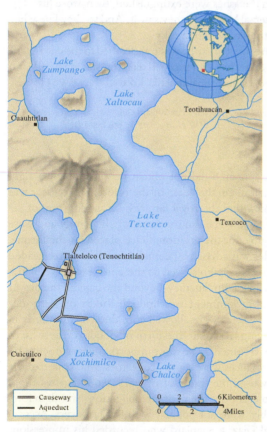

Map 6.3 The Valley of Mexico Under Aztec Rule. The Aztecs were one of the most advanced peoples in pre-Columbian Central America. Their capital at Tenochtitlán—Tlaltelolco (tuh-lahl-teh-LOH-koh)—was located at the site of modern-day Mexico City. Of the five lakes shown here, only Lake Texcoco remains today.

 What forms of agriculture were practiced in the Valley of Mexico, and why?

MARKETS AND MERCHANDISE IN AZTEC MEXICO

Interaction & Exchange **ONE OF OUR MOST VALUABLE DESCRIPTIONS** of Aztec civilization is *The Conquest of New Spain*, written by Bernal Díaz, a Spaniard who visited Mexico in 1519. In the following passage, Díaz describes the great market at Tenochtitlán.

Bernal Díaz, *The Conquest of New Spain*

Let us begin with the dealers in gold, silver, and precious stones, feathers, cloaks, and embroidered goods, and male and female slaves who are also sold there. They bring as many slaves to be sold in that market as the Portuguese bring Negroes from Guinea. Some are brought there attached to long poles by means of collars round their necks to prevent them from escaping, but others are left loose. Next there were those who sold coarser cloth, and cotton goods and fabrics made of twisted thread, and there were chocolate merchants with their chocolate. In this way you could see every kind of merchandise to be found anywhere in New Spain, laid out in the same way as goods are laid out in my own district of Medina del Campo, a center for fairs, where each line of stalls has its own particular sort. So it was in this great market. There were those who sold sisal cloth and ropes and the sandals they wear on their feet, which are made from the same plant. All these were kept in one part of the market, in the place assigned to them, and in another part were skins of tigers and lions, otters, jackals, and deer, badgers, mountain cats, and other wild animals, some tanned and some untanned, and other classes of merchandise.

There were sellers of kidney beans and sage and other vegetables and herbs in another place, and in yet another they were selling fowls, and birds with great dewlaps, also rabbits, hares, deer, young ducks, little dogs, and other such creatures. Then there were the fruiterers; and the women who sold cooked food, flour and honey cake, and tripe, had their part of the market. Then came pottery of all kinds, from big water jars to little jugs, displayed in its own place, also honey, honey paste, and other sweets like nougat. Elsewhere they sold timber too, boards, cradles, beams, blocks, and benches, all in a quarter of their own.

Then there were the sellers of pitch pine for torches, and other things of that kind, and I must also mention, with all apologies, that they sold many canoe loads of human excrement, which they kept in the creeks near the market. This was for the manufacture of salt and the curing of skins, which they say cannot be done without it. I know that many gentlemen will laugh at this, but I assure them it is true. I may add that on all the roads they have shelters made of reeds or straw or grass so that they can retire when they wish to do so, and purge their bowels unseen by passersby, and also in order that their excrement shall not be lost.

 Which of the items offered for sale in this account might also have been available in a market in Asia, Egypt, or Europe? What types of goods mentioned here appear to be unique to the Americas?

Source: From *The Conquest of New Spain* by Bernal Díaz. Copyright © 1975. (Harmondsworth: Penguin), pp. 232–233.

---

society enjoyed more legal rights than women in some other traditional civilizations, they were still not equal to men. Women were permitted to own and inherit property and to enter into contracts. Marriage was usually monogamous, although noble families sometimes practiced **polygyny** (having more than one wife at a time). Wedding partners were normally selected from within the lineage group but not the immediate family. As in most societies at the time, parents usually selected their child's spouse, often for purposes of political or social advancement.

Classes in Aztec society were rigidly stratified. Commoners were not permitted to enter the nobility, although some occasionally rose to senior positions in the army or the priesthood as the result of exemplary service. As in medieval Europe, such occupations often provided a route of upward mobility for ambitious commoners. A woman of noble standing would sometimes marry a commoner because the children of such a union would inherit her higher status, and she could expect to be treated better by her husband's family, who would be proud of the marriage relationship.

Land of the Feathered Serpent: Aztec Religion and Culture
The Aztecs, like their contemporaries throughout Mesoamerica, lived in an environment populated by a multitude of gods.

Scholars have identified more than a hundred deities in the Aztec pantheon; some of them were nature spirits, like the rain god, Tlaloc (tuh-lah-LOHK), and some were patron deities, like the symbol of the Aztecs themselves, Huitzilopochtli. A supreme deity, called Ometeotl (oh-met-tee-AH-tul), represented the all-powerful and omnipresent forces of the heavens, but he was rather remote, and other figures, notably the feathered serpent Quetzalcoatl, had a more direct impact on the lives of the people. Representing the forces of creation, virtue, and learning and culture, Quetzalcoatl bears a distinct similarity to Shiva in Hindu belief. According to Aztec tradition, this god-like being had left his homeland in the Valley of Mexico in the tenth century, promising to return in triumph (see Historians Debate: "Why Did the Maya Decline?" Section 6-2e, p. 170).

Aztec cosmology was based on a belief in the existence of two worlds, the material and the divine. The earth was the material world and took the form of a flat disk surrounded by water on all sides. The divine world, which consisted of both heaven and hell, was the abode of the gods. Human beings could aspire to a form of heavenly salvation but first had to pass through a transitional stage, somewhat like Christian purgatory, before reaching their final destination, where the soul was finally freed from the body.

Quetzalcoatl. The first representation of the demigod Quetzalcoatl appeared in stone images, shown here, that were placed along the walls of the so-called Quetzalcoatl Pyramid at Teotihuacán during the first millennium CE.

To prepare for the final day of judgment, as well as to help them engage in proper behavior through life, all citizens underwent religious training at temple schools during adolescence and took part in various rituals throughout their lives. The most devout were encouraged to study for the priesthood. Once accepted, they served at temples ranging from local branches at the *calpulli* level to the highest shrines in the ceremonial precinct at Tenochtitlán. In some respects, however, Aztec society may have been undergoing a process of secularization. By late Aztec times, athletic contests at the ball court had apparently lost some of their religious significance. Gambling was increasingly common, and wagering on the results of the matches was widespread. One province reportedly sent 16,000 rubber balls to the capital city of Tenochtitlán as its annual tribute to the royal court.

Aztec religion contained a distinct element of fatalism that was inherent in the creation myth, which described an unceasing struggle between the forces of good and evil throughout the universe. This struggle led to the creation and destruction of four worlds, or suns. The world was now living in the time of the fifth sun. But that world, too, was destined to end with the destruction of this earth and all that is within it:

> Even jade is shattered,
> Even gold is crushed,
> Even quetzal plumes are torn. . . .
> One does not live forever on this earth:
> We endure only for an instant![3]

In an effort to postpone the day of reckoning, the Aztecs practiced human sacrifice. The Aztecs believed that by appeasing the sun god, Huitzilopochtli, with sacrifices, they could delay the final destruction of their world. Victims were prepared for the ceremony through elaborate rituals and then brought to the holy shrine, where their hearts were ripped out of their chests and presented to the gods as a holy offering. It was an honor to be chosen for sacrifice, and captives were often used as sacrificial victims, since they represented valor, the trait the

Aztecs prized most (see "Aztec Religion Through Spanish Eyes").

Art and Culture Like the art of the Olmecs, most Aztec architecture, art, and sculpture had religious significance. At the center of the capital city of Tenochtitlán was the sacred precinct, dominated by the massive pyramid dedicated to Huitzilopochtli and the rain god, Tlaloc. According to Bernal Díaz, at its base the pyramid was equal to the plots of six large European town houses and tapered from there to the top, which was surmounted by a platform containing shrines to the gods and an altar for performing human sacrifices. The entire pyramid was covered with brightly colored paintings and sculptures.

Although little Aztec painting survives, it was evidently of high quality. Díaz compared the best work with that of Michelangelo. Artisans worked with stone and with soft metals such as gold and silver, which they cast using the lost wax technique. They did not have the knowledge for making implements in bronze or iron, however. Stoneworking consisted primarily of representations of the gods and basreliefs depicting religious ceremonies. Among the most famous is the massive disk called the Stone of the Fifth Sun, carved for use at the central pyramid at Tenochtitlán.

The Aztecs had devised a form of writing based on hieroglyphs that represented an object or a concept. The symbols had no phonetic significance and did not constitute a writing system

The Stone of the Fifth Sun. This basalt disk, which weighs 26 tons, recorded the Aztec view of the cosmos. It portrays the perpetual struggle between forces of good and evil in the universe; in the center is an intimidating image of the sun god clutching human hearts with his talons. Having previously traversed the creation and destruction of four worlds, the Aztecs believed they were living in the world of the fifth and final sun—hence this stone carving, which was found in the central pyramid at Tenochtitlán. Werner Forman/Art Resource, NY

AZTEC RELIGION THROUGH SPANISH EYES

Religion & Philosophy

WHEN THE FIRST EUROPEAN EXPLORERS arrived in Mexico in the early sixteenth century, they reported their impressions of Aztec society in diaries and letters to their compatriots back home. The following passage from Father Diego Duran's *The Aztecs: The History of the Indies of New Spain* describes the ritual of human sacrifice as a central part of Aztec religion. The Aztecs believed that only the gift of human hearts would appease their god Huitzilopochtli and prevent him from bringing disaster to their civilization. Although some modern-day scholars doubt the accuracy of such reports, it is now widely accepted that human sacrifice was a common practice in many Amerindian societies, as it had once been in other parts of the world as well.

Diego Duran, *The Aztecs: The History of the Indies of New Spain*

When the day of the feast arrived, Moteczoma and Tlacaelel blackened their bodies with soot and applied it in such a way that it caught the light. . . . They placed crowns of fine feathers, adorned with gold and precious stones, upon their heads, and on each arm they wore a sheath of gold reaching from the elbow to the shoulder. On their feet were richly worked jaguar skin sandals, inlaid with gold and gems. They also were robed in splendid royal mantles. . . . Jeweled plugs were attached to holes in their noses, and both these lords carried flint knives in their hands.

The king and Tlacaelel now appeared before the assembly and went to stand upon the stone which was the likeness and image of the sun, one having ascended by one staircase and the other by another. The five priests of sacrifice followed them. They were to hold down the feet, hands and heads of the victims, and they were painted all over with red ocher, even their loincloths and tunics. Upon their heads they wore paper crowns surmounted by little shields which hung to the middle of their foreheads, also painted in ocher. On the top of their heads they wore long stiff feathers which had been tied to their hair and which stood straight up. On their feet were very common, worthless sandals. . . .

The five priests entered and claimed the prisoner who stood first in the line at the skull rack. Each prisoner they took to the place where the king stood and, when they had forced him to stand upon the stone which was the figure and likeness of the sun, they threw him upon his back. One took him by the right arm, another by the left, one by his left foot, another by his right, while the fifth priest tied his neck with a cord and held him down so that he could not move.

The king lifted the knife on high and made a gash in his breast. Having opened it he extracted the heart and raised it high with his hand as an offering to the sun. When the heart had cooled he tossed it into the circular depression, taking some of the blood in his hand and sprinkling it in the direction of the sun. In this way the sacrificers killed four, one by one; then Tlacaelel came and killed another four in his turn. And so, four by four, the prisoners were slain, till every last man that had been brought from the Mixteca had perished.

 What other societies encountered in this book engaged in human sacrifices as an aspect of their religious practices?

Source: From Diego Duran, *The Aztecs: The History of the Indies of New Spain*, Doris Heyden and Fernando Horcasitas, trans. (New York: Orion Press, 1964), pp. 120–121.

as such but could give the sense of a message and were probably used by civilian or religious officials as notes or memorandums for their orations. Although many of the notes simply recorded dates in the complex calendar that had evolved since Olmec times, others provide insight into the daily lives of the Aztec peoples. A trained class of scribes carefully painted the notes on paper made from the inner bark of fig trees. Unfortunately, many of these notes were destroyed by the Spaniards as part of their effort to eradicate all aspects of Aztec religion and culture.

6–3 PEOPLES AND SOCIETIES IN EARLY NORTH AMERICA

Q **Focus Question:** What were the main characteristics of the first human societies in North America, and how did they resemble or differ from their counterparts in Mesoamerica?

To the north of the great civilizations in ancient Mesoamerica lay the vast continent of North America, where other communities of Amerindians were also beginning to master the art of agriculture and to build organized societies. From early times, many of these peoples maintained active contacts with other human societies to the south, and in many ways their culture bore some resemblance to the advanced civilizations in Mesoamerica, but geographical and climatic differences resulted in the creation of societies that differed in vital respects.

Although human beings had occupied much of the continent of North America during the early phase of human settlement, the switch to farming as a means of survival did not occur until the third millennium BCE at the earliest, and much later in most areas of the continent. Until that time, most Amerindian communities lived by hunting, fishing, or foraging. As the supply of large animals began to diminish, they turned to smaller game and to fishing and foraging for wild plants, fruits, and nuts.

6-3a The Eastern Woodlands

It was probably during the third millennium BCE that peoples in the Eastern Woodlands (the land in eastern North America from the Great Lakes to the Gulf of Mexico) began to cultivate indigenous plants for food in a systematic way. As wild game and food became scarce, some communities began to place more emphasis on cultivating crops. This shift first occurred in the Mississippi River Valley from Ohio, Indiana, and Illinois down to the Gulf of Mexico. Among the most commonly cultivated crops were maize, squash, beans, and various grasses.

As the population in the area increased, people began to congregate in villages, and sedentary communities began to develop in the alluvial lowlands, where the soil could be cultivated for many years at a time because of the nutrients deposited by the river water.

Village councils were established to adjudicate disputes, and in a few cases, several villages banded together under the authority of a local chieftain. Urban centers began to appear, some of them inhabited by ten thousand people or more. At the same time, regional trade increased. The people of the **Hopewell culture** in Ohio ranged from the shores of Lake Superior to the Appalachian Mountains and the Gulf of Mexico in search of metals, shells, obsidian, and manufactured items to support their economic needs and religious beliefs.

6-3b Cahokia

At the site of Cahokia, near the modern city of East Saint Louis, Illinois, archaeologists found a burial mound more than 98 feet high with a base larger than that of the Great Pyramid in Egypt. A hundred smaller mounds were also found in the vicinity. The town itself, which covered almost 300 acres and was surrounded by a wooden stockade, was apparently the administrative capital of much of the surrounding territory until its decline in the 1200s. With a population of more than 20,000, it was reportedly the largest city in North America until Philadelphia surpassed that number in the early nineteenth century. Cahokia carried on extensive trade with other communities throughout the region, and there are some signs of regular contacts with the civilizations in Mesoamerica, such as the presence of ball courts in the Central American style. But wars were not uncommon, leading the Iroquois, who inhabited much of the modern states of Pennsylvania and New York as well as parts of southern Canada, to create a tribal alliance called the League of Iroquois.

6-3c The Ancient Pueblo Peoples

West of the Mississippi River basin, most Amerindian peoples lived by hunting or food gathering. During the first millennium CE, knowledge of agriculture gradually spread up the rivers to the Great Plains, and farming was practiced as far west as southwestern Colorado, where an agricultural community was established in an area extending from northern New Mexico and Arizona to southwestern Colorado and parts of southern Utah. Although they apparently never discovered the wheel or used beasts of burden, these Ancient Pueblo peoples (formerly known by the Navajo name "Anasazi," or "alien ancient ones") created a system of roads that facilitated an extensive

exchange of technology, products, and ideas throughout the region. By the ninth century, they had mastered the art of irrigation, which allowed them to expand their productive efforts to squash and beans, and had established an important urban center at Chaco Canyon, in southern New Mexico, where they built a walled city with dozens of three-story adobe communal houses, today called **pueblos**, with timbered roofs. Community religious functions were carried out in two large circular chambers called *kivas* (KEE-vuhs). Clothing was made from hides or cotton cloth. At its height, **Pueblo Bonito** contained several hundred compounds housing several thousand residents.

In the mid-twelfth century, the Ancient Pueblo peoples moved north to Mesa Verde, in southwestern Colorado. At first, they settled on top of the mesa, where maize had been cultivated since as early as the seventh century CE, but eventually—for reasons that are still unclear—they migrated onto the cliffs of surrounding canyons.

Sometime during the late thirteenth century, however, Mesa Verde was also abandoned, and the inhabitants migrated

Cliff Palace at Mesa Verde. Mesa Verde is one of the best-developed sites of the Ancient Pueblo peoples in southwestern North America. At one time they were farmers who tilled the soil atop the mesas, but eventually they were forced to build their settlements in more protected locations. At Cliff Palace, shown here, adobe houses were hidden on the perpendicular face of the mesa. Access was achieved only by a perilous descent via indented finger- and toeholds on the rock face.

southward. Their descendants, the Zuni and the Hopi, now occupy pueblos in central Arizona and New Mexico (thus leading them to adopt their new name). For years, archaeologists surmised that a severe drought was the cause of the migration, but new evidence has raised doubts that decreasing rainfall, by itself, was a sufficient explanation. An increase in internecine warfare, perhaps brought about by climatic changes, may also have played a role in the decision to relocate. Some archaeologists point to evidence that cannibalism was practiced at Pueblo Bonito and suggest that migrants from the south may have arrived in the area, provoking bitter rivalries within Ancient Pueblo society. In any event, with increasing aridity and the importation of the horse by the Spanish in the sixteenth century, hunting revived, and mounted nomads like the Apache and the Navajo came to dominate much of the Southwest. Prior to their relocation, however, the Pueblo Bonito peoples clearly maintained commercial contacts with their counterparts in Mexico and even as far south as the Pacific Coast of South America. Jars containing the residue of fermented chocolate have been found in the area, suggesting that trade with peoples in Mesoamerica, where cacao trees were cultivated, was common.

6–4 THE FIRST CIVILIZATIONS IN SOUTH AMERICA

 Focus Question: What role did the environment play in the evolution of societies in the Americas?

South America is a vast continent, characterized by extremes in climate and geography. The north is dominated by the mighty Amazon River, which flows through dense tropical rain forests carrying a larger flow of water than any other river system in the world (see Map 6.4). Farther to the south, the forests are replaced by prairies and steppes stretching westward to the Andes Mountains, which extend the entire length of the continent, from the Isthmus of Panama to the Strait of Magellan. Along the Pacific coast, on the western slopes of the Andes, are some of the driest desert regions in the world.

South America has been inhabited by human beings for more than 12,000 years. Wall paintings discovered at the so-called Cavern of the Painted Rock in the Amazon region suggest that Stone Age peoples were living in the area at least 11,000 years ago, and a site at Monte Verde, along the central coast of Chile, has been dated to 10,500 BCE. Early peoples lived by hunting, fishing, and food gathering, but there are indications that irrigated farming was being practiced on the western slopes of the Andes Mountains more than 5,000 years ago.

6–4a Caral

By the third millennium BCE, complex societies had begun to emerge in the coastal regions of modern-day Peru and Ecuador. Some settlements were located along the coast, but the remnants of farming communities watered by canals have also been found in the valleys of rivers flowing down to the sea from the Andes Mountains. Fish, reeds, and various other maritime

Map 6.4 Early Peoples and Cultures of Central and South America. This map shows regions of early human settlements in Central and South America. Urban conglomerations appear in Mesoamerica (see inset) and along the western coast of South America.

 Why do you think urban centers appeared in these areas?

products were traded to inland peoples for agricultural produce, wool, and salt.

The most vivid example of this process can be seen along the Pacific coast of modern-day Peru. By 3500 BCE—more than a thousand years earlier than the earliest known cities in Mesoamerica—the first permanent settlements appeared in the region. At Caral, a highly publicized site located 14 miles inland from the coast, the remnants of a 4,500-year-old city sit on the crest of a 60-foot-high plateau just above the fertile valley of the Supe River. Several pyramids similar to those built in Mesoamerica were erected at the site, along with plazas, sunken altars, residential areas, and structures that were evidently used for astronomical observation (see illustration "Caral: The First City," p. 178). Nearly twenty similar settlements are scattered over an area of 66 hectares on both sides of the Supe River as it makes it way westward to the sea.

The inhabitants of these ancient settlements raised corn, squash, beans, and tomatoes in the river valley below, and they provided such agricultural produce, as well as cotton and salt, to fishing communities along the nearby coast, where the

William J. Duiker

Caral: The First City? Archaeologists today debate whether maritime or river valley communities were the most prevalent antecedents of modern urban centers of civilization. Along the Pacific coast of South America in what today is the state of Peru, the answer apparently was both. On a desolate plateau just adjacent to the fertile banks of the Supe River, the ceremonial center of Caral began to emerge at least 5,000 years ago. Note the upright stone in front of the pyramid, suggesting that the inhabitants were fascinated by the heavenly bodies, and had begun to make astronomical calculations in an effort to plan their daily activities. A few miles to the west, peoples living along the coast established their own settlement, known as Aspero, based on the fruits of the sea. For centuries, the two settlements survived in a symbiotic relationship, providing each other with foodstuffs and articles of daily use necessary for their survival. Together they composed one of the oldest centers of civilization in South America, if not in the world at large. Caral and Aspero are believed to be among the first permanent settlements to arise in the Western Hemisphere.

cotton material was used to make fishnets. In return, they received maritime products and reeds for baskets. They were sophisticated farmers, as evidenced by the remnants of ancient irrigation canals found in the vicinity. Some maritime trade was apparently conducted along the Pacific coast, as evidenced by the presence of *Spondylus* shells from Ecuador (used for religious ceremonies) and various plants not found in the vicinity.

The exact nature of these early communities is not yet clear. Indeed, it is not known whether these early settlements were actual villages or merely ceremonial centers, although there is convincing evidence of the existence of distinct social classes, a ruling elite, specialized labor, and organized religious beliefs, as well as cultural activities such as music and crafts. There are even indications of the appearance of a primitive writing system (see "Inka Culture," Section 6-4c, p. 182).

Although the reasons for eventual decline are not yet clear, this culture apparently reached its height during the first millennium BCE with the emergence of the Chavín style, named for a site near the modern city of Chavín de Huantar (chah-VEEN day HWAHN-tar). The ceremonial precinct at the site contained an impressive stone temple complete with interior galleries, a stone-block ceiling, and a system of underground canals that probably channeled water into the temple complex for ceremonial purposes. Evidence of metallurgy has also been found, with objects made of copper and gold.

6–4b Moche

Chavín society had broken down by 200 BCE, but early in the first millennium CE, another advanced civilization appeared in northern Peru, in the valley of the Moche River, which flows from the foothills of the Andes into the Pacific Ocean. It occupied an area of more than 2,500 square miles, and its capital city, large enough to contain more than 15,000 people, was dominated by two massive adobe pyramids, each nearly 100 feet high. The larger one, known today as the Pyramid of the Sun, covered a total of 15 acres. The smaller one, built on the side of a mountain called Cerro Blanco and known as the Pyramid of the Moon, was adorned with painted murals depicting battles, ritual sacrifices, and various local deities. The most common image that appears on the pyramid is that of Ai Apaec, the Moche creator god and the giver of life. Ai Apaec was also the god of sacrifice, and sacrificial ceremonies were routinely carried out at the apex of the pyramid to give thanks to the mountain for providing precious water resources to the community (see illustration "Ai Apaec: The Decapitator God" in the Comparative Essay).

Artifacts found at Moche (moh-CHAY), especially the metalwork and stone and ceramic figures, exhibit a high quality of artisanship. They were imitated at river valley sites throughout the surrounding area, which suggests that the influence of the Moche rulers may have extended as far as 400 miles along the coast. The artifacts also indicate that the people at Moche, like those in Central America, were preoccupied with warfare. Paintings and pottery as well as other artifacts in stone, metal, and ceramics frequently portray warriors, prisoners, and sacrificial victims. The Moche were also fascinated by the heavens, and much of their art consisted of celestial symbols and astronomical constellations.

Environmental Problems The Moche River Valley is extremely arid, normally receiving less than an inch of rain annually. The peoples in the area compensated by building a sophisticated irrigation system to carry water from the river to the parched fields. By the eighth century, however, Moche civilization was in a state of collapse, the irrigation canals had been abandoned, and the remaining population had left the area and moved farther inland or suffered from severe malnutrition.

What had happened to bring Moche culture to this untimely end? Archaeologists speculate that environmental disruptions

CHRONOLOGY	Early South America
Monte Verde	10,500 BCE
First organized societies in the Andes	c. 3500 BCE
Agriculture first widely practiced	c. 3200 BCE
Founding of Caral	c. 2500 BCE
Chavín style	First millennium BCE
Moche civilization	c. 150–800 CE
Wari culture	c. 500–1000 CE
Civilization of Chimor	c. 1100–1450
Inka takeover in central Andes	1400s

COMPARATIVE ESSAY

History and the Environment

Earth & Environment Ai Apaec was the founding deity of the Moche peoples. His abode was on Cerro Blanco, the mountain that today towers over the ruins of the capital city on the coast of northern Peru. In times of drought or flood, Ai Apaec presided over sacrificial ceremonies at the nearby Pyramid of the Moon to beseech the heavenly forces in the mountain to provide precious water to the parched fields below. In the end, Ai Apaec's labors were in vain, because eventually the Moche civilization was brought to an end by a series of disastrous droughts and floods—known as the El Niño effect—in the eighth century CE. Moche was by no means the only civilization to be brought to an end by dramatic changes in the natural environment. Climatic change or natural disaster almost certainly led to the decline and fall of the Indus Valley civilization, and of the Mayan city-states in Mesoamerica as well. A lengthy drought may have damaged the wheat-growing regions in North Africa and contributed to the collapse of the Roman Empire itself.

Sometimes the problems may have been self-inflicted, as in the case of Mesopotamia and the Maya, where overuse of the land may have led to erosion or leached the soil of nutrients. Whatever the case, historians have become increasingly aware that climatic change or environmental conditions may have been a contributing factor in the fate of several of the great civilizations—including Medieval Europe and the Tang Dynasty in China—throughout the ancient world. In the case of the Moche, massive flooding brought about by the El Niño effect (environmental conditions triggered by changes in water temperature in the Pacific Ocean) led to the collapse of a great civilization.

Climatic changes, of course, have not always been detrimental to the health and prosperity of human beings. A warming trend that took place at the end of the last ice age eventually made much of the world more habitable for farming peoples about ten thousand years ago. The effects of El Niño may be beneficial to people living in some areas and disastrous in others. But human misuse of land and water resources is always dangerous to settled societies, especially those living in fragile environments.

Q *Many ancient civilizations throughout the world were weakened or destroyed by changes taking place in the environment. What are some examples in the pre-Columbian Americas?*

William J. Duiker

Ai Apaec: The Decapitator God. Among the most familiar figures along the walls of the Pyramid of the Moon at Moche is the face of Ai Apaec, the creator god in Moche mythology. Ai Apaec presided over ceremonies held at the site, and researchers believe that many of the human victims (war captives seized by the Moche during wars fought with their neighbors) were sacrificed as a plea to the mountain deity for relief from climatic disasters such as droughts or floods. The image of Ai Apaec, whose spider-like tentacles were allegedly designed to suck the blood of sacrificial victims, must have been a terrifying sight to all inhabitants of the city who observed it.

in the sixth and seventh centuries, perhaps brought on by changes in the temperature of the Pacific Ocean known as **El Niño**, led to alternating periods of drought and flooding of coastal regions, which caused the irrigated fields to silt up (see Comparative Essay "History and the Environment"). The warm water created by El Niño conditions also killed local marine life, severely damaging the local fishing industry.

Wari and Chimor A few hundred miles to the south of Moche, a people known as the Wari (WAH-ree) culture began to expand from their former home in the Andes foothills and established communities along the coast in the vicinity of modern Lima, Peru. As the state of Moche declined, the Wari gradually spread northward in the eighth century and began to occupy many of the urban sites in the Moche Valley. According to some scholars, they may even have made use of the Moche's sacred buildings and appropriated their religious symbolism. In the process, the Wari created the most extensive land empire yet seen in South America. In the end, however, they too succumbed to the challenge posed by unstable environmental conditions.

Around 1100, a new power, the kingdom of Chimor (chee-MAWR), with its capital at Chan Chan (CHAHN CHAHN), at the mouth of the Moche River, emerged in the area. Built almost entirely of adobe, the city of Chan Chan housed an estimated 30,000 residents in an area of more than 12 square miles that included a number of palace compounds surrounded by walls nearly 30 feet high. One compound contained an intricate labyrinth that wound its way progressively inward until it ended in a central chamber, probably occupied by the ruler. Like the Moche before them, the people of Chimor—the Chimú (chee-MOO)—relied on irrigation to funnel the water from the river into their fields. An elaborate system of canals brought the water through hundreds of miles of hilly terrain to the fields near the coast. Nevertheless, by the fifteenth century, Chimor, too, had disappeared, a victim of floods and a series of earthquakes that destroyed the intricate irrigation system that had been the basis of its survival.

While they existed, these early civilizations in the Andes were by no means isolated from other societies in the region. As early as 2000 BCE, local peoples had been venturing into the Pacific Ocean on wind-powered rafts constructed of woven reeds or balsa wood. By the late first millennium CE, seafarers from the coast of Ecuador had established a vast trading network that extended southward to central Peru and as far north as western Mexico, more than 2,000 miles away. Items transported included jewelry, beads, and metal goods. In all likelihood, technological exchanges were an important byproduct of the relationship.

Reed Boats of South America. Boats constructed of reeds are among the earliest form of sea travel worldwide, and examples dating back several thousand years have been found in Africa, the Persian Gulf, Southeast Asia, and South America. One form of reed boat, long and thin and shaped like a cigar, was used for both fishing and commerce, and is still in use along the Pacific coast of South America. In the photograph shown here, a string of reed boats are drying in the sun in the fishing village of Huanchaco, along the northern coast of Peru.

Transportation by land, however, was more difficult. Although roads were constructed to facilitate communication between communities, the forbidding terrain in the mountains was a serious obstacle, and the only draft animal on the entire continent was the llama, which is considerably less hardy than

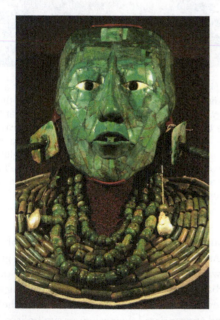

Jade and Gold Funeral Masks. Early civilizations in the Americas, as elsewhere, often placed precious artifacts in the royal tombs of their deceased rulers. The jade and gold mined in Mesoamerica and the continent of South America were transformed into stunning burial masks, as seen here. The jade funeral mask of Lord Pacal (left), a seventh-century ruler of Palenque, was placed in his tomb in the hope that its spiritual energy would propel Pacal into the afterlife, thereby merging him with the divine in the Mayan cosmos. The hammered gold mask from the Chimor culture (right), successors to the Moche civilization in what is present-day Peru, is reminiscent of the famous death mask found at Mycenae, in central Greece (see Chapter 4). (left) Carver Mostardi/Alamy; (right) HIP/Art Resource, NY

the cattle, horses, and water buffalo used in much of Asia. Such problems undoubtedly hampered the development of regular contacts with distant societies in the Americas, as well as the exchange of goods and ideas that had lubricated the rise of civilizations from China to the Mediterranean Sea.

6–4c The Inka

The Chimor kingdom was eventually succeeded in the late fifteenth century by an invading force from the mountains far to the south. In the late fourteenth century, the Inka were a small community in the area of Cuzco (KOOS-koh), a city located at an altitude of 10,000 feet in the mountains of southern Peru. In the 1440s, however, under the leadership of their powerful ruler Pachakuti (pah-chah-KOO-tee) (sometimes called Pachacutec, or "he who transforms the world"), the Inka launched a campaign of conquest that eventually brought the entire region under their authority. Under Pachakuti and his immediate successors,

Paracas Royal Mummy. The ancient residents of coastal Chile developed complex methods for mummifying their dead more than four thousand years ago, and this practice continued up through Inka times. In Peru, the Paracas (pah-RAH-kus) culture (200 BCE–500 CE) bundled up its rulers in extensive layers of sumptuously embroidered textiles. The body was placed in the fetal position, adorned with articles of value such as a crown of feathers, animal skins, and gold and bone jewelry. The mummy was then interred in a chamber with other deceased members of the community. Food offerings of maize and peanuts accompanied the mummy for sustenance in the afterlife.

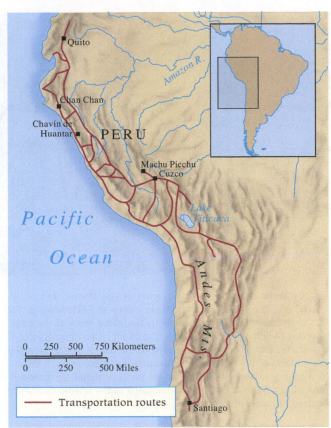

DEA/M. Seemuller/Getty Images

Map 6.5 The Inka Empire About 1500 CE. The Inka were the last civilization to flourish in South America before the arrival of the Spanish. The impressive system of roads constructed to facilitate communication shows the extent of Inka control throughout the Andes Mountains.

Q *In what modern countries was the Inka state located?*

Topa Inka (TOH-puh INK-uh) and Huayna Inka (WY-nuh INK-uh) (the word *Inka* means "ruler"), the boundaries of the empire were extended as far as Ecuador, central Chile, and the edge of the Amazon basin.

The Four Quarters: Inka Politics and Society Pachakuti created a highly centralized state (see Map 6.5). With a stunning concern for mathematical precision, he divided his empire, comprising over 20,000 square miles and called Tahuantinsuyu (tuh-HWAHN-tin-SOO-yoo), or "the world of the four quarters," into provinces and districts. Each province contained about ten thousand residents (at least in theory) and was ruled by a governor related to the royal family. Excess inhabitants were transferred to other locations. The capital of Cuzco was divided into four quarters, or residential areas, and the social status and economic functions of the residents of each quarter were rigidly defined.

The state was built on forced labor. Often entire communities of workers were moved from one part of the country to another to open virgin lands or engage in massive construction projects. Under Pachakuti, Cuzco was transformed from a city of mud and thatch into an imposing metropolis of stone. The walls, built

The Great Walls of Cuzco. On a hillside overlooking the modern city of Cuzco, Peru, is a walled complex known locally as Saksaywaman. The walls of the complex—which apparently contained many of the most important buildings in the one-time Inka capital—are composed of large stones carved to fit together without the use of mortar. How the Inka builders of the wall managed to obtain such precision in their stone carving is a question that has not yet been definitely answered by archaeologists, but is certainly a testimonial to the artistic excellence achieved in Inka culture.

of close-fitting stones without the use of mortar, were a wonder to early European visitors. The most impressive structure in the city was a temple dedicated to the sun. According to a Spanish observer, "All four walls of the temple were covered from top to bottom with plates and slabs of gold."[4] Equally impressive are the ruins of the abandoned city of Machu Picchu (MAH-choo PEE-choo), built on a lofty hilltop far above the Urubamba River.

Another major construction project was a system of 24,800 miles of highways and roads (known to the Inka as the "capac nan," or "the great road") that extended for more than 3,000 miles from the border of modern Colombia to a point south of modern Santiago, Chile. Two major roadways extended in a north-south direction, one through the Andes Mountains and the other along the coast, with connecting routes between them. Rest houses and storage depots were placed along the roads. Suspension bridges made of braided fiber and fastened to stone abutments on opposite banks were built over ravines and waterways. Use of the highways was restricted to official and military purposes. Trained runners carried messages rapidly from one way station to another, enabling information to travel up to 140 miles in a single day. Parts of the road are still in use.

In rural areas, the population lived mainly by farming. In the mountains, the most common form was terraced agriculture, watered by irrigation systems that carried precise amounts of water into the fields, which were planted with maize, potatoes, and other crops. The plots were tilled by collective labor regulated by the state. Like other aspects of Inkan society, marriage was strictly regulated, and men and women were required to select a marriage partner from within the immediate tribal group. For women, there was one escape from a life of domestic

servitude: fortunate maidens were selected to serve as "chosen virgins" in temples throughout the country (see "Virgins with Red Cheeks"). Noblewomen were eligible to compete for service in the Temple of the Sun at Cuzco, while commoners might hope to serve in temples in the provincial capitals. Punishment for breaking the vow of chastity was harsh, and few evidently took the risk.

Inka Culture Like many other civilizations in pre-Columbian Latin America, the Inka state was built on war. Soldiers for the 200,000-man Inka army, the largest and best armed in the region, were raised by universal male conscription. Military units were moved rapidly along the highway system and were bivouacked in the rest houses located along the roadside. Because the Inka had no wheeled vehicles, supplies were carried on the backs of llamas. Once an area was placed under Inka authority, the local inhabitants were instructed in the Quechua (KEH-chuh-wuh) language, which became the lingua franca of

The *Quipu*. Not having a writing system, the Inka tallied the various data of their kingdom on strands of knotted yarn. Highly skilled and esteemed, official secretaries recorded population census data, crop and household inventories, government inspector reports, crime investigations, taxes, legal decisions and contracts, and all the official statistics of the realm by an intricate system of tying knots on a circular grouping of strings of yarn. The use of knotted yarn as a means of recording data was apparently not unique to the Inka.

VIRGINS WITH RED CHEEKS

Family & Society

A LETTER FROM A PERUVIAN CHIEF to King Philip III of Spain written four hundred years ago gives us a firsthand account of the nature of traditional Inkan society. The purpose of author Huaman Poma was both to justify the history and culture of the Inka peoples and to record their sufferings under Spanish domination. In his letter, Poma describes Inkan daily life from birth to death in minute detail. He explains the different tasks assigned to men and women, beginning with their early education. Whereas boys were taught to watch the flocks and trap animals, girls were taught to dye, spin, and weave cloth and perform other domestic chores. Most interesting, perhaps, was the emphasis that the Inka placed on virginity, as is evident in the document presented here. The Inka's tradition of temple virgins is reminiscent of similar practices in ancient Rome, where young girls from noble families were chosen as priestesses to tend the sacred fire in the Temple of Vesta for thirty years. If an Inkan temple virgin lost her virginity, she was condemned to be buried alive in an underground chamber.

Huaman Poma, Letter to a King

During the time of the Incas certain women, who were called *accla* or "the chosen," were destined for lifelong virginity. Mostly they were confined in houses and they belonged to one of two main categories, namely sacred virgins and common virgins.

The so-called "virgins with red cheeks" entered upon their duties at the age of twenty and were dedicated to the service of the Sun, the Moon, and the Day-Star. In their whole life they were never allowed to speak to a man.

The virgins of the Inca's own shrine of Huanacauri were known for their beauty as well as their chastity. The other principal shrines had similar girls in attendance. At the less important shrines there were the older virgins who occupied themselves with spinning and weaving the silklike clothes worn by their idols. There was a still lower class of virgins, over forty years of age and no longer very beautiful, who performed unimportant religious duties and worked in the fields or as ordinary seamstresses.

Daughters of noble families who had grown into old maids were adept at making girdles, headbands, string bags, and similar articles in the intervals of their pious observances.

Girls who had musical talent were selected to sing or play the flute and drum at Court, weddings and other ceremonies, and all the innumerable festivals of the Inca year.

There was yet another class of *accla* or "chosen," only some of whom kept their virginity and others not. These were the Inca's beautiful attendants and concubines, who were drawn from noble families and lived in his palaces. They made clothing for him out of material finer than taffeta or silk. They also prepared a maize spirit of extraordinary richness, which was matured for an entire month, and they cooked delicious dishes for the Inca. They also lay with him, but never with any other man.

 According to this selection, one of the chief duties of a woman in Inkan society was to spin and weave. In what other traditional societies was textile making a woman's work? Why do you think this was the case?

Source: From *Letter to a King* by Guaman Poma de Ayala. Translated and edited by Christopher Dilke. Published by E. P. Dutton, New York, 1978.

---

the state, and were introduced to the state religion. Like most other faiths in the Western Hemisphere, the Inka religion was polytheistic, with separate deities for the heavens and the earth, and it relied on human sacrifice to appease the gods and win their support. Pachamama, the "mother of the earth," was common to all religions throughout the Andes.

The Inka had no writing system but kept records using a system of knotted strings called *quipu* (KEE-poo), maintained by professionally trained officials, that were able to record all data of a numerical nature. Strings of *quipu* have recently been discovered at a warehouse south of Lima, and were apparently used to record the amounts and types of agricultural products stored at the site. Meaning was achieved by varying the colors and the number of knots on each string. What could not be recorded in such a manner was committed to memory and then recited when needed. The practice was apparently not invented by the Inka. Fragments of *quipu* have been found at Caral and dated at approximately five thousand years ago. Nor apparently was the experiment limited to the Americas. A passage in the Chinese classic *The Way of the Tao* declares, "Let the people revert to communication by knotted cords" (see Chapter 3).

As in the case of the Aztecs and the Maya, the lack of a fully developed writing system did not prevent the Inka from realizing a high level of cultural achievement. Their ability to construct buildings and walls of large stones without the use of mortar—notably in their one-time capital of Cuzco, as well as the spectacular summer palace deep in the Andes at Machu Picchu—testifies to their skill in architecture. The Inka also had a highly developed tradition of court theater, including both tragic and comic works. There was also some poetry, composed in blank verse and often accompanied by music played on reed instruments.

6–4d Stateless Societies in South America

East of the Andes Mountains in South America, other Amerindian societies were beginning to make the transition to agriculture. Perhaps the most prominent were the Arawak (AR-uh-wahk), a people living along the Orinoco River in modern Venezuela. Having begun to cultivate manioc (a tuber also known as *cassava* or *yuca*, the source of tapioca) along the banks of the river, they gradually migrated down to the coast and then proceeded to move eastward along the northern coast of the continent. Some occupied the islands of the Caribbean Sea.

Machu Picchu. Situated in the Andes in modern Peru, Machu Picchu reflects the glory of Inka civilization. To farm such rugged terrain, the Inka constructed terraces and stone aqueducts. To span vast ravines, they built suspension bridges made of braided fiber and fastened them to stone abutments on the opposite banks. The most revered of the many temples and stone altars at Machu Picchu was the thronelike "hitching post of the sun," so called because of its close proximity to the sun god.

Carol C. Coffin

In their new island habitat, they lived by a mixture of fishing, hunting, and cultivating maize, beans, manioc, and squash, as well as other crops such as peanuts, peppers, and pineapples. As the population increased, a pattern of political organization above the village level appeared, along with recognizable social classes headed by a chieftain (*cacique*) whose authority included control over the economy. The Arawak practiced human sacrifice, and some urban centers contained ball courts, suggesting the possibility of contacts with Mesoamerica.

Eventually, new peoples from South America began to migrate into the islands of the Caribbean Sea. Known as Caribs, they tended to be more warlike than their predecessors and often drove the previous arrivals to seek refuge on islands farther to the north. A Carib community survives today on the island of Dominica, in the Lesser Antilles.

In most such societies, where clear-cut class stratifications had not as yet taken place, men and women were considered of equal status. Men were responsible for hunting, warfare, and dealing with outsiders, while women were accountable for the crops, the distribution of food, maintaining the household, and bearing and raising the children. Their roles were complementary and were often viewed as a divine division of labor. In such cases, women in the stateless societies of North America held positions of greater respect than their counterparts in the river valley civilizations of the ancient world.

While the Arawak and the Carib peoples eventually left their original homeland in the northern sections of South America and migrated into the Caribbean islands, others remained. Small groups of hunter-gatherers continue today to live in virtual isolation throughout the vast Amazon River basin. Yet although conditions along the Amazon and its tributaries often appear to impose limits on the forms of economic and cultural activity practiced by local inhabitants, this was not always the case. One of the most intriguing puzzles in pre-Columbian South American archaeology is the recently discovered evidence of substantial human activity that took place in parts of the Amazon River Valley. Scholars had long been skeptical that advanced societies could take shape in the region because the soil was believed to lack adequate nutrients to support a large population. Recent archaeological evidence, however, suggests that in some areas where decaying organic matter produces a rich soil suitable for farming—such as the region near the modern river port of Santarem—large agricultural societies may once have existed. More information about this previously unknown culture must await further archaeological evidence.

CHAPTER SUMMARY

The first human beings did not arrive in the Americas until quite late in the prehistorical period. For the next several millennia, their descendants were forced to respond to the challenges of the environment in total isolation from other parts of the world. Nevertheless, around 5000 BCE, farming settlements began to appear in river valleys and upland areas in both Central and South America. Not long afterward—as measured in historical time—organized communities embarked on the long march toward creating advanced technological societies. Although the total number of people living in the Americas is a matter of debate, estimates range from 10 million to as many as 90 million people.

What is perhaps most striking about the developments in the Western Hemisphere is how closely they paralleled those of other civilizations. Irrigated agriculture, long-distance trade, urbanization, and the development of a writing

system were all hallmarks of the emergence of advanced societies of the classical type.

Some of the parallels, of course, were less appealing. States in the Western Hemisphere were every bit as addicted to warfare as their counterparts elsewhere. The widespread use of human sacrifice is reminiscent of similar practices in other ancient societies. Not much is yet known about relations between men and women in the Americas, but it appears that gender roles were as sharply delineated there as in much of Asia and the Mediterranean world.

In some respects, the societies that emerged in the Americas were not as advanced technologically as their counterparts elsewhere. They were not familiar with the process of smelting iron, for example, and they had not yet invented wheeled vehicles. Their writing systems were still in their infancy. Several possible reasons have been advanced to explain this technological gap. Geographic isolation—not only from people of other continents but also, in some cases, from each other—deprived them of the diffusion of ideas that had enabled other societies to learn from their neighbors. Contacts among societies in the Americas were made much more difficult because of the topography and the diversity of the environment.

In some ways, too, they were not as blessed by nature. As the sociologist Jared Diamond has pointed out, the Americas did not possess many indigenous varieties of edible grasses that could encourage hunter-gatherers to take up farming. Nor were there abundant large mammals that could easily be domesticated for food and transport (horses had disappeared from the Western Hemisphere before the arrival of *Homo sapiens sapiens* at the end of the last ice age). It was not until the arrival of the Europeans that such familiar attributes of civilization became widely available for human use in the Americas.[5]

These disadvantages can help explain some of the problems that the early peoples of the Americas encountered in their efforts to master their environments. It is interesting to note that the spread of agriculture and increasing urbanization had already begun to produce a rising incidence of infectious diseases. It is also significant that in the Americas, as elsewhere, many of the first civilizations formed by the human species appear to have been brought to an end as much by environmental changes and disease as by war. In the next chapter, we shall return to Asia, where new civilizations were in the process of replacing the ancient empires.

CHAPTER TIMELINE

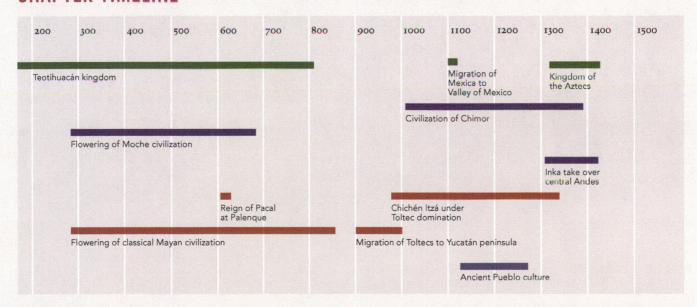

CHAPTER REVIEW

Upon Reflection

Q How did geographic and climatic factors affect the rise and fall of early societies in the Americas? Were similar factors at work among contemporary societies in other parts of the world?

Q What are some of the reasons advanced for the collapse of Mayan civilization in the late first millennium CE? Which do archaeologists find the most persuasive?

Q What common features linked the emerging societies in the Americas during the pre-Columbian period? Does it appear that technological and cultural achievements passed from one society to another as frequently as in other parts of the world?

Key Terms

Amerindians (p. 163)
chinampas (p. 165)
calpullis (p. 173)
polygyny (p. 173)
Hopewell culture (p. 176)

pueblos (p. 176)
Pueblo Bonito (p. 176)
El Niño (p. 179)
quipu (p. 183)

Chapter Notes

1. Quoted in S. Morley and G. W. Brainerd, *The Ancient Maya* (Stanford, Calif., 1983), p. 513.
2. B. Díaz, *The Conquest of New Spain* (Harmondsworth, England, 1975), p. 210.
3. Quoted in M. D. Coe, D. Snow, and E. P. Benson, *Atlas of Ancient America* (New York, 1988), p. 149. Courtesy of Michael Coe.
4. G. de la Vega (El Inca), *Royal Commentaries of the Incas and General History of Peru*, pt. 1, trans. H. V. Livermore (Austin, Tex., 1966), p. 180.
5. J. Diamond, *Guns, Germs, and Steel: The Fates of Human Societies* (New York, 1997), pp. 187–188.

MindTap® is a fully online personalized learning experience built upon Cengage Learning content. MindTap® combines student learning tools—readings, multimedia, activities, and assessments—into a singular Learning Path that guides students through the course and helps students develop the critical thinking, analysis, and communication skills that are essential to academic and professional success.

CHAPTER 7

FERMENT IN THE MIDDLE EAST: THE RISE OF ISLAM

Chapter Outline and Focus Questions

Muhammad rises to heaven. OR 2265 Ascent of the Prophet Muhammad to Heaven/Mirak, Aqa (fl.c.1520-76)/BRITISH LIBRARY/British Library, London, UK/Bridgeman Images

Critical Thinking

Q *In what ways did the arrival of Islam change or maintain the political, social, and cultural conditions that had existed in the area before Muhammad?*

Connections to Today

Q *Do the tactics and the motives that led to the crusades provide any lessons for the conduct of foreign policy by the United States and its allies toward the Middle East today? If so, what are those lessons?*

IN THE YEAR 570, in the Arabian city of Mecca, there was born a child named Muhammad (moh-HAM-id or muh-HAHM-ud) whose life changed the course of world history. The son of a merchant, Muhammad grew to maturity in a time of transition. The Roman Empire, which had once been able to impose its hegemony over the Middle East, was only a distant memory. The region was now divided into many squabbling states, and the people adhered to many different faiths.

Concerned at the corrupt and decadent society of his day, Muhammad took to wandering in the hills outside Mecca, where on one of these occasions he experienced visions that he was convinced had been inspired by Allah (AH-lah). Eventually, they would be transcribed into the Qur'an (kuh-RAN or kuh-RAHN)— the holy book of Islam—and provide inspiration to millions of people throughout the world. According to popular belief, Muhammad, mounted on his faithful steed Buraq and, accompanied by the angel Gabriel, embarked on a mystical "night journey" to heaven, where Allah introduced him to paradise and hell so that on his return to earth he could instruct the faithful on their prospects in the next world (see chapter-opening illustration, "Muhammad Rises to Heaven").

Within a few decades of Muhammad's death, the Middle East was united once again. As armies under the command of Muhammad's followers swept through the Middle East to the gates of India and the shores of the Mediterranean Sea, Arab beliefs and customs, as reflected through the prism of Muhammad's teachings, transformed the societies and cultures of the peoples living in the new empire. Although the distinctive political and cultural forces that had long characterized the region began to reassert themselves, conditions in all areas affected by these events would never be the same again.

7–1 THE RISE OF ISLAM

 Focus Question: What were the main tenets of Islam, and how does the religion compare with Judaism and Christianity?

The Arabs are a Semitic-speaking people of southwestern Asia with a long history. They were mentioned in Greek sources of the fifth century BCE and even earlier in the Old Testament. The Greek historian Herodotus had applied the name *Arab* to the entire peninsula, calling it Arabia. In 106 BCE, the Romans extended their authority into the Arabian Peninsula, transforming it into a province of their growing empire.

During Roman times, the region was inhabited primarily by the **Bedouin** (BED-oo-un *or* BED-wuhn) Arabs, nomadic peoples who came originally from the northern part of the peninsula. Bedouin society was organized on a tribal basis. The ruling member of the tribe was called the *sheikh* (SHAYK *or* SHEEK) and was selected from one of the leading families by a council of elders called the *majlis* (MAHJ-liss). The *sheikh* ruled the tribe with the consent of the council. Each tribe was autonomous but felt a general sense of allegiance to the larger unity of all the clans

in the region. In early times, the Bedouins had supported themselves primarily by sheepherding or by raiding passing caravans, but after the domestication of the camel during the second millennium BCE, the Bedouins began to participate in the caravan trade themselves and became major carriers of goods between the Persian Gulf and the Mediterranean Sea.

The Arabs of pre-Islamic times were polytheistic, with a supreme god known as Allah presiding over a community of spirits. It was a communal faith, involving all members of the tribe, and had no priesthood. Spirits were believed to inhabit natural objects, such as trees, rivers, and mountains, while the supreme deity was symbolized by a sacred stone. Each tribe possessed its own stone, but by the time of Muhammad, a massive black meteorite, housed in a central shrine called the Ka'aba (KAH-buh) in the commercial city of Mecca, had come to possess especially sacred qualities.

In the fifth and sixth centuries CE, the economic importance of the Arabian Peninsula began to increase. As a result of the political disorder in Mesopotamia—a consequence of the constant wars between the Eastern Roman (Byzantine) and Sassanian Persian Empires—and in Egypt, the trade routes that ran directly across the peninsula or down the Red Sea became increasingly perilous, and a third route, which passed from the Mediterranean through Mecca to Yemen and then by ship across the Indian Ocean, became more popular. The communities in that part of the peninsula benefited from the change and took a larger share of the caravan trade between the Mediterranean and the countries on the other side of the Indian Ocean. As a consequence, relations between the Bedouins of the desert and the increasingly wealthy merchant class of the towns began to become strained.

The Ka'aba in Mecca. The Ka'aba, the shrine containing a black meteorite in the Arabian city of Mecca, is the most sacred site of the Islamic faith. Wherever Muslims pray, they are instructed to face Mecca; each thus becomes a spoke of the Ka'aba, the holy center of the wheel of Islam. All Muslims are encouraged to visit the Ka'aba, now dwarfed by skyscrapers erected to provide temporary housing for the faithful, at least once in their lifetime if they are able to do so. Called the *hajj*, this pilgrimage to Mecca represents the ultimate in spiritual fulfillment for every Muslim.

7–1a The Role of Muhammad

Into this world came Muhammad (also known as Mohammed), a man whose spiritual visions unified the Arab world (see Map 7.1) with a speed no one would have suspected possible. Unfortunately, there is almost no verifiable evidence relating to Muhammad's life. As a result, historians must rely on a limited number of sources, including the Qur'an and testimonials about his life by his followers (the *Hadith*). These sources were extensively revised after his death, however, and may have been shaped so as to favor the interests of his successors. Consequently, to many historians of the Middle East, the first years of Islam remain a matter of debate and conjecture.

Born in Mecca to a merchant family and orphaned at the age of six, Muhammad (570–632) grew up to become a caravan manager and eventually married a rich widow, Khadija (kah-DEE-juh), who was also his employer. A member of the local Hashemite (HASH-uh-myt) clan of the Quraishi (koo-RY-shee)

tribe, he lived in Mecca as a merchant for several years but, according to tradition, was troubled by the growing gap between the Bedouin values of honesty and generosity and the acquisitive behavior of the affluent commercial elites in the city. Deeply concerned, he began to visit the nearby hills to meditate in isolation. It was there that he encountered the angel Gabriel, who commanded him to preach the revelations that he would be given.

It is said that Muhammad was acquainted with Jewish and Christian beliefs and came to believe that while Allah had already revealed himself in part through Moses and Jesus—and thus through the Hebraic and Christian traditions—the final revelations were now being given to him. Out of his revelations, which were eventually dictated to scribes, came the Qur'an (meaning "recitation"; also spelled Koran), the holy scriptures of Islam (meaning "submission," implying submission to the will of Allah). The Qur'an contained the guidelines by which followers of Allah, known as Muslims (practitioners of Islam), were to live. Like the Christians and the Jews, Muslims (also known as Moslems) were a "people of the Book," believers in a faith based on scripture.

After returning home, Muhammad set out to comply with Gabriel's command by preaching to the residents of Mecca about his revelations. At first, many were convinced that he was a madman or a charlatan. Others were concerned that his vigorous attacks on traditional beliefs and the corrupt society around him might severely shake the social and political order. After three years of proselytizing, he had only thirty followers.

Discouraged, perhaps, by the systematic persecution of his followers, which was allegedly undertaken with a brutality reminiscent of the cruelties suffered by early Christians, in 622 Muhammad and his closest supporters (mostly from his own Hashemite clan) left the city and retreated north to the rival city of Yathrib, later renamed Medina (muh-DEE-nuh), or "city of the Prophet." That flight, known in history as the **Hegira** (huh-JY-ruh *or* HEH-juh-ruh) (*Hijrah*), marks the first date on the official calendar of Islam. At Medina, Muhammad failed in his original purpose—to convert the Jewish community in Medina to his beliefs. But he was successful in winning support from many residents of the city as well as from Bedouins in the surrounding countryside. From this mixture, he formed the first Muslim community—the **umma** (UM-mah). Returning to his birthplace at the head of

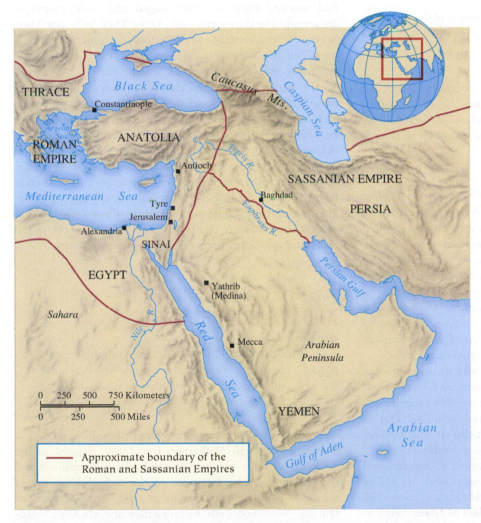

Map 7.1 The Middle East in the Time of Muhammad. When Islam began to spread throughout the Middle East in the early seventh century, the dominant states in the region were the Roman Empire in the eastern Mediterranean and the Sassanian Empire in Persia.

Q *What were the major territorial divisions existing at the time and the key sites connected to the rise of Islam?*

as *Muhammad: Messenger of God* (1976), was designed by the Syrian-American filmmaker Moustapha Akka to fill that gap. The film places emphasis on factual accuracy rather than on glitz, and therefore lacks some of the emotional punch of some familiar biblical epics, but it is beautifully produced and includes a number of swashbuckling battle scenes. Because of the Muslim stricture against showing the face of Muhammad, he does not appear on screen, but by voice only.

Q *Why do Muslims object to the portrayal of the Prophet Muhammad in works of art?*

a considerable military force, Muhammad conquered Mecca and converted the townspeople to the new faith. In 630, he made a symbolic visit to the Ka'aba, where he declared it a sacred shrine of Islam and ordered the destruction of the idols of the traditional faith (see Film & History).

7–1b The Teachings of Muhammad

Like Christianity and Judaism, Islam is monotheistic. Allah is the all-powerful being who created the universe and everything in it. Islam is also concerned with salvation and offers the hope of an afterlife. Those who hope to achieve it must subject themselves to the will of Allah. Unlike Christianity, Islam makes no claim to the divinity of its founder. Muhammad, like Abraham, Moses, and other figures of the Old Testament, was a prophet, but he was also a man like other men. Because, according to the Qur'an, earlier prophets had corrupted his revelations, Allah sent his complete revelation through Muhammad.

At the heart of Islam is the Qur'an, with its basic message that there is no God but Allah and Muhammad is his Prophet. Consisting of 114 *suras* (SUR-uhz) (chapters) drawn together by a committee established after Muhammad's death, the Qur'an is not only the sacred book of Islam but also an ethical guidebook and a code of law and political theory combined.

As it evolved, Islam developed a number of fundamental tenets. Of primary importance is the need to obey the will of Allah. This means following a basic ethical code that consists of what are popularly termed the **Five Pillars of Islam**: belief in Allah and Muhammad as his Prophet; standard prayer five times a day and public prayer on Friday at midday to worship Allah; observance of the holy month of **Ramadan** (RAH-muh-dan), including fasting from dawn to sunset; making a pilgrimage—known as the *hajj* (HAJ)—to Mecca at least once in one's lifetime,

if possible (see Film & History); and giving alms, called *zakat* (zuh-KAHT), to the poor and unfortunate. The faithful who observe the law are guaranteed a place in an eternal paradise (a vision of a luxurious and cool garden shared by some versions of Eastern Christianity) with the sensuous delights so obviously lacking in the Arabian Desert.

Islam is not just a set of religious beliefs but a way of life as well. After the death of Muhammad, a panel of Muslim scholars, known as the **ulama** (OO-luh-mah *or* oo-LAH-muh), drew up a law code, called the **Shari'a** (shah-REE-uh), to provide believers with a set of prescriptions to regulate their daily lives. Much of the *Shari'a* was drawn from existing legal regulations or from the **Hadith** (hah-DEETH), a collection of the sayings of the Prophet that was used to supplement the revelations contained in the holy scriptures.

Believers are subject to strict behavioral requirements. In addition to the Five Pillars, Muslims are forbidden to gamble, eat pork, drink alcoholic beverages, or engage in dishonest behavior. Sexual mores are also strict. Contacts between unmarried men and women are discouraged, and ideally, marriages are arranged by the parents (see "Draw Their Veils over Their Bosoms"). In accordance with Bedouin custom, polygyny is permitted, but Muhammad attempted to limit the practice by restricting males to no more than four wives.

The degree to which the traditional account of the exposition and inner meaning of the Qur'an can stand up to historical analysis is a matter of debate. As explained earlier, the circumstances surrounding the life of Muhammad and his role in founding the religion of Islam remain highly speculative, and many Muslims may be concerned that the consequences of rigorous examination might undercut key tenets of the Muslim faith. One problem is that the earliest known versions of the Qur'an available today do not contain the diacritical marks that modern Arabic uses to clarify meaning, so much of the sacred text is ambiguous and open to varying interpretations.

7–2 THE ARAB EMPIRE AND ITS SUCCESSORS

 Focus Question: Why did the Arabs undergo such a rapid expansion in the seventh and eighth centuries, and why were they so successful in creating an empire?

The death of Muhammad presented his followers with a dilemma. Although Muhammad had not claimed divine qualities, Muslims saw no separation between political and religious authority. Submission to the will of Allah meant submission to his Prophet, Muhammad. According to the Qur'an, "Whoso obeyeth the messenger obeyeth Allah."[1] Muhammad's charismatic authority and political skills had been at the heart of his success. But Muslims have never agreed on whether he named a successor, and although he had several daughters, he left no sons. In the male-oriented society of his day, who would lead the community of the faithful?

"DRAW THEIR VEILS OVER THEIR BOSOMS"

Religion & Philosophy BEFORE THE ISLAMIC ERA, many upper-class women greeted men on the street, entertained their husband's friends at home, went on pilgrimages to Mecca, and even accompanied their husbands to battle. Such women were neither veiled nor secluded. Muhammad, however, specified that his own wives, who (according to the Qur'an) were "not like any other women," should be modestly attired and should be addressed by men from behind a curtain. Over the centuries, Muslim theologians, fearful that female sexuality could threaten the established order, interpreted Muhammad's references to "modest attire" and curtains to mean that all Muslim women should remain in segregated seclusion and conceal their bodies. In fact, one strict scholar in fourteenth-century Cairo went so far as to prescribe that, ideally, a woman should leave her home only three times in her life: on entering her husband's home after marriage, after the death of her parents, and after her own death.

In traditional Islamic societies, veiling and seclusion were more prevalent among urban women than among their rural counterparts. The latter, who worked in the fields and rarely saw people outside their extended family, were less restricted. In this excerpt from the Qur'an, women are instructed to "guard their modesty" and "draw veils over their bosoms." Nowhere in the Qur'an, however, does it stipulate that women should be sequestered or covered from head to toe.

Qur'an, Sura 24: "The Light"

And say to the believing women
That they should lower

Their gaze and guard
Their modesty: that they
Should not display their
Beauty and ornaments except
What [must ordinarily] appear
Thereof: that they should
Draw their veils over
Their bosoms and not display
Their beauty except
To their husbands, their fathers,
Their husbands' fathers, their sons,
Their husbands' sons,
Their brothers or their brothers' sons,
Or their sisters' sons,
Or their women, or the slaves
Whom their right hands
Possess, or male servants
Free of physical needs,
Or small children who
Have no sense of the shame
Of sex; and that they
Should not strike their feet
In order to draw attention
To their hidden ornaments.

 How does the role of women in Islam compare with what we have seen in other traditional societies, such as India, China, and the Americas?

Source: The Holy Quran, 24:32.

Shortly after Muhammad's death, a number of his closest followers selected Abu Bakr (ah-boo BAHK-ur), a wealthy merchant from Medina who was Muhammad's father-in-law and one of his first supporters, as **caliph** (KAY-liff) (*khalifa*, literally "successor"). The caliph was the temporal leader of the Islamic community and was also considered, in general terms, to be a religious leader, or *imam* (ih-MAHM). Under Abu Bakr's prudent leadership, the movement succeeded in suppressing factional tendencies among some of the Bedouin tribes in the peninsula and began to direct its attention to wider fields. Muhammad had used the Arabic tribal custom of the *razzia* (RAZZ-ee-uh), or raid, in the struggle against his enemies. Now his successors turned to the same custom to expand the authority of the movement.

When historians of the Middle East today discuss the expansion of Islam after the death of Muhammad, the Arabic term *jihad* (jee-HAHD) is often used to describe the process. The word appears in the Qur'an on several occasions, and it appears to have had multiple meanings, much as the word *crusade* does in English. Sometimes *jihad* is used in the sense of "striving in the way of the Lord," as a means of exhorting believers

to struggle against the evil within themselves. In other cases, however, it has been translated as "holy war," justifying hostile action against the enemies of Islam. In that sense, the word can be used to describe the expansion of the world of Islam into the realm of the unbelievers (see "The Spread of the Muslim Faith," p. 192). Islamic terrorist movements of the present day clearly view *jihad* in the latter sense, an interpretation that many other Muslims vigorously reject. Because the word is so heavily laden with emotional connotations, it clearly should be used sparingly and with care.

7–2a Creation of an Empire

Once the Arabs had become unified under Muhammad's successor, they began directing against neighboring peoples the energy they had formerly directed against each other. The Byzantine and Sassanian Empires were the first to feel the strength of the newly united Arabs, now aroused to a peak of zeal by their common faith. In 636, the Muslims defeated the Byzantine army on the Yarmuk (yahr-MOOK) River, north of the Dead Sea. Four years later, they took possession of the Byzantine province of Syria. In 640, they conquered Cairo. To the east, the Arabs

THE SPREAD OF THE MUSLIM FAITH

Religion & Philosophy — **LIKE CHRISTIANITY,** Islam is not an exclusive religion, intended solely for members of a particular social or ethnic group, but is universalist in form, with all humans eligible to join the ranks of the believers. As a result, the sacred books of both religions—the Bible and the Qur'an—contain passages that encourage the spread of faith by whatever means are necessary and appropriate. In this selection from the Qur'an, Muslims are called upon to take part in the proselytizing effort, sometimes known in Arabic as *jihad*. While the vast majority of Muslims today believe that conversion to Islam should only take place by peaceful means, militants cite this passage from Chapter 47 as justification for their decision to make war on "unbelievers."

The Qur'an: Chapter 47, "Muhammad, Revealed at Medina"

Allah will bring to nothing the deeds of those who disbelieve and debar others from His path. As for the faithful who do good works and believe in what is revealed to Muhammad—which is the truth from their Lord—He will forgive them their sins and ennoble their state.

This, because the unbelievers follow falsehood, while the faithful follow the truth from their Lord. Thus Allah coins their sayings for mankind.

When you meet the unbelievers in the battlefield strike off their heads and, when you have laid them low, bind your captives firmly. Then grant them their freedom or take ransom from them, until War shall lay down her armour.

Thus shall you so. Had Allah willed, He could Himself have punished them; but He has ordained it thus that He might test you, the one by the other.

As for those who are slain in the cause of Allah, He will not allow their works to perish. He will vouchsafe them guidance and ennoble their state; He will admit them to the Paradise He has made known to them.

Believers, if you help Allah, Allah will help you and make you strong. But the unbelievers shall be consigned to perdition. He will bring their deeds to nothing. Because they opposed His revelations, He will frustrate their works.

Have they never journeyed through the land and seen what was the end of those who have gone before them? Allah destroyed them utterly. A similar fate awaits the unbelievers because Allah is the protector of the faithful; because the unbelievers have no protector.

Allah will admit those who embrace the true faith and do good works to gardens watered by running streams. The unbelievers take their fill of pleasure and eat as the beasts eat: but Hell shall be their home. . . .

This is the Paradise which the righteous have been promised. There shall flow in it rivers of unpolluted water, and rivers of milk forever fresh; rivers of delectable wine and rivers of clearest honey. They shall eat therein of every fruit and receive forgiveness from their Lord. Is this like the lot of those who shall abide in Hell forever and drink scalding water which will tear their bowels? . . .

Know that there is no god but Allah. Implore Him to forgive your sins and to forgive the true believers, men and women. Allah knows your busy haunts and resting places.

 According to this passage, what is the fate of those who adhere to the teachings of the Prophet Muhammad? How should unbelievers be treated?

Source: From *The Koran*, trans. N. J. Dawood (Penguin Classics, 1956, 5th rev. ed. 1990). Copyright © N. J. Dawood.

---

defeated a Persian force in 637 and then went on to conquer the entire empire of the Sassanids by 650. In the meantime, the rest of Egypt and other areas of North Africa were also brought under Arab authority (see Chapter 8).

HISTORIANS DEBATE — **What Was the Secret of Arab Success?** What accounts for this rapid expansion of the Arabs after the rise of Islam in the early seventh century? Historians have proposed various explanations, ranging from a prolonged drought on the Arabian Peninsula, to the use of the Arabian camel as an instrument of war, to the desire of Islam's leaders to channel the energies of their new converts. Others have suggested that the Byzantine Empire had been weakened by a plague epidemic that had not affected the desert regions farther to the east. Still another hypothesis is that the expansion was deliberately planned by the ruling elites in Mecca to extend their trade routes and bring surplus-producing regions under their control. Whatever the case, Islam's ability

to unify the Bedouin peoples certainly played a role. Although the Arab triumph was made substantially easier by the ongoing conflict between the Byzantine and Persian Empires, which had weakened both powers, the strength and mobility of the Bedouin armies with their much vaunted cavalry should not be overlooked. Led by a series of brilliant generals, the Arabs assembled a large, highly motivated army whose valor was enhanced by the belief that Muslim warriors who died in battle were guaranteed a place in paradise. This is clearly a case where the multitudes had been inspired by a message, and were prepared to carry that message to the ends of the earth.

Administering an Empire Once the army had prevailed, Arab civilian administration of the conquered areas was applied. Although hostile sources traditionally portrayed the takeover in violent terms, many historians today adopt a more nuanced approach, pointing out that Arab policy toward non-believers varied from place to place. Sometimes, due to a shortage of

William J. Duiker

The Camel: Islam's Secret Weapon. The one-humped Arabian camel, technically known as the dromedary, was first domesticated in the Horn of Africa about 5,000 years ago. By the beginning of the first millennium BCE it was introduced in the Middle East, where it became popular as a beast of burden and—after the rise of Islam—as an instrument of war, where its adaptability to desert conditions made it superior to the horse. Even today, camels are prized throughout the region, where fleet-footed varieties like the one shown here command high prices for their prowess on the race track.

trained Arab administrators, government was left to local officials, who sometimes applied pressure on non-believers to convert to Islam. Officially, however, conversion to Islam was voluntary, in accordance with the maxim in the Qur'an that "there shall be no compulsion in religion."[2] Those who chose not to convert, however, were required to submit to Muslim rule and to pay a head tax in return for exemption from military service, which was required of all Muslim males. Under such conditions, the local populations often regarded Arab rule as preferable to Byzantine rule or that of the Sassanid dynasty in Persia. Furthermore, the simple and direct character of the new religion and its egalitarian qualities (all people were viewed as equal in the eyes of Allah) were very likely attractive to peoples throughout the region.

7–2b The Rise of the Umayyads

The main challenge to the growing empire sometimes came from within. Some of Muhammad's followers had not agreed with the selection of Abu Bakr as the first caliph and promoted the candidacy of Ali, Muhammad's cousin and son-in-law, as an alternative. Ali's claim was ignored by other leaders, however, and after Abu Bakr's death, the office passed to Umar (oo-MAR), another of Muhammad's followers. In 656, Umar's successor, Uthman (ooth-MAHN), was assassinated, and Ali, who happened to be in Medina at the time, was finally selected for the position. But according to tradition, Ali's rivals were convinced that he had been implicated in the death of his predecessor, and a factional struggle broke out within the Muslim leadership. In 661, Ali himself was assassinated, and Mu'awiya (moo-AH-wee-yah), the governor of Syria and one of Ali's chief rivals, replaced him in office. Mu'awiya thereupon made the caliphate (KAY-luh-fayt)

hereditary in his own family, called the Umayyads (oo-MY-ads), who were a branch of the Quraishi clan. The new regime, with its capital at Damascus, remained in power for nearly a century.

The factional struggle within Islam did not bring an end to Arab expansion. At the beginning of the eighth century, new attacks were launched at both the western and the eastern ends of the Mediterranean world (see Map 7.2). Arab armies advanced across North Africa, displacing Byzantine rule and conquering the Berbers, a primarily pastoral people living along the Mediterranean coast and in the mountains in the interior. Although resistance continued for years, the local inhabitants were eventually converted to Islam (see Chapter 8).

Muslim fleets also attacked several islands in the eastern Mediterranean. Then, around 710, Arab forces, supplemented by Berber allies under their commander, Tariq (tuh-REEK), crossed the Strait of Gibraltar and occupied southern Spain (thus the modern name of the Rock of Gibraltar—*Jebel Tariq*, or "Tariq's Mountain"). The Visigothic kingdom, already weakened by internecine warfare (see Chapters 5 and 12), quickly collapsed, and by 725, most of the Iberian Peninsula had become a Muslim state with its center in Andalusia (an-duh-LOO-zhuh). Seven years later, an Arab force, making a foray into southern France, was defeated by the army of Charles Martel between Tours (TOOR) and Poitiers (pwah-TYAY). For the first time, Arab horsemen had met their match against a disciplined Frankish infantry. Some historians think that internal exhaustion would have forced the invaders to retreat even without their defeat at the hands of the Franks, the Germanic people who had established a kingdom in what is now France. In any event, the Battle of Tours (or Poitiers) would be the high-water mark of Arab expansion in Europe.

As Islamic power spread westward into the Mediterranean basin, the primary adversary for Arab forces was the Byzantine Empire. Because the Byzantines possessed a powerful fleet, many of the battles would inevitably take place at sea, where the Arab ships were initially at a substantial disadvantage, since the peoples of the Arabian Peninsula—lacking protected harbors and sources of wood and iron for ships—had little experience in maritime warfare. They were quick to learn, however (see "The Wealth of Araby: Trade and Cities in the Middle East," Section 7-3b, p. 202), and were soon competing on an equal basis with their opponents. Before the end of the seventh century, Arab fleets were able to seize a number of islands in the Mediterranean. In 717, a Muslim force launched an attack on Constantinople with the hope of destroying the Byzantine Empire. But the Byzantines' use of Greek fire, a petroleum-based compound containing quicklime and sulfur, destroyed the Muslim fleet, thereby saving the empire and indirectly Christian Europe, since the fall of Constantinople would have opened the door to an Arab invasion of eastern Europe. The Byzantine Empire and Islam now established an uneasy frontier in southern Asia Minor.

Arab power also extended to the east, consolidating Islamic rule in Mesopotamia and Persia and northward into Central Asia. But factional disputes continued to plague the empire. Many Muslims of non-Arab extraction resented the favoritism toward Arabs shown by local administrators. In some cases, resentment led to revolt, as in southern Iraq, where Ali's second son, Hussein, disputed the legitimacy of the Umayyads and incited his supporters—to

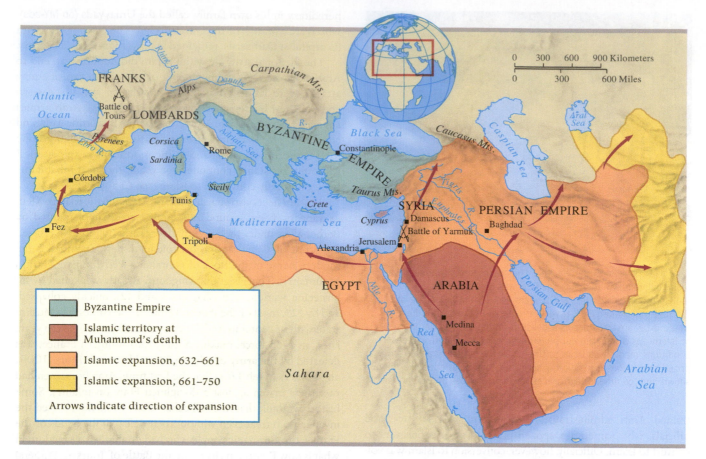

Map 7.2 The Expansion of Islam. This map traces the expansion of the Islamic faith from its origins in the Arabian Peninsula. Muhammad's followers carried the religion as far west as Spain and southern France and eastward to India and Southeast Asia.

Q *In which of these areas is the Muslim faith still the dominant religion?*

be known in the future as **Shi'ites** (SHEE-yts) (from the Arabic phrase *shi'at Ali*, "partisans of Ali")—to rise up against Umayyad rule in 680. Hussein's forces, many of whom were migrants from Persia, were defeated, and with the death of Hussein in the battle, a schism between Shi'ite and Arab Muslims had been created that continues to this day.

Umayyad rule created resentment, not only in Mesopotamia but also in Persia, where Arab migrants began to replace local aristocrats in position of influence, and in North Africa, where Berber resistance continued, especially in the mountainous areas south of the coastal plains. According to critics, the Umayyads may have contributed to their own demise by their decadent behavior. One caliph allegedly swam in a pool of wine and then imbibed enough of the contents to lower the level significantly. Finally, in 750, a revolt led by Abu al-Abbas (ah-boo al-ah-BUSS), a descendant of Muhammad's uncle, led to the overthrow of the Umayyads and the establishment of the Abbasid (uh-BAH-sid *or* AB-uh-sid) dynasty (750–1258) in what is now Iraq.

7–2c The Abbasids

The Abbasid caliphs brought political, economic, and cultural change to the world of Islam. While seeking to implant their

own version of religious orthodoxy, to be known as **Sunni** (SOON-nee), or "the law," they opened schools—known as **madrasas**—to popularize their teachings. They also tried to break down the distinctions between Arab and non-Arab Muslims. All Muslims were now allowed to hold both civil and military offices. This change helped open Islamic culture to the influences of the occupied civilizations. Some Arabs began to intermarry with the peoples they had conquered. In many parts of the Islamic world, notably North Africa and the eastern Mediterranean, most Muslim converts began to consider themselves Arabs. In 762, the Abbasids built a new capital city at Baghdad, on the Tigris River far to the east of the Umayyad capital at Damascus. The new capital was strategically positioned to take advantage of river traffic to the Persian Gulf and also lay astride the caravan route from the Mediterranean to Central Asia. The move eastward allowed Persian influence to come to the fore, encouraging a new cultural orientation. Under the Abbasids, judges, merchants, and government officials, rather than warriors, were regarded as the ideal citizens.

Abbasid Rule The new Abbasid caliphate experienced a period of splendid rule well into the ninth century. Best known of the caliphs of the time was Harun al-Rashid (hah-ROON al-rah-

SHEED) (r. 786–809), or Harun "the Upright," whose reign is often described as the golden age of the Abbasid caliphate. His son al-Ma'mun (al-muh-MOON) (r. 813–833) was a patron of learning who founded an astronomical observatory and established a foundation for translating Classical Greek works (see "Philosophy and Science," Section 7-3d, p. 204). This was also a period of growing economic prosperity. The Arabs had conquered many of the richest provinces of the Roman Empire and now controlled the routes to the east (see Map 7.3). Baghdad became the center of an enormous commercial market that extended into Europe, Central Asia, and Africa, greatly adding to the wealth of the Islamic world and promoting an exchange of culture, ideas, and technology from one end of the known world to the other. Paper was introduced from China and eventually passed on to North Africa and Europe. Crops from India and Southeast Asia, including rice, sugar, sorghum, and cotton, moved toward the west, while glass, wine, and indigo dye were introduced into China.

Although the Abbasids initially sought to lessen the gap between the elites and the majority of the population, their effort had little success, since under their rule the caliphs became more regal. More kings than spiritual leaders, described by such august phrases as the "caliph of God," they ruled by autocratic means similar to those used by the kings and emperors in neighboring civilizations. A thirteenth-century Chinese author, who compiled a world geography based on accounts by Chinese travelers, left the following description of one of the later caliphs:

The king wears a turban of silk brocade and foreign cotton stuff [buckram]. On each new moon and full moon he puts on an eight-sided flat-topped headdress of pure gold, set with the most precious jewels in the world. His robe is of silk brocade and is bound around him with a jade girdle. On his feet he wears golden shoes. . . . The king's throne is set with pearls and precious stones, and the steps of the throne are covered with pure gold.[3]

As the caliph took on more of the trappings of a hereditary autocrat, the bureaucracy assisting him in administering the expanding empire grew more complex as well. The caliph was advised by a council—called a *diwan* (di-WAHN)—headed by a prime minister, known as a **vizier** (veh-ZEER) (*wazir*). The caliph did not attend meetings of the *diwan* in the normal manner but sat behind a screen and then communicated his divine will to the vizier. Some historians have ascribed the change in the caliphate to Persian influence, which gradually permeated the empire after the capital was moved to Baghdad. Persian influence was indeed strong (the mother of the caliph al-Ma'mun, for example, was a Persian), but more likely, the increase in pomp and circumstance was a natural consequence of the growing power and prosperity of the empire.

Instability and Division Nevertheless, an element of instability lurked beneath the surface. The lack of spiritual authority may have weakened the caliphate and given impetus to potential rivals, and disputes over the succession were

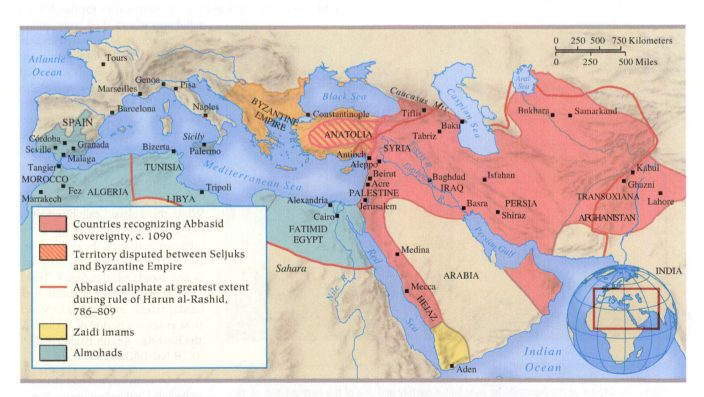

Map 7.3 The Abbasid Caliphate at the Height of Its Power. The Abbasids arose in the eighth century as the defenders of the Muslim faith and established their capital at Baghdad. With its prowess as a trading state, the caliphate was the most powerful and extensive state in the region for several centuries. The "Zaidi imams" indicated on the map were a group of dissident Shi'ites who established an independent kingdom on the southern tip of the Arabian Peninsula.

Q *Which of the major urban centers shown on this map were under the influence of Islam?*

common. At Harun's death, the rivalry between his two sons, Amin and al-Ma'mun, led to civil war and the destruction of Baghdad. As described by the tenth-century Muslim historian al-Mas'udi (al-muh-SOO-dee), "Mansions were destroyed, most remarkable monuments obliterated; prices soared. . . . Brother turned his sword against brother, son against father, as some fought for Amin, others for Ma'mun. Houses and palaces fueled the flames; property was put to the sack."[4]

Wealth contributed to financial corruption. By awarding important positions to court favorites, the Abbasid caliphs began to undermine the foundations of their own power and eventually became mere figureheads. Under Harun al-Rashid, members of his Hashemite clan received large pensions from the state treasury, and his wife Zubaida (zoo-BY-duh) reportedly spent huge sums while shopping on a pilgrimage to Mecca. One powerful family, the Barmakids, amassed vast wealth and power until Harun al-Rashid eliminated the entire clan in a fit of jealousy.

The life of luxury enjoyed by the caliph and other political and economic elites in Baghdad seemingly undermined the stern fiber of Arab society as well as the strict moral code of Islam. Strictures against sexual promiscuity were widely ignored, and caliphs were rumored to maintain thousands of concubines in their harems. Divorce was common, homosexuality was widely practiced, and alcohol was consumed in public despite Islamic law's prohibition against imbibing spirits.

The process of disintegration was accelerated by changes that were taking place within the armed forces and the bureaucracy of the empire. Given the shortage of qualified Arabs for key positions in the army and the administration, the caliphate began to recruit officials from among the non-Arab peoples in the empire, such as Persians and Turks from Central Asia. These people gradually became a dominant force in the army and administration.

Environmental problems added to the regime's difficulties. The Tigris and Euphrates river system, lifeblood of Mesopotamia for three millennia, was beginning to silt up. Bureaucratic inertia now made things worse, as many of the country's canals became virtually unusable, leading to widespread food shortages.

The fragmentation of the Islamic empire accelerated in the tenth century. Morocco became independent, and in 973, a new Shi'ite dynasty under the Fatimids (FAT-uh-mids) was established in Egypt with its capital at Cairo. With increasing disarray in the empire, the Islamic world was held together only by the common commitment to the Arabic language and the Qur'an.

The Seljuk Turks In the eleventh century, the Abbasid caliphate faced yet another serious threat in the form of the Seljuk (SEL-jook) Turks. When the nomadic Xiongnu Empire fell apart early in the first millennium CE (see Chapter 3), Turkic-speaking people in the area gradually migrated westward into Xinjiang and Central Asia. Some of them converted to Islam in the process. Eventually, one group, known as the Seljuk Turks, began to serve as military mercenaries for the Abbasid caliphate, where they were known for their ability as mounted archers. Moving gradually into Persia and Armenia as the Abbasids weakened, the Seljuk Turks grew in number until by the eleventh century, they were able to occupy the eastern provinces of the Abbasid Empire. In 1055, a Turkish leader captured Baghdad and assumed command of the empire with the title of **sultan** (SUL-tun) ("holder of power"). While the Abbasid caliph remained the chief representative of Sunni religious authority, the real military and political power of the state was in the hands of the Seljuk Turks. The latter did not establish their headquarters in Baghdad, which now entered a period of decline. As the historian Khatib Baghdadi (kah-TEEB bag-DAD-ee) described:

There is no city in the world equal to Baghdad in the abundance of its riches, the importance of its business, the number of its scholars and important people, the distinctions of its leaders and its

The Great Mosque of Samarra. The ninth-century mosque of Samarra, located north of Baghdad in present-day Iraq, is the largest mosque in the Islamic world. Rising from the center of the city of Samarra, the capital of the Abbasids for over half a century and one of the largest cities of its time, the imposing tower shown here is 156 feet in height. Its circular ramp may have inspired artists in medieval Europe as they imagined the ancient cultures of Mesopotamia. As a twelfth-century Muslim adventurer noted in his account, *The Travels of Ibn Jubayr,* "Pleased is he who looks upon it." Although the mosque is now in ruins, its spiral tower still signals the presence of Islam to the faithful across the broad valley of the Tigris and Euphrates Rivers.

Josef Polleross/The Image Works

common people, the extent of its palaces, inhabitants, streets, avenues, alleys, mosques, baths, docks and caravansaries, the purity of its air, the sweetness of its water, the freshness of its dew and its shade, the temperateness of its summer and winter, the healthfulness of its spring and fall, and its great swarming crowds. The buildings and the inhabitants were most numerous during the time of Harun al-Rashid, when the city and its surrounding areas were full of cooled rooms, thriving places, fertile pastures, rich watering-places for ships. Then the riots began, an uninterrupted series of misfortunes befell the inhabitants, its flourishing conditions came to ruin to such extent that, before our time and the century preceding ours, it found itself, because of the perturbation and the decadence it was experiencing, in complete opposition to all capitals and in contradiction to all inhabited countries.[5]

Baghdad would revive, but it would no longer be the "Gift of God" of Harun al-Rashid.

By the last decades of the eleventh century, the Seljuks were exerting military pressure on Egypt and the Byzantine Empire. In 1071, when the Byzantines foolishly challenged the Turks, their army was routed at Manzikert (MANZ-ih-kurt), near Lake Van in eastern Turkey, and the victors took over much of the Anatolian peninsula (see Map 7.4). In dire straits, the Byzantine Empire turned to the west for help, setting in motion the papal pleas that led to the **crusades** (see next section).

In Europe, and undoubtedly within the Muslim world itself, the arrival of the Turks was initially regarded as a disaster. The Turks were viewed as barbarians who destroyed civilizations and oppressed populations. In fact, in many respects, Turkish rule in the Middle East was probably beneficial. After converting to Islam, the Turkish rulers temporarily brought an end to the fraternal squabbles between Sunni and Shi'ite Muslims while supporting the Sunnis. They put their energies into revitalizing Islamic law and institutions and provided much-needed political stability to the empire, which helped restore its former prosperity. Under Seljuk rule, Muslims began to organize themselves into autonomous brotherhoods, whose relatively tolerant practices characterized Islamic religious attitudes until the end of the nineteenth century, when increased competition with Europe led to confrontation with the West.

Seljuk political domination over the old Abbasid Empire, however, provoked resentment on the part of many Persian Shi'ites, who viewed the Turks as usurping foreigners who had betrayed the true faith of Islam. Among the regime's most feared enemies was Hasan al-Sabahh (hah-SAHN al-SAH-bah), a Cairo-trained Persian who formed a rebel group, popularly known as "assassins" (guardians), who for several decades terrorized government officials and other leading political and religious figures from their base in the mountains south of the Caspian Sea. Like their modern-day equivalents, the members of the terrorist organization known as al-Qaeda, Sabahh's followers were highly motivated and were adept at infiltrating the enemy's camp to carry out their clandestine activities. The organization was finally eliminated by the invading Mongols in the thirteenth century.

7–2d The Crusades

Just before the end of the eleventh century, the Byzantine emperor Alexius I desperately called for assistance from other Christian states in Europe to protect his empire against the invading Seljuk Turks. As part of his appeal, he said that the Muslims were desecrating Christian shrines in the Holy Land and molesting Christian pilgrims en route to the shrines. In actuality, the Muslims had never threatened the shrines or cut off Christian access to them. But tension between Christendom and Islam was on the rise, and the Byzantine emperor's appeal received a ready response in Europe. Beginning in 1096 and continuing into the thirteenth century, a series of Christian raids on Islamic territories known as the crusades brought the Holy Land and adjacent areas on the Mediterranean coast from Antioch to the Sinai Peninsula under Christian rule (see Chapter 12).

At first, Muslim rulers in the area were taken aback by the invading crusaders, whose armored cavalry presented a new challenge to local warriors, and their response was ineffectual. The Seljuk Turks by that time were preoccupied with events taking place farther to the east and took no action themselves. But in 1169, Sunni Muslims under the leadership of Saladin (SAL-uh-din or Salah al-Din), vizier to the last

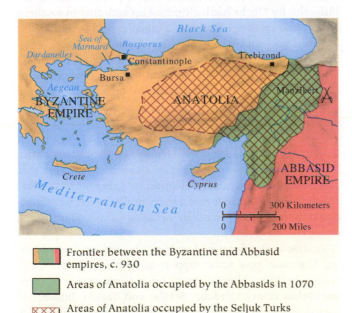

Map 7.4 The Turkish Occupation of Anatolia. This map shows the expansion of Turkic-speaking peoples into the Anatolian peninsula. The Seljuk Turks seized much of the peninsula after the Battle of Manzikert in 1071. In the late thirteenth century, Seljuk power collapsed and was replaced by another Turkic-speaking people, the Ottoman Turks, who began to consolidate their power in the northwestern part of Anatolia. The Ottomans established their capital at Bursa in 1335 and eventually at Constantinople in 1453 (see Chapter 16).

Q **What role did the expansion of the Seljuk Turks play in the origins of the crusades?**

Frontier between the Byzantine and Abbasid empires, c. 930

Areas of Anatolia occupied by the Abbasids in 1070

Areas of Anatolia occupied by the Seljuk Turks in the early thirteenth century

Fatimid caliph, brought an end to the Fatimid dynasty. Proclaiming himself sultan, Saladin succeeded in establishing his control over both Egypt and Syria, thereby confronting the Christian states in the area with united Muslim power on two fronts. In 1187, Saladin's army invaded the kingdom of Jerusalem and destroyed the Christian forces concentrated there. Further operations reduced Christian occupation in the area to a handful of fortresses along the northern coast. Unlike the Christians of the First Crusade, who had slaughtered much of the population of Jerusalem when they captured the city, Saladin did not permit a massacre of the civilian population and even tolerated the continuation of Christian religious services in conquered territories. For a time, Christian occupation forces even carried on a lively trade relationship with Muslim communities in the region.

The Christians returned for another try a few years after the fall of Jerusalem, but the campaign succeeded only in securing some of the coastal cities. Although the Christians would retain a toehold on the coast for much of the thirteenth century (Acre, their last stronghold, fell to the Muslims in 1291), they were no longer a significant force in Middle Eastern affairs. In retrospect, the crusades had only minimal importance in the history of the Middle East, although they may have served to unite the forces of Islam against the foreign invaders, thus creating a residue of distrust toward Christians that continues to resonate through the Islamic world today. Far more important in their impact were the Mongols, a pastoral people who swept out of the Gobi Desert in the early thirteenth century to seize control over much of the known world (see Chapter 10). Beginning with the advances of Genghis Khan (JING-uss or GENG-uss KAHN) in northern China, Mongol armies later spread across Central Asia, and in 1258, under the leadership of Hulegu (HOO-lay-goo), brother of the more famous Khubilai Khan (KOO-bluh KAHN), they seized Persia and Mesopotamia, bringing an end to the caliphate at Baghdad.

7–2e The Mongols

Unlike the Seljuk Turks, the Mongols were not Muslims, and they found it difficult to adapt to the settled conditions that they found in the major cities in the Middle East. Their treatment of the local population in conquered territories was brutal and destructive to the economy. Much of the local population was massacred, cities were razed to the ground, and dams and other irrigation works were destroyed, reducing prosperous agricultural societies to the point of mass starvation. The Mongols advanced as far as the Red Sea, but their attempt to seize Egypt failed, in part because of the effective resistance posed by the Mamluks (MAM-looks) (or Mamelukes, a military class originally composed of Turkish slaves), who had recently overthrown the administration set up by Saladin and seized power for themselves.

Eventually, the Mongol rulers in the Middle East began to assimilate with the culture of the peoples they had conquered. Mongol elites converted to Islam, Persian influence became predominant at court, and the cities began to be rebuilt. By the fourteenth century, the Mongol empire had begun to split into separate kingdoms and then to disintegrate. In the meantime, however, the old Islamic empire originally established by the Arabs in the seventh and eighth centuries had long since come to an end. The new center of Islamic civilization was in Cairo, now about to promote a renaissance in Muslim culture under the sponsorship of the Mamluks.

To the north, another new force appeared on the horizon with the rise of the Ottoman Turks on the Anatolian peninsula, superseding the Seljuks, who had previously ruled in the area. In 1453, the Ottoman ruler Mehmet II seized Constantinople and brought an end to the Byzantine Empire. Then the Ottomans began to turn their attention to the rest of the Middle East (see Chapter 16).

7–2f Andalusia: A Muslim Outpost in Europe

After the decline of Baghdad, perhaps the brightest star in the Muslim firmament was in Spain, where a member of the Umayyad dynasty had managed to establish himself after his family's rule in the Middle East had been overthrown in 750 CE. Abd al-Rathman (AHB-d al-rahkh-MAHN) had escaped the carnage in Damascus and made his way to Spain, where Muslim power had recently replaced that of the Visigoths. By 756, he had legitimized his authority in southern Spain—known to the Arabs as *al-Andaluz* and to Europeans as Andalusia—and taken the title of *emir* (EH-meer) (commander), with his capital at Córdoba (KOR-duh-buh). There he and his successors sought to build a vibrant new center for Islamic culture in the region. With the primacy of Baghdad now at an end, Andalusian rulers established a new caliphate in 929 (see "A Pilgrimage to Mecca").

Now that the seizure of Crete, Sardinia, Sicily, and the Balearic Islands had turned the Mediterranean Sea into a Muslim lake, Andalusia became part of a vast trade network that stretched all the way from the Strait of Gibraltar to the Red Sea and beyond. Valuable new agricultural products were introduced to the Iberian Peninsula, including cotton, sugar, olives, citrus, and the date palm.

Andalusia also flourished as an artistic and intellectual center. The court gave active support to writers and artists, creating a brilliant culture focused on the emergence of three world-class cities—Córdoba, Seville, and Toledo. Intellectual leaders arrived in the area from all parts of the Islamic world, bringing their knowledge of medicine, astronomy, mathematics, and philosophy. With the establishment of a paper factory near Valencia, the means of disseminating such information dramatically improved, and the libraries of Andalusia became the wonder of their time (see "Philosophy and Science," Section 7-3d, p. 204). Other wonders of the East that now began to become known in western Europe were glass mirrors and the private bath.

One major reason for the rise of Andalusia as a hub of artistic and intellectual activity was the atmosphere of tolerance in social relations fostered by the state. Although Islam was firmly established as the official faith and non-Muslims were required

A PILGRIMAGE TO MECCA

Religion & Philosophy

THE PILGRIMAGE TO MECCA, one of the Five Pillars of Islam, is the duty of every Muslim. Ibn Jubayr, a twelfth-century Spanish Muslim who was an ardent proponent of the view that Andalusian Islam had now become the leading force in global Islam with the decline of the Abbasids, left a description of his trip in his journal. The work is famous for its vivid and abundant detail. In this almost lyrical passage, Ibn Jubayr tells of reaching his final destination, the Ka'aba at Mecca, containing the Black Stone. The Qarmata were an extremist religious sect in ninth- and tenth-century Mesopotamia.

Ibn Jubayr, *The Travels of Ibn Jubayr*

The blessed Black Stone is encased in the corner [of the Ka'aba] facing east. The depth to which it penetrates it is not known, but it is said to extend two cubits into the wall. Its breadth is two-thirds of a span, its length one span and a finger joint. It has four pieces, joined together, and it is said that it was the Qarmata—may God curse them—who broke it. Its edges have been braced with a sheet of silver whose white shines brightly against the black sheen and polished brilliance of the Stone, presenting the observer a striking spectacle which will hold his gaze. The Stone, when kissed, has a softness and moistness which so enchants the mouth that he who puts his lips to it would wish them never to be removed. This is one of the special favors of Divine Providence, and it is enough that the Prophet—may God bless and preserve him—declare it to be a covenant of God on each. May God profit us by the kissing and touching of it. By His favor may all who yearn fervently for it be brought to it. In the sound piece of the stone, to the right of him who presents himself to kiss it, is a small white spot that shines and appears like a mole on the blessed surface. Concerning this white mole, there is a tradition that he who looks upon it clears his vision, and when kissing it one should direct one's lips as closely as one can to the place of the mole.

 What are the other Pillars of Islam? How does each task contribute to making a good Muslim?

Source: Excerpt from *The Travels of Ibn Jubayr*, J. R. C. Broadhurst, trans. (London: Jonathan Cape Ltd., 1952).

---

to pay a special tax and prohibited from proselytizing for their faith, the policy of *convivência* (con-vee-VEN-cee-uh) (commingling) provided an environment in which many Christians and Jews were able to maintain their religious beliefs and even obtain favors from the court.

A Time of Troubles Unfortunately, the primacy of Andalusia as a cultural center was short-lived. By the end of the tenth century, factionalism was beginning to undermine the foundations of the emirate. In 1009, the royal palace at Córdoba was totally destroyed in a civil war. Twenty years later, the caliphate itself disappeared as the emirate dissolved into a patchwork of city-states.

In the meantime, the Christian kingdoms that had managed to establish themselves in the north of the Iberian Peninsula were consolidating their position and beginning to expand southward. In 1085, Alfonso VI, the Christian king of Castile, seized Toledo, one of Andalusia's main intellectual centers. The new rulers continued to foster the artistic and intellectual activities of their predecessors, leading eventually to the spread of such ideas northward to the great cities and universities of central and western Europe. To recoup their losses, the Muslim rulers in Seville called on fellow Muslims, the Almoravids (al-MOR-uh-vids)—a Berber dynasty in Morocco—for help in halting the Christian advance. Berber mercenaries defeated Castilian forces at Badajoz (bah-duh-HOHZ) in 1086 but then remained in the area to establish their own rule over remaining Muslim-held areas in southern Spain.

A warrior culture with little tolerance for heterodox ideas, the Almoravids quickly brought an end to the era of religious tolerance and intellectual achievement. But the presence of Andalusia's new warlike rulers was unable to stem the tide of Christian advance. In 1215, Pope Innocent III called for a new crusade to destroy Muslim rule in southern Spain. Over the next two hundred years, Christian armies advanced relentlessly southward, seizing the cities of Seville and Córdoba. But a single redoubt of Abd al-Rathman's glorious achievement remained: the remote mountain city of Granada (greh-NAH-duh), with its imposing hilltop fortress, the Alhambra (al-HAM-bruh).

HISTORIANS DEBATE **Moorish Spain: An Era of "Cultural Tolerance"?** In standard interpretations of European history, Western historians have usually described the *Reconquista* (ray-con-KEES-tuh) (reconquest) of southern Spain by the Christian kingdoms in the north as a positive development that freed the Spanish people

0 100 200 300 Kilometers
0 100 200 Miles

Pyrenees
CASTILE · ARAGON
Toledo · Valencia
Badajoz
Córdoba
Seville · Granada
Atlantic Ocean
Mediterranean Sea
AFRICA

☐ Christian-held areas

Spain in the Eleventh Century

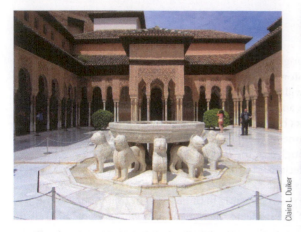

Claire L. Duiker

William J. Duiker

The Alhambra in Granada. Islamic civilization reached its zenith with the fourteenth-century castle known as the Alhambra, in southern Spain. Sitting high above the city of Granada, the castle is forbidding from the exterior, but behind its walls lies a magical world. The Lion Court (left) in the ruler's private quarters is world renowned for its lion fountain and surrounding arcade with elegant columns and carvings. Like the Hindus in India, the Muslims of the Middle East and Spain lived in a hot, dry climate, making water a highly prized commodity both literally and psychologically. The quiet, refreshing coolness of water became a vital component of Muslim architecture, displayed here in magnificent gardens featuring fountains and reflecting pools (right photo).

from centuries of oppressive Muslim rule. In recent years, however, it has become fashionable to point to the Moorish era in Spain (the term *Moors* is often used to refer to the Muslims in Spain) as a period of "cultural tolerance," a time of diversity that was followed by the bloody era of the Spanish Inquisition, when the Catholic Church persecuted Muslims, Jews, and Christian heretics for their refusal to accept the true faith. This interpretation has been especially popular since the terrorist attacks in

September 2001, as revisionist scholars seek to present a favorable image of Islam to counter the popular perception that all Muslims are sympathetic to terrorism against the West.

Some historians, however, argue that this portrayal of the Moorish era as a period of "cultural tolerance" overstates the case. They point out that even under the relatively benign rule of Abd al-Rathman true religious tolerance was never achieved and that, in any case, any such era came to end with the arrival of the Almoravids and the Almohads (AL-moh-hads), a Berber dynasty that supplanted the Almoravids in Andalusia in the twelfth century. For historian J. S. Elliot, the era was, at best, one of "cultural interaction," which was eventually followed by a hardening of attitudes on both sides of the cultural spectrum. If there was an era of religious diversity in Spain under Muslim rule, it was all too brief.

CHRONOLOGY	Islam: The First Millennium
Life of Muhammad	570–632
Flight to Medina	622
Conquest of Mecca	630
Fall of Cairo	640
Defeat of Persians	650
Election of Ali to caliphate	656
Muslim entry into Spain	c. 710
Abbasid caliphate	750–1258
Construction of city of Baghdad	762
Reign of Harun al-Rashid	786–809
Umayyad caliphate in Spain	929–1031
Founding of Fatimid dynasty in Egypt	973
Capture of Baghdad by Seljuk Turks	1055
Seizure of Anatolia by Seljuk Turks	1071
First Crusade	1096
Saladin destroys Fatimid kingdom	1169
Mongols seize Baghdad	1258
Ottoman Turks capture Constantinople	1453

7–3 ISLAMIC CIVILIZATION

 Focus Question: What were the main features of Islamic society and culture during its era of early growth?

As Thomas Lippman, author of *Understanding Islam*, has remarked, the Muslim religion is based on behavior as well as belief. Although this generalization applies in broad terms to most major religions, it seems to be particularly true of Islam. To be a Muslim is not simply to worship Allah but also to live according to his law as revealed in the Qur'an, which is viewed as fundamental and immutable doctrine, not to be revised by human beings. As Allah has decreed, so must human beings behave. Therefore, Islamic doctrine must be consulted to determine questions of politics, economic behavior, civil and criminal law, and social ethics.

Of course, to live entirely by God's law is difficult, if not impossible. While pure behavior lived according to the teachings

SAGE ADVICE FROM FATHER TO SON

Politics & Government

TAHIR IBN HUSAYN (tah-HEER IB-un HOO-sayn) was born into an aristocratic family in Central Asia and became a key political adviser to al-Ma'mun, the Abbasid caliph of Baghdad in the early ninth century. Appointed in 821 to a senior position in Khurusan (kor-uh-SAHN), a district near the city of Herat in what is today Afghanistan, he wrote the following letter to his son, giving advice on how to wield authority most effectively. The letter so impressed al-Ma'mun that he had it widely distributed throughout his bureaucracy.

Letter of Tahir Ibn Husayn

Look carefully into the matter of the land-tax which the subjects have an obligation to pay. . . . Divide it among the taxpayers with justice and fairness with equal treatment for all. Do not remove any part of the obligation to pay the tax from any noble person just because of his nobility or any rich person because of his richness or from any of your secretaries or personal retainers. Do not require from anyone more than he can bear, or exact more than the usual rate. . . .

[The ruler should also devote himself] to looking after the affairs of the poor and destitute, those who are unable to bring their complaints of ill-treatment to you personally and those of wretched estate who do not know how to set about claiming their rights. . . . Turn your attention to those who have suffered injuries and their orphans and widows and provide them with allowances from the state treasury,

following the example of the Commander of the Faithful, may God exalt him, in showing compassion for them and giving them financial support, so that God may thereby bring some alleviation into their daily lives and by means of it bring you the spiritual food of His blessing and an increase of His favor. Give pensions from the state treasury to the blind, and give higher allowances to those who know of the Qur'an, or most of it by heart. Set up hospices where sick Muslims can find shelter, and appoint custodians for these places who will treat the patients with kindness and physicians who will cure their illnesses. . . .

Keep an eye on the officials at your court and on your secretaries. Give them each a fixed time each day when they can bring you their official correspondence and any documents requiring the ruler's signature. They can let you know about the needs of the various officials and about all the affairs of the provinces you rule over. Then devote all your faculties, ears, eyes, understanding and intellect, to the business they set before you: consider it and think about it repeatedly. Finally take those actions which seem to be in accordance with good judgment and justice.

 How does Tahir's advice compare with that given in the political treatise Arthasastra, *discussed in Chapter 2? Would his advice serve as an effective model for political leadership today?*

Source: H. Keller (ed.), Ibn Abi Tahir Kitab Baghdad (Leipzig, 1908), cited in H. Kennedy, *When Baghdad Ruled the Muslim World: The Rise and Fall of Islam's Greatest Dynasty* (Cambridge, MA, 2004), pp. 204–205.

---

of Muhammad has been relatively infrequent in the Islamic world, the social pressure to do so is probably stronger than within other major religions. Moreover, many issues of social organization and human behavior were not addressed in the Qur'an or in the *Hadith* or *Shari'a*. There was therefore some room for differing interpretations of Holy scripture in accordance with individual preference and local practice. Still, the Islamic world is and has probably always been more homogeneous in terms of its political institutions, religious beliefs, and social practices than most of its contemporary civilizations.

7-3a Political Structures

For early converts, establishing political institutions and practices that conformed to Islamic doctrine was a daunting task. In the first place, the will of Allah, as revealed to his Prophet, was not precise about the relationship between religious and political authority, simply decreeing that human beings should "conduct their affairs by mutual consent." On a more practical plane, establishing political institutions for a large and multicultural empire presented a challenge for the Arabs, whose own political structures were relatively rudimentary and relevant only to small pastoral communities (see "Sage Advice from Father to Son").

During the life of Muhammad, the problem could be ignored, since he was generally accepted as both the religious and the political leader of the Islamic community—the *umma*. His death, however, raised the question of how a successor should be chosen and what authority that person should have. As we have seen, Muhammad's immediate successors were called caliphs. Their authority was purely temporal, although they were also considered in general terms to be religious leaders, with the title of *imam*. At first, each caliph was selected informally by leading members of the *umma*. Soon succession became hereditary in the Umayyad clan, but their authority was still qualified, at least in theory, by the idea that they should consult with other leaders. The issue was further clouded by the bitter dispute over succession that led ultimately to the split between Shi'ites and Sunni within the Islamic world.

7-3b The Wealth of Araby: Trade and Cities in the Middle East

As we have noted, the Abbasid era was probably one of the most prosperous periods in the history of the Middle East. Trade flourished, not only in the Islamic world but also with China (now in a period of efflorescence during the Tang and

Song Dynasties; see Chapter 10), with the Byzantine Empire, and with the trading societies in Southeast Asia (see Chapter 9). Trade goods were carried both by ship and by the camel caravans that traversed the arid land from Morocco in the far west to the countries beyond the Caspian Sea. From West Africa came gold and slaves; from China, silk and porcelain; from East Africa, gold, ivory, and rhinoceros horn; and from the lands of South Asia, sandalwood, cotton, wheat, sugar, and spices. Within the empire, Egypt contributed grain; Iraq, linens, dates, and precious stones; Spain, leather goods, olives, and wine; and western India, pepper and various textile goods. The exchange of goods was facilitated by the development of banking and the use of currency and letters of credit (see Comparative Essay "Trade and Civilization").

One of the key reasons for the Arab empire's emergence as a major participant in the regional trade network was its success in mastering the latest in naval technology. Arab ships known as dhow—with hulls of teakwood and lateen sails appropriate for the sailing conditions in the Indian Ocean and beyond—were guided to their destinations by the astrolabe (an invention of the Greeks) and the compass (invented in China). Soon Muslim fleets were a familiar feature in the sea lanes from the western Mediterranean to the coast of southern China. In the process, Muslim merchants gradually replaced their Jewish or Persian counterparts in port cities throughout the region. Sailors throughout the Middle East continue to use the dhow to transport cargo, although many of them have now been motorized. In some instances, however (as is the case with the dhow in Zanzibar harbor), they still operate under sail.

Under these conditions, urban areas flourished. While the Abbasids were in power, Baghdad was probably the greatest city in the empire, but after the rise of the Fatimids in Egypt, the focus of trade shifted to Cairo, described by the traveler Leo Africanus as "one of the greatest and most famous cities in all the whole world, filled with stately and admirable palaces and colleges, and most sumptuous temples."[6] Other great commercial cities included Basra at the head of the Persian Gulf, Aden at the southern tip of the Arabian Peninsula, Damascus in modern Syria, and Marrakech in Morocco. In the cities, the inhabitants were generally segregated by religion, with Muslims, Jews, and Christians living in separate neighborhoods. But all were equally subject to the most common threats to urban life—fire, flood, and disease.

The most impressive urban buildings were usually the palace for the caliph or the local governor and the great mosque. Houses were often constructed of stone or brick on a timber frame. The larger houses were often built around an interior courtyard where the residents could retreat from the dust, noise, and heat of the city streets. Sometimes domestic animals such as goats or sheep would be stabled there. The houses of

William J. Duiker

The Dhow: Workhorse of the Indian Ocean. The dhow, a generic term for various types of sailing ships found in the Arabian Sea or along the east coast of Africa, has been the classic vessel for transporting goods in the Indian Ocean for over two millennia. Their lateen sails and narrow hulls composed of teak planking make them ideal for catching the monsoon winds that blow seasonally across the ocean between the Asian landmass and the coast of East Africa. Shown here is a traditional wind-powered cargo ship being unloaded at the East African city of Zanzibar. Today, many of the dhow used as cargo ships are motorized and are thus no longer subject to the whims of the yearly monsoon winds. Wind-powered vessels of this type, however, remain common throughout the region.

the wealthy were often multistoried, with balconies and windows covered with latticework to provide privacy. The poor in both urban and rural areas lived in simpler houses composed of clay or unfired bricks. The Bedouins lived in tents that could be dismantled and moved according to their needs.

The Arab empire was clearly more urbanized than most other areas of the known world at the time. Yet the bulk of the population continued to live in the countryside, supported by farming or herding animals. Farm productivity increased steadily throughout much of the empire, aided by reservoirs, new crops, and advanced water management techniques such as underground irrigation canals that had first been invented in the region thousands of years previously. During the early stages, most of the farmland was owned by independent peasants, but eventually some concentration of land in the hands of wealthy owners began to take place. Some lands were owned by the state or the court and were cultivated by slave labor, but plantation agriculture was not as common as it would be later in many areas of the world. In the valleys of rivers such as the Tigris, the Euphrates, and the Nile, the majority of the farmers were probably independent peasants. A Chinese account described life along the Nile:

The peasants work their fields without fear of inundation or droughts; a sufficiency of water for irrigation is supplied by a river whose source is not known. During the seasons when no cultivation is in progress, the level of the river remains even with the banks; with the beginning of cultivation it

COMPARATIVE ESSAY

Trade and Civilization

Interaction & Exchange In 2002, archaeologists unearthed the site of an ancient Egyptian port city on the shores of the Red Sea. Established sometime during the first millennium BCE, the city of Berenike linked the Nile River Valley with ports as far away as the island of Java in Southeast Asia. The discovery of Berenike is only the latest piece of evidence confirming the importance of interregional trade in the ancient world. The exchange of goods between far-flung societies became a powerful engine behind the rise of advanced civilizations throughout the ancient world. Raw materials such as copper, tin, and obsidian; items of daily necessity such as salt, fish, and other foodstuffs; and luxury goods including gold, silk, and precious stones passed from one end of the Eurasian supercontinent to the other, across the desert from the Mediterranean Sea to sub-Saharan Africa. A similar network extended throughout much of the Americas. Less well known but also important was the maritime trade that stretched from the Mediterranean across the Indian Ocean to port cities on the distant coasts of Southeast and East Asia.

During the first millennium CE, the level of interdependence among human societies intensified as three major trade routes—across the Indian Ocean, along the Silk Road, and by caravan across the Sahara—created the framework of a single system of trade. The new global network was not only commercial but informational as well, transmitting technology and ideas, such as the emerging religions of Buddhism, Christianity, and Islam, to new destinations.

There was a close relationship between missionary activities and trade. Buddhist merchants first brought the teachings of Siddhartha Gautama to China, and Muslim traders carried Muhammad's words to Southeast Asia and sub-Saharan Africa. Indian traders carried Hindu beliefs and political institutions to Southeast Asia.

What caused the rapid expansion of trade during this period? One key factor was the introduction of technology to facilitate transportation. The development of the compass, improved techniques in mapmaking and shipbuilding, and greater knowledge of wind patterns all contributed to the expansion of maritime trade. Caravan trade, once carried by wheeled chariots or on the backs of oxen, now used the camel as the preferred beast of burden through the deserts of Africa, Central Asia, and the Middle East.

Art Directors & TRIP/Alamy

Arab Trading Ship in the Indian Ocean.

Another reason for the expansion of commerce during this period was the appearance of several multinational empires that created zones of stability and affluence in key areas of the Eurasian landmass. Most important were the emergence of the Abbasid Empire in the Middle East and the prosperity of China during the Tang and Song Dynasties (see Chapter 10). The Mongol invasions in the thirteenth century temporarily disrupted the process but then established a new era of stability that fostered long-distance trade throughout the world.

The importance of interregional trade as a crucial factor in promoting the growth of human civilizations can be highlighted by comparing the social, cultural, and technological achievements of active trading states with those communities that have traditionally been cut off from contacts with the outside world. We shall encounter many of these communities in later chapters. Even in the Western Hemisphere, where regional trade linked societies from the great plains of North America to the Andes Mountains in present-day Peru, geographic barriers limited the exchange of inventions and ideas, placing these societies at a distinct disadvantage when the first contacts with peoples across the oceans occurred at the beginning of the modern era.

Q *What were the chief factors that led to the expansion of interregional trade during the first millennium CE? What role did Islamic peoples play in this process?*

rises day by day. Then it is that an official is appointed to watch the river and to await the highest water level, when he summons the people, who then plough and sow their fields. When they have had enough water, the river returns to its former level.[7]

Eating habits varied in accordance with economic standing and religious preference. Muslims did not eat pork, but those who could afford it often served other meats, including mutton, goat, poultry, or fish. Fruit, spices, and various sweets were delicacies. The poor were generally forced to survive on boiled millet or peas with an occasional lump of meat or fat. Bread—white or whole meal—could be found on tables throughout the region except in the deserts, where boiled grain was the staple food. Pasta was probably first introduced to the Italians by Arab traders operating in Sicily.

7–3c Islamic Society

In some ways, Arab society was probably one of the most egalitarian of its time. Both the principles of Islam, which held that all were equal in the eyes of Allah, and the importance of trade to the prosperity of the state certainly contributed to this egalitarianism. Although there was a fairly well defined upper class, consisting of the ruling families, senior officials, tribal elites, and the wealthiest merchants, there was no hereditary nobility as in many contemporary societies, and merchants enjoyed a degree of respect that they did not receive in Europe, China, or India.

Not all benefited from the high degree of social mobility in the Islamic world, however. Slavery was widespread. Since a Muslim could not be enslaved, the supply came from sub-Saharan Africa or from non-Islamic populations elsewhere in Asia. Most slaves were employed in the army (which was sometimes a road to power, as in the case of the Mamluks) or as domestic servants, who were occasionally permitted to purchase their freedom. The slaves who worked the large estates experienced the worst living conditions and rose in revolt on several occasions.

The Islamic principle of human equality also fell short, as in most other societies of its day, in the treatment of women. Although the Qur'an instructed men to treat women with respect, and women did have the right to own and inherit property, the male was dominant in Muslim society. Polygyny was permitted, and the right of divorce was in practice restricted to the husband, although some schools of legal thought permitted women to stipulate that their husband could have only one wife or to seek a separation in certain specific circumstances. Adultery and homosexuality were stringently forbidden, although such prohibitions were frequently ignored in practice.

Islamic custom also stipulated that women be cloistered in their homes and prohibited from social contacts with males outside their own family. In accordance with the reference in the Qur'an requiring women to "guard their modesty," the practice of covering the face and body of women whenever they appeared in public prevailed in many Muslim societies. For example, in the picture from a cultural display in the Persian Gulf state of Oman that is shown here, the bride covers her face during a traditional wedding ceremony (see illustration "A Marriage Ceremony").

A prominent example of this custom is the harem, introduced at the Abbasid court during the reign of Harun al-Rashid. Members of the royal harem were drawn from non-Muslim female populations throughout the empire. The custom of requiring women to cover virtually all parts of their body when appearing in public was common in urban areas and continues to be practiced in many Islamic societies today. It should be noted, however, that these customs owed more to traditional Arab practice than to Qur'anic law (see "The Gift of the Robe").

A Marriage Ceremony. In much of the Middle East, women were expected to avoid contact with males outside the bounds of the family. On those occasions when a public appearance was required, custom decreed that women should cover their bodies and faces in accordance with the stipulations of the Qur'an. In this cultural display of a wedding ceremony at the Khasab Museum in Khasab, Oman, the bride wears a mask to hide her face from the direct view of those in attendance.

7–3d The Culture of Islam

The Arabs were heirs to many elements of the remaining Greco-Roman culture of the Roman Empire, and they assimilated Byzantine and Persian culture just as readily. In the eighth and ninth centuries, numerous Greek, Syrian, and Persian scientific and philosophical works were translated into Arabic and eventually found their way to Europe. As the chief language in the southern Mediterranean and the Middle East, Arabic became an international language. Later, Persian and Turkish also came to be important in administration and culture.

The spread of Islam led to the emergence of a new culture throughout the Arab empire. This was true in all fields of endeavor, from literature to art and architecture. But pre-Islamic traditions were not extinguished and frequently combined with Muslim motifs, resulting in creative works of great imagination and originality.

Philosophy and Science During the centuries following the rise of the Arab empire, it was the Islamic world that was most responsible for preserving and spreading the scientific and philosophical achievements of ancient civilizations. At a time when ancient Greek philosophy was largely unknown in Europe, key works by Aristotle, Plato, and other Greek philosophers were translated into Arabic and stored in a "house of wisdom" in Baghdad, where they were read and studied by Muslim scholars. Eventually, many of these works were translated into Latin and were brought to Europe, where they exercised a profound influence on the later course of Christianity and Western philosophy.

The process began in the sixth century CE, when the devout Byzantine ruler Justinian (see Chapter 13) shut down the Platonic Academy in Athens, declaring that it promoted heretical ideas. Many of the scholars at the Academy fled to

THE GIFT OF THE ROBE

Interaction & Exchange **IBN BATTUTA** (IB-un ba-TOO-tuh) (1304–1377), a travel writer born in the Moroccan city of Tangier, is often described as the Muslim equivalent of his famous Italian counterpart Marco Polo. Over the course of a quarter of a century, he voyaged widely throughout Africa and Asia, logging over 75,000 miles in the process. The fascinating personal account of his travels is a prime source of information about his times. In the excerpt presented here, he describes a visit to the city of Balkh (BAHLK), one of the fabled caravan stops on the Silk Road as it passed through Central Asia.

The Travels of Ibn Battuta

After a journey of a day and a half over a sandy desert in which there was no house, we arrived at the city of Balkh, which now lies in ruins. It has not been rebuilt since its destruction by the cursed Jengiz Khān. The situation of its buildings is not very discernible, although its extent may be traced. It is now in ruins, and without society.

Its mosque was one of the largest and handsomest in the world. Its pillars were incomparable: three of which were destroyed by Jengiz Khān, because it had been told him, that the wealth of the mosque lay concealed under them, provided as a fund for its repairs. When, however, he had destroyed them, nothing of the kind was to be found: the rest, therefore he left as they were.

The story about this treasure arose from the following circumstance. It is said, that one of the Califs of the house of Abbas was very much enraged at the inhabitants of Balkh, on account of some accident which had happened, and, on this account, sent a person to collect a heavy fine from them. Upon this occasion, the women and children of the city betook themselves to the wife of their then governor, who, out of her own money, built this mosque; and to her they made a grievous complaint. She accordingly sent to the officer, who had been commissioned to collect the fine, a robe very richly embroidered and adorned with jewels, much greater in value than the amount of the fine imposed. This, she requested might be sent to the Calif as a present from herself, to be accepted instead of the fine. The officer accordingly took the robe, and sent it to the Calif; who, when he saw it, was surprised at her liberality, and said: This woman must not be allowed to exceed myself in generosity. He then sent back the robe, and remitted the fine. When the robe was returned to her, she asked, whether a look of the Calif had fallen upon it; and being told that it had, she replied: No robe shall ever come upon me, upon which the look of any man, except my own husband, has fallen. She then ordered it to be cut up and sold; and with the price of it she built the mosque, with the cell and structure in the front of it. Still, from the price of the robe there remained a third, which she commanded to be buried under one of its pillars, in order to meet any future expenses which might be necessary for its repairs. Upon Jengiz Khān's hearing this story, he ordered these pillars to be destroyed; but, as already remarked, he found nothing.

 Would a Muslim observer have considered the actions of the governor's wife described here to be meritorious? Why or why not?

Source: S. Lee (trans.), *The Travels of Ibn Battuta in the Near East, Asia, and Africa, 1325–1354* (Mineola, NY, 2004), pp. 93–94.

Baghdad, where their ideas and the Classical texts they brought with them soon aroused local interest and were translated into Persian or Arabic. Later such works were supplemented by acquisitions in Constantinople and possibly also from the famous library at Alexandria.

The academies where such translations were carried out—often by families specializing in the task—were not true universities like those that would later appear in Europe but were private operations under the sponsorship of a great patron, many of them highly cultivated Persians living in Baghdad or other major cities. Dissemination of the translated works was stimulated by the arrival of paper in the Middle East, brought by Buddhist pilgrims from China passing along the Silk Road. Knowledge of the new technique of block printing—also a recent invention in China (see Chapter 10)—arrived in the Middle East at this time as well. Paper was much cheaper to manufacture than papyrus, and by the end of the eighth century, the first paper factories were up and running in Baghdad. Libraries and booksellers soon appeared, leading one recent scholar to suggest that Abbasid society was the first "book culture."

What motives inspired this ambitious literary preservation project? At the outset, it may have simply been an effort to provide philosophical confirmation for existing religious beliefs as derived from the Qur'an. Perhaps, also, the purpose was to train administrators for newly conquered lands in Europe by acquainting them with conditions in those areas. Eventually, however, more adventurous minds began to use the Classical texts not only to seek greater knowledge of the divine will but also to seek a better understanding of the laws of nature.

Such was the case with the physician and intellectual Ibn Sina (IB-un SEE-nuh) (980–1037), known in the West as Avicenna (av-i-SENN-uh), who in his own philosophical writings cited Aristotle to the effect that the world operated not only at the will of Allah but also by its own natural laws, laws that could be ascertained by human reason. Avicenna, a native of Balkh, was once imprisoned as punishment for publishing heterodox ideas, but the popularity of his writings caused them to spread nonetheless throughout the Islamic world and beyond.

Although Islamic scholars are justly praised for preserving much of Classical knowledge for the West, they also made

بالمواضع الضرورة وبسط ما يعدل في الملابس والمأكل والمشارب في الحركات ... ساد علي آله النجوم والصلحان ... ومات وله ثمانون وخمسون سنة

Preserving the Wisdom of the Greeks. After the fall of the Roman Empire, the philosophical works of ancient Greece were virtually forgotten in Europe or were banned as heretical by the Byzantine Empire. It was thanks to Muslim scholars, who stored copies and translations in libraries in Baghdad, Alexandria, and elsewhere in the Arab world, that many Classical Greek writings survived. Here young Muslim scholars are being trained in the Greek language so that they can translate Classical Greek literature into Arabic. Later the works were translated back into Western languages and served as the catalyst for an intellectual revival in medieval and Renaissance Europe. MS Ahmed III 3206 Aristotle teaching, illustration from 'Kitab Mukhtar al-Hikam wa-Mahasin al-Kilam' by Al-Mubashir (pen & ink and gouache on paper)/Turkish School, (13th century)/Topkapi Palace Museum, Istanbul, Turkey/Bridgeman Images

After its translation into Latin, Avicenna's work became a basic medical textbook for medieval European university students.

Ultimately, though, the spurt of interest in Classical philosophy and science throughout much of the Muslim world proved somewhat abortive. The suggestion that reason could build a bridge to faith aroused the ire of traditional Muslim scholars, and although Classical works by such ancient writers as Euclid, Ptolemy, and Archimedes continued to be translated, the influence of Greek philosophy began to wane in Baghdad by the end of the eleventh century and did not recover. Madrasas (the schools set up under Abbasid rule) were designed simply to provide instruction in Islamic doctrine and not to improve understanding of the world of Nature. At the same time, the new technique of printing did not spread, perhaps because it allegedly lacked the aesthetic qualities of cursive script or was viewed as inappropriate for the dissemination of the words of Allah.

A similar pattern occurred in Spain, where philosophers such as Averroës (uh-VERR-oh-eez), whose Arabic name was Ibn Rushd (IB-un RUSH-ed *or* IB-un RUSHT), and Maimonides (my-MAH-nuh-deez) (Musa Ibn Maymun, a Jew who often wrote in Arabic) undertook their own translations and wrote in support of Avicenna's defense of the role of human reason. Both were born in Córdoba in the early twelfth century but were persecuted for their ideas by the Almohads, who had replaced the Almoravids in Andalusia, and both men ended their days in exile in North Africa.

By then, however, Christian rulers such as Alfonso X in Castile and Frederick II in Sicily were beginning to sponsor their own translations of Classical Greek works from Arabic into Latin, whence they made their way to the many new universities sprouting up all over western Europe. The end result of this period of cultural interaction would be an intellectual revolution that would transform the world of medieval Europe to its very core.

considerable advances of their own. Nowhere is this more evident than in mathematics and the natural sciences. Islamic scholars adopted and passed on the numerical system of India, including the use of zero, and a ninth-century Persian mathematician founded the mathematical discipline of algebra (*al-jabr*, "the reduction"). Simplified "Arabic" numerals had begun to replace cumbersome Roman numerals in Italy by the thirteenth century.

In astronomy, Muslims set up an observatory at Baghdad to study the position of the stars. They were aware that the earth was round and in the ninth century produced a world map based on the tradition of the Greco-Roman astronomer Ptolemy (see Comparative Illustration "A Twelfth-Century Map of the World"). Aided by the astrolabe, an instrument designed to enable sailors to track their position by means of the stars, Muslim fleets and caravans opened up new trading routes connecting the Islamic world with other civilizations, and Muslim travelers such as al-Mas'udi and Ibn Battuta provide modern readers with their most accurate descriptions of political and social conditions throughout the Middle East.

Muslim scholars also made many new discoveries in optics and chemistry and, with the assistance of texts on anatomy by the ancient Greek physician Galen (c. 180–200 CE), developed medicine as a distinctive field of scientific inquiry. Avicenna compiled a medical encyclopedia that, among other things, emphasized the contagious nature of certain diseases and showed how they could be spread by contaminated water supplies.

Islamic Literature The literature of the Middle East is diverse, reflecting the many distinct cultures of the region. The Arabic and Persian works in particular represent a significant contribution to world literature. Arabic poetry prior to Muhammad extolled the Bedouin experience of tribal life, courage in battle, hunting, sports, and respect for the animals of the desert, especially the camel. Pre-Muslim Persia also boasted a long literary tradition, most of it oral and later written down using the Arabic alphabet. Lacking the desert tradition of the Arabs, Persian writers focused on legends of past kings, Zoroastrian religious themes, romances, fables, and folktales. The transcendent literary monument of

COMPARATIVE ILLUSTRATION

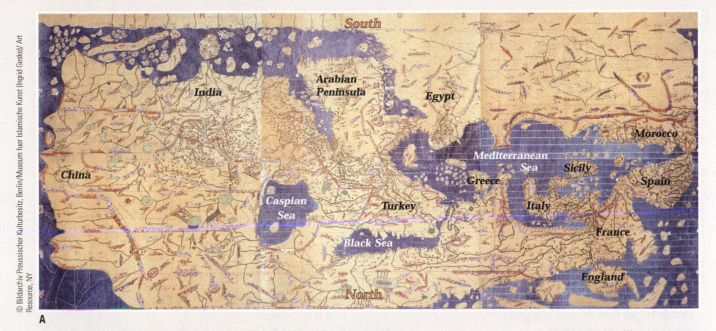

A

B

Science & Technology

A Twelfth-Century Map of the World. The twelfth-century Muslim geographer Al-Idrisi received his education in the Spanish city of Córdoba while it was under Islamic rule. Later he served at the court of the Norman king of Sicily, Roger II, where he created an atlas of the world based on Arab and European sources. In the Muslim tradition at the time, north and south were inverted from modern practice. Al-Idrisi's map, shown in A, depicts the world as it was known at that time, stretching from the Spanish peninsula on the right to the civilization of China on the far left. It is also a testimonial to the vast extension of the power and influence of Islam in the five centuries since the death of Muhammad in 632. Maps drawn by Al-Idrisi's European contemporaries were still highly stylized, with the Christian holy city of Jerusalem placed at the center of the world, as in the map shown in B.

Q *How much of the world shown on the map above was explored by Muslim fleets?*

early Persian literature is *The Book of Lords*, an early-sixth-century compilation of poetry about Persian myths and legendary heroes.

Islam brought major changes to the culture of the Middle East, not least to literature. Muslims regarded the Qur'an as their greatest literary work, but pre-Islamic traditions continued to influence writers throughout the region. Poetry is the Persian art par excellence. *The Book of Kings*, a ten-volume epic poem by the Persian poet Ferdowzi (fur-DOW-see) (940–1020), is one of the greatest achievements of Persian literature. It traces the history of the country from legendary times to the arrival of Islam. Iranian schoolchildren still learn its verses, which serve to reaffirm pride in their ancient heritage. But

love poetry remained popular. One notable example was Rabe'a of Qozdar (rah-BAY-uh of kuz-DAHR), Persia's first known woman poet, whose writings in the second half of the tenth century expressed her anguish at the suffering love brings.

In the West, the most famous works of Middle Eastern literature are undoubtedly the *Rubaiyat* of Omar Khayyam (OH-mar ky-YAHM) and *Tales from 1001 Nights* (also called *The Arabian Nights*). Although these two works are not especially popular with Middle Eastern readers, they appealed to the taste of nineteenth-century Europeans, who developed a taste for stories set in exotic foreign places—a classic example of the tendency of

THE PASSIONS OF A SUFI MYSTIC

Sufism was an unorthodox form of Islam that flourished in many parts of the Muslim world. It preached the importance of a highly personal relationship between Allah and the individual believer. Sufi orders began to assume considerable influence by the thirteenth century, perhaps because of the disintegration of the Abbasid Empire and heightened instability throughout the Islamic world. Sufi missionaries played a major role in efforts to spread Islam to India and Central Asia. In this poem, the thirteenth-century Persian poet Rumi describes the mystical relationship achieved by means of passionate music and dance.

Rumi, *Call to the Dance*

Come!
But don't join us without music.
We have a celebration here.
Rise and beat the drums.
We are Mansur who said "I am God!"
We are in ecstasy—
Drunk, but not from wine made of grapes.
Whatever your thoughts are about us,
We are far, far from them.
This is the night of the same
When we whirl to ecstasy.
There is light now,

There is light, there is light.
This is true love,
Which means farewell to the mind.
There is farewell today, farewell.
Tonight each flaming heart is a friend of music.
Longing for your lips,
My heart pours out of my mouth.
Hush!
You are made of feeling and thought and passion;
The rest is nothing but flesh and bone.
We are the soul of the world,
Not heavy or sagging like the body.
We are the spirit's treasure,
Not bound to this earth, to time or space.
How can they talk to us of prayer rugs and piety?
We are the hunter and the hunted,
Autumn and spring,
Night and day,
Visible and hidden.
Love is our mother.
We were born of Love.

 How does this poem celebrate the spiritual side of life? Why might such writings be attacked as contrary to Islamic doctrine?

Source: *Persian Literature*, Ehsan Yarshatar, ed., 1988.

Western observers to regard the customs and cultures of non-Western societies as strange or exotic.

Omar Khayyam's poetry, which he often composed orally over wine at a neighborhood tavern, is simple and down to earth. Key themes are the impermanence of life, the impossibility of knowing God, and disbelief in an afterlife. Among his most popular verses is the famous couplet: "Here with a loaf of bread beneath the bough, / A flask of wine, a book of verse, and thou." Ironically, recent translations of his work appeal to modern attitudes of skepticism and minimalist simplicity that may make him even more popular in the West:

In youth I studied for a little while;
Later I boasted of my mastery.
Yet this was all the lesson that I learned:
We come from dust, and with the wind are gone....
Drink wine by moonlight, darling, for the moon
Will shine long after this, and find us not.[8]

Like Omar Khayyam's verse, *The Arabian Nights* was loosely translated into European languages and adapted to Western tastes. A composite of folktales, fables, and romances of Indian and indigenous origin, the stories interweave the natural with the supernatural. The earliest stories were told orally and were later transcribed, with many later additions, in Arabic and Persian versions. The famous story of Aladdin and the Magic

Lamp, for example, was an eighteenth-century addition. Nevertheless, *The Arabian Nights* has entertained readers for centuries, allowing them to enter a land of wish fulfillment through extraordinary plots, sensuality, comic and tragic situations, and a cast of unforgettable characters.

Sadi (sah-DEE) (1210–1292), considered the Persian Shakespeare, remains to this day the favorite author in Iran. His *Rose Garden* is a collection of entertaining stories written in prose sprinkled with verse. He is also renowned for his sonnetlike love poems, which set a model for generations to come. Sadi was a master of the pithy maxim:

A cat is a lion in catching mice
But a mouse in combat with a tiger.

He has found eternal happiness who lived a good life,
Because, after his end, good repute will keep his name alive.

When thou fightest with anyone, consider
Whether thou wilt have to flee from him or he from thee.[9]

Such maxims are typical of the Middle East, where the proverb, a one-line witty observation on the vagaries of life, has long been popular. Proverbs are not only a distinctive feature of Middle Eastern verse, especially Persian, but are also a part of daily life—a scholar recently recovered more than four thousand in one Lebanese village, including the following: "He who has

IBN KHALDUN: ISLAM'S GREATEST HISTORIAN

Art & Ideas — Ibn Khaldun (1332–1406), born of an official family in Tunis, is generally recognized as the greatest of Muslim historians. Many years spent in the cosmopolitan city of Granada exposed him to ancient Greek science and philosophy, while a lifetime of travel and service in official capacities familiarized him with political conditions in the real world. His most famous work, the *Muqaddimah* (Introduction), has been widely praised for its striking modern sensitivity to the role of climate and geography on historical events. In this introductory passage, the author presents his interpretation of the primary tasks of the historian. It is well worth reading by practitioners of the craft today.

From the *Muqaddimah*

It should be known that history is a discipline that has a great number of approaches. Its useful aspects are very many. Its goal is distinguished.

History makes us acquainted with the conditions of past nations as they are reflected in their national character. It makes us acquainted with the biographies of the prophets and with the dynasties and policies of rulers. Whoever so desires may thus achieve the useful result of being able to imitate historical examples in religious and worldly matters.

The (writing of history) requires numerous sources and much varied knowledge. It also requires a good speculative mind and thoroughness, which lead the historian to the truth and keep him from slips and errors. If he trusts historical information in its plain transmitted form and has no clear knowledge of the principles resulting from custom, the fundamental facts of politics, the nature of civilization, or the conditions governing human social organization, and if, furthermore, he does not evaluate remote or ancient material through comparison with near or contemporary material, he often cannot avoid stumbling and slipping and deviating from the path of truth. Historians, Qur'an commentators and leading transmitters have committed frequent errors in the stories and events they reported. They accepted them in the plain transmitted form, without regard for its value. They did not check them with the principles underlying such historical situations, nor did they compare them with similar material. Also, they did not probe with the yardstick of philosophy, with the help of knowledge of the nature of things, or with the help of speculation and historical insight. Therefore, they strayed from the truth and found themselves lost in the desert of baseless assumptions and errors.

This is especially the case with figures, either of sums of money or of soldiers, whenever they occur in stories. They offer good opportunity for false information and constitute a vehicle for nonsensical statements. They must be controlled and checked with the help of known fundamental facts.

Source: Ibn Khaldun, *The Muqaddimah: An Introduction to History* (trans. Franz Rosenthal), Princeton University Press, classics edition 2015.

money can eat sherbet in Hell." From Persia comes the cynical aphorism: "Trust in God, but tie up your camel."

Some Arabic and Persian literature reflected the deep spiritual and ethical concerns of the Qur'an. The thirteenth-century poet Rumi (ROO-mee), for example, embraced **Sufism** (SOO-fiz-uhm), a form of religious belief that called for a mystical relationship between Allah and human beings (the term *Sufism* stems from the Arabic word for "wool," referring to the rough wool garments that its adherents wore). Converted to Sufism by a wandering dervish (dervishes, from the word for "poor" in Persian, sought to achieve a mystical union with Allah through dancing and chanting in an ecstatic trance), Rumi abandoned orthodox Islam to embrace God directly through ecstatic love. Realizing that love transcends intellect, he sought to reach God through a trance attained by the whirling dance of the dervish, set to mesmerizing music. As he twirled, the poet extemporized some of the most passionate lyrical verse ever conceived. His faith and art remain an important force in Islamic society today (see "The Passions of a Sufi Mystic").

The Islamic world also made a major contribution to historical writing, another discipline that was stimulated by the introduction of paper manufacturing. The first great Islamic historian was al-Mas'udi. Born in Baghdad in 896, he wrote about both the Muslim and the non-Muslim world, traveling widely in the process.

His *Meadows of Gold* is the source of much of our knowledge about the golden age of the Abbasid caliphate. Translations of his work reveal a wide-ranging mind and a keen intellect, combined with a human touch that practitioners of the art in our century might find reason to emulate. Equaling al-Mas'udi in talent and reputation was the fourteenth-century historian Ibn Khaldun (IB-un kal-DOON). Combining scholarship with government service, Ibn Khaldun was one of the first historians to attempt a philosophy of history (see "Ibn Khaldun: Islam's Greatest Historian").

Islamic Art and Architecture The art of Islam is a blend of Arab, Turkish, and Persian traditions. Although local influences can be discerned throughout the region, the Arabs, with their new religion and their writing system, served as a unifying force. Fascinated by the mathematics and astronomy they inherited from the Romans or the Babylonians, they developed a sense of rhythm and abstraction that found expression in their use of repetitive geometric ornamentation. The Turks made their own contribution with the use of abstraction in figurative and nonfigurative designs, while the Persians added their lyrical poetic mysticism.

The ultimate expression of Islamic art is to be found in magnificent architectural monuments beginning in the late seventh century. The first great example is the Dome of the Rock, built in 691 to proclaim the spiritual and political legitimacy of the new religion to the ancient world. Set in the sacred heart of Jerusalem on Muhammad's holy rock and touching both the Western Wall of the Jews and the city's oldest Christian church, the Dome of the Rock remains one of the most revered Islamic monuments. Constructed on Byzantine lines with an octagonal shape and marble columns and ornamentation, the interior reflects Persian motifs with mosaics of precious stones. Although rebuilt several times and incorporating influences from both East and West, this first monument to Islam represents the birth of a new art.

At first, desert Arabs, whether nomads or conquering armies, prayed in an open court, shaded along the *qibla* (KIB-luh) (the wall facing the holy city of Mecca) by a thatched roof supported by rows of palm trunks. There was also a ditch where the faithful could wash off the dust of the desert prior to prayer. As Islam became better established, enormous mosques, such as the one earlier discussed at Samarra (see illustration "The Great Mosque of Samarra," Section 7-2c, p. 196), were constructed, but they were still modeled on the open court, which would be surrounded on all four sides with pillars supporting a wooden roof over the prayer area facing the *qibla* wall. Set in that wall was a niche, or **mihrab** (MEER-uhb), containing a decorated panel pointing to Mecca and representing Allah.

No discussion of mosques would be complete without mentioning the famous ninth-century mosque at Córdoba in southern Spain, which is still in remarkable condition. Its 514 columns supporting double horseshoe arches transform this architectural wonder into a unique forest of trees pointing upward, contributing to a light and airy effect. The unparalleled sumptuousness and elegance make the Córdoba mosque one of the wonders of world art, let alone Islamic art.

Since the Muslim religion combines spiritual and political power in one, palaces also reflected the glory of Islam. Beginning in the eighth century with the spectacular castles of Syria, the rulers constructed large brick domiciles reminiscent of Roman design, with protective walls, gates, and baths. With a central courtyard surrounded by two-story arcades and massive gate-towers, they resembled fortresses as much as palaces. The most impressive remaining Islamic palace is the fourteenth-century Alhambra in Spain. The extensive succession of courtyards, rooms, gardens, and fountains created a fairytale castle perched high above the city of Granada. Every inch of surface is decorated in intricate floral and semiabstract patterns; much of the decoration is done in carved plasterwork so fine that it resembles lace (see illustration "The Qur'an as Sculptured Design," p. 212).

Since antiquity, one of the primary occupations of women has been the spinning and weaving of cloth to make clothing and other useful items for their families. In countless villages in the Middle East, the art of rug weaving has been passed down from mother to daughter over the centuries. Girls as young as four years old took part in the process by helping to spin and prepare the wool shorn from the family sheep. Eventually their slender fingers would be producing fine carpets. Originating in the pre-Muslim era, knotted woolen rugs were initially used to insulate stone palaces against the cold as well as to warm shepherds' tents. Eventually, they were applied to religious purposes, since every practicing Muslim is required to pray five times a day on clean ground. Small rugs served as prayer mats for individual use, while larger

The Dome of the Rock. One of the first architectural structures in the Islamic world, as well as one of the finest, the Dome of the Rock is topped with an opulent golden dome that still dominates the skyline of Jerusalem. Built by seventh-century artisans proficient in the Byzantine style, it boasts colored marble columns, glass and tile mosaics, and inscriptions from the Qur'an. Beneath the structure is a rock reputed to be the site of Adam's burial place, as well as the spot where Abraham prepared to sacrifice his son as recounted in the Bible. According to Muslims, the Prophet Muhammad began his night journey to heaven here. This magnificent building symbolizes the presence of Islam in a city historically identified with Judaism and Christianity.

William J. Duiker

Claire L. Duiker

Yvonne V. Duiker

The Recycled Mosque. The Great Mosque at Córdoba was erected on the site of a Christian church built by the Visigoths. Earlier the same site had been dedicated to the Roman god Janus. In the eighth century, the Muslims incorporated parts of the Visigothic church into their new mosque, aggrandizing it over the centuries. After the Muslims were driven from Spain, the mosque reverted to Christianity, and in 1523, a soaring cathedral sprouted from its spine. Inside, the mosque and the cathedral seem to blend well aesthetically, a prototype for harmonious religious coexistence. In the interior, a series of arched columns provide the entire structure with an effect of mass as well as lightness (upper photo). Above the Christian worshipper in the *mihrab* chamber today rises a glittering dome in the Arab style (lower photo). Throughout history, societies have all too often destroyed past architectural wonders, robbing older marble glories to erect new marvels. It is rare and wonderful that the Great Mosque has survived as a testimonial to the continuing struggle to achieve religious tolerance.

and more elaborate ones were given by rulers as rewards for political favors. Bedouins in the Arabian Desert covered their sandy floors with rugs to create a cozy environment in their tents.

Skilled artisanship represented an extra enticement to prospective bridegrooms, and rugs often became an important part of a woman's dowry to her future husband. After the

wedding, the wife would continue to make rugs for home use, as well as for sale to augment the family income. Eventually, rugs began to be manufactured in workshops by professional artisans, who reproduced the designs from detailed painted diagrams.

Representation of the Prophet Muhammad, in painting or in any other art form, has traditionally been strongly

The Qur'an as Sculptured Design.
Muslim sculptors and artists, reflecting the traditional view that any visual representation of the Prophet Muhammad was blasphemous, turned to geometric patterns, as well as to flowers and animals, as a means of fulfilling their creative urges. The predominant motif, however, was the reproduction of Qur'anic verses in the Arabic script. Calligraphy, which was almost as important in the Middle East as it was in traditional China, used the Arabic script to decorate all of the Islamic arts, from painting to pottery, tile and ironwork, and wall decorations such as this carved plaster panel in a courtyard of the Alhambra palace in Spain. Since a recitation from the Qur'an was an important component of the daily devotional activities for all practicing Muslims, elaborate scriptural panels such as this one perfectly blended the spiritual and the artistic realms.

William J. Duiker

discouraged. Although no passage of the Qur'an forbids representational painting, the *Hadith* warned against any attempt to imitate God through artistic creation or idolatry, and this has been interpreted as an outright ban on any such depictions. Accordingly, with the exception of Persian miniatures, where an earlier style involving human representation survived for a while, most decorations on all forms of Islamic art consisted of Arabic script and natural plant and figurative motifs. Repeated continuously in naturalistic or semiabstract geometrical patterns called arabesques, these decorations completely covered the surface and left no area undecorated. This dense decor was also evident in brick, mosaic, and stucco ornamentation and culminated in the magnificent tile work of later centuries.

CHAPTER SUMMARY

After the collapse of Roman power in the west, the Eastern Roman Empire, centered on Constantinople, continued to dominate much of the eastern Mediterranean and eventually emerged as the unique Christian civilization known as the Byzantine Empire, which flourished for hundreds of years (see Chapter 13). The seventh century, however, saw the emergence of a new force—Islam—that blossomed in the Arabian Peninsula and spread rapidly throughout the Middle East. In the eyes of some Europeans during the Middle Ages, the Arab empire was a malevolent force that posed a serious threat to the security of Christianity. Their fears were not entirely misplaced, for within a century after the death of Islam's founder, Muhammad, Arab armies overran Christian states in North Africa and the Iberian Peninsula, and Turkish Muslims moved eastward onto the fringes of the Indian subcontinent.

But although the teachings of Muhammad brought war and conquest to much of the known world, they also brought hope and a sense of political and economic stability to peoples throughout the region. Thus, for many people in the medieval Mediterranean world, the arrival of Islam was a welcome event. Islam brought a code of law and a written language to societies that had previously lacked them. Finally, by creating a revitalized trade network stretching from West Africa to East Asia, it established a vehicle for the exchange of technology and ideas that brought untold wealth to thousands and a better life to millions.

Like other empires in the region, the Arab empire did not last. It fell victim to a combination of internal and external pressures, and by the end of the thirteenth century, it was no more than a memory. But it left a powerful legacy in Islam, which remains one of the great religions of the world. In succeeding centuries, Islam began to penetrate into new areas beyond the edge of the Sahara and across the Indian Ocean into the islands of the Indonesian archipelago.

CHAPTER TIMELINE

CHAPTER REVIEW

Upon Reflection

Q By what process was Arab power expanded throughout the Middle East and North Africa in the years following the death of Muhammad? What was the impact of that expansion on the subject peoples?

Q What role did the Abbasid Empire play in promoting the establishment of a trade network extending from East Asia to the Mediterranean Sea and beyond? Is it reasonable to say that the Muslim world was the linchpin of global trade during this period?

Q What circumstances do some historians refer to when they say that the Muslim governments in Spain provided an example of religious tolerance?

Key Terms

Bedouin (p. 188)
sheikh (p. 188)
majlis (p. 188)
Hegira (p. 189)
umma (p. 189)
Five Pillars of Islam (p. 190)
Ramadan (p. 190)
ulama (p. 190)
Shari'a (p. 190)
Hadith (p. 190)
caliph (p. 191)

imam (p. 191)
jihad (p. 191)
Shi'ites (p. 194)
Sunni (p. 194)
madrasas (p. 194)
vizier (p. 195)
sultan (p. 196)
crusades (p. 197)
emir (p. 198)
Sufism (p. 209)
mihrab (p. 210)

Chapter Notes

1. M. M. Pickthall, trans., *The Meaning of the Glorious Koran* (New York, 1953), p. 89.
2. Quoted in T. W. Lippman, *Understanding Islam: An Introduction to the Moslem World* (New York, 1982), p. 118.
3. F. Hirth and W. W. Rockhill, trans., *Chau Ju-kua: His Work on the Chinese and Arab Trade in the Twelfth and Thirteenth Centuries, Entitled "Chu-fan-chi"* (New York, 1966), p. 115.
4. al-Mas'udi, *The Meadows of Gold: The Abbasids*, ed. P. Lunde and C. Stone (London, 1989), p. 151.
5. Quoted in G. Wiet, *Baghdad: Metropolis of the Abassid Caliphate*, trans. S. Feiler (Norman, Okla., 1971), pp. 118–119.
6. L. Africanus, *The History and Description of Africa and of the Notable Things Therein Contained* (New York, n.d.), pp. 820–821.
7. Hirth and Rockhill, *Chau Ju-kua*, p. 116.
8. E. Yarshater, ed., *Persian Literature* (Albany, N.Y., 1988), pp. 154–159.
9. E. Rehatsek, trans., *The Gulistan or Rose Garden of Sa'di* (New York, 1964), pp. 65, 67, 71.

MindTap® is a fully online personalized learning experience built upon Cengage Learning content. MindTap® combines student learning tools—readings, multimedia, activities, and assessments—into a singular Learning Path that guides students through the course and helps students develop the critical thinking, analysis, and communication skills that are essential to academic and professional success.

Chapter Outline and Focus Questions

8-1 *The Emergence of Civilization*

Q How did the advent of farming and pastoralism affect the various peoples of Africa? How did the consequences of the agricultural revolution in Africa compare with its consequences in Eurasia and America?

8-2 *The Coming of Islam*

Q What effects did the coming of Islam have on African religion, society, political structures, trade, and culture?

8-3 *States and Noncentralized Societies in Central and Southern Africa*

Q What role did migration play in the evolution of early African societies? How did the impact of these migrations compare with similar population movements elsewhere?

8-4 *African Society*

Q What role did lineage groups, women, and slavery play in African societies? In what ways did African societies in various parts of the continent differ? What accounted for these differences?

8-5 *African Culture*

Q What are some of the chief characteristics of African sculpture and carvings, music, and architecture, and what purpose did these forms of creative expression serve in African society?

The temple at Great Zimbabwe. Nick Greaves/Alamy

Critical Thinking

Q *In what parts of Africa did the first states and city-states emerge? What conditions led to their appearance?*

Connections to Today

Q *How does the discussion in the Comparative Essay "The Migration of Peoples" in this chapter relate to migratory movements of people around the world today? Is large-scale migration a natural process? If so, should it be allowed to run its course, or should it be restricted in some ways?*

IN 1871, THE GERMAN EXPLORER Karl Mauch began to search southern Africa's central plateau for the colossal stone ruins of a legendary lost civilization. In late August, he found what he had been looking for. He recorded the moment in his diary: "Presently I stood before it and beheld a wall of a height of about 20 feet of granite bricks. Very close by there was a place where a kind of footpath led over rubble into the interior. Following this path I stumbled over masses of rubble and parts of walls and dense thickets. I stopped in front of a towerlike structure. Altogether it rose to a height of about 30 feet." Mauch was convinced that "a civilized nation must once have lived here." Like many other nineteenth-century Europeans, however, Mauch was equally convinced that the Africans who had lived there could never have built such splendid structures as the ones he had found at Great Zimbabwe. To Mauch and other archaeologists, Great Zimbabwe must have been the work of "a northern race closely akin to the Phoenician and Egyptian." It was not until the twentieth century that Europeans would overcome their prejudices and finally admit that Africans south of Egypt had also developed advanced civilizations with spectacular achievements.

The continent of Africa has played a central role in the long evolution of humankind. It was in Africa that the first hominids appeared more than 3 million years ago. It was probably in Africa that the immediate ancestors of modern human beings—*Homo sapiens*—emerged. The domestication of animals and perhaps the initial stages of the agricultural revolution may have occurred first in Africa. Certainly, one of the first states appeared in Africa, in the Nile Valley in the northeastern corner of the continent, in the form of the kingdom of the pharaohs. Recent evidence suggests that Egyptian civilization was significantly influenced by cultural developments taking place to the south, in Nubia, in modern Sudan. Egypt in turn exercised a profound influence on scientific and cultural developments throughout the eastern Mediterranean region, including the civilization of the Greeks.

After the decline of the Egyptian empire during the first millennium BCE, the focus of social change began to shift from the lower Nile Valley to other areas of the continent: to West Africa, where a series of major trading states began to take part in the caravan trade with the Mediterranean through the vast wastes of the Sahara; to the region of the upper Nile River, where the states of Kush and Axum dominated trade for several centuries; and to the eastern coast from the Horn of Africa (formally known as Cape Guardafui) to the straits between the continent and the island of Madagascar, where African peoples began to play an active role in the commercial traffic in the Indian Ocean. In the meantime, a gradual movement of agricultural peoples brought Iron Age farming to the central portion of the continent, leading eventually to the creation of several states in the Congo River basin and the plateau region south of the Zambezi River.

Thus, since ancient times, the peoples of Africa have played a significant role in the changing human experience. Yet the landmass of Africa is so vast and its topography so diverse that communication within the continent and between Africans and peoples living elsewhere in the world has often been more difficult than in many other regions. As a consequence, while some parts of the continent were directly exposed to the currents of change sweeping across Eurasia and were influenced by them to varying degrees, other regions were virtually isolated from the "great tradition" cultures discussed in Part I of this book and, like the cultures of the Americas, developed in their own directions, rendering generalizations about Africa difficult, if not impossible, to make.

8-1 THE EMERGENCE OF CIVILIZATION

 Focus Questions: How did the advent of farming and pastoralism affect the various peoples of Africa? How did the consequences of the agricultural revolution in Africa compare with its consequences in Eurasia and America?

After Asia, Africa is the largest of the continents (see Map 8.1). It stretches nearly 5,000 miles from the Cape of Good Hope in the south to the Mediterranean in the north and extends a similar distance from Cape Verde on the west coast to the Horn of Africa on the Indian Ocean.

8-1a The Land

Africa is as physically diverse as it is vast. The northern coast, washed by the Mediterranean Sea, is mountainous for much of its length. South of the mountains lies the greatest desert on earth, the Sahara, which stretches from the Atlantic to the Indian Ocean. To the east is the Nile River, heart of the ancient Egyptian civilization. Beyond that lies the Red Sea, separating Africa from Asia.

The Sahara acts as a great divide separating the northern coast from the rest of the continent. Africa south of the Sahara contains a number of major regions. In the west is the so-called hump of Africa, which juts like a massive shoulder into the Atlantic Ocean. Here the Sahara gradually gives way to grasslands in the interior and then to tropical rain forests along the coast. This region, dominated by the Niger River, is rich in natural resources and was the home of many ancient civilizations.

Far to the east, bordering the Indian Ocean, is a very different terrain of snowcapped mountains, upland plateaus, and lakes. Much of this region is grassland populated by wild beasts, which has caused many Westerners to view it as "safari country." Here, in the East African Rift Valley in the lake district of modern Kenya, early hominids began their long trek toward civilization several million years ago.

Directly to the west lies the Congo basin, with its rain forests watered by the mighty Congo River. The forests of equatorial Africa then fade gradually into the hills, plateaus, and deserts of the south. This rich land contains some of the most valuable mineral resources known today.

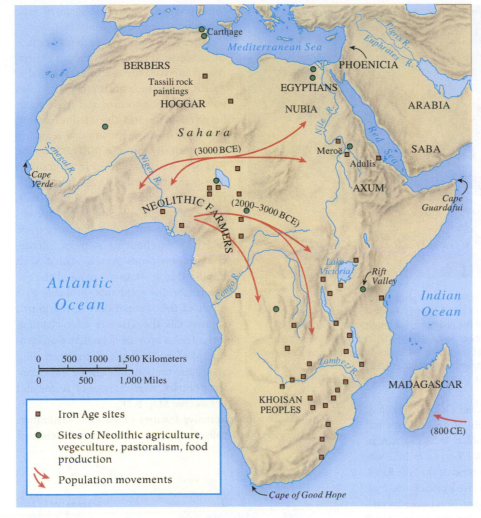

Map 8.1 **Ancient Africa.** Modern human beings, the primate species known as *Homo sapiens*, first evolved on the continent of Africa. Some key sites of early human settlement are shown on this map.

 Which are the main river systems on the continent of Africa?

8–1b The First Farmers

It is not certain when agriculture was first practiced on the continent of Africa. Until recently, historians assumed that crops were first cultivated in the lower Nile Valley (the northern part near the Mediterranean) about seven or eight thousand years ago, when wheat and barley were introduced, possibly from the Middle East. Eventually, as explained in Chapter 1, this area gave rise to the civilization of ancient Egypt.

Recent evidence, however, suggests that this hypothesis may need some revision. South of Egypt, near the junction of the White Nile and the Blue Nile, is an area historically known as Nubia (see Chapter 1). By the ninth millennium BCE, peoples living in this area began to domesticate animals, first wild cattle and then sheep and goats, which had apparently originated in the Middle East. In areas where the climate permitted, they supplemented their diet by gathering wild grains and soon learned how to cultivate grains such as sorghum and millet, while also growing gourds and melons.

Eventually, the practice of agriculture began to spread westward across the Sahara. At that time, the world's climate was much cooler and wetter than it is today, but a warm, humid climate prevailed in parts of the Sahara, creating lakes and ponds, as well as vast grasslands (known as savannas) replete with game. Hence, indigenous peoples living in the area were able to provide for themselves by hunting, food gathering, and fishing. By the seventh and sixth millennia BCE, however, conditions were becoming increasingly arid, forcing them to find new means of support. Rock paintings found in what are today some of the most uninhabitable parts of the region (see illustration that accompanies Comparative Essay "The Migration of Peoples," Section 8–1e, p. 222) show that by the fourth millennium BCE fishing and pastoralism in the heart of the Sahara were being supplemented by the limited cultivation of grain crops, including a drought-resistant form of dry rice.

Thus, the peoples of northern Africa, from Nubia westward into the heart of the Sahara, were among the earliest in the world to adopt settled agriculture as a means of subsistence. Shards of pottery found at archaeological sites in the area suggest that they were also among the first to manufacture clay pots, which allowed them to consume their cereals in the form of porridge rather than as bread baked from flour. By 5000 BCE, they were cultivating cotton plants for the purpose of manufacturing textiles.

After 3000 BCE, the desiccation (drying up) of the Sahara intensified, and the lakes began to dry up, forcing many local inhabitants to migrate eastward toward the Nile River and southward into the grasslands. As a result, farming began to spread into the savannas on the southern fringes of the desert and eventually into the tropical forest areas to the south, where crops were no longer limited to drought-resistant cereals but could include tropical fruits and tubers. In the meantime, the foundation was being laid for the emergence of an advanced civilization in Egypt along the banks of the Nile River (see Chapter 1).

8–1c Axum and Meroë

To the south of Egypt in Nubia, the kingdom of Kush had emerged as a major trading state by the end of the second millennium BCE (see Chapter 1). Kush adopted many of its political institutions and much of its culture from the kingdom of the pharaohs farther to the north and—at a time of Egyptian weakness in the eighth century BCE—even managed to seize the

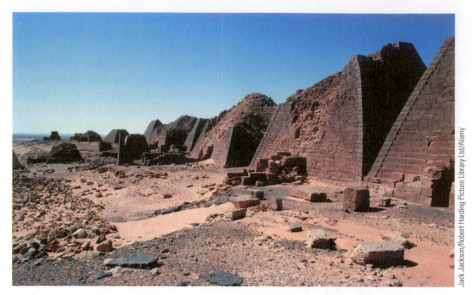

The Pyramids at Meroë. The kingdom of Kush borrowed much of its culture from the Egyptian empire to the north, while placing its own imprint on all imports. Kushite rulers, for example, modeled their political institutions after those of the pharaohs, but governmental authority was somewhat more centralized, and monarchical power was apparently limited by the influence of priests and the local aristocracy. The pyramids at Meroë, on the banks of the Nile River, are another example. Younger, smaller, unpointed at the top, and more standardized in size and shape than their famous counterparts at Giza, they remain a dramatic reminder of the glory of ancient Kush.

city of Memphis and much of the Nile River Delta. Eventually, however, the Kushite rulers were driven out of lower Egypt and forced to retreat back to their original habitat in Nubia, where a new capital was established at Meroë (MER-oh-ee *or* MER-uh-wee), near the Fourth Cataract in the great bend of the Nile River.

The new capital was located near extensive iron deposits and, once smelting techniques had been developed, iron evidently provided the basis for much of the area's growing prosperity. Meroë eventually became a cultural center and a major trading hub for iron goods and other manufactures for the entire region. The prosperity of the area is attested to by the remnants of a number of pyramids, similar in design but smaller in size than their Egyptian counterparts, which were constructed to serve as tombs for the deceased rulers of the ruling dynasty. Recently, other pyramids, some as short as 3 feet high, have been located along the banks of the river, suggesting that local elites mimicked the ruling family in what one archaeologist called "the democratization of pyramids."

By the third century CE, however, a competitor to Meroë's regional economic prominence began to arise a few hundred miles to the southeast, in the mountainous highlands of what today is known as Ethiopia. The founders of Axum (AHK-soom) claimed descent from migrants who arrived in Africa from the kingdom of Saba (SAH-buh) (also known as Sheba), across the Red Sea on the southern tip of the Arabian Peninsula. During antiquity, Saba was a major trading state, serving as a transit point for goods carried from South Asia into the lands surrounding the Mediterranean. Biblical sources credited the "queen of Sheba" with vast wealth and resources. In fact, much of that wealth had originated much farther to the east and passed through Saba en route to the countries adjacent to the Mediterranean. Whether migrants from Saba were responsible for founding Axum is sheer conjecture, but a similarity in architectural styles suggests that

there probably was some form of relationship between the two states.

After Saba declined, perhaps because of the desiccation of the Arabian Desert, Axum survived for centuries. Like Saba, Axum owed much of its prosperity to its location on the commercial trade route between India and the Mediterranean, and ships from Egypt stopped regularly at the port of Adulis (a-DOO-luss) on the Red Sea. Axum exported ivory, frankincense, myrrh, and slaves, while its primary imports were textiles, metal goods, wine, and olive oil. For a time, Axum competed for control of the ivory trade with the neighboring state of Meroë, and hunters from Axum armed with imported iron weapons scoured the entire region for elephants. Probably as a result of this competition, in the fourth century CE, the Axumite ruler, claiming he had been provoked, launched an invasion of Meroë and conquered it, creating an empire that, in the view of some contemporaries, rivaled those of Rome and Persia (see Map 8.2).

One of the most distinctive features of Axumite civilization was its religion. Originally, the rulers of Axum (who claimed

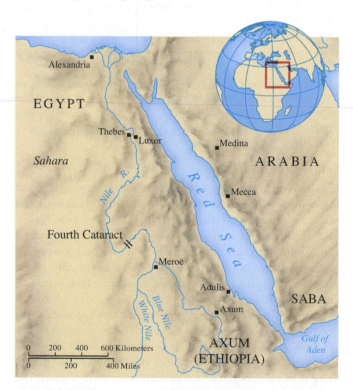

Map 8.2 Ancient Ethiopia and Nubia. The first civilizations to appear on the African continent emerged in the Nile River Valley. Early in the first century CE, the state of Axum emerged in what is today the state of Ethiopia.

Q *Where are the major urban settlements in the region, as shown on this map?*

FAULT LINE IN THE DESERT

Interaction & Exchange Little is known regarding Antonius Malfante (an-TOH-nee-uss mal-FAHN-tay), the Italian adventurer who in 1447 wrote this letter describing his travels along the trade route used by the Hausa (HOW-suh) city-states of northern Nigeria. In this passage, he astutely described the various peoples who inhabited the Sahara: Arabs, Jews, Berbers, Tuaregs (TWAH-regs) (a subgroup of the Berber peoples), and African blacks, who coexisted in uneasy proximity as they struggled to survive in the stark conditions of the desert. The mutual hostility between settled and pastoral peoples in the area continues today.

Antonius Malfante, Letter to Genoa

Though I am a Christian, no one ever addressed an insulting word to me. They said they had never seen a Christian before. It is true that on my first arrival they were scornful of me, because they all wished to see me, saying with wonder, "This Christian has a countenance like ours"—for they believed that Christians had disguised faces. Their curiosity was soon satisfied, and now I can go alone anywhere, with no one to say an evil word to me.

There are many Jews, who lead a good life here, for they are under the protection of the several rulers, each of whom defends his own clients. Thus, they enjoy very secure social standing. Trade is in their hands, and many of them are to be trusted with the greatest confidence.

This locality is a mart of the country of the Moors [Berbers] to which merchants come to sell their goods: gold is carried hither, and bought by those who come up from the coast. . . .

It never rains here: if it did, the houses, being built of salt in the place of reeds, would be destroyed. It is scarcely ever cold here: in summer the heat is extreme, wherefore they are almost all blacks. The children of both sexes go naked up to the age of fifteen. These people observe the religion and law of Muhammad.

In the lands of the blacks, as well as here, dwell the Philistines [the Tuaregs], who live, like the Arabs, in tents. They are without number, and hold sway over the land of Gazola from the borders of Egypt to the shores of the Ocean, as far as Massa and Safi, and over all the neighboring towns of the blacks. They are fair, strong in body and very handsome in appearance. They ride without stirrups, with simple spurs. They are governed by kings, whose heirs are the sons of their sisters—for such is their law. They keep their mouths and noses covered. I have seen many of them here, and have asked them through an interpreter why they cover their mouths and noses thus. They replied: "We have inherited this custom from our ancestors." They are sworn enemies of the Jews, who do not dare to pass hither. Their faith is that of the Blacks. Their sustenance is milk and flesh, no corn or barley, but much rice. Their sheep, cattle, and camels are without number. One breed of camel, white as snow, can cover in one day a distance which would take a horseman four days to travel. Great warriors, these people are continually at war amongst themselves.

The states which are under their rule border upon the land of the blacks . . . which have inhabitants of the faith of Muhammad. In all, the great majority are blacks, but there are a small number of whites. . . .

 What occupations does Malfante mention? To what degree are they identified with specific peoples living in the area?

Source: From *Western African History*, Vol. I by Robert O. Collins (Princeton, NJ: Markus Weiner Press, 1990), pp. 24–26.

---

descent from King Solomon through the visit of the queen of Sheba to Israel in biblical times) followed the religion of Saba. But in the fourth century CE, Axumite rulers adopted Christianity, possibly as the result of contacts with Egypt. This commitment to the Egyptian form of Christianity—often called **Coptic** (KAHP-tik) from the local language of the day—was retained even after the collapse of Axum and the expansion of Islam through the area in later centuries. Later, Axum (renamed Ethiopia) would be identified by some Europeans as the "hermit kingdom" and the home of Prester John, a legendary Christian king of East Africa.

8–1d The Sahara and Its Environs

Meroë and Axum were part of the ancient trading network that extended from the shores of the Mediterranean Sea to the Indian Ocean and were affected in various ways by the cross-cultural contacts that took place throughout that region. Elsewhere in Africa, somewhat different patterns prevailed; they varied from area to area, depending on the geography and climate.

Historians do not know when goods first began to be exchanged across the Sahara in a north-south direction, but during the first millennium BCE, the commercial center of Carthage on the Mediterranean had become a focal point of the trans-Saharan trade. The **Berbers**, an ethnic group indigenous to western parts of North Africa (see Chapter 7), served as intermediaries, carrying food products and manufactured goods from Carthage across the desert and exchanging them for salt, gold and copper, skins, various agricultural products, and perhaps slaves. According to the Greek historian Herodotus, Carthaginian fleets had for centuries also been actively searching for markets along the east African coast.

This trade initiated a process of cultural exchange that would exert a significant impact on the peoples of tropical Africa. Among other things, it may have spread the knowledge of iron-working south of the desert. Although historians once believed that ironworking knowledge reached sub-Saharan Africa from Meroë in the first centuries CE, recent finds suggest that the peoples along the Niger River were smelting iron five or six hundred years earlier. Some scholars believe that the technique developed independently there, but others surmise that it was introduced by the Berbers, who had learned it from the Carthaginians (see "Fault Line in the Desert").

Nok Pottery Head. The Nok peoples of the Niger River are the oldest known culture in West Africa to have created sculpture. This is a typical terra-cotta head of the Nok culture produced between 500 BCE and 200 CE. Discovered by accident in the twentieth century by tin miners, these heads feature perforated eyes set in triangles or circles, stylized eyebrows, open thick lips, broad noses with wide nostrils, and large ears. Perhaps the large facial openings permitted the hot air to escape as the heads were fired. Although the function of these statues is not known for certain, they were likely connected with religious rituals or devotion to ancestors.

Whatever the case, the **Nok** (NAHK) **culture** in northern Nigeria eventually became one of the most active ironworking societies in Africa. Excavations have unearthed numerous terra-cotta and metal figures, as well as stone and iron farm implements, dating back as far as 500 BCE. The remains of smelting furnaces confirm that the iron was produced locally.

Early in the first millennium CE, the introduction of the camel from across the Red Sea in the Middle East provided a major stimulus to the trans-Saharan trade. With its ability to store considerable amounts of food and water, the camel was far better equipped to handle the arduous conditions of the desert than the donkey and the wheeled cart, which had been used previously. The camel caravans of the Berbers, arduously threading their way from the shores of the Mediterranean through the heart of the Sahara, became so essential to the local trade network that they became known as the "fleets of the desert."

The Garamantes Not all the peoples involved in trade across the Sahara were nomadic. Recent exploratory work in the Libyan Desert has revealed the existence of an ancient kingdom that for over a thousand years transported goods between societies along the Mediterranean Sea and sub-Saharan West Africa. The Garamantes (gar-uh-MAN-teez), as they were known to the Romans, carried salt, glass, metal, olive oil, and wine southward in return for gold, slaves, and various tropical products. To provide food for their communities in the heart of the desert, they constructed a complex irrigation system consisting of several thousand miles of underground channels. The technique is reminiscent of similar systems in Persia and Central Asia (see Chapter 7). Scholars believe that the kingdom declined as a result of the fall of the Roman Empire, which led to a drop in the exchange of goods throughout the area, and the desiccation of the desert. As the historian Felipe Fernández-Armesto has noted in his provocative study *Civilizations*, advanced societies do not easily thrive in desert conditions.[1]

8–1e East Africa

South of Axum, along the shores of the Indian Ocean and in the inland plateau that stretches from the mountains of Ethiopia through the lake district of Central Africa, lived a mixture of peoples. Some originally depended on hunting and food gathering, whereas others followed pastoral pursuits.

Beginning in the third millennium BCE, farming peoples speaking dialects of the Bantu (BAN-too) family of languages began to migrate from their original homeland in what today is Nigeria (see Comparative Essay "The Migration of Peoples," p. 222). Eventually, they reached East Africa, where they may have been responsible for introducing the widespread cultivation of crops and knowledge of ironworking, although there are signs of some limited iron smelting in the area before their arrival.

The Bantu settled in rural communities based on subsistence farming. The primary crops were millet and sorghum, along with yams, melons, and beans. In addition to stone implements, they often used iron tools, usually manufactured in a local smelter, to till the land. Some people kept domestic animals such as cattle, sheep, goats, or chickens or supplemented their diets by hunting and food gathering. Because the population was minimal and an ample supply of cultivable land was available, most settlements were relatively small, although there was apparently a readily visible set of class distinctions within the local population (see "A Chinese View of Africa").

As early as the era of the New Kingdom in the second millennium BCE, Egyptian ships had plied the waters off the East African coast in search of gold, ivory, palm oil, and perhaps slaves. By the first century CE, the region was an established part of a trading network that included the Mediterranean and the Red Sea. In that century, a Greek seafarer from Alexandria wrote an account of his travels down the coast from Cape Guardafui (GWAR-duh-fwee *or* GWAR-duh-foo-ee) at the tip of the Horn of Africa to the Strait of Madagascar (ma-duh-GAS-kur), thousands of miles to the south. Called the *Periplus* (PER-ih-pluss), this work

Scala/Art Resource, NY

A CHINESE VIEW OF AFRICA

Interaction & Exchange

THIS PASSAGE FROM CHAU JU-KUA'S thirteenth-century treatise on geography describes various aspects of life along the eastern coast of Africa in what is now Somalia, including the urban architecture. The author was an inspector of foreign trade in the city of Quanzhou (sometimes called Zayton) on the southern coast of China. His account was compiled from reports of seafarers. Note the varied uses that the local people make of a whale carcass.

Chau Ju-kua on East Africa

The inhabitants of the Chung-li country [the Somali coast] go bareheaded and barefooted; they wrap themselves in cotton stuffs, but they dare not wear jackets, for the wearing of jackets and turbans is a privilege reserved to the ministers and the king's courtiers. The king lives in a brick house covered with glazed tiles, but the people live in huts made of palm leaves and covered with grass-thatched roofs. Their daily food consists of baked flour cakes, sheep's and camel's milk. There are great numbers of cattle, sheep, and camels. . . .

There are many sorcerers among them who are able to change themselves into birds, beasts, or aquatic animals, and by these means keep the ignorant people in a state of terror. If some of them in trading with some foreign ship have a quarrel, the sorcerers pronounce a charm over the ship so that it can neither go forward nor backward, and they only release the ship when it has settled the dispute. The government has formally forbidden this practice.

When one of the inhabitants dies, and they are about to bury him in his coffin, his kinsfolk from near and far come to condole. Each person, flourishing a sword in his hand, goes in and asks the mourners the cause of the person's death. If he was killed by the hand of man, each one says, we will revenge him on the murderer with these swords. Should the mourners reply that he was not killed by any one, but that he came to his end by the will of Heaven, they throw away their swords and break into violent wailing.

Every year there are driven on the coast a great many dead fish measuring two hundred feet in length and twenty feet through the body. The people do not eat the flesh of these fish, but they cut out their brains, marrow, and eyes, from which they get oil. They mix this oil with lime to caulk their boats, and use it also in lamps. The poor people use the ribs of these fish to make rafters, the backbones for door leaves, and they cut off vertebrae to make mortars with.

 What does this passage offer in terms of information about housing and consumption habits in East Africa?

Source: *Chau Ju-Kua: His Work on the Chinese and Arab Trade in the Twelfth and Thirteenth Centuries, entitled Chu-fan-chi*, translated from the Chinese and annotated by Friedrich Hirth and W. W. Rockhill. (St. Petersburg. Printing Office of the Imperial Academy of Sciences, Vass. Ostr., Kinth Liao, 12. 1911), pp. 130–131.

provides descriptions of the peoples and settlements along the African coast and the trade goods they supplied.

According to the *Periplus*, the port of Rhapta (RAHP-tuh) (probably modern Dar es Salaam) was a commercial metropolis, exporting ivory, rhinoceros horn, and tortoise shell and importing glass, wine, grain, and metal goods such as weapons and tools. The identity of the peoples taking part in this trade is not clear, but it seems likely that the area was inhabited primarily by a mixture of local peoples supplemented by a small number of immigrants from the Arabian Peninsula. Out of this mixture would eventually emerge a cosmopolitan **Swahili** (swah-HEE-lee) culture (see "East Africa: The Land of the Zanj," Section 8-2d, p. 225) that continues to exist in coastal areas today. Beyond Rhapta was "unexplored ocean." Some contemporary observers believed that the Indian and Atlantic Oceans were connected. Others were convinced that the Indian Ocean was an enclosed sea and that the continent of Africa could not be circumnavigated. Adverse winds and currents from the straits dividing Madagascar from Africa down to the southern tip of the continent made sailing conditions there difficult.

Trade across the Indian Ocean and down the coast of East Africa, facilitated by the monsoon winds, would gradually become one of the most lucrative sources of commercial profit in the ancient and medieval worlds. Although the origins of the trade remain shrouded in mystery, traders eventually came by sea from as far away as China and mainland Southeast Asia. Early in the first millennium CE, Malay (mah-LAY) peoples bringing cinnamon to the Middle East from the Indonesian archipelago began to cross the Indian Ocean directly and landed on the southeastern coast of Africa. Eventually, a Malay settlement was established on the island of Madagascar, where the population is still of mixed Malay-African origin. Historians suspect that Malay immigrants were responsible for introducing such Southeast Asian foods as the banana and the yam to Africa, although recent archaeological evidence suggests that such plants may have arrived in Africa as early as the third millennium BCE. The banana, with its high yield and ability to grow in uncultivated rain forest, became the preferred crop of many Bantu peoples.

The Migration of Peoples

Interaction & Exchange About 80,000 years ago, a small band of humans crossed the Sinai Peninsula from Africa and began to spread out across the Eurasian supercontinent. Thus began a migration of peoples that continued with accelerating speed throughout the ancient era and beyond. By 40,000 BCE, their descendants had spread across Eurasia as far as China and eastern Siberia and had even settled the distant continent of Australia.

Who were these peoples, and what provoked their decision to change their habitat? Undoubtedly, the first migrants were foragers or hunters in search of wild game, but with the advent of agriculture and the domestication of animals about 12,000 years ago, other peoples began to migrate vast distances in search of fertile farming and pasturelands.

The ever-changing climate was undoubtedly a major factor driving the process. Around 8,000 years ago, farming peoples, perhaps motivated by drought conditions in the Middle East, began to migrate into Greece and the Balkans, spreading a knowledge of agriculture as they advanced. Beginning in the fourth millennium BCE, the drying up of rich pasturelands in the Sahara forced the local inhabitants to migrate eastward toward the Nile River Valley and the grasslands of East Africa. At about the same time, Indo-European-speaking pastoral peoples left the region of the Black Sea and moved gradually into central Europe in search of new pastures. They were eventually followed by nomadic groups from Central Asia who began to occupy lands along the frontiers of the Roman Empire, while other bands of nomads threatened the plains of northern China from the Gobi Desert. In the meantime, Bantu-speaking farmers had migrated from the Niger River southward into the rain forests of Central Africa and beyond. Similar movements took place in Southeast Asia and the Americas.

This steady flow of migrating peoples often had a destabilizing effect on sedentary societies in their path. Nomadic incursions represented a constant menace to the security of China, Egypt, and the Roman Empire and ultimately brought them to an end. But these vast movements of peoples often had beneficial effects as well, spreading new technologies and means of livelihood. Although some migrants, like the Huns, came for plunder and left havoc in their wake, other groups, like the Celtic peoples and the Bantus, prospered in their new environments.

Erich Lessing/Art Resource, NY

Rock Paintings of the Sahara. Even before the Egyptians built their pyramids at Giza, other peoples far to the west in the vast wastes of the Sahara were creating their own art forms. These rock paintings, some of which date back to the fourth millennium BCE and are reminiscent of similar examples from Europe, Asia, and Australia, provide a valuable record of a society that supported itself by a combination of farming, hunting, and herding animals. After the introduction of the horse from Arabia around 1200 BCE, subsequent rock paintings depicted chariots and horseback riding. Eventually, camels began to appear in the paintings, a consequence of the increasing desiccation of the Sahara.

The most famous of all nomadic invasions is a case in point. In the thirteenth century CE, the Mongols left their homeland in the Gobi Desert, advancing westward into the Russian steppes and southward into China and Central Asia, leaving death and devastation in their wake. At the height of their empire, the Mongols controlled virtually all of Eurasia except its western and southern fringes, thereby creating a zone of stability in which a global trade and informational network could thrive that stretched from China to the shores of the Mediterranean.

 What have been some of the key reasons for the migration of large numbers of people throughout human history? Is the process still under way in our own day?

8–2 THE COMING OF ISLAM

Q **Focus Question:** What effects did the coming of Islam have on African religion, society, political structures, trade, and culture?

As Chapter 7 described, the rise of Islam during the first half of the seventh century CE had ramifications far beyond the Arabian Peninsula. Arab armies swept across North Africa, incorporating it into the Arab empire and isolating the Christian state of Axum to the south. Although East Africa and West Africa south of the Sahara were not occupied by the Arab forces, Islam began to penetrate these areas as well.

8–2a African Religious Beliefs and the Advent of Islam

When Islam arrived, most societies in Africa already had well-developed systems of religious belief. Like other aspects of life, early African religious beliefs varied considerably, but certain characteristics appear to have been shared throughout much of the continent. One of these common features was **pantheism**, belief in a single creator god from whom all things came. Sometimes the creator god was accompanied by a whole pantheon of lesser deities. The Ashanti (uh-SHAN-tee *or* uh-SHAHN-tee) people of Ghana (GAH-nuh) in West Africa believed in a supreme being called Nyame (NY-AH-may), whose sons were lesser gods. Each son served a different purpose: one was the rainmaker, another was the source of compassion, and a third was responsible for the sunshine. This heavenly hierarchy paralleled earthly arrangements: worship of Nyame was the exclusive preserve of the king through his priests; lesser officials and the common people worshiped Nyame's sons, who might intercede with their father on behalf of ordinary Africans.

Belief in an afterlife was closely connected to the importance of ancestors and the **lineage group**, or clan, in many African societies. Each lineage (LIH-nee-ij) group could trace itself back to a founding ancestor or group of ancestors. These ancestral souls would not be extinguished as long as the lineage group continued to perform rituals in their name. The rituals could also benefit the lineage group on earth, for the ancestral souls, being closer to the gods, had the power to influence the lives of their descendants, for good or evil.

Such beliefs were challenged but not always replaced in those parts of the continent affected by the arrival of Islam. In some ways, the tenets of Islam were in conflict with traditional beliefs and customs. Although the concept of a single transcendent deity did not always present problems, Islam's rejection of spirit

worship and a priestly class sometimes ran counter to local beliefs and was often ignored in practice. Similarly, as various Muslim travelers observed, Islam's insistence on the separation of the sexes contrasted with the relatively informal relationships that prevailed in many African societies and was probably slow to take root. In the long run, imported ideas were synthesized with indigenous beliefs to create a unique brand of Africanized Islam.

8–2b The Arabs in North Africa

In 641, Arab forces advanced into Egypt, seized the delta of the Nile River, and brought two centuries of Byzantine rule to an end. To guard against attacks from the Byzantine fleet, the Arabs eventually built a new capital at Cairo, inland from the previous Byzantine capital of Alexandria, and began to consolidate their control over the entire region (see Chapter 7).

On their arrival in Egypt, the Arab conquerors were probably welcomed by many, if not the majority, of the local inhabitants. Although Egypt had been a thriving commercial center under the Byzantines, the average Egyptian had not shared in this prosperity. Tax rates were generally high, and Christians were subjected to periodic persecution by the Byzantines, who viewed the local Coptic faith and other sects in the area as heresies. Although the new rulers continued to obtain much of their revenue from taxing the local farming population, tax rates were generally lower than they had been under the corrupt Byzantine government, and conversion to Islam brought exemption from taxation. During the next generations, many Egyptians converted to the Muslim faith, but Islam did not move into the upper Nile Valley until several hundred years later. As Islam

Leptis Magna: Graveyard of Empires. Among the more poignant testimonials to the cruel vicissitudes of history are the abandoned shells of magnificent Byzantine churches and cathedrals scattered along the coast of North Africa. Destroyed by Arab armies during their march westward toward the Strait of Gibraltar, many of them lie virtually forgotten, with their forlorn remains bleaching in the hot sun of an African sky. Among the more stirring examples are the ruins of a Byzantine cathedral that was built in the ancient Roman city of Leptis Magna on the coast of modern Libya. Originally erected within the walls of the one-time Roman Forum, it was abandoned by the conquering Arabs and fell victim to the drifting sands. In recent years it was revived as a tourist attraction by the regime of Libyan dictator Muammar Gaddhafi, but is now threatened again with destruction as a casualty of the Libyan civil war.

Photograph by William J. Duiker

BEWARE THE TROGLODYTES!

Family & Society

IN AFRICA, as elsewhere, relations between pastoral peoples and settled populations living in cities or in crowded river valleys were frequently marked by distrust and conflict. Such was certainly the case in the city of Meroë in the upper Nile Valley, where the residents viewed the nomadic peoples in the surrounding hills and deserts with a mixture of curiosity and foreboding. In the following selection, the second century BCE Greek historian Agatharchides (a-ga-THAR-kuh-deez) describes the so-called Troglodyte (TRAH-gluh-dyt) people living in the mountains east of the Nile River.

On the Erythraean Sea

Now, the Troglodytes are called "Nomads" by the Greeks and live a wandering life supported by their herds in groups ruled by tyrants. Together with their children they have their women in common except for the one belonging to the tyrant. Against a person who has sexual relations with her the chief levies as a fine a specified number of sheep.

This is their way of life. When it is winter in their country—this is at the time of the Etesian winds—and the god inundates their land with heavy rains, they draw their sustenance from blood and milk, which they mix together and stir in jars which have been slightly heated. When summer comes, however, they live in the marshlands, fighting among themselves over the pasture. They eat those of their animals that are old and sick after they have been slaughtered by butchers whom they call "Unclean."

For armament the tribe of Troglodytes called Megabari have circular shields made of raw ox-hide and clubs tipped with iron knobs, but the others have bows and spears.

They do not fight with each other, as the Greeks do, over land or some other pretext but over the pasturage as it sprouts up at various times. In their feuds, they first pelt each other with stones until some are wounded. Then for the remainder of the battle they resort to a contest of bows and arrows. In a short time many die as they shoot accurately because of their practice in this pursuit and their aiming at a target bare of defensive weapons. The older women, however, put an end to the battle by rushing in between them and meeting with respect. For it is their custom not to strike these women on any account so that immediately upon their appearance the men cease shooting.

They do not, he says, sleep as do other men. They possess a large number of animals which accompany them, and they ring cowbells from the horns of all the males in order that their sound might drive off wild beasts. At nightfall, they collect their herds into byres and cover these with hurdles made from palm branches. Their women and children mount up on one of these. The men, however, light fires in a circle and sing additional tales and thus ward off sleep, since in many situations discipline imposed by nature is able to conquer nature.

 Does the author of this passage describe the customs of the Troglodytes in an impartial manner, or do you detect a subtle attitude of disapproval or condescension?

Source: Agatharchides of Cnidus, *On the Erythraen Sea*, trans. S. Burstein (London, 1989), fragments 62–64, as cited in S. Burstein (ed.), *Ancient African Civilizations: Kush and Axum* (Princeton, 1998), pp. 47–50.

---

spread southward, it was adopted by many lowland peoples, but it had less success in the mountains of Ethiopia, where Coptic Christianity continued to win adherents.

In the meantime, Arab rule was gradually being extended westward along the Mediterranean coast, replacing the Byzantines, who had occupied much of the coast after the collapse of the Roman Empire. In 690 CE, they seized the city of Carthage and sought to extend their control over the entire region, which they called *al-Maghrib* (al MAH-greb), or "the West." At first, the local Berber peoples—who were tough fighters—resisted their new conquerors and limited Arab rule to towns and lowland coastal areas. But Arab persistence eventually paid off, and by the early eighth century, the entire North African coast as far west as the Strait of Gibraltar was under Muslim rule. The Arabs were now poised to cross the strait and expand into southern Europe and to push south beyond the fringes of the Sahara.

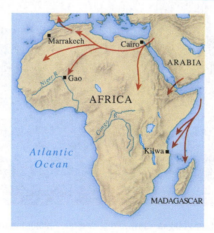

The Spread of Islam in Africa

8–2c The Kingdom of Ethiopia: A Christian Island in a Muslim Sea

By the end of the sixth century CE, the kingdom of Axum, long a dominant force in the trade network through the Red Sea, was in a state of decline. Overexploitation of farmland had played a role in the process, as had a shift in trade routes away from the Red Sea to the Arabian Peninsula and Persian Gulf. By the beginning of the ninth century, the capital had been moved farther into the mountainous interior, and Axum was gradually transformed from a maritime power into an isolated agricultural society.

The rise of Islam on the Arabian Peninsula hastened this process, as the Arab world increasingly began to serve as the focus of the regional trade passing through the area. By the eighth century, a number of Muslim trading states had been established on the African coast of the Red Sea, a development that contributed to the transformation of Axum into a landlocked society with primarily agricultural interests. At first, relations between Christian Axum and its Muslim neighbors were relatively peaceful, as the larger and more powerful Axumite kingdom attempted with some success to compel the coastal Islamic states to accept a tributary relationship. Axum's role in the local commercial network temporarily revived, and the area became a prime source for ivory, gold, resins such as frankincense and myrrh, and slaves. Slaves came primarily from the south, where Axum had been attempting to subjugate restive tribal peoples living in the Amharic (am-HAR-ik) plateau beyond its southern border (see "Beware the Troglodytes!").

Beginning in the twelfth century, however, relations between Axum and its neighbors deteriorated as the Muslim states along the coast began to move inland to gain control over the growing trade in slaves and ivory. Axum responded with force and at first had some success in reasserting its hegemony over the area. But in the early fourteenth century, the Muslim state of Adal (a-DAHL), located at the juncture of the Indian Ocean and the Red Sea, launched a new attack on the Christian kingdom.

Axum also underwent significant internal change during this period. The Zagwe (ZAH-gweh) dynasty, which seized control of the country in the mid-twelfth century, centralized the government and extended the Christian faith throughout the kingdom, now known as Ethiopia (see Comparative Illustration "Rock Architecture," p. 226). Military commanders or civilian officials who had personal or kinship ties with the royal court established vast landed estates to maintain security and facilitate the

CHRONOLOGY	Early Africa
Origins of agriculture in Africa	c. 9000–5000 BCE
Desiccation of the Sahara begins	c. 5000 BCE
Kingdom of Kush in Nubia	c. 1070 BCE–350 BCE
Iron Age begins	c. Sixth century BCE
Beginning of trans-Saharan trade	c. First millennium BCE
Rise of Meroë	c. 300 BCE
Rise of Axum	First century CE
Arrival of Malays on Madagascar	Second century CE
Arrival of Bantu in East Africa	Early centuries CE
Conquest of Meroë by Axum	Fourth century CE
Origins of Ghana	Fifth century CE
Arab takeover of lower Nile Valley	641 CE
Development of Swahili culture	c. First millennium CE
Spread of Islam across North Africa	Seventh century CE
Spread of Islam in Horn of Africa	Ninth century CE
Decline of Ghana	Twelfth century CE
Kingdom of Zimbabwe	c. 1100–c. 1450
Establishment of Zagwe dynasty in Ethiopia	c. 1150
Rise of Mali	c. 1250

collection of taxes from the local population. In the meantime, Christian missionaries established monasteries and churches to propagate the faith in outlying areas. Close relations were reestablished with leaders of the Coptic church in Egypt and with Christian officials in the Holy Land. This process was continued by the Solomonids (sah-luh-MAHN-idz), who succeeded the Zagwe dynasty in 1270. But by the early fifteenth century, the state had become deeply involved in an expanding conflict with Muslim Adal to the east, a conflict that lasted for over a century and gradually took on the characteristics of a holy war.

8–2d East Africa: The Land of the Zanj

The rise of Islam also had a lasting impact on the coast of East Africa, which the Greeks had called Azania and the Arabs called Zanj (ZANJ) referring to the "burnt skin" of the indigenous population. According to Swahili oral traditions, during the seventh and eighth centuries peoples from the Arabian Peninsula and the Persian Gulf began to settle at ports along the coast and on the small islands offshore. Then, in the middle of the tenth century, a Persian from the city of Shiraz sailed to the area with his six sons. As

The Swahili Coast

his small fleet stopped along the coast, each son disembarked on one of the coastal islands and founded a small community; these settlements eventually grew into important commercial centers including Mombasa (mahm-BAH-suh), Pemba (PEM-buh), Zanzibar (ZAN-zi-bar) (literally, "the coast of the Zanj"), and Kilwa (KIL-wuh). Although this oral tradition undoubtedly underestimates the role played by the indigenous population in the emergence of the region as a major participant in the trade network centered on the Indian Ocean, it probably also reflects the degree to which African merchants—who often served as middlemen between the peoples of the interior and the traders arriving from ports all around the Indian Ocean—saw themselves as part of that important commercial network.

In any case, by the ninth and tenth centuries, a string of trading ports had appeared stretching from Mogadishu (moh-guh-DEE-shoo) (today the capital of Somalia) in the north to Kilwa (south of present-day Dar es Salaam) in the south. Kilwa became especially important because it was near the southern limit for a ship hoping to complete the round-trip journey in a single season. Goods such as ivory, gold, and rhinoceros horn were exported across the Indian Ocean to countries as far away as China, while imports included iron goods, glassware, Indian textiles, and Chinese porcelain. Merchants in these cities often amassed considerable profit, as evidenced by their lavish stone palaces, some of which still stand in the modern cities of Mombasa and Zanzibar. Though now in ruins, Kilwa was one of the most magnificent cities of its day. The fourteenth-century Arab traveler Ibn Battuta

COMPARATIVE ILLUSTRATION

Rock Architecture. As we have seen, one of the earliest forms of religious architecture in India was the rock chamber (see Section 2-4b, p. 59). One of the most famous examples is the eighth-century temple at Ellora, in central India. Named after Shiva's holy mountain in the Himalayas, the temple is approximately the size of the Parthenon in Athens but was literally carved out of a hillside, with its exquisite sculptures open to the sky (image A).

This form of architecture also found expression in parts of Africa. In 1200 CE, Christian monks in Ethiopia began to construct a remarkable series of eleven churches carved out of solid volcanic rock (image B). After a 40-foot trench was formed by removing the bedrock, the central block of stone was hewed into the shape of a Greek cross; then it was hollowed out and decorated. These churches, which are still in use today, testify to the fervor of Ethiopian Christianity, which plays a major role in preserving the country's cultural and national identity.

Q *Why do you think some early cultures made frequent use of the concept of rock architecture, while others did not? Why do you think the process was discontinued?*

A

William J. Duiker

B

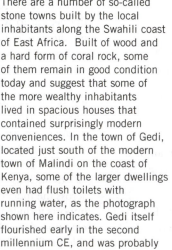

Werner Forman/Art Resource, NY

William J. Duiker

A House with Modern Conveniences. There are a number of so-called stone towns built by the local inhabitants along the Swahili coast of East Africa. Built of wood and a hard form of coral rock, some of them remain in good condition today and suggest that some of the more wealthy inhabitants lived in spacious houses that contained surprisingly modern conveniences. In the town of Gedi, located just south of the modern town of Malindi on the coast of Kenya, some of the larger dwellings even had flush toilets with running water, as the photograph shown here indicates. Gedi itself flourished early in the second millennium CE, and was probably destroyed by nomadic invaders from the north.

(IB-un ba-TOO-tuh) described it as "amongst the most beautiful of cities and most elegantly built. All of it is of wood, and the ceilings of its houses are of *al-dis* [reeds]."[2] One particularly impressive structure was the Husini Kubwa (hoo-SEE-nee KOOB-wuh), a massive palace with vaulted roofs capped with domes and elaborate stone carvings, surrounding an inner courtyard. Ordinary townspeople and the residents in smaller towns did not live in such luxurious conditions, of course, but even so, affluent urban residents lived in spacious stone buildings, with indoor plumbing and consumer goods imported from as far away as China and southern Europe.

Most of the coastal states were self-governing, although sometimes several towns were grouped together under a single dominant authority. Government revenue came primarily from taxes imposed on commerce. Some trade went on between these coastal city-states and the peoples of the interior, who provided gold

The Great Mosque of Kilwa. The city of Kilwa, located on an island south of the present-day city of Dar es Salaam, was a longtime major center of Muslim culture along the coast of East Africa, and its mosque was one of the most impressive stone structures on the entire African continent. Today the city has been abandoned, but the ruins of its mosque serve as a testimonial to the renowned achievements of Swahili civilization, which was vividly described by such tireless Muslim travelers as al-Mas'udi and Ibn Battuta.

and iron, ivory, and various agricultural goods and animal products in return for textiles, manufactured articles, and weapons. Relations with domestic suppliers apparently varied, and the coastal merchants sometimes resorted to force to obtain goods from the inland peoples. A Portuguese visitor recounted that "the men [of Mombasa] are oft-times at war and but seldom at peace with those of the mainland, and they carry on trade with them, bringing thence great store of honey, wax, and ivory."[3]

By the twelfth and thirteenth centuries, a cosmopolitan culture, eventually known as Swahili, from the Arabic *sahel* (sah-HEL), meaning "coast," began to emerge throughout the seaboard area. Intermarriage between the small number of immigrants and the local population eventually led to the emergence of a ruling class of mixed heritage, some of whom had Arab or Persian ancestors. By this time, too, many members of the ruling class had converted to Islam. Middle Eastern urban architectural styles and other aspects of Arab culture were implanted within a society still predominantly African. Arabic words and phrases were combined with Bantu grammatical structures to form a distinct language, also known as Swahili; it is the national language of Kenya and Tanzania today.

8–2e The States of West Africa

During the eighth century, merchants from the Maghrib began to carry

Muslim beliefs to the savanna areas south of the Sahara. At first, conversion took place on an individual basis and primarily among local merchants, rather than through official encouragement. The first rulers to convert to Islam were the royal family of Gao (GAH-oh) at the end of the tenth century. Five hundred years later, most of the population in the grasslands south of the Sahara had accepted Islam.

The expansion of Islam into West Africa had a major impact on the political system. By introducing Arabic as the first written language in the region and Muslim law codes and administrative practices from the Middle East, Islam provided local rulers with the tools to increase their authority and the efficiency of their governments. Moreover, as Islam gradually spread throughout the region, a common religion united previously diverse peoples into a more coherent community.

When Islam arrived in the grasslands south of the Sahara, the region was beginning to undergo significant political and social change. As a partial consequence of the initiation of a new wet phase throughout the region in the early fourth century, a number of major trading states were in the making, and they eventually transformed the Sahara into one of the leading avenues of world trade, crisscrossed by caravan routes leading to destinations as far away as the Atlantic Ocean, the Mediterranean, and the Red Sea (see Map 8.3).

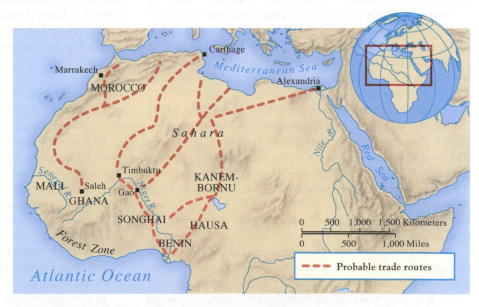

Map 8.3 Trans-Saharan Trade Routes. Trade across the Sahara began during the first millennium BCE. With the arrival of the camel from the Middle East, trade expanded dramatically.

 What were the major cities involved in the trade, as shown on this map?

THE GOLD RUSH, AFRICAN STYLE

Interaction & Trade

Attractive to the eye, malleable in shape, and resistant to corrosion, gold has been a valuable commodity in human societies since ancient times. Because of its relative rarity in the natural world, efforts to locate sources of the precious metal have often resulted in the establishment of contacts between previously unacquainted peoples. The commercial transaction described here has been recounted by the ancient Greek historian Herodotus.

Herodotus, *The Histories*

The Carthaginians also tell us they trade with a race of men who live in a part of Libya beyond the Pillars of Hercules [the Strait of Gibraltar]. On reaching this country, they unload their goods, arrange them tidily along the beach, and then, returning to their boats, raise a smoke. Seeing the smoke, the natives come down to the beach, place on the ground a certain quantity of gold in exchange for the goods, and go off again to a distance. The Carthaginians then come ashore and take a look at the gold; and if they think it represents a fair price for their wares, they collect it and go away; if, on the other hand, it seems too little, they go back aboard and wait, and the natives come and add to the gold until they are satisfied. There is perfect honesty on both sides; the Carthaginians never touch the gold until it equals in value what they offered for sale, and the natives never touch the goods until the gold has been taken away.

Source: Herodotus, *The Histories*, trans. A. de Sélincourt (Baltimore, 1964), p. 307.

Ghana The first of these great commercial states was Ghana, which emerged in the fifth century CE in the upper Niger Valley, a grassland region between the Sahara and the tropical forests along the West African coast. (The modern state of Ghana, which takes its name from this early trading society, is located in the forest region to the south.) The majority of the people in the area were farmers living in villages under the authority of a local chieftain. Gradually, these local communities were united to form the kingdom of Ghana.

Although the people of the region had traditionally lived from agriculture, a primary reason for Ghana's growing importance was gold. The heartland of the state was located near one of the richest gold-producing areas in all of Africa. Ghanaian merchants transported the gold to Morocco, whence it was distributed throughout the known world. The exchange of goods became quite ritualized (see "The Gold Rush, African Style"). Later, Ghana became known to Arabic-speaking peoples in North Africa as "the land of gold." Actually, the name was misleading, for the gold did not come from Ghana but from a neighboring people, who sold it to merchants from Ghana.

Eventually, other exports from Ghana found their way to the bazaars of the Mediterranean coast and beyond—ivory, ostrich feathers, hides, leather goods, and ultimately slaves. The origins of the slave trade in the area probably go back to the first millennium BCE, when Berber tribesmen seized African villagers in the regions south of the Sahara and sold them to buyers in Europe and the Middle East. In return, Ghana imported metal goods (especially weapons), textiles, horses, and salt.

Much of the trade across the desert was still conducted by the nomadic Berbers, but Ghanaian merchants played an active role as intermediaries, trading tropical products such as bananas, kola nuts, and palm oil from the forest states of Guinea along the Atlantic coast to the south. By the eighth and ninth centuries, much of this trade was conducted by Muslim merchants, who purchased the goods from local traders (using iron and copper coins or cowrie shells from Southeast Asia as the primary means of exchange) and then sold them to Berbers, who carried them across the desert. The merchants who carried on this trade often became quite wealthy and lived in splendor in cities like Saleh (SAH-luh), the capital of Ghana. So did the king, of course, who taxed the merchants as well as the farmers and the producers.

Like other West African monarchs, the king of Ghana ruled by divine right and was assisted by a hereditary aristocracy composed of the leading members of the prominent clans, who also served as district chiefs responsible for maintaining law and order and collecting taxes. The king was responsible for maintaining the security of his kingdom, serving as an intermediary with local deities, and functioning as the chief law officer to adjudicate disputes. The kings of Ghana did not convert to Islam themselves, although they welcomed Muslim merchants and apparently did not discourage their subjects from adopting the new faith (see "Royalty and Religion in Ghana").

Mali The Empire of Ghana flourished for several hundred years, but by the twelfth century, weakened by ruinous wars with Berber marauders, it had begun to decline. The downfall of Ghana was a partial consequence of the emergence of the powerful Almoravid (al-MOR-uh-vid) dynasty in Morocco. The Almoravids were not only active in protecting the Moorish kingdoms in Andalusia (see Chapter 7), but also began to expand their activities southward in the desert from their new capital of Marrakech (mar-uh-KESH), a trading center founded in the eleventh century at a caravan stop near the Atlas Mountains. Attacks by mounted Berber forces on the weakening state of Ghana began shortly after, and it collapsed by the end of the following century.

In the ashes of the kingdom of Ghana rose a number of new trading societies, including large territorial empires like Mali (MAHL-ee) and Songhai (song-GY) in the west, Kanem-Bornu (KAH-nuhm-BOR-noo) in the east, and small commercial

ROYALTY AND RELIGION IN GHANA

AFTER ITS FIRST APPEARANCE IN WEST AFRICA in the decades following the death of Muhammad, Islam competed with indigenous African religions for followers. Eventually, several local rulers converted to the Muslim faith. This passage by the Arab geographer al-Bakri (al-BAHK-ree) reflects religious tolerance in the state of Ghana during the eleventh century under a non-Muslim ruler with many Muslim subjects.

Al-Bakri's Description of Royalty in Ghana

The king's residence comprises a palace and conical huts, the whole surrounded by a fence like a wall. Around the royal town are huts and groves of thorn trees where live the magicians who control their religious rites. These groves, where they keep their idols and bury their kings, are protected by guards who permit no one to enter or find out what goes on in them.

None of those who belong to the imperial religion may wear tailored garments except the king himself and the heir-presumptive, his sister's son. The rest of the people wear wrappers of cotton, silk or brocade according to their means.

Most of the men shave their beards and the women their heads. The king adorns himself with female ornaments around the neck and arms. On his head he wears gold-embroidered caps covered with turbans of finest cotton. He gives audience to the people for the redressing of grievances in a hut around which are placed 10 horses covered in golden cloth. Behind him stand 10 slaves carrying shields and swords mounted with gold. On his right are the sons of vassal kings, their heads plaited with gold and wearing costly garments. On the ground around him are seated his ministers, whilst the governor of the city sits before him. On guard at the door are dogs of fine pedigree, wearing collars adorned with gold and silver. The royal audience is announced by the beating of a drum, called *daba*, made out of a long piece of hollowed-out wood. When the people have gathered, his coreligionists draw near upon their knees sprinkling dust upon their heads as a sign of respect, whilst the Muslims clap hands as their form of greeting.

 Why might an African ruler find it advantageous to adopt the Muslim faith? What kinds of changes would the adoption of Islam entail for the peoples living in West Africa?

Source: Adapted from translation quoted in J. S. Trimingham, *A History of Islam and West Africa,* copyright 1970 by Oxford University Press.

---

city-states like the Hausa states, located in what is today northern Nigeria (see Map 8.4).

The greatest of the empires that emerged after the destruction of Ghana was Mali. Extending from the Atlantic coast inland as far as the trading cities of Timbuktu (tim-buk-TOO) and Gao on the Niger River, Mali built its wealth and power on the gold trade. But the heartland of Mali was situated south of the Sahara in the savanna region, where there was sufficient moisture for farmers to grow such crops as sorghum, millet, and rice. The farmers lived in villages ruled by a local chieftain, called a *mansa* (MAHN-suh), who served as both religious and administrative leader and was responsible for forwarding tax revenues from the village to higher levels of government.

The primary wealth of the country was accumulated in the cities. Here lived the merchants, who were primarily of local origin, although many were now practicing Muslims. Commercial activities were taxed but were apparently so lucrative

The Great Gate at Marrakech. The Moroccan city of Marrakech, founded in the ninth century CE, was a major northern terminus of the trans-Saharan trade and one of the chief commercial centers in pre-modern Africa. Widely praised by such famous travelers as Ibn Battuta, the city was an architectural marvel in that all its major public buildings were constructed of red sandstone. Shown here is the Great Gate to the city, through which camel caravans passed en route to and from the vast desert. In the Berber language, Marrakech means "pass without making a noise," a necessity for caravan traders who had to be alert to the danger of thieves in the vicinity.

William J. Duiker

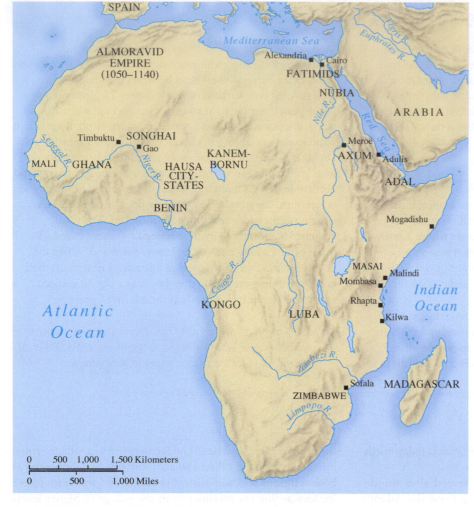

Map 8.4 The Emergence of States in Africa. By the end of the first millennium CE, organized states had begun to appear in various parts of Africa. The extensive empires of Ghana, Mali, and Songhai emerged at different times and did not exist simultaneously.

Q *Why did organized states appear at these particular spots and not in other areas of Africa?*

that both the merchants and the kings prospered. One of the most powerful kings of Mali was Mansa Musa (MAHN-suh MOO-suh) (r. 1312–1337), a ruler whose primary contribution to his people was probably not economic prosperity but the Muslim faith. Mansa Musa strongly encouraged the building of mosques and the study of the Qur'an in his kingdom and imported scholars and books to introduce his subjects to the message of Allah.

The city of Timbuktu ("well of Bouctu," a Taureg woman who lived in the area) is the most storied of the cities that emerged under the kingdom of Mali. It was founded by Berber tribal groups in 1100 CE as a seasonal camp for caravan traders on the Niger River. Under Mansa Musa and his successors, the city gradually emerged as a major intellectual and cultural center in West Africa and the site of a renowned mosque, as well as schools of Islamic law, literature, and the sciences. Still, it was trade that drove the commerce of the city. As one Muslim historian later commented, "For Timbuktu, the great wealth was from salt. . . . Timbuktu would never have grown as important as it did if it hadn't been the main entrepôt for the merchants of Djenné, which sent here a large number of businessmen and men of letters."[4]

Art Collection/Alamy

Mansa Musa. Mansa Musa, king of the West African state of Mali, was one of the richest and most powerful rulers of his day. During a famous pilgrimage to Mecca, he arrived in Cairo with a hundred camels laden with gold and gave away so much gold that its value depreciated there for several years. To promote the Islamic faith in his country, he bought homes in Cairo and Mecca to house pilgrims en route to the holy shrine, and he brought back to Mali a renowned Arab architect to build mosques in the trading centers of Gao and Timbuktu. His fame spread to Europe as well, evidenced by this Spanish map of 1375, which depicts Mansa Musa seated on his throne in Mali, holding an impressive gold nugget.

8–3 STATES AND NONCENTRALIZED SOCIETIES IN CENTRAL AND SOUTHERN AFRICA

 Focus Questions: What role did migration play in the evolution of early African societies? How did the impact of these migrations compare with similar population movements elsewhere?

In the southern half of the African continent, from the great basin of the Congo River to the Cape of Good Hope, states formed somewhat more slowly than in the north. Until the eleventh century CE, most of the peoples in this region lived in what are sometimes called **noncentralized societies**, characterized by autonomous villages organized by clans and ruled by a local chieftain or clan head. Beginning in the eleventh century, in some parts of southern Africa, these independent villages gradually began to consolidate. Out of these groupings came the first states.

8–3a The Congo River Valley

One area where this process occurred was the Congo River Valley, where the combination of fertile land and nearby deposits of copper and iron enabled the inhabitants to enjoy an agricultural surplus and engage in regional commerce. Two new states in particular underwent this transition. Sometime during the fourteenth century, the kingdom of Luba (LOOB-uh) was founded in the center of the continent, in a rich agricultural and fishing area near the shores of Lake Kisale. Luba had a relatively centralized government, in which the king appointed provincial governors, who were responsible for collecting tribute from the village chiefs. At about the same time, the kingdom of Kongo was formed just south of the mouth of the Congo River on the Atlantic coast.

These new states were primarily agricultural, although both had a thriving manufacturing sector and took an active part in the growing exchange of goods throughout the region. As time passed, both began to expand southward to absorb the mixed farming and pastoral peoples in the area of modern Angola. In the drier grassland area to the south, other small communities continued to support themselves by herding, hunting, or food gathering. A Portuguese sailor who encountered them in the late sixteenth century reported:

> These people are herdsmen and cultivators. . . . Their main crop is millet, which they grind between two stones or in wooden mortars to make flour. . . . Their wealth consists mainly in their huge number of dehorned cows. . . . They live together in small villages, in houses made of reed mats, which do not keep out the rain.[5]

8–3b Zimbabwe

Farther to the east, the situation was somewhat different. In the grassland regions immediately to the south of the Zambezi (zam-BEE-zee) River, a mixed economy involving farming, cattle herding, and commercial pursuits had begun to develop during the early centuries of the first millennium CE. Characteristically, villages in this area were constructed inside walled enclosures to protect the animals at night. The most famous of these communities was Zimbabwe (zim-BAHB-way), located on the plateau of the same name between the Zambezi and Limpopo Rivers. From the twelfth century to the middle of the fifteenth, Zimbabwe was the most powerful and most prosperous state in the region and played a major role in the gold trade with the Swahili trading communities on the eastern coast.

The ruins of Zimbabwe's capital, known today as Great Zimbabwe (*Zimbabwe* means "stone house" in the Bantu language), provide a vivid illustration of the kingdom's power and influence. Strategically situated between substantial gold reserves to the west and a small river leading to the coast, Great Zimbabwe was well placed to benefit from the expansion of trade between the coast and the interior. The town sits on a hill overlooking the river and is surrounded by stone walls, which enclosed an area large enough to hold over ten thousand residents. Like the Inka in South America (see Chapter 6), the local people stacked stone blocks without mortar to build their walls. The houses of the wealthy were built of cement on stone foundations, while those of the common people were of dried mud with thatched roofs. In the valley below is the royal palace, surrounded by a stone wall 30 feet high (see illustration on opening page of chapter). Artifacts found at the site include household implements and ornaments made of gold and copper, as well as jewelry and porcelain imported from China.

Most of the royal wealth probably came from two sources: the ownership of cattle and the king's ability to levy heavy taxes on the gold that passed through the kingdom en route to the coast. By the middle of the fifteenth century, however, the city was apparently abandoned, possibly because of environmental damage caused by overgrazing. With the decline of Zimbabwe, the focus of economic power began to shift northward to the valley of the Zambezi River.

8–3c Southern Africa

South of the East African plateau and the Congo basin is a vast land of hills, grasslands, and arid desert stretching almost to the Cape of Good Hope at the tip of the continent. As Bantu-speaking farmers spread southward during the final centuries of the first millennium BCE, they began to encounter Neolithic peoples in the area who still lived primarily by hunting and foraging.

Available evidence suggests that early relations between these two peoples were relatively harmonious. Intermarriage between members of the two groups was apparently not unusual, and many of the hunter-gatherers were gradually absorbed into what became a dominantly Bantu-speaking pastoral and agricultural society that spread throughout much of southern Africa during the first millennium CE.

The Khoi and the San Two such peoples were the Khoi (KOI) and the San (SAHN). The two were related because of their language, known as Khoisan (KOI-sahn), distinguished by the use of "clicking" sounds. The Khoi were herders, while the San were hunter-gatherers who lived in small family communities of twenty to twenty-five members throughout southern Africa from Namibia in the west to the Drakensberg Mountains near the southeastern coast. Archaeologists have studied rock paintings found in caves throughout the area in their efforts to learn more about the early life of the San. These multicolored paintings, which predate the coming of the Europeans, were drawn with a brush made of small feathers fastened to a reed. They depict various aspects of the San's lifestyle, including their hunting techniques and religious rituals.

HISTORIANS DEBATE 8–3d Africa: A Continent Without History?

Until the second half of the twentieth century, the prevailing view among Western historians was that Africa was a continent without history, a land of scattered villages isolated from the main currents of world affairs. But in the decades after the end of World War II, a new generation of historians trained in African studies, spurred on in part by the appearance in 1959 of Basil Davidson's path-breaking work, *Lost Cities of Africa*, began to contest that view. Their studies have demonstrated that throughout history not only were many African societies actively in contact with peoples beyond their shores, but also that they created a number of advanced civilizations of their own.

Although the paucity of written sources continues to be a challenge for historians, other sources have been used with increasing success to throw light on the African historical experience. African peoples were at the forefront of the agricultural revolution in the ninth and eighth millennia BCE, and although some parts of the continent remained isolated from the main currents of world history, a number of other African societies began as early as the first millennium CE to play an active role in the expanding global trade network, which stretched from the Mediterranean Sea deep into the Sahara. Another major commercial trade route ran from the Arabian Peninsula down the coast of East Africa along the shores of the Indian Ocean. Thus, it is becoming increasingly clear that from the dawn of history the peoples of Africa have made a significant contribution to the human experience.

8–4 AFRICAN SOCIETY

Focus Questions: What role did lineage groups, women, and slavery play in African societies? In what ways did African societies in various parts of the continent differ? What accounted for these differences?

As noted earlier, generalizing about social organization, cultural development, and daily life in traditional Africa is difficult because of the extreme diversity of the continent and its inhabitants. One-quarter of all the languages in the world are spoken in Africa, and five of the major language families are located there. Ethnic divisions are equally pronounced. Because many of these languages did not have a system of writing until fairly recently, historians must rely on accounts by occasional visitors, such as al-Mas'udi and Ibn Battuta. Such travelers, however, tended to come into contact mostly with the wealthy and the powerful, leaving us to speculate about what life was like for ordinary Africans during this early period.

8–4a Urban Life

African towns often began as fortified walled villages and gradually evolved into larger communities serving several purposes. Here, of course, were the center of government and the teeming markets filled with goods from distant regions. Here also were artisans skilled in metalworking or woodworking, pottery making, and other crafts. Unlike the rural areas, where a village was usually composed of a single lineage group or clan, the towns drew their residents from several clans, although individual clans usually lived in their own compounds and were governed by their own clan heads.

In the states of West Africa, the focal point of the major towns was the royal precinct. The relationship between the ruler and the merchant class differed from the situation in most Asian societies, where the royal family and the aristocracy were largely isolated from the remainder of the population. In Africa, the chasm between the king and the common people was not so great. Often the ruler would hold an audience to allow people to voice their complaints or to welcome visitors from foreign countries. In the city-states of the East African coast, the rulers were often wealthy merchants who, as in the case of the town of Kilwa, "did not possess more country than the city itself."[6]

This is not to say that the king was not elevated above all others in status. In wealthier states, the walls of the audience chamber would be covered with sheets of beaten silver and gold, and the king would be surrounded by hundreds of armed soldiers and some of his trusted advisers. Nevertheless, the symbiotic relationship between the ruler and merchant class served to reduce the gap between the king and his subjects. The relationship was mutually beneficial, since the merchants received honors and favors from the palace while the king's coffers were filled with taxes paid by the merchants. Certainly, it was to the king's benefit to maintain law and order in his domain so that the merchants could ply their trade. As Ibn Battuta observed, among the good qualities of the peoples of West Africa was the prevalence of peace in the region. "The . . . traveller may proceed alone among them," he remarked, "without the least fear of a thief or robber."[7]

8–4b Village Life

The vast majority of Africans lived in small rural villages. Their identities were established by their membership in a nuclear family and a lineage group. At the basic level was the nuclear family of parents and preadult children; sometimes it included an elderly grandparent and other family dependents as well. They lived in small, round huts constructed of packed mud and topped with a conical thatch roof. In most African

Home Sweet Home: A Traditional House in South Africa. The conical mud-and-thatch hut is a familiar site throughout much of rural Africa today. Built of widely available local materials, such one-room dwellings are generally inexpensive and easy to build, and have been a common form of housing on the continent for thousands of years. In this Xhosa village in South Africa, some of the local residents live in modern houses in a nearby town, but maintain such traditional huts like the one shown here to perform their ancestral ceremonies. According to villagers, the conical shape of the dwelling is designed as a means of keeping out evil spirits.

Photograph by Yvonne V. Duiker

into the mines to extract gold because of their smaller physiques.

But there were some key differences between the role of women in Africa and elsewhere. In many African societies, lineage was **matrilinear** rather than **patrilinear**. As Ibn Battuta observed during his travels in West Africa, "[T]he sister's son always succeeds to property in preference to the son."[8] He said he had never encountered this custom before except among the unbelievers of the Malabar coast in India. Women were often permitted to inherit property, and the husband was often expected to move into his wife's house.

Relations between the sexes were also sometimes more relaxed than in China or India, with none of the taboos characteristic of those societies. Again, in the words of Ibn Battuta, himself a Muslim:

As to their women, they are not shy with regard to the men, nor do they veil themselves from them, although they constantly accompany them at prayers. . . . It is a custom among them, that many may have a mistress, . . . who may come and associate with him, even in the presence of her own husband and of his wife. In like manner, a man will enter his own house, and see the friend of his wife with her alone, and talking with her, without the least emotion or attempt to disturb them; he will only come in and sit down on one side, till the man goes.[9]

When Ibn Battuta asked an African acquaintance about these customs, the latter responded, "This is our custom; nor is there any suspicion from our being in society together." Ibn Battuta noted his astonishment at such a "thoughtless" answer and did not accept further invitations to visit his friend's house.[10]

Such informal attitudes toward the relationship between the sexes were not found everywhere in Africa and were probably curtailed as many Africans converted to Islam (see "Women and Islam in North Africa," p. 234). But it is a testimony to the tenacity of traditional customs that the relatively puritanical views about the role of women in society brought by Muslims from the Middle East made little impression even among Muslim families in West Africa.

8-4d Slavery

African slavery is often associated with the period after 1500. Indeed, the slave trade did reach enormous proportions in the seventeenth and eighteenth centuries, when European slave ships transported millions of unfortunate victims abroad to Europe or the Americas (see Chapter 14).

Slavery did not originate with the coming of the Europeans, however. It had been practiced in Africa since ancient times and probably originated when prisoners of war were forced into perpetual servitude. Slavery was common in ancient Egypt and became especially prevalent during the New Kingdom, when

societies, these nuclear family units were combined into larger kinship communities known as households or lineage groups.

The lineage group was similar in many respects to the clan in China or the *jati* in India in that it was normally based on kinship ties, although sometimes outsiders such as neighbors or other dependents may have been admitted to membership. Throughout the precolonial era, lineages served, in the words of one historian, as the "basic building blocks" of African society. The authority of the leading members of the lineage group was substantial. As in China, the elders had considerable power over the economic functions of the other people in the group, which provided mutual support for all members.

A village would usually be composed of a single lineage group, although some communities may have consisted of several unrelated families. At the head of the village was the familiar "big man," who was often assisted by a council of representatives of the various households in the community. Often the "big man" was believed to possess supernatural powers, and as the village grew in size and power, he might eventually be transformed into a local chieftain or monarch.

8-4c The Role of Women

Although generalizations are risky, we can say that women were usually subordinate to men in Africa, as in most early societies. In some cases, they were valued for the work they could do or for their role in increasing the size of the lineage group. Polygyny was not uncommon, particularly in Muslim societies. Women often worked in the fields while the men of the village tended the cattle or went on hunting expeditions. In some communities, the women specialized in commercial activities. In one area in southern Africa, young girls were sent

WOMEN AND ISLAM IN NORTH AFRICA

 Family & Society

IN MUSLIM SOCIETIES IN NORTH AFRICA, as elsewhere, women were required to cover their bodies to avoid tempting men, but Islam's puritanical insistence on the separation of the sexes contrasted with the relatively informal relationships that prevailed in many African societies. In this excerpt from *The History and Description of Africa*, Leo Africanus describes the customs along the Mediterranean coast of Africa. A resident of Spain of Muslim parentage who was captured by Christian corsairs in 1518 and later served under Pope Leo X, Leo Africanus undertook many visits to Africa.

Leo Africanus, *The History and Description of Africa*

Their women (according to the guise of that country) go very gorgeously attired: they wear linen gowns dyed black, with exceeding wide sleeves, over which sometimes they cast a mantle of the same color or of blue, the corners of which mantle are very [attractively] fastened about their shoulders with a fine silver clasp. Likewise they have rings hanging at their ears, which for the most part are made of silver; they wear many rings also upon their fingers. Moreover they usually wear about their thighs and ankles certain scarfs and rings, after the fashion of the Africans. They cover their faces with certain masks having only two holes for the eyes to peep out at. If any man chance to meet with them, they presently hide their faces, passing by him with silence, except it be some of their allies or kinsfolks; for unto them they always [uncover] their faces, neither is there any use of the said mask so long as they be in presence. These Arabians when they travel any journey (as they oftentimes do) they set their women upon certain saddles made handsomely of wicker for the same purpose, and fastened to their camel backs, neither be they anything too wide, but fit only for a woman to sit in. When they go to the wars each man carries his wife with him, to the end that she may cheer up her good man, and give him encouragement. Their damsels which are unmarried do usually paint their faces, breasts, arms, hands, and fingers with a kind of counterfeit color: which is accounted a most decent custom among them.

Q *Which of the practices described here are dictated by the social regulations of Islam? Does the author approve of the behavior of African women as described in this passage?*

Source: From *The History and Description of Africa*, by Leo Africanus (New York: Burt Franklin), pp. 158–159.

---

slaving expeditions brought back thousands of captives from the upper Nile to be used in labor gangs, for tribute, and even as human sacrifices.

Slavery persisted during the early period of state building, well past the tenth century CE. Berber tribes may have regularly raided agricultural communities south of the Sahara for captives who were transported northward and eventually sold throughout the Mediterranean. Some were enrolled as soldiers, while others, often women, were put to work as domestic servants in the homes of the well-to-do. The use of captives for forced labor or exchange was apparently also common in African societies farther to the south and along the eastern coast.

Life was difficult for the average slave. The least fortunate were probably those who worked on plantations owned by the royal family or other wealthy landowners. Those pressed into service as soldiers were sometimes more fortunate, since in Muslim societies in the Middle East, they might at some point win their freedom. Many slaves were employed in the royal household or as domestic servants in private homes. In general, these slaves probably had the most tolerable existence. Although they ordinarily were not permitted to purchase their freedom, their living conditions were often decent and sometimes practically indistinguishable from those of the free individuals in the household. In some societies in North Africa, slaves reportedly made up as much as 75 percent of the entire population. Elsewhere, the percentage was much lower, in some cases less than 10 percent.

8–5 AFRICAN CULTURE

 Focus Question: What are some of the chief characteristics of African sculpture and carvings, music, and architecture, and what purpose did these forms of creative expression serve in African society?

In early Africa, as in much of the rest of the world at the time, creative expression, whether in the form of painting, literature, or music, was above all a means of serving religion and the social order. Though to the uninitiated a wooden mask or the bronze and iron statuary of southern Nigeria is simply a work of art, to the artist it was often a means of expressing religious convictions and communal concerns. Indeed, some African historians reject the use of the term *art* to describe such artifacts because they were produced for spiritual or moral rather than aesthetic purposes.

8–5a Painting and Sculpture

The oldest extant art forms in Africa are rock paintings. The most famous examples are in the Tassili Mountains in the central Sahara, where the earliest paintings may date back as far as 5000 BCE, though the majority are a millennium or so younger. Some of the later paintings depict the two-horse chariots used to transport goods prior to the introduction of the camel. Rock paintings are also found elsewhere in the continent, including the Nile Valley and eastern and southern Africa. Those of the

San peoples of southern Africa are especially interesting for their illustrations of ritual ceremonies in which village shamans induce rain, propitiate the spirits, or cure illnesses.

More familiar, perhaps, are African wood carvings and sculpture. Mentioned in the account of the traveler Ibn Battuta as early as the fourteenth century, these remarkable statues, masks, and headdresses were carved from living trees, after the artist had made a sacrifice to the tree's spirit. These masks and headdresses were worn by costumed singers and dancers in performances to the various spirits, revealing the identification and intimacy of the African with the natural world. The "Fang" masks of Equatorial Africa, for example, were used both for initiation ceremonies as well as for entertainment on festive occasions. Masks decorated in white clay were meant to convey the embodied spirits of the deceased so as to protect the village from evil forces.

In the thirteenth and fourteenth centuries CE, metalworkers at Ife (EE-fay) in what is now southern Nigeria produced handsome bronze and iron statues using the lost-wax method, in which melted wax in a mold is replaced by molten metal. The Ife sculptures may in turn have influenced artists in Benin (bay-NEEN), in West Africa, who produced equally impressive works in bronze during the same period. The Benin sculptures include bronze heads, relief plaques depicting life at court, ornaments, and figures of various animals.

Westerners once regarded African wood carvings and metal sculpture as a form of "primitive art," but the label is not appropriate. The metal sculpture of Benin, for example, is highly sophisticated, and some of the best works are considered masterpieces. Such works were often created by artists in the employ of the royal court.

8–5b Music

Like sculpture and wood carving, African music and dance often served a religious function. With their characteristic heavy rhythmic beat, dances were a means of communicating with the spirits, and the frenzied movements that are often identified with African dance were intended to represent the spirits acting through humans.

African music during the traditional period varied from one society to another. A wide variety of instruments were used, including drums and other percussion instruments, xylophones, bells, horns and flutes, and stringed instruments like the fiddle, harp, and zither. Still, the music throughout the continent had sufficient common characteristics to justify a few generalizations. In the first place, a strong rhythmic pattern was an important feature of most African music, although the desired effect was achieved through a wide variety of means, including gourds, pots, bells, sticks beaten together, and hand clapping as well as drums.

Another important feature of African music was the integration of voice and instrument into a total musical experience. Musical instruments and the human voice were often woven together to tell a story, and instruments, such as the famous "talking drum," were often used to represent the voice. Choral music and individual voices were frequently used in a pattern of repetition and variation, sometimes known as "call and response." Through this technique, the audience participated in the music by uttering a single phrase over and over as a choral

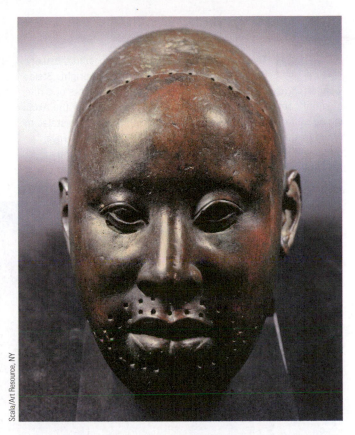

Scala/Art Resource, NY

African Metalwork. The rulers of emerging West African states frequently commissioned royal artifacts to adorn their palaces and promote their temporal grandeur. Elaborate stools, weaponry, shields, and sculpted heads of members of the royal family served to commemorate the ruler's reign and preserve his memory for later generations. This regal thirteenth-century brass head attests to the technical excellence and sophistication of Ife metalworkers. The small holes along the scalp and the mouth permitted either hair, a veil, or a crown to be attached to the head, which itself was often attached to a wooden mannequin dressed in elaborate robes for display during memorial services.

response to the changing call sung by the soloist. This tradition was carried by slaves to the Americas and survives to this day in the gospel music sung in many African American congregations. Sometimes instrumental music achieved a similar result.

Much music was produced in the context of social rituals, such as weddings and funerals, religious ceremonies, and official inaugurations. It could also serve an educational purpose by passing on to the young people information about the history and social traditions of the community. In the absence of written languages in sub-Saharan Africa (except for the Arabic script, used in Muslim societies in East and West Africa), music served as the primary means of transmitting folk legends and religious traditions from generation to generation. Oral tradition, which was usually undertaken by a priestly class or a specialized class of storytellers, served a similar function.

8–5c Architecture

No aspect of African artistic creativity is more varied than architecture. From the pyramids along the Nile to the ruins of Great Zimbabwe south of the Zambezi River, from the

COMPARATIVE ILLUSTRATION

The Stele. A stele is a stone slab or pillar, usually decorated or inscribed and placed upright. Stelae were often used to commemorate the accomplishments of a ruler or significant figure. Shown in image A is the tallest of the Axum stelae still standing, in present-day Ethiopia. The stone stelae in Axum in the fourth century BCE marked the location of royal tombs with inscriptions commemorating the glories of the kings. An earlier famous stele, seen in image B, is the obelisk at Luxor in southern Egypt. A similar kind of stone pillar, shown in image C, was erected in India during the reign of Ashoka in the third century BCE (see Chapter 2) to commemorate events in the life of the Buddha. Archaeologists have also found stelae in ancient China, Greece, and Mexico.

 Why do you think the stele was so widely used during early times as a symbol of royal power?

A   **B**   **C**

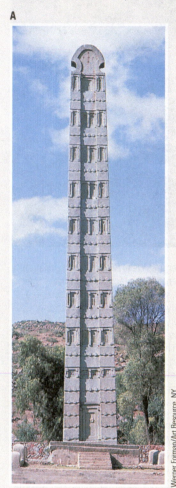

Werner Forman/Art Resource, NY

William J. Duiker

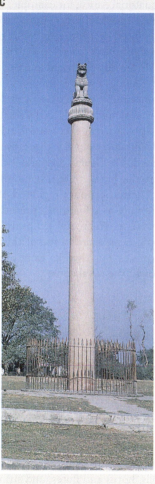

Borromeo/Art Resource, NY

Moorish palaces at Zanzibar to the turreted mud mosques of West Africa, African architecture shows a striking diversity of approach and technique that is unmatched in other areas of creative endeavor.

The earliest surviving architectural form found in Africa is the pyramid. The kingdom of Meroë apparently adopted the pyramidal form from Egypt during the last centuries of the first millennium BCE. Although used for the same purpose as their earlier counterparts at Giza, the pyramids at Meroë were distinctive in style; they were much smaller and were topped with a flat platform rather than rising to a point. Remains of temples with massive carved pillars at Meroë also reflect Egyptian influence.

Farther to the south, the kingdom of Axum was developing its own architectural traditions. Most distinctive were the carved stone pillars, known as stelae (STEE-lee; singular STEE-luh) (see Comparative Illustration "The Stele") that were used to mark the tombs of dead kings. Some stood as high as 100 feet. The advent of Christianity eventually had an impact on Axumite architecture. During the Zagwe dynasty, churches carved out of solid rock were constructed throughout the country. The earliest may have been built in the eighth century CE. Stylistically, they combined indigenous techniques inherited from the pre-Christian period with elements borrowed from Christian churches in the Holy Land (see Comparative Illustration "Rock Architecture," Section 8-2c, p. 226).

A WEST AFRICAN ORAL TRADITION

LIKE OTHER GREAT EPICS OF WORLD LITERATURE, the West African *Epic of Son-Jara* describes the ordeals of a male protagonist as he hurdles superhuman obstacles while fulfilling his heroic destiny. It is interesting, however, to observe the role played by women in the epic hero's calamitous journey. Although he is often opposed by evil witches and temptresses, he can also be assisted in foiling his foes by a courageous woman. Penelope in the *Odyssey* outwits her enemies, as does Sita in the Ramayana and Draupadi in the Mahabharata.

In this pivotal passage, Son-Jara's sister, Sugulun Kulunkan, offers to seduce his enemy Sumamuru in order to obtain the Manden secret, or magic spell, needed to control the kingdom of Mali. Sumamuru divulges his all-powerful secret and is rebuked by his mother; both son and mother then disown each other with the trenchant symbols of the slashed breast and cut cloth. After each line of verse recited by the bard, an assistant would respond with the endorsement "true." This practice is perhaps the distant ancestor of today's African American custom, called "call and response," of following each line of religious oratory with "Amen."

The Epic of Son-Jara

Son-Jara's flesh-and-blood sister, Sugulun Kulunkan,
She said, "O Magan Son-Jara,
"One person cannot fight this war.
"Let me go seek Sumamuru.
"Were I then to reach him,
"To you I will deliver him,
"So that the folk of the Manden be yours,
"And all the Mandenland you shield."
Sugulun Kulunkan arose,
And went up to the gates of Sumamuru's fortress:
. . .
"Come open the gates, Susu Mountain Sumamuru!
"Come make me your bed companion!"
Sumamuru came to the gates:
"What manner of person are you?"
"It is I, Sugulun Kulunkan!"

"Well, now, Sugulun Kulunkan,
"If you have come to trap me,
"To turn me over to some person,
"Know that none can ever vanquish me.
"I have found the Manden secret,
"And made the Manden sacrifice,
"And in five score millet stalks placed it,
"And buried them here in the earth.
"'Tis I who found the Manden secret,
"And made the Manden sacrifice,
"And in a red piebald bull did place it,
"And buried it here in the earth.
"Know that none can vanquish me.
"'Tis I who found the Manden secret
"And made a sacrifice to it,
"And in a pure white cock did place it.
"Were you to kill it,
"And uproot some barren groundnut plants,
"And strip them of their leaves,
"And spread them round the fortress,
"And uproot more barren peanut plants,
"And fling them into the fortress,
"Only then can I be vanquished."
His mother sprang forward at that:
"Heh! Susu Mountain Sumamuru!
"Never tell all to a woman,
"To a one-night woman!
"The woman is not safe, Sumamuru."
Sumamuru sprang towards his mother,
And came and seized his mother,
And slashed off her breast with a knife, magasi!
She went and got the old menstrual cloth.
"Ah! Sumamuru!" she swore.
"If your birth was ever a fact,
"I have cut your old menstrual cloth!"

Q *What purpose did the call and response serve in such epics? What effect would the technique have on the audience?*

Source: From *The Epic of Son-Jara: A West African Tradition*, text by Fa-Digi Sisoko, notes, translation, and new introduction by John William Johnson (Bloomington: Indiana University Press, 1992), pp. 91–92.

In West Africa, buildings constructed in stone were apparently a rarity until the emergence of states during the first millennium CE. At that time, the royal palace and other buildings of civic importance were often built of stone or cement, while the houses of the majority of the population continued to be constructed of dried mud. On his visit to the state of Guinea on the West African coast, the sixteenth-century traveler Leo Africanus noted that the houses of the ruler and other elites were built of chalk with roofs of straw. Even then, however, well into the state-building period, mosques were often built of mud.

Along the east coast, the architecture of the elite tended to reflect Middle Eastern styles. In the coastal towns and islands from Mogadishu to Kilwa, the houses of the wealthy were built of stone and reflected Arabic influence. As elsewhere, the common people lived in huts of mud, thatch, or palm leaves. Mosques were normally built of stone.

The most famous stone buildings in sub-Saharan Africa are those at Great Zimbabwe. Constructed without mortar, the outer wall and public buildings at Great Zimbabwe are an impressive monument to the architectural creativity of the peoples of the region.

8–5d Literature

Literature in the sense of written works did not exist in sub-Saharan Africa during the early traditional period, except in regions where Islam had brought the Arabic script from the Middle East. But African societies compensated for the absence of a written language with a rich tradition of oral lore. The **bard**, a professional storyteller, was an ancient African institution by which history was transmitted orally from generation to generation. In many West African societies, bards were highly esteemed and served as counselors to kings as well as protectors of local tradition. Bards were revered for their oratory and singing skills, phenomenal memory, and astute interpretation of history. As one African scholar wrote, the death of a bard was equivalent to the burning of a library.

Bards served several necessary functions in society. They were chroniclers of history, preservers of social customs and proper conduct, and entertainers who possessed a monopoly over the playing of several musical instruments, which accompanied their narratives. Because of their unique position above normal society, bards often played the role of mediator between hostile families or clans in a community. They were also credited with possessing occult powers and could read divinations and give blessings and curses. Traditionally, bards also served as advisers to the king, sometimes inciting him to action (such as going to battle) through the passion of their poetry. When captured by the enemy, bards were often treated with respect and released or compelled to serve the victor with their art.

One of the most famous West African poems is *The Epic of Son-Jara*. Passed down orally by bards for more than seven hundred years, it relates the heroic exploits of Son-Jara (sun-GAR-uh) (also known as Sunjata or Sundiata), the founder of Mali's empire and its ruler from 1230 to 1255. Although Mansa Musa is famous throughout the world because of his flamboyant pilgrimage to Mecca in the fourteenth century, Son-Jara is more celebrated in West Africa because of the dynamic and unbroken oral traditions of the West African peoples (see "A West African Oral Tradition," p. 237).

Like the bards, women were appreciated for their storytelling talents, as well as for their role as purveyors of the moral values and religious beliefs of African societies. In societies that lacked a written tradition, women represented the glue that held the community together. Through the recitation of fables, proverbs, poems, and songs, mothers conditioned the communal bonding and moral fiber of succeeding generations in a way that was rarely encountered in the patriarchal societies of Europe, Asia, and the Middle East. Such activities were not only vital aspects of education in traditional Africa but also offered a welcome respite from the drudgery of everyday life and a spark to develop the imagination and artistic awareness of the young. Renowned for its many proverbs, Africa also offers the following: "A good story is like a garden carried in the pocket."

CHAPTER SUMMARY

Thanks to the dedicated work of a generation of archaeologists, anthropologists, and historians, we have a much better understanding of the evolution of human societies in Africa than we did a few decades ago. Intensive efforts by archaeologists have demonstrated beyond reasonable doubt that the first hominids lived there. Recently discovered evidence suggests that farming may have been practiced in Africa more than 11,000 years ago.

Less is known about more recent African history, partly because of the paucity of written records. Still, historians have established that the first civilizations had begun to take shape in sub-Saharan Africa by the first millennium CE, while the continent as a whole was an active participant in emerging regional and global trade with the Mediterranean world and across the Indian Ocean.

Thus, the peoples of Africa were not as isolated from the main currents of human history as was once assumed. Although the state-building process in sub-Saharan Africa was still in its early stages compared with the ancient civilizations of India, China, and Mesopotamia, in many respects these new states were as impressive and as sophisticated as their counterparts elsewhere in the world.

In the fifteenth century, a new factor was added to the equation. Urged on by the tireless efforts of Prince Henry the Navigator, Portuguese fleets began to probe southward along the coast of West Africa. At first, their sponsors were in search of gold and slaves, but at the end of the century, Vasco da Gama's voyage around the Cape of Good Hope signaled Portugal's determination to dominate the commerce of the Indian Ocean in the future. The new situation posed a challenge to the peoples of Africa, whose nascent states and technology would be severely tested by the rapacious demands of the Europeans (see Chapter 14).

CHAPTER TIMELINE

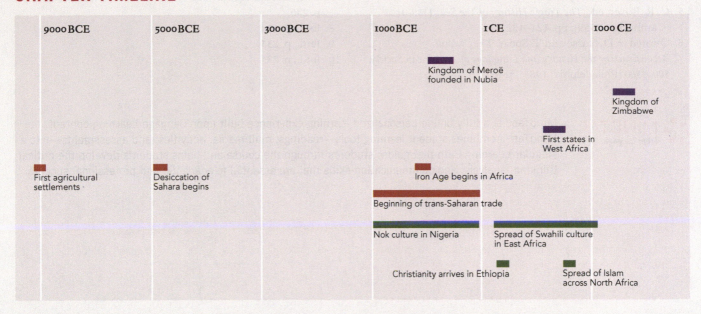

9000 BCE	5000 BCE	3000 BCE	1000 BCE	1 CE	1000 CE

Kingdom of Meroë founded in Nubia

Kingdom of Zimbabwe

First states in West Africa

First agricultural settlements

Desiccation of Sahara begins

Iron Age begins in Africa

Beginning of trans-Saharan trade

Nok culture in Nigeria

Spread of Swahili culture in East Africa

Christianity arrives in Ethiopia

Spread of Islam across North Africa

CHAPTER REVIEW

Upon Reflection

Q Where and under what conditions was agriculture first practiced on the continent of Africa? What effect did the advent of farming have on the formation of human communities there?

Q Although geographic barriers posed a challenge for African peoples in establishing communications with societies beyond their shores, by the end of the first millennium CE the continent had become an active player in the global trade network. What areas of Africa took part in this commercial expansion, and what products were exchanged?

Q The migration of the Bantu-speaking peoples was one of the most extensive population movements in world history. Trace the Bantu migration from its point of origin and discuss how it affected the later history of the continent.

Key Terms

Coptic (p. 219)
Berbers (p. 219)
Nok culture (p. 220)
Swahili (p. 221)
pantheism (p. 223)
lineage group (p. 223)

mansa (p. 229)
noncentralized societies (p. 231)
matrilinear (p. 233)
patrilinear (p. 233)
bard (p. 238)

Chapter Notes

1. F. Fernández-Armesto, *Civilizations* (London, 2000), pp. 66–68.
2. S. Hamdun and N. King, eds., *Ibn Battuta in Africa* (London, 1975), p. 19.

3. *The Book of Duarte Barbosa* (Nedeln, Liechtenstein, 1967), p. 28.
4. Sidi Salem Ould Elhadj, "The Pachalik arma de Tombouctou, 1591–1826," cited in M. de Villiers and

S. Hirtle, *Timbuktu: The Sahara's Fabled City of Gold* (New York, 2007), p. 68.

5. C. R. Boxer, ed., *The Tragic History of the Sea, 1589–1622* (Cambridge, 1959), pp. 121–122.

6. Quoted in D. Nurse and T. Spear, *The Swahili: Reconstructing the History and Language of an African Society, 800–1500* (Philadelphia, 1985), p. 84.

7. S. Lee (tr. and ed.), *The Travels of Ibn Battuta in the Near East, Asia and Africa, 1325–1354* (Mineola, N.Y., 2004), p. 240.

8. Ibid., p. 234.

9. Ibid., p. 235.

10. Ibid., p. 235.

Chapter Outline and Focus Questions

9-1 The Silk Road

Q What were some of the chief destinations along the Silk Road, and what kinds of products and ideas traveled along the route?

9-2 India After the Mauryas

Q How did Buddhism change in the centuries after Siddhartha Gautama's death, and why did the religion ultimately decline in popularity in India?

9-3 The Arrival of Islam

Q How did Islam arrive in the Indian subcontinent, and why were Muslim peoples able to establish states there?

9-4 Society and Culture

Q What impact did Muslim rule have on Indian society? To what degree did the indigenous population convert to the new religion, and why?

9-5 The Golden Region: Early Southeast Asia

Q What were the main characteristics of Southeast Asian social and economic life, culture, and religion before 1500 CE?

One of the two massive carved statues of the Buddha formerly at Bamiyan. Thomas J. Abercrombie/National Geographic Creative

Critical Thinking

Q *New religions had a significant impact on the social and cultural life of peoples living in southern Asia during the period covered in this chapter. What factors caused the spread of these religions in the first place? What changes occurred as a result of the introduction of these new faiths? Were the religions themselves affected by their spread into new regions of Asia?*

Connections to Today

Q *What does the Comparative Essay entitled "Caste, Class, and Family," (Section 9-4c, page 255) tell us about the role that nuclear and joint families tend to play in human societies? Do the examples cited provide any lessons for the present day?*

WHILE TRAVELING from his native China to India along the Silk Road in the early fifth century CE, the Buddhist monk Fa Xian (fah SHEE-ahn) stopped en route at a town called Bamiyan (BAH-mee-ahn), a rest stop located deep in the mountains of what is today known as Afghanistan. At that time, Bamiyan was a major center of Buddhist studies, with dozens of temples and monasteries filled with students, all overlooked by two giant standing statues of the Buddha hewn directly out of the side of a massive cliff. Fa Xian was thrilled at the sight. "The law of Buddha," he remarked with satisfaction in his account of the experience, "is progressing and flourishing." He then continued southward to India, where he spent several years visiting Buddhist sites throughout the country. Because little of the literature from that period survives, Fa Xian's observations are a valuable resource for our knowledge of the daily lives of the Indian people.

The India that Fa Xian visited was no longer the unified land it had been under the Mauryan (MOWR-yun) dynasty. The overthrow of the Mauryas in the early second century BCE had been followed by several hundred years of divided rule, when the subcontinent was divided into a number of separate kingdoms and principalities. The dominant force in the north was the Kushan (KOO-shan) state, established by Indo-European-speaking pastoral peoples who had been driven out of what is now China's Xinjiang province by the Xiongnu in the second or first century BCE (see Chapter 3). The Kushans penetrated into the mountains north of the Indus River, where they eventually formed a kingdom with its capital at Bactria, not far from modern Kabul (KAH-bul). Over the next two centuries, the Kushans established their supremacy along the Indus River and in the central Ganges Valley.

Meanwhile, to the south, a number of kingdoms arose among the Dravidian-speaking peoples of the Deccan Plateau, which had been only partly under Mauryan rule. The most famous of these kingdoms was Chola (CHOH-luh) (sometimes spelled Cola) on the southeastern coast. Chola developed into a major trading power and sent merchant fleets eastward across the Bay of Bengal, where they introduced Indian culture as well as Indian goods to the peoples of Southeast Asia. In the fourth century CE, Chola was overthrown by the Pallavas (puh-LAH-vuhz), who ruled from their capital at Kanchipuram (KAHN-chee-poo-rum), known today as Kanchi (KAHN-chee), just southwest of modern Chennai (CHEN-ny) (Madras), for the next four hundred years.

9–1 THE SILK ROAD

 Focus Question: What were some of the chief destinations along the Silk Road, and what kinds of products and ideas traveled along the route?

Shortly after the fall of the Mauryas, the Kushan kingdom, with its power base beyond the Khyber Pass in modern Afghanistan, became the dominant political force in northern India (see Chapter 2). Prior to being evicted from their original habitat by the Xiongnu, they had engaged in the silk trade with China from their base near Khotan (koh-TAHN), located on the southern route through the Taklimakan (tah-kluh-muh-KAHN) Desert. Now, having consolidated their position astride the main trade routes across the northern half of the Indian subcontinent, the Kushans thrived on the commerce that passed through the area (see Map 9.1). Although most of the trade was local, some of it passed between the Roman Empire and China and was transported along the route now known as the Silk Road, one segment of which passed through the mountains northwest of India (see Chapter 10). From there, goods such as raw silk and precious stones

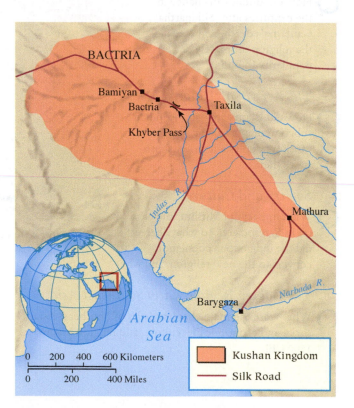

Map 9.1 The Kushan Kingdom and the Silk Road. After the collapse of the Mauryan Empire, a new state formed by recent migrants from the north arose north of the Indus River Valley. For the next four centuries, the Kushan kingdom played a major role in regional trade via the Silk Road until it declined in the third century CE.

 What were the major products shipped along the Silk Road? Which countries beyond the borders of this map took an active part in trade along the Silk Road?

A PORTRAIT OF MEDIEVAL INDIA

Interaction & Exchange **MUCH OF WHAT WE KNOW ABOUT LIFE** in medieval India comes from the accounts of Chinese missionaries who visited the subcontinent in search of documents recording the teachings of the Buddha. In this selection, the Buddhist monk Fa Xian, who spent several years there in the fifth century CE, reports on conditions in the kingdom of Mathura (MAH-too-ruh) (Mo-tu-lo), a vassal state in western India that was part of the Gupta Empire. Although he could not have been pleased that the Gupta monarchs in India had adopted the Hindu faith, he found that the people were contented and prosperous except for the outcastes, whom he called Chandalas.

Fa Xian, *The Travels of Fa Xian*

Going southeast . . . somewhat less than 80 *joyanas* [about 640 miles], we passed very many temples one after another, with some myriad of priests in them. Having passed these places, we arrived at a certain country. This country is called Mo-tu-lo. Once more we followed the Puna river. On the sides of the river, both right and left, are twenty *sangharamas* [monasteries] with perhaps 3,000 priests. The law of Buddha is progressing and flourishing. Beyond the deserts are the countries of western India. The kings of these countries are all firm believers in the law of Buddha. They remove their caps of state when they make offerings to the priests. The members of the royal household and the chief ministers personally direct the food giving; when the distribution of food is over, they spread a carpet on the ground opposite the chief seat (the president's seat) and sit down before it. They dare not sit on couches in the presence of the priests. The rules relating to the almsgiving of kings have been handed down from the time of Buddha till now. Southward from this is the so-called middle country (Madhyadesa). The climate of this country is warm and equable, without frost or snow. The people are very well off, without poll tax or official restrictions. Only those who till the royal lands return a portion of profit of the land. If they desire to go, they go; if they like to stop, they stop. The kings govern without corporal punishment; criminals are fined, according to circumstances, lightly or heavily. Even in cases of repeated rebellion they only cut off the right hand. The king's personal attendants, who guard him on the right and left, have fixed salaries. Throughout the country the people kill no living thing nor drink wine, nor do they eat garlic or onions, with the exception of Chandalas only. The Chandalas are named "evil men" and dwell apart from others; if they enter a town or market, they sound a piece of wood in order to separate themselves; then men, knowing who they are, avoid coming in contact with them. In this country they do not keep swine nor fowls, and do not deal in cattle; they have no shambles [slaughterhouses] or wine shops in their marketplaces. In selling they use cowrie shells. The Chandalas only hunt and sell flesh.

 To what degree do the practices described here appear to conform to the principles established by Siddhartha Gautama in his teachings? Would political advisers such as Kautilya and the Chinese philosopher Mencius have approved of the government's policies?

Source: "Fu-kwo-ki," in Hiuen Tsang, Si-Yu Ki: *Buddhist Records of the Western World*, translated by Samuel Beal (London: Trubner & Co., 1886).

---

were shipped to Rome through the Persian Gulf or the Red Sea. The importance of the trade with the Mediterranean region is attested to by the fact that gold and silver coins minted by the Kushan state were often imprinted with the figures of Iranian and Greek deities.

Trade between India and Europe had begun even before the rise of the Roman Empire, but it expanded rapidly in the first century CE, when sailors mastered the pattern of the monsoon winds in the Indian Ocean (from the southwest in the summer and the northeast in the winter). Commerce between the Mediterranean and the Indian Ocean, as described in the *Periplus*, a first-century CE account by a Greek merchant, was extensive and often profitable, and it resulted in the establishment of several small trading settlements along the Indian coast. Rome imported ivory, indigo, textiles, precious stones, and pepper from India and silk from China. The Romans sometimes paid cash for these goods but also exported silver, wine, perfume, slaves, and glass and cloth from Egypt. Overall, Rome appears to have imported much more than it sold to the Far East.

The Silk Road was a conduit not only of material goods but also of technology and of ideas. The first Indian monks to visit China may have traveled over the road during the second century CE. By the time of Fa Xian, Buddhist monks from China were beginning to arrive in increasing numbers to visit holy sites in India. The visits not only enriched the study of Buddhism in the two countries but also led to a fruitful exchange of ideas and technological advances in astronomy, mathematics, and linguistics. According to one scholar, the importation of Buddhist writings from India encouraged the development of printing in China, while the Chinese obtained lessons in health care from monks returned from the Asian subcontinent.

Indeed, the emergence of the Kushan kingdom as a major commercial power was due not only to its role as an intermediary in the Rome-China trade but also to the rising popularity of Buddhism. During the second century CE, Kanishka (kuh-NISH-kuh), the greatest of the Kushan monarchs, began to patronize Buddhism. Under Kanishka and his successors, an intimate and mutually beneficial relationship was established between Buddhist monasteries and the local merchant community in thriving urban centers like Taxila (tak-SUH-luh) and Varanasi (vah-RAH-nah-see). Merchants were eager to build stupas and donate money to monasteries in return for social prestige and the implied promise of a better life in this world or the hereafter.

For their part, the wealthy monasteries ceased to be simple communities where monks could find a refuge from the material cares of the world; instead they became major consumers of luxury goods provided by their affluent patrons. Monasteries and their inhabitants became increasingly involved in the economic life of society, and Buddhist architecture began to be richly decorated with precious stones and glass purchased from local merchants or imported from abroad. The process was very similar to the changes that would later occur in the Christian church in medieval Europe.

It was from the Kushan kingdom that Buddhism began its long journey across the wastes of Central Asia to China and other societies in eastern Asia. As trade between the two regions increased, merchants and missionaries flowed from Bactria over the trade routes snaking through the mountains toward the northeast. At various stopping points on the trail, pilgrims erected statues and decorated mountain caves with magnificent frescoes depicting the life of the Buddha and his message to his followers. One of the most prominent of these centers was at Bamiyan, not far from modern-day Kabul, where believers carved two mammoth statues of the Buddha out of a sheer sandstone cliff. According to the Chinese pilgrim Fa Xian (see "A Portrait of Medieval India," p. 243), when he visited the area in 400 CE, more than a thousand monks were attending a religious ceremony at the site.

9–2 INDIA AFTER THE MAURYAS

 Focus Question: How did Buddhism change in the centuries after Siddhartha Gautama's death, and why did the religion ultimately decline in popularity in India?

Weakened by wars with Persia and the collapse of the Han dynasty in China, the Kushan kingdom came to an end under uncertain conditions sometime in the third century CE. In 320, a new state was established in the central Ganges Valley by a local raja named Chandragupta (chun-druh-GOOP-tuh) (no relation to Chandragupta Maurya, the founder of the Mauryan dynasty). Chandragupta located his capital at Pataliputra (pah-tah-lee-POO-truh), the site of the now decaying palace of the Mauryas. Under his successor, Samudragupta (suh-moo-druh-GOOP-tuh), the territory under Gupta (GOOP-tuh) rule was extended into surrounding areas, and eventually the new kingdom became the dominant political force throughout northern India. It also established a loose suzerainty over the Dravidian state of Pallava to the south, thus becoming the greatest state in the subcontinent since the decline of the Mauryan Empire. Under a succession of powerful, efficient, and highly

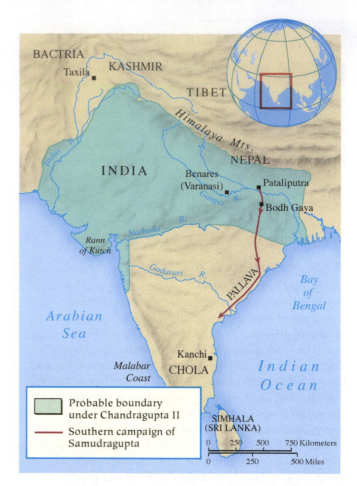

Map 9.2 The Gupta Empire. This map shows the extent of the Gupta Empire, the only major state to arise in the Indian subcontinent during the first millennium CE. The arrow indicates the military campaign into southern India led by King Samudragupta.

 How did the Gupta Empire differ in territorial extent from its great predecessor, the Mauryan Empire?

cultured monarchs, notably Samudragupta (r. 335–375 CE) and Chandragupta II (r. 375–415 CE), India enjoyed a new "classical age" of civilization (see Map 9.2).

9–2a The Gupta Dynasty: A New Golden Age?

Historians of India have traditionally viewed the Gupta era as a time of prosperity and thriving commerce with China, Southeast Asia, and the Mediterranean. Great cities, notable for their temples and Buddhist monasteries as well as for their economic prosperity, rose along the main trade routes throughout the subcontinent. The religious trade also prospered as pilgrims from across India and as far away as China came to visit the major religious centers.

As in the Mauryan Empire, much of the trade in the Gupta Empire was managed or regulated by the government. The Guptas owned mines and vast crown lands and earned massive profits from their commercial dealings. But there was also a large private sector, dominated by *jati* (caste) guilds that

Kushan kingdom	c. 150 BCE–c. 200 CE
Gupta dynasty	320–600s
Chandragupta I	r. 320–c. 335
Samudragupta	r. 335–375
Chandragupta II	r. 375–415
Arrival of Fa Xian in India	c. 406
First Buddhist temples at Ellora	Seventh century
Travels of Xuan Zang in India	630–643
Conquest of Sind by Arab armies	c. 711
Reign of Mahmud of Ghazni	997–1030
Delhi sultanate	1206–1527
Mongol invasion of northern India	1221
Invasion of Tamerlane	1398

monopolized key sectors of the economy. A money economy had probably been in operation since the second century BCE, when copper and gold coins had been introduced from the Middle East. This in turn led to the development of banking. Nevertheless, there are indications that the circulation of coins was limited and that cowrie shells continued to be used for local trade. The Chinese missionary Xuan Zang (SHOO-wen ZAHNG), who visited India in the first half of the seventh century, remarked that most commercial transactions were conducted by barter.[1]

But the good fortunes of the Guptas proved to be relatively short-lived. Beginning in the late fifth century CE, incursions by nomadic warriors from the northwest gradually reduced the power of the empire. Soon northern India was once more divided into myriad small kingdoms engaged in seemingly constant conflict. In the south, however, emerging states like Chola and Pallava prospered from their advantageous position athwart the regional trade network stretching from the Red Sea eastward into Southeast Asia (see "Foreign Trade," Section 9-4b, p. 256).

9–2b The Transformation of Buddhism

The Chinese pilgrims who traveled to India during the Gupta era encountered a Buddhism that had changed in a number of ways in the centuries since the time of Siddhartha Gautama. They also found a doctrine that was beginning to decline in popularity in the face of the rise of Hinduism, as the Brahmanical religious beliefs of the Aryan people would eventually be called.

The transformation in Buddhism had come about in part because the earliest written sources were transcribed two centuries after Siddhartha's death and in part because his message was reinterpreted as it became part of the everyday life of the people. Abstract concepts of a Nirvana that cannot be described began to be replaced, at least in the popular mind, with more concrete visions of heavenly salvation, and

Siddhartha was increasingly regarded as a divinity rather than as a sage.

As a sign of that transformation, the face of the Buddha began to be displayed in sacred sculptures, along with clear suggestions that, like Jesus, he was of divine birth (Comparative Illustration "The Buddha and Jesus," Section 2-4b, p. 62). The Buddha's teachings that all four classes were equal gave way to the familiar Brahmanical conviction that some people, by reason of previous reincarnations, were closer to Nirvana than others.

Theravada These developments led to a split in the movement. Purists emphasized what they insisted were the original teachings of the Buddha, describing themselves as the school of **Theravada** (thay-ruh-VAH-duh), or "the teachings of the elders." Followers of Theravada, many of them located in southern India and on the island of Sri Lanka, considered Buddhism a way of life, not a salvationist creed. Theravada stressed the importance of strict adherence to personal behavior and the quest for understanding as a means of release from the wheel of life.

Mahayana In the meantime, another interpretation of Buddhist doctrine was emerging in the northwest. Here Buddhist believers, perhaps hoping to compete with other salvationist faiths circulating in the region, began to promote the view that Nirvana could be achieved through devotion and not just through painstaking attention to one's behavior. According to advocates of this school, eventually to be known as **Mahayana** (mah-huh-YAH-nuh) ("greater vehicle"), Theravada teachings were too demanding or too strict for ordinary people to follow and therefore favored the wealthy, who were more apt to have the time and resources to spend weeks or months away from their everyday occupations. Mahayana Buddhists referred to their rivals as **Hinayana** (hee-nuh-YAH-nuh), or "lesser vehicle," because in Theravada fewer would reach enlightenment. Mahayana thus attempted to provide hope for the masses in their efforts to reach Nirvana, but to the followers of Theravada, it did so at the expense of an insistence on proper behavior.

To advocates of the Mahayana school, salvation could also come from the intercession of a **bodhisattva** (boh-duh-SUT-vuh) ("he who possesses the essence of Buddhahood"). According to Mahayana beliefs, some individuals who had achieved *bodhi* and were thus eligible to enter the state of Nirvana after death chose instead, because of their great compassion, to remain on earth in spirit form to help all human beings achieve release from the life cycle. Followers of Theravada, who believed the concept of bodhisattva applied only to Siddhartha Gautama himself, denounced such ideas as "the teaching of demons." But to their proponents, such ideas extended the hope of salvation to the masses. Mahayana Buddhists revered the saintly individuals who, according to tradition, had become bodhisattvas at death and erected temples in their honor where the local population could pray and render offerings. The most famous bodhisattva was Avalokitesvara (uh-VAH-loh-kee-TESH-vuh-rah), a mythic figure whose name in Sanskrit means "Lord of Compassion." Perhaps because of the identification of Avalokitesvara with the concept of mercy, in China he was gradually transformed into a female figure known as Guan Yin (gwahn YIN).

A final distinguishing characteristic of Mahayana Buddhism was its reinterpretation of Buddhism as a religion rather than as a philosophy. Although Mahayana had philosophical aspects, its adherents increasingly regarded the Buddha as a divine figure, and an elaborate Buddhist cosmology developed. Nirvana was not a form of extinction but a true heaven with many rest stations along the way for the faithful.

Under Kushan rule, Mahayana achieved considerable popularity in northern India and for a while even made inroads in such Theravada strongholds as the island of Sri Lanka (sree LAHN-kuh). But in the end, neither Mahayana nor Theravada was able to retain its popularity in Indian society. By the seventh century CE, Theravada had declined rapidly on the subcontinent, although it retained its foothold in Sri Lanka and across the Bay of Bengal in Southeast Asia, where it remained an influential force to modern times (see Map 9.3). Mahayana prospered in the northwest for centuries, but eventually it was supplanted by a revived Hinduism and later by a new arrival, Islam. But Mahayana too would find better fortunes abroad, as it was carried over the Silk Road or by sea to China and then to Korea and Japan (see Chapters 10 and 11). In all three countries, Buddhism has coexisted with Confucian doctrine and indigenous beliefs to the present.

9–2c The Decline of Buddhism in India

Why was Buddhism unable to retain its popularity in its native India, although it became a major force elsewhere in Asia? Some have speculated that in denying the existence of the soul, Buddhism ran counter to traditional Indian belief. Perhaps, too, one of Buddhism's strengths was also a weakness. In rejecting the class divisions that defined the Indian way of life, Buddhism appealed to those very groups who lacked an accepted place in Indian society, such as the untouchables. But at the same time, it represented a threat to those with a higher status. Moreover, by emphasizing the responsibility of each person to seek an individual path to Nirvana, Buddhism undermined the strong social bonds of the Indian class system.

Buddhism at the Crossroads of Culture. One of the consequences of Alexander the Great's ambition to conquer the known world was the introduction of Greek artistic styles into Central Asia. By the first century CE, as the Buddhist faith spread throughout the region, freestanding statues of the Buddha in monastic robes reminiscent of Greek togas became increasingly popular. During the Gupta era in northern India (320–600s CE), such statues reached a pinnacle of artistic achievement, serving as a model for sculptors from the subcontinent into the islands of Southeast Asia. This fifth-century life-size rendering of the Buddha in red sandstone was found in Mathura, once a thriving religious center in the upper Ganges River Valley. Although the head is missing, the portrayal in stone nonetheless displays a unique blend of sensuality and transcendence, while the cotton toga, which clings tightly to the body, reflects the high quality of Indian cotton goods at the time. Yvonne V. Duiker

Perhaps a final factor in the decline of Buddhism was the transformation of Brahmanism into a revised faith known as **Hinduism**. In its early development, Brahmanism had been highly elitist (see "The Education of a Brahmin," p. 248). Not only was observance of court ritual a monopoly of the *brahmin* class, but the major route to individual salvation, asceticism, was hardly realistic for the average Indian. In the centuries after the fall of the Mauryas, however, a growing emphasis on devotion—*bhakti* (BAHK-tee)—as a religious observance brought the possibility of improving one's *karma* by means of ritual acts within the reach of Indians of all classes. Perhaps Hindu devotionalism rose precisely to combat the inroads of Buddhism and reduce the latter's appeal among the Indian population. The Chinese Buddhist missionary Fa Xian reported that mutual hostility between the Buddhists and the *brahmins* in the Gupta era was quite strong:

> Leaving the southern gate of the capital city, on the east side of the road is a place where Buddha once dwelt. Whilst here he bit [a piece from] the willow stick and fixed it in the earth; immediately it grew up seven feet high, neither more nor less. The unbelievers and Brahmans, filled with jealousy, cut it down and scattered the leaves far and wide, but yet it always sprang up again in the same place as before.[2]

For a while, Buddhism was probably able to stave off the Hindu challenge by its own salvationist creed of Mahayana, which also emphasized the role of devotion, but the days of Buddhism as a dominant faith in the subcontinent were numbered. By the eighth century CE, Hindu missionaries spread throughout southern India, where their presence was spearheaded by new temples dedicated to Shiva at Kanchipuram (Kanchi), the site of a famous Buddhist monastery, and at Mamallapuram (muh-MAH-luh-poor-um).

HISTORIANS DEBATE ## 9–2d When Did the Indians Become Hindus?

When did Brahmanism—the faith originally brought to India by the Aryan peoples in the second millennium BCE—evolve into Hinduism, the religion practiced by the majority of the Indian people today? That question has aroused considerable interest among historians of India in

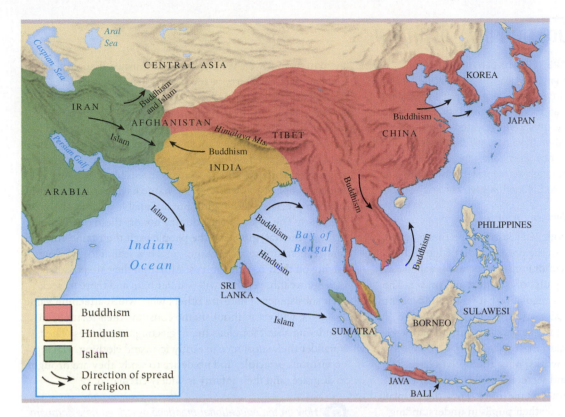

Map 9.3 The Spread of Religions in Southern and Eastern Asia, 600–1900 CE. Between 600 and 1900, three of the world's great religions—Buddhism, Hinduism, and Islam—continued to spread from their original sources to various parts of southern and eastern Asia.

 Which religion had the greatest impact? How might the existence of major trade routes help explain the spread of these religions?

Mamallapuram Shore Temple. Mamallapuram ("The City of the Great Warrior") was so named by one of the powerful kings of the Pallavan kingdom on the eastern coast of South India. From this port, ships embarked on naval expeditions to Sri Lanka and far-off destinations in Southeast Asia. Although the site was originally identified with the Hindu deity Vishnu, in the eighth century CE a Pallavan monarch built this shore temple in honor of Vishnu's rival deity, Shiva. It stands as a visual confirmation of the revival of the Hindu faith in southern India at the time. Centuries of wind and rain have eroded the ornate carvings that originally covered the large granite blocks. William J. Duiker

THE EDUCATION OF A *BRAHMIN*

Religion & Philosophy

ALTHOUGH THE SEVENTH-CENTURY CHINESE TRAVELER Xuan Zang was a Buddhist, he faithfully recorded his impressions of the Hindu religion in his memoirs. Here he describes the education of a *brahmin*, the highest class in Indian society. *Brahmin* youths were educated at what were called *ashramas* (ash-RAHM-uhz), where they received instruction in medicine, science, astronomy, and the Vedas. Their Buddhist counterparts were taught at monasteries, including a famous one at Sarnath, where Siddhartha gave his first sermon.

Xuan Zang, *Records of Western Countries*

The Brahmans study the four *Veda Sastras*. The first is called *Shau* [longevity]; it relates to the preservation of life and the regulation of the natural condition. The second is called *Sse* [sacrifice]; it relates to the [rules of] sacrifice and prayer. The third is called *Ping* [peace or regulation]; it relates to decorum, casting of lots, military affairs, and army regulations. The fourth is called *Shue* [secret mysteries]; it relates to various branches of science, incantations, medicine.

The teachers [of these works] must themselves have closely studied the deep and secret principles they contain, and penetrated to their remotest meaning. They then explain their general sense, and guide their pupils in understanding the words that are difficult. They urge them on and skillfully conduct them. They add luster to their poor knowledge, and stimulate the desponding. If they find that their pupils are satisfied with their acquirements, and so wish to escape to attend to their worldly duties, then they use means to keep them in their power. When they have finished their education, and have attained thirty years of age, then their character is formed and their knowledge ripe. When they have secured an occupation they first of all thank their master for his attention. There are some, deeply versed in antiquity, who devote themselves to elegant studies, and live apart from the world, and retain the simplicity of their character. These rise above mundane presents, and are as insensible to renown as to the contempt of the world. Their name having spread afar, the rulers appreciate them highly, but are unable to draw them to the court. The chief of the country honors them on account of their [mental] gifts, and the people exalt their fame and render them universal homage. . . . They search for wisdom, relying on their own resources. Although they are possessed of large wealth, yet they will wander here and there to seek their subsistence. There are others who, whilst attaching value to letters, will yet without shame consume their fortunes in wandering about for pleasure, neglecting their duties. They squander their substance in costly food and clothing. Having no virtuous principle, and no desire to study, they are brought to disgrace, and their infamy is widely circulated.

 How do the educational practices described here compare with the training provided to young men in other traditional societies in Europe, Asia, and the Americas? What, if anything, was distinctive about the educational system in India?

Source: From Hiuen Tsang, *Si-Yu Ki: Buddhist Records of the Western World*, translated by Samuel Beal (London: Trubner & Co., 1886).

---

recent years. Of course, the question does not have a single precise answer because the issue is partly a matter of definition, while the transition itself was undoubtedly a gradual process.

Some observers point to the advent of Muslim rule in the northern parts of the subcontinent in the late first millennium CE (see Section 9-3, "The Arrival of Islam"), when the indigenous people, labeled "Hindus" by the new arrivals, began to develop a greater sense of their distinct ethnic and cultural identity. Others point to the colonial era, when British colonial policies reinforced an Indian sense of being "the Other" and provoked them to rise to the defense of their cultural and historical heritage.

But perhaps the most decisive transition took place during the first millennium CE, when the Brahmanical emphasis on court sacrifice and asceticism was gradually replaced by a more populist tradition focused on personal worship, known as *puja* (POO-juh), and the achievement of individual goals. In that interpretation, the change from Brahmanism to a faith more accessible to the mass of the population may initially have been stimulated by the egalitarian tendencies of early Buddhism. In any event, by the end of the first millennium CE, the religious faith originally known as Brahmanism had fought off the challenges of alternative belief systems while transforming itself into the religion of the majority of the Indian people.

What were the primary characteristics of this new popular religion? In addition to the familiar trinity of gods, all of whom had wives with readily identifiable roles and personalities, the Hindu pantheon was now inhabited by countless minor deities (such as Ganesha, the god of good fortune), each again with his or her own specific function. The rich variety and the earthy character of many of these deities is somewhat misleading, however, for Hindus regard the multitude of gods simply as different manifestations of one ultimate reality. The various deities also provide a way for ordinary Indians to personify their religious feelings. Even though some individuals continued to express their devotion through the practice of asceticism, most sought to satisfy their own individual religious needs through devotion, which they expressed through ritual ceremonies and offerings at a temple. Such offerings were not only a way of seeking salvation, but also a means of satisfying all the aspiration of daily life.

Ganesha: The God of Good Fortune. One of the best examples of a popular deity in Hindu religious belief is Ganesha, described in Indian literature as a son of the deity Shiva who was accidentally beheaded by his father in a fit of anger. When Shiva repented of his action, he provided his son with the head of an elephant. Beginning in the fourth and fifth centuries CE, Ganesha became a popular subject of devotion, especially in the state of Maharashtra and the city of Bombay (today Mumbai), where a religious holiday is annually celebrated in his name. Even today, Ganesha is widely revered as the god of good fortune, as well as a patron of the arts and sciences, and his image is regularly approached by wives hoping to give birth to a child.

9-3 THE ARRIVAL OF ISLAM

Q **Focus Question:** How did Islam arrive in the Indian subcontinent, and why were Muslim peoples able to establish states there?

While India was still undergoing a transition after the collapse of the Gupta Empire, a new and dynamic force in the form of Islam was arising in the Arabian Peninsula to the west. As we have seen, during the seventh and eighth centuries, Arab armies carried the new faith westward to the Iberian Peninsula and eastward across the arid wastelands of Persia and into the rugged mountains of the Hindu Kush. Islam first reached India through the Arabs in the eighth century, but a second onslaught in the tenth and eleventh centuries by Turkic-speaking converts had a more lasting effect (see Map 9.3).

Although Arab merchants had been active along the Indian coasts for centuries, Arab armies did not reach India until the early eighth century. When Indian pirates attacked Arab shipping near the delta of the Indus River, the Muslim ruler in Mesopotamia demanded an apology from the ruler of Sind (SINNED), a Hindu state in the Indus Valley. When the latter refused, Muslim forces conquered lower Sind in 711 and then moved northward into the Punjab (pun-JAHB), bringing Arab rule into the frontier regions of the subcontinent for the first time.

9-3a The Empire of Mahmud of Ghazni

For the next three centuries, Islam made no further advances into India. But a second phase began at the end of the tenth century with the rise of the state of Ghazni (GAHZ-nee), located in the area of the old Kushan kingdom in present-day Afghanistan. The new kingdom was founded in 962 when Turkic-speaking slaves seized power from the Samanids, a Persian dynasty. When the founder of the new state died in 997, his son, Mahmud (MAHKH-mood) of Ghazni (r. 997–1030), succeeded him. Brilliant and ambitious, Mahmud used his patrimony as a base of operations for sporadic forays against neighboring Hindu kingdoms to the southeast. Before his death in 1030, he was able to extend his rule throughout the upper Indus Valley and as far south as the Indian Ocean (see Map 9.4). In wealth and cultural brilliance, his court at Ghazni rivaled that of the Abbasid Dynasty in Baghdad. But he was not universally admired. Describing Mahmud's conquests in northwestern India, the contemporary historian al-Biruni (al-buh-ROO-nee) wrote:

> Mahmud utterly ruined the prosperity of the country, and performed wonderful exploits by which the Hindus became like atoms scattered in all directions, and like a tale of old in the mouth of the people. Their scattered remains cherish, of course, the most inveterate aversion towards all Muslims. This is the reason, too, why Hindu sciences have retired far away from those parts of the country conquered by us, and have fled to places which our hand cannot yet reach, to Kashmir, Benares, and other places.[3]

Resistance against the advances of Mahmud and his successors into northern India was led by the Rajputs (RAHJ-pootz), aristocratic Hindu clans who were probably descended from tribal groups that had penetrated into northwestern India from Central Asia in earlier centuries. The Rajputs possessed a strong military tradition and fought bravely, but their military tactics, based on infantry supported by elephants, were no match for the fearsome cavalry of the invaders, whose ability to strike with lightning speed contrasted sharply with the slow-footed forces of their adversaries. Moreover, the incessant squabbling among the Rajput leaders put them at a disadvantage against the single-minded intensity and religious fervor of Mahmud's armies. Although the power of Ghazni declined after his death, a successor state in the area resumed the advance in the late twelfth century, and soon after 1200, Muslim power, in the form of a new Delhi (DEL-ee) sultanate, had been extended over the entire plain of northern India.

9-3b The Delhi Sultanate

South of the Ganges River Valley, Muslim influence spread more slowly and in fact had little immediate impact. Muslim traders

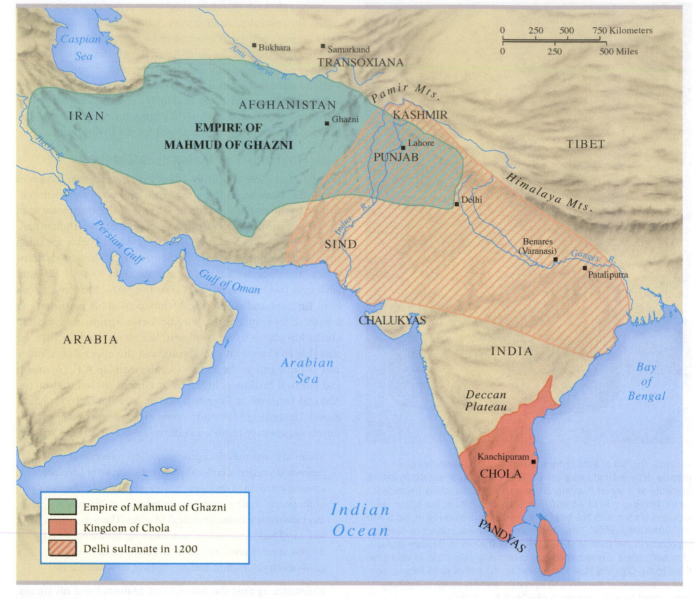

Map 9.4 India, 1000–1200. Beginning in the tenth century, Turkic-speaking peoples invaded northwestern India and introduced Islam to the peoples in the area. Most famous was the empire of Mahmud of Ghazni.

Q *Locate the major trade routes passing through the area. What geographic features explain the location of those routes?*

made some converts along the western coast, and Muslim rulers launched occasional forays into the Deccan Plateau, but the latter had little success, even though the area was divided among a number of warring kingdoms, including the Cholas along the eastern coast and the Pandyas (PUHN-dee-ahz) far to the south.

One reason the Delhi sultanate failed to take advantage of the disarray of its rivals was the threat posed by the Mongols on the northwestern frontier (see Chapter 10). Mongol armies unleashed by the great tribal warrior Genghis Khan occupied Baghdad and destroyed the Abbasid caliphate in the 1250s, while other forces occupied the Punjab around Lahore (luh-HOR), from which they threatened Delhi on several occasions. For the next half-century, the attention

of the sultanate was focused on the Mongols. That threat finally declined in the early fourteenth century with the gradual breakup of the Mongol Empire, and a new Islamic state emerged in the form of the Tughluq (tug-LUK) dynasty (1320–1413), which extended its power into the Deccan Plateau. In praise of his sovereign, the Tughluq monarch Ala-ud-din (uh-LAH-ud-DEEN), the poet Amir Khusrau (ah-MEER KOOS-roh) exclaimed:

Happy be Hindustan, with its splendor of religion,
Where Islamic law enjoys perfect honor and dignity;
In learning Delhi now rivals Bukhara;
Islam has been made manifest by the rulers.
From Ghazni to the very shore of the ocean
You see Islam in its glory.[4]

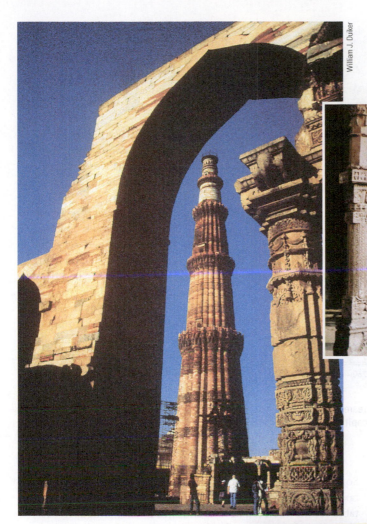

The Kutub Minar. To commemorate their victory in 1192, the Muslim conquerors of northern India constructed a magnificent mosque on the site of the city of Delhi's largest Hindu temple. Much of the material for the mosque came from twenty-seven local Hindu and Jain shrines. Pillars used for the mosque were plastered over to cover up the highly intricate carvings used for the previous Hindu temple (see right photo). Adjacent to the mosque soars the Kutub Minar (KUH-tub mee-NAHR), or "Tower of Victory," an imposing symbol of the new conquering faith. Originally 238 feet high, the tower's inscription proclaimed its mission to cast the long shadow of Allah over the realm of the Hindus.

Such happiness was not destined to endure, however. During the latter half of the fourteenth century, the Tughluq dynasty gradually fell into decline. In 1398, a new military force crossed the Indus River from the northwest, raided the capital of Delhi, and then withdrew. According to some contemporary historians, as many as 100,000 Hindu prisoners were massacred before the gates of the city. Such was India's first encounter with Tamerlane (TAM-ur-layn).

9–3c Tamerlane

Tamerlane (b. 1330s), also known as Timur-i-lang (Timur the Lame), was the ruler of a Mongol khanate based in Samarkand (SAM-ur-kand) to the north of the Pamir (pah-MEER) Mountains. His kingdom had been founded on the ruins of the Mongol Empire, which had begun to disintegrate as a result of succession struggles in the thirteenth

Samarkand, Gem of the Empire. The city of Samarkand has a long history. Originating during the first millennium BCE as a caravan stop on the Silk Road, it was later occupied by Alexander the Great, the Abbasids, and the Mongols before becoming the capital of Tamerlane's expanding empire. Tamerlane expended great sums in creating a city worthy of his imperial ambitions. Shown here is the great square, known as the Registan. Site of a mosque, a library, and a Muslim university, all built in the exuberant Persian style, Samarkand was the jumping-off point for trade with China far to the east.

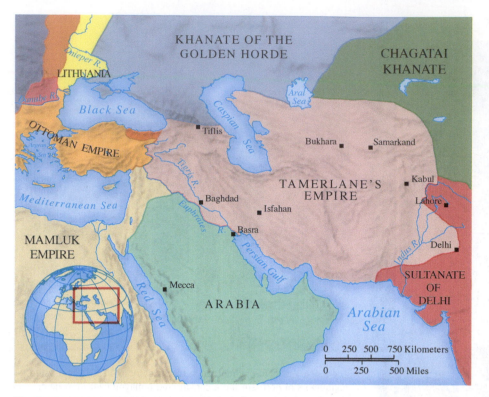

Map 9.5 **The Empire of Tamerlane.** In the fourteenth century, Tamerlane, a feared conqueror of Mongolian extraction, established a brief empire in Central Asia with his capital at Samarkand.

Q *Which of the states in this map were part of Muslim civilization?*

century. The son of a local aristocrat and of mixed Turko-Mongolian heritage, Tamerlane seized power in Samarkand in 1369 and immediately launched a program of conquest. During the 1380s, he brought the entire region east of the Caspian Sea under his authority and then conquered Baghdad and occupied Mesopotamia (see Map 9.5). After his brief foray into northern India, he turned to the west and raided the Anatolian peninsula. Defeating the army of the Ottoman Turks, he advanced almost as far as the Bosporus before withdrawing. "The last of the great nomadic conquerors," as one modern historian described him, died in 1405 in a final military campaign.

The passing of Tamerlane removed a major menace from the diverse states of the Indian subcontinent. But the respite from external challenge was not long. By the end of the fifteenth century, two new challenges had appeared from beyond the horizon: the Mughals, a newly emerging nomadic power beyond the Khyber Pass in the north, and the Portuguese traders, who arrived by sea from the eastern coast of Africa in search of gold and spices. Both, in different ways, would exert a major impact on the later course of Indian civilization.

9–4 SOCIETY AND CULTURE

Q **Focus Questions:** What impact did Muslim rule have on Indian society? To what degree did the indigenous population convert to the new religion, and why?

The establishment of Muslim rule over the northern parts of the subcontinent had a significant impact on the society and culture of the Indian people.

9–4a Religion

Like their counterparts in other areas that came under Islamic rule, some Muslim rulers in India were relatively tolerant of other faiths and used peaceful means, if any, to encourage nonbelievers to convert to Islam. Even the more enlightened, however, could be fierce when their religious zeal was aroused. One ruler, on being informed that a Hindu fair had been held near Delhi, ordered the promoters of the event put to death. Hindu temples were razed, and mosques were erected in their place. Eventually, however, most Muslim rulers realized that not all non-believers could be converted and recognized the necessity of accepting what to them were alien and repugnant religions. While Hindu religious practices were generally tolerated, all non-Muslims were compelled to pay a tax to the state. Some Hindus probably converted to Islam to avoid paying the tax, but they were then expected to make the traditional charitable contribution required of Muslims in all Islamic societies.

Over time, millions of Indians did turn to the Muslim faith. Some were individuals or groups in the employ of the Muslim ruling class, such as government officials, artisans, or merchants catering to the needs of the court. But many others were probably peasants from the *sudra* class or even untouchables who found in the egalitarian message of Islam a way of removing the stigma of low-class status in the Hindu social hierarchy.

Seldom have two major religions been so strikingly different. Where Hinduism tolerated a belief in the existence of several deities (although admittedly they were all considered by some to be manifestations of one supreme god), Islam was uncompromisingly monotheistic. Where Hinduism was hierarchical, Islam was egalitarian. Where Hinduism featured a priestly class to serve as an intermediary with the ultimate force of the universe, Islam permitted no one to come between believers and their god. Such differences contributed to the mutual hostility that developed between the adherents of the two faiths in the Indian subcontinent, but more mundane issues, such as the Muslim habit of eating beef and the idolatry and sexual frankness of Hindu art, were probably a greater source of antagonism at the popular level (see "The Islamic Conquest of India").

In other cases, the two peoples borrowed from each other. Some Muslim rulers found the Indian idea of divine kingship appealing. In their turn, Hindu rajas learned by bitter experience the superiority of cavalry mounted on horses instead of

THE ISLAMIC CONQUEST OF INDIA

ONE CONSEQUENCE OF THE MUSLIM CONQUEST of northern India was the imposition of many Islamic customs on Hindu society. In this excerpt, the eleventh-century Central Asian scholar Abu Rayham Biruni—sometimes known as al-Biruni—describes the conquest of north India by Mahmud of Ghazni and the impact of Islamic beliefs on the conquered population. Biruni had accompanied Mahmud on his campaigns. The author's contempt for Hindu beliefs and practices is apparent, as is his conviction that the relationship between the indigenous population and the Muslim occupiers is inherently hostile.

A Muslim Ruler Suppresses Hindu Practices

[The Hindus] totally differ from us in religion, as we believe in nothing in which they believe, and vice versa. On the whole, there is very little disputing about theological topics among themselves; at the utmost, they fight with words, but they will never stake their soul or body or their property on religious controversy. On the contrary, all their fanaticism is directed against those who do not belong to them—against all foreigners. They call them *mleccha*, i.e., impure, and forbid having any connection with them, be it by intermarriage or any other kind of relationship, or by sitting, eating, and drinking with them, because thereby, they think, they would be polluted. . . . They are not allowed to receive anybody who does not belong to them, even if he wished it, or was inclined to their religion. This too, renders any connection with them quite impossible and constitutes the widest gulf between us and them . . .

But then came Islam; the Persian empire perished, and the repugnance of the Hindus against foreigners increased more and more when the Muslims began to make their inroads into their country, for Muhammad Ibn Qasim entered Sindh [in 711], . . . sometimes fighting sword in hand, sometimes gaining his ends by treaties, leaving to the people their ancient belief, except in the case of those who wanted to become Muslims. All these events planted a deeply rooted hatred in their hearts.

 How does the description of the Muslim conquest of India, as described here, compare with the approaches adopted by Muslim rulers in African and Asian societies as described in Chapters 7 and 8?

Source: A. T. Embree (ed.), *Sources of Indian Tradition*, Vol. I, 2nd ed. (New York, 1988), pp. 437–438, citing E. C. Sachau (tr.), *Alberuni's India*, pp. 19–22.

---

elephants, the primary assault weapon in early India. Some upper-class Hindu males were attracted to the Muslim tradition of *purdah* (PUR-duh *or* POOR-duh) and began to keep their women in seclusion (termed locally "behind the curtain") from everyday society. Hindu sources claimed that one reason for adopting the custom was to protect Hindu women from the roving eyes of foreigners. But it is likely that many Indian families adopted the practice for reasons of prestige or because they were convinced that *purdah* was a practical means of protecting female virtue. Adult Indian women had already begun to cover their heads with a scarf during the Gupta era.

All in all, Muslim rule probably did not have a significant impact on the lives of most Indian women (see Comparative Essay "Caste, Class, and Family," p. 255). *Purdah* was more commonly practiced among high castes than among the lower castes. Though it was probably of little consolation, relations between the genders were relatively egalitarian in poor and low-class families, as men and women worked together on press gangs or in the fields. Muslim customs apparently had little effect on the Hindu tradition of *sati* (widow burning) (see "The Practice of *Sati*," p. 254). In fact, in many respects, Muslim women had more rights than their Hindu counterparts. They had more property rights than Hindu women and were legally permitted to divorce under certain conditions and to remarry after the death of their husband. The primary role for Indian women in general, however, was to produce children. Sons were preferred over daughters, not only because they alone could conduct ancestral rites but also because a

daughter was a financial liability. A father had to provide a costly dowry for his daughter when she married, yet after the wedding, she would transfer her labor and assets to her husband's family. Still, women shared with men a position in the Indian religious pantheon. The cult of the mother-goddess, which had originated in the Harappan era, revived during the Gupta era stronger than ever. The Hindu female deity known as Devi (DAY-vee) was celebrated by both men and women as the source of cosmic power, bestower of wishes, and symbol of fertility.

Overall, the Muslims continued to view themselves as foreign conquerors and generally maintained a strict separation between the Muslim ruling class and the mass of the Hindu population. Although a few Hindus rose to important positions in the local bureaucracy, most high posts in the central government and the provinces were reserved for Muslims. Only with the founding of the Mughal Dynasty was a serious effort undertaken to reconcile the differences.

One result of this effort was the religion of the Sikhs (SEEKS *or* see-ikhz) ("disciples"). Founded by the guru Nanak (NAH-nuhk) in the early sixteenth century in the Punjab, Sikhism attempted to integrate the best of the two faiths in a single religion. Sikhism originated in the devotionalist movement in Hinduism, which taught that God was the single true reality. All else is illusion. But Nanak rejected the Hindu tradition of asceticism and mortification of the flesh and, like Muhammad, taught his disciples to participate in the world. Sikhism achieved considerable popularity in northwestern India, where

THE PRACTICE OF *SATI*

Family & Society

IN THE COURSE OF HIS EXTENSIVE TRAVELS throughout Africa and Asia, the Muslim diarist Ibn Battuta—whom we first encountered in Chapters 7 and 8—spent several months in Muslim-held territories in India. In the following excerpt, he describes the Hindu practice of *sati*, in which a widow immolates herself on her deceased husband's funeral pyre as a means of expressing her fealty to her lord and master.

The Travels of Ibn Battuta

In this part, I also saw those women who burn themselves when their husbands die. The woman adorns herself, and is accompanied by a cavalcade of the infidel Hindus and Brahmans, with drums, trumpets, and men, following her, both Moslems and Infidels for mere pastime. The fire had been already kindled, and into it they threw the dead husband. The wife then threw herself upon him, and both were entirely burnt. A woman's burning herself, however, with her husband is not considered as absolutely necessary among them, but it is encouraged; and when a woman burns herself with her husband, her family is considered as being ennobled, and supposed to be worthy of trust. But when she does not burn herself, she is ever after clothed coarsely, and remains in constraint among her relations, on account of her want of fidelity to her husband.

The woman who burns herself with her husband is generally surrounded by women, who bid her farewell, and commission her with salutations for their former friends, while she laughs, plays, or dances to the very time in which she is to be burnt.

Some of the Hindus, moreover, drown themselves in the river Ganges to which they perform pilgrimages; and into which they pour the ashes of those who have been burnt. When any one intends to drown himself, he opens his mind on the subject to one of his companions, and says: You are not to suppose that I do this for the sake of anything worldly; my only motive is to draw near to Kisaī, which is a name of God with them. And when he is drowned, they draw him out of the water, burn the body, and pour the ashes into the Ganges.

 Why do historians evaluate documents such as this one with caution? Are there reasons to doubt the reliability of a report by a Muslim on conditions in Hindu civilization? What evidence do you find in this selection that Ibn Battuta was approaching Hindu society from the perspective of his own experience and applying the values of his own culture?

Source: S. Lee (trans.), *The Travels of Ibn Battuta in the Near East, Asia, and Africa, 1325–1354* (Mineola, NY, 2004), pp. 108–110.

Islam and Hinduism confronted each other directly, and eventually evolved into a militant faith that fiercely protected its adherents against its two larger rivals. In the end, Sikhism did not reconcile Hinduism and Islam but provided an alternative to them.

Class and Caste One complication for both Muslims and Hindus as they tried to come to terms with the existence of a mixed society was the problem of class and caste (see Comparative Essay "Caste, Class, and Family"). Could non-Hindus form castes, and if so, how were these castes related to the Hindu castes? Where did the Turkic-speaking elites who made up the ruling class in many of the Islamic states fit into the equation?

The problem was resolved in a pragmatic manner that probably followed an earlier tradition of assimilating non-Hindu tribal groups into the system. Members of the Turkic-speaking ruling groups formed social groups that were roughly equivalent to the Hindu *brahmin* or *kshatriya* class. During the Delhi sultanate in the north, members of the local Rajput nobility who converted to Islam were occasionally permitted to join such class groupings. Ordinary Indians who converted to Islam also formed Muslim castes, although at a lower level on the social scale. Many who did so were probably artisans who converted en masse to obtain the privileges that conversion could bring.

In most of India, then, Muslim rule did not substantially disrupt the class and caste system, although it may have become more fluid than was formerly the case. One perceptive European visitor in the early sixteenth century reported that in Malabar (MAL-uh-bar), along the southwestern coast, there were separate castes for fishing, pottery making, weaving, carpentry and metalworking, salt mining, sorcery, and labor on the plantations. There were separate castes for doing the laundry, one for the elite and the other for the common people.

9–4b Economy and Daily Life

India's landed and commercial elites lived in the cities, often in conditions of considerable opulence. The rulers, of course, possessed the most wealth. One maharaja of a relatively small state in southern India, for example, had more than 100,000 soldiers in his pay along with 900 elephants and 20,000 horses. Another maintained a thousand high-caste women to serve as sweepers of his palace. Each carried a broom and a brass basin containing a mixture of cow dung and water and followed him from one house to another, plastering the path where he was to tread. Most urban dwellers did not live in

COMPARATIVE ESSAY

Caste, Class, and Family

Family & Society Why have men and women played such different roles throughout human history? Why have some societies historically adopted the nuclear family, while others preferred the joint family or the clan? Such questions are controversial and often subject to vigorous debate, yet they are crucial to our understanding of the human experience.

As we know, the first human beings practiced hunting and foraging, living in small bands composed of one or more lineage groups and moving from place to place in search of sustenance. Individual members of the community were assigned different economic and social roles—usually with men as the hunters and women as the food gatherers—but such roles were not rigidly defined. The concept of private property did not exist, and all members shared the goods possessed by the community according to need.

The agricultural revolution brought about dramatic changes in human social organizations. Although women, as food gatherers, may have been the first farmers, men—now increasingly deprived of their traditional role as hunters—began to replace them in the fields. As communities gradually adopted a sedentary lifestyle, women were increasingly assigned to domestic tasks in the home while raising the children. As farming communities grew in size and prosperity, vocational specialization and the concept of private property appeared, leading to the family as a legal entity and the emergence of a class system composed of elites, commoners, and slaves. Women were deemed inferior to men and placed in a subordinate status.

This trend toward job specialization and a rigid class system was less developed in pastoral societies, some of which still practiced a nomadic style of life and shared communal goods on a roughly equal basis within the community. Even within sedentary societies, there was considerable variety in the nature of social organizations. In some areas, the nuclear family consisted of parents and their dependent children. Other societies, however, adopted (either in theory or in practice) the idea of the joint family (ideally consisting of

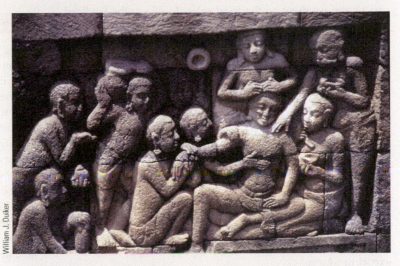

William J. Duiker

The Good Life. On the walls of the Buddhist temple of Borobudur are a series of bas-reliefs in stone depicting the path to enlightenment. The lower levels depict the pleasures of the material world. Shown here is a woman of leisure, assisted by her maidservants, at her toilette.

three generations of a family living under one roof) and sometimes, even going a step further, linked several families under the larger grouping of the caste or the clan. Prominent examples of the latter tendency include India and China, although the degree to which reality conformed to such concepts is a matter of debate.

Such large social organizations, where they occurred, often established a rigid hierarchy of status within the community, including the subordination of women. At the same time, they sometimes played a useful role in society, providing a safety net or a ladder of upward mobility for disadvantaged members of the group, as well as a source of stability in societies where legitimate and effective authority at the central level was lacking.

 What were some of the unique aspects of community and family life in traditional India? What do you think accounts for these unique characteristics?

such style, although, according to the Chinese Buddhist missionary Xuan Zang, many urban dwellers lived their lives in relative comfort:

> Their houses are surrounded by low walls. . . . The earth being soft and muddy, the walls of the towns are mostly built of brick or tiles. The towers on the walls are constructed of wood or

bamboo; the houses have balconies and belvederes, which are made of wood, with a coating of lime or mortar, and covered with tiles. The different buildings have the same form as those in China; rushes, or dry branches, or tiles, or boards are used for covering them. The walls are covered with lime and mud, mixed with cow's dung for purity. At different seasons they scatter flowers about. Such are some of their different customs.[5]

Agriculture The majority of India's population (estimated at slightly more than 100 million by the year 1000), however, lived on the land. Most were peasants who tilled small plots with a wooden plow pulled by oxen and paid a percentage of the harvest to their landlord. The landlord in turn forwarded part of the payment to the local ruler. In effect, the landlord functioned as a tax collector for the king, who retained ultimate ownership of all farmland in his domain. At best, most peasants lived at the subsistence level. At worst, they were forced into debt and fell victim to moneylenders who charged exorbitant rates of interest.

In the north and in the upland regions of the Deccan Plateau, the primary grain crops were wheat and barley. In the Ganges Valley and the southern coastal plains, the main crop was rice. Vegetables were grown everywhere, and southern India produced many spices and fruits, as well as sugarcane and cotton, both of which were gradually transported westward by the Arabs. Sugarcane was first cultivated in Southeast Asia, while the cotton plant apparently originated in the Indus River Valley and spread from there. Spices such as cinnamon, pepper, ginger, sandalwood, cardamom, and cumin were also major export products.

Foreign Trade Agriculture, of course, was not the only source of wealth in India. Since ancient times, the subcontinent had served as a major entrepôt for trade between the Middle East and the Pacific basin, as well as the source of other goods shipped throughout the known world. Although civil strife and piracy, heavy taxation of the business community by local rulers to finance their fratricidal wars, and increased customs duties between principalities may have contributed to a decline in internal trade, the level of foreign trade remained high, particularly in the Dravidian-speaking kingdoms in the south and along the northwestern coast, which were located along the traditional trade routes to the Middle East and the Mediterranean Sea. Much of this foreign trade was carried on by wealthy Hindu castes with close ties to the royal courts. But there were other participants as well, including such non-Hindu minorities as the Muslims, Jews from the Middle East, the Parsis (PAR-seez), and the Jains. The Parsis, expatriates from Persia who practiced the Zoroastrian religion, dominated banking and the textile industry in the cities bordering the Rann of Kutch (RUN of KUTCH). Later they would become a major economic force in the modern city of Mumbai (Bombay). The Jains became prominent in trade and manufacturing even though their faith emphasized simplicity and the rejection of materialism.

According to early European travelers, merchants often lived quite well. One Portuguese observer described the "Moorish" population in Bengal as follows:

> They have girdles of cloth, and over them silk scarves; they carry in their girdles daggers garnished with silver and gold, according to the rank of the person who carries them; on their fingers many rings set with rich jewels, and cotton turbans on their heads. They are luxurious, eat well and spend freely, and have many other extravagances as well. They bathe often

in great tanks which they have in their houses. Everyone has three or four wives or as many as he can maintain. They keep them carefully shut up, and treat them very well, giving them great store of gold, silver and apparel of fine silk.[6]

HISTORIANS DEBATE **The Indian Economy: Promise Unfulfilled?**
Outside these relatively small, specialized trading communities, most manufacturing and commerce were in the hands of petty traders and artisans, who were generally limited to local markets. This failure to build on the promise of antiquity has led some historians to ask why India failed to produce an expansion of commerce and growth of cities similar to the developments that began in Europe during the High Middle Ages or even in China during the Song Dynasty (see Chapter 10). Some have pointed to the traditionally low status of artisans and merchants in Indian society, symbolized by the comment in the *Arthasastra* that merchants were "thieves that are not called by the name of thief."[7] Yet commercial activities were frowned on in many areas in Europe throughout the Middle Ages, a fact that did not prevent the emergence of capitalist societies in much of the West.

Another factor may have been the monopoly on foreign trade held by the government in many areas of India. More important, perhaps, was the impact of the class and caste system, which reduced the ability of entrepreneurs to expand their activities and have dealings with other members of the commercial and manufacturing community. Successful artisans, for example, normally could not set up as merchants to market their products, nor could merchants compete for buyers outside their normal area of operations. The complex interlocking relationships among the various classes in a given region were a powerful factor inhibiting the development of a thriving commercial sector in medieval India.

Science and Technology Still, Indian thinkers played an important role during this period in promoting knowledge of the sciences throughout the Eurasian world. One example is the fifth-century astronomer Aryabhata (AHR-yuh-BAH-tuh), who accurately calculated the value of pi and measured the length of the solar year at slightly more than 365 days. Indian writings on astronomy, mathematics, and medicine were influential elsewhere in the region, while, as noted in Chapter 7, the Indian system of numbers, including the concept of zero, was introduced into the Middle East and ultimately replaced the Roman numerals then in use in medieval Europe.

9–4c The Wonder of Indian Culture

The era between the Mauryas and the Mughals in India was a period of cultural evolution as Indian writers and artists built on the literary and artistic achievements of their predecessors. This is not to say, however, that Indian culture rested on its ancient laurels. To the contrary, it was an era of tremendous innovation in all fields of creative endeavor.

Art and Architecture At the end of antiquity, the primary forms of religious architecture were the Buddhist cave temples

William J. Duiker

The Beauty of Sigiriya. Closely linked to Indian art and culture are a series of surviving paintings at the sixth-century rock fortress at Sigiriya, on the island of Sri Lanka. Portraits of dancers and serving girls from the king's harem were painted high up along the cliff wall. Many of these paintings dealt with secular subjects and therefore were destroyed by Buddhist monks when they returned to the area after the king's death. Thankfully, a few of these graceful, languid maidens–such as the one shown here–were left unharmed to captivate viewers over the centuries.

and monasteries. The next millennium witnessed the evolution of religious architecture from underground cavity to monumental structure.

The twenty-eight caves of Ajanta (uh-JUHN-tuh) in the Deccan Plateau (see Chapter 2) are among India's greatest artistic achievements. They are as impressive for their sculptures and paintings as for their architecture. Except for a few examples from the second century BCE, most of the caves were carved out of solid rock over an incredibly short period of eighteen years, from 460 to 478 CE. In contrast to the early unadorned temple halls, these caves were exuberantly decorated with ornate pillars, friezes, beamed ceilings, and statues of the Buddha and bodhisattvas. Several caves served as monasteries, which by then had been transformed from simple holes in the wall to large complexes with living apartments, halls, and shrines to the Buddha. Other temples, such as the one at Ellora (eh-LOR-uh), were carved directly out of the mountains (see Comparative Illustration "Rock Architecture," Section 8-2c, p. 226).

All of the inner surfaces of the caves, including the ceilings, sculptures, walls, door frames, and pillars, were painted in vivid colors. Perhaps best known are the wall paintings, which illustrate the

various lives and incarnations of the Buddha. These paintings are in an admirable state of preservation, making it possible to reconstruct the customs, dress, house interiors, and physical characteristics of the peoples of fifth-century India. Similar rock paintings focusing on secular subjects can be found at Sigiriya (see-gee-REE-uh), a fifth-century royal palace on the island of Sri Lanka. As a defensive measure, the palace was located on top of a gigantic volcanic rock.

Among the most impressive rock carvings in southern India are the cave temples at Mamallapuram (also known as Mahabalipuram), south of the modern city of Chennai (Madras). The sculpture, called *Descent of the Ganges River*, depicts the role played by Shiva in intercepting the heavenly waters of the Ganges and allowing them to fall gently on the earth. Mamallapuram also boasts an eighth-century shore temple (see illustration "Mamallapuram Shore Temple," Section 9-2c, p. 247), which is one of the earliest surviving freestanding structures in the subcontinent.

From the eighth century until the time of the Mughals, Indian architects built a multitude of magnificent Hindu temples, now constructed exclusively aboveground. Each temple consisted of a central shrine surmounted by a sizable tower, a hall for worshipers, a vestibule, and a porch, all set in a rectangular courtyard that might also contain other minor shrines. Temples became progressively more ornate until the eleventh century, when sculpture began to dominate the structure. The towers became higher and the temple complexes more intricate, some becoming virtual walled compounds set one within the other and resembling small towns.

William J. Duiker

Descent of the Ganges River. One of India's most outstanding sculptures is found at Mamallapuram, an eighth-century Hindu temple on the eastern coast south of Chennai (Madras). This open relief, known as the *Descent of the Ganges River*, is about 20 feet high and 80 feet long. It portrays Shiva's effort to deflect the waters of the heavenly River Ganges on his head to spare the earth from destruction. Although it presents a rich panorama of gods, animals, and men, the gentle elephants in particular delight one and all.

The greatest example of medieval Hindu temple art, however, is probably Khajuraho (khah-joo-RAH-hoh). Of the original eighty-five temples, dating from the tenth century, twenty-five remain standing today. All of the towers are buttressed at various levels on the sides, giving the whole a sense of unity and creating a vertical movement similar to Mount Kailasa (ky-LAH-suh) in the Himalayas, sacred to Hindus. Everywhere the viewer is entertained by voluptuous temple dancers bringing life to the massive structures. One is removing a thorn from her foot, another is applying eye makeup, and yet another is wringing out her hair.

In the Deccan Plateau, a different style prevailed. The southern temple style was marked by massive oblong stone towers, some 200 feet high. The towers were often covered with a profusion of sculpted figures and were visible for miles. The walls surrounding the temple complex were also surmounted with impressive gate towers, known as *gopuras* (GOH-pur-uhz). Craftsmen in the southern states also won plaudits for the high quality of their bronze statues, many of them portraying Indian deities such as Shiva and Vishnu and designed for use in Hindu religious rituals and ceremonies. Unlike the famous ritual bronzes of ancient China, Indian bronze work relied on the lost-wax method described in Chapter 3.

Literature During this period, Indian authors produced a prodigious number of written works, both religious and secular. Indian religious poetry was written in Sanskrit and also in the languages of southern India. As Hinduism was transformed from a contemplative to a more devotional religion, its poetry became more ardent and erotic and prompted a sense of divine ecstasy. Much of the religious verse extolled the lives and heroic acts of Shiva, Vishnu, Rama, and Krishna by repeating the same themes over and over. In the eighth century, a tradition of poet-saints inspired by intense mystical devotion to a particular deity emerged in southern India. Many were women who sought to escape the drudgery of domestic toil through an imagined sexual union with the god-lover.

The great secular literature of traditional India was also written in Sanskrit in the form of poetry, drama, and prose. Some of the best medieval Indian poetry is found in single-stanza poems, which create an entire emotional scene in just a few lines. Witness this poem by the poet Amaru (am-uh-ROO):

> *We'll see what comes of it, I thought,*
> *and I hardened my heart against her.*
> *What, won't the villain speak to me? She*
> *thought, flying into a rage.*
> *And there we stood, sedulously refusing to look one*
> *another in the face,*
> *Until at last I managed an unconvincing laugh,*
> *and her tears robbed me of my resolution.*[8]

One of India's most famous authors was Kalidasa (kahlee-DAH-suh), who lived during the Gupta dynasty. Although little is known of him, including his dates, he probably wrote for the court of Chandragupta II (r. 375–415). Even today, Kalidasa's hundred-verse creation *The Cloud Messenger* remains one of the most popular Sanskrit poems. But Kalidasa was also a

Dancing Shiva. From the tenth to the twelfth centuries CE, the southern kingdom of Chola excelled in the use of the lost-wax technique to make portable bronze statues of Hindu gods. Bathed, clothed, and decorated with flowers, these Chola bronzes were then paraded in religious ceremonies. One of the most numerous and iconic of these bronze deities was the dancing Shiva. As shown here, the statue portrays Shiva performing a cosmic dance in which he simultaneously creates and destroys the universe. While his upper right hand creates the cosmos, his upper left hand reduces it in flames. With his right foot, Shiva crushes the back of the dwarf of ignorance. Shiva's dancing statues visually convey to his followers the message of his power and compassion.

great dramatist. He wrote three plays, all dramatic romances that blend the erotic with the heroic and the comic. *Shakuntala*, perhaps the best-known play in all Indian literature, tells the story of a king who, while out hunting, falls in love with the maiden Shakuntala. He asks her to marry him and offers her a ring of betrothal but is suddenly recalled to his kingdom on urgent business. Shakuntala, who is pregnant, goes to him, but the king has been cursed by a hermit and no longer recognizes her. With the help of the gods, the king eventually recalls their love and is reunited with Shakuntala and their son.

Kalidasa was one of the greatest Indian dramatists, but he was by no means the only one. Sanskrit plays typically contained one to ten acts. They were performed in theaters in the palaces or in court temples by troupes of actors of both sexes who were trained and supported by the royal family. The plots were usually taken from Indian legends of gods and kings. No scenery or props were used, but costumes and makeup were elaborate. The theaters had to be small because much of the drama was conveyed through intricate gestures and dance conventions. There were many different positions for various parts of the body, including one hundred for the hands alone.

Like poetry, prose developed in India from the Vedic period. The use of prose was well established by the sixth and seventh centuries CE. This is truly astonishing considering that the novel did not appear until the tenth century in Japan and until the seventeenth century in Europe. One of the greatest masters of Sanskrit prose was Dandin (DUN-din), who lived during the seventh century. In *The Ten Princes*, he created a fantastic and exciting world that fuses history and fiction. His keen powers of observation, details of low life, and humor give his writing considerable vitality.

Music Another area of Indian creativity that developed during this era was music. Ancient Indian music had come from the chanting of the Vedic hymns and thus had a strong metaphysical and spiritual flavor. The actual physical vibrations of music (*nada*) were believed to be related to the spiritual world. An off-key or sloppy rendition of a sacred text could upset the harmony and balance of the entire universe.

In form, Indian classical music is based on a scale, called a *raga* (RAH-guh). There are dozens, if not hundreds, of separate scales, which are grouped into separate categories depending on the time of day during which they are to be performed. The performers use a stringed instrument called a *sitar* (si-TAHR) and various types of wind instruments and drums. The performers select a basic *raga* and then are free to improvise the melodic structure and rhythm. A good performer never performs a particular *raga* the same way twice. As with jazz music in the West, the audience is concerned not so much with faithful reproduction as with the performer's creativity.

9–5 THE GOLDEN REGION: EARLY SOUTHEAST ASIA

 Focus Question: What were the main characteristics of Southeast Asian social and economic life, culture, and religion before 1500 CE?

Between China and India lies the region that today is called Southeast Asia. It has two major components: a mainland region extending southward from the Chinese border down to the tip of the Malay Peninsula and an extensive archipelago, most of which is part of present-day Indonesia and the Philippines. Travel among the islands and toward regions to the west, north, and east was not difficult, so Southeast Asia has historically served as a vast land bridge for the movement of peoples between China, the Indian subcontinent, and the more than 25,000 islands of the South Pacific. The first arrivals probably appeared as long as 70,000 years ago, as part of the initial exodus of *Homo sapiens* from Africa. The final destination for some of these peoples was Australia, where their descendants, known today as aborigines, still live.

Mainland Southeast Asia consists of several north-south mountain ranges, separated by river valleys that run in a southerly or southeasterly direction. Much of the population of the region consists of descendants of migrants who came down the valleys from China or Tibet centuries ago in search of new homelands. One of the earliest were **Malayo-Polynesian** (muh-LAY-oh-pah-leh-NEE-zhun) speakers who had previously lived along the southeastern coast of China. Then came the Thai (TY) from southwestern China and the Burmese from the Tibetan highlands. Once in Southeast Asia, most of these migrants settled in the fertile deltas of the rivers—the Irrawaddy (ir-uh-WAH-dee) and the Salween (SAL-ween) in Burma, the Chao Phraya (chow PRY-uh) in Thailand, and the Red River and the Mekong (MAY-kahng) in Vietnam. Some of the Malayo-Polynesian speakers eventually moved down the Malay Peninsula or into the islands of the Indonesian archipelago. The ethnic Vietnamese people, as we shall see in Chapter 11, were a special case.

Although the river valleys facilitated north-south travel on the Southeast Asian mainland, movement between east and west was relatively difficult. The mountains are densely forested and infested with malaria-carrying mosquitoes. Consequently, the lowland peoples in the river valleys were often isolated from each other and had only limited contacts with upland peoples in the mountains. These geographic barriers may help explain why mainland Southeast Asia is one of the few regions in Asia that was never unified under a single government. Communication among peoples living in the Malay Peninsula and the southern islands, however, was relatively easy.

9–5a Paddy Fields and Spices: The States of Southeast Asia

The first states of Southeast Asia began gradually to emerge in the first millennium CE and can be broadly divided between agricultural and trading societies. The distinction between farming and commerce was a product of the environment. The agricultural societies—notably, Vietnam, Thailand, Angkor (AN-kor) in what is now Cambodia, and the Burmese state of Pagan (puh-GAHN)—were situated in fertile river deltas that were conducive to the development of a wet rice economy (see Map 9.6). As in India and China, the cultivation of wet rice led to an expanding population and eventually to the formation of states. Although all produced some goods for regional markets, they were not situated in areas that naturally produced large qualities of export goods, such as spices and other tropical products. As a result, they were not tempted to turn to commerce as the prime source of national income. The emerging societies on the Malay Peninsula and the Indonesian archipelago, on the other hand, were not only rich in the highly desired spices and aromatic woods so fervently prized in regional markets, but they were also located at the nexus of trade routes stretching between the South China Sea and the Indian Ocean. As a result, they early in time became actively involved in the regional trade that passed between China and the Indian subcontinent.

The Mainland States One exception to this general rule was the kingdom of Funan (FOO-nan), which arose in the fertile

Map 9.6 Southeast Asia in the Thirteenth Century. This map shows the major states that arose in Southeast Asia after the year 1000 CE. Some, such as Angkor and Dai Viet, were predominantly agricultural. Others, such as Srivijaya and Champa, were commercial.

Q *How did geography influence whether states were primarily agricultural or commercial?*

valley of the lower Mekong River in the second century CE. At that time, much of the regional trade between India and the South China Sea moved across the narrow neck of the Malay Peninsula. With access to copper, tin, and iron, as well as a variety of tropical agricultural products, Funan played an active role in this process, and Oc Eo (ohk-EEOH), on the Gulf of Thailand, became one of the primary commercial ports in the region. Funan declined in the fifth century, when trade began to pass through the Strait of Malacca (muh-LAK-uh), and it was eventually replaced by the great kingdom of Angkor.

Angkor was the most powerful state to emerge in mainland Southeast Asia before the sixteenth century (see "The Kingdom of Angkor"). The remains of its capital city, Angkor Thom (AN-kor TOHM), give a sense of the magnificence of Angkor civilization. The city center formed a square 2 miles on each side. Its massive stone walls were several feet thick and were surrounded

by a moat. Four main gates led into the city, which at its height had a substantial population, much of it located in suburban areas outside the extensive city wall. Like its predecessor Funan, the wealth of Angkor was based on both agriculture and trade, although it heavily depended upon the cultivation of wet rice, which had been introduced to the Mekong River Valley from China in the third millennium BCE. Other products were honey, textiles, fish, and salt. By the fourteenth century, however, Angkor had begun to decline, a product of incessant wars with its neighbors, drought, overpopulation, and the silting up of its irrigation system, and in 1432, Angkor Thom was destroyed by the Thai, who had migrated into the region from southwestern China in the thirteenth century and established their capital at Ayuthaya (ah-yoo-TY-yuh), in lower Thailand, in 1351.

As the Thai expanded southward, however, their main competition came from the west, where the Burmese peoples had formed their own agricultural society in the valleys of the Salween and Irrawaddy Rivers. Like the Thai, they were relatively recent arrivals in the area, having migrated southward from the highlands of Tibet beginning in the seventh century CE. After subjugating weaker societies already living in the area, in the eleventh century they founded the first great Burmese state, the kingdom of Pagan. Like the Thai, they quickly converted to Buddhism and adopted many aspects of Indian political institutions and culture. For a while, they were a major force in the western part of Southeast Asia, but attacks from the Mongols in the late thirteenth century (see Chapter 10) weakened Pagan, and the resulting vacuum may have benefited the Thai as they moved into areas occupied by Burmese migrants in the Chao Phraya Valley.

The Malay World In the Malay Peninsula and the Indonesian archipelago, a different pattern emerged. For centuries, this area had been linked to regional trade networks and, as

Rice Culture in Southeast Asia. Rice was first cultivated in southern Asia seven or eight thousand years ago. It is a labor-intensive crop that requires many workers to plant the seedlings and organize the distribution of water. Initially, the fields are flooded to facilitate the rooting of the rice seedlings and add nutrients to the soil. In this photograph, workers are performing the backbreaking task of transplanting rice seedlings in a flooded field in modern Vietnam.

The significance of rice in Southeast Asia is reflected in the fact that all cultures in the region have traditionally venerated its sacred nature by creating elaborate rituals to the rice goddess. In Indonesia, the worship of Dewi Sri has long been essential to assure a good harvest.

THE KINGDOM OF ANGKOR

Interaction & Exchange

ANGKOR WAS THE GREATEST KINGDOM of its time in Southeast Asia. This passage was written in the thirteenth century by the Chinese customs inspector Chau Ju-kua (zhow RU-gwah), in the city of Quanzhou (CHWAHN-JOE) (sometimes called Zaiton) on the southern coast of China. His account, compiled from reports of seafarers, includes a brief description of the capital city, Angkor Thom, which is still one of the great archaeological sites of the region. Angkor was already in decline when Chau Ju-kua described the kingdom, and the capital was abandoned in 1432.

Chau Ju-kua, *Records of Foreign Nations*

The officials and the common people dwell in houses with sides of bamboo matting and thatched with reeds. Only the king resides in a palace of hewn stone. It has a granite lotus pond of extraordinary beauty with golden bridges, some three hundred odd feet long. The palace buildings are solidly built and richly ornamented. The throne on which the king sits is made of gharu wood and the seven precious substances; the dais is jewelled, with supports of veined wood [possibly ebony]; the screen [behind the throne] is of ivory.

When all the ministers of state have audience, they first make three full prostrations at the foot of the throne; they then kneel and remain thus, with hands crossed on their breasts, in a circle round the king, and discuss the affairs of state. When they have finished, they make another prostration and retire. . . .

[The people] are devout Buddhists. There are serving [in the temples] some three hundred foreign women; they dance and offer food to the Buddha. They are called *a-nan* or slave dancing girls.

As to their customs, lewdness is not considered criminal; theft is punished by cutting off a hand and a foot and by branding on the chest.

The incantations of the Buddhist and Taoist priests [of this country] have magical powers. Among the former those who wear yellow robes may marry, while those who dress in red lead ascetic lives in temples. The Taoists clothe themselves with leaves; they have a deity called P'o-to-li which they worship with great devotion.

[The people of this country] hold the right hand to be clean, the left unclean, so when they wish to mix their rice with any kind of meat broth, they use the right hand to do so and also to eat with.

The soil is rich and loamy; the fields have no bounds. Each one takes as much as he can cultivate. Rice and cereals are cheap; for every tael [1.3 ounces] of lead one can buy two bushels of rice.

The native products comprise elephants' tusks, the *chan* and *su* [varieties of gharu wood], good yellow wax, kingfisher's feathers, . . . resin, foreign oils, ginger peel, goldcolored incense, . . . raw silk and cotton fabrics.

The foreign traders offer in exchange for these gold, silver, porcelainware, sugar, preserves, and vinegar.

Q *Because of the paucity of written records about Angkor society, documents such as this one from a Chinese source are important for the knowledge they provide about local conditions. What does this excerpt tell us about the political system, religious beliefs, and land use in thirteenth-century Angkor?*

Source: Excerpt from Chau Ju-kua: *His Work on the Chinese and Arab Trade in the Twelfth and Thirteenth Centuries,* entitled *Chu-fan-chi,* Friedrich Hirth and W. W. Rockhill, eds., copyright © 1966 by Paragon Reprint.

---

long-distance shipping gradually became more commonplace, much of its wealth had come from the export of tropical products to China, India, and the Middle East. Because the river valleys in the archipelago were generally shorter, the emerging polities in the region tended to be smaller and more decentralized than on the mainland. Nevertheless, the Malay peoples living in the regions were active seafarers, and as the trade networks expanded, the islands of the Indonesian archipelago eventually gave rise to two of the region's most notable trading societies—Srivijaya (sree-vih-JAH-yuh) on the island of Sumatra, and the Javanese kingdom of Majapahit (mah-jah-PAH-hit). Both were major participants in what might be called the "spice road," a maritime equivalent of the Silk Road on the Asian mainland. As the wealth of China, the Arab empire, and then of continental Europe increased, so did the demand for the products of Southeast Asia. Merchant fleets from India and the Arabian Peninsula sailed to the Indonesian islands to buy cloves, pepper, nutmeg, cinnamon, precious woods, and other exotic products coveted by the wealthy. In

the eighth century, Srivijaya, which had been established along the eastern coast of Sumatra around 670, became a powerful commercial state that dominated the trade passing through the Strait of Malacca, at that time the most convenient route from East Asia into the Indian Ocean. The rulers of Srivijaya had helped bring the route to prominence by controlling the pirates who had previously plagued shipping in the strait. Another inducement was Srivijaya's capital at Palembang (pah-lem-BAHNG), a deepwater port where sailors could wait out the monsoon season before making their return voyage. In 1025, however, Chola, one of the kingdoms of southern India and a commercial rival of Srivijaya, inflicted a devastating defeat on the island kingdom. Although Srivijaya survived, it was unable to regain its former dominance, in part because the main trade route had shifted to the east, through the Strait of Sunda (SOON-duh) and directly out into the Indian Ocean. In the late thirteenth century, this shift in trade patterns led to the founding of the new kingdom of Majapahit on the island of Java. In the mid-fourteenth century, Majapahit succeeded in uniting most of the archipelago and perhaps even part of the Southeast Asian mainland under its rule.

Between China and India Given the location of Southeast Asia between China and India, it is not surprising that both of those major civilizations influenced developments within the region. In 111 BCE, the young Vietnamese kingdom, located in the Red River Valley, was conquered by the Han dynasty and remained under Chinese control for more than a millennium (see Chapter 11). Other parts of the region were exposed to varying degrees of Chinese influence, depending on the importance of their trade with the Celestial Empire.

For their part, the Indian states never exerted much political control over Southeast Asia, but their influence was pervasive nonetheless. The first contacts had taken place by the fourth century BCE, when Indian merchants began sailing to Southeast Asia; they were soon followed by Buddhist and Hindu missionaries. Indian influence can be seen in many aspects of Southeast Asian culture, from political and social institutions and religious belief to art and architecture, language, and literature. Basing themselves on models from the Dravidian kingdoms of southern India, Southeast Asian kings claimed to possess special godlike qualities that set them apart from ordinary people. In societies such as Angkor, Indian religious influence was paramount, while the most prominent royal advisers constituted a *brahmin* class on the Indian model. In Pagan and Angkor, some division of the population into separate classes based on occupation and

ethnic background seems to have occurred, although these divisions do not seem to have developed the rigidity of the Indian class system.

India also supplied Southeast Asians with a writing system. The societies of the region had no written scripts for their spoken languages before the arrival of the Indian merchants and missionaries. Indian phonetic symbols were borrowed and used to record the spoken language. Initially, Southeast Asian literature was written in the Indian Sanskrit but eventually came to be written in the local languages. At the same time, Southeast Asian authors borrowed popular Indian themes, such as stories from the Buddhist scriptures and tales from the Ramayana.

Local forms of cultural expression, however, were by no means abandoned. A popular form of entertainment among

CHRONOLOGY	Early Southeast Asia
Chinese conquest of Vietnam	111 BCE
Arrival of Burmese peoples	c. seventh century CE
Formation of Srivijaya	c. 670
Construction of Borobudur	c. eighth century
Creation of Angkor kingdom	c. ninth century
Thai migrations into Southeast Asia	c. thirteenth century
Rise of Majapahit empire	1292
Fall of Angkor kingdom	1432

William J. Duiker

Angkor Wat. The Khmer (kuh-MEER) rulers of Angkor constructed a number of remarkable temples and palaces. Devised as either Hindu or Buddhist shrines, the temples also reflected the power and sanctity of the king. This twelfth-century temple known as Angkor Wat is renowned both for its spectacular architecture and for the thousands of fine bas-reliefs relating Hindu legends and Khmer history. Most memorable are the heavenly dancing maidens and the royal processions with elephants and soldiers.

the common people, the *wayang kulit* (WAH-yahng KOO-lit), or shadow play, may have come originally from India or possibly China, but it became a distinctive art form in Java and other islands of the Indonesian archipelago. In a shadow play, flat leather puppets were manipulated behind an illuminated screen while the narrator recited tales from the Indian classics. The plays were often accompanied by a gamelan (GA-muh-lan), an orchestra composed primarily of percussion instruments such as gongs and drums that apparently originated in Java.

9–5b Daily Life

Because of the diversity of ethnic backgrounds, religions, and cultures, making generalizations about daily life in Southeast Asia during the early historical period is as difficult as it is in Africa. Southeast Asian societies were somewhat more egalitarian and less hierarchical than was the case in nearby regions, and the rigid social distinctions that prevailed in India were less deeply rooted. For example, although the local populations in societies like Angkor and Pagan were classified according to a variety of economic functions, the dividing lines between classes were not as rigid and imbued with religious significance as they were in the Indian subcontinent.

Social Structures Still, traditional societies in the region possessed some clearly hierarchical characteristics. At the top of the social ladder were the hereditary aristocrats, who monopolized both political power and economic wealth and enjoyed a borrowed aura of charisma by virtue of their proximity to the ruler. Some elites lived in the capital, the main source of power, wealth, and foreign influence in the country. Others lived outside the major cities, where they were responsible for maintaining public order and forwarding agricultural taxes to the central government. Some regional elites possessed family ties to the royal family, while others were local potentates who had their own power base, and whose loyalty to the ruling dynasty was contingent upon benefits received.

Below the elite classes lived the mass of the population, composed of farmers, fishers, artisans, and merchants. In most mainland societies, the vast majority were probably rice farmers, living at a bare level of subsistence and paying heavy rents or taxes to a landlord or a local ruler. Some were considered free subjects, while others were indentured to a higher official with ties to the central government. Few of them were actively engaged in commerce except as a consumer of various necessities.

In the Malay world, social relations were generally less formal. Most of the people in the region, whether engaged in farming, fishing, or the crafts, lived in small *kampongs* (KAHM-pahngs) (Malay for "villages") in wooden houses built on stilts to avoid flooding during the monsoon season. Some of the farmers were probably sharecroppers who paid a part of their harvest to a landlord, but the tradition of free farming was strong. Unlike the situation in the mainland states, many were involved in growing or mining products for export, such as tropical food products, precious woods, tin, and precious gems. Most of the regional trade was carried on by local merchants, who purchased products from local growers and then transported them to the major port cities (see "Chinese Traders in the

Philippines," p. 264). During the early state-building era, roads were few and relatively primitive, so most of the trade was transported by small boats down rivers to the major ports along the coast. There the goods were loaded onto larger ships for delivery outside the region. Growers of export goods in areas near the coast were thus indirectly involved in the regional trade network but received few economic benefits from the relationship.

Women and the Family The women of Southeast Asia during this era have been described as the most fortunate in the world. Although most women worked side by side with men in the fields, as in Africa they often played an active role in trading activities. Not only did this lead to a higher literacy rate among women than among their male counterparts, but it also allowed them more financial independence than their counterparts in China and India, a fact that was noticed by the Chinese traveler Zhou Daguan (JOE dah-GWAHN) at the end of the thirteenth century: "In Cambodia it is the women who take charge of trade. For this reason a Chinese arriving in the country loses no time in getting himself a mate, for he will find her commercial instincts a great asset."[9]

Although, as elsewhere, warfare was normally part of the male domain, women sometimes played a role as bodyguards as well. According to Zhou Daguan, women were used to protect the royal family in Angkor, as well as in kingdoms located on the islands of Java and Sumatra. While there is no evidence that such female units ever engaged in battle, they did give rise to wondrous tales of "amazon" warriors in the writings of foreign travelers such as the fourteenth-century Muslim adventurer Ibn Battuta.

One reason for the enhanced status of women in traditional Southeast Asia is that the nuclear family was more common than the joint family system prevalent in China and the Indian subcontinent. Throughout the region, wealth in marriage was passed from the male to the female, in contrast to the dowry system applied in China and India. In most societies, virginity was usually not a valued commodity in brokering a marriage, and divorce proceedings could be initiated by either party. Still, most marriages were monogamous, and marital fidelity was taken seriously.

The relative availability of cultivable land in the region may help explain the absence of joint families. Joint families under patriarchal leadership tend to be found in areas where land is scarce and individual families must work together to conserve resources and maximize income. With the exception of a few crowded river valleys, few areas in Southeast Asia had a high population density per acre of cultivable land. Throughout most of the area, water was plentiful, and the land was relatively fertile. In parts of Indonesia, much of the diet could be supplied by the bountiful produce of wild fruit trees—bananas, coconuts, mangoes, and a variety of other tropical fruits.

9–5c World of the Spirits: Religious Belief

Indian religions also had a profound effect on Southeast Asia. Traditional religious beliefs in the region took the familiar form of spirit worship and animism that we have seen in other cultures. Southeast Asians believed that spirits dwelled in the

CHINESE TRADERS IN THE PHILIPPINES

Interaction & Exchange

FROM EARLY TIMES, the peoples living in the islands south of the East Asian mainland played an active role in the regional trade network between the Chinese coast and the Indian Ocean. This excerpt from a thirteenth-century Chinese account describes the nature of the commercial exchanges that took place between Chinese merchants and the indigenous population in the Philippine Islands. The author of the account, Chau Ju-kua, was a superintendent of trade in South China. His description of the indigenous peoples in the Philippines is one of the few sources on such communities before the arrival of European ships in the sixteenth century.

A Description of Barbarian Peoples

The country of Ma-i [Philippine archipelago] is to the north of P'o-ni [Borneo]. Over a thousand families are settled together along both banks of a creek (or, gully). The natives cover themselves with a sheet of cotton cloth, or hide the lower part of the body with a loincloth.

There are bronze images of gods, of unknown origin, scattered about in the grassy wilderness. Pirates seldom come to this country.

When trading ships enter the anchorage, they stop in front of the officials' place, for that is the place for bartering of the country. After a ship has been boarded, the natives mix freely with the ship's folk. The chiefs are in the habit of using white umbrellas, for which reason the traders offer them as gifts.

The custom of the trade is for the savage traders to assemble in crowds and carry the goods away with them in baskets; and, even if one cannot at first know them, and can but slowly distinguish the men who remove the goods, there will yet be no loss. The savage traders will after this carry these goods on to other islands for barter, and, as a rule, it takes them as much as eight or nine months till they return, when they repay the traders on shipboard with what they have obtained (for the goods). Some, however, do not return within the proper term, for which reason vessels trading with Ma-i are the latest in reaching home. . . .

The products of the country consist of yellow wax, cotton, pearls, tortoise-shell, medicinal betel-nuts and *yü-ta* cloth [abaca textiles]; and (the foreign) traders barter for these porcelain, trade-gold, iron censers, lead, coloured glass beads, and iron needles. . . .

The San-sü (or "Three Islands"), belong to the Ma-i; their names are Kia-ma-yen (Calamián Island Group between Mindoro and Palawan), Pa-lau-yu (Palawan), and Pa-ki-nung (Busuanga Island, largest of the Calamián Islands), and each has its own tribes scattered over the islands. When ships arrive there, the natives come out to trade with them; the generic name (of these islands) is San-sü.

Their local customs are about the same as those of Ma-i. Each tribe consists of about a thousand families. The country contains many lofty ridges, and ranges of cliffs rise steep as the walls of a house.

The natives build wattled huts perched in lofty and dangerous spots, and since the hills contain no springs, the women may be seen carrying on their heads two or three jars one above the other in which they fetch water from the streams, and with their burdens mount the hills with the same ease as if they were walking on level ground. . . .

Whenever foreign traders arrive at any of the settlements, they live on board ship before venturing to go on shore, their ships being moored in mid-stream, announcing their presence to the natives by beating drums. Upon this the savage traders race for the ship in small boats, carrying cotton, yellow wax, native cloth, cocoanut-heart mats, which they offer for barter. If the prices (of goods they may wish to purchase) cannot be agreed upon, the chief of the (local) traders must go in person, in order to come to an understanding, which being reached the natives are offered presents of silk umbrellas, porcelain, and rattan baskets; but the foreigners still retain on board one or two (natives) as hostages. After that they go on shore to traffic, which being ended they return the hostages. A ship will not remain at anchor longer than three or four days, after which it proceeds to another place; for the savage settlements along the coast of San-sü are not connected by a common jurisdiction (i.e., are all independent).

 How does the trading process take place in this account? How does each side seek to guarantee satisfaction?

Source: From *Chau Ju-kua, His Work on the Chinese and Arab Trade in the Twelfth and Thirteenth Centuries, entitled Chu-fan-chi,* trans. F. Hirth and W. W. Rockhill (St. Petersburg: Printing Office of the Imperial Academy of Sciences, 1911), pp. 159–162.

---

mountains, rivers, streams, and other sacred places in their environment. Mountains were particularly sacred, since they were considered to be the abode of ancestral spirits, the place to which the souls of all the departed would retire after death.

When Hindu and Buddhist ideas began to penetrate the area early in the first millennium CE, they exerted a strong appeal among local elites. Not only did the new doctrines offer a more convincing explanation of the nature of the cosmos, but they also provided local rulers with a means of enhancing their prestige and power and conferred an aura of legitimacy on their relations with their subjects. In the Javanese kingdoms and in Angkor, Hindu gods such as Vishnu and Shiva provided a new and more sophisticated veneer for existing beliefs in nature deities and ancestral spirits. In Angkor, the king's duties included performing sacred rituals on the mountain in the capital city; in time, the ritual became a state cult uniting Hindu gods with local nature deities and ancestral spirits in a complex pantheon.

This state cult, financed by the royal court, eventually led to the construction of temples throughout the country. Many of these temples housed thousands of priests and retainers

William J. Duiker

Mount Agung: Sacred Mountain of Bali. In many traditional Asian societies, as in Classical Greece, mountains were viewed as the abode of the gods, and temples were built in the shape of a mountain to create an earthly representation of a heavenly paradise. But mountains could hold dangers as well. Such is certainly the case with the Indonesian archipelago in Southeast Asia, an island chain formed by volcanic eruptions along a major fault line in the earth's crust. Shown here is beautiful Mount Agung (AH-goong), on the Indonesian island of Bali, still viewed as the local equivalent of sacred Mount Meru (MAY-roo) in India. In Balinese cosmology, the sea is the home of evil spirits, while humans occupy the profane world in between. An active volcano, Agung erupted in 1964, killing thousands of islanders in a cloud of volcanic ash.

and amassed great wealth, including vast estates farmed by local peasants. It has been estimated that there were as many as 300,000 priests in Angkor at the height of its power. This vast wealth, which was often exempt from taxes, may be one explanation for Angkor's gradual decline in the thirteenth and fourteenth centuries. Initially, the spread of Hindu and Buddhist doctrines was essentially an elite phenomenon. Although the common people participated in the state cult and helped construct the temples, they did not give up their traditional beliefs in local deities and ancestral spirits. A major transformation began in the eleventh century, however, when Theravada Buddhism began to penetrate the mainland kingdom of Pagan from the island of Sri Lanka. From Pagan, it spread rapidly to other areas in Southeast Asia and eventually became the religion of the masses throughout the mainland west of the Annamite Mountains (see "The Spread of Buddhism in Southeast Asia").

THE SPREAD OF BUDDHISM IN SOUTHEAST ASIA

Religion & Philosophy   **LIKE FA XIAN AND XUAN ZANG, I-TSING** (635–713) was a Chinese monk who traveled to India in order to study Buddhist teachings. En route home after two decades in South Asia, he stopped at a number of ports in Southeast Asia, including Bhoga (today's Palembang) on the Indonesian island of Sumatra. As this passage indicates, Buddhism had already established a firm beachhead in the region, since many of the local elites had adopted the faith, presumably as a result of contacts with other Buddhist pilgrims and traders from the South Asian subcontinent. Other parts of the region had converted to Brahmanism. Later, both faiths would be replaced by Islam and Christianity.

A Record of the Buddhist Religion as Practised in India and the Malay Archipelago

This [East India] is the place where we embark when returning to China. Sailing from here two months in the south-east direction we come to Ka-cha [Acheh]. By this time a ship from Bhoga [Palembang] will have arrived there. This is generally in the first or second month of the year. But those who go to the Simhala Island [Ceylon] must sail in the southwest direction. They say that the island is 700 yoganas off. We stay in Ka-cha till winter, then start on board ship for the south, and we come after a month to a country of Malayau, which has now become Bhoga; there are many states (under it). The time of

arrival is generally in the first or second month. We stay there till the middle of summer and we sail to the north; in about a month we reach Kwang-fu (Kwang-tung). The first half of the year will be passed by this time.

When we are helped by the power of our (former) good actions, the journey everywhere is as easy and enjoyable as if we went through a market, but, on the other hand, when we have not much influence of Karma, we are often exposed to danger as if (a young one) in a reclining nest. I have thus shortly described the route and the way home, hoping that the wise may still expand their knowledge by hearing more.

Many kings and chieftains in the islands of the Southern Ocean admire and believe (Buddhism), and their hearts are set upon accumulating good actions. In the fortified city of Bhoga Buddhist priests number more than 1,000, whose minds are bent on learning and good practices. They investigate and study all the subjects that exist just as in the Middle Kingdom (Madhya-desa, India); the rules and ceremonies are not at all different. If a Chinese priest wishes to go to the West in order to hear (lectures) and read (the original), he had better stay here one or two years and practice the proper rules and then proceed to Central India.

 Does the author of this account appear to believe that the majority of the population in Acheh consists of fervent disciples of the Buddhist faith? Why or why not?

Source: From I-tsing, *A Record of the Buddhist Religion as Practised in India and the Malay Archipelago*, trans. J. Takakusu (Oxford: Clarendon, 1896), pp. xxxiv–xxxv.

Theravada's appeal to the peoples of Southeast Asia is reminiscent of the original attraction of Buddhist thought centuries earlier on the Indian subcontinent. By teaching that individuals could seek Nirvana through their own actions rather than through the intercession of the ruler or a priest, Theravada was more accessible to the masses than the state cults promoted by the rulers. During the next centuries, Theravada gradually undermined the influence of state-supported religions and became the dominant faith in several mainland societies, including Burma, Thailand, Laos, and Cambodia. In the process, however, it was gradually appropriated by local rulers, who portrayed themselves as "immanent Buddhas," higher than ordinary mortals on the scale of human existence.

Theravada did not penetrate far into the Malay Peninsula or the Indonesian island chain, perhaps because it entered Southeast Asia through Burma farther to the north. But the Malay world found its own popular alternative to state religions when Islam began to enter the area through the arrival of merchants from India and the Middle East in the thirteenth and fourteenth centuries. Because the Muslim expansion into Southeast Asia took place for the most part after 1500, its emergence as a major force in the region will be discussed later in this book (see Chapter 14).

Not surprisingly, Indian influence extended to the Buddhist and Hindu temples of Southeast Asia. Temple architecture reflecting Gupta or southern Indian styles began to appear in Southeast Asia during the first centuries CE. Most famous is the Buddhist temple at Borobudur (boh-roh-buh-DOOR), in central Java. Begun in the late eighth century at the behest of a king of Sailendra (SY-len-druh) (an agricultural kingdom based in eastern Java), Borobudur is a massive stupa with nine terraces. Sculpted on the sides of each terrace are bas-reliefs depicting the nine stages in the life of Siddhartha Gautama, from childhood to his final release from the chain of human existence. Surmounted by hollow bell-like towers containing

William J. Duiker

John Van Hasselt-Corbis/Getty Images

The Temple of Borobudur. The colossal pyramid temple at Borobudur, on the island of Java, is one of the greatest Buddhist monuments. Constructed in the eighth century CE, it depicts the path to spiritual enlightenment in stone. Sculptures and relief portrayals of the life of the Buddha at the lower level depict the world of desire. At higher elevations, they give way to empty bell towers (see right photo) and culminate at the summit with an empty and closed stupa, signifying the final state of Nirvana. Shortly after it was built, Borobudur was abandoned when a new ruler switched his allegiance to Hinduism and ordered the erection of the Hindu temple of Prambanan nearby. Buried for a thousand years under volcanic ash and jungle, Borobudur was rediscovered in the nineteenth century and has recently been restored to its former splendor.

representations of the Buddha and capped by a single stupa, the structure dominates the landscape for miles around.

Second only to Borobudur in technical excellence and even more massive in size are the ruins of the old capital city of Angkor Thom. The temple of Angkor Wat (AN-kor WAHT) is the most famous and arguably the most beautiful of all the existing structures at Angkor Thom. Built on the model of the legendary Mount Meru (the home of the gods in Hindu tradition), it combines Indian architectural techniques with native inspiration in a structure of impressive delicacy and grace.

In existence for more than six hundred years, Angkor Thom serves as a bridge between the Hindu and Buddhist architectural styles. The last of its great temples, known as the Bayon (BAY-on), followed the earlier Hindu model but was topped with sculpted towers containing four-sided representations of a bodhisattva, searching, it is said, for souls to save. Shortly after the Bayon was built, Theravada Buddhist societies in Burma and Thailand began to create a new Buddhist architecture based on the concept of a massive stupa surmounted by a spire. Most famous, perhaps, is the Shwedagon (SCHWEE-da-gahn) Pagoda in Yangon (YAN-gon) (Rangoon), capital of modern Myanmar (Burma), which is covered with gold leaf contributed by devout Buddhists from around the country.

9–5d Expansion into the Pacific

One of the great maritime feats of human history was the penetration of the islands of the Pacific Ocean by Malayo-Polynesian-speaking peoples. By 2000 BCE, these seafarers had migrated as far as the Bismarck Archipelago, northeast of the island of New Guinea, where they encountered Melanesian peoples whose ancestors had taken part in the first wave of human settlement into the region 30,000 years previously.

From there, the Polynesian peoples—as they are now familiarly known—continued their explorations eastward in large sailing canoes up to 100 feet long that carried more than forty people and many of their food staples, such as chickens, chili peppers, and a tuber called taro, the source of poi. Stopping in Fiji, Samoa, and the Cook Islands during the first millennium CE, their descendants pressed onward, eventually reaching Tahiti, Hawaii, and even Easter Island, one of the most remote sites of human habitation in the world. Eventually, one group of Polynesians, now known as the Maori (MAU-ree), sailed southwestward from the island of Rarotonga and settled in New Zealand, off the coast of Australia. The final frontier of human settlement had been breached.

Giant Heads of Easter Island. When the Malayo-Polynesian-speaking peoples spread out from their homeland into the islands of the Pacific, they eventually settled in areas as distant as Hawaii and Easter Island. Some of these peoples first arrived on Easter Island in the fifth century CE and soon began to erect giant stone statues. It is thought that they were erected by rival chiefdoms for reasons of prestige. Some scholars estimate that the process of moving the statues from the quarry (shown here) by rolling them on a bed of rounded logs eventually devastated the forests and caused the total erosion of the landscape. As a result, almost the entire population was wiped out.

During the more than 1,500 years from the fall of the Mauryas to the rise of the Mughals, Indian civilization faced a number of severe challenges. One challenge was primarily external and took the form of a continuous threat from beyond the mountains in the northwest. As a result of the foreign conquest of northern India, Islam was introduced into the region. The new religion soon became a serious rival to traditional beliefs among the people of India. Another challenge had internal causes, stemming from the tradition of factionalism and internal rivalry that had marked relations within the aristocracy since the Aryan influx in the second millennium BCE (see Chapter 2). Despite the abortive efforts of the Guptas, that tradition continued almost without interruption down to the founding of the Mughal Empire in the sixteenth century.

During the same period that Indian civilization faced these challenges at home, it was having a profound impact on the emerging states of Southeast Asia. Situated at the crossroads between two oceans and two great civilizations, Southeast Asia has long served as a bridge linking peoples and cultures, and as complex societies began to develop in the area, it is not surprising that they were strongly influenced by the older civilizations of neighboring China and India.

At the same time, the Southeast Asian peoples put their own unique stamp on the ideas that they adopted and eventually rejected those that were inappropriate to local conditions.

The result was a region characterized by an almost unparalleled cultural richness and diversity, reflecting influences from as far away as the Middle East yet preserving indigenous elements that were deeply rooted in the local culture. Unfortunately, that very diversity posed potential problems for the peoples of Southeast Asia as they faced a new challenge from beyond the horizon. We shall deal with that challenge when we return to the region later in the book. In the meantime, we must turn our attention to the other major civilization that spread its shadow over the societies of southern Asia—China.

CHAPTER TIMELINE

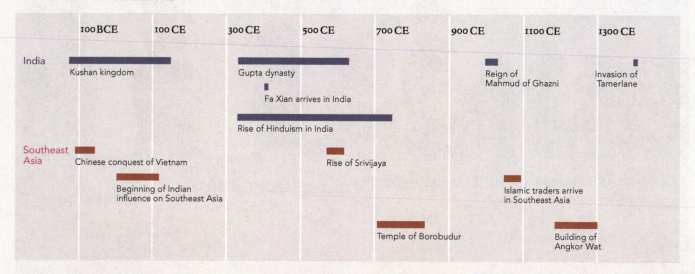

| | 100 BCE | 100 CE | 300 CE | 500 CE | 700 CE | 900 CE | 1100 CE | 1300 CE |

India
Kushan kingdom
Gupta dynasty
Fa Xian arrives in India
Rise of Hinduism in India
Reign of Mahmud of Ghazni
Invasion of Tamerlane

Southeast Asia
Chinese conquest of Vietnam
Beginning of Indian influence on Southeast Asia
Rise of Srivijaya
Islamic traders arrive in Southeast Asia
Temple of Borobudur
Building of Angkor Wat

CHAPTER REVIEW

Upon Reflection

Q How does the religion known today as Hinduism compare in its essential respects with the Brahmanical faith from which it emerged in the first millennium CE? What may explain the differences?

Q The Indian social system has been characterized by the existence of extensive lineage groups—known as *jati*—that are larger than the traditional joint and nuclear families found in many other societies. What are the most prominent features of such lineage groups, and why have they endured for so long in Indian society?

Q Many of the states that were formed in Southeast Asia during the first millennium CE absorbed strong influences from merchants and missionaries arriving from India. What political, social, and religious characteristics of Indian civilization were adopted by the indigenous states in Southeast Asia, and how were they applied in their new environment?

Key Terms

Theravada (p. 245)
Mahayana (p. 245)
Hinayana (p. 245)
bodhisattva (p. 245)
Hinduism (p. 246)

bhakti (p. 246)
puja (p. 248)
purdah (p. 253)
Malayo-Polynesian (p. 259)

Chapter Notes

1. Hiuen Tsiang, *Si-Yu-Ki: Buddhist Records of the Western World*, trans. S. Beal (London, 1982), pp. 89–90.
2. "Fo-Kwo-Ki" (Travels of Fa Xian), ch. 20, p. 43, in ibid.
3. E. C. Sachau, *Alberoni's India* (London, 1914), vol. 1, p. 22.
4. Quoted in S. M. Ikram, *Muslim Civilization in India* (New York, 1964), p. 68.
5. Hiuen Tsiang, *Si-Yu-Ki*, pp. 73–74.
6. D. Barbosa, *The Book of Duarte Barbosa* (Nedeln, Liechtenstein, 1967), pp. 147–148.
7. Quoted in R. Lannoy, *The Speaking Tree: A Study of Indian Culture and Society* (London, 1971), p. 232.
8. Quoted in A. L. Basham, *The Wonder That Was India* (London, 1954), p. 426.
9. Quoted in S. Hughes and B. Hughes, *Women in World History*, vol. 1 (Armonk, N.Y., 1995), p. 217.

THE FLOWERING OF TRADITIONAL CHINA

Chapter Outline and Focus Questions

10–1 China's Golden Age: The Sui, the Tang, and the Song

Q What major changes in political structures and social and economic life occurred during the Sui, Tang, and Song Dynasties? To what degree do these changes compare with contemporary events in India and the Middle East?

10–2 Explosion in Central Asia: The Mongol Empire

Q Why were the Mongols able to amass an empire, and what were the main characteristics of their rule in China?

10–3 The Ming Dynasty

Q What were the chief initiatives taken by the early rulers of the Ming Dynasty to enhance the role of China in the world? Why did the imperial court order the famous voyages of Zheng He, and why were they discontinued?

10–4 In Search of the Way

Q What roles did Buddhism, Daoism, and Neo-Confucianism play in Chinese intellectual life in the period between the Sui dynasty and the Ming?

10–5 Changing Social Conditions in Traditional China

Q In what ways did social conditions in Chinese society evolve during the period from the Tang to the Ming Dynasties? Do you see any parallel with similar events elsewhere in the world?

10–6 The Apogee of Chinese Culture

Q What were the main achievements in Chinese literature and art in the period between the Tang Dynasty and the Ming, and what technological innovations and intellectual developments contributed to these achievements?

Detail of a Chinese scroll, Going up the River at the Spring Festival. Werner Forman/Art Resource, NY

Critical Thinking

Q *The civilization of ancient China fell under the onslaught of nomadic invasions, as did some of its counterparts elsewhere in the world. But China, unlike other classical empires, was later able to reconstitute itself on the same political and cultural foundations. How do you account for the difference?*

Connections to Today

Q *The Comparative Essay "The Spread of Technology," (Section 11-1f, p. 280) suggests that active participation in the global trade network helped medieval societies compete more effectively in the international marketplace. Do you feel that this argument could be made about societies today?*

ON HIS FIRST VISIT to the city, the traveler was mightily impressed. Its streets were so straight and wide that he could see through the city from one end to the other. Along the wide boulevards were beautiful palaces and inns in great profusion. The city was laid out in squares like a chessboard, and within each square were spacious courts and gardens. Truly, said the visitor, this must be one of the largest and wealthiest cities on earth—a city "planned out to a degree of precision and beauty impossible to describe."[1]

The visitor was Marco Polo (MAR-koh POH-loh), and the city was Khanbaliq (kahn-bah-LEEK) (later known as Beijing), capital of the Yuan (YOO-enn or YWAHN) dynasty (1279–1368) and one of the great urban centers of the Chinese Empire. Marco Polo was an Italian merchant who had traveled to China in the late thirteenth century and then served as an official at the court of Khubilai Khan (KOO-blah KAHN). Polo's diary, published after his return to Italy almost twenty years later, astonished readers with tales of this magnificent but unknown civilization far to the east. In fact, many of his European contemporaries were skeptical of his claims and suspected that he was a charlatan seeking to win fame and fortune with a fictional account of his travels to fantastic lands. Even today, some observers doubt that Marco Polo actually ever visited China.

Many contemporary readers of Marco Polo's memoirs in other parts of the world, however, would have found his account of the wonders of the East more credible, for evidence of the greatness of the Chinese Empire—then under the domination of a fearsome Central Asian people called Mongols—was all around them. Indeed, after the decline of the Abbasids in the eleventh and twelfth centuries, China had clearly emerged as the richest and most powerful empire on the Eurasian supercontinent.

10–1 CHINA'S GOLDEN AGE: THE SUI, THE TANG, AND THE SONG

 Focus Questions: What major changes in political structures and social and economic life occurred during the Sui, the Tang, and the Song Dynasties? To what degree do they compare with contemporary events in India and the Middle East?

After the collapse of the Han dynasty at the beginning of the third century BCE, China fell into an extended period of division and civil war. Taking advantage of the absence of organized government in China, nomadic forces from the Gobi Desert penetrated south of the Great Wall and established their own rule over northern China. In the Yangzi Valley and farther to the south, native Chinese rule was maintained, but constant civil war and instability led later historians to refer to the period as the "era of the six dynasties."

10–1a A Time of Troubles: China After the Han

The collapse of the Han Empire had a marked effect on the Chinese psyche. The Confucian principles that emphasized hard work, the subordination of the individual to community interests, and belief in the essentially rational order of the universe came under severe challenge, and many Chinese began to turn to more messianic creeds that emphasized the supernatural or the promise of earthly or heavenly salvation. Intellectuals began to reject the stuffy moralism and complacency of State Confucianism and sought emotional satisfaction in hedonistic pursuits or philosophical Daoism.

Eccentric behavior and a preference for philosophical Daoism became a common response to a corrupt age. A group of writers known as the "seven sages of the bamboo forest" exemplified the period. Among the best known was the poet Liu Ling (lyoo LING), whose odd behavior is described in this oft-quoted passage:

> Liu Ling was an inveterate drinker and indulged himself to the full. Sometimes he stripped off his clothes and sat in his room stark naked. Some men saw him and rebuked him. Liu Ling said, "Heaven and earth are my dwelling, and my house is my trousers. Why are you all coming into my trousers?"[2]

But neither popular beliefs in the supernatural nor philosophical Daoism could satisfy deeper emotional needs or provide solace in time of sorrow or the hope of a better life in the hereafter. Buddhism filled that gap.

Buddhism was brought to China in the first or second century BCE, probably by missionaries and merchants traveling over the Silk Road, and soon began to make inroads among the local population, especially in the north, where the rulers of non-Chinese governments were receptive to the new doctrine. Although the intellectual hairsplitting that often accompanied discussion of the Buddha's message in India was too esoteric for Chinese tastes, in the difficult years surrounding the decline of the Han dynasty, Buddhist ideas, especially those of the Mahayana school, began to find adherents among intellectuals and ordinary people alike. As Buddhism increased in popularity, it was frequently attacked by supporters of Confucianism and Daoism for its foreign origins. Some Confucian adherents even claimed that Siddhartha Gautama had been a disciple of Lao Tzu. But such sniping did not halt the progress of Buddhism, and eventually the new faith was assimilated into Chinese culture, assisted by the efforts of such tireless advocates as the missionaries Fa Xian and Xuan Zang and the support of ruling elites in both northern and southern China (see "The Rise and Decline of Buddhism and Daoism," Section 10–4a, p. 289).

10–1b The Sui Dynasty

After nearly four centuries of internal division, China was unified once again in 581 when Yang Jian (yahng JEE-YEN), a member of a respected aristocratic family in northern China, founded a new dynasty, known as the Sui (SWAY) (581–618). Yang Jian, who is also known by his reign title of Sui Wendi (SWAY wen-DEE), established his capital at the historic metropolis of Chang'an (CHENG-AHN) and began to extend his authority throughout the heartland of China.

Like many of his predecessors, the new emperor sought to create a unifying ideology for the state to enhance its efficiency. But where Liu Bang, the founder of the Han dynasty, had adopted Confucianism as the official doctrine to knit the empire together, Yang Jian turned to Daoism and Buddhism. He founded monasteries for both doctrines in the capital and appointed Buddhist monks to key positions as political advisers.

Yang Jian was a builder as well as a conqueror, ordering the construction of a new canal from the capital to the confluence of the Wei and Yellow Rivers nearly 100 miles to the east. His son, Emperor Sui Yangdi (SWAY yahng-DEE), continued the process, and the 1,400-mile-long Grand Canal, linking the two great rivers of China, the Yellow and the Yangzi, was essentially completed during his reign. The new canal facilitated the shipment of grain and other commodities from the rice-rich southern provinces to the densely populated north. The canal also served other purposes, such as speeding communications between the two regions and permitting the rapid dispatch of troops to troubled provinces. His flotilla, composed of "dragon boats, . . . red battle cruisers, multi-decked transports, lesser vessels of bamboo slats," must have been an impressive sight to onlookers.[3]

The Grand Canal. Built over centuries, the Grand Canal is one of the engineering wonders of the world and a crucial conduit for carrying goods between northern and southern China. In this stylized painting, "dragon boats" carry the emperor and his retinue on an inspection tour of the canal and its adjacent territories.

The Granger Collection, NYC

Despite such efforts to project the majesty of the imperial personage, the Sui dynasty came to an end immediately after Sui Yangdi's death. The Sui emperor was a tyrannical ruler, and his expensive military campaigns aroused widespread unrest. After his return from a failed campaign against Korea in 618, the emperor was murdered in his palace. One of his generals, Li Yuan (lee YWAHN), took advantage of the instability that ensued and declared the foundation of a new dynasty, known as the Tang (TAHNG). Building on the successes of its predecessor, the Tang lasted for three hundred years, until the year 907.

10–1c The Tang Dynasty

Li Yuan ruled for a brief period and then was elbowed aside by his son, who assumed the reign title Tang Taizong (tahng ty-ZOONG). Under his vigorous leadership, the new dynasty launched a program of internal renewal and external expansion that would make it one of the greatest dynasties in the long history of China (see Map 10.1). The northwest was pacified and given the name of Xinjiang, or "new region," sparking an increase in the traffic of goods and ideas across what would eventually be termed the "Silk Road" (see "The Silk Road," Section 10-1f, p. 280). After a long conflict with Tibet, Chinese control was extended for the first time over that vast and desolate plateau as well. In the meantime, the southern provinces below the Yangzi were fully assimilated into the Chinese Empire, and the imperial court established commercial and diplomatic relations with the states of Southeast Asia. With reason, China now claimed to be the foremost power in East Asia, and the emperor demanded fealty and tribute from all his fellow rulers beyond the frontier. Korea accepted tribute status and attempted to adopt the Chinese model, and the Japanese dispatched official missions to China to learn more about its customs and institutions (see Chapter 11).

One key to the success of the Tang Dynasty in reuniting China after several centuries of internal division was the decision to revive many of the Confucian principles and practices that had been abandoned after the fall of the Han. Although the process took many years and did not reach its culmination until the advent of the Song Dynasty in the tenth century, Tang rulers began to draw on the principles of State Confucianism originally established during the Han as a means of centralizing power at court and weakening the power of the aristocrats (see "Political Structures: The Triumph of Confucianism," Section 10-1e, p. 276).

The Controversial Empress Wu Perhaps the individual most responsible for this development was Wu Zhao (c. 624–705), popularly known as Wu Zetian, or simply "Empress Wu." Selected by Emperor Tang Taizong as one of his many concubines, she rose to a position of influence after his death in 649 and became the chief consort of his successor, Emperor Gaozong. At first she was content to exert her influence at court discretely, but when Gaozong became seriously ill in 660, she was able to win appointment as regent. After he died, she strengthened her hold on power and in 690 declared herself Empress of China.

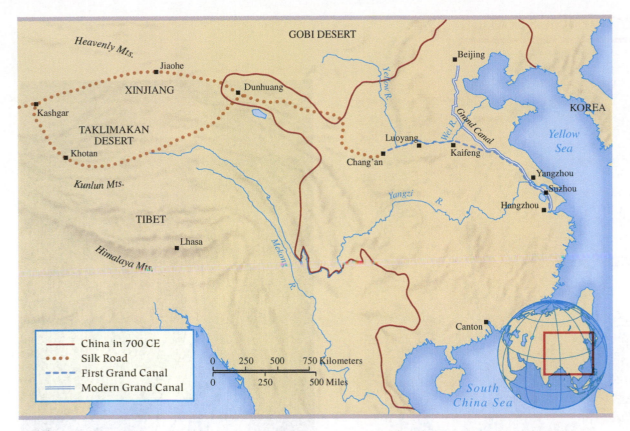

Map 10.1 China Under the Tang. The era of the Tang Dynasty was one of the greatest periods in the long history of China. Tang influence spread from heartland China into neighboring regions, including Central and Southeast Asia.

Q *Why was the Grand Canal built, and what was its main function during this period?*

To bolster her claim to legitimacy as China's first female ruler, Empress Wu cited a Buddhist sutra to the effect that a woman would eventually rule the world after the death of Siddhartha Gautama. For her presumption, she has been vilified by generations of Chinese historians, but in recent years some scholars have claimed that she was actually a quite capable ruler, taking measures to reform the agricultural system, undercut the power of the landed aristocracy, and strengthen the civil service system by selecting examination graduates for senior positions in government, while simultaneously improving women's rights. While few deny her ruthlessness in eliminating rivals, some modern historians contend that her actions laid the groundwork for the "golden age" of Tang China that took root in the eighth century CE.

It was also under Empress Wu and her successors that the Tang achieved a flowering of Chinese culture. Many modern observers feel that the era represents the apogee of Chinese creativity in poetry and sculpture. One reason for this explosion of culture was the influence of Buddhism, which affected art, literature, and philosophy, as well as religion and politics (see Comparative Illustration "The Two Worlds of Tang China," p. 274). Monasteries sprang up throughout China, and Buddhist monks served as advisers at the Tang imperial court. Even Empress Wu, whose policies generally reflected the growing influence of State Confucian ideology, was an avid supporter of

Buddhism. The city of Chang'an, now restored to the glory it had known as the capital of the Han dynasty, once again became the seat of the empire. With a population estimated at nearly 2 million, it was possibly the greatest city in the world of its time. The city was filled with temples and palaces, and its markets

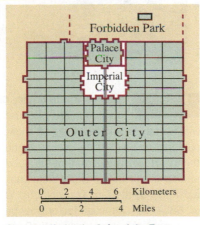

Chang'an Under the Sui and the Tang

teemed with goods from all over the known world (see "The Good Life in the High Tang," p. 275).

The Fall of The Tang But the Tang, like the Han, sowed the seeds of their own destruction. Tang rulers could not prevent the rise of internal forces that would ultimately weaken the dynasty and bring it to an end. Two familiar problems were court intrigue and official corruption. Xuanzong (shwahn-ZOONG) (r. 712–756), one of the great Tang emperors and a renowned

A

B

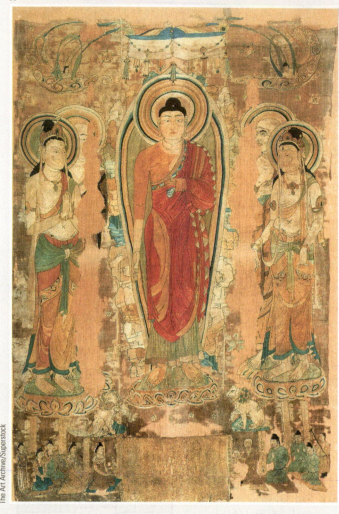

The Two Worlds of Tang China. In Tang Dynasty China, the arts often reflected influences from a wide variety of cultures. Image A shows an eighth-century wall painting from a cliffside cave at Dunhuang, a major rest stop on the Silk Road. The portrait of the Buddha clearly reflects Indian influence. Illustration B is a stone rubbing of Confucius based on a painting by the Tang Dynasty artist Wu Daozi (woo DOW-zuh) (c. 685–758). Although the original painting is not extant, this block print of a stone copy of Wu Daozi's work, showing Confucius in his flowing robe, reflects the indigenous style for which the painter was famous. It became the iconic portrait of the Master for millions of later Chinese. The Chinese government recently commissioned a copy based on Wu's original painting to serve as the standard portrait of Confucius for people around the world.

 How do the two portraits shown here differ in the way their creators seek to present the character and the underlying philosophy of the Buddha and Confucius?

patron of the arts, was dominated in later life by one of his favorite concubines, the beautiful Yang Guifei (yahng gway-FAY). One of her protégés, the military adventurer An Lushan (ahn loo-SHAHN), launched a rebellion against the dynasty in 755 and briefly seized the capital of Chang'an. The revolt was eventually suppressed, and Yang Guifei, who has traditionally been viewed as one of the great villains of Chinese history, was put to death. But Emperor Xuanzong, and indeed the Tang Dynasty itself, never fully recovered from the catastrophe. The loss of power by the central government led to chronic instability along the northern and western frontiers, where local military commanders ruled virtually without central government interference. Climatologists also speculate that a prolonged drought that affected much of the world (see Chapter 6) may

THE GOOD LIFE IN THE HIGH TANG

Art & Ideas

AT THE HEIGHT OF THE TANG DYNASTY, China was at the apex of its power and magnificence. Here the Tang poet Du Fu (DOO FOO) (Tu Fu) describes a gala festival in the capital of Chang'an attended by the favored elite. The author's distaste for the spectacle of arrogance and waste is expressed in muted sarcasm.

Du Fu, *A Poem*

> Third day of the third month
> The very air seems new
> In Ch'ang-an along the water
> Many beautiful girls . . .
> Firm, plump contours,
> Flesh and bone proportioned.
> Dresses of gauze brocade
> Mirror the end of spring
> Peacocks crimped in thread of gold
> Unicorns in silver . . . .
> Some are kin to the imperial favorite
> Among them the Lady of Kuo and the Lady of Ch'in [Qin].
> Camel-humps of purple meat
> Brought in shining pans
> The white meat of raw fish

> Served on crystal platters
> Don't tempt the sated palate.
> All that is cut with fancy and
> Prepared with care—left untouched.
> Eunuchs, reins a-flying Disturb no dust
> Bring the "eight chef d'oeuvres"
> From the palace kitchens.
> Music of strings and pipes . . .
> Accompanying the feasting
> Moving the many guests
> All of rank and importance.
> Last comes a horseman
> See him haughtily
> Dismount near the screen
> And step on the flowery carpet. . . .
> The chancellor is so powerful
> His mere touch will scorch.
> Watch you don't come near
> Lest you displease him.

 Why does the author of this poem appear to be so angry at the festival goers described here?

Source: A. F. Wright and D. Twitchett, *Perspectives on the T'ang*, (New Haven, 1973) Yale University Press. Used with permission.

---

have played a role in the decline of the dynasty. It was an eerie repetition of the final decades of the Han.

The end finally came in the early tenth century, when border troubles with northern nomadic peoples called the Khitan (Kee-TAN) increased, leading to the collapse of the dynasty in 907. The Tang had followed the classic Chinese strategy of "using a barbarian to oppose a barbarian" by allying with a trading people called the Uighurs (WEE-gurz), a Turkic-speaking people who had taken over many of the caravan routes along the Silk Road, against their old rivals. But then another nomadic people called the Kirghiz (keer-GEEZ) defeated the Uighurs and turned on the Tang government in its moment of weakness and overthrew it.

10–1d The Song Dynasty

China slipped once again into disunity. This time, the period of foreign invasion and division was much shorter. In 960, a new dynasty, known as the Song (SOONG) (960–1279), rose to power. From the start, however, the Song rulers encountered more problems in defending their territory than their predecessors. Although the founding emperor, Song Taizu (soong TY-DZOO), was able to co-opt many of the powerful military commanders whose rivalry had brought the Tang Dynasty to an end, he was unable to reconquer the northwestern part of the country from the nomadic Khitan peoples. The emperor therefore established his capital farther to the east, at Kaifeng, where the

Grand Canal intersected the Yellow River. Later, when pressures from the nomads in the north increased, the court was forced to move the capital even farther south, to Hangzhou (HAHNG-joe), on the coast just south of the Yangzi River delta; the emperors who ruled from Hangzhou are known as the southern Song (1127–1279). The Song also lost control over Tibet. Despite its political and military weaknesses, the dynasty nevertheless ruled during a period of economic expansion, prosperity, and cultural achievement and is therefore considered among the more successful Chinese dynasties. The population of the empire had risen to an estimated 40 million people, slightly more than that of the continent of Europe.

Yet the Song were never able to surmount the external challenge from the north, and that failure eventually brought about the end of the dynasty. During its final decades, the Song rulers were forced to pay tribute to the Jurchen (roor-ZHEN) peoples from Manchuria (man-CHUR-ee-uh). In the early thirteenth century, the Song, ignoring precedent and the fate of the Tang, formed an alliance with the Mongols, a new and obscure nomadic people from the Gobi Desert. As under the Tang, the decision proved to be a disaster. Within a few years, the Mongols had become a much more serious threat to China than the Jurchen. After defeating the Jurchen, the Mongols turned their attention to the Song, advancing on Chinese territory from both the north and the west. By this time, the Song empire had been weakened by internal factionalism and a loss of tax revenues.

After a series of river battles and sieges marked by the use of catapults and gunpowder, the Song were defeated, and the conquerors announced the creation of a new Yuan (Mongol) dynasty. Ironically, the Mongols had first learned about gunpowder from the Chinese.

10–1e Political Structures: The Triumph of Confucianism

During the nearly seven hundred years from the Sui to the end of the Song, a mature political system based on principles originally established during the Qin and Han dynasties gradually emerged in China. After the Tang Dynasty's brief flirtation with Buddhism, State Confucianism became the ideological cement that held the system together. The development of this system took several centuries, and it did not reach its height until the period of the Song Dynasty.

Equal Opportunity in China: The Civil Service Examination At the apex of the government hierarchy was the **Grand Council**, assisted by a secretariat and a chancellery; it included representatives from all three authorities—civil, military, and censorate. Under the Grand Council was the Department of State Affairs, composed of ministries responsible for justice, military affairs, personnel, public works, revenue, and rites (ritual). This department was in effect the equivalent of a modern cabinet.

The Tang Dynasty adopted the practice of selecting some officials through periodic civil service examinations. The effectiveness of this merit system was limited, however, because the examination was administered only in the capital city and because the process was dominated by the great aristocratic clans, who had mastered the technique of preparing candidates for the exams. According to one source, fully one-third of those who succeeded on the imperial examinations during the Tang era came from the great families.

CHRONOLOGY	Medieval China
Arrival of Buddhism in China	c. first century BCE
Fall of the Han dynasty	220 BCE
Sui dynasty	581–618
Tang Dynasty	618–907
Li Bo and Du Fu	700s
Emperor Xuanzong	712–756
Song Dynasty	960–1279
Wang Anshi	1021–1086
Southern Song Dynasty	1127–1279
Life of Genghis Khan	c. 1162–1227
Mongol conquest of China	1279
Reign of Khubilai Khan	1260–1294
Fall of the Yuan dynasty	1368
Ming Dynasty	1369–1644

The Song were more successful at limiting aristocratic control over the bureaucracy, in part because the power of the nobility had been irreparably weakened during the final years of the Tang Dynasty and did not recover during the interregnum that followed its collapse. Song officials also sought to strengthen the power of the central administration by making the civil service examination system the primary route to an official career (see "Equal Opportunity in China: The Civil Service Examination," and "Choosing the Best and Brightest"). To reduce the power of the noble families, relatives of individuals serving in the imperial court, as well as eunuchs, were prohibited from taking the examinations. But if the Song rulers' objective was to make the bureaucracy more subservient to the court, they may have been disappointed. The rising professionalism of the bureaucracy, which numbered about ten thousand in the imperial capital, with an equal number at the local level, provided it with an esprit de corps and an influence that sometimes enabled it to resist the whims of individual emperors.

Under the Song, the examination system attained the form that it would retain in later centuries. In general, three levels of examinations were administered. The first was a qualifying examination given annually at the provincial capital. Candidates who succeeded in this first stage were normally not given positions in the bureaucracy except at the local level. Many stopped at this level and accepted positions as village teachers to train other candidates. Those who wished to secure an official position could take a second examination given at the capital every three years. Some went on to take the final examination, which was given in the imperial palace once every three years. Those who passed were eligible for high positions in the central bureaucracy or for appointments as district magistrates.

During the early Tang, the examinations included questions on Buddhist and Daoist as well as Confucian texts, but by Song times, the popularity of Buddhist and Daoist ideas had declined among the elite, and examinations were based entirely on the Confucian classics (see Opposing Viewpoints "Confucianism and Its Enemies: An Ideological Dispute in Medieval China," p. 278). Candidates were expected to memorize passages and to be able to define the moral lessons they contained. The system guaranteed that successful candidates—and therefore officials—would have received a full dose of Confucian political and social ethics. Whether they followed those ethics, of course, was another matter. Some students brought crib notes into the examination hall (one enterprising candidate concealed an entire Confucian text in the lining of his cloak). For those candidates who succeeded, official arrogance, bureaucratic infighting, corruption, and legalistic interpretations of government regulations were as prevalent in medieval China as in bureaucracies the world over.

The Song authorities tried to open up the system to provide an equal opportunity to the poor as well as to the affluent. Training academies were set up at the provincial and district levels (see "Equal Opportunity in China: The Civil Service Examination," and "Choosing the Best and Brightest"). Without such academies, only those individuals fortunate enough to receive training in the classics in family-run schools would have had the expertise to pass the examinations. Still, in most years,

CHOOSING THE BEST AND BRIGHTEST

Politics & Government

WANG ANSHI (WAHNG anh-SHEE) (1021–1086) was a prominent government official in Song Dynasty China. As a senior adviser at court, he sought to implement a series of reforms designed to improve the operations of the Chinese state, and thus enhance the well-being of the population. One key tenet of his program was to appoint honest and competent officials to key positions in the bureaucracy. In the great tradition of Chinese statecraft, Wang agreed with the proposition that it was good men, and not just laws, that created the best civil society. Current practice, however, placed primary emphasis on the ability of candidates to memorize passages from the ancient classics. In his view, what was more important was for candidates to understand the general principles of governing and behavior, principles that could be gleaned from the writings of ancient times without the need for rote memorization.

Memorial to Emperor Renzong (1058)

The most urgent need of the present time is to secure capable men. Only when we can produce a large number of capable men in the empire will it be possible to select a sufficient number of persons qualified to serve in the government. And only when we get capable men in the government will there be no difficulty in assessing what may be done, in view of the time and circumstances, and in consideration of the human distress that may be occasioned, gradually to change the decadent laws of the empire in order to approach the ideas of the ancient kings. The empire today is the same as the empire of the ancient kings. There were numerous capable men in their times. Why is there a dearth of such men today? It is because, as has been said, we do not train and cultivate men in the proper way. . . .

What is the way to select officials? The ancient kings selected men only from the local villages and through the local schools. The people were asked to recommend those they considered to be virtuous and able, sending up their nominations to the court, which investigated each one. Only if the men recommended proved truly virtuous and able would they be appointed to official posts commensurate with their individual virtue and ability. . . . Today, although we have schools in each prefecture and district, they amount to no more than school buildings. There are no officers of instruction and guidance; nothing is done to train and develop human talent. In recent years, teaching has been based on the essays required for the civil service examinations, but this kind of essay cannot be learned without resorting to extensive memorization and strenuous study, upon which students must spend their efforts the whole day long. Such proficiency as they attain is at best of no use in the government of the empire, and at most the empire can make no use of them. . . .

In addition, candidates are examined in such fields as the Nine Classics, the Five Classics, specialization [in one classic], and the study of law. The court has already become concerned over the uselessness of this type of knowledge and has stressed the need for an understanding of general principles [as set forth in the classics]. . . . When we consider the men selected through "understanding of the classics," however, it is still those who memorize, recite, and have some knowledge of literary composition who are able to pass the examination, while those who can apply them [the classics] to the government of the empire are not always brought in through this kind of selection.

 Does Wang Anshi cite examples from ancient times to strengthen his complaint about the current nature of training for a career in officialdom? Do his criticisms have relevance for our own day?

Source: William Theodore de Bary and Irene Bloom, *Sources of Chinese Tradition*, Vol. 1, 2nd ed. (New York: Columbia University Press, 1999), pp. 612–616. Reprinted with permission of the publisher.

---

the majority of candidates came from the landed gentry, nonaristocratic landowners who controlled much of the wealth in the countryside. Because the gentry prized education and became the primary upholders of the Confucian tradition, they were often called the **scholar-gentry**.

Despite such weaknesses, the civil service examination system was an impressive achievement for its day and probably provided a more efficient government and more opportunity for upward mobility than were found in any other civilization of its time. Most Western governments, for example, began to recruit officials on the basis of merit only in the nineteenth century. Furthermore, by regulating the content of the examinations, the system helped provide China with a cultural uniformity lacking in empires elsewhere in Asia.

The court also attempted to curb official misbehavior through the censorate. Specially trained officials known as censors were assigned to investigate possible cases of official wrongdoing and report directly to the court. The censorate was supposed to be independent of outside pressures to ensure that its members would feel free to report wrongdoing wherever it occurred. In practice, censors who displeased high court officials were often removed or even subjected to more serious forms of punishment, which reduced the effectiveness of the system.

Local Government The Song Dynasty maintained the local government institutions that it had inherited from its predecessors. At the base of the government pyramid was the district

Confucianism and Its Enemies: An Ideological Dispute in Medieval China

Religion & Philosophy | **DURING THE INTERREGNUM BETWEEN THE FALL OF THE HAN DYNASTY** in 220 BCE and the rise of the Tang four hundred years later, Daoist critics lampooned the hypocrisy of the "Confucian gentleman" and the Master's emphasis on ritual and the maintenance of proper relations among individuals in society. In the first selection, a third-century Daoist launches an attack on the pompous and hypocritical Confucian gentleman who feigns high moral principles while secretly engaging in corrupt and licentious behavior.

By the eighth century, the tables had turned and Confucian concepts were making a comeback at court. In the second selection, Han Yu (hahn YOO) (768–824), a key figure in the emergence of Neo-Confucian thought as the official ideology of the state, composes a memorial to the emperor containing a withering analysis of the dangers involved in allowing Daoist and Buddhist ideas to prosper among the common people. His tone is much more direct than that of most such memorials and probably reflects his confidence that the emperor would be receptive to his views.

Biography of a Great Man

What the world calls a gentleman [*chun-tzu*] is someone who is solely concerned with moral law [*fa*], and cultivates exclusively the rules of propriety [*li*]. His hand holds the emblem of jade [authority]; his foot follows the straight line of the rule. He likes to think that his actions set a permanent example; he likes to think that his words are everlasting models. In his youth, he has a reputation in the villages of his locality; in his later years, he is well known in the neighboring districts. Upward, he aspires to the dignity of the Three Dukes; downward, he does not disdain the post of governor of the nine provinces.

Have you ever seen the lice that inhabit a pair of trousers? They jump into the depths of the seams, hiding themselves in the cotton wadding, and believe they have a pleasant place to live. Walking, they do not risk going beyond the edge of the seam; moving, they are careful not to emerge from the trouser leg; and they think they have kept to the rules of etiquette. But

when the trousers are ironed, the flames invade the hills, the fire spreads, the villages are set on fire and the towns burned down; then the lice that inhabit the trousers cannot escape.

What difference is there between the gentleman who lives within a narrow world and the lice that inhabit trouser legs?

Han Yu, *Memorial Discussing the Buddha's Bone*

I am of the opinion that Buddhism is nothing more than a religion of the outlying tribes. Since the Eastern Han it has made inroads into the heartland, but such a thing never existed in high antiquity. . . . [I]n those days the world enjoyed perfect peace; the common people were secure in their happiness and lived to ripe old age. Yet at this time there was no Buddhism in the heartland.

The Buddhist religion appeared only in the reign of Emperor Ming of the Han, and Emperor Ming sat on the throne for only eighteen years. After him, turmoil and destruction were continuous, and fate gave no long reigns. . . . Consideration of these cases leads us to understand that the Buddha does not merit devotion. . . .

When you first took the throne, Your Majesty did not permit people to take vows to become monks, nuns, or Daoist priests; you further did not permit the foundation of new monasteries and Daoist temples. . . . [H]ow can you give them free rein and make them prosper even more than before?

I recently heard that Your Majesty has commanded a group of monks to welcome the Buddha's bone in Feng-xiang; then . . . it will be carried with ceremony into the palace precincts. . . . How could such a sagely and enlightened ruler as yourself bring himself to have faith in this sort of thing?

Nevertheless, the common people are foolish and ignorant, easy to lead into error and hard to enlighten. If Your Majesty behaves like this, they will assume that you serve the Buddha from genuine feeling . . .

 Which author appears to make the better case for his chosen ideological preference?

Sources: Excerpt from ed. and translator, Stephen Owen, *An Anthology of Chinese Literature: Beginnings to 1911* (New York: W.W Norton, 1996), pp. 598–601. From *Chinese Civilization and Bureaucracy*, by Etienne Balasz, p. 238. Copyright © 1964 by Yale University Press.

(or county), governed by a magistrate. The magistrate, assisted by his staff of three or four officials and several other menial employees, was responsible for maintaining law and order and collecting taxes within his jurisdiction. A district could exceed 100,000 people. Below the district was the basic unit of Chinese government, the village. Because villages were so numerous in China, the central government did not appoint an official at that level and allowed the villages to administer themselves. Village government was normally in the hands of a council

of elders, most often assisted by a chief. The council, usually composed of the heads of influential families in the village, maintained the local irrigation and transportation network, adjudicated local disputes, organized and maintained a militia, and assisted in collecting taxes (usually paid in grain) and delivering them to the district magistrate.

As a rule, most Chinese had little involvement with government matters. When they had to deal with the government, they almost always turned to their village officials. Although the district magistrate was empowered to settle local civil disputes, most villagers preferred to resolve problems among themselves. It was expected that the magistrate and his staff would supplement their income by charging for such services, a practice that reduced the costs of the central government but also provided an opportunity for bribes, a problem that continued to plague the Chinese bureaucracy down to modern times.

10–1f The Economy

During the long period between the Sui and the Song, the Chinese economy, like the government, grew considerably in size and complexity. China was still an agricultural society, but commerce and manufacturing began to occupy a much larger percentage of the country's national product. The urban sector of the economy was becoming increasingly important, new social classes were beginning to appear, and the economic focus of the empire was beginning to shift from the Yellow River valley in the north to the Yangzi River valley in the center—a process that was encouraged both by the expansion of cultivation in the Yangzi delta and by the control increasingly exerted over the north by nomadic peoples during the Song.

Land Reform The economic revival began shortly after the rise of the Tang. During the long period of internal division, land had become concentrated in the hands of noble families, and most peasants were reduced to serfdom or slavery. Under Empress Wu (see above), the Tang Dynasty tried to reduce the power of the landed nobility and maximize tax revenues by adopting the ancient "well-field" system, in which land was allocated to farmers for life in return for an annual tax payment and three weeks of conscript labor.

At first, the new system was vigorously enforced and led to increased rural prosperity and government revenue. But eventually the rich and the politically influential, including some of the largest Buddhist monasteries, learned to manipulate the system for their own benefit and accumulated huge tracts of land. The growing population, bolstered by a rise in food production and the extended period of social stability, also put steady pressure on the system. Finally, the government abandoned the effort to equalize landholdings and returned the land to private hands while attempting to prevent inequalities through the tax system. The failure to resolve the land problem—along with the climatic changes mentioned earlier—contributed to the fall of the Tang Dynasty in the early tenth century, although the reversion of farmlands to private hands did result in more efficient production in some instances as well as an expansion of the long-distance trade in food products.

The Song tried to resolve the land problem by returning to the successful programs of the early Tang and reducing the power of the wealthy landed aristocrats. During the late eleventh century, the reformist official Wang Anshi (1021–1086) attempted to limit the size of landholdings through progressive land taxes and provided cheap credit to poor farmers to help them avoid bankruptcy. His reforms met with some success, but other developments probably contributed more to the general agricultural prosperity under the Song. These included the opening of new lands in the Yangzi River valley, improvements in irrigation techniques such as the chain pump (a circular chain of square pallets on a treadmill that enabled farmers to lift considerable amounts of water or mud to a higher level), and the introduction of a new strain of quick-growing rice from Southeast Asia, which permitted farmers in warmer regions to plant and harvest two crops each year. It was during the Song Dynasty that rice became the main food crop for the Chinese people.

An Increase in Manufacturing Major changes also took place in the Chinese urban economy, which witnessed significant growth in manufacturing and trade. This process began under the Tang Dynasty, but it was not entirely a product of deliberate state policy. In fact, early Tang rulers shared some of the traditional prejudice against commercial activities that had been prevalent under the Han and enacted a number of regulations that restricted trade and industry. As under the Han, the state maintained monopolies over key commodities such as salt.

Despite the restrictive policies of the state, the manufacturing sector grew steadily larger and more complex, helped by several new technological developments (see Comparative Essay "The Spread of Technology," p. 280). During the Tang, the Chinese mastered the art of manufacturing steel by mixing cast iron and wrought iron. The blast furnace was heated to a high temperature by burning coal, which had been used as a fuel in China from about the fourth century BCE. The resulting product was used in the manufacture of swords, sickles, and even suits of armor. By the eleventh century, more than 35,000 tons of steel were being produced annually. The introduction of cotton from India offered new opportunities in textile production. Gunpowder was invented by the Chinese during the Tang Dynasty and used primarily for explosives and a primitive flamethrower; it reached the West via the Arabs in the twelfth century.

The Expansion of Commerce The nature of trade was also changing. In the past, most long-distance trade had been undertaken by state monopolies. By the time of the Song, private commerce was being actively encouraged, and many merchants engaged in shipping as well as in wholesale and retail trade. The construction of the Grand Canal, as well as the expansion of the road system under the Tang, facilitated a dramatic increase in the regional trade network. Guilds began to appear, along with a new money economy. Paper currency, such as the banknote from the Shanghai Museum that appears in the illustration on page 280 began to be used in the eighth and ninth centuries (see illustration "The First Paper Currency," p. 280). Credit (at first called "flying money") also made its first appearance during the Tang. With the increased circulation of paper money, banking began to develop as merchants found that strings of copper coins were too cumbersome for their increasingly complex operations. Unfortunately, early issues of paper currency were not backed by metal coinage and led to price inflation. Equally useful, if more prosaic, was the invention of the abacus, an early form of calculator that simplified the computations needed for commercial transactions.

The Spread of Technology

Science & Technology From the invention of stone tools and the discovery of fire to the introduction of agriculture and the writing system, mastery of technology has been a driving force in the history of human evolution. But why do some human societies appear to be much more advanced in their use of technology than others? People living on the island of New Guinea, for example, began cultivating local crops like taro and bananas as early as ten thousand years ago but never took the next steps toward creating a complex society until the arrival of Europeans many millennia later. Advanced societies had begun to emerge in the Western Hemisphere during the Classical era, but none had discovered the use of the wheel or the smelting of metals for tool making. Writing was in its infancy there.

Technological advances appear to take place for two reasons: need and opportunity. Farming peoples throughout the world needed to control the flow of water, so in areas where water was scarce or unevenly distributed, they learned to practice irrigation to make resources available throughout the region. Peoples living in the Pacific Ocean learned how to read the stars and the ocean currents in order to navigate from island to island. Sometimes, however, opportunity strikes by accident (as in the legendary story of the Chinese princess who dropped a silkworm cocoon in her cup of hot tea, thereby initiating a series of discoveries that resulted in the manufacture of silk) or when new technology is introduced from a neighboring region (as when the discovery of tin in Anatolia launched the Bronze Age throughout the Middle East).

The most important factor enabling societies to keep abreast of the latest advances in technology, it would appear, is participation in the global trade and communications network. In this respect, the relative ease of communications between the Mediterranean Sea and the Indus River Valley represented a major advantage for the Abbasid Empire, as the peoples living there had rapid access to all the resources and technological advances in that part of the world. China was more isolated from other major civilizations by distance, but with its size and high level of cultural achievement, it was almost a continent in itself and was able to communicate with countries to the west via the Silk Road and the South China Sea.

Societies that were not linked to this vast network were at an enormous disadvantage in keeping up with new developments in technology. The peoples of New Guinea, at the far end of the Indonesian islands, had little or no contact

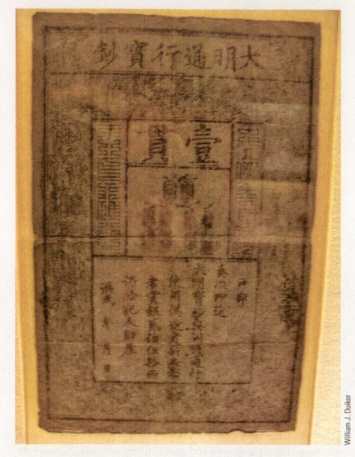

The First Paper Currency

William J. Duiker

with the outside world. In the Western Hemisphere, a trade network did begin to take shape between societies in the Andes and their counterparts in Mesoamerica. But because of difficulties in communication (see Chapter 6), contacts were more intermittent. As a result, technological developments taking place in distant Eurasia did not reach the Americas until the arrival of the conquistadors.

 In what ways did China contribute to the spread of technology and ideas throughout the world during the period from the Sui dynasty to the beginning of the Ming Dynasty? How did China benefit from the process?

The Silk Road Long-distance trade, both overland and by sea, expanded under the Tang Dynasty. Trade with countries and peoples to the west had been carried on for centuries (see Chapter 3), but it had declined dramatically between the fourth and sixth centuries BCE as a result of the collapse of the Han and Roman

Empires. It began to revive with the rise of the Tang and the simultaneous unification of much of the Middle East under the Arabs. During the Tang era, the route that we call the Silk Road reached its zenith, as Chinese military forts were established at strategic points along the edge of the Taklimakan Desert all the way to the borders of Central Asia. Along the Silk Road to China came raw hides, furs, and horses. Chinese aristocrats, their appetite for material consumption stimulated by the affluence of Chinese society during much of the Tang and Song periods, were fascinated by the exotic goods and the flora and fauna of the desert and the tropical lands of the South Seas. Much of the trade was carried by the Turkic-speaking Uighurs or Iranian-speaking Sogdians (SAHG-dee-unz) from Central Asia. During the Tang, Uighur caravans of two-humped Bactrian camels (a hardy variety native to Iran and regions to the northeast) carried goods back and forth between China and the countries of South Asia and the Middle East (see illustration "Tang Camel," Section 10-6b, p. 298). Bolts of silk, a textile which was in great demand throughout the region, became a popular means of currency.

In actuality, the Silk Road was composed of a number of separate routes. The first to be used, probably because of the jade found in the mountains south of Khotan (koh-TAHN), ran along the southern rim of the Taklimakan (tah-kluh-muh-KAHN) Desert via Kashgar (KASH-gahr) and thence through the Pamir (pah-MEER) Mountains into Bactria. The first Buddhist missionaries traveled this route between India and China. Eventually, however, this area began to dry up, and traders were forced to seek other routes. From a climatic standpoint, the best route for the Silk Road was to the north of the Tian Shan (TEE-en SHAHN) (Heavenly Mountains), where moisture-laden northwesterly winds created pastures where animals could graze. But the area

was frequently infested by bandits who preyed on unwary travelers. Most caravans therefore followed the southern route, which passed along the northern fringes of the Taklimakan Desert to Kashgar and down into northwestern India. Travelers avoided the direct route through the desert (in the Uighur language, the name means "go in and you won't come out") and trudged from oasis to oasis along the southern slopes of the Tian Shan following a route littered by animal bones. The oases were created by the water runoff from winter snows in the mountains and dried up in the searing heat of the desert summer.

The eastern terminus of the Silk Road was the city of Chang'an, perhaps the wealthiest city in the world during the Tang era. The city's days as China's foremost metropolis were numbered, however. Chronic droughts throughout the region made it more and more difficult to supply the city with food, and the growing power of Turkic-speaking peoples such as the Uighurs in the hinterlands made the city increasingly vulnerable to attack by rebel forces. During the later Tang, the imperial court was periodically shifted to the old secondary capital of Luoyang (LWOH-yahng). The Song Dynasty, a product of the steady drift of the national center of gravity toward the south, was forced to abandon Chang'an altogether as a historic symbol of imperial greatness and a link to the riches of the far west.

The Maritime Route With the collapse of the Tang Dynasty in the tenth century, the Silk Road became so hazardous that shipping goods by sea was seen as an appealing alternative. China had long been engaged in sea trade with other countries in the region, but most of the commerce was originally in the hands of Korean, Japanese, Southeast Asian, or Middle Eastern merchants. Under the Song, however, Chinese maritime activities were stimulated by the invention of the compass and technical improvements in shipbuilding such as the widespread use of the sternpost rudder and the lug sail (which enabled ships to sail close to the wind). If Marco Polo's observations can be believed, by the thirteenth century, Chinese junks had as many as four masts and could carry several hundred men, many more than contemporary ships in the West. The Chinese governor of Canton in the early twelfth century remarked:

According to the government regulations concerning sea-going ships, the larger ones can carry several hundred men, and the smaller ones may have more than a hundred men on board. . . . The ships' pilots are acquainted with the configuration of the coasts; at night they steer by the stars, and in the daytime by the

Jiaohe: Outpost of the Chinese Empire. The oasis settlement of Jiaohe, located at the confluence of two rivers on a plateau in Chinese Central Asia, had been a stopping point on the silk road since the first millennium BCE, and was first occupied by Chinese military forces during the Han dynasty. During the Tang Dynasty, when merchants carried goods and ideas between the Chinese heartland and countries far to the west, the town's inhabitants were primarily of the Buddhist faith. Shown here are the remnants of a Buddhist temple, with an image of the Buddha set in a niche along the central wall of the building. Like all other structures in the town, the temple was constructed of sun-dried brick. Eventually the community was occupied by Uighurs, who brought the Muslim faith. Jiaohe was abandoned after the Mongols swept through the area in the thirteenth century, but later a new settlement arose in the nearby Turfan depression, the lowest point of altitude in China.

William J. Duiker

Sun. In dark weather they look at the south-pointing needle. They also use a line a hundred feet long with a hook at the end, which they let down to take samples of mud from the sea-bottom; by its appearance and smell they can determine their whereabouts.[4]

A wide variety of goods passed through Chinese ports. The Chinese exported tea, silk, and porcelain to the countries beyond the South China Sea, receiving exotic woods, precious stones, cotton from India, and various tropical goods in exchange. Silk was probably the most desirable commodity of trade, as the quality of Chinese silk was generally recognized as far superior to that produced by other countries in the area. Seaports on the southern coast of China also exported sweet oranges, lemons, and peaches in return for grapes, walnuts, and pomegranates. The major port of exit in southern China was Canton (also known as Guangzhou), where an estimated 100,000 merchants lived. Their activities were controlled by an imperial commissioner sent from the capital.

Some of this trade was a product of the tribute system, which the Chinese rulers used as an element of their foreign policy. The Chinese viewed the outside world as they viewed their own society—in a hierarchical manner. Rulers of smaller countries along the periphery were viewed as "younger brothers" of the Chinese emperor and owed fealty to him. Foreign rulers who accepted the relationship were required to pay tribute and to promise not to harbor enemies of the Chinese Empire. But the foreign rulers also benefited from the relationship. Not only did it confer legitimacy on them, but they often received magnificent gifts from their "elder brother" as a reward for good behavior. Merchants from their countries also gained access to the vast Chinese market.

10–2 EXPLOSION IN CENTRAL ASIA: THE MONGOL EMPIRE

 Focus Question: Why were the Mongols able to amass an empire, and what were the main characteristics of their rule in China?

The Mongols, who succeeded the Song as the rulers of China in the late thirteenth century, rose to power in Asia with stunning rapidity. In the 1160s, when Genghis Khan (JING-uss *or* GENG-uss KAHN) (also known as Chinggis Khan), the founder of Mongol greatness, was born, the Mongols were a relatively obscure pastoral people in the area of modern-day Outer Mongolia. Like most of the nomadic peoples in the region, they were organized loosely into clans and tribes and even lacked a common name for themselves. Rivalry among the various tribes over pastureland, livestock, and booty was intense and increased at the end of the twelfth century as a result of a growing population and the consequent overgrazing of pastures. Since they had no source of subsistence besides their herds, the Mongols were, in the words of one historian, in a "state of stress."

This challenge was met by the great Mongol chieftain Genghis Khan (c. 1162–1227), whose original name was Temuchin

(TEM-yuh-jin) (or Temujin). When Temuchin was still a child, his father, an impoverished noble of his tribe, was murdered by a rival, and the boy was forced to seek refuge in the wilderness. Described by one historian as tall, adroit, and vigorous, young Temuchin gradually unified the Mongol tribes through his prowess and the power of his personality. In 1206, he was elected Genghis Khan ("universal ruler") at a massive tribal meeting in the Gobi Desert. From that time on, he devoted himself to military pursuits. Mongol nomads were now forced to pay taxes and were subject to military conscription. "Man's highest joy," Genghis Khan reportedly remarked, "is in victory: to conquer one's enemies, to pursue them, to deprive them of their possessions, to make their beloved weep, to ride on their horses, and to embrace their wives and daughters."[5]

The army that Genghis Khan unleashed on the world was not exceptionally large—totaling less than 130,000 in 1227, at a time when the total Mongol population numbered between 1 million and 2 million. But their mastery of military tactics set the Mongols apart from their rivals. Their tireless flying columns of mounted warriors surrounded their enemies and harassed them like cattle, luring them into pursuit and then ambushing them with flank attacks. John Plano Carpini (PLAN-oh car-PEE-nee), a contemporary Franciscan friar, remarked:

> As soon as they discover the enemy they charge and each one unleashes three or four arrows. If they see that they can't

Genghis Khan. Founder of the Mongol Empire, Temuchin (later to be known as Genghis Khan) died in 1227, long before Mongol warriors defeated the armies of the Song and established the Yuan dynasty in China in 1279. In this portrait by a Chinese court artist, the ruler appears in a stylized version, looking much like other Chinese emperors from the period. Painters in many societies used similar techniques to render their subjects in a manner more familiar to prospective observers.

A LETTER TO THE POPE

Interaction & Exchange

IN 1245, POPE INNOCENT IV dispatched the Franciscan friar John Plano Carpini to the Mongol headquarters at Karakorum to appeal to the great khan Kuyuk (koo-YOOK) to cease his attacks on Christians. After a considerable wait, Carpini was given the following reply, which could not have pleased the pope. The letter was discovered recently in the Vatican archives.

A Letter from Kuyuk Khan to Pope Innocent IV

By the power of the Eternal Heaven, We are the all-embracing Khan of all the Great Nations. It is our command:

This is a decree, sent to the great Pope that he may know and pay heed.

After holding counsel with the monarchs under your suzerainty, you have sent us an offer of subordination, which we have accepted from the hands of your envoy.

If you should act up to your word, then you, the great Pope, should come in person with the monarchs to pay us homage and we should thereupon instruct you concerning the commands of the Yasak.

Furthermore, you have said it would be well for us to become Christians. You write to me in person about this matter, and have addressed to me a request. This, your request, we cannot understand.

Furthermore, you have written me these words: "You have attacked all the territories of the Magyars and other Christians, at which I am astonished. Tell me, what was their crime?" These, your words, we likewise cannot understand. Jenghiz Khan and Ogatai Khakan revealed the commands of Heaven. But those whom you name would not believe the commands of Heaven. Those of whom you speak showed themselves highly presumptuous and slew our envoys. Therefore, in accordance with the commands of the Eternal Heaven the inhabitants of the aforesaid countries have been slain and annihilated. If not by the command of Heaven, how can anyone slay or conquer out of his own strength?

And when you say: "I am a Christian. I pray to God. I arraign and despise others," how do you know who is pleasing to God and to whom He allots His grace? How can you know it, that you speak such words?

Thanks to the power of the Eternal Heaven, all lands have been given to us from sunrise to sunset. How could anyone act other than in accordance with the commands of Heaven? Now your own upright heart must tell you: "We will become subject to you, and will place our powers at your disposal." You in person, at the head of the monarchs, all of you, without exception, must come to tender us service and pay us homage, then only will we recognize your submission. But if you do not obey the commands of Heaven, and run counter to our orders, we shall know that you are our foe.

That is what we have to tell you. If you fail to act in accordance therewith, how can we foresee what will happen to you? Heaven alone knows.

 Based on the account given here, what message was the pope seeking to convey to the great khan in Karakorum? What was the nature of the latter's reply?

Source: From Prawdin, Michael, *The Mongol Empire: Its Rise and Legacy* (Free Press, 1961), pp. 280–281.

---

break him, they retreat in order to entice the enemy to pursue, thus luring him into an ambush prepared in advance. . . . Their military stratagems are numerous. At the moment of an enemy cavalry attack, they place prisoners and foreign auxiliaries in the forefront of their own position, while positioning the bulk of their own troops on the right and left wings to envelop the adversary, thus giving the enemy the impression that they are more numerous than in reality.[6]

In the years after the election of Temuchin as universal ruler, the Mongols defeated tribal groups to their west and then turned their attention to the non-Chinese kingdoms of northern China. There they discovered that their adversaries were armed with a weapon called a fire-lance, an early form of flamethrower. Gunpowder had been invented in China during the late Tang period, and by the early thirteenth century, a fire-lance had been developed that could spew out flames and projectiles a distance of 30 or 40 yards, inflicting considerable damage on the enemy.

Before the end of the thirteenth century, the fire-lance had evolved into the much more effective handgun and cannon.

These inventions came too late to save China from the Mongols, however, and were transmitted to Europe by the early fourteenth century by foreigners employed by the Mongol rulers of China.

While some Mongol armies were engaged in the conquest of northern China, others traveled farther afield and advanced as far as central Europe. Only the death of Genghis Khan in 1227 may have prevented an all-out Mongol attack on western Europe (see "A Letter to the Pope"). In 1231, the Mongols attacked Persia and then defeated the Abbasids at Baghdad in 1258 (see Chapter 7). Mongol forces attacked the Song from the west in the 1260s and finally defeated the remnants of the Song navy in 1279. Once again, as had occurred after the fall of the Han dynasty, the heartland of China was placed under alien rule.

By then, the Mongol Empire was quite different from what it had been under its founder. Prior to the conquests of Genghis Khan, the Mongols had been purely nomadic. They spent their winters in the southern plains, where they found suitable pastures for their cattle, and traveled north in the summer to wooded areas where the water was sufficient. They lived in round, felt-covered tents (called yurts), which were lightly constructed so that they could be easily transported. For food, the Mongols depended on milk and meat from their herds and game from hunting.

To administer the new empire, Genghis Khan had set up a capital city at Karakorum (khah-rah-KOR-um), in present-day Outer Mongolia, but prohibited his fellow Mongols from practicing sedentary occupations or living in cities. But under his successors, the Mongols began to adapt to their conquered areas. As one khan remarked, quoting his Chinese adviser, "Although you inherited the Chinese Empire on horseback, you cannot rule it from that position." Mongol aristocrats began to enter administrative positions, while commoners took up sedentary occupations as farmers or merchants.[7]

The territorial nature of the empire also changed. Following tribal custom, at the death of the ruling khan, the territory was distributed among his heirs. The once-united empire of Genghis Khan was thus divided into several separate **khanates**

The Mongol Conquest of China

(KHAH-nayts), each under the autonomous rule of one of his sons by his principal wife. One of his sons was awarded the khanate of Chaghadai (chag-huh-DY) in Central Asia with its capital at Samarkand; another ruled Persia from the conquered city of Baghdad; a third took charge of the khanate of Kipchak (KIP-chahk), commonly known as the Golden Horde. But it was one of his grandsons, named Khubilai Khan (1215–1294), who completed the conquest of the Song and established a new Chinese dynasty, called the Yuan (from a phrase in the *Book of Changes* referring to the "original creative force" of the universe). Khubilai moved the capital of China northward from Hangzhou to Khanbaliq ("city of the khan"), which was located on a major trunk route from the Great Wall to the plains of northern China (see Map 10.2). Later the city would be known by the Chinese name Beijing (bay-ZHING), or Peking (pee-KING) ("northern capital").

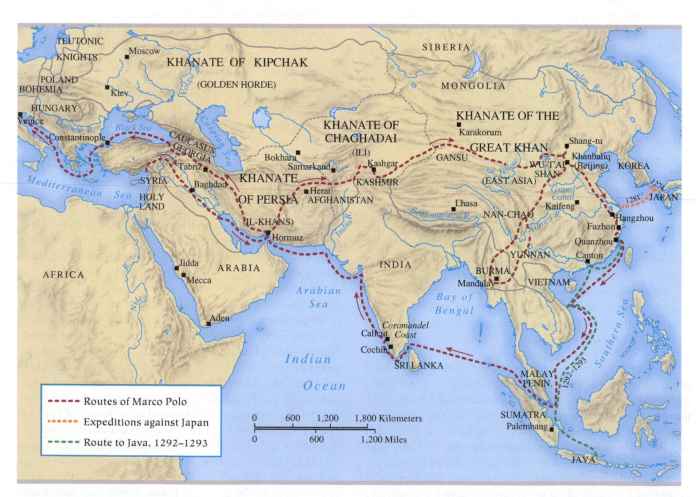

Map 10.2 Asia Under the Mongols. This map traces the expansion of Mongol power throughout Eurasia in the thirteenth century. After the death of Genghis Khan in 1227, the empire was divided into four separate khanates.

Q *Why was the Mongol Empire divided into four separate khanates?*

10-2a Mongol Rule in China

At first, China's new rulers exhibited impressive vitality. Under the leadership of the talented Khubilai Khan, the Yuan continued to flex their muscles by attempting to expand their empire. Mongol armies advanced into the Red River Valley and reconquered Vietnam, which had declared its independence after the fall of the Tang three hundred years earlier. Mongol fleets were launched against Malay kingdoms in Java and Sumatra and also against the islands of Japan. Only the expedition against Vietnam succeeded, however, and even that success was temporary. The Vietnamese counterattacked and eventually drove the Mongols back across the border. The attempted conquest of Japan was even more disastrous, as a massive storm destroyed the Mongol fleet, killing thousands (see Chapter 11). Yuan rulers belatedly discovered that familiar tactics such as cavalry charges and siege warfare were less effective in distant lands composed of unfamiliar terrain.

The Mongols had more success in governing China. After a failed attempt to administer their conquest as they had ruled their own tribal society (some advisers reportedly even suggested that the plowed fields be transformed into pastures), Mongol rulers adapted to the Chinese political system and made use of local talents in the bureaucracy. The tripartite division of the administration into civilian, military, and censorate was retained, as were the six ministries. The civil service system, which had been abolished in the north in 1237 and in the south forty years later, was revived in the early fourteenth century. The state cult of Confucius was also restored, although Khubilai Khan himself remained a Buddhist.

But there were some key differences. Culturally, the Mongols were nothing like the Chinese and remained a separate class with their own laws. The highest positions in the bureaucracy were usually staffed by Mongols. Although some leading Mongols followed their ruler in converting to Buddhism, most commoners retained their traditional religion. Even those who adopted Buddhism chose the Lamaist (LAH-muh-ist) variety from Tibet, which emphasized divination and magic.

Despite these differences, the Mongols were able to rule China for nearly a century. The people of the north, after all, were used to foreign rule, and although those living farther to the south may have resented their alien conquerors, they probably came to respect the stability, unity, and economic prosperity that the Mongols initially brought to China, where they continued the relatively tolerant economic policies of the southern Song. By bringing much of the Eurasian landmass under a single rule, they encouraged long-distance trade, particularly along the Silk Road, where additional guard posts and an expanded official presence in many of the oasis towns made travel for merchants—many of whom were now Muslims from Central Asia—much safer than had been the case before. To promote internal trade, the Grand Canal was extended from the Yellow River to the capital. Adjacent to the canal, a paved highway was constructed that extended all the way from the Song capital of Hangzhou to its Mongol counterpart at Khanbaliq.

The capital was a magnificent city. According to the Italian merchant Marco Polo, who resided there during the reign of Khubilai Khan, it was 24 miles in diameter and surrounded by thick walls of earth penetrated by a dozen massive gates (see

FILM & HISTORY

The saga of Marco Polo's travels through Asia during the Middle Ages have excited readers for centuries. Filmmakers in Hollywood were not slow to catch on, and in 1938 they produced a blockbuster called *The Adventures of Marco Polo*, starring the current leading man Gary Cooper, and supported by a cast of primarily Western actors. In 2007, the Hallmark Channel tried again with more success. Except for the aging emperor Khubilai Khan, most of the actors in a remake entitled simply *Marco Polo* were of Asian background, and due credit was ascribed to the Chinese for their technological accomplishments.

Q *Marco Polo is not the only famous traveler to write a journal about his experiences in far-flung parts of the world. What other such chroniclers have we already encountered in this book?*

Everett Collection

Film & History). He was even more impressed by the old Song capital of Hangzhou, which he described as a noble city where the delights were so abundant that an inhabitant might imagine himself in paradise.[8]

Ironically, while many of their subjects prospered, the Mongols themselves often did not. Burdened by low wages and heavy military obligations that left them little time for their herds, many Mongol warriors became so impoverished that they were forced to sell their sons and daughters into slavery. In the end, the Yuan fell victim to the same fate that had afflicted other powerful dynasties in China. In fact, it was one of the shortest-lived of the great

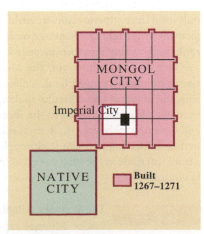

Khanbaliq (Beijing) Under the Mongols

dynasties, lasting less than a century. Excessive spending on foreign conquest, inadequate tax revenues, factionalism and corruption at court and in the bureaucracy, and growing internal instability, brought about in part by a famine in central China in the 1340s, all contributed to the dynasty's demise. Khubilai Khan's successors lacked his administrative genius, and by the middle of the next century, the Yuan dynasty in China, like the Mongol khanates elsewhere in Central Asia, had begun to decline rapidly (see Chapter 13).

The immediate instrument of Mongol defeat was Zhu Yuanzhang (JOO yoo-wen-JAHNG), the son of a poor peasant in the lower Yangzi Valley. After losing most of his family in the famine of the 1340s, Zhu became an itinerant monk and then the leader of a gang of bandits. In the 1360s, unrest spread throughout the country, and after defeating a number of rivals, Zhu put an end to the disintegrating Yuan regime and declared the foundation of the new Ming (MING) ("bright") Dynasty (1369–1644).

10-2b The Mongols' Place in History

The Mongols were the last, and arguably the greatest, of the nomadic peoples who came thundering out of the steppes of Central Asia, pillaging and conquering the territories of their adversaries. What caused this extraordinary burst of energy, and why were the Mongols so much more successful than their predecessors? Historians are divided. Some have suggested that drought and overpopulation may have depleted the available pasture on the steppes, yet another example of the unseen impact of environmental changes on human history. Others have cited the ambition and genius of Genghis Khan, who was able to arouse a sense of personal loyalty unusual in a society where commitments were ordinarily of a tribal nature. Still others point to his reliance on the organizational unit known as the *ordos* (OR-dohz), described by the historian Samuel Adshead as "a system of restructuring tribes into decimal units whose top level of leadership was organized on bureaucratic lines."[9] Although the *ordos* system had been used by the Xiongnu and other nomadic peoples before them, the Mongols applied it to create disciplined military units that were especially effective against the relatively freewheeling tactics of their rivals on the steppes and devastating against the relatively immobile armies of the sedentary states in their path. Once organized, the Mongols used their superior horsemanship and blitzkrieg tactics effectively, while taking advantage of divisions within the enemy ranks and borrowing more advanced military technology.

Once in power, however, the Mongols' underlying weaknesses eventually proved fatal. Unlike some of their predecessors, the Mongols had difficulty making the transition from the nomadic life of the steppes to the sedentary life of the villages, and their unwieldy system of royal succession led to instability in their leadership ranks. Still, although the Mongol era was just a brief interlude in the long sweep of human history, it was rich in consequences.

HISTORIANS DEBATE **The Mongols: A Reputation Undeserved?** The era of Mongol expansion has usually been portrayed as a tragic period in human history. The Mongols'

conquests resulted in widespread death and suffering throughout the world. Nations and empires were humbled, cities destroyed, and irrigation systems laid waste. Then, just when the ravages of the era appeared to come to an end, bubonic plague, probably carried by lice hidden in the saddlebags of Mongol horsemen, decimated the population of Europe and the Middle East (see Chapter 13). Some regions lost as much as one-third of their population to massacre or starvation.

Few modern historians would dispute the brutality that characterized Mongol expansion. But some now point out that beyond the legacy of death and destruction, the Mongols also brought an era of widespread peace, known as the *Pax Mongolica* (PAKS *or* PAHKS mahn-GOH-lik-uh), to much of the Eurasian supercontinent and inaugurated what one scholar has described as "the idea of the unified conceptualization of the globe," creating a "basic information circuit" that spread commodities, ideas, and inventions from one end of the Eurasian supercontinent to the other. That being said, there is no denying that the Mongol invasions resulted in widespread suffering and misfortune to millions of people in their path. If there was a Mongol peace, it was, for many, the peace of death. In any event, such conditions were not destined to last.

10-3 THE MING DYNASTY

 Focus Questions: What were the chief initiatives taken by the early rulers of the Ming Dynasty to enhance the role of China in the world? Why did the imperial court order the famous voyages of Zheng He, and why were they discontinued?

The Ming inaugurated a new era of greatness in Chinese history. Under a series of strong rulers, China extended its rule into Mongolia and Central Asia. The Ming even briefly reconquered Vietnam, which, after a thousand years of Chinese rule, had reclaimed its independence following the collapse of the Tang Dynasty in the tenth century. Along the northern frontier, the Emperor Yongle (YOONG-luh) (r. 1402–1424) strengthened the Great Wall and pacified the nomadic tribes that had troubled China in previous centuries (see Comparative Illustration "The Great Walls of China"). A tributary relationship was established with the Choson (Yi) Dynasty in Korea.

The internal achievements of the Ming were equally impressive. When they replaced the Mongols in the fourteenth century, the Ming turned to traditional Confucian institutions as a means of ruling their vast empire. These included the six ministries at the apex of the bureaucracy, the use of the civil service examinations to select members of the bureaucracy, and the division of the empire into provinces, districts, and counties. As before, Chinese villages were relatively autonomous, and local councils of elders continued to be responsible for adjudicating disputes, initiating local construction and irrigation projects, mustering a militia, and assessing and collecting taxes.

The society that was governed by this vast hierarchy of officials was a far cry from the predominantly agrarian society

COMPARATIVE ILLUSTRATION

William J. Duiker

William J. Duiker

The Great Walls of China. Although the Great Wall is popularly believed to be more than two thousand years old, the part of the wall that is most frequently visited by tourists today was a reconstruction undertaken during the early Ming Dynasty to protect against invasion from the north. Part of that wall, which was built to protect the imperial capital of Beijing, is shown in A. The original walls, which stretched from the shores of the Pacific Ocean to the deserts of Central Asia, were often composed of loose stone, dirt, or piled rubble. The section shown in B is located north of the Turfan Depression in Xinjiang Province.

 What were the major reasons for building the Great Wall? To what degree was the wall successful in achieving these objectives?

---

that had been ruled by the Han. In the burgeoning cities near the coast and along the Yangzi River Valley, factories and workshops were vastly increasing the variety and output of their manufactured goods. The population had doubled, and new crops had been introduced, greatly expanding the food output of the empire.

10–3a The Voyages of Zheng He

In 1405, in a splendid display of Chinese maritime might, Emperor Yongle sent a fleet of Chinese trading ships under the eunuch admiral Zheng He (JEHNG-huh) through the Strait of Malacca and out into the Indian Ocean. There they traveled as far west as the east coast of Africa, stopping on the way at ports in South Asia. The size of the fleet was impressive: nearly 28,000 sailors on sixty-two ships, some of them junks larger by far than any other oceangoing vessels

the world had yet seen (although the actual size of the larger ships is in dispute). China seemed about to become a direct participant in the vast trade network that extended as far west as the Atlantic Ocean, thereby culminating the process of opening China to the wider world that had begun with the Tang Dynasty.

HISTORIANS DEBATE **Why Were Zheng He's Voyages Undertaken, and Why Were They Abandoned?** Why the expeditions were undertaken has been a matter of much debate. Some historians point to Yongle's native curiosity and note that the expedition—and the six others that followed it—returned not only with goods and a plethora of information about the outside world but also with some items unknown in China (the emperor was especially intrigued by the giraffes brought back from East Africa and placed them in the imperial zoo, where they were identified by soothsayers with the advent of good government). Others argue more persuasively that economic profit, or what in our day is called "power projection" was the main reason. In their view, the voyages were probably aimed at solidifying China's hegemonic role and strengthening its alliances with trading partners, while simultaneously clearing the southern seas of pirates who preyed on merchant shipping throughout the region.

Whatever the case, the voyages resulted in a dramatic increase in Chinese knowledge about the world and the nature of ocean travel. They also brought massive profits for their sponsors, some of whom were allies of Admiral Zheng He at court. This undoubtedly aroused resentment among conservatives within the bureaucracy, some of whom viewed commercial activities with a characteristic measure of Confucian disdain. One disgruntled critic commented that an end to the voyages would provide the Chinese people with a respite "so that they can devote themselves to husbandry [agriculture] and schooling."

Shortly after Yongle's death, the voyages were discontinued, never to be revived. Ironically, the turn inward had been initiated, perhaps inadvertently, by Emperor Yongle himself when he decided to move the Ming capital from Nanjing (nahn-JING), in central China, where the ships were built and the voyages launched, back to the old Mongol capital in Beijing, where official eyes were firmly focused on the threat from the north. As a means of reducing that threat, Yongle ordered the strengthening of sections of the Great Wall north of the new capital, along with the resettlement of thousands of families to the region

from the fertile Yangzi Valley. The emperor presumably had not intended to set forces in motion that would divert the country from its contacts with the external world. After all, he had been the driving force behind Zheng He's voyages. But the end result was a shift in the balance of power from central China, where it had been since the southern Song Dynasty, back to northern China, where it had originated and would remain for the rest of the Ming era. China would not look outward again for more than four centuries.

For historians, why Yongle's successors discontinued Zheng He's explorations and turned their attention back to domestic concerns has long been a puzzle. Some speculate that court intrigues or the replacement of one emperor by another is not a sufficient explanation. More likely, they argue, Ming officials concluded that when local rulers throughout the South Seas had been sufficiently intimidated to accept a tributary relationship with their "elder brother" in China, the voyages—which had been prohibitively expensive—were no longer necessary. Whatever the case, the decision had long-term consequences and affected China's relationships with the rest of Asia for several centuries.

One recent theory that has added a new element to the equation contends that the Chinese fleets did not limit their explorations to the Indian Ocean but actually circled the earth and discovered the existence of the Western Hemisphere in the process. Although that theory has won few scholarly adherents, the voyages, and their abrupt discontinuance, remain one of the most fascinating enigmas in the history of China.

The World in Chinese Eyes. In 1406 the Chinese admiral Zheng He left the coast of China on the first of his many voyages to the Indian Ocean. He was not sailing into the unknown. Taking advantage of geographical knowledge obtained from Islamic and Mongolian sources, Chinese cartographers of the early Ming era had already produced world maps that included information on the continent of Africa and the vast territories that comprised the Eurasian supercontinent. The earliest of such maps is the *Comprehensive Map of the Great Ming Dynasty*. Drawn up sometime in the fourteenth century, it reflected the knowledge gleaned by seafarers over many generations. In the map shown here, China appears to the right, while the continents of Africa and Europe are compressed on the edge of the map at the far left. Photograph by David Trochos

10–4 IN SEARCH OF THE WAY

Q Focus Question: What roles did Buddhism, Daoism, and Neo-Confucianism play in Chinese intellectual life in the period between the Sui dynasty and the Ming?

By the time of the Sui dynasty, Buddhism and Daoism had emerged as major rivals of Confucianism as the ruling ideology of the state. But during the last half of the Tang, Confucianism revived and once again became dominant at court, a position it would retain to the end of the dynastic period in the early twentieth century. Buddhist and Daoist beliefs, however, remained popular at the local level.

10–4a The Rise and Decline of Buddhism and Daoism

As noted earlier, Buddhism arrived in China with travelers from India and found its first adherents within the merchant community and among intellectuals intrigued by the new ideas. During the chaotic centuries following the collapse of the Han dynasty, Buddhism and Daoism appealed to those who were searching for more emotional and spiritual satisfaction than Confucianism could provide. Both faiths reached beyond the common people and found support among the ruling classes as well. The capital of Chang'an even had a small Christian church after Christianity was introduced to China by Syrian merchants in the sixth century BCE.

The Sinification of Buddhism As Buddhism attracted more followers, it began to take on Chinese characteristics and divided into a number of separate sects. Some, like the **Chan** (Zen in Japanese) sect, called for mind training and a strict regimen as a means of seeking enlightenment, a technique that reflected Daoist ideas and appealed to many intellectuals. Others, like the **Pure Land** sect, stressed the role of devotion, an approach that was more appealing to ordinary Chinese, who lacked the time and inclination for strict monastic discipline. Still others were mystical sects, like **Tantrism** (TUHN-tri-zem), which emphasized the importance of magical symbols and ritual in seeking a preferred way to enlightenment. Some Buddhist groups, like their Daoist counterparts, had political objectives. The **White Lotus** sect, founded in 1133, often adopted the form of a rebel movement, seeking political reform or the overthrow of a dynasty and forecasting a new era when a "savior Buddha" would come to earth to herald the advent of a new age. Most believers, however, assimilated Buddhism into their daily lives, where it joined Confucian ideology and spirit worship as an element in the highly eclectic and tolerant Chinese worldview.

The burgeoning popularity of Buddhism continued into the early years of the Tang Dynasty. Early Tang rulers lent their support to the Buddhist monasteries that had been established throughout the country. Buddhist scriptures were regularly included in the civil service examinations, and Buddhist and Daoist advisers replaced shamans and Confucian scholar-officials as advisers at court. But ultimately, Buddhism and Daoism lost

William J. Duiker

Buddhist Sculpture at Longmen. The Silk Road was an avenue for ideas as well as trade. Over the centuries, Christian, Buddhist, and Muslim teachings came to China across the sandy wastes of the Taklimakan Desert. In the seventh century, the Tang emperor Gaozong (gow-ZOONG) commissioned this massive cliffside carving as part of a large complex of cave art devoted to the Buddha at Longmen (LAHNG-mun) in central China. Bold and grandiose in its construction, this towering statue of the Buddha, surrounded by temple guardians and bodhisattvas, reflects the glory of the Tang Dynasty.

favor at court and were increasingly subjected to official persecution. Part of the reason was xenophobia. Envious Daoists and Confucianists made a point of criticizing the foreign origins of Buddhist doctrines, which one prominent Confucian scholar characterized as nothing but "silly relics." To deflect such criticism, Buddhists attempted to make the doctrine more Chinese, equating the Indian concept of *dharma* (law) with the Chinese concept of *Dao* (the Way). Emperor Tang Taizong ordered the Buddhist monk Xuan Zang to translate Lao Tzu's classic, *The Way of the Dao*, into Sanskrit, reportedly to show visitors from India that China had its own equivalent to the Buddhist scriptures. But another reason for this change of heart may have been financial. The great Buddhist monasteries had accumulated thousands of acres of land and serfs that were exempt from paying taxes to the state. Such wealth contributed to the corruption of the monks and other Buddhist officials and in turn aroused popular resentment and official disapproval. As the state attempted to eliminate the great landholdings of the aristocracy, the large monasteries also attracted its attention. During the later Tang, countless temples and monasteries were destroyed, and more than 100,000 monks were compelled to leave the monasteries and return to secular life.

Buddhism Under Threat There were probably deeper cultural and ideological reasons for the growing antagonism between Buddhism and the state. By preaching the illusory nature of the material world, Buddhism was denying the very essence of Confucian teachings—the necessity for filial piety and hard work. By encouraging young Chinese to abandon their rice fields and seek refuge and wisdom in the monasteries, Buddhism was undermining the foundation stones of Chinese society—the family unit and the work ethic. In the final analysis, Buddhism was incompatible with the activist element in Chinese society, an orientation that was most effectively expressed by State Confucianism. In the competition with Confucianism for support by the state, Buddhism, like Daoism, was almost certain to lose, at least in the more this-worldly, secure, and prosperous milieu of Tang and Song China. The

two doctrines continued to win converts at the local level, but official support ceased. In the meantime, Buddhism was under attack in Central Asia as well. In the eighth century, the Uighur kingdom adopted **Manichaeanism** (ma-nuh-KEE-uh-nizm), an offshoot of the ancient Zoroastrian religion with some influence from Christianity. Manichaeanism spread rapidly throughout the area and may have been a reason for the European belief that a Christian king (the legendary Prester John) ruled somewhere in Asia. By the tenth century, however, Islam was beginning to move east along the Silk Road, posing a severe threat to both Manichaean and Buddhist centers in the area. As its lifeline to the Indian subcontinent along the Silk Road was severed, Chinese Buddhism lost access to its spiritual roots and became increasingly subject to the pull of indigenous intellectual and social currents.

10–4b Neo-Confucianism: The Investigation of Things

Into the vacuum left by the decline of Buddhism and Daoism stepped a revived Confucianism. As during the Han dynasty, the teachings of "master Kung" were used to buttress the power and majesty of the state. The emperor continued to be seen as an intermediary between Heaven and earth, while his legitimacy was based not on the hereditary principle but on his talent and virtue, a central component of Confucian doctrine since the era of the "hundred schools" of philosophy in ancient times.

At the same time, however, it was a new form of Confucianism that had been significantly altered by its competition with Buddhist and Daoist teachings. Challenged by Buddhist and Daoist ideas about the nature of the universe, Confucian thinkers began to flesh out the spare metaphysical structure of classical Confucian doctrine with a set of sophisticated theories about the nature of the cosmos and humans' place in it. Although the origins of this effort can be traced to the early Tang period, it reached fruition during the intellectually prolific Song Dynasty, when it became the dominant ideology of the state.

The fundamental purpose of **Neo-Confucianism**, as the new doctrine was called, was to unite the metaphysical speculations of Buddhism and Daoism with the pragmatic Confucian approach to society. In response to Buddhism and Daoism, Neo-Confucianism maintained that the world is real, not illusory, and that fulfillment comes from participation, not withdrawal.

The primary contributor to this intellectual effort was the philosopher Zhu Xi (JOO SHEE). Raised during the southern Song era, Zhu Xi accepted the division of the world into a material world and a transcendent world, called by Neo-Confucianists the **Supreme Ultimate**, or *Tai Ji* (TY JEE). The Supreme Ultimate was roughly equivalent to the *Dao*, or Way, in classical Confucian philosophy. To Zhu Xi, this Supreme Ultimate was a set of abstract principles governed by the law of *yin* and *yang* and the five elements.

Human beings served as a link between the two halves of this bifurcated universe. Although human beings live in the material world, each individual has an identity that is linked with the Supreme Ultimate, and the goal of individual action is to transcend the material world in a Buddhist sense to achieve an essential identity with the Supreme Ultimate. According to Zhu Xi and his

The Big Goose Pagoda. When the Buddhist pilgrim Xuan Zang returned to China from India in the mid-seventh century BCE, he settled in the capital of Chang'an, where, under orders from the Tang emperor, he began to translate Buddhist texts in his possession from Sanskrit into Chinese. The Big Goose Pagoda, shown here, was erected shortly afterward to house them. Originally known as the Pagoda of the Classics, the structure consists of seven stories and is more than 240 feet high.

William J. Duiker

followers, the means of transcending the material world is self-cultivation, which is achieved by the "investigation of things."

The School of Mind During the remainder of the Song Dynasty and into the early years of the Ming, Zhu Xi's ideas became the central core of Confucian ideology and a favorite source of questions for the civil service examinations. But during the mid-Ming era, his ideas came under attack from a Confucian scholar named Wang Yangming (WAHNG yahng-MING). Wang and his supporters disagreed with Zhu Xi's focus on learning through an investigation of the outside world and asserted that the correct way to transcend the material world was through an understanding of self. According to this so-called **School of Mind**, the mind and the universe were a single unit. Knowledge was thus intuitive rather than empirical and was obtained through internal self-searching rather than through an investigation of the outside world. The debate is reminiscent of a similar disagreement between followers of the ancient Greek philosophers Plato and Aristotle. Plato had argued that all knowledge comes from within, while Aristotle argued that knowledge resulted from an examination of the external world. Wang Yangming's ideas attracted many followers during the Ming Dynasty, and the school briefly rivaled that of Zhu Xi in popularity among Confucian scholars. Nevertheless, it never won official acceptance, probably because it was too much like Buddhism in denying the importance of a life of participation and social action.

For the average Chinese, of course, an instinctive faith in the existence of household deities or nature spirits continued to take precedence over the intellectual ruminations of Buddhist monks or Confucian scholars. But a prevailing belief in the concept of *karma* and possible rebirth in a next life was one important legacy of the Buddhist connection, while a new manifestation of the Confucian concept of hierarchy was the village god—often believed to live in a prominent tree in the vicinity—who protected the community from wandering evil spirits.

10–5 CHANGING SOCIAL CONDITIONS IN TRADITIONAL CHINA

 Focus Questions: In what ways did social conditions in China evolve during the period from the Tang to the Ming Dynasties? Do you see any parallel with similar events elsewhere in the world?

The political and economic changes that took place from the end of the Han to the rise of the Ming Dynasty affected Chinese society in several ways. For one thing, China became much more complex. Whereas previously the country had been almost exclusively rural, with a small urban class of merchants, artisans, and workers almost entirely dependent on the state, the cities had now grown into an important, if statistically still insignificant, part of the population. Urban life, too, had changed. Cities were no longer primarily administrative centers dominated by officials and their families but now included a much broader mix of officials, merchants, artisans, peddlers,

and entertainers. Unlike European cities, however, Chinese cities did not possess special privileges that protected their residents from the rapacity of the central government.

In the countryside, equally significant changes were taking place as the relatively rigid demarcation between the landed aristocracy and the mass of the rural population gave way to a more complex mixture of landed gentry, free farmers, sharecroppers, and landless laborers. There was also a class of "base people," consisting of actors, butchers, and prostitutes, who possessed only limited legal rights and were not permitted to take the civil service examination.

10–5a The Rise of the Gentry

Under the early Tang, powerful noble families not only possessed a significant part of the national wealth, but also dominated high positions in the imperial government, just as they had at the end of the Han dynasty four hundred years earlier. Some Tang rulers, such as Empress Wu in the late seventh century, sought to limit the power of the great families by recruiting officials through the civil service examinations, but in the end it was the expansion of regional power—often under non-Chinese military governors—after the An Lushan revolt that sounded the death knell to the aristocratic system.

During the Song Dynasty, the landed gentry (see "Equal Opportunity in China: The Civil Service Examination," Section 10-1e, p. 276) emerged as the most influential force in Chinese society. From that time on, the scholar-gentry class, as it is often called, controlled much of the wealth in the rural areas and produced the majority of the candidates for the bureaucracy. By virtue of their possession of land and specialized knowledge of the Confucian classics, the scholar-gentry had replaced the aristocracy as the political and economic elite of Chinese society. Unlike the aristocracy, however, they did not form an exclusive class separated by the accident of birth from the remainder of the population. Upward and downward mobility between the scholar-gentry class and the remainder of the population was not uncommon and may have been a key factor in the stability and longevity of the system. A position in the bureaucracy opened the doors to wealth and prestige for the individual and his family, but it was no guarantee of success, and the fortunes of individual families might experience a rapid rise and fall.

For affluent Chinese in this era, life offered many more pleasures than had been available to their forebears. As a result of increased contacts with the outside world first brought about as the result of the rise of the Silk Road under the Tang Dynasty, the country was much more cosmopolitan than it had been in previous centuries. In the large commercial cities such as Chang'an, Hangzhou, and Guangzhou, merchants from Central Asia and the Middle East mingled with their Chinese counterparts, introducing their hosts to new forms of entertainment, such as playing cards and chess (brought from India, although an early form had been invented in China during the Zhou dynasty). There were also new forms of transportation, such as the paddlewheel boat and horseback riding (made possible by the introduction of the stirrup); better means of communication (block printing was first invented in the eighth century BCE); and new tastes for the palate introduced from lands beyond the frontier. Tables

A CONFUCIAN WEDDING CEREMONY

Family & Society

DURING THE TWELFTH CENTURY, the philosopher Zhu Xi attempted to reinvigorate Confucian teachings in a contemporary setting that would make them more accessible to a broad audience. His goal was militantly Confucian—to combat both popular Buddhist doctrines and the superstitious practices of the common people. With his new moral code, Zhu Xi hoped to put Chinese society back on the Confucian track, with its emphasis on proper behavior. He therefore set forth the proper rituals required to carry out the special days that marked the lives of all Chinese: entry into adolescence, marriage, and funeral and ancestral rites. In the following selection, he prescribes the proper protocol for the Confucian wedding ceremony.

Zhu Xi's *Family Rituals*
4. Welcoming in Person

On the day before the wedding, the bride's family sends people to lay out the dowry furnishings in the groom's chamber. At dawn the groom's family sets places in the chamber. Meanwhile, the bride's family sets up places outside. As the sun goes down, the groom puts on full attire. After the presiding man makes a report at the offering hall, he pledges the groom and orders him to go to fetch the bride. The groom goes out and mounts his horse. When he gets to the bride's home he waits at his place. The presiding man of the bride's family makes a report at the offering hall, after which he pledges the bride and instructs her. Then he goes out to greet the groom. When the groom enters, he presents a goose. The duenna takes the girl out to climb into the conveyance. The groom mounts his horse and leads the way for the bridal vehicle. When they arrive at his house he leads the bride in and they take their seats. After the eating and drinking are done, the groom leaves the chamber. On reentering, he takes off his clothes and the candles are removed.

5. The Bride Is Presented to Her Parents-in-Law

The next day, having risen at dawn, the bride meets her parents-in-law, who entertain her. Then the bride is presented to the elders. If she is the wife of the eldest son, she serves food to her parents-in-law. Then the parents-in-law feast the bride.

6. Presentation at the Family Shrine

On the third day the presiding man takes the bride to be presented at the offering hall.

7. The Groom Is Presented to the Wife's Parents

The day after that the groom goes to see his wife's parents. Afterward he is presented to his wife's relatives. The bride's family entertains the groom, as in ordinary etiquette.

 What was Zhu Xi's apparent purpose in describing proper etiquette in this manner? How would adherence to such rigid rituals contribute to becoming a good Confucian?

Source: Excerpted from *Confucianism and Family Rituals in Imperial China: A Social History of Writing About Rites*, "A Welcoming in Person," translated and edited by P. B. Ebrey. Copyright © Princeton University Press, 1991.

and chairs, as well as chopsticks (known in China as "fast ones"), came into common usage in the home during the Song era. Tea had been introduced from the Burmese frontier by monks as early as the Han dynasty, and brandy and other concentrated spirits produced by the distillation of alcohol made their appearance in the seventh century. Tea began to emerge as a popular drink and took on ritual significance among intellectuals, poets, and Buddhist monks who believed that it could stimulate the brain cells and focus the mind. The turn inward that took place during the fifteenth century slowed down this process, but did not bring it to a halt.

10–5b Village and Family

Despite the changes described above, during the Ming Dynasty, the vast majority of the Chinese people still lived off the land in villages ranging in size from a few dozen residents to several thousand. A farmer's life was bounded by his village. Although many communities were connected to the outside world by roads or rivers, the average Chinese rarely left the confines of his native village except for an occasional visit to a nearby market town. This isolation was psychological as well as physical, for most Chinese identified with their immediate environment and had difficulty envisioning themselves living beyond the bamboo hedges or mud walls that marked the limit of their horizon.

An even more basic unit than the village in the lives of most Chinese, of course, was the family. The ideal was the joint family with at least three generations under one roof. Because rice farming was heavily labor-intensive, the tradition of the joint family was especially prevalent in the south. When a son married, he was expected to bring his new wife back to live in his parents' home. Often the parents added a new wing to the house for the new family. Women who did not marry remained in the home where they grew up.

Chinese village architecture reflected these traditions. Most family dwellings were simple, consisting of one or at most two rooms. They were usually constructed of dried mud, stone, or brick, depending on available materials and the prosperity of the family. Roofs were of thatch or tile, and the floors were usually of packed dirt. Large houses were often built in a square around an inner courtyard, thus guaranteeing privacy from the outside world.

Within the family unit, the proper forms of etiquette were essential (see "A Confucian Wedding Ceremony"). The eldest male theoretically ruled as an autocrat. He was responsible for presiding over ancestral rites at an altar, usually in the main

THE SAINTLY MISS WU

Family & Society

THE IDEA THAT A WIFE SHOULD SACRIFICE her wants to the needs of her husband and family was deeply embedded in traditional Chinese society. Widows in particular had few rights, and their remarriage was strongly condemned. In this account from a story by Hung Mai (hoong MY), a twelfth-century writer, the widowed Miss Wu wins the respect of the entire community by faithfully serving her mother-in-law.

Hung Mai, *A Song Family Saga*

Miss Wu served her mother-in-law very filially. Her mother-in-law had an eye ailment and felt sorry for her daughter-in-law's solitary and poverty-stricken situation, so she suggested that they call in a son-in-law for her and thereby get an adoptive heir. Miss Wu announced in tears, "A woman does not serve two husbands. I will support you. Don't talk this way." Her mother-in-law, seeing that she was determined, did not press her. Miss Wu did spinning, washing, sewing, cooking, and cleaning for her neighbors, earning perhaps a hundred cash a day, all of which she gave to her mother-in-law to cover the cost of firewood and food. If she was given any meat, she would wrap it up to take home. . . .

Once when her mother-in-law was cooking rice, a neighbor called to her, and to avoid overcooking the rice she dumped it into a pan. Owing to her bad eyes, however, she mistakenly put it in the dirty chamber pot. When Miss Wu returned and saw it, she did not say a word. She went to a neighbor to borrow some cooked rice for her mother-in-law and took the dirty rice and washed it to eat herself.

One day in the daytime neighbors saw [Miss Wu] ascending into the sky amid colored clouds. Startled, they told her mother-in-law, who said, "Don't be foolish. She just came back from pounding rice for someone, and is lying down on the bed. Go and look." They went to the room and peeked in and saw her sound asleep. Amazed, they left.

When Miss Wu woke up, her mother-in-law told her what happened, and she said, "I just dreamed of two young boys in blue clothes holding documents and riding on the clouds. They grabbed my clothes and said the Emperor of Heaven had summoned me. They took me to the gate of heaven and I was brought in to see the emperor, who was seated beside a balustrade. He said 'Although you are just a lowly ignorant village woman, you are able to serve your old mother-in-law sincerely and work hard. You really deserve respect.' He gave me a cup of aromatic wine and a string of cash, saying, 'I will supply you. From now on you will not need to work for others.' I bowed to thank him and came back, accompanied by the two boys. Then I woke up."

There was in fact a thousand cash on the bed, and the room was filled with a fragrance. They then realized that the neighbors' vision had been a spirit journey. From this point on even more people asked her to work for them, and she never refused. But the money that had been given to her she kept for her mother-in-law's use. Whatever they used promptly reappeared, so the thousand cash was never exhausted. The mother-in-law also regained her sight in both eyes.

 What is the moral of this story? How do the supernatural elements in the account strengthen the lesson intended by the author?

Source: From *The Inner Quarters: Marriage and the Lives of Chinese Women in the Sung Period*, Patricia Ebrey (Berkeley: University of California Press, 1993), pp. 197–198.

room of the house. He had traditional legal rights over his wife, and if she did not provide him with a male heir, he was permitted to take a second wife. She, however, had no recourse to divorce. As the old saying went, "Marry a chicken, follow the chicken; marry a dog, follow the dog." Wealthy Chinese might keep concubines, who lived in a separate room in the house and sometimes competed with the legal wife for precedence.

In accordance with Confucian tradition, children were expected, above all, to obey their father, who not only determined his children's careers but also selected their marriage partners. Filial piety was viewed as an absolute moral good, above virtually all other moral obligations. Even today, duty to one's parents is considered important in traditional Chinese families, and the tombstones of deceased Chinese are often decorated with tile paintings depicting the filial acts that they performed during their lifetime.

10–5c The Role of Women

Although the tradition of male superiority continued from ancient times, conditions were changing. During the Tang Dynasty, a number of women—including, of course, the notorious Empress Wu—were active in politics, and several were prominent in the entertainment world. Nevertheless, it is doubtful that such limited achievement among the elite trickled down to the mass of the population. Female children were considered less desirable than males because they could not undertake heavy work in the fields or carry on the family traditions. Women were not permitted to take the civil service examinations. Poor families often sold their daughters to wealthy villagers to serve as concubines, and female infanticide was not uncommon in times of famine to ensure that there would be food for the remainder of the family. Concubines had few legal rights; female domestic servants, even fewer.

In any event, any progress in women's rights was reversed under the Song and successive dynasties, when Chinese social customs began to reflect a more rigid interpretation of Confucian orthodoxy (see "The Saintly Miss Wu"). During the Song era, two new practices emerged that changed the equation for women seeking to obtain a successful marriage contract. First, a new form of dowry appeared. Whereas previously the prospective husband offered the bride's family a bride price, now the bride's parents were expected to pay the groom's family a dowry. With the prosperity that characterized Chinese society during much of the Song era, affluent parents sought to buy a satisfactory husband for their daughter, preferably one with a higher social standing and good prospects for an official career (see illustration "A Young Chinese Bride and Her Dowry").

A second source of marital bait during the Song period was the promise of a bride with tiny bound feet. The process of **foot binding**, carried out on girls aged five to thirteen, was excruciatingly painful, as it bent and compressed the foot to half its normal size by imprisoning it in restrictive bandages. But the procedure was often performed by ambitious mothers intent on assuring that their daughters would have the best possible prospects for marriage. A zealous mother would also want her daughter to have a competitive edge in dealing with the other wives and concubines of her future husband. Bound feet represented submissiveness and self-discipline, two of the required attributes of an ideal Confucian wife.

Throughout northern China, foot binding became common under the Song for women of all social classes. It was less widespread in southern China, where the cultivation of wet rice could not be carried out with bandaged feet; there it tended to be limited to the scholar-gentry class. Still, most Chinese women with bound feet contributed to the labor force to supplement the family income. Tattooing the body was also not uncommon, in contrast to earlier times, when it had only been applied to criminals as a means of identification and humiliation.

As in most traditional cultures, there were exceptions to the low status of women in Chinese society. Women had substantial property rights and retained control over their dowries even after divorce or the death of the husband. Women were actively involved in commerce, especially in the major cities, where they ran restaurants and guesthouses, or served as owners or clerks of textile shops catering to female customers. Some were employed in silk factories, or—as a thirteenth century scroll on the various stages of sericulture graphically demonstrates—even engaged in the production of woven silk in the home (see illustration "The Preparation of Silk"). Wives were frequently an influential force within the family as well, often handling the accounts and taking primary responsibility for raising the children.

A Young Chinese Bride and Her Dowry. A Chinese bride had to leave her parental home and move to her husband's house, thereby also transferring her filial allegiance to her in-laws. For this reason, the mother-son relationship was the most important one in a Chinese woman's life. With the expansion of the gentry class during the Song Dynasty, young men who passed the civil service examination became the most sought-after marriage prospects, requiring that the families of young women offer a substantial dowry as an enticement to the groom's family. But some women were destined for more distant homes. In this Persian miniature, a Chinese bride destined to marry a Turkish bridegroom travels along the Silk Road, leading a procession that is transporting her dowry of prized Chinese porcelain to her new home.

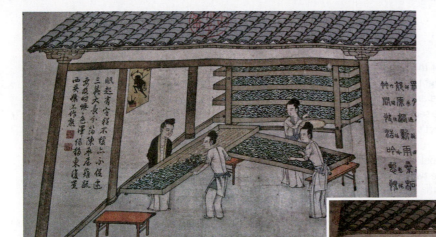

The Preparation of Silk. Since antiquity, the Chinese have fashioned textiles out of silk. The Shang dynasty produced both hemp and silk cloth, whereas wool, cotton, and hemp were prominent in other parts of the world. Early Chinese dynasties used it for a variety of reasons: as clothing for elites, as currency along the Silk Road, and as a tax from peasants. Although much silk was produced in factories, it was also a cottage industry in the home, with women playing the primary role in the process. Shown here are two paintings from a Yuan dynasty scroll portraying the various stages in the manufacture of silk yarn. On the left, women workers separate silk leaves; on the right, they feed leaves to the silkworms.
Photographs by William J. Duiker/Yuan dynasty scroll on stages of sericulture, Freer Gallery of Art, Washington, D.C.

10–6 THE APOGEE OF CHINESE CULTURE

 Focus Question: What were the main achievements in Chinese literature and art in the period between the Tang Dynasty and the Ming, and what technological innovations and intellectual developments contributed to these achievements?

The period between the Tang and the Ming Dynasties was in many ways the great age of achievement in Chinese literature and art. Enriched by Buddhist and Daoist images and themes, Chinese poetry and painting reached the pinnacle of their creativity. Porcelain emerged as the highest form of Chinese ceramics, and sculpture flourished under the influence of styles imported from India and Central Asia.

10–6a Literature

The development of Chinese literature was stimulated by two technological innovations: the invention of paper during the Han dynasty (see Chapter 3) and the invention of woodblock printing during the Tang. At first, paper was used for clothing, wrapping material, toilet tissue, and even armor, but by the first century BCE, it was being used for writing as well.

In the seventh century BCE, the Chinese developed the technique of carving an entire page of text into a wooden block, inking it, and then pressing it onto a sheet of paper. Ordinarily, a text was printed on a long sheet of paper like a scroll. Then the paper was folded and stitched together to form a book. The earliest printed book known today is a Buddhist text published in 868 BCE; it is more than 16 feet long. Although the Chinese eventually developed movable type as well, block printing continued to be used until relatively modern times because of the large number of Chinese characters needed to produce a lengthy text. Even with printing, books remained too expensive for most Chinese, but they did help popularize all forms of literary writing among the educated elite. Although literature was primarily a male occupation, a few women achieved prominence as a result of their creative prowess.

During the post-Han era, historical writing and essays continued to be favorite forms of literary activity. Each dynasty produced an official dynastic history of its predecessor to elucidate sober maxims about the qualities of good and evil in human nature, and local gazetteers added to the general knowledge about the various regions. Encyclopedias brought together in a single location information and documents about all aspects of Chinese life.

The Importance of Poetry During the Tang and the Song Dynasties, it was in poetry, above all, that Chinese writers most effectively expressed their literary talents. Chinese poems celebrated the beauty of nature, the changes of the seasons, and the joys of friendship and drink; others expressed sorrow at the brevity of life, old age, and parting. Given the frequency of imperial banishment and the requirement that officials serve away from their home district (an official means of preventing nepotism),

TWO TANG POETS

LI BO WAS ONE OF THE GREAT POETS of the Tang Dynasty. The first selection, "Quiet Night Thoughts," is probably the best known poem in China and has been memorized by schoolchildren for centuries. The second poem, "Drinking Alone in Moonlight," reflects the poet's carefree attitude toward life.

Du Fu, Li Bo's prime competitor as the greatest poet of the Tang Dynasty, was often the more reflective of the two. In "Spring Prospect," the poet has been imprisoned in the capital after a rebellion against the dynasty has left the city in ruins.

Li Bo, "Quiet Night Thoughts on a Quiet Night"

Beside my bed the moon shines brightly
It almost looks like frost on the ground.
When I lift my head, I see the bright moon;
When I lower my head, I think of my old home.

Li Bo, "Drinking Alone Beneath the Moon"

A jug of wine among the flowers,
I drink alone—without friends or family.
I lift my cup to the bright moon.
With my shadow, we make a threesome.
But the moon is unable to drink,
And my shadow trails behind me.

So I join the moon and my shadow,
And we happily greet the end of spring.
I sing, and the moon sways to my song;
I dance, and my shadow trails behind.
When I'm sober we share our joys,
When I'm drunk, we go our separate ways:
Forever joined, we wander without care,
Until we meet in the Milky Way!

Du Fu, "Spring Prospect"

The city has fallen. Only the mountains and rivers have survived,
The grass and trees grow thickly to greet the spring.
Touched by the sight, even the flowers shed their tears;
Reluctant to leave, the birds are heavy of heart.
The beacon fires have been burning for three months;
A letter from home would be as precious as gold.
The hairs on my white head have grown so thin;
That they can barely hold a hairpin!

 Historians often contrast these two famous poets in terms of their personalities and their approach to life. Can you see any differences in their points of view as conveyed in these short poems?

---

it is little wonder that separation from friends and family was an important theme. Love poems existed but were neither as intense as Western verse nor as sensual as Indian poetry.

Two eighth-century Tang poets, Li Bo (LEE BOH), sometimes known as Li Bai or Li Taibo, and Du Fu, symbolized the genius of the era as well as the two most popular styles (see "Two Tang Poets").

The two poets were a study in contrasts. Where Li Bo was a carefree Daoist, whose writing often centered on nature and shifted easily between moods of revelry and melancholy, Du Fu was a sober Confucian. His poems often dealt with historical issues or ethical themes, befitting a scholar-official living during the chaotic times of the late Tang. Many of his works reflect a concern with social injustice and the plight of the unfortunate rarely to be found in the writings of his contemporaries. Few of the poems from the pen of the great writers of the Tang and Song Dynasties, however, were written for or ever reached the average Chinese peasant, the vast majority of whom were essentially illiterate. The millions of Chinese peasants and artisans living in rural villages and market towns acquired their knowledge of Chinese history, Confucian moralisms, and even Buddhist scripture from stories, plays, and songs passed down by storytellers, wandering minstrels, and itinerant monks in a rich oral tradition. One exception is the popular poem "Song of Lasting Pain" by the Tang poet Bo Ju-yi (BOH joo-YEE) (772–846), whose poignant portrayal of the emperor's consort Yang Guifei resonates among Chinese readers down to the present day.

The Chinese Novel During the Yuan dynasty, new forms of literary creativity, including popular theater and the novel, began to appear. The two most famous novels were *Romance of the Three Kingdoms* and *Tale of the Marshes.* The former had been told orally for centuries, appearing in written form during the Song as a scriptbook for storytellers. It was first printed in 1321 but was not published for mass consumption until 1522. Each new edition was altered in some way, making the final edition a composite effort of generations of the Chinese imagination. The plot recounts the power struggle that took place among competing groups after the fall of the Han dynasty. Packed with court intrigues, descriptions of peasant life, and gripping battles, *Romance of the Three Kingdoms* stands as a magnificent epic, China's counterpart to the Mahabharata.

Tale of the Marshes is an often violent tale of outlaw heroes who at the end of the northern Song banded together to oppose government taxes and official oppression. They rob those in power in order to share with the poor. *Tale of the Marshes* is the first prose fiction that describes the daily ordeal of ordinary Chinese people in their own language. Unlike the picaresque novel in the West, *Tale of the Marshes* does not limit itself to the exploits of one hero, offering instead 108 different story lines.

This multitude of plots is a natural outgrowth of the tradition of the professional storyteller, who attempts to keep the audience's attention by recounting as many adventures as the market will bear.

Popular Culture By the Song Dynasty, China had 60 million people, 1 million in Hangzhou alone. With the growth of cities came an increased demand for popular entertainment. Although the Tang Dynasty had imposed a curfew on urban residents, the Song did not. The city gates and bridges were closed at dark, but food stalls and entertainment continued through the night. At fairgrounds throughout the year, one could find comedians, musicians, boxers, fencers, wrestlers, acrobats, puppets and marionettes, shadow plays, and especially storytellers. Many of these arts had come from India centuries before and were now the favorite forms of amusement of the Chinese people.

10–6b Art

Although painting flourished in China under the Han and reached a level of artistic excellence under the Tang, little remains from those periods. From the celebrated Tang Dynasty artist Wu Daozi, for example, little remains today except for copies of paintings and rubbings as seen in the image in Section 10-1c, which was purchased at the Shaanxi History Museum in Xian (see Comparative Illustration "The Two Worlds of Tang China," Section 10-1c, p. 274). Many scroll paintings by artists of the Song and the Yuan dynasties, however, have survived, and are considered the apogee of painting in traditional China.

Like literature, Chinese painting found part of its inspiration in Buddhist and Daoist sources. Some of the best surviving examples of the Tang period are the Buddhist wall paintings in the caves at Dunhuang (doon-HWAHNG), in Central Asia. These paintings were commissioned by Buddhist merchants who stopped at Dunhuang and, while awaiting permission to enter China, wished to give thanks for surviving the rigors of the Silk Road. The entrances to the caves were filled with stones after the tenth century, when Muslim zealots began to destroy Buddhist images throughout Central Asia, and have only recently been uncovered. Like the few surviving Tang scroll paintings, these wall paintings display a love of color and refinement that are reminiscent of styles in India and Persia.

Daoism ultimately had a greater influence than Buddhism on Chinese painting. From early times, Chinese artists removed themselves to the mountains to write and paint and find the *Dao*, or Way, in nature. In the fifth century, one Chinese painter, too old to travel, began to paint mountain scenes from memory and announced that depicting nature could function as a substitute for contemplating nature itself. Painting, he said, could be the means of realizing the *Dao*. This explains in part the emphasis on nature in traditional Chinese painting. The word for *landscape* in Chinese means "mountain-water," and the Daoist search for balance between earth and water, hard and soft, *yang* and *yin*, is at play in the tradition of Chinese painting. To enhance the effect, poems were added to the paintings, underscoring the fusion of the visual and the verbal in Chinese art. Many artists were proficient in both media, the poem inspiring the painting and vice versa.

To represent the totality of nature, Chinese artists attempted to reveal the quintessential forms of the landscape. Rather than depicting the actual realistic shape of a specific mountain, they tried to portray the "idea" of a mountain. Empty spaces were left in the paintings because in the Daoist vision, one cannot know the whole truth. Daoist influence was also evident in the tendency to portray human beings as insignificant in the midst of nature. In contrast to the focus on the human body and personality in Western art, Chinese art presented people as tiny figures fishing in a small boat, meditating on a cliff, or wandering up a hillside trail, coexisting with but not dominating nature.

The Chinese displayed their paintings on long scrolls of silk or paper that were attached to a wooden cylindrical bar at the

Private Collection/The Bridgeman Images

Willows and Distant Mountains. In contrast to the focus on the human personality that is found in Western art, traditional Chinese painting often presented people as the insignificant figures coexisting within the totality of nature. Ma Yuan (1190–1235), descended from a family of painters, continued this long tradition of "mountain-water" landscapes in the painting shown here. Although they are dwarfed by the immensity of the surrounding mountains, these five tiny figures seem in harmony with nature as they go about their daily lives.

bottom. Varying in length from 3 to 20 feet, the paintings were unfolded slowly so that the eye could enjoy each segment, one after the other, beginning at the bottom with water or a village and moving upward into the hills to the mountain peaks and the sky.

By the tenth century, some Chinese painters began to eliminate color from their paintings, preferring the challenge of capturing the distilled essence of the landscape in washes of black ink on white silk. Borrowing from calligraphy, traditionally a sophisticated and revered art, they emphasized the brush stroke and created black-and-white landscapes characterized by a gravity of mood and dominated by overpowering mountains. Other artists turned toward more expressionist and experimental painting. These so-called literati artists were scholars and administrators, highly educated and adept at music, poetry, and painting. For them, the purpose of painting was not representation but expression. No longer did painters wish to evoke the feeling of wandering in nature. Rather, they tried to reveal to the viewer their own mind and feelings. Like many Western painters in the nineteenth and twentieth centuries, many of these artists were misunderstood by the public and painted only for themselves and one another.

Second only to painting in creativity was the field of ceramics, notably the manufacture of porcelain. Made of fine clay baked at unusually high temperatures in a kiln, porcelain was first produced during the period after the fall of the Han and became popular during the Tang era (see illustration "Tang Camel"). During the Song, porcelain came into its own. Most renowned perhaps are the celadons (SEH-luh-dahnz), in a delicate gray-green (see Chapter 11), but Song artists also excelled in other colors and techniques. As in painting, Song delicacy and grace contrasted with the bold and often crude styles popular under the Tang. The translucency of Chinese porcelain resulted from a technique that did not reach Europe until the eighteenth century. During the Yuan and the Ming, new styles appeared. Most notable is the cobalt blue-and-white porcelain usually identified with the Ming Dynasty, which actually originated during the Yuan (see illustration "World-Class China Ware," Section 17-2d p. 493). The Ming also produced a multicolored porcelain—often in green, yellow, and red—covered with exotic designs.

Tang Camel. During the Tang Dynasty, trade between China, India, and the Middle East along the famous Silk Road increased rapidly and introduced new Central Asian motifs to Chinese culture. As seen in this sturdy example, the Bactrian two-humped camel played a major role in carrying goods along the trade route, since its ability to withstand long periods without water enabled it to survive the grueling trek across the Central Asian deserts. Created as tomb figures, and therefore preserved for us today, are numerous ceramic studies of horses and camels, along with officials, court ladies, and servants painted in brilliant gold, green, and blue lead glazes. The Philadelphia Museum of Art/Art Resource, NY

CHAPTER SUMMARY

Traditionally, Chinese historians believed that Chinese history was cyclical, driven by the dynamic interplay of the forces of good and evil, *yang* and *yin*, growth and decay. Beyond the forces of conflict and change lay the essential continuity of Chinese history, based on the timeless principles established by Confucius and other thinkers during the Zhou dynasty in antiquity.

This view of the dynamic forces of Chinese history was long accepted as valid by historians in the West and led many to assert that Chinese history was unique and could not be placed in a European or universal framework. Whereas Western history was linear, leading steadily away from the past, China's history

always returned to its moorings and was rooted in the values and institutions of antiquity.

In recent years, however, this traditional view of a changeless China has come under increasing challenge from historians who see patterns of change that made the China of the late fourteenth century a very different place from the country that had existed at the rise of the Tang Dynasty in 600. To these

scholars, China had passed through its own version of the "middle ages" and was on the verge of beginning a linear evolution into a posttraditional society.

As we have seen, China in the early Ming era was much changed since the end of the Han dynasty more than a thousand years earlier. The industrial and commercial sector had grown considerably in size, complexity, and technological capacity. In the countryside, the concentration of political and economic power in the hands of the aristocracy had been replaced by a more stable and more equitable mixture of landed gentry, freehold farmers, and sharecroppers. The civil service provided an avenue of upward mobility that had not been available under the Han, and the state tolerated a diversity of beliefs that responded to the emotional needs and preferences of the Chinese people.

In many respects, China's achievements were unsurpassed throughout the world and marked a major advance beyond antiquity.

Yet there were also some key similarities between the China of the Ming and the China of late

antiquity. Ming China was still a predominantly agrarian society, with wealth based primarily on the ownership of land. Commercial activities flourished but remained under a high level of government regulation and by no means represented a major proportion of the national income. China also remained a relatively centralized empire based on an official ideology that stressed the virtue of hard work, social conformity, and hierarchy. In foreign affairs, the long frontier struggle with the nomadic peoples along the northern and western frontiers continued unabated.

Thus, the change that China experienced during its medieval era can probably be best described as one of change within continuity, an evolutionary working out of trends that had first become visible during the Han dynasty or even earlier. The result was a civilization that was the envy of its neighbors and of the known world. It also influenced other states in the region, including Japan, Korea, and Vietnam. It is to these societies along the Chinese rimlands that we now turn.

CHAPTER TIMELINE

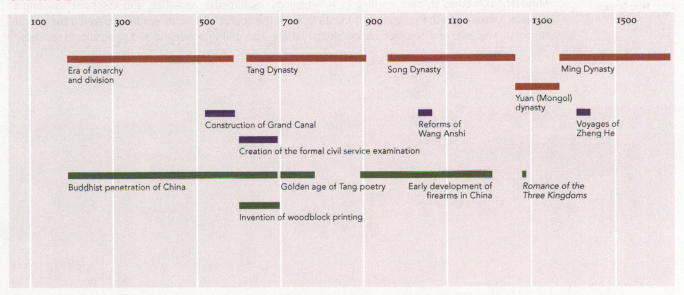

CHAPTER REVIEW

Upon Reflection

Q Why is the Tang Dynasty often described as the greatest and most glorious era in Chinese history, and do you think that its reputation is justified?

Q What impact did the era of Mongol rule have on societies that were affected by it? Do you agree that some of the ultimate consequences were beneficial in their effects on world history? If so, why?

Q What are the arguments on both sides of the debate over whether Chinese society underwent fundamental changes during the period discussed in this chapter? Which arguments do you find more persuasive, and why?

Key Terms

Grand Council (p. 276)
scholar-gentry (p. 277)
khanates (p. 284)
Chan (p. 289)
Pure Land (p. 289)
Tantrism (p. 289)

White Lotus (p. 289)
Manichaeanism (p. 290)
Neo-Confucianism (p. 290)
Supreme Ultimate (p. 290)
School of Mind (p. 291)
foot binding (p. 294)

Chapter Notes

1. *The Travels of Marco Polo* (New York, n.d.), p. 128.
2. Quoted in A. F. Wright, *Buddhism in Chinese History* (Stanford, Calif., 1959), p. 30.
3. Quoted in A. F. Wright, *The Sui Dynasty* (New York, 1978), p. 180.
4. Chu-yu, *P'ing-chow Table Talks*, quoted in R. Temple, *The Genius of China: 3,000 Years of Science, Discovery, and Invention* (New York, 1986), p. 150.
5. Quoted in J. K. Fairbank, E. O. Reischauer, and A. M. Craig, *East Asia: Tradition and Transformation* (Boston, 1973), p. 164.
6. Quoted in R. Grousset, *L'Empire des Steppes* (Paris, 1939), p. 285.
7. A. M. Khazanov, *Nomads and the Outside World* (Cambridge, 1983), p. 241.
8. *The Travels of Marco Polo* (New York, n.d.), p. 229.
9. S. A. M. Adshead, *China in World History* (New York, 2000), p. 132.

 **MINDTAP** From Cengage

THE EAST ASIAN RIMLANDS: EARLY JAPAN, KOREA, AND VIETNAM

Chapter Outline and Focus Questions

11-1 *Japan: Land of the Rising Sun*

Q How did Japan's geographic location affect the course of early Japanese history, and how did it influence the political structures and social institutions that arose there?

11-2 *Korea: Bridge to the East*

Q What were the main characteristics of economic and social life in early Korea?

11-3 *Vietnam: The Smaller Dragon*

Q What were the main developments in Vietnamese history before 1500? Why were the Vietnamese able to restore their national independence after a millennium of Chinese rule?

The Jade Mountain Temple on Returned Sword Lake, Hanoi. William J. Duiker

Critical Thinking

Q *How did Chinese civilization influence the societies that arose in Japan, Korea, and Vietnam during their early history?*

Connections to Today

Q *The fact that Japan is an island nation has had a significant effect on how the Japanese people see their role in the world. How do you think the fact that the United States is a continental nation affects the attitude of the American people in today's world?*

THERE IS A SMALL body of water in the heart of the Vietnamese national capital of Hanoi (ha-NOY) that is known affectionately to local city-dwellers as Returned Sword Lake. The lake owes its name to a legend that Le Loi (LAY LOY), founder of the later Le (LAY) dynasty in the fifteenth century, drew a magic sword from the lake that enabled him to achieve a great victory over Chinese occupation forces. Thus, to many Vietnamese the lake symbolizes their nation's historical resistance to domination by its powerful northern neighbor.

Ironically, however, a temple that was later erected on an island on the lake reflects the strong influence that China continued to exert on traditional Vietnamese culture. After Le Loi's victory, according to the legend, the sword was returned to the water, and the Vietnamese ruler accepted a tributary relationship to his "elder brother," the Chinese emperor in Beijing. China's philosophy, political institutions, and social mores served as hallmarks for the Vietnamese people down to the early years of the twentieth century. That is why Vietnam was for centuries known as "the smaller dragon."

Le Loi's deferential attitude toward his larger neighbor should not surprise us. During ancient times, China was the most technologically advanced society in East Asia. To its north and west were pastoral peoples whose military exploits were often impressive but whose political and cultural attainments were still limited, at least by comparison with the great river valley civilizations of the day. South of the Yangzi River were a number of other agricultural societies that were beginning to follow a pattern of development similar to that of China, although somewhat later in time. One of these was the land of Yueh (YWEH), an area extending from the delta of the Yangzi River southward to the Red River Valley in what is today the northern part of Vietnam. The Yueh peoples had created a relatively advanced agricultural civilization that was gradually integrated into the Chinese empire during the Qin and Han dynasties. To the east was the Korean peninsula and the islands of Japan, where organized societies were beginning to take shape beginning in the first millennium BCE.

All of these early agricultural societies were eventually influenced to some degree by their great neighbor, China. Vietnam, then limited in size to its original homeland in the Red River Valley, remained under Chinese rule for a thousand years. The Korean people managed to create their own independent states but were influenced by and in many ways followed the cultural example of their larger neighbor, China. Only Japan retained both its political independence and its cultural uniqueness. Yet even the Japanese were strongly influenced by the glittering culture of their powerful neighbor, and today many Japanese institutions and customs still bear the imprint of several centuries of borrowing from China. In this chapter, we will take a closer look at these emerging societies along the Chinese rimlands and consider how their cultural achievements reflected or contrasted with those of the Chinese Empire.

11–1 JAPAN: LAND OF THE RISING SUN

 Focus Question: How did Japan's geographic location affect the course of early Japanese history, and how did it influence the political structures and social institutions that arose there?

Geography accounts for many of the historical differences between Chinese and Japanese society. Whereas China is a continental civilization, Japan is an island country. It consists of four main islands (see Map 11.1): Hokkaido (hoh-KY-doh)

Map 11.1 Early Japan. This map shows key cities in Japan during the early development of the Japanese state.

 Where was the original heartland of Japanese civilization on the main island of Honshu?

in the north, the main island of Honshu (hahn-SHOO) in the center, and the two smaller islands of Kyushu (KYOO-shoo) and Shikoku (shee-KOH-koo) in the southwest. Its total land area is about 146,000 square miles, about the size of the state of Montana. Japan's main islands are at approximately the same latitude as the eastern seaboard of the United States.

Like the eastern United States, Japan is blessed with a temperate climate. It is slightly warmer on the east coast, which is washed by the Pacific Current sweeping up from the south, and has a number of natural harbors that provide protection from the winds and high waves of the Pacific Ocean. As a consequence, in recent times, the majority of the Japanese people have tended to live along the east coast, especially in the flat plains surrounding the cities of Tokyo (TOH-kee-oh), Osaka (oh-SAH-kuh), and Kyoto (KYOH-toh). In these favorable environmental conditions, Japanese farmers have been able to harvest two crops of rice annually since early times.

By no means, however, is Japan an agricultural paradise. Like China, much of the country is mountainous, with only about 20 percent of the total land area suitable for cultivation. These mountains are of volcanic origin, since the Japanese islands are located at the juncture of the Asian and Pacific tectonic plates. This location is both an advantage and a disadvantage. Volcanic soils are extremely fertile, which helps explain the exceptionally high productivity of Japanese farmers. At the same time, the area is prone to earthquakes, such as the famous quake of 1923, which destroyed almost the entire city of Tokyo. In 2011, a massive earthquake slightly offshore triggered a tsunami that devastated large areas along the eastern coast of northern Honshu island.

The fact that Japan is an island country has had a significant impact on Japanese history. As we have seen, the continental character of Chinese civilization, with its constant threat of invasion from the north, had a number of consequences for

Chinese history. One effect was to make the Chinese more sensitive to the preservation of their culture from destruction at the hands of non-Chinese invaders. As one fourth-century CE Chinese ruler remarked when he was forced to move his capital southward under pressure from nomadic incursions, "The King takes All Under Heaven as his home."[1] Proud of their own considerable cultural achievements and their dominant position throughout the region, the Chinese have traditionally been reluctant to dilute the purity of their culture with foreign innovations. Culture more than race is a determinant of the Chinese sense of identity.

By contrast, the island character of Japan probably had the effect of strengthening the Japanese sense of ethnic and cultural distinctiveness. Although the Japanese view of themselves as the most ethnically homogeneous people in East Asia may not be entirely accurate (the modern Japanese probably represent a mix of peoples, much like their neighbors on the continent), their sense of racial and cultural homogeneity has enabled them to import ideas from abroad without worrying that the borrowings will destroy the uniqueness of their own culture.

11-1a A Gift from the Gods: Prehistoric Japan

According to an ancient legend recorded in historical chronicles written in the eighth century CE, the islands of Japan were formed as a result of the marriage of the god Izanagi (ee-zah-NAH-gee) and the goddess Izanami (ee-zah-NAH-mee). After giving birth to Japan, Izanami gave birth to a sun goddess whose name was Amaterasu (ah-mah-teh-RAH-soo). A descendant of Amaterasu later descended to earth and became the founder of the Japanese nation. This Japanese creation myth is reminiscent of similar beliefs in other ancient societies, which often saw themselves as the product of a union of deities. What is interesting about the Japanese version is that it has survived into modern times as an explanation for the uniqueness of the Japanese people and the divinity of the Japanese emperor, who is still believed by some Japanese to be a direct descendant of the sun goddess Amaterasu.

Modern scholars have a more prosaic explanation for the origins of Japanese civilization. According to archaeological evidence, the Japanese islands have been occupied by human beings for at least 100,000 years. The earliest known Neolithic inhabitants, known as the Jomon (JOH-mahn) people (named for the cord pattern of their pottery), lived in the islands as early as 8000 BCE. They lived by hunting, fishing, and food gathering.

Agriculture probably appeared in Japan sometime during the first millennium BCE, although some archaeologists believe that the Jomon people had learned to cultivate some food crops considerably earlier than that. By about 800 BCE, rice cultivation had been introduced, possibly by immigrants from the mainland by way of the Korean peninsula. Until recently, historians believed that these immigrants drove out the existing inhabitants of the area and gave rise to the emerging Yayoi (yah-YOH-ee) culture (named for the site near Tokyo where pottery from the period was found). It is now thought, however, that Yayoi culture was a product of a mixture between the Jomon people and the new arrivals. In any event, it seems clear that

the Yayoi peoples were the ancestors of the vast majority of present-day Japanese.

At first, the Yayoi lived primarily on the southern island of Kyushu, but eventually they migrated northward onto the main island of Honshu, assimilating with the indigenous inhabitants of the area, some of whose descendants, known as the Ainu (Y-nyoo), still live in the northern islands. Finally, in the first centuries CE, the Yayoi settled in the Yamato (YAH-mah-toh) plain in the vicinity of the modern cities of Osaka and Kyoto. Japanese legend recounts the story of a "divine warrior," Jimmu (JIH-moo), who led his people eastward from the island of Kyushu to establish a kingdom in the Yamato plain.

In central Honshu, the Yayoi set up a tribal society based on a number of clans, called *uji* (oo-JEE). Each *uji* was ruled by a hereditary chieftain, who provided protection to the local population in return for a proportion of the annual harvest. The population itself was divided between a small aristocratic class and the majority, composed of rice farmers, artisans, and other household servants of the aristocrats. Yayoi society was highly decentralized, although eventually the chieftain of the dominant clan in the Yamato region, who claimed to be descended from the sun goddess Amaterasu, achieved a kind of titular primacy. There is no evidence, however, of a central ruler equivalent in power to the Chinese rulers of the Shang and the Zhou eras.

11-1b The Rise of the Japanese State

Although the inhabitants of the Japanese islands had been aware of China for centuries, they paid relatively little attention to their more advanced neighbor until the early seventh century, when the rise of the centralized and expansionistic Tang dynasty presented a challenge. When the Tang began to meddle in the affairs of the Korean peninsula, Yamato rulers sought to deal with the potential threat in two ways. First, they sought alliances with the Korean states (see "The Three Kingdoms," Section 11-2a, p. 317). Second, they attempted to centralize their authority so that they could mount a more effective resistance in the event of a Chinese invasion. The key figure in this effort was Shotoku Taishi (shoh-TOH-koo ty-EE-shee) (572–622), a leading aristocrat in one of the dominant clans in the Yamato region. Prince Shotoku sent missions to the Tang capital of Chang'an to learn about the political institutions already in use in the relatively centralized Tang kingdom (see Map 11.2).

Emulating the Chinese Model Shotoku Taishi then launched a series of reforms to create a new system based roughly on the Chinese model. In the so-called seventeen-article constitution, he called for the creation of a centralized government under a supreme ruler and a merit system for selecting and ranking public officials (see "The Seventeen-Article Constitution," p. 304). His objective was to limit the powers of the hereditary nobility and enhance the prestige and authority of the Yamato ruler, who claimed divine status and was now emerging as the symbol of the unique character of the Japanese nation. In reality, there is evidence that places the origins of the Yamato clan on the Korean peninsula.

THE SEVENTEEN-ARTICLE CONSTITUTION

Politics & Government

THE FOLLOWING EXCERPT from the *Nihon Shoki* (*Chronicles of Japan*) is a passage from the seventeen-article constitution promulgated in 604 CE. Although the opening section reflects Chinese influence in its emphasis on social harmony, there is also a strong focus on obedience and hierarchy. The constitution was put into practice during the reign of the famous Prince Shotoku.

The Chronicles of Japan

I. Harmony is to be cherished, and opposition for opposition's sake must be avoided as a matter of principle.... [T]here are some who disobey their lords and fathers, or who dispute with their neighboring villages. If those above are harmonious and those below are cordial, their discussion will be guided by a spirit of conciliation, and reason shall naturally prevail. There will be nothing that cannot be accomplished.

II. [R]evere the three treasures. The three treasures, consisting of Buddha, the Doctrine, and the Monastic Order, are... the supreme objects of worship in all countries. Can any man in any age ever fail to respect these teachings? Few men are utterly devoid of goodness, and men can be taught to follow the teachings. Unless they take refuge in the three treasures, there is no way of rectifying their misdeeds.

III. When an imperial command is given, obey it with reverence. The sovereign is likened to heaven, and his subjects are likened to earth. With heaven providing the cover and earth supporting it, the four seasons proceed in orderly fashion.... If earth attempts to overtake the functions of heaven, it destroys everything.... If there is no reverence shown to the imperial command, ruin will automatically result....

VII. Every man must be given his clearly delineated responsibility. If a wise man is entrusted with office, the sound of praise arises. If a wicked man holds office, disturbances become frequent.... In all things, great or small, find the right man, and the country will be well governed.... In this manner, the state will be lasting....

Q *What are the key components of this constitution, the first in the history of Japan? To what degree do its provisions conform to Chinese Confucian principles?*

Source: Excerpt from *Sources of Japanese History*, David Lu, ed. (New York: McGraw-Hill, 1974), I, p. 7.

Map 11.2 Japan's Relations with China and Korea. This map shows the Japanese islands at the time of the Yamato state. Maritime routes taken by Japanese traders and missionaries to China are indicated.

Q *Where did Japanese traders travel after reaching the mainland?*

After Shotoku Taishi's death in 622, his successors continued to introduce reforms to make the government more efficient. In the series of so-called **Taika reforms**—*taika* (TY-kuh) means "great change"—that began in the mid-seventh century, the Grand Council of State was established, presiding over a cabinet of eight ministries. To the traditional six ministries of Tang China were added ministers representing the central secretariat and the imperial household. Official communications were to be based on the Chinese written language. The islands of Japan were divided into administrative districts on the Chinese pattern. The rural village, composed ideally of fifty households, was the basic unit of government. The village chief was responsible for "the maintenance of the household registers, the assigning of the sowing of crops and the cultivation of mulberry trees, the prevention of offenses, and the requisitioning of taxes and forced labor." A law code was introduced, and a new tax system was established; now all farmland technically belonged to the state, so taxes were paid directly to the central government rather than through the local nobility, as had previously been the case.

As a result of their new acquaintance with China, the Japanese also developed a strong interest in Buddhism. Some of the first Japanese to travel to China during this period were Buddhist pilgrims hoping to learn more about the exciting new doctrine and bring back scriptures. By the seventh century CE, Buddhism had become quite popular among the aristocrats, who endowed wealthy monasteries that became active in Japanese politics. At first, the new faith did not penetrate to the masses, but eventually, popular sects such as the Pure Land sect, an import from China, won many adherents among the common people.

The Nara Period Initial efforts to build a new state modeled roughly after the Tang state were successful. After Shotoku Taishi's death in 622, political influence fell into the hands of the powerful Fujiwara (foo-jee-WAH-rah) clan, which managed to marry into the ruling family and continue the reforms Shotoku had begun. In 710, a new capital, laid out on a grid similar to the great Tang city of Chang'an, was established at Nara (NAH-rah), on the eastern edge of the Yamato plain. The Yamato ruler began to use the title "son of Heaven" in the Chinese fashion. In deference to the belief in the ruling family's divine character, the mandate remained in perpetuity in the imperial house rather than being bestowed on an individual who was selected by heaven because of his talent and virtue, as was the case in China. It was apparently at this time, as well, that the Yamato began to refer to their country as Japan ("Sun's origin") when dealing with the Tang court. Eventually the new name replaced the Tang's previous use of the term *Wa*, or "dwarf country," to refer to the peoples of Japan.

Had these reforms succeeded, Japan might have followed the Chinese pattern and developed a centralized bureaucratic government. But as time passed, the central government proved unable to curb the power of the aristocracy. Unlike the situation in Tang China, the civil service examinations in Japan were not open to commoners but were restricted to individuals of noble birth. Leading officials were awarded large tracts of land, and they and other powerful families were able to keep the taxes from the lands for themselves. Increasingly starved for revenue, the central government steadily lost power and influence. There would be no empire in Japan similar to that created by the Tang Dynasty in China.

The Heian Period The influence of powerful Buddhist monasteries in the city of Nara soon became oppressive, and in 794, the emperor moved the capital to his family's original power base at nearby Heian (hay-AHN), on the site of present-day Kyoto. Like its predecessor, the new capital was laid out in the now familiar Chang'an

The Yamato Plain

checkerboard pattern, but on a larger scale than at Nara. Now increasingly self-confident, the rulers ceased to emulate the Tang and sent no more missions to Chang'an. The influence of Buddhism was restricted by prohibiting the establishment of monasteries inside the new capital. At Heian, the emperor—as the royal line descended from the sun goddess was now styled—continued to rule in name, but actual power was in the hands of the Fujiwara clan, which had managed through intermarriage to link its fortunes closely with the imperial family. A senior member of the clan began to serve as regent (in practice, the chief executive of the government) for the emperor.

What was occurring was a return to the decentralization that had existed prior to Shotoku Taishi. The central government's attempts to impose taxes directly on the rice lands failed, and rural areas came under the control of powerful families whose wealth was based on the ownership of tax-exempt farmland called *shoen* (SHOH-en). To avoid paying taxes, peasants would often surrender their lands to a local aristocrat, who would then allow the peasants to cultivate the lands in return for the payment of rent. To obtain protection from government officials, these local aristocrats might in turn grant title of their lands to a more powerful aristocrat with influence at court. In return, these individuals would receive inheritable rights to a portion of the income from the estate.

With the decline of central power at Heian, local aristocrats tended to take justice into their own hands and increasingly used military force to protect their interests. A new class of military retainers called the **samurai** (SAM-uh-ry) emerged whose purpose was to protect the security and property of their patron (see "Japan's Warrior Class"). They frequently drew

A Worship Hall in Nara. Buddhist temple compounds in Japan traditionally offered visitors an escape from the tensions of the outside world. The temple site normally included an entrance gate, a central courtyard, a worship hall, a pagoda, and a cloister, as well as support buildings for the monks. The pagoda, a multitiered tower, harbored a sacred relic of the Buddha and served as the East Asian version of the Indian stupa. The worship hall corresponded to the Vedic carved chapel. Here we see the Todaiji (toh-DY-jee) worship hall in Nara. Originally constructed in the mid-eighth century CE, it is reputed to be the largest wooden structure in the world and is the centerpiece of a vast temple complex on the outskirts of the old capital city.

William J. Duiker

JAPAN'S WARRIOR CLASS

Politics & Government

THE SAMURAI WAS THE JAPANESE EQUIVALENT of the medieval European knight. Like the knights, the samurai fought on horseback and were expected to adhere to a strict moral code. Although this selection comes from a document dating only to the 1500s, a distinct mounted warrior class had already begun to emerge in Japan as early as the tenth century. This passage shows the importance of hierarchy and duty in a society influenced by the doctrine of Confucius.

The Way of the Samurai

The master once said: … Generation after generation men have taken their livelihood from tilling the soil, or devised and manufactured tools, or produced profit from mutual trade, so that people's needs were satisfied. Thus, the occupations of farmer, artisan, and merchant necessarily grew up as complementary to one another. However, the samurai eats food without growing it, uses utensils without manufacturing them, and profits without buying or selling…. The samurai is one who does not cultivate, does not manufacture, and does not engage in trade, but it cannot be that he has no function at all as a samurai….

If one deeply fixes [one's] attention on what I have said and examines closely one's own function, it will become clear what the business of the samurai is. The business of the samurai consists in reflecting on his own station in life, in discharging loyal service to his master if he has one, in deepening his fidelity in associations with friends, and, with due consideration of his own position, in devoting himself to duty above all…. The samurai dispenses with the business of the farmer, artisan, and merchant and confines himself to practicing this Way; should there be someone in the three classes of the common people who transgresses against these moral principles, the samurai summarily punishes him and thus upholds proper moral principles in the land…. Outwardly he stands in physical readiness for any call to service, and inwardly he strives to fulfill the Way of the lord and subject, friend and friend, father and son, older and younger brother, and husband and wife. Within his heart he keeps to the ways of peace, but without he keeps his weapons ready for use. The three classes of the common people make him their teacher and respect him. By following his teachings, they are enabled to understand what is fundamental and what is secondary.

Herein lies the Way of the samurai, the means by which he earns his clothing, food, and shelter; and by which his heart is put at ease, and he is enabled to pay back at length his obligation to his lord and the kindness of his parents. Were there no such duty, it would be as though one were to steal the kindness of one's parents, greedily devour the income of one's master, and make one's whole life a career of robbery and brigandage. This would be very grievous.

 In what ways were the duties of a samurai similar to those of an Indian warrior, as expressed by Krishna in Chapter 2? How do they compare with the responsibilities of a Confucian "gentleman" in China? What might account for the similarities and differences?

Source: From *Sources of Japanese Tradition*, Vol. 2, 2e, pgs. 192–194, by William Theodore de Bary, Carol Gluck, and Arthur E. Tiedemann. Copyright © 2005 by Columbia University Press. Reprinted with permission of the publisher.

---

their leaders from disappointed aristocratic office seekers, who thus began to occupy a prestigious position in local society, where they often served an administrative as well as a military function. The samurai lived a life of simplicity and self-sacrifice and were expected to maintain an intense and unquestioning loyalty to their lord. Bonds of loyalty were also quite strong among members of the samurai class, and homosexuality was common. Like the knights of medieval Europe, the samurai fought on horseback (although a samurai carried a sword and a bow and arrows rather than lance and shield) and were supposed to live by a strict warrior code, known in Japan as **Bushido** (BOO-shee-doh), or "way of the warrior." As time went on, they became a major force and almost a surrogate government in much of the Japanese countryside.

The Kamakura Shogunate and After By the end of the twelfth century, as rivalries among noble families led to almost constant civil war, centralizing forces again asserted themselves. This time the instrument was a powerful noble from a warrior clan named Minamoto Yoritomo (mee-nah-MOH-toh yoh-ree-TOH-moh) (1142–1199), who defeated several rivals and set up his power base on the Kamakura (kah-mah-KOO-rah) peninsula, south of the modern city of Tokyo. To strengthen the state, he created a more centralized government—the *bakufu* (buh-KOO-foo *or* bah-KOO-fuh) or "tent government"—under a powerful military leader known as the **shogun** (SHOH-gun) (general). The shogun attempted to increase the powers of the central government while reducing rival aristocratic clans to vassal status. This **shogunate system**, in which the emperor was the titular authority while the shogun exercised actual power, served as the political system in Japan until the second half of the nineteenth century.

The shogunate (SHOH-gun-ut *or* SHOH-gun-ayt) system worked effectively, and it was fortunate that it did, because during the next century, Japan faced the most serious challenge it had confronted yet. The Mongols, who had destroyed the Song Dynasty in China, were now attempting to assert their hegemony throughout all of Asia (see Chapter 10). In 1266, Emperor Khubilai Khan demanded tribute from Japan. When

The Burning of the Palace. The Kamakura era is represented in this action-packed thirteenth-century scene from the *Scroll of the Heiji Period*, which depicts the burning of a retired emperor's palace in the middle of the night. Servants and ladies of the court flee the massive flames; confusion and violence reign. The determined faces of the samurai warriors only add to the ferocity of the attack.

the Japanese refused, he invaded with an army of more than 30,000 troops. Bad weather and difficult conditions forced a retreat, but the Mongols tried again in 1281. An army nearly 150,000 strong landed on the northern coast of Kyushu. The Japanese were able to contain them for two months until virtually the entire Mongol fleet was destroyed by a massive typhoon—a "divine wind," or *kamikaze* (kah-mi-KAH-zee). Japan would not face a foreign invader again until American forces landed on the Japanese islands in the summer of 1945.

Resistance to the Mongols had put a heavy strain on the system, however, and in 1333, the Kamakura Shogunate was overthrown by a coalition of powerful clans. A new shogun, supplied by the Ashikaga (ah-shee-KAH-guh) family, arose in Kyoto and attempted to continue the shogunate system. But the Ashikaga were unable to restore the centralized power of their predecessors. With the central government reduced to a shell, the power of the local landed aristocracy increased to an unprecedented degree. Heads of great noble families, now called **daimyo** (DYM-yoh) ("great names"), controlled vast landed estates that owed no taxes to the government or to the court in Kyoto. As clan rivalries continued, the daimyo relied increasingly on the samurai for protection, and political power came into the hands of a loose coalition of noble families.

By the end of the fifteenth century, Japan was again close to anarchy. A disastrous civil conflict known as the Onin War (1467–1477) led to the virtual destruction of the capital city of Kyoto and the disintegration of the shogunate. With the disappearance of central authority, powerful aristocrats in rural areas now seized total control over large territories and ruled as independent lords. Territorial rivalries and claims of precedence led to almost constant warfare in this period of "warring states," as it is called (in obvious parallel with a similar era during the Zhou dynasty in China). The trend back toward central authority did not begin until the last quarter of the sixteenth century.

HISTORIANS DEBATE **Was Japan a Feudal Society?** That question has aroused vigorous debate among historians in recent years. Few would dispute that political, social, and economic conditions in Japan were similar in a number of respects to those in medieval Europe, where the term was first applied (see Comparative Essay "Feudal Orders Around the World," p. 308 as well as Chapter 12). But some European historians worry that the term *feudalism* has been overused; they argue that it should be narrowly defined, based on conditions that existed in Europe during a specific time period.

For the student of world history, the term obviously has some comparative value, in that the broad political and economic conditions that are normally considered to be characteristic of a feudal society can be found in a number of areas around the world. Still, it is important to remember that, under the surface, there were often profound differences between one "feudal" society and another. With that in mind, the term can be a highly useful teaching tool for world historians.

11–1c Economic and Social Structures

From the time the Yayoi culture was first established on the Japanese islands, Japan was a predominantly agrarian society. Although Japan lacked the spacious valleys and deltas of the river valley societies, its inhabitants were able to take advantage

Feudal Orders Around the World

Politics & Government When we use the word *feudalism*, we usually think of European knights on horseback clad in armor and wielding a sword and lance. Between 800 and 1500, however, a form of social organization that modern historians have called feudalism developed in different parts of the world. Historians use the term to refer to a decentralized political order in which local lords owed loyalty and provided military service to a king or more powerful lord. In Europe, a feudal order based on lords and vassals arose between 800 and 900 and flourished for the next four hundred years.

In Japan, a feudal order much like that found in Europe developed between 800 and 1500. By the end of the ninth century, powerful nobles in the countryside, while owing a loose loyalty to the Japanese emperor, began to exercise political and legal power in their own extensive lands. To protect their property and security, these nobles retained samurai, warriors who owed loyalty to the nobles and provided military service for them. Like knights in Europe, the samurai followed a warrior code and fought on horseback, clad in armor, but they carried a sword and bow and arrow rather than a sword and lance.

In some respects, the political relationships among the Indian states beginning in the fifth century took on the character of the feudal relationships that emerged in Europe in the Middle Ages. Like medieval European lords, local Indian rajas were technically vassals of the king, but unlike the European situation, the relationship was not a contractual one. Still, the Indian model became highly complex, with vassals characterized as "inner" or "outer," depending on their physical or political proximity to the king, and vassals described as "greater" or "lesser," depending on their power and influence. As in Europe, the vassals themselves often had vassals.

In the Valley of Mexico between 1300 and 1500, the Aztecs developed a political system that bore some similarities to the Japanese, Indian, and European feudal orders. Although the Aztec king was a powerful, authoritarian ruler, the local rulers of lands outside the capital city were allowed considerable freedom. They did pay tribute to the king, however, and also provided him with military forces. Weapons differed from those used in Europe and Japan: Aztec warriors were armed with sharp knives made of stone and spears of wood fitted with razor-sharp blades cut from stone.

 What were the key characteristics of the political order we know as feudalism? To what degree can Japanese conditions be considered "feudal"?

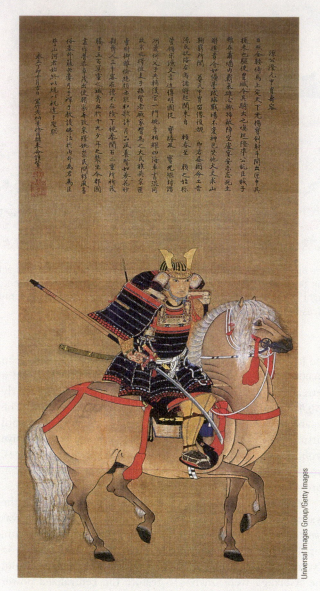

Universal Images Group/Getty Images

Samurai. During the Kamakura period, painters began to depict the adventures of the new warrior class. Here is an imposing mounted samurai warrior, the Japanese equivalent of the medieval knight in fief-holding Europe. Like his European counterpart, the samurai was supposed to live by a strict moral code and was expected to maintain an unquestioning loyalty to his liege lord. Above all, a samurai's life was one of simplicity and self-sacrifice.

LIFE IN THE LAND OF WA

Family & Society Some of the earliest descriptions of Japan come from Chinese sources. The following passage from the *History of the Wei Dynasty* was written in the late third century CE. *Wa* is a derogatory word meaning "dwarf," frequently used in China to refer to the Japanese people. The author of this passage, while remarking on the strange habits of the Japanese, writes without condescension.

History of the Wei Dynasty

The people of Wa make their abode in the mountainous islands located in the middle of the ocean....

All men, old or young, are covered by tattoos.... They are considered an ornament.... Men allow their hair to cover both of their ears and wear head-bands. They wear loincloths wrapped around their bodies and seldom use stitches. Women gather their hair at the ends and tie it in a knot and then pin it to the tops of their heads. They make their clothes in one piece, and cut an opening in the center for their heads. They plant wet-field rice,... [nettles], and mulberry trees. They

raise cocoons and reel the silk off the cocoons. They produce clothing made of... coarse silk, and of cotton.... They fight with halberds, shields, and wooden bows.... Their arrows are made of bamboo, and iron and bone points make up the arrowhead.

People ... live long, some reaching one hundred years of age.... Normally men of high echelon have four or five wives, and the plebeians may have two or three. When the law is violated, the light offender loses his wife and children by confiscation, and the grave offender has his household and kin exterminated. There are class distinctions within the nobility and the base, and some are vassals of others. There are mansions and granaries erected for the purpose of collecting taxes....

 What does this document tell us about the nature of Japanese society in the third century CE? What does it tell us about the author's point of view?

Source: *Sources of Japanese History*, edited by David Lu, © 1974 McGraw-Hill, New York, Vol. I, p. 10.

---

of their limited amount of tillable land and plentiful rainfall to create a society based on the cultivation of wet rice.

Trade and Manufacturing As in China, commerce was slow to develop as an independent force in Japan. During ancient times, each *uji* had a local artisan class, composed of weavers, carpenters, and ironworkers, but trade was essentially local and was regulated by the local clan leaders. With the rise of the Yamato state, a money economy gradually began to develop, but most internal trade was still conducted through barter until the twelfth century, when metal coins introduced from China became more popular.

Trade and manufacturing began to develop more rapidly during the Kamakura period, with the appearance of quarterly markets in the larger towns and the emergence of such industries as paper, iron casting, and porcelain. Foreign trade, mainly with Korea and China, began during the eleventh century. Japan exported raw materials, paintings, swords, and other manufactured items in return for silk, porcelain, books, and copper cash. Some Japanese traders were so aggressive in pressing their interests that authorities in China and Korea attempted to limit the number of Japanese commercial missions that could visit each year. Such restrictions were often ignored, however, and encouraged some Japanese traders to turn to piracy.

Significantly, manufacturing and commerce developed rapidly during the more decentralized period of the Ashikaga Shogunate and the era of the warring states, perhaps because of the rapid growth in the wealth and autonomy of local daimyo families. Market towns, now operating on a full money economy, began to appear, and local manufacturers formed guilds to

protect their mutual interests. Sometimes local peasants would bring homemade goods, such as silk or hemp clothing, household items, or food, to sell at the markets. In general, however, trade and manufacturing remained under the control of the local daimyo, who would often provide tax breaks to local guilds in return for other benefits. Although Japan remained a primarily agricultural society, it was on the verge of a major advance in manufacturing.

Daily Life One of the first descriptions of the life of the Japanese people comes from a Chinese dynastic history from the third century CE. It describes lords and peasants living in an agricultural society that was based on the cultivation of wet rice. Laws had been enacted to punish offenders, local trade was conducted in markets, and government granaries stored the grain that was paid as taxes (see "Life in the Land of Wa").

Life for the common people probably changed very little over the next several hundred years. Most were peasants, who worked on land owned by their lord or, in some cases, by the state or by Buddhist monasteries. By no means, however, were all peasants equal either economically or socially. Although in ancient times, all land was owned by the state and peasants working the land were taxed at an equal rate depending on the nature of the crop, after the Yamato era, variations began to develop. At the top were local officials, who were often well-to-do peasants. They were responsible for organizing collective labor services and collecting tax grain from the peasants and were in turn exempt from such obligations themselves (see Comparative Illustration "The Longhouse," p. 310).

COMPARATIVE ILLUSTRATION

The Longhouse. Many early peoples built longhouses of wood and thatch to store their goods and carry on community activities. Many such structures were erected on heavy pilings to protect the interior from floods, insects, or wild animals. In illustration A is a model of a sixth-century CE warehouse in Osaka, Japan. The original was apparently used by local residents to store grain and other foodstuffs. In illustration B is a reconstruction of a similar structure built originally by Vikings in Denmark. The longhouses in illustration C are still occupied by families living on Nias, a small island off the coast of Sumatra. The outer walls were built to resemble the hulls of Dutch galleons that plied the seas near Nias during the seventeenth and eighteenth centuries.

Q *The longhouse served as a communal structure in many human communities in early times. What types of structures serve communities in modern societies?*

B

William J. Duiker

C

A

William J. Duiker

William J. Duiker

The majority of the peasants were under the authority of these local officials. In general, peasants were free to dispose of their harvest as they saw fit after paying their tax quota, but in practical terms, their freedom was limited. Those who were unable to pay the tax sank to the level of *genin* (GAY-nin), or landless laborers, who could be bought and sold by their proprietors like slaves along with the land on which they worked. Some fled to escape such a fate and attempted to survive by clearing plots of land in the mountains or by becoming bandits.

In addition to the *genin*, the bottom of the social scale was occupied by the *eta* (AY-tuh), a class of hereditary slaves who, like the outcastes in India, were responsible for what were considered degrading occupations, such as curing leather and burying the dead. The origins of the *eta* are not entirely clear, but they probably were descendants of prisoners of war, criminals, or mountain dwellers who were not related to the dominant Yamato peoples. As we shall see, the *eta* are still a distinctive part of Japanese society, and although their full legal rights are guaranteed under the current constitution, discrimination against them is not uncommon.

CHRONOLOGY	Formation of the Japanese State
Shotoku Taishi	572–622
Era of Taika reforms	Mid-seventh century
Nara period	710–784
Heian (Kyoto) period	794–1185
Murasaki Shikibu	978–c. 1016
Minamoto Yoritomo	1142–1199
Kamakura Shogunate	1185–1333
Mongol invasions	Late thirteenth century
Ashikaga period	1333–1600
Onin War	1467–1477

Daily life for ordinary people in early Japan resembled that of their counterparts throughout much of Asia. The vast majority lived in small villages, several of which normally made up a single *shoen*. Housing was simple. Most lived in small two-room houses of timber, mud, or thatch, with dirt floors covered by straw or woven mats—the origin, perhaps, of the well-known *tatami* (tuh-TAH-mee), or woven-mat floor, of more modern times. Their diet consisted of rice (if some was left after the payment of the grain tax), wild grasses, millet, roots, and some fish and birds. Life must have been difficult at best; as one eighth-century poet lamented:

> Here I lie on straw
> Spread on bare earth,
> With my parents at my pillow,
> My wife and children at my feet,
> All huddled in grief and tears.
> No fire sends up smoke
> At the cooking place,
> And in the cauldron
> A spider spins its web.[2]

The Role of Women Evidence about the relations between men and women in early Japan presents a mixed picture (see Film & History). The Chinese dynastic history reports that "in their meetings and daily living, there is no distinction between … men and women." It notes that a woman "adept in the ways of shamanism" had briefly ruled Japan in the third century CE. But it also remarks that polygyny was common, with nobles normally having four or five wives and commoners two or three.[3] An eighth-century law code guaranteed the inheritance rights of women, and wives abandoned by their husbands were permitted to obtain a divorce and remarry. A husband could divorce his wife if she did not produce a male child, committed adultery, disobeyed her in-laws, talked too much, engaged in theft, was jealous, or had a serious illness.

When Buddhism was introduced, women were initially relegated to a subordinate position in the new faith. Although they were permitted to take up monastic life—many widows entered a monastery at the death of their husbands—they were not permitted to visit Buddhist holy places, nor were they even (in the accepted wisdom) equal with men in the afterlife. One Buddhist commentary from the late thirteenth century said that a woman could not attain enlightenment because "her sin is grievous, and so she is not allowed to enter the lofty palace of the great Brahma, nor to look upon the clouds which hover over his ministers and people."[4] Other Buddhist scholars were more egalitarian: "Learning the Law of Buddha and achieving release from illusion have nothing to do with whether one happens to be a man or a woman."[5] Such views ultimately prevailed, and women were eventually allowed to participate fully in Buddhist activities in medieval Japan.

Although women did not possess the full legal and social rights of their male counterparts, they played an active role at various levels of Japanese society. Aristocratic women were prominent at court, and some, such as the author known as Lady Murasaki (978–c. 1016), won renown for their artistic or literary talents (see "Seduction of the Akashi Lady," p. 312). Though few commoners could aspire to such prominence, women often appear in the scroll paintings of the period along with men,

⊿ FILM & HISTORY

The film *Rashomon* (1950), directed by the celebrated filmmaker Akira Kurosawa, was one of a number of Japanese movies that won international plaudits in the period shortly after World War II. Like many other Japanese films of the era, it explored key aspects of human nature, often through the lens of snippets of life in medieval Japan. What made *Rashomon* unique was its portrayal of the elusive nature of truth, as the events surrounding the rape and murder of a young Japanese woman are presented through the eyes of a number of the participants.

Q *Japanese movie director Akira Kurosawa is notorious for having introduced a new cinematic technique in his 1950 film* Rashomon. *What was this technique, and can you think of any movies that you have seen that have successfully adopted it?*

The Kobal Collection at Art Resource, NY

doing the spring planting, threshing and hulling the rice, and acting as carriers, peddlers, salespersons, and entertainers.

11–1d In Search of the Pure Land: Religion in Early Japan

In Japan, as elsewhere, religious belief began with the worship of nature spirits. Early Japanese worshiped spirits called *kami* (KAH-mi) who resided in trees, rivers and streams, and mountains. They also believed in ancestral spirits present in the atmosphere. In Japan, these beliefs eventually evolved into a kind of state religion

SEDUCTION OF THE AKASHI LADY

Family & Society

OUT OF THE JAPANESE TRADITION of female introspective prose appeared one of the world's truly great novels, *The Tale of Genji*, written around the year 1000 by the diarist and court author Murasaki Shikibu (MOO-rah-SAH-kee SHEE-kee-boo), known as Lady Murasaki. The novel has influenced Japanese writing for more than a thousand years and even today is revered for its artistic refinement and sensitivity. A panoramic portrayal of court life in tenth-century Japan, it traces the life and loves of the courtier Genji as he strives to retain the favor of those in power while simultaneously pursuing his cult of love and beauty. The remarkable character of Genji is revealed to the reader through myriad psychological observations. In this excerpt, Genji has just seduced a lady at court and now feels misgivings at having betrayed his child bride. A *koto* is a Japanese stringed instrument similar to a zither.

Lady Murasaki, *The Tale of Genji*

A curtain string brushed against a koto, to tell him that she had been passing a quiet evening at her music.

"And will you not play for me on the koto of which I have heard so much?" …

This lady had not been prepared for an incursion and could not cope with it. She fled to an inner room. How she could have contrived to bar it he could not tell, but it was very firmly barred indeed. Though he did not exactly force his way through, it is not to be imagined that he left matters as they were. Delicate, slender—she was almost too beautiful. Pleasure was mingled with pity at the thought that he was imposing himself upon her. She was even more pleasing than reports from afar had had her. The autumn night, usually so long, was over in a trice. Not wishing to be seen, he hurried out, leaving affectionate assurances behind.

Genji called in secret from time to time. The two houses being some distance apart, he feared being seen by fishers, who were known to relish a good rumor, and sometimes several days would elapse between his visits....

Genji dreaded having Murasaki [his bride] learn of the affair. He still loved her more than anyone, and he did not want her to make even joking reference to it. She was a quiet, docile lady, but she had more than once been unhappy with him. Why, for the sake of brief pleasure, had he caused her pain? He wished it were all his to do over again. The sight of the Akashi lady only brought new longing for the other lady.

He got off a more earnest and affectionate letter than usual, at the end of which he said: "I am in anguish at the thought that, because of foolish occurrences for which I have been responsible but have had little heart, I might appear in a guise distasteful to you. There has been a strange, fleeting encounter. That I should volunteer this story will make you see, I hope, how little I wish to have secrets from you. Let the gods be my judges.

*"It was but the fisherman's brush with the salty sea pine.
Followed by a tide of tears of longing."*

Her reply was gentle and unreproachful, and at the end of it she said: "That you should have deigned to tell me a dreamlike story which you could not keep to yourself calls to mind numbers of earlier instances.

*"Naive of me, perhaps; yet we did make our vows.
And now see the waves that wash the Mountain of Waiting!"*

It was the one note of reproach in a quiet, undemanding letter. He found it hard to put down, and for some nights he stayed away from the house in the hills.

 Why does this thousand-year-old passage still resonate with readers today?

Source: From *The Tale of the Genji* by Lady Murasaki, translated by Edward G. Seidensticker, copyright © 1976 by Edward G. Seidensticker (New York: Alfred A. Knopf).

---

called **Shinto** (SHIN-toh) (the Sacred Way or Way of the Gods) that is still practiced today. Shinto still serves as an ideological and emotional force that knits the Japanese into a single people and nation.

Shinto does not have a complex metaphysical superstructure or an elaborate moral code. It does require certain ritual acts, usually undertaken at a shrine, and a process of purification, which may have originated in primitive concerns about death, childbirth, illness, and menstruation. This traditional concern about physical purity may help explain the strong Japanese concern for personal cleanliness and the practice of denying women entrance to the holy places.

Another feature of Shinto is its stress on the beauty of nature and the importance of nature itself in Japanese life. Shinto shrines are usually located in places of exceptional beauty and are often dedicated to a nearby physical feature. As time passed, such primitive beliefs contributed to the characteristic Japanese love of nature. In this sense, early Shinto beliefs have been incorporated into the lives of all Japanese.

In time, Shinto evolved into a state doctrine that was linked with belief in the divinity of the emperor and the sacredness of the Japanese nation. A national shrine was established at Ise (EE-say), north of the early capital of Nara, where the emperor annually paid tribute to the sun goddess. But although Shinto had evolved well beyond its primitive origins, like its counterparts elsewhere, it could not satisfy all the religious and emotional needs of the Japanese people. For those needs, the Japanese turned to Buddhism.

As we have seen, Buddhism was introduced into Japan from China during the sixth century CE and had begun to spread beyond the court to the general population by the eighth century.

11–1e Sources of Traditional Japanese Culture

Nowhere is the Japanese genius for blending indigenous and imported elements into an effective whole better demonstrated than in the national culture. In such widely diverse fields as art, architecture, sculpture, and literature, the Japanese from early times showed an impressive ability to borrow selectively from abroad without destroying essential native elements.

Growing contact with China during the rise of the Yamato state stimulated Japanese artists. Missions sent to China and Korea during the seventh and eighth centuries returned with examples of Tang literature, sculpture, and painting, all of which influenced the Japanese.

The Japanese Stone Lantern. One of the most familiar artifacts found at Japanese Buddhist temples is the stone lantern. In Buddhist teachings, a burning lamp symbolizes Siddhartha Gautama himself as he brings light to humanity as a means of banishing ignorance. The first stone lanterns were brought to the Japanese islands from China in the sixth or seventh centuries CE and were originally used as votive lights to accompany symbolic offerings at Buddhist temples. Eventually they took on a secular purpose as a decorative element in private gardens and tea houses. The lanterns here are located at the Taiji Buddhist temple in Nara, Japan.

Literature Borrowing from Chinese models was somewhat complicated, however, since the early Japanese had no system for recording their own spoken language and initially adopted the Chinese pictographic language for writing. The challenge was complicated by the fact that spoken Japanese is not part of the Sino-Tibetan family of languages. But resourceful Japanese soon adapted the Chinese written characters so that they could be used for recording the Japanese language. In some cases, Chinese characters were given Japanese pronunciations. But Chinese characters could not easily be used to record Japanese words, which normally contain more than one syllable. Sometimes the Japanese simply used Chinese characters as phonetic symbols that were combined to form Japanese words. Later they simplified the characters into phonetic symbols that were used alongside Chinese characters. This hybrid system continues to be used today.

At first, most educated Japanese preferred to write in Chinese, and a court literature—consisting of essays, poetry, and official histories—appeared in the classical Chinese language. But spoken Japanese never totally disappeared among the educated classes and eventually became the instrument of a unique literature. With the lessening of Chinese cultural influence in the tenth century, Japanese verse resurfaced. Between the tenth and fifteenth centuries, twenty imperial anthologies of poetry were compiled. Initially, they were written primarily by courtiers, but with the fall of the Heian court and the rise of the warrior and merchant classes, all literate segments of society began to produce poetry.

As in China, most Japanese saw no contradiction between worshiping both the Buddha and their local nature gods (*kami*), many of whom were considered later manifestations of the Buddha. Most of the Buddhist sects that had achieved popularity in China were established in Japan, and many of them attracted powerful patrons at court. Great monasteries were built that competed in wealth and influence with the noble families that had traditionally ruled the country.

Perhaps the two most influential Buddhist sects were the Pure Land (in Japanese, Jodo) sect and **Zen** (in Chinese, Chan or Ch'an). The Pure Land sect, which taught that devotion alone could lead to enlightenment and release, was very popular among the common people, for whom monastic life was one of the few routes to upward mobility. Among the aristocracy, the most influential school was Zen, which exerted a significant impact on Japanese life and culture during the era of the warring states. With its emphasis on austerity, self-discipline, and communion with nature, Zen complemented many traditional beliefs in Japanese society and became an important component of the samurai warrior's code.

In Zen teachings, there were various ways to achieve enlightenment—*satori* (suh-TAWR-ee) in Japanese. Some stressed that it could be achieved suddenly. One monk, for example, reportedly achieved *satori* by listening to the sound of a bamboo stick striking against roof tiles; another did so by carefully watching the opening of peach blossoms in the spring. But other practitioners, sometimes called adepts, said that enlightenment could come only through studying the scriptures and arduous self-discipline, known as *zazen* (ZAH-ZEN), or "seated Zen." Seated Zen involved a lengthy process of meditation that cleansed the mind of all thoughts so that it could concentrate on the essential.

Japanese poetry is unique. It expresses its themes in a simple form, a characteristic stemming from traditional Japanese aesthetics, Zen religion, and the language itself. The aim of the Japanese poet was to create a mood, perhaps the melancholic effect of gently falling cherry blossoms or leaves. With a few specific references, the poet suggested a whole world, just as Zen Buddhism sought enlightenment from a sudden perception. Poets often alluded to earlier poems by repeating their images with small changes, a technique that was viewed not as plagiarism but as an elaboration on the meaning of the earlier poem.

By the fourteenth century, the technique of the "linked verse" had become the most popular form of Japanese poetry. Known as *haiku* (HY-koo), it is composed of seventeen syllables divided into lines of five, seven, and five syllables, respectively. The poems usually focused on images from nature and the mutability of life. Often the poetry was written by several individuals alternately composing verses and linking them together into long sequences of hundreds and even thousands of lines. The following example, by three poets named Sogi (SOH-gee), Shohaku (shoh-HAH-koo), and Socho (SOH-choh), is one of the most famous of the period:

> Snow clinging to slope,   Sogi
>   On mist-enshrouded mountains
>   At evening time.
> In the distance flows   Shohaku
>   Through plum-scented villages.
> Willows cluster   Socho
>   In the river breeze
>   As spring appears.[6]

Poetry served a unique function at the Heian court, where it was the initial means of communication between lovers. By custom, aristocratic women were isolated from all contact with men outside their immediate family and spent their days hidden behind screens. Some amused themselves by writing poetry. When courtship began, poetic exchanges were the only means a woman had to attract her prospective lover, who would be enticed solely by her poetic art.

During the Heian period, male courtiers wrote in Chinese, believing that Chinese civilization was superior and worthy of emulation. Like the Chinese, they viewed prose fiction as "vulgar gossip." Nevertheless, from the ninth century to the twelfth, Japanese women were prolific writers of prose fiction in Japanese (see "Seduction of the Akashi Lady," p. 312). Excluded from school, they learned to read and write at home and wrote diaries and stories to pass the time. Some of the most talented women were invited to court as authors in residence.

The famous classical Japanese drama known as *No* (NOH) also originated during this period. *No* developed out of a variety of entertainment forms, such as dancing and juggling, that were part of the native tradition or had been imported from China and other regions of Asia. The plots were normally based on stories from Japanese history or legend. Eventually, *No* evolved into a highly stylized drama in which the performers wore masks and danced to the accompaniment of instrumental music. Like much of Japanese culture, *No* was restrained, graceful, and refined.

Art and Architecture In art and architecture, as in literature, the Japanese pursued their interest in beauty, simplicity, and nature. To some degree, Japanese artists and architects were influenced by Chinese forms. As they became familiar with Chinese architecture, Japanese rulers and aristocrats tried to emulate the splendor of Tang civilization and began constructing their palaces and temples in Chinese style.

The Golden Pavilion in Kyoto. Gardens, water, and architecture combine to create a magnificent setting for the Golden Pavilion. Constructed in the fourteenth century as a retreat where the shoguns could withdraw from their administrative duties, the pavilion derived its name from the gold foil that covered its exterior. Completely destroyed by an arsonist in 1950 as a protest against the commercialism of modern Buddhism, it was rebuilt and reopened in 1987. The use of water as a backdrop is especially noteworthy in Chinese and Japanese landscapes, as well as in the Middle East.

During the Heian period (794–1185), the search for beauty was reflected in various art forms, such as narrative hand scrolls, screens, sliding door panels, fans, and lacquer decoration. As in the case of literature, nature themes dominated—seashore scenes, a spring rain, moon and mist, flowering wisteria and cherry blossoms. All were intended to evoke an emotional response on the part of the viewer. Japanese painting suggested the frail beauty of nature by presenting it on a smaller scale. The majestic mountain in a Chinese painting became a more intimate Japanese landscape with rolling hills and a rice field. Faces were rarely shown, and human drama was indicated by a woman lying prostrate or hiding her face in her sleeve. Tension was shown by two people talking at a great distance or with their backs to one another.

During the Kamakura period (1185–1333), the hand scroll with its physical realism and action-packed paintings of the new warrior class achieved great popularity. Reflecting these chaotic times, the art of portraiture flourished, and a scroll would include a full

Guardian Kings. Larger than life and intimidating in its presence, this thirteenth-century wooden statue departs from the refined atmosphere of the Heian court and pulsates with the masculine energy of the Kamakura period. Placed strategically at the entrance to Buddhist shrines, guardian kings such as this one protected the temple and the faithful. In contrast to the refined atmosphere of the Fujiwara court, the Kamakura era was a warrior's world.

philosophy found expression in the Japanese garden, the tea ceremony, the art of flower arranging, pottery and ceramics, and miniature plant display—the famous *bonsai* (bon-SY), literally "pot scenery."

Landscapes served as an important means of expression in both Japanese art and architecture. Japanese gardens were initially modeled on Chinese examples. Early court texts during the Heian period emphasized the importance of including a stream or pond when creating a garden. The landscape surrounding the fourteenth-century Golden Pavilion in Kyoto displays a harmony of garden, water, and architecture that makes it one of the treasures of the world. Because of the shortage of water in the city, later gardens concentrated on rock composition, using white pebbles to represent water (see Comparative Illustration "In the Garden," p. 316).

Like the Japanese garden, the tea ceremony represents the fusion of Zen and aesthetics. Developed in the fifteenth century, it was practiced in a simple room devoid of external ornament except for a *tatami* floor, sliding doors, and an alcove with a writing desk and asymmetrical shelves. The participants could therefore focus completely on the activity of pouring and drinking tea. "Tea and Zen have the same flavor" goes the Japanese saying. Considered the ultimate symbol of spiritual deliverance, the tea ceremony continues to have great aesthetic value and moral significance today as well as in traditional times.

11–1f Japan and the Chinese Model

Few major societies in Asia have been as isolated as Japan. Cut off from the mainland by 120 miles of frequently turbulent ocean, the Japanese had only minimal contact with the outside world during most of their early development.

Whether or not this isolation was ultimately beneficial to Japanese society cannot be determined. On the one hand, lack of knowledge of developments taking place elsewhere probably delayed the process of change in Japan. On the other hand, the Japanese were spared the destructive invasions that afflicted other ancient civilizations. Certainly, once the Japanese became acquainted with Chinese culture at the height of the Tang era, they were quick to take advantage of the opportunity. In the space of a few decades, the young state adopted many aspects of Chinese society and culture and thereby introduced major changes into Japanese life.

Nevertheless, Japanese political institutions failed to follow all aspects of the Chinese pattern. Despite Prince Shotoku's effort to make effective use of the imperial traditions of Tang China, the decentralizing forces in Japanese society remained dominant throughout the period under discussion in this chapter. Adoption of the Confucian civil service examination did not lead to a breakdown of Japanese social divisions; instead, the examination was administered in a manner that preserved and strengthened them. Although Buddhist and Daoist doctrines made a significant contribution to Japanese religious practices, Shinto beliefs continued to play a major role in shaping the Japanese worldview.

Why Japan did not follow the Chinese road to centralized authority has been a subject of debate among historians. Some

gallery of warriors and holy men in starkly realistic detail, including such unflattering features as stubble, worry lines on a forehead, and crooked teeth. Japanese sculptors also produced naturalistic wooden statues of generals, nobles, and saints. By far the most distinctive were the fierce heavenly "guardian kings," who still intimidate the viewer today (see illustration "Guardian Kings").

Zen Buddhism, an import from China in the thirteenth century, also influenced Japanese aesthetics. With its emphasis on immediate enlightenment without recourse to intellectual analysis and elaborate ritual, Zen reinforced the Japanese predilection for simplicity and self-discipline. During this era, Zen

Religion & Philosophy

In the Garden. In traditional China and Japan, gardens were meant to free the observer's mind from mundane concerns, offering spiritual refreshment in the quiet of nature. Chinese gardens were designed to reconstruct an orderly microcosm of nature, where the harassed Confucian official could find spiritual renewal. Wandering through constantly changing perspectives of ponds, trees, rocks, and pavilions, he could imagine himself immersed in a monumental landscape. In the garden in Suzhou in image A, the rocks represent towering mountains to suggest a Daoist sense of withdrawal and eternity, reducing the viewer to a tiny speck in the grand flow of life.

In Japan, the traditional garden reflected the Zen Buddhist philosophy of simplicity, restraint, allusion, and tranquility. In the garden in image B, at the Ryoanji (RYOH-ahn-jee) temple in Kyoto, the rocks are meant to suggest mountains rising from a sea of pebbles. Such gardens served as an aid to meditation, inspiring the viewer to join with comrades in composing "linked verse" (see poetry by Sogi, Shohaku, and Socho, Section 11-1e, p. 314).

 How do gardens in traditional China and Japan differ in form and purpose from gardens in Western societies? Why do you think this is the case?

A

William J. Duiker

B

William J. Duiker

argue that the answer lies in differing cultural traditions, while others suggest that Chinese institutions and values were introduced too rapidly to be assimilated effectively by Japanese society. One factor may have been the absence of a foreign threat (except for the brief incursion by the Mongols). A recent view holds that diseases (such as smallpox and measles) imported inadvertently from China led to a marked decline in the population of the islands, reducing food output and preventing the population from coalescing in more compact urban centers.

In any event, Japan was not the only society in Asia to assimilate ideas from abroad while at the same time preserving customs and institutions inherited from the past. Across the Sea of Japan to the west and several thousand miles to the southwest, other Asian peoples were embarked on a similar journey. We now turn to their experience.

11–2 KOREA: BRIDGE TO THE EAST

Q **Focus Question:** What were the main characteristics of economic and social life in early Korea?

Few of the societies on the periphery of China have been as directly influenced by the Chinese model as Korea. The relationship between China and the peoples living on the Korean

peninsula has frequently been characterized by tension and conflict, however, and Koreans have often resented what they perceive to be Chinese chauvinism and arrogance.

A graphic example of this attitude has occurred in recent years as officials and historians in both countries have presented differing interpretations of the early history of the Korean people. The Korean peninsula was probably first settled by Altaic-speaking fishing and hunting peoples from neighboring Manchuria during the Neolithic Age. Because the area, which is slightly larger than the state of Minnesota, is relatively mountainous (only about one-fifth of the peninsula is adaptable to cultivation), farming was apparently not practiced until about 2000 BCE. At that time, the peoples living in the area began to form organized communities.

It is this period that gives rise to disagreement. In 2004, Chinese official sources claimed that the first organized kingdom in the area, known as Koguryo (koh-GOOR-yoh) (37 BCE– 668 CE), occupied a wide swath of Manchuria as well as the northern section of the Korean peninsula and was thus an integral part of Chinese history. Korean scholars, basing their contentions on a combination of legend and limited historical evidence, countered that the first kingdom established on the peninsula, known as Gojoseon (goh-joh-SHAWN), was created by the ruler Dangun (dan-GOON) in 2333 BCE, and that both he and his subjects in the surrounding area were ethnically Korean.

It was at that time, these scholars maintain, that the Bronze Age got under way in northeastern Asia.

Although this dispute has not yet been resolved, most scholars today do agree that in 109 BCE, the northern part of the peninsula came under direct Chinese influence. During the next several generations, the area was ruled by the Han dynasty, which divided the territory into provinces and introduced Chinese institutions. With the decline of the Han in the third century CE, power gradually shifted to local leaders, who drove out the Chinese administrators but continued to absorb Chinese cultural influences. Eventually, three separate kingdoms emerged on the peninsula: Koguryo in the north, Paekche (bayk-JEE) in the southwest, and Silla (SIL-uh) in the southeast.

Korea's Three Kingdoms

11–2a The Three Kingdoms

From the fourth to the seventh centuries, the three kingdoms were bitter rivals for influence and territory on the peninsula. At the same time, all began to adopt Chinese political and cultural institutions. Koguryo was the first among the kingdoms to introduce Buddhism in the late fourth century CE. The first Confucian academy on the peninsula was established in the capital at Pyongyang (pyahng-YANG). All three kingdoms also appear to have accepted a tributary relationship with one or another of the squabbling states that emerged in China after the fall of the Han. The kingdom of Silla, less exposed than its two rivals to Chinese influence, was at first the weakest of the three, but eventually it emerged as the dominant power on the peninsula. To pacify the haughty Chinese, who continued to claim a degree of suzerainty with the kingdoms on the peninsula, Silla accepted tributary status under the Tang Dynasty. In the meantime, any remaining Japanese colonies in the south were eliminated.

With the country unified for the first time, the rulers of Silla attempted to use Chinese political institutions and ideology to forge a centralized state. As the state religion, Buddhism grew in popularity, and Korean monks followed the paths of their Japanese counterparts on journeys to Buddhist sites in China. Chinese architecture and art became dominant in the capital at Kyongju (KEE-yahng-joo) and other urban centers, and the written Chinese language became the official means of legal communication. Korean skilled workers made their own contributions in the fields of science and technology, especially in the area of metallurgy, ceramics, and astronomy (the earliest observatory in East Asia was established there in the seventh century). But the effort by Silla rulers to replicate the Chinese model faced strong headwinds, as powerful

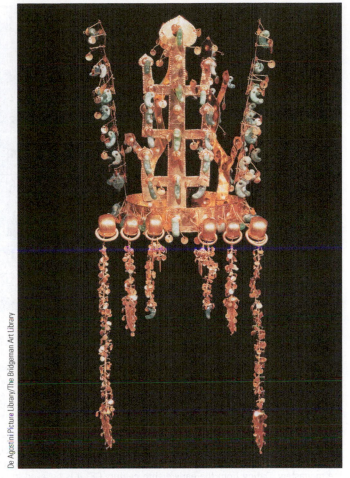

De Agostini Picture Library/The Bridgeman Art Library

Korean Royal Crown. The Silla Dynasty was renowned for the high quality of its gold, jewelry, crowns, and sword sheaths. Shown here is a jewel-inlaid royal crown of the fifth century CE that was excavated from a royal tomb in eastern Korea. Although much Silla artwork reflects Chinese influence, royal crowns located in Silla tombs often contain antler-like motifs, reflecting the animistic traditions of Korea's pre-Chinese past. The comma-shaped jewels symbolize the king's Heaven-sanctioned authority on earth.

aristocratic families, long dominant in the southeastern part of the peninsula, were still influential at court. They were able to prevent the adoption of the Tang civil service examination system and resisted the distribution of manorial lands to the poor. But squabbling among noble families steadily increased, and after the assassination of the king of Silla in 780, civil war erupted.

11–2b The Rise of the Koryo Dynasty

When the Silla Dynasty collapsed in the early tenth century, a new dynasty called Koryo (KAWR-yoh) (the root of the modern name of the country in English) arose in the north. The new kingdom followed the Silla example by turning to Chinese political institutions in an effort to strengthen its power and unify the peninsula. The civil service examination system was introduced in 958, but as in Japan, the bureaucracy continued to be dominated by influential aristocratic families.

Pulguksa Bell Tower. Among the greatest architectural achievements on the Korean peninsula is the Pulguksa (Monastery of the Land of Buddha), built near Kyongju, the ancient capital of Silla, in the eighth century CE. Shown here is the bell tower, located in the midst of beautiful parklands on the monastery grounds. In 1966, a scroll was discovered inside a stone stupa adjacent to the monastery. Dating from the early eighth century CE, it is believed to be the oldest printed text extant in the world today.

The Koryo dynasty managed to retain power for four hundred years, protected from invasion by the absence of a strong dynasty in neighboring China. Under the Koryo, industry and commerce slowly began to develop, but as in China, agriculture was the prime source of wealth. In theory, all land was the property of the king, but in actuality, noble families controlled their holdings. The lands were worked by peasants who were subject to burdens similar to those of European serfs. At the bottom of society was a class of *chonmin* (CHAWN-min), or "base people," composed of slaves, artisans, and other specialized workers.

From a cultural perspective, the Koryo era was one of high achievement. Buddhist monasteries, run by sects introduced from China, including Pure Land and Zen, controlled vast territories, while their monks served as royal advisers at court. At first, Buddhist themes dominated in Korean art and sculpture, and the entire Tripitaka (tri-pih-TAH-kah) (the "three baskets," or sections, of the Buddhist canon) was printed using wooden blocks. Eventually, however, with the appearance of landscape painting and porcelain, Confucian themes began to predominate.

11–2c Resisting the Mongols

Like its predecessor in Silla, the kingdom of Koryo was unable to overcome the power of the nobility and the absence

of a reliable tax base. In the thirteenth century, the Mongols seized the northern part of the country and assimilated it into the Yuan empire. The weakened kingdom of Koryo became a tributary of the great khan in Khanbaliq (see Chapter 10).

The era of Mongol rule was one of profound suffering for the Korean people, especially the thousands of peasants and artisans who were compelled to perform conscript labor to help build the ships in preparation for Khubilai Khan's invasion of Japan. On the positive side, the Mongols introduced many new ideas and technology from China and farther afield. The Koryo dynasty had managed to survive, but only by accepting Mongol authority, and when the power of the Mongols declined, the kingdom declined with it. With the rise to power of the Ming in China, Koryo collapsed, and power was seized by the military commander Yi Song-gye (YEE-song-YEE), who declared the founding of the new Choson (also known as Yi [YEE]) Dynasty in 1392. Once again, the Korean people were in charge of their own destiny.

Always aware of potential threats emanating from more powerful neighbors, the Choson kingdom was actively interested in events taking place elsewhere in the region and was quick to follow up on technological advances taking place in China. Koreans were among the first to adopt the new invention of block printing, and Korean cartographers hastened to

Korean Celadon Ware. Although Chinese ceramics were generally praised as the most desired of their kind in eastern Asia, other countries in the region, such as Korea, Thailand, and Vietnam, produced high-quality products as well. This was especially the case during the so-called Ming Gap, when the Ming Dynasty unilaterally banned Chinese commercial activities throughout the remainder of Asia. Korea was noted for its so-called celadon inlay ware, in which liquid inlay materials were inscribed into a clay vessel before firing. Korean workers produced a number of such vessels during the Koryo kingdom.

draw up regional and world maps based on Chinese originals. The famous "Kangnido" world map, based on Chinese models but produced in Korea in 1402, is considered to be the second oldest surviving map drawn up in Asia (see illustration "The World in Chinese Eyes," Section 10-3a, p. 288).

11–3 VIETNAM: THE SMALLER DRAGON

 Focus Questions: What were the main developments in Vietnamese history before 1500? Why were the Vietnamese able to restore their national independence after a millennium of Chinese rule?

While the Korean people were attempting to establish their own identity in the shadow of the powerful Chinese Empire, the peoples of Vietnam, on China's southern frontier, were seeking to do the same. The Vietnamese (known as the Yueh in Chinese, from the peoples of that name inhabiting the southeastern coast of mainland China) began to practice irrigated agriculture in the flooded regions of the Red River Delta at an early date and entered the Bronze Age sometime during the second millennium BCE. By about 200 BCE, a young state had begun to form in the area but immediately encountered the expanding power of the Qin dynasty (see Chapter 3). The Vietnamese were not easy to subdue, however, and the collapse of the Qin temporarily enabled them to preserve their independence (see "The First Vietnam War"). Nevertheless, a century later, they were absorbed into the Han Empire.

At first, the Han were satisfied to rule the delta as an autonomous region under the administration of the local landed aristocracy. But Chinese taxes were oppressive, and in 39 CE, a revolt led by the Trung sisters (widows of local nobles who had been executed by the Chinese) briefly brought Han rule to an end. The Chinese soon suppressed the rebellion, however, and began

THE FIRST VIETNAM WAR

Politics & Government **IN THE THIRD CENTURY BCE,** the armies of the Chinese state of Qin (Ch'in) invaded the Red River Delta to launch an attack on the small Vietnamese state located there. As this passage from a Han dynasty philosophical text shows, the Vietnamese were not easy to conquer, and the new state soon declared its independence from the Qin. It was a lesson that was too often forgotten by would-be conquerors in later centuries.

Masters of Huai Nan

Ch'in Shih Huang Ti [the first emperor of Qin] was interested in the rhinoceros horn, the elephant tusks, the kingfisher plumes, and the pearls of the land of Yueh [Viet]; he therefore sent Commissioner T'u Sui at the head of five hundred thousand men divided into five armies.... For three years the sword and the crossbow were in constant readiness. Superintendent Lu was sent; there was no means of assuring the transport of supplies so he employed soldiers to dig a canal for sending grain, thereby making it possible to wage war on the people of Yueh. The lord of Western Ou, I Hsu Sung, was killed; consequently, the Yueh people entered the

wilderness and lived there with the animals; none consented to be a slave of Ch'in; choosing from among themselves men of valor, they made them their leaders and attacked the Ch'in by night, inflicting on them a great defeat and killing Commissioner T'u Sui; the dead and wounded were many. After this, the emperor deported convicts to hold the garrisons against the Yueh people.

The Yueh people fled into the depths of the mountains and forests, and it was not possible to fight them. The soldiers were kept in garrisons to watch over the abandoned territories. This went on for a long time, and the soldiers grew weary. Then the Yueh came out and attacked; the Ch'in soldiers suffered a great defeat. Subsequently, convicts were sent to hold the garrisons against the Yueh.

 How would the ancient Chinese military strategist Sun Tzu, mentioned in Chapter 3, have advised the Qin military commanders to carry out their operations? Would he have approved of the tactics adopted by the Vietnamese? Why or why not?

Source: From Keith W. Taylor, *The Birth of Vietnam* (Berkeley, 1983), p. 18.

COMPARATIVE ILLUSTRATION

Vietnam: On the Fault Line of Asia. Waves of cultural influence from the great civilizations in China and India washed steadily over Southeast Asia beginning during the first millennium CE. Nowhere was this process more in evidence than in the region of modern-day Vietnam, where Indian influence in the southern state of Champa contrasted with the influx of Chinese political institutions, philosophy, and culture to the north in the Red River Valley. The most visual example of this clash of culture appears in the field of architecture. As seen in image A, an eleventh-century shrine-tower originally dedicated to the Indian deity Shiva in the city of

Nha Trang clearly displays the influence of Indian models, while the distinctive one-pillar pagoda shown in image B reflects Chinese influence. The latter was built at the order of an eleventh-century Vietnamese monarch who had dreamed that the Buddhist goddess of mercy, known in China as Guan Yin, while seated on a lotus, had promised him a son. Shortly after the dream the emperor fathered a son. In gratitude he constructed this pagoda on one pillar, resembling a lotus blossom, the Buddhist symbol of purity, rising out of the mud.

A

B

William J. Duiker

William J. Duiker

to rule the area directly through officials dispatched from China. The first Chinese officials to serve in the region became exasperated at the uncultured ways of the locals, who wandered around "naked without shame."[7] In time, however, these foreign officials began to intermarry with the local nobility and form a Sino-Vietnamese ruling class who, though trained in Chinese culture, began to identify with the cause of Vietnamese autonomy.

For nearly a thousand years, the Vietnamese were exposed to the art, architecture, literature, philosophy, and written language of China as the Chinese attempted to integrate the area culturally as well as politically and administratively into their empire. It was a classic example of the Chinese effort to introduce advanced Confucian civilization to the "backward peoples" along the perimeter. To all intents and purposes, the Red River Delta, then known to the Chinese as the "pacified South," or Annam (ahn-NAHM), became a part of China.

11–3a The Rise of Great Viet

Despite Chinese efforts to assimilate Vietnam, the Vietnamese sense of ethnic and cultural identity proved inextinguishable, and in 939, the Vietnamese took advantage of the collapse of the Tang Dynasty in China to overthrow Chinese rule.

The new Vietnamese state, which called itself Dai Viet (dy VEE-et) (Great Viet), now sought to become a dynamic new force on the Southeast Asian mainland. Although the economic foundations of Vietnamese society had traditionally been founded on the cultivation of rice in the sediment-rich Red River Delta, Vietnamese merchants now became active participants in the commercial expansion that was taking place throughout the region. For centuries, the Vietnamese had been in active competition for territory and markets with the trading state of Champa (CHAHM-puh) to the south; by the end of the fifteenth century, economic competition increasingly turned to outright military hostilities.

Located along the central coast of what is now modern Vietnam, Champa was a trading society based on Indian cultural traditions that had originally been founded in 192 CE (see Comparative Illustration "Vietnam: On the Fault Line of Asia"). Over the next several centuries, it played an active role in the regional trade network, both as an intermediary between China and the remainder of Southeast Asia and as an exporter of forest products (see Chapter 9). By the beginning of the fifteenth century, the states of Dai Viet and Champa had gone to war on numerous occasions, but the decentralized Cham state, whose power base was centered on a number of

A PLEA TO THE NEW EMPEROR

LIKE MANY OTHER SOCIETIES IN PREMODERN East and Southeast Asia, the kingdom of Vietnam regularly paid tribute to the imperial court in China. The arrangement was often beneficial to both sides, as the tributary states received a form of international recognition from the relationship, as well as trading privileges in the massive Chinese market. China, for its part, assured itself that neighboring areas would not harbor dissident elements hostile to its own security.

In this document, contained in a historical chronicle written by Le Tac (LAY-tac) in the fourteenth century, a claimant to the Vietnamese throne seeks recognition in 1295 from the new emperor of the Yuan (Mongol) dynasty in China. Note how the Vietnamese ruler stresses his hope that the new emperor in Beijing, Timur Khan, will adopt a policy of peace and friendship with his southern neighbor. Timur's predecessor, the great Khubilai Khan, had sent Chinese troops to invade Vietnam a few years previously in a bid to place the country back under Chinese rule.

Le Tac, *Essay on Annam*

The Dragon flies in the heavens; new life has come to the Golden Throne. Many embassies have flocked to the Palace to express their sincere congratulations.

One man has ascended the Throne and ten thousand kingdoms are at peace. In great awe I observe that, under His Imperial Majesty's rule, peace and culture flourish within the Empire. His benevolence and virtue permeate the lands beyond the sea as they do at home. Always faithful to the kingly way, He embraces with the same kindness far lands and near. He lays aside military concerns and promotes cultural achievements. He restrains the ardor of his troops and puts an end to all combat. He enlarges His own indulgence and benevolence. He illuminates the virtue and merit of His Ancestors. The sound of thunder has ceased; it has changed into a rain of Imperial blessings. His investiture of tributary kings has been granted with a heavenly generosity. For the people it is a true rebirth, for the Universe a true springtime. I and my people happily live in peace and rejoice to hear the news of His ascendance to the Throne. My glances are directed toward the Northern sky; my heart also turns toward the extreme North, toward the Imperial Dwelling. From this country so remote in the South which I govern, I wish and desire that the longevity of the Emperor may be as great as the mountains of the South are high.

 What message does the new ruler of Vietnam seem to be sending to his counterpart in Beijing? Why does he feel that this message is important in the mutual relations between the two countries?

Source: From Le Tac, An-nam chi-luoc (Hue, University of Hue, 1961), p. 126 [Vietnamese version]; pp. 83–84 [Chinese version]. English translation by T. B. Lam. The translated document appears in Benda and Larkin, *The World of Southeast Asia* (New York: Harper & Row, 1967), pp. 148–149.

---

small river estuaries along the coast of the South China Sea, was in the end no match for its more powerful rival and in 1471 it met its final destruction. The Vietnamese then launched their historic "march to the south," establishing agricultural settlements in the newly conquered Cham territories. By the seventeenth century, the Vietnamese had reached the Gulf of Siam.

The Vietnamese, however, faced a serious challenge from the north. Although the Song Dynasty in China, beset with its own problems on the northern frontier, had accepted the Dai Viet ruler's offer of tribute status, both the Yuan and Ming Dynasties attempted to reintegrate the Red River Delta into the Chinese Empire. The first effort was made in the late thirteenth century by the Mongols, who attempted on two occasions to conquer the Vietnamese. After a series of bloody battles, during which the Vietnamese displayed an impressive capacity for guerrilla warfare, the

The Kingdom of Dai Viet, 1100

invaders were driven out (see "A Plea to the New Emperor"). A little over a century later, however, the Ming Dynasty tried again, and for twenty years Vietnam was once more under Chinese rule. In 1428, the Vietnamese finally evicted the Chinese, an experience that has ever since contributed to the strong sense of Vietnamese identity.

The Chinese Legacy Despite their stubborn resistance to Chinese rule, after the restoration of independence in the tenth century, Vietnamese rulers quickly discovered the convenience of the Confucian model in administering a river valley society and therefore attempted to follow Chinese practice in forming their own state. The ruler styled himself an emperor like his counterpart to the north (although he prudently termed himself a king in his direct dealings with the Chinese court), adopted Chinese court rituals, claimed the mandate of Heaven, and arrogated to himself the same authority and privileges in his dealings with his subjects. But unlike a Chinese emperor, who had no particular symbolic role as defender of the Chinese people or Chinese culture, a Vietnamese monarch was viewed, above all, as the symbol and defender of Vietnamese independence.

Like their Chinese counterparts, Vietnamese rulers fought to preserve their authority from the challenges of powerful aristocratic families and turned to the Chinese bureaucratic model, including civil service examinations, as a means of doing so. Under the pressure of strong monarchs, the concept of merit eventually took hold, and the power of the landed aristocracy was weakened if not entirely broken. The Vietnamese adopted much of the Chinese administrative structure, including the six ministries, the censorate, and the various levels of provincial and local administration.

Another aspect of the Chinese legacy was the spread of Buddhist, Daoist, and Confucian ideas, which supplemented the traditional belief in nature spirits. Buddhist precepts became popular among the local population, who integrated the new faith into their existing belief system by founding Buddhist temples dedicated to the local village deity in the hope of guaranteeing an abundant harvest. Upper-class Vietnamese educated in the Confucian classics tended to follow the more agnostic Confucian doctrine, but some joined Buddhist monasteries. Daoism also flourished at all levels of society and, as in China, provided a structure for animistic beliefs and practices that still predominated at the village level.

During the early period of independence, Vietnamese culture also borrowed liberally from its larger neighbor. Educated Vietnamese tried their hand at Chinese poetry, wrote dynastic histories in the Chinese style, and followed Chinese models in sculpture, architecture, and porcelain. Many of the notable buildings of the medieval period, such as the Temple of Literature and the famous One-Pillar Pagoda in Hanoi, are classic examples of Chinese architecture.

But there were signs that Vietnamese creativity would eventually transcend the bounds of Chinese cultural norms. Although most classical writing was undertaken in literary Chinese, the only form of literary expression deemed suitable by Confucian conservatives, an adaptation of Chinese written characters, called *chu nom* (CHOO nahm) ("southern characters"), was devised to provide a written system for spoken Vietnamese. In use by the early ninth century, it eventually began to be used for the composition of essays and poetry in the Vietnamese language. Such pioneering efforts would lead in later centuries to the emergence of a vigorous national literature totally independent of Chinese forms.

11–3b Society and Family Life

Vietnamese social institutions and customs were also strongly influenced by those of China. As in China, the introduction of a Confucian system and the adoption of civil service examinations undermined the role of the old landed aristocrats and led eventually to their replacement by the scholar-gentry class. Also as in China, the examinations were open to most males,

regardless of family background, which opened the door to a degree of social mobility unknown in most of the other states in the region. Candidates for the bureaucracy read many of the same Confucian classics and absorbed the same ethical principles as their counterparts in China. At the same time, they were also exposed to the classic works of Vietnamese history, which strengthened their sense that Vietnam was a distinct culture similar to, but separate from, that of China.

The vast majority of the Vietnamese people, however, were peasants. Most were small landholders or sharecroppers who rented their plots from wealthier farmers, but large estates were rare due to the systematic efforts of the central government to prevent the rise of a powerful local landed elite.

Family life in Vietnam was similar in many respects to that in China. The Confucian concept of family took hold during the period of Chinese rule, along with the related concepts of filial piety and gender inequality. Perhaps the most striking difference between family traditions in China and Vietnam was that Vietnamese women possessed more rights both in practice and by law. Since ancient times, wives had been permitted to own property and initiate divorce proceedings. One consequence of Chinese rule was a growing emphasis on male dominance, but the tradition of women's rights was never totally extinguished and was legally recognized in a law code promulgated in 1460.

Moreover, Vietnam had a strong historical tradition associating heroic women with the defense of the homeland. The Trung sisters were the first but by no means the only example. In the following passage, a Vietnamese historian of the eighteenth century recounts their story:

> The imperial court was far away; local officials were greedy and oppressive. At that time the country of one hundred sons was the country of the women of Lord To. The ladies [the Trung sisters] used the female arts against their irreconcilable foe; skirts and hairpins sang of patriotic righteousness, uttered a solemn oath at the inner door of the ladies' quarters, expelled the governor, and seized the capital.… Were they not grand heroines? … Our two ladies brought forward an army of all the people, and, establishing a royal court that settled affairs in the territories of the sixty-five strongholds, shook their skirts over the Hundred Yueh [the Vietnamese people].[8]

CHRONOLOGY	Early Korea and Vietnam
Foundation of Gojoseon state in Korea	c. 2333 BCE
Chinese conquest of Korea and Vietnam	Second and first centuries BCE
Trung Sisters' Revolt	39 CE
Founding of Champa	192
Era of Three Kingdoms in Korea	300s–600s
Restoration of Vietnamese independence	939
Mongol invasions of Korea and Vietnam	1257–1285
Founding of Choson (Yi) Dynasty in Korea	1392
Vietnamese conquest of Champa	1471

CHAPTER SUMMARY

Like many other great civilizations, the Chinese were traditionally convinced of the superiority of their culture and, when the opportunity arose, sought to introduce it to neighboring peoples. Although the latter were viewed in China with a measure of condescension, the adoption of Confucian teachings suggested the possibility of redemption. As the Master had remarked in the *Analects*, "By nature, people are basically alike; in practice they are far apart."[9] As a result, Chinese policies in the region were often shaped by the desire to introduce Chinese values and institutions to non-Chinese peoples living on the periphery.

As this chapter has shown, when conditions were right, China's "civilizing mission" sometimes had some marked success. All three countries that we have dealt with here borrowed liberally from the Chinese model. At the same time, all adapted Chinese institutions and values to the conditions prevailing in their own societies. Though all expressed admiration and respect for China's achievement, all sought to keep Chinese power at a distance.

As an island nation, Japan was the most successful of the three in protecting its political sovereignty and its cultural identity. Both Korea and Vietnam were compelled on various occasions to defend their independence by force of arms. That experience may have shaped their strong sense of national distinctiveness, as we shall discuss further in a later chapter.

The appeal of Chinese institutions can undoubtedly be explained by the fact that Japan, Korea, and Vietnam were all agrarian societies, much like their larger neighbor. But it is undoubtedly significant that the aspect of Chinese political culture that was least amenable to adoption abroad was the civil service examination system. The Confucian concept of meritocracy ran directly counter to the strong aristocratic tradition that flourished in all three societies during their early stage of development. Even when the system was adopted, it was put to quite different uses. Only in Vietnam did the concept of merit eventually triumph over that of birth, as strong rulers of Dai Viet attempted to initiate the Chinese model as a means of creating a centralized system of government.

CHAPTER TIMELINE

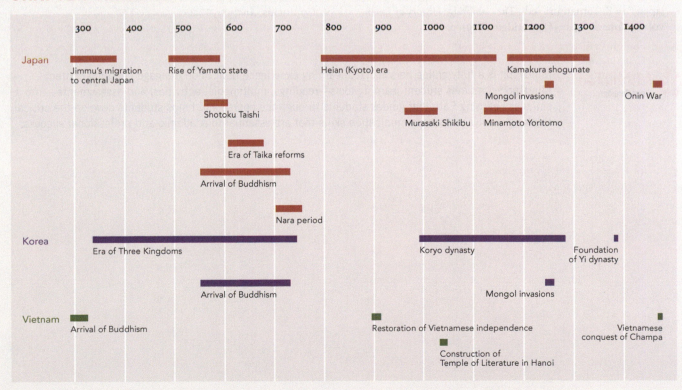

CHAPTER REVIEW

Upon Reflection

Q To what degree did the institutions and values of medieval Japan conform to the Chinese model? What factors explain the key differences?

Q How did the Korean peninsula fit into the overall history of East Asia during the period under discussion in this chapter and the previous chapter?

Q In what ways was Vietnam's relationship with China during the early historical period similar to the relationship between China and the other two major civilizations in the region—Japan and Korea? In what ways was the Vietnamese relationship with China different?

Key Terms

uji (p. 303)
Taika reforms (p. 304)
samurai (p. 305)
Bushido (p. 306)
bakufu (p. 306)
shogun (p. 306)
shogunate system (p. 306)
daimyo (p. 307)
genin (p. 310)

eta (p. 310)
kami (p. 311)
Shinto (p. 312)
Zen (p. 313)
satori (p. 313)
bonsai (p. 315)
chonmin (p. 318)
chu nom (p. 322)

Chapter Notes

1. Cited in C. Holcombe, *The Genesis of East Asia, 221 BC–AD 907* (Honolulu, 2001), p. 41.
2. Quoted in D. J. Lu, *Sources of Japanese History*, vol. 1 (New York, 1974), p. 7.
3. From "The History of Wei," quoted in ibid., p. 10.
4. From "On the Salvation of Women," quoted in ibid., p. 127.
5. Quoted in B. Ruch, "The Other Side of Culture in Medieval Japan," in K. Yamamura, ed., *The Cambridge History of Japan*, vol. 3, *Medieval Japan* (Cambridge, 1990), p. 506.

6. Excerpt from *The Cambridge History of Japan*, Vol. III, edited by Koza Yamamura, excerpt from "A Sample of Linked Verse" by H. Paul Verley, from p. 480. Copyright © 1990 Cambridge University Press.
7. K. W. Taylor, *The Birth of Vietnam* (Berkeley, Calif., 1983), p. 76.
8. Quoted in ibid., pp. 336–337.
9. Confucius, *Analects*, 17:2.

 **MINDTAP** From Cengage

MindTap® is a fully online personalized learning experience built upon Cengage Learning content. MindTap® combines student learning tools—readings, multimedia, activities, and assessments—into a singular Learning Path that guides students through the course and helps students develop the critical thinking, analysis, and communication skills that are essential to academic and professional success.

Chapter Outline
and Focus Questions

12–1 *The Emergence of Europe in the Early Middle Ages*

Q What contributions did the Romans, the Christian church, and the Germanic peoples make to the new civilization that emerged in Europe after the collapse of the Western Roman Empire? What was the significance of Charlemagne's coronation as emperor?

12–2 *Europe in the High Middle Ages*

Q What roles did aristocrats, peasants, and townspeople play in medieval European civilization, and how did their lifestyles differ? How did cities in Europe compare with those in China and the Middle East? What were the main aspects of the political, economic, spiritual, and cultural revivals that took place in Europe during the High Middle Ages?

12–3 *Medieval Europe and the World*

Q In what ways did Europeans begin to relate to peoples in other parts of the world after 1000 CE? What were the reasons for the crusades, and who or what benefited the most from them?

Critical Thinking

Q *In what ways was the civilization that developed in Europe in the Middle Ages similar to those in China and the Middle East? How were they different?*

Connections to Today

Q *Do you think there is a relationship between the crusades in the Middle Ages and contemporary events in the Middle East, including the Persian Gulf War and the activities of al-Qaeda and ISIS? If so, what do you think the relationship is?*

The coronation of Charlemagne by Pope Leo III, as depicted in a medieval French manuscript.
Scala/Art Resource, NY

IN 800, CHARLEMAGNE, the king of the Franks, journeyed to Rome to help Pope Leo III, head of the Catholic Church, who was barely clinging to power in the face of rebellious Romans. On Christmas Day, Charlemagne and his family, attended by Romans and Franks, crowded into Saint Peter's Basilica to hear Mass. Quite unexpectedly, according to a Frankish writer, "as the king rose from praying before the tomb of the blessed apostle Peter, Pope Leo placed a golden crown on his head." The people in the church shouted, "Long life and victory to Charles Augustus, crowned by God the great and peace-loving Emperor of the Romans." Seemingly, the Roman Empire in the west had been reborn, and Charles had become the first Roman emperor since 476. But this "Roman emperor" was actually a German king, and he had been crowned by the head of the western Christian church. In truth, the coronation of Charlemagne was a sign not of the rebirth of the Roman Empire but of the emergence of a new European civilization that came into being in western Europe after the collapse of the Western Roman Empire.

This new civilization—European civilization—was formed by the coming together of three major elements: the legacy of the Romans, the Christian church, and the Germanic peoples who moved in and settled the western empire. European civilization developed during a period that historians call the Middle Ages, or the medieval period, which lasted from about 500 to about 1300. To the historians who first used the phrase, the Middle Ages was a middle period between the ancient world and the modern world. During the Early Middle Ages, from about 500 to 1000 CE, the Roman world of the western empire was slowly transformed into a new Christian European society.

12-1 THE EMERGENCE OF EUROPE IN THE EARLY MIDDLE AGES

 Focus Questions: What contributions did the Romans, the Christian church, and the Germanic peoples make to the new civilization that emerged in Europe after the collapse of the Western Roman Empire? What was the significance of Charlemagne's coronation as emperor?

As we saw in Chapter 10, China descended into political chaos and civil wars after the end of the Han Empire, and it was almost four hundred years before a new imperial dynasty established political order. Similarly, after the collapse of the Western Roman Empire in the fifth century, it would also take hundreds of years to establish a new society.

12-1a The New Germanic Kingdoms

The Germanic peoples were an important component of the new European civilization. Already by the third century CE, they had begun to move into the lands of the Roman Empire. As imperial authority vanished in the fifth century, a number of German kings set up new states. By 500, the Western Roman Empire had been replaced politically by a series of states ruled by German kings.

The fusion of Romans and Germans took different forms in the various Germanic kingdoms. The kingdom of the Ostrogoths (AHSS-truh-gahths) in Italy (see Map 12.1) managed to preserve the Roman tradition of government. After establishing his control over Italy, the Ostrogothic king Theodoric (thee-AHD-uh-rik) (493–526) kept the entire structure of imperial Roman government, although he used separate systems of rule for Romans and Ostrogoths. The Roman population of Italy lived under Roman law administered by Roman officials. The Ostrogoths were governed by their own customs and their

own officials. Theodoric's system made possible a degree of stability by encouraging the living together of Germans and Romans.

Like the kingdom of the Ostrogoths in Italy, the kingdom of the Visigoths (VIZ-uh-gahths) in Spain inherited and continued to maintain much of the Roman structure of government. In both states, the Roman population was allowed to maintain Roman institutions while being largely excluded from power as a Germanic warrior caste came to dominate the considerably larger native population. Over a period of time, the Visigoths and the native peoples began to fuse together.

Roman influence was weaker in Britain. When the Roman armies abandoned Britain at the beginning of the fifth century, the Angles and Saxons, Germanic tribes from Denmark and northern Germany, moved in and settled there. Eventually, these peoples succeeded in carving out small kingdoms throughout the island, Kent in southeast England being one of them.

The Kingdom of the Franks One of the most prominent German states on the European continent was the kingdom of the Franks. The establishment of a Frankish kingdom was the work of Clovis (KLOH-viss) (c. 482–511), a member of the Merovingian (meh-ruh-VIN-jee-un) dynasty who became a Catholic Christian around 500. He was not the first German king to convert to Christianity, but the others had joined the Arian (AR-ee-un) sect of Christianity, a group who believed that Jesus was the son of God, thus subordinate to God the father, and that only God the father had existed for all of eternity. God and Jesus were thus not coequals. The Christian church in Rome, which had become known as the Roman Catholic Church, regarded the Arians as heretics, people who believed in teachings different from the official church doctrine. To Catholics, Jesus was human, but of the "same substance" as God and therefore also truly God. Clovis found that his conversion to Catholic Christianity gained him the support of the Roman Catholic Church, which was only too eager to obtain the friendship of a major Germanic ruler who was a Catholic Christian.

By 510, Clovis had established a powerful new Frankish kingdom stretching from the Pyrenees in the west to German lands in the east (modern France and western Germany). After Clovis's death, however, his sons divided his newly created kingdom, as was the Frankish custom. During the sixth and seventh centuries, the once-united Frankish kingdom came to be divided into three major areas: Neustria (NOO-stree-uh), in northern Gaul; Austrasia (awss-TRAY-zhuh), consisting of the ancient Frankish lands on both sides of the Rhine; and the former kingdom of Burgundy.

The Society of the Germanic Peoples As Germans and Romans intermarried and began to form a new society, some of the social customs of the Germanic peoples came to play an important role. The crucial social bond among the Germanic peoples was the family, especially the extended family of husbands, wives, children, brothers, sisters, cousins, and grandparents. The German family structure was quite simple.

Political Divisions of Britain

- Angles
- Saxons
- Jutes
- Britons

Map 12.1 The Germanic Kingdoms of the Old Western Empire. Germanic tribes filled the power vacuum caused by the collapse of the Western Roman Empire, founding states that blended elements of Germanic customs and laws with those of Roman culture, including large-scale conversions to Christianity. The Franks established the most durable of these Germanic states.

Q *How did the movements of Franks during this period correspond to the borders of present-day France?*

the Roman system, as in our own, a crime such as murder was considered an offense against society or the state and was handled by a court that heard evidence and arrived at a decision. Germanic law was personal. An injury to one person by another could lead to a blood feud in which the family of the injured party took revenge on the family of the wrongdoer. Feuds could involve savage acts of revenge, such as hacking off hands or feet or gouging out eyes. Because this system could easily get out of control, an alternative system arose that made use of a fine called **wergeld** (WUR-geld), which was paid by a wrongdoer to the family of the person injured or killed. *Wergeld*, which literally means "man money," was the value of a person in monetary terms. That value varied considerably according to social status. An offense against a nobleman, for example, cost considerably more than one against a freeman or a slave.

Germanic law also provided a means of determining guilt or innocence: the ordeal. The ordeal was based on the idea of divine intervention: divine forces (whether pagan or Christian) would not allow an innocent person to be harmed (see "Germanic Customary Law: The Ordeal," p. 328).

12–1b The Role of the Christian Church

By the end of the fourth century, Christianity had become the predominant religion of the Roman Empire. As the official Roman state disintegrated, the Christian church played an increasingly important role in the growth of the new European civilization.

The Organization of the Church By the fourth century, the Christian church had developed a system of government. A bishop, whose area of jurisdiction was known as a bishopric, or **diocese**, headed the Christian community in each city; the bishoprics of each Roman province were joined together under the direction of an archbishop. The bishops of four great cities—Rome, Jerusalem, Alexandria, and Antioch—held positions of special power in church affairs because the churches in these cities all asserted that they had been founded by the

Males were dominant and made all the important decisions. A woman obeyed her father until she married and then fell under the legal domination of her husband. For most women in the new Germanic kingdoms, their legal status reflected the material conditions of their lives. Most women had life expectancies of only thirty or forty years, and perhaps 15 percent of women died in their childbearing years, no doubt due to complications associated with childbirth. For most women, life consisted of domestic labor: providing food and clothing for the household, caring for the children, and assisting with farming chores.

The German conception of family affected the way Germanic law treated the problem of crime and punishment. In

GERMANIC CUSTOMARY LAW: THE ORDEAL

Family & Society

IN GERMANIC CUSTOMARY LAW, the ordeal was a means by which accused persons might clear themselves. Although the ordeal took different forms, all involved a physical trial of some sort, such as holding a red-hot iron. It was believed that God would protect the innocent and allow them to come through the ordeal unharmed. This sixth-century account by Gregory of Tours describes an ordeal by hot water.

Gregory of Tours, *An Ordeal of Hot Water* (c. 580)

An Arian presbyter disputing with a deacon of our religion made venomous assertions against the Son of God and the Holy Ghost, as is the habit of that sect [the Arians]. But when the deacon had discoursed a long time concerning the reasonableness of our faith and the heretic, blinded by the fog of unbelief, continued to reject the truth, . . . the former said: "Why weary ourselves with long discussions? Let acts approve the truth; let a kettle be heated over the fire and someone's ring be thrown into the boiling water. Let him who shall take it from the heated liquid be approved as a follower of the truth, and afterward let the other party be converted to the knowledge of the truth. And do you also understand, O heretic, that this our party will fulfill the conditions with the aid of the Holy Ghost; you shalt confess that there is no discordance, no dissimilarity in the Holy Trinity." The heretic consented to the proposition and they separated after appointing the next morning for the trial. But the fervor of faith in which the deacon had first made this suggestion began to cool through the instigation of the enemy. Rising with the dawn he bathed his arm in oil and smeared it with ointment. But nevertheless he made the round of the sacred places and called in prayer on the Lord. . . . About the third hour they met in the marketplace. The people came together to see the show. A fire was lighted, the kettle was placed upon it, and when it grew very hot the ring was thrown into the boiling water. The deacon invited the heretic to take it out of the water first. But he promptly refused, saying, "You who did propose this trial are the one to take it out." The deacon all of a tremble bared his arm. And when the heretic presbyter saw it besmeared with ointment he cried out: "With magic arts you have thought to protect yourself, that you have made use of these salves, but what you have done will not avail." While they were thus quarreling there came up a deacon from Ravenna named Iacinthus and inquired what the trouble was about. When he learned the truth he drew his arm out from under his robe at once and plunged his right hand into the kettle. Now the ring that had been thrown in was a little thing and very light so that it was thrown about by the water as chaff would be blown about by the wind; and searching for it a long time he found it after about an hour. Meanwhile the flame beneath the kettle blazed up mightily so that the greater heat might make it difficult for the ring to be followed by the hand; but the deacon extracted it at length and suffered no harm, protesting rather that at the bottom the kettle was cold while at the top it was just pleasantly warm. When the heretic beheld this he was greatly confused and audaciously thrust his hand into the kettle saying, "My faith will aid me." As soon as his hand had been thrust in all the flesh was boiled off the bones clear up to the elbow. And so the dispute ended.

 What was the purpose of the ordeal of hot water? What does it reveal about the nature of the society that used it?

Source: From *Translations and Reprints from the Original Sources of European History*, Series I, Vol. 4, No. 4, by A. C. Howland, copyright 1897 by Department of History, University of Pennsylvania Press.

original apostles sent out by Jesus. Soon, however, one of them—the bishop of Rome—claimed that he was the sole leader of the western Christian church. According to church tradition, Jesus had given the keys to the kingdom of heaven to Peter, who was considered the chief apostle and the first bishop of Rome. Subsequent bishops of Rome were considered Peter's successors and came to be known as popes (from the Latin word *papa*, meaning "father"). By the sixth century, the popes had been successful in extending papal authority over the Christian church in the west and converting the pagan peoples of Germanic Europe. Their primary instrument of conversion was the monastic movement.

The Monks and their Missions A **monk** (in Latin, *monachus*, meaning "one who lives alone") was a man who sought to live a life divorced from the world, cut off from ordinary human society, in order to pursue an ideal of total dedication to God. As the monastic ideal spread, a new form of **monasticism** based on living together in a community soon became the dominant form. Saint Benedict (c. 480–c. 543), who founded a monastic house for which he wrote a set of rules, established the basic form of monastic life in the western Christian church.

Benedict's rules divided each day into a series of activities, with primary emphasis on prayer and manual labor. Physical work of some kind was required of all monks for several hours a day as a means to reach God because idleness was "the enemy of the soul." At the very heart of community practice was prayer, the proper "work of God." Although this included private meditation and reading, all monks gathered together seven times during the day for common prayer and chanting of psalms. The Benedictine life was a communal one. Monks ate, worked, slept, and worshiped together.

Each Benedictine monastery was strictly ruled by an **abbot**, or "father" of the monastery, who had complete authority over

Saint Benedict. Benedict was the author of a set of rules that was instrumental in the development of monastic groups in the Catholic Church. In this sixth-century Latin manuscript miniature, an abbot is shown offering codes and possessions to Saint Benedict.

his fellow monks. Unquestioning obedience to the will of the abbot was expected of every monk. Each Benedictine monastery held lands that enabled it to be a self-sustaining community, isolated from and independent of the world surrounding it. Within the monastery, however, monks were to fulfill their vow of poverty: "Let all things be common to all, as it is written, lest anyone should say that anything is his own."[1] Only men could be monks, but women, called **nuns**, also began to withdraw from the world to dedicate themselves to God.

Monasticism played an indispensable role in early medieval civilization. Monks became the new heroes of Christian civilization, and their dedication to God became the highest ideal of Christian life. They were the social workers of their communities: monks provided schools for the young, hospitality for travelers, and hospitals for the sick. Monks also copied Latin works and passed on the legacy of the ancient world to the new European civilization. Monasteries became centers of learning wherever they were located. Moreover, the monks were important in spreading Christianity to the entire European world. English and Irish monks were

Charlemagne's Empire

Legend:
- Frankish kingdom, 768
- Territories gained by Charlemagne

particularly enthusiastic missionaries, who undertook the conversion of pagan peoples, especially in Germany.

One of the most famous of the Christian missionaries in the fifth century was Saint Patrick (c. 390–461). Son of a Romano-British Christian, Patrick was kidnapped as a young man by Irish raiders and kept as a slave in Ireland. After his escape to Gaul, he became a monk and chose to return to Ireland to convert the Irish to Christianity. Irish tradition ascribes to Patrick the title of "founder of Irish Christianity," a testament to his apparent success.

Women played an important role in the monastic missionary movement and the conversion of the Germanic kingdoms. Some served as **abbesses** (an abbess was the head of a monastery for nuns, known as a convent); many abbesses came from aristocratic families, especially in Anglo-Saxon England. In the kingdom of Northumbria, for example, Saint Hilda founded the monastery of Whitby in 657. As abbess, she was responsible for making learning an important part of the life of the monastery.

12-1c Charlemagne and the Carolingians

During the seventh and eighth centuries, as the kings of the Frankish kingdom gradually lost their power, the mayors of the palace—the chief officers of the king's household—assumed more control of the kingdom. One of these mayors, Pepin (PEP-in or pay-PANH), finally took the logical step of assuming the kingship of the Frankish state for himself and his family. Upon his death in 768, his son came to the throne of the Frankish kingdom.

This new king was the dynamic and powerful ruler known to history as Charles the Great (768–814), or Charlemagne (SHAR-luh-mayn) (from the Latin for Charles the Great, *Carolus Magnus*). He was determined and decisive, intelligent and inquisitive, a strong statesman, and a pious Christian. Although unable to read or write himself, he was a wise patron of learning. In a series of military campaigns, he greatly expanded the territory he had inherited and created what came to be known as the Carolingian (kar-uh-LIN-jun) Empire. At its height, Charlemagne's empire covered much of western and central Europe; not until the time of Napoleon in the nineteenth century would an empire of its size be seen again in Europe (see "The Achievements of Charlemagne," p. 330).

Charlemagne continued the efforts of his father in organizing the

THE ACHIEVEMENTS OF CHARLEMAGNE

Politics & Government

EINHARD (YN-HART), the biographer of Charlemagne, was born in the valley of the Main River in Germany about 775. Raised and educated in the monastery of Fulda, an important center of learning, he arrived at the court of Charlemagne in 791 or 792. Although he did not achieve high office under Charlemagne, he served as private secretary to Louis the Pious, Charlemagne's son and successor. In this selection, Einhard discusses some of Charlemagne's accomplishments.

Einhard, *Life of Charlemagne*

Such are the wars, most skillfully planned and successfully fought, which this most powerful king waged during the forty-seven years of his reign. He so largely increased the Frank kingdom, which was already great and strong when he received it at his father's hands, that more than double its former territory was added to it. . . . He subdued all the wild and barbarous tribes dwelling in Germany between the Rhine and the Vistula, the Ocean and the Danube, all of which speak very much the same language, but differ widely from one another in customs and dress. . . .

He added to the glory of his reign by gaining the good will of several kings and nations;. . . . The Emperors of Constantinople [the Byzantine emperors] sought friendship and alliance with Charles by several embassies; and even when the Greeks [the Byzantines] suspected him of designing to take the empire from them, because of his assumption of the title Emperor, they made a close alliance with him, that he might have no cause of offense. In fact, the power of the Franks was always viewed with a jealous eye, whence the Greek proverb, "Have the Frank for your friend, but not for your neighbor."

This King . . . undertook also very many works calculated to adorn and benefit his kingdom, and brought several of them to completion. Among these, the most deserving of mention are the basilica of the Holy Mother of God at Aix-la-Chapelle [Aachen], built in the most admirable manner, and a bridge over the Rhine River at Mainz, half a mile long, the breadth of the river at this point. . . . Above all, sacred buildings were the object of his care throughout his whole kingdom; and whenever he found them falling to ruin from age, he commanded the priests and fathers who had charge of them to repair them. . . . Thus did Charles defend and increase as well as beautify his kingdom. . . .

He cherished with the greatest fervor and devotion the principles of the Christian religion, which had been instilled into him from infancy. Hence it was that he built the beautiful church at Aix-la-Chapelle, which he adorned with gold and silver and lamps, and with rails and doors of solid brass. . . . He was a constant worshiper at this church as long as his health permitted, going morning and evening, even after nightfall, besides attending mass. . . .

He was very forward in caring for the poor, so much so that he not only made a point of giving in his own country and his own kingdom, but when he discovered that there were Christians living in poverty in Syria, Egypt, and Africa, at Jerusalem, Alexandria, and Carthage, he . . . used to send money over the seas to them. . . . He sent great and countless gifts to the popes, and [one of his aims] was to defend and protect the Church of St. Peter, and to beautify and enrich it out of his own store above all other churches.

 How long did Einhard know Charlemagne? Does this excerpt reflect close, personal knowledge of the man, his court, and his works or hearsay and legend?

Source: From Einhard, *The Life of Charlemagne*, translated by S. E. Turner, pp. 50–54. Copyright © 1960 by The University of Michigan. Translated from the *Monumenta Germanie*.

Carolingian kingdom. Besides his household staff, Charlemagne's administration of the empire depended on the use of counts as the king's chief representatives in local areas. As an important check on the power of the counts, Charlemagne established the *missi dominici* (MISS-ee doh-MIN-i-chee) ("messengers of the lord king"), two men who were sent out to local districts to ensure that the counts were executing the king's wishes. They had the power to remove counts if they were abusing their power, thus making the *missi* an important instrument in bolstering royal power.

HISTORIANS DEBATE **What Was the Significance of Charlemagne?**
As Charlemagne's power grew, so did his prestige as the most powerful Christian ruler of what one monk called the "kingdom of Europe." In 800, Charlemagne

acquired a new title: emperor of the Romans. The significance of this imperial coronation has been much debated by historians. We are not even sure if the pope or Charlemagne initiated the idea when they met in the summer of 799 in Paderborn in German lands or whether Charles was pleased or displeased. The crowning of an emperor by a pope is significant in beginning a new era of the relationship between popes and emperors in the Middle Ages.

In any case, Charlemagne's coronation as Roman emperor demonstrated the strength, even after three hundred years, of the concept of an enduring Roman Empire. More important, it symbolized the fusion of Roman, Christian, and Germanic elements. Did this fusion constitute the foundations of European civilization? A Germanic king had been crowned emperor of the Romans by the spiritual leader of western Christendom.

Charlemagne had created an empire that stretched from the North Sea to Italy and from the Atlantic Ocean to the Danube River. This differed significantly from the Roman Empire, which encompassed much of the Mediterranean world. Had a new civilization emerged? And should Charlemagne be regarded, as one of his biographers has argued, as the "father of Europe"?[2]

Other historians argue that there was only a weak sense of community in Europe before 1000. As one has stated, "Europe was not born in the early Middle Ages. . . . There was no common European culture, and certainly not any Europewide economy."[3]

12–1d The World of Lords and Vassals

The Carolingian Empire began to disintegrate soon after Charlemagne's death in 814, and less than thirty years later, in 843, it was divided among his grandsons into three major sections: the western Frankish lands, which formed the core of the eventual kingdom of France; the eastern lands, which eventually became Germany; and a "middle kingdom" extending from the North Sea to the Mediterranean. The territories of the middle kingdom became a source of incessant struggle between the other two Frankish rulers and their heirs. At the same time, powerful nobles gained even more dominance in their local territories while the Carolingian rulers fought each other, and incursions by outsiders into various parts of the Carolingian world furthered the process of disintegration.

Invasions of the Ninth and Tenth Centuries

In the ninth and tenth centuries, western Europe was beset by a wave of invasions. Muslims attacked the southern coasts of Europe and sent raiding parties into southern France. The Magyars (MAG-yarz), a people from western Asia, moved into central Europe at the end of the ninth century and settled on the plains of Hungary, launching forays from there into western Europe. Finally crushed at the Battle of Lechfeld (LEK-feld) in Germany in 955, the Magyars converted to Christianity, settled down, and established the kingdom of Hungary.

The most far-reaching attacks of the time came from the Northmen or Norsemen of Scandinavia, also known to us as the Vikings. The Vikings were warriors whose love of adventure and search for booty and new avenues of trade may have spurred them to invade other areas of Europe. Viking ships were the best of the period. Long and narrow with beautifully carved arched prows, the Viking "dragon ships" each carried about fifty men. Their shallow draft enabled them to sail up European rivers and attack places at some distance inland. In the ninth century, Vikings sacked villages and towns, destroyed churches, and easily defeated small local armies. Viking attacks were terrifying, and many a clergyman pleaded with his parishioners to change their behavior and appease God's anger to avert the attacks, as in this sermon by an English archbishop in 1014:

> Things have not gone well now for a long time at home or abroad, but there has been devastation and persecution in every district again and again, and the English have been

for a long time now completely defeated and too greatly disheartened through God's anger; and the pirates [Vikings] so strong with God's consent that often in battle one puts to flight ten, and sometimes less, sometimes more, all because of our sins. . . . We pay them continually and they humiliate us daily; they ravage and they burn, plunder, and rob and carry on board; and lo, what else is there in all these events except God's anger clear and visible over this people?[4]

By the middle of the ninth century, the Norsemen had begun to build winter settlements in different areas of Europe. By 850, groups from Norway had settled in Ireland, and Danes occupied northeastern England by 878. Beginning in 911, the ruler of the western Frankish lands gave one band of Vikings land at the mouth of the Seine (SEN) River, a territory that came to be known as Normandy. This policy of settling the Vikings and converting them to Christianity was a deliberate one; by their conversion to Christianity, the Vikings were soon made a part of European civilization.

HISTORIANS DEBATE **What Was Feudalism?** The disintegration of central authority in the Carolingian world and the invasions by Muslims, Magyars, and Vikings led to the emergence of a new type of relationship between free individuals. When governments ceased to be able to defend their subjects, it became important to find some powerful lord who could offer protection in return for service. The contract sworn between a lord and his subordinate is the basis for what earlier generations of historians called *feudalism*, which they defined as a political and military system that applied to much of Europe in the Early Middle Ages.

In the 1970s, some historians denounced the use of the term *feudalism*, considering it an oversimplied model and not useful in describing medieval society. A later work maintained that historians had taken the feudal legal and social relations of the eleventh and twelfth centuries to falsely describe developments in the ninth and tenth centuries. Moreover, many historians argue that there were large differences from region to region in the relationshp of service and duty based on land. To many historians today feudalism was never a cohesive system, and they prefer to avoid using the term.

The Development of Fief-Holding

With the breakdown of royal governments, powerful nobles took control of large areas of land in many parts of western Europe. They needed men to fight for them, so the practice arose of giving grants of land to **vassals** who in return would fight for their lord. The Frankish army had originally consisted of foot soldiers, dressed in coats of mail and armed with swords. But in the eighth century, larger horses began to be used, along with the stirrup, which was introduced by nomadic horsemen from Asia. Earlier, horsemen had been throwers of spears. Now they wore armor in the form of coats of mail (the larger horse could carry the weight) and wielded long lances that enabled them to act as battering rams (the stirrups kept them on their horses). For almost five hundred years, heavily armored cavalry, or *knights*, as they were called, dominated warfare in Europe. The knights

The Vikings Attack England. The illustration on the left, from an eleventh-century English manuscript, depicts a band of armed Vikings invading England. Two ships have already reached the shore, and a few Vikings are shown walking down a long gangplank onto English soil. On the right is a replica of a well-preserved Viking ship found at Oseberg, Norway. The Oseberg ship was one of the largest Viking ships of its day.

came to have the greatest social prestige and formed the backbone of the European aristocracy.

Of course, it was expensive to have a horse, armor, and weapons. It also took time and much practice to learn to wield these instruments skillfully from horseback. Consequently, a lord who wanted men to fight for him had to grant each vassal a piece of land that provided for the support of the vassal and his family. In return for the land, the vassal provided his lord with his fighting skills. Each needed the other. In the society of the Early Middle Ages, where there was little trade and wealth was based primarily on land, land became the most important gift a lord could give to a vassal in return for his loyalty and military service.

In some areas of Europe, the grant of land made to a vassal became known as a **fief** (FEEF). A fief was a piece of land held from the lord by a vassal in return for military service, but vassals who held such grants of land came to exercise rights of jurisdiction or political and legal authority within these fiefs. As the Carolingian world disintegrated politically under the impact of internal dissension and invasions, an increasing number of powerful lords arose who were now responsible for keeping order.

The Practice of Fief-Holding Fief-holding also became increasingly complicated with the development of **subinfeudation** (sub-in-fyoo-DAY-shun). The vassals of a king, who were themselves great lords, might also have vassals who would owe them military service in return for a grant of land taken from their estates. Those vassals, in turn, might likewise have vassals, who at such a level would be simple knights with barely enough land to provide their equipment. The lord-vassal relationship, then, bound together both greater and lesser landowners. At all levels, the lord-vassal relationship was always an honorable relationship between free men and did not imply any sense of servitude.

Fief-holding came to be characterized by a set of practices that determined the relationship between a lord and his vassal. The major obligation of a vassal to his lord was to perform military service, usually about forty days a year. A vassal was also required to appear at his lord's court when summoned to give advice to the lord. He might also be asked to sit in judgment in a legal case, since the important vassals of a lord were peers and only they could judge each other. Finally, vassals were also responsible for aids, or financial payments to the lord on a number of occasions, including the knighting of the lord's eldest son, the marriage of his eldest daughter, and the ransom of the lord's person if he were captured (see Comparative Essay "Feudal Orders Around the World," Section 11-1b, p. 308).

In turn, a lord had responsibilities toward his vassals. His major obligation was to protect his vassal, either by defending him militarily or by taking his side in a court of law. The lord was also responsible for the maintenance of the vassal, usually by granting him a fief.

The Manorial System The landholding class of nobles and knights contained a military elite whose ability to function as warriors depended on having the leisure time to pursue the arts of war. Landed estates, located on the fiefs given to a vassal by his lord and worked by a dependent peasant class, provided the economic sustenance that made this way of life possible. A **manor** was an agricultural estate operated by a lord and worked by peasants (see Map 12.2). Although a large class of free peasants continued to exist, increasing numbers of free peasants became **serfs**, who were bound to the land and required to provide labor services, pay rents, and be subject to the lord's jurisdiction. By the ninth century, probably 60 percent of the population of western Europe had become serfs.

Labor services involved working the lord's **demesne** (duh-MAYN or duh-MEEN), the land retained by the lord, which might consist of one-third to one-half of the cultivated lands scattered throughout the manor. The rest would be used by the peasants for themselves. Building barns and digging ditches were also part of the labor services. Serfs usually worked about three days a week for their lord and paid rents by giving the lord a share of every product they raised.

Serfs were legally bound to the lord's lands and could not leave without his permission. Although free to marry, serfs could not marry anyone outside their manor without the lord's approval. Moreover, lords sometimes exercised public rights or political authority on their lands, which gave them the right to try peasants in their own courts.

12–2 EUROPE IN THE HIGH MIDDLE AGES

 Focus Questions: What roles did aristocrats, peasants, and townspeople play in medieval European civilization, and how did their lifestyles differ? How did cities in Europe compare with those in China and the Middle East? What were the main aspects of the political, economic, spiritual, and cultural revivals that took place in Europe during the High Middle Ages?

The new European civilization that had emerged in the Early Middle Ages began to flourish in the High Middle Ages (1000–1300). New agricultural practices that increased the food supply spurred commercial and urban expansion. Both lords and vassals recovered from the invasions and internal dissension of the Early Middle Ages, and medieval kings began to exert a centralizing authority. The recovery of the Catholic Church made it a forceful presence in every area of life. The High Middle Ages also gave birth to a cultural revival.

12–2a Land and People

In the Early Middle Ages, Europe had a relatively small population of about 38 million, but in the High Middle Ages, the number of people nearly doubled to 74 million. What accounted for this dramatic increase? For one thing, conditions in Europe were more settled and more peaceful after the invasions of the Early Middle Ages had ended. For another, agricultural production surged after 1000.

The New Agriculture During the High Middle Ages, Europeans began to farm in new ways. An improvement in climate resulted in better growing conditions, but an important factor in increasing food production was the expansion of cultivated or arable land, accomplished by clearing forested areas. Peasants of the eleventh and twelfth centuries cut down trees and drained swamps until by the thirteenth century, Europeans had more acreage available for farming than at any time before or since.

Map 12.2 A Typical Manor. The manorial system created small, tightly knit communities in which peasants were economically and physically bound to their lord. Crops were rotated, with roughly one-third of the fields lying fallow (untilled) at any one time, which helped replenish soil nutrients.

How does the area of the lord's demesne, his manor house, other buildings, garden, and orchard compare with that of the peasant holdings in the village?

Technological changes also furthered the development of farming. The Middle Ages saw an explosion of laborsaving devices, many of which were made from iron, which was mined in different areas of Europe. Iron was used to make scythes, axes, and hoes for use on farms as well as saws, hammers, and nails for building purposes. Iron was crucial in making the *carruca* (kuh-ROO-kuh), a heavy, wheeled plow with an iron plowshare pulled by teams of horses, which could turn over the heavy clay soil north of the Alps.

Besides using horsepower, the High Middle Ages harnessed the power of water and wind to do jobs formerly done by human or animal power. Although the watermill had been invented as early as the second century BCE, it did not come into widespread use until the High Middle Ages. Located along streams, watermills were used to grind grain into flour. Often dams were constructed to increase the waterpower. The development of the cam enabled millwrights to mechanize entire industries; waterpower was used in certain phases of cloth production and to run trip-hammers for the working of metals. The Chinese had made use of the cam in operating trip-hammers for hulling rice by the third century CE but apparently had not extended its use to other industries.

Where rivers were unavailable or not easily dammed, Europeans developed windmills to use the power of the wind. Historians are uncertain whether windmills were imported into Europe (they were invented in Persia) or designed independently by Europeans. In either case, by the end of the twelfth century, they were beginning to dot the European landscape. The watermill and windmill were the most important devices for the harnessing of power before the invention of the steam engine in the eighteenth century.

The shift from a two-field to a three-field system also contributed to the increase in food production (see Comparative Illustration "The New Agriculture in the Medieval World"). In the Early Middle Ages, peasants had planted one field while another of equal size was allowed to lie fallow (untilled) to regain its fertility. Now estates were divided into three parts. One field was planted in the fall with winter grains, such as rye and wheat, while spring grains, such as oats or barley, and vegetables, such as peas or beans, were planted in the second field. The third was allowed to lie fallow. By rotating the use of the fields, only one-third rather than one-half of the land lay fallow at any time. The rotation of crops also kept the soil from being exhausted so quickly, and more crops could now be grown.

Daily Life of the Peasantry The lifestyle of the peasants was quite simple. Their cottages were built with wood frames with walls made of laths or sticks; the spaces between the laths were stuffed with straw and rubble and then plastered over with clay. Roofs were often thatched with reeds or straw. The houses of poorer peasants consisted of a single room, but others had at least two rooms—a main room for cooking, eating, and other activities and another room for sleeping.

Peasant women occupied an important but difficult position in manorial society. As mothers, they were expected to carry and bear their children, as well as provide for their socialization and religious training. Peasant women also bore responsibility for doing the spinning and weaving that provided the household's clothes, tending the family's vegetable garden and chickens, and providing the meals. They also brewed ale for use in the household and for sale to help household finances. A woman's ability to manage the household might determine whether a peasant family would starve or survive in difficult times. At the same time, peasant women often worked with men in the fields, especially at harvest time. Indeed, as one historian has noted, peasant marriage was an "economic partnership" in which both husbands and wives contributed their own distinctive labor.

Though simple, a peasant's daily diet was adequate when food was available. The staple of the peasant diet, and the medieval diet in general, was bread. Women made the dough for the bread at home and then brought their loaves to be baked in community ovens, which were owned by the lord of the manor. Peasant bread was highly nutritious, containing not only wheat and rye but also barley, millet, and oats, giving it a dark appearance and a very heavy, hard texture. Bread was supplemented by numerous vegetables from the household gardens, cheese from cow's or goat's milk, nuts and berries from woodlands, and fruits, such as apples, pears, and cherries. Chickens provided eggs and sometimes meat.

The Nobility of the Middle Ages In the High Middle Ages, European society, like that of Japan during the same period, was dominated by men whose chief concern was warfare. Like the Japanese samurai, many Western nobles loved war. As one nobleman wrote:

> And well I like to hear the call of "Help" and see the wounded fall
> Loudly for mercy praying,
> And see the dead, both great and small,
> Pierced by sharp spearheads one and all.[5]

The men of war were the lords and vassals of medieval society.

The lords were the kings, dukes, counts, barons, and viscounts (and even bishops and archbishops) who had extensive landholdings and wielded considerable political influence. They formed an **aristocracy** or nobility of people who held real political, economic, and social power. Both the great lords and ordinary knights were warriors, and the institution of knighthood united them. But there were also social divisions among them based on extremes of wealth and landholdings.

In the eleventh and twelfth centuries, in part under the influence of the church, an ideal of civilized behavior called **chivalry** (SHIV-uhl-ree) gradually evolved among the nobility. Chivalry represented a code of ethics that knights were supposed to uphold. In addition to defending the church and the defenseless, knights were expected to treat captives as honored guests instead of throwing them in dungeons. Chivalry also implied that knights should fight only for glory, but the ideals of chivalry were not always taken seriously.

Although aristocratic women could legally hold property, most women remained under the control of men—their fathers until they married and their husbands after that. Nevertheless, these women had many opportunities for playing important roles. Because the lord was often away at war or at court, the

COMPARATIVE ILLUSTRATION

The New Agriculture in the Medieval World. New agricultural methods and techniques in the Middle Ages enabled peasants in both Europe and China to increase food production. This general improvement in diet was a factor in supporting noticeably larger populations in both areas. A thirteenth-century illustration (B) shows a group of English peasants harvesting grain. Overseeing their work is a bailiff, or manager, who supervised the work of the peasants. A thirteenth-century painting (A) shows Chinese peasants harvesting rice, which became the staple food in China.

Q *How important were staple foods (such as wheat and rice) to the diet and health of people in Europe and China during the Middle Ages?*

A

The Art Archive at Art Resource, NY

B

The Art Archive at Art Resource, NY

lady of the castle had to manage the estate. Households could include large numbers of officials and servants, so this was no small responsibility. Maintaining the financial accounts alone took considerable financial knowledge. The lady of the castle was also responsible for overseeing the food supply and maintaining all the other supplies needed for the smooth operation of the household.

Although women were legally expected to show deference to their husbands, many advised or dominated their husbands. Perhaps the most famous was Eleanor of Aquitaine (c. 1122–1204). Married to King Louis VII of France, Eleanor accompanied her husband on a crusade, but her alleged affair with her uncle during the crusade led Louis to have their marriage annulled. Eleanor then married Henry, duke of Normandy and

count of Anjou (AHN-zhoo), who became King Henry II of England (1154–1189). She took an active role in politics, even assisting her sons in rebelling against Henry in 1173 and 1174 (see Film & History, p. 336).

12–2b The New World of Trade and Cities

Medieval Europe was overwhelmingly agrarian, with most people living in small villages. In the eleventh and twelfth centuries, however, new elements were introduced that began to transform the economic foundation of European civilization: a revival of trade, the emergence of specialized craftspeople and artisans, and the growth and development of towns. These changes were made possible by the new agricultural practices and subsequent increase in food production, which freed some

European families from the need to produce their own food. Merchants and craftspeople could now buy their necessities. The increase in agricultural production also had an impact on the development of trade. Crop surpluses made possible the export of food and the development of local markets and eventually regional markets to handle new trade possibilities.

The Revival of Trade The revival of trade was a gradual process. During the chaotic conditions of the Early Middle Ages, large-scale trade had declined in western Europe except for Byzantine contacts with Italy and the Jewish traders who moved back and forth between the Muslim and Christian worlds. By the end of the tenth century, however, people were emerging in Europe with both the skills and the products for commercial activity. Cities in Italy took the lead in this revival of trade. Venice, for example, emerged as a town by the end of the eighth century, developed a mercantile fleet, and by the end of the

Flanders as a Trade Center

tenth century had become the chief western trading center for Byzantine and Islamic commerce.

While the northern Italian cities were busy trading in the Mediterranean, the towns of Flanders were doing likewise in northern Europe. Flanders, the area along the coast of present-day Belgium and northern France, was known for its high-quality woolen cloth. The location of Flanders made it an ideal center for the traders of northern Europe. Merchants from England, Scandinavia, France, and Germany converged there to trade their goods for woolen cloth. Flanders prospered in the eleventh and twelfth centuries, and such Flemish towns as Bruges (BROOZH) and Ghent (GENT) became centers of the medieval cloth trade.

By the twelfth century, a regular exchange of goods had developed between Flanders and Italy, the two major centers of northern and southern European trade. To encourage this trade, the counts of Champagne in northern France began to hold a series of six fairs annually in the chief towns of their territory. At these fairs, northern merchants brought the furs, woolen cloth, tin, and honey of northern Europe and exchanged them for the cloth and swords of northern Italy and the silks, sugar, and spices of the East (see Opposing Viewpoints "Two Views of Trade and Merchants").

As trade increased, both gold and silver came to be in demand at fairs and trading markets of all kinds. Slowly, a money economy began to emerge. New trading companies and banking firms were set up to manage the exchange and sale of goods. New techniques, including double-entry bookkeeping, commercial contracts, and insurance, also appeared to facilitate the expansion of businesses. All of these new practices were part of a commercial revolution based on the growth of **capitalism**, an economic system in which commerce and industry are controlled by private owners who invest in trade and goods in order to make profits.

Trade Outside Europe In the High Middle Ages, Italian merchants became even more daring in their trade activities. They established trading posts in Cairo, Damascus, and a number of Black Sea ports, where they acquired spices, silks, jewelry, dyestuffs, and other goods brought by Muslim merchants from India, China, and Southeast Asia.

The spread of the Mongol Empire in the thirteenth century (see Chapter 10) also opened the door to Italian merchants in the markets of Central Asia, India, and China. As nomads who relied on trade with settled communities, the Mongols maintained safe trade routes for merchants moving through their lands. Two Venetian merchants, the brothers Niccolò and Maffeo Polo, began to travel in the Mongol Empire around 1260.

The creation of the crusader states in Syria and Palestine in the twelfth and thirteenth centuries (discussed later in this chapter) was especially favorable to Italian merchants. In return for taking

Two Views of Trade and Merchants

Interaction & Exchange **THE REVIVAL OF TRADE IN EUROPE WAS A GRADUAL PROCESS,** but by the High Middle Ages, it had begun to expand dramatically. During the medieval period, trade already flourished in other parts of the world, especially in the Islamic world and in China. Nevertheless, many people in these societies, including rulers, nobles, and religious leaders, had some reservations about the success of merchants. The first selection is taken from an account of the life of Godric, a twelfth-century European merchant who became a saint. The second selection is from the *Prolegomena*, the first part of a universal history written by Ibn Khaldun, a Muslim historian who traveled widely in the Muslim world in the fourteenth century.

Life of Saint Godric

At first, he lived as a peddler for four years in Lincolnshire, going on foot and carrying the smallest wares; then he traveled abroad, first to St. Andrews in Scotland and then for the first time to Rome. On his return, having formed a familiar friendship with certain other young men who were eager for merchandise, he began to launch upon bolder courses, and to coast frequently by sea to the foreign lands that lay around him. Thus, sailing often to and fro between Scotland and Britain, he traded in many divers wares and, amid these occupations, learned much worldly wisdom. . . .

Thus aspiring ever higher and higher, and yearning upward with his whole heart, at length his great labors and cares bore much fruit of worldly gain. For he labored not only as a merchant but also as a shipman . . . to Denmark and to Flanders and Scotland; in all which lands he found certain rare, and therefore more precious, wares, which he carried to other parts wherein he knew them to be least familiar, and coveted by the inhabitants beyond the price of gold itself; wherefore he exchanged these wares for others coveted by men of other lands; and thus he chaffered [traded] most freely and assiduously. Hence he made great profit in all his bargains, and gathered much wealth in the sweat of his brow; for he sold dear in one place the wares which he had bought elsewhere at a small price.

And now he had lived sixteen years as a merchant, and began to think of spending on charity, to God's honor and

service, the goods which he had so laboriously acquired. He therefore took the cross as a pilgrim to Jerusalem. . . . [When he had returned to England] Godric, that he might follow Christ the more freely, sold all his possessions and distributed them among the poor [and began to live the life of a hermit].

Ibn Khaldun, *Prolegomena*

As for trade, although it be a natural means of livelihood, yet most of the methods it employs are tricks aimed at making a profit by securing the difference between the buying and selling prices, and by appropriating the surplus. This is why [religious] Law allows the use of such methods, which, although they come under the heading of gambling, yet do not constitute the taking without return of other people's goods. . . .

Should their standard of living, however, rise, so that they begin to enjoy more than the bare necessities, the effect will be to breed in them a desire for repose and tranquility. They will therefore cooperate to secure superfluities; their food and clothing will increase in quantity and refinement; they will enlarge their houses and plan their towns for defense. A further improvement in their conditions will lead to habits of luxury, resulting in extreme refinement in cooking and the preparation of food; in choosing rich clothing of the finest silk; in raising lofty mansions and castles and furnishing them luxuriously, and so on. At this stage the crafts develop and reach their height. Lofty castles and mansions are built and decorated sumptuously, water is drawn to them and a great diversity takes place in the way of dress, furniture, vessels, and household equipment. Such are the townsmen, who earn their living in industry or trade.

 What did the biographer of Godric and Ibn Khaldun see as valuable in mercantile activity? What reservations did they have about trade? How are the two perspectives alike? How are they different, and how do you explain the differences? What generalizations can you make about Christian and Muslim attitudes toward trade?

Sources: Life of Saint Godric from Reginald of Durham, "Life of St. Godric," in G. G. Coulton, ed., *Social Life in Britain from the Conquest to the Reformation* (Cambridge: Cambridge University Press, 1918), pp. 415–420. From *An Arab Philosophy of History*, ed. and trans. by Charles Issawi (New York: Darwin Press, 1987).

the crusaders to the east, Italian merchant fleets received trading concessions in Syria and Palestine. Venice, for example, which profited the most from this trade, was given a quarter, soon known as "a little Venice in the east," in Tyre on the coast of what is now Lebanon. Such quarters here and in other cities soon became bases for carrying on lucrative trade.

The Growth of Cities The revival of trade led to a revival of cities. Towns had greatly declined in the Early Middle Ages, especially in Europe north of the Alps. Old Roman cities continued to exist but had dwindled in size and population. With the revival of trade, merchants began to settle in these old cities, followed by craftspeople or artisans, people who on manors or elsewhere had developed skills and now saw an opportunity to ply their trade and make goods that could be sold by the merchants. In the course of the eleventh and twelfth centuries, the old Roman cities came alive with new populations and growth.

Beginning in the late tenth century, many new cities or towns were also founded, particularly in northern Europe. Usually, a group of merchants established a settlement near some fortified stronghold, such as a castle or monastery. (This explains why so many place names in Europe end in *borough, burgh, burg,* or *bourg,* all of which mean "fortress" or "walled enclosure.") Castles were particularly favored because they were generally located along trade routes; the lords of the castle also offered protection. If the settlement prospered and expanded, new walls were built to protect it.

Although lords wanted to treat towns and townspeople as they would their vassals and serfs, cities had totally different needs and a different perspective. Townspeople needed mobility to trade. Consequently, these merchants and artisans (who came to be called *burghers* or *bourgeois,* from the same root as *borough* and *burg*) needed their own unique laws to meet their requirements and were willing to pay for them. In many instances, lords and kings saw that they could also make money and were willing to sell to the townspeople the liberties they were beginning to demand, including the right to bequeath goods and sell property, freedom from any military obligation to the lord, and written urban laws that guaranteed their freedom. Some towns also obtained the right to govern themselves by choosing their own officials and administering their own courts of law.

Where townspeople experienced difficulties in obtaining privileges, they often swore an oath, forming an association called a **commune**, and resorted to force against their lay or ecclesiastical lords. Communes made their first appearance in northern Italy, in towns that were governed by their bishops, whom the emperors used as their chief administrators. In the eleventh century, city residents swore communal associations with the bishops' noble vassals and overthrew the authority of the bishops by force. Communes took over the rights of government and created new offices for self-rule. Although communes were also sworn in northern Europe, townspeople did not have the support of rural nobles, and revolts against lay lords were usually suppressed. When they succeeded, communes received the right to choose their own officials and run their own cities. Unlike the towns in Italy, however, where the decline of the emperor's authority ensured that the northern Italian cities could function as self-governing republics, towns in France and England, like their counterparts in the Islamic and Chinese empires, did not become independent city-states but remained ultimately subject to royal authority.

Medieval cities in Europe, then, possessed varying degrees of self-government, depending on the amount of control retained over them by the lord or king in whose territory they were located. Nevertheless, all towns, regardless of the degree of outside control, evolved institutions of government for running the affairs of the community. Only males who were born in the city or had lived there for a specific length of time could be citizens. In many cities, these citizens elected members of a city council who served as judges and city officials and passed laws.

Medieval cities remained relatively small in comparison with either ancient or modern cities (see Comparative Essay "Cities in the Medieval World"). A large trading city might have about 5,000 inhabitants. By 1200, London was the largest city in England with 30,000 people. On the Continent north of the Alps, only a few urban centers of commerce, such as Bruges and Ghent, had populations close to 40,000. Italian cities tended to be larger, with Venice, Florence, Genoa, Milan, and Naples numbering almost 100,000. Even the largest European city, however, seemed small beside the Byzantine capital of Constantinople or the Arab cities of Damascus, Baghdad, and Cairo.

Daily Life in the Medieval City Medieval towns were surrounded by stone walls that were expensive to build, so the space within was precious. Consequently, most medieval cities featured narrow, winding streets with houses crowded against each other and second and third stories extending out over the streets. Because dwellings were built mostly of wood before the fourteenth century and candles and wood fires were used for light and heat, fire was a constant threat. Medieval cities burned rapidly once a fire started.

Most of the people who lived in cities were merchants involved in trade and artisans engaged in manufacturing a wide range of products, such as cloth, metalwork, shoes, and leather

Shops in a Medieval Town. Most urban residents were merchants involved in trade and artisans who manufactured a wide variety of products. Master craftsmen had their workshops in the ground-level rooms of their homes. In this illustration, two well-dressed burghers are touring the shopping district of a French town. Tailors, furriers, a barber, and a grocer (from left to right) are visible at work in their shops.

Snark/Art Resource, NY

Cities in the Medieval World

Interaction & Exchange The exchange of goods between societies was a feature of both the ancient and medieval worlds. Trade routes crisscrossed the lands of the medieval world, and with increased trade came the growth of cities. In Europe, towns had dwindled after the collapse of the Western Roman Empire, but with the revival of trade in the eleventh and twelfth centuries, the cities came back to life. This revival occurred first in the old Roman cities, but soon new cities arose as merchants and artisans sought additional centers for their activities. As cities grew, so did the number of fortified houses, town halls, and churches whose towers punctuated the urban European skyline. Nevertheless, in the Middle Ages, cities in western Europe, especially north of the Alps, remained relatively small. Even the larger cities of Italy, with populations of 100,000, seemed insignificant in comparison with Constantinople and the great cities of the Middle East and China.

With a population of possibly 300,000 people, Constantinople, the capital city of the Byzantine Empire (see Chapter 13), was the largest city in Europe in the Early and High Middle Ages, and until the twelfth century, it was Europe's greatest commercial center, important for the exchange of goods between West and East. In addition to palaces, cathedrals, and monastic buildings, Constantinople also had numerous gardens and orchards that occupied large areas inside its fortified walls. Despite the extensive open and cultivated spaces, the city was not self-sufficient and relied on imports of food under close government direction.

As trade flourished in the Islamic world, cities prospered. When the Abbasids were in power, Baghdad, with a population close to 700,000, was probably the largest city in the empire and one of the greatest cities in the world. After the rise of the Fatimids in Egypt, however, the focus of trade shifted to Cairo. Islamic cities had a distinctive physical appearance. Usually, the most impressive urban buildings were the palaces for the caliphs or the local governors and the great mosques for worship. There were also public buildings with fountains and secluded courtyards, public baths, and bazaars. The bazaar, a covered market, was a crucial part of every Muslim settlement and an important trading center where goods from throughout the known world were available. Food prepared for sale at the market was carefully supervised. A rule in one Muslim city stated, "Grilled meats should only be made with fresh meat and not with meat coming from a sick animal and bought for its cheapness." The merchants were among the greatest beneficiaries of the growth of cities in the Islamic world.

During the medieval period, cities in China were the largest in the world. The southern port of Hangzhou had at least a million residents by 1000, and a number of other cities,

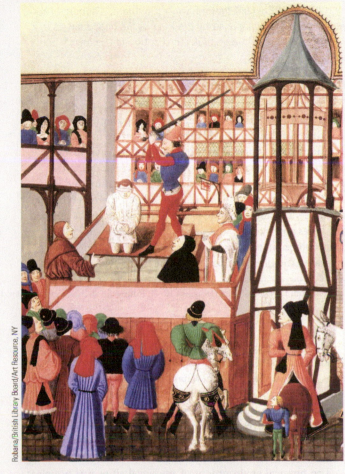

Robana/British Library Board/Art Resource, NY

Crime and Punishment in the Medieval City. Violence was a common feature of medieval life. Criminals, if apprehended, were punished quickly and severely, and public executions, like the one seen here, were considered a deterrent to crime.

including Chang'an and Kaifeng, may also have reached that size. Chinese cities were known for their broad canals and wide, tree-lined streets. They were no longer administrative centers dominated by officials and their families but now included a broader mix of officials, merchants, artisans, and entertainers. The prosperity of Chinese cities was well known. Marco Polo, in describing Hangzhou to unbelieving Europeans in the late thirteenth century, said, "So many pleasures can be found that one fancies himself to be in Paradise."

 Based on a comparison of these medieval cities, which of these civilizations do you think was the most advanced? Why?

POLLUTION IN A MEDIEVAL CITY

Earth & Environment

ENVIRONMENTAL POLLUTION IS NOT NEW. Medieval cities and towns had their own problems with filthy living conditions. This excerpt is taken from an order sent by the king of England to the town of Boutham, a suburb of York, which was then being used by the king as his headquarters in a war with the Scots. It demands rectification of the town's pitiful physical conditions.

The King's Command to Boutham

To the bailiffs of the abbot of St. Mary's, York, at Boutham. Whereas it is sufficiently evident that the pavement of the said town of Boutham is so very greatly broke up that all and singular passing and going through that town sustain immoderate damages and grievances, and in addition the air is so corrupted and infected by the pigsties situated in the king's highways and in the lanes of that town and by the swine feeding and frequently wandering about in the streets and lanes and by dung and dunghills and many other foul things placed in the streets and lanes, that great repugnance overtakes the king's ministers staying in that town and also others there dwelling and passing through; the advantage of more wholesome air is impeded; the state of men is grievously injured, and other unbearable inconveniences and many other injuries are known to proceed from such corruption, to the nuisance of the king's ministers aforesaid and of others there dwelling and passing through, and to the peril of their lives. . . . The king, being unwilling longer to tolerate such great and unbearable defects there, orders the bailiffs to cause the pavement to be suitably repaired within their liberty before All Saints next, and to cause the pigsties, aforesaid streets and lanes to be cleansed from all dung and dunghills, and to cause proclamation to be made throughout their bailiwick forbidding any one, under pain of grievous forfeiture, to cause or permit their swine to feed or wander outside his house in the king's streets or the lanes aforesaid.

 What does the king's command to Boutham illustrate about the physical environment of medieval cities? What factors or human habits contributed to the degradation of the medieval urban environment?

Source: From *English Historical Documents III*, H. Rothwell, ed. (London: Methuen, 1975).

---

goods. Generally, merchants and artisans had their own sections within a city. The merchant area included warehouses, inns, and taverns. Artisan sections were usually divided along craft lines. From the twelfth century on, craftspeople began to organize themselves into **guilds**, and by the thirteenth century, there were individual guilds for virtually every craft. Each craft had its own street where its activity was pursued.

The physical environment of medieval cities was not pleasant. They were dirty and smelled of animal and human wastes deposited in backyard privies or on the streets (see "Pollution in a Medieval City"). The rivers near most cities were polluted with wastes, especially from the tanning and butchering industries. Because of the pollution, cities did not use the rivers for drinking water but relied instead on wells.

Private and public baths also existed in medieval towns. Paris, for example, had thirty-two public baths for men and women. City laws did not allow lepers and people with "bad reputations" to use them. This did not, however, prevent public baths from being known for permissiveness due to public nudity. One contemporary commented on what occurred in public bathhouses: "Shameful things. Men make a point of staying all night in the public baths and women at the break of day come in and through 'ignorance' find themselves in the men's rooms."[6]

In medieval cities, women, in addition to supervising the household, purchasing food and preparing meals, raising the children, and managing the family finances, also often helped their husbands in their trades. Some women also developed their own trades, such as brewing ale or making glass, to earn extra money. When some master craftspeople died, their widows even carried on their trades. Some women in medieval towns were thus able to lead lives of considerable independence and made important contributions to the market economy. Nevertheless, women often made less than men and faced obstacles that kept them from more rewarding opportunities. For example, women in textile production usually were given the most menial jobs. Many were forced to become domestic servants and given room and board in return for cooking, cleaning, and other domestic services.

12–2c Evolution of the European Kingdoms

The recovery and growth of European civilization in the High Middle Ages also affected the state. Although lords and vassals seemed forever mired in endless petty conflicts, some medieval kings inaugurated the process of developing new kinds of monarchical states that were based on the centralization of power rather than the decentralized political order that was characteristic of fief-holding. By the thirteenth century, European monarchs were solidifying their governmental institutions in pursuit of greater power.

England in the High Middle Ages In late September 1066, an army of heavily armed knights under William of Normandy landed on the coast of England, and a few weeks later, on October 14, they soundly defeated King Harold and his Anglo-Saxon foot soldiers in the Battle of Hastings. William (1066–1087) was crowned king of England at Christmastime in London and promptly began a process of combining Anglo-Saxon and Norman institutions that would change England forever. Many of the Norman knights were given parcels of land that they held as fiefs from the new English king. William made all nobles swear an oath of loyalty to him as sole ruler of England and insisted that all people owed loyalty to the king. The Normans also took over existing Anglo-Saxon institutions, such as the office of sheriff. William took a census and more fully developed the system of taxation and royal courts begun by the Anglo-Saxon kings of the tenth and eleventh centuries. All in all, William of Normandy established a strong, centralized monarchy.

The Norman Conquest had numerous repercussions. Because the new king of England was still the duke of Normandy, he was both a king (of England) and at the same time a vassal to a king (of France), but a vassal who was now far more powerful than his lord. This connection with France kept England heavily involved in European affairs throughout the High Middle Ages.

In the twelfth century, the power of the English monarchy was greatly enlarged during the reign of Henry II (1154–1189; see Film & History, Section 12-2a, p. 336). The new king was particularly successful in strengthening the power of the royal courts. Henry expanded the number of criminal cases to be tried in the king's court and also devised means for taking property cases from local courts to the royal courts. Henry's goals were clear: expanding the power of the royal courts increased the king's power and, of course, brought revenues into his coffers. Moreover, since the royal courts were now found throughout England, a body of **common law** (law that was common to the whole kingdom) began to replace the different law codes that often varied from place to place.

The Norman Conquest of England. The Bayeux (bah-YUH *or* bah-YUR) tapestry, a magnificent wall hanging of woolen embroidery on a linen backing, was made by English needlewomen before 1082 for Bayeux Cathedral. It depicts scenes from the Norman invasion of England. The first segment (left) shows the Norman fleet beginning its journey to England. The second segment (below) shows the Norman cavalry charging the shield wall of the Saxon infantry during the Battle of Hastings.

Henry was less successful at imposing royal control over the church and became involved in a famous struggle between church and state. Henry claimed the right to punish clergymen in the royal courts, but Thomas à Becket, as archbishop of Canterbury, the highest-ranking English cleric, claimed that only church courts could try clerics. Attempts at compromise failed, and the angry king publicly expressed the desire to be rid of Becket: "Who will free me of this priest?" he screamed. Four knights took the challenge, went to Canterbury, and murdered the archbishop in the cathedral. Faced with public outrage, Henry was forced to allow the right of appeal from English church courts to the papal court.

Many English nobles came to resent the growth of the king's power and rose in rebellion during the reign of King John (1199–1216). At Runnymede in 1215, John was forced to accept Magna Carta (Great Charter) guaranteeing feudal liberties. Feudal custom had always recognized that the relationship between king and vassals was based on mutual rights and obligations. Magna Carta gave written recognition to that fact and was used in later years to support the idea that a monarch's power was limited.

During the reign of Edward I (1272–1307), an institution of great importance in the development of representative government—the English Parliament—emerged. Originally, the word *parliament* was applied to meetings of the king's Great Council, in which the greater barons and chief prelates of the church met with the king's judges and principal advisers to deal with judicial affairs. But needing money, in 1295 Edward invited two knights from every county and two residents from each town to meet with the Great Council to consent to new taxes. This was the first Parliament.

Thus, the English Parliament came to be composed of two knights from every county and two burgesses from every borough as well as the barons and ecclesiastical lords. Eventually, the barons and church lords formed the House of Lords; the knights and burgesses, the House of Commons. The Parliaments of Edward I approved taxes, discussed politics, passed laws, and handled judicial business. The law of the realm was beginning to be determined not by the king alone but by the king in consultation with representatives of various groups that constituted the community.

Growth of the French Kingdom

The Carolingian Empire had been divided into three major sections in 843. The western Frankish lands formed the core of the eventual kingdom of France. In 987, after the death of the last Carolingian king, the western Frankish nobles chose Hugh Capet (YOO ka-PAY) as the new king, thus establishing the Capetian (kuh-PEE-shun) dynasty of French kings. Although they carried the title of kings, the Capetians had little real power. They controlled as the royal domain only the lands around Paris known as the Île-de-France (EEL-duh-fronhss). As kings of France, the Capetians were formally the overlords of the great lords of France, such as the dukes of Normandy, Brittany, Burgundy, and Aquitaine. In reality, however, many of the dukes were considerably more powerful than the Capetian kings. All in all, it would take the Capetian dynasty hundreds of years to create a truly centralized monarchical authority in France.

The reign of King Philip II Augustus (1180–1223) was an important turning point in the growth of the French monarchy. Philip II waged war against the Plantagenet (plan-TAJ-uhnet) rulers of England, who also ruled the French territories of Normandy, Maine, Anjou, and Aquitaine, and was successful in gaining control of most of these territories, thereby enlarging the power of the French monarchy (see Map 12.3). To administer justice and collect royal revenues in his new territories, Philip appointed new royal officials, thus inaugurating a French royal bureaucracy in the thirteenth century.

Capetian rulers after Philip II continued to add lands to the royal domain. Philip IV the Fair (1285–1314) was especially effective in strengthening the French monarchy. He reinforced the royal bureaucracy and also brought a French parliament into being by asking representatives of the three estates, or classes—the clergy (First Estate), the nobles (Second Estate), and the townspeople (Third Estate)—to meet with him. They did so in 1302, inaugurating the Estates-General, the first French parliament, although it had little real power. By the end of the thirteenth century, France was the largest, wealthiest, and best-governed monarchical state in Europe.

Christian Reconquest: The Iberian Kingdoms

Much of Spain had been part of the Islamic world since the eighth century. From the tenth century, however, the most noticeable feature of Spanish history was the weakening of Muslim power and the beginning of a Christian reconquest that lasted until the final expulsion of the Muslims at the end of the fifteenth century.

A number of small Christian kingdoms were established in northern Spain in the eleventh century, and within a hundred years, they had been consolidated into the Christian kingdoms of Castile (ka-STEEL), Navarre, Aragon, and Portugal, which first emerged as a separate kingdom in 1139.

In the thirteenth century, Aragon, Castile, and Portugal made significant conquests of Muslim territory in the southern half of Spain. The Muslims remained ensconced only in the kingdom of Granada in the southeast of the Iberian Peninsula, which remained an independent Muslim state until its final conquest by the forces of Ferdinand and Isabella of Aragon and Castile in 1492.

The Spanish kingdoms followed no consistent policy in their treatment of the conquered Muslim population. In Aragon, Muslim farmers continued to work the land but were forced to pay very high rents. In Castile, King Alfonso X (1252–1284), who called himself the "King of Three Religions," encouraged the continued development of a cosmopolitan culture shared by Christians, Jews, and Muslims.

The Lands of the Holy Roman Empire

In the tenth century, the powerful dukes of the Saxons became kings of the eastern Frankish kingdom (or Germany, as it came to be called). The best known of the Saxon kings of Germany was Otto I (936–973), who intervened in Italian politics and for his efforts was crowned emperor of the Romans by the pope in 962, reviving a title that had not been used since the time of Charlemagne.

Map 12.3 Europe in the High Middle Ages. Although the nobility dominated much of European society in the High Middle Ages, kings began the process of extending their power in more effective ways, creating the monarchies that would form the European states.

 Which were the strongest monarchical states by 1300? Why?

In the eleventh century, German kings created a strong monarchy and a powerful empire by leading armies into Italy. To strengthen their grip, they relied on their ability to control the church and select bishops, whom they could then use as royal administrators. But the struggle between church and state during the reign of Henry IV (1056–1106) weakened the king's ability to use church officials in this way (see "Reform of the Papacy," Section 12-2d, p. 345). The German kings also tried to bolster their power by using their position as emperors to exploit the resources of Italy. But this strategy tended to backfire; many a German king lost armies in Italy in pursuit of a dream of empire, and no German dynasty demonstrates this better than the Hohenstaufens (hoh-en-SHTOW-fens).

The two most famous members of the Hohenstaufen dynasty, Frederick I Barbarossa (bar-buh-ROH-suh) (1152–1190) and Frederick II (1212–1250), tried to create a new kind of empire. Previous German kings had focused on building a strong German kingdom, but Frederick I planned to get his chief revenues from Italy as the center of a "holy empire," as he called

it (hence the name *Holy Roman Empire*). But his attempt to conquer northern Italy ran into severe problems. The pope opposed him, fearful that the emperor wanted to absorb Rome and the Papal States into his empire. The cities of northern Italy, which had become used to their freedom, were also unwilling to be Frederick's subjects. An alliance of these northern Italian cities, with the support of the pope, defeated the emperor's forces in 1176.

The main goal of Frederick II was the establishment of a strong centralized state in Italy dominated by the kingdom in Sicily, which he had inherited from his mother. Frederick's major task was to gain control of northern Italy. In the attempt, however, he became involved in a deadly conflict with the popes, who feared that a single ruler of northern and southern Italy would mean the end of papal power in the center of the peninsula. Furthermore, the northern Italian cities were unwilling to give up their freedom. Frederick nevertheless waged a long and bitter struggle, winning many battles but ultimately losing the war.

The struggle between popes and emperors had dire consequences for the Holy Roman Empire. By spending their time fighting in Italy, the German emperors left Germany in the hands of powerful German lords who ignored the emperor and created their own independent kingdoms. This ensured that the German monarchy would remain weak and incapable of establishing a centralized monarchical state; thus, the German Holy Roman Emperor had no real power over either Germany or Italy. Unlike France and England, neither Germany nor Italy had a centralized national monarchy in the Middle Ages. Both of these regions consisted of many small, independent states, a situation that changed little until the nineteenth century.

The Slavic Peoples of Central and Eastern Europe

The Slavs were originally a single people in central Europe, but they gradually divided into three major groups: western, southern, and eastern (see Map 12.4). The western Slavs eventually formed the Polish and Bohemian kingdoms. German Christian missionaries converted both the Czechs in Bohemia and the Slavs in Poland by the tenth century. German Christians also converted the non-Slavic kingdom of Hungary, which emerged after the Magyars settled down after their defeat in 955. The Poles, Czechs, and Hungarians all accepted Catholic or western Christianity and became closely tied to the Roman Catholic Church and its Latin culture.

The southern and eastern Slavic populations took a different path: the Slavic peoples of Moravia were converted to the Orthodox Christianity of the Byzantine Empire (see Chapter 13) by two Byzantine missionary brothers, Cyril and Methodius, who began their activities in 863. The southern Slavic peoples included the Croats, Serbs, and Bulgarians. For the most part, they too embraced Eastern Orthodoxy, although the Croats came to accept the Roman Catholic faith. The adoption of Eastern Orthodoxy by the Serbs and Bulgarians tied their cultural life to the Byzantine state.

The eastern Slavic peoples, from whom the modern Russians and Ukrainians are descended, had settled in the territory of present-day Ukraine and European Russia. There, beginning in the late eighth century, they began to encounter Swedish Vikings who moved down the extensive network of rivers into the lands of the eastern Slavs in search of booty and new trade routes (see "A Muslim's Description of the Rus"). These Vikings built trading settlements and eventually came to dominate the native peoples, who called them "the Rus" (ROOSS *or* ROOSH), from which the name Russia is derived.

The Development of Russia: Impact of the Mongols

A Viking leader named Oleg (c. 873–913) settled in Kiev (KEE-yev) at the beginning of the tenth century and founded the Rus state known as the principality of Kiev. His successors extended their control over the eastern Slavs and expanded the territory of Kiev until it included the area between the Baltic and Black Seas and the Danube and Volga Rivers. By marrying Slavic wives, the Viking ruling class was gradually assimilated into the Slavic population.

The growth of the principality of Kiev attracted religious missionaries, especially from the Byzantine Empire. One Rus ruler, Vladimir (VLAD-ih-meer) (c. 980–1015), married the Byzantine emperor's sister and in 987 officially accepted Christianity for himself and his people. By the end of the tenth century, Byzantine Christianity had become the model for Russian religious life.

The Kievan Rus state prospered and reached its high point in the first half of the eleventh century. But civil wars and new invasions by Asian nomads caused the principality of Kiev to collapse, and its sack by north Russian princes in 1169 brought an end to the first Russian state, which had remained closely tied to the Byzantine

Map 12.4 The Migrations of the Slavs. Originally from east-central Europe, the Slavic people broke into three groups. The western Slavs converted to Catholic Christianity, while most of the eastern and southern Slavs, under the influence of the Byzantine Empire, embraced the Eastern Orthodox faith.

 What connections do these Slavic migrations have with what we today characterize as eastern Europe?

A MUSLIM'S DESCRIPTION OF THE RUS

Family & Society | **DESPITE THE DIFFICULTIES** that travel presented, early medieval civilization did witness some contact among the various cultures. This might occur through trade, diplomacy, or the conquest and migration of peoples. This document is a description of the Swedish Rus, who eventually merged with the native Slavic peoples to form the principality of Kiev, commonly regarded as the first Russian state. It was written by Ibn Fadlan, a Muslim diplomat sent from Baghdad in 921 to a settlement on the Volga River. His comments on the filthiness of the Rus reflect the Muslim emphasis on cleanliness.

Ibn Fadlan, *The Rus*

I saw the Rus folk when they arrived on their trading mission and settled at the river Atul (Volga). Never had I seen people of more perfect physique. They are tall as date palms, and reddish in color. They wear neither coat nor kaftan, but each man carried a cape which covers one half of his body, leaving one hand free. No one is ever parted from his axe, sword, and knife. Their swords are Frankish in design, broad, flat, and fluted. Each man has a number of trees, figures, and the like from the fingernails to the neck. Each woman carried on her bosom a container made of iron, silver, copper, or gold—its size and substance depending on her man's wealth.

[The Rus] are the filthiest of God's creatures. They do not wash after discharging their natural functions, neither do they wash their hands after meals. They are as lousy as donkeys. They arrive from their distant lands and lay their ships alongside the banks of the Atul, which is a great river, and there they build big houses on its shores. Ten or twenty of them may live together in one house, and each of them has a couch of his own where he sits and diverts himself with the pretty slave girls whom he had brought along for sale. He will make love with one of them while a comrade looks on; sometimes they indulge in a communal orgy, and, if a customer should turn up to buy a girl, the Rus man will not let her go till he has finished with her.

They wash their hands and faces every day in incredibly filthy water. Every morning the girl brings her master a large bowl of water in which he washes his hands and face and hair, then blows his nose into it and spits into it. When he has finished the girl takes the bowl to his neighbor—who repeats the performance. Thus, the bowl goes the rounds of the entire household. . . .

If one of the Rus folk falls sick they put him in a tent by himself and leave bread and water for him. They do not visit him, however, or speak to him, especially if he is a serf. Should he recover he rejoins the others; if he dies they burn him. But if he happens to be a serf they leave him for the dogs and vultures to devour. If they catch a robber they hang him to a tree until he is torn to shreds by wind and weather.

 What was Ibn Fadlan's impression of the Rus? Why do you think he was so critical of their behavior?

Source: From *The Vikings*, by Johannes Bronsted, translated by Kalle Skov (Penguin Books, 1965).

Empire, not to Europe. In the thirteenth century, the Mongols conquered Russia and cut it off even more from Europe.

The Mongols had exploded onto the scene in the thirteenth century, moving east into China and west into the Middle East and central Europe. Although they conquered Russia, they were not numerous enough to settle the vast Russian lands. They occupied only part of Russia but required Russian princes to pay tribute to them. One Russian prince soon emerged as more powerful than the others. Alexander Nevsky (NYEF-skee), prince of Novgorod (NAHV-guhrahd), defeated a German invading army in northwestern Russia in 1242. His cooperation with the Mongols won him their favor. The khan, leader of the western part of the Mongol Empire, rewarded Alexander Nevsky with the title of grand-prince, enabling his descendants to become the princes of Moscow and eventually leaders of all Russia.

12–2d Christianity and Medieval Civilization

Christianity was an integral part of the fabric of European society and the consciousness of Europe. Papal directives affected the actions of kings and princes alike, and Christian teachings and practices touched the lives of all Europeans.

Reform of the Papacy Since the fifth century, the popes of the Catholic Church had reigned supreme over church affairs. They had also come to exercise control over the territories in central Italy that came to be known as the Papal States, which kept the popes involved in political matters, often at the expense of their spiritual obligations. At the same time, the church became increasingly entangled in the evolving feudal relationships. High officials of the church, such as bishops and abbots, came to hold their offices as fiefs from nobles. As vassals, they were obliged to carry out the usual duties, including military service. Of course, lords assumed the right to choose their vassals and thus came to appoint bishops and abbots. Because lords often chose their vassals from other noble families for political reasons, these bishops and abbots were often worldly figures who cared little about their spiritual responsibilities.

By the eleventh century, church leaders realized the need to free the church from the interference of lords in the appointment of church officials. **Lay investiture** was the practice by which secular rulers both chose nominees to church offices and invested them with (bestowed on them) the symbols of their office. Pope Gregory VII (1073–1085) decided to fight this

England		
Norman Conquest	1066	
William the Conqueror	1066–1087	
Henry II	1154–1189	
John	1199–1216	
Magna Carta	1215	
Edward I	1272–1307	
First Parliament	1295	
France		
Philip II Augustus	1180–1223	
Philip IV	1285–1314	
First Estates-General	1302	
Germany and the Holy Roman Empire		
Otto I	936–973	
Henry IV	1056–1106	
Frederick I	1152–1190	
Northern Italian cities defeat Frederick	1176	
Frederick II	1212–1250	
The Eastern World		
Alexander Nevsky, prince of Novgorod	c. 1220–1263	
Mongol conquest of Russia	1230s	

practice. Gregory claimed that he, as pope, was God's "vicar on earth" and that the pope's authority extended over all of Christendom, including its rulers. In 1075, he issued a decree forbidding high-ranking clerics from receiving their investiture from lay leaders.

Gregory soon found himself in conflict with the German king over his actions. King Henry IV was also a determined man who had appointed high-ranking clerics, especially bishops, as his vassals in order to use them as administrators. Henry had no intention of obeying a decree that challenged the very heart of his administration.

The struggle between Henry IV and Gregory VII, which is known as the Investiture Controversy, was one of the great conflicts between church and state in the High Middle Ages. It dragged on until a new German king and a new pope reached a compromise in 1122 called the Concordat of Worms (kun-KOR-dat of WURMZ or VORMPS). Under this agreement, church officials first elected a bishop in Germany. After election, the nominee paid homage to the king as his lord, who then invested him with the symbols of temporal office. A representative of the pope, however, then invested the new bishop with the symbols of his spiritual office.

The Church Supreme: The Papal Monarchy
The popes of the twelfth century did not abandon the reform ideals of Pope Gregory VII, but they were more inclined to consolidate their power and build a strong administrative system. During the papacy of Pope Innocent III (1198–1216), the Catholic Church reached the height of its power. At the beginning of his pontificate, in a letter to a priest, the pope made a clear statement of his views on papal supremacy:

> As God, the creator of the universe, set two great lights in the firmament of heaven, the greater light to rule the day, and the lesser light to rule the night, so He set two great dignities in the firmament of the universal church, . . . the greater to rule the day, that is, souls, and the lesser to rule the night, that is, bodies. These dignities are the papal authority and the royal power. And just as the moon gets her light from the sun, and is inferior to the sun . . . so the royal power gets the splendor of its dignity from the papal authority.[7]

Innocent III's actions were those of a man who believed that he, as pope, was the supreme judge of European affairs. To achieve his political ends, he did not hesitate to use the spiritual weapons at his command, especially the **interdict**, which forbade priests to dispense the **sacraments** of the church in the hope that the people, deprived of the comforts of religion, would exert pressure against their ruler. Apparently, Pope Innocent's interdicts worked: for example, one of them forced the king of France, Philip Augustus, to take back his wife and queen after Philip had tried to have his marriage annulled.

New Religious Orders and New Spiritual Ideals Between 1050 and 1150, a wave of religious enthusiasm seized Europe, leading to a spectacular growth in the number of monasteries and the emergence of new monastic orders. Most important was the Cistercian (sis-TUR-shun) order, founded in 1098 by a group of monks dissatisfied with the moral degeneration and lack of strict discipline at their own Benedictine monastery. The Cistercians were strict. They ate a simple diet and possessed only a single robe apiece. More time for prayer and manual labor was provided by shortening the number of hours spent at religious services. The Cistercians played a major role in developing a new, activist spiritual model for twelfth-century Europe. A Benedictine monk often spent hours in prayer to honor God. The Cistercian ideal had a different emphasis: "Arise, soldier of Christ, arise! Get up off the ground and return to the battle from which you have fled! Fight more boldly after your flight, and triumph in glory!"[8] These were the words of Saint Bernard of Clairvaux (klayr-VOH) (1090–1153), who more than any other person embodied the new spiritual ideal of Cistercian monasticism. He has been called the most widely respected holy man of the twelfth century. Bernard was an outstanding preacher, wholly dedicated to the service of God. His reputation reportedly influenced many young men to join the Cistercian order.

Women were also actively involved in the spiritual movements of the age. The number of women joining religious houses grew dramatically in the High Middle Ages. Most nuns were from the ranks of the landed aristocracy. Convents were convenient for families unable or unwilling to find husbands for their daughters and for aristocratic women who did not wish to marry. Female intellectuals found them a haven for their

The Holy Office, as the papal Inquisition was formally called, was a court established by the church to find and try heretics. Anyone accused of heresy who refused to confess was considered guilty and was turned over to the state for execution. So were relapsed heretics—those who confessed, did penance, and then reverted to heresy again. Most heretics, however, were put in prison or made to do various forms of penance. To the Christians of the thirteenth century, who believed that there was only one path to salvation, heresy was a crime against God and against humanity. In their minds, force should be used to save souls from damnation.

A Group of Nuns. Although still viewed by the medieval church as inferior to men, women were as susceptible to the spiritual fervor of the twelfth century as men, and female monasticism grew accordingly. This manuscript illustration shows at the left a group of nuns welcoming a novice (dressed in white) to their order. At the right, a nun receives a sick person on a stretcher for the order's hospital care.

activities. Most of the learned women of the Middle Ages were nuns. One of the most distinguished was Hildegard of Bingen (HIL-duh-gard of BING-un) (1098–1179), who became abbess of a convent at Disibodenberg in western Germany.

Hildegard shared in the religious enthusiasm of the twelfth century. Soon after becoming abbess, she began to write an account of the mystical visions she had experienced for years. "A great flash of light from heaven pierced my brain and . . . in that instant my mind was imbued with the meaning of the sacred books," she wrote in a description typical of the world's mystical literature. Eventually, she produced three books based on her visions. Hildegard gained considerable renown as a mystic and prophet, and popes, emperors, kings, dukes, and bishops eagerly sought her advice.

In the thirteenth century, two new religious orders emerged that had a profound impact on the lives of ordinary people. Like their founder, Saint Francis of Assisi (uh-SEE-zee) (1182–1226), the Franciscans lived among the people, preaching repentance and aiding the poor. Their calls for a return to the simplicity and poverty of the early church, reinforced by their own example, were especially effective and made them very popular.

The Dominican order arose out of the desire of a Spanish priest, Dominic de Guzmán (DAH-muh-nik duh gooz-MAHN) (1170–1221), to defend church teachings from **heresy**—beliefs contrary to official church doctrine. Unlike Francis, Dominic was an intellectual who was appalled by the growth of heresy. He came to believe that a new religious order of men who lived lives of poverty but were learned and capable of preaching effectively would best be able to attack heresy. The Dominicans became especially well known for their roles as the inquisitors of the papal Inquisition.

Popular Religion in the High Middle Ages We have witnessed the actions of popes, bishops, and monks. But what of ordinary clergy and laypeople? What were their religious hopes and fears? What were their spiritual aspirations?

The sacraments of the Catholic Church ensured that the church was an integral part of people's lives, from birth to death. There were (and still are) seven sacraments, administered only by the clergy. Sacraments, such as baptism and the Eucharist (YOO-kuh-rest) (the Lord's Supper), were viewed as outward symbols of an inward grace and were considered imperative for a Christian's salvation (see "The Miraculous Power of the Sacraments," p. 348). Therefore, the clergy were seen to have a key role in the attainment of salvation.

Other church practices were also important to ordinary people. Saints were seen as men and women who, through their holiness, had achieved a special position in heaven, enabling them to act as intercessors with God. The saints' ability to protect poor souls enabled them to take on great importance at the popular level. Jesus's apostles were, of course, recognized throughout Europe as saints, but there were also numerous local saints who were of special significance to a single area. New cults developed rapidly, especially in the intense religious atmosphere of the eleventh and twelfth centuries. The English, for example, introduced Saint Nicholas, the patron saint of children, who is known today as Santa Claus.

In the High Middle Ages, the Virgin Mary, the mother of Jesus, occupied the foremost position among the saints. Mary was viewed as the most important mediator with her son, Jesus, the judge of all sinners. Moreover, from the eleventh century on, a fascination with Mary as Jesus's human mother became more evident. A sign of Mary's importance was the growing number of churches all over Europe that were dedicated to Our Lady in the twelfth and thirteenth centuries, including the cathedral of Notre-Dame in Paris.

THE MIRACULOUS POWER OF THE SACRAMENTS

Religion & Philosophy In the Middle Ages, the sacraments of the Catholic Church came to be associated with miraculous occurrences. Many stories emerged, telling of the wondrous workings of the sacraments. Wandering priests then spread these tales to laypeople. The first excerpt below is taken from a collection called *The Dialogues Concerning Miracles*, put together by a Cistercian monk in the thirteenth century. The second excerpt is taken from the work of a Dominican priest in the thirteenth century.

Caesar of Heisterbach

In Hemmenrode a certain aged priest, Henry by name, died a few years ago. He was a holy and just man, and had been for many years sacristan in that monastery. When he was celebrating the mass one day at the altar of St. John the Baptist, in the choir of the lay brethren, a certain one of the lay brethren standing near saw, in the hands of the priest, the Saviour (Jesus) in the form of a man. Nevertheless the priest himself did not see it. One of the elders of that convent related this to me.

Stephen of Bourbon

I have heard that a certain rustic, wishing to become wealthy and having many hives of bees, asked certain evil men how he could get rich and increase the number of his bees. He was told by some one that if he retained the sacred host [sacrament of the Eucharist or Lord's Supper] on Easter and placed it in some one of his hives, he would entice away all of his neighbor's bees, which, leaving their own hives, would come to the place where the body of our Lord was and there would make honey. So he did this.

Then all the bees came to the hive where the body of Christ was, and just as if they felt sorrow for the irreverence

done to it, by their labor they began to construct a little church and to erect foundations, and bases, and columns, and an altar; then with the greatest reverence they place the body of our Lord upon the altar. And within their little beehive they formed the little church with wonderful and most beautiful workmanship. The bees of the vicinity, leaving their hives, came to that one; and over that work they sang in their own manner certain wonderful melodies like hymns.

The rustic, hearing this, marveled. But waiting until the fitting time for collecting the honey, he found nothing in his hives. Finding himself impoverished through the means by which he had expected to be enriched, he went to the hive where he had placed the host, and where he saw the bees had come together. But when he approached, just as if they wished to vindicate the insult to our Savior, the bees rushed upon the rustic and stung him so severely that he escaped with difficulty and in great agony. Going to the priest, he related all that he had done, and what the bees had done.

The priest, by the advice of the bishop, collected his parishioners and made a procession to that place. Then the bees, leaving the hive, rose in the air, making sweet melody. Raising the hive, they found inside the noble structure of that little church and the body of our Lord placed upon the altar. Then, returning thanks, they bore to their own church that little church of the bees, constructed with such skill and elegance, and place it on the altar.

By this deed those who do not reverence, but offer insult instead, to the sacred body of Christ, or the sacred place where it is, ought to be put to great confusion.

 What do these two stories tell us about popular religious beliefs in the thirteenth century?

Source: James Harvey Robinson, *Readings in European History* (Boston: Ginn and Company, 1904), pp. 355–356.

Emphasis on the role of the saints was closely tied to the use of relics, which also increased noticeably in the High Middle Ages. Relics were usually the bones of saints or objects intimately connected to saints that were considered worthy of veneration by the faithful. A twelfth-century English monk began his description of the abbey's relics by saying that "there is kept there a thing more precious than gold, . . . the right arm of St. Oswald. . . . This we have seen with our own eyes and have kissed, and have handled with our own hands. . . . There are kept here also part of his ribs and of the soil on which he fell."[9] The monk went on to list additional relics possessed by the abbey, including two pieces of Jesus's swaddling clothes, pieces of Jesus's manger, and part of the five loaves of bread with which Jesus fed five thousand people. Because the holiness of the saint was considered to be inherent in his relics, these objects were believed to be capable of healing people or producing other miracles.

12–2e The Culture of the High Middle Ages

The High Middle Ages was a time of extraordinary intellectual and artistic vitality. It witnessed the birth of universities and a building spree that left Europe bedecked with churches and cathedrals.

The Rise of Universities The university as we know it—with faculty, students, and degrees—was a product of the High Middle Ages. The word *university* is derived from the Latin word *universitas* (yoo-nee-VAYR-see-tahss), meaning a corporation or guild, and referred to either a corporation of teachers or a corporation of students. Medieval universities were educational guilds or corporations that produced educated and trained individuals.

The first European university appeared in Bologna (boh-LOHN-yuh), Italy, where a great teacher named Irnerius

UNIVERSITY STUDENTS AND VIOLENCE AT OXFORD

Art & Ideas   **MEDIEVAL UNIVERSITIES SHARED** in the violent atmosphere of their age. Town and gown quarrels often resulted in bloody conflicts, especially during the universities' formative period. This selection is taken from an anonymous description of a student riot at Oxford at the end of the thirteenth century.

A Student Riot at Oxford

They [the townsmen] seized and imprisoned all scholars on whom they could lay hands, invaded their inns [halls of residence], made havoc of their goods and trampled their books under foot. In the face of such provocation the proctors [university officials] sent their assistants about the town, forbidding the students to leave their inns. But all commands and exhortations were in vain. By nine o'clock next morning, bands of scholars were parading the streets in martial array. If the proctors failed to restrain them, the mayor was equally powerless to restrain his townsmen. The great bell of St. Martin's rang out an alarm; oxhorns were sounded in the streets; messengers were sent into the country to collect rustic allies. The clerks [students and teachers], who numbered 3,000 in all, began their attack simultaneously in various quarters. They broke open warehouses in the Spicery, the Cutlery and elsewhere. Armed with bow and arrows, swords and bucklers, slings and stones, they fell upon their opponents. Three they slew, and wounded fifty or more. One band . . . took up a position in High Street between the Churches of St. Mary and All Saints', and attacked the house of a certain Edward Hales. This Hales was a longstanding enemy of the clerks. There were no half measures with him. He seized his crossbow, and from an upper chamber sent an unerring shaft into the eye of the pugnacious rector. The death of their valiant leader caused the clerks to lose heart. They fled, closely pursued by the townsmen and country-folk. Some were struck down in the streets, and others who had taken refuge in the churches were dragged out and driven mercilessly to prison, lashed with thongs and goaded with iron spikes.

Complaints of murder, violence and robbery were lodged straightway with the king by both parties. The townsmen claimed 3,000 pounds' damage. The commissioners, however, appointed to decide the matter, condemned them to pay 200 marks, removed the bailiffs, and banished twelve of the most turbulent citizens from Oxford.

 Who do you think was responsible for this conflict between town and gown? Why? Why do you think the king supported the university?

Source: From *The Story of Oxford* by Cecil Headlam, 1907.

(1088–1125), who taught Roman law, attracted students from all over Europe. Most of them were laymen, usually older individuals who were administrators for kings and princes and were eager to learn more about law so that they could apply it in their own jobs. To protect themselves, students at Bologna formed a guild or *universitas*, which was recognized by Emperor Frederick Barbarossa and given a charter in 1158. Kings, popes, and princes soon competed to found new universities, and by the end of the Middle Ages, there were eighty universities in Europe, most of them in England, France, Italy, and Germany (see "University Students and Violence at Oxford").

University students (all men—women did not attend universities in the Middle Ages) began their studies with the traditional **liberal arts** curriculum, which consisted of grammar, rhetoric, logic, arithmetic, geometry, music, and astronomy. Teaching was done by the lecture method. The word *lecture* is derived from the Latin verb for "read." Before the development of the printing press in the fifteenth century, books were expensive and few students could afford them, so teachers read from a basic text (such as a collection of laws if the subject was law) and then added their explanations. No exams were given after a series of lectures, but when a student applied for a degree, he was given a comprehensive oral examination by a committee of teachers. The exam was taken after a four- or six-year period of study. The first degree a student could earn was a bachelor of arts; later he might receive a master of arts degree.

After completing the liberal arts curriculum, a student could go on to study law, medicine, or theology. This last was the most highly regarded subject at the medieval university. The study of any of these three disciplines could take a decade or more. A student who passed his final oral examinations was granted a doctor's degree, which officially enabled him to teach his subject. Students who received degrees from medieval universities could pursue other careers besides teaching that proved to be much more lucrative. A law degree was necessary for those who wished to serve as advisers to kings and princes. The growing administrative bureaucracies of popes and kings also demanded a supply of clerks with a university education who could keep records and draw up official documents. Universities provided the teachers, administrators, lawyers, and doctors for medieval society.

Development of Scholasticism The importance of Christianity in medieval society made it certain that theology would play a central role in the European intellectual world. Theology, the formal study of religion, was "queen of the sciences" in the new universities.

Beginning in the eleventh century, the effort to apply reason or logical analysis to the church's basic theological doctrines had a significant impact on the study of theology. The philosophical and theological system of the medieval schools is known as **scholasticism** (skoh-LAS-tih-sizm). Scholasticism tried to reconcile faith and reason, to demonstrate that what was accepted on faith was in harmony with what could be learned by reason.

The overriding task of scholasticism was to harmonize Christian teachings with the work of the Greek philosopher Aristotle. In the twelfth century, due largely to the work of Muslim and Jewish scholars in Spain, western Europe was introduced to a large number of Greek scientific and philosophical works, including the works of Aristotle. But Aristotle's works threw many theologians into consternation. Aristotle was so highly regarded that he was called "the Philosopher," yet he had arrived at his conclusions by rational thought, not by faith, and some of his doctrines, such as the eternal universe, contradicted the teachings of the church. The most famous attempt to reconcile Aristotle and the doctrines of Christianity was that of Saint Thomas Aquinas (uh-KWY-nuss).

Aquinas (1225–1274) is best known for his *Summa Theologica* (SOO-muh tay-oh-LAH-jee-kuh) (*Summa of Theology*—a summa was a compendium of knowledge that attempted to bring together all the received learning of the preceding centuries on a given subject). Aquinas's masterpiece was organized according to the dialectical method of the scholastics. Aquinas first posed a question, cited sources that offered opposing opinions on the question, and then resolved the matter by arriving at his own conclusions. In this fashion, Aquinas raised and discussed some six hundred articles.

Aquinas's reputation derives from his masterful attempt to reconcile faith and reason. He took it for granted that there were truths derived by reason and truths derived by faith. He was certain, however, that the two truths could not be in conflict. The natural mind, unaided by faith, could arrive at truths concerning the physical universe. Without the help of God's grace, however, reason alone could not grasp spiritual truths, such as the Trinity (the manifestation of God in three separate yet identical persons—Father, Son, and Holy Spirit) or the Incarnation (Jesus's simultaneous identity as God and human).

Romanesque Architecture

The eleventh and twelfth centuries witnessed an explosion of building, both private and public. The construction of castles and churches absorbed most of the surplus resources of medieval society and at the same time reflected its basic preoccupations, God and warfare. The churches were by far the most conspicuous of the public buildings.

Barrel Vaulting. The eleventh and twelfth centuries witnessed an enormous amount of church construction. Utilizing the basilica shape, master builders replaced flat wooden roofs with long, round stone vaults known as barrel vaults. As this illustration of a Romanesque church in Vienne, France, indicates, the barrel vault limited the size of a church and left little room for windows.

The cathedrals of the eleventh and twelfth centuries were built in the **Romanesque** (roh-man-ESK) style, prominent examples of which can be found in Germany, France, and Spain. Romanesque churches were normally built in the basilica shape used in the construction of churches in the Late Roman Empire. Basilicas were rectangular churches with flat wooden roofs. Romanesque builders made a significant innovation by replacing the flat wooden roof with a long, round stone vault called a barrel vault (or a cross vault where two barrel vaults intersected). Although barrel and cross vaults were technically difficult to create, they were considered aesthetically more pleasing than flat wooden roofs and were also less apt to catch fire.

Because stone roofs were extremely heavy, Romanesque churches required massive pillars and walls to hold them up. This left little space for windows, and Romanesque churches were correspondingly dark on the inside. Their massive walls and pillars gave Romanesque churches a sense of solidity and almost the impression of a fortress.

The Gothic Cathedral

Begun in the twelfth century and brought to perfection in the thirteenth, the **Gothic** cathedral remains one of the greatest artistic triumphs of the High Middle Ages. Soaring skyward, as if to reach heaven, it was a fitting symbol for medieval people's preoccupation with God.

Two fundamental innovations of the twelfth century made Gothic cathedrals possible. The combination of ribbed vaults and pointed arches replaced the barrel vaults of Romanesque churches and enabled builders to make Gothic churches higher than Romanesque ones. The use of pointed arches and ribbed vaults created an impression of upward movement, a sense of weightless upward thrust that implied the energy of God. Another technical innovation, the flying buttress, a heavy arched pier of stone built onto the outside of the walls, made it possible to distribute the weight of the church's vaulted ceilings outward and down and thus eliminate the heavy walls used in Romanesque churches to hold the weight of the massive barrel vaults. Thus, Gothic cathedrals could be built with thin walls containing magnificent stained-glass windows, which created a play of light inside that varied with the sun at different times of the day. The extensive use of colored light in Gothic cathedrals was not accidental but was executed by people who believed that natural light was a symbol of the divine light of God.

The first fully Gothic church was the abbey of Saint-Denis (san-duh-NEE) near Paris, inspired by its famous Abbot Suger (soo-ZHAYR) (1122–1151) and built between 1140 and 1150. By the mid-thirteenth century, French Gothic architecture, most brilliantly executed in cathedrals in Paris (Notre-Dame), Reims, Amiens, and Chartres, had spread to virtually all of Europe.

A Gothic cathedral was the work of the entire community. All classes contributed to its construction. Master masons, who were both architects and engineers, designed them, and stonemasons and other craftspeople were paid a daily wage and provided the skilled labor to build them. A Gothic cathedral symbolized the chief preoccupation of a medieval Christian community, its dedication to a spiritual ideal. As we have observed before, the largest buildings of an era reflect the values of its society. The Gothic cathedral, with its towers soaring toward heaven, gave witness to an age when a spiritual impulse underlay most aspects of its existence.

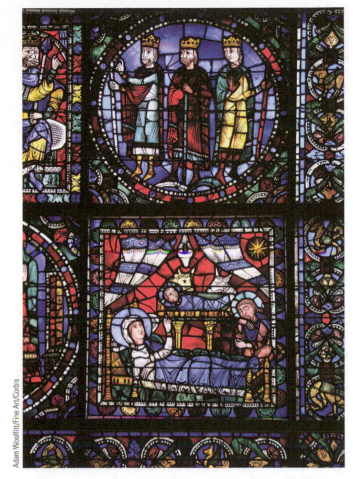

Adam Woolfitt/Fine Art/Corbis

Chartres Cathedral: Stained-Glass Window. The stained glass of Gothic cathedrals is remarkable for the beauty and variety of its colors. Stained-glass windows depicted a remarkable variety of scenes. The windows of Chartres Cathedral, for example, present the saints, views of the everyday activities of ordinary men and women, and, as in this panel, scenes from the life of Jesus.

The Gothic Cathedral. The Gothic cathedral was one of the great artistic triumphs of the High Middle Ages. Shown here is the cathedral of Notre-Dame in Paris. Begun in 1163, it was not completed until the beginning of the fourteenth century.

12–3 MEDIEVAL EUROPE AND THE WORLD

 Focus Questions: In what ways did Europeans begin to relate to peoples in other parts of the world after 1000 CE? What were the reasons for the crusades, and who or what benefited the most from them?

As it developed, European civilization remained largely confined to its home continent, although Europe was never completely isolated. Some Europeans, especially merchants, had contacts with parts of Asia and Africa. The goods of those lands made their way into medieval castles, and the works of Muslim philosophers were read in medieval universities. The Vikings were also daring explorers. After 860, they sailed westward in

Tkachuk/Shutterstock.com

their long ships across the North Atlantic Ocean, reaching Iceland in 874. Erik the Red, a Viking exiled from Iceland, traveled even farther west and discovered Greenland in 985. Some Vikings even reached North America, landing in Newfoundland, the only known Viking site in North America, but it proved to be short-lived as Viking expansion drew to a close by the tenth century. Only at the end of the eleventh century did Europeans begin their first concerted attempt to expand beyond the frontiers of Europe by conquering the land of Palestine.

12–3a The Early Crusades

The crusades were based on the idea of a holy war against infidels (unbelievers). Christian wrath against Muslims had already found some expression in the attempt to wrest Spain from the Moors and the success of the Normans in reclaiming Sicily. At the end of the eleventh century, Christian Europe found itself with a glorious opportunity when the Byzantine emperor, Alexius I, asked Pope Urban II for help against the Seljuk Turks (see Chapter 13). The pope saw this as a chance to rally the warriors of Europe for the liberation of Jerusalem and the Holy Land of Palestine from the infidels. The Holy City of Jerusalem—where Jesus had lived and died—had long been the focus of Christian pilgrimages. At the Council of Clermont in southern France toward the end of 1095, Urban challenged Christians to take up their weapons and join in a holy war to recover the Holy Land. The pope promised remission of sins: "All who die by the way, whether by land or by sea, or in battle against the pagans, shall have immediate remission of sins. This I grant them through the power of God with which I am invested."[10] The enthusiastic crowd cried out in response: "It is the will of God, it is the will of God."

The initial response to Urban's speech reveals how appealing many people found this combined call to military arms and religious fervor. A self-appointed leader, Peter the Hermit, who preached of his visions of the Holy City of Jerusalem, convinced a large mob, some of them nobles but most of them poor and many of them peasants, to undertake a crusade to liberate the city. One person who encountered Peter described him in these words: "Outdoors he wore a woolen tunic, which revealed his ankles, and above it a hood; he wore a cloak to cover his upper body, a bit of his arms, but his feet were bare. He drank wine and ate fish, but scarcely ever ate bread. This man, partly because of his reputation, partly because of his preaching, [assembled] a very large army."[11]

This "People's Crusade" or "Crusade of the Poor" moved through the Balkans, terrorizing natives and looting for their food and supplies. Their misplaced religious enthusiasm led to another tragic byproduct as well, the persecution of the Jews, long pictured by the church as the murderers of Christ. As a contemporary chronicler described it, "They persecuted the hated race of the Jews wherever they were found." Two bands of people's crusaders, led by Peter the Hermit, managed to reach Constantinople. The Byzantine emperor wisely shipped them over to Asia Minor, where the Turks massacred the undisciplined and poorly armed mob.

HISTORIANS DEBATE **What Motivated the Crusaders?** Pope Urban II did not share the wishful thinking of the peasant crusaders but was more inclined to trust knights who had been well trained in the art of war. The warriors of western Europe, particularly France, formed the first crusading armies. But was Urban motivated by a desire to free Jerusalem from the infidels in a just war? One historian maintains that the pope thought of the crusade as "an attempt to consolidate papal empowerment and expand Rome's sphere of influence," in order to "meet the needs of the papacy."

Historians have long debated the motives of the crusaders. Many historians today maintain that the knights who made up this first serious crusading host were motivated by religious fervor and an opportunity to gain salvation—had the pope not offered a full remission of sins for those who participated in these "armed pilgrimages." But were there other attractions as well? Some historians argue that some of the crusaders sought adventure and welcomed a legitimate opportunity to pursue their favorite pastime—fighting—as well as an opportunity to gain territory, riches, status, and possibly a title. An older generation of historians had believed that from the perspective of the pope and European monarchs, the crusades offered a way to rid Europe of contentious young nobles who disturbed the peace and wasted lives and energy fighting each other. The Catholic Church had tried earlier to limit the ongoing bloodletting, but without a great deal of success. Historians recently, however, have made a strong case against this old argument and maintain that the crusaders were wealthy and pious nobles who even risked their wealth to pursue a just cause of helping their fellow Christians in the east.

The First Crusade In the First Crusade, begun in 1096, three organized bands of noble warriros, most of them French, made their way to the east. The crusading army probably numbered several thousand cavalry and as many as ten thousand infantry. After the capture of Antioch in 1098, much of the crusading host proceeded down the Palestinian coast, evading the well-defended coastal cities, and reached Jerusalem in June 1099. After a five-week siege, the Holy City was taken amid a horrible massacre of the inhabitants—men, women, and children.

After further conquest of Palestinian lands, the crusaders ignored the wishes

Crusader Kingdoms in Palestine

The First Crusade: The Capture of Jerusalem. Recruited from the noble class of western Europe, the first crusading army had taken Antioch by 1098. Working down the coast of Palestine, the crusaders captured Jerusalem in 1099. Shown here in a fifteenth-century manuscript illustration is a fanciful re-creation of the looting after Jerusalem's capture by the Christian crusaders.

of the Byzantine emperor and organized four Latin crusader states. Because Muslim forces surrounded the crusader kingdoms, they grew increasingly dependent on the Italian commercial cities for supplies from Europe. Some Italian cities, such as Genoa, Pisa, and especially Venice, benefited in the process.

The Second Crusade But it was not easy for the crusader kingdoms to maintain themselves. Already by the 1120s, the Muslims had begun to strike back. The fall of one of the Latin kingdoms in 1144 led to renewed calls for another crusade, especially from the monastic firebrand Saint Bernard of Clairvaux. He exclaimed, "Now, on account of our sins, the enemies of the cross have begun to show their faces. . . . What are you doing, you servants of the cross? Will you throw to the dogs that which is most holy? Will you cast pearls before swine?"[12] Bernard even managed to enlist two powerful rulers, but their Second Crusade proved to be a total failure.

The Third Crusade The Third Crusade was a reaction to the fall of the Holy City of Jerusalem in 1187 to the Muslim forces under Saladin. Now all of Christendom was ablaze with calls for a new crusade. Three major monarchs agreed to lead their forces in person: Emperor Frederick Barbarossa of Germany,

Richard I the Lionhearted of England (1189–1199), and Philip II Augustus, king of France. Some of the crusaders finally arrived in the Holy Land by 1189 only to encounter problems. Frederick Barbarossa drowned while swimming in a local river, and his army quickly disintegrated. The English and French arrived by sea and met with success against the coastal cities, where they had the support of their fleets, but when they moved inland, they failed miserably. Eventually, after Philip went home, Richard the Lionhearted negotiated a settlement whereby Saladin agreed to allow Christian pilgrims free access to Jerusalem.

12–3b The Later Crusades

After the death of Saladin in 1193, Pope Innocent III initiated the Fourth Crusade. On its way east, the crusading army became involved in a dispute over the succession to the Byzantine throne. Although some historians believe the Venetian leaders of the Fourth Crusade saw an opportunity to neutralize their greatest commercial competitor, the Byzantine Empire, it is more likely that a series of unfortunate circumstances and misunderstandings led the western crusaders to sack the great capital city of Constantinople in 1204 and set up the new Latin Empire of Constantinople (see Chapter 13). Not until 1261 did a Byzantine army recapture Constantinople. In the meantime, additional crusades were undertaken to reconquer the Holy Land. All of them were largely disasters, and by the end of the thirteenth century, the European military effort to capture Palestine was recognized as a complete failure.

HISTORIANS DEBATE 12–3c What Were the Effects of the Crusades?

Whether the crusades had much effect on European civilization is debatable. The crusaders made little long-term impact on the Middle East, where the only visible remnants of their conquests were their castles. There may have been some broadening of perspective that comes from the exchange between two cultures, but the interaction of Christian Europe with the Muslim world was actually both more intense and more meaningful in Spain and Sicily than in the Holy Land. Nevertheless, some historians believe that there was some influence of the crusades on Europe's intellectual development with the absorption of the advanced science and learning of the Islamic world.

Did the crusades help stabilize European society by removing large numbers of young warriors who would have fought each other in Europe? Some historians think so and believe that

Western monarchs established their control more easily as a result. However, as we have seen, historians today doubt this and argue that it was the wealthy and pious nobles who risked their lives and fortunes to help their fellow Christians. Taking the cross as a religious incentive was important to many nobles. As one prayed, "Lord, take me from wars between Christians in which I have spent much of my life; let me die in your service so I may share your kingdom in Paradise"[13]

There is no doubt that the crusades did contribute to the economic growth of the Italian port cities, especially Genoa, Pisa, and Venice. But it is important to remember that the growing wealth and population of twelfth-century Europe had made the crusades possible in the first place. The crusades may have enhanced Italian trade in the Mediterranean, but they certainly did not cause the revival of trade. Even without the crusades, Italian merchants would have pursued new trade contacts with the eastern world. Moreover, there was little economic gain for many crusaders, most of whom did not settle in the east but returned home after their initial success. Many faced economic ruin after selling their lands to finance their expeditions.

Did the crusades have side effects that would haunt European society for generations? The crusades did not lead, as some historians have suggested, to the decline of the Muslim world, which had little interest in the crusades during the Middle Ages; after all, once united, the Muslim world had ended the crusader states in the Middle East. Not until the twentieth century, after believers in Western imperialism redefined the crusades as the first effort of Western colonialism, did many in the Islamic world begin to view the crusades as the first attempt of Western powers to colonize the Middle East, helping to lead to the troubled relationship between the Muslim world and the West today.

Another possible side effect is more apparent. The first widespread attacks on the Jews began with the crusades. As some Christians argued, to undertake holy wars against infidel Muslims while the "murderers of Christ" ran free at home was unthinkable. With the crusades, the massacre of Jews became a regular feature of medieval European life.

CHAPTER SUMMARY

After the collapse of the Han dynasty in the third century CE, China experienced nearly four centuries of internal chaos until the Tang Dynasty in the seventh century CE attempted to follow the pattern of the Han dynasty and restore the power of the Chinese Empire. The fall of the Western Roman Empire in the fifth century brought a quite different result as three new civilizations emerged out of the collapse of Roman power in the Mediterranean. A new world of Islam emerged in the east; it occupied large parts of the old Roman Empire and created its own flourishing civilization. As we shall see in Chapter 13, the eastern part of the old Roman Empire, increasingly Greek in culture, continued to survive as the Christian Byzantine Empire. At the same time, a new Christian European civilization

was establishing its roots in the West. By the eleventh and twelfth centuries, these three heirs of Rome began their own conflict for control of the lands of the eastern Mediterranean.

The coronation of Charlemagne, the descendant of a Germanic tribe converted to Christianity, as emperor of the Romans in 800 symbolized the fusion of the three chief components of the new European civilization: the German tribes, the Roman legacy, and the Christian church. Charlemagne's Carolingian Empire fostered the idea of a distinct European identity.

With the disintegration of that empire, however, power fell into the hands of many different lords, who came to constitute a nobility that dominated Europe's political, economic, and social life. But within this world of castles and private power, during the High Middle Ages kings gradually began to develop the machinery of government and accumulate political authority. Although they could not know it then, the actions of these medieval monarchs laid the foundation for the European states that in one form or another have dominated the European political scene ever since.

European civilization began to flourish in the High Middle Ages. The revival of trade, the expansion of towns and cities, and the development of a money economy did not mean the end of a predominantly rural European society, but they did open the door to new ways to make a living and new opportunities for people to expand and enrich their lives. At the same time, the High Middle Ages also gave birth to a cultural revival that led to new centers of learning in the universities, to the use of reason to systematize the study of theology, and to a dramatic increase in the number and size of churches.

The Catholic Church shared in the challenge of new growth by reforming itself and striking out on a path toward greater papal power, both within the church and over European society. The High Middle Ages witnessed a spiritual renewal that enhanced papal leadership and the religious life of the clergy and laity. At the same time, this spiritual renewal also gave rise to the crusading "holy warrior," thereby creating an animosity between Christians and Muslims that still has repercussions to this day.

CHAPTER TIMELINE

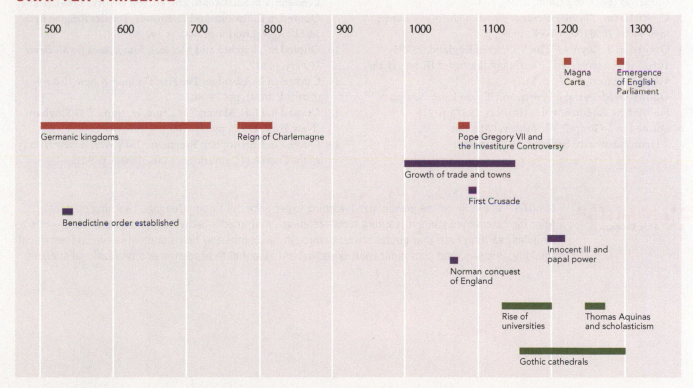

| 500 | 600 | 700 | 800 | 900 | 1000 | 1100 | 1200 | 1300 |

Germanic kingdoms

Reign of Charlemagne

Magna Carta

Emergence of English Parliament

Pope Gregory VII and the Investiture Controversy

Growth of trade and towns

Benedictine order established

First Crusade

Innocent III and papal power

Norman conquest of England

Rise of universities

Thomas Aquinas and scholasticism

Gothic cathedrals

CHAPTER REVIEW

Upon Reflection

Q What impact did the Vikings have on the history and culture of medieval Europe?

Q What are the major political developments in Europe during the Middle Ages, and how do they compare to developments in Asia, Africa, and the Middle East?

Q The medieval Catholic Church developed in the High Middle Ages at two levels—an institutional level and a popular religion level. What were the most important features of each level?

Key Terms

wergeld (p. 327)
diocese (p. 327)
monk (p. 328)
monasticism (p. 328)
abbot (p. 328)
nuns (p. 329)
abbesses (p. 329)
vassals (p. 331)
fief (p. 332)
subinfeudation (p. 332)
manor (p. 333)
serfs (p. 333)
demesne (p. 333)
aristocracy (p. 334)

chivalry (p. 334)
capitalism (p. 336)
commune (p. 338)
guilds (p. 340)
common law (p. 341)
lay investiture (p. 345)
interdict (p. 346)
sacraments (p. 346)
heresy (p. 347)
liberal arts (p. 349)
scholasticism (p. 350)
Romanesque (p. 350)
Gothic (p. 350)

Chapter Notes

1. Quoted in N. F. Cantor, ed., *The Medieval World, 300–1300* (New York, 1963), p. 104.
2. A. Barbero, *Charlemagne: Father of a Continent*, trans. A. Cameron (Berkeley, Calif., 2004), p. 4.
3. C. Wickham, *The Inheritance of Rome: A History of Europe from 400 to 1000* (New York, 2009), p. 4.
4. Quoted in S. Keynes, "The Vikings in England, c. 790–1016," in P. Sawyer, ed., *The Oxford Illustrated History of the Vikings* (Oxford, 1997), p. 81.
5. Quoted in M. Perry, J. Peden, and T. von Laue, *Sources of the Western Tradition*, vol. 1 (Boston, 1987), p. 218.
6. Quoted in J. Gimpel, *The Medieval Machine* (Harmondsworth, England, 1977), p. 92.
7. O. J. Thatcher and E. H. McNeal, eds., *A Source Book for Medieval History* (New York, 1905), p. 208.
8. Quoted in R. H. C. Davis, *A History of Medieval Europe from Constantine to Saint Louis*, 2nd ed. (New York, 1988), p. 252.
9. Quoted in R. Brooke and C. Brooke, *Popular Religion in the Middle Ages* (London, 1984), p. 19.
10. Quoted in Thatcher and McNeal, *Source Book for Medieval History*, p. 517.
11. Quoted in T. Asbridge, *The First Crusade: A New History* (Oxford, 2004), pp. 79–80.
12. Quoted in H. E. Mayer, *The Crusades*, trans. J. Gillingham (New York, 1972), pp. 99–100.
13. Quoted in Christopher Tyerman, *God's War: A New History of the Crusades* (Cambridge, Mass., 2006), p. 921.

MindTap® is a fully online personalized learning experience built upon Cengage Learning content. MindTap® combines student learning tools—readings, multimedia, activities, and assessments—into a singular Learning Path that guides students through the course and helps students develop the critical thinking, analysis, and communication skills that are essential to academic and professional success.

CHAPTER 13

THE BYZANTINE EMPIRE AND CRISIS AND RECOVERY IN THE WEST

Chapter Outline and Focus Questions

13–1 *From Eastern Roman to Byzantine Empire*

Q How did the Byzantine Empire that had emerged by the eighth century differ from the empire of Justinian and from the Germanic kingdoms in the West? How were they alike?

13–2 *The Zenith of Byzantine Civilization (750–1025)*

Q What were the chief developments in the Byzantine Empire between 750 and 1025?

13–3 *The Decline and Fall of the Byzantine Empire (1025–1453)*

Q What impact did the crusades have on the Byzantine Empire? How and why did Constantinople and the Byzantine Empire fall?

13–4 *The Crises of the Fourteenth Century in the West*

Q What impact did the Black Death have on Europe and Asia in the fourteenth century? What problems did Europeans face during the fourteenth century, and what impact did these crises have on European economic, social, and religious life?

13–5 *Recovery: The Renaissance*

Q What were the main features of the Renaissance in Europe, and how did it differ from the Middle Ages?

Justinian and Theodora. Scala/Art Resource, NY

Critical Thinking

Q *In what ways did the Byzantine, European, and Islamic civilizations resemble and differ from each other? Were their relationships generally based on cooperation or conflict?*

Connections to Today

Q *How is the concept of the Renaissance relevant to the early twenty-first century?*

AT THE SAME TIME that medieval European civilization was emerging in the West, the Eastern part of the Late Roman Empire, increasingly Greek in culture, continued to survive. While serving as a buffer between Europe and the peoples to the East, especially the growing empire of Islam, the Late Roman Empire in the East (Byzantine Empire) also preserved the intellectual and legal accomplishments of the Greeks and Romans.

In its early decades, the Eastern Roman Empire was beset by crises. Soon after the beginning of his reign, the emperor Justinian was faced with a serious revolt in the capital city of Constantinople. In 532, two factions, called the Blues and the Greens because they supported chariot teams bearing those colors when they competed in the Hippodrome (a huge amphitheater), joined together and rioted to protest the emperor's taxation policies. The riots soon became a revolt as insurgents burned and looted the center of the city, shouting "*Nika!*" (victory), the word normally used to cheer on their favorite teams.

Aristocratic factions joined the revolt and put forward a nobleman named Hypatius as a new emperor. Justinian seemed ready to flee, but his wife, the empress Theodora, strengthened his resolve by declaring, according to the historian Procopius, "If now, it is your wish to save yourself, O Emperor, there is no difficulty. For we have much money, and there is the sea, here the boats. However, consider whether it will not come about after you have been saved that you would gladly exchange that safety for death. As for myself, I approve a certain ancient saying that royalty is a good burial-shroud."[1] Shamed by his wife's words, Justinian resolved to fight. He ordered troops, newly returned from fighting the Persians, to attack a large crowd that had gathered in the Hippodrome to acclaim Hypatius as emperor. In the ensuing massacre, the imperial troops slaughtered 30,000 of the insurgents, about 5 percent of the city's population. After crushing the Nika Revolt, Justinian began a massive rebuilding program and continued the autocratic reign that established the foundations of the Byzantine Empire (as it came to be known beginning in the eighth century).

Despite the early empire's reversals, the Macedonian emperors in the ninth, tenth, and eleventh centuries enlarged the empire, achieved economic prosperity, and expanded its cultural influence to Eastern Europe and Russia. But after the Macedonian Dynasty ended in 1056 CE, the empire began a slow but steady decline. Involvement in the crusades proved especially disastrous, leading to the occupation of Constantinople by Western crusading forces in 1204. Byzantine rule was restored in 1261, and the empire survived in a weakened condition for another 190 years until the Ottoman Turks finally conquered it in 1453.

In the fourteenth century, Europe, too, sustained a series of crises and reversals after flourishing during the three centuries of the High Middle Ages. Unlike the Byzantine Empire, however, European civilization rebounded in the fifteenth century, experiencing an artistic and intellectual revival in the Renaissance as well as a renewal of monarchical authority among the Western European states. Europe was poised to begin its dramatic entry into world affairs.

13–1 FROM EASTERN ROMAN TO BYZANTINE EMPIRE

 Focus Questions: How did the Byzantine Empire that had emerged by the eighth century differ from the empire of Justinian and from the Germanic kingdoms in the West? How were they alike?

As noted earlier, the Western and Eastern parts of the Roman Empire began to drift apart in the fourth century. As the Germanic peoples moved into the Western part of the empire and established various kingdoms over the course of the fifth century, the Late Roman Empire in the East solidified and prospered.

Constantinople, the imperial capital, viewed itself not only as the center of a world empire but also as a special Christian city. The inhabitants believed that the city was under the protection of God and the Virgin Mary. One thirteenth-century Byzantine said: "About our city you shall know: until the end she will fear no nation whatsoever, for no one will entrap or capture her, not by any means, for she has been given to the Mother of God and no one will snatch her out of Her hands. Many nations will break their horns against her walls and withdraw with shame."[2] The Byzantines saw their state as a Christian empire protected by God and the Virgin Mary.

13–1a The Reign of Justinian (527–565)

In the sixth century, the empire in the East came under the control of one of its most remarkable rulers, the emperor Justinian (juh-STIN-ee-un). As the nephew and heir of the previous emperor, Justinian had been well trained in imperial administration. He was determined to reestablish the Roman Empire in the entire Mediterranean world and began his attempt to reconquer the West in 533.

Justinian's army under Belisarius (bell-uh-SAH-ree-uss), probably the best general of the late Roman world, presented a formidable force. Belisarius sailed to North Africa and quickly defeated the Vandals in two major battles. From North Africa, he led his forces onto the Italian peninsula after occupying Sicily in 535. But it was not until 552 that the Ostrogoths were finally defeated. The struggle devastated Italy, which suffered more from Justinian's reconquest than from all of the previous barbarian invasions.

Justinian has long been criticized for overextending his resources and bankrupting the empire. Historians now think, however, that a devastating plague in 542 and long-term economic factors were far more damaging to the Eastern Roman Empire than Justinian's conquests. Before he died, Justinian appeared to have achieved his goals. He had restored the imperial Mediterranean world; his empire included Italy, part of Spain, North Africa, Asia Minor, Palestine, and Syria (see Map 13.1). But the conquest of the Western empire proved fleeting. Only three years after Justinian's death, another Germanic people, the Lombards, entered Italy. Although the Eastern empire maintained the fiction of Italy as a province, its forces were limited to small pockets here and there.

The Codification of Roman Law Though his conquests proved short-lived, Justinian made a lasting contribution to Western civilization through his codification of Roman law. The Eastern empire was heir to a vast quantity of materials connected to the development of Roman law. These included laws passed by the senate and assemblies, legal commentaries of jurists, decisions of praetors, and the edicts of emperors. Justinian had been well trained in imperial government and was thoroughly acquainted with Roman law. He wished to codify and simplify this mass of materials.

To accomplish his goal, Justinian authorized the jurist Trebonian to make a systematic compilation of imperial edicts. The result was the Code of Law, the first part of the *Corpus Iuris Civilis* (KOR-pus YOOR-iss SIV-i-liss) (Body of Civil Law), completed in 529. Four years later, two other parts of the *Corpus* appeared: the *Digest*, a compendium of writings of Roman jurists, and the *Institutes*, a brief summary of the chief principles of Roman law that could be used as a textbook. The fourth part of the *Corpus* was the *Novels*, a compilation of the most important new edicts issued during Justinian's reign.

Justinian's codification of Roman law became the basis of imperial law in the Byzantine Empire until its end in 1453. More important, however, since it was written in Latin (it was, in fact, the last product of Eastern Roman culture to be written in Latin, which was soon replaced by Greek), it was also eventually used in the West and in fact became the basis of the legal system of all of continental Europe.

The Empress Theodora Theodora (thee-uh-DOR-uh) was the daughter of the "keeper of bears" for the games at Constantinople, who died when Theodora was a child. Theodora followed in her mother's footsteps by becoming an actress, which at that time was considered a lower-class activity. Often actresses also worked as prostitutes, and Theodora was no exception. At the age of twenty-five, she met Justinian, who was forty. His uncle, the emperor Justin, had to change the law to allow an aristocratic senator to marry a woman who had been an actress. After his uncle died in 527, Justinian became emperor and Theodora empress, a remarkable achievement for a woman from the lower classes.

Justinian and Theodora were close and loving companions. She also influenced her husband in both church and state affairs. A strong-willed and intelligent woman, she proved especially valuable in 532, when her steely resolve during the Nika Revolt convinced Justinian to fight and crush the protesters rather than to flee. Theodora also helped establish a number of churches and monasteries, including a convent for former prostitutes.

Map 13.1 The Eastern Roman Empire in the Time of Justinian. The Eastern Roman emperor Justinian briefly restored much of the Mediterranean portion of the old Roman Empire. His general, Belisarius, conquered the Vandals in North Africa quite easily but wrested Italy from the Ostrogoths only after a long and devastating struggle.

Q *Look back at Map 5.3, Section 5-2b, p. 143. What former Roman territories lay outside Justinian's control?*

The Emperor Justinian and His Court. As the seat of late Roman power in Italy, the town of Ravenna was adorned with examples of late Roman art. The Church of San Vitale at Ravenna contains some of the finest examples of sixth-century mosaics. Small pieces of colored glass were set in mortar on the wall to form these figures and their surroundings. The emperor is seen as both head of state (he wears a jeweled crown and a purple robe) and head of the church (he carries a gold bowl symbolizing the body of Jesus).

The Emperor's Building Program After the riots destroyed much of Constantinople, Justinian rebuilt the city and gave it the appearance it would keep for almost a thousand years (see

Map 13.2 Constantinople. In the Middle Ages, Constantinople was the largest European city and a nexus of trade between East and West. Emperor Justinian oversaw a massive building program that produced important architectural monuments such as Hagia Sophia.

Q *What natural and human-built aspects of the city helped protect it from invasion?*

Map 13.2). Earlier, Emperor Theodosius (thee-uh-DOH-shuss) II (408–450) had constructed an enormous defensive wall to protect the capital on its land side. The city was dominated by an immense palace complex, a huge arena known as the Hippodrome, and hundreds of churches. No residential district was particularly fashionable; palaces, tenements, and slums ranged alongside one another. Justinian added many new buildings. His public works projects included roads, bridges, walls, public baths, law courts, and colossal underground reservoirs to hold the city's water supply. He also built hospitals, schools, monasteries, and churches. Churches were his special passion, and in Constantinople he built or rebuilt thirty-four of them. His greatest achievement was the famous Hagia Sophia (HAG-ee-uh soh-FEE-uh), the Church of the Holy Wisdom.

Completed in 537, Hagia Sophia was designed by two Greek scientists who departed radically from the simple, flat-roofed basilica of Western architecture. The center of Hagia Sophia consisted of four huge piers crowned by an enormous dome, which seemed to be floating in space. This effect was emphasized by Procopius (pruh-KOH-pee-uss), the court historian, who at Justinian's request wrote a treatise on the emperor's building projects: "From the lightness of the building,

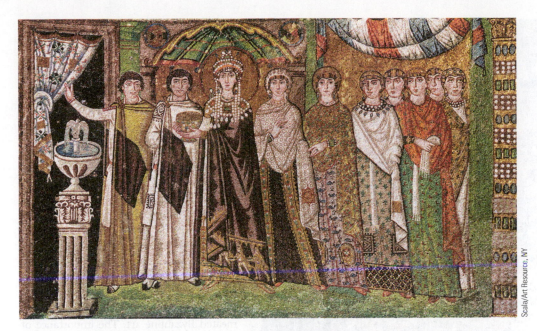

Theodora and Attendants. This mosaic, located on the south wall of the apse of the Church of San Vitale (Justinian is on the north wall), depicts Theodora and her attendants. Her presence on the wall of this church indicates the important role she played in the late Roman state. At the bottom of her robe is a scene of the Three Wise Men, an indication that Theodora was special enough to have belonged in the company of the three kings who visited the newborn Jesus.

it does not appear to rest upon a solid foundation, but to cover the place beneath as though it were suspended from heaven by the fabled golden chain." In part, this impression was created by putting forty-two windows around the base of the dome, which allowed an incredible play of light within the cathedral. Light served to remind the worshipers of God; as Procopius commented:

> Whoever enters there to worship perceives at once that it is not by any human strength or skill, but by the favor of God that this work has been perfected; his mind rises sublime to commune with God, feeling that He cannot be far off, but must especially love to dwell in the place which He has chosen; and this takes place not only when a man sees it for the first time, but it always makes the same impression upon him, as though he had never beheld it before.[3]

As darkness is illuminated by invisible light, so too, it was believed, the world is illuminated by invisible spirit.

The royal palace complex, Hagia Sophia, and the Hippodrome were the three greatest buildings in Constantinople. This last was a huge amphitheater, constructed of brick covered by marble, holding as many as 60,000 spectators. Although gladiator fights were held there, the main events were the chariot races; twenty-four would usually be presented in one day. The citizens of Constantinople were passionate fans of chariot racing. Successful charioteers were acclaimed as heroes and honored with public statues. Crowds in the Hippodrome also took on political significance. Being a member of the two chief factions of charioteers—the Blues or the Greens—was the only real outlet for political expression. Even emperors had to be aware of their demands and attitudes: the loss of a race in the Hippodrome frequently resulted in bloody riots that could threaten the emperor's power.

13–1b A New Kind of Empire

Justinian's accomplishments had been spectacular, but when he died, he left the Eastern Roman Empire with serious problems: too much distant territory to protect, an empty treasury, a smaller population after a devastating plague, and renewed threats to the frontiers. The seventh century proved to be an important turning point in the history of the empire.

Problems of the Seventh Century In the first half of the century, during the reign of Heraclius (he-ruh-KLY-uss *or* huh-RAK-lee-uss) (610–641), the empire faced attacks from the Persians to the East and the Slavs to the north. A new system of defense was put in place, using a new and larger administrative unit, the *theme*, which combined civilian and military offices in the hands of the same person. Thus, the civil governor was also the military leader of the area. Although this innovation helped the empire survive, it also fostered an increased militarization of the empire. By the mid-seventh century, it had become apparent that a restored Mediterranean empire was simply beyond the resources of the Eastern empire, which now increasingly turned its back on the Latin West. A renewed series of external threats in the second half of the seventh century strengthened this development.

The most serious challenge to the empire was the rise of Islam, which unified the Arab tribes and created a powerful new force that swept through the region (see Chapter 7). The defeat of an Eastern Roman army near the Yarmuk River in 636 meant the loss of the provinces of Syria and Palestine. The Arabs also moved into the old Persian Empire and conquered

Interior View of Hagia Sophia. Pictured here is the interior of the Church of the Holy Wisdom in Constantinople (modern Istanbul), constructed under Justinian by Anthemius of Tralles (an-THEE-mee-uss of TRAL-leez) and Isidore of Miletus (IH-zuh-dor of mih-LEE-tuss). Some of the stones used in the construction of the church had been plundered from the famous Classical Temple of Diana, near Ephesus, in Asia Minor (modern Turkey). This view gives an idea of how the windows around the base of the dome produced a special play of light within the cathedral. The pulpits and plaques bearing inscriptions from the Qur'an were introduced when the Turks converted this church to a mosque in the fifteenth century.

that would last until 1453 (Constantinople was built on the site of an older city named Byzantium—hence the name *Byzantine*).

The Byzantine Empire in the Eighth Century The Byzantine Empire was a Greek state. Justinian's *Corpus Iuris Civilis* had been the last official work published in Latin. Increasingly, Latin fell into disuse as Greek became not only the common language of the Byzantine Empire but its official language as well.

The Byzantine Empire was also a Christian state, built on a faith in Jesus that was shared in a profound way by almost all its citizens. An enormous amount of artistic talent was poured into the construction of churches, church ceremonies, and church decoration. Spiritual principles deeply permeated Byzantine art. The importance of religion to the Byzantines explains why theological disputes took on an exaggerated form. The most famous of these disputes, the so-called iconoclastic controversy, threatened the stability of the empire in the first half of the eighth century.

Beginning in the sixth century, the use of religious images, especially in the form of icons or pictures of sacred figures, became so widespread that charges of idolatry, the worship of images, began to be heard. The use of images or icons had been justified by the argument that icons were not worshiped but were simply used to help illiterate people understand their religion. This argument failed to stop the **iconoclasts**, as the opponents of icons were called.

Iconoclasm was not unique to the Byzantine Empire. In the neighboring Islamic empire, religious art did not include any physical representations of Muhammad (see Comparative Illustration "Religious Imagery in the Medieval World"). Iconoclasm would also play a role among some of the new religious groups that emerged in the Protestant Reformation in sixteenth-century Europe (see Chapter 15).

it. An Arab attempt to besiege Constantinople that began in 674 failed, in large part due to the use of Greek fire against the Arab fleets. Greek fire was a petroleum-based compound containing quicklime and sulfur. Because it would burn under water, the Byzantines created the equivalent of modern flamethrowers by using tubes to blow Greek fire onto wooden ships, with frightening effect. Arabs and Eastern Roman forces now faced each other along a frontier in southern Asia Minor.

Problems also arose along the northern frontier, especially in the Balkans, where an Asiatic people known as the Bulgars had arrived earlier in the sixth century. In 679, the Bulgars defeated the Eastern Roman forces and took possession of the lower Danube Valley, setting up a strong Bulgarian kingdom.

By the beginning of the eighth century, the Eastern Roman Empire was greatly diminished in size, consisting only of a portion of the Balkans and Asia Minor. It was now an Eastern Mediterranean state. These external challenges had important internal repercussions as well. By the eighth century, the Eastern Roman Empire had been transformed into what historians call the Byzantine Empire, a civilization with its own unique character

The Byzantine Empire, c. 750

A

Art Resource, NY

B

Erich Lessing/Art Resource, NY

COMPARATIVE ILLUSTRATION

Art & Ideas **Religious Imagery in the Medieval World.** The Middle Ages was a golden age of religious art, reflecting the important role of religion itself in medieval society. These three illustrations show different aspects of medieval religious imagery. In Europe, much Christian art appeared in illuminated manuscripts. Illustration A shows a page depicting the figure of Jesus from *The Book of Kells*, a richly decorated manuscript of the Christian gospels produced by the monks of Iona in the British Isles. Byzantine art was also deeply religious, as was especially evident in icons. Illustration B is an icon of the Virgin and Child (Mary and Jesus) from the monastery of Saint Catherine at Mount Sinai in Egypt dating to around the year 600. Painted on wood, this icon shows the enthroned Virgin and Child between Saints Theodore and George with two angels behind them looking upward to a beam of light containing the hand of God. The figures are not realistic; the goal of the icon was to bridge the gap between the divine and the outer material world. Artists in the Muslim world faced a different challenge—Muslims warned against imitating God by creating pictures of living beings, thus effectively prohibiting the representation of humans, especially Muhammad. Islamic religious artists therefore used decorative motifs based on geometric patterns and the Arabic script. The scriptural panel in illustration C is an artistic presentation of a verse from the Qur'an, thus blending the spiritual and artistic spheres.

C

Vanni Archive/Art Resource, NY

Q *How is the importance of religious imagery in the Middle Ages evident in these three illustrations?*

Beginning in 730, the Byzantine emperor Leo III (717–741) outlawed the use of icons. Strong resistance ensued, especially from monks. Leo also used the iconoclastic controversy to add to the prestige of the patriarch of Constantinople, the highest church official in the East and second in dignity only to the bishop of Rome. The Roman popes were opposed to the iconoclastic edicts, and their opposition created considerable dissension between the popes and the Byzantine emperors. Late in the eighth century, the Byzantine rulers reversed their stand on the use of images, but not before considerable damage had been done to the unity of the Christian church. Although the final separation between Roman Catholicism and Greek Orthodoxy (as the Christian church in the Byzantine Empire was called) did not occur until 1054, the iconoclastic controversy was important in moving both sides in that direction.

The Byzantine Emperor The emperor occupied a crucial position in the Byzantine state. Portrayed as chosen by God, the Byzantine emperor was crowned in elaborate sacred ceremonies, and his subjects were expected to prostrate themselves in his presence. The wives of the emperors also played significant roles in the court rituals that upheld imperial authority.

The importance of court ritual is apparent in the *Book of Ceremonies*, a tenth-century compendium of imperial ceremonies and court rituals. Court ritual could be very complicated and included a variety of activities. Everyday rituals included the daily opening of the imperial palace: imperial officials, all arranged in order of rank, waited until the palace doors were officially opened; then they marched into the palace in a procession. A similar ceremony was held for the opening of the palace in the afternoon. In addition to these regular daily ceremonies, special ceremonies involving specific rituals were held on many occasions, including the emperor's birthday, the promotion of officials, imperial marriages, and commemorations of important military battles. The emperor was also required to participate in the ceremonies held regularly in the churches on important saints' days and during church festivals.

The power of the Byzantine emperor was considered absolute and was limited in practice only by assassination. A rather unusual ruling class assisted the emperors. Civil servants and high churchmen essentially stemmed from the same ranks of the urban society of Constantinople. They received the same education and often followed the same careers in civil service

until they went their separate ways into church and government offices. A strong bureaucracy was one of the most basic features of the Byzantine Empire.

The Byzantine Empire was characterized by what might be called a permanent war economy. Byzantine emperors maintained the late Roman policy of state regulation of economic affairs. Of course, this practice was easy to justify: the survival of the empire depended on careful shepherding of economic resources and the maintenance of the army. Thus, the state encouraged agricultural production, regulated the guilds or corporations responsible for industrial production and the various stages of manufacturing, and controlled commerce by making trade in grain and silk, the two most valuable products, government monopolies.

In addition, because of their many foreign enemies, Byzantine emperors spent considerable energy on war and preparation for war. Manuals on war, providing instruction in the ways of fighting, were a common type of Byzantine literature (see "A Byzantine Emperor Gives Military Advice"). Byzantine armies, often led by the emperors, were well trained and equipped with the latest weapons. The Byzantines, however, often preferred to secure their goals through diplomacy rather than fighting. Our word *byzantine*—often defined as "extremely complicated" or "carried on by underhanded methods"—stems from the complex and crafty instructions that Byzantine rulers sent to their envoys.

Because the emperor appointed the patriarch, he also exercised control over both church and state. The Byzantines believed that God had commanded their state to preserve the true faith, Orthodox Christianity. Emperor, clergy, and civic officials were all bound together in service to this ideal. It can be said that spiritual values truly held the Byzantine state together.

By 750, it was apparent that two of Rome's heirs, the Germanic kingdoms and the Byzantine Empire, were moving in different directions. Nevertheless, Byzantine influence on the Western world was significant. The images of a Roman imperial state that continued to haunt the West lived on in Byzantium. As noted, the legal system of the West came to owe much to Justinian's codification of Roman law. In addition, the Byzantine Empire served in part as a buffer state, protecting the West for a long time from incursions from the East.

Intellectual Life The intellectual life of the Byzantine Empire was greatly influenced by the traditions of Classical civilization. Scholars actively strived to preserve the works of the ancient Greeks and based a great deal of their own literature on Classical models. Although the Byzantines produced a substantial body of literature, much of it was of a very practical nature, focusing on legal, military, and administrative matters. The most outstanding literary achievements of the empire's early centuries, however, were historical and religious works. Many of the latter were theological treatises, often of an extremely combative nature because of the intense theological controversies. More popular were biographies of saints, which traced the adventures of religious figures who after many struggles achieved a life of virtue.

The empire's best-known historian was Procopius (c. 500–c. 562), court historian during the reign of Justinian.

CHRONOLOGY	The Eastern Roman/Byzantine Empire to 750
Justinian codifies Roman law	529–533
Reconquest of Italy by Justinian	535–552
Completion of Hagia Sophia	537
Attacks on the empire in the reign of Heraclius	610–641
Arab defeat of the Byzantines at Yarmuk	636
Defeat by the Bulgars; losses in the Balkans	679
Leo III and iconoclasm	717–741

A BYZANTINE EMPEROR GIVES MILITARY ADVICE

Politics & Government

TO AN EMPIRE SURROUNDED BY ENEMIES on all sides, military prowess was an absolute necessity. Both Byzantine emperors and the ruling elite, however, also realized that military forces alone would not suffice and consequently fostered the art of diplomacy and military intelligence. This document is from an early seventh-century work known as the *Strategikon* (stra-TEE-jih-kahn), a manual of strategy written by the emperor Maurice (582–602), himself a strong military leader who led his troops into battle. The work is based on the assumption that a detailed knowledge of the habits and fighting skills of their enemies would give the Byzantines an advantage if they had to fight them.

Maurice, *Strategikon*

The light-haired races [Germanic peoples] place great value on freedom. They are bold and undaunted in battle. Daring and impetuous as they are, they consider any timidity and even a short retreat as a disgrace. They calmly despise death as they fight violently in hand-to-hand combat either on horseback or on foot. If they are hard pressed in cavalry actions, they dismount at a single prearranged sign and line up on foot. Although only a few against many horsemen, they do not shrink from the fight. They are armed with shields, lances, and short swords slung from their shoulders. They prefer fighting on foot and rapid charges.

Whether on foot or on horseback, they draw up for battle, not in any fixed measure and formation, or in regiments or divisions, but according to tribes, their kinship with one another, and common interest. Often, as a result, when things are not going well and their friends have been killed, they will risk their lives fighting to avenge them. In combat they make the front of their battle line even and dense. Either on horseback or on foot they are impetuous and undisciplined in charging, as if they were the only people in the world who are not cowards. They are disobedient to their leaders. They are not interested in anything that is at all complicated and pay little attention to external security and their own advantage. They despise good order, especially on horseback. They are easily corrupted by money, greedy as they are.

They are hurt by suffering and fatigue. Although they possess bold and daring spirits, their bodies are pampered and soft, and they are not able to bear pain calmly. In addition, they are hurt by heat, cold, rain, lack of provisions, especially of wine, and postponement of battle. When it comes to a cavalry battle, they are hindered by uneven and wooded terrain. They are easily ambushed along the flanks and to the rear of their battle line, for they do not concern themselves at all with scouts and the other security measures. Their ranks are easily broken by a simulated flight and a sudden turning back against them.. . . .

Above all, therefore, in warring against them one must avoid engaging in pitched battles, especially in the early stages. Instead, make use of well-planned ambushes, sneak attacks, and stratagems. Delay things and ruin their opportunities. Pretend to come to agreements with them. Aim at reducing their boldness and zeal by shortage of provisions or the discomfort of heat or cold. This can be done when our army has pitched camp on rugged and difficult ground. On such terrain this enemy cannot attack successfully because they are using lances. But if a favorable opportunity for a regular battle occurs, line up the army as set forth in the book on formations.

 What did Maurice identify as the strengths and weaknesses of the Germanic peoples? Based on his analysis of their traits, what did he advise his military forces to do if they faced the Germans in battle?

Source: George T. Dennis, trans. *Maurice's Strategikon: Handbook of Byzantine Military Strategy*, Book 11 (Philadelphia: University of Pennsylvania Press, 1984), pp. 118–119.

Procopius served as secretary to the great general Belisarius and accompanied him on his wars on behalf of Justinian. Procopius's best historical work, the *Wars*, is a firsthand account of Justinian's wars of reconquest in the Western Mediterranean and his wars against the Persians in the East. Deliberately modeled after the work of his hero, the Greek historian Thucydides (see Chapter 4), Procopius's narrative features vivid descriptions of battle scenes, clear judgment, and noteworthy objectivity.

Life in Constantinople: The Importance of Trade With a population in the hundreds of thousands, Constantinople was the largest city in Europe during the Middle Ages. Until the twelfth century, Constantinople was also Europe's greatest commercial center. The city was the chief entrepôt for the exchange of products between West and East, and trade formed the basis for its fabulous prosperity. Foreign merchants, however, largely carried on this trade. As one contemporary said:

> All sorts of merchants come here from the land of Babylon, from . . . Persia, Media, and all the sovereignty of the land of Egypt, from the lands of Canaan, and from the empire of Russia, from Hungaria, Khazaria [the Caspian region], and the land of Lombardy and Sepharad [Spain]. It is a busy city, and merchants come to it from every country by sea or land, and there is none like it in the world except Baghdad, the great city of Islam.[4]

Highly desired in Europe were the products of the East: silk from China, spices from Southeast Asia and India, jewelry and ivory from India (used by artisans for church items), wheat and furs from southern Russia, and flax and honey from the Balkans. Many of these Eastern goods were then shipped to the Mediterranean area and northern Europe. Despite the Germanic incursions, trade with Europe did not entirely end.

Moreover, imported raw materials were used in Constantinople for local industries. During Justinian's reign, two Christian monks smuggled silkworms from China to begin a silk industry. The state had a monopoly on the production of silk cloth, and the workshops themselves were housed in Constantinople's royal palace complex. European demand for silk cloth made it the city's most lucrative product. It is interesting to note that the upper classes, including emperors and empresses, were not discouraged from making money through trade and manufacturing. Indeed, one empress even manufactured perfumes in her bedroom.

13–2 THE ZENITH OF BYZANTINE CIVILIZATION (750–1025)

 Focus Question: What were the chief developments in the Byzantine Empire between 750 and 1025?

In the seventh and eighth centuries, the Byzantine Empire lost much of its territory to Slavs, Bulgars, and Muslims. By 750, the empire consisted only of Asia Minor, some lands in the Balkans, and the southern coast of Italy. Although Byzantium was beset with internal dissension and invasions in the ninth century, it was able to deal with them and not only endured but even expanded, reaching its high point in the tenth century, which some historians have called the golden age of Byzantine civilization.

13–2a The Beginning of a Revival

During the reign of Michael III (842–867), the Byzantine Empire began to experience a revival. Iconoclasm was finally abolished in 843, and reforms were made in education, church life, the military, and the peasant economy. There was a noticeable intellectual renewal. But the empire was still plagued by persistent problems. The Bulgars mounted new attacks, and the Arabs continued to harass the periphery. Moreover, a new religious dispute with political repercussions erupted over differences between the pope as leader of the Western Christian church and the patriarch of Constantinople as leader of the Eastern Christian church. Patriarch Photius (FOH-shuss) condemned the pope as a heretic for accepting a revised form of the Nicene Creed stating that the Holy Spirit proceeded from the Father and the Son instead of from the Father alone. A council of Eastern bishops followed Photius's wishes and excommunicated the pope, creating the so-called Photian schism. Although the differences were later papered over, this controversy

inserted a greater wedge between the Eastern and Western Christian churches.

13–2b The Macedonian Dynasty

The problems that arose during Michael's reign were effectively dealt with by a new dynasty of Byzantine emperors known as the Macedonians (867–1056). The founder of the dynasty, Basil I (867–886), was a Macedonian of uncertain background who came to Constantinople to improve his lot in life. After impressing Emperor Michael III with his wrestling skills, he married the emperor's mistress and was made co-emperor. One year later, he arranged the murder of Michael and then became sole ruler, establishing a dynasty that would last almost two hundred years.

The Macedonian Dynasty managed to hold off Byzantium's external enemies and reestablish domestic order. Supported by the church, the emperors thought of the Byzantine Empire as a continuation of the Christian Roman Empire of late antiquity. Although for diplomatic reasons they occasionally recognized the imperial titles of earlier Western emperors, such as Charlemagne and Otto I, they still regarded them as little more than barbarian parvenus.

Economic and Religious Policies The Macedonian emperors could boast of a remarkable number of achievements in the late ninth and tenth centuries. They worked to strengthen the position of the free farmers, who felt threatened by the attempts of landed aristocrats to expand their estates at the farmers' expense. The emperors were well aware that the free farmers made up the rank and file of the Byzantine cavalry and provided the military strength of the empire. Nevertheless, despite their efforts, the Macedonian emperors found that it was not easy to control the power of the landed nobles, and many free farmers continued to lose their lands to the nobles.

The Macedonian emperors also fostered a burst of economic prosperity by expanding trade relations with Western Europe, especially by selling silks and metalwork, and the city of Constantinople flourished. Foreign visitors continued to be astounded by its size, wealth, and physical surroundings. To Western Europeans, it was the stuff of legends and fables (see "A Western View of the Byzantine Empire").

In this period of prosperity, Byzantine cultural influence expanded due to the active missionary efforts of Eastern Byzantine Christians. Eastern Orthodox Christianity was spread to Eastern European peoples, such as the Bulgars and Serbs. Perhaps the greatest missionary success occurred when the prince of Kiev in Russia converted to Christianity in 987. From the end of the tenth century on, Byzantine Christianity became the model for Russian religious life, just as Byzantine imperial ideals came to influence the outward forms of Russian political life.

Political and Military Achievements Under the Macedonian rulers, Byzantium enjoyed a strong civil service, talented emperors, and military advances. Well-educated, competent aristocrats

A WESTERN VIEW OF THE BYZANTINE EMPIRE

Politics & Government

BISHOP LIUDPRAND OF CREMONA undertook diplomatic missions to Constantinople on behalf of two Western kings, Berengar of Italy and Otto I of Germany. This selection is taken from his description of his mission to the Byzantine emperor Constantine VII in 949 as an envoy for Berengar, king of Italy from 950 until his overthrow by Otto I of Germany in 964. Liudprand had mixed feelings about Byzantium: admiration, yet also envy and hostility because of its superior wealth.

Liudprand of Cremona, *Antapodosis*

Next to the imperial residence at Constantinople there is a palace of remarkable size and beauty. . . . In order to receive some Spanish envoys, who had recently arrived, as well as myself . . ., Constantine gave orders that this palace should be got ready. . . .

Before the emperor's seat stood a tree, made of bronze gilded over, whose branches were filled with birds, also made of gilded bronze, which uttered different cries, each according to its varying species. The throne itself was so marvelously fashioned that at one moment it seemed a low structure, and at another it rose high into the air. It was of immense size and was guarded by lions, made either of bronze or of wood covered over with gold, who beat the ground with their tails and gave a dreadful roar with open mouth and quivering tongue. Leaning upon the shoulders of two eunuchs I was brought into the emperor's presence. At my approach the lions began to roar and the birds to cry out, each according to its kind; but I was neither terrified nor surprised, for I had previously made enquiry about all these things from people who were well acquainted with them. So after I had three times [bowed] to the emperor with my face upon the ground, I lifted my head, and behold!

The man whom just before I had seen sitting on a moderately elevated seat had now changed his raiment and was sitting on the level of the ceiling. How it was done I could not imagine, unless perhaps he was lifted up by some such sort of device as we use for raising the timbers of a wine press. On that occasion he did not address me personally, . . . but by the intermediary of a secretary he enquired about Berengar's doings and asked after his health. I made a fitting reply and then, at a nod from the interpreter, left his presence and retired to my lodging.

It would give me some pleasure also to record here what I did then for Berengar. . . . The Spanish envoys . . . had brought handsome gifts from their masters to the emperor Constantine. I for my part had brought nothing from Berengar except a letter and that was full of lies. I was very greatly disturbed and shamed at this and began to consider anxiously what I had better do. . . . It finally occurred to me that I might offer the gifts, which on my account I had brought for the emperor, as coming from Berengar, and trick out my humble present with fine words. I therefore presented him with nine excellent cuirasses, seven excellent shields . . ., some swords, spears, and spits, and what was more precious to the emperor than anything, four carzimasia; that being the Greek name for young eunuchs who have had both their testicles and their penis removed. This operation is performed by traders who take the boys into Spain and make a huge profit.

Q *What impressions of the Byzantine court do you get from Liudprand's account? What is the modern meaning of the word byzantine? How does this account help explain the modern meaning of the word?*

Source: Excerpt from *Works of Liudprand of Cremona* by F. A. Wright, 1930, Routledge and Kegan Paul Publishers.

---

from Constantinople staffed the Byzantine civil service and oversaw the collection of taxes, domestic administration, and foreign policy. At the same time, the Macedonian Dynasty produced some truly outstanding emperors skilled in administration and law, including Leo VI and Constantine VII. Leo VI (886–912), known as Leo the Wise, was an accomplished scholar who composed works on politics and theology, systematized rules for regulating both trade and court officials, and arranged for a new codification of all Byzantine law. Constantine VII (945–959) wrote a detailed treatise on foreign policy to instruct his officials, as well as his son, on

The Byzantine Empire, 1025

running the empire wisely. Constantine also worked to reduce the tax burden on the peasants.

In the tenth century, competent emperors combined with a number of talented generals to mobilize the empire's military resources and take the offensive. Especially important was Basil II (976–1025), who campaigned regularly against the Bulgars. Although his first campaign was a failure, he continued his efforts until he defeated the Bulgars and annexed Bulgaria to the empire (see "The Achievements of Basil II," p. 368). After his final victory over the Bulgars in 1014, Basil blinded

THE ACHIEVEMENTS OF BASIL II

Politics & Government

BASIL II CAME TO POWER at the age of eighteen and during his long reign greatly enlarged the Byzantine Empire. An alliance with the Russian prince Vladimir was instrumental in bringing Orthodox Christianity to the Russians. We know a great deal about Basil II from an account by Michael Psellus (1018–c.1081), one of the foremost Byzantine historians. He wrote the *Chronographia*, a series of biographies of the Byzantine emperors from 976 to 1078, much of it based on his own observations. In this selection, Psellus discusses the qualities of Basil as a leader.

Michael Psellus, *Chronographia*

Having purged the empire of the barbarians [Bulgars] he dealt with his own subjects and completely subjugated them too—I think "subjugate" is the right word to describe it. He decided to abandon his former policy, and after the great families had been humiliated and put on an equal footing with the rest, Basil found himself playing the game of power-politics with considerable success. He surrounded himself with favorites who were neither remarkable for brilliance of intellect, nor of noble lineage, nor too learned. . . . [W]ith them he was accustomed to share the secrets of state. . . .

By humbling the pride or jealousy of his people, Basil made his own road to power an easy one. He was careful, moreover, to close the exit-doors on the monies contributed to the treasury. So a huge sum of money was built up, partly by the exercise of strict economy, partly by fresh additions from abroad. . . . He himself took no pleasure in any of it: quite the reverse indeed, for the majority of the precious stones, . . . were hidden away in his underground vaults. . . .

On his expedition against the barbarians, Basil did not follow the customary procedure of other emperors, setting out at the middle of spring and returning home at the end of summer. For him the time to return was when the task in hand was accomplished. He endured the rigors of winter and the heat of summer with equal indifference. He disciplined himself against thirst. In fact, all his natural desires were kept under stern control, and the man was as hard as steel. . . . He professed to conduct his wars and draw up the troops in line of battle, himself planning each campaign, but he preferred not to engage in combat personally. A sudden retreat might otherwise prove embarrassing. . . .

Basil's character was two-fold, for he readily adapted himself no less to the crises of war than to the calm of peace. Really, if the truth be told, he was more of a villain in wartime, more of an emperor in time of peace. Outbursts of wrath he controlled and like the proverbial "fire under the ashes," kept anger hid in his heart, but if his orders were disobeyed in war, on his return to the palace he would kindle his wrath and reveal it. Terrible then was the vengeance he took on the miscreant. Generally, he persisted in his opinions, but there were occasions when he did change his mind. . . . He was slow to adopt any course of action, but never would he willingly alter the decision, once it was [made]. Consequently, his attitude to friends was unvaried, unless perchance he was compelled by necessity to revise his opinion of them. Similarly, where he had burst out in anger against someone, he did not quickly moderate his wrath. Whatever estimate he formed, indeed, was to him an irrevocable and divinely inspired judgment.

 Based on this account, what were the personal qualities that made Basil II successful, and how would you characterize the nature of the Byzantine government? Compare the achievements of Basil II with those of Charlemagne as described by Einhard in "The Achievements of Charlemagne" (Section 12-1c, p. 330). How were the two rulers alike? How were they different? How do you explain the differences?

Source: E. R. A. Sewter, trans. *The Chronographia of Michael Psellus* (Yale University Press, 1953), pp. 23–27.

14,000 Bulgar captives before allowing them to return to their homes. The Byzantines went on to add the islands of Crete and Cyprus to the empire and to defeat the Muslim forces in Syria, expanding the empire to the upper Euphrates. By the end of Basil's reign in 1025, the Byzantine Empire was the largest it had been since the beginning of the seventh century.

13–2c Women in the Byzantine Empire

In Byzantium, as in European society, women were regarded as inferior to men and, at times, even considered to be the instrument of the devil. In general, women were expected to remain at home. They could leave to shop, visit parents, and take part in civic celebrations, but they were supposed to wear veils on these occasions.

Women were generally expected to fulfill three major functions: to marry and bear children, to maintain the household, and to weave clothes for their families. Thus, a good wife was seen as a special gift to her husband. Contrary to these ideal female roles, some women in the Byzantine world worked outside the home as artisans and sellers, especially of foodstuffs, in the markets of Constantinople. Others served as midwives, bakers, cooks, and dancers, although some dancers also worked as prostitutes.

Upper-class women had greater opportunities to play important roles in the empire. Some aristocratic wives funded the establishment of monasteries, occupied important positions at court, and patronized the arts. Imperial wives could exercise considerable political power as regents for their sons; some

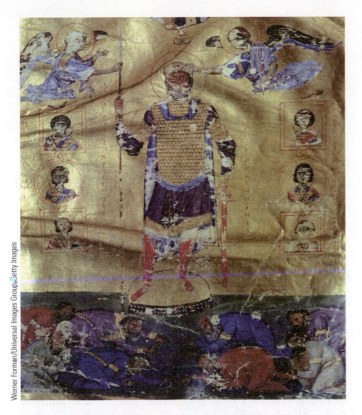

Basil the Bulgar-Slayer. Basil II became known as the Bulgar-slayer after his devastating victory over the Bulgars in 1014. This frontispiece illustration from a religious prayer book shows the warrior Basil standing on top of bodies of the conquered Bulgarians. Both angels and warrior-saints are shown protecting the emperor.

even became empresses in their own right. Irene, for example, served as regent for her son until 797 when she blinded and deposed him; she then ruled in her own right until she was overthrown in 802.

13-3 THE DECLINE AND FALL OF THE BYZANTINE EMPIRE (1025–1453)

Q Focus Questions: What impact did the crusades have on the Byzantine Empire? How and why did Constantinople and the Byzantine Empire fall?

The Macedonian Dynasty of the tenth and eleventh centuries had restored much of the power of the Byzantine Empire; its incompetent successors, however, reversed most of the gains.

13-3a New Challenges and New Responses

After the Macedonian Dynasty was extinguished in 1056, the empire was beset by internal struggles for power between ambitious military leaders and aristocratic families who bought the support of the great landowners of Anatolia by allowing them greater control over their peasants. This policy was

self-destructive, however, because the peasant-warrior was an important source of military strength in the Byzantine state. By the middle of the eleventh century, the Byzantine army began to decline; with fewer peasant recruits, military leaders also began to rely more on mercenaries.

A Christian Schism The growing division between the Roman Catholic Church of the West and the Eastern Orthodox Church of the Byzantine Empire also weakened the Byzantine state. The Eastern Orthodox Church was unwilling to accept the pope's claim that he was the sole head of the Christian church. This dispute reached a climax in 1054 when Pope Leo IX and Patriarch Michael Cerularius (sayr-yuh-LAR-ee-uss), head of the Byzantine church, formally excommunicated each other, initiating a schism between the two branches of Christianity that has not been healed to this day.

Islam and the Seljuk Turks The Byzantine Empire faced external threats to its security as well. In the West, the Normans were menacing the remaining Byzantine possessions in Italy. A much greater threat, however, came from the world of Islam. By the mid-tenth century, the Islamic empire led by the Abbasid caliphate in Baghdad (see Chapter 7) was disintegrating. An attempt was made around that time to unify the Islamic world under the direction of a Shi'ite Dynasty known as the Fatimids. Originating in North Africa, they conquered Egypt and founded the new city of Cairo as their capital. In establishing a Shi'ite caliphate, they became rivals to the Sunni caliphate of Baghdad and divided the Islamic world.

The Fatimid Dynasty prospered and soon surpassed the Abbasid caliphate as the dynamic center of Islam. Benefiting from their position in the heart of the Nile Delta, the Fatimids played a major role in the regional trade passing from the Mediterranean to the Red Sea and beyond. They were tolerant in matters of religion and created a strong army by using nonnative peoples as mercenaries. One of these peoples, the Seljuk Turks, soon posed a threat to the Fatimids themselves.

A nomadic people from Central Asia, the Seljuk Turks had been converted to Islam. As their numbers increased, they moved into the Eastern provinces of the Abbasid Empire, and in 1055 they captured Baghdad and occupied the rest of the empire. When they moved into Asia Minor—the heartland of the Byzantine Empire and its main source of food and manpower—the Byzantines were forced to react. Emperor Romanus IV led an army of recruits and mercenaries into Asia Minor in 1071 and met Turkish forces at Manzikert (MANZ-ih-kurt), where the Byzantines were soundly defeated. Seljuk Turks then went on to occupy much of Anatolia, where many peasants, already disgusted by their exploitation at the hands of Byzantine landowners, readily accepted Turkish control (see Map 7.4, Section 7-2c, p. 197).

A New Dynasty After the loss at Manzikert, factional fighting erupted over the imperial title until Alexius Comnenus (kahm-NEE-nuss) (1081–1118) seized the throne and established a dynasty that breathed new life into the Byzantine Empire. Under Alexius, the Byzantines were victorious on the Greek Adriatic coast against the Normans, defeated their enemies in the Balkans, and stopped the Turks in Anatolia. In the twelfth century, the Byzantine Empire experienced a cultural revival and a period of prosperity, fueled by an expansion of trade. The era was also marked by the increased importance of aristocratic families, especially those from a military background. In fact, Alexius's power was built on an alliance of the Comnenus family with other aristocratic families. But both the Comneni Dynasty and the revival of the twelfth century were ultimately threatened by Byzantium's encounters with crusaders from the West.

13–3b Impact of the Crusades

Lacking the resources to undertake additional campaigns against the Turks, Emperor Alexius turned to the West for military assistance and asked Pope Urban II for help against the Seljuk Turks. Instead of the military aid the emperor had expected, the pope set in motion the First Crusade (see Chapter 12), a decision that created enormous difficulties for the Byzantines. To pursue the goal of liberating Palestine from the Muslims, Western crusading armies would have to go through Byzantine lands to reach their objective. Alexius, and especially his daughter, Anna Comnena (who was also the Byzantine Empire's only female historian), were fearful that "to all appearances they were on pilgrimage; in reality they planned to dethrone Alexius and seize the capital."[5]

The Byzantines became cautious; Alexius requested that the military leaders of the First Crusade take an oath of loyalty to him and promise that any territory they conquered would be under Byzantine control. The crusaders ignored the emperor's wishes, and after conquering Antioch, Jerusalem, and additional Palestinian lands, they organized the four crusading states of Edessa, Antioch, Tripoli, and Jerusalem. The Byzantines now had to worry not only about the Turks in Anatolia but also about Westerners in the crusading states. The Second and Third Crusades posed similar difficulties for the Byzantine emperors.

With the crusades, the Byzantine Empire also became better acquainted with Westerners and Western customs. In the mid-twelfth century, the Byzantine emperor Manuel I (1140–1183) introduced the Western practice of knightly jousting to the Byzantine aristocracy. The Byzantine emperors also conferred trading concessions on the Italian city-states of Venice, Pisa, and Genoa, and in the course of the century, probably 60,000 Western Europeans came to live in Constantinople. But the presence of Westerners and Western practices also led to a growing hostility. Byzantine writers began to denounce Western attitudes, and Westerners often expressed jealousy of Constantinople's wealth. In 1171, Emperor Manuel I expelled the Venetians and seized their goods and ships, arousing in Venice a desire for revenge that was no doubt a factor in the disastrous Fourth Crusade in 1204.

The Latin Empire of Constantinople After the death of Saladin in 1193 (see Chapter 7), Pope Innocent III launched the Fourth Crusade. Judging the moment auspicious, Innocent encouraged the nobility of Europe to don the crusader's mantle. The Venetians agreed to transport the crusaders to the East but diverted them from the Holy Land by persuading them to first capture Zara, a Christian port on the Dalmatian coast. The crusading army thus became enmeshed in Byzantine politics.

At the start of the thirteenth century, the Byzantine Empire was experiencing yet another struggle for the imperial throne. One contender, Alexius, son of the overthrown Emperor Isaac II, appealed to the crusaders in Zara for assistance, offering to pay them 200,000 marks in silver (the Venetians were getting 85,000 as a transport fee) and to reconcile the Eastern Orthodox Church with the Roman Catholic Church. The crusade leaders now diverted their forces to Constantinople. When the crusading army arrived, the deposed Isaac II was reestablished with his son, Alexius IV, as co-emperor. Unfortunately, the emperors were unable to pay the promised sum. Relations between the crusaders and the Byzantines deteriorated, leading to an attack on Constantinople by the crusaders in the spring of 1204. On April 12, they stormed and sacked the city (see "Christian Crusaders Capture Constantinople"). Christian crusaders took gold, silver, jewelry, and precious furs, while the Catholic clergy accompanying the crusaders stole as many relics as they could find.

The Byzantine Empire now disintegrated into a series of petty states ruled by crusading barons and Byzantine princes. The chief state was the new Latin Empire of Constantinople led by Count Baldwin of Flanders as emperor. The Venetians seized the island of Crete and assumed control of Constantinople's trade. Why had the Western crusaders succeeded so easily when Persians, Bulgars, and Arabs had failed for centuries to conquer Constantinople? Although the crusaders were no doubt motivated by greed and a lust for conquest, they were also convinced that they were acting in God's cause. After all, a Catholic patriarch (a Venetian) had now been installed in Constantinople, and the reconciliation of Eastern Orthodoxy with Catholic Christianity had been accomplished. Nor should we overlook the military superiority of the French warriors and the superb organizational skills of the Venetians; together, they formed a powerful and highly effective union.

Revival of the Byzantine Empire Although he vehemently protested the diversion of the crusade from the Holy Land and even excommunicated all who participated in the crusade, Pope Innocent III belatedly accepted as "God's work" the conversion of Greek Byzantium to Latin Christianity. Some have argued that Innocent did realize, however, that the use of force to reunite the churches virtually guaranteed the failure of any permanent reunion. All too soon, this proved correct. The West was unable to maintain the Latin Empire, for the Western rulers of the newly created principalities were soon engrossed in fighting each other. Some parts of the Byzantine Empire had managed to survive under Byzantine princes.

CHRISTIAN CRUSADERS CAPTURE CONSTANTINOPLE

Politics & Government | **POPE INNOCENT III INAUGURATED** the Fourth Crusade after Saladin's empire began to disintegrate. Tragically, however, the crusading army of mostly French nobles was diverted to Constantinople to intervene in Byzantine politics. In 1204, the Christian crusaders stormed and sacked one of Christendom's greatest cities. This description of the division of the spoils after the conquest of Constantinople is taken from a contemporary account by a participant in the struggle.

Geoffrey de Villehardouin, *The Conquest of Constantinople*

Then it was proclaimed throughout the host by Marquis Boniface of Montferrat, who was lord of the host, and by the barons, and by the doge of Venice, that all the booty should be collected and brought together, as had been covenanted under oath and pains of excommunication. Three churches were appointed for the receiving of the spoils, and guards were set to have them in charge, both Franks [the French] and Venetians, the most upright that could be found.

Then each began to bring in such booty as he had taken and to collect it together. And some brought in loyally, and some in evil sort, because covetousness, which is the root of all evil hindered them. So from that time forth the covetous began to keep things back, and our Lord began to love them less. Ah God! how loyally they had borne themselves up to now! And well had the Lord God shown them that in all things He was ready to honor and exalt them above all people. But often do the good suffer for the sins of the wicked.

The spoils and the booty were collected together, and you must know that all was not brought into the common stock, for not a few kept things back, in spite of the excommunication of the pope. That which was brought to the churches was divided, in equal parts between the Franks and the Venetians, according to the sworn covenant. And you must know further that the pilgrims, after the division had been made, paid out of their share fifty thousand marks of silver to the Venetians, and then divided, at least one hundred thousand marks between themselves, among their own people. . . .

And as to theft, and those who were convicted thereof, you must know that stern justice was meted out to such as were found guilty, and not a few were hanged. The count of St. Paul hung one of his knights, who had kept back certain spoils, with his shield to his neck; but many there were both great and small, who kept back part of the spoils, and it was never known. Well may you be assured that the booty was very great, for if it had not been for what was stolen, and for the part given to the Venetians, there would have been at least four hundred thousand marks of silver, and at least ten thousand horses. Thus were divided the spoils of Constantinople, as you have heard.

Q *What does this document reveal about the crusading ideals and practices of the Europeans?*

Source: From Hutton Webster, *Readings in Medieval and Modern History* (Boston: D. C. Heath & Co., 1917), pp. 116–117.

In 1259, Michael Paleologus (pay-lee-AWL-uh-guss), a Greek military leader, took control of the kingdom of Nicaea in Western Asia Minor, led a Byzantine army to recapture Constantinople two years later, and then established a new Byzantine dynasty, the Paleologi.

The Byzantine Empire had been saved, but it was no longer a Mediterranean power. The restored empire was a badly truncated entity, consisting of the city of Constantinople and its surrounding territory, some lands in Asia Minor, and part of Thessalonica. It was surrounded by enemies— Bulgarians, Mongols, Turks, and Westerners, especially the resentful Venetians. And there was still internal opposition to Michael VIII. But the emperor survived and began a badly needed restoration of Constantinople.

Even in its reduced size, the empire limped along for another 190 years,

The Fall of Constantinople, 1453

and Constantinople remained an active economic center. Scholars continued to study the classics, and new churches and monasteries were built. Yet civil strife persisted as rival claimants struggled over the throne, and enemies continued to multiply. The threat from the Turks finally doomed the aged empire.

13–3c The Ottoman Turks and the Fall of Constantinople

Beginning in northeastern Asia Minor in the thirteenth century, the Ottoman Turks spread rapidly, seizing the lands of the Seljuk Turks and the Byzantine Empire. In 1345, they bypassed Constantinople and pushed into the Balkans. Under Sultan Murad (moo-RAHD), Ottoman forces moved through Bulgaria and into the lands of the Serbs; in 1389, at the Battle of Kosovo

The Fall of Constantinople. Few events in the history of the Ottoman Empire are more dramatic than the conquest of Constantinople in 1453. Although the Venetian painter Palma Giovane did not witness the conquest itself, he tried to capture the drama in his opulent reconstruction of the first attack by the Turks on the legendary city. This painting was one of a series done for the Doge's Palace in Venice.

(KAWSS-suh-voh), Ottoman forces defeated the Serbs. By the beginning of the fifteenth century, the Byzantine Empire had been reduced to little more than Constantinople, now surrounded on all sides by the Ottomans. When Mehmet (meh-MET) II came to the throne in 1451 at the age of only nineteen, he was determined to capture Constantinople and complete the demise of the Byzantine Empire.

The siege began in April when Mehmet moved his army— probably about 80,000 men—within striking distance of the 13-mile-long land walls along the western edge of the city. The pope and the Italian city-states of Venice and Genoa promised aid, but most of it was too little and too late. The city probably had 6,000 to 8,000 soldiers mobilized for its defense. On April 2, Emperor Constantine XI (1449–1453), the last Byzantine emperor, ordered that a floating chain or boom be stretched across the Golden Horn, the inlet that forms the city's harbor, to prevent a naval attack from the north. Mehmet's forces, however, took control of the tip of the peninsula north

of the Golden Horn and then pulled their ships overland across the peninsula from the Bosporus and placed them into the water behind the chains. The Ottoman fleet in the Horn built a pontoon bridge and set up artillery, forcing the Byzantines to defend the city on all sides.

The Ottomans' main attack, however, came against the land walls. On April 6, the artillery onslaught began. The Ottoman invaders had a distinct advantage with their cannons. One of them, constructed by a Hungarian engineer, had a 26-foot barrel that fired stone balls weighing 1,200 pounds. It took 60 oxen and 2,000 men to pull the great cannon into position. On May 29, Mehmet decided on a final assault, focused against the areas where the walls had been breached. When Ottoman forces broke into the city, the emperor became one of the first casualties. Irregular Ottoman forces began to loot the city before regular troops were able to stop them. About 4,000 defenders were killed, and thousands of the inhabitants were sold into slavery. Early in the afternoon,

Mehmet II rode into the city, exalted the power of Allah from the pulpit in the cathedral of Hagia Sophia, and ordered that it be converted into a mosque. He soon began rebuilding the city as the capital of the Ottoman Empire. The Byzantine Empire had come to an end.

HISTORIANS DEBATE **13–3d Why Did the Eastern Roman Empire (Byzantine Empire) Last a Thousand Years Longer Than the Western Roman Empire?**

Historians have long debated why the Eastern Roman Empire lasted a thousand years longer than the Roman Empire in the West. Some have emphasized the political strengths of the Eastern Empire. A relatively stable monarchy was reinforced by a strong bureaucracy that helped to avoid political instability even when there were deadly conflicts over the occupant of the imperial throne. Then, too, as we have seen, a permanent war economy as well as the preoccupation of many emperors with military affairs and astute diplomacy kept the Byzantines well prepared when facing a considerable number of enemies.

Other historians have argued for the importance of the capital city of Constantinople. Its location surrounded by sea and land walls protected it (until 1453) from potential enemies at the heart of the empire. Some historians have also emphasized that Constantinople was in a good strategic position for trading activities. The volume of trade thus assured the fabled prosperity of the empire over a long period of time.

Finally, some historians have also noted that the Eastern world in the Mediterranean was always more prosperous and literate than the Western Mediterranean world, giving the Byzantine Empire a distinct advantage.

CHRONOLOGY	The Byzantine Empire, 750–1453
Revival under Michael III	842–867
Macedonian Dynasty	867–1056
Basil I	867–886
Leo VI	886–912
Constantine VII	945–959
Basil II	976–1025
Schism between Eastern Orthodox Church and Roman Catholic Church	1054
Turkish defeat of the Byzantines at Manzikert	1071
Revival under Alexius Comnenus	1081–1118
Manuel Comnenus	1140–1183
Latin Empire of Constantinople	1204–1261
Revival of Byzantine Empire	1261
Turkish defeat of Serbs at Kosovo	1389
Constantine XI, the last Byzantine emperor	1449–1453
Fall of the empire	1453

13–4 THE CRISES OF THE FOURTEENTH CENTURY IN THE WEST

 Focus Questions: What impact did the Black Death have on Europe and Asia in the fourteenth century? What problems did Europeans face during the fourteenth century, and what impact did these crises have on European economic, social, and religious life?

At the beginning of the fourteenth century, changes in global weather patterns ushered in what has been called a "little ice age." Shortened growing seasons and disastrous weather conditions, including heavy storms and constant rain, led to widespread famine and hunger. Soon an even greater catastrophe struck.

13–4a The Black Death: From Asia to Europe

In the mid-fourteenth century, a disaster known as the **Black Death** struck in Asia, North Africa, and Europe. Bubonic plague was the most common and most important form of plague in the diffusion of the Black Death and was spread by black rats infested with fleas who were host to the deadly bacterium *Yersinia pestis* (yur-SIN-ee-uh PES-tiss).

Role of the Mongols This great plague originated in Asia. After disappearing from Europe and the Middle East in the Middle Ages, bubonic plague continued to haunt areas of southwestern China. In the early 1300s, rats accompanying Mongol troops spread the plague into central China and by 1331 to northeastern China. In one province near Beijing, it was reported that 90 percent of the population died. Overall, China's population may have declined from 120 million in the mid-1300s to 80 million by 1400.

In the thirteenth century, the Mongols had brought much of the Eurasian landmass under a single rule, which in turn facilitated long-distance trade, particularly along the Silk Road, now dominated by Muslim merchants from Central Asia (see Chapter 10). The spread of people and goods throughout this Eurasian landmass also facilitated the spread of the plague.

In the 1330s, the plague had spread to Central Asia; by 1339 it had reached Samarkand, a caravan stop on the Silk Road. From Central Asia, trading caravans brought the plague to Caffa, on the Black Sea, in 1346 and to Constantinople by the following year (see Comparative Essay "The Role of Disease in History," p. 374). Its arrival in the Byzantine Empire was noted in a work by Emperor John VI, who lost a son: "Upon arrival in Constantinople she [the empress] found Andronikos, the youngest born, dead from the invading plague, which . . . attacked almost all the sea coasts of the world and killed most of their people."[6] By 1348, the plague had spread to Egypt and also to Mecca, Damascus, and other parts of the Middle East. The Muslim historian Ibn Khaldun (IB-un kahl-DOON), writing in the fourteenth century, commented, "Civilization in the East and West was visited by a destructive plague which devastated nations

The Role of Disease in History

Interaction & Exchange When Hernán Cortés and his fellow conquistadors arrived in Mesoamerica in 1519, the local inhabitants were frightened of the horses and the firearms that accompanied the Spaniards. What they did not know was that the most dangerous enemies brought by these strange new arrivals were invisible—the disease-bearing microbes that would soon kill them by the millions.

Diseases have been the scourge of animal species since the dawn of prehistory, making the lives of human beings, in the words of the English philosopher Thomas Hobbes, "nasty, brutish, and short." With the increasing sophistication of forensic evidence, archaeologists today are able to determine from recently discovered human remains that our immediate ancestors were plagued by such familiar ailments as anemia, arthritis, tuberculosis, and malaria.

With the explosive growth of the human population brought about by the agricultural revolution, the problems posed by the presence of disease intensified. As people began to congregate in villages and cities, bacteria settled in their piles of refuse and were carried by lice in their clothing. The domestication of animals made humans more vulnerable to diseases carried by their livestock. As population density increased, the danger of widespread epidemics increased with it.

As time went on, succeeding generations gradually developed partial or complete immunity to many of these diseases, which became chronic rather than fatal to their victims, as occurred with malaria in parts of Africa, for example, and chickenpox in the Americas. But when a disease was introduced to a particular society that had not previously been exposed to it, the consequences were often devastating. The most dramatic example was the famous

Snark/Art Resource, NY

Mass Burial of Plague Victims. The Black Death had spread to northern Europe by the end of 1348. Shown here is a mass burial of victims of the plague in Tournai, located in modern Belgium. As is evident in the illustration, at this stage of the plague, there was still time to make coffins for the victims' burial. Later, as the plague intensified, the dead were thrown into open pits.

Black Death, the plague that ravaged Europe and China during the fourteenth century, killing one-fourth to one-half of the inhabitants in the affected regions (and even greater numbers in certain areas). Smallpox had the same impact in the Americas after the arrival of Christopher Columbus, and malaria was fatal to many Europeans on their arrival in West Africa. How were these diseases transmitted? In most instances, they followed the trade routes. Such was the case with the Black Death, which was initially carried by fleas living in the saddlebags of Mongol warriors as they advanced toward Europe in the thirteenth and fourteenth centuries and thereafter by rats in the holds of cargo ships. Smallpox and other diseases were brought to the Americas by the conquistadors. Epidemics, then, are a price that humans pay for having developed the network of rapid communication that has accompanied the evolution of human society.

 What role has disease played in human history?

and caused populations to vanish. It swallowed up many of the good things of civilization and wiped them out."[7] Egypt was particularly devastated by the plague; it has been estimated that the population of Egypt did not return to its pre-1347 level until the nineteenth century.

The Black Death in Europe The Black Death of the mid-fourteenth century was the most devastating natural disaster in European history, ravaging Europe's population and causing

economic, social, political, and cultural upheaval. Contemporary chroniclers lamented that parents attempted to flee, abandoning their children; one related the words of a child left behind: "Oh father, why have you abandoned me? . . . Mother where have you gone?"[8]

The plague reached Europe in October 1347 when Genoese merchants brought it from Caffa to the island of Sicily off the coast of Italy. One contemporary wrote, "As it happened, among those who escaped from Caffa by boat, there were a

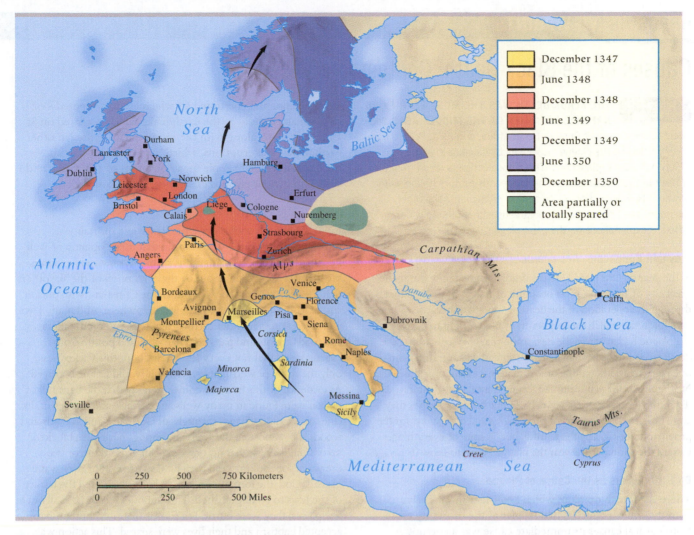

Map 13.3 Spread of the Black Death. The plague entered Europe through Sicily in 1347 and within three years had killed between one-quarter and one-half of the population. Outbreaks continued into the early eighteenth century, and the European population took two hundred years to return to the level it had reached before the Black Death.

few sailors who had been infected with the poisonous disease. Some boats were bound for Genoa, others went to Venice and other Christian areas. When the sailors reached these places and mixed with the people there, it was as if they had brought evil spirits with them."[9] The plague quickly spread to southern Italy and then to southern France by the end of the year (see Map 13.3). Diffusion of the Black Death followed commercial trade routes. In 1348, it spread through Spain, France, and the Low Countries and into Germany. By the end of that year, it had moved to England. By the end of the next, the plague had reached northern Europe and Scandinavia. Eastern Europe and Russia were affected by 1351.

Mortality figures for the Black Death were incredibly high. Especially hard hit were Italy's crowded cities, where 50 to 60 percent of the people died. One citizen of Florence wrote, "A great many breathed their last in the public streets, day and night; a large number perished in their homes, and it was only by the stench of their decaying bodies that they proclaimed their deaths to their neighbors. Everywhere the city was teeming with corpses."[10] In England and Germany,

entire villages simply disappeared. It has been estimated that out of a total European population of 75 million, as many as 38 million people may have died of the plague between 1347 and 1351.

As contemporaries attempted to explain the Black Death and mitigate its harshness, some turned to extreme sorts of behavior. Many believed that the plague either had been sent by God as a punishment for humans' sins or had been caused by the devil (see Opposing Viewpoints "Causes of the Black Death: Contemporary Views," p. 376). Some, known as flagellants (FLAJ-uh-lunts), resorted to extreme measures to gain God's forgiveness. Groups of flagellants, both men and women, wandered from town to town, flogging each other with whips to beg the forgiveness of God whom they believed had sent the plague to punish humans for their sinful ways. One contemporary chronicler described a flagellant procession:

The penitents went about, coming first out of Germany. They were men who did public penance and scourged themselves with whips of hard knotted leather with little iron

Causes of the Black Death: Contemporary Views

Interaction & Exchange **THE BLACK DEATH WAS THE MOST TERRIFYING NATURAL CALAMITY OF THE MIDDLE AGES** and affected wide areas of Europe, North Africa, and Asia. People were often baffled by the plague, especially by its causes, and gave widely different explanations. The first selection is taken from the preface to the *Decameron* by the fourteenth-century Italian writer Giovanni Boccaccio (joh-VAH-nee boh-KAH-choh). The other selections are from contemporary treatises that offered widely different explanations for the great plague.

Giovanni Boccaccio, *Decameron*

In the year of Our Lord 1348 the deadly plague broke out in the great city of Florence, most beautiful of Italian cities. Whether through the operation of the heavenly bodies or because of our own iniquities which the just wrath of God sought to correct, the plague had arisen in the East some years before, causing the death of countless human beings. It spread without stop from one place to another, until, unfortunately, it swept over the West. Neither knowledge nor human foresight availed against it.. . . Nor did humble supplications serve. Not once but many times they were ordained in the form of processions and other ways for the propitiation of God by the faithful, but, in spite of everything, toward the spring of the year the plague began to show its ravages.

On Earthquakes as the Cause of Plague

There is a fourth opinion, which I consider more likely than the others, which is that insofar as the mortality arose from natural causes its immediate cause was a corrupt and poisonous earthy exhalation, which infected the air in various parts of the world and, when breathed in by people, suffocated them and suddenly snuffed them out.. . .

It is a matter of scientific fact that earthquakes are caused by the exhalation of fumes enclosed in the bowels of the earth. When the fumes batter against the sides of the earth, and cannot get out, the earth is shaken and moves. I say that

it is the vapor and corrupted air which has been vented—or so to speak purged—in the earthquake which occurred on St Paul's day, 1347, along with the corrupted air vented in other earthquakes and eruptions, which has infected the air above the earth and killed people in various parts of the world; and I can bring various reasons in support of this conclusion.

Herman Gigas on Well Poisoning

In 1347 there was such a great pestilence and mortality throughout almost the whole world that in the opinion of well-informed men scarcely a tenth of mankind survived.. . . Some say that it was brought about by the corruption of the air; others that the Jews planned to wipe out all the Christians with poison and had poisoned wells and springs everywhere. And many Jews confessed as much under torture: that they had bred spiders and toads in pots and pans, and had obtained poison from overseas; and that not every Jew knew about this wickedness, only the more powerful ones, so that it would not be betrayed. As evidence of this heinous crime, men say that the bags full of poison were found in many wells and springs, and as a result, in cities, towns and villages throughout Germany, and in fields and woods too, almost all the wells and springs have been blocked up or built over, so that no one can drink from them or use the water for cooking, and men have to use rain or river water instead. God, the lord of vengeance, has not suffered the malice of the Jews to go unpunished. Throughout Germany, in all but a few places, they were burnt. For fear of that punishment many accepted baptism and their lives were spared. This action was taken against the Jews in 1349.

 What were the different explanations for the causes of the Black Death? How do you explain the differences, and what do these explanations tell you about the level of scientific knowledge in the Later Middle Ages? Why do you think Jews became scapegoats?

Sources: From *The Decameron* by Giovanni Boccaccio, trans. by Frances Winwar, p. xxii. Reprinted by permission of the Limited Editions Club. From Rosemary Horrox, ed., *The Black Death*, pp. 177–178, 207. Copyright © 1994 University of Manchester Press.

spikes. Some made themselves bleed very badly between the shoulder blades and some foolish women had cloths ready to catch the blood and smear it on their eyes, saying it was miraculous blood. While they were doing penance, they sang very mournful songs about the nativity and the passion of Our Lord. The object of this penance was to put a stop to the mortality, for in that time . . . at least a third of all the people in the world died.[11]

The flagellants attracted attention and created mass hysteria wherever they went. The Catholic Church, however, became

alarmed when flagellant groups began to kill Jews and attack clergy who opposed them. Pope Clement VI condemned the flagellants in October 1349 and urged the public authorities to crush them. By the end of 1350, most of the flagellant movement had been destroyed.

An outbreak of virulent anti-Semitism also accompanied the Black Death. Jews were accused of causing the plague by poisoning town wells. The worst **pogroms** (POH-grums) (massacres) against this minority were carried out in Germany, where more than sixty major Jewish communities had been exterminated by 1351. Many Jews fled Eastward to Russia and especially to Poland, where the king offered them protection. Eastern Europe became home to large Jewish communities.

13–4b Economic Dislocation and Social Upheaval

The deaths of so many people in the fourteenth century had severe economic consequences. Trade declined, and some industries suffered greatly. Florence's woolen industry, one of the giants, had produced 70,000 to 80,000 pieces of cloth in 1338; in 1378, it was yielding only 24,000 pieces.

Both peasants and noble landlords were also affected. A shortage of workers caused a dramatic rise in the price of labor, while the decline in the number of people lowered the demand for food, resulting in falling prices. Landlords were now paying more for labor at the same time that their rental income was declining. Concurrently, the decline in the number of peasants after the Black Death made it easier for some to convert their labor services to rent, thus freeing them from serfdom. But there were limits to how much the peasants could advance. They faced the same economic hurdles as the lords, who also attempted to impose wage restrictions and reinstate old forms of labor service. New governmental taxes also hurt. Peasant complaints became widespread and soon gave rise to rural revolts.

The English Peasants' Revolt of 1381 was the most prominent. The immediate cause of the revolt was the monarchy's attempt to raise revenues by imposing a poll tax, a flat charge on each adult member of the population. Peasants in Eastern England refused to pay the tax and expelled the collectors forcibly from their villages. Rebellion spread as peasants burned down the manor houses of aristocrats, lawyers, and government officials. Soon, however, the young king, Richard II (1377–1399), with the assistance of aristocrats, arrested hundreds of the rebels and ended the revolt. The poll tax was eliminated, however, and in the end most of the rebels were pardoned.

Although the peasant revolts sometimes resulted in short-term gains for the participants, the uprisings were relatively easily crushed and their gains quickly lost. Accustomed to ruling, the established classes easily combined and stifled dissent. Nevertheless, the revolts of the fourteenth century had introduced a new element to European life; henceforth, social unrest would be a characteristic of European history.

13–4c Political Instability

Famine, plague, economic turmoil, and social upheaval were not the only problems of the fourteenth century. War and political instability must also be added to the list. And of all the struggles that ensued, the Hundred Years' War was the most violent.

The Hundred Years' War In the thirteenth century, England still held one small possession in France known as the duchy of Gascony. As duke of Gascony, the English king pledged loyalty as a vassal to the French king, but when King Philip VI of France

(1328–1350) seized Gascony in 1337, the duke of Gascony—King Edward III of England (1327–1377)—declared war on Philip.

The war began in a burst of knightly enthusiasm. The French army of 1337 still relied largely on heavily armed noble cavalrymen, who looked with contempt on foot soldiers and crossbowmen, whom they regarded as social inferiors. The English, too, used heavily armed cavalry, but they relied even more on large numbers of paid foot soldiers. Armed with pikes, many of these soldiers had also adopted the longbow. The longbow was first used by the Welsh, but the English, recognizing the power of the longbow used against them, soon adopted its use. A well-trained longbowman could shoot ten to twelve arrows per minute, a more rapid speed of fire than the more powerful crossbow. And the arrows could pierce the armor of a knight at ranges of more than 250 yards. Although the English made use of heavily armed cavalry, they relied even more on large numbers of foot soldiers.

The first major battle of the war occurred in 1346 at Crécy (kray-SEE), just south of Flanders. The larger French army followed no battle plan but simply attacked the English lines in a disorderly fashion. The arrows of the English archers decimated the French cavalry. As the chronicler Froissart (frwah-SAR) described it, "The English [with their longbows] continued to shoot into the thickest part of the crowd, wasting none of their arrows. They impaled or wounded horses and riders, who fell to the ground in great distress, unable to get up again without the help of several men."[12] It was a stunning victory for the English and the foot soldier.

The Battle of Crécy. This fifteenth-century manuscript illustration depicts the Battle of Crécy, the first of several military disasters suffered by the French in the Hundred Years' War, and shows why the English preferred the longbow to the crossbow. At the left, the French crossbowmen stop shooting and prime their weapons by cranking the handle, while English archers continue to shoot their longbows (a skilled archer could launch ten arrows a minute).

Bibliotheque Nationale, Paris, France/The Bridgeman Art Library

The Battle of Crécy was not decisive, however. The English simply did not possess the resources to subjugate all of France, but they continued to try. The English king, Henry V (1413–1422), was especially eager to achieve victory. At the Battle of Agincourt (AH-zhen-koor) in 1415, the heavy, armor-plated French knights attempted to attack across a field turned to mud by heavy rain; the result was a disastrous French defeat and the death of 1,500 French nobles. The English had become the masters of northern France.

The seemingly hopeless French cause fell into the hands of the dauphin (DAH-fin *or* doh-FAN) Charles, the heir to the throne, who governed the southern two-thirds of French lands. Charles's cause seemed doomed until a French peasant woman quite unexpectedly saved the timid monarch. Born in 1412, the daughter of well-to-do peasants, Joan of Arc was a deeply religious person who came to believe that her favorite saints had commanded her to free France. In February 1429, Joan made her way to the dauphin's court and persuaded Charles to allow her to accompany a French army to Orléans (or-lay-AHN). Apparently inspired by the faith of the peasant girl known as "the Maid of Orléans," the French armies found new confidence in themselves and liberated the city. Joan had brought the war to a decisive turning point.

But she did not live to see the war concluded. Captured in 1430, Joan was turned over by the English to the Inquisition, which tried her on charges of witchcraft. In the fifteenth century, spiritual visions were thought to be inspired by either God or the devil. Joan was condemned to death as a heretic and burned at the stake in 1431.

Joan of Arc's accomplishments proved decisive. Although the war dragged on for another two decades, defeats of English armies in Normandy and Aquitaine led to French victory by 1453. Important to the French success was the use of the cannon, a new weapon made possible by the invention of gunpowder. The Chinese had invented gunpower in the tenth century and devised a simple cannon by the thirteenth. The Mongols greatly improved this technology, developing more accurate cannons and cannonballs; both spread to the Middle East in the thirteenth century and to Europe by the fourteenth. The use of gunpowder eventually brought drastic changes to European warfare by making castles, city walls, and armored knights obsolete.

Political Disintegration By the fourteenth century, the feudal order had begun to break down. With money from taxes, kings could now hire professional soldiers, who tended to be more reliable than feudal knights anyway. Fourteenth-century kings had their own problems as well. Many dynasties in Europe were unable to produce male heirs, while the founders of new dynasties had to fight for their positions as factions of nobles, trying to gain advantages for themselves, supported opposing candidates. Rulers encountered financial problems too. Hiring professional soldiers left them always short of cash, adding yet another element of uncertainty and confusion to fourteenth-century politics.

13–4d The Decline of the Church

The papacy of the Roman Catholic Church reached the height of its power in the thirteenth century. But crises in the fourteenth century led to a serious decline for the church. By that time, the monarchies of Europe were no longer willing to accept papal claims of temporal supremacy, as is evident in the struggle between Pope Boniface VIII (1294–1303) and King Philip IV (1285–1314) of France. In his desire to acquire new revenues, Philip claimed the right to tax the clergy of France, but Boniface VIII insisted that the clergy of any state could not pay taxes to their secular ruler without the pope's consent. In no uncertain terms he argued that popes were supreme over both the church and the state.

Philip IV refused to accept the pope's position and sent a small contingent of French forces to capture Boniface and bring him back to France for trial. The pope escaped but soon died from the shock of his experience. To ensure his position and avoid any future papal threat, Philip IV engineered the election of a Frenchman, Clement V (1305–1314), as pope. Using the excuse of turbulence in the city of Rome, the new pope took up residence in Avignon (ah-veen-YOHN) on the East bank of the Rhone River.

From 1305 to 1377, the popes resided in Avignon, leading to an increase in antipapal sentiment. The city of Rome was the traditional capital of the universal church. The pope was the bishop of Rome, and it was unseemly that the head of the Catholic Church should reside in Avignon instead of Rome. Moreover, the splendor in which the pope and cardinals were living in Avignon led to highly vocal criticism of both clergy and papacy. At last, Pope Gregory XI (1370–1378), perceiving the disastrous decline in papal prestige, returned to Rome in 1377.

The Great Schism and Cries for Reform Gregory XI died in Rome the spring after his return. When the college of cardinals met to elect a new pope, the citizens of Rome, fearful that the French majority would choose another Frenchman who would move the papacy back to Avignon, threatened that the cardinals would not leave Rome alive unless they elected a Roman or an Italian as pope. Indeed, the guards of the conclave warned the cardinals that they "ran the risk of being torn in pieces" if they did not choose an Italian. Wisely, the terrified cardinals duly elected the Italian archbishop of Bari as Pope Urban VI (1378–1389). Five months later, a group of dissenting cardinals—the French ones—declared Urban's election invalid and chose one of their number, a Frenchman, who took the title of Clement VII and promptly returned to Avignon. Because Urban remained in Rome, there were now two popes, beginning a crisis that has been called the Great Schism of the church.

The Great Schism divided Europe. France and its allies supported the pope in Avignon, whereas France's enemy England and its allies supported the pope in Rome. The Great Schism was also damaging to the faith of Christian believers in the institution of the Catholic Church. The pope was widely believed to be the true leader of Christendom; when both lines of popes denounced the other as the Antichrist, people's faith in the papacy and the church was undermined.

Meanwhile, the crises in the Catholic Church produced cries for reform. The Great Schism led large numbers of churchmen to take up the theory of **conciliarism**, or the belief that only a general council of the church, and not the pope, could bring reform to the church in its "head and members." These cries for change finally led to a church council that met at Constance in Switzerland in 1417. After the competing popes resigned or were deposed, a new pope was elected who was acceptable to all parties.

Although the Council of Constance ended the Great Schism, the council's efforts to reform the church were less successful. By the mid-fifteenth century, the papacy had reasserted its authority and ended the conciliar movement. At the same time, however, as a result of these crises, the church had lost much of its temporal power. Even worse, the papacy and the church had also lost much of their moral prestige.

13–5 RECOVERY: THE RENAISSANCE

 Focus Question: What were the main features of the Renaissance in Europe, and how did it differ from the Middle Ages?

People who lived in Italy between 1350 and 1550 or so believed that they were witnessing a rebirth of Classical antiquity—the world of the Greeks and Romans. To them, this marked a new age, which historians later called the **Renaissance** (French for "rebirth") and viewed as a distinct period of European history, which began in Italy and then spread to the rest of Europe.

Renaissance Italy was largely an urban society. The city-states became the centers of Italian political, economic, and social life. Within this new urban society, a secular spirit emerged as increasing wealth created new possibilities for the enjoyment of worldly things.

The Renaissance was also an age of recovery from the disasters of the fourteenth century, including the Black Death, political disorder, and economic recession. In pursuing that recovery, Italian intellectuals became intensely interested in the glories of their own past, the Greco-Roman culture of antiquity.

A new view of human beings emerged as people in the Italian Renaissance began to emphasize individual ability. The fifteenth-century Florentine architect Leon Battista Alberti (LAY-un buh-TEESS-tuh al-BAYR-tee) expressed the new philosophy succinctly: "Men can do all things if they will."[13] This high regard for human worth and for individual potentiality gave rise to a new social ideal of the well-rounded personality or "universal person"—*I'uomo universale* (WOH-moh OO-nee-ver-SAH-lay)—who was capable of achievements in many areas of life.

13–5a The Intellectual Renaissance

The emergence and growth of individualism and secularism as characteristics of the Italian Renaissance are most noticeable in the intellectual and artistic realms. The most important literary movement associated with the Renaissance was humanism.

Renaissance humanism was an intellectual movement based on the study of the classics, the literary works of Greece and Rome. Humanists studied the liberal arts—grammar, rhetoric, poetry, moral philosophy or ethics, and history—all based on the writings of ancient Greek and Roman authors. We call these subjects the humanities.

Petrarch (PEE-trark *or* PET-trark) (1304–1374), who has often been called the father of Italian Renaissance humanism, did more than any other individual in the fourteenth century to foster its development. Petrarch sought to find forgotten Latin manuscripts and set in motion a ransacking of monastic libraries throughout Europe. He also began the humanist emphasis on the use of pure Classical Latin. Humanists used the works of Cicero as a model for prose and those of Virgil for poetry. As Petrarch said, "Christ is my God; Cicero is the prince of the language."

In Florence, the humanist movement took a new direction at the beginning of the fifteenth century. Fourteenth-century humanists such as Petrarch had described the intellectual life as one of solitude. They rejected family and a life of action in the community. Now, however, the humanists who worked as secretaries for the city council of Florence took a new interest in civic life. They came to believe that it was the duty of an intellectual to live an active life for one's state. Humanists came to believe that their study of the humanities should be put to the service of the state. It is no accident that humanists served as secretaries in Italian city-states or at courts of princes or popes.

Also evident in the humanism of the first half of the fifteenth century was a growing interest in Classical Greek civilization. One of the first Italian humanists to gain a thorough knowledge of Greek was Leonardo Bruni (leh-ah-NAHR-doh BROO-nee), who became an enthusiastic pupil of the Byzantine scholar Manuel Chrysoloras (man-WEL kriss-uh-LAHR-uss), who taught in Florence from 1396 to 1400.

HISTORIANS DEBATE **Was There a Renaissance for Women?** Historians have disagreed over the benefits of the Renaissance for women. Some maintain that during the Middle Ages upper-class women in particular had greater freedom to satisfy their emotional needs, whereas upper-class women in the Renaissance experienced a contraction of both social and personal options as they became even more subject to male authority. Other historians have argued that although conditions remained bleak for most women, some women, especially those in courtly, religious, and intellectual environments, found ways to develop a new sense of themselves as women. This may be especially true of women who were educated in the humanist fashion and went on to establish literary careers.

Isotta Nogarola (ee-ZAHT-uh noh-guh-ROH-luh), born to a noble family in Verona, mastered Latin and wrote numerous letters and treatises that brought her praise from male Italian intellectuals. Cassandra Fedele (FAY-duh-lee) of Venice, who learned both Latin and Greek from humanist tutors hired by her family, became prominent in Venice for her public recitations of orations. Laura Cereta (say-REE-tuh) was educated in Latin by her father, a physician from Brescia. In a series of letters, Laura defended the ability of women to pursue scholarly pursuits.

Masaccio, *Tribute Money.* With the frescoes of Masaccio, regarded by many as the first great works of Early Renaissance art, a new realistic style of painting was born. *Tribute Money* was one of a series of frescoes that Masaccio painted in the Brancacci Chapel of the Church of Santa Maria del Carmine in Florence. In *Tribute Money,* Masaccio depicted the biblical story of Jesus's confrontation by a tax collector at the entrance to the town of Capernaum (seen at the center). Jesus sent Peter to collect a coin from the mouth of a fish from Lake Galilee (seen at the left); Peter then paid the tax collector (seen at the right). In illustrating this story from the Bible, Masaccio used a rational system of perspective to create a realistic relationship between the figures and their background; the figures themselves are realistic. As one Renaissance observer said, "The works made before Masaccio's day can be said to be painted, while his are living, real, and natural."

13–5b The Artistic Renaissance

Renaissance artists sought to imitate nature in their works of art. Their search for naturalism became an end in itself: to persuade onlookers of the reality of the object or event they were portraying. At the same time, the new artistic standards reflected the new attitude of mind in which human beings became the focus of attention, the "center and measure of all things," as one artist proclaimed.

The frescoes by Masaccio (muh-ZAH-choh) (1401–1428) in Florence have long been regarded as the first masterpieces of Early Renaissance art. With his use of monumental figures, a more realistic relationship between figures and landscape, and the visual representation of the laws of perspective, a new realistic style of painting was born. Onlookers became aware of a world of reality that appeared to be a continuation of their own. Masaccio's massive, three-dimensional human figures provided a model for later generations of Florentine artists.

This new Renaissance style was absorbed and modified by other Florentine painters in the fifteenth century. Especially important were two major developments. One emphasized the technical side of painting—understanding the laws of perspective and the geometrical organization of outdoor space and light. The second development was the investigation of movement and anatomical structure. The realistic portrayal of the human nude became one of the foremost preoccupations of Italian Renaissance artists.

A new style in architecture also emerged when Filippo Brunelleschi (fee-LEE-poh BROO-nuh-LESS-kee) (1377–1446),

inspired by Roman models, created an interior in the Church of San Lorenzo in Florence that was very different from that of the great medieval cathedrals. San Lorenzo's Classical columns, rounded arches, and coffered ceiling created an environment that did not overwhelm the worshipers physically and psychologically, as Gothic cathedrals did, but comforted them as a space created to fit human, not divine, measurements. Like painters and sculptors, Renaissance architects sought to reflect a human-centered world.

By the end of the fifteenth century, Italian artists had mastered the new techniques for scientific observation of the world around them and were now ready to move into new forms of creative expression. This marked the shift to the High Renaissance, which was dominated by the work of three artistic giants, Leonardo da Vinci (leh-ah-NAHR-doh dah VEEN-chee) (1452–1519), Raphael (RAFF-ee-ul) (1483–1520), and Michelangelo (my-kuh-LAN-juh-loh) (1475–1564). Leonardo carried on the fifteenth-century experimental tradition by studying everything and even dissecting human bodies in order to see how nature worked. But Leonardo stressed the need to advance beyond such realism and initiated the High Renaissance's preoccupation with the idealization of nature, an attempt to generalize from realistic portrayal to an ideal form.

At twenty-five, Raphael was already regarded as one of Italy's best painters. He was acclaimed for his numerous madonnas, in which he attempted to achieve an ideal of beauty far surpassing human standards. He is well known for his frescoes in the

Leonardo da Vinci, *The Last Supper*. Leonardo da Vinci was the impetus behind the High Renaissance concern for the idealization of nature, moving from a realistic portrayal of the human figure to an idealized form. Evident in Leonardo's *Last Supper* is his effort to depict a person's character and inner nature by the use of gesture and movement. Unfortunately, Leonardo used an experimental technique in this fresco, which soon led to its physical deterioration.

Raphael, *School of Athens*. Raphael arrived in Rome in 1508 and began to paint a series of frescoes commissioned by Pope Julius II for the papal apartments at the Vatican. In *School of Athens,* painted in 1510 or 1511, Raphael created an imaginary gathering of ancient philosophers. In the center stand Plato and Aristotle. At the left is Pythagoras, showing his system of proportions on a slate. At the right is Ptolemy, holding a celestial globe.

THE GENIUS OF MICHELANGELO

DURING THE RENAISSANCE, ARTISTS CAME to be viewed as creative geniuses with almost divine qualities. One individual who helped create this image was himself a painter. Giorgio Vasari (JOR-joh vuh-ZAHR-ee) was an avid admirer of Italy's great artists and wrote a series of brief biographies of them. This excerpt is taken from his account of Michelangelo.

Giorgio Vasari, *Lives of the Artists*

Michelangelo was much inclined to the labors of art, seeing that everything, however difficult, succeeded with him, he having had from nature a genius very apt and ardent in the noble arts of design. Moreover, in order to be entirely perfect, innumerable times he made anatomical studies, dissecting men's bodies in order to see the principles of their construction and the arrangement of the bones, muscles, veins and nerves; the various movements and all the postures of the human body; and not of men only, but also of animals, and particularly of horses,. . .Of all these he desired to learn the principles and laws in so far as touched his art, and this knowledge he so demonstrated in the works that fell to him to handle that those who attend to no other study than this do now know more. He so executed his works, whether with the brush or with the chisel, that they are almost inimitable, and he gave to his labors such grace and loveliness that he surpassed and vanquished the ancients. He was able to wrest things out of the greatest difficulties with such facility that they do not appear wrought with effort, although whoever draws his works after him finds it very hard to imitate them.

The genius of Michelangelo was recognized in his lifetime, and not, as happens to many, after death, for several of the popes always wished to have him near them, and also Suleiman, emperor of the Turks, Francis of Valois, king of France, the emperor Charles V, the signory of Venice, and finally Duke Cosimo de' Medici. All offered him honorable salaries, for no other reason but to avail themselves of his great genius. This does not happen except to men of great worth, such as he was. It is well known that all the three arts of painting, sculpture, and architecture were so perfect in him, that it is not found that among persons ancient or modern, in all the many years that the sun had been whirling round, God has granted this to any other but Michelangelo.

He had imagination of such a kind, and so perfect, and the things conceived by him in idea were such, that often, through not being able to express with the hands conceptions so terrible and grand, he abandoned his works—nay, destroyed many of them.

 How do you think Vasari's comments on Leonardo fostered the image of the Renaissance artist as a "creative genius with almost divine qualities"?

Source: Hutton Webster, *Readings in Medieval and Modern History* (Boston, 1917), pp. 191–192.

Vatican Palace, which reveal a world of balance, harmony, and order—the underlying principles of the art of Classical Greece and Rome.

Michelangelo, an accomplished painter, sculptor, and architect, was fiercely driven by a desire to create, and he worked with great passion and energy on a remarkable number of projects. Michelangelo was influenced by Neoplatonism, especially evident in his figures on the ceiling of the Sistine Chapel. These muscular figures reveal an ideal type of human being with perfect proportions. In good Neoplatonic fashion, their beauty is meant to be a reflection of divine beauty; the more beautiful the body, the more God-like the figure. Another manifestation of Michelangelo's search for ideal beauty was his *David*, a colossal marble statue commissioned by the government of Florence in 1501 and completed in 1504.

The Artist and Social Status As in the Middle Ages, Early Renaissance artists were still largely viewed as artisans. Since guilds depended on commissions for their projects, patrons played an important role in the art of the Early Renaissance. The wealthy upper classes determined both the content and the purpose of the paintings and pieces of sculpture they commissioned.

By the end of the fifteenth century, a transformation in the position of the artist had occurred. Especially talented individuals, such as Leonardo, Raphael, and Michelangelo, were

Michelangelo, *David*. This statue of David, cut from an 18-foot-high piece of marble, exalts the beauty of the human body and is a fitting symbol of the Italian Renaissance's affirmation of human power. Completed in 1504, *David* was moved by Florentine authorities to a special location in front of the Palazzo Vecchio, the seat of the Florentine government.
Scala/Art Resource, NY

Map 13.4 **Europe in the Second Half of the Fifteenth Century.** By the second half of the fifteenth century, monarchs in Western Europe, particularly France, Spain, and England, had begun the process of modern state building. With varying success, they reined in the power of the church and nobles, increased their ability to levy taxes, and established effective government bureaucracies.

 What aspects of Europe's political boundaries help explain why France and the Holy Roman Empire were often at war with each other?

no longer regarded as artisans but as artistic geniuses with creative energies akin to the divine (see "The Genius of Michelangelo"). Artists were heroes, individuals who were praised more for their creativity than for their competence as craftspeople. Michelangelo, for example, was frequently addressed as "Il Divino"—the Divine One. As society excused their eccentricities and valued their creative genius, the artists of the High Renaissance became the first to embody the modern concept of the artist.

13–5c The State in the Renaissance

In the second half of the fifteenth century, attempts were made to reestablish the centralized power of monarchical governments after the political disasters of the

Italian States in the Renaissance

fourteenth century. Some historians called these states the "new monarchies," especially those of France, England, and Spain (see Map 13.4).

The Italian States The Italian states provided the earliest examples of state building in the fifteenth century. During the Middle Ages, Italy had failed to develop a centralized territorial state, and by the fifteenth century, five major powers dominated the Italian peninsula: the duchy of Milan, the republics of Florence and Venice, the Papal States, and the kingdom of Naples.

Milan, Florence, and Venice proved especially adept at building strong, centralized states. Under a series of dukes, Milan became a highly centralized territorial state in which the rulers devised systems of taxation that generated enormous revenues for the government. The maritime republic of Venice remained an extremely stable political entity governed by a small oligarchy of merchant-aristocrats. Its commercial empire brought in vast revenues and gave it the status of an international power. In Florence, Cosimo de' Medici (KAH-zee-moh duh MED-ih-chee) took control of the merchant oligarchy in 1434. Through lavish patronage and careful courting of political allies, he and his family dominated the city at a time when Florence was the center of the cultural Renaissance.

As strong as these Italian states became, they still could not compete with the powerful monarchical states to the north and West. Beginning in 1494, Italy became a battlefield for the great power struggle between the French and Spanish monarchies, a conflict that led to Spanish domination of Italy in the sixteenth century.

Machiavelli and Political Power in the Renaissance No one gave better expression to the Renaissance preoccupation with political power than Niccoló Machiavelli (nee-koh-LOH mahk-ee-uh-VEL-ee) (1469–1527), an Italian who wrote *The Prince* (1513), one of the most influential works on political power in the Western world. Machiavelli's major concerns in *The Prince* were the acquisition, maintenance, and expansion of political power as the means to restore and maintain order. In the Middle Ages, many political theorists stressed the ethical side of a prince's activity—how a ruler ought to behave based on Christian moral principles. Machiavelli bluntly contradicted this approach: "For the gap between how people actually behave and how they ought to behave is so great that anyone who ignores everyday reality in order to live up to an ideal will soon discover he had been taught how to destroy himself, not how to preserve himself."[14] Machiavelli considered his approach far more realistic than that of his medieval forebears. He maintained that political activity should not be restricted by moral considerations. The prince acts on behalf of the state and for the sake of the state must be willing to let his conscience sleep. Machiavelli was among the first Western thinkers to abandon morality as the basis for the analysis of political activity (see Opposing Viewpoints "The Renaissance Prince: The Views of Machiavelli and Erasmus").

Western Europe The Hundred Years' War left France prostrate. But it had also engendered a certain degree of French national feeling toward a common enemy that the kings could use to reestablish monarchical power. The development of a French territorial state was greatly advanced by King Louis XI (1461–1483), known as the Spider because of his wily and devious ways. Louis strengthened the use of the *taille* (TY)—an annual direct tax usually on land or property—as a permanent tax imposed by royal authority, giving him a sound, regular source of income, which created the foundations of a strong French monarchy.

The Hundred Years' War had also strongly affected the English. The cost of the war in its final years and the losses to the labor force strained the English economy. At the end of the war, England faced even greater turmoil when a civil war, known as the War of the Roses, erupted and aristocratic factions fought over the monarchy until 1485, when Henry Tudor established a new dynasty.

As the first Tudor king, Henry VII (1485–1509) worked to establish a strong monarchical government. Henry ended the petty wars of the nobility by abolishing their private armies. He was also very thrifty. By not overburdening the nobility and the middle class with taxes, Henry won their favor, and they provided him much support.

Spain, too, experienced the growth of a strong national monarchy by the end of the fifteenth century. During the Middle Ages, several independent Christian kingdoms had emerged in the course of the long reconquest of the Iberian Peninsula from the Muslims. Two of the strongest were Aragon and Castile. The marriage of Isabella of Castile (1474–1504) and Ferdinand of Aragon (1479–1516) in 1469 was a major step toward unifying Spain. The two rulers worked to strengthen royal control of government. They filled the royal council, which supervised the administration of the government, with middle-class lawyers. Trained in Roman law, these officials operated on the belief that the monarchy embodied the power of the state. Ferdinand and Isabella also reorganized the military forces of Spain, making the new Spanish army the best in Europe by the sixteenth century.

Central and Eastern Europe Unlike France, England, and Spain, the Holy Roman Empire failed to develop a strong monarchical authority. The failure of the German emperors in the thirteenth century ended any chance of centralized authority, and Germany became a land of hundreds of virtually independent states. After 1438, the position of Holy Roman Emperor was held by members of the Habsburg (HAPS-burg) Dynasty. Having gradually acquired a number of possessions along the Danube, known collectively as Austria, the house of Habsburg had become one of the wealthiest landholders in the empire and by the mid-fifteenth century had begun to play an important role in European affairs.

In Eastern Europe, rulers struggled to achieve the centralization of the territorial states. Religious differences troubled the area as Roman Catholics, Eastern Orthodox Christians, and other groups, including the Mongols, confronted each other. In Poland, the nobles gained the upper hand and established the right to elect their kings, a policy that drastically weakened royal authority.

Since the thirteenth century, Russia had been under the domination of the Mongols. Gradually, the princes of Moscow rose to prominence by using their close relationship to the Mongol khans to increase their wealth and expand their possessions. During the reign of the great Prince Ivan III (1462–1505), a new Russian state was born. Ivan annexed other Russian principalities and took advantage of dissension among the Mongols to throw off their yoke by 1480.

The Renaissance Prince: The Views of Machiavelli and Erasmus

Politics & Government

AT THE BEGINNING OF THE SIXTEENTH CENTURY, two writers produced very different views of political power and how a ruler should conduct affairs of state. In this selection from Chapter 17 of *The Prince*, Machiavelli analyzes whether it is better for a ruler to be loved than to be feared. Three years later, the Dutch intellectual Erasmus, leader of the Christian humanists (see Chapter 15), also wrote a treatise on political power, entitled *Education of a Christian Prince*. As is evident in this excerpt from his treatise, Erasmus followed in the footsteps of medieval theorists regarding power by insisting that a true prince should think only of his moral obligations to the people he rules.

Machiavelli, *The Prince* (1513)

This leads us to a question that is in dispute: Is it better to be loved than feared, or vice versa? My reply is one ought to be both loved and feared; but, since it is difficult to accomplish both at the same time, I maintain it is much safer to be feared than loved, if you have to do without one of the two. For of men one can, in general, say this: They are ungrateful, fickle, deceptive and deceiving, avoiders of danger, eager to gain. As long as you serve their interests, they are devoted to you. . . . But as soon as you need help, they turn against you. Any ruler who relies simply on their promises and makes no other preparations, will be destroyed. For you will find that those whose support you buy, who do not rally to you because they admire your strength of character and nobility of soul, these are people you pay for, but they are never yours, and in the end you cannot get the benefit of your investment. Men are less nervous of offending someone who makes himself lovable, than someone who makes himself frightening. For love attaches men by ties of obligation, which, since men are wicked, they break whenever their interests are at stake. But fear restrains men because they are afraid of punishment, and this fear never leaves them. Still, a ruler should make himself feared in such a way that, if he does not inspire love, at least he does not provoke hatred. For it is perfectly possible to be feared and not hated. You will only be hated if you seize the property or the women of your subjects and citizens. Whenever you have to kill someone, make sure that you have a suitable excuse and an obvious reason; but, above all else, keep your hands off other people's property; for men are quicker to forget the death of their father than the loss of their inheritance.. . .

Erasmus, *Education of a Christian Prince* (1516)

A good prince . . . is a living likeness of God, who is at once good and powerful. His goodness makes him want to help all; his power makes him able to do so. On the other hand, an evil prince, who is like a plague to his country, is the incarnation of the devil, who has great power joined with his wickedness. All his resources to the very last, he uses for the undoing of the human race.. . .

[A good prince is one] who holds the life of each individual dearer than his own; who works and strives night and day for just one end—to be the best he can for everyone; with whom rewards are ready for all good men . . . for so much does he want to be of real help to his people, without thought of recompense, that if necessary he would not hesitate to look out for their welfare at great risk to himself; who considers his wealth to lie in the advantage of his country; who is ever on the watch so that everyone else may sleep deeply; who grants no leisure to himself so that he may spend his life in the peace of his country; who worries himself with continual cares so that his subjects may have peace and quiet.. . . He does everything and allows everything that will bring everlasting peace to his country, for he realizes that war is the source of all misfortunes to the state.

 What does Machiavelli have to say about being loved rather than feared? How does this view contrast with that of Erasmus on the characteristics of a good ruler? Which viewpoint do you consider more modern? Why? Which viewpoint do you think is correct? Why?

Sources: Machiavelli, The Prince (1513). From *The Prince* by Machiavelli, translated by David Wootton, pp. 51–52. Erasmus, Education of a Christian Prince (1516). From *The Education of a Christian Prince*, by Erasmus, translated by L. K. Born. Copyright © 1936 by Columbia University Press.

After the collapse of Roman power in the West, the Late Roman Empire in the East or the Eastern Roman Empire, centered on Constantinople, continued in the Eastern Mediterranean and eventually emerged as the Byzantine Empire, which flourished for hundreds of years. While a new Christian civilization arose in Western Europe, the Byzantine Empire created its own unique Christian civilization. And while Western Europe struggled in the Early Middle Ages, the Byzantine world continued to prosper and flourish. Especially during the ninth, tenth, and eleventh centuries, under the Macedonian emperors, the Byzantine Empire expanded and achieved an economic prosperity that was evident to foreign visitors who were awed by the size, wealth, and physical surroundings of Constantinople.

During its heyday, Byzantium was a multicultural and multiethnic empire that ruled a remarkable number of peoples who spoke different languages. Byzantine cultural and religious forms spread to the Balkans, parts of central Europe, and Russia. Byzantine scholars eventually spread the study of the Greek language to Italy, fostering the Renaissance humanists' interest in Classical Greek civilization. The Byzantine Empire also interacted with the world of Islam to its East and the new European civilization of the West. Both interactions proved costly and ultimately fatal. Although European civilization and Byzantine civilization shared a common bond in Christianity, it proved incapable of keeping

them in harmony politically. Indeed, the West's crusades to Palestine, ostensibly for religious motives, led to Western control of the Byzantine Empire from 1204 to 1261. Although the empire was restored, it had been significantly weakened and could only limp along until its interaction with its other neighbor—the Muslim world—led to its demise in 1453 when the Ottoman Turks conquered the city of Constantinople and made it the center of their new empire.

While Byzantium was declining in the twelfth and thirteenth centuries, Europe was achieving new levels of growth and optimism. In the fourteenth century, however, Europe too experienced a time of troubles, as it was devastated by the Black Death, economic dislocation, political chaos, and religious decline. But in the fifteenth century, while Constantinople and the remnants of the Byzantine Empire finally fell to the world of Islam, Europe experienced a dramatic revival. Elements of recovery during the Renaissance made the fifteenth century a period of significant artistic, intellectual, and political change in Europe. By the second half of the fifteenth century, as we shall see in the next chapter, the growth of strong, centralized monarchical states made possible the dramatic expansion of Europe into other parts of the world.

CHAPTER TIMELINE

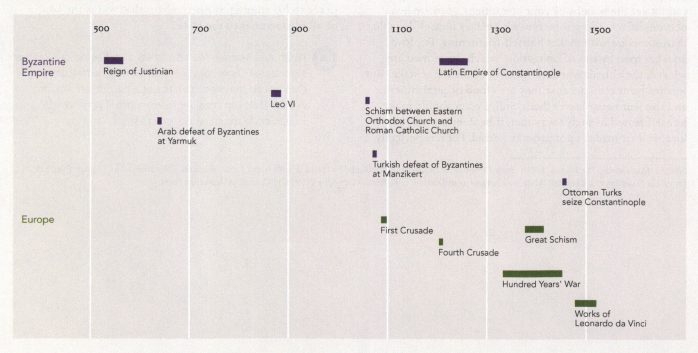

CHAPTER REVIEW

Upon Reflection

Q What were Justinian's major goals, and how did he try to accomplish them? How successful was he in achieving his goals?

Q Why does the chapter use the phrase "zenith of Byzantine civilization" to describe the period from 750 to 1025?

Q Compare developments in the Byzantine world and Europe in the fourteenth and fifteenth centuries. What are the similarities and differences?

Key Terms

iconoclasts (p. 362)
iconoclasm (p. 362)
Black Death (p. 373)
pogroms (p. 376)

conciliarism (p. 378)
Renaissance (p. 379)
Renaissance humanism (p. 379)
taille (p. 384)

Chapter Notes

1. Quoted in P. Cesaretti, *Theodora: Empress of Byzantium*, trans. R. M. Frongia (New York, 2004), p. 197.
2. Quoted in J. Harris, *Constantinople: Capital of Byzantium* (New York, 2007), p. 40.
3. Procopius, *Buildings of Justinian* (London, 1897), pp. 9, 6–7.
4. Quoted in Harris, *Constantinople*, p. 118.
5. A. Cameron, *The Byzantines* (Oxford, 2006), p. 45.
6. Quoted in C. S. Bartsocas, "Two Fourteenth-Century Descriptions of the 'Black Death,'" *Journal of the History of Medicine* (October 1966), p. 395.
7. Quoted in M. Dols, *The Black Death in the Middle East* (Princeton, N.J., 1977), p. 270.
8. Quoted in D. J. Herlihy, *The Black Death and the Transformation of the West*, ed. S. K. Cohn Jr. (Cambridge, Mass., 1997), p. 9.

9. Quoted in R. Horrox, *The Black Death* (Manchester, England, 1994), p. 16.
10. G. Boccaccio, *The Decameron*, trans. F. Winwar (New York, 1955), p. xiii.
11. J. Froissart, *Chronicles*, ed. and trans. G. Brereton (Harmondsworth, England, 1968), p. 111.
12. Ibid., p. 89.
13. Quoted in J. Burckhardt, *The Civilization of the Renaissance in Italy*, trans. S. G. C. Middlemore (London, 1960), p. 81.
14. N. Machiavelli, *The Prince*, trans. D. Wootton (Indianapolis, Ind., 1995), p. 48.

 **MINDTAP** From Cengage   MindTap® is a fully online personalized learning experience built upon Cengage Learning content. MindTap® combines student learning tools—readings, multimedia, activities, and assessments—into a singular Learning Path that guides students through the course and helps students develop the critical thinking, analysis, and communication skills that are essential to academic and professional success.

THE EMERGENCE OF NEW WORLD PATTERNS (1500–1800)

HISTORIANS OFTEN REFER to the period from the sixteenth through the eighteenth centuries as the early modern era. During these years, several factors were at work that created the conditions of our own time.

From a global perspective, perhaps the most noteworthy event of the period was the extension of the maritime trade network throughout the entire populated world. Traders from the Middle East had spearheaded the process with their voyages to East Asia and southern Africa in the first millennium CE; the Chinese had followed suit with Zheng He's groundbreaking voyages to India and East Africa mentioned in Chapter 10. By the end of the fifteenth century, a thriving trade network stretched from the Middle East through the Indian Ocean and all the way to China and the islands of Japan. It was at this time that a resurgent Europe suddenly exploded onto the world scene when the Portuguese discovered a maritime route to the East and Spanish adventurers opened up the first European contacts with the peoples of the Western Hemisphere. Although the Europeans were late to the game, they were quick learners, and over the next three centuries they gradually managed to dominate much of the shipping on international trade routes.

Some contemporary historians argue that it was this sudden burst of energy from Europe that created the first truly global economic network. Although it is true that European explorers were responsible for opening up communications with the vast new world of the Americas, other historians contend that it was the rise of the Arab empire in the Middle East and the Mongol expansion a few centuries later that played the greatest role in creating a widespread communications network by enabling goods and ideas to travel from one end of the Eurasian supercontinent to the other.

Whatever the truth of this debate, there are still many reasons for considering the end of the fifteenth century to be a crucial date in world history. By marking the end of the long isolation of the Western Hemisphere from the rest of the inhabited world, it led to the creation of the first truly global network of ideas and commodities, which would introduce plants, ideas, and (unfortunately) new diseases to all humanity (see Comparative Essay "The Columbian Exchange," Section 14-3e, p. 407). In turn, the era gave birth to a stunning increase in trade and manufacturing that stimulated major political, economic, and social changes not only in Europe but in other parts of the world as well.

But the period from 1500 to 1800 was not only an incubation period for the modern world, it was also the launching pad for an era of European domination that would reach fruition in the nineteenth century. To understand why the West emerged as the leading force in the world at that time, it is necessary to grasp what factors were at work in Europe that differentiated its actions from those of other major civilizations around the globe. For example, historians have identified improvements in navigation, shipbuilding, and weaponry as essential elements in promoting the European Age of Exploration. As we have seen, many of these technological advances were based on earlier discoveries that had taken place elsewhere—in China, India, and the Middle East—and had then been brought to Europe on Muslim

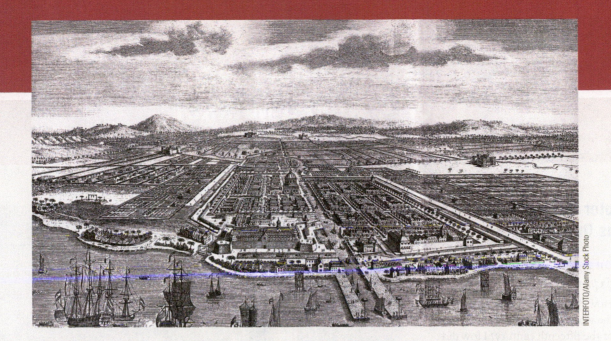

ships or along the trade routes through Central Asia. But it was the determination of the Europeans to make practical use of the discoveries of others that was the decisive factor in the equation, thus enabling them to dominate international sea lanes and ultimately to create vast colonial empires in the Western Hemisphere.

What explains the sudden explosion of Europe across the international scene? As was the case with Arab expansion several hundred years previously, European expansion was not fueled solely by economic considerations, but by religious motives as well. In the fifteenth century, the world of Christendom was in the midst of a major period of conflict with the forces of Islam, a rivalry that had been exacerbated by the conquest of the Byzantine Empire by the Ottoman Turks in 1453 (see Chapter 13). Although the claims of Portuguese and Spanish adventurers that their activities were motivated primarily by a desire to bring the word of God to non-Christian peoples certainly included a considerable measure of hypocrisy, there seems no reason to doubt that religious motives played a meaningful role in the process.

While Europe was on the cusp of a dynamic era of political, economic, and cultural expansion, conditions in other parts of the world were less conducive to these economic and political developments. In China, for example, the Ming Dynasty, after launching a major effort to extend its power and influence throughout the Indian Ocean, suddenly abandoned the quest and turned inward. Smugly confident of its superiority to all potential rivals, it continued to rely on a prosperous agricultural sector as the economic foundation of the empire. In the societies of India and the Middle East, manufacturing and commerce had played a vital role since the emergence of the Indian Ocean trade network in the first centuries CE. But beginning in the eleventh century, the area had suffered through an extended period of political instability, marked by invasions by nomadic peoples from Central Asia. The emergence of the Ottoman Empire, as well as the rise to power of the Mughal Dynasty in India, signaled the revival of Islam as a major force within the region, but the relative lack of interest shown by Ottoman and Mughal elites in manufacturing, technology, and commerce placed them at a significant disadvantage in their competition with Christian rivals.

In the early modern era, then, Europe was best placed to take advantage of the technological innovations that had become increasingly available. Whereas other regions were still beset by internal obstacles or had deliberately turned inward to seek their destiny, Europe now turned outward to seek a new and dominant position in the world. This does not imply, however, that significant changes were not taking place in other parts of the world as well, and many of these changes had relatively little to do with the situation in the West. As we shall see, the impact of European expansion on the rest of the world was still limited at the end of the eighteenth century. Although European political authority was firmly established in a few key areas, such as the Spice Islands and Latin America, traditional societies remained relatively intact in most regions of Africa and Asia. And processes at work in these societies were often operating independently of events in Europe and would later give birth to forces that acted to restrict or shape the Western impact. One of these forces was the progressive emergence of centralized states, some of them built on the concept of ethnic unity.

NEW ENCOUNTERS: THE CREATION OF A WORLD MARKET

Chapter Outline and Focus Questions

The Vasco da Gama pillar at Malindi. William J. Duiker

Critical Thinking

Q *Christopher Columbus has recently become a controversial figure in world history. Why do you think this is so, and how would you evaluate his contribution to the modern world?*

Connections to Today

Q *In hindsight, do you think that European explorers can be held accountable for transmitting Old World diseases to the peoples of the Western Hemisphere?*

WHEN THE PORTUGUESE FLEET arrived at the town of Calicut (KAL-ih-kuht) (now known as Kozhikode), on the western coast of India, in the spring of 1498, the fleet commander Vasco da Gama (VAHSH-koh dah GAHM-uh) ordered a landing party to go ashore to contact the local authorities. The first to greet them, a Muslim merchant from Tunisia, said, "May the Devil take thee! What brought thee hither?" "Christians and spices," replied the visitors. "A lucky venture, a lucky venture," replied the Muslim. "Plenty of rubies, plenty of emeralds! You owe great thanks to God, for having brought you to a country holding such riches!"[1]

Such words undoubtedly delighted the Portuguese, who explored the immediate vicinity of the town and soon convinced themselves that the local population appeared to be Christians originally converted by the apostle Thomas in the first century CE. Although it later turned out that they were mistaken—the local faith was a form of Hinduism—their spirits were probably not seriously dampened, for the conversion of the indigenous population was likely of less immediate importance than gold and glory to sailors who had gone through considerable hardship to become the first Europeans since the ancient Greeks to sail across the Indian Ocean. They left two months later with a cargo of spices and the determination to return soon with a second and larger fleet.

Vasco da Gama's maiden voyage to India inaugurated an extended period of European expansion into Asia, led by merchant adventurers and missionaries, that lasted several hundred years and had effects that are still felt today. His tiny fleet had rounded the Cape of Good Hope and sailed up the eastern coast of Africa, where they encountered an Arab navigator in the port of Malindi who promised to take them across the Indian Ocean to seek the riches of Asia. To memorialize the occasion and mark the spot for their return, the Portuguese erected a pillar of coral stone mounted by a cross that still stands on the site today (see illustration "The Vasco da Gama Pillar at Malindi").

Da Gama's voyage was a fateful one, for it eventually resulted in a Western takeover of existing trade routes in the Indian Ocean and the establishment of colonies throughout the region, as well as in Africa and Latin America. In later years, Western historians would begin to describe these events as an "Age of Discovery" that significantly broadened the maritime trade network and set the stage for the emergence of the modern world.

As we now know, of course, the voyages of Vasco da Gama and his European successors were a "discovery" only in the sense that Europeans for the first time began to take part in a regional trade network that had been in existence for centuries, and was already flourishing at a time when European maritime commerce was still essentially restricted to the Mediterranean Sea and the stormy waters of the North Atlantic Ocean. By the early fifteenth century, Chinese fleets under Zheng He had roamed the Indian Ocean, linking China with societies as distant as the Middle East and the coast of East Africa. By then, ships regularly passed between India, Southeast Asia, eastern Africa, and the Middle East, bringing goods from one part of the region to another. At the same time, Muslim caravans snaked across the Sahara from the Mediterranean to the civilizations that flourished along the banks of the Niger River.

The Europeans, then, were not trailblazers, but latecomers to the process. It was, after all, a Muslim from North Africa who greeted the Portuguese on their first appearance off the coast of India. In this chapter, we turn our attention to the stunning expansion in the scope and volume of commercial and cultural contacts that took place in the generations preceding and following Vasco da Gama's historic voyage to India, as well as to the factors that brought about this expansion.

14–1 AN AGE OF EXPLORATION AND EXPANSION

 Focus Questions: How did Muslim merchants expand the world trade network at the end of the fifteenth century? How did their achievements extend the era of commercial expansion that took place under the Mongols during the thirteenth and fourteenth centuries?

Western historians have customarily regarded the voyage of Vasco da Gama as a crucial step in the opening of trade routes to the East. In the sense that the voyage was a harbinger of future European participation in the spice trade, and that a new maritime route between the Atlantic and the Indian Oceans had been discovered, this view undoubtedly has merit. In fact, however, as has been pointed out in earlier chapters, the Indian Ocean had been a busy thoroughfare for centuries. The spice trade had been carried on by sea in the region since the days of the legendary Queen of Sheba, and Arab dhows, Indian sailing ships, and Chinese junks had sailed throughout the area in search of cloves and nutmeg and other precious items since the Tang Dynasty (see Chapter 10).

14–1a Islam and the Spice Trade

By the fourteenth century, a growing portion of the spice trade was being transported in Muslim ships sailing from ports in India or the Middle East. Muslims, either Arabs or Indian converts, had taken part in the Indian Ocean trade for centuries, and by the thirteenth century, Islam had established a presence in seaports on the islands of Sumatra and Java and was gradually moving inland. In 1292, the Venetian traveler Marco Polo observed that Muslims were engaging in missionary activity in northern Sumatra: "This kingdom is so much frequented by the Saracen merchants that they have converted the natives to the Law of Mahomet—I mean the townspeople only, for the hill people live for all the world like beasts, and eat human flesh, as well as other kinds of flesh, clean or unclean."[2]

But the major impetus for the spread of Islam in Southeast Asia came in the early fifteenth century, with the foundation of a new sultanate at Malacca (muh-LAK-uh), on the strait that today bears the same name. The founder was Paramesvara (pahr-uhmuss-VAHR-uh), a vassal of the Hindu state of Majapahit (mahjah-PAH-hit) on Java. Paramesvara's original base of operations had been at Palembang (pah-lem-BAHNG), on the island of Sumatra, but in 1390, he moved his base to Tumasik (tuh-MAH-sik) (modern Singapore), at the tip of the Malay

The Strait of Malacca

Peninsula, hoping to enhance his ability to play a role in the commerce passing through the region. Under pressure from the expanding power of the Thai state of Ayuthaya (ah-yoo-TY-yuh) (see "Southeast Asia in the Era of the Spice Trade," Section 14-5, p. 414) in the early fifteenth century, Paramesvara moved once again to Malacca. The latter's potential strategic importance was confirmed in the sixteenth century by a visitor from Portugal, who noted that Malacca "is a city that was made for commerce; . . . the trade and commerce between the different nations for a thousand leagues on every hand must come to Malacca."[3]

Shortly after its founding, Malacca was visited by a Chinese fleet under the command of Admiral Zheng He (see Chapter 10). To protect his patrimony from local rivals, Paramesvara agreed to become a tributary of the Chinese empire and cemented the new relationship by making an official visit to the Ming imperial court in Beijing. He also converted to Islam, undoubtedly with a view to enhancing Malacca's ability to participate in the trade that passed through the strait, much of which was dominated by Muslim merchants. Blessed by its fortunate location, within a few years Malacca had become the leading economic power in the region and helped promote the spread of Islam to trading ports throughout the islands of Southeast Asia, including Java, Borneo, Sulawesi (soo-lah-WAY-see), and the Philippines. Adoption of the Muslim faith was eased by the popularity of Sufism, a brand of Islam that expressed a marked tolerance for mysticism and local religious beliefs (see Chapter 7).

14–1b The Spread of Islam in West Africa

In the meantime, Muslim commercial and religious influence continued to expand south of the Sahara into the Niger River Valley in West Africa. The area had been penetrated by traders from across the Sahara since ancient times, and contacts undoubtedly increased after the establishment of Muslim control over the Mediterranean coastal regions. Muslim traders—first Arabs and later African converts—crossed the desert carrying Islamic values, political culture, and legal traditions along with their goods. The early stage of

state formation in Africa had culminated with the kingdom of Mali, symbolized by the renowned Mansa Musa, whose pilgrimage to Mecca in the fourteenth century had left an indelible impression on observers (see Chapter 8).

The Empire of Songhai With the decline of Mali in the late fifteenth century, a new power eventually appeared: the empire of Songhai (song-GY). The founder of Songhai was Sonni Ali (Sonni the Great), a local chieftain from Gao, a major trading entrepôt (ON-truh-poh) on the Niger River east of Timbuktu. After seizing power in 1464, he set out to destroy the remnants of the Mali Empire and restore the formidable empire of his predecessors. Rumored to possess magical powers, Sonni Ali was criticized by Muslim scholars for supporting traditional religious practices, but under his rule, Songhai emerged as a major trading state in the region (see Map 14.1). When he died in 1492, his son ascended to the throne but was deposed shortly thereafter by one of his military commanders, who seized power as king under the name Askia Mohammed (r. 1493–1528).

Under the new ruler, a fervent Muslim, Songhai increasingly relied on Islamic institutions and ideology to strengthen national unity and centralize its authority. Askia Mohammed himself embarked on a pilgrimage to Mecca and was recognized by the caliph of Cairo as the Muslim ruler of the Niger River Valley. On his return from Mecca, he tried to revive Timbuktu as a major center of Islamic learning but had less success in converting his predominantly animist subjects. He did preside over a significant increase in trans-Saharan trade in gold, salt, and slaves, which provided a steady source of income to Songhai and other states in the region (see "The Great City of Timbuktu"). Gold, the source of which was located

Map 14.1 The Songhai Empire. Songhai was the last of the great states to dominate the Niger River Valley prior to the European takeover in the nineteenth century.

 What were the predecessors of the Songhai Empire in the region? Why is the area so important in African history?

THE GREAT CITY OF TIMBUKTU

Interaction & Exchange

AFTER ITS FOUNDING IN THE TWELFTH CENTURY, Timbuktu became a great center of Islamic learning and a fabled city of mystery and riches to Europeans. By the sixteenth century, Timbuktu had become a major commercial hub for all trade passing through the Sahara as routes to the gold fields farther to the east declined as a result of Tuareg raids and increasing aridity. This description of the city was written in 1526 by Leo Africanus, a Muslim from the Islamic state of Granada who had once lived in Rome and was one of the great travelers of his time. By then, Timbuktu had become a vibrant multiracial city marked by widespread literacy and tolerant social mores.

Leo Africanus, *History and Description of Africa*

Here are many shops of artificers and merchants, and especially of such as weave linen and cotton cloth. And hither do the Barbary merchants bring cloth of Europe. All the women of this region, except the maid-servants, go with their faces covered, and sell all necessary victuals. The inhabitants, and especially strangers there residing, are exceeding rich, insomuch that the king that now is, married both his daughters to rich merchants. Here are many wells containing sweet water; and so often as the river Niger overfloweth, they convey the water thereof by certain sluices into the town. Corn, cattle, milk, and butter this region yieldeth in great abundance: but salt is very scarce here; for it is brought hither by land from Taghaza which is 500 miles distant. When I myself was here, I saw one camel's load of salt sold for 80 ducats. The rich king of Timbuktu hath many plates and scepters of gold, some whereof weigh 1,300 pounds: and

he keeps a magnificent and well-furnished court. When he travelleth any whither he rideth upon a camel which is led by some of his noblemen; and so he doth likewise when he goeth forth to warfare, and all his soldiers ride upon horses. Whoever will speak unto this king must first fall down before his feet, and then taking up earth must first sprinkle it upon his own head and shoulders: which custom is ordinarily observed by . . . ambassadors from other princes. He hath always 3,000 horsemen, and a number of footmen that shoot poisoned arrows, attending upon him. They have often skirmishes with those that refuse to pay tribute, and so many as they take, they sell unto the merchants of Timbuktu. Here are very few horses bred, and the merchants and courtiers keep certain little nags which they use to travel upon: but their best horses are brought out of Barbary. . . . Here are great store of doctors, judges, priests, and other learned men, that are bountifully maintained at the king's cost and charges, and hither are brought divers manuscripts or written books out of Barbary, which are sold for more money than any other merchandise. The coin of Timbuktu is of gold without any stamp or superscription but in matters of small value they use certain shells brought hither out of the kingdom of Persia, 400 of which are worth a ducat: and 6⅔ pieces of their gold coin weigh an ounce. The inhabitants are people of gentle and cheerful disposition, and spend a great part of the night singing and dancing through all the streets of the city.

 What role did the city of Timbuktu play in regional commerce, according to this author? What were the chief means of payment?

Source: From *The History and Description of Africa*, by Leo Africanus (New York: Burt Franklin).

The City of Timbuktu. The city of Timbuktu sat astride one of the major trade routes that passed through the Sahara between the kingdoms of West Africa and the Mediterranean Sea. Caravans transported food and various manufactured articles southward in exchange for salt, gold, copper, skins, agricultural goods, and slaves. Salt was at such a premium in Timbuktu that a young Moroccan wrote in 1513 that one camel's load brought 500 miles by caravan sold for 80 gold ducats, while a horse sold for only 40 ducats. Timbuktu became a prosperous city and a great center of Islamic scholarship. By 1550, it had three universities connected to its principal mosques and 180 Qur'anic schools. This pen-and-ink sketch was done by the French traveler René Caillie in 1828, when the city was long past its peak of prosperity and renown.

FOR GOD, GOLD, AND GLORY IN THE AGE OF EXPLORATION

Much has been written by modern historians about the motives behind the European "Age of Exploration." Some researchers stress the desire for fame and riches, while others point to the importance of the missionary effort to spread the message of Christianity. As this letter from King Manuel of Portugal to the king and queen of Castile suggests, the motives for European expansion were not always subject to simple interpretation. As the slogan often voiced by participants in the Spanish conquest of the Americas suggests, the motives behind the process were a complex mixture of "God, Gold, and Glory," and not necessarily in that order.

Letter from King Manuel of Portugal

Your Highnesses already know that we had ordered Vasco da Gama, a nobleman of our household, and his brother Paulo da Gama, with four vessels to make discoveries by sea, and that two years have now elapsed since their departure. And as the principal motive of this enterprise has been . . . the service of God our Lord . . . it pleased Him in His mercy to speed them on their route. From a message which has now been brought to this city by one of the captains, we learn that they did reach and discover India and other kingdoms and lordships bordering upon it; that they entered and navigated its sea, finding large cities, large edifices and rivers, and great populations, among whom is carried on all the trade in spices and precious stones, which are forwarded in ships . . . to Mecca, and thence to Cairo, whence they are dispersed throughout the world. Of these they have brought a quantity, including cinnamon, cloves, ginger, nutmeg, and pepper . . . also many fine stones of all sorts, such as rubies and others.

And they also came to a country in which there are mines of gold, of which, as of the spices and precious stones, they did not bring as much as they could have done, for they took no merchandise with them.

As we are aware that your Highnesses will hear of these things with much pleasure and satisfaction, we thought well to give this information. And your Highnesses may believe, in accordance with what we have learnt concerning the Christian people whom these explorers reached, that it will be possible, notwithstanding that they are not as yet strong in the faith or possessed of a thorough knowledge of it, to do much in the service of God and the exaltation of the Holy Faith, once they shall have been converted and fully fortified in it. And when they shall have thus been fortified in the faith there will be an opportunity for destroying the Moors of those parts. Moreover, we hope, with the help of God, that the great trade which now enriches the Moors of those parts, through whose hands it passes without the intervention of other persons or peoples, shall, in consequence of our regulations be diverted to the natives and ships of our own kingdom, so that henceforth all Christendom, in this part of Europe, shall be able, in a large measure, to provide itself with these spices and precious stones. . . . This . . . will cause our designs and intentions to be pushed with more ardour . . . the war upon the Moors of the territories conquered by us in these parts . . .

 Based on what you have learned in this chapter, how would you rate the various motives for European expansion as identified in this document?

Source: Letter from King Manuel of Portugal to their Highnesses Ferdinand and Isabella of Castile, from *A Journal of the First Voyage of Vasco da Gama, 1497–1499* (London: Hakluyt Society, 1898), tr. E .G. Ravenstein, pp. 113–114, and cited in Nigel Cliff, *The Last Crusade: The Epic Voyages of Vasco da Gama* (New York: Harper, 2011), pp. 277–278.

---

south of the city of Jenne, was used as the local currency, as well as cowrie shells from the Indian Ocean. Despite the efforts of Askia Mohammed and his successors, however, centrifugal forces within Songhai, brought on by rivalries at court, chronic drought, and bouts of the plague, led to civil disorder and eventually led to its breakup. The end came in 1591, when Moroccan forces armed with firearms conquered the city of Gao in a bid to gain control over the gold trade in the region. At that point, the city of Timbuktu, and the trade route that had enabled its rise, began a long period of decline, as other forces began to make their entrance into the region.

14–1c A New Player: Europe

The rise of Songhai in the mid-fifteenth century coincides with the appearance of a new competitor in the region. Europeans had long been attracted to the East. Myths and legends of an exotic land of great riches, sparked by the dramatic account of the Venetian adventurer Marco Polo, were widespread in the Middle Ages. But

the conquests of the Ottoman Turks in Anatolia and the Mediterranean Sea temporarily reduced Western traffic to Asia. With the closing of the overland routes, a number of people in Europe became interested in the possibility of reaching Asia by sea.

As we have seen in Chapter 13, by the mid-fifteenth century Europe was in the process of recovering from the turmoil of the recent past. A new spirit of adventure and confidence, combined with political consolidation and a vigorous economic recovery, stimulated a growing desire among Europeans to look for wealth and trading opportunities beyond their frontiers. As one Spanish conquistador (kahn-KEESS-tuh-dor) explained, he and his kind went to the Americas to "serve God and His Majesty, to give light to those who were in darkness, and to grow rich, as all men desire to do."[4]

That statement alludes to another major reason for the overseas voyages—religious zeal. For centuries, Christian zealots had dreamed of spreading the word of Jesus beyond the bounds of Europe to Africa, the Middle East, and beyond. John Plano

Carpini, the Franciscan friar dispatched in 1245 by the Vatican to the Mongol capital at Karakorum, had initiated the process by appealing to his hosts to convert to the Christian faith. Two centuries later, that crusading mentality reasserted itself in Portugal and Spain, where conflict with regional Muslim powers had intensified religious rivalries. Contemporaries of Prince Henry the Navigator of Portugal (see below), an outspoken advocate of European expansion into the continent of Africa, said that he was motivated by his zeal to spread the Christian message to pagan peoples beyond the confines of Europe. Although most scholars believe that the religious motive was secondary to economic considerations, it would be foolish to overlook the genuine desire on the part of both explorers and conquistadors, let alone missionaries, to convert the heathen to Christianity. Hernán Cortés (hayr-NAHN kor-TAYSS *or* kor-TEZ), the conqueror of Mexico, asked his Spanish rulers if it was not their duty to ensure that the native Mexicans were "introduced into and instructed in the holy Catholic faith."[5] Thus spiritual and secular motives were closely intertwined in the sixteenth century. No doubt dreams of personal grandeur and glory, along with intellectual curiosity and a spirit of adventure, also played a role in European expansion.

The Means If "Christians and spices," as Vasco da Gama alleged, were the primary motives, what made the voyages possible? Perhaps first and foremost, by the end of the fifteenth century, European states had achieved a level of knowledge and technology that enabled them to carry out ambitious ocean voyages well beyond the confines of continental Europe. Although the highly schematic and symbolic maps popular in the medieval era (see Chapter 7) were of little help to sailors, detailed charts made by medieval navigators and mathematicians in the thirteenth and fourteenth centuries, known as *portolani* (pohr-tuh-LAH-nee), were more useful. With details on coastal contours, distances between ports (thus the name), and compass readings, they proved of great value for voyages in European waters. But because the *portolani* were drawn on a flat surface and took no account of the curvature of the earth, they were of little use for longer overseas voyages. Only when seafarers began to venture beyond the coasts of Europe did they begin to accumulate information about the actual shape of the earth and how to measure it. By the end of the fifteenth century, cartography had developed to the point that Europeans possessed fairly accurate maps of the known world.

In addition, Europeans had developed remarkably seaworthy ships as well as new navigational techniques. European shipbuilders had mastered the use of the sternpost rudder, an import from China (previous rudders had been located on

COMPARATIVE ILLUSTRATION

European Warships During the Age of Exploration. Prior to the fifteenth century, most European ships were either small craft with triangular, lateen sails used in the Mediterranean or slow, unwieldy square-rigged vessels operating in the North Atlantic. By the sixteenth century, European naval architects began to build caravels (A), ships that combined the maneuverability and speed offered by lateen sails (widely used by sailors in the Indian Ocean) with the carrying capacity and seaworthiness of the square-riggers. For a century, caravels were the feared "raiders of the oceans." Eventually, as naval technology progressed, European warships developed in size and firepower, as the illustration of Portuguese carracks in Illustration B shows.

Q *What were the key characteristics of these different types of ships, and how did they affect their performance on the high seas?*

A

Album/Oronoz/Album/Superstock

B

DEA/G. Dagli Orti/Getty Images

the right side of the vessel, thus giving birth to the term "starboard," or "steer board"), and had learned how to combine the use of lateen sails (commonly used in the Indian Ocean) with the square rig familiar in northern European waters. With these innovations, they could construct **caravels** (KER-uh-velz), ships mobile enough to sail against the wind and engage in naval warfare and also large enough to be armed with heavy cannons and carry a substantial amount of goods over long distances (see Comparative Illustration, "European Warships During the Age of Exploration," p. 395). Previously, sailors had used a quadrant and their knowledge of the position of the polestar to ascertain their latitude. Below the equator, however, this technique was useless. Only with the assistance of new navigational aids such as the compass (a Chinese invention) and the astrolabe, an astronomical

instrument reportedly developed from ancient Greek examples by Arab sailors (see Chapter 7), were they able to explore the high seas with confidence.

A final spur to exploration was the growing knowledge of the wind patterns in the Atlantic Ocean (see Map 14.2). The first European fleets sailing southward along the coast of West Africa had found their efforts to return hindered by the strong winds that blew steadily from the north along the coast. During the mid-fifteenth century, however, sailors had learned to tack out into the ocean, where they were able to catch westerly winds in the vicinity of the Azores that brought them back to the coast of western Europe. Christopher Columbus used this technique in his voyages to the Americas, and others relied on their new knowledge of the winds to round the continent of Africa in search of spices.

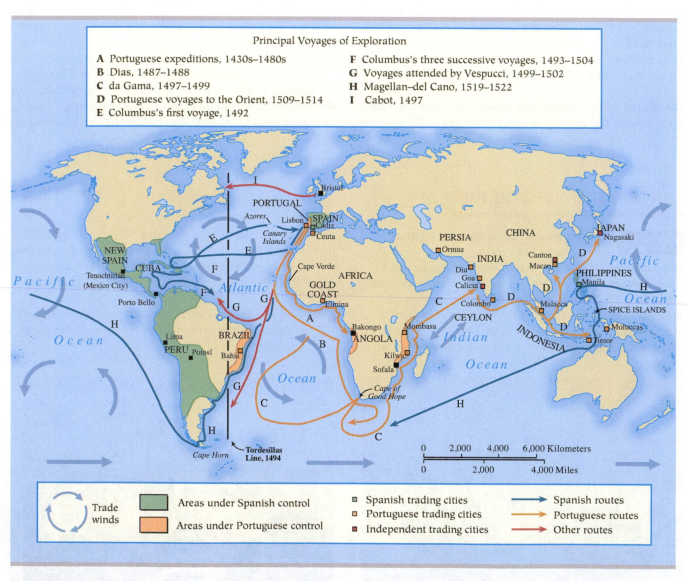

Principal Voyages of Exploration

A Portuguese expeditions, 1430s–1480s
B Dias, 1487–1488
C da Gama, 1497–1499
D Portuguese voyages to the Orient, 1509–1514
E Columbus's first voyage, 1492

F Columbus's three successive voyages, 1493–1504
G Voyages attended by Vespucci, 1499–1502
H Magellan–del Cano, 1519–1522
I Cabot, 1497

Map 14.2 European Voyages and Possessions in the Sixteenth and Seventeenth Centuries. This map indicates the most important voyages launched by Europeans during their momentous Age of Exploration in the sixteenth and seventeenth centuries.

Q *Why did Vasco da Gama sail so far into the South Atlantic on his voyage to Asia?*

14–2 THE PORTUGUESE MARITIME EMPIRE

Focus Questions: Why were the Portuguese so successful in taking over the spice trade? Why was their period of hegemony in Asia so brief?

Portugal took the lead when it began exploring the western coast of Africa under the sponsorship of Prince Henry the Navigator (1394–1460). Henry had three objectives: acquiring new trade opportunities for his kingdom (especially in the gold trade with West Africa), weakening the Muslim states in Spain and West Africa, and extending the realm of Christianity. In 1419, he founded a school for navigators on the southwestern coast of Portugal. Shortly thereafter, Portuguese fleets began probing southward along the western coast of Africa in search of gold, which had for centuries been carried northward from its source

An Ivory Mask from Benin. By the end of the fifteenth century, the West African state of Benin had developed into an extensive and powerful empire enjoying trade with many of its neighbors, as well as with the state of Portugal. With the latter it traded ivory, forest products, and slaves in exchange for textiles and other European manufactured goods. This life-size ivory mask was probably intended to be worn by the king of Benin as a belt ornament in a gesture of gratitude to his mother, who had allegedly used her magical powers to help defeat his enemies. On the crest of the crown are carvings of Portuguese figures, providing one of the first examples in African art of the new trade relationship between that continent and Europe.

south of the Sahara. In 1441, Portuguese ships reached the Senegal River, just north of Cape Verde. They found no gold but brought home a cargo of black Africans, most of whom were sold as slaves to wealthy buyers elsewhere in Europe. Within a few years, about a thousand slaves a year were shipped from the area back to Lisbon. Although obtaining slaves had not been one of their original motives for exploring the west coast of Africa, the Portuguese had inadvertently found a way to circumvent the traditional trans-Saharan slave route from Central Africa to the Mediterranean.

Continuing southward, in 1471 the Portuguese discovered a source of gold along the southern coast of the hump of West Africa (an area that would henceforth be known to Europeans as the Gold Coast). A few years later, they established contact with the inland state of Benin, north of the Gold Coast. To facilitate trade in gold, ivory, and slaves (not all slaves were brought back to Lisbon; some were bartered to local merchants for gold), the Portuguese leased land from local rulers and built stone forts along the coast. Trade was slow to develop at first, however, because the Portuguese initially did not have many products that appealed to potential African buyers.

14–2a En Route to India

Hearing reports of a route to India around the southern tip of Africa, Portuguese sea captains continued their probing. A few years later, contacts were established with the kingdom of Kongo, near the mouth of the Congo River. Then, in 1487, Bartolomeu Dias (bar-toh-loh-MAY-oo DEE-uhs) took advantage of westerly winds in the South Atlantic to round the Cape of Good Hope, but fearing a mutiny from his crew, he returned home without continuing further. Ten years later, a fleet under the command of Vasco da Gama rounded the cape and stopped at several ports controlled by Muslim merchants along the coast of East Africa, including Sofala, Kilwa, and Mombasa. At the coastal town of Malindi, they befriended the local ruler and erected the pillar shown on the opening page of this chapter to identify the spot for their return voyage (see illustration, "The Vasco da Gama Pillar at Malindi," p. 390). Then, having located a Muslim navigator who was familiar with seafaring in the region, da Gama's fleet crossed the Arabian Sea and arrived off the port of Calicut, on the southwestern coast of India, on May 18, 1498. The Portuguese crown had sponsored da Gama's voyage with the clear objective of destroying the Muslim monopoly over the spice trade, a monopoly that had been intensified by the Ottoman conquest of Constantinople in 1453 (see "For God, Gold, and Glory in the Age of Exploration," p. 394). Calicut was a major entrepôt on the long route from the Spice Islands to the Mediterranean

The Spice Islands

Image credit (rotated, beside mask image): The Trustees of the British Museum/Art Resource, NY

Sea, but the ill-informed Europeans believed it was the source of the spices themselves. Purchasing as much in the way of spices as his ships could carry, after three months in India, da Gama set out for home. Although he lost two ships along the way, the remaining vessels returned to Europe with their holds filled with ginger and cinnamon, a cargo that earned the investors a profit of several thousand percent.

14–2b The Search for the Source of Spices

Encouraged by the results of Vasco da Gama's maiden voyage, the Portuguese set out to gain control of the spice trade. In 1510, Admiral Afonso de Albuquerque (ah-FAHN-soh day AL-buh-kur-kee) established his headquarters at Goa (GOH-uh), on the western coast of India south of present-day Mumbai, formerly called Bombay. Over the next few years, they established a series of fortresses and trading posts along the coasts of western India, the Persian Gulf, and East Africa in a bid to dominate the trade network of the Indian Ocean. From these ports, the Portuguese raided Arab shippers, provoking the following comment from an Arab source: "[The Portuguese] took about seven vessels, killing those on board and making some prisoner. This was their first action, may God curse them."[6] In 1511, Albuquerque attacked Malacca itself.

For Albuquerque, control of Malacca would serve two purposes. It could help destroy the Arab spice trade network by blocking passage through the Strait of Malacca, and it could also provide the Portuguese with a way station en route to the Spice Islands (known today as the Moluccas) and other points east. After a short but bloody battle, the Portuguese seized the city and put the local Arab population to the sword. They then proceeded to erect the normal accoutrements of the day—a fort, a "factory" (warehouse), and a church.

From Malacca, the Portuguese launched expeditions farther east, to China in 1514 and the Moluccas (muh-LUHK-uhz). There they signed a treaty with a local sultan for the purchase and export of cloves to the European market. Within a few years, they had managed to seize control of much of the spice trade from Muslim traders and had garnered substantial profits for the Portuguese monarchy.

Why were the Portuguese so successful? Basically, it was a matter of guns and seamanship. The first Portuguese fleet to arrive in Indian waters was relatively modest in size. It consisted of three ships and twenty guns, a force sufficient for self-defense and intimidation but not for serious military operations. Most sixteenth-century Portuguese fleets were more heavily armed and were capable of inflicting severe defeats if necessary on local naval and land forces. The Portuguese by no means possessed a monopoly on the use of firearms and explosives, but their highly maneuverable, light ships enabled them to maintain their distance while bombarding the enemy with their powerful cannons. Such tactics gave them a military superiority over lightly armed rivals that they were able to exploit until the arrival of other European forces several decades later.

14–2c New Rivals Enter the Scene

Portugal's efforts to dominate the spice trade network were never totally successful, however. After some early disastrous defeats at sea, Muslim rivals sought to recover the initiative, harassing Portuguese fleets from seaports on the Arabian Peninsula and the coast of Africa and thereby preventing the latter from obtaining a monopoly on trade within the region. For their part, the Portuguese lacked both the numbers and the wealth to overcome local resistance and colonize the Asian regions. Moreover, their massive investments in ships and laborers for their empire (hundreds of ships and hundreds of thousands of workers in shipyards and overseas bases) proved very costly. Disease, shipwrecks, and battles took a heavy toll. The empire was simply too large and Portugal too small to maintain it, and by the end of the sixteenth century, the Portuguese were being severely challenged by European rivals.

The Spanish First on the scene was Spain. Queen Isabella of Spain had already signaled her intent to enter the competition in 1492 when she sponsored the voyage of Christopher Columbus into the Atlantic

Bukha Fort. As the Portuguese carried out their expansion across the Indian Ocean en route to the Spice Islands, they sought permanent bases along the way to serve as ports of call for their ships to obtain provisions and trade goods. One such base was in the Strait of Hormuz, where they erected several forts at the end of the sixteenth century to control the entrance into the Persian Gulf and replenish their food and water supplies. Shown here is Bukha Fort, erected along the shore of the Musandam Peninsula with a distinctive pear-shaped tower designed to deflect enemy cannon fire. Portuguese success was brief, however. In the early seventeenth century, the area was seized by local Omani Arabs, who used the fortifications to prevent entrance into the Gulf by hostile European powers. Today the restored fort serves as a museum.

William J. Duiker

DIVIDING UP THE SPOILS OF EXPLORATION

Interaction & Exchange **WHEN ADVENTURERS FROM PORTUGAL AND SPAIN** set off in opposite directions to find a route to the fabled "Spice Islands" on the other side of the globe, they created an awkward dilemma for themselves—how to divide up the territories along the different routes to the East. In the Treaty of Tordesillas, signed in 1494, they agreed to establish a vertical line west of Africa in the middle of the Atlantic Ocean, thus assigning all of the lands to the west to the Spanish, while those to the east were given to Portugal. Most of the Western Hemisphere—except for the eastern hump of the future Brazil—was thus placed in the Spanish sphere of influence.

But what line should be drawn on the other side of the world, where the two journeys would ultimately intersect, presumably somewhere near the Spice Islands themselves? That problem was not resolved in 1494, and as it turned out, domination over the spice trade was the subject of violent dispute involving several European nations over the next three centuries. In the end, ownership over the spice trade was decided at the point of a gun, not by the pen of the diplomat.

The Treaty of Tordesillas (June 7, 1494)

That, whereas a certain controversy exists between the said lords, their constituents, as to what lands, of all those discovered in the ocean sea up to the present day, the date of this treaty, pertain to each one of the said parts respectively; therefore, for the sake of peace and concord, and for the preservation of the relationship and love of the said King of Portugal for the said King and Queen of Castile, Aragon, etc., it being the pleasure of their Highnesses, they their said representatives, acting in their name and by virtue of their powers herein described, covenanted and agreed that a boundary or straight line be determined and drawn north and south, from pole to pole, on the said ocean sea, from the Arctic to the Antarctic pole. This boundary or line shall be drawn straight, as aforesaid, at a distance of three hundred and seventy leagues west of the Cape Verde Islands, being calculated by degrees, or by any other manner as may be considered the best and readiest, provided the distance shall be no greater than abovesaid. And all lands, both islands and mainlands, found and discovered already, or to be found and discovered hereafter, by the said King of Portugal and by his vessels on this side of the said line and bound determined as above, toward the east, in either north or south latitude, on the eastern side of the said bound, provided the said bound is not crossed, shall belong to, and remain in the possession of, and pertain forever to, the said King of Portugal and his successors. And all other lands, both islands and mainlands, found or to be found hereafter, discovered or to be discovered hereafter, which have been discovered or shall be discovered by the said King and Queen of Castile, Aragon, etc., and by their vessels, on the western side of the said bound, determined as above, after having passed the said bound toward the west, in either its north or south latitude, shall belong to, and remain in the possession of, and pertain forever to, the said King and Queen of Castile, Leon, etc., and to their successors.

 Why did Spain and Portugal encounter difficulty when seeking to divide up the newly discovered territories in the Pacific Ocean?

Source: From F. G. Davenport, ed., *European Treaties Bearing on the History of the United States and Its Dependencies to 1648* (Washington, D.C.: Carnegie Institution of Washington, 1917), p. 95.

Ocean in search of a westward route to the Indies (see map "Cape Horn and the Strait of Magellan"). That led to a dispute between the two Iberian nations over the rights to newly conquered territories. In 1494, in an effort to head off potential conflict between the two countries, the Treaty of Tordesillas (tor-day-SEE-yass) divided the newly discovered world into separate Portuguese and Spanish spheres of influence (see "Dividing Up the Spoils of Exploration"). Thereafter, the route east around the Cape of Good Hope was reserved for the Portuguese, while the route across the Atlantic (except for the eastern hump of South America) was assigned to Spain (see Map 14.2).

Columbus's later voyages eventually convinced influential figures at the Spanish court that the lands he had reached were not the Indies but an unknown

Cape Horn and the Strait of Magellan

land that possessed its own attractions. Still seeking a route to the Spice Islands, in 1519 Spain dispatched a fleet under the command of the Portuguese adventurer Ferdinand Magellan that sailed around the southern tip of South America, proceeded across the Pacific Ocean, and landed on the island of Cebu in the Philippine Islands. Although Magellan and some forty of his crew were killed there in a skirmish with the local population, one of the two remaining ships sailed on to Tidor, in the Moluccas, and thence around the world via the Cape of Good Hope. In the words of a contemporary historian, having completed the first circumference of the earth, they arrived in Cádiz "with precious cargo and fifteen men surviving out of a fleet of five sail."[7]

As it turned out, the Spanish, who were increasingly preoccupied with the territories newly discovered by Columbus, could not follow up on Magellan's accomplishment, and in 1529 they sold their rights in Tidor to the Portuguese. But Magellan's voyage was not a total loss to the Spanish, who soon consolidated their control over the Philippines and transformed it into a major way station in the carrying trade across the Pacific. Spanish galleons learned to follow the Pacific trade winds by carrying silk and other luxury goods from China to Acapulco in exchange for silver from the mines of Mexico.

The English and the Dutch The primary threat to the Portuguese toehold in Southeast Asia came from the English and the Dutch. In 1591, the first English expedition to the Indies through the Indian Ocean arrived in London with a cargo of pepper. Nine years later, a private joint-stock company, the East India Company, was founded to provide a stable source of capital for future voyages. In 1608, an English fleet landed at Surat (SOOR-et), on the northwestern coast of India. Trade with Southeast Asia soon followed.

The Dutch, bitter trade rivals to the English, were equally determined to show the flag in the region. Seven years after the first Dutch fleet arrived in India in 1595, the Dutch East India Company (Vereenigde Oost-Indische Compagnie, or VOC) was established under government sponsorship and began to compete actively for access to the spice trade. In 1611, a Dutch fleet made history by sailing directly east on the "roaring forties" (the powerful westerly winds circling the globe at that southern latitude) from South Africa to the Indonesian archipelago. In 1641, the Dutch seized the entrepôt of Malacca, one of the linchpins of Portugal's trading empire in Asia, and became a dominant force in controlling

the spice trade. An early eighteenth-century engraving by the Dutch author and naturalist Francis Valentijn depicts the harbor of Malacca filled with the ships of many nations. On a hill above the town, a new Protestant church in the Dutch style replaces a Catholic counterpart originally erected by the Portuguese a century earlier (see illustration "The Port of Malacca in 1726").

14–3 THE CONQUEST OF THE "NEW WORLD"

 Focus Question: How did Portugal and Spain acquire their empires in the Americas, and why were they so much more successful in setting down deep roots there than was the case in Asia?

Although the Portuguese had successfully defeated their Spanish rivals in obtaining access to the spice trade in the Indies, the latter, aided by their greater resources, were on the verge of establishing a far grander overseas empire.

14–3a The Voyages

An important figure in the history of Spanish exploration was an Italian from Genoa, Christopher Columbus (1451–1506). Like many knowledgeable Europeans, Columbus was aware that the world was round, but he was also convinced that the circumference of the earth was smaller than some of his contemporaries believed. He therefore argued that Asia could easily be reached by sailing due west instead of eastward around Africa. After his plan was rejected by the Portuguese, he persuaded Queen Isabella of Castile to finance his exploratory expedition, which left Spain in early August 1492 and reached land somewhere in the islands of the Bahamas ten weeks later. For the next few weeks, his three ships explored the coastline of Cuba and the northern shores of the neighboring island of Hispaniola (his-puhn-YOH-luh or ees-pahn-YAH-luh). Columbus believed that he had reached Asia and in three subsequent voyages (1493, 1498, and 1502) sought in vain to find a route through the outer islands to the Asian mainland. In his four voyages, Columbus reached all the major islands of the Caribbean, which he called the Indies, as well as Honduras in Central America.

Although Columbus clung for the rest of his life to his belief that he had reached Asia,

The Port of Malacca in 1726. In 1641, the Dutch took over the seaport of Malacca from the Portuguese. Over the next several decades, the new owners gradually replaced their Catholic rivals in controlling the spice trade between Europe and the Indies. One of the most prominent chroniclers of this process was the Dutch naturalist and author Francis Valentijn. Born in 1666, he spent many years in the Dutch East Indies and wrote a highly respected study of the Indonesian archipelago. His engraving of Malacca, shown here with European ships floating in the harbor, appeared shortly before his death in 1727. In the early nineteenth century, Malacca was ceded by treaty to Great Britain.

Photograph by William J. Duiker/Engraving of the city of Malacca by Francis Valentijn

other navigators soon realized that he had discovered a new frontier altogether and joined the race to what Europeans began to call the "New World." A Venetian seafarer, John Cabot, explored the New England coastline of the Americas under a license from King Henry VII of England. The continent of South America was discovered accidentally by the Portuguese sea captain Pedro Cabral (PAY-droh kuh-BRAHL) in 1500. Amerigo Vespucci (ahm-ay-REE-goh vess-POO-chee), a Florentine, accompanied several of Cabral's voyages and wrote a series of letters describing the geography of the lands he observed. The publication of these letters led eventually to the use of the name "America" (after Amerigo) for the new lands.

The Arrival of Hernán Cortés in Mexico

14–3b The Conquests

The newly discovered territories that Europeans referred to as the New World actually contained flourishing civilizations populated by millions of people (see Chapter 6). But the Americas were new to the Europeans, who quickly saw opportunities for conquest and exploitation. With Portugal clearly in the lead in the race to exploit the riches of the Indies, the importance of these lands was magnified in the minds of the Spanish, especially those who saw a chance to win fame and fortune for themselves and their families.

The Spanish **conquistadors** ("conquerors"), as they were called, were a hardy lot of mostly upper-class individuals motivated by a typical sixteenth-century blend of glory, greed, and religious zeal. Their superior weapons, organizational skills, and determination brought them incredible success in their new environment. In 1519, a Spanish expedition under the command of Hernán Cortés landed at Veracruz, on the Gulf of Mexico. Marching to Tenochtitlán (teh-nahch-teet-LAHN) at the head of a small contingent of troops, Cortés received a friendly welcome from the Aztec monarch Moctezuma Xocoyotzin (mahk-tuh-ZOO-muh shoh-koh-YAHT-seen) (often called Montezuma), who may have initially believed that his visitor was a representative of Quetzalcoatl (KWET-sul-koh-AHT-ul), the legendary and godlike feathered serpent of the Amerindian peoples (see Chapter 6). The king and his subjects were astounded to see men on horseback, for the horse had disappeared from the Americas at least ten thousand years earlier.

But tensions soon erupted between the Spaniards and the Aztecs, provoked in part by demands by Cortés that the

Aztecs renounce their native beliefs and accept Christianity. When the Spanish took Moctezuma hostage and began to destroy Aztec religious shrines, the local population revolted and drove the invaders from the city. Receiving assistance from the Aztec tribute state of Tlaxcallan (tuh-lah-SKAH-lahn), Cortés managed to fight his way back into the city. Meanwhile, the Aztecs were beginning to suffer the first effects of the diseases brought by the Europeans, which would eventually wipe out the majority of the local population. In a battle that to many Aztecs must have seemed to symbolize the dying of the legendary fifth sun, the Aztecs were finally vanquished. Within months, their magnificent city and its temples, believed by the conquerors to be the work of Satan, had been destroyed (see Comparative Illustration "The Spaniards Conquer a New World," p. 402).

A similar fate awaited the powerful Inka Empire in South America. Between 1531 and 1536, another expedition, led by a hardened and somewhat corrupt soldier, Francisco Pizarro (frahn-SEES-koh puh-ZAHR-oh) (1470–1541), destroyed Inka power high in the Peruvian Andes. The Spanish conquests were undoubtedly facilitated by the prior arrival of European diseases, which had decimated the local population. Although it took another three decades before the western part of Latin America was brought under Spanish control, already by 1535, the Spanish had created a system of colonial administration that made the New World—at least in European eyes—an extension of the old.

The Catholic Cathedral at Cuzco. After the total destruction of the Inka Empire, the Spanish conquistadors rebuilt the Inkan capital of Cuzco in their own image. Among the many changes that they implemented, the sacred Inkan pyramid in the heart of the city was dismantled and an impressive Spanish Baroque cathedral was erected on its base. As a final humiliation, many of the materials originally used for the pyramid were later put to use in building its replacement.

North Wind/North Wind Picture Archives

guzmā.   michvacā.

Ibero-Amerikanisches Institut/Art Resource, NY

B

COMPARATIVE ILLUSTRATION

Politics & Government **The Spaniards Conquer a New World.** The perspective that the Spanish brought to their arrival in the Americas was quite different from that of the indigenous peoples. In the European painting shown in illustration A, the encounter was a peaceful one, and the upturned eyes of Columbus and his fellow voyagers imply that their motives were spiritual rather than material. Illustration B, drawn by an Aztec artist, expresses a dramatically different point of view, as the Spanish invaders, assisted by their Indian allies, use superior weapons against the bows and arrows of their adversaries to bring about the conquest of Mexico.

Q *What does the Aztec painting presented here show the viewer about the nature of the conflict between the two contending armies?*

The Portuguese in Brazil Although the Spanish had taken the lead in planting their flag in the Western Hemisphere, they were not alone. After the Portuguese sea captain Pedro Cabral inadvertently discovered the eastern coast of Latin America in 1500 while en route to the Indies, the Portuguese crown established the colony of Brazil in the area, basing its claim on the Treaty of Tordesillas, which had allocated that territory to the Portuguese sphere of influence (see "Dividing Up the Spoils of Exploration," Section 14-2c, p. 399). Like their Spanish rivals, the Portuguese initially viewed their new colony as a source of gold and silver, but they soon discovered that profits could be made in other ways as well. A formal administrative system was instituted in Brazil in 1549, and Portuguese migrants

CHRONOLOGY	Spanish and Portuguese Activities in the Americas
Christopher Columbus's first voyage to the Americas	1492
Portuguese fleet arrives in Brazil	1500
Columbus's last voyages	1502–1504
Spanish conquest of Mexico	1519–1522
Francisco Pizarro's conquest of the Inkas	1531–1536
Viceroyalty of New Spain established	1535
Formal colonial administrative system established in Brazil	1549

arrived to establish plantations to produce sugar, coffee, and other tropical products for export to Europe.

14–3c Governing the Empires

While Portugal set out to strengthen its control over Brazil, Spain began to construct a colonial empire that included Central America, most of South America, and parts of North America. Within the lands of Central and South America, a new civilization arose that we have come to call Latin America (see Map 14.3).

Latin America rapidly became a multiracial society. Already by 1501, Spanish rulers allowed intermarriage between Europeans and the inhabitants of the Americas, whom the Europeans called Indians. Their offspring became known as **mestizos** (mess-TEE-zohz). In addition, over a period of three centuries, possibly as many as 8 million African slaves were brought to Spanish and Portuguese America to work the plantations that were established (see Section 14-4c, "The Slave Trade," p. 408). **Mulattoes** (muh-LAH-tohz)—the offspring of Africans and Europeans—joined mestizos and descendants of whites, Africans, and local Indians to produce a unique multiracial society in Latin America.

The State and the Church in Colonial Latin America Although the colonial empires of Portuguese Brazil and Spanish America lasted more than three hundred years, the difficulties of communication and travel between the Americas and Europe made it virtually impossible for the home-country monarchs to provide close regulation of their empires. This left colonial officials in Latin America with much autonomy in implementing imperial policies. Nevertheless, the Iberians tried to keep the most important posts of colonial government in the hands of Europeans.

To rule their American empires, the kings of Spain and Portugal appointed **viceroys**, who ruled over a bureaucracy staffed primarily by Europeans, known as *peninsulares*. The first Spanish viceroyalty was established for New Spain (Mexico) in 1535. Another was organized in Peru in 1543, and later two additional ones—New Granada and La Plata—were added. Viceroyalties were in turn subdivided into smaller units, where **creoles**—American-born descendants of Europeans—often held prominent positions.

From the beginning, Spanish and Portuguese rulers were determined to convert the indigenous peoples of the Western Hemisphere to Christianity. Catholic missionaries fanned out to different parts of the Spanish Empire, where they brought Indians together into villages where they could be converted to Christianity, taught a trade, and encouraged to grow crops (see Film & History, p. 405). The Catholic Church also built hospitals, orphanages, and schools to instruct Indian students in the rudiments of reading, writing, and arithmetic.

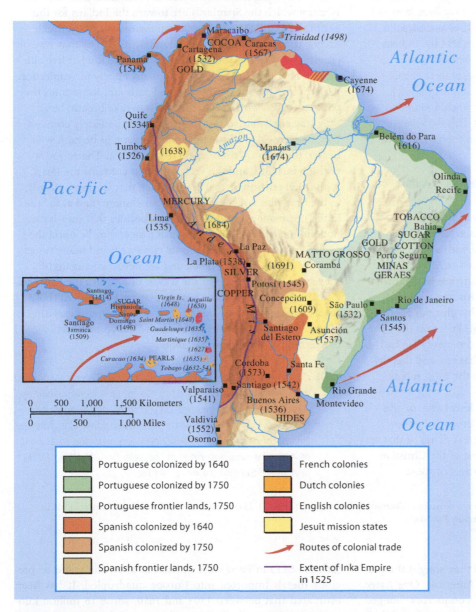

Map 14.3 Latin America from c. 1500 to 1750. From the sixteenth century, Latin America was largely the colonial preserve of the Spanish, although Portugal dominated Brazil. The Latin American colonies supplied the Spanish and Portuguese with gold, silver, sugar, tobacco, cotton, and animal hides.

Q *How do you explain the ability of Europeans to dominate such large areas of Latin America?*

Exploiting the Riches of the Americas The most vital task for administrators in the Americas was to enable the home countries to profit economically from their colonies in Latin America. In the minds of Europeans, the chief source of national and

The March of Civilization

Interaction & Exchange

AS EUROPEANS BEGAN TO EXPLORE NEW PARTS OF THE WORLD IN THE FIFTEENTH CENTURY, they were convinced that it was their duty to introduce civilized ways to the heathen peoples they encountered. This attitude is reflected in the first selection, which describes the Spanish captain Vasco Núñez de Balboa (BAHS-koh NOON-yez day bal-BOH-uh) in 1513, when from a hill on the Isthmus of Panama he first laid eyes on the Pacific Ocean.

Bartolomé de Las Casas (1474–1566) was a Dominican monk who participated in the conquest of Cuba and received land and Indians in return for his efforts. But in 1514, he underwent a radical transformation that led him to believe that the Indians had been cruelly mistreated by his fellow Spaniards. He spent the remaining years of his life fighting for the Indians. The second selection is taken from his most influential work, *Brevísima Relación de la Destrucción de las Indias*, known to English readers as *The Tears of the Indians*. This work was largely responsible for the reputation of the Spanish conquistadors as cruel and murderous fanatics.

Gonzalo Fernández de Ovieda, *Historia General y Natural de las Indias*

On Tuesday, the twenty-fifth of September of the year 1513, at ten o'clock in the morning, Captain Vasco Núñez, having gone ahead of his company, climbed a hill with a bare summit, and from the top of this hill saw the South Sea. Of all the Christians in his company, he was the first to see it. He turned back toward his people, full of joy, lifting his hands and his eyes to Heaven, praising Jesus Christ and his glorious Mother the Virgin, Our Lady. Then he fell upon his knees on the ground and gave great thanks to God for the mercy He had shown him, in allowing him to discover that sea, and thereby to render so great a service to God and to the most serene Catholic Kings of Castile, our sovereigns. . . .

And he told all the people with him to kneel also, to give the same thanks to God, and to beg Him fervently to allow them to see and discover the secrets and great riches of that sea and coast, for the greater glory and increase of the Christian faith, for the conversion of the Indians, natives of those southern regions, and for the fame and prosperity of the royal throne of Castile and of its sovereigns present and to come. All the people cheerfully and willingly did as they were bidden; and the Captain made them fell a big tree and make from it a tall cross, which they erected in that same place, at the top of the hill from which the South Sea had first been seen.

Bartolomé de Las Casas, *The Tears of the Indians*

There is nothing more detestable or more cruel than the tyranny which the Spaniards use toward the Indians for the getting of pearl. Surely the infernal torments cannot much exceed the anguish that they endure, by reason of that way of cruelty; for they put them under water some four or five ells deep, where they are forced without any liberty of respiration, to gather up the shells wherein the Pearls are; sometimes they come up again with nets full of shells to take breath, but if they stay any while to rest themselves, immediately comes a hangman row'd in a little boat, who as soon as he hath well beaten them, drags them again to their labor. Their food is nothing but filth, and the very same that contains the Pearl, with small portion of that bread which that Country affords; in the first whereof there is little nourishment; and as for the latter, it is made with great difficulty, besides that they have not enough of that neither for sustenance; they lie upon the ground in fetters, lest they should run away; and many times they are drown'd in this labor, and are never seen again till they swim upon the top of the waves; oftentimes they also are devoured by certain sea monsters, that are frequent in those seas. Consider whether this hard usage of the poor creatures be consistent with the precepts which God commands concerning charity to our neighbor. . . .

 Can the sentiments expressed by Vasco Núñez be reconciled with the treatment accorded to the Indians as described by Las Casas? Which selection do you think better describes the behavior of the Spaniards in the Americas? Compare the treatment of the Indians described here with the treatment of African slaves described in the selection "A Slave Market in Africa," Section 14-4c, p. 411.

Source: From *The Age of Reconnaissance* by J. H. Parry (International Thomson Publishing, 1969), pp. 233–234. From *The Tears of the Indians*, Bartolomé de Las Casas. Copyright © 1970 by The John Lilburne Company Publishers.

personal wealth was gold and silver, and they sought the precious metals wherever they went in the Americas. One Aztec observer commented that the Spanish conquerors "longed and lusted for gold. Their bodies swelled with greed, and their hunger was ravenous; they hungered like pigs for that gold."[8] Rich silver deposits were found and exploited in Mexico and in southern Peru (modern Bolivia). When the mines at Potosí (poh-toh-SEE) in Peru were opened in 1545, the value of precious metals imported into Europe quadrupled. It has been estimated that between 1503 and 1650, some 16 million kilograms (17,500 tons) of silver and 185,000 kilograms (200 tons) of gold entered the port of Seville in Spain.

Although the pursuit of gold and silver offered prospects of fantastic financial rewards to the conquistadors and their

descendants, agriculture ultimately proved to be a more abiding source of prosperity for Latin America. To their initial disappointment, the newly discovered lands produced few of the familiar spices they had sought in Asia, but they soon discovered that the region contained a multitude of other products unknown in the Old World (see Comparative Essay "The Columbian Exchange," Section 14-3e, p. 407). At the same tme, the climate of the Americas was also conducive for growing valuable products like sugar and coffee. The American colonies became important sources of new imports for Spain and Portugal as sugar, tobacco, chocolate, precious woods, animal hides, and a number of other natural products made their way to Europe. In turn, the mother countries supplied their colonists with manufactured goods (see Map 14.4). Both Spain and Portugal closely regulated the trade of their American colonies to keep others out, but the English and the French eventually became too powerful to be excluded from this lucrative Latin American market.

To produce these goods, colonial authorities initially tried to rely on local sources of human labor. Spanish policy toward the Indians was a combination of confusion, misguided paternalism, and cruel exploitation. Confusion arose over the nature of the Indians. Queen Isabella declared the Indians to be subjects of Castile

and instituted the *encomienda* **system**, under which European settlers received grants of land and could collect tribute from the indigenous peoples and use them as laborers. In return, the holders of an *encomienda* (en-koh-MYEN-duh) were supposed to protect the Indians and supervise their spiritual and material needs. In practice, this meant that the settlers were free to implement the system as they pleased. Three thousand miles from Spain, Spanish settlers largely ignored their government and brutally used the Indians to pursue their own economic interests (see Opposing Viewpoints "The March of Civilization"). Indians were put to work on sugar plantations and in the lucrative gold and silver mines.

Forced labor, starvation, and especially disease took a fearful toll on Indian lives. With little or no natural resistance to European diseases, the Indians were ravaged by smallpox, measles, and typhus brought by the explorers and the conquistadors. Although scholarly estimates vary drastically, a reasonable guess is that at least half of the local population in some areas died of European diseases. On Hispaniola alone, out of an initial population of 100,000 when Columbus arrived in 1493, only 300 Indians survived by 1570. In 1542, largely in response to the publications of Bartolomé de Las Casas (bahr-toh-loh-MAY day lahs KAH-sahs), a Dominican monk who championed the Indians, the government abolished the *encomienda* system and provided more protection for the Indians. By then, however, the indigenous population had been decimated by disease, causing the Spanish—and eventually the Portuguese as well—to import African slaves to replace the Indians in the sugar fields.

14-3d The Competition Intensifies

The success of the Spanish and the Portuguese in exploiting the riches of the Americas soon attracted competition from other European trading states. In 1607, after an abortive effort to establish a base near Cape Hatteras had failed, the English set up their first permanent settlement at Jamestown, near the Chesapeake Bay. Within a few years, other European states had followed suit, and by the end of the seventeenth century, they had occupied much of the eastern seaboard of North America (see Chapter 18).

But the major area of competition was in South America and the Caribbean islands, where the lure of profits from the sugar trade was difficult to resist. The Dutch formed their own West India Company in 1621 to compete with Spanish and Portuguese interests and briefly took control of the sugar plantations on the east coast of Brazil. The French and the English focused their efforts on the Caribbean, where their privateers preyed on Spanish galleons carrying silver from the Americas back to Seville. They also competed actively for control of several of the Caribbean islands, where sugar plantations were producing fabulous profits for their new European owners. A number of the islands in the region shifted control several times over the course of the seventeenth and eighteenth centuries.

HISTORIANS DEBATE · 14-3e Christopher Columbus: Hero or Villain?

For centuries, the explorer Christopher Columbus has generally been viewed by most observers in a positive light. By discovering the Western Hemisphere, he opened up the world and laid the

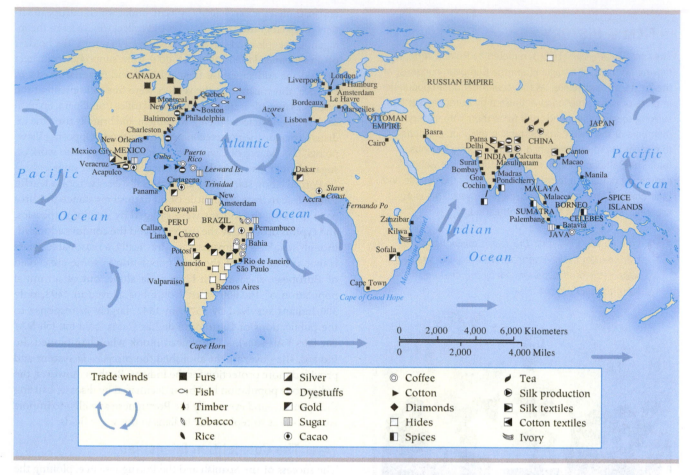

Map 14.4 Patterns of World Trade Between 1500 and 1800. This map shows the major products that were traded by European merchants throughout the world during the era of European exploration.

Q *What were the primary sources of gold and silver, so sought after by Columbus and his successors?*

foundations for the modern global economy. Recently, however, some historians have begun to challenge the prevailing image of Columbus as a heroic figure in world history and view him instead as a symbol of European colonial repression and a prime mover in the virtual extinction of the peoples and cultures of the Americas (see Comparative Essay "The Columbian Exchange").

Certainly, they have a point. As we have seen, the immediate consequences of Columbus's voyages were tragic for countless peoples in the Western Hemisphere. And as historical studies have shown, Columbus, who was himself not an entirely sympathetic figure, viewed the indigenous peoples that he encountered with condescension, describing them to his sponsors as naïve innocents who could be exploited for the purpose of bringing wealth and power to Spain. As a consequence, his men frequently treated the local population brutally.

But is it fair to blame Columbus for possessing many of the character traits and prejudices common to his era? To do so is to demand that an individual transcend the limitations of his time and adopt the values of another generation several hundred years into the future—something that few, if any, would be able to achieve. Perhaps it is better to note simply that Columbus and his contemporaries showed relatively little understanding and sympathy for the cultural values of peoples who lived beyond the borders of their own civilization, a limitation that would probably apply to one degree or another to all generations, including our own. Whether Columbus was a hero or a villain will remain a matter of debate. That he and his contemporaries played a key role in the emergence of the modern world is a matter on which there can be no doubt.

14–4 AFRICA IN TRANSITION

Q **Focus Question:** What were the main features of the African slave trade, and how did European participation in that trade affect traditional African practices?

Although the primary objective of the Portuguese in rounding the Cape of Good Hope was to find a sea route to the Spice Islands, they soon discovered that profits were to be made en route, along the eastern coast of Africa.

14–4a The Portuguese in Africa

In the early sixteenth century, a Portuguese fleet commanded by Francisco de Almeida (fran-SEESH-koh duh ahl-MAY-duh)

COMPARATIVE ESSAY

The Columbian Exchange

Interaction & Exchange In the Western world, the discovery of the Americas has traditionally been viewed in a largely positive sense, as the first step in a process that expanded the global trade network and eventually led to increased economic well-being and the spread of civilization throughout the world. In recent years, however, that view has come under sharp attack from some observers, who point out that for the peoples of the Americas, the primary legacy of the European conquest was not improved living standards but harsh colonial exploitation and the spread of pestilential diseases that devastated local populations.

Certainly, the record of the European conquistadors leaves much to be desired, and the voyages of Columbus were not of universal benefit to his contemporaries or to later generations. They not only resulted in the destruction of vibrant civilizations in the Americas but also led ultimately to the enslavement of millions of Africans, who were separated from their families and shipped to a far-off world in deplorable, inhuman conditions.

But to focus solely on the evils committed in the name of exploration and civilization misses a larger point and obscures the long-term ramifications of the events taking place. The age of European expansion that began in the fifteenth century was only the latest in a series of population movements that included the spread of nomadic peoples across Central Asia and the expansion of Islam out of the Middle East after the death of the prophet Muhammad. In fact, the migration of peoples in search of a better livelihood has been a central theme in the evolution of the human race since the dawn of prehistory. Virtually all of the migrations involved acts of unimaginable cruelty and the forcible displacement of peoples and societies.

In retrospect, it seems clear that the consequences of such broad population movements are too complex to be summed up in moral or ideological simplifications. The Mongol invasions and the expansion of Islam are two examples of movements that brought benefits as well as costs for the peoples who were affected. By the same token, the European conquest of the Americas not only brought the destruction of cultures and dangerous new diseases but also initiated the exchange of plant and animal species that have ultimately

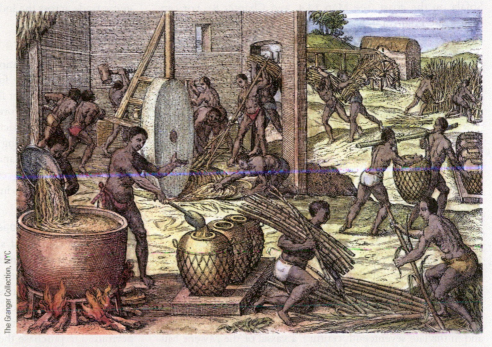

A sugar plantation on the island of Hispaniola

fed millions and been of widespread benefit to peoples throughout the globe. The introduction of the horse, the cow, and various grain crops vastly increased food production in the Americas. The cultivation of corn, manioc, and the potato, all of them products of the Western Hemisphere, has had the same effect in Asia, Africa, and Europe. The **Columbian Exchange**, as it is sometimes labeled, has had far-reaching consequences that transcend facile moral judgments.

The opening of the Americas had other long-term ramifications as well. The importation of vast amounts of gold and silver into Europe was a crucial factor in the growth of commercial capitalism that helped to finance the Industrial Revolution and set the stage for the global economy of the modern era (see Chapter 19).

Viewed in that context, the Columbian Exchange, whatever its moral failings, ultimately brought tangible benefits to peoples throughout the world. For some, the costs were high, and it can be argued that the indigenous peoples of the Americas might have better managed the transformation on their own. But the "iron law" of history operates at its own speed and does not wait for laggards. For good or ill, the Columbian Exchange marks a major stage in the transition between the traditional and the modern world.

 How can the costs and benefits of the Columbian Exchange be measured? What standards would you apply in attempting to measure them?

seized a number of East African port cities, including Kilwa, Sofala, and Mombasa, and built forts along the coast in an effort to control the trade in the area. Above all, the Portuguese wanted to monopolize the trade in gold, which was mined in the hills along the upper Zambezi River and then shipped to Sofala on the coast (see Map 14.4, and Chapter 8). For centuries, the gold trade had been monopolized by local Bantu-speaking Shona peoples at Zimbabwe. In the fifteenth century, it had come under the control of a Shona dynasty known as the Mwene Mutapa (MWAY-nay moo-TAH-puh).

The Mwene Mutapa had originally controlled the region south of the Zambezi River and may have been the builders of the impressive city known today as Great Zimbabwe, but sometime in the fifteenth century, they moved northeastward to the valley of the Zambezi. Here they encountered the arriving Portuguese, who had begun to move inland to gain access to the lucrative gold trade and had established ports on the Zambezi River. The Portuguese opened treaty relations with the Mwene Mutapa, and Jesuit priests were eventually posted to the court in 1561. At first, the Mwene Mutapa found the Europeans useful as an ally against local rivals, but by the end of the sixteenth century, the Portuguese had established a protectorate and forced the local ruler to grant title to large tracts of land to European officials and private individuals living in the area. Eventually, those lands would be integrated into the colony of Mozambique. The Portuguese, however, lacked the personnel and the capital to dominate local trade, and in the late seventeenth century, a vassal of the Mwene Mutapa succeeded in driving them from the plateau; his descendants maintained control of the area for the next two hundred years.

North of the Zambezi River, Bantu-speaking peoples were coming under pressure not only from the Portuguese but also from pastoralists migrating southward from the southern Sudan. The latter were frequently aggressive and began to occupy the rift valley and parts of the lake district that had previously been controlled by Bantu-speaking farmers. In some cases, the conflict between farmers and pastoralists was fairly clear-cut. In Rwanda and Burundi, immediately west of Lake Victoria, farming Hutu peoples defended their hilltop communities against roving Tutsi pastoralists occupying the surrounding lowlands.

14-4b The Dutch in South Africa

The first Europeans to settle in southern Africa were the Dutch. After an unsuccessful attempt to seize the Portuguese settlement on the island of Mozambique off the East African coast, in 1652 the Dutch set up a way station at the Cape of Good Hope to serve as a base for their fleets en route to the East Indies. At first, the new settlement was intended simply to provide food and other provisions to Dutch ships, but eventually it developed into a permanent colony. Dutch farmers, known as **Boers** and speaking a Dutch dialect that evolved into Afrikaans, began to settle in the sparsely occupied areas outside the city of Cape Town. The temperate climate and the absence of tropical diseases made the territory near the cape almost the only land south of the Sahara that the Europeans found suitable for habitation.

The Dutch, like their chief rivals, the English and the French, also took advantage of the decline of the Songhai Empire to become active in the West African trade in the mid-sixteenth century, encroaching particularly on the Portuguese spheres of influence. During the mid-seventeenth century, the Dutch seized a number of Portuguese forts along the West African coast while at the same time taking over the bulk of the Portuguese trade across the Indian Ocean.

14-4c The Slave Trade

The European exploration of the African coastline had little immediate significance for most peoples living in the interior of the continent, except for a few who engaged in direct or indirect trade with the foreigners. But for peoples living on or near the coast, the impact was often great indeed. As the trade in slaves increased during the sixteenth, seventeenth, and eighteenth centuries, thousands and then millions of men, women, and even children were removed from their homes and forcibly exported to plantations in the Western Hemisphere.

The Arrival of the Europeans As we saw in Chapter 8, there were different forms of slavery in Africa before the arrival of the Europeans. For centuries, slaves—often captives seized in battle or in raids between neighboring villages—had been used in many African societies as agricultural laborers, household servants, or concubines. Many served as domestic servants or as wageless workers for the local ruler, and some were permitted to purchase their freedom under certain conditions. After the expansion of Islam south of the Sahara in the eighth century, a vigorous traffic in slaves developed, as Arab merchants traded for slaves along routes snaking across the Sahara or up the Nile River Valley. Under Askia Mohammad and his successors, Songhai became active in the process, launching raids in non-Muslim areas and selling their captives to Arab merchants for shipment to the Middle East, where they were put to use as domestic servants or as workers on plantations throughout the region. Slavery also existed in many European countries, where a few slaves from Africa or Slavic-speaking peoples captured in war in the regions near the Black Sea (the English word *slave* derives from "Slav") were used for domestic purposes or as agricultural workers in the lands adjacent to the Mediterranean. Merchants from Genoa routinely traded captives that had been seized along the coast of the Black Sea to their Arab counterparts in return for spices.

With the arrival of the Europeans in Africa in the fifteenth century, the African slave trade changed dramatically, although the change did not occur immediately. At first, the Portuguese simply replaced European slaves with African ones. During the second half of the fifteenth century, about a thousand slaves were taken to Portugal each year; the vast majority were apparently destined to serve as domestic servants for affluent families throughout Europe. But the discovery of the Western Hemisphere in the 1490s and the subsequent planting of sugarcane in South America and on the islands of the Caribbean changed the situation dramatically.

Cane sugar was native to Indonesia and had first been introduced to Europeans from the Middle East during the crusades. By the fifteenth century, sugar cane was grown (often by slaves from Africa or the region of the Black Sea) in modest amounts on the islands of Cyprus and Sicily and in the southern regions of the Iberian Peninsula. But when the Ottoman Empire seized much of the eastern Mediterranean (see Chapter 16), the Europeans needed to seek out new areas suitable for cultivation. In 1490, the Portuguese established sugar plantations worked by African laborers at São Tomé, an island off the central coast of Africa. Demand increased as sugar gradually replaced honey as a sweetener, especially in northern Europe.

But the primary impetus to the sugar industry came from the colonization of the Americas. During the sixteenth century, plantations were established along the eastern coast of Brazil and on several islands in the Caribbean ("The Competition Intensifies," Section 14-3d, p. 405). Because the cultivation of cane sugar is an arduous process demanding both skill and large quantities of labor, the new plantations required more workers than could be provided by the importation of Europeans (mostly prisoners) or by the Indian population in the Americas, many of whom rapidly died of diseases imported from Europe and Africa. Since the climate and soil of much of West Africa were not especially conducive to the cultivation of sugar (cane sugar requires access to ample water and a frost-free environment), African slaves began to be shipped to Brazil and the

Caribbean to work on the plantations. The first were sent from Portugal, but in 1518, a Spanish ship carried the first boatload of African slaves directly from Africa to the Americas.

The Middle Passage During the next two centuries, the trade in slaves increased by massive proportions (see Map 14.5). An estimated 275,000 enslaved Africans were exported to other countries during the sixteenth century, more than two-thirds of them to the Americas. The total climbed beyond a million in the seventeenth century and jumped to 6 million in the eighteenth century, when the trade spread from West and Central Africa to East Africa. Even during the nineteenth century, when Great Britain and a number of other European countries attempted to end the slave trade, nearly 2 million humans were exported. It has been estimated that altogether as many as 10 million African slaves were transported to the Americas between the early sixteenth and the late nineteenth centuries. As many as 2 million were exported to other areas during the same period.

One reason for these astonishing numbers, of course, was the tragically high death rate. In what is often called the **Middle Passage**, the arduous voyage from Africa to the Americas, losses were frequently appalling. Although figures

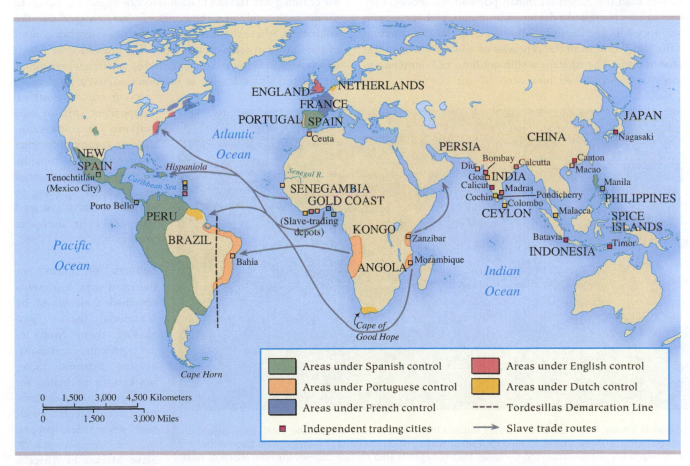

Map 14.5 The Slave Trade. Beginning in the sixteenth century, the trade in African slaves to the Americas became a major source of profit to European merchants. This map traces the routes taken by slave-trading ships, as well as the territories and ports of call of European powers in the seventeenth century.

Q *What were the major destinations for the slave trade?*

on the number of slaves who died on the journey are almost entirely speculative, during the first shipments, up to one-third of the human cargo may have died of disease or malnourishment. Even among crew members, mortality rates were sometimes as high as one in four. Later merchants became more efficient and reduced losses to about 10 percent. Still, the future slaves were treated inhumanely, chained together in the holds of ships reeking with the stench of human waste and diseases carried by vermin.

Slavery in the Americas Ironically, African slaves who survived the brutal voyage fared somewhat better than whites after their arrival. Mortality rates for Europeans in the West Indies were ten to twenty times higher than in Europe, and death rates for those newly arrived in the islands averaged more than 125 per 1,000 annually. But the figure for Africans, many of whom had developed at least a partial immunity to yellow fever, was only about 30 per 1,000.

The reason for the staggering death rates was clearly more than maltreatment, although that was certainly a factor. As we have seen, the transmission of diseases from one continent to another brought high death rates among those lacking immunity. African slaves were somewhat less susceptible to European diseases than the American Indian populations. Indeed, they seem to have possessed a degree of immunity, perhaps because their ancestors had developed antibodies to diseases common to the Old World from the centuries of contact via the trans-Saharan trade. The Africans would not have had immunity to native American diseases, however.

The mortality rates were higher for immigrants than for individuals born in the Americas, who as children gradually developed at least a partial immunity to many diseases. Death rates for native-born slaves tended to be significantly lower than for recent arrivals, which raises the question of why the slave population did not begin to rise after the initial impact of settlement had worn off. The answer appears to be a matter of economics. In the first place, only half as many women were enslaved as men, birthrates for women living in slavery were low, and infant mortality was high. In the second place, as long as the price of slaves was low, many slave owners in the West Indies apparently believed that purchasing a new slave was less expensive than raising a child from birth to working age at adolescence. After the price of slaves began to rise during the eighteenth century, plantation owners started to devote more efforts to replenishing the supply of workers by natural methods.

One of the lesser-known facts about slavery in the Americas is that many Africans did not accept their brutal life on the sugar, cotton, and tobacco plantations and took measures to avoid it. Work on sugar plantations was especially onerous, as slaves imported from Africa were forced to cut the sugarcane in the heat of the tropical sun and then bring it to the mill for crushing and transformation into raw sugar. Desperate to escape such conditions, thousands of slaves escaped into the wilderness, where they set up communities safe from control of the European colonial authorities. The most successful such efforts were in Brazil and on the island of Jamaica, where camps for escaped slaves, known as **maroons**, survived for decades carrying out an existence independent of colonial authority. In some cases, maroon communities even won recognition from the local colonial authorities in return for agreeing to return recently escaped slaves to their European masters.

Sources of Slaves For the most part, Europeans obtained their slaves by traditional means, purchasing them from local African merchants at the infamous slave markets in exchange for gold, guns, or other European manufactured goods such as textiles, copper, or iron utensils (see "A Slave Market in Africa"). The "third leg" of this so-called **Triangular Trade** took place when slave owners in the Americas

Gateway to Slavery. Of the 12 million slaves shipped from Africa to other parts of the world, some passed through Gorée (GOR-ay) prison, located on a small island just off the coast of Senegal, near Cape Verde. Beginning in the sixteenth century, European traders began to ship African captives from the region of West Africa to the Americas to be used as slave labor on sugar plantations. Although the number of individuals shipped from Gorée was relatively small, the prison has been promoted as a poignant symbol of the cruelty afflicted by the slave trade on millions of innocent Africans. As a sign on a doorway in the prison reads: "From this door, they would embark on a voyage with no return, eyes fixed on an infinity of suffering." The modern African city of Dakar looms in the distance.

A SLAVE MARKET IN AFRICA

Family & Society | **TRAFFIC IN SLAVES** had been carried on in Africa since the kingdom of the pharaohs in ancient Egypt. But the slave trade increased dramatically after the arrival of European ships off the coast of West Africa. The following passage by a Dutch observer describes a slave market in Africa and the conditions on the ships that carried the slaves to the Americas.

Slavery in Africa: A Firsthand Report

When these slaves come to Fida, they are put in prison all together; and when we treat concerning buying them, they are brought out into a large plain. There, by our surgeons, whose province it is, they are thoroughly examined, even to the smallest member, and that naked too, both men and women, without the least distinction or modesty. Those that are approved as good are set on one side; and the lame or faulty are set by as invalids. . . .

The invalids and the maimed being thrown out, . . . the remainder are numbered, and it is entered who delivered them. In the meanwhile, a burning iron, with the arms or name of the companies, lies in the fire, with which ours are marked on the breast. This is done that we may distinguish them from the slaves of the English, French, or others (which are also marked with their mark), and to prevent the Negroes exchanging them for worse, at which they have a good hand.

I doubt not but this trade seems very barbarous to you, but since it is followed by mere necessity, it must go on; but we take all possible care that they are not burned too hard, especially the women, who are more tender than the men.

When we have agreed with the owners of the slaves, they are returned to their prison. There from that time forward they are kept at our charge, costing us two pence a day a slave; which serves to subsist them, like our criminals, on bread and water. To save charges, we send them on board our ships at the very first opportunity, before which their masters strip them of all they have on their backs so that they come aboard stark naked, women as well as men. In this condition they are obliged to continue, if the master of the ship is not so charitable (which he commonly is) as to bestow something on them to cover their nakedness.

You would really wonder to see how these slaves live on board, for though their number sometimes amounts to six or seven hundred, yet by the careful management of our masters of ships, they are so regulated that it seems incredible. And in this particular our nation exceeds all other Europeans, for the French, Portuguese and English slave ships are always foul and stinking; on the contrary, ours are for the most part clean and neat.

The slaves are fed three times a day with indifferent good victuals, and much better than they eat in their own country. Their lodging place is divided into two parts, one of which is appointed for the men, the other for the women, each sex being kept apart. Here they lie as close together as it is possible for them to be crowded.

 Q *What is the author's overall point of view toward the institution of slavery? Does he justify the practice? How does he compare Dutch behavior with that of other European countries involved in the slave trade?*

Source: From The Great Travelers, vol. I, Milton Rugoff, ed. Copyright © 1960 by Simon & Schuster.

---

paid for their slaves with sugar or its byproducts (such as rum and molasses) exported to buyers in Europe. At first, local slave traders obtained their supply from nearby regions, but as demand increased, they had to move further inland to find their victims. In a few cases, local rulers became concerned about the impact of the slave trade on the political and social well-being of their societies (see "A Plea Between Friends," p. 412). As a general rule, however, the local monarchs viewed the slave trade as a source of income, and many launched forays against defenseless villages in search of unsuspecting victims.

Historians once thought that Europeans controlled the terms of the slave trade and were thus able to obtain victims at bargain prices. Recently, however, it has become clear that African intermediaries—private merchants, local elites, and trading state monopolies—were very active in the process and were often able to dictate the price, volume, and availability of slaves to European purchasers. The majority of the slaves sold to European buyers were males; females, who were in great demand in Africa and on the trans-Saharan trade, tended to be reserved for those markets. The slave merchants were often paid in various types of imported goods, including East Asian textiles (highly desired for their bright colors and durability), furniture, and other manufactured products. Until the end of the seventeenth century, the Portuguese preferred gold to slaves and would sometimes pay for the gold by selling slaves to African kingdoms that were short of labor. In fact, not until the beginning of the eighteenth century did slaves surpass gold and ivory as the continent's leading exports.

The Effects of the Slave Trade The effects of the slave trade varied from area to area. It might be assumed that apart from the tragic effects on the lives of individual victims and their families, the practice would have led to the depopulation of vast areas of the continent. This did occur in some areas, notably in modern Angola, south of the mouth of the Congo River, and in thinly populated regions in East Africa, but it was less true in West Africa. There high birthrates were often

A PLEA BETWEEN FRIENDS

KING AFONSO I OF THE STATE OF KONGO was one of Portugal's chief African allies during the early sixteenth century. A convert to Christianity, he used his relationship with the Portuguese to extend the territory of his kingdom at the expense of neighboring states in the region. Captives obtained during his military campaigns were sold to merchants and then exported abroad as slaves. As the demand for slaves increased, however, traders began to trap and enslave Afonso's own subjects, while flooding the country with goods from abroad that undermined his royal authority.

In this letter, written in 1526, Afonso appealed to his "brother" sovereign, Dom João III, king of Portugal, to prevent such unscrupulous merchants from seizing his subjects and selling them as slaves to European sea captains. The letter is a vivid testimonial to how the slave trade destabilized African societies on or near the coast during the sixteenth and seventeenth centuries.

A Letter to King João

[1526] Sir, your Highness [of Portugal] should know how our Kingdom is being lost in so many ways that it is convenient to provide for the necessary remedy, since this is caused by the excessive freedom given by your factors and officials to the men and merchants who are allowed to come to this Kingdom to set up shops with goods and many things which have been prohibited by us, and which they spread throughout our Kingdoms and Domains in such an abundance that many of our vassals, whom we had in obedience, do not comply because they have the things in greater abundance than we ourselves; and it was with these things that we had them content and subjected under our vassalage and jurisdiction, so

it is doing a great harm not only to the service of God, but the security and peace of our Kingdoms and State as well.

And we cannot reckon how great the damage is, since the mentioned merchants are taking every day our natives, sons of the land and the sons of our noblemen and vassals and our relatives, because the thieves and men of bad conscience grab them wishing to have the things and wares of this Kingdom which they are ambitious of; they grab them and get them to be sold; and so great, Sir, is the corruption and licentiousness that our country is being completely depopulated, and Your Highness should not agree with this nor accept it as in your service. And to avoid it we need from those [your] Kingdoms no more than some priests and a few people to teach in schools, and no other goods except wine and flour for the holy sacrament. That is why we beg of Your Highness to help and assist us in this matter, commanding your factors that they should not send here either merchants or wares, because it is *our will that in these Kingdoms there should not be any trade of slaves nor outlet for them.* Concerning what is referred above, again we beg of Your Highness to agree with it, since otherwise we cannot remedy such an obvious damage. Pray Our Lord in His mercy to have Your Highness under His guard and let you do for ever the things of His service. I kiss your hand many times.

At our town of Congo, written on the sixth day of July.
João Teixeira did it in 1526.
The King, Dom Afonso.

[On the back of this letter the following can be read: "To the most powerful and excellent prince Dom João, King our Brother."]

 In what ways were the European merchants destabilizing the kingdom of Kongo? What remedy did Afonso propose?

Source: From *The African Past: Chronicles from Antiquity to Modern Times* by Basil Davidson (Boston: Little, Brown and Company, 1964), pp. 191–192.

---

able to counterbalance the loss of able-bodied adults, and the introduction of new crops from the Americas, such as maize, peanuts, and manioc, led to an increase in food production that made it possible to support a larger population. One of the many cruel ironies of history is that while the institution of slavery was a tragedy for many, it benefited others.

Still, there is no denying the reality that from a moral point of view, the slave trade represented a tragic loss for millions of Africans, not only for the individual victims but also for their families. One of the more poignant aspects of the trade is that as many as 20 percent of those sold to European slavers were children, a statistic that may be partly explained by the fact that many European countries enacted regulations that permitted more children than adults to be transported aboard the ships.

Beyond the effects on individual Africans and their families, the slave trade also had a corrosive impact on the structure of society as a whole. Another consequence of the arrival

of the Europeans was the introduction of firearms into the African continent. As the European demand for slaves steadily increased, African slave traders began to use their newly purchased guns to raid neighboring villages in search of captives, initiating a chain of violence that rapidly extended into the interior and created a climate of fear and insecurity throughout the region. Old polities were undermined, and new regimes ruled by rapacious "merchant princes" began to proliferate on the coast.

How did Europeans justify cruelty of such epidemic proportions? In some cases, they rationalized that slave traders were only carrying on a tradition that had existed for centuries throughout the Mediterranean and African world. In others, they eased their consciences by noting that slaves brought from Africa would now be exposed to the Christian faith and would be able to replace American Indian workers, many of whom were considered too physically fragile for the heavy human labor involved in cutting sugarcane.

CHRONOLOGY The Penetration of Africa

CHRONOLOGY	The Penetration of Africa	
Life of Prince Henry the Navigator		1394–1460
Portuguese ships reach the Senegal River		1441
Bartolomeu Dias sails around the tip of Africa		1487
First boatload of slaves to the Americas		1518
Dutch way station established at the Cape of Good Hope		1652
Ashanti kingdom established in West Africa		1680
Portuguese expelled from Mombasa		1698

14–4d Political and Social Structures in a Changing Continent

Of course, the Western economic penetration of Africa had other dislocating effects. As in other parts of the non-Western world, the importation of manufactured goods from Europe undermined the foundations of local cottage industries and impoverished countless families. The demand for slaves and the introduction of firearms intensified political instability and civil strife. At the same time, the impact of the Europeans should not be exaggerated. Only in a few isolated areas, such as South Africa and Mozambique, were permanent European settlements established. Elsewhere, at the insistence of African rulers and merchants, European influence generally did not penetrate beyond the coastal regions.

Nevertheless, inland areas were often affected by events taking place elsewhere. In the western Sahara, for example, the diversion of trade routes toward the coast led to the weakening of the old Songhai trading empire and its eventual conquest by a vigorous new Moroccan dynasty in the late sixteenth century. Morocco had long hoped to expand its influence into the Sahara in order to seize control over the commerce in gold and salt, and in 1590, Moroccan forces defeated Songhai's army at Gao, on the Niger River, and then occupied the great caravan center of Timbuktu. Even after the departure of the invaders, Songhai was beyond recovery, and the next two centuries were marked by ongoing strife between divergent states and intense competition between Muslims in the cities and towns and adherents of traditional African religions in rural areas.

European influence had a more direct impact along the coast of West Africa, especially in the vicinity of European forts such as Dakar and Sierra Leone, but no European colonies were established there before 1800. Most of the numerous African states in the area from Cape Verde to the delta of the Niger River were sufficiently strong to resist Western encroachments, and they often allied with each other to force European purchasers to respect their monopoly over trading operations. Some, like the powerful Ashanti kingdom, established in 1680 on the Gold Coast, profited substantially from the rise in seaborne commerce. Some states, particularly along the so-called Slave Coast, in what is now Benin and Togo, or in the densely populated Niger River Delta, took an active part in the slave trade. The demands of slavery and the temptations

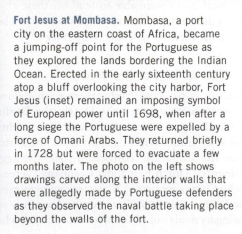

Fort Jesus at Mombasa. Mombasa, a port city on the eastern coast of Africa, became a jumping-off point for the Portuguese as they explored the lands bordering the Indian Ocean. Erected in the early sixteenth century atop a bluff overlooking the city harbor, Fort Jesus (inset) remained an imposing symbol of European power until 1698, when after a long siege the Portuguese were expelled by a force of Omani Arabs. They returned briefly in 1728 but were forced to evacuate a few months later. The photo on the left shows drawings carved along the interior walls that were allegedly made by Portuguese defenders as they observed the naval battle taking place beyond the walls of the fort.

William J. Duiker

of economic profit, however, also contributed to the increase in conflict among the states in the area.

This was especially true in the region of the Congo River, where Portuguese activities eventually led to the splintering of the state of Kongo and two centuries of rivalry and internal strife among the successor states in the area. A similar pattern developed in East Africa, where Portuguese activities led to the decline and eventual collapse of the Mwene Mutapa. Northward along the coast, in present-day Kenya and Tanzania, African rulers, assisted by Arab forces from Oman and Muscat in the Arabian Peninsula, expelled the Portuguese from Mombasa in 1698. Swahili culture now regained some of the dynamism it had possessed before the arrival of Vasco da Gama and his successors. But with much shipping now diverted southward to the route around the Cape of Good Hope, the commerce of the area never completely recovered and was increasingly dependent on the export of slaves and ivory obtained through contacts with African states in the interior.

14-5 SOUTHEAST ASIA IN THE ERA OF THE SPICE TRADE

 Focus Question: What were the main characteristics of Southeast Asian societies, and how were they affected by the coming of Islam and the Europeans?

As we noted in Chapters 9 and 10, Southeast Asia was affected in various ways by the expansion of the global trade network that began to accelerate in the early fifteenth century with the arrival of Chinese fleets under the command of Admiral Zheng He. Although the Chinese presence soon receded, that of Islam, introduced by merchants from India and the Middle East, soon began to make serious inroads, notably in the Malay Peninsula and in coastal areas in the Indonesian archipelago. In 1511, however, the seizure of the Malaccan sultanate by a Portuguese fleet introduced a new presence into the region, while inaugurating a period of intense conflict among various European competitors for access to the spice trade. At first, the rulers of most of the local states were able to fend off these challenges and maintain their independence. As we shall see in a later chapter, however, the reprieve was only temporary.

14-5a The Arrival of the West

Where the Portuguese trod, others soon followed. By the early seventeenth century, the Dutch, the English, and the French had begun to join the scramble for rights to the lucrative spice trade. Within a short time, the Dutch appeared to seize the advantage. Formed in 1602, the aggressive and well-financed Dutch East India Company (Vereenigde Oost-Indische Compagnie, or VOC) possessed ten times the capital of the English East India Company and not only succeeded in elbowing its rivals out of the spice trade but also had begun to consolidate political and military control over the area. On the island of Java, where they established a fort at Batavia (today's Jakarta) in 1619 (see Part III opener illustration, p. 389), the Dutch found that it was necessary to bring the inland regions under their control to protect their position on the coast. Rather than establishing a formal colony, however, they tried to rule as much as possible through the local landed aristocracy. On Java and the neighboring island of Sumatra, the VOC established pepper plantations, which soon produced massive profits for Dutch merchants in Amsterdam. Elsewhere they attempted to monopolize the clove trade by limiting cultivation of the crop to one island. By the end of the eighteenth century, the Dutch had succeeded in bringing much of the Indonesian archipelago under their control.

The arrival of the Europeans initially had somewhat less impact on the states of mainland Southeast Asia, where cohesive monarchies in Burma (modern Myanmar), Thailand (then known as Ayuthaya), and Vietnam (then known as Dai Viet) vigorously resisted foreign interference in their domestic affairs. Local ruling elites were interested in exploiting trade opportunities, however, and by the seventeenth century, several European nations had begun to compete actively for commercial and missionary privileges within the region. As was the case in other parts of the world, Europeans eventually became involved in local factional disputes as a means of obtaining political and economic advantages. In Burma, for example, the English and the French supported rival groups in the internal struggles of the monarchy until a new dynasty emerged and threw the foreigners out. A similar process took place at the Thai capital of Ayuthaya, which managed to survive the pressure from European interests but was eventually destroyed by a Burmese army in 1767.

In Vietnam, the appearance of Western merchants and missionaries coincided with a period of internal conflict among ruling groups in the country. After their arrival in the mid-seventeenth century, the European powers characteristically began to intervene in local politics, with the Portuguese and the Dutch supporting rival factions. By the end of the century,

CHRONOLOGY	The Spice Trade	
Vasco da Gama lands at Calicut in southwestern India		1498
Albuquerque establishes base at Goa		1510
Portuguese seize Malacca		1511
Portuguese ships land in southern China		1514
Magellan's voyage around the world		1519–1522
English East India Company established		1600
Dutch East India Company established		1602
English arrive at Surat in northwestern India		1608
Dutch fort established at Batavia		1619
Dutch seize Malacca from the Portuguese		1641
Burmese sack of Ayuthaya		1767

however, it became clear that economic opportunities were limited in Vietnam, and most European states abandoned their trading stations in the area (see illustration "The Japanese Bridge at Hoi An," Section 17-3b, p. 495). French missionaries attempted to remain, but their efforts were hampered by the local authorities, who viewed the Catholic insistence that converts give their primary loyalty to the pope as a threat to the legal status and prestige of the Vietnamese emperor.

14–5b State and Society in Precolonial Southeast Asia

Between 1500 and 1800, Southeast Asia experienced the last flowering of traditional culture before the advent of European rule in the nineteenth century. Although the arrival of the Europeans had an immediate and direct impact in some areas, notably in the Philippines and parts of the Malay world, in most areas Western influence was still relatively limited. Europeans occasionally dabbled in local politics and commerce, but they generally were not a decisive factor in the evolution of local political or social systems.

Nevertheless, Southeast Asian societies were changing in several subtle ways—in their trade patterns, their means of livelihood, and their religious beliefs. In some ways, these changes accentuated the differences between individual states in the region. Yet beneath these differences was an underlying commonality of life for most people. Despite the diversity of cultures and religious beliefs in the area, Southeast Asians were in most respects closer to each other than they were to peoples outside the region. For the most part, the states and peoples of Southeast Asia were still in control of their own destiny.

Religion and Kingship Buddhism and Islam continued to earn the allegiance of most of the population of the states in Southeast Asia, although Christianity began to make some inroads, especially in port cities directly occupied by Europeans, such as Malacca and Batavia, and in the Philippines. Buddhism was dominant in lowland areas on the mainland, from Burma to Vietnam. Muslim influence was prevalent mainly on the Malay Peninsula and along the northern coasts of Java and Sumatra, where local merchants encountered their Muslim counterparts from foreign lands on a regular basis. Elsewhere, traditional religious beliefs continued to survive, especially in inland areas, where the local populations either ignored the new doctrines or integrated them into their traditional forms of spirit worship. Buddhists in rural Burma and Thailand, for example, might also believe in nature spirits. On Java and Sumatra, where Islam was slow to penetrate into the interior, the result was a division between devout Muslims in the cities and essentially animist peasants in the upland rural villages.

Both Buddhism and Islam brought other changes in their train—temple education for Buddhists and schools for Islamic scholars (known as *pesantren* in Indonesia). They also imposed new religious and moral restrictions on human behavior such as refraining from eating pork and drinking wine for Muslims. Because Islam discouraged the traditional tattooing of the body, Muslim converts turned to the technique of decorating textiles called *batik* (buh-TEEK). Buddhism and Islam also helped shape Southeast Asian political institutions. The Buddhist style of kingship took shape between the eleventh and the fifteenth centuries as Theravada teachings spread throughout the area. It became the predominant political system in the Buddhist states of mainland Southeast Asia—Burma, Ayuthaya, Laos, and Cambodia. Perhaps the most prominent feature of the Buddhist model was the godlike character of the monarch, who was considered by virtue of his *karma* to be innately superior to other human beings and served as a link between human society and the cosmos. Court rituals stressed the sacred nature of the monarch, and even the palace was modeled after the symbolic design of the Hindu universe. In its center was an architectural rendering of sacred Mount Meru, the legendary home of the gods (see "Idolaters and Heathens in Old Siam," p. 416).

On the island of Java, kingship often took the form of a blend of Buddhist and Islamic political traditions. Like their mainland counterparts, Javanese monarchs originally possessed a sacred quality and maintained the balance between the sacred and the material world, but as Islam penetrated the Indonesian islands in the fifteenth and sixteenth centuries, the monarchs began to lose their semidivine status. On the Malay Peninsula and along the coast of the Indonesian archipelago, a more purely Islamic model prevailed. In this pattern, the head of state was a sultan, who was viewed as a mortal, although he still possessed some magical qualities. The sultan served as a defender of the faith and staffed his bureaucracy mainly with aristocrats, but he also frequently relied on the Muslim community of scholars—the *ulama*—and was expected, at least in theory, to rule according to the *Shari'a*. A display in the museum at the restored Sultan's Palace in Malacca shows the local sultan sitting on a raised dais before his advisers and assembled guests (see illustration "The Sultan of Malacca and His Court," p. 417).

Economy and Society During the early period of European penetration, the economy of most Southeast Asian societies was based primarily on agriculture, as it had been for thousands of years. Still, manufacturing and commercial activities were on the rise, as the region increasingly served as a focal point in a widespread trading network between East Asia and the Indian Ocean. By the sixteenth century, commerce was beginning to affect daily life, especially in the cities that were starting to proliferate along the coasts or on navigable rivers. In part, this was because agriculture itself was becoming more commercialized as cash crops like sugar and spices replaced subsistence farming of rice or other cereals in some areas. Spices, of course, were the mainstay of the interregional trade, but other products were exchanged as well. The region exported tin (mined in Malaya since the tenth century), copper, gold, tropical fruits and other agricultural products, cloth, gems, and luxury goods in exchange for manufactured goods, ceramics, and high-quality textiles such as silk from China. Although on balance the region was an importer of manufactured goods, it produced some high-quality goods of its own. The ceramics of Vietnam and Thailand, though not made with the high-temperature firing techniques used in China, were still of good quality. The

IDOLATERS AND HEATHENS IN OLD SIAM

Religion & Philosophy

MANY EARLY CHRISTIAN TRAVELERS to the states and societies of southern Asia were offended by the "heathen" religious beliefs and practices that they encountered in the region. In some cases, however, such visitors found much to admire as well. In this account, Joost Schouten, an official of the Dutch East India Company in the early seventeenth century, described what he observed during a visit to Ayuthaya, the capital of the kingdom of Siam, in surprisingly favorable terms. Indeed, the sense of tolerance and voluntarism that characterized Buddhist practices at the time continue to be appealing to our modern eyes.

William J. Duiker

The Thai Capital at Ayuthaya. The longest-lasting Thai capital was at Ayuthaya, which was one of the finest cities in Asia from the fourteenth century to the eighteenth century. After the Burmese invasion in 1767, most of Ayuthaya's inhabitants were killed, and all official Thai records were destroyed. Here the remains of some Buddhist stupas, erected in a ceremonial precinct in the center of the city, remind us of the greatness of Thai civilization.

Joost Schouten, *A True Description of the Kingdom of Siam*

The *Siammers*, as also the Neighboring Nations, are all Idolaters and Heathens, so that they have every where great and little Temples and Cloysters for the services of their Gods; and the dwellings of their Priests. These Edifices are builded of Wood and Stone very Artificial and sumptuous, with guilded [gilded] Towers and Pyramids; each of the Temples and Cloysters being filled with an incredible amount of *Idols*, of diverse materials and greatness, gilded, adorned and beautified very rich and admirable; some of the Idols are four, six, eight, and ten fathoms long; In these Temples and Cloysters there are many Priests and Religious Men disciplined, and very obedient to their superiours. . . . All the Clergy . . . are clothed, without any remarkable difference, in yellow linen clothes, having their heads all shorn. The learnedst amongst these are professed Priests. . . . These are prohibited the natural use of Women, upon pain of being burned; but they may always, and at pleasure upon declaration of their frailty or weakness, quit their frocks, and betake themselves to another life, which happens often amongst them. They live upon the Alms and bounty of the King and great Ones, as also on the fruit which their Church Lands bring forth; but principally out of the sweet [sweat] and labours of the Commonalty, who unanimously share with them, they sending every morning some Priests and Clerks out of their Cloysters, with begging bags to receive these donations and charity: Besides these Priests, there are a sort of old Nuns shown, lodged in Chappels near the greatest Temples, who assist very devoutly in all their preachings, singings, ceremonies,

and other Church services, but all voluntary, being tied to no rules or prescriptions. These Heathens do generally believe, (however differing in many particulars) that there is one upper God, with many lesser Deities in Heaven, who created all things; that the Souls of Men are immortal, and shall be rewarded or punished according to their merits and actions; the good dwelling with the God(s) in bliss, whilest the wicket are tormented by the Devils that seduced them. . . . The Priests carry themselves very moderately to those of a contrary Religion, condemning no opinions, but believe that all, though of differing tenets, living vertuously, may be saved, all services which are performed with zeal being acceptable to the great God, especially theirs, they being convinced of its truth and innocency. This constancy of theirs makes them not easily to be drawn to any other perswasion, which hath been sufficiently attempted by the *Portugals*, whose industrious Priests omitted nothing for their conversion, and by the Mohametans who are no less zealous in their way, though with little or no success by either of them, and yet the Christians, as also the Mohametans, are both permitted the free exercise of their Religions in their Countrey. . . .

 Why does the writer of this document declare that it is difficult to convert the peoples of Siam to other religions, such as Islam or Christianity?

Source: From Francois Caron and Joost Schouten, *A True Description of the Mighty Kingdoms of Japan and Siam* (London: The Argonaut Press, 1935), pp. 104, 106, 109.

In general, Southeast Asians probably enjoyed a somewhat higher living standard than their contemporaries elsewhere in Asia, and hunger was not a widespread problem. Several factors help explain this relative prosperity. In the first place, the region has been blessed with a salubrious climate. The uniformly high temperatures and the abundant rainfall lead to the proliferation of tropical fruits and enable farmers to grow two or even three crops of rice each year. Second, although the soil in some areas is poor, the alluvial deltas on the mainland are fertile, and the volcanoes of Sumatra and Java periodically spew forth rich volcanic ash that renews the mineral resources of the soil on both islands. Fi-

The Sultan of Malacca and His Court. Before the conquest of Malacca by the Portuguese in 1511, the city and its surroundings were ruled by a Muslim sultan, who ruled from a spacious palace that has now been restored as a museum. In the display shown in this illustration, the sultan, seated on a raised dias, attends to official business in the Royal Audience Hall, with his advisers and other officials seated at his feet. It was also in this hall that he greeted visiting merchants as well as emissaries from other countries in the region.

Portuguese traveler Duarte Barbosa (DWAR-tay bar-BOH-suh) observed that the Javanese were skilled cabinetmakers, weapons manufacturers, shipbuilders, and locksmiths. The royal courts were both the main producers and the primary consumers of luxury goods, most of which were produced by highly skilled slaves in the employ of the court.

nally, most of Southeast Asia was relatively thinly populated. According to one estimate, the population of the entire region in 1600 was about 20 million, or about 14 persons per square mile, well below levels elsewhere in Asia. Only in a few areas such as the Red River Delta in northern Vietnam was overpopulation a serious problem.

CHAPTER SUMMARY

Beginning in the fifteenth century, the pace of international commerce throughout the world increased dramatically. Chinese fleets embarked on several visits to the Indian Ocean while Muslim traders extended their activities into the Spice Islands and sub-Saharan West Africa. Then the Europeans burst onto the world scene. Beginning with the seemingly modest ventures of the Portuguese ships that sailed southward along the West African coast, the process accelerated with the epoch-making voyages of Christopher Columbus to the Americas and Vasco da Gama to the Indian Ocean in the 1490s. Soon a number of other European states had entered the fray, helping to create a global trade network that distributed foodstuffs, textiles, spices, and precious minerals from one end of the globe to the other.

In less than three hundred years, the expansion of the global trade network changed the face of the world. In some areas, such as the Americas and the Spice Islands, it led to the destruction of indigenous civilizations and the establishment of European colonies. In others, as in Africa, South Asia, and mainland Southeast Asia, it left native regimes intact, but had a strong impact on local societies and regional trade patterns. In some areas, it led to an irreversible decline in traditional institutions and values, setting in motion a corrosive process that has not been reversed to this day.

At the time, most European observers viewed the process in a favorable light. Not only did it lead to an expansion of world trade and foster the exchange of new crops and discoveries between the Old and New Worlds, but it also introduced Christianity to what were known as "heathen peoples" around the globe. Some modern historians have been much more critical of the process, concluding that European activities during the sixteenth and seventeenth centuries created a "tributary mode of production" based on European profits from unequal terms of trade that foreshadowed the exploitative relationship characteristic of the later colonial period. Other scholars have questioned that contention, however, and argue that although Western commercial operations had a significant impact on global trade patterns, they did not—at least not before the nineteenth century—usher in an era of Western dominance over the rest of the world. Muslim merchants were long able to evade European efforts to eliminate them from the spice trade, while local traders, some of them migrants from China and South Asia, dominated commercial activities in many of the port cities within the region. In the meantime, the trans-Saharan caravan trade was relatively unaffected by European merchant shipping along the West African coast. Only in the late nineteenth century did Europeans begin to penetrate into the heart of the continent.

In the meantime, traditional empires continued to hold sway over many of the lands washed by the Muslim faith. Beyond the Himalayas, Chinese emperors in their new northern capital of Beijing retained proud dominion over all the vast territory of continental East Asia. We shall deal with these regions, and how they confronted the challenges of a changing world, in Chapters 16 and 17.

CHAPTER TIMELINE

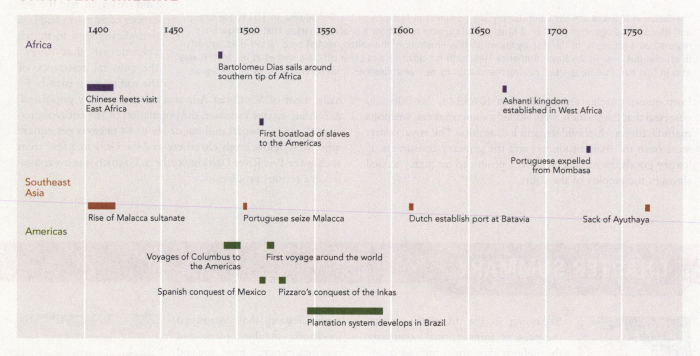

	1400	1450	1500	1550	1600	1650	1700	1750

Africa
- Chinese fleets visit East Africa
- Bartolomeu Dias sails around southern tip of Africa
- First boatload of slaves to the Americas
- Ashanti kingdom established in West Africa
- Portuguese expelled from Mombasa

Southeast Asia
- Rise of Malacca sultanate
- Portuguese seize Malacca
- Dutch establish port at Batavia
- Sack of Ayuthaya

Americas
- Voyages of Columbus to the Americas
- First voyage around the world
- Spanish conquest of Mexico
- Pizarro's conquest of the Inkas
- Plantation system develops in Brazil

CHAPTER REVIEW

Upon Reflection

Q What were some of the key features of the Columbian Exchange, and what effects did they have on the world trade network?

Q How did the expansion of European power during the Age of Exploration compare with the expansion of the Islamic empires in the Middle East a few centuries earlier?

Q Why were the Spanish conquistadors able to complete their conquest of Latin America so quickly when their contemporaries failed to do so in Africa and Southeast Asia?

Key Terms

portolani (p. 395)
caravels (p. 396)
conquistadors (p. 401)
mestizos (p. 403)
mulattoes (p. 403)
viceroys (p. 403)
creoles (p. 403)

encomienda **system** (p. 405)
encomienda (p. 405)
Columbian Exchange (p. 407)
Boers (p. 408)
Middle Passage (p. 409)
maroons (p. 410)
Triangular Trade (p. 410)

Chapter Notes

1. From *A Journal of the First Voyage of Vasco da Gama* (London, 1898), cited in J. H. Parry, *The European Reconnaissance: Selected Documents* (New York, 1968), p. 82.
2. H. J. Benda and J. A. Larkin, eds., *The World of Southeast Asia: Selected Historical Readings* (New York, 1967), p. 13.
3. Parry, *European Reconnaissance*, quoting from A. Cortesão, *The Summa Oriental of Tomé Pires* (London, 1944), vol. 2, pp. 283, 287.
4. Quoted in J. H. Parry, *The Age of Reconnaissance: Discovery, Exploration, and Settlement, 1450 to 1650* (New York, 1963), p. 33.
5. Quoted in R. B. Reed, "The Expansion of Europe," in R. DeMolen, ed., *The Meaning of the Renaissance and Reformation* (Boston, 1974), p. 308.
6. K. N. Chaudhuri, *Trade and Civilization in the Indian Ocean: An Economic History from the Rise of Islam to 1750* (Cambridge, 1985), p. 65.
7. Quoted in Parry, *Age of Reconnaissance*, pp. 176–177.
8. Quoted in M. Leon-Portilla, ed., *The Broken Spears: The Aztec Account of the Conquest of Mexico* (Boston, 1969), p. 51.

 **MINDTAP** From Cengage

MindTap® is a fully online personalized learning experience built upon Cengage Learning content. MindTap® combines student learning tools—readings, multimedia, activities, and assessments—into a singular Learning Path that guides students through the course and helps students develop the critical thinking, analysis, and communication skills that are essential to academic and professional success.

CHAPTER 15

EUROPE TRANSFORMED: REFORM AND STATE BUILDING

Chapter Outline and Focus Questions

15-1 *The Reformation of the Sixteenth Century*

Q What were the main tenets of Lutheranism, Calvinism, and Anabaptism, and how did they differ from each other and from Catholicism?

15-2 *Europe in Crisis, 1560–1650*

Q Why is the period between 1560 and 1650 in Europe considered an age of crisis, and how did the turmoil contribute to the artistic developments of the period?

15-3 *Response to Crisis: The Practice of Absolutism*

Q What was absolutism, and what were the main characteristics of the absolute monarchies that emerged in France, Prussia, Austria, and Russia?

15-4 *England and Limited Monarchy*

Q How and why did England avoid the path of absolutism?

15-5 *The Flourishing of European Culture*

Q How did the artistic and literary achievements of this era reflect the political and economic developments of the period?

A nineteenth-century engraving showing Luther before the Diet of Worms. BPK, Berlin/Art Resource, NY

Critical Thinking

Q *What was the relationship between European overseas expansion (as traced in Chapter 14) and political, economic, and social developments in Europe?*

Connections to Today

Q *How does the exercise of state power in the seventeenth century compare with the exercise of state power in the twenty-first century? What, if anything, has changed?*

ON APRIL 18, 1521, A LOWLY MONK stood before the emperor and princes of Germany in the city of Worms (VAWRMZ). He had been called before this august diet (a deliberating council) to answer charges of heresy, charges that could threaten his very life. The monk was confronted with a pile of his books and asked if he wished to defend them all or reject a part. Courageously, Martin Luther defended them all and asked to be shown where any part was in error on the basis of "Scripture and plain reason." The emperor was outraged by Luther's response and made his own position clear the next day: "Not only I, but you of this noble German nation, would be forever disgraced if by our negligence not only heresy but the very suspicion of heresy were to survive. After having heard yesterday the obstinate defense of Luther, I regret that I have so long delayed in proceeding against him and his false teaching. I will have no more to do with him." Luther's appearance at Worms set the stage for a serious challenge to the authority of the Catholic Church. This was by no means the first crisis in the church's 1,500-year history, but its consequences were more far-reaching than anyone at Worms in 1521 could have imagined.

After the disintegrative patterns of the fourteenth century, Europe began a remarkable recovery that encompassed a revival of arts and letters in the fifteenth century, known as the Renaissance, and a religious renaissance in the sixteenth century, known as the Reformation. The resulting religious division of Europe (Catholics versus Protestants) was instrumental in triggering a series of wars that dominated much of European history from 1560 to 1650 and exacerbated the economic and social crises that were besetting the region.

One of the responses to the crises of the seventeenth century was a search for order. The most general trend was an extension of monarchical power as a stabilizing force. This development, which historians have called **absolutism** or *absolute monarchy*, was most evident in France during the flamboyant reign of Louis XIV, regarded by some as the perfect embodiment of an absolute monarch.

But absolutism was not the only response to the search for order in the seventeenth century. Other states, such as England, reacted very differently to domestic crisis, and yet another system emerged in which monarchs were limited by the power of their representative assemblies. Absolute and limited monarchy were the two poles of seventeenth-century state building.

15–1 THE REFORMATION OF THE SIXTEENTH CENTURY

 Focus Question: What were the main tenets of Lutheranism, Calvinism, and Anabaptism, and how did they differ from each other and from Catholicism?

The **Protestant Reformation** is the name given to the religious reform movement that divided the Western Christian church into Catholic and Protestant groups. Although the Reformation

began with Martin Luther in the early sixteenth century, several earlier developments had set the stage for religious change.

15–1a Background to the Reformation

Changes in the fifteenth century—the age of the Renaissance—helped prepare the way for the dramatic upheavals in sixteenth-century Europe.

The Growth of State Power In the first half of the fifteenth century, European states had continued the disintegrative patterns of the previous century. In the second half of that century, however, recovery had set in, and attempts had been made to reestablish the centralized power of monarchical governments. To characterize the results, some historians have used the label "Renaissance states"; others have spoken of the "**new monarchies**," especially those of France, England, and Spain at the end of the fifteenth century (see Chapter 13).

What was new about these Renaissance monarchs was their concentration of royal authority, their attempts to suppress the nobility, their efforts to control the church in their lands, and their desire to obtain new sources of revenue in order to increase royal power and enhance the military forces at their disposal. Like the rulers of fifteenth-century Italian states, the Renaissance monarchs were often crafty men obsessed with the acquisition and expansion of political power. Of course, none of these characteristics was entirely new; a number of medieval monarchs, especially in the thirteenth century, had exhibited them. Nevertheless, the Renaissance period marks a significant expansion of centralized royal authority and a new preoccupation with the acquisition, maintenance, and expansion of political power.

Social Changes in the Renaissance Social changes in the fifteenth century also helped to create an environment in which the Reformation of the sixteenth century could occur. After the severe economic reversals and social upheavals of the fourteenth century, the European economy gradually recovered as manufacturing and trade increased in volume. The Italians and especially the Venetians expanded their wealthy commercial empire, rivaled only by the increasingly powerful Hanseatic (han-see-AT-ik) League, a commercial and military alliance of north German coastal towns. Not until the sixteenth century, when overseas discoveries gave new importance to the states facing the Atlantic, did the Italian city-states begin to suffer from the competitive advantages of the more powerful national territorial states.

As noted in Chapter 12, society in the Middle Ages was divided into three estates: the clergy, or First Estate, whose preeminence was grounded in the belief that people should be guided to spiritual ends; the nobility, or Second Estate, whose privileges rested on the principle that nobles provided security and justice for society; and the peasants and inhabitants of the towns and cities, the Third Estate. Although this social order continued into the Renaissance, some changes also became evident.

Throughout much of Europe, the landholding nobles faced declining real incomes during most of the fourteenth and

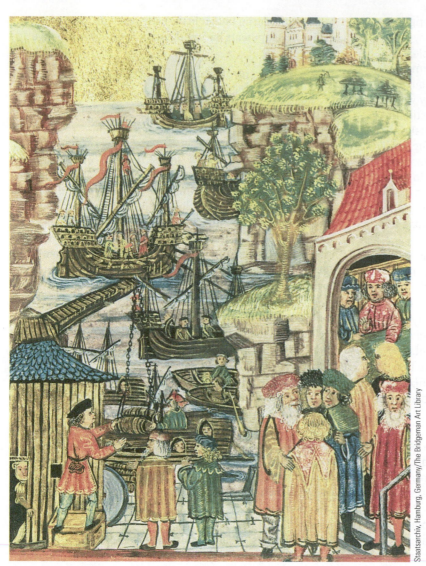

Harbor Scene at Hamburg. Hamburg was a founding member of the Hanseatic League. This illustration from a fifteenth-century treatise on the laws of the city shows a busy port with ships of all sizes. At the left, a crane is used to unload barrels. In the building at the right, customs officials collect their dues. Merchants and townspeople are shown talking at dockside.

century, the grievances of peasants, especially in Germany, led many of them to support religious reform movements.

Inhabitants of towns and cities, originally merchants and artisans, constituted the remainder of the Third Estate. But by the fifteenth century, the Renaissance town or city had become more complex. At the top of urban society were the patricians, whose wealth from capitalistic enterprises in trade, industry, and banking enabled them to dominate their urban communities economically, socially, and politically. Below them were the petty burghers—the shopkeepers, artisans, guild-masters, and guildsmen—who were largely concerned with providing goods and services for local consumption. Below these two groups were the propertyless workers earning pitiful wages and the unemployed, living squalid and miserable lives. These poor city-dwellers made up 30 to 40 percent of the urban population. The pitiful conditions of the lower groups in urban society often led them to support calls for radical religious reform in the sixteenth century.

The Impact of Printing The Renaissance witnessed the development of printing, which made an immediate impact on European intellectual life and thought. Printing from hand-carved wooden blocks had been done in the West since the twelfth century and in China even before that. What was new in the fifteenth century in Europe was multiple printing with movable metal type. The development of printing from movable type was a gradual process that culminated sometime between 1445 and 1450; Johannes Gutenberg (yoh-HAH-nuss GOO-ten-bayrk) of Mainz (MYNTS) played an important role in bringing the process to completion. Gutenberg's Bible, completed in 1455 or 1456, was the first true book produced from movable type.

By 1500, there were more than a thousand printers in Europe, who collectively had published almost 40,000 titles (between 8 million and 10 million copies). Probably half of these books were religious—Bibles and biblical commentaries, books of devotion, and sermons. Next in importance were the Latin and Greek classics, medieval grammars, legal handbooks, and works on philosophy.

The printing of books encouraged scholarly research and the desire to attain knowledge. Printing also stimulated the development of an ever-expanding lay reading public, a development that had an enormous impact on European society. Indeed, the printing press enabled the new religious ideas of the Reformation to spread as rapidly as they did in the sixteenth century.

Prelude to Reformation During the second half of the fifteenth century, the new Classical learning of the Italian Renaissance spread to the European countries north of the Alps

fifteenth centuries. Many members of the old nobility survived, however, and new blood also infused their ranks. In 1500, the nobles, old and new, who constituted between 2 and 3 percent of the population in most countries, still dominated society, as they had in the Middle Ages, holding important political posts and serving as advisers to the king.

Except in the heavily urban areas of northern Italy and Flanders, peasants made up the overwhelming mass of the Third Estate—they constituted 85 to 90 percent of the total European population. Serfdom had decreased as the manorial system continued its decline. Increasingly, the labor dues owed by peasants to their lord were converted into rents paid in money. By 1500, especially in western Europe, more and more peasants were becoming legally free. At the same time, peasants in many areas resented their social superiors and sought to keep a greater share of the benefits from their labor. In the sixteenth and spawned a movement called **Christian humanism** or **northern Renaissance humanism**, whose major goal was the reform of Christianity. The Christian humanists believed in the ability of human beings to reason and improve themselves and thought that through education in the sources of Classical, and especially Christian, antiquity, they could instill an inner piety or an inward religious feeling that would bring about a reform of the church and society. To change society, they must first change the human beings who compose it.

The most influential of all the Christian humanists was Desiderius Erasmus (dez-i-DEER-ee-uss i-RAZZ-mus) (1466–1536), who formulated and popularized the reform program of Christian humanism. He called his conception of religion "the philosophy of Christ," by which he meant that Christianity should be a guiding philosophy for the direction of daily life rather than the system of dogmatic beliefs and practices that the medieval church seemed to stress. In other words, he emphasized inner piety and de-emphasized the external forms of religion (such as the sacraments, pilgrimages, fasts, and relics). To Erasmus, the reform of the church meant spreading an understanding of the philosophy of Jesus, providing enlightened education in the sources of early Christianity, and criticizing the abuses in the church. No doubt his work helped prepare the way for the Reformation; as contemporaries proclaimed, "Erasmus laid the egg that Luther hatched."

Church and Religion on the Eve of the Reformation

Considerable corruption in the Catholic Church was another factor that led people to want reform. Between 1450 and 1520, a series of popes—called the Renaissance popes—largely failed to meet the church's spiritual needs. The popes were supposed to be the spiritual leaders of the Catholic Church, but as rulers of the Papal States, they were all too often involved in worldly concerns. Julius II (1503–1513), the fiery "warrior-pope," personally led armies against his enemies, much to the disgust of pious Christians, who thought the pope's role was to serve as a spiritual leader. As one intellectual wrote, "How, O bishop standing in the room of the Apostles, dare you teach the people the things that pertain to war?" Many high church officials were also concerned with accumulating wealth and used their church offices as opportunities to advance their careers and their fortunes, and many ordinary parish priests seemed ignorant of their spiritual duties.

While many leaders of the church were failing to meet their responsibilities, many ordinary people were clamoring for meaningful religious expression and certainty of salvation. As a result, for some the process of salvation became almost mechanical. As more and more people sought certainty of salvation through veneration of relics (bones or other objects intimately associated with the saints), collections of **relics** grew. Frederick the Wise, elector (one of the seven German princes who chose the Holy Roman Emperor) of Saxony and Martin Luther's prince, had amassed nearly 19,000 relics to which were attached **indulgences** that could reduce a person's time in purgatory by nearly 2 million years. (An indulgence is a remission, after death, of all or part of the punishment due to sin.) Other people sought certainty of salvation in more spiritual terms by participating in the popular mystical movement known as the Modern Devotion, which downplayed religious dogma and stressed the need to follow the teachings of Jesus.

What is striking about the revival of religious piety in the fifteenth century—whether expressed through such external forces as the veneration of relics and the buying of indulgences or the mystical path—was its adherence to the orthodox beliefs and practices of the Catholic Church. The agitation for certainty of salvation and spiritual peace occurred within the framework of the "holy mother Church." But disillusionment grew as the devout experienced the inability of many clergy to live up to their expectations. The deepening of religious life, especially in the second half of the fifteenth century, found little echo among the worldly-wise clergy, and this environment helps explain the tremendous and immediate impact of Luther's ideas.

15–1b Martin Luther and the Reformation in Germany

Martin Luther (1483–1546) was a monk and a professor at the University of Wittenberg (VIT-ten-bayrk), where he lectured on the Bible. Probably sometime between 1513 and 1516, through his study of the Bible, he arrived at an answer to a problem—the assurance of salvation—that had disturbed him since his entry into the monastery.

Catholic doctrine had emphasized that both faith and good works were required for a Christian to achieve personal salvation. In Luther's eyes, human beings, weak and powerless in the sight of an almighty God, could never do enough good works to merit salvation. Through his study of the Bible, Luther came to believe that humans are saved not through their good works but through faith in the promises of God, made possible by the sacrifice of Jesus on the cross. This doctrine of salvation, or justification by grace through faith alone, became the primary doctrine of the Protestant Reformation (**justification by faith** is the act by which a person is made deserving of salvation). Because Luther had arrived at this doctrine from his study of the Bible, the Bible became for Luther, as for all other Protestants, the chief guide to religious truth.

Luther did not see himself as a revolutionary innovator or a heretic, but he was greatly upset by the widespread selling of indulgences. Especially offensive in his eyes was the monk Johann Tetzel, who hawked indulgences with the slogan "As soon as the coin in the coffer [money box] rings, the soul from purgatory springs." Greatly angered, in 1517 he issued a stunning indictment of the abuses in the sale of indulgences, known as the Ninety-Five Theses (see "Luther and the Ninety-Five Theses," p. 424). Thousands of copies were printed and quickly spread to all parts of Germany.

By 1520, Luther had begun to move toward a more definite break with the Catholic Church and called on the German princes to overthrow the papacy in Germany and establish a reformed German church. Through all his calls for change, Luther expounded more and more on his new doctrine of

LUTHER AND THE NINETY-FIVE THESES

Religion & Philosophy — **TO MOST HISTORIANS**, the publication of Luther's Ninety-Five Theses marks the beginning of the Reformation. To Luther, they were simply a response to what he considered blatant abuses committed by sellers of indulgences. Although written in Latin, the theses were soon translated into German and disseminated widely across Germany. They made an immense impression on Germans already dissatisfied with the ecclesiastical and financial policies of the papacy.

Martin Luther, Selections from the Ninety-Five Theses

5. The Pope has neither the will nor the power to remit any penalties beyond those he has imposed either at his own discretion or by canon law.

20. Therefore the Pope, by his plenary remission of all penalties, does not mean "all" in the absolute sense, but only those imposed by himself.

21. Hence those preachers of Indulgences are wrong when they say that a man is absolved and saved from every penalty by the Pope's Indulgences. It is mere human talk to preach that the soul flies out [of purgatory] immediately [when] the money clinks in the collection box.

28. It is certainly possible that when the money clinks in the collection box greed and avarice can increase; but the intercession of the Church depends on the will of God alone.

50. Christians should be taught that if the Pope knew the exactions of the preachers of Indulgences, he would rather have the basilica of St. Peter reduced to ashes than built with the skin, flesh, and bones of his sheep [the indulgences that so distressed Luther were being sold to raise money for the construction of the new St. Peter's Basilica in Rome].

81. This wanton preaching of pardons makes it difficult even for learned men to redeem respect due to the Pope from the slanders or at least the shrewd questionings of the laity.

82. For example: "Why does not the Pope empty purgatory for the sake of most holy love and the supreme need of souls? This would be the most righteous of reasons, if he can redeem innumerable souls for sordid money with which to build a basilica, the most trivial of reasons."

86. Again: "Since the Pope's wealth is larger than that of the crassest Crassi of our time, why does he not build this one basilica of St. Peter with his own money, rather than with that of the faithful poor?"

90. To suppress these most conscientious questionings of the laity by authority only, instead of refuting them by reason, is to expose the Church and the Pope to the ridicule of their enemies, and to make Christian people unhappy.

94. Christians should be exhorted to seek earnestly to follow Christ, their Head, through penalties, deaths, and hells.

95. And let them thus be more confident of entering heaven through many tribulations rather than through a false assurance of peace.

 What were the major ideas of Luther's Ninety-Five Theses? Why did they have such a strong appeal in Germany?

Source: From *Martin Luther*, by E. G. Rupp and Benjamin Drewery.

---

salvation. It is faith alone, he said, not good works, that justifies and brings salvation through Christ.

Unable to accept Luther's ideas, the church excommunicated him in January 1521. He was also summoned to appear before the Reichstag (RYKHSS-tahk) (imperial diet) of the Holy Roman Empire, convened by the newly elected Emperor Charles V (1519–1556). Ordered to recant the heresies he had espoused, Luther refused and made the famous reply that became the battle cry of the Reformation:

> Unless I am convicted by Scripture and plain reason—I do not accept the authority of popes and councils, for they have contradicted each other—my conscience is captive to the Word of God. I cannot and I will not recant anything, for to go against conscience is neither right nor safe. Here I stand, I cannot do otherwise. God help me. Amen.[1]

Members of the Reichstag were outraged and demanded that Luther be arrested and delivered to the emperor. But Luther's ruler, Elector Frederick of Saxony, stepped in and protected him (see Film & History).

During the next few years, Luther's movement began to grow and spread. As it made an impact on the common people, it also created new challenges. This was especially true of the Peasants' War that erupted in 1524. Social discontent created by their pitiful conditions became entangled with religious revolt as the German peasants looked to Martin Luther for support. But when the peasants took up arms and revolted against their landlords, Luther turned against them and called on the German princes, who in Luther's eyes were ordained by God to maintain peace and order, to crush the rebels. By May 1525, the German princes had ruthlessly suppressed the peasant hordes. By this time, Luther found himself dependent on the state authorities for the growth of his reformed church.

Luther now succeeded in gaining the support of many of the rulers of the three hundred or so German states that made up the Holy Roman Empire. These rulers quickly took control of the churches in their territories. The Lutheran churches in Germany (and later in Scandinavia) became territorial or state churches in which the state supervised the affairs of the church. As part of the development of these state-dominated churches,

Watch *Luther* (2003), which depicts the early life and career of Martin Luther, largely from a Lutheran point of view. The movie focuses on some of the major events in Luther's early life, such as his years in a monastery; his study for a doctorate in theology at the University of Wittenberg; the writing of his Ninety-Five Theses; and his dramatic stand at the Diet of Worms. The movie is based more on legends about Luther than on a strict adherence to the historical facts.

Q *What historical errors can you find in this portrayal of Luther's career? Does the film reveal what made Luther a rebel? Why or why not?*

Photos 12/Alamy Stock Photo

Luther also instituted new religious services to replace the Catholic Mass. These focused on reading the Bible, preaching the word of God, and singing hymns. Following his own denunciation of clerical celibacy, Luther married a former nun, Katherina von Bora, in 1525. Their union provided a model of married and family life for the new Protestant minister.

Politics and Religion in the German Reformation From its very beginning, the fate of Luther's movement was closely tied to political affairs. In 1519, Charles I, king of Spain and the grandson of Emperor Maximilian, was elected Holy Roman Emperor as Charles V. Charles V ruled over an immense empire, consisting of Spain and its overseas possessions, the traditional Austrian Habsburg lands, Bohemia, Hungary, the Low Countries, and the kingdom of Naples in southern Italy. Politically, Charles wanted to maintain his enormous empire; religiously, he hoped to preserve the unity of his empire in the Catholic faith. A number of problems, however, kept him preoccupied and cost him both his dream and his health.

Moreover, the internal political situation in the Holy Roman Empire was not in Charles's favor. Although all the German states owed loyalty to the emperor, during the Middle Ages these states had become quite independent of imperial authority. By the time Charles V was able to bring military forces to Germany in 1546, Lutheranism had become well established and the Lutheran princes were well organized. Unable to defeat them, Charles was forced to negotiate a truce. An end to religious warfare in Germany came in 1555 with the Peace of

Joerg P. Anders/Art Resource, NY

A Reformation Woodcut. In the 1520s, after Luther's return to Wittenberg, his teachings began to spread rapidly, ending ultimately in a reform movement supported by state authorities. Pamphlets containing picturesque woodcuts were important in the spread of Luther's ideas. In the woodcut shown here, the crucified Jesus attends Luther's service on the left, while on the right the pope is at a table selling indulgences.

Augsburg (OUKS-boork). The division of Christianity was formally acknowledged; Lutheran states were to have the same legal rights as Catholic states. Although the German states were now free to choose between Catholicism and Lutheranism, the peace settlement did not recognize the principle of religious toleration for individuals. The right of each German ruler to determine the religion of his subjects was accepted, but not the right of the subjects to choose their own religion. With the Peace of Augsburg, what had at first been merely feared was now certain: the ideal of Christian unity was lost. The rapid spread of new Protestant groups made this a certainty for all of Europe.

15–1c The Spread of the Protestant Reformation

Switzerland was home to two major Reformation movements, Zwinglianism and Calvinism. Ulrich Zwingli (OOL-rikh TSFING-lee) (1484–1531) was ordained a priest in 1506 and accepted an appointment as a cathedral priest in the Great Minster of Zürich (ZOOR-ik *or* TSIH-rikh) in 1518. Zwingli's preaching of the Gospel caused such unrest that in 1523 the city council held a public disputation (debate) in the town hall. Zwingli's party was accorded the victory, and over the next two years, evangelical reforms were promulgated in Zürich by a city council strongly influenced by Zwingli. Relics and images were abolished; all paintings and decorations were removed from the churches and replaced by whitewashed walls. The Mass was replaced by a new liturgy consisting of Scripture reading, prayer, and sermons. Monasticism, pilgrimages, the veneration of saints, clerical celibacy, and the pope's authority were all abolished as remnants of papal Christianity.

As his movement began to spread to other cities in Switzerland, Zwingli sought an alliance with Martin Luther and the German reformers. Although both the German and the Swiss reformers realized the need for unity to defend against the opposition of the Catholic authorities, they were unable to agree on the interpretation of the Lord's Supper, the sacrament of Communion (see Opposing Viewpoints "A Reformation Debate: Conflict at Marburg"). Zwingli believed that the scriptural words "This is my body, this is my blood" should be taken figuratively, not literally, and refused to accept Luther's insistence on the real presence of the body and blood of Jesus "in, with, and under the bread and wine." In October 1531, war erupted between the Swiss Protestant and Catholic states. Zürich's army was routed, and Zwingli was found wounded on the battlefield. His enemies killed him, cut up his body, burned the pieces, and scattered the ashes. The leadership of Swiss Protestantism now passed to John Calvin, the systematic theologian and organizer of the Protestant movement.

Calvin and Calvinism John Calvin (1509–1564) was educated in his native France, but after converting to Protestantism, he was forced to flee to the safety of Switzerland. In 1536, he published the first edition of the *Institutes of the Christian Religion*, a masterful synthesis of Protestant thought that immediately secured his reputation as one of the new leaders of Protestantism.

John Calvin. After a conversion experience, John Calvin abandoned his life as a humanist and became a reformer. In 1536, Calvin began working to reform the city of Geneva, where he remained until his death in 1564. This is a seventeenth-century portrait of Calvin done by a member of the Swiss school.

Société de l'Histoire du Protestantisme Francais, Paris/Giraudon/The Bridgeman Art Library

On most important doctrines, Calvin stood very close to Luther. He adhered to the doctrine of justification by faith alone to explain how humans achieved salvation. But Calvin also placed much emphasis on the absolute sovereignty or all-powerful nature of God—what Calvin called the "power, grace, and glory of God." One of the ideas derived from his emphasis on the absolute sovereignty of God—**predestination**—gave a unique cast to Calvin's teachings. This "eternal decree," as Calvin called it, meant that God had predestined some people to be saved (the elect) and others to be damned (the reprobate). According to Calvin, "He has once for all determined, both whom He would admit to salvation, and whom He would condemn to destruction."[2] Although Calvin stressed that there could be no absolute certainty of salvation, his followers did not always make this distinction. The practical psychological effect of predestination was to give later Calvinists an unshakable conviction that they were doing God's work on earth, making Calvinism a dynamic and activist faith.

In 1536, Calvin began working to reform the city of Geneva. He was able to fashion a tightly organized church order that

A Reformation Debate: Conflict at Marburg

Religion & Philosophy **DEBATES PLAYED A CRUCIAL ROLE IN THE REFORMATION PERIOD.** They were a primary instrument for introducing the Reformation in innumerable cities as well as a means of resolving differences among like-minded Protestant groups. This selection contains an excerpt from the vivacious and often brutal debate between Luther and Zwingli over the sacrament of the Lord's Supper at Marburg in 1529. The two protagonists failed to reach agreement.

The Marburg Colloquy, 1529

The Hessian Chancellor Feige: My gracious prince and lord [Landgrave Philip of Hesse] has summoned you for the express and urgent purpose of settling the dispute over the sacrament of the Lord's Supper. . . . Let everyone on both sides present his arguments in a spirit of moderation. . . . Now then, Doctor Luther, you may proceed.

Luther: Noble prince, gracious lord! Undoubtedly the colloquy is well intentioned. . . . Although I have no intention of changing my mind, which is firmly made up, I will nevertheless present the grounds of my belief and show where the others are in error. . . . Your basic contentions are these: In the last analysis you wish to prove that a body cannot be in two places at once, and you produce arguments about the unlimited body which are based on natural reason. I do not question how Christ can be God and man and how the two natures can be joined. For God is more powerful than all our ideas, and we must submit to his word.

Prove that Christ's body is not there where the Scripture says, "This is my body!" Rational proofs I will not listen to. . . . It is God who commands, "Take, eat, this is my body." I request, therefore, valid scriptural proof to the contrary.

Zwingli: I insist that the words of the Lord's Supper must be figurative. This is ever apparent, and even required by the article of faith: "taken up into heaven, seated at the right hand of the Father." Otherwise, it would be absurd to look for him in the Lord's Supper at the same time that Christ is telling us that he is in heaven. One and the same body cannot possibly be in different places. . . .

Luther: I call upon you as before: your basic contentions are shaky. Give way, and give glory to God!

Zwingli: And we call upon you to give glory to God and to quit begging the question! The issue at stake is this: Where is the proof of your position? I am willing to consider your words carefully—no harm meant! You're trying to outwit me. . . . You'll have to sing another tune.

Luther: You're being obnoxious.

Zwingli: (*excitedly*) Don't you believe that Christ was attempting in John 6 to help those who did not understand?

Luther: You're trying to dominate things! You insist on passing judgment! Leave that to someone else! . . . It is your point that must be proved, not mine. But let us stop this sort of thing. It serves no purpose.

Zwingli: It certainly does! It is for you to prove that the passage in John 6 speaks of a physical repast.

Luther: You express yourself poorly and make about as much progress as a cane standing in a corner. You're going nowhere.

Zwingli: No, no, no! This is the passage that will break your neck!

Luther: Don't be so sure of yourself. Necks don't break this way. You're in Hesse, not Switzerland.

 How did the positions of Zwingli and Luther on the sacrament of the Lord's Supper differ? What was the purpose of this debate? Based on this example, why did many Reformation debates lead to further hostility rather than compromise and unity between religious and sectarian opponents? What implications did this have for the future of the Protestant Reformation?

Source: "The Marburg Colloquy," edited by Donald Ziegler, from *Great Debates of the Reformation*, edited by Donald Ziegler, copyright © 1969 by Donald Ziegler.

---

employed both clergy and laymen in the service of the church. The Consistory, a special body for enforcing moral discipline, functioned as a court to oversee the moral life, daily behavior, and doctrinal orthodoxy of Genevans and to admonish and correct deviants. Citizens in Geneva were punished for such varied "crimes" as dancing, singing obscene songs, drunkenness, swearing, and playing cards.

Calvin's success in Geneva enabled the city to become a vibrant center of Protestantism. Following Calvin's lead, missionaries trained in Geneva were sent to all parts of Europe.

Calvinism became established in France, the Netherlands, Scotland, and central and eastern Europe, and by the mid-sixteenth century, Calvin's Geneva stood as the fortress of the Reformation.

The English Reformation The English Reformation was rooted in politics, not religion. King Henry VIII (1509–1547) had a strong desire to divorce his first wife, Catherine of Aragon, with whom he had a daughter, Mary, but no male heir. The king wanted to marry Anne Boleyn (BUH-lin *or* buh-LIN), with

Marriage in the Early Modern World

Family & Society Marriage is an ancient institution. In China, myths about the beginnings of Chinese civilization maintained that the rite of marriage began with the primordial couple Fuxi and Nugun and that marriage actually preceded such discoveries as fire, farming, and medicine. In the early modern world, family and marriage were inseparable and were at the center of all civilizations.

In the early modern period, the family was still at the heart of Europe's social organization. For the most part, people viewed the family in traditional terms, as a patriarchal institution in which the husband dominated his wife and children. The upper classes in particular thought of the family as a "house," an association whose collective interests were more important than those of its individual members. Parents (especially the fathers) generally selected marriage partners for their children, based on the interests of the family. When the son of a French noble asked about his upcoming marriage, his father responded, "Mind your own business." Details were worked out well in advance, sometimes when children were only two or three years old, and were set out in a legally binding contract. An important negotiating point was the size of the dowry, money presented by the bride's family to the groom upon marriage. The dowry could be a large sum, and all families were expected to provide dowries for their daughters.

Arranged marriages were not unique to Europe but were common throughout the world. In China, marriages were normally arranged for the benefit of the family, often by a go-between, and the groom and bride were usually not consulted. Frequently, they did not meet until the marriage ceremony. Love was obviously not a reason for marriage and in fact was often viewed as a detriment because it could distract the married couple from their responsibility to the larger family unit. In Japan too, marriages were arranged, often by the heads of dominant families in rural areas, and the new wife moved in with the family of her husband. In India, not only were marriages arranged, but it was not uncommon for women to be married before the age of ten. In colonial Latin America, parents selected marriage partners for their children and often chose a dwelling for the couple as well. In many areas, before members of the lower classes could marry, they had to offer gifts to the powerful noble landowners in the region and obtain their permission. These nobles often refused to allow women to marry in order to keep them as servants.

Arranged marriages were the logical result of a social system in which men dominated and women's primary role was to bear children, manage the household, and work in the field. Not until the nineteenth century did a feminist

Marriage Ceremonies. At the left is a detail of a marriage ceremony in Italy from a fresco painted by Dominico di Bartolo in 1443. At the right is a seventeenth-century Mughal painting showing Shah Jahan, the Mughal emperor (with halo). He is riding to the wedding celebration of his son, who rides before him.

Iberfoto/Iberfoto/Superstock

The Granger Collection, NYC

movement emerge in Europe to improve the rights of women. By the beginning of the twentieth century, that movement had spread to other parts of the world. The New Culture Movement in China, for example, advocated the free choice of spouses. Although the trend throughout the world is toward allowing people to choose their mates, in some areas, especially in rural communities, families remain active in choosing marriage partners.

 In what ways were marriage practices similar in the West and the East during the early modern period? Were there any significant differences?

whom he had fallen in love. Impatient with the pope's unwillingness to grant him an annulment of his marriage, Henry turned to England's own church courts. As archbishop of Canterbury and head of the highest church court in England, Thomas Cranmer ruled in May 1533 that the king's marriage to Catherine was "absolutely void." At the beginning of June, Anne was crowned queen, and three months later, a child was born; much to the king's disappointment, the baby was a girl (the future Queen Elizabeth I).

In 1534, at Henry's request, Parliament moved to finalize the break of the Church of England with Rome. The Act of Supremacy of 1534 declared that the king was "the only supreme head on earth of the Church of England," a position that gave him control of doctrine, clerical appointments, and discipline. Although Henry VIII had broken with the papacy, little change occurred in matters of doctrine, theology, and ceremony. Some of his supporters, including Archbishop Cranmer, sought a religious reformation as well as an administrative one, but Henry was unyielding. But he died in 1547 and was succeeded by his son, the underage and sickly Edward VI (1547–1553), and during Edward's reign, Cranmer and others inclined toward Protestant doctrines were able to move the Church of England (or Anglican Church) in a more Protestant direction. New acts of Parliament gave the clergy the right to marry and created a new Protestant church service.

Edward VI was succeeded by Mary (1553–1558), a Catholic who attempted to return England to Catholicism. Her actions aroused much anger, however, especially when "bloody Mary" burned more than three hundred Protestant heretics. By the end of Mary's reign, England was more Protestant than it had been at the beginning.

The Anabaptists The Anabaptists were the radical reformers of the Protestant Reformation. To Anabaptists, the true Christian church was a voluntary association of believers who had undergone spiritual rebirth and had then been baptized into the church. Anabaptists advocated adult rather than infant baptism. They also wanted to return to the practices and spirit of early Christianity and considered all believers to be equal. Each church chose its own minister, who might be any member of the community since all Christians were considered priests (though women were often excluded).

Finally, unlike the Catholics and other Protestants, most Anabaptists believed in the complete separation of church and state. Government was to be excluded from the realm of religion and could not exercise political jurisdiction over real Christians. Anabaptists refused to hold political office or bear arms because many took the commandment "Thou shall not kill" literally. Their political beliefs as much as their religious beliefs caused the Anabaptists to be regarded as dangerous radicals who threatened the very fabric of sixteenth-century society. Indeed, the chief thing Protestants and Catholics could agree on was the need to persecute Anabaptists.

15–1d The Social Impact of the Protestant Reformation

The Protestants were especially important in developing a new view of the family. Because Protestantism had eliminated any idea of special holiness for celibacy and had abolished both monasticism and a celibate clergy, the family could be placed at the center of human life, and a new stress on "mutual love between man and wife" could be extolled (see Comparative Essay "Marriage in the Early Modern World").

But were doctrine and reality the same? Most often, reality reflected the traditional roles of husband as the ruler and wife as the obedient servant whose chief duty was to please her husband. Luther stated it clearly:

> The rule remains with the husband, and the wife is compelled to obey him by God's command. He rules the home and the state, wages war, defends his possessions, tills the soil, builds, plants, etc. The woman on the other hand is like a nail driven into the wall . . . so the wife should stay at home and look after the affairs of the household, as one who has been deprived of the ability of administering those affairs that are outside and that concern the state. She does not go beyond her most personal duties.[3]

Obedience to her husband was not a wife's only role; her other important duty was to bear children. To Calvin and Luther, this function of women was part of the divine plan, and for most Protestant women, family life was their only destiny (see "A Protestant Woman," p. 430). Overall, the Protestant Reformation did not noticeably alter women's subordinate place in society.

15–1e The Catholic Reformation

By the mid-sixteenth century, Lutheranism had become established in Germany and Scandinavia and Calvinism in Scotland, Switzerland, France, the Netherlands, and eastern Europe. In England, the split from Rome had resulted in the creation of a national church. The situation in Europe

A PROTESTANT WOMAN

Family & Society **IN THE INITIAL ZEAL OF THE PROTESTANT REFORMATION,** women were frequently allowed to play untraditional roles. Catherine Zell of Germany (c. 1497–1562) first preached beside her husband in 1527. After the death of her two children, she devoted the rest of her life to helping her husband and their Anabaptist faith. This selection is taken from one of her letters to a young Lutheran minister who had criticized her activities.

A Letter from Catherine Zell to Ludwig Rabus of Memmingen

I, Catherine Zell, wife of the late lamented Mathew Zell, who served in Strasbourg, where I was born and reared and still live, wish you peace and enhancement in God's grace. . . .

From my earliest years I turned to the Lord, who taught and guided me, and I have at all times, in accordance with my understanding and His grace, embraced the interests of His church and earnestly sought Jesus. Even in youth this brought me the regard and affection of clergymen and others much concerned with the church, which is why the pious Mathew Zell wanted me as a companion in marriage; and I, in turn, to serve the glory of Christ, gave devotion and help to my husband, both in his ministry and in keeping his house. . . . Ever since I was ten years old I have been a student and a sort of church mother, much given to attending sermons. I have loved and frequented the company of learned men, and I conversed much with them, not about dancing, masquerades, and worldly pleasures but about the kingdom of God. . . .

Consider the poor Anabaptists, who are so furiously and ferociously persecuted. Must the authorities everywhere be incited against them, as the hunter drives his dog against wild animals? Against those who acknowledge Christ the Lord in very much the same way we do and over which we broke with the papacy? Just because they cannot agree with us on lesser things, is this any reason to persecute them and in them Christ, in whom they fervently believe and have often professed in misery, in prison, and under the torments of fire and water?

Governments may punish criminals, but they should not force and govern belief, which is a matter for the heart and conscience not for temporal authorities. . . . When the authorities pursue one, they soon bring forth tears, and towns and villages are emptied.

 What new ideas did Catherine Zell bring to the Reformation? Why did people react so strongly against them?

Source: Excerpt from *Not in God's Image: Women in History From the Greeks to the Victorians* by Julia O'Faolain and Lauro Martines. Copyright © 1973 by Julia O'Faolain and Lauro Martines.

---

did not look particularly favorable for the Roman Catholic Church, although Protestants in many places were still a minority (see Map 15.1).

HISTORIANS DEBATE **Catholic Reformation or Counter-Reformation?** There is no doubt that the Catholic Church underwent a revitalization in the sixteenth century. But was this reformation a **Catholic Reformation** or a Counter-Reformation? Some historians prefer the term *Counter-Reformation* to focus on the aspects that were a direct reaction against the Protestant movement. Historians who prefer the term *Catholic Reformation* point out that elements of reform were already present in the Catholic Church at the end of the fifteenth century and the beginning of the sixteenth century. Especially noticeable were the calls for reform from the religious orders of the Franciscans, Dominicans, and Augustinians. Members of these groups put particular emphasis on preaching to laypeople. Another example was the Oratory of Divine Love, first organized in Italy in 1497 as an informal group of clergy and laymen who worked to foster reform by emphasizing personal spiritual development and outward acts of charity. The Oratory's members included a Spanish archbishop, Cardinal Ximenes (khee-MAY-ness), who was especially active in using Christian humanism to reform the church in Spain.

No doubt, both positions on the nature of the reformation of the Catholic Church contain elements of truth. The Catholic Reformation revived the best features of medieval Catholicism and then adjusted them to meet new conditions, as is most apparent in the emergence of a new mysticism, closely tied to the traditions of Catholic piety, and the revival of monasticism through the regeneration of older religious orders and the founding of new orders.

The Society of Jesus Of all the new religious orders, the most important was the Society of Jesus, known as the Jesuits, founded by a Spanish nobleman, Ignatius of Loyola (if-NAY-schuss of loi-OH-luh) (1491–1556). Loyola brought together a small group of individuals who were recognized as a religious order by the pope in 1540. The new order was grounded on the principles of absolute obedience to the papacy, a strict hierarchical order for the society, the use of education to achieve its goals, and a dedication to engage in "conflict for God." A special vow of absolute obedience to the pope made the Jesuits an important instrument for papal policy.

Another prominent Jesuit activity was the propagation of the Catholic faith among non-Christians. Francis Xavier (ZAY-vee-ur) (1506–1552), one of the original members of the Society of Jesus, carried the message of Catholic Christianity to the East. After attracting tens of thousands of converts in

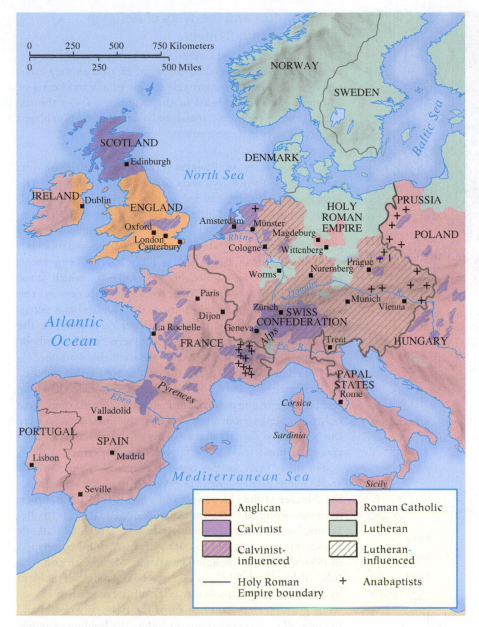

Chinese pride in their own culture, the Jesuits attempted to draw parallels between Christian and Confucian concepts and to show the similarities between Christian morality and Confucian ethics. For their part, the missionaries were much impressed with many aspects of Chinese civilization, and reports of their experiences heightened European curiosity about this great society on the other side of the world.

The Jesuits were also determined to carry the Catholic banner and fight Protestantism. Jesuit missionaries succeeded in restoring Catholicism to parts of Germany and eastern Europe. Poland was largely won back for the Catholic Church through Jesuit efforts.

A Reformed Papacy A reformed papacy was another important factor in the development of the Catholic Reformation. The involvement of Renaissance popes in dubious finances and Italian political and military affairs had created numerous sources of corruption. It took the jolt of the Protestant Reformation to bring about serious reform. Pope Paul III (1534–1549) perceived the need for change and took the audacious step of appointing a reform commission to ascertain the church's ills. The commission's report in 1537 blamed the church's problems on the corrupt policies of popes and cardinals. Paul III also formally recognized the Jesuits and summoned the Council of Trent.

The Council of Trent In March 1545, a group of high church officials met in the city of Trent on the border between Germany and Italy and initiated the Council of Trent, which met intermittently from 1545 to 1563 in three major sessions. The final decrees of the Council of Trent reaffirmed traditional Catholic teachings in opposition to Protestant beliefs. Scripture and tradition were affirmed as equal authorities in religious matters; only the church could interpret Scripture. Both faith and good works were declared necessary for salvation. Belief in purgatory and in the use of indulgences was strengthened, although the selling of indulgences was prohibited.

After the Council of Trent, the Roman Catholic Church possessed a clear body of doctrine and a unified structure under the acknowledged supremacy of the popes. Although the

Map 15.1 Catholics and Protestants in Europe by 1560. The Reformation continued to evolve beyond the basic split of the Lutherans from the Catholics. Several Protestant sects broke away from the teachings of Martin Luther, each with a separate creed and different ways of worship. In England, Henry VIII broke with the Catholic Church for political and dynastic reasons.

Q *Which areas of Europe were solidly Catholic, which were solidly Lutheran, and which were neither?*

India, he traveled to Malacca and the Moluccas before finally reaching Japan in 1549. He spoke highly of the Japanese: "They are a people of excellent morals—good in general and not malicious."[4] Thousands of Japanese, especially in the southernmost islands, became Christians. In 1552, Xavier set out for China but died of fever before he reached the mainland.

Although conversion efforts in Japan proved short-lived, Jesuit activity in China, especially that of the Italian Matteo Ricci (ma-TAY-oh REE-chee), was more long-lasting. Recognizing the

Ignatius of Loyola. The Jesuits became the most important new religious order of the Catholic Reformation. Shown here in a sixteenth-century painting by an unknown artist is Ignatius of Loyola, founder of the Society of Jesus. Loyola is seen kneeling before Pope Paul III, who officially recognized the Jesuits in 1540.

Roman Catholic Church had become one Christian denomination among many, the church entered a new phase of its history with a spirit of confidence.

CHRONOLOGY	Key Events of the Reformation Era
Luther's Ninety-Five Theses	1517
Excommunication of Luther	1521
Act of Supremacy in England	1534
Pontificate of Paul III	1534–1549
John Calvin's *Institutes of the Christian Religion*	1536
Society of Jesus (Jesuits) recognized as a religious order	1540
Council of Trent	1545–1563
Peace of Augsburg	1555

15–2 EUROPE IN CRISIS, 1560–1650

 Focus Question: Why is the period between 1560 and 1650 in Europe considered an age of crisis, and how did the turmoil contribute to the artistic developments of the period?

Between 1560 and 1650, Europe experienced religious wars, revolutions and constitutional crises, economic and social disintegration, and a witchcraft craze. It was truly an age of crisis.

15–2a Politics and the Wars of Religion in the Sixteenth Century

By 1560, Calvinism and Catholicism had become activist religions dedicated to spreading the word of God as they interpreted it. Although their struggle for the minds and hearts of Europeans was at the heart of the religious wars of the sixteenth century, economic, social, and political forces also played important roles in these conflicts.

The French Wars of Religion (1562–1598) Religion was central to the French civil wars of the sixteenth century. The growth of Calvinism had led to persecution by the French kings, but the latter did little to stop the spread of Calvinism. Huguenots (HYOO-guh-nots), as the French Calvinists were called, constituted only about 7 percent of the population, but 40 to 50 percent of the French nobility became Huguenots, including the house of Bourbon (boor-BOHN), which stood next to the Valois (val-WAH) in the royal line of succession. The conversion of so many nobles made the Huguenots a potentially dangerous political threat to monarchical power. Still, the Calvinist minority was greatly outnumbered by the Catholic majority, and the Valois monarchy was staunchly Catholic.

The religious issue was not the only factor that contributed to the French civil wars. Towns and provinces, which had long resisted the growing power of monarchical centralization, were only too willing to join a revolt against the monarchy. So were the nobles, and the fact that so many of them were Calvinists created an important base of opposition to the crown.

For thirty years, battles raged in France between Catholic and Calvinist parties. Finally, in 1589, Henry of Navarre, the political leader of the Huguenots and a member of the Bourbon dynasty, succeeded to the throne as Henry IV (1589–1610). Realizing, however, that he would never be accepted by Catholic France, Henry converted to Catholicism. With his coronation in 1594, the Wars of Religion had finally come to an end. The Edict of Nantes (NAHNT) in 1598 solved the religious problem by acknowledging Catholicism as the official religion of France while guaranteeing the Huguenots the right to worship and to enjoy all political privileges, including the holding of public offices.

Philip II and Militant Catholicism The greatest advocate of militant Catholicism in the second half of the sixteenth century was King Philip II of Spain (1556–1598), the son and heir of Charles V. Philip's reign ushered in an age of Spanish greatness, both politically and culturally. Philip had inherited from his father Spain, the Netherlands, and possessions in Italy and the Americas. To strengthen his control, Philip insisted on strict conformity to Catholicism and strong monarchical authority. Achieving the latter was not an easy task, because each of the lands of his empire had its own structure of government.

The Catholic faith was crucial to the Spanish people and their ruler. Driven by a heritage of crusading fervor, Spain saw itself as a nation of people chosen by God to save Catholic Christianity from the Protestant heretics. Philip II, the "most Catholic king," became the champion of Catholicism throughout

Europe. Spain's leadership of a "holy league" against Turkish encroachments in the Mediterranean resulted in a stunning victory over the Turkish fleet in the Battle of Lepanto (LEH-pahn-toh *or* LIH-pan-toh) in 1571. But Philip's problems with the Netherlands and the English Queen Elizabeth led to his greatest misfortunes.

Philip's attempt to strengthen his control in the Spanish Netherlands, which consisted of seventeen provinces (modern Netherlands and Belgium), soon led to a revolt. The nobles, who stood to lose the most politically, strongly opposed Philip's efforts. Religion also became a major catalyst for rebellion when Philip attempted to crush Calvinism. Violence erupted in 1566, and the revolt became organized, especially in the northern provinces, where the Dutch, under the leadership of William of Nassau, the prince of Orange, offered growing resistance. The struggle dragged on for decades until 1609, when a twelve-year truce ended the war, virtually recognizing the independence of the northern provinces. These seven northern provinces, which called themselves the United Provinces of the Netherlands, became the core of the modern Dutch state.

To most Europeans at the beginning of the seventeenth century, Spain still seemed the greatest power of the age, but the reality was quite different. The Spanish treasury was empty, the armed forces were obsolescent, and the government was inefficient. Spain continued to play the role of a great power, but much power had shifted to England.

The England of Elizabeth When Elizabeth Tudor, the daughter of Henry VIII and Anne Boleyn, ascended the throne in 1558, England was home to fewer than 4 million people. Yet during her reign (1558–1603), the small island kingdom became the leader of the Protestant nations of Europe and laid the foundations for a world empire.

Intelligent, cautious, and self-confident, Elizabeth moved quickly to solve the difficult religious problem she inherited from her half-sister, Queen Mary. Elizabeth's religious policy was based on moderation and compromise. She repealed the Catholic laws of Mary's reign, and a new Act of Supremacy designated Elizabeth as "the only supreme governor" of both church and state. The Church of England under Elizabeth was basically Protestant, but it was of a moderate bent that kept most people satisfied.

Elizabeth proved as adept in government and foreign policy as in religious affairs (see "Queen Elizabeth I: "I Have the Heart of a King," p. 434). Assisted by competent officials, she handled Parliament with much skill. Caution and moderation also dictated Elizabeth's foreign policy. Nevertheless, Elizabeth was gradually drawn into conflict with Spain. Having resisted for years the idea of invading England as too impractical, Philip II of Spain was finally persuaded to do so by advisers who assured him that the people of England would rise against their queen when the Spaniards arrived. A successful invasion of England would mean the overthrow of heresy and the return of England

Procession of Queen Elizabeth I. Intelligent and learned, Elizabeth Tudor was familiar with Latin and Greek and spoke several European languages. Served by able administrators, Elizabeth ruled for nearly forty-five years and generally avoided open military action against any major power. This picture, painted near the end of her reign, shows the queen in a ceremonial procession.

QUEEN ELIZABETH I: "I HAVE THE HEART OF A KING"

Politics & Government | **QUEEN ELIZABETH I RULED ENGLAND** from 1558 to 1603 with a consummate skill that contemporaries considered unusual in a woman. Though shrewd and paternalistic, Elizabeth's power, like that of other sixteenth-century monarchs, depended on the favor of her people. When England was faced with the threat of an invasion by the armada of Philip II, Elizabeth sought to rally her troops with a speech in Tilbury, a town on the Thames River. This selection is taken from her speech.

Queen Elizabeth I, Speech at Tilbury

My loving people, we have been persuaded by some, that are careful of our safety, to take heed how we commit ourselves to armed multitudes, for fear of treachery; but I assure you, I do not desire to live to distrust my faithful and loving people. Let tyrants fear; I have always so behaved myself that, under God, I have placed my chiefest strength and safeguard in the loyal hearts and good will of my subjects. And therefore I am come amongst you at this time, not as for my recreation or sport, but being resolved, in the midst and heat of the battle, to live or die amongst you all; to lay down, for my God, and

for my kingdom, and for my people, my honor and my blood, even the dust. I know I have but the body of a weak and feeble woman; but I have the heart of a king, and of a king of England, too; and think foul scorn that Parma or Spain, or any prince of Europe, should dare to invade the borders of my realms: to which, rather than any dishonor should grow by me, I myself will take up arms; I myself will be your general, judge, and rewarder of every one of your virtues in the field. I know already, by your forwardness, that you have deserved rewards and crowns; and we do assure you, on the word of a prince, they shall be duly paid you. In the mean my lieutenant general shall be in my stead, than whom never princes commanded a more noble and worthy subject; not doubting by your obedience to my general, by your concern in the camp and by your valor in the field, we shall shortly have a famous victory over the enemies of my God, of my kingdom, and of my people.

 What qualities evident in Elizabeth's speech would have endeared her to her listeners? How was her popularity connected to the events of the late sixteenth century?

Source: From Elizabeth I's Speech at Tillbury in 1588 to the troops.

---

to Catholicism. Philip ordered preparations for a fleet of warships, the *armada*, to spearhead the invasion of England.

The armada was a disaster. The Spanish fleet that finally set sail had neither the ships nor the manpower that Philip had planned to send. Battered by a number of encounters with the English, the Spanish fleet sailed back to Spain by a northward route around Scotland and Ireland, where it was further pounded by storms. Although the English and Spanish would continue their war for another sixteen years, the defeat of the armada guaranteed for the time being that England would remain a Protestant country.

15–2b Economic and Social Crises

The period of European history from 1560 to 1650 witnessed severe economic and social crises as well as political upheaval. Economic contraction began to be evident in some parts of Europe by the 1620s. In the 1630s and 1640s, as imports of silver from the Americas declined, economic recession intensified, especially in the Mediterranean area. Once the industrial and financial center of Europe in the age of the Renaissance, Italy was now facing economic difficulties.

Population Decline Population trends of the sixteenth and seventeenth centuries also reveal Europe's worsening conditions. The population of Europe increased from 60 million in 1500 to 85 million by 1600, the first major recovery of the European population since the devastation of the Black Death in the mid-fourteenth century. By 1650, however, records indicate that

the population had declined, especially in central and southern Europe. Europe's longtime adversaries—war, famine, and plague—continued to affect population levels. After the middle of the sixteenth century, another "little ice age," when average temperatures fell, reduced harvests and led to food shortages. Europe's problems created social tensions, some of which became manifested in an obsession with witches.

Witchcraft Mania Hysteria over witchcraft affected the lives of many Europeans in the sixteenth and seventeenth centuries. Perhaps more than 100,000 people were prosecuted throughout Europe on charges of witchcraft. As more and more people were brought to trial, the fear of witches, as well as the fear of being accused of witchcraft, escalated to frightening levels (see "A Witchcraft Trial in France").

Common people—usually those who were poor and without property—were more likely to be accused of witchcraft. Indeed, where lists are available, those mentioned most often are milkmaids, peasant women, and servant girls. In the witchcraft trials of the sixteenth and seventeenth centuries, more than 75 percent of the accused were women, most of them single or widowed and many over fifty years old.

That women were most often the victims of the witch hunt has led some scholars to argue that the witch hunt was really a woman hunt or "genderized mass murder," arguing that men hunted witches because they caused disorder and were sexual beings in a patriarchal society. Other scholars have rejected this approach and argue first, that men were also accused of

A WITCHCRAFT TRIAL IN FRANCE

Family & Society

PERSECUTIONS FOR WITCHCRAFT reached their high point in the sixteenth and seventeenth centuries, when tens of thousands of people were brought to trial. In this excerpt from the minutes of a trial in France in 1652, we can see why the accused witch stood little chance of exonerating herself.

The Trial of Suzanne Gaudry

28 May, 1652. . . . Interrogation of Suzanne Gaudry, prisoner at the court of Rieux. . . . [During interrogations on May 28 and May 29, the prisoner confessed to a number of activities involving the devil.]

Deliberation of the Court—June 3, 1652

The undersigned advocates of the Court have seen these interrogations and answers. They say that the aforementioned Suzanne Gaudry confesses that she is a witch, that she had given herself to the devil, that she had renounced God, Lent, and baptism, that she has been marked on the shoulder, that she has cohabited with the devil and that she has been to the dances,. . . .

Third Interrogation, June 27

This prisoner being led into the chamber, she was examined to know if things were not as she had said and confessed at the beginning of her imprisonment.

—Answers no, and that what she has said was done so by force.

Pressed to say the truth, that otherwise she would be subjected to torture . . .

—Answers that she is not a witch. . . .

She was placed in the hands of the officer in charge of torture . . .

The Torture

On this same day, being at the place of torture.

This prisoner, before being strapped down, was admonished to maintain herself in her first confessions. . . .

—Says that she denies everything she has said, ... Feeling herself being strapped down, says that she is not a witch, . . . and being a little stretched [on the rack] screams ceaselessly that she is not a witch.

Asked if she did not confess that she had been a witch for twenty-six years.

—Says that she said it, that she retracts it, crying that she is not a witch. . . .

The mark having been probed by the officer, . . . it was adjudged by the aforesaid doctor and officer truly to be the mark of the devil.

Being more tightly stretched upon the torture rack, urged to maintain her confessions.

—Said that it was true that she is a witch . . . Asked how long she has been in subjugation to the devil.

—Answers that it was twenty years ago that the devil appeared to her, being in her lodgings in the form of a man dressed in a little cowhide and black breeches. . . .

Verdict

July 9, 1652. In the light of the interrogations, answers, and investigations made into the charge against Suzanne Gaudry, . . . seeing by her own confessions that she is said to have made a pact with the devil, received the mark from him, . . . and that following this, she . . . had let herself be known carnally by him, in which she received satisfaction. Also, seeing that she is said to have been a part of nocturnal carols and dances.

For expiation of which the advice of the undersigned is that the office of Rieux can legitimately condemn the aforesaid Suzanne Gaudry to death, tying her to a gallows, and strangling her to death, then burning her body and burying it here in the environs of the woods.

 Why were women, particularly older women, especially vulnerable to accusations of witchcraft? What "proofs" are offered here that Suzanne Gaudry had consorted with the devil? What does this account tell us about the spread of witchcraft persecutions in the seventeenth century?

Source: From *Witchcraft in Europe, 1100–1700: A Documentary History* by Alan Kors and Edward Peters, pp. 266–275. Copyright © 1972 by The University of Pennsylvania Press.

witchcraft, and second, that women accused other women of witchcraft. These scholars believe that people in the sixteenth and seventeenth centuries believed in witchcraft as a constant threat in their society.

Despite scholarly differences about the nature of the witch hunts, there is no doubt that women were the primary victims. Current estimates are that there were 100,000 to 110,000 witch trials between 1450 and 1750 with about 50 percent of the trials leading to executions. Of those executed, 75 to 80 percent were women, many of them older women.

That women should be the chief victims of witchcraft trials was hardly accidental. Nicholas Rémy (nee-koh-LAH ray-MEE), a witchcraft judge in France in the 1590s, found it "not unreasonable that this scum of humanity, i.e., witches, should be drawn chiefly from the feminine sex." To another judge, it came as no surprise that witches would confess to sexual experiences with Satan: "The Devil uses them so, because he knows that women love carnal pleasures, and he means to bind them to his allegiance by such agreeable provocations."[5]

By the mid-seventeenth century, the witchcraft hysteria had begun to subside. As governments grew stronger, fewer magistrates were willing to accept the unsettling and divisive conditions generated by the trials of witches. Moreover, by the end of the seventeenth century and the beginning of the eighteenth, more and more people were questioning their old attitudes toward religion and found it especially contrary to reason to believe in the old view of a world haunted by evil spirits.

Economic Trends in the Seventeenth Century In the course of the seventeenth century, new economic trends also emerged. **Mercantilism** is the name historians apply to the economic practices of the seventeenth century. According to the mercantilists, the prosperity of a nation depended on a plentiful supply of bullion (gold and silver). For this reason, it was desirable to achieve a favorable balance of trade in which goods exported were of greater value than those imported, promoting an influx of gold and silver payments that would increase the quantity of bullion. Furthermore, to encourage exports, governments should stimulate and protect export industries and trade by granting trade monopolies, encouraging investment in new industries through subsidies, importing foreign artisans, and improving transportation systems by building roads, bridges, and canals. By imposing high tariffs on foreign goods, they could reduce imports and prevent them from competing with domestic industries. Colonies were also deemed valuable as sources of raw materials and markets for finished goods.

Mercantilist theory on the role of colonies was matched in practice by Europe's overseas expansion. With the development of colonies and trading posts in the Americas and the East, Europeans embarked on an adventure in international commerce in the seventeenth century. Although some historians speak of a nascent world economy, we should remember that local, regional, and intra-European trade still predominated. At the end of the seventeenth century, for example, English imports totaled 360,000 tons, but only 5,000 tons came from the East Indies. What made the transoceanic trade rewarding, however, was not the volume but the value of its goods. Dutch, English, and French merchants were bringing back products that were still consumed largely by the wealthy but were beginning to make their way into the lives of artisans and merchants. Pepper and spices from the Indies, West Indian and Brazilian sugar, and Asian coffee and tea were becoming more readily available to European consumers.

The commercial expansion of the sixteenth and seventeenth centuries was made easier by new forms of commercial organization, especially the **joint-stock company**. Individuals bought shares in a company and received dividends on their investment while a board of directors ran the company and made the important business decisions. The return on investments could be spectacular. During its first ten years, investors received 30 percent annually on their money from the Dutch East India Company, which opened the Spice Islands and Southeast Asia to Dutch activity. The joint-stock company made it easier to raise large amounts of capital for world trading ventures.

Despite the growth of commercial capitalism, most of the European economy still depended on an agricultural system that had experienced few changes since the thirteenth century. At least 80 percent of Europeans still worked on the land. Almost all of the peasants in western Europe were free of serfdom, although many still owed a variety of feudal dues to the nobility. Despite the expanding markets and rising prices, European peasants saw little or no improvement in their lot as they faced increased rents and fees and higher taxes imposed by the state.

15–2c Seventeenth-Century Crises: Revolution and War

During the first half of the seventeenth century, a series of rebellions and civil wars rocked the domestic stability of many European governments. A devastating war that affected much of Europe also added to the sense of crisis.

The Thirty Years' War (1618–1648) The Thirty Years' War began in 1618 in the Germanic lands of the Holy Roman Empire as a struggle between Catholic forces, led by the Habsburg Holy Roman Emperors, and Protestant—primarily Calvinist—nobles in Bohemia who rebelled against Habsburg authority (see Map 15.2). What began as a struggle over religious issues soon became a wider conflict perpetuated by political motivations as both minor and major European powers—Denmark, Sweden, France, and Spain—entered the war. The competition for European leadership between the Bourbon dynasty of France and the Habsburg dynasties of Spain and the Holy Roman Empire was an especially important factor. Nevertheless, most of the battles were fought on German soil, with considerable damage. The Thirty Years' War was undoubtedly the most destructive conflict Europe had yet experienced (see "The Destruction of Magdeburg in the Thirty Years' War," p. 438).

The war in Germany was officially ended in 1648 by the Peace of Westphalia, which proclaimed that all German states, including the Calvinist ones, were free to determine their own religion. The major contenders gained new territories, and France emerged as the dominant nation in Europe. The more than three hundred entities that made up the Holy Roman Empire were recognized as independent states, and each was given the power to conduct its own foreign policy; this brought an end to the Holy Roman Empire and ensured German disunity for another two hundred years. The Peace of Westphalia made it clear that political motives, not religious convictions, had become the guiding force in public affairs.

HISTORIANS DEBATE **Was There A Military Revolution?** By the seventeenth century, war played an increasingly important role in European affairs. Military power was considered essential to a ruler's reputation and power; thus, the pressure to build an effective military machine was intense. Some historians believe that the changes that occurred in the science of warfare between 1560 and 1650 warranted the title of military revolution.

Medieval warfare, with its mounted knights and supplementary archers, had been transformed in the Renaissance by the employment of infantry armed with pikes and halberds

Map 15.2 Europe in the Seventeenth Century. This map shows Europe at the time of the Thirty Years' War (1618–1648). Although the struggle began in Bohemia and much of the fighting took place in the Germanic lands of the Holy Roman Empire, the conflict became a Europe-wide struggle. Compare this map with Map 15.1 (Section 15-1e, p. 431).

 Which countries engaged in the war were predominantly Protestant, which were Catholic, and which were mixed?

(long-handled weapons combining an axe with a spike) and arranged in massed rectangles known as squadrons or battalions. The use of firearms required adjustments to the size and shape of the massed infantry and made the cavalry less effective.

It was Gustavus Adolphus (goo-STAY-vus uh-DAHL-fuss), the king of Sweden (1611–1632), who developed the first standing army of conscripts, notable for the flexibility of its tactics. The infantry brigades of Gustavus's army were composed of equal numbers of musketeers and pikemen, standing six men deep. They employed the salvo, in which all rows of the infantry fired at once instead of row by row. These salvos of fire, which cut up the massed ranks of the opposing infantry squadrons, were followed by a pike charge, giving the infantry a primarily offensive deployment. Gustavus also used his cavalry in a more mobile fashion. After shooting a pistol volley, they charged the enemy with their swords. Additional flexibility was obtained by

using lighter artillery pieces that were more easily moved during battle. All of these innovations required coordination, careful training, and better discipline, forcing rulers to move away from undisciplined mercenary forces. Naturally, the success of Gustavus Adolphus led to imitation.

Some historians have questioned the use of the phrase "military revolution" to describe the military changes from 1560 to 1660, arguing instead that military developments were gradual. In any case, for the rest of the seventeenth century, warfare continued to change. Standing armies, based partly on conscription, grew ever larger and more expensive. Standing armies necessitated better-disciplined and better-trained soldiers and led to the education of officers in military schools. Armies also introduced the use of linear rather than square formations to provide greater flexibility and mobility in tactics. There was also an increased use of firearms as the musket with

THE DESTRUCTION OF MAGDEBURG IN THE THIRTY YEARS' WAR

Politics & Government

AFTER KING GUSTAVUS ADOLPHUS OF SWEDEN entered the war, he was finally joined by German Protestant forces after the fall of the Protestant city of Magdeburg to the imperial forces. In the following excerpt, a writer of this period gives a vivid description of what happened to Magdeburg and its inhabitants.

An Account of the Destruction of Magdeburg

Thus it came about that the city and all its inhabitants fell into the hands of the enemy, whose violence and cruelty were due in part to their common hatred of the adherents of the Augsburg Confession [Lutherans], and in part to their being embittered by the chain shot which had been fired at them and by the derision and insults that the Magdeburgers had heaped upon them from the ramparts.

Then was there naught but beating and burning, plundering, torture, and murder. Most especially was every one of the enemy bent on securing much booty. When a marauding party entered a house, if its master had anything to give he might thereby purchase respite and protection for himself and his family till the next man, who also wanted something should come along. It was only when everything had been brought forth and there was nothing left to give that the real trouble commenced. Then, what with blows and threats of shooting, stabbing, and hanging, the poor people were so terrified that if they had had anything left they would have brought it forth if it had been buried in the earth or hidden away in a thousand castles. In this frenzied rage, the great and splendid city that had stood like a fair princess in the land was now, in its hour of direst need and unutterable distress and woe, given over to the flames, and thousands of innocent men, women, and children, in the midst of a horrible din of heartrending shrieks and cries, were tortured and put to death in so cruel and shameful a manner that no words would suffice to describe, nor no tears to bewail it . . .

Thus, in a single day this noble and famous city, the pride of the whole country, went up in fire and smoke; and the remnant of its citizens, with their wives and children, were taken prisoner and driven away by the enemy with a noise of weeping and wailing that could be heard from afar, while the cinders and ashes from the town were carried by the wind to . . . distant places . . .

In addition to all this, quantities of sumptuous and irreplaceable house furnishings and movable property of all kinds, such as books, manuscripts, paintings, memorials of all sorts . . . which money could not buy, were either burned or carried away by the soldiers as booty. The most magnificent garments, hangings, silk stuffs, gold and silver lace, linen of all sorts, and other household goods were bought by the army sutlers for a mere song and peddled about by the cart load all throughout the archbishopric of Magdeburg. . . . Gold chains and rings, jewels, and every kind of gold and silver utensils were to be bought from the common soldiers for a tenth of their real value . . .

 What does this document reveal about the effect of war on ordinary Europeans? Compare this description with the descriptions of the treatment of civilians in other wars. Does this author exaggerate, or is this description similar to the others?

Source: James Harvey Robinson, *Readings in European History*, Vol. 2 (Boston: Ginn and Company, 1906), pp. 211–212.

---

attached bayonet increasingly replaced the pike in the ranks of the infantry. A naval arms race in the seventeenth century led to more and bigger warships or capital ships known as "ships of the line."

Larger armies and navies could be maintained only by levying heavier taxes, making war a greater economic burden and an ever more important part of the early modern European state. The creation of large bureaucracies to supervise the military resources of the state led to growth in the power of state governments.

CHRONOLOGY	Europe in Crisis, 1560–1650: Key Events	
Reign of Philip II		1556–1598
French Wars of Religion		1562–1598
Outbreak of revolt in the Netherlands		1566
Defeat of the Spanish armada		1588
Edict of Nantes		1598
Truce between Spain and the Netherlands		1609–1621
Thirty Years' War		1618–1648
Peace of Westphalia		1648

15–3 RESPONSE TO CRISIS: THE PRACTICE OF ABSOLUTISM

 Focus Question: What was absolutism, and what were the main characteristics of the absolute monarchies that emerged in France, Prussia, Austria, and Russia?

Many people responded to the crises of the seventeenth century by searching for order. An increase in monarchical power became an obvious means for achieving stability. The result

COMPARATIVE ILLUSTRATION

Sun Kings, West and East. At the end of the seventeenth century, two powerful rulers in different parts of the world held sway in kingdoms that dominated the affairs of the regions around them. Both rulers saw themselves as favored by divine authority—Louis XIV of France as a divine-right monarch and Kangxi (GANG-zhee) of China as possessing the mandate of Heaven. Thus, both rulers saw themselves not as divine beings but as divinely ordained beings whose job was to govern organized societies. In image A, Louis, who ruled France from 1643 to 1715, is seen in a portrait by Hyacinthe Rigaud (ee-ah-SANT ree-GOH) that captures the king's sense of royal dignity and grandeur. One person at court said of the king: "Louis XIV's vanity was without limit or restraint." In image B, Kangxi, who ruled China from 1661 to 1722, is seen in a portrait that shows him seated in majesty on his imperial throne. A dedicated ruler, Kangxi once wrote, "One act of negligence may cause sorrow all through the country, and one moment of negligence may result in trouble for hundreds and thousands of generations."

Q *Although these rulers practiced very different religions, why did they justify their powers in such a similar fashion?*

A

RMN-Grand Palais/Art Resource, NY

B

Hu Weibiao/Panorama/The Image Works

was what historians have called absolutism or absolute monarchy, in which the sovereign power or ultimate authority in the state rested in the hands of a king who claimed to rule by divine right—the idea that kings received their power from God and were responsible to no one but God. Late-sixteenth-century political theorists believed that sovereign power consisted of the authority to make laws, levy taxes, administer justice, control the state's administrative system, and determine foreign policy.

15–3a France Under Louis XIV

France during the reign of Louis XIV (1643–1715) has traditionally been regarded as the best example of the practice of absolute or **divine-right monarchy** in the seventeenth century (see Comparative Illustration "Sun Kings, West and East,"). French culture, language, and manners reached into all levels of European society. French diplomacy and wars overwhelmed the political affairs of western and central Europe. The court of Louis XIV was also imitated elsewhere in Europe.

Political Institutions One of the keys to Louis's power was his control of the central policymaking machinery of government because it was part of his own court and household. The royal court, located in the magnificent palace at Versailles (vayr-SY), outside Paris, served three purposes simultaneously: it was the personal household of the king, the location of central governmental machinery, and the place where powerful subjects came to find favors and offices for themselves and their clients. The greatest danger to Louis's personal rule came from the very high nobles and princes of the blood (the royal princes), who considered it their natural function to assert the policymaking role of royal ministers. Louis eliminated this threat by removing them from the royal council, the chief administrative body of the king, and enticing them to his court, where he could keep them preoccupied with court life and out of politics. Instead of the high nobility and royal princes, Louis relied for his ministers on nobles who came from relatively new aristocratic families. His ministers were expected to be subservient: "I had no intention of sharing my authority with them," Louis said.

Court life at Versailles itself became highly ritualized with Louis at the center of it all. The king had little privacy; only when he visited his wife or mother or mistress was he free of the noble courtiers who swarmed about the palace. Most daily ceremonies were carefully staged, including those attending Louis's rising from bed, dining, praying, attending Mass, and going to bed. A mob of nobles aspired to assist the king in carrying out these solemn activities. It was considered a great honor for a noble to be chosen to hand the king his shirt while dressing. Court etiquette was also a complex matter. Nobles and royal princes were arranged in an elaborate order of seniority and expected to follow certain rules of precedence. Who could sit down and on what kind of chair was a subject of much debate.

Louis's domination of his ministers and secretaries gave him control of the central policymaking machinery of government and thus authority over the traditional areas of monarchical power: the formulation of foreign policy, the making of war and peace, the assertion of the secular power of the crown against any religious authority, and the ability to levy taxes to fulfill these functions. Louis had considerably less success with the internal administration of the kingdom, however. The traditional groups and institutions of French society—the nobles, officials, town councils, guilds, and representative estates in some provinces—were simply too powerful for the king to have direct control over the lives of his subjects. As a result, control of the provinces and the people was achieved largely by bribing the individuals responsible for carrying out the king's policies.

The Economy and the Military The cost of building palaces, maintaining his court, and pursuing his wars made finances a crucial issue for Louis XIV. He was most fortunate in having the services of Jean-Baptiste Colbert (ZHAHN-bap-TEEST kohl-BAYR) (1619–1683) as his controller general of finances. Colbert sought to increase the wealth and power of France through general adherence to mercantilism, which advocated government intervention in economic activities for the benefit of the state. To decrease imports and increase exports, Colbert granted subsidies to individuals who established new industries. To improve communications and the transportation of goods internally, he built roads and canals. To decrease imports directly, Colbert raised tariffs on foreign goods.

The increase in royal power that Louis pursued led the king to develop a professional army numbering 100,000 men in peacetime and 400,000 in time of war. To achieve the prestige

Interior of Versailles: The Hall of Mirrors. Pictured here is the exquisite Hall of Mirrors at Versailles. Located on the second floor, the hall overlooks the park below. Three hundred and fifty-seven mirrors were placed on the wall opposite the windows in order to create an illusion of even greater width. Careful planning went into every detail of the interior decoration. Even the doorknobs were specially designed to reflect the magnificence of Versailles. This photo shows the Hall of Mirrors after the restoration work that was completed in June 2007, a project that took three years, cost 12 million euros (more than $16 million), and included the restoration of the Bohemian crystal chandeliers.

RMN-Grand Palais/Art Resource, NY

and military glory befitting an absolute king as well as to ensure the domination of his Bourbon dynasty over European affairs, Louis waged four wars between 1667 and 1713. His ambitions roused much of Europe to form coalitions against him to prevent the certain destruction of the European balance of power by Bourbon hegemony. Although Louis added some territory to France's northeastern frontier and established a member of his own Bourbon dynasty on the throne of Spain, he also left France impoverished and surrounded by enemies.

15–3b Absolutism in Central and Eastern Europe

During the seventeenth century, a development of great importance for the modern Western world took place with the appearance in central and eastern Europe of three new powers: Prussia, Austria, and Russia.

Prussia Frederick William the Great Elector (1640–1688) laid the foundation for the Prussian state. Realizing that the land he had inherited, known as Brandenburg-Prussia, was a small, open territory with no natural frontiers for defense, Frederick William built an army of 40,000 men, making it the fourth largest in Europe. To sustain the army, Frederick William established the General War Commissariat to levy taxes for the army and oversee its growth. The Commissariat soon evolved into an agency for civil government as well. The new bureaucratic machine became the elector's chief instrument to govern the state. Many of its officials were members of the Prussian landed aristocracy, the Junkers (YOONG-kers), who also served as officers in the all-important army.

In 1701, Frederick William's son Frederick officially gained the title of king. Elector Frederick III became King Frederick I, and Brandenburg-Prussia simply Prussia. In the eighteenth century, Prussia emerged as a great power in Europe.

Austria The Austrian Habsburgs had long played a significant role in European politics as Holy Roman Emperors. By the end of the Thirty Years' War, the Habsburg hopes of creating an empire in Germany had been dashed. In the seventeenth century, the house of Austria created a new empire in eastern and southeastern Europe.

The nucleus of the new Austrian Empire remained the traditional Austrian hereditary possessions: Lower and Upper Austria, Carinthia, Carniola, Styria, and Tyrol. To these had been added the kingdom of Bohemia and parts of northwestern Hungary. After the defeat of the Turks in 1687 (see Chapter 16), Austria took control of all of Hungary, Transylvania, Croatia, and Slovenia, thus establishing the Austrian Empire in southeastern Europe. By the beginning of the eighteenth century, the house of Austria had assembled an empire of considerable size.

The Austrian monarchy, however, never became a highly centralized, absolutist state, primarily because it contained so many different national groups. The Austrian Empire remained a collection of territories held together by the Habsburg emperor, who was archduke of Austria, king of Bohemia, and king of Hungary. Each of these regions, however, had its own laws and political life.

From Muscovy to Russia A new Russian state had emerged in the fifteenth century under the leadership of the principality of Muscovy and its grand dukes. In the sixteenth century, Ivan IV (1533–1584) became the first ruler to take the title of *tsar* (the Russian word for "Caesar"). Ivan expanded the territories of Russia eastward and crushed the power of the Russian nobility. He was known as Ivan the Terrible because of his ruthless deeds, among them stabbing his son to death in a heated argument. When Ivan's dynasty came to an end in 1598, fifteen years of anarchy ensued until the Zemsky Sobor (ZEM-skee suh-BOR), or national assembly, chose Michael Romanov (ROH-muh-nahf) as the new tsar, establishing a dynasty that lasted more than four hundred years. One of its most prominent members was Peter the Great.

Peter the Great (1689–1725) was an unusual character. A strong man towering 6 feet 9 inches tall, Peter enjoyed low humor—belching contests and crude jokes—and vicious punishments, including floggings, impalings, and roastings. Peter got a firsthand view of the West when he made a trip there in 1697–1698 and returned to Russia with a firm determination to westernize Russia. He was especially eager to borrow European technology in order to create the army and navy he needed to make Russia a great power.

As could be expected, one of Peter's first priorities was the reorganization of the army and the creation of a navy. Employing both Russians and Europeans as officers, he conscripted peasants for twenty-five-year stints of service to build a standing army of 210,000 men and at the same time formed the first navy Russia had ever had.

To impose the rule of the central government more effectively throughout the land, Peter divided Russia into provinces. Although he hoped to create a "police state," by which he meant a well-ordered community governed in accordance with law, few of his bureaucrats shared his concept of loyalty to the state. Peter hoped to evoke a sense of civic duty among his people, but his own forceful personality created an atmosphere of fear that prevented any such sentiment.

This use of force was also evident when Peter began to introduce Western customs, practices, and manners into Russia shortly after his return from the West in 1698. Because Europeans at that time did not wear beards or traditional long-skirted coats, Russian beards had to be shaved and coats shortened, a reform Peter personally enforced at court by shaving off his nobles' beards and cutting their coats at the knees with his own hands. Outside the court, barbers and tailors planted at town gates enforced the edicts by cutting the beards and cloaks of those who entered or left. Many Russians, as a result, regarded the tsar as a tyrant.

The object of Peter's domestic reforms was to make Russia into a great state and military power. His primary goal was to "open a window to the west," meaning an ice-free port easily accessible to Europe. This could only be achieved on the Baltic, but at that time, the Baltic coast was controlled by Sweden, the most important power in northern Europe. A long and hard-fought war with Sweden won Peter the lands he sought. In 1703, Peter began the construction of a new city, Saint Petersburg, his window to the west and a symbol that Russia was looking westward to Europe. By the time Peter died in 1725, Russia had become a great military power and an important European state.

Peter the Great. Peter the Great wished to westernize Russia, especially in the realm of technical skills. His goal was the creation of a strong army and navy and the acquisition of new territory in order to make Russia a great power. Jean Marc Nattier, a French artist, painted this portrait of the tsar dressed in military armor in 1717. Portrait of Peter the Great against a background of the Battle of Poltava, Danhauer, Gottfried (c.1680–1733/7) (attr. to)/Tretyakov Gallery, Moscow, Russia/Bridgeman Images

15–4 ENGLAND AND LIMITED MONARCHY

 Focus Question: How and why did England avoid the path of absolutism?

Not all states were absolutist in the seventeenth century. One of the most prominent examples of resistance to absolute monarchy came in England, where king and Parliament struggled to determine the roles each should play in governing England.

15–4a Conflict Between King and Parliament

With the death of the childless Queen Elizabeth I in 1603, the Tudor dynasty became extinct, and the Stuart line of rulers was inaugurated with the accession to the throne of Elizabeth's cousin, King James VI of Scotland, who became James I (1603–1625) of England. James espoused the divine right of kings, a viewpoint that alienated Parliament, which had grown accustomed under the Tudors to act on the premise that monarch and Parliament together ruled England as a "balanced polity." Then, too, the **Puritans**—Protestants within the Anglican

Church who, inspired by Calvinist theology, wished to eliminate every trace of Roman Catholicism from the Church of England—were alienated by the king's strong defense of the Anglican Church. Many of England's gentry, mostly well-to-do landowners, had become Puritans and formed an important and substantial part of the House of Commons, the lower house of Parliament. It was not wise to alienate these men.

The conflict that had begun during the reign of James came to a head during the reign of his son Charles I (1625–1649). Like his father, Charles believed in divine-right monarchy, and religious differences also added to the hostility between Charles I and Parliament. The king's attempt to impose more ritual on the Anglican Church struck the Puritans as a return to Catholic practices. When Charles tried to force the Puritans to accept his religious policies, thousands of them went off to the "howling wildernesses" of America.

15–4b Civil War and Commonwealth

Grievances mounted until England finally slipped into a civil war (1642–1648) won by the parliamentary forces, due largely to the New Model Army of Oliver Cromwell, the only real military genius of the war. The New Model Army was composed primarily of more extreme Puritans known as the Independents, who, in typical Calvinist fashion, believed they were doing battle for God. As Cromwell wrote in one of his military reports, "Sir, this is none other but the hand of God; and to Him alone belongs the glory." We might give some credit to Cromwell; his soldiers were well trained in the new military tactics of the seventeenth century.

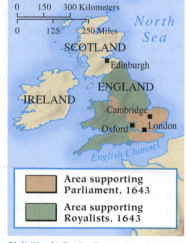

Civil War in England

After the execution of Charles I on January 30, 1649, Parliament abolished the monarchy and the House of Lords and proclaimed England a republic or commonwealth. But Cromwell and his army, unable to work effectively with Parliament, dispersed it by force and established a military dictatorship. After Cromwell's death in 1658, the army decided that military rule was no longer feasible and restored the monarchy in the person of Charles II, the son of Charles I.

15–4c Restoration and a Glorious Revolution

Charles was sympathetic to Catholicism, and Parliament's suspicions were aroused in 1672 when Charles took the audacious step of issuing the Declaration of Indulgence, which suspended the laws that Parliament had passed against Catholics and Puritans after the restoration of the monarchy. Parliament forced the king to suspend the declaration.

France	
Louis XIV	1643–1715
Brandenburg-Prussia	
Frederick William the Great Elector	1640–1688
Elector Frederick III (King Frederick I)	1688–1713
Russia	
Ivan IV the Terrible	1533–1584
Peter the Great	1689–1725
First trip to the West	1697–1698
Construction of Saint Petersburg begins	1703
England	
Civil wars	1642–1648
Commonwealth	1649–1653
Charles II	1660–1685
Declaration of Indulgence	1672
James II	1685–1688
Glorious Revolution	1688
Bill of Rights	1689

The accession of James II (1685–1688) to the crown virtually guaranteed a new constitutional crisis for England. An open and devout Catholic, his attempt to further Catholic interests made religion once more a primary cause of conflict between king and Parliament. James named Catholics to high positions in the government, army, navy, and universities. Parliamentary outcries against James's policies stopped short of rebellion because members knew that he was an old man and that his successors were his Protestant daughters Mary and Anne, born to his first wife. But on June 10, 1688, a son was born to James II's second wife, also a Catholic. Suddenly, the specter of a Catholic hereditary monarchy loomed large. A group of prominent English noblemen invited the Dutch chief executive, William of Orange, husband of James's daughter Mary, to invade England. William and Mary raised an army and invaded England while James, his wife, and their infant son fled to France. With little bloodshed, England had undergone its "Glorious Revolution."

In January 1689, Parliament offered the throne to William and Mary, who accepted it along with the provisions of a bill of rights (see "The Bill of Rights," p. 444). The Bill of Rights affirmed Parliament's right to make laws and levy taxes. The rights of citizens to keep arms and have a jury trial were also confirmed. By deposing one king and establishing another, Parliament had destroyed the divine-right theory of kingship (William was, after all, king by grace of Parliament, not God) and asserted its right to participate in the government. Parliament did not have complete control of the government, but it now had the right to participate in affairs of state. Over the next century, it would gradually prove to be the real authority in the English system of **limited (constitutional) monarchy**.

15–5 THE FLOURISHING OF EUROPEAN CULTURE

Q **Focus Question:** How did the artistic and literary achievements of this era reflect the political and economic developments of the period?

Despite religious wars and the growth of absolutism, European culture continued to flourish. The era was blessed with a number of prominent artists and writers.

15–5a Art: The Baroque

The artistic movement known as the **Baroque** (buh-ROHK) dominated the Western artistic world for a century and a half. The Baroque began in Italy in the last quarter of the sixteenth century and spread to the rest of Europe and Latin America. Baroque artists sought to harmonize the Classical ideals of Renaissance art with the spiritual feelings of the sixteenth-century religious revival.

RMN-Grand Palais/Art Resource, NY

Peter Paul Rubens, *The Landing of Marie de' Medici at Marseilles*. The Flemish painter Peter Paul Rubens played a key role in spreading the Baroque style from Italy to other parts of Europe. In *The Landing of Marie de' Medici at Marseilles*, Rubens made a dramatic use of light and color, bodies in motion, and luxurious nudes to heighten the emotional intensity of the scene. This was one of a cycle of twenty-one paintings dedicated to the queen mother of France.

THE BILL OF RIGHTS

Politics & Government

IN 1688, THE ENGLISH EXPERIENCED a bloodless revolution in which the Stuart king, James II, was replaced by Mary, James's daughter, and her husband, William of Orange. After William and Mary had assumed power, Parliament passed the Bill of Rights, which set out the rights of Parliament and laid the foundation for a constitutional monarchy.

The Bill of Rights

Whereas the said late King James II having abdicated the government, and the throne being thereby vacant, his Highness the prince of Orange (whom it hath pleased Almighty God to make the glorious instrument of delivering this kingdom from popery and arbitrary power) did (by the device of the lords spiritual and temporal, and diverse principal persons of the Commons) cause letters to be written to the lords spiritual and temporal, being Protestants, and other letters to the several counties, cities, universities, boroughs, and Cinque Ports, for the choosing of such persons to represent them, as were of right to be sent to parliament, to meet and sit at Westminster upon the two and twentieth day of January, in this year 1689, in order to such an establishment as that their religion, laws, and liberties might not again be in danger of being subverted; upon which letters elections have been accordingly made.

And thereupon the said lords spiritual and temporal and Commons, pursuant to their respective letters and elections, being now assembled in a full and free representation of this nation, taking into their most serious consideration the best means for attaining the ends aforesaid, do in the first place (as their ancestors in like case have usually done), for the vindication and assertion of their ancient rights and liberties, declare:

1. That the pretended power of suspending laws, or the execution of laws, by regal authority, without consent of parliament is illegal.
2. That the pretended power of dispensing with the laws, or the execution of law by regal authority, as it hath been assumed and exercised of late, is illegal.

Source: From *The Statutes: Revised Edition* (London: Eyre & Spotiswoode, 1871), Vol. 2, pp. 10–12.

3. That the commission for erecting the late court of commissioners for ecclesiastical causes, and all other commissions and courts of like nature, are illegal and pernicious.
4. That levying money for or to the use of the crown by pretense of prerogative, without grant of parliament, for longer time or in other manner than the same is or shall be granted, is illegal.
5. That it is the right of the subjects to petition the king, and all commitments and prosecutions for such petitioning are illegal.
6. That the raising or keeping a standing army within the kingdom in time of peace, unless it be with consent of parliament, is against law.
7. That the subjects which are Protestants may have arms for their defense suitable to their conditions, and as allowed by law.
8. That election of members of parliament ought to be free.
9. That the freedom of speech, and debates or proceedings in parliament, ought not to be impeached or questioned in any court or place out of parliament.
10. That excessive bail ought not to be required, nor excessive fines imposed, nor cruel and unusual punishments inflicted.
11. That jurors ought to be duly impaneled and returned, and jurors which pass upon men in trials for high treason ought to be freeholders.
12. That all grants and promises of fines and forfeitures of particular persons before conviction are illegal and void.
13. And that for redress of all grievances, and for the amending, strengthening, and preserving of the laws, parliament ought to be held frequently.

 How did the Bill of Rights lay the foundation for a constitutional monarchy in England?

In large part, Baroque art and architecture reflected the search for power that was characteristic of much of the seventeenth century. Baroque churches and palaces featured richly ornamented facades, sweeping staircases, and an overall splendor meant to impress people. Kings and princes wanted not only their subjects but also other kings and princes to be in awe of their power.

Baroque painting was known for its use of dramatic effects to arouse the emotions. This style was especially evident in the works of Peter Paul Rubens (1577–1640) of Flanders, a prolific artist and an important figure in the spread of the Baroque from Italy to other parts of Europe. In his artistic masterpieces, bodies in violent motion, heavily fleshed nudes, a dramatic use

of light and shadow, and rich sensuous pigments converge to express highly intense emotions.

Perhaps the greatest figure of the Baroque was the Italian architect and sculptor Gian Lorenzo Bernini (JAHN loh-RENT-zoh bur-NEE-nee) (1598–1680), who completed Saint Peter's Basilica at the Vatican and designed the vast colonnade enclosing the piazza in front of it. Action, exuberance, profusion, and dramatic effects mark the work of Bernini in the interior of Saint Peter's, where his *Throne of Saint Peter* hovers in midair, held by the hands of the four great doctors of the Catholic Church. Above the chair, rays of golden light drive a mass of clouds and angels toward the spectator. In his most striking sculptural work, the *Ecstasy of Saint Theresa*, Bernini depicts a moment of mystical experience in the life of the sixteenth-century Spanish saint. The elegant draperies and the expression on her face create a sensuously real portrayal of physical ecstasy.

15–5b Art: Dutch Realism

A brilliant flowering of Dutch painting paralleled the supremacy of Dutch commerce in the seventeenth century. Wealthy patricians and burghers of Dutch urban society commissioned works of art for their guild halls, town halls, and private dwellings. The subject matter of many Dutch paintings reflected the interests of this bourgeois society: portraits of themselves, group portraits of their military companies and guilds, landscapes, seascapes, genre scenes, still lifes, and the interiors of their residences. Unlike Baroque artists, Dutch painters were primarily interested in the realistic portrayal of secular everyday life.

This interest in painting scenes of everyday life is evident in the work of Judith Leyster (LESS-tur) (c. 1609–1660), who established her own independent painting career, a remarkable achievement for a woman in seventeenth-century Europe. Leyster became the first female member of the painters' Guild of Saint Luke in Haarlem, which enabled her to set up her own workshop and take on three male pupils. Musicians playing their instruments, women sewing, children laughing while playing games, and actors performing all form the subject matter of Leyster's portrayals of everyday Dutch life.

15–5c A Golden Age of Literature in England

In England, writing for the stage reached new heights between 1580 and 1640. The golden age of English literature is often called the Elizabethan era because much of the English cultural flowering occurred during Elizabeth's reign. Elizabethan literature exhibits the exuberance and pride associated with English exploits at the time (see "William Shakespeare: In Praise of England," p. 446). Of all the forms of Elizabethan literature, none expressed the energy and intellectual versatility of the era better than drama. And no dramatist is more famous or more accomplished than William Shakespeare (1564–1614).

Shakespeare was a "complete man of the theater." Although best known for writing plays, he was also an actor and a shareholder in the chief acting company of the time, the Lord Chamberlain's Company, which played in various London theaters. Shakespeare is to this day hailed as a genius. A master of the English language, he imbued its words with power and majesty. And his technical proficiency was matched by incredible insight into human psychology. Whether writing tragedies or comedies, Shakespeare exhibited a remarkable understanding of the human condition.

Scala/Art Resource, NY

Gian Lorenzo Bernini, *Ecstasy of Saint Theresa.* One of the great artists of the Baroque period was the Italian sculptor and architect Gian Lorenzo Bernini. The *Ecstasy of Saint Theresa*, created for the Cornaro Chapel in the Church of Santa Maria della Vittoria in Rome, was one of Bernini's most famous sculptures. Bernini sought to convey visually Theresa's mystical experience when, according to her description, an angel pierced her heart repeatedly with a golden arrow.

National Gallery of Art, Washington, DC

Judith Leyster, *Self-Portrait.* Although Judith Leyster was a well-known artist to her Dutch contemporaries, her fame diminished soon after her death. In the late nineteenth century, a Dutch art historian rediscovered her work. In her *Self-Portrait*, painted in 1635, she is seen pausing in her work in front of one of the scenes of daily life that made her such a popular artist in her own day.

WILLIAM SHAKESPEARE: IN PRAISE OF ENGLAND

Art & Ideas

WILLIAM SHAKESPEARE is one of the most famous playwrights of the Western world. He is a universal genius, outclassing all others in his psychological insights, depth of characterization, imaginative skills, and versatility. His historical plays reflect the patriotic enthusiasm of the English in the Elizabethan era, as this excerpt from *Richard II* illustrates.

William Shakespeare, *Richard II*

This royal throne of kings, this sceptred isle,
This earth of majesty, this seat of Mars,
This other Eden, demi-Paradise,
This fortress built by Nature for herself
Against infection and the hand of war,
This happy breed of men, this little world,
This precious stone set in the silver sea,
Which serves it in the office of a wall
Or as a moat defensive to a house
Against the envy of less happier lands—
This blessed plot, this earth, this realm, this England,
This nurse, this teeming womb of royal kings,
Feared by their breed and famous by their birth,

Renowned for their deeds as far from home,
For Christian service and true chivalry,
As is the sepulcher in stubborn Jewry [the Holy Sepulcher in
    Jerusalem and the enduring Jewish community there]
Of the world's ransom, blessed Mary's Son—
This land of such dear souls, this dear dear land,
Dear for her reputation through the world,
Is now leased out, I die pronouncing it,
Like a tenement or pelting farm.
England, bound in with the triumphant sea,
Whose rocky shore beats back the envious siege
Of watery Neptune, is now bound in with shame,
With inky blots and rotten parchment bonds.
That England, that was wont to conquer others,
Hath made a shameful conquest of itself.
Ah, would the scandal vanish with my life,
How happy then were my ensuing death!

 Why is William Shakespeare aptly described as not merely a playwright but a "complete man of the theater"? Which countries might Shakespeare have meant by the phrase "the envy of less happier lands"?

Source: Excerpt from "Richard II" in *Shakespeare: The Complete Works* by G. B. Harrison, copyright © 1968 by Harcourt Brace & Company and renewed 1980 by G. B. Harrison.

CHAPTER SUMMARY

In the last chapter, we observed how the movement of Europeans beyond Europe began to change the shape of world history. But what had made this development possible? After all, the Reformation of the sixteenth century, initially begun by Martin Luther, had brought about the religious division of Europe into Protestant and Catholic camps. By the middle of the sixteenth century, it was apparent that the religious passions of the Reformation era had brought an end to the religious unity of medieval Europe. The religious division (Catholics versus Protestants) was instrumental in beginning a series of religious wars that were complicated by economic, social, and political forces that also played a role.

The crises of the sixteenth and seventeenth centuries soon led to a search for a stable, secular order of politics and made possible the emergence of a system of nation-states in which

power politics took on increasing significance. Within those states, there slowly emerged some of the machinery that made possible a growing centralization of power. In those states called absolutist, strong monarchs with the assistance of their aristocracies took the lead in providing the leadership for greater centralization. In this so-called age of absolutism, Louis XIV, the Sun King of France, was the model for other rulers. Strong monarchy also prevailed in central and eastern Europe, where three new powers made their appearance: Prussia, Austria, and Russia.

But not all European states followed the pattern of absolute monarchy. Especially important were developments in England, where a series of struggles between the king and Parliament took place in the seventeenth century. In the long run, the landed aristocracy gained power at the expense of the monarchs, thereby laying the foundations for a constitutional government in which Parliament provided the focus for the institutions of centralized power.

In all the major European states, a growing concern for power and dynamic expansion led to larger armies and greater conflict, stronger economies, and more powerful governments. From a global point of view, Europeans—with their strong governments, prosperous economies, and strengthened military forces—were beginning to dominate other parts of the world, leading to a growing belief in the superiority of their civilization.

Yet despite Europeans' increasing domination of global trade markets, they had not achieved their goal of diminishing the power of Islam, first pursued during the crusades. In fact, as we shall see in the next chapter, in the midst of European expansion and exploration, three new and powerful Muslim empires were taking shape in the Middle East and South Asia.

CHAPTER TIMELINE

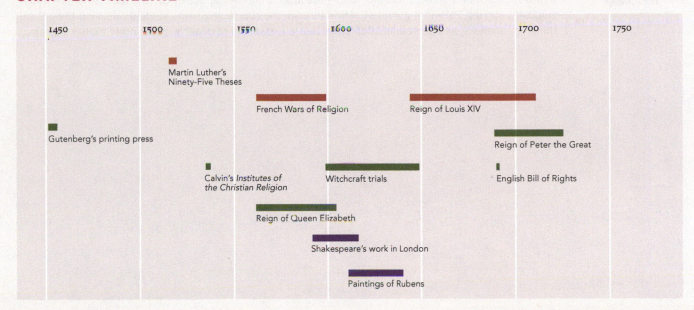

| 1450 | 1500 | 1550 | 1600 | 1650 | 1700 | 1750 |

Martin Luther's Ninety-Five Theses

French Wars of Religion

Reign of Louis XIV

Gutenberg's printing press

Reign of Peter the Great

Calvin's *Institutes of the Christian Religion*

Witchcraft trials

English Bill of Rights

Reign of Queen Elizabeth

Shakespeare's work in London

Paintings of Rubens

CHAPTER REVIEW

Upon Reflection

Q What role did politics play in the success of the Protestant Reformation?

Q What did Louis XIV hope to accomplish through his domestic and foreign policies? To what extent did he succeed?

Q Compare and contrast the development of states in Europe and the world of Islam (see Chapter 16). What are the similarities and differences in these developments? How do you explain the similarities and differences?

Key Terms

absolutism (p. 421)
Protestant Reformation (p. 421)
new monarchies (p. 421)
Christian humanism (northern Renaissance humanism) (p. 423)
relics (p. 423)
indulgences (p. 423)
justification by faith (p. 423)

predestination (p. 426)
Catholic Reformation (p. 430)
mercantilism (p. 436)
joint-stock company (p. 436)
divine-right monarchy (p. 439)
Puritans (p. 442)
limited (constitutional) monarchy (p. 443)
Baroque (p. 443)

Chapter Notes

1. Quoted in R. Bainton, *Here I Stand: A Life of Martin Luther* (New York, 1950), p. 144.
2. J. Calvin, *Institutes of the Christian Religion*, trans. J. Allen (Philadelphia, 1936), vol. 1, p. 228; vol. 2, p. 181.
3. Quoted in B. S. Anderson and J. P. Zinsser, *A History of Their Own: Women in Europe from Prehistory to the Present* (New York, 1988), vol. 1, p. 259.
4. Quoted in J. O'Malley, *The First Jesuits* (Cambridge, Mass., 1993), p. 76.
5. Quoted in J. Klaits, *Servants of Satan: The Age of Witch Hunts* (Bloomington, Ind., 1985), p. 68.

MindTap® is a fully online personalized learning experience built upon Cengage Learning content. MindTap® combines student learning tools—readings, multimedia, activities, and assessments—into a singular Learning Path that guides students through the course and helps students develop the critical thinking, analysis, and communication skills that are essential to academic and professional success.

Chapter Outline and Focus Questions

16–1 *The Ottoman Empire*

Q What were the chief reasons for the success of the Ottoman Turks in consolidating their influence throughout the Middle East and the Balkans? Why were they more successful at the effort than their predecessors, the Byzantine Empire?

16–2 *The Safavids*

Q What problems did the Safavid Empire face, and how did its rulers attempt to solve them? How did their successes and failures compare with those of the other Muslim empires?

16–3 *The Grandeur of the Mughals*

Q What role did Islam play in the Mughal Empire, and how did the Mughals' approach to religion compare with that of the Ottomans and the Safavids? What might explain the similarities and differences?

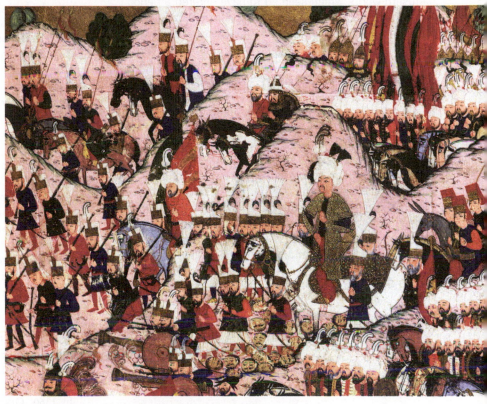

Turks fight Christians at the Battle of Mohács. Universal Images Group/Art Resource, NY

Critical Thinking

Q *What were the main characteristics of each of the Muslim empires, and in what ways did they resemble each other? How were they distinct from their European counterparts?*

Connections to Today

Q *How would you compare the position of Islam in the world today with its position in the era described in this chapter?*

THE OTTOMAN ARMY, led by Sultan Suleyman the Magnificent, arrived at Mohács, on the plains of Hungary, on an August morning in 1526. The Turkish force numbered about 100,000 men, and its weapons included three hundred new long-range cannons. Facing them was a somewhat larger European force, clothed in heavy armor but armed with only one hundred older cannons, along with a detachment of Hungarian cavalry.

The battle began at noon and was over in two hours. The Hungarian cavalry units had been destroyed, and 20,000 foot soldiers from the European army had drowned in a nearby swamp. The Ottomans had lost fewer than two hundred men. Two weeks later, they seized the Hungarian capital at Buda and prepared to lay siege to the nearby

Austrian city of Vienna. Europe was in a panic, but Mohács was to be the high point of Turkish expansion in Europe.

In launching their Age of Exploration, European rulers had hoped that by controlling global markets, they could cripple the power of Islam and reduce its threat to the security of Europe. But the dream of Christian nations to extend their political and economic dominance around the globe at the expense of their Muslim rivals was destined to prove abortive, at least for the time being. On the contrary, the Muslim world, which seemed to have entered a period of decline with the collapse of the Abbasid caliphate during the era of the Mongols, managed to revive in the shadow of Europe's Age of Exploration, a period that witnessed the rise of three great Muslim empires. These powerful Muslim states—of the Ottomans, the Safavids, and the Mughals—dominated the Middle East and the South Asian subcontinent and brought a measure of stability to a region that had been in turmoil for centuries. One of them—the Ottoman Empire—managed to impose its rule over much of eastern Europe and establish its own dominant position throughout the Mediterranean world.

The stability brought to the region by these three great Muslim states, however, was not long-lived. By the end of the eighteenth century, the Safavid empire had collapsed, while much of India and the Middle East had come under severe European pressure and had returned to a state of anarchy. The Ottoman Empire was still substantially intact, but it no longer threatened the Christian nations in Europe, and some observers were convinced that it was in a state of irreversible decline.

16–1 THE OTTOMAN EMPIRE

 Focus Questions: What were the chief reasons for the success of the Ottoman Turks in consolidating their influence throughout the Middle East and the Balkans? Why were they more successful at the effort than their predecessors, the Byzantine Empire?

The Ottoman Turks were among the Turkic-speaking nomadic peoples who had spread westward from Central Asia in the ninth, tenth, and eleventh centuries. The first to appear in the Middle East were the Seljuk Turks, who initially attempted to revive the declining Abbasid caliphate in Baghdad. Later they established themselves in the Anatolian peninsula as the successors to the Byzantine Empire. Turks served as warriors or administrators, while the peasants who tilled the farmland were mainly Greek.

16–1a The Rise of the Ottoman Turks

In the late thirteenth century, a new group of Turks under the tribal leader Osman (os-MAHN) (r. 1280–1326) began to consolidate power in the northwestern corner of the Anatolian peninsula. That land had been given to them by the Seljuk rulers as a reward for helping drive out the Mongols in the late thirteenth century. At first, the Osman Turks were relatively peaceful and engaged in pastoral pursuits, but as the Seljuk empire began to crumble in the early fourteenth century, the Osman Turks began to expand and founded the Osmanli (os-MAHN-lee) dynasty, with its capital at Bursa (BURR-suh). The Osmanlis later came to be known as the Ottomans.

A key advantage for the Ottomans was their location in the northwestern corner of the peninsula. From there they were able to expand westward and eventually take over the Bosporus and the Dardanelles, between the Mediterranean and the Black Seas. The Byzantine Empire, of course, had controlled the area for centuries, serving as a buffer between the Muslim Middle East and the Latin West. The Byzantines, however, had been severely weakened by the sack of Constantinople in the Fourth Crusade in 1204 and the occupation of much of the empire by western Europeans for the next half century. In 1345, Ottoman forces under their leader Orkhan (or-KHAHN) I (r. 1326–1360) crossed the Bosporus for the first time to support a usurper against the Byzantine emperor in Constantinople. Setting up their first European base at Gallipoli (gah-LIP-poh-lee) at the Mediterranean entrance to the Dardanelles, Turkish forces expanded gradually into the Balkans and allied with fractious Serbian and Bulgar forces against the Byzantines. In these unstable conditions, the Ottomans gradually established permanent settlements throughout the area, where Turkish provincial governors, called **beys** (BAYS) (from the Turkish *beg*, "knight"), collected taxes from the local Slavic peasants after driving out the previous landlords. The Ottoman leader now began to claim the title of sultan (SUL-tun) or sovereign of his domain.

In 1360, Orkhan was succeeded by his son Murad (moo-RAHD) I, who consolidated Ottoman power in the Balkans, set up a capital at Edirne (eh-DEER-nay) (see Map 16.1), and gradually reduced the Byzantine emperor to a vassal. Murad did not initially attempt to conquer Constantinople because his forces were composed mostly of the traditional Turkish cavalry and lacked the ability to breach the strong walls of the city. Instead, he began to build up a strong military administration based on the recruitment of Christians into an elite guard. Called **janissaries** (JAN-nih-say-reez) (from the Turkish *yeni cheri*, "new troops"), they were recruited from the local Christian population in the Balkans and then converted to Islam and trained as foot soldiers or administrators. One of the major advantages of the janissaries (an elite core of eight thousand troops) was that they were directly subordinated to the sultanate and therefore owed their loyalty to the person of the sultan. Other military forces were organized by the beys and were thus loyal to their local tribal leaders.

The janissary corps also represented a response to changes in warfare. As the knowledge of firearms spread from China in the late fourteenth century, the Turks began to master the new technology, including siege cannons and muskets (see Comparative Essay "The Changing Face of War," p. 452). The traditional nomadic cavalry charge was now outmoded and was superseded by infantry forces armed with muskets. Thus, the janissaries provided a well-armed infantry that served both as an elite guard to protect the palace and as a means of extending Turkish control in the Balkans. With his new forces, Murad defeated the Serbs at the famous Battle of Kosovo (KAWSS-suh-voh) in 1389 and ended Serbian hegemony in the area.

16–1b Expansion of the Empire

Under Murad's successor, Bayazid (by-uh-ZEED) I (r. 1389–1402), the Ottomans advanced northward, annexed Bulgaria, and slaughtered the French cavalry at a major battle on the Danube. A defeat at Ankara (AN-kuh-ruh) at the hands of the Mongol warrior Tamerlane (see Chapter 9) in 1402 proved to be only a temporary setback. When Mehmet (meh-MET) II (r. 1451–1481) succeeded to the throne, he was determined to capture Constantinople. Already in control of the Dardanelles, he ordered the construction of a major fortress on the Bosporus just north of the city, which put the Turks in a position to strangle the Byzantines.

The Fall of Constantinople The last Byzantine emperor desperately called for help from the Europeans, but only the Genoese came to his defense. With 80,000 troops ranged against only 6,000 to 8,000 defenders, Mehmet laid siege to Constantinople in 1453. In their attack on the city, the Turks made use

Map 16.1 The Ottoman Empire. This map shows the territorial growth of the Ottoman Empire from the eve of the conquest of Constantinople in 1453 to the end of the seventeenth century, when a defeat at the hands of Austria led to the loss of a substantial portion of central Europe.

Q *Where did the Ottomans come from?*

COMPARATIVE ESSAY

The Changing Face of War

Science & Technology

"War," as the renowned French historian Fernand Braudel once observed, "has always been a matter of arms and techniques. Improved techniques can radically alter the course of events." Braudel's remark was directed to the situation in the Mediterranean region during the sixteenth century, when the adoption of artillery changed the face of warfare and gave enormous advantages to the countries—such as the Ottoman Empire—that took advantage of the new technological revolution in firearms. But it can just as easily be applied to the present day, when some powerful states possess weapons capable of reaching across oceans and continents, while weaker adversaries must adopt strategies and tactics to compensate for their disadvantages in terms of arms technology.

One crucial aspect of military superiority, then, lies in the nature of weaponry. From the invention of the bow and arrow to the advent of the atomic era, the possession of superior instruments of war has provided a distinct advantage against a poorly armed enemy. It was at least partly the possession of bronze weapons, for example, that enabled the invading Hyksos to conquer Egypt during the second millennium BCE.

Mobility is another factor of vital importance. During the second millennium BCE, horse-drawn chariots revolutionized the art of war from the Mediterranean Sea to the Yellow River Valley in northern China. Later, the invention of the stirrup enabled mounted warriors to shoot arrows from horseback, a technique applied with great effect by the Mongols as they devastated civilizations across the Eurasian supercontinent.

To protect themselves from marauding warriors, settled societies began to erect massive walls around their cities and fortresses. That in turn led to the invention of siege weapons like the catapult and the battering ram. The Mongols allegedly even came up with an early form of chemical warfare, hurling human bodies infected with the plague into the bastions of their enemies.

The invention of explosives launched the next great revolution in warfare. First used as a weapon of war by the Tang dynasty in China, explosives were brought to the West by the Turks, who used them with great effectiveness in

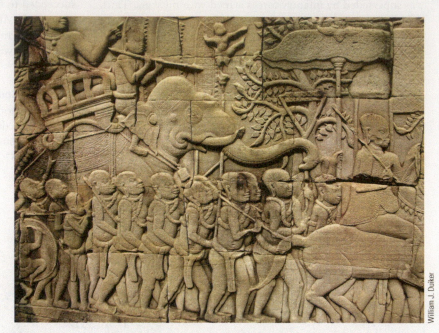

Angkor Troops advancing against their enemies in Champa.

William J. Duiker

the fifteenth century against the Byzantine Empire. But the Europeans quickly mastered the new technology and took it to new heights, inventing handheld firearms and mounting iron cannons on their warships. The latter represented a significant advantage to European fleets as they began to compete with rivals for control of the Indian and Pacific Oceans.

The twentieth century saw revolutionary new developments in the art of warfare, from armed vehicles to airplanes to nuclear arms. But as weapons grow ever more fearsome, they are more dangerous to use, resulting in the paradox of the Vietnam War, when lightly armed Viet Cong guerrilla units were able to fight the world's mightiest army to a virtual standstill. The lessons of Vietnam have been effectively absorbed in our own day, as lightly armed insurgents rely on terror and assassination to promote their goals against more powerful enemies. As the Chinese military strategist Sun Tzu had long ago observed, victory in war often goes to the smartest, not the strongest.

 Why were the Europeans, rather than other peoples, able to make effective use of firearms to expand their influence throughout the world?

of massive cannons with 26-foot barrels that could launch stone balls weighing up to 1,200 pounds each. The Byzantines stretched heavy chains across the Golden Horn, the inlet that forms the city's harbor, to prevent a naval attack from the north and prepared to make their final stand behind the 13-mile-long wall along the western edge of the city. But Mehmet's forces seized the tip of the peninsula north of the Golden Horn and then dragged their ships overland across the peninsula from the Bosporus and put them into the water behind the chains. Finally, the walls were breached; the Byzantine emperor died in the final battle. Mehmet II, standing before the palace of the emperor, paused to reflect on the passing nature of human glory. But it was not long before he and the Ottomans were again on the march.

The Advance Into Western Asia and Africa

With their new capital at Constantinople, eventually renamed Istanbul, the Ottoman Turks had become a dominant force in the Balkans and the Anatolian peninsula. They now began to advance to the east against the Shi'ite kingdom of the Safavids (sah-FAH-weeds) in Persia (see Section 16-2, "The Safavids," p. 460), which had been promoting rebellion among the Anatolian tribal population and disrupting Turkish trade through the Middle East. After defeating the Safavids at a major battle in 1514, Emperor Selim (seh-LEEM) I (r. 1512–1520) consolidated Turkish control over Mesopotamia and then turned his attention to the Mamluks (MAM-looks) in Egypt, who had failed to support the Ottomans in their struggle against the Safavids. Ottoman troops defeated the Mamluks in Syria in 1516; Cairo fell a year later. Now controlling several of the holy cities of Islam, including Jerusalem, Mecca, and Medina, Selim declared himself the new caliph, or successor to Muhammad. During the next few years, Turkish armies and fleets advanced westward along the African coast, occupying Tripoli, Tunis, and Algeria and eventually penetrating almost to the Strait of Gibraltar (see Map 16.1). In their advance, the invaders had taken advantage of the progressive disintegration of the Nasrid (NAS-rid) dynasty in Morocco, which had been in decline for decades and had lost its last foothold on the European continent when Granada fell to Spain in 1492.

The impact of Turkish rule on the peoples of North Africa was relatively light. Like their predecessors, the Turks were Muslims, and they preferred where possible to administer their conquered regions through local rulers. The central government utilized appointed **pashas** (PAH-shuz) who were directly responsible to Istanbul; the pashas collected taxes, paying a fixed percentage as tribute to the central government, and maintained law and order. The Turks ruled from coastal cities such as Algiers, Tunis, and Tripoli and made no attempt to control the interior beyond maintaining the trade routes through the Sahara to the commercial centers along the Niger River. Meanwhile, local pirates along the Barbary Coast—the northern coast of Africa from Egypt to the Atlantic Ocean—competed with their Christian rivals in raiding the shipping that passed through the Mediterranean.

By the seventeenth century, the links between the imperial court in Istanbul and its appointed representatives in the Turkish regencies in North Africa had begun to weaken. Some of the pashas were dethroned by local elites, while others, such as the bey of Tunis, became hereditary rulers. Even Egypt, whose agricultural wealth and control over the route to the Red Sea made it to the Turks the most important country in the area, gradually became autonomous under a new official class of janissaries. Many of them became wealthy landowners by exploiting their official positions and collecting tax revenues far in excess of what they had to remit to Istanbul. In the early eighteenth century, the Mamluks returned to power, although the Turkish government managed to retain some control by means of a viceroy appointed from Istanbul.

Turkish Expansion in Europe

After their conquest of Constantinople in 1453, the Ottoman Turks tried to complete their conquest of the Balkans, where they had been established since the fourteenth century. Although they were successful in taking the Romanian territory of Wallachia (wah-LAY-kee-uh) in 1476, the resistance of the Hungarians initially kept the Turks from advancing up the Danube Valley. From 1480 to 1520, internal problems and the need to consolidate their eastern frontiers kept the Turks from any further attacks on Europe.

Suleyman (SOO-lay-mahn) I the Magnificent (r. 1520–1566) (also known as "the lawgiver" in deference to his role in strengthening the Ottoman legal system) brought the Turks back to Europe's attention. Advancing up the Danube, the Turks seized Belgrade in 1521 and won a major victory over the Hungarians at the Battle of Mohács (MOH-hach) on the Danube in 1526. Subsequently, the Turks overran most of Hungary, moved into Austria, and advanced as far as Vienna, where they were finally driven back in 1529. An equally bitter struggle was taking place at sea, where Turkish fleets advanced as far as the Balearic islands, off the coast of Spain, thus threatening to turn the Mediterranean into a "Turkish lake." Unlike the situation in the Indian Ocean, where highly armed Portuguese sailing ships put the Ottomans at a disadvantage, Turkish fleets composed primarily of oared vessels could be used to good advantage in the more closed quarters along the shores of the Mediterranean.

Europe eventually got the message, and a large Turkish fleet was destroyed by the Spanish at Lepanto, off the coast of Greece, in 1571. Despite the defeat, the Turks continued to hold nominal suzerainty over the southern shores of the Mediterranean. One year after Lepanto, the Turks reconstituted their fleet and seized the island of Cyprus. Responding to the joy expressed in Europe over the naval victory at Lepanto, the **grand vizier** (veh-ZEER) (Turkish *vezir*), or chief minister (under the sultan), in Constantinople remarked to the Venetian ambassador, "There is a big difference between our loss and yours. In taking Cyprus, we have cut off one of your arms. In sinking our fleet you only shaved our beard. A lost arm cannot be replaced, but a shorn beard grows back quickly to its prior magnificence."[1]

Although Christians in Europe frequently called for new crusades against the "infidel" Turks, by the beginning of the seventeenth century the Ottoman Empire was being treated like any other European power by European rulers seeking alliances and trade concessions. During the first half of the seventeenth century, the Ottoman Empire was viewed in Europe as a "sleeping giant." Involved in domestic bloodletting and heavily threatened by a challenge from Persia, the Ottomans were content with the status quo in eastern Europe. But under a new line of grand viziers in the second half of the seventeenth century, the Ottoman Empire again took the offensive. By mid-1683, the Ottomans had marched through the Hungarian plain and once again laid siege to Vienna. Repulsed by a mixed army of Austrians, Poles, Bavarians, and Saxons, the Turks retreated and were pushed out of Hungary by a new European coalition. Although they retained the core of their empire, the Ottoman Turks would never again be a threat to Europe and, by the beginning of the eighteenth century, they faced new challenges from the ever-expanding Austrian Empire in southeastern Europe and the new Russian giant to the north.

A PORTRAIT OF SULEYMAN THE MAGNIFICENT

Politics & Government Suleyman I was perhaps the greatest of all Ottoman sultans. Like King Louis XIV of France and Emperor Kangxi of China, he presided over his domain at the peak of its military and cultural achievement. This description of him was written by Ghislain de Busbecq (GEE-lan duh booz-BEK), the Habsburg ambassador to Constantinople. Busbecq observed Suleyman at first hand and, as this selection indicates, was highly impressed by the Turkish ruler.

Ghislain de Busbecq, *The Turkish Letters*

The Sultan was seated on a rather low sofa, no more than a foot from the ground and spread with many costly coverlets and cushions embroidered with exquisite work. Near him were his bow and arrows. His expression, as I have said, is anything but smiling, and has a sternness which, though sad, is full of majesty. On our arrival we were introduced into his presence by his chamberlains, who held our arms—a practice which has always been observed since a Croatian sought an interview and murdered the Sultan Amurath in a revenge for the slaughter of his master, Marcus the Despot of Serbia. After going through the pretense of kissing his hand, we were led to the wall facing him backwards, so as not to turn our backs or any part of them toward him. He then listened to the recital of my message, but, as it did not correspond [to] his expectations (for the demands of my imperial master [the Habsburg emperor Ferdinand I] were full of dignity and independence, and, therefore, far from acceptable to one who thought that his slightest wishes ought to be obeyed), he assumed an expression of disdain, and merely answered "*Giusel, giusel,*" that is, "Well, well." We were then dismissed to our lodging. . . .

You will probably wish me to describe the impression which Suleyman made upon me. He is beginning to feel the weight of years, but his dignity of demeanor and his general physical appearance are worthy of the ruler of so vast an empire. He has always been frugal and temperate, and was so even in his youth, when he might have erred without incurring blame in the eyes of the Turks. Even in his earlier years he did not indulge in wine or in those unnatural vices to which the Turks are often addicted. Even his bitterest critics can find nothing more serious to allege against him than his undue submission to his wife and its result in his somewhat precipitate action in putting Mustapha [his firstborn son, by another wife] to death, which is generally imputed to her employment of love potions and incantations. It is generally agreed that ever since he promoted her to the rank of his lawful wife, he has possessed no concubines, although there is no law to prevent his doing so. He is a strict guardian of his religion and its ceremonies, being not less desirous of upholding his faith than of extending his dominions. For his age—he has almost reached his sixtieth year—he enjoys quite good health, though his bad complexion may be due to some hidden malady; and indeed it is generally believed that he has an incurable ulcer or gangrene on his leg. This defect of complexion he remedies by painting his face with a coating of red powder, when he wishes departing ambassadors to take with them a strong impression of his good health; for he fancies that it contributes to inspire greater fear in foreign potentates if they think that he is well and strong.

 What were the main achievements of Suleyman that caused him to be called "the Magnificent"? Is this description the work of an admirer or a critic? Why do you think so?

Source: O.G. De Busbecq, *The Turkish Letters* translated by E. S. Forster.

16–1c The Nature of Turkish Rule

Like other Muslim empires in Persia and India, the Ottoman political system was the result of the evolution of tribal institutions into a sedentary empire. At the apex of the Ottoman system was the sultan, who was the supreme authority in both a political and a military sense. The origins of this system can be traced back to the bey, who was only a tribal leader, a first among equals, who could claim loyalty from his chiefs so long as he could provide booty and grazing lands for his subordinates. Disputes were settled by tribal law; Muslim law was secondary. Tribal leaders collected taxes—or booty—from areas under their control and sent one-fifth on to the bey. Both administrative and military power were centralized under the bey, and the capital was wherever the bey and his administration happened to be.

The Role of the Sultan But the rise of empire brought about changes and an adaptation to Byzantine traditions of rule, much as Abbasid political practices had been affected by Persian monarchical tradition at an earlier time in Baghdad. The status and prestige of the sultan now increased relative to the subordinate tribal leaders, and with Suleyman the Magnificent—perhaps the Ottoman Empire's greatest ruler—the position took on the trappings of imperial rule (see "A Portrait of Suleyman the Magnificent"). Court rituals were inherited from the Byzantines and Persians, and a centralized administrative system was adopted that increasingly isolated the sultan in his palace. The position of the sultan was hereditary, with a son, although not necessarily the eldest, always succeeding the father. This practice led to chronic succession struggles upon the death of individual sultans, and the losers

The Sultan's Chambers in Topkapi Palace. After his conquest of Constantinople in 1453, Mehmet II constructed the extensive palace compound known as Topkapi as his royal residence and the seat of the new government. Set on a high promontory overlooking the Bosporus and the Sea of Marmara, this self-contained city housed over four thousand people and included a royal harem, dormitories, libraries, schools, mosques, a hospital, and gardens with fountains. Shown here (left) is the sultan's imperial throne room. The walls of the harem are covered with magnificent tile work designs, including this design of colorful flowers in vases (right). Ottoman artists were renowned for the high quality of their glazed tile art, produced in many colors including their own secret "tomato red," which adorned palaces as well as mosques.

were often executed or imprisoned. Potential heirs to the throne were assigned as provincial governors to provide them with experience.

The Harem The heart of the sultan's power was in the Topkapi (tahp-KAH-pee) Palace in the center of Istanbul. Topkapi (meaning "cannon gate") was constructed in 1459 by Mehmet II and served as an administrative center as well as the private residence of the sultan and his family. Eventually, it had a staff of 20,000 employees. The private domain of the sultan was called the **harem** ("sacred place"). Here he resided with his concubines. Normally, a sultan did not marry but chose several concubines as his favorites; they were accorded this status after they gave birth to sons. When a son became a sultan, his mother became known as the queen mother and served as adviser to the throne. This tradition, initiated by the influential wife of Suleyman the Magnificent, often resulted in considerable authority for the queen mother in affairs of state.

Like the janissaries, members of the harem were often of slave origin and formed an elite element in Ottoman society. Since the enslavement of Muslims was forbidden, slaves were taken among non-Islamic peoples. Some concubines were prisoners selected for the position, while others were purchased or offered to the sultan as gifts. They were then trained and educated like the janissaries in a system called *devshirme* (dev-SHEER-may) ("collection"). *Devshirme* had originated in the practice of requiring local clan leaders to provide prisoners to the sultan as part of their tax obligation. Talented males were given special training for eventual placement in military or administrative positions, while their female counterparts were trained for service in the harem, with instruction in reading, the Qur'an, sewing and embroidery, and musical performance. They were ranked according to their status, and some were permitted to leave the harem to marry officials. If they were later divorced, they were sometimes allowed to return to the harem.

Unique to the Ottoman Empire from the fifteenth century onward was the exclusive use of slaves to reproduce its royal heirs. Contrary to myth, few of the women of the imperial harem were used for sexual purposes, as the majority were relatives of the sultan's extended family—sisters, daughters, widowed mothers, and in-laws, with their own personal slaves and entourages. Contemporary European observers compared the atmosphere in the Topkapi harem to a Christian nunnery, with its hierarchical organization, enforced chastity, and rule of silence.

Because of their proximity to the sultan, the women of the harem often wielded so much political power that the era has been called the "sultanate of women." Queen mothers administered the imperial household and engaged in diplomatic relations with other countries while controlling the marital alliances of their daughters with senior civilian and military officials or members of other royal families in the region. One princess was married seven separate times from the age of two after her previous husbands died either in battle or by execution.

Administration of the Government The sultan ruled through an imperial council that met four days a week and was chaired by the grand vizier. The sultan often attended behind a screen,

A Janissary officer recruiting devsirme for Sultan Suleyman I (1495–1566), from the 'Suleymanname' (Mss Hazine. 1517 f.31v), 1558 (ink & gold leaf on vellum), Ali Amir Beg (fl. 1558)/Topkapi Palace Museum, Istanbul, Turkey/The Bridgeman Art Library

Recruitment of the Children. The Ottoman Empire, like its Chinese counterpart, sought to recruit its officials on the basis of merit. Through the system called *devshirme* ("collection"), youthful candidates were selected from the non-Muslim population in villages throughout the empire. In this painting, an imperial officer is counting coins to pay for the children's travel expenses to Istanbul, where they will undergo extensive academic and military training. Note the concern of two of the mothers and a priest as they question the official, who undoubtedly underwent the process himself as a child. As they leave their family and friends, the children carry their worldly possessions in bags slung over their shoulders.

whence he could privately indicate his desires to the grand vizier. The latter presided over the imperial bureaucracy. Like the palace guard, the bureaucrats were not an exclusive group but were chosen at least partly by merit from a palace school for training officials. Most officials were Muslims by birth, but some talented janissaries became senior members of the bureaucracy, and almost all the later grand viziers came from the *devshirme* system.

Local administration during the imperial period was a product of Turkish tribal tradition and was similar in some respects to fief-holding in Europe. The empire was divided into provinces and districts governed by officials who, like their tribal predecessors, combined both civil and military functions. They were assisted by bureaucrats trained in the palace school in Istanbul. Senior officials were assigned land in fief by the sultan

and were then responsible for collecting taxes and supplying armies to the empire. These lands were then farmed out to the local cavalry elite called the *sipahis* (suh-PAH-heez), who obtained their salaries by exacting a tax from all peasants in their fiefdoms. These local officials were not hereditary aristocrats, but sons often inherited their fathers' landholdings, and the vast majority were descendants of the beys who had formed the tribal elites before the imperial period.

16–1d Religion and Society in the Ottoman World

Like most Turkic-speaking peoples in the Anatolian peninsula and throughout the Middle East, the Ottoman ruling elites were Sunni Muslims. Ottoman sultans had claimed the title of caliph ("defender of the faith") since the early sixteenth century and thus were theoretically responsible for guiding the flock and maintaining Islamic law, the *Shari'a*. In practice, the sultan assigned these duties to a supreme religious authority, who administered the law and maintained a system of schools for educating Muslims.

Islamic law and customs were applied to all Muslims in the empire. Although most Turkic-speaking people were Sunni Muslims, some communities were attracted to Sufism (see Chapter 7) or other heterodox doctrines. The government tolerated such activities as long as their practitioners remained loyal to the empire, but in the early sixteenth century, unrest among these groups—some of whom converted to the Shi'ite version of Islam—outraged the conservative *ulama* and eventually led to war against the Safavids (see Section 16-2, "The Safavids," p. 460).

The Treatment of Minorities Non-Muslims—mostly Orthodox Christians (Greeks and Slavs), Jews, and Armenian Christians—formed a significant minority within the empire, which treated them with relative tolerance. Non-Muslims were compelled to pay a head tax (as compensation for their exemption from military service), and they were permitted to practice their religion or convert to Islam (people who were already Muslim were prohibited from adopting another faith). Most of the population in European areas of the empire remained Christian, but in some places, such as the Balkan territory now known as Bosnia and Herzegovina, substantial numbers converted to Islam.

Each religious group within the empire was organized as an administrative unit called a **millet** (mi-LET) ("nation" or "community"). Each group, including the Muslims themselves, had its own patriarch, priest, or grand rabbi who dealt as an intermediary with the government and administered the community according to its own laws. The leaders of the individual *millets* were responsible to the sultan and his officials for the behavior of the subjects under their care and collected taxes for transmission to the government. Each *millet* established its own system of justice, set its own educational policies, and provided welfare for the needy.

Social Classes The subjects of the Ottoman Empire were also divided by occupation and place of residence. In addition to the ruling class, there were four main occupational groups: peasants, artisans, merchants, and pastoral peoples. The first

Reign of Osman I	1280–1326
Ottoman Turks cross the Bosporus	1345
Murad I consolidates Turkish power in the Balkans	1360
Ottomans defeat the Serbian army at Kosovo	1389
Tamerlane defeats the Ottoman army at Ankara	1402
Reign of Mehmet II the Conqueror	1451–1481
Turkish conquest of Constantinople	1453
Turks defeat the Mamluks in Syria and seize Cairo	1516–1517
Reign of Suleyman I the Magnificent	1520–1566
Defeat of the Hungarians at Battle of Mohács	1526
Defeat of the Turks at Vienna	1529
Battle of Lepanto	1571
Second siege of Vienna	1683

three were classified as "urban" residents. Peasants tilled land that was leased to them by the state (ultimate ownership of all land resided with the sultan), but the land was deeded to them, so they were able to pass it on to their heirs. They were not allowed to sell the land and thus in practice were forced to remain on the soil. Taxes were based on the amount of land the peasants possessed and were paid to the local sipahis, who held the district in fief.

Nomadic peoples were placed in a separate *millet* and were subject to their own regulations and laws. They were divided into the traditional nomadic classifications of tribes, clans, and "tents" (individual families) and were governed by their hereditary chiefs, the beys. As we have seen, the beys were responsible for administration and for collecting taxes for the state.

Artisans were organized according to craft guilds. Each guild, headed by a council of elders, was responsible not only for dealing with the governmental authorities but also for providing financial services, social security, and training for its members. Outside the ruling elite, merchants were the most privileged class in Ottoman society. They were largely exempt from government regulations and taxes and were therefore able in many cases to amass large fortunes. Charging interest was technically illegal under Islamic law, but the rules were often ignored in practice. In the absence of regulations, merchants often established monopolies and charged high prices, which caused them to be bitterly resented by other subjects of the empire.

The Position of Women Women in the Ottoman Empire were subject to the same restrictions that afflicted their counterparts in other Muslim societies, but their position was ameliorated to some degree by a variety of factors. In the first place, non-Muslims were subject to the laws and customs of their own religions; thus, Orthodox Christian, Armenian Christian, and Jewish women were spared some of the restrictions applied to their Muslim sisters (although they were then subject to restrictions imposed by their own faith). In the second place, Islamic laws as applied in the Ottoman Empire defined the

legal position of women comparatively tolerantly, perhaps because Turkish tribal tradition had adopted a more egalitarian view of gender roles than was the case in the sedentary societies around them. Women were permitted to own and inherit property, including their dowries. They could not be forced into marriage and in certain cases were permitted to seek a divorce. As we have seen, women often exercised considerable influence in the palace and in a few instances even served as senior officials, such as governors of provinces.

HISTORIANS DEBATE

16–1e The Ottoman Empire: A Civilization in Decline?

By the late seventeenth century, the expansionist tendencies of earlier eras had largely disappeared, and the empire began to lose many of its territorial gains in the region. Many observers have interpreted these conditions as symptoms of a civilization in decline, and indeed many contemporary internal critics agreed with that assessment. Recently, however, some historians have taken issue with this paradigm, maintaining that in many respects the empire remained relatively healthy up to the early twentieth century, when the final collapse occurred.

The issue is partly a matter of the interpretation of facts. In a number of respects, the dynamic forces that had dominated during the early stages of growth were no longer present. In the first place, the quality of leadership had begun to decline. Talented early leaders like Mehmet II and Suleyman the Magnificent gave way to incompetent sultans who lacked interest in the affairs of state and turned responsibility for governing over to administrators or members of the harem. Palace intrigue was the result.

Secondly, the administrative system began to break down as talented officials selected through the relatively meritocratic *devshirme* system were gradually transformed into a privileged and often degenerate hereditary caste. Local administrators were corrupted and taxes rose as the central bureaucracy lost its links with rural areas. Constant wars depleted the treasury, and transport and communications were neglected. Interest in science and technology, once a hallmark of the Arab Empire, was in decline. In addition, the empire was beset by economic difficulties caused by the diversion of trade routes away from the eastern Mediterranean and the price inflation brought about by the influx of cheap American silver.

Most important, perhaps, was the failure of the Ottomans to take an interest in the technological advances that were being introduced as a result of the scientific revolution in Europe. The adoption of printed books produced from movable type, for example, was resisted vigorously by conservative Muslim clerics who argued that they were objectionable on religious and aesthetic grounds. Similarly, the use of mechanical clocks to keep accurate time was opposed in favor of the traditional use of the water clock and the sundial. Imports of military technology lagged as well, and the vaunted Ottoman superiority in cannonry gradually disappeared. At root, the Ottomans lacked an interest in events taking place elsewhere in the world and adopted instead an attitude of smug complacency based on the alleged superiority of traditional Islamic civilization.

A TURKISH DISCOURSE ON COFFEE

Interchange & Exchange

COFFEE WAS INTRODUCED to Turkey from the Arabian Peninsula in the mid-sixteenth century and reportedly came to Europe during the Turkish siege of Vienna in 1527. The following account was written by Katib Chelebi (kah-TEEB CHEL-uh-bee), a seventeenth-century Turkish author who compiled an extensive encyclopedia and bibliography. In *The Balance of Truth*, he described how coffee entered the empire and the problems it caused for public morality. In the Muslim world, as in Europe and later in colonial America, rebellious elements often met in coffeehouses to promote antigovernment activities. Chelebi died in Istanbul in 1657, reportedly while drinking a cup of coffee.

Katib Chelebi, *The Balance of Truth*

[Coffee] originated in Yemen and has spread, like tobacco, over the world. Certain sheikhs, who lived with their dervishes [ascetic followers] in the mountains of Yemen, used to crush and eat the berries . . . of a certain tree. Some would roast them and drink their water. Coffee is a cold dry food, suited to the ascetic life and sedative of lust. . . .

It came to Asia Minor by sea, about 1543, and met with a hostile reception, *fetwas* [decrees] being delivered against it. For they said, apart from its being roasted, the fact that it is drunk in gatherings, passed from hand to hand, is suggestive of loose living. It is related of Abul-Suud Efendi that he had holes bored in the ships that brought it, plunging their cargoes of coffee into the sea. But these strictures and prohibitions availed nothing. . . . One coffeehouse was opened after another, and men would gather together, with great eagerness and enthusiasm, to drink. Drug addicts in particular, finding it a life-giving thing, which increased their pleasure, were willing to die for a cup.

Storytellers and musicians diverted the people from their employments, and working for one's living fell into disfavor. Moreover the people, from prince to beggar, amused themselves with knifing one another. Toward the end of 1633, the late Ghazi Gultan Murad, becoming aware of the situation, promulgated an edict, out of regard and compassion for the people, to this effect: Coffeehouses throughout the Guarded Domains shall be dismantled and not opened hereafter. Since then, the coffeehouses of the capital have been as desolate as the heart of the ignorant. . . . But in cities and towns outside Istanbul, they are opened just as before. As has been said above, such things do not admit of a perpetual ban.

 Why did coffee come to be regarded as a dangerous substance in the Ottoman Empire? Were the authorities successful in suppressing its consumption?

Source: From *The Balance of Truth* by Katib Chelebi, translated by G. L. Lewis, copyright 1927.

Ottoman society was by no means totally isolated from the outside world. As familiarity with European civilization gradually increased, some cosmopolitan officials and merchants began to mimic the habits and lifestyles of their European counterparts, dressing in the European fashion, purchasing Western furniture and art objects, and ignoring Muslim strictures against the consumption of alcohol and sexual activities outside marriage. Coffee and tobacco had been introduced into polite Ottoman society by the late sixteenth and seventeenth centuries, and eventually cafés for the consumption of both began to appear in the major cities (see "A Turkish Discourse on Coffee"). But such behavior aroused concern in some quarters. One sultan in the early seventeenth century issued a decree prohibiting the consumption of both coffee and tobacco, arguing (correctly, no doubt) that many cafés were nests of antigovernment intrigue. He even began to wander incognito through the streets of Istanbul at night. Any of his subjects detected in immoral or illegal acts were summarily executed and their bodies left on the streets as an example to others.

Despite these limitations—and notwithstanding the concerns expressed by the sultan over the seditious activities supposedly carried out in Istanbul's coffeehouses—the Ottoman Empire compiled an impressive record of longevity, enduring over a period that lasted almost five hundred years. By creating a centralized administrative system based on a unified ideology that yet tolerated a high degree of ethnic and cultural diversity, the Ottomans managed to bring to the region of the eastern Mediterranean an era of relative peace and stability that had not been achieved since the days of the pharaohs—and has not been repeated since.

16–1f Ottoman Art

The Ottoman sultans were enthusiastic patrons of the arts and maintained large ateliers of artisans and artists, primarily at the Topkapi Palace in Istanbul but also in other important cities of the vast empire. The period from Mehmet II in the fifteenth century to the early eighteenth century witnessed a flourishing of pottery, rugs, silk and other textiles, jewelry, arms and armor, and calligraphy. All adorned the palaces of the new rulers, testifying to their opulence and exquisite taste. The artists came from all parts of the realm and beyond. Besides Turks, there were Persians, Greeks, Armenians, Hungarians, and Italians, all vying for the esteem and generous rewards of the sultans and fearing that losing favor might mean losing their heads! In the second half of the sixteenth century, Istanbul alone listed more than 150 craft guilds, ample proof of the artistic activity of the era.

A

Fergus O'Brien/The Image Bank/Getty Images

B

William J. Duiker

Hagia Sophia and the Suleymaniye Mosque.

The magnificent mosques built under the patronage of Suleyman the Magnificent are a great legacy of the Ottoman Empire and a fitting supplement to Hagia Sophia, the cathedral built by the Byzantine emperor Justinian in the sixth century CE and later turned into a mosque by Mehmet II. Towering under a central dome, these mosques seem to defy gravity and, like European Gothic cathedrals, convey a sense of weightlessness. The Suleymaniye Mosque (in A), constructed in the mid-sixteenth century on a design by the great architect Sinan, borrowed many elements from its great predecessor (in B) and today is one of the most impressive and most graceful in Istanbul. A far cry from the seventh-century desert mosques constructed of palm trunks, the Ottoman mosques stand among the architectural wonders of the world.

 How would you compare the mosques built by the architect Sinan and his successors with the Gothic cathedrals that were being built at the same time in Europe? What do you think accounts for the differences?

Architecture By far the greatest contribution of the Ottoman Empire to world art was its architecture, especially the magnificent mosques of the second half of the sixteenth century. Traditionally, prayer halls in mosques had been subdivided by numerous pillars that supported small individual domes, creating a private, forestlike atmosphere. The Turks, however, modeled their new mosques on the open floor plan of the Byzantine church of Hagia Sophia and began to push the pillars toward the outer wall to create a prayer hall with an uninterrupted central area under one large dome. With this plan, large numbers of believers could worship in unison in accordance with Muslim preference. By the mid-sixteenth

century, the greatest of all Ottoman architects, Mimar Sinan (si-NAHN), began erecting the first of his eighty-one mosques with an uncluttered prayer area topped by an imposing dome. and framed with towering narrow minarets. The interiors were characterized by delicate plasterwork and tile decoration that transformed the mosque into a monumental oasis of spirituality, opulence, and power. Sinan's masterpieces, such as the Suleymaniye (soo-lay-MAHN-ee-eh) and the Blue Mosque of Istanbul, were always part of a large socioreligious compound that included a library, school, hospital, mausoleums, and even bazaars, all of equally magnificent construction (see Comparative Illustration "Hagia Sophia and the Suleymaniye Mosque").

Textiles The sixteenth century also witnessed the flourishing of textiles and rugs. The Byzantine emperor Justinian had introduced the cultivation of silkworms to the West in the sixth century, and the silk industry resurfaced under the Ottomans. Its capital was at Bursa, where factories produced silks for wall hangings, soft covers, and especially court costumes. Perhaps even more famous than Turkish silk are the rugs. But whereas silks were produced under the patronage of the sultans, rugs were a peasant industry. Each village boasted its own distinctive design and color scheme for the rugs it produced.

16–2 THE SAFAVIDS

 Focus Questions: What problems did the Safavid Empire face, and how did its rulers attempt to solve them? How did their successes and failures compare with those in the other Muslim empires?

After the collapse of the empire of Tamerlane in the early fifteenth century, the area extending from Persia into Central Asia lapsed into anarchy. The Uzbeks (ooz-BEKS), Turkic-speaking peoples from Central Asia, were the chief political and military force in the area. From their capital at Bokhara (boh-KAHR-uh or boo-KAH-ruh), they maintained a semblance of control over the fluid tribal alignments until the emergence of the Safavid Dynasty in Persia at the beginning of the sixteenth century.

16–2a The Rise of the Safavids

The Safavid Dynasty was founded by Shah Ismail (IS-mah-eel) (r. 1487–1524), a descendant of Sheikh Safi al-Din (SAH-fee ul-DIN) (hence the name *Safavid*) (1252–1334), who traced his origins to Ali, the fourth *imam* of the Muslim faith. In the early fourteenth century, Safi had been the leader of a community of Turkic-speaking people in Azerbaijan, near the Caspian Sea. Safi's community was one of many Sufi mystical religious groups throughout the area. In time, the doctrine spread among nomadic groups throughout the Middle East and was transformed into the more activist Shi'ite faith. Its adherents were known as "red heads" because of their distinctive red cap with twelve folds, meant to symbolize allegiance to the twelve *imams* of the Shi'ite faith.

In 1501, Ismail seized much of the lands of the old Abbasid Empire and proclaimed himself shah of a new Persian state, to be called Iran in deference to the ancient term derived from the ethnic word "Aryan." Baghdad was subdued in 1508, as were the Uzbeks in Bokhara shortly thereafter. Ismail now promoted the Shi'ite faith among the primarily Sunni local population and sent Shi'ite preachers into Anatolia to proselytize and promote rebellion among Turkish tribal peoples in the Ottoman Empire. In retaliation, the Ottoman sultan, Selim I (see above), advanced against the Safavids in Persia and won a major battle near Tabriz (tah-BREEZ) in 1514. But Selim could

not maintain control of the area, and Ismail regained Tabriz a few years later.

The Ottomans returned to the attack in the 1580s and forced the new Safavid shah, Abbas (uh-BAHS) I (r. 1587–1629), to sign a punitive peace in which he accepted the loss of much territory. The capital was subsequently moved for defensive reasons from Tabriz in the northwest to Isfahan (is-fah-HAHN) in the south. Still, it was under Shah Abbas ("the Great") that the Safavids reached the zenith of their glory. He established a system similar to the janissaries in Turkey to train administrators to replace the traditional warrior elite. He also used the interval of peace to strengthen his army, now armed with modern weapons, and in the early seventeenth century, he attempted to regain the lost territories. Although he had some initial success, war resumed in the 1620s, and a lasting peace was not achieved until 1638 (see Map 16.2).

16–2b Decline and Collapse of the Dynasty

By centralizing power in his hands and broadening the nation's economy, Abbas the Great managed to consolidate his power base, and for a time after his death in 1629, Iran remained stable and vigorous. But succession conflicts plagued the dynasty. Partly as a result, the influence of the more militant Shi'ites began to increase at court and in Safavid society at large. The intellectual freedom that had characterized the empire at its height was increasingly curtailed under the pressure of religious orthodoxy, and Iranian women, who had enjoyed considerable freedom and influence during the early period, were forced to withdraw into seclusion and behind the veil. Meanwhile, attempts to suppress the religious beliefs of minorities led to increased popular unrest. In the early eighteenth century, Afghan warriors took advantage of local revolts to seize the capital of Isfahan, forcing the remnants of the Safavid ruling family to retreat to Azerbaijan, their original homeland. As the Ottomans seized territories along the western border, the empire finally collapsed in 1723. Eventually, order was restored by the military adventurer Nadir Shah Afshar (NAH-der shah ahf-SHAR), who launched an extended series of campaigns that restored the country's borders and even occupied the Mughal capital of Delhi (see "The Shadows Lengthen," Section 16-3c, p. 468). After his death, the Zand dynasty ruled until the end of the eighteenth century.

CHRONOLOGY	The Safavids	
Ismail seizes lands of present-day Iran and Iraq and becomes shah of Persia		1501
Ismail conquers Baghdad and defeats the Uzbeks		1508
Reign of Shah Abbas I		1587–1629
Truce achieved between Ottomans and Safavids		1638
Collapse of the Safavid Empire		1723

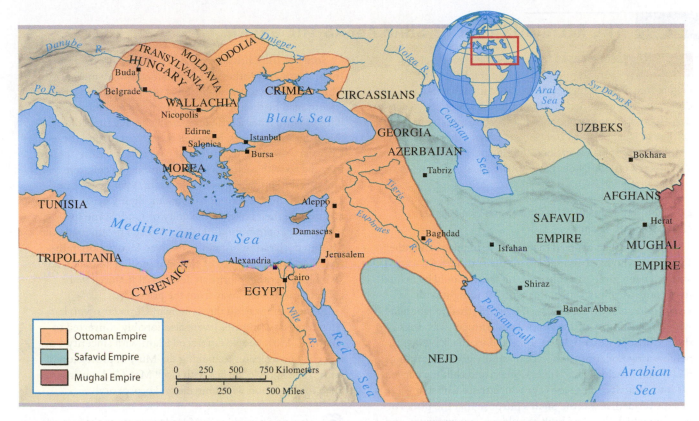

Map 16.2 The Ottoman and Safavid Empires, c. 1683. During the seventeenth century, the Ottoman and Safavid Empires contested vigorously for hegemony in the eastern Mediterranean and the Middle East. This map shows the territories controlled by each state in the late seventeenth century.

 Which states shared control over the ancient lands in the Tigris and Euphrates Valleys? In what modern-day countries are those territories?

16–2c Safavid Politics and Society

Like the Ottoman Empire, Iran under the Safavids was a mixed society. The dynasty had come to power with the support of Turkic-speaking nomadic tribal groups, and leading elements from those groups retained considerable influence within the empire. But the majority of the population were Iranian, descendants of migrating peoples who had arrived in the area in the first millennium BCE; most of them were farmers or townspeople, with attitudes inherited from the relatively sophisticated and urbanized culture of pre-Safavid Persia. Faced with the problem of integrating unruly Turkic-speaking tribal peoples with the sedentary Persian-speaking population of the urban areas, the Safavids used the Shi'ite faith as a unifying force (see "The Religious Zeal of Shah Abbas the Great," p. 462). The shah himself acquired an almost divine quality and claimed to be the spiritual leader of all Islam. Shi'ism was declared the state religion.

Although there was a landed aristocracy, aristocratic power and influence were firmly controlled by strong-minded shahs, who confiscated aristocratic estates when possible and brought them under the control of the crown. Appointment to senior positions in the bureaucracy was by merit rather than birth. To avoid encouraging competition between Turkish and non-Turkish elements, Shah Abbas I hired a number of foreigners from neighboring countries for positions in his government.

The Safavid shahs took a direct interest in the local economy and actively engaged in commercial and manufacturing activities, although there was also a large and affluent urban bourgeoisie, many of them of Armenian or Indian extraction. The currency was reformed and exports such as silk product, horses, and almonds were promoted. Although the road system was quite poor, most goods traveled by caravan. The government provided accommodations for weary travelers and, at least in times of strong rulers, kept the roads relatively clear of thieves and bandits.

At its height, Safavid Iran was a worthy successor of the great Persian empires of the past, although it was probably not as wealthy as its neighbors to the east and west, the Mughals and the Ottomans. Hemmed in by the seapower of the Europeans to the south and by the land power of the Ottomans to the west, the Safavids had no navy and were forced to divert overland trade with Europe through southern Russia to avoid an Ottoman blockade. Still, the brocades, carpets, and leather

THE RELIGIOUS ZEAL OF SHAH ABBAS THE GREAT

Religion & Philosophy **SHAH ABBAS I**, probably the greatest of the Safavid rulers, expanded the borders of his empire into areas of the southern Caucasus inhabited by Christians and other non-Muslim peoples. After Persian control was assured, he instructed that the local peoples be urged to convert to Islam for their own protection and the glory of God. In this passage, his biographer, the Persian historian Eskander Beg Monshi (es-KAHN-der bayg MAHN-shee), recounts the story of that effort.

Eskander Beg Monshi, "The Conversion of a Number of Christians to Islam"

This year the Shah decreed that those Armenians and other Christians who had been settled in [the southern Caucasus] and had been given agricultural land there should be invited to become Muslims. Life in this world is fraught with vicissitudes, and the Shah was concerned [that] in a period when the authority of the central government was weak, these Christians . . . might be subjected to attack by the neighboring Lor tribes (who are naturally given to causing injury and mischief), and their women and children carried off into captivity. In the areas in which these Christian groups resided, it was the Shah's purpose that the places of worship which they had built should become mosques, and the muezzin's call should be heard in them, so that these Christians might assume the guise of Muslims, and their future status accordingly be assured. . . .

Some of the Christians, guided by God's grace, embraced Islam voluntarily; others found it difficult to abandon their Christian faith and felt revulsion at the idea. They were encouraged by their monks and priests to remain steadfast in their faith. After a little pressure had been applied to the monks and priests, however, they desisted, and these Christians saw no alternative but to embrace Islam, though they did so with reluctance. The women and children embraced Islam with great enthusiasm, vying with one another in their eagerness to abandon their Christian faith and declare their belief in the unity of God. Some five thousand people embraced Islam. As each group made the Muslim declaration of faith, it received instruction in the Koran and the principles of the religious law of Islam, and all bibles and other Christian devotional material were collected and taken away from the priests.

In the same way, all the Armenian Christians who had been moved to [the area] were also forcibly converted to Islam. . . . Most people embraced Islam with sincerity, but some felt an aversion to making the Muslim profession of faith. True knowledge lies with God! May God reward the Shah for his action with long life and prosperity!

 How do Shah Abbas's efforts to convert nonbelievers to Islam compare with similar programs by Muslim rulers in India, as described in Chapter 9? What did the author of this selection think about the conversions?

Source: From Eskander Beg Monshi in *History of Shah Abbas the Great*, Vol. II by Roger M. Savory by Westview Press, 1978.

---

goods of Persia were highly prized throughout the world. A school of philosophy that sought truth in a fusion of rationalist and intuitive methods flourished in the sixteenth and seventeenth centuries, and Safavid science, medicine, and mathematics were the equal of other societies in the region.

16–2d Safavid Art and Literature

Persia witnessed an extraordinary flowering of the arts during the reign of Shah Abbas I. His new capital, Isfahan, was a grandiose planned city with wide visual perspectives and a sense of order almost unique in the region. Shah Abbas ordered his architects to position his palaces, mosques, and bazaars around a massive rectangular polo ground. Much of the original city is still in good condition and remains the gem of modern Iran. The immense mosques are richly decorated with elaborate blue tiles. The palaces are delicate structures with unusual slender wooden columns. These architectural wonders of Isfahan epitomize the grandeur, delicacy, and color that defined the Safavid golden age. To adorn the splendid buildings, Safavid artisans created imaginative metalwork,

tile decorations, and original and delicate glass vessels. The ceramics of the period, imitating Chinese prototypes of celadon or blue-and-white Ming design, largely ignored traditional Persian designs.

The greatest area of productivity, however, was in textiles. Silk weaving based on new techniques became a national industry. The silks depicted birds, animals, and flowers in a brilliant mass of color with silver and gold threads. Above all, carpet weaving flourished, stimulated by the great demand for Persian carpets in the West. Still highly prized all over the world, these seventeenth-century carpets reflect the grandeur and artistry of the Safavid Dynasty.

The long tradition of Persian painting continued into the Safavid era, but changed dramatically in two ways during the second half of the sixteenth century. First, taking advantage of the growing official toleration of portraiture, painters began to highlight the inner character of their subjects. Second, since royal patronage was not always forthcoming, artists sought to attract a larger audience by producing individual paintings that promoted their own distinctive styles and proudly bore their own signature.

The Royal Academy of Isfahan. Along with institutions such as libraries and hospitals, theological schools were often included in the mosque compound. One of the most sumptuous was the Royal Academy of Isfahan, built by the shah of Persia in the early eighteenth century. This view shows the large courtyard surrounded by arcades of student rooms, reminiscent of the arrangement of monks' cells in European cloisters.

George Holton/Science Source

Image copyright © The Metropolitan Museum of Art. Image source: Art Resource, NY

Two Lovers. Riza-i-Abbasi (ree-ZAH-yah-BAH-see) (1565–1635), the most renowned painter of the Safavid era, won praise for his exquisite portraits of courtiers and lovers. This delicate painting of a couple embracing conveys passion with a refined elegance. His style influenced later artists, who adapted it to other media, such as dazzling silk fabrics and the Persian carpets still much sought after all over the world. Especially popular were his colorful tile wall decorations depicting scenes of elegant peoples in flowing robes and turbans.

16–3 THE GRANDEUR OF THE MUGHALS

 Focus Questions: What role did Islam play in the Mughal Empire, and how did the Mughals' approach to religion compare with that of the Ottomans and the Safavids? What might explain the similarities and differences?

In retrospect, the period from the sixteenth to the eighteenth century can be viewed both as a high point of traditional culture in India and as the first stage of perhaps its biggest challenge. The era began with the creation of one of the subcontinent's greatest empires, that of the Mughals (MOO-guls). Mughal rulers, although foreigners and Muslims like many of their immediate predecessors, nevertheless brought India to a peak of political power and cultural achievement. For the first time since the Mauryan dynasty, almost the entire subcontinent was united under a single government, with a common culture, at least on the surface, that inspired admiration and envy throughout the region.

16–3a Babur: Founder of the Mughal Dynasty

When the Portuguese fleet led by Vasco da Gama arrived at the port of Calicut in the spring of 1498 (see Chapter 14), the Indian subcontinent was still divided into a number of Hindu and Muslim kingdoms. But it was on the verge of a new era of unity that would be brought about by a foreign dynasty called the Mughals. Like so many other rulers of northern India, the founders of the Mughal Empire were not natives of India but came from the mountainous region north of the Ganges River. The founder of the dynasty, known to history as Babur (BAH-burr) (1483–1530), had an illustrious pedigree. His father was descended from the great Asian conqueror Tamerlane, his mother from the Mongol conqueror Genghis Khan.

Babur had inherited a fragment of Tamerlane's empire in an upland valley of the Syr Darya (SEER DAHR-yuh) River (see Map 16.2). Driven south by the rising power of the Uzbeks

THE MUGHAL CONQUEST OF NORTHERN INDIA

Politics & Government Babur, the founder of the great Mughal dynasty, began his career by allying with one Indian prince against another and then turned on his ally to put himself in power, a tactic that had been used by the Ottomans and the Mongols before him (see Chapter 10). In this excerpt from his memoirs, Babur describes his triumph over the powerful army of his Indian enemy, the Sultan Ibrâhim.

Babur, *Memoirs*

They made one or two very poor charges on our right and left divisions. My troops making use of their bows, plied them with arrows, and drove them in upon their center. The troops on the right and the left of their center, being huddled together in one place, such confusion ensued, that the enemy, while totally unable to advance, found also no road by which they could flee. The sun had mounted spear-high when the onset of battle began, and the combat lasted till midday, when the enemy were completely broken and routed, and my friends victorious and exulting. By the grace and mercy of Almighty God, this arduous undertaking was rendered easy for me, and this mighty army, in the space of half a day, laid in the dust. Five or six thousand men were discovered lying slain, in one spot, near Ibrâhim. We reckoned that the number lying slain, in different parts of this field of battle, amounted to fifteen or sixteen thousand men. On reaching Agra, we found, from the accounts of the natives of Hindustân, that forty or fifty thousand men had fallen in this field. After routing the enemy, we continued the pursuit, slaughtering, and making them prisoners. . . .

It was now afternoon prayers when Tahir Taberi, the younger brother of Khalîfeh, having found Ibrâhim lying dead amidst a number of slain, cut off his head, and brought it in. . . .

In consideration of my confidence in Divine aid, the Most High God did not suffer the distress and hardships that I had undergone to be thrown away, but defeated my formidable enemy, and made me the conqueror of the noble country of Hindustân. This success I do not ascribe to my own strength, nor did this good fortune flow from my own efforts, but from the fountain of the favor and mercy of God.

 What did the Mughals' military tactics have in common with those used by the Ottomans and the Mongols as they expanded their empires? Why were these tactics successful?

Source: *The Memoirs of Zehir-ed-din Muhammed Baber,* translated by John Leyden and William Erskine (London: Longman and Cadell, 1826)

---

and then the Safavid Dynasty in Persia, Babur and his warriors seized Kabul in 1504 and, thirteen years later, crossed the Khyber Pass into India.

Following a pattern that we have seen before, Babur began his rise to power by offering to help an ailing dynasty against its opponents. Although his own forces were far less numerous than those of his adversaries, he possessed advanced weapons, including artillery, and used them to great effect. His use of mobile cavalry was particularly successful against his enemy's massed forces supplemented by mounted elephants. In 1526, with only 12,000 troops against an enemy force nearly ten times that size, Babur captured Delhi (DEL-ee) and established his power in the plains of northern India (see "The Mughal Conquest of Northern India"). Over the next several years, he continued his conquests in northern India until his death in 1530 at the age of forty-seven.

Babur's success was due in part to his vigor and his charismatic personality, which earned him the undying loyalty of his followers. His son and successor, Humayun (hoo-MY-yoon) (r. 1530–1556), was, in the words of one British historian, "intelligent but lazy." Whether or not this is a fair characterization, Humayun clearly lacked the will to consolidate his father's conquests and the personality to inspire loyalty among his subjects. In 1540, he was forced to flee to Persia, where he lived in exile for sixteen years. Finally, with the aid of the Safavid shah of Persia, he returned to India and reconquered Delhi in 1555 but died the following year in a household accident, reportedly from injuries suffered in a fall after smoking a pipeful of opium.

Humayun was succeeded by his son Akbar (AK-bar) (r. 1556–1605). Born while his father was living in exile, Akbar was only fourteen when he mounted the throne. Illiterate but highly intelligent and industrious, Akbar set out to extend his domain, then limited to the Punjab (puhn-JAHB) and the upper Ganges River Valley. "A monarch," he remarked, "should be ever intent on conquest, otherwise his neighbors rise in arms against him. The army should be exercised in warfare, lest from want of training they become self-indulgent."[2] By the end of his life, he had brought Mughal rule to most of the subcontinent, from the Himalaya Mountains to the Godavari (goh-DAH-vuh-ree) River in central India and from Kashmir to the mouths of the Brahmaputra (brah-muh-POO-truh) and the Ganges. In so doing, Akbar had created the greatest Indian empire since the Mauryan dynasty nearly two thousand years earlier (see Map 16.3).

16–3b Akbar and Indo-Muslim Civilization

Although Akbar was probably the greatest of the conquering Mughal monarchs, like his famous predecessor Ashoka, he is best known for the humane character of his rule. Above all,

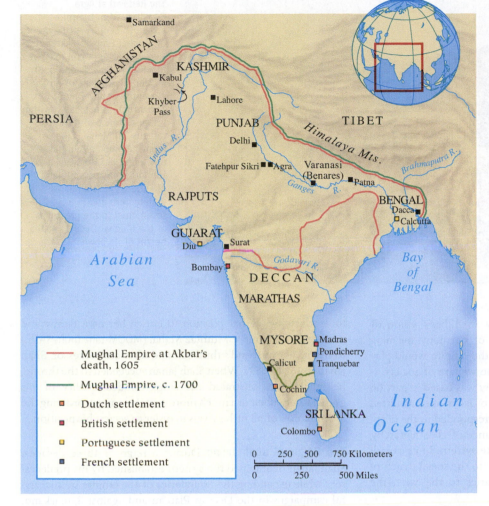

Map 16.3 The Mughal Empire. This map shows the expansion of the Mughal Empire from the death of Akbar in 1605 to the reign of Aurangzeb at the end of the seventeenth century.

Q *In which cities on the map were European settlements located? When did each group of Europeans arrive, and how did the settlements spread?*

he accepted the diversity of Indian society and took steps to reconcile his Muslim and Hindu subjects.

Religion and the State Though raised an orthodox Muslim, Akbar had been exposed to other beliefs during his childhood and had little patience with the pedantic views of Muslim scholars at court. As emperor, he displayed a keen interest in other religions, not only tolerating Hindu practices in his own domains but also welcoming the expression of Christian views by his Jesuit advisers. Akbar put his policy of religious tolerance into practice by taking a Hindu princess as one of his wives, and the success of this marriage may well have had an effect on his religious convictions. He patronized classical Indian arts and architecture and abolished many of the restrictions faced by Hindus in a Muslim-dominated society.

During his later years, Akbar became steadily more hostile to Islam. To the dismay of many Muslims at court, he sponsored

a new form of worship called the Divine Faith (*Din-i-Ilahi*), which combined characteristics of several religions with a central belief in the infallibility of all decisions reached by the emperor. Some historians have maintained that Akbar totally abandoned Islam and adopted a Persian model of imperial divinity. But others have pointed out that the emperor was claiming only divine guidance, not divine status, and suggest that the new ideology was designed to cement the loyalty of officials to the person of the monarch. Whatever the case, the new faith aroused deep hostility in Muslim circles and vanished rapidly after his death.

Administrative Reforms Akbar also extended his innovations to the imperial administration. The empire was divided into provinces, and the administration of each province was modeled after the central government, with separate departments for military, financial, commercial, and legal affairs. Senior officials in each department reported directly to their counterparts in the capital city of Agra.

Although the upper ranks of the government continued to be dominated by nonnative Muslims, a substantial proportion of lower-ranking officials were Hindus, and a few Hindus were appointed to positions of importance. At first, most officials were paid salaries, but later they were ordinarily assigned sections of agricultural land for their temporary use; they kept a portion of the taxes paid by the local peasants in lieu of a salary. These local officials, known as *zamindars* (zuh-meen-DAHRZ), were expected to forward the rest of the taxes from the lands under their control to the central government, which also derived much of its revenue from the exploitation of substantial crown lands. *Zamindars* often recruited a number of military and civilian retainers and accumulated considerable power in their localities.

The same tolerance that marked Akbar's attitude toward religion and administration extended to the Mughal legal system. While Muslims were subject to the Islamic codes (the *Shari'a*), Hindu law (the *Dharmashastra*) applied to areas settled by Hindus, who after 1579 were no longer required to pay the unpopular *jizya* (JIZ-yuh), or poll tax on non-Muslims. Punishments for crime were relatively mild, at least by the standards of the day, and justice was administered in a relatively impartial and efficient manner.

The Red Fort at Agra. Constructed in the mid-sixteenth century at the order of Mughal Emperor Akbar, the Red Fort at Agra is a massive block of red sandstone built on the foundations of an eleventh-century Rajput fort. The structure is located within visual distance of the more famous Taj Mahal. Like so many ceremonial buildings erected under the Mughals, the fort represents a blend of Hindu and Islamic architecture and is a testimonial to the greatness of the Mughal Dynasty at the height of its power.

William J. Duiker

A Harmonious Society A key element in Akbar's vision of the ideal social order was the concept of harmony, meaning that each individual and group within the empire would play their assigned role and contribute to the welfare of society as a whole. This concept of social harmony was based in part on his vision of a world shaped by the laws of Islam as transmitted by Muhammad (*Shari'a*), but it also corresponded to the deep-seated indigenous belief in the importance of class hierarchy, as expressed in the Indian class and caste system. In its overall conception, it bears a clear resemblance to the social structure adopted by the Mughals' contemporaries to the west, the Ottoman Empire.

Overall, Akbar's reign was a time of peace and prosperity. Although all Indian peasants were required to pay about one-third of their annual harvest to the state through the *zamindars*, in general the system was applied fairly, and when drought struck in the 1590s, the taxes were reduced or even suspended altogether. Thanks to a long period of relative peace and political stability, commerce and manufacturing flourished. Foreign trade, in particular, thrived as Indian goods, notably textiles, tropical food products, spices, and precious stones, were exported in exchange for gold and silver. Tariffs on imports were low. Much of the foreign commerce was handled by Arab traders, since the Indians, like their Mughal rulers, did not care for travel by sea. Internal trade, however, was dominated by large merchant castes, which also were active in banking and handicrafts.

16–3c Akbar's Successors

Akbar died in 1605 and was succeeded by his son Jahangir (juh-HAHN-geer) (r. 1605–1628). During the early years of his reign, Jahangir continued to strengthen central control over the vast empire. Eventually, however, his grip began to weaken (according to his memoirs, he "only wanted a bottle of wine and a piece of meat to make merry"), and the court fell under the influence of one of his wives, the Persian-born Nur Jahan (NOOR juh-HAHN) (see "The Power Behind the Throne"). The empress

took advantage of her position to enrich her own family and arranged for her niece Mumtaz Mahal (MOOM-tahz muh-HAHL) to marry her husband's third son and ultimate successor, Shah Jahan (r. 1628–1657). When Shah Jahan succeeded to the throne, he quickly demonstrated the single-minded quality of his grandfather (albeit in a much more brutal manner), ordering the assassination of all of his rivals in order to secure his position.

The Reign of Shah Jahan During a reign of three decades, Shah Jahan maintained the system established by his predecessors while expanding the boundaries of the empire by successful campaigns in the Deccan Plateau and against Samarkand, north of the Hindu Kush. But Shah Jahan's rule was marred by his failure to deal with the growing domestic problems. He had inherited a nearly empty treasury because of Empress Nur Jahan's penchant for luxury and ambitious charity projects. Though the majority of his subjects lived in grinding poverty, Shah Jahan's frequent military campaigns and expensive building projects put a heavy strain on the imperial finances and compelled him to raise taxes. At the same time, the government did little to improve rural conditions. In a country where transport was primitive (it often took three months to travel the 600 miles between Patna, in the middle of the Ganges River Valley, and Delhi) and drought conditions frequent, the dynasty made few efforts to increase agricultural efficiency or to improve the roads or the irrigation network, although a grand trunk road was eventually constructed between the capital Agra (AH-gruh) and Lahore (luh-HOHR), a growing city several hundred miles to the northwest. A Dutch merchant in Gujarat (goo-juh-RAHT) described conditions during a famine in the mid-seventeenth century:

As the famine increased, men abandoned towns and villages and wandered helplessly. It was easy to recognize their condition: eyes sunk deep in head, lips pale and covered with slime, the skin hard, with the bones showing through, the belly nothing but a pouch hanging down empty, knuckles and

THE POWER BEHIND THE THRONE

Politics & Government

DURING HIS REIGN AS MUGHAL EMPEROR, Jahangir (1605–1628) was addicted to alcohol and opium. Because of his weakened condition, his Persian wife, Nur Jahan, began to rule on his behalf. She also groomed his young son Khurram to rule as the future emperor Shah Jahan and arranged for him to marry her own niece, Mumtaz Mahal, thereby cementing her influence over two successive Mughal rulers. During this period, Nur Jahan was the de facto ruler of India, exerting her influence in both internal and foreign affairs during an era of peace and prosperity. Although the extent of her influence was often criticized at court, her performance impressed many European observers, as these remarks by an English visitor attest.

Nur Jahan, Empress of Mughal India

If anyone with a request to make at Court obtains an audience or is allowed to speak, the King hears him indeed, but will give no definite answer of Yes or No, referring him promptly to Asaf Khan, who in the same way will dispose of no important matter without communicating with his sister, the Queen, and who regulates his attitude in such a way that the authority of neither of them may be diminished. Anyone then who obtains a favour must thank them for it, and not the King. . . .

Her abilities were uncommon; for she rendered herself absolute, in a government in which women are thought incapable of bearing any part. Their power, it is true, is sometimes exerted in the harem; but, like the virtues of the magnet, it is silent and unperceived. Nur Jahan stood forth in public; she broke through all restraint and custom, and acquired power by her own address, more than by the weakness of Jahangir. . . .

Her former and present supporters have been well rewarded, so that now most of the men who are near the King owe their promotion to her, and are consequently under . . . obligations to her. . . . Many misunderstandings result, for the King's orders or grants of appointments, etc., are not certainties, being of no value until they have been approved by the Queen.

Q *Based on this description, how does the position that Nur Jahan occupied in Mughul government compare with the roles played by other female political figures in China, Africa, and Europe? What do all of these women have in common?*

Source: *Nur Jahan: Empress of Mughal India*, by Ellison Banks Findly. Oxford University Print on Demand, 1993.

---

kneecaps showing prominently. One would cry and howl for hunger, while another lay stretched on the ground dying in misery; wherever you went, you saw nothing but corpses.[3]

In 1648, Shah Jahan moved his capital from Agra to Delhi and built the famous Red Fort in his new capital city. But he is best known for the Taj Mahal (tahj muh-HAHL) in Agra, widely considered to be the most beautiful building in India, if not in the entire world. The story is a romantic one—that the Taj was built by the emperor in memory of his wife Mumtaz Mahal, who had died giving birth to her thirteenth child at the age of thirty-nine. But the reality has a less attractive side: the expense of the building, which employed 20,000 masons over twenty years, forced the government to raise agricultural taxes, further impoverishing many Indian peasants.

Jahangir the Magnificent. In 1615, the English ambassador to the Mughal court presented an official portrait of King James I to Shah Jahangir, who returned the favor with a portrait of himself. Thus was established a long tradition of exchanging paintings between the two empires. As it turned out, the practice altered the style of Mughal portraiture, which had previously shown the emperor in action, hunting, participating at official functions, or engaging in battle. Henceforth, portraits of the ruler followed European practice by focusing on the opulence and spiritual power of the empire. In this painting, Jahangir has chosen spiritual over earthly power by offering a book to a sheikh while ignoring the Ottoman sultan, King James I, and the Hindu artist who painted the picture. Even the cherubs, a European artifice, are dazzled by the shah's divine character, which is further demonstrated by an enormous halo.

bpk, Berlin/Museum fuer Islamische Kunst/Georg Niedermeiser/Art Resource, NY

The Taj Mahal: Symbol of the Exotic East. The Taj Mahal, completed in 1653, was built by the Mughal emperor Shah Jahan as a tomb to glorify the memory of his beloved wife, Mumtaz Mahal. Raised on a marble platform above the Jumna River, the Taj is dramatically framed by contrasting twin red sandstone mosques, magnificent gardens, and a long reflecting pool that mirrors and magnifies its beauty. The effect is one of monumental size, near blinding brilliance, and delicate lightness, a startling contrast to the heavier and more masculine Baroque style then popular in Europe. The entire exterior and interior surface of the Taj is decorated with cut-stone geometric patterns, delicate black stone tracery, or intricate inlay of colored precious stones in floral and Qur'anic arabesques.

The Rule of Aurangzeb Succession struggles returned to haunt the dynasty in the mid-1650s when Shah Jahan's illness led to a struggle for power between his sons Dara Shikoh (DA-ruh SHIH-koh) and Aurangzeb (ow-rang-ZEB). Dara Shikoh was described by his contemporaries as progressive and humane, although possessed of a violent temper and a strong sense of mysticism. But he apparently lacked political acumen and was outmaneuvered by Aurangzeb (r. 1658–1707), who had Dara Shikoh put to death and then imprisoned his father in the fort at Agra.

Aurangzeb is one of the most controversial individuals in the history of India. A man of high principle, he attempted to eliminate many of what he considered India's social evils, prohibiting the immolation of widows on their husband's funeral pyre (*sati*), the castration of eunuchs, and the exaction of illegal taxes. With less success, he tried to forbid gambling, drinking, and prostitution. But Aurangzeb, a devout and somewhat doctrinaire Muslim, also adopted a number of measures that reversed the policies of religious tolerance established by his predecessors. The building of new Hindu temples was prohibited, and the Hindu poll tax was restored. Forced conversions to Islam were resumed, and non-Muslims were driven from the court. Aurangzeb's heavy-handed religious policies led to considerable domestic unrest and to a revival of Hindu fervor during the last years of his reign. A number of revolts also broke out against imperial authority.

The Shadows Lengthen During the eighteenth century, Mughal power was threatened from both within and without. Fueled by the growing power and autonomy of the local gentry and merchants, rebellious groups in provinces throughout the empire, from the Deccan to the Punjab, began to reassert local authority and reduce the power of the Mughal emperor to that of a "tinsel sovereign." Increasingly divided, India was vulnerable to attack from abroad. In 1739, Delhi was sacked by the Persians, who left it in ashes and carried off its splendid Peacock Throne.

A number of obvious reasons for the virtual collapse of the Mughal Empire can be identified, including the draining of the imperial treasury and the decline in competence of the Mughal rulers. By 1700, the Europeans, who at first were no more than an irritant, had begun to seize control of regional trade routes and to meddle in the internal politics of the subcontinent (see Section 16-3d, "The Impact of European Power in India").

It should be noted, however, that even at its height under Akbar, the empire was less a centralized state than a loosely knit collection of heterogeneous principalities held together by the authority of the throne, which tried to combine Persian concepts of kingship with the Indian tradition of decentralized power. Decline set in when centrifugal forces gradually began to predominate over centripetal ones.

Ironically, one element in this process was the very success of the system, which led to the rapid expansion of wealth and autonomous power at the local level. As local elites increased their wealth and influence, they became less willing to accept the authority and financial demands from Delhi. The reassertion of Muslim orthodoxy under Aurangzeb and his successors simply exacerbated the problem by irritating many of the emperor's Hindu subjects. This process was hastened by the growing European military and economic presence along the periphery of the empire.

The Capture of Port Hoogly

Interaction & Exchange

IN 1632, THE MUGHAL RULER, SHAH JAHAN, ORDERED AN ATTACK on the city of Hoogly (HOOG-lee), a fortified Portuguese trading post on the northeastern coast of India. For the Portuguese, who had profited from half a century of triangular trade between India, China, and various countries in the Middle East and Southeast Asia, the loss of Hoogly at the hands of the Mughals hastened the decline of their influence in the region. Presented here are two contemporary versions of the battle. The first, from the *Padshahnama* (pad-shah-NAHM-uh) (*Book of Kings*), relates the course of events from the Mughal point of view. The second account is by John Cabral, a Jesuit missionary who was resident in Hoogly at the time.

The *Padshahnama*

During the reign of the Bengalis, a group of Frankish [European] merchants . . . settled in a place one *kos* from Satgaon . . . and, on the pretext that they needed a place for trading, they received permission from the Bengalis to construct a few edifices. Over time, due to the indifference of the governors of Bengal, many Franks gathered there and built dwellings of the utmost splendor and strength, fortified with cannons, guns, and other instruments of war. It was not long before it became a large settlement and was named Hoogly. . . . The Franks' ships trafficked at this port, and commerce was established, causing the market at the port of Satgaon to slump. . . . Of the peasants of those places, they converted some to Christianity by force and others through greed and sent them off to Europe in their ships. . . .

Since the improper actions of the Christians of Hoogly Port toward the Muslims was accurately reflected in the mirror of the mind of the Emperor before his accession to the throne, when the imperial banners cast their shadows over Bengal, and inasmuch as he was always inclined to propagate the true religion and eliminate infidelity, it was decided that when he gained control over this region he would eradicate the corruption of these abominators from the realm.

John Cabral, *Travels of Sebastian Manrique, 1629–1649*

Hugli continued at peace all the time of the great King Jahangir. For, as this Prince, by what he showed, was more attached to Christ than to Mohammad and was a Moor in name and dress only. . . . Sultan Khurram was in everything unlike his father, especially as regards the latter's leaning towards Christianity. . . . He declared himself the mortal enemy of the Christian name and the restorer of the law of Mohammad. . . . He sent a *firman* [order] to the Viceroy of Bengal, commanding him without reply or delay, to march upon the Bandel of Hugli and put it to fire and the sword. He added that, in doing so, he would render a signal service to God, to Mohammad, and to him. . . .

Consequently, on a Friday, September 24, 1632. . . . all the people [the Portuguese] embarked with the utmost secrecy. . . . Learning what was going on, and wishing to be able to boast that they had taken Hugli by storm, they [the imperialists] made a general attack on the Bandel by Saturday noon. They began by setting fire to a mine, but lost in it more men than we. Finally, however, they were masters of the Bandel.

 How do these two accounts of the Battle of Hoogly differ? Is there any way to reconcile the two into a single narrative?

Sources: From *King of the World: A Mughal Manuscript from the Royal Library, Windsor Castle*, trans. by Wheeler Thackston, text by Milo Cleveland Beach and Ebba Koch (London: Thames and Hudson, 1997), p. 59.

16–3d The Impact of European Power in India

As we have seen, the first Europeans to arrive were the Portuguese. Although they sought to establish a virtual monopoly over regional trade in the Indian Ocean, they did not seek to penetrate the interior of the subcontinent but focused on establishing way stations en route to China and the Spice Islands. The situation changed at the end of the sixteenth century when the English and the Dutch entered the scene. Soon both powers were in active competition with Portugal and with each other for trading privileges in the region (see Opposing Viewpoints "The Capture of Port Hoogly").

Penetration of the new market was not easy for the Europeans because they initially had little to offer their hosts, who had been conducting a thriving trade with peoples throughout the Indian Ocean regional market for centuries. On the other hand, the Mughals expressed little interest in the sea and left the practice of maritime commerce to foreign shippers. As a result, European merchants focused on taking part in the carrying trade between one Asian port and another. The Portuguese, for example, carried high-quality textile goods from India to Africa in exchange for gold from the mines in Zimbabwe. With their profits, they paid for spices to be transported back to Europe. Eventually, goods such as textiles and spices were paid for with gold and silver bullion mined in Latin America.

The experience of the English was a prime example. When in 1608 the first English fleet arrived at Surat (SOOR-et), a thriving port on the northwestern coast of India, the English request for trading privileges was rejected by Emperor Jahangir, at the suggestion of the Portuguese advisers already in residence at the imperial court. Needing lightweight Indian cloth to trade for spices in the East Indies, the English persisted, and in 1616, they were finally permitted to install their own ambassador at the imperial court in Agra. Three years later, the first English factory, or warehouse, was established at Surat.

During the next several decades, the English presence in India steadily increased as Mughal power waned. By mid-century, additional English trading posts had been established at Bombay ("good bay" in Portuguese) on the west coast of the peninsula, at Fort William (now the great city of Calcutta, recently renamed Kolkata) on the Hoogly River near the Bay of Bengal, and at Madras (muh-DRAS or muh-DRAHS) (now Chennai) on the southeastern coast. From there, English ships carried high-quality Indian-made cotton goods back home to the British Isles, where they began to compete effectively with locally produced woolen products, or to the East Indies, where they were bartered for spices to be shipped back to England.

English success in India attracted rivals, including the Dutch and the French. The Dutch eventually abandoned their interests in India to concentrate on the spice trade, but the French were more persistent and seized Madras in 1746. For a brief period, the French competed successfully for trade privileges with the British, but the military genius of Sir Robert Clive (CLYV), an aggressive British administrator and empire builder who eventually became the chief representative of the East India Company in the subcontinent, combined with the refusal of the French government to provide financial support for French actions in India eventually left the latter with only a fort at Pondicherry (pon-dir-CHEH-ree) and a handful of other tiny enclaves on the southeastern coast (see Chapter 18).

In the meantime, Clive began to consolidate British control in Bengal (ben-GAHL), where the local Indian ruler had attacked Fort William and imprisoned the local British population in the infamous Black Hole of Calcutta (an underground prison for holding the prisoners, many of whom died in captivity). In 1757, a small British force numbering about three thousand defeated a Mughal-led army over ten times that size in the Battle of Plassey. As part of the spoils of victory, the British East India Company exacted from the now-decrepit Mughal court the authority to collect taxes from extensive lands in the area surrounding Calcutta. Less than ten years later, British forces seized the reigning Mughal emperor in a skirmish at Buxar (buk-SAHR), and the British began to consolidate their economic and administrative control over Indian territory through the surrogate power of the now powerless Mughal court (see Map 16.4).

To officials of the East India Company, the expansion of their authority into the interior of the subcontinent probably seemed like a simple commercial decision, a move designed to seek guaranteed revenues to pay for the increasingly expensive military operations in India. To historians, it marks a major step in the gradual transfer of all of the Indian subcontinent to the British East India Company and later, in 1858, to the British crown. The process was more haphazard than deliberate. Under a new governor general, Warren Hastings, the British

attempted to consolidate areas under their control and defeat such rivals as the rising Hindu Marathas (muh-RAH-tuhz), who exploited the decline of the Mughals to expand their own territories in Maharashtra (mah-huh-RAHSH-truh).

The Economic Consequences of Conquest The British East India Company's takeover of vast landholdings, notably in the eastern Indian states of Orissa (uh-RIH-suh) and Bengal, may have been a windfall for enterprising British officials, but it had serious consequences for the Indian economy. In the first place, it resulted in the transfer of capital from the local Indian aristocracy to company officials, most of whom sent their profits back to Britain. Second, it eventually hastened the destruction of India's once healthy textile industry. At first, exports of high-quality Indian cotton goods skyrocketed, as the attractive local muslins and colorful calicoes began to replace the traditional woolen garments previously in fashion in Europe. Eventually, however, rising costs for imported Indian textiles, combined with stiff resistance from the woolen industry, produced dramatic changes in British textile production. Imports of cheap raw cotton from fields newly planted in the Americas, combined with revolutionary new inventions in the spinning and weaving process, transformed the British Isles during the eighteenth century into the center of global textile production. Inexpensive British machine-made textiles were now imported duty-free into India to compete against local goods, many of which were produced on hand looms in Indian villages, thus putting millions out of work.

Finally, British expansion in India hurt the peasants. As the British took over the administration of the land tax, they began to apply British law, which allowed the lands of those unable to pay the tax to be confiscated. In the 1770s, a series of famines led to the death of an estimated one-third of the population in the areas under company administration. The British government attempted to resolve the problem by assigning tax lands to the local revenue collectors (*zamindars*) in the hope of transforming them into English-style rural gentry, but many collectors themselves fell into bankruptcy and sold their lands to absentee bankers while the now landless peasants remained in abject poverty. It was hardly an auspicious beginning to "civilized" British rule.

Resistance to the British As a result of such conditions, Britain's rise to power in India did not go unchallenged. Although Mughal authority was by now virtually moribund, local forces took matters into their own hands. Astute Indian commanders avoided pitched battles with the well-armed British troops but harassed and ambushed them in the manner of guerrillas in our time. Said Haidar Ali (HY-dur AH-lee), one of Britain's primary rivals for control in southern India:

> You will in time understand my mode of warfare. Shall I risk my cavalry which cost a thousand rupees each horse, against your cannon ball which cost two pice? No! I will march your troops until their legs swell to the size of their bodies. You shall not have a blade of grass, nor a drop of water. I will hear of you every time your drum beats, but you shall not know where I am once a month. I will give your army battle, but it must be when I please, and not when you choose.[4]

Ms Fr 2810 f.84v, *Pepper Harvest in Coilum, Southern India*, illustration from the *Livre des Merveilles du Monde*, c.1410–12 (tempera on vellum)/Boucicaut Master, (fl.1390–1430) (and workshop)/INDIVISION CHARMET/Bibliothèque Nationale, Paris, France/Bridgeman Images

A Pepper Plantation. During the Age of Exploration, pepper was one of the spices most sought by European adventurers. Unlike cloves and nutmeg, it was found in other areas of Asia besides the Indonesian archipelago. Shown here is a medieval European portrayal of a pepper plantation in southern India. The illustration appeared in a fifteenth-century edition of *The Travels of Marco Polo*.

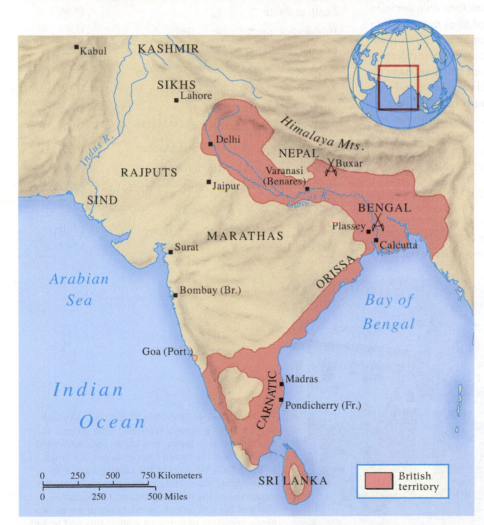

Map 16.4 India in 1805. By the early nineteenth century, much of the Indian subcontinent had fallen under British domination.

Q *Where was the capital of the Mughal Empire located?*

Unfortunately for India, not all its commanders were as astute as Haidar Ali. In the last years of the eighteenth century, when the East India Company's authority came into the capable hands of Lord Cornwallis and his successor, Lord Mornington, the future marquess of Wellesley, the stage was set for the final consolidation of British rule over the subcontinent.

HISTORIANS DEBATE 16–3e

The Mughal Dynasty: A "Gunpowder Empire"?

To some recent historians, the success of the Mughals, like that of the Ottomans and the Safavids, was due to their mastery of the techniques of modern warfare, especially the use of firearms. In this view, firearms played a central role in the ability of all three empires to overcome their rivals and rise to regional hegemony. Accordingly, some scholars have labeled them "gunpowder empires." Although technical prowess in the art of warfare was undoubtedly a key element in their success, we should not forget that other factors, such as dynamic leadership, political acumen, and the possession of an ardent following motivated by religious zeal (at least in the case of the Safavids in Iran) were equally important in their drive to power and ability to retain it.

In the case of the Mughals, the "gunpowder empire" thesis has been challenged by historian Douglas Streusand, who argues that the Mughals used "the carrot and the stick" to extend their authority, relying not just on heavy artillery but also on other forms of siege warfare and the offer of negotiations. Once in power, the Mughals created an empire that appeared highly centralized from the outside but was actually a collection of semiautonomous principalities ruled by provincial elites and linked together by the overarching majesty of the Mughal emperor—and not simply by the barrel of a gun. Even today, many Indians regard Akbar as the country's greatest ruler, a tribute not only to his military success but also to the humane policies adopted during his reign.

Unlike the Ottoman Turks, however, the Mughals were inconsistent in applying a policy of tolerance for the non-Muslim peoples within their borders. Although Akbar promoted a policy of inclusion for all of his subjects, many of his successors, notably Aurangzeb, adopted a policy of actively converting peoples of other faiths to the reigning ideology of Islam. Not surprisingly under the pressure of the European incursion, the empire began to disintegrate, as Hindu insurgent groups sought to to break away from Mughal rule and seek their own destinies.

In other respects, the Mughals suffered from the same limitations that afflicted their counterpart empires in Isfahan and Istanbul. Smugly confident in the superiority of their culture to that of their potential rivals, they expressed little interest in the dramatic changes taking place in the fields of science and technology. Eventually, even their vaunted superiority in the art of war abandoned them, as they failed to realize the importance of adopting modern naval technology and tactics, a tragic mistake that placed them at a disadvantage in an era when naval warfare was becoming the key to national survival.

16–3f Society Under the Mughals: A Synthesis of Cultures

The Mughals were the last of the great traditional Indian dynasties. Like so many of their predecessors since the fall of the Guptas nearly a thousand years before, the Mughals were Muslims. But like the Ottoman Turks, the best Mughal rulers did not simply impose Islamic institutions and beliefs on the predominantly Hindu population; they combined Muslim with Hindu and even Persian concepts and cultural values in a unique social and cultural synthesis that even today seems to epitomize the greatness of Indian civilization. The new faith of Sikhism, founded in the early sixteenth century in an effort to blend both faiths (see Chapter 9), undoubtedly benefited from the mood of syncretism promoted by the Mughal court.

To be sure, Hindus sometimes attempted to defend themselves and their religious practices against the efforts of some

CHRONOLOGY	The Mughal Era
Arrival of Vasco da Gama at Calicut	1498
Babur seizes Delhi	1526
Death of Babur	1530
Humayun recovers throne in Delhi	1555
Death of Humayun and accession of Akbar	1556
Death of Akbar and accession of Jahangir	1605
Arrival of English at Surat	1608
English embassy to Agra	1616
Reign of Emperor Shah Jahan	1628–1657
Foundation of English factory at Madras	1639
Aurangzeb succeeds to the throne	1658
Death of Aurangzeb	1707
Sack of Delhi by the Persians	1739
French capture Madras	1746
Battle of Plassey	1757

The Astronomical Observatory of Jai Singh. Although Mughal elites generally expressed little interest in science and technology, one Indian ruler who broke the mold was the Hindu ruler of Jaipur, Jai Singh. In the 1720s, he ordered the construction of an astronomical observatory in his palace to study the movement of the heavenly bodies. Unfortunately, much of the equipment—some of which are shown here—consisted of outdated instruments and lacked the capacity to compete with the accurate telescopic observations then being carried out in Europe. The observatory was closed a few years later and is now merely a curiosity. William J. Duiker

Mughal monarchs to impose the Islamic religion and Islamic mores on the indigenous population. In some cases, despite official prohibitions, Hindu men forcibly married Muslim women and then converted them to the native faith, while converts to Islam normally lost all of their inheritance rights within the Indian family. Government orders to destroy Hindu temples were often ignored by local officials, sometimes as the result of bribery or intimidation. Although the founding emperor Babur expressed little admiration for the country he had subjected to his rule, ultimately Indian practices had an influence on the Mughal elites, as many Mughal chieftains married Indian women and adopted Indian forms of dress.

In some areas, Emperor Akbar's tireless effort to bring about a blend of Middle Eastern and South Asian religious and cultural values paid rich dividends, as substantial numbers of Indians decided to convert to the Muslim faith during the centuries of Mughal rule. Some were undoubtedly attracted to the egalitarian characteristics of Islam, but others found that the mystical and devotional qualities promoted by Sufi missionaries corresponded to similar traditions among the local population. This was especially true in Bengal, on the eastern edge of the Indian subcontinent, where Hindu practices were not as well established and where forms of religious devotionalism had long been popular among the population.

The Economy Although much of the local population in the subcontinent lived in the grip of grinding poverty, punctuated by occasional periods of widespread famine, the first centuries of Mughal rule were in some respects a period of relative prosperity for the region. India was a leading participant in the growing foreign trade that crisscrossed the Indian Ocean from the Red Sea and the Persian Gulf to the Strait of Malacca and the Indonesian archipelago. High-quality cloth from India was especially prized, and the country's textile industry made it, in the words of one historian, "the industrial workshop of the world."

Long-term stability led to increasing commercialization and the spread of wealth to new groups within Indian society. The Mughal era saw the emergence of an affluent landed gentry and a prosperous merchant class. Members of prestigious castes from the pre-Mughal period reaped many of the benefits of the increasing wealth, but some of these changes transcended caste boundaries and led to the emergence of new groups who achieved status and wealth on the basis of economic achievement rather than traditional kinship ties. During the late eighteenth century, this economic prosperity was shaken by the decline of the Mughal Empire and the increasing European presence. But many prominent Indians reacted by establishing commercial relationships with the foreigners. For a time, such relationships often worked to the Indians' benefit. Later, as we shall see, they would have cause to regret the arrangement.

The Position of Women Deciding whether Mughal rule had much effect on the lives of ordinary Indians is somewhat problematic. The treatment of women is a good example.

Women had traditionally played an active role in Mongol tribal society—many actually fought on the battlefield alongside the men—and Babur and his successors often relied on the women in their families for political advice. Women from aristocratic families were often awarded honorific titles, received salaries, and were permitted to own land and engage in business. Women at court sometimes received an education, and Emperor Akbar reportedly established a girls' school at Fatehpur Sikri to provide teachers for his own daughters. Aristocratic women often expressed their creative talents by writing poetry, painting, or playing music. Women of all castes were adept at spinning thread, either for their own use or to sell to weavers to augment the family income. Weaving was carried out in the home by all members of the families of the weaving subcaste. They sold simple cloth to local villages and fine cotton, silk, and wool to the Mughal court. By Akbar's reign, the textile manufacturing was of such high quality and so well established that India sold cloth to much of the world: Arabia, the coast of East Africa, Egypt, Southeast Asia, and Europe.

To a certain degree, these Mughal attitudes toward women may have had an impact on Indian society. Women were allowed to inherit land, and some even possessed *zamindar* rights. Women from mercantile castes sometimes took an active role in business activities. At the same time, however, as Muslims, the Mughals subjected women to certain restrictions under Islamic law. On the whole, these Mughal practices coincided with and even accentuated existing tendencies in Indian society. The Muslim practice of isolating women and preventing them from associating with men outside the home (*purdah*) was adopted by many upper-class Hindus as a means of enhancing their status or protecting their women from unwelcome advances by Muslims in positions of authority. In other ways, Hindu practices were unaffected. The custom of *sati* continued to be practiced despite efforts by the Mughals to abolish it, and child marriage (most women were betrothed before the age of ten) remained common. Women were still instructed to obey their husbands without question and to remain chaste.

16–3g Mughal Culture

The era of the Mughals was one of synthesis in culture as well as in politics and religion. The Mughals combined Islamic themes with Persian and indigenous motifs to produce a unique Indo-Muslim style that enriched and embellished Indian art and culture. The Mughal emperors were zealous patrons of the arts and enticed painters, poets, and artisans from as far away as the Mediterranean. Apparently, the generosity of the Mughals made it difficult to refuse a trip to India. It was said that they would reward a poet with his weight in gold.

Architecture Undoubtedly, the Mughals' most visible achievement was in architecture. Here they integrated Persian and Indian styles in a new and sometimes breathtakingly beautiful form best symbolized by the Taj Mahal, built by the emperor Shah Jahan in the mid-seventeenth century (see illustration

The Palace of the Winds at Jaipur. Built by the maharaja of Jaipur (JY-poor) in 1799, this imposing building, part of a palace complex, is today actually only a facade. Behind the intricate pink sandstone window screens, the women of the palace were able to observe city life while at the same time remaining invisible to prying eyes. The palace, like most of the buildings in the city of Jaipur, was constructed of sandstone, a product of the nearby desert of Rajasthan (RAH-juh-stahn).

"The Taj Mahal: Symbol of the Exotic East," p. 468). Although the human and economic cost of the Taj tarnishes the romantic legend of its construction, there is no denying the beauty of the building. It had evolved from a style that originated several decades earlier with the tomb of Humayun, which was built by his widow in Agra in 1565 during the reign of Akbar. Ironically, after he was deposed by his son Aurangzeb, Shah Jahan spent his last years imprisoned in a room in the Red Fort at Agra; from his windows, he could see the beautiful memorial to his beloved wife.

The Taj was by no means the only magnificent building erected during the Mughal era. Akbar, in the words of a contemporary, "dresses the work of his mind and heart in the garment of stone and clay." His first palace at Agra, the Red Fort, was begun in 1565. A few years later, he ordered the construction of a new palace at Fatehpur Sikri, 26 miles to the west. The new palace was built in honor of a Sufi mystic who had correctly forecast the birth of a son to the emperor. In gratitude, Akbar decided to build a new capital city and palace on the site of the mystic's home (see illustration "The Construction of Fatehpur Sikri"). Over a period of fifteen years, from 1571 to 1586, a magnificent new city in red sandstone was constructed. Although the city was abandoned before completion and now stands almost untouched, it is a popular destination for tourists and pilgrims.

Painting The other major artistic achievement of the Mughal period was painting. Painting had never been one of the great attainments of Indian culture due in part to the fact that paper had not been introduced to India from Persia until the latter part of the fourteenth century, so traditionally painting had been done on palm leaves, which had severely hampered artistic creativity. By the fifteenth century, Indian painting had made the transition from palm leaf to paper, and the new medium eventually stimulated a burst of creativity, particularly in the genre of miniatures, or book illustrations.

As in so many other areas of endeavor, painting in Mughal India resulted from the blending of Indian and Persian cultures. Akbar in particular was so enamored with the new medium that he established a state workshop at Fatehpur Sikri for two hundred artists, mostly Hindus, who worked under the guidance of the Persian masters to create the Mughal school of painting.

Akbar's encouragement to depict the human figure in Mughal painting outraged orthodox Muslims at court, but he argued that the painter, "in sketching anything that has life . . . must come to feel that he cannot bestow individuality upon his work, and is thus forced to think of God, the Giver of Life, and will thus increase in knowledge."[5]

Painting during Akbar's reign followed the trend toward realism and historical narrative that had originated in the Ottoman Empire. For example, Akbar had the illustrated *Book of Akbar* made to record his military exploits and court activities. Many of the paintings of Akbar's life portray him in action in the real world. After his death, his son and grandson continued the patronage of the arts.

Literature The development of Indian literature was held back by the absence of printing, which was not introduced until the end of the Mughal era. Literary works were inscribed by calligraphers, and one historian has estimated that the library of Agra contained more than 24,000 volumes. Poetry, in particular, flourished under the Mughals, who established poets laureate at court. Poems were written in the Persian style and in the Persian language. In fact, Persian became the official language of the court until the sack of Delhi in 1739. At the time, the Indians' anger at their conquerors led them to adopt Urdu as the new language for the court and for poetry. By that time, Indian verse on the Persian model had already lost its original vitality and simplicity and had become more artificial in the manner of court literature everywhere.

Another aspect of the long Mughal reign was a Hindu revival of devotional literature, much of it dedicated to Krishna and Rama. The retelling of the Ramayana in the vernacular, beginning in the southern Tamil languages in the eleventh century and spreading slowly northward, culminated in the

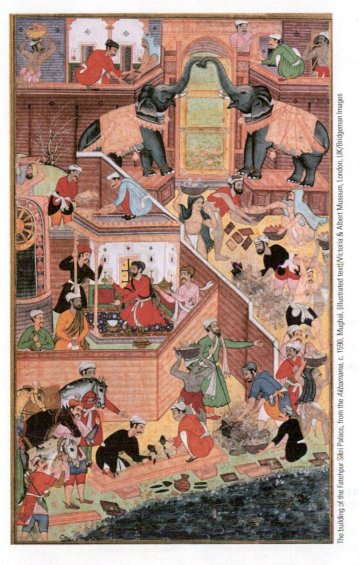

The building of the Fatehpur Sikri Palace, from the *Akbarnama*, c. 1590, Mughal, (illustrated text)/Victoria & Albert Museum, London, UK/Bridgeman Images

The Construction of Fatehpur Sikri. In this contemporary Mughal painting, artisans are completing construction of the Elephant Gate at Akbar's new capital of Fatehpur Sikri (fah-tay-POOR SIK-ree). Because both the Ottoman Empire and Mughal India used Persian as their court language, they learned to appreciate the illuminated manuscript techniques produced by Safavid workshops in Persia and adapted them to their own cultural heritage. Emperor Akbar, the greatest Mughal ruler, enthusiastically embraced the art of bookmaking, peopling his royal workshops with more than one hundred artists. The illustrated manuscripts from Mughal India rival those of Safavid Persia in brilliance and imagination and provide fascinating historical details of military campaigns and court ceremonies, as well as scenes from daily life.

sixteenth-century Hindi version by the great poet Tulsidas (tool-see-DAHSS) (1532–1623). His *Ramcaritmanas* (RAM-kah-rit-MAH-nuz) presents the devotional story with a deified Rama and Sita. Tulsidas's genius was in combining the conflicting cults of Vishnu and Shiva into a unified and overwhelming love for the divine, which he expressed in some of the most moving of all Indian poetry. The *Ramcaritmanas* has eclipsed its two-thousand-year-old Sanskrit ancestor in popularity and even became the basis of an Indian television series in the late 1980s.

CHAPTER SUMMARY

The three empires discussed in this chapter exhibited a number of striking similarities. First of all, they were Muslim in their religious affiliation, although the Safavids were Shi'ite rather than Sunni, a distinction that often led to mutual tensions and conflict. More important, perhaps, they were all of nomadic origin, and the political and social institutions that they adopted carried the imprint of their preimperial past. Once they achieved imperial power, however, all three ruling dynasties displayed an impressive capacity to administer a large empire and brought a degree of stability to peoples who had all too often lived in conditions of internal division and war.

The rise of these powerful Muslim states coincided with the opening period of European expansion at the end of the fifteenth century and the beginning of the sixteenth. The military and political talents of these empires helped protect much of the Muslim world from the resurgent forces of Christianity. In fact, the Ottoman Turks carried their empire into the heart of Christian Europe and briefly reached the gates of the great city of Vienna. By the end of the eighteenth century, however, the Safavid Dynasty had imploded, and the powerful Mughal Empire was in a state of virtual collapse. Only the Ottoman Empire was still functioning.

Yet it too had lost much of its early expansionistic vigor and was showing signs of internal decay.

The reasons for the decline of these empires have inspired considerable debate among historians. One factor was undoubtedly the expansion of European power into the Indian Ocean and the Middle East. But internal causes were probably more important in the long run. All three empires experienced growing factionalism within the ruling elite, incompetent leadership, and the emergence of divisive forces in the empire at large—factors that have marked the passing of traditional empires since early times. Climate change (the region was reportedly hotter and drier after the beginning of the seventeenth century) may have been a contributing factor. Paradoxically, one of the greatest strengths of these empires— their mastery of gunpowder—may have simultaneously been

a serious weakness in that it allowed them to develop a complacent sense of security. With little incentive to turn their attention to new developments in science and technology, they were increasingly vulnerable to attack by the advanced nations of the West.

The Muslim empires, however, were not the only states in the Old World that were able to resist the first outward thrust of European expansion. Farther to the east, the mature civilizations in China and Japan faced down a similar challenge from Western merchants and missionaries. Unlike their counterparts in South Asia and the Middle East, as the nineteenth century dawned, they continued to thrive.

CHAPTER TIMELINE

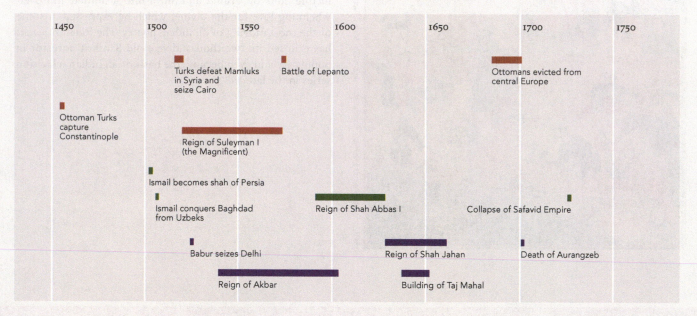

| 1450 | 1500 | 1550 | 1600 | 1650 | 1700 | 1750 |

Turks defeat Mamluks in Syria and seize Cairo

Battle of Lepanto

Ottomans evicted from central Europe

Ottoman Turks capture Constantinople

Reign of Suleyman I (the Magnificent)

Ismail becomes shah of Persia

Ismail conquers Baghdad from Uzbeks

Reign of Shah Abbas I

Collapse of Safavid Empire

Babur seizes Delhi

Reign of Shah Jahan

Death of Aurangzeb

Reign of Akbar

Building of Taj Mahal

CHAPTER REVIEW

Upon Reflection

Q How did the social policies adopted by the Ottomans compare with those of the Mughals and the Safavids? What similarities and differences do you detect, and what might account for them?

Q What is meant by the phrase "gunpowder empires," and to what degree did the Muslim states discussed here conform to

this description? Can the concept be applied to other parts of the world as well?

Q What role did women play in the Ottoman, Safavid, and Mughal Empires? What might explain the similarities and differences? How did the treatment of women in these states compare with their treatment in other parts of the world?

Key Terms

beys (p. 450)
janissaries (p. 450)
pashas (p. 453)
grand vizier (p. 453)
harem (p. 455)

devshirme (p. 455)
sipahis (p. 456)
millet (p. 456)
zamindars (p. 465)

Chapter Notes

1. Cited in Christophe Courau, "Turquie: Sublime Porte de 1'Europe," in *Historia* (October 2005), p. 15.
2. Quoted in V. A. Smith, *The Oxford History of India* (Oxford, 1967), p. 341.
3. Quoted in M. Edwardes, *A History of India: From the Earliest Times to the Present Day* (London, 1961), p. 188.
4. Quoted in ibid., p. 220.
5. Quoted in R. C. Craven, *Indian Art: A Concise History* (New York, 1976), p. 205.

MindTap® is a fully online personalized learning experience built upon Cengage Learning content. MindTap® combines student learning tools—readings, multimedia, activities, and assessments—into a singular Learning Path that guides students through the course and helps students develop the critical thinking, analysis, and communication skills that are essential to academic and professional success.

Chapter Outline and Focus Questions

17-1 *China at Its Apex*

Q Why were the Manchus so successful at establishing a foreign dynasty in China, and what were the main characteristics of Manchu rule?

17-2 *Changing China*

Q How did the economy and society change during the Ming and Qing eras, and to what degree did these changes seem to be leading toward an industrial revolution on the European model?

17-3 *Tokugawa Japan*

Q How did the society and economy of Japan change during the Tokugawa era, and how did Japanese culture reflect those changes?

17-4 *Korea and Vietnam*

Q To what degree did developments in Korea during this period reflect conditions in China and Japan? What were the unique aspects of Vietnamese civilization?

Critical Thinking

Q *How did China and Japan respond to the coming of the Europeans, and what explains the differences? What impact did European contacts have on these two East Asian civilizations through the end of the eighteenth century?*

Connections to Today

Q *The world population was increasing dramatically in parts of the world during the eighteenth century, just as it is today. What were the main reasons for this expansion, and what lessons does it suggest for dealing with the issue in our own day?*

Emperor Kangxi. Hu Weibiao/Panorama/The Image Works

IN DECEMBER 1717, Emperor Kangxi (KANG-shee) returned from a hunting trip north of the Great Wall and began to suffer from dizzy spells. Conscious of his approaching date with mortality—he was now nearly seventy years of age—the emperor called together his sons and leading government officials in the imperial palace and issued an edict summing up his ideas on the art of statecraft. Rulers, he declared, should sincerely revere Heaven's laws as their fundamental strategy for governing the country. Among other things, those laws required that the ruler show concern for the welfare of the people, practice diligence, protect the state from its enemies, choose able advisers, and strike a careful balance between leniency and strictness, principle and expedience. That, he concluded, was all there was to it.[1]

Any potential successor to the throne in Beijing would have been well advised to attend to the emperor's advice. Kangxi was not only one of the longest reigning of all China's rulers but also one of the wisest. His era was one of peace and prosperity, and after half a century of rule, the empire was now at the zenith of its power and influence. As his life approached its end, Heaven must indeed have been pleased at the quality of his stewardship, for the emperor's edict clearly reflected the genius of Confucian teachings at their best and, with its emphasis on prudence, compassion, and tolerance, has a timeless quality that applies to our age as well as to one of the golden ages in the history of China.

There is an element of irony in this remark, since Kangxi, who reigned during one of the most glorious eras in the long history of China, was not Chinese by birth, but a member of the Manchu minority. Under the Ming Dynasty (see Chapter 10), the empire had expanded its borders to a degree not seen since the Han and the Tang Dynasties, and its culture was the envy of its neighbors, earning the admiration of many European visitors, including Jesuit priests and Enlightenment philosophes (see Chapter 18). By the middle of the seventeenth century, however, Ming society was under severe stress, and in the year 1644, the last Ming ruler was overthrown by the Manchus, a semi-pastoral people whose homeland was north of the Great Wall and who created a new dynasty, called the Qing. Kangxi was the greatest of the Qing emperors.

During this extended period of history, China appeared to many observers to be an unchanging society patterned after the Confucian vision of a "golden age" in the remote past. China's rulers, including those of the Qing Dynasty, referred constantly to tradition as a model for imperial institutions and cultural values. Yet although few observers could have been aware of it at the time, China was changing—and rather rapidly. The China of the Han, and even of the Tang and the Song, was a tantalizing vision of the past.

A similar process was under way in neighboring Japan. In the early seventeenth century, the vigorous new Tokugawa (toh-koo-GAH-wah) Shogunate rose to power and managed to revitalize the traditional system in a somewhat more centralized form that enabled it to survive for another 250 years. But major structural changes were taking place in Japanese society, and by the nineteenth century, tensions were growing as the gap between theory and reality widened.

One of the many factors contributing to the quickening pace of change in both countries was contact with the West, which began with the arrival of Portuguese ships in Chinese and Japanese waters in the first half of the sixteenth century. After initially welcoming the new arrivals, Chinese and Japanese rulers soon came to fear the corrosive effects of Western ideas and practices and sought to protect their traditional societies from external intrusion. But neither could forever resist the importunities of Western trading nations, nor were they able to inhibit the societal shifts that were taking place within their borders. When the doors to the West were finally reopened in the mid-nineteenth century, both societies were ripe for radical change.

17–1 CHINA AT ITS APEX

 Focus Question: Why were the Manchus so successful at establishing a foreign dynasty in China, and what were the main characteristics of Manchu rule?

In 1514, a Portuguese fleet dropped anchor off the coast of China, just south of the Pearl River estuary and present-day Hong Kong. It was the first direct contact between the Chinese Empire and the West since the arrival of the Venetian adventurer Marco Polo two centuries earlier, and it opened an era that would eventually change the face of China and, indeed, all the world.

17–1a The Later Ming

Marco Polo had reported on the magnificence of China after visiting Beijing (bay-ZHING) during the reign of Khubilai Khan, the great Mongol ruler. By the time the Portuguese fleet arrived off the coast of China, of course, the Yuan dynasty had long since disintegrated. It had gradually weakened after the death of Khubilai Khan and was finally overthrown in 1368 by a massive peasant rebellion under the leadership of Zhu Yuanzhang (JOO yoo-wen-JAHNG), who had declared himself the founding emperor of a new Ming (Bright) Dynasty (1369–1644), with his capital at Nanjing (nahn-JING) in central China.

As we have seen, the Ming inaugurated a period of territorial expansion westward into Central Asia and southward into Vietnam while consolidating control over China's vast heartland. It had also embarked on a brief era of maritime expansion, when the admiral Zheng He (JEHNG-huh) led a series of voyages that spread Chinese influence far into the Indian Ocean. In 1433, however, those voyages were suddenly discontinued, as the dynasty turned its attention to domestic concerns (see Chapter 10). To underline the new policy, Emperor Yongle (YOONG-luh) transplanted his capital to Beijing, where he ordered the construction of a new imperial home—known as the Imperial City—on the grounds of Khubilai's old palace under the Yuan dynasty.

The Imperial City in Beijing. During the fifteenth century, the Ming Dynasty erected an immense imperial city on the remnants of the palace of Khubilai Khan in Beijing. Surrounded by 6½ miles of walls, the enclosed compound is divided into a maze of private apartments and offices; it also includes an imposing ceremonial quadrangle with stately halls for imperial audiences and banquets. Because it was off-limits to commoners, the compound was known as the Forbidden City. Today the Imperial City is open to visitors, including even the throne room and the private apartments of the imperial family.

Among the most active and the most effective were highly educated Jesuits, who were familiar with European philosophical and scientific developments. Court officials were particularly impressed by the visitors' ability to predict the exact time of a solar eclipse, an event that the Chinese viewed with extreme reverence.

Recognizing the Chinese pride in their own culture, the Jesuits attempted to draw parallels between Christian and Confucian concepts (for example, they identified the Western concept of God with the Chinese character for Heaven) and to show the similarities between Christian morality and Confucian ethics. European inventions such as the clock, the prism, and various astronomical and musical instruments impressed Chinese officials, hitherto deeply imbued with a sense of the superiority of Chinese civilization, and helped Western ideas win acceptance at court. An elderly Chinese scholar expressed his wonder at the miracle of eyeglasses:

> *White glass from across the Western Seas*
> *Is imported through Macao:*
> *Fashioned into lenses big as coins,*
> *They encompass the eyes in a double frame.*
> *I put them on—it suddenly becomes clear;*
> *I can see the very tips of things!*
> *And read fine print by the dim-lit window*
> *Just like in my youth.*[2]

For their part, the missionaries were much impressed with many aspects of Chinese civilization, and reports of their experiences heightened European curiosity about this great society on the other side of the world (see "The Art of Printing," Section 17-2d, p. 492). By the late seventeenth century, European philosophers and political thinkers had begun to praise Chinese civilization and to hold up Confucian institutions and values as a mirror to criticize their counterparts in the West.

First Contacts with the West Despite the Ming's retreat from active participation in maritime trade, when the Portuguese arrived in 1514, China was in command of a vast empire that stretched from the steppes of Central Asia to the China Sea, from the Gobi Desert to the tropical rain forests of Southeast Asia. From the lofty perspective of the imperial throne in Beijing, the Europeans could only have seemed like an unusually exotic form of barbarian to be inserted within the familiar framework of the tributary system, the hierarchical arrangement in which rulers of all other countries were regarded as "younger brothers" of the Son of Heaven. Indeed, the bellicose and uncultured behavior of the Portuguese initially so outraged Chinese officials that they expelled the Europeans. After further negotiations, however, Chinese officials relented and authorized the Portuguese to occupy the tiny territory of Macao (muh-KOW) as a means of retaining sporadic contacts with the Celestial Empire.

As a result, the arrival of the Portuguese did not have much impact on Chinese society. Direct trade between Europe and China was limited, and Portuguese ships became involved in the regional trade network, carrying silk from China to Japan in return for Japanese silver. Eventually, the Spanish also began to participate, using the Philippines as an anchor in the galleon trade between China and the great silver mines in the Americas.

More influential than trade, perhaps, were the ideas introduced by Christian missionaries, who first received permission to reside in China in the last quarter of the sixteenth century.

The Ming Brought to Earth During the late sixteenth century, the Ming began to decline as a series of weak rulers led to an era of corruption, concentration of land ownership, and ultimately peasant rebellions and tribal unrest along the northern frontier. The inflow of vast amounts of foreign silver to pay for Chinese goods led to an alarming increase in inflation. Then the arrival of the English and the Dutch, whose ships preyed on the Spanish galleon trade between Asia and the Americas, disrupted the silver trade; silver imports plummeted, severely straining the Chinese economy by raising the value of the metal relative to that of copper. Crop yields declined due to harsh weather—linked to the "little ice age" of the early seventeenth century—and the resulting scarcity made it difficult for the government to provide food in times of imminent starvation. High taxes, necessitated in part because corrupt officials siphoned off revenues, led to rural unrest and violent protests among urban workers. A folk song of the period, addressed to the "Lord of Heaven," complained:

Old skymaster,
You're getting on, your ears are deaf, your eyes are gone.
Can't see people, can't hear words.
Glory for those who kill and burn;
For those who fast and read the scriptures,
Starvation.
Fall down, old master sky, how can you be so high?
How can you be so high? Come down to earth.[3]

As always, internal problems were accompanied by disturbances along the northern frontier. Following long precedent, the Ming had attempted to pacify the frontier tribes by forging alliances with them, arranging marriages between them and the local aristocracy, and granting trade privileges. One of the alliances was with the Manchus (man-CHOOZ)—also known as the Jurchen (roor-ZHEN)—the descendants of a non-Chinese people who had briefly established a kingdom in northern China during the early thirteenth century. The Manchus, a mixed agricultural and hunting people, lived northeast of the Great Wall in the area known today as Manchuria (man-CHUR-ee-uh).

At first, the Manchus were satisfied with consolidating their territory and made little effort to extend their rule south of the Great Wall. But during the first decades of the seventeenth century, the problems of the Ming Dynasty began to come to a head. A major epidemic devastated the population in many areas of the country. The suffering brought on by the epidemic and widespread drought conditions helped spark a vast peasant revolt led by the formal postal worker Li Zicheng (lee zuh-CHENG) (1604–1651). With the imperial court now increasingly preoccupied by tribal attacks along the frontier (see Map 17.1), in the 1630s, Li managed to extend the revolt throughout the country, and his forces finally occupied the capital, Beijing, in 1644. The last Ming emperor committed suicide by hanging himself from a tree in the palace gardens.

But the rebels were unable to hold their conquest. Emboldened by the overthrow of the dynasty, the Manchus—now assisted by military commanders who had deserted from the Ming—managed to seize Beijing. Li Zicheng's army rapidly disintegrated, and the Manchus declared a new dynasty: the Qing (CHING) (or Pure), which lasted from 1644 until 1911. Once again, China was under foreign rule.

17–1b The Greatness of the Qing

The accession of the Manchus to power in Beijing was not universally applauded. Their ruthless policies and insensitivity to Chinese customs soon provoked resistance. Some Ming loyalists fled to Southeast Asia, but others sought to resist the new rulers from inside the country. To make it easier to identify rebels, the government ordered all Chinese to adopt Manchu dress and hairstyles. All Chinese males were to shave their foreheads and braid their hair into a queue (KYOO); those who refused were to be executed. As a popular saying put it, "Lose your hair or lose your head."[4]

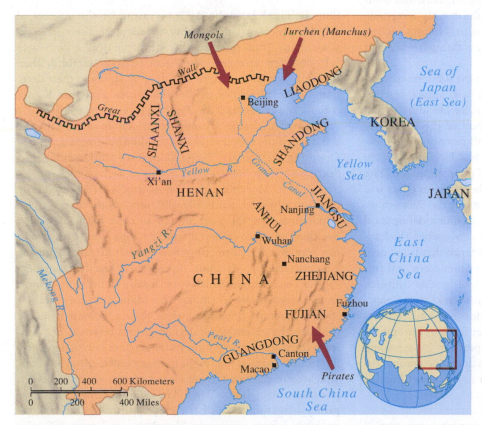

Map 17.1 China and Its Enemies During the Late Ming Era. During the seventeenth century, the Ming Dynasty faced challenges on two fronts: from China's traditional adversaries, nomadic groups north of the Great Wall, and from new arrivals, European merchants who had begun to press for trading privileges along the southern coast.

 How did these threats differ from those faced by previous dynasties in China?

But the Manchus eventually proved to be more adept at adapting to Chinese conditions than their predecessors, the Mongols. Unlike the latter, who had tried to impose their own methods of ruling, the Manchus adopted the Chinese political system (although, as we shall see, they retained their distinct position within it) and were gradually accepted by many Chinese as the legitimate rulers of the country.

Like all of China's great dynasties, the Qing was blessed with a series of strong early rulers who pacified the country, rectified many of the most obvious social and economic inequities, and restored peace and prosperity to the country. For the Ming Dynasty, these strong emperors had been Zhu Yuanzhang and Yongle; under the Qing, they would be Kangxi and Qianlong (CHAN-loong). The two Qing monarchs ruled China from the middle of the seventeenth century to the end of the eighteenth and were responsible for much of the greatness of Manchu China.

The Reign of Kangxi

Kangxi (r. 1661–1722) was arguably the greatest ruler in Chinese history. Ascending to the throne at the age of seven, he was blessed with diligence, political astuteness, and a strong character and began to take charge of Qing administration while still an adolescent. During the six decades of his reign, Kangxi not only stabilized imperial rule by pacifying the restive peoples along the northern and western frontiers but also managed to make the dynasty acceptable to the general population. As an active patron of arts and letters, he cultivated the support of scholars through a number of major projects.

During Kangxi's reign, the activities of the Western missionaries, Dominicans and Franciscans as well as Jesuits, reached their height. An intellectually curious ruler like the Mughal emperor Akbar, Kangxi was quite tolerant of the Christians, and several Jesuit missionaries became influential at court. Several hundred court officials converted to Christianity, as did an estimated 300,000 among the general population (see "The Debate over Christianity," p. 483). But the Christian effort was ultimately undermined by squabbling among the Western religious orders over the Jesuit policy of accommodating local beliefs and practices in order to facilitate conversion. The Jesuits had acquiesced to the emperor's insistence that traditional Confucian rituals such as ancestor veneration were civil ceremonies and thus could be undertaken by Christian converts. Jealous Dominicans and Franciscans complained to the pope, who issued an edict ordering all missionaries and converts to conform to the official orthodoxy set forth in Europe. At first, Kangxi attempted to resolve the problem by appealing directly to the Vatican, but the pope was uncompromising. After Kangxi's death, his successor began to suppress Christian activities throughout China.

The Reign of Qianlong

Kangxi's achievements were carried on by his successors, Yongzheng (YOONG-jehng) (r. 1722–1736) and Qianlong (r. 1736–1795). Like Kangxi, Qianlong was known for his diligence, tolerance, and intellectual curiosity, and he too combined vigorous military action against the unruly tribes along the frontier with active efforts to promote economic prosperity, administrative efficiency, and scholarship and artistic excellence. The result was continued growth for the Manchu Empire throughout much of the eighteenth century.

But it was also under Qianlong that the first signs of the internal decay of the Manchu Dynasty began to appear. The clues were familiar ones. Qing military campaigns along the frontier were expensive and placed heavy demands on the imperial treasury. As the emperor aged, he became less astute in selecting his subordinates and fell under the influence of corrupt elements at court, including the notorious Manchu official Heshen (HEH-shen). Funds officially destined for military or other official use were increasingly siphoned off by Heshen or his favorites, arousing resentment among military and civilian officials.

Corruption at the center led inevitably to unrest in rural areas, where higher taxes, bureaucratic venality, and rising pressure on the land because of the growing population had produced economic hardship. In central China, discontented peasants who had recently been resettled on infertile land launched a revolt known as the White Lotus Rebellion (1796–1804). The revolt was eventually suppressed, but at great expense.

Qing Political Institutions

One reason for the success of the Manchus was their ability to adapt to their new environment. They retained the Ming political system with relatively few changes. They also tried to establish their legitimacy as China's rightful rulers by stressing their devotion to the principles of Confucianism. Emperor Kangxi ostentatiously studied the Confucian classics and issued a "sacred edict" that proclaimed to the entire empire the importance of the moral values established by "the Master" (see Opposing Viewpoints "Some Confucian Commandments," Section 17-3d, p. 500).

Still, the Manchus, like the Mongols, were ethnically, linguistically, and culturally different from their subject population. The Qing attempted to cope with this reality by adopting a two-pronged strategy. One part of this strategy was aimed at protecting their distinct identity within an alien society. The Manchus, representing less than 2 percent of the entire population, were legally defined as distinct from everyone else in China. The Manchu nobles retained their aristocratic privileges, while their economic base was protected by extensive landholdings and revenues provided from the state treasury. Other Manchus were assigned farmland and organized into eight military units, called **banners**, which were stationed as separate units in various strategic positions throughout China. These "bannermen" were the primary fighting force of the empire. Ethnic Chinese were prohibited from settling in Manchuria and were still compelled to wear their hair in a queue as a sign of submission to the ruling dynasty.

At the same time that the Qing attempted to preserve their identity, they recognized the need to bring ethnic Chinese into

The Debate over Christianity

The arrival of a number of Christian missionaries at the Ming imperial court in Beijing caused a major tumult among Chinese officials there. While some were attracted to the new faith, others expressed alarm that these strange new ideas could corrupt traditional neo-Confucian doctrine. As the following passages indicate, both supporters and opponents had only a rudimentary understanding of Christian teachings and the Western culture from which they had sprung.

Xu Guangqi: A Memorial in Defense of the [Western] Teaching (1616)

Because the teaching of the men from afar [i.e., Christian missionaries from Europe] is most correct, and because your humble servant knows from experience that it is right, he earnestly begs to memorialize the throne, to the end that blessings may last forever and peace may be handed on to all generations. . . .

[Y]our servant . . . has studied with and learned from these [Western] tributary officials, and I know that they are most honest and solid. There is nothing whatsoever about them that is dubious. Truly, they are all disciples of the sages. Their way is very correct, their discipline strict, their learning very broad, their knowledge superior, their affections true, and their views very stable. . . .

Now in their countries, men of the church all cultivate personal virtue in order to serve the Lord of Heaven. . . . This teaching has as its basic tenet serving the Lord on High; to save the body and soul is the most essential principle, while one's practice should consist in loyalty, filial piety, love, and compassion. The way to begin is to choose good and repent, and the way to advance and improve is to confess and reform. True blessing in Heaven is the glorious reward of doing good, while eternal retribution in hell is the bitter recompense of doing evil. . . .

Now there are more than thirty countries in the West, and they have accepted and practiced this teaching for a thousand and several hundred years, right up to the present time, great and small living together in harmony, superior and inferior at peace with each other. The borders are not guarded, and the rulers of the states are all of the same family. . . . As for revolt and rebellion, not even once has there been such a thing or such people. . . .

Yang Guangxian: I Cannot Do Otherwise (1665)

According to a book by [the Christian scholar] Li Zubo, the Qing dynasty is nothing but an offshoot of Judea; our ancient Chinese rulers, sages, and teachers were but the offshoots of a heterodox sect; and our classics and the teachings of the sages propounded generation after generation are no more than the remnants of a heterodox teaching. How can we abide these calumnies! They really aim to inveigle the people of the Qing into rebelling against the Qing and following this heterodox sect, which would lead all-under-Heaven to abandon respect for rulers and fathers. . . .

Our Confucian teaching is based on the Five Relationships (between parent and child, ruler and minister, husband and wife, older and younger brothers, and friends), whilst the Lord of Heaven Jesus was crucified because he plotted against his own country, showing that he did not recognize the relationship between ruler and subject. Mary, the mother of Jesus had a husband named Joseph, but she said Jesus was not conceived by him.

Those who follow this teaching [Christianity] are not allowed to worship their ancestors and ancestral tablets. They do not recognize the relationship of parent and child. Their teachers oppose the Buddhists and Daoists, who do recognize the relationship between ruler and subject and father and son. Jesus did not recognize the relationship between ruler and subject and parent and child. . . . What arrant nonsense! . . .

 To what degree do you feel that the authors of these two passages misrepresent Christian teachings and the influence that such ideas have had in European society?

Source: W. T. de Bary and R. Lufrano, *Sources of Chinese Tradition: From 1600 Through the Twentieth Century*, Vol. II (New York: Columbia University Press, 2000), pp. 148–151.

the top ranks of imperial administration. Their solution was to create a system, known as **diarchy** (DY-ahr-kee), in which all important administrative positions were shared equally by Chinese and Manchus. Of the six members of the grand secretariat, three were Manchu and three were Chinese. Each of the six ministries had an equal number of Chinese and Manchu members, and Manchus and Chinese also shared responsibilities at the provincial level. Below the provinces, Chinese were dominant. Although the system did not work perfectly, the Manchus' willingness to share power did win the allegiance of many Chinese. Meanwhile, the Manchus themselves, despite official efforts to preserve their separate language and culture,

William J. Duiker

The Temple of Heaven. This temple, located in the capital city of Beijing, is one of the most significant historical structures in China. Built in 1420 at the order of the Ming emperor Yongle, it was the site of the emperor's annual appeal to Heaven for a good harvest. In this important ceremony, the emperor demonstrated to his subjects that he was their protector and would ward off the evil forces in nature. Yongle's temple burned to the ground in 1889 but was immediately rebuilt following the original design.

found it imperative to adopt many of the beliefs and rituals of their hosts, and were increasingly assimilated into Chinese civilization.

The new rulers also tinkered with the civil service examination system. In an effort to make it more equitable, quotas were established for each major ethnic group and each province to prevent the positions from being monopolized by candidates from certain provinces in central China that had traditionally produced large numbers of officials. In practice, however, the examination system probably became less equitable during the Manchu era because increasingly positions were assigned to candidates who had purchased their degree instead of competing through the system. Moreover, positions were becoming harder to obtain because their number did not rise fast enough to match the unprecedented increase in population under Qing rule.

China on the Eve of the Western Onslaught In some ways, China was at the height of its power and glory in the mid-eighteenth century. But as we have seen, it was also during this

period that the first signs of serious trouble for the Qing Dynasty began to appear.

Unfortunately for China, the decline of the Qing occurred just as China's modest relationship with the West was about to give way to a new era of military confrontation and increased pressure for trade. The first challenges came in the north, where Russian traders seeking skins and furs began to penetrate the region between Siberian Russia and Manchuria. Earlier the Ming Dynasty had attempted to deal with the Russians by the traditional method of placing them in a tributary relationship and playing them off against other non-Chinese groups in the area. But the tsar refused to play by Chinese rules. His envoys to Beijing ignored the tribute system and refused to perform the **kowtow** (the ritual of prostration and touching the forehead to the ground), the classical symbol of fealty demanded of all foreign ambassadors to the Chinese court. Formal diplomatic relations were finally established in 1689, when the Treaty of Nerchinsk (ner-CHINSK), negotiated with the aid of Jesuit missionaries resident at the Qing court, settled the boundary dispute and provided for regular trade between the two countries. Through such arrangements, the Manchus were able not only to pacify the northern frontier but also to extend their rule over Xinjiang (SHIN-jyahng) and Tibet to the west and southwest (see Map 17.2 p. 485). In the meantime, tributary relations were established with such neighboring countries as Korea, Burma, Vietnam, and Ayuthaya.

Dealing with the foreigners who arrived by sea was more difficult. By the end of the seventeenth century, the English had replaced the Portuguese as the dominant force in European trade. Operating through the East India Company, which served as both a trading unit and the administrator of

CHRONOLOGY	China During the Early Modern Era
Rise of the Ming Dynasty	1369
Voyages of Zheng He	1405–1433
Portuguese arrive in southern China	1514
Matteo Ricci arrives in China	1601
Li Zicheng occupies Beijing	1644
Manchus seize China	1644
Reign of Kangxi	1661–1722
Treaty of Nerchinsk	1689
First English trading post at Canton	1699
Reign of Qianlong	1736–1795
Lord Macartney's mission to China	1793
White Lotus Rebellion	1796–1804

English territories in Asia, the English established their first trading post at Canton (KAN-tun) in 1699. Over the next decades, trade with China, notably the export of tea and silk to England, increased rapidly. To limit contact between Chinese and Europeans, the Qing licensed Chinese trading firms at Canton to be the exclusive conduit for trade with the West. Eventually, the Qing confined the Europeans to a small island just outside the city walls and permitted them to reside there only from October through March.

For a while, the British tolerated this system, which brought considerable profit to the East India Company and its shareholders. But by the end of the eighteenth century, the British had begun to demand that they be allowed access to other cities along the Chinese coast and that the country be opened to British manufactured goods. The British government and traders alike were restive at the uneven balance of trade between the two countries, which forced the British to ship vast amounts of silver bullion to China in exchange for its silk, porcelain, and tea. In 1793, a mission under Lord Macartney visited Beijing to press for liberalization of trade restrictions. A compromise was reached on the kowtow (Macartney was permitted to bend on one knee, as was the British custom), but Qianlong expressed no interest in British manufactured products (see "The Tribute System in Action," p. 487). An exasperated Macartney compared the Chinese Empire to "an old, crazy, first-rate man-of-war" that had once awed its neighbors "merely by her bulk and appearance" but was now destined under incompetent leadership to be "dashed to pieces on the shore."[5] With his contemptuous dismissal of the British request, the emperor had inadvertently sowed the seeds for a century of humiliation.

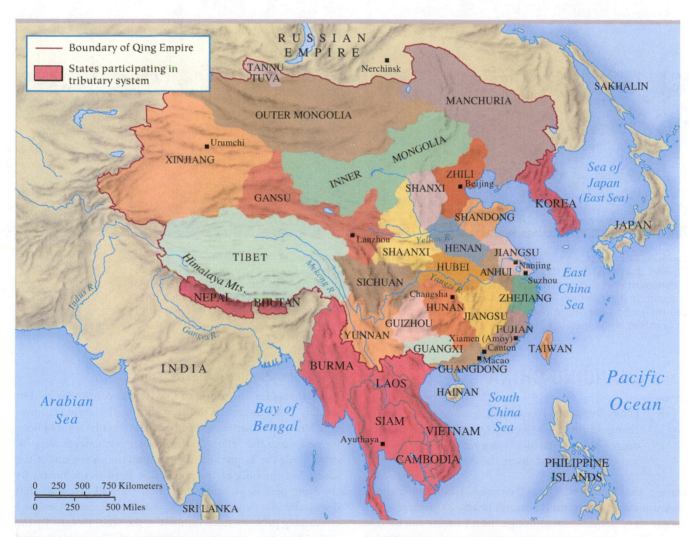

Map 17.2 The Qing Empire in the Eighteenth Century. The boundaries of the Chinese Empire at the height of the Qing Dynasty in the eighteenth century are shown on this map.

Q *What areas were linked in tributary status to the Chinese Empire, and how did they benefit the empire?*

European Warehouses at Canton. Aggravated by the growing presence of foreigners in the eighteenth century, the Chinese court severely restricted the movement of European traders in China. They were permitted to live only in a compound near Canton during the seven months of the trading season and could go into the city only three times a month. In this painting, foreign flags (including, from the left, those of the United States, Sweden, Great Britain, and Holland) fly over the warehouses and residences of the foreign community while Chinese sampans and junks sit anchored in the river.

DEA/A. DAGLI ORTI/Getty Images

17–2 CHANGING CHINA

 Focus Question: How did the economy and society change during the Ming and Qing eras, and to what degree did these changes seem to be leading toward an industrial revolution on the European model?

During the Ming and Qing Dynasties, China remained a predominantly agricultural society; nearly 85 percent of its people were farmers. But although most Chinese still lived in rural villages, the economy was undergoing changes that led to the emergence of a vibrant and rapidly growing industrial and commercial sector. A number of cities, notably along the coast or along the major river systems, began to prosper under the impact of growing contacts between China and the outside world.

17–2a The Population Explosion

In the first place, the center of gravity was continuing to shift steadily from the north to the south. In the early centuries of Chinese civilization, the bulk of the population had been located along the Yellow River. Smaller settlements were located along the Yangzi and in the mountainous regions of the south, but the bulk of the population lived in the north. By the Song period, however, that emphasis had begun to shift drastically as a result of climatic changes, deforestation, and continuing pressure from nomads in the Gobi Desert. By the early Qing, the economic breadbasket of China was located along the Yangzi River or in the mountains to the south. One concrete indication of this shift occurred during the Ming Dynasty, when Emperor Yongle ordered the renovation of the Grand Canal to facilitate the shipment of rice from the Yangzi delta to the food-starved north.

THE TRIBUTE SYSTEM IN ACTION

Interaction & Exchange

IN 1793, THE BRITISH EMISSARY Lord Macartney visited the Qing Empire to request the opening of formal diplomatic and trading relations between his country and China. Emperor Qianlong's reply, addressed to King George III of Britain, illustrates how the imperial court in Beijing viewed the world. King George could not have been pleased. The document provides a good example of the complacency with which the Celestial Empire viewed the world beyond its borders.

A Decree of Emperor Qianlong

An Imperial Edict to the King of England: You . . . are so inclined toward our civilization that you have sent a special envoy across the seas to bring to our Court your memorial of congratulations on the occasion of my birthday and to present your native products as an expression of your thoughtfulness. On perusing your memorial, so simply worded and sincerely conceived, I am impressed by your genuine respectfulness and friendliness and greatly pleased.

As to the request made in your memorial . . . to send one of your nationals to stay at the Celestial Court to take care of your country's trade with China, this is not in harmony with the state system of our dynasty and will definitely not be permitted. Traditionally people of the European nations who wished to render some service under the Celestial Court have been permitted to come to the capital. But after their arrival they are obliged to wear Chinese court costumes, are placed in a certain residence, and are never allowed to return to their own countries. This is the established rule of the Celestial Dynasty with which presumably you . . . are familiar. Now you . . . wish to send one of your nationals to live in the capital, but he is not like the Europeans who come to Peking [Beijing] as Chinese employees, live there, and never return home again, nor can he be allowed to go and come and maintain any correspondence. . . . Moreover the territory under the control of the Celestial Court is very large and wide. There are well-established regulations governing tributary envoys from the outer states to Peking, giving them provisions [of food and traveling expenses] by our post-houses and limiting their going and coming. There has never been a precedent for letting them do whatever they like. Now if you . . . wish to have a representative in Peking, his language will be unintelligible and his dress different from the regulations; there is no place to accommodate him. . . .

The Celestial Court has pacified and possessed the territory within the four seas. Its sole aim is to do its utmost to achieve good government and to manage political affairs, attaching no value to strange jewels and precious objects. . . . As a matter of fact, the virtue and prestige of the Celestial Dynasty having spread far and wide, the kings of the myriad nations come by land and sea with all sorts of precious things. Consequently there is nothing we lack, as your principal envoy and others have themselves observed. We have never set much store on strange or ingenious objects, nor do we need any more of your country's manufactures.

 What reasons did the emperor give for refusing Macartney's request to have a permanent British ambassador in Beijing? How did the tribute system differ from the principles of international relations as practiced in the West?

Source: Reprinted by permission of the publisher from *China's Response to the West: A Documentary Survey, 1839–1923*, by Ssu-yu Teng and John King Fairbank, p. 19, Cambridge, Mass.: Harvard University Press, Copyright © 1954, 1979 by the President and Fellows of Harvard College. Copyright renewed 1982 by Ssu-yu Teng and John King Fairbank.

Moreover, the population was beginning to increase rapidly. For centuries, China's population had remained within a range of 50 to 100 million, rising in times of peace and prosperity and falling in periods of foreign invasion and internal strife. During the Ming and the early Qing, however, the population increased from an estimated 70 to 80 million in 1390 to more than 300 million at the end of the eighteenth century. There were probably several reasons for this population increase: the relatively long period of peace and stability under the early Qing; the introduction of new crops from the Americas, including peanuts, sweet potatoes, and maize; and the planting of a new species of faster-growing rice from Southeast Asia (see Comparative Essay, "Population Explosion," p. 488).

Of course, this population increase meant much greater pressure on the land, smaller farms, and a razor-thin margin of safety in the event of a natural disaster. The imperial court attempted to deal with the problem through various means, most notably by preventing the concentration of land in the hands of wealthy landowners. Nevertheless, by the eighteenth century, almost all the land that could be irrigated was already under cultivation, and the problems of rural hunger and landlessness were becoming increasingly serious.

17-2b Seeds of Industrialization

Another change that took place during the early modern period in China was the steady growth of manufacturing and commerce. Taking advantage of the long era of peace and prosperity, merchants and manufacturers began to expand their operations beyond their immediate provinces. Commercial networks began to operate on a regional and sometimes even a national basis as trade in silk, metal and

Population Explosion

Earth & Environment Between 1700 and 1800, Europe, China, and to a lesser degree India and the Ottoman Empire experienced a dramatic growth in population. In Europe, the population grew from 120 million people to almost 200 million by 1800; in China, from less than 200 million to more than 300 million during the same period.

Four developments in particular contributed to this population explosion. First, better growing conditions, made possible by an improvement in climate, affected wide areas of the world and enabled people to produce more food. Both China and Europe experienced warmer summers beginning in the early eighteenth century. Second, by the eighteenth century, people had begun to develop immunities to the epidemic diseases that had caused widespread loss of life between 1500 and 1700. The increase in travel by ship after 1500 had led to devastating epidemics. For example, the arrival of Europeans in Mexico introduced smallpox, measles, and chickenpox to a native population that had no immunities to European diseases. In 1500, between 11 and 20 million people lived in the area of Mexico; by 1650, only 1.5 million remained. Gradually, however, people developed resistance to these diseases.

A third factor in the population increase was the introduction of new foods. As a result of the Columbian Exchange (see Comparative Essay, "The Columbian Exchange," Section 14-3e, p. 407), American food crops,

such as corn, potatoes, and sweet potatoes, were transported to other parts of the world, where they became important food sources. China imported a new species of rice from Southeast Asia that had a shorter harvest cycle than existing varieties. These new foods provided additional sources of nutrition that enabled more people to live for a longer time. At the same time, land development and canal building in the eighteenth century enabled government authorities to move food supplies to areas threatened with crop failure and famine.

Finally, the use of new weapons based on gunpowder allowed states to control larger territories and ensure a new degree of order. The early rulers of the Qing Dynasty, for example, pacified the Chinese Empire and ensured a long period of peace and stability. Absolute monarchs achieved similar goals in a number of European states. Less violence resulted in fewer deaths at the same time that an increase in food supplies and a decrease in deaths from diseases were occurring, thus making possible in the eighteenth century the beginning of the world population explosion that persists to this day.

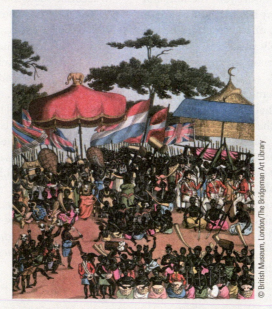

© British Museum, London/The Bridgeman Art Library

Festival of the Yam. The spread of a few major food crops made possible new sources of nutrition to feed more people. The importance of the yam to the Ashanti people of West Africa is evident in this celebration of a yam festival at harvest time in 1817.

 What were the main reasons for the dramatic expansion in the world population during the early modern era?

---

wood products, porcelain, cotton goods, and cash crops like cotton and tobacco developed rapidly. Foreign trade also expanded after the Ming court in 1567 suspended its prohibition on such activities. In response, Chinese merchants began to set up extensive contacts with countries in Southeast Asia. As Chinese tea, silk, and porcelain became ever more popular in other parts of the world, the trade surplus grew as the country's exports greatly outnumbered its imports. Silver bullion, carried to the Philippines by Spanish galleons from the Americas, flooded into Chinese coffers. As the economy expanded, Chinese officials encouraged the importation of silver as a means of supplementing the inadequate supply of bronze coinage, but eventually the glut of silver in the marketplace

caused price distortions that may have contributed to the fall of the Ming Dynasty.

HISTORIANS DEBATE **The Qing Economy: Ready for Takeoff?** For many years, it was a common belief among Western historians that conditions in traditional China were not conducive to the onset of an industrial revolution along the European model. In recent years, however, some have suggested that because of the impressive advances achieved during the early Qing Dynasty, by the end of the eighteenth century China was poised to make the transition from an agricultural to a predominantly manufacturing and commercial economy—a transition that began to take place in western Europe with the onset of the Industrial Revolution at the end of the eighteenth century (see Chapter 19).

Certainly, in many respects, the Chinese economy in the mid-Qing era was as advanced as any of its counterparts around the world. China's achievements in technology over the past centuries were unsurpassed, and the population as a whole was among the most prosperous in the world. A perceptive observer at the time might well have concluded that the Manchu Empire would be highly competitive with the most advanced nations around the globe for the indefinite future.

Nevertheless, a number of factors raise doubts that China in the mid-Qing era was poised to advance rapidly into the industrial age. In the first place, the mercantile class was not as independent in China as in some European societies. Trade and manufacturing in China remained under the firm control of the state. In addition, political and social prejudices against commercial activity remained strong, and the road to success was still seen as resulting from a career in officialdom. Reflecting an ancient preference for agriculture over manufacturing and trade, the state levied heavy taxes on manufacturing and commerce while attempting to keep agricultural taxes low.

To a considerable degree, these views were shared by the population at large, as the scholar-gentry continued to dominate intellectual fashions in China throughout the early Qing period. Chinese elites in general had little interest in the natural sciences or economic activities and often viewed them as a threat to their own dominant status within Chinese society as a whole. The commercial middle class, lacking social status and an independent position in society, had little say in intellectual matters and relatively little influence at court.

At the root of such attitudes was the lingering influence of Neo-Confucianism, which remained the official state doctrine in China down to the end of the Qing Dynasty. Although the founding fathers of Neo-Confucianism had originally focused on the "investigation of things," as time passed its practitioners tended to emphasize the elucidation of moral principles rather than the expansion of scientific knowledge. As the historian Toby Huff has noted, the civil service examination contained no questions on science or technology, while Chinese interest in European scientific advances in areas like astronomy was limited to a few officials at court. Though the Chinese economy was gradually being transformed from an agricultural to a commercial and industrial giant, scholars tended to look back to antiquity, rather than to empirical science, as the prime source for knowledge of the natural world and human events. The result was an intellectual environment that valued continuity over change and tradition over innovation. In effect, although the conditions for a transition to a modern industrial economy were present in early Qing China, the motivation to do so was lacking.

The Chinese indifference to foreign trade provides a good example. Although the early Ming emperor Yongle had expressed a strong interest in expanding Chinese contacts with the external world (see Chapter 10), his successors tended to focus on internal concerns and for a time even sought to prohibit trade with foreign countries in a bid to bring an end to the chronic pirate attacks taking place along the coast. Interest in geography and the shape of the world also declined, despite advances in Chinese mapmaking as discussed in Chapter 10.

The Chinese reaction to European clock-making techniques provides an additional case study. In the early seventeenth century, the Jesuit priest Matteo Ricci introduced advanced European clocks driven by weights or springs. The emperor was fascinated and found the clocks more reliable than Chinese timekeepers, but the population at large did not adopt the Western invention. Although European timepieces became a popular novelty at court, the Chinese expressed little curiosity about the technology involved, provoking one European observer to remark that playthings like cuckoo clocks "will be received here with much greater interest than scientific instruments or *objets d'art.*"[6]

© Peabody Essex Museum, Salem, Massachusetts, USA/The Bridgeman Art Library

Haggling over the Price of Tea. An important item in the China trade of the eighteenth and early nineteenth centuries was tea, which had become extremely popular in Great Britain. The painting depicts the various stages of growing, processing, and marketing tea leaves. In the background, workers are removing tender young leaves from the bushes. In the foreground, British and Chinese merchants bargain over the price. After being dried, the leaves are packed into chests and loaded on vessels for shipment abroad.

17–2c Daily Life in Qing China

Despite the changes in the economy, daily life in China under the Ming and early Qing Dynasties continued for the most part to follow traditional patterns.

The Family Chinese society continued to be organized around the family. As in earlier periods, the ideal family unit in Qing China was the joint family, in which three or four generations lived under the same roof. When sons married, they brought their wives to live with them in their family homestead. Prosperous families would add a separate section to the house to accommodate the new family unit. Unmarried daughters would also remain in the house. Aging parents and grandparents remained under the same roof until they died and were cared for by younger members of the household. This ideal did not always correspond to reality, however, since many families did not possess sufficient land to support a large household. One historian has estimated that only about 40 percent of Chinese families actually lived in joint families.

Still, the family retained its importance in early Qing times for the same reasons as in earlier eras. As a labor-intensive society based primarily on the cultivation of rice, China needed large families to help with the harvest and to provide security for parents too old to work in the fields. Sons were especially prized, not only because they had strong backs but also because they would raise their own families under the parental roof. With few opportunities for employment outside the family, sons had little choice but to remain with their parents and help on the land. Within the family, the oldest male was in charge, and theoretically his wishes had to be obeyed by all family members (see "A Last Will and Testament," p. 491). These values were reiterated in Emperor Kangxi's Sacred Edict, which listed filial piety and loyalty to the family as its first two maxims.

For many Chinese, the effects of these values were also apparent in the choice of a marriage partner. Arranged marriages were the norm, and the primary consideration in selecting a spouse was whether the union would benefit the family unit as a whole. The couple usually had no say in the matter and might not even meet until the marriage ceremony. Not only were romantic feelings between the couple considered unimportant in marriage, but they were often viewed as undesirable because they could draw the attention of the husband and wife away from their primary responsibility to the larger family unit.

Although this emphasis on filial piety might seem to represent a blatant disregard for individual rights, the obligations were not all on the side of the children. The father was expected to provide support for his wife and children and, like the ruler, was supposed to treat those in his care with respect and compassion. All too often, however, the male head of the family was able to exact his privileges without performing his responsibilities in return.

Beyond the joint family was the clan, which was an extended kinship unit consisting of dozens or even hundreds of joint and nuclear families linked by a clan council of elders and a variety of other common social and religious functions. The clan served several useful purposes. Some possessed lands that could be rented out to poorer families, or richer families within the clan might provide land for the poor. Since there was no general state-supported educational system, sons of poor families might be invited to study in a school established in the home of a more prosperous relative. If the young man succeeded in becoming an official, he would be expected to provide favors and prestige for the clan as a whole.

Like joint families, clans were not universal, and millions of Chinese had none. They may have originated among the great landed families of the Tang era and managed to survive despite periodic efforts by the imperial court to weaken and destroy them. In many cases, clan solidarity was weakened by intralineage conflicts or differing levels of status and economic achievement. Nevertheless, in the early modern period, they were still an influential force at the local level and were particularly prevalent in the south.

The Role of Women In traditional China, the role of women had always been inferior to that of men. A sixteenth-century Spanish visitor to South China observed that Chinese women were "very secluded and virtuous, and it was a very rare thing for us to see a woman in the cities and large towns, unless it was an old crone."[7] Women were more visible, he said, in rural areas, where they frequently could be seen working in the fields.

The concept of female inferiority had deep roots in Chinese history. This view was embodied in the belief that only a male could carry on sacred family rituals and that men alone had the talent to govern others. Only males could aspire to a career in government or scholarship. Within the family system, the wife was clearly subordinated to the husband. Legally, she could not divorce her husband or inherit property. The husband, however, could divorce his wife if she did not produce male heirs, or he could take a second wife as well as a concubine for his pleasure. Life was especially difficult for a widow: she had to raise her children on a single income or fight off her dead husband's greedy relatives, who would try to coerce her to remarry because, by law, they would then inherit all of her previous property and her original dowry. Female children were also less desirable because of their limited physical strength and because their parents would have to pay a dowry to the parents of their future husbands. Female children normally did not receive an education, and in times when food was in short supply, daughters might even be put to death.

Though women were clearly inferior to men in theory, this was not always the case in practice. Capable women often compensated for their legal inferiority by playing a strong role within the family. Women were often in charge of educating the children and handling the family budget. Some privileged women also received training in the Confucian classics, although their schooling was generally for a shorter time and less rigorous than that of their male counterparts. A few produced significant works of art and poetry.

All in all, however, life for women in traditional China was undoubtedly difficult. In Chinese novels, women were treated as scullery maids or love objects. They were frequently under the domination of both their husband and their mother-in-law,

A LAST WILL AND TESTAMENT

THE MING DYNASTY OFFICIAL YANG JISHENG (YAHNG jee-SHENG) is remembered by historians of China primarily for his admirable courage in speaking out against the corruption of powerful forces at the imperial court. The reward for his courage was torture and eventual execution. On learning of his fate, Yang wrote from prison to his family on how to comport themselves in a proper Confucian manner. His "Final Instructions" were widely circulated during the late Ming and early Qing dynasties as a model for managing family affairs.

First, he pleaded with his wife not to commit suicide after his execution; in his day, widows often did so to proclaim their fidelity and chastity—a poignant parallel with the tradition of sati in India. Unfortunately, on the day of his execution, she hanged herself in the town marketplace. Second, he advised his two sons to devote themselves to studying for the civil service examination in preparation for a prestigious official career. Following the common practice of his day, he counseled them to focus on memorizing the text rather than on absorbing the inner message of the classics, a widely followed tendency that reduced the essential teachings of Confucius and his followers to a dry scholasticism.

Yang Jisheng, "Final Instructions"

To the Wife

My only regret will be that my two sons are both young. In studying they have both made progress, and in the future they will both succeed. I only fear that [my death will] adversely affect their [future]. My one daughter is not yet married; without someone to teach, guide, and take care of her, I am afraid she will be ridiculed. If I should happen to die, I leave you behind to teach and guide my sons and daughter into adulthood. If each is able to complete their household and establish their objectives, then it will be as if I am still alive. . . .

[My concubine] Erzhen is still young and moreover has no children. After I have died, see that she marries someone else.

Give her an allotment of clothing and jewelry. . . . You must not have her stay at home and maintain widowhood. . . .

As for second elder sister and fourth elder sister, I'd like you always to look after them. As for fifth elder sister and sixth elder sister, when our father's concubine dies you should also become close to them. . . . The remaining household affairs I am sure you will deal with well.

To the Sons

You two are young in years. I fear that if you come to the notice of slick, sleazy people, they will try to tempt and defraud you. Some will ask you to dinner, some will tempt you to gamble, some will present you with objects you desire, some will tempt you with beautiful women. As soon as you enter their snare, you will suffer losses to them. Not only will the patrimony be completely dissipated, they'll also keep you from becoming a proper person. . . .

Preparing for the examinations is simply a matter of memorizing a great deal and composing a great deal. From the basic classics of the Four Books, memorize one thousand selections and read one hundred essays, one hundred policy inquiries, fifty declarations, and eighty judgments. If you have extra energy, read one hundred selections from the Five Classics and one hundred sections of better ancient prose. Every day compose one section of text, and every month write three essays and two policy inquiries. It is crucial to remember that you must not pass a single day without a teacher. If you have no teacher, then you have no strictness and no fear. . . . If you pass the local examinations or become a jinshi [obtain a doctorate], considering my bitter [experiences] it is best if you do not become an official. If you do become an official, you must be upright and honest, loyal and trustworthy, wholeheartedly serving the country to the best of your ability.

 How did Yang Jisheng advise his sons to prepare for a career in the bureaucracy? How did he use his own official career as an example of proper behavior?

Source: From *Under Confucian Eyes: Writings on Gender in Chinese History*, ed. by Susan Mann and Yu-Yin Cheng (Berkeley: University of California Press, 2001), pp. 122–127.

---

and in some cases the bullying was so brutal that suicide seemed to be the only way out.

17–2d Cultural Developments

During the late Ming and early Qing Dynasties, traditional culture in China reached new heights of achievement. With the rise of a wealthy urban class, the demand for art, porcelain, textiles, and literature increased dramatically.

The Rise of the Chinese Novel During the Ming Dynasty, a new form of literature arose that eventually evolved into the modern Chinese novel. Although considered less respectable than poetry and nonfiction prose, these groundbreaking works

(often written anonymously or under pseudonyms) were enormously popular, especially among well-to-do urban dwellers. Rapid advances in printing were a major factor in spreading the availability of books to the general population (see "The Art of Printing," p. 492).

Written in a colloquial but realistic style, the new fiction produced vivid portraits of Chinese society. Many of the stories sympathized with society's downtrodden—often helpless maidens—and dealt with such crucial issues as love, money, marriage, and power. Adding to the realism were sexually explicit passages that depicted the private side of Chinese life. Readers delighted in sensuous tales that, no matter how pornographic, always professed a moral lesson; the villains

THE ART OF PRINTING

Art & Ideas

EUROPEANS OBTAINED much of their early information about China from the Jesuits who served at the Ming court in the sixteenth and seventeenth centuries. The Italian Jesuit Matteo Ricci (ma-TAY-oh REE-chee) (1552–1610), who arrived in China in 1601, found much to admire in Chinese civilization. Here Ricci expresses a keen interest in Chinese printing methods, which at that time were well in advance of the techniques used in the West. Later Christian missionaries expressed strong interest in Confucian philosophy and Chinese ideas of statecraft.

Matteo Ricci, *The Diary of Matthew Ricci*

The art of printing was practiced in China at a date somewhat earlier than that assigned to the beginning of printing in Europe, which was about 1405. It is quite certain that the Chinese knew the art of printing at least five centuries ago, and some of them assert that printing was known to their people before the beginning of the Christian era, about 50 BCE. Their method of printing differs widely from that employed in Europe, and our method would be quite impracticable for them because of the exceedingly large number of Chinese characters and symbols....

Their method of making printed books is quite ingenious. The text is written in ink, with a brush made of very fine hair, on a sheet of paper which is inverted and pasted on a wooden tablet. When the paper has become thoroughly dry, its surface is scraped off quickly and with great skill, until nothing but a fine tissue bearing the characters remains on the wooden tablet. Then, with a steel graver, the workman cuts away the surface following the outlines of the characters until these alone stand out in low relief. From such a block a skilled printer can make copies with incredible speed, turning out as many as fifteen hundred copies in a single day. . . . This scheme of engraving wooden blocks is well adapted for the large and complex nature of the Chinese characters, but I do not think it would lend itself very aptly to our European type, which could hardly be engraved upon wood because of its small dimensions.

Their method of printing has one decided advantage, namely, that once these tablets are made, they can be preserved and used for making changes in the text as often as one wishes. Additions and subtractions can also be made as the tablets can be readily patched. . . . We have derived great benefit from this method of Chinese printing, as we employ the domestic help in our homes to strike off copies of the books on religious and scientific subjects which we translate into Chinese from the languages in which they were written originally. In truth, the whole method is so simple that one is tempted to try it for himself after once having watched the process. The simplicity of Chinese printing is what accounts for the exceedingly large numbers of books in circulation here and the ridiculously low prices at which they are sold.

 How did the Chinese method of printing differ from that used in Europe at that time? What were the advantages of the Chinese system?

Source: From *China in the Sixteenth Century*, by Matthew Ricci, translated by Louis J. Gallagher. Copyright © 1942 and renewed 1970 by Louis J. Gallagher, S. J.

---

were punished and the virtuous rewarded. During the more puritanical Qing era, a number of the more erotic works were censored or banned and found refuge in Japan, where several have recently been rediscovered by scholars.

Gold Vase Plum, known in English translation as *The Golden Lotus*, presents a cutting exposé of the decadent aspects of late Ming society. Considered by many the first realistic social novel—preceding its European counterparts by two centuries—*The Golden Lotus* depicts the depraved life of a wealthy landlord who cruelly manipulates those around him for sex, money, and power. In a rare exception in Chinese fiction, the villain is not punished for his evil ways; justice is served instead by the misfortunes that befall his descendants.

The Dream of the Red Chamber is generally considered China's most distinguished popular novel. Published in 1791, some 150 years after *The Golden Lotus*, it tells of the tragic love of two young people caught in the financial and moral disintegration of a powerful Chinese clan. The hero and the heroine, both sensitive and spoiled, represent the inevitable decline of the Chia family and come to an equally inevitable tragic end, she in death and he in an unhappy marriage to another.

The Art of the Ming and the Qing During the Ming and the early Qing, China produced its last outpouring of traditional artistic brilliance. Although most of the creative work was modeled on past examples, the art of this period is impressive for its technical perfection and impressive quantity.

In architecture, the most outstanding example is the Imperial City in Beijing, which, on the order of Ming emperor Yongle, was constructed on the remnants of the old imperial palace of the Yuan dynasty. His successors continued to add to the palace, but the basic design has not changed since the Ming era. Surrounded by high walls, the immense compound is divided into a maze of private apartments and offices and an imposing ceremonial quadrangle with a series of stately halls for imperial audiences and banquets. The grandiose scale, richly carved marble, spacious gardens, and graceful upturned roofs also contribute to the splendor of the "Forbidden City."

The decorative arts flourished in this period, especially intricately carved lacquerware and boldly shaped and colored cloisonné (kloi-zuh-NAY *or* KLWAH-zuh-nay), a type of enamelwork in which thin metal bands separate areas of colored enamel. Silk production reached its zenith, and the best-quality silks were highly prized in Europe, where chinoiserie (sheen-wah-zuh-REE *or* shee-nwahz-REE), as Chinese art of all kinds was called, was in vogue. Perhaps the most famous of all the achievements of the Ming era was the blue-and-white porcelain, still prized by collectors throughout the world. Of unsurpassed luminosity, this porcelain was used by Ming emperors to promote the prestige of their opulent and powerful empire. One variety caused such a sensation in the Netherlands that the Dutch began to manufacture their own blue-and-white porcelain at a new factory set up in Delft.

During the Qing Dynasty, Chinese artists produced great quantities of paintings to grace the walls of elite Chinese compounds. The commercial city of Yangzhou (YAHNG-Joh) on the Grand Canal emerged as an active artistic center. Inside the Forbidden City in Beijing, court painters worked alongside Jesuit artists and experimented with Western techniques. In general, however, European art, dismissed by some local artists as "mere craftsmanship," did not greatly influence Chinese painting at this time. Scholarly painters and the literati totally rejected foreign techniques and became obsessed with traditional Chinese styles. As a result, Qing painting became progressively more repetitive and stale. Ironically, the Qing Dynasty thus represents both the apogee of traditional Chinese art and the beginning of its decline.

World-Class China Ware. Ming porcelain was desired throughout the world for its delicate blue-and-white floral decorations. The blue coloring was produced with cobalt that had originally been brought from the Middle East along the Silk Road and was known in China as "Mohammedan blue." In the early seventeenth century, the first Ming porcelain arrived in the Netherlands, where it was called *kraak* because it had been loaded on two Portuguese ships known as carracks seized by the Dutch fleet. It took Dutch artisans more than a century to learn how to produce a porcelain as fine as the examples brought from China.

William J. Duiker

The Ming Tombs: Chinese Feng Shui in Action. When Emperor Yongle moved the capital of China from Nanjing to Beijing in the fifteenth century, the location of the Ming Dynasty's imperial tombs was moved as well. The last thirteen rulers of the dynasty were interred at a new location north of the new Imperial City. The site was selected with care, according to the hallowed principles of *feng shui* (literally "wind and water"), being placed on the southern slope of forested mountains that would protect the site from cold north winds. Entry into the complex took place by a wide avenue lined with stone statues of guardian animals and senior officials. As this statue of a Bactrian camel demonstrates, the lure of the Silk Road still pertained in late Ming Dynasty China.

William J. Duiker/Freer Gallery of Art, Smithsonian Institution, Washington, D.C.

17–3 TOKUGAWA JAPAN

Q Focus Question: How did the society and economy of Japan change during the Tokugawa era, and how did Japanese culture reflect those changes?

At the end of the fifteenth century, the traditional Japanese system was at a point of near anarchy. With the decline in the authority of the Ashikaga (ah-shee-KAH-guh) Shogunate at Kyoto (KYOH-toh), clan rivalries had exploded into an era of warring states similar to the period of the same name in Zhou dynasty China. Even at the local level, power was frequently diffuse. For a typical daimyo (DYM-yoh) (great lord), the domain had become little more than a coalition of fief-holders held together by a loose allegiance to the manor lord. Prince Shotoku's dream of a united Japan seemed only a distant memory (see Chapter 11). In actuality, Japan was on the verge of an extended era of national unification and peace under the rule of its greatest shogunate, the Tokugawa.

17–3a The Three Great Unifiers

The process began in the mid-sixteenth century with the emergence of three very powerful political figures: Oda Nobunaga (1568–1582), Toyotomi Hideyoshi (1582–1598), and Tokugawa Ieyasu (1598–1616). In 1568, Oda Nobunaga (OH-dah noh-buh-NAH-guh), the son of a samurai (SAM-uh-ry) and a military commander under the Ashikaga Shogunate, seized the imperial capital of Kyoto and placed the reigning shogun under his domination. During the next few years, the brutal and ambitious Nobunaga attempted to consolidate his rule throughout the central plains by defeating his rivals and suppressing the power of the Buddhist estates, but he was killed by one of his generals in 1582 before the process was complete. He was succeeded by Toyotomi Hideyoshi (toh-yoh-TOH-mee hee-day-YOH-shee), a farmer's son who had worked his way up through the ranks to become a military commander. Originally lacking a family name of his own, he eventually adopted the name Toyotomi ("abundant provider") to embellish his reputation for improving the material standards of his domain. Hideyoshi placed his capital at Osaka (oh-SAH-kuh), where he built a castle to accommodate his headquarters, and gradually extended his power outward to the southern islands of Shikoku (shee-KOH-koo) and Kyushu (KYOO-shoo) (see Map 17.3). By 1590, he had persuaded most of the daimyo on the Japanese islands to accept his authority and created a national currency. Then he invaded Korea in an abortive effort to export his rule to the Asian mainland (see Section 17-4a, "Korea: In a Dangerous Neighborhood," p. 504).

Despite their efforts, however, neither Nobunaga nor Hideyoshi was able to eliminate the power of the local daimyo. Both were compelled to form alliances with some daimyo in order to destroy other more powerful rivals. At the conclusion of his conquests in 1590, Toyotomi Hideyoshi could claim to be the supreme proprietor of all registered lands in areas under his authority. But he then reassigned those lands as fiefs to the local daimyo, who declared their allegiance to him. The daimyo in turn began to pacify the countryside, carrying out extensive "sword hunts" to disarm the population and attracting samurai to their service. The Japanese tradition of decentralized rule had not yet been overcome.

After Hideyoshi's death in 1598, Tokugawa Ieyasu (toh-koo-GAH-wah ee-yeh-YAH-soo), the powerful daimyo of Edo (EH-doh)—modern Tokyo—moved to fill the vacuum. Neither Hideyoshi nor Oda Nobunaga had claimed the title of shogun (SHOH-gun), but Ieyasu named himself shogun in 1603, initiating the most powerful and long-lasting of all Japanese shogunates. The Tokugawa rulers completed the restoration of central authority begun by Nobunaga and Hideyoshi and remained in power until 1868, when a war dismantled the entire system. As a contemporary phrased it, "Oda pounds the national rice cake, Hideyoshi kneads it, and in the end Ieyasu sits down and eats it."[8]

17–3b Opening to the West

The unification of Japan took place almost simultaneously with the coming of the Europeans. Portuguese traders sailing

Map 17.3 Tokugawa Japan. This map shows the Japanese islands during the long era of the Tokugawa Shogunate. Key cities, including the shogun's capital of Edo (Tokyo), are shown.

 Where was the imperial court located?

A Japanese Castle. In imitation of European castle architecture, the Japanese perfected a new type of fortress-palace in the early seventeenth century. Strategically placed high on a hilltop, constructed of heavy stone with tiny windows, and fortified by numerous watchtowers and massive walls, these strongholds were impregnable to arrows and catapults. They served as a residence for the local daimyo, while the castle compound also housed his army and contained the seat of local government. Osaka Castle was built by Toyotomi Hideyoshi essentially as a massive stage set to proclaim his power and grandeur. In 1615, the powerful warlord Tokugawa Ieyasu seized the castle, and it remained in his family's control for nearly 250 years.

in a Chinese junk that may have been blown off course by a typhoon had landed on the islands in 1543. Within a few years, Portuguese ships were stopping at Japanese ports on a regular basis to take part in the regional trade between Japan, China, and Southeast Asia. The first Jesuit missionary, Francis Xavier (ZAY-vee-ur), arrived in 1549.

Initially, the visitors were welcomed. Although Japanese leaders were somewhat ambivalent about establishing relations with countries in the outside world, Japanese traders were active in the regional trade network, and when the Ming court sought to prohibit all maritime trade in the 1530s, Japanese merchants countered by engaging in piracy or smuggling along the Chinese coast, despite efforts by leaders in both countries to stop them. Some ventured even farther afield, establishing their presence at trading ports throughout Southeast Asia, where they quickly earned the reputation as ferocious competitors.

The arrival of the Europeans added a new dimension to the equation. The curious Japanese (the Japanese were "very desirous of knowledge," said Francis Xavier) were fascinated by tobacco, clocks, spectacles, and other European goods, and local daimyo were especially interested in purchasing all types of European weapons and armaments. Oda Nobunaga and Toyotomi Hideyoshi found the new firearms helpful in defeating their enemies and unifying the islands. The effect on Japanese military architecture was particularly striking as local lords began to erect castles on the European model. Many of these castles, such as Hideyoshi's castle at Osaka, still exist today (see illustration, "A Japanese Castle,").

The missionaries also had some success. Though confused by misleading translations of sacred concepts in both cultures (Francis Xavier was notoriously poor at learning foreign languages), they converted a number of local daimyo, some of whom may have been motivated in part by the desire for commercial profits. By the end of the sixteenth century, thousands of Japanese in the southernmost islands of Kyushu and Shikoku had become Christians. One converted daimyo ceded the superb natural harbor of the modern city of Nagasaki (nah-gah-SAH-kee) to the Society of Jesus, which proceeded to use

The Japanese Bridge at Hoi An. Europeans were not the only people who sailed from from native shores in the pursuit of commercial profits during the Age of Exploration. Even prior to the arrival of the first Portuguese fleets in East Asian waters, merchants from all over the region had established a vigorous trading network stretching from Japan into the Indian Ocean. Among the active participants were the Japanese. Shown here is a bridge erected in the port city of Hoi An on the central coast of Vietnam. The bridge spanned a creek entering the harbor and separated the Japanese section of town from other neighborhoods inhabited by merchants from other countries. Japanese merchants shipped a variety of tropical goods from the area, as well as local porcelain.

TOYOTOMI HIDEYOSHI EXPELS THE MISSIONARIES

Religion & Philosophy — **WHEN CHRISTIAN MISSIONARIES** in sixteenth-century Japan began to interfere in local politics and criticize traditional religious practices, Toyotomi Hideyoshi issued an edict calling for their expulsion. In this letter to the Portuguese viceroy in Asia, Hideyoshi explains his decision. Note his conviction that the followers of the Buddha, Confucius, and Shinto all believe in the same God and his criticism of Christianity for rejecting all other faiths.

Toyotomi Hideyoshi, Letter to the Viceroy of the Indies

Ours is the land of the Gods, and God is mind. Everything in nature comes into existence because of mind. Without God there can be no spirituality. Without God there can be no way. God rules in times of prosperity as in times of decline. God is positive and negative and unfathomable. Thus, God is the root and source of all existence. This God is spoken of by Buddhism in India, Confucianism in China, and Shinto in Japan. To know Shinto is to know Buddhism as well as Confucianism.

As long as man lives in this world, Humanity will be a basic principle. Were it not for Humanity and Righteousness, the sovereign would not be a sovereign, nor a minister of a state a minister. It is through the practice of Humanity and Righteousness that the foundations of our relationships between sovereign and minister, parent and child, and husband and wife are established. If you are interested in the profound philosophy of God and Buddha, request an explanation and it will be given to you. In your land one doctrine is taught to the exclusion of others, and you are not yet informed of the [Confucian] philosophy of Humanity and Righteousness. Thus, there is no respect for God and Buddha and no distinction between sovereign and ministers. Through heresies you intend to destroy the righteous law. Hereafter, do not expound, in ignorance of right and wrong, unreasonable and wanton doctrines. A few years ago the so-called Fathers came to my country seeking to bewitch our men and women, both of the laity and clergy. At that time punishment was administered to them, and it will be repeated if they should return to our domain to propagate their faith. It will not matter what sect or denomination they represent—they shall be destroyed. It will then be too late to repent. If you entertain any desire of establishing amity with this land, the seas have been rid of the pirate menace, and merchants are permitted to come and go. Remember this.

 What reason did Hideyoshi give for prohibiting the practice of Christianity in Japan? How did his religious beliefs, as expressed in this document, differ from those of other religions like Christianity and Islam?

Source: From *Sources of Japanese Tradition*, Vol. 1, pgs. 316–317, by Ryusaku Tsunoda, William Theodore de Bary, and Donald Keene. Copyright © 1958 Columbia University Press. Reprinted with permission of the publisher.

the new settlement for both missionary and trading purposes. But papal claims to the loyalty of all Japanese Christians and the European habit of intervening in local politics soon began to arouse suspicion in official circles. Missionaries added to the problem by deliberately destroying local idols and shrines and turning some temples into Christian schools or churches.

Expulsion of the Christians Inevitably, the local authorities reacted. In 1587, Toyotomi Hideyoshi issued an edict prohibiting further Christian activities within his domains. Japan, he declared, was "the land of the Gods," and the destruction of shrines by the foreigners was "something unheard of in previous ages." To "corrupt and stir up the lower classes" to commit such sacrileges, he declared, was "outrageous."[9] The parties responsible (the Jesuits) were ordered to leave the country within twenty days. Hideyoshi was careful to distinguish missionary from trading activities, however, and merchants were permitted to continue their operations (see "Toyotomi Hideyoshi Expels the Missionaries").

The Jesuits protested the expulsion, and eventually Hideyoshi relented, permitting them to continue proselytizing as long as they were discreet. But he refused to repeal the edicts, and when the aggressive activities of newly arrived Spanish Franciscans aroused his ire, he ordered the execution of nine missionaries and a number of their Japanese converts. When the missionaries continued to interfere in local politics (some even tried to incite the daimyo in the southern islands against the shogunate government in Edo), Tokugawa Ieyasu completed the process by ordering the eviction of all missionaries in 1612. The persecution of Japanese Christians intensified, leading to an abortive revolt by Christian peasants on the island of Kyushu in 1637, which was bloodily suppressed.

At first, Japanese authorities hoped to maintain commercial relations with European countries even while suppressing the Western religion, but eventually they decided to regulate foreign trade more closely and closed the two major foreign factories on the island of Hirado (heh-RAH-doh) and at Nagasaki. The sole remaining opening to the West was at the island of Deshima (deh-SHEE-muh *or* den-JEE-muh) in Nagasaki harbor, where in 1609 a small Dutch community was permitted to engage in limited trade with Japan (the Dutch, unlike the Portuguese and the Spanish, had not allowed missionary activities to interfere with their commercial interests). Dutch ships were permitted to dock at Nagasaki harbor only once a year and, after close inspection, were allowed to remain for two or three months. Nor were the Japanese free to engage in foreign trade, as the *bakufu* (buh-KOO foo *or* bah KOO fuh)—the central government—sought to restrict the ability of local authorities

Deshima: A Dutch Enclave in Nagasaki, Japan. Shown here is a model of what was once a Dutch enclave on a small island in Nagasaki harbor, in southern Japan. As the photograph indicates, conditions on the island were quite confining, and the Dutch physician Engelbert Kaempfer complained that he and his countrymen were forced to live in "almost perpetual imprisonment." But the true importance of Deshima was its capacity to serve as a conduit for the importation of manuals about Western technology into Japan. Under encouragement from the Tokugawa Shogunate, Japanese officials assiduously absorbed such information, which would serve them in good stead when contacts with the outside world resumed in the nineteenth century.

to carry out commercial transactions with foreign merchants. Skittish about maintaining official contacts with European nations because of their tendency to interfere in Japanese domestic affairs, shogunate officials were willing to approve a limited amount of trade with European merchants, but resisted efforts to lure them into the establishment of formal diplomatic relations with European governments. A small amount of commerce took place with China and other parts of Asia, but Japanese subjects of the shogunate were forbidden to leave the country on penalty of death.

17–3c The Tokugawa "Great Peace"

Once in power, the Tokugawa attempted to strengthen the system that had governed Japan for more than three hundred years. They followed precedent in ruling through the *bakufu*, composed now of a coalition of daimyo, and a council of elders. But the system was more centralized than it had been previously. Now the shogunate government played a dual role. It set national policy on behalf of the emperor in Kyoto while simultaneously governing the shogun's own domain, which included about one-quarter of the national territory as well as the three great cities of Edo, Kyoto, and Osaka. As before, the state was divided into separate territories, called domains (*han*), which were ruled by a total of about 250 individual daimyo lords. The daimyo themselves were divided into two types: the *fudai* (FOO-dy) **daimyo** (inside daimyo), who were mostly small daimyo that were directly subordinate to the shogunate, and the *tozama* (toh-ZAH-mah) **daimyo** (outside daimyo), who were larger, more independent lords that

were usually more distant from the center of shogunate power in Edo.

Daimyo and Samurai In theory, the daimyo were essentially autonomous, since they were able to support themselves from taxes on their lands (the shogunate received its own revenues from its extensive landholdings). In actuality, the shogunate was able to guarantee daimyo loyalties by compelling daimyo lords to maintain two residences, one in their own domains and the other at Edo, and to leave their families in Edo as hostages for the daimyo's good behavior. Keeping up two residences also placed the Japanese nobility in a difficult economic position. Some were able to defray the high costs by concentrating on cash crops such as sugar, fish, and forestry products, but most were rice producers, and their revenues remained roughly the same throughout the period. The daimyo were also able to protect their economic interests by depriving their samurai retainers of their proprietary rights over the land and transforming them into salaried officials. The fief thus became a stipend, and the personal relationship between the daimyo and his retainers gradually gave way to a bureaucratic authority.

The Tokugawa also tinkered with the social system by limiting the size of the samurai class and reclassifying samurai who supported themselves by tilling the land as commoners. In fact, with the long period of peace brought about by Tokugawa rule, the samurai gradually ceased to be a warrior class and were required to live in the castle towns. As a gesture to their glorious past, samurai were still permitted to wear their two swords, and a rigid separation was maintained between persons of samurai status and the nonaristocratic segment of the population. The Jesuit missionary Francis Xavier observed that "on no account would a poverty-stricken gentleman marry with someone outside the gentry, even if he were given great sums to do so."[10]

Seeds of Capitalism The long period of peace under the Tokugawa Shogunate made possible a dramatic rise in commerce and manufacturing, especially in the growing cities. By the mid-eighteenth century, Edo, with a population of more than one million, was one of the largest cities in the world. The growth of trade and industry was stimulated by a rising standard of living—driven in part by technological advances in agriculture and an expansion of arable land—and the voracious appetites of the aristocrats for new products. The daimyo's need for income also contributed as many of them began to promote the sale of local goods from their domains, such as textiles, forestry products, sugar, and sake (SAH-kee) (fermented rice wine).

Most of this commercial expansion took place in the major cities and the castle towns, where the merchants and artisans lived along with the samurai, who were clustered in neighborhoods surrounding the daimyo's castle. Banking flourished, and paper money became the normal medium of exchange in commercial transactions. Merchants formed guilds not only to control market conditions but also to facilitate government oversight and the collection of taxes. Under the benign, if somewhat contemptuous, supervision of Japan's noble rulers, a Japanese merchant class gradually began to emerge from the shadows to play a significant role in the life of the Japanese nation. Some historians view the Tokugawa era as the first stage in the rise of an indigenous form of capitalism, based loosely on the Western model.

Eventually, the increased pace of industrial activity spread beyond the cities into rural areas. As in Great Britain, cotton was a major factor. Cotton had been introduced to China during the Song Dynasty and had spread to Korea and Japan shortly thereafter. Traditionally, however, cotton cloth had been too expensive for the common people, who instead wore clothing made of hemp. Imports increased during the sixteenth century, however, when cotton cloth began to be used for uniforms, matchlock fuses, and sails. Eventually, technological advances reduced the cost, and specialized communities for producing cotton cloth began to appear in the countryside and were gradually transformed into towns. By the eighteenth century, cotton had firmly replaced hemp as the cloth of choice for most Japanese.

The expansion of trade was facilitated by the construction of a new and expanded system of roads and bridges ordered by Tokugawa Ieyasu himself. The main trunk road—known as the Tokaido, or "East Coast Highway"—connected the imperial city in Kyoto with the administrative capital of Edo, and fifty-three post stations were established along the route to provide travelers with food stalls and rest facilities to ease their journey to their destinations.

Not everyone benefited from the economic changes of the seventeenth and eighteenth centuries, however, notably the samurai, who were barred by tradition and prejudice from commercial activities. Although some profited from their transformation into a managerial class on the daimyo domains, most still relied on their revenues from rice lands, which were often insufficient to cover their rising expenses; consequently, they fell heavily into debt. Others were released from servitude to their lord and became "masterless samurai." Occasionally, these unemployed warriors—known as *ronin* (ROH-nihn), or "wave men"—revolted or plotted against the local authorities. In one episode, made famous in song and story as "The Forty-Seven *Ronin*," the masterless samurai of a local lord who had been forced to commit suicide by a shogunate official later assassinated the official in revenge. Although their act received wide popular acclaim, the *ronin* were later forced to take their own lives.

Land Problems The effects of economic developments on the rural population during the Tokugawa era are harder to estimate. Some farm families benefited by exploiting the growing demand for cash crops. But not all prospered. Most peasants continued to rely on rice cultivation and were whip-sawed between declining profits and rising costs and taxes (as daimyo expenses increased, land taxes often took up to 50 percent of

The Tokaido: Japan's East Coast Highway. This seventeenth-century handscroll by an anonymous artist shows the movement of goods along the Tokaido—the main trunk road stretching from the imperial city of Kyoto to the Shogunate's administration capital in Edo—on the east coast of Japan. As this section of the handscroll indicates, a number of post stations were established en route to provide accommodations to travelers along the route. In the nineteenth century, the famous Japanese artist Ando Hiroshige would immortalize these post stations with a series of colorful block prints.

William J. Duiker/Freer Gallery of Art, Smithsonian Institution, Washington, D.C.

CHRONOLOGY	**Japan and Korea During the Early Modern Era**
First phonetic alphabet in Korea	Fifteenth century
Portuguese merchants arrive in Japan	1543
Francis Xavier arrives in Japan	1549
Rule of Oda Nobunaga	1568–1582
Seizure of Kyoto	1568
Rule of Toyotomi Hideyoshi	1582–1598
Edict prohibiting Christianity in Japan	1587
Japan invades Korea	1592
Death of Hideyoshi and withdrawal of the Japanese army from Korea	1598
Rule of Tokugawa Ieyasu	1598–1616
Creation of Tokugawa Shogunate	1603
Dutch granted permission to trade at Nagasaki	1609
Order evicting Christian missionaries	1612
Korea declares fealty to China	1630s

the annual harvest). Many were forced to become tenants or to work as wage laborers on the farms of wealthy neighbors or in village industries. When rural conditions in some areas became desperate, peasant revolts erupted. According to one estimate, nearly seven thousand disturbances took place during the Tokugawa era. Peasant disturbances became a more or less routine means of protesting against rising taxes and official corruption or of demanding "benevolence" from the manor lord in times of natural disaster.

Some historians take issue with this grim picture and point out that Japanese peasants did not suffer the same level of hardship as was taking place among their counterparts in neighboring China. In the first place, an increase in the amount of land under cultivation, combined with improved agricultural technology, led to increased yields. Secondly, Japan experienced a relatively low rate of population growth during the Tokugawa era. Although the reasons for that phenomenon are not entirely clear, Honda Toshiaki (HAHN-duh toh-SHEE-ah-kee), a late-eighteenth-century demographer, ascribed the primary cause to a combination of late marriage, abortion, and infanticide. As he described the situation:

> Aware that if they have many children they will not have any property to leave them, [husbands and wives] confer and decide that rather than rear children who in later years will have great difficulty in making a decent living, it is better to take precautions before they are born and not add another mouth to feed. If they do have a child, they secretly destroy it, calling the process by the euphemism of "thinning out."[11]

17–3d Life in the Village

The changes that took place during the Tokugawa era had a major impact on the lives of ordinary Japanese. In some respects, the result was an increase in the power of the central government at the village level. The shogunate increasingly relied on Confucian maxims advocating obedience and hierarchy to enhance its authority with the general population. Decrees from the *bakufu* instructed the peasants on all aspects of their lives, including their eating habits and their behavior (see Opposing Viewpoints "Some Confucian Commandments," p. 500). At the same time, the increased power of the government led to more autonomy from the local daimyo for the peasants. Villages now had more control over their local affairs and were responsible to the central government as much as to the nearby manor lord, although land taxes were still paid to the daimyo.

At the same time, the Tokugawa era saw the emergence of the nuclear family (*ie*) as the basic unit in Japanese society. In previous times, Japanese peasants had few legal rights. Most were too poor to keep their conjugal family unit intact or to pass property on to their children. Many lived at the manorial residence or worked as servants in the households of more affluent villagers. Now, with farm income on the rise, the nuclear family took on the same form as in China, although without the joint family concept. The Japanese system of inheritance was based on primogeniture (pry-moh-JEN-ih-chur). Family property was passed on to the eldest son, although younger sons often received land from their parents to set up their own families after marriage.

The Role of Women Another result of the changes under the Tokugawa was that women were somewhat more restricted than they had been previously. The rights of females were especially restricted in the samurai class, where Confucian values were highly influential. Male heads of households had broad authority over property, marriage, and divorce; wives were expected to obey their husbands on pain of death. Males often took concubines or homosexual partners, while females were expected to remain chaste. The male offspring of samurai parents studied the Confucian classics in schools established by the daimyo, while females were reared at home, where only the fortunate might receive a rudimentary training in reading and writing Chinese characters. Some women, however, became accomplished poets and painters since, in aristocratic circles, female literacy was prized for enhancing the refinement, social graces, and moral virtue of the home. Under the Tokugawa, it was the obligation of the wife in elite families to reflect her husband's rank and status through a strict code of comportment and dress.

Women were similarly at a disadvantage among the common people. Marriages were arranged, and as in China, the new wife moved in with the family of her husband. A wife who did not meet the expectations of her spouse or his family was likely to be divorced. Still, gender relations were more egalitarian than among the nobility. Women were generally valued as childbearers and homemakers, and both sexes worked in the fields. Coeducational schools were established in villages and market towns, and about one-quarter of the students were female. Poor families, however, often put infant daughters to death or sold them into prostitution and the "floating world" of entertainment (see "The Literature of the New Middle Class," p. 501). During the late Tokugawa era, peasant women became

Some Confucian Commandments

Family & Society

ALTHOUGH THE QING DYNASTY WAS OF FOREIGN ORIGIN, its rulers found Confucian maxims convenient for maintaining the social order. In 1670, the great emperor Kangxi issued the Sacred Edict to popularize Confucian values among the common people. The edict was read publicly at periodic intervals in every village in China and set the standard for behavior throughout the empire. Like the Qing Dynasty in China, the Tokugawa shoguns attempted to keep their subjects in line with decrees that carefully prescribed all kinds of behavior. Yet a subtle difference in tone can be detected between these two documents. Whereas Kangxi's edict tended to encourage positive behavior, the decree of the Tokugawa Shogunate focused more on actions that were prohibited or discouraged.

Kangxi's Sacred Edict

1. Esteem most highly filial piety and brotherly submission, in order to give due importance to the social relations.
2. Behave with generosity toward your kindred, in order to illustrate harmony and benignity.
3. Show that you prize moderation and economy, in order to prevent the lavish waste of your means.
4. Extirpate strange principles, in order to exalt the correct doctrine.
5. Lecture on the laws, in order to warn the ignorant and obstinate.
6. Labor diligently at your proper callings, in order to stabilize the will of the people.
7. Instruct sons and younger brothers, in order to prevent them from doing what is wrong.
8. Put a stop to false accusations, in order to preserve the honest and good.
9. Fully remit your taxes, in order to avoid being pressed for payment.
10. Remove enmity and anger, in order to show the importance due to the person and life.

Maxims for Peasant Behavior in Tokugawa Japan

1. Young people are forbidden to congregate in great numbers.
2. Entertainments unsuited to peasants, such as playing the samisen or reciting ballad dramas, are forbidden.
3. Staging sumo matches is forbidden for the next five years.
4. The edict on frugality issued by the han at the end of last year must be observed.
5. If a person has to leave the village for business or pleasure, that person must return by ten at night.
6. Father and son are forbidden to stay overnight at another person's house. An exception is to be made if it is to nurse a sick person.
7. Corvée [obligatory labor] assigned by the han must be performed faithfully.
8. Children who practice filial piety must be rewarded.
9. One must never get drunk and cause trouble for others.
10. Peasants who neglect farm work and cultivate their paddies and upland fields in a slovenly and careless fashion must be punished.
11. Fights and quarrels are forbidden in the village.
12. The deteriorating customs and morals of the village must be rectified.
13. Peasants who are suffering from poverty must be identified and helped.
14. This village has a proud history compared to other villages, but in recent years bad times have come upon us. Everyone must rise at six in the morning, cut grass, and work hard to revitalize the village.
15. The punishments to be meted out to violators of the village code and gifts to be awarded the deserving are to be decided during the last assembly meeting of the year.

 In what ways did Kangxi's set of commandments conform to the principles of State Confucianism? How do Kangxi's standards compare with those applied in Japan?

Sources: From *Popular Culture in Late Imperial China* by David Johnson et al. Copyright © 1985 The Regents of the University of California. From Chi Nakane and Oishi Shinsabura, *Tokugawa Japan: The Social and Economic Antecedents of Modern Japan* (Japan, University of Tokyo, 1990), pp. 51–52. Translated by Conrad Totman. Copyright 1992 by Columbia University Press.

more outspoken and active in social protests and in some cases played a major role in provoking demonstrations against government exactions or exploitation by landlords or merchants.

Such attitudes toward women operated within the context of the increasingly rigid stratification of Japanese society. Deeply conservative in their social policies, the Tokugawa rulers established strict legal distinctions between the four main classes in Japan (warriors, artisans, peasants, and merchants).

Intermarriage between classes was forbidden in theory, although sometimes the prohibitions were ignored in practice. Below these classes were Japan's outcasts, the *eta* (AY-tuh). Formerly, they were permitted to escape their status, at least in theory. The Tokugawa made their status hereditary and enacted severe discriminatory laws against them, regulating their place of residence, their dress, and even their hairstyles.

17-3e Tokugawa Culture

Under the Tokugawa, the tensions between the old society and the emerging new one were starkly reflected in the arena of culture. On the one hand, the classical culture, influenced by Confucian themes, Buddhist quietism, and the samurai warrior tradition, continued to flourish under the patronage of the shogunate. On the other, a vital new set of cultural values began to appear, especially in the cities. This innovative era witnessed the rise of mass entertainment and a popular literature written by and for the townspeople. With the development of wood-block printing in the early seventeenth century, literature became available to the common people, literacy levels rose, and lending libraries increased the accessibility of printed works. In contrast to the previous mood of doom and gloom, the new prose was cheerful and even frivolous, its primary aim being to divert and amuse.

The Literature of the New Middle Class The best examples of this new urban fiction are the works of Saikaku (Sy-KAH-koo) (1642–1693), considered one of Japan's finest novelists. Saikaku's greatest novel, *Five Women Who Loved Love*, relates the amorous exploits of five women of the merchant class. Based partly on real-life experiences, it broke from the Confucian ethic that stressed a wife's fidelity to her husband and portrayed women who were willing to die for love—and all but one eventually did. Despite the tragic circumstances, the tone of the novel is upbeat and sometimes comic, and the author's wry comments prevent the reader from becoming emotionally involved with the heroines' misfortunes. In addition to heterosexual novels for the merchant class, Saikaku also wrote of homosexual liaisons among the samurai.

In the theater, the rise of Kabuki (kuh-BOO-kee) threatened the long dominance of the *No* (NOH) play, replacing the somewhat restrained and elegant thematic and stylistic approach of the classical drama with a new emphasis on violence, music, and dramatic gestures. Significantly, the new drama emerged not from the rarefied world of the court but from the new world of entertainment and amusement (see Comparative Illustration "Popular Culture: East and West," p. 502). Its very commercial success, however, led to difficulties with the government, which periodically attempted to restrict or even suppress it. Early Kabuki was often performed by prostitutes, and shogunate officials, fearing that such activities could have a corrupting effect on the nation's morals, prohibited women from appearing on the stage; at the same time, they attempted to create a new professional class of male actors to impersonate female characters on stage. The decree had a mixed effect, however, because it encouraged homosexual activities, which had been popular among the samurai and in Buddhist monasteries since medieval times. Yet the use of male actors also promoted a greater emphasis on physical activities such as acrobatics and swordplay and furthered the evolution of Kabuki into a mature dramatic art.

In contrast to the popular literature of the Tokugawa period, poetry persevered in its more serious tradition. Although linked verse, so popular in the fourteenth and fifteenth centuries, found a more lighthearted expression in the sixteenth century, the most exquisite poetry was produced in the seventeenth century by the greatest of all Japanese poets, Basho (BAH-shoh) (1644–1694). He was concerned with the search for the meaning of existence and the poetic expression of his experience. Basho's genius lies in his sudden juxtaposition of a general or eternal condition with an immediate perception, a spark that instantly reveals a moment of truth. Thanks to his love of Daoism and Zen Buddhism, Basho found answers to his quest for the meaning of life in nature, and his poems are grounded in seasonal imagery. The following are among his most famous poems:

> The ancient pond
> A frog leaps in
> The sound of the water.
> On the withered branch
> A crow has alighted—
> The end of autumn.

His last poem, dictated to a disciple only three days before his death, succinctly expressed his frustration with the unfinished business of life:

> On a journey, ailing—
> my dreams roam about
> on a withered moor.

Like all great artists, Basho made his poems seem effortless and simple. He speaks directly to everyone, everywhere.

Tokugawa Art The arts also reflected the dynamism and changes in Japanese culture under the Tokugawa regime. The shogun's order that all daimyo and their families live every other year in Edo set off a burst of building as provincial rulers competed to erect the most magnificent mansion. Furthermore, the shoguns themselves constructed splendid castles adorned with sumptuous, almost ostentatious décor and furnishings. And the prosperity of the newly rising merchant class added fuel to the fire. Japanese paintings, architecture, textiles, and ceramics all flourished during this affluent era.

Court painters filled magnificent multipaneled screens with gold foil, which was also used to cover walls and even ceilings. This lavish use of gold foil mirrored the grandeur of the new Japanese rulers but also served a practical purpose: it reflected light in the dark castle rooms, where windows were kept small for defensive purposes. In contrast to the almost gaudy splendors of court painting, however, some Japanese artists of the late sixteenth century returned to the tradition of black ink wash. No longer copying the Chinese, these masterpieces expressed Japanese themes and techniques. In *Pine Forest* by Tohaku (toh-HAH-koo), a pair of six-panel screens depicting pine trees, 85 percent of the paper is left blank, suggesting mist and the quiet of an autumn dawn.

Although Japan was isolated from the Western world during much of the Tokugawa era, Japanese art was enriched by ideas from other cultures. Japanese pottery makers borrowed both techniques and designs from Korea to produce handsome ceramics. The passion for "Dutch learning"

COMPARATIVE ILLUSTRATION

Popular Culture: East and West. By the seventeenth century, a popular culture distinct from the elite culture of the nobility was beginning to emerge in the urban worlds of both the East and the West. Image A shows a festival scene from the pleasure district of Kyoto known as the Gion. Spectators on a balcony are enjoying a colorful parade of floats and costumed performers. The festival originated as a celebration of the passing of a deadly epidemic in medieval Japan. Image B shows is a scene from the celebration of Carnival on the Piazza Sante Croce in Florence, Italy. Carnival was a period of festivities before Lent, celebrated primarily in Roman Catholic countries. It became an occasion for indulgence in food, drink, games, and practical jokes as a prelude to the austerity of the forty-day Lenten season from Ash Wednesday to Easter.

Q *Do festivals such as these still exist in our own day? What purpose might they serve?*

A

Newark Museum/Art Resource, NY

B

Scala/Art Resource, NY

Arrival of the Portuguese at Nagasaki. Portuguese traders, dressed in billowing pantaloons and broad-brimmed hats, landed in Japan by accident in 1543. In a few years, they were arriving regularly, taking part in a regional trade network involving Japan, China, and Southeast Asia. In these panels done in black lacquer and gold leaf, we see a late-sixteenth-century Japanese interpretation of the landing of Portuguese merchants at Nagasaki. Normally, Japanese screens are read from right to left, but this one is read left to right. Having arrived by ship, the Portuguese proceed in splendor to the Jesuit priests waiting in a church on the right.

inspired Japanese to study Western medicine, astronomy, and languages and also led to experimentation with oil painting and Western ideas of perspective and the interplay of light and dark. Some painters depicted the "southern barbarians," with their strange ships and costumes, large noses, and plumed hats. Europeans desired Japanese lacquerware and metalwork, inlaid with ivory and mother-of-pearl, and especially the ceramics, which were now as highly prized as those of the Chinese.

Perhaps the most famous of all Japanese art of the Tokugawa era is the woodblock print. Genre painting, or representations of daily life, began in the sixteenth century and found its new mass-produced form in the eighteenth-century woodblock print. The now literate mercantile class was eager for illustrated texts of the amusing and bawdy tales that had circulated in oral tradition. At first, these prints were done in black and white, but later they included vibrant colors. The self-confidence of the age is dramatically captured in these prints, which represent a collective self-portrait of the late Tokugawa urban classes. Some prints depict entire city blocks filled with people, trades, and festivals, while others show the interiors of houses; thus, they provide us with excellent visual documentation of the times. Others portray the "floating world" of the entertainment quarter, with scenes of carefree revelers enjoying the pleasures of life.

One of the most renowned of the numerous block-print artists was Utamaro (OO-tah-mah-roh) (1754–1806), who painted erotic and sardonic women in everyday poses, such as walking down the street, cooking, or drying their bodies

after a bath. Hokusai (HOH-kuh-sy) (1760–1849) was famous for *Thirty-Six Views of Mount Fuji*, a new and bold interpretation of the Japanese landscape. Finally, Ando Hiroshige (AHN-doh hee-roh-SHEE-gay) (1797–1858) developed the genre of the travelogue print in his *Fifty-Three Stations of the Tokaido Road*, which presented ordinary scenes of daily life, both in the country and in the cities, all enveloped in a lyrical, quiet mood.

Why did a new popular culture begin to appear in Tokugawa Japan while traditional values continued to prevail in neighboring China? One factor was the rapid growth of the cities as the main point of convergence for all the dynamic forces taking place in Japanese society. But other factors may have been at work as well. Despite the patent efforts of the Tokugawa rulers to promote traditional Confucian values, Confucian doctrine had historically occupied a relatively weak position in Japanese society. In China, the scholar-gentry class served as the defenders and propagators of traditional orthodoxy, but the samurai, who were steeped in warrior values and had little exposure to Confucian learning, did not play a similar role in Japan. Tokugawa policies also contributed. Whereas the scholar-gentry class in Qing China continued to reside in the villages, serving as members of the local council or as instructors in local schools, the samurai class in Japan was deliberately isolated from the remainder of the population by government fiat and class privilege. The result was an ideological and cultural vacuum that would eventually be filled by the growing population of merchants and artisans in the major cities.

Hokusai: From *Thirty-Six Views of Mount Fuji*. Along with Ando Hiroshige, Matsushika Hokusai became enormously popular in nineteenth-century Japan because of his colorful block prints portraying the people and the geography of the country. His series entitled *Thirty-Six Views of Mount Fuji* were among his admired works, not least because of the symbolic importance that symmetrical mount in Japanese culture. Long considered to be the home of the gods, Fuji became the focus of a sect of Shintoism, and even today thousands of Japanese make a pilgrimage to the peak of the mountain to view the sunrise over the eastern sea. The print shown here is entitled *Tama River in Musashi Province*.

17–4 KOREA AND VIETNAM

 Focus Questions: To what degree did developments in Korea during this period reflect conditions in China and Japan? What were the unique aspects of Vietnamese civilization?

On the fringes of the East Asian mainland, two of China's close neighbors sought to preserve their fragile independence from the expansionistic tendencies of the powerful Ming and Qing Dynasties.

17–4a Korea: In a Dangerous Neighborhood

While Japan under the Tokugawa Shogunate moved steadily out from the shadows of the Chinese Empire by creating a unique society with its own special characteristics, the Choson Dynasty in Korea continued to pattern itself, at least on the surface, after the Chinese model. The dynasty had been founded by the military commander Yi Song Gye (YEE song yee) in the late fourteenth century and immediately set out to establish close political and cultural relations with the Ming Dynasty. From their new capital at Seoul (SOHL), located on the Han

(HAHN) River in the center of the peninsula, the Choson rulers accepted a tributary relationship with their powerful neighbor and engaged in the wholesale adoption of Chinese institutions and values. As in China, the civil service examinations tested candidates on their knowledge of the Confucian classics, and success was viewed as an essential step toward upward mobility.

There were differences, however. As in Japan, the dynasty continued to restrict entry into the bureaucracy to members of the aristocratic class, known in Korea as the *yangban* (YAHNG-ban) (or "two groups," civilian and military). At the same time, the peasantry remained in serflike conditions, working on government estates or on the manor holdings of the landed elite. A class of slaves, called *chonmin* (CHAWN-min), labored on government plantations or served in certain occupations, such as butchers and entertainers, considered beneath the dignity of other groups in the population.

Eventually, Korean society began to show signs of independence from Chinese orthodoxy. In the fifteenth century, a phonetic alphabet for writing the Korean spoken language (*hangul*) was devised. Although it was initially held in contempt by the elites and used primarily as a teaching device, eventually it became the medium for private correspondence and the publishing of fiction for a popular audience. At the same time, changes were taking place in the economy, where rising agricultural production contributed to a population increase and the appearance of a small urban industrial and commercial sector, and in society, where the long domination of the *yangban* class began to weaken. As their numbers increased and their power and influence declined, some *yangban* became merchants or even moved into the ranks of the peasantry, further blurring the distinction between the aristocratic class and the common people.

Meanwhile, the Choson Dynasty faced continual challenges to its independence from its neighbors. Throughout much of the sixteenth century, the main threat came from the north, where Manchu forces harassed Korean lands just south of the Yalu (YAH-loo) River (see Map 17.3, Section 17-3a, p. 494). By the 1580s, however, the larger threat came from the east in the form of a newly united Japan. During much of the sixteenth century, leading Japanese daimyo had been involved in a protracted civil war, as Oda Nobunaga, Toyotomi Hideyoshi, and Tokugawa Ieyasu strove to solidify their control over the islands. Of the three, only Hideyoshi lusted for an empire beyond the seas. Although born to a commoner family, he harbored visions of grandeur and in the late 1580s announced plans to attack the Ming Empire. When the Korean king Sonjo (SOHN-joe) (1567–1608) refused Hideyoshi's offer of an alliance, in 1592 the latter launched an invasion of the Korean peninsula.

At first the campaign went well, and Japanese forces, wreaking death and devastation throughout the countryside, advanced as far as the Korean capital at Seoul. But eventually the Koreans, under the inspired leadership of the military commander Yi Sunshin (YEE-soon-SHIN) (1545–1598), who designed fast but heavily armed ships that could destroy the more cumbersome landing craft of the invading forces, managed to repel the attack and safeguard their independence. The respite was brief, however. By the 1630s, a new threat from the Manchus had emerged from across the northern border. A Manchu force invaded northern Korea in the 1630s and eventually compelled the Choson Dynasty to promise allegiance to the new imperial government in Beijing. Korea was relatively untouched by the arrival of European merchants and missionaries, although information about Christianity was brought to the peninsula by Koreans returning from tribute missions to China, and a small Catholic community was established there in the late eighteenth century.

17–4b Vietnam: The Perils of Empire

Vietnam—or Dai Viet (dy VEE-et), as it was known at the time—managed to avoid the fate of many of its neighbors during the seventeenth and eighteenth centuries. Isolated from the major maritime routes that passed through the region, the country was only peripherally involved in the spice trade with the West and did not suffer the humiliation of losing territory to European colonial powers. In fact, Dai Viet had followed an imperialist path of its own, defeating the trading state of Champa to the south in 1471 and imposing its suzerainty over the rump of the old Angkor empire—today known as Cambodia. The state of Dai Viet then extended from the Chinese border to the shores of the Gulf of Siam.

But expansion undermined the cultural integrity of traditional Vietnamese society, as those migrants who settled in the marshy Mekong River delta developed a "frontier spirit" far removed from the communal values long practiced in the old national heartland of the Red River Valley. By the seventeenth century, a civil war had split Dai Viet into two squabbling territories in the north and south, providing European powers with the opportunity to meddle in the country's internal affairs to their own benefit. In 1802, with the assistance of a French adventurer long active in the region, a member of the southern royal family managed to reunite the country under the new Nguyen (NGWEN) dynasty, which lasted until 1945.

To placate China, the country was renamed Vietnam (South Viet), and the new imperial capital was placed in the city of Hué (HWAY), a small river port roughly equidistant from the two rich river valleys that provided the country with its chief sustenance, wet rice. The founder of the new dynasty, who took the reign title of Gia Long, fended off French efforts to promote Christianity among his subjects and sought to promote traditional Confucian values among an increasingly diverse population.

CHAPTER SUMMARY

When the first European ships began to appear off the coasts of China and Japan in the course of the sixteenth century, the new arrivals were welcomed, if only as curiosities. Eventually, several European nations established trade relations with the nations in the region, and Christian missionaries of various religious orders were active in both countries and in Korea and Vietnam as well. But their welcome was short-lived. Europeans eventually began to be perceived as detrimental to law and order, and during the seventeenth century, the majority of the foreign merchants and missionaries were evicted from all four countries. From that time until the beginning of the nineteenth century, the nations of East Asia were relatively little affected by events taking place beyond their borders.

That fact led many observers to assume that the societies of East Asia were essentially

stagnant, characterized by agrarian institutions and values reminiscent of those of the feudal era in Europe. As we have seen, however, that picture is misleading, for conditions in the region, and especially in China and Japan, were evolving and by the early nineteenth century were quite different from what they had been three centuries earlier.

Ironically, these changes were especially marked in Tokugawa Japan, a seemingly "closed" country, but one where traditional classes and institutions were under increasing strain, not only from the emergence of a new merchant class but also from the centralizing tendencies of the powerful Tokugawa Shogunate. On the mainland as well, the popular image in the West of a "changeless China" was increasingly divorced from reality, as social and economic conditions were marked by a growing complexity, giving birth to tensions that by the middle of the nineteenth century would strain the Qing Dynasty to its very core.

By the beginning of the nineteenth century, then, powerful tensions, reflecting a growing gap between the ideal and reality, were at work in Chinese and Japanese society. Under these conditions, both countries were soon forced to face a new challenge from the aggressive power of an industrializing Europe.

CHAPTER TIMELINE

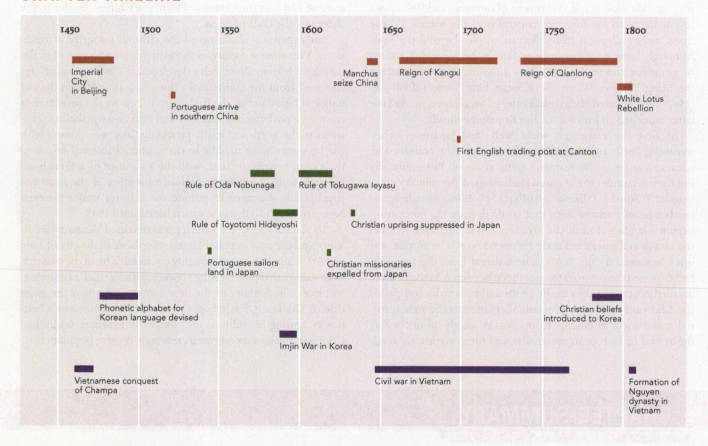

| 1450 | 1500 | 1550 | 1600 | 1650 | 1700 | 1750 | 1800 |

Imperial City in Beijing

Portuguese arrive in southern China

Manchus seize China

Reign of Kangxi

Reign of Qianlong

White Lotus Rebellion

First English trading post at Canton

Rule of Oda Nobunaga

Rule of Tokugawa Ieyasu

Rule of Toyotomi Hideyoshi

Christian uprising suppressed in Japan

Portuguese sailors land in Japan

Christian missionaries expelled from Japan

Phonetic alphabet for Korean language devised

Christian beliefs introduced to Korea

Imjin War in Korea

Vietnamese conquest of Champa

Civil war in Vietnam

Formation of Nguyen dynasty in Vietnam

CHAPTER REVIEW

Upon Reflection

Q What factors at the end of the eighteenth century might have served to promote or to impede China's transition to an advanced industrial and market economy? How did these factors compare with those facing Great Britain at the end of the eighteenth century?

Q To what degree were conditions in Tokugawa Japan conducive to the launching of an Industrial Revolution on the European model?

Q What was the nature of Sino-Korean relations during the early modern era? How did they compare with Chinese policies toward Vietnam?

Key Terms

banners (p. 482)

dyarchy (p. 483)

kowtow (p. 484)

fudai daimyo (p. 497)

tozama daimyo (p. 497)

ronin (p. 498)

yangban (p. 504)

Chapter Notes

1. J. D. Spence, *Emperor of China: Self-Portrait of K'ang Hsi* (New York, 1974), pp. 143–144.

2. Quoted in R. Strassberg, *The World of K'ang Shang-jen: A Man of Letters in Early Ch'ing China* (New York, 1983), p. 275.

3. Quoted in F. Wakeman Jr., *The Great Enterprise: The Manchu Reconstruction of Imperial Order in Seventeenth-Century China* (Berkeley, Calif., 1985), p. 16.

4. L. Struve, *The Southern Ming, 1644–1662* (New Haven, Conn., 1984), p. 61.

5. J. L. Cranmer-Byng, *An Embassy to China: Lord Macartney's Journal, 1793–1794* (London, 1912), p. 340.

6. Quoted in D. J. Boorstin, *The Discoverers: A History of Man's Search to Know His World and Himself* (New York, 1983), p. 63.

7. Quoted in C. R. Boxer, ed., *South China in the Sixteenth Century* (London, 1953), p. 265.

8. Quoted in C. Nakane and S. Oishi, eds., *Tokugawa Japan* (Tokyo, 1990), p. 14.

9. Quoted in J. Elisonas, "Christianity and the Daimyo," in J. W. Hall, ed., *The Cambridge History of Japan*, vol. 4 (Cambridge, 1991), p. 360.

10. Quoted in J. H. Parry, *European Reconnaissance: Selected Documents* (New York, 1968), p. 144.

11. Quoted in D. Keene, *The Japanese Discovery of Europe, 1720–1830*, rev. ed. (Stanford, Calif., 1969), p. 114.

 **MINDTAP** From Cengage

MindTap® is a fully online personalized learning experience built upon Cengage Learning content. MindTap® combines student learning tools—readings, multimedia, activities, and assessments—into a singular Learning Path that guides students through the course and helps students develop the critical thinking, analysis, and communication skills that are essential to academic and professional success.

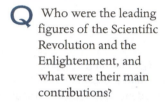

CHAPTER 18

THE WEST ON THE EVE OF A NEW WORLD ORDER

Chapter Outline and Focus Questions

18–1 *Toward a New Heaven and a New Earth: An Intellectual Revolution in the West*

Q Who were the leading figures of the Scientific Revolution and the Enlightenment, and what were their main contributions?

18–2 *Economic Changes and the Social Order*

Q What changes occurred in the European economy in the eighteenth century, and to what degree were these changes reflected in social patterns?

18–3 *Colonial Empires and Revolution in the Americas*

Q What colonies did the British and French establish in the Americas, and how did their methods of administering their colonies differ?

18–4 *Toward a New Political Order*

Q What do historians mean by the term *enlightened absolutism*, and to what degree did eighteenth-century Prussia, Austria, and Russia exhibit its characteristics?

18–5 *The French Revolution*

Q What were the causes, the main events, and the results of the French Revolution?

18–6 *The Age of Napoleon*

Q Which aspects of the French Revolution did Napoleon preserve, and which did he destroy?

The crowd in Paris after the storming of the Bastille on July 14th 1789. INTERFOTO/Alamy

Critical Thinking

Q *In what ways were the American Revolution, the French Revolution, and the seventeenth-century English revolutions alike? In what ways were they different?*

Connections to Today

Q *What are the similarities and differences between the French Revolution and contemporary revolutions?*

IN PARIS ON THE MORNING of July 14, 1789, a mob of eight thousand men and women in search of weapons streamed toward the Bastille (bass-STEEL), a royal armory filled with arms and ammunition. The Bastille was also a state prison, and although it held only seven prisoners at the time, in the eyes of these angry Parisians, it was a glaring symbol of the government's despotic policies. The armory was defended by the marquis de Launay (mar-KEE duh loh-NAY) and a small garrison of 114 men. The attack began in earnest in the early afternoon, and after three hours of fighting, de Launay and the garrison surrendered. Angered by the loss of ninety-eight of their members, the victorious mob beat de Launay to death, cut off his head, and carried it aloft in triumph through the streets. When King Louis XVI was told the news of the fall of the Bastille by the duc de La Rochefoucauld-Liancourt (dook duh lah-RUSH-foo-koh-lee-ahn-KOOR), he exclaimed, "Why, this is a revolt." "No, Sire," replied the duc. "It is a revolution."

The French Revolution of 1789 was a key factor in the emergence of a new world order. Historians have often considered the eighteenth century the final phase of an old Europe that would be forever changed by the violent upheaval and reordering of society associated with the French Revolution. Before the Revolution, the old order—still largely agrarian, dominated by kings and landed aristocrats, and grounded in privileges for nobles, clergy, towns, and provinces—seemed content to continue a basic pattern that had prevailed since medieval times. As the century drew to a close, however, a new intellectual ethos based on rationalism and secularism emerged, and demographic, economic, social, and political patterns were beginning to change in ways that proclaimed the arrival of a new and more modern order.

The French Revolution demolished the institutions of the old regime and established a new order based on individual rights, representative institutions, and a concept of loyalty to the nation rather than to the monarch. The revolutionary upheavals of the era, especially in France, gave rise to new liberal and national political ideals, summarized in the French revolutionary slogan "Liberty! Equality! Fraternity!" that transformed France and then spread to other European countries and the rest of the world.

18–1 TOWARD A NEW HEAVEN AND A NEW EARTH: AN INTELLECTUAL REVOLUTION IN THE WEST

 Focus Question: Who were the leading figures of the Scientific Revolution and the Enlightenment, and what were their main contributions?

In the seventeenth century, a group of scientists set the Western world on a new path known as the **Scientific Revolution**, which exposed Europeans to a new way of viewing the universe and their place in it. The Scientific Revolution affected only a small number of Europe's educated elite. But in the eighteenth century, this changed dramatically as a group of intellectuals popularized the ideas of the Scientific Revolution and used them to undertake a dramatic reexamination of all aspects of life. The widespread impact of these ideas on their society has caused historians ever since to call the eighteenth century in Europe the Age of Enlightenment.

18–1a The Scientific Revolution

The Scientific Revolution ultimately challenged conceptions and beliefs about the nature of the external world that had become dominant by the Late Middle Ages.

Toward a New Heaven: A Revolution in Astronomy The philosophers of the Middle Ages had used the ideas of Aristotle, Ptolemy (the greatest astronomer of antiquity, who lived in the second century CE), and Christianity to form the Ptolemaic (tahl-uh-MAY-ik) or **geocentric theory** of the universe. In this conception, the universe was seen as a series of concentric spheres with a fixed or motionless earth at its center. Composed of material substance, the earth was imperfect and constantly changing. The spheres that surrounded the earth were made of a crystalline, transparent substance and moved in circular orbits around the earth. The heavenly bodies, which in 1500 were believed to number ten, were pure orbs of light, embedded in the moving, concentric spheres. Working outward from the earth, the first eight spheres contained the moon, Mercury, Venus, the sun, Mars, Jupiter, Saturn, and the fixed stars. The ninth sphere imparted to the eighth sphere of the fixed stars its daily motion, while the tenth sphere was frequently described as the prime mover that moved itself and imparted motion to the other spheres. Beyond the tenth sphere was the Empyrean Heaven—the location of God and all the saved souls. Thus, God and the saved souls were at one end of the universe, and humans were at the center. They had power over the earth, but their real purpose was to achieve salvation.

Nicolaus Copernicus (NEE-koh-lowss kuh-PURR-nuh-kuss) (1473–1543), a native of Poland, was a mathematician who felt that Ptolemy's geocentric system failed to accord with the observed motions of the heavenly bodies and hoped that his **heliocentric** (sun-centered) **theory** would offer a more accurate explanation. Copernicus argued that the sun was motionless at the center of the universe. The planets revolved around the sun in the order of Mercury, Venus, the earth, Mars, Jupiter, and Saturn. The moon, however, revolved around the earth. Moreover, what appeared to be the movement of the sun around the earth was really explained by the daily rotation of the earth on its axis and the journey of the earth around the sun each year. But Copernicus did not reject the idea that the heavenly spheres moved in circular orbits.

Johannes Kepler (yoh-HAHN-us KEP-lur) (1571–1630) took the next step in destroying the geocentric conception and supporting the Copernican system. A brilliant German mathematician and astronomer, Kepler arrived at laws of planetary motion that confirmed Copernicus's heliocentric theory. In his first law, however, he contradicted Copernicus by showing that the orbits

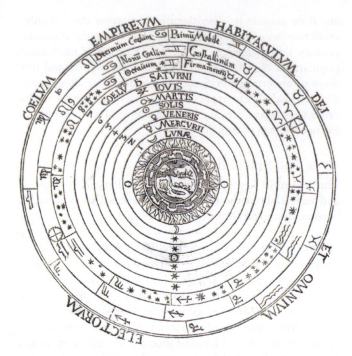

Medieval Conception of the Universe. As this sixteenth-century illustration shows, the medieval cosmological view placed the earth at the center of the universe, surrounded by a series of concentric spheres. The earth was imperfect and constantly changing, whereas the heavenly bodies that surrounded it were perfect and incorruptible. Beyond the tenth and final sphere was heaven, where God and all the saved souls were located. (The circles read, from the center outward: 1. Moon, 2. Mercury, 3. Venus, 4. Sun, 5. Mars, 6. Jupiter, 7. Saturn, 8. Firmament (of the Stars), 9. Crystalline Sphere, 10. Prime Mover; and around the outside, Empyrean Heaven—Home of God and All the Elect, that is, saved souls.)

Image Select/Art Resource, NY

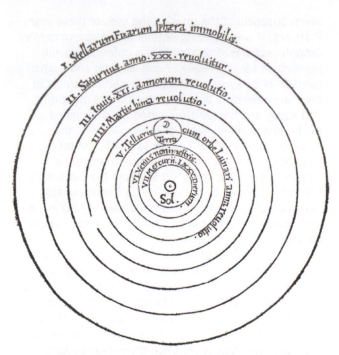

The Copernican System. The Copernican system was presented in *On the Revolutions of the Heavenly Spheres,* published shortly before Copernicus's death. As shown in this illustration from the first edition of the book, Copernicus maintained that the sun was the center of the universe and that the planets, including the earth, revolved around it. Moreover, the earth rotated daily on its axis. (The circles read, from the center outward: Sun; VII. Mercury, orbit of 80 days; VI. Venus; V. Earth, with the moon, orbit of one year; IIII. Mars, orbit of 2 years; III. Jupiter, orbit of 12 years; II. Saturn, orbit of 30 years; I. Immobile Sphere of the Fixed Stars.)

Image Select/Art Resource, NY

of the planets around the sun were not circular but elliptical, with the sun at one focus of the ellipse rather than at the center.

Kepler's work destroyed the basic structure of the Ptolemaic system. People could now think in new terms of the actual paths of planets revolving around the sun in elliptical orbits. But important questions remained unanswered. For example, what were the planets made of? An Italian scientist achieved the next important breakthrough to a new cosmology by answering that question.

Galileo Galilei (gal-li-LAY-oh GAL-li-lay) (1564–1642) taught mathematics and was the first European to make systematic observations of the heavens by means of a telescope, inaugurating a new age in astronomy. Galileo turned his telescope to the skies and made a remarkable series of discoveries: mountains on the moon, four moons revolving around Jupiter, and sunspots. Galileo's observations seemed to destroy yet another aspect of the traditional cosmology in that the universe seemed to be composed of material similar to that of earth rather than a perfect and unchanging substance.

Galileo's revelations, published in *The Starry Messenger* in 1610, made Europeans aware of a new picture of the universe. But the Catholic Church condemned Copernicanism and ordered Galileo to abandon the Copernican thesis. The church attacked the Copernican system because it threatened not only

Scripture but also an entire conception of the universe. The heavens were no longer a spiritual world but a world of matter.

By the 1630s and 1640s, most astronomers had come to accept the new heliocentric conception of the universe. Nevertheless, no one yet had explained motion in the universe and tied together the ideas of Copernicus, Galileo, and Kepler. This would be the work of an Englishman who has long been considered the greatest genius of the Scientific Revolution.

Isaac Newton (1642–1727) taught at Cambridge University, where he wrote his major work, *Mathematical Principles of Natural Philosophy,* known simply as the *Principia* (prin-SIP-ee-uh) by the first word of its Latin title. In the first book of the *Principia,* Newton defined the three laws of motion that govern the planetary bodies, as well as objects on earth. Crucial to his whole argument was the universal law of gravitation, which explained why the planetary bodies did not go off in straight lines but continued in elliptical orbits about the sun. In mathematical terms, Newton explained that every object in the universe is attracted to every other object by a force called gravity.

Newton had demonstrated that one mathematically proven universal law could explain all motion in the universe. At the same time, the Newtonian synthesis created a new cosmology in which the universe was seen as one huge, regulated, and uniform machine that operated according to natural laws in absolute time, space, and motion. Newton's **world-machine** concept dominated the modern worldview until the twentieth century, when Albert Einstein's concept of relativity created a new picture of the universe.

Toward a New Earth: Descartes and Rationalism The new conception of the universe contained in the cosmological revolution of the sixteenth and seventeenth centuries inevitably had an impact on the Western view of humankind. Nowhere is this more evident than in the work of the French philosopher René Descartes (ruh-NAY day-KART) (1596–1650). The starting point for Descartes's new system was doubt. As Descartes explained at the beginning of his most famous work, *Discourse on Method*, written in 1637, he decided to set aside all that he had learned and begin again. One fact seemed to Descartes beyond doubt—his own existence:

> I immediately became aware that while I was thus disposed to think that all was false, it was absolutely necessary that I who thus thought should be something; and noting that this truth *I think, therefore I am*, was so steadfast and so assured that the suppositions of the skeptics, to whatever extreme they might all be carried, could not avail to shake it, I concluded that I might without scruple accept it as being the first principle of the philosophy I was seeking.[1]

With this emphasis on the mind, Descartes asserted that he would accept only things that his reason said were true.

From his first postulate, Descartes deduced an additional principle, the separation of mind and matter. Descartes argued that since "the mind cannot be doubted but the body and material world can, the two must be radically different." From this came an absolute dualism between mind and matter, or what has also been called **Cartesian dualism**. Using mind or human reason and its best instrument, mathematics, humans can understand the material world because it is pure mechanism, a machine that is governed by its own physical laws because it was created by God—the great geometrician.

Descartes's separation of mind and matter allowed scientists to view matter as dead or inert, as something that was totally separate from themselves and could be investigated independently by reason. The split between mind and body led Westerners to equate their identity with mind and reason rather than with the whole organism. Descartes has rightly been called the father of modern **rationalism**.

Europe, China, and Scientific Revolutions An interesting question that arises is why the Scientific Revolution occurred in Europe and not in China. In the Middle Ages, China had been the most technologically advanced civilization in the world. After 1500, that distinction passed to the West (see Comparative Essay "The Scientific Revolution," p. 512). Historians are not sure why. Some have contrasted the sense of order in Chinese society with the competitive spirit existing in Europe. Others have emphasized China's ideological viewpoint that favored living in harmony with nature rather than trying to dominate it. One historian has even suggested that China's civil service system drew the "best and the brightest" into government service, to the detriment of other occupations.

18-1b Background to the Enlightenment

The impetus for political and social change in the eighteenth century stemmed in part from the **Enlightenment**. The Enlightenment was a movement of intellectuals who were greatly impressed with the accomplishments of the Scientific Revolution. When they used the word *reason*—one of their favorite words—they were advocating the application of the **scientific method** to the understanding of all life. All institutions and all systems of thought were subject to the rational, scientific way of thinking if people would only free themselves from the shackles of past, worthless traditions, especially religious ones. If Isaac Newton could discover the natural laws regulating the world of nature, they too, by using reason, could find the laws that governed human society. This belief in turn led them to hope that they could make progress toward a better society than the one they had inherited. *Reason, natural law, hope, progress*—these were the buzzwords in the heady atmosphere of eighteenth-century Europe.

Major sources of inspiration for the Enlightenment were Isaac Newton and his fellow Englishman John Locke (1632–1704). Newton had contended that the world and everything in it worked like a giant machine. Enchanted by the grand design of this world-machine, the intellectuals of the Enlightenment were convinced that by following Newton's rules of reasoning, they could discover the natural laws that governed politics, economics, justice, and religion.

John Locke's theory of knowledge also made a great impact. In his *Essay Concerning Human Understanding*, written in 1690, Locke denied the existence of innate ideas and argued instead that every person was born with a *tabula rasa* (TAB-yuh-luh RAH-suh), a blank mind:

> Let us then suppose the mind to be, as we say, white paper, void of all characters, without any ideas. How comes it to be furnished? Whence comes it by that vast store which the busy and boundless fancy of man has painted on it with an almost endless variety? Whence has it all the materials of reason and knowledge? To this I answer, in one word, from experience. . . . Our observation, employed either about external sensible objects or about the internal operations of our minds perceived and reflected on by ourselves, is that which supplies our understanding with all the materials of thinking.[2]

By denying innate ideas, Locke's philosophy implied that people were molded by their environment, by whatever they perceived through their senses from their surrounding world. Thus, by altering the environment and subjecting people to proper influences, they could be changed and a new society created. And how should the environment be changed? Newton had paved the way: reason enabled enlightened people to discover the natural laws to which all institutions should conform.

18-1c The Philosophes and Their Ideas

The intellectuals of the Enlightenment were known by the French term *philosophes* (fee-loh-ZAHFS), although they were not all French and few were philosophers in the strict sense of the term. The **philosophes** were literary people, professors,

COMPARATIVE ESSAY

The Scientific Revolution

Science & Technology

When Catholic missionaries arrived in China in the sixteenth century, they marveled at the sophistication of Chinese civilization and its many accomplishments, including woodblock printing and the civil service examination system. In turn, their hosts were impressed with European inventions such as the spring-driven clock and eyeglasses.

It is not surprising that visitors from the West were impressed with what they saw in China, for that country had long been at the forefront of human achievement. After the sixteenth century, however, Europe would take the lead in the advance of science and technology, a phenomenon that would ultimately bring about the Industrial Revolution and set in motion a transformation of human society.

Why did Europe suddenly become the engine for rapid change in the seventeenth and eighteenth centuries? One factor was the change in the European worldview, the shift from a metaphysical to a materialist perspective and the growing inclination among European intellectuals to question first principles. In contrast to China, where, for example, the "investigation of things" proposed by Song Dynasty thinkers had been used to analyze and confirm principles first established by Confucius and his contemporaries, empirical scientists in early modern Europe rejected received religious ideas, developed a

The Telescope—a European Invention

new conception of the universe, and sought ways to improve material conditions around them.

Why were European thinkers more interested in practical applications of their discoveries than their counterparts elsewhere? No doubt the literate mercantile and propertied elites of Europe were attracted to the new science because it offered new ways to exploit resources for profit. Some of the early scientists made it easier for these groups to accept the new ideas by showing how they could be applied directly to specific industrial and technological needs. Galileo, for example, consciously sought an alliance between science and the material interests of the educated elite when he assured his listeners that the science of mechanics would be quite useful "when it becomes necessary to build bridges or other structures over water, something occurring mainly in affairs of great importance."

Finally, the political changes that were beginning to take place in Europe during this period may also have contributed. Many European states enlarged their bureaucratic machinery and consolidated their governments in order to collect the revenues and amass the armies needed to compete militarily with rivals. Political leaders desperately sought ways to enhance their wealth and power and grasped eagerly at whatever tools were available to guarantee their survival and prosperity.

 Why did the Scientific Revolution emerge in Europe and not in China?

journalists, economists, political scientists, and, above all, social reformers. They came from both the nobility and the middle class, and a few even stemmed from lower-middle-class origins. Although it was a truly international and cosmopolitan movement, the Enlightenment also enhanced the dominant role being played by French culture; Paris was its recognized capital. Most of the leaders of the Enlightenment were French. The French philosophes, in turn, affected intellectuals elsewhere and created a movement that touched the entire Western world, including the British and Spanish colonies in America (see Map 18.1). (The terms *British* and *Great Britain* came to be used after 1707 when the United Kingdom of Great Britain came into existence, uniting the governments of England and Scotland, as well as Wales, which had been joined to England previously.)

To the philosophes, the role of philosophy was not just to discuss the world but to change it. The philosophes believed that reason was a scientific method, and it relied on an appeal to facts. A spirit of rational criticism was to be applied to everything, including religion and politics. Spanning almost a century, the Enlightenment evolved with each succeeding generation, becoming more radical as new thinkers built on the contributions of their predecessors. A few individuals, however, dominated the landscape so completely that we can gain insight into the core ideas of the philosophes by focusing on the three French giants—Montesquieu, Voltaire, and Diderot.

Montesquieu Charles de Secondat (SHARL duh suh-KAHN-da), the baron de Montesquieu (MOHN-tess-kyoo) (1689–1755),

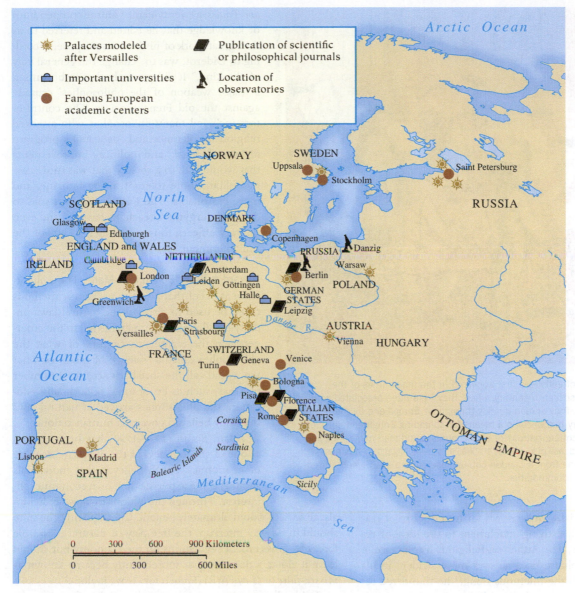

Map 18.1 The Enlightenment in Europe. "Have the courage to use your own intelligence!" The words of the German philosopher Immanuel Kant (i-MAHN-yoo-el KAHNT) epitomize the role of the individual in using reason to understand all aspects of life—the natural world and the sphere of human nature, behavior, and institutions.

 Which countries or regions were at the center of the Enlightenment, and what reasons could account for peripheral regions being less involved?

came from the French nobility. His most famous work, *The Spirit of the Laws*, was published in 1748. In this comparative study of governments, Montesquieu attempted to apply the scientific method to the social and political arena to ascertain the "natural laws" governing the social and political relationships of human beings. Montesquieu distinguished three basic kinds of governments: republic, monarchy, and despotism.

Montesquieu used England as an example of monarchy, and it was his analysis of England's constitution that led to his most lasting contribution to political thought—the importance of checks and balances achieved by means of a **separation of powers**. He believed that England's system, with its separate executive, legislative, and judicial branches that served to limit and control each other, provided the greatest freedom and security for a state. The translation of his work into English two years after publication ensured that it would be read by American political leaders, who eventually incorporated its principles into the U.S. Constitution.

Voltaire The greatest figure of the Enlightenment was François-Marie Arouet (frahn-SWAH-ma-REE ahr-WEH), known simply as Voltaire (vohl-TAYR) (1694–1778). Son of a prosperous middle-class family from Paris, he studied law, although he achieved his first success as a playwright. Voltaire was a prolific author and wrote an almost endless stream of pamphlets, novels, plays, letters, philosophical essays, and histories.

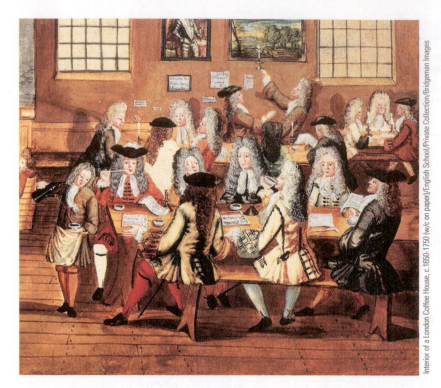

A London Coffeehouse. Coffeehouses first appeared in the major cities of the Ottoman Empire in the sixteenth century, where they were often associated with antigovernment activity. They spread quickly throughout Europe and by the beginning of the eighteenth century had become a means for spreading Enlightenment ideas. In addition to drinking coffee, patrons of coffeehouses could read magazines and newspapers, exchange ideas, play chess, smoke, and even engage in business transactions. In this scene from a London coffeehouse around 1705, well-attired gentlemen make bids on commodities.

Voltaire was especially well known for his criticism of traditional religion and his strong attachment to the ideal of religious toleration (see "The Attack on Religious Intolerance"). As he grew older, Voltaire became ever more strident in his denunciations. "Crush the infamous thing," he thundered repeatedly—the infamous thing being religious fanaticism, intolerance, and superstition.

Throughout his life, Voltaire championed not only religious tolerance but also **deism**, a religious outlook shared by most other philosophes. Deism was built on the Newtonian world-machine, which implied the existence of a mechanic (God) who had created the universe. To Voltaire and most other philosophes, the universe was like a clock, and God was the clock-maker who had created it, set it in motion, and allowed it to run according to its own natural laws.

Diderot Denis Diderot (duh-NEE dee-DROH) (1713–1784), the son of a skilled craftsman from eastern France, became a writer so that he could be free to study and read in many subjects and languages. One of Diderot's favorite topics was Christianity, which he condemned as fanatical and unreasonable. Of all religions, Christianity, he averred, was the worst, "the most absurd and the most atrocious in its dogma."

Diderot's most famous contribution to the Enlightenment was the *Encyclopedia, or Classified Dictionary of the Sciences, Arts,* *and Trades*, a twenty-eight-volume compendium of knowledge that he edited and referred to as the "great work of his life." Its purpose, according to Diderot, was to "change the general way of thinking." It did precisely that in becoming a major weapon of the philosophes' crusade against the old French society. The contributors included many philosophes who attacked religious intolerance and advocated a program for social, legal, and political improvements that would lead to a society that was more cosmopolitan, more tolerant, more humane, and more reasonable. The *Encyclopedia* was sold to doctors, clergymen, teachers, lawyers, and even military officers, thus spreading the ideas of the Enlightenment.

Toward a New "Science of Man" The Enlightenment belief that Newton's scientific methods could be used to discover the natural laws underlying all areas of human life led to the emergence in the eighteenth century of what the philosophes called a "science of man," or what we would call the social sciences. In a number of areas, such as economics, politics, and education, the philosophes arrived at natural laws that they believed governed human actions.

Adam Smith (1723–1790) has been viewed as one of the founders of the modern discipline of economics. Smith believed that individuals should be free to pursue their own economic self-interest. Through the actions of these individuals, all society would ultimately benefit. Consequently, the state should in no way interrupt the free play of natural economic forces by government regulations on the economy but should leave it alone, a doctrine that subsequently became known as *laissez-faire* (less-ay-FAYR) (French for "leave it alone").

Smith allotted government only three basic functions: to protect society from invasion (via an army), defend its citizens from injustice (by means of a police force), and keep up certain public works, such as roads and canals, that private individuals could not afford.

The Later Enlightenment By the late 1760s, a new generation of philosophes who had grown up with the worldview of the Enlightenment began to move beyond their predecessors' beliefs. Most famous was Jean-Jacques Rousseau (ZHAHNH-ZHAHK roo-SOH) (1712–1778), whose political beliefs were presented in two major works. In his *Discourse on the Origins of the Inequality of Mankind*, Rousseau argued that people had adopted laws and governors in order to preserve their private property. In the process, they had become enslaved by government. What, then, should people do to regain their freedom? In his celebrated treatise *The Social Contract*, published in 1762, Rousseau found an answer in the concept of the social contract, whereby an entire society agreed to be governed by its general will. Each individual might have a particular will

THE ATTACK ON RELIGIOUS INTOLERANCE

Religion & Philosophy **ALTHOUGH VOLTAIRE'S IDEAS ON RELIGION** were not original, his lucid prose, biting satire, and clever wit caused his works to be widely read and all the more influential. These two selections present different sides of Voltaire's attack on religious intolerance. The first is from his straightforward treatise *The Ignorant Philosopher*, and the second is from his only real literary masterpiece, the novel *Candide*, where he used humor to make the same fundamental point about religious intolerance.

Voltaire, *The Ignorant Philosopher*

The contagion of fanaticism then still subsists. . . . The author of the Treatise upon Toleration has not mentioned the shocking executions wherein so many unhappy victims perished in the valleys of Piedmont. He has passed over in silence the massacre of six hundred inhabitants of Valtelina, men, women, and children, who were murdered by the Catholics in the month of September, 1620. I will not say it was with the consent and assistance of the archbishop of Milan, Charles Borome, who was made a saint. Some passionate writers have averred this fact, which I am very far from believing; but I say, there is scarce any city or borough in Europe where blood has not been spilt for religious quarrels; I say, that the human species has been perceptibly diminished because women and girls were massacred as well as men; I say, that Europe would have had a third larger population if there had been no theological disputes. In fine, I say, that so far from forgetting these abominable times, we should frequently take a view of them, to inspire an eternal horror for them; and that it is for our age to make reparation by toleration, for this long collection of crimes, which has taken place through the want of toleration, during sixteen barbarous centuries.

Let it not then be said, that there are no traces left of that shocking fanaticism, of the want of toleration; they are still everywhere to be met with, even in those countries that are esteemed the most humane. The Lutheran and Calvinist preachers, were they masters, would, perhaps, be as little inclined to pity, as obdurate, as insolent as they upbraid their antagonists with being.

Voltaire, *Candide*

At last [Candide] approached a man who had just been addressing a big audience for a whole hour on the subject of charity. The orator peered at him and said:

"What is your business here? Do you support the Good Old Cause?"

"There is no effect without a cause," replied Candide modestly. "All things are necessarily connected and arranged for the best. It was my fate to be driven from Lady Cunégonde's presence and made to run the gauntlet, and now I have to beg my bread until I can earn it. Things could not have happened otherwise."

"Do you believe that the Pope is Antichrist, my friend?" said the minister.

"I have never heard anyone say so," replied Candide; "but whether he is or he isn't, I want some food."

"You don't deserve to eat," said the other. "Be off with you, you villain, you wretch! Don't come near me again or you'll suffer for it."

The minister's wife looked out of the window at that moment, and seeing a man who was not sure that the Pope was Antichrist, emptied over his head a chamber pot, which shows to what lengths ladies are driven by religious zeal.

 Compare the two approaches that Voltaire uses to address the problem of religious intolerance. Which do you think is more effective? Why?

Source: From *Absolutism to Revolution: 1648–1848*, 2/E by Herbert Rowen. Copyright © 1968 by Macmillan College Publishing Company, Inc.

---

contrary to the general will, but if the individual put his particular will (self-interest) above the general will, he should be forced to abide by the general will. "This means nothing less than that he will be forced to be free," said Rousseau, because the general will, being ethical and not just political, represented what the entire community ought to do.

Another influential treatise by Rousseau was his novel *Émile*, one of the Enlightenment's most important works on education. Rousseau's fundamental concern was that education should foster, rather than restrict, children's natural instincts. Rousseau's own experiences had shown him the importance of the emotions. What he sought was a balance between heart and mind, between emotion and reason.

But Rousseau did not necessarily practice what he preached. His own children were sent to orphanages, where many children died at a young age. Rousseau also viewed women as "naturally different" from men. In *Émile*, Sophie, Émile's intended wife, was educated for her role as wife and mother by learning obedience and the nurturing skills that would enable her to provide loving care for her husband and children. Not everyone in the eighteenth century agreed with Rousseau, however.

The "Woman Question" in the Enlightenment For centuries, many male intellectuals had argued that the nature of women made them inferior to men and made male domination of women necessary and right. These biases restricted women's access to education. Despite these educational limitations, many women made notable contributions to the Scientific Revolution. Maria Winkelmann (VINK-ul-mahn) in Germany,

THE RIGHTS OF WOMEN

Art & Ideas **MARY WOLLSTONECRAFT** responded to an unhappy childhood in a large family by seeking to lead an independent life. Few occupations were available for middle-class women in her day, but she survived by working as a teacher, chaperone, and governess to aristocratic children. All the while, she wrote and developed her ideas on the rights of women. This selection is taken from her *Vindication of the Rights of Woman*, written in 1792. This work led to her reputation as the foremost British feminist thinker of the eighteenth century.

Mary Wollstonecraft, *Vindication of the Rights of Woman*

It is a melancholy truth—yet such is the blessed effect of civilization—the most respectable women are the most oppressed; and, unless they have understandings far superior to the common run of understandings, taking in both sexes, they must, from being treated like contemptible beings, become contemptible. How many women thus waste life away the prey of discontent, who might have practiced as physicians, regulated a farm, managed a shop, and stood erect, supported by their own industry, instead of hanging their heads surcharged with the dew of sensibility, that consumes the beauty to which it at first gave luster. . . .

Proud of their weakness, however, [women] must always be protected, guarded from care, and all the rough toils that dignify the mind. If this be the fiat of fate, if they will make themselves insignificant and contemptible, sweetly to waste "life away," let them not expect to be valued when their beauty fades, for it is the fate of the fairest flowers to be admired and pulled to pieces by the careless hand that plucked them. In how many ways do I wish, from the purest benevolence, to impress this truth on my sex; yet I fear that they will not listen to a truth that dear-bought experience has brought home to many an agitated bosom, nor willingly resign the privileges of rank and sex for the privileges of humanity, to which those have no claim who do not discharge its duties. . . .

Would men but generously snap our chains, and be content with rational fellowship instead of slavish obedience, they would find us more observant daughters, more affectionate sisters, more faithful wives, and more reasonable mothers—in a word, better citizens. We should then love them with true affection, because we should learn to respect ourselves; and the peace of mind of a worthy man would not be interrupted by the idle vanity of his wife.

 What picture did Wollstonecraft paint of the women of her day? Why were they in such a deplorable state? Why did Wollstonecraft suggest that both women and men were at fault for the "slavish" situation of females?

Source: From *First Feminists: British Women, 1578–1799* by Moira Ferguson. Copyright © 1985 Indiana University Press.

for example, was an outstanding practicing astronomer. Nevertheless, when she applied for a position as assistant astronomer at the Berlin Academy, for which she was highly qualified, she was denied the post by the academy's members, who feared that hiring a woman would set a bad precedent ("mouths would gape"). Winkelmann's difficulties with the Berlin Academy were typical of the obstacles women faced in being accepted in scientific work, which was considered a male preserve.

Female thinkers in the eighteenth century disagreed with this attitude and offered suggestions for improving conditions for women. The strongest statement for the rights of women was advanced by the English writer Mary Wollstonecraft (WULL-stun-kraft) (1759–1797), viewed by many as the founder of modern European **feminism**.

In her *Vindication of the Rights of Woman*, written in 1792, Wollstonecraft pointed out two contradictions in the views of women held by such Enlightenment thinkers as Rousseau. To argue that women must obey men, she said, was contrary to the beliefs of the same individuals that a system based on the arbitrary power of monarchs over their subjects or slave owners over their slaves was wrong. The subjection of women to men was equally wrong. In addition, she argued, the Enlightenment was based on an ideal of reason innate in all human beings. If women have reason, then they should have the same rights as men to obtain an education and engage in economic and political life (see "The Rights of Women").

18–1d Culture in an Enlightened Age

Although the Baroque style that had dominated the seventeenth century continued to be popular, by the 1730s, a new style affecting decoration and architecture known as **Rococo** (ruh-KOH-koh) had spread throughout Europe. Unlike the Baroque, which stressed power, grandeur, and movement, Rococo emphasized grace, charm, and gentle action. Rococo rejected strict geometrical patterns and had a fondness for curves; it liked to follow the wandering lines of natural objects, such as seashells and flowers. It made much use of interlaced designs colored in gold with delicate contours and graceful arcs. Highly secular, its lightness and charm spoke of the pursuit of pleasure, happiness, and love.

Some of Rococo's appeal is evident in the work of Antoine Watteau (AHN-twahn wah-TOH) (1684–1721), who created a specific type of Rococo art. His paintings portrayed a lyrical view of aristocratic life, refined, sensual, and civilized, with gentlemen

Antoine Watteau, *Return from Cythera*. Antoine Watteau was one of the most gifted painters in eighteenth-century France. His portrayal of aristocratic life reveals a world of elegance, wealth, and pleasure. In this painting, which is considered his masterpiece, Watteau depicts a group of aristocratic lovers about to depart from the island of Cythera, where they have paid homage to Venus, the goddess of love. Luxuriously dressed, they move from the woodlands to a golden barge that is waiting to take them from the island.

and ladies in elegant dress—reflecting a world of upper-class pleasure and joy. Underneath that exterior, however, was an element of sadness as the artist revealed the fragility and transitory nature of pleasure, love, and life. Watteau relied upon the use of color rather than representational form to highlight his subjects. Later artists, such as Jean-Honoré Fragonard (FRA-go-NARD) (1732–1806), continued Watteau's use of color and subject matter.

Another aspect of Rococo was that its decorative work could easily be paired with Baroque architecture. The palace at Versailles had made an enormous impact on Europe. "Keeping up with the Bourbons" became important as European rulers built grandiose palaces. While imitating Versailles in size, they were not so much modeled after the French classical style as they were after the seventeenth-century Italian Baroque, as modified by a series of brilliant German and Austrian sculptor-architects. This Baroque-Rococo architectural style typified eighteenth-century palaces and church buildings, and often the same architects designed both. This is evident in the work of one of the greatest architects of the eighteenth century,

Jean-Honoré Fragonard, *The Swing*. Fragonard captured the frivolity and decadence of France's aristocracy. In this painting, Fragonard portrays a young lady being pushed on a swing as her suitor sits below her. The lush environs and curvilinear landscape epitomize Rococo's love of nature, while the delicate light and color of the lady's dress highlight the playful moment of her kicking off her shoe.

Vierzehnheiligen. Pictured here is the interior of the Vierzehnheiligen, the famous pilgrimage church in Bad Staffelstein, Bavaria, designed by Johann Balthasar Neumann. Elaborate detail, blazing light, rich colors, and opulent decoration were brought together to create a work of stunning beauty. The pilgrim in search of holiness is struck by an incredible richness of detail. Persuaded by joy rather than fear, the believer is lifted toward heaven on a cloud of rapture.

Johann Balthasar Neumann (yoh-HAHN BAHL-tuh-zahr NOI-mahn) (1687–1753). One of Neumann's masterpieces was the pilgrimage church known as the Vierzehnheiligen (feer-tsayn-HY-li-gen) (Fourteen Saints) in southern Germany. Secular and spiritual merge in its lavish and fanciful ornamentation; light, bright colors; and elaborate, rich detail. The church is designed without any straight lines, only ovals and circles, contrasting the traditional rectilinear nave, creating a fluidity of motion reflected in the curvilinear gilding on the ceiling.

High Culture Historians have grown accustomed to distinguishing between a civilization's high culture and its popular culture. **High culture** is the literary and artistic culture of the educated and wealthy ruling classes; **popular culture** is the written and unwritten culture of the masses, most of which has traditionally been passed down orally.

By the eighteenth century, the two forms were beginning to blend, owing to the expansion of both the reading public and publishing. Whereas French publishers issued 300 titles in 1750,

about 1,600 were being published yearly in the 1780s. Although the majority of these titles were still intended for small groups of the educated elite, many were directed to the new reading public of the middle classes, which included women and even urban artisans.

An important aspect of the growth of publishing and reading in the eighteenth century was the development of magazines for the general public. Great Britain saw 25 different periodicals published in 1700, 103 in 1760, and 158 in 1780. Along with magazines came daily newspapers. The first was printed in London in 1702, but by 1780, thirty-seven other English towns had their own newspapers.

Popular Culture The distinguishing characteristic of popular culture is its collective nature. Group activity was especially common in the *festival*, a broad name used to cover a variety of celebrations: community festivals in Catholic Europe that celebrated the feast day of the local patron saint; annual festivals, such as Christmas and Easter, that went back to medieval Christianity; and the ultimate festival, Carnival, which was celebrated in the Mediterranean world of Spain, Italy, and France as well as in Germany and Austria.

Carnival began after Christmas and lasted until the start of Lent, the forty-day period of fasting and purification leading up to Easter. Because people were expected to abstain from meat, sex, and most recreations during Lent, Carnival was a time of great indulgence, when heavy consumption of food and drink was the norm. It was a time of intense sexual activity as well.

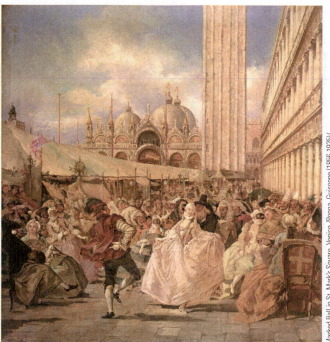

Carnival. The Carnival of Venice, Italy, begun in the middle ages, is depicted here in an eighteenth-century painting. The carnival in Venice was one of Europe's most elaborate and famous festivals. In this scene from the Carnival, attendees are portrayed eating, drinking, and dancing in their finest attire and masks in the Piazza San Marco.

Songs with double meanings that would ordinarily be considered offensive could be sung publicly at this time of year. A float of Florentine "keymakers," for example, sang this ditty to the ladies: "Our tools are fine, new and useful. We always carry them with us. They are good for anything. If you want to touch them, you can."[3]

18–2 ECONOMIC CHANGES AND THE SOCIAL ORDER

Focus Question: What changes occurred in the European economy in the eighteenth century, and to what degree were these changes reflected in social patterns?

The eighteenth century in Europe witnessed the beginning of economic changes that ultimately had a strong impact on the rest of the world.

18–2a New Economic Patterns

Europe's population began to grow around 1750 and continued to increase steadily. The total European population was probably around 120 million in 1700, 140 million in 1750, and 190 million in 1790. A falling death rate was perhaps the most important reason for this population growth. Of great significance in lowering death rates was the disappearance of bubonic plague, but so was diet. More plentiful food and better transportation of food supplies led to improved nutrition and relief from devastating famines (see Historians Debate "Was There an Agricultural Revolution?").

Textiles were the most important product of European industry in the eighteenth century. Most were still produced by master artisans in guild workshops, but in many areas, textile production was beginning to shift to the countryside where the "putting-out" or "domestic" system was used. A merchant-capitalist entrepreneur bought the raw materials, mostly wool and flax, and "put them out" to rural workers who spun the raw material into yarn and then wove it into cloth on simple looms. The capitalist entrepreneurs sold the finished product, made a profit, and used it to purchase materials to manufacture more. This system became known as the **cottage industry** because the spinners and weavers worked at spinning wheels and looms in the cottages where they lived.

In the eighteenth century, overseas trade boomed. Some historians speak of the emergence of a true global economy, pointing to the patterns of trade that interlocked Europe, Africa, the East, and the Americas (see Map 18.2). In one trade pattern, gold and silver flowed into Spain from its colonial American empire. Much of this gold and silver made its way to Britain, France, and the Netherlands in return for manufactured goods. The British, French, and Dutch merchants then used their profits to buy tea, spices, silk, and cotton goods from China and India to sell in Europe. The plantations of the Western Hemisphere were another important source of trading activity. The plantations produced coffee, tobacco, sugar, and cotton, which

were shipped to Europe. In a third pattern of trade, British merchant ships carried British manufactured goods to Africa, where they were traded for cargoes of slaves, which were then shipped to Virginia and paid for with tobacco, which was in turn shipped back to Britain, where it was processed and then sold in Germany for cash.

As a result of the growth in trade, historians have argued that during the eighteenth century, England and parts of northern Europe experienced a "consumer revolution," where ordinary people partook in a large increase in the consumption of consumer goods. Expensive porcelain had been imported from China for centuries; however, by the eighteenth century factories on the Continent and in England had bypassed Chinese production. Large showrooms opened in London; the most noticeable was that of Josiah Wedgewood. By the late eighteenth century, Wedgewood exported nearly 80 percent of its wares. In addition to porcelain, imports of inexpensive Indian fabric increased the sale of clothing. By the end of the eighteenth century, most ordinary families could consume former luxury goods such as tea, sugar, tobacco, furniture, cutlery, and clothing.

Commercial capitalism resulted in enormous prosperity for some European countries. By 1700, Spain, Portugal, and the Dutch Republic, which had earlier monopolized overseas trade, found themselves increasingly overshadowed by France and England, which built hugely profitable colonial empires in the course of the eighteenth century. After the French lost the Seven Years' War in 1763, Britain emerged as the world's strongest overseas trading nation, and London became the world's greatest port.

HISTORIANS DEBATE **Was There an Agricultural Revolution?** Did improvements in agricultural practices and methods in the eighteenth century lead to an **agricultural revolution**? The topic is much debated. Some historians have noted the beginning of agrarian changes already in the seventeenth century, especially in the Low Countries. Others, however, have questioned the use of the term, arguing that significant changes occurred only in England and that even there the upward trend in agricultural production was not maintained after 1750. Traditional interpretations of the agricultural revolution are characterized by four interrelated factors: more farmland, increased crop yields per acre, healthier and more abundant livestock, and an improved climate.

Historians dispute the increase of the amount of land under cultivation and the rate at which more land entered cultivation. One argument for greater land availability was the abandoning of the old open-field system, in which part of the land was allowed to lie fallow to renew it and plow it for weeds. The formerly empty fields were now planted with new crops, such as alfalfa, turnips, and clover, which stored nitrogen in their roots and thereby restored the soil's fertility, allowing for a greater yield of crops. Historians also argue that one of the reasons why output increased during this time was due to land reclamation, especially in eastern England. However, the increase of the new crops served another purpose: they provided winter fodder for livestock, enabling landlords to maintain an ever-larger number of animals.

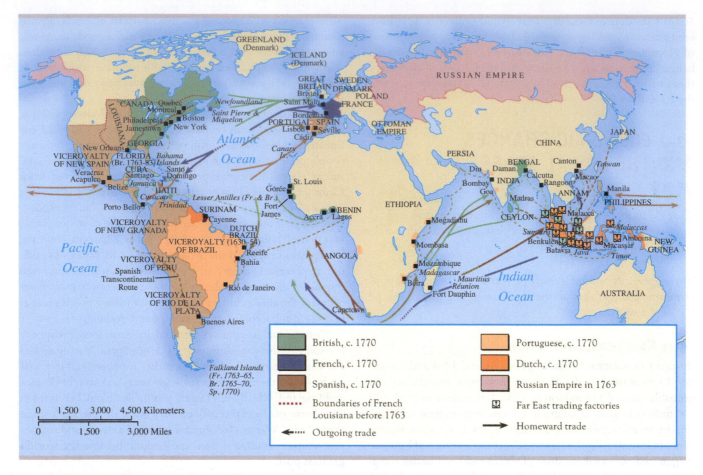

Map 18.2 Global Trade Patterns of the European States in the Eighteenth Century. New patterns of trade interlocked Europe, Africa, the East, and the Americas. Dutch, English, French, Spanish, and Portuguese colonies had been established in North and South America, and the ships of these nations followed the trade routes across the Atlantic, Pacific, and Indian Oceans.

 With what regions did Britain conduct most of its trade?

The eighteenth century witnessed greater yields of meat and vegetables. The more numerous livestock increased the amount of meat in the European diet and enhanced food production by making available more animal manure, which was used to fertilize fields and produce larger yields per acre. Landed aristocrats with an interest in the scientific experimentation of the age also adopted innovations that increased yields. Importation of vegetables from America, the potato and maize (Indian corn), increased food yields. Although they were not grown in quantity until after 1700, both had been brought to Europe from America in the sixteenth century. The potato became a staple in Germany, the Low Countries, and especially Ireland, where repression by English landlords forced large numbers of poor peasants to survive on small plots of marginal land.

Another argument on the agriculture revolution is whether or not the new crops and agricultural inventions increased food production while lowering the agricultural workforce, consequently altering the size and scale of farms and displacing agricultural workers. The new agricultural techniques were considered best suited to large-scale farms. Large landowners or yeomen farmers enclosed the old open fields, combining many small holdings into larger units. The end of the open-field system led to the demise of the cooperative farming of the village community. As crop yields increased, food prices began to decline, leaving landlords with the prospect of lowered profits; their response was to enact legislation. Historians are still debating the causes of this legislation and whether or not it forced more innovative farming practices, leading to higher food yields.

Historians also debate the role of climate in food production during the eighteenth century. Climatologists believe that the "little ice age" of the seventeenth century declined in the eighteenth, especially evident in moderate summers that provided more ideal growing conditions.

18–2b European Society in the Eighteenth Century

The patterns of Europe's social organization, first established in the Middle Ages, continued well into the eighteenth century. Society was still divided into the traditional orders or estates determined by heredity.

Because society was still mostly rural in the eighteenth century, the peasantry constituted the largest social group, about 85 percent of Europe's population. There were rather wide differences within this group, however, especially between free peasants and serfs. In eastern Germany, eastern Europe, and Russia, serfs remained tied to the lands of their noble landlords. In contrast, peasants in Britain, northern Italy, the Low Countries, Spain, most of France, and some areas of western Germany were largely free.

The nobles, who constituted only 2 to 3 percent of the European population, played a dominating role in society. Being born a noble automatically guaranteed a place at the top of the social order, with all its attendant special privileges and rights. Nobles, for example, were exempt from many forms of taxation. Since medieval times, landed aristocrats had functioned as military officers, and eighteenth-century nobles held most of the important offices in the administrative machinery of state and controlled much of the life of their local districts.

Townspeople were still a distinct minority of the total population except in the Dutch Republic, Britain, and parts of Italy. At the end of the eighteenth century, about one-sixth of the French population lived in towns of two thousand people or more. The biggest city in Europe was London, with a million inhabitants; Paris was a little more than half that size.

Many cities in western and even central Europe had a long tradition of **patrician** oligarchies that continued to control their communities by dominating town and city councils. Just below the patricians stood an upper crust of the middle classes:

nonnoble officeholders, financiers and bankers, merchants, wealthy *rentiers* (rahn-TYAYS) who lived off their investments, and important professionals, including lawyers. Another large urban group was the lower middle class, made up of master artisans, shopkeepers, and small traders. Below them were the laborers or working classes and a large group of unskilled workers who served as servants, maids, and cooks at pitifully low wages.

18–3 COLONIAL EMPIRES AND REVOLUTION IN THE AMERICAS

 Focus Question: What colonies did the British and French establish in the Americas, and how did their methods of administering their colonies differ?

In the sixteenth century, Spain and Portugal had established large colonial empires in the Americas (see Chapter 14). Portugal continued to profit from its empire in Brazil. The Spanish also maintained an enormous South American empire, but Spain's importance as a commercial power declined rapidly in the seventeenth century because of a drop in the output of the silver mines and the poverty of the Spanish monarchy. By the beginning of the seventeenth century, both Portugal and Spain found themselves facing new challenges to their American empires from the Dutch, English, and French, who increasingly sought to create their own colonial empires in the Western Hemisphere, both within the West Indies and on the North American continent.

18–3a The West Indies

Both the French and British colonial empires in the Americas ultimately included large parts of the West Indies. The British held Barbados, Jamaica, and Bermuda, and the French possessed Saint-Dominigue, Martinique, and Guadeloupe. On these tropical islands, both the British and the French used African slaves to work plantations that produced tobacco, cotton, coffee, and sugar, all products increasingly in demand in Europe.

The "sugar factories," as the sugar plantations in the Caribbean were called, played an especially prominent role. By the last two decades of the eighteenth century, Jamaica, one of Britain's most important colonies, was producing 50,000 tons of sugar annually with the slave labor of 200,000 blacks. The French colony of Saint-Dominique (later Haiti) had 500,000 slaves working on three thousand plantations during the same period. This colony produced 100,000 tons of sugar a year, but at the expense of a high death rate from the brutal treatment of the slaves. It is not surprising that Saint-Dominique saw the first successful slave uprising in 1793.

18–3b British North America

Although Spain had claimed all of North America as part of its American overseas empire, other nations largely ignored its claim, following the English argument that "prescription

Conversation in a Park, portrait of the artist and his wife, Margaret Burr (1728-98) at the time of their marriage, 1746 (oil on canvas), Gainsborough, Thomas (1727-88) / Louvre, Paris, France / Peter Willi / The Bridgeman Art Library

The Aristocratic Way of Life. The eighteenth-century country house fulfilled the desire among British aristocrats for both elegance and greater privacy. Thomas Gainsborough's *Conversation in the Park*, shown here, captures the relaxed life of two aristocrats in the park of their country estate.

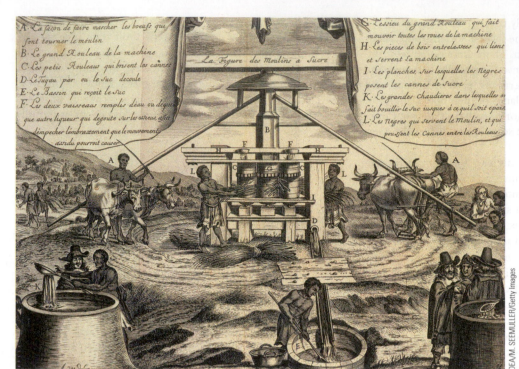

The handwritten labels in the illustration read:

A. La façon de faire marcher les boeufs qui font tourner le moulin.

B. Le grand Rouleau de la machine.

C. Les petis Rouleaux qui brisent les cannes.

D. Le Tuyau par ou le Suc decoule.

E. Le Bassin qui reçoit le Suc.

F. Les deux vaisseaux remplis d'eau ou d'aque que autre liqueur qui degoute sur les essieux, afin d'empecher l'embrazement que le mouvement assidu pourroit causer.

La Figure des Moulins a Sucre

G. L'essieu du grand Rouleau qui fait mouvoir toutes les roues de la machine.

H. Les pieces de bois entrelassees qui lient et serrent la machine.

I. Les planches, sur lesquelles les Negres posent les cannes de Sucre.

K. Les grandes chaudieres dans laquelle on fait bouillir le suc iusques à ce qu'il soit epais.

L. Les Negres qui servent le Moulin, et qui poussent les Cannes entre les Rouleaux.

A Sugar Mill in the West Indies. Cane sugar was one of the most valuable products produced in the West Indies. By 1700, sugar was replacing honey as a sweetener for increasing numbers of Europeans. This seventeenth-century French illustration shows the operation of a sugar mill in the French West Indies.

DEA/M. SEEMÜLLER/Getty Images

without possession availeth nothing." The Dutch had been among the first to establish settlements on the North American continent. Their activities began after 1609 when Henry Hudson, an English explorer hired by the Dutch, discovered the river that bears his name. Within a few years, the Dutch had established the mainland colony of New Netherland, which stretched from the mouth of the Hudson River as far north as Albany, New York. Present-day names such as Staten Island and Harlem remind us that it was the Dutch who initially settled the Hudson River Valley. In the second half of the seventeenth century, competition from the English and French and years of warfare with those rivals led to the decline of the Dutch commercial empire. In 1664, the English seized the colony of New Netherland and renamed it New York.

In the meantime, the English had begun to establish their own colonies in North America. In 1606 the Virginia Company of London sponsored the first permanent English settlement in America. A ship carrying 105 passengers departed England in December 1606, landing in America in 1607, in Jamestown, in what is now Virginia. The settlers barely survived, making it clear that colonizing American lands was not necessarily conducive to quick profits. In Massachusetts, however, the desire to practice one's own religion, combined with economic interests, could lead to successful colonization, as the Massachusetts Bay Company demonstrated. The Massachusetts colony had 4,000 settlers in its early years, but by 1660 their numbers had swelled to 40,000. Almost all settlers were Puritans, a religious group whose members believed in religious reforms of the Church of England. Puritans did not believe in abandoning the Church of England but sought religious reforms. Other English settlers, such as the Pigrims in Plymouth County, settled as religious separatists, breaking from the Church of England. By the end of the seventeenth century, the English had established control over most of the eastern seaboard of the present United States.

British North America came to consist of thirteen colonies. They were thickly populated, containing about 1.5 million people by 1750, and were also prosperous. Supposedly run by the British Board of Trade, the Royal Council, and Parliament, these thirteen colonies had legislatures that tended to act independently. Merchants in such port cities as Boston, Philadelphia, New York, and Charleston resented and resisted regulation from the British government.

Both the North American and the West Indian colonies of Britain were assigned roles in keeping with mercantilist theory. They provided raw materials for the mother country while buying the latter's manufactured goods. Navigation acts regulated what could be taken from and sold to the colonies. Theoretically, the system was supposed to provide a balance of trade favorable to the mother country.

18–3c French North America

The French also established a colonial empire in North America. In 1534, the French explorer Jacques Cartier (ZHAHK kar-TYAY) had discovered the Saint Lawrence River and laid claim to Canada as a French possession. Not until Samuel de Champlain (sa-my-ELL duh shahm-PLAN or SHAM-playn) established a settlement at Quebec in 1608, however, did the French take a serious interest in Canada as a colony. In 1663, Canada was made the property of the French crown and administered by a French governor like a French province.

French North America was run autocratically as a vast trading area, where valuable furs, leather, fish, and timber were acquired. The inability of the French state to persuade its people to emigrate to its Canadian possessions, however, left the territory thinly populated. In the mid-eighteenth century, there were only about 15,000 French Canadians, most of whom were hunters, trappers, missionaries, or explorers. The French also failed to provide adequate men or money for the venture, allowing their wars in Europe to take precedence over the conquest of the North American continent. Already in 1713, by the Treaty of Utrecht, the French began to cede some of their American possessions to their British rival. As a result of the Seven Years' War, they surrendered the rest of their Canadian lands to Britain in 1763.

18–3d The Seven Years' War: Global War

The philosophes condemned war as a foolish waste of life and resources in stupid quarrels of no value to humankind. Despite their words, the rivalry among states that led to costly struggles remained unchanged in the European world of the eighteenth century. Europe consisted of a number of self-governing, individual states that were largely guided by the self-interest of the ruler. And as Frederick the Great of Prussia said, "The fundamental rule of governments is the principle of extending their territories."

By far the most dramatic confrontation occurred in the Seven Years' War. Although it began in Europe, it soon turned into a global conflict fought in Europe, India, and North America. In Europe, the British and Prussians fought the Austrians, Russians, and French. With his superb army and military skill, Frederick the Great of Prussia was able for some time to defeat the Austrian, French, and Russian armies. Eventually, however, his forces were gradually worn down and faced utter defeat until a new Russian tsar withdrew Russian troops from the conflict. A stalemate ensued, ending the European conflict in 1763.

The struggle between Britain and France in the rest of the world had more decisive results. In India, local rulers allied with British and French troops fought a number of battles. Ultimately, the British under Robert Clive won out, not because they had better forces but because they were more persistent. By the Treaty of Paris in 1763, the French withdrew and left India to the British.

The greatest conflicts of the Seven Years' War took place in North America, where it was known as the French and Indian War. British and French rivalry led to a number of confrontations. The French had more troops in North America but less naval support. The defeat of French fleets in 1759 left the French unable to reinforce their garrisons. That year, British forces under General Wolfe defeated the French under General Montcalm on the Plains of Abraham, outside Quebec. The British went on to seize Montreal, the Great Lakes area, and the Ohio Valley. The French were forced to make peace. In the Treaty of Paris, they ceded Canada and the lands east of the Mississippi to Britain. Their ally Spain transferred Spanish Florida to British control; in return, the French gave their Louisiana territory to the Spanish. By 1763, Great Britain had become the world's greatest colonial power. British victories cost Great Britain substantially, the national debt of Great Britain rose from 75 million pounds in 1756 to 133 million pounds in 1763. Great Britain's attempts to raise revenue by taxing the American colonies led to the American Revolution (see Section 18–3e "The American

Robert Clive in India. Robert Clive was the leader of the army of the British East India Company. He had been commanded to fight the ruler of Bengal in order to gain trading privileges. After the Battle of Plassey in 1757, Clive and the East India Company took control of Bengal. In this painting by Edward Penny, Clive is shown receiving a grant of money for his injured soldiers from the local nabob or governor of Bengal.

Revolution"). France financed the war by loans instead of raising taxes. The loss of France's empire was soon followed by an even greater internal upheaval (see Section 18–5 "The French Revolution," p. 527).

18–3e The American Revolution

By the mid-eighteenth century, increasing trade and industry had led to a growing middle class in Britain that favored expansion of trade and world empire. These people found a spokesman in William Pitt the Elder (1708–1778), who became prime minister in 1757 and began to expand the British Empire. In North America, after the end of the Seven Years' War in 1763, Britain controlled Canada and the lands east of the Mississippi.

The Americans and the British had different conceptions of how the empire should be governed, however. In eighteenth-century Britain, the king or queen and Parliament shared power, with Parliament gradually gaining the upper hand. The monarch chose ministers who were responsible to the crown and who set policy and guided Parliament. Parliament had the power to make laws, levy taxes, pass budgets, and indirectly influence the monarch's ministers. The British envisioned that Parliament would be the supreme authority performing these functions throughout the empire. But the Americans had their own representative assemblies. They believed that neither king nor Parliament should interfere in their internal affairs and that no tax could be levied without the consent of their own assemblies. After the Seven Years' War, when British policymakers sought to obtain new revenues from the colonies to pay for British army expenses in defending the colonies, the colonists resisted. An attempt to levy new taxes by the Stamp Act of 1765 led to riots and the law's quick repeal.

Crisis followed crisis in the 1770s until 1776, when the colonists decided to declare their independence from the British Empire. On July 4, 1776, the Second Continental Congress approved a declaration of independence written by Thomas Jefferson (1743–1826). A stirring political document, the Declaration of Independence affirmed the Enlightenment's natural rights of "life, liberty, and the pursuit of happiness" and declared the colonies to be "free and independent states absolved from all allegiance to the British crown." The war for American independence had formally begun.

Of great importance to the colonies' cause was the support of foreign countries that were eager to gain revenge for earlier defeats at the hands of the British. French officers and soldiers served under General Rochameau (ROH-sham-BOW), fighting bravely with George Washington (1732–1799) during the siege of Yorktown. When the British army of General Cornwallis was forced to surrender to a combined American and French army and French fleet under Washington at Yorktown in 1781, the British decided to call it quits. The Treaty of Paris, signed in 1783, recognized the independence of the American colonies and granted the Americans control of the territory from the Appalachians to the Mississippi River.

Birth of a New Nation The thirteen American colonies had gained their independence, but a fear of concentrated power and concern for their own interests caused them to have little enthusiasm for establishing a united nation with a strong central government, and so the Articles of Confederation, ratified in 1781, did not create one. A movement for a different form of national government soon arose. In the summer of 1787, fifty-five delegates attended a convention in Philadelphia to revise the Articles of Confederation. The convention's delegates—wealthy, politically experienced, and well educated—rejected revision and decided instead to devise a new constitution.

The proposed United States Constitution established a central government distinct from and superior to the governments of the individual states. The central or federal government was divided into three branches, each with some power to check the functioning of the others. A president would serve as the chief executive with the power to execute laws, veto the legislature's acts, supervise foreign affairs, and direct military forces. Legislative power was vested in the second branch of government, a bicameral legislature composed of the Senate, elected by the state legislatures, and the House of Representatives, elected directly by the people. A supreme court and other courts "as deemed necessary" by Congress provided the third branch of government. They would enforce the Constitution as the "supreme law of the land."

The Constitution was approved by the states—by a slim margin. Important to its success was a promise to add a bill of rights to the Constitution as the new government's first piece of business. Accordingly, in March 1789, the new Congress enacted the first ten amendments to the Constitution, known ever since as the Bill of Rights. These guaranteed freedom of religion, speech, press, petition, and assembly, as well as the right to bear arms, protection against unreasonable searches and arrests, trial by jury, due process of law, and protection of property rights. Many of these rights were derived from the **natural rights** philosophy of the eighteenth-century philosophes and the American colonists. Is it any wonder that many European intellectuals saw the American Revolution as the embodiment of the Enlightenment's political dreams?

18–4 TOWARD A NEW POLITICAL ORDER

 Focus Question: What do historians mean by the term *enlightened absolutism*, and to what degree did eighteenth-century Prussia, Austria, and Russia exhibit its characteristics?

There is no doubt that Enlightenment thought had some impact on the political development of European states in the eighteenth century. The philosophes believed in natural rights, which were thought to be privileges that ought not to be withheld from any person. These natural rights included equality before the law, freedom of religious worship, freedom of speech and press, and the right to assemble, hold property, and seek happiness.

But how were these natural rights to be established and preserved? Most philosophes believed that people needed to be ruled by an enlightened ruler. What made rulers enlightened? They must allow religious toleration, freedom of speech and press, and the rights of private property. They must foster the arts, sciences, and education. Above all, they must obey the laws and enforce them fairly for all subjects. Only strong monarchs seemed capable of overcoming vested interests and effecting the reforms society needed. Reforms then should come from above (from absolute rulers) rather than from below (from the people).

Many historians once assumed that a new type of monarchy emerged in the later eighteenth century, which they called *enlightened despotism* or **enlightened absolutism**. Monarchs such as Frederick II of Prussia, Catherine the Great of Russia, and Joseph II of Austria supposedly followed the advice of the philosophes and ruled by enlightened principles. Recently, however, scholars have questioned the usefulness of the concept of enlightened absolutism. We can determine the extent to which it can be applied by examining the major "enlightened absolutists" of the late eighteenth century.

18–4a Prussia: The Army and the Bureaucracy

Frederick II, known as Frederick the Great (1740–1786), was one of the best-educated and most cultured monarchs of the eighteenth century (see "Frederick the Great and His Father," p. 525). He was well versed in Enlightenment thought and even invited Voltaire to live at his court for several years. A believer

FREDERICK THE GREAT AND HIS FATHER

Politics & Government

AS A YOUNG MAN, THE FUTURE FREDERICK THE GREAT was quite different from his strict and austere father, Frederick William I. Possessing a high regard for French culture, poetry, and flute playing, Frederick resisted his father's wishes that he immerse himself in governmental and military affairs. Eventually, Frederick capitulated to his father's will and accepted the need to master affairs of state. These letters, written when Frederick was sixteen, illustrate the difficulties in their relationship.

Frederick to His Father, Frederick William I (September 11, 1728)

I have not ventured for a long time to present myself before my dear papa, partly because I was advised against it, but chiefly because I anticipated an even worse reception than usual and feared to vex my dear papa still further by the favor I have now to ask; so I have preferred to put it in writing.

I beg my dear papa that he will be kindly disposed toward me. I do assure him that after long examination of my conscience I do not find the slightest thing with which to reproach myself; but if, against my wish and will, I have vexed my dear papa, I hereby beg most humbly for forgiveness, and hope that my dear papa will give over the fearful hate which has appeared so plainly in his whole behavior and to which I cannot accustom myself. I have always thought hitherto that I had a kind father, but now I see the contrary. However, I will take courage and hope that my dear papa will think this all over and take me again into his favor. Meantime I assure him that I will never, my life long, willingly fail him, and in spite of his disfavor I am still, with most dutiful and childlike respect, my dear papa's

> Most obedient and faithful servant and son,
> Frederick

Frederick William I to His Son Frederick

A bad, obstinate boy, who does not love his father; for when one does one's best, and especially when one loves one's father, one does what he wishes not only when he is standing by but when he is not there to see. Moreover you know very well that I cannot stand an effeminate fellow who has no manly tastes, who cannot ride or shoot (to his shame be it said!), is untidy about his person, and wears his hair curled like a fool instead of cutting it; and that I have condemned all these things a thousand times, and yet there is no sign of improvement. For the rest, haughty, offish as a country lout, conversing with none but a favored few instead of being affable and popular, grimacing like a fool, and never following my wishes out of love for me but only when forced into it, caring for nothing but to have his own way, and thinking nothing else is of any importance. This is my answer.

> Frederick William

 Based on these documents, why was the relationship between Frederick II and his father such a difficult one? What does this troubled relationship tell you about the effects of ruling on the great monarchs of Europe and their families? What new duties and concerns of rulers (like Frederick William) may have reshaped relations between kings and sons?

Source: From *Readings in European History*, vol. 2, by James Harvey Robinson (Lexington, Mass.: Ginn and Co., 1906).

---

in the king as the "first servant of the state," Frederick the Great was a conscientious ruler who enlarged the Prussian army (to 200,000 men) and kept a strict watch over the bureaucracy. The Prussian army, because of its size and excellent reputation, was the most important institution in the state. Its officers, who were members of the nobility or landed aristocracy, had a strong sense of service to the king or state. As Prussian nobles, they believed in duty, obedience, and sacrifice. The bureaucracy also had its own code in which the supreme values were obedience, honor, and service to the king as the highest duty.

For a time, Frederick seemed quite willing to make enlightened reforms. He abolished the use of torture except in treason and murder cases and also granted limited freedom of speech and press, as well as religious toleration. He did exclude the Jews, levying special taxes on the Jewish subjects and barring them from civil service. Frederick attempted to improve the lives of the peasants by increasing agricultural productivity—he imported clover and potatoes from Western Europe, and the iron plow, while draining swamps in the lower Oder Valley. At the same time, however, he kept Prussia's rigid social structure and serfdom intact and avoided any additional reforms.

18-4b The Austrian Empire of the Habsburgs

The Austrian Empire had become one of the great European states by the beginning of the eighteenth century. Yet it was difficult to rule because it was a sprawling conglomerate of nationalities, languages, religions, and cultures (see Map 18.3). Empress Maria Theresa (1740–1780) managed to make administrative reforms that helped centralize the Austrian Empire, but they were done for practical reasons—to strengthen the power of the Habsburg state—and were accompanied by an enlargement and modernization of the armed forces. Maria Theresa remained staunchly conservative and was not open to the wider reform calls of the philosophes. But her successor was.

Joseph II (1780–1790) believed in the need to sweep away anything standing in the path of reason. As he said, "I have made Philosophy the lawmaker of my empire; her logical

Map 18.3 **Europe in 1763.** By the middle of the eighteenth century, five major powers dominated Europe—Prussia, Austria, Russia, Britain, and France. Each sought to enhance its power both domestically, through a bureaucracy that collected taxes and ran the military, and internationally, by capturing territory or preventing other powers from capturing territory.

 Given the distribution of Prussian and Habsburg holdings, in what areas of Europe were they most likely to compete for land and power?

applications are going to transform Austria." Joseph's reform program was far-reaching. He abolished serfdom, supported public education, abrogated the death penalty, and established the principle of equality of all before the law. Joseph carried out drastic religious reforms as well, including complete religious toleration.

Joseph's reform program proved overwhelming for Austria, however. He alienated the nobility by freeing the serfs and alienated the church by his attacks on the monastic establishment. Joseph realized his failure when he wrote the epitaph for his own gravestone: "Here lies Joseph II, who was unfortunate in everything that he undertook." His successors undid many of his reforms.

18–4c Russia Under Catherine the Great

Catherine II the Great (1762–1796) was an enlightened despot who was familiar with the works of the philosophes and seemed to favor enlightened reforms. She invited the French philosophe Diderot to Russia and, when he arrived, urged him to speak frankly "as man to man." He did, outlining a far-reaching program of political and financial reform. But Catherine was skeptical about impractical theories, which, she said, "would have turned everything in my kingdom upside down." She did consider the idea of a new law code that would recognize the principle of the equality of all people in the eyes of the law. But in the end she did nothing, knowing that her success depended on the support of the Russian nobility. In 1785, she gave the nobles a charter that exempted them from taxes.

Catherine's policy of favoring the landed nobility led to even worse conditions for the Russian peasants and a rebellion. Incited by an illiterate Cossack, Emelyan Pugachev (yim-yil-YAHN poo-guh-CHAHF), the rebellion began in 1773 and spread across southern Russia. But the rebellion soon faltered. Pugachev was captured, tortured, and executed. The rebellion collapsed completely, and Catherine responded with even stronger measures against the peasantry.

Above all, Catherine proved a worthy successor to Peter the Great in her policies of territorial expansion westward into Poland and southward to the Black Sea. Russia spread southward by defeating the Turks. Russian expansion westward occurred

CHRONOLOGY	Enlightened Absolutism in Eighteenth-Century Europe	
Prussia		
Frederick II the Great		1740–1786
Austrian Empire		
Maria Theresa		1740–1780
Joseph II		1780–1790
Russia		
Catherine II the Great		1762–1796
Pugachev's rebellion		1773–1775
Charter of the Nobility		1785

at the expense of neighboring Poland. In three partitions of Poland, Russia gained about 50 percent of Polish territory.

18–4d Enlightened Absolutism Reconsidered

Of the rulers we have discussed, only Joseph II sought truly radical changes based on Enlightenment ideas. Both Frederick II and Catherine II liked to talk about enlightened reforms, and they even attempted some. But the policies of neither seemed seriously affected by Enlightenment thought. Necessities of state and maintenance of the existing system took precedence over reform. Indeed, many historians maintain that Joseph, Frederick, and Catherine were all primarily guided by a concern for the power and well-being of their states. In the final analysis, heightened state power was used to create armies and wage wars to gain more power.

It would be foolish, however, to overlook the fact that the ability of enlightened rulers to make reforms was also limited by political and social realities. Everywhere in Europe, the hereditary aristocracy was still the most powerful class in society. Enlightened reforms were often limited to administrative and judicial measures that did not seriously undermine the powerful interests of the European nobility. As the chief beneficiaries of a system based on traditional rights and privileges for their class, they were not willing to support a political ideology that trumpeted the principle of equal rights for all. The first serious challenge to their supremacy would come in the French Revolution, an event that blew open the door to the modern world of politics.

18–5 THE FRENCH REVOLUTION

 Focus Question: What were the causes, the main events, and the results of the French Revolution?

The year 1789 witnessed two far-reaching events, the beginning of a new United States of America under its revamped constitution and the eruption of the French Revolution. Compared to the American Revolution a decade earlier, the French Revolution was more complex, more violent, and far more radical in its attempt to reconstruct both a new political order and a new social order.

18–5a Background to the French Revolution

The root causes of the French Revolution must be sought in the condition of French society. Before the Revolution, France was a society grounded in privilege and inequality. During the eighteenth century, the population had increased by 44 percent from 18 million to 26 million. It was a young country, with 36 percent under the age of twenty, and 40 percent between twenty and forty. It was divided, as it had been since the Middle Ages, into three orders or estates.

Social Structure of the Old Regime The First Estate consisted of the clergy and numbered about 130,000 people who owned approximately 10 percent of the land. Clergy were exempt from the *taille* (TY), France's chief tax. The church was very wealthy; income from church property and other investments produced almost 300 million *livres* annually—half the income of the royal crown. Clergy were also radically divided: the higher clergy, stemming from aristocratic families, shared the interests of the nobility and lived in palaces and townhouses, while the parish priests were often poor and from the class of commoners.

The Second Estate consisted of the nobility, composed of about 350,000 people who owned about 25 to 30 percent of the land. The nobility had continued to play an important and even crucial role in French society in the eighteenth century, holding many of the leading positions in the government, the military, the law courts, and the higher church offices. The nobles sought to expand their power at the expense of the monarchy and to maintain their control over positions in the military, church, and government. Moreover, the possession of privileges remained a hallmark of the nobility. Common to all nobles were tax exemptions, especially from the *taille*.

The Third Estate, or the commoners of society, constituted the overwhelming majority of the French population. They were divided by vast differences in occupation, level of education, and wealth. The peasants, who constituted 75 to 80 percent of the total population, were by far the largest segment of the Third Estate. They owned 35 to 40 percent of the land, although their landholdings varied from area to area and more than half had little or no land on which to survive. The landless peasants were day laborers who increasingly migrated to Paris in search of work; they were the first to suffer in hard times. Serfdom no longer existed on any large scale in France, but French peasants still had obligations to their local landlords that they deeply resented. These "relics of feudalism," or aristocratic privileges, had survived from an earlier age and included the payment of fees for the use of village facilities, such as the flour mill, community oven, and winepress.

Another part of the Third Estate consisted of skilled craftspeople, shopkeepers, and other wage earners in the cities. In the eighteenth century, these urban groups suffered a noticeable decline in purchasing power as consumer prices rose faster than wages. Their daily struggle for survival led many of these people to play an important role in the Revolution, especially in Paris.

About 8 percent of the population, or 2.3 million people, constituted the bourgeoisie or middle class, who owned about 20 to 25 percent of the land. This group included merchants, industrialists, and bankers who controlled the resources of trade, manufacturing, and finance and benefited from the economic prosperity after 1730. The bourgeoisie also included professional people—lawyers, holders of public offices, doctors, and writers. Many members of the bourgeoisie had their own set of grievances because they were often excluded from the social and political privileges monopolized by nobles.

Moreover, the new political ideas of the Enlightenment proved attractive to both the aristocracy and the bourgeoisie. Both elites, long accustomed to a new socioeconomic reality based on wealth and economic achievement, were increasingly frustrated by a monarchical system resting on privileges and on an old and rigid social order based on the concept of estates. The opposition of these elites to the **old order** led them ultimately to take drastic action against the monarchical **old regime**. In a real sense, the Revolution had its origins in political grievances.

Other Problems Facing the French Monarchy Although France had enjoyed fifty years of economic expansion in the first half of the eighteenth century, in the late 1780s bad harvests in 1787 and 1788 and the beginnings of a manufacturing depression had resulted in food shortages, rising prices for food and other goods, and unemployment in the cities. The number of poor, estimated at almost one-third of the population, reached crisis proportions on the eve of the Revolution.

The French monarchy seemed incapable of dealing with the new social realities. Louis XVI (1774–1792) had become king in

1774 at the age of twenty; he knew little about the operations of the French government and lacked the energy to deal decisively with state affairs. His wife, Marie Antoinette (ma-REE ahn-twahn-NET), was an Austrian princess who devoted much of her time to court intrigues (see Film & History). As France's crises worsened, neither Louis nor his queen seemed able to fathom the depths of despair and discontent that soon led to violent revolution.

The immediate cause of the French Revolution was the near collapse of government finances. France experienced a depression from 1778 to 1787 as a result of a loss of overseas markets and overproduction. Prices of grain and wine fell by 40 and 50 percent. Peasants faced increasing uncertainty as rent prices remained high due to a rapidly growing population. Poor harvests in 1788 and 1789 sent prices of wheat and rye soaring—leaving many people desperate. Costly wars and royal extravagance drove French governmental expenditures ever higher. The government responded by borrowing. Poor taxation policy contributed to the high debt, with most of the monarchy's funds coming from the peasantry. Unlike Britain, where the Bank of England financed the borrowing of money at low interest rates, France had no central bank, and instead relied on private loans (see "The State of French Finances," p. 529). By 1788, the interest on the debt alone constituted half of government spending. Financial lenders, fearful they would never be repaid, were refusing to lend additional amounts.

On the verge of a complete financial collapse, the government of Louis XVI was finally forced to call a meeting of the Estates-General, the French parliamentary body that had not met since 1614. The Estates-General consisted of representatives from the three orders of French society. In the elections for the Estates-General, the government had ruled that the Third Estate should get double representation (it did, after all, constitute 97 percent of the population). Consequently, while both the First Estate (the clergy) and the Second Estate (the nobility) had about three hundred delegates each, the Third Estate had almost six hundred representatives, most of whom were lawyers from French towns.

18–5b From Estates-General to National Assembly

The Estates-General opened at Versailles on May 5, 1789. It was troubled from the start with the question of whether voting should be by order or by head (each delegate having one vote). Traditionally, each order would vote as a group and have one vote. That meant that the First and Second Estates could outvote the Third Estate two to one. The Third Estate demanded that each deputy have one vote. With the assistance of liberal nobles and clerics, that would give the Third Estate a majority. When the First Estate declared in favor of voting by order, the Third Estate responded dramatically. On June 17, 1789, the Third Estate declared itself the "National Assembly" and decided to draw up a constitution. This was the first step in the French Revolution because the Third Estate had no legal right to act as the National Assembly. But this audacious act was soon in jeopardy, as the king sided with the First Estate and threatened to dissolve the Estates-General. Louis XVI now prepared to use force.

The common people, however, saved the Third Estate from the king's forces. On July 14, a mob of Parisians stormed the Bastille, a royal armory, and proceeded to dismantle it, brick by brick.

THE STATE OF FRENCH FINANCES

Politics & Government

IN 1781, JACQUES NECKER (ZHAHK neh-KAIR), the assistant to Louis XVI's controller general of finance (Necker could not be named controller general due to his Swiss birth and Protestant faith), published an account of the French monarchy's finances. Although Necker denied that the monarchy was in debt and hid France's enormous interest payments, his efforts to expose the inadequacies of the monarchy's monetary policies were the first real steps toward financial reform. His efforts, however, could not prevent the financial crisis that engulfed the French monarchy.

Jacques Necker, *Preface to the King's Accounts* (1781)

Sire,

[I] offer Your Majesty . . . a public account of . . . the current state of His Majesty's finances. . . .

If one examines the great credit that England enjoys and which is currently its greatest strength in the war, one should not attribute that entirely to the nature of its government; because, regardless of the authority of the monarch of France, since his interests are known always to rest on the foundation of faithfulness and justice, he could easily make all forget that he has the power to dismiss those principles; it is up to Your Majesty, with his strength of character and virtue, to make this truth felt through experience.

But another cause of the great credit of England is . . . the public renown to which the status of its finances is subject. That status is presented to Parliament each year, and printed afterward; and thus all lenders have regular knowledge of the balance being maintained between revenue and expenditure, they are never troubled by suspicions and imaginary fears. . . .

In France, a great mystery is always made of the status of the finances; or, if they are occasionally discussed, it is in the preambles of edicts and always when we want to borrow; but those words, too often the same to be true, have necessarily lost their authority and experienced men no longer believe them without the guarantee, so to speak, of the moral character of the minister of finance. It is vital to found confidence on a more solid base. I admit that, under certain circumstances, it has been possible to profit from the veil cast over the financial situation to obtain, in the midst of disorder, some mediocre credit that was not warranted; but this momentary advantage, which sustained a misleading illusion and favored the indifference of the administration, was soon followed by unhappy transactions, the memory of which lasts longer and which will take long to correct. . . .

The sovereign of a realm like that of France can always, when he wants to do so, maintain the balance between expenditures and ordinary revenue; the diminution of the former, always seconded by the wishes of the public, is in his hands; and when circumstances require, increasing taxes is within his power; but the most dangerous, and the most unjust of resources, is to seek momentary aid with blind confidence and take loans without insuring the interest, or to raise revenues, or to economize.

Such administration, which is seductive because it postpones the moment of difficulty, only increases ills and digs itself deeper into the hole; while another kind of conduct, simpler and more frank, multiplies the means available to the Sovereign and forever protects it from any sort of injustice.

It is thus this broad view of administration on the part of His Majesty which has permitted us to offer a public account of the state of his finances; and I hope that, for the good of the realm and his power, this happy institution will not be temporary.

 What did Necker believe were the main differences between the French and British systems of public finance?

Source: From Mason, *The French Revolution*, 1e. © 1999 Cengage Learning.

Louis XVI was soon informed that the royal troops were unreliable. Louis's acceptance of that reality signaled the collapse of royal authority; the king could no longer enforce his will.

At the same time, popular revolts broke out throughout France, both in the cities and in the countryside (see Comparative Illustration "Revolution and Revolt in France and China," p. 530). Behind the popular uprising was a growing resentment of the entire landholding system, with its fees and obligations. The fall of the Bastille and the king's apparent capitulation to the demands of the Third Estate now led peasants to take matters into their own hands. The peasant rebellions that occurred throughout France had a great impact on the National Assembly meeting at Versailles.

18–5c Destruction of the Old Regime

One of the first acts of the National Assembly was to abolish the rights of landlords and the fiscal exemptions of nobles, clergy, towns, and provinces. Three weeks later, the National Assembly adopted the Declaration of the Rights of Man and the Citizen (see Opposing Viewpoints "The Natural Rights of the French People: Two Views," p. 531). This charter of basic liberties proclaimed freedom and equal rights for all men and access to public office based on talent. All citizens were to have the right to take part in the legislative process. Freedom of speech and the press were coupled with the outlawing of arbitrary arrests.

The declaration also raised another important issue. Did its ideal of equal rights for "all men" also include women? Many deputies insisted that it did, provided that, as one said, "women do not hope to exercise political rights and functions." Olympe de Gouges (oh-LAMP duh GOOZH), a playwright, refused to accept this exclusion of women from political rights. Echoing the words of the official declaration, she penned the Declaration

COMPARATIVE ILLUSTRATION

A

Politics & Government

Revolution and Revolt in France and China. Both France and China experienced revolutionary upheaval at the end of the eighteenth century and well into the nineteenth. In both countries, common people often played an important role. Image B shows a scene from the storming of the Bastille in Paris in 1789. This early action by the people of Paris ultimately led to the overthrow of the French monarchy. Image A shows a scene from one of the struggles during the Taiping Rebellion, a major peasant revolt in the mid-nineteenth century in China. An imperial Chinese army is shown recapturing the city of Nanjing from Taiping rebels in 1864.

Q *What role did common people play in revolutionary upheavals in France and China in the eighteenth and nineteenth centuries?*

B

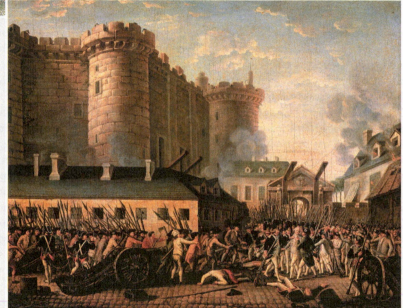

of the Rights of Woman and the Female Citizen, in which she insisted that women should have all the same rights as men (see Opposing Viewpoints "The Natural Rights of the French People: Two Views"). The National Assembly ignored her demands.

Because the Catholic Church was seen as an important pillar of the old order, it too was reformed. Most of the lands of the church were seized. The new Civil Constitution of the Clergy was put into effect in 1790. Both bishops and priests were to be elected by the people and paid by the state. The Catholic Church, still an important institution in the life of the French people, now became an enemy of the Revolution.

By 1791, the National Assembly had completed a new constitution that established a limited constitutional monarchy. There was still a monarch (now called "king of the French"), but the new Legislative Assembly was to make the laws. The Legislative Assembly, in which sovereign power was vested, was to sit for two years and consist of 745 representatives, or deputies,

chosen by an indirect system of election that preserved power in the hands of the more affluent members of society. A small group of 50,000 electors chose the deputies.

By 1791, the old order had been destroyed. The new order, however, had many opponents—Catholic priests, nobles, lower classes hurt by a rise in the cost of living, peasants who remained opposed to dues that had still not been abandoned, and political clubs like the Jacobins (JAK-uh-binz) that offered more radical solutions to France's problems. The king also made things difficult for the new government when he sought to flee France in June 1791 and almost succeeded. Louis XVI, however, stopped for several unplanned rests to have his meals prepared and missed his military escort. Once recognized in Varennes, he could have escaped but waited too long for a larger military escort. The National Guardsmen and members of the National Assembly arrived instead and brought him back to Paris. The flight to Varennes shattered the illusion of a loyal king. In this unsettled situation, under a discredited and seemingly disloyal

The Natural Rights of the French People: Two Views

Politics & Government | **ONE OF THE IMPORTANT DOCUMENTS OF THE FRENCH REVOLUTION**, the Declaration of the Rights of Man and the Citizen, was adopted on August 26, 1789, by the National Assembly. The declaration affirmed that "men are born and remain free and equal in rights," that government must protect these natural rights, and that political power is derived from the people.

Olympe de Gouges (the pen name used by Marie Gouze) was a butcher's daughter who wrote plays and pamphlets. She argued that the Declaration of the Rights of Man and the Citizen did not apply to women and composed her own Declaration of the Rights of Woman and the Female Citizen in 1791.

Declaration of the Rights of Man and the Citizen

1. Men are born and remain free and equal in rights. Social distinctions can only be founded upon the general good.
2. The aim of all political association is the preservation of the natural and imprescriptible rights of man. These rights are liberty, property, security, and resistance to oppression.
3. The principle of all sovereignty resides essentially in the nation. No body or individual may exercise any authority which does not proceed directly from the nation.
4. Liberty consists in being able to do everything which injures no one else. . . .
6. Law is the expression of the general will. Every citizen has a right to participate personally or through his representative in its formation. It must be the same for all, whether it protects or punishes. All citizens being equal in the eyes of the law are equally eligible to all dignities and to all public positions and occupations according to their abilities and without distinction except that of their virtues and talents.
7. No person shall be accused, arrested, or imprisoned except in the cases and according to the forms prescribed by law. . . .
10. No one shall be disturbed on account of his opinions, including his religious views, provided their manifestation does not disturb the public order established by law.
11. The free communication of ideas and opinions is one of the most precious of the rights of man. Every citizen may, accordingly, speak, write and print with freedom, being responsible, however, for such abuses of this freedom as shall be defined by law.
12. The security of the rights of man and of the citizen requires public military force. These forces are, therefore, established for the good of all and not for the personal advantage of those to whom they shall be entrusted. . . .
14. All the citizens have a right to decide either personally or by their representatives as to the necessity of the public contribution, to grant this freely, to know to what uses it is put, and to fix the proportion, the mode of assessment, and of collection, and the duration of the taxes.
15. Society has the right to require of every public agent an account of his administration.
16. A society in which the observance of the law is not assured nor the separation of powers defined has no constitution at all.
17. Property being an inviolable and sacred right, no one shall be deprived thereof except where public necessity, legally determined, shall clearly demand it, and then only on condition that the owner shall have been previously and equitably indemnified.

Declaration of the Rights of Woman and the Female Citizen

Mothers, daughters, sisters and representatives of the nation demand to be constituted into a national assembly. Believing that ignorance, omission, or scorn for the rights of woman are the only causes of public misfortunes and of the corruption of governments, the women have resolved to set forth in a solemn declaration the natural, inalienable, and sacred rights of woman in order that this declaration, constantly exposed before all the members of the society, will ceaselessly remind them of their rights and duties. . . .

Consequently, the sex that is as superior in beauty as it is in courage during the sufferings of maternity recognizes and declares in the presence and under the auspices of the Supreme Being, the following Rights of Woman and of Female Citizens.

1. Woman is born free and lives equal to man in her rights. Social distinctions can be based only on the common utility.
2. The purpose of any political association is the conservation of the natural and imprescriptible rights of woman and man; these rights are liberty, property, security, and especially resistance to oppression.
3. The principle of all sovereignty rests essentially with the nation, which is nothing but the union of woman and man; no body and no individual can exercise any authority which does not come expressly from [the nation].
4. Liberty and justice consist of restoring all that belongs to others; thus, the only limits on the exercise of the natural rights of woman are perpetual male tyranny; these limits are to be reformed by the laws of nature and reason. . . .
6. The law must be the expression of the general will; all female and male citizens must contribute either personally

(Continued)

or through their representatives to its formation; it must be the same for all: male and female citizens, being equal in the eyes of the law, must be equally admitted to all honors, positions, and public employment according to their capacity and without other distinctions besides those of their virtues and talents.

7. No woman is an exception; she is accused, arrested, and detained in cases determined by law. Women, like men, obey this rigorous law. . . .

10. No one is to be disquieted for his very basic opinions; woman has the right to mount the scaffold; she must equally have the right to mount the rostrum, provided that her demonstrations do not disturb the legally established public order.

11. The free communication of thought and opinions is one of the most precious rights of woman, since that liberty assured the recognition of children by their fathers. . . .

12. The guarantee of the rights of woman and the female citizen implies a major benefit; this guarantee must be instituted for the advantage of all, and not for the particular benefit of those to whom it is entrusted. . . .

14. Female and male citizens have the right to verify, either by themselves or through their representatives, the necessity of the public contribution. This can only apply to women

if they are granted an equal share, not only of wealth, but also of public administration, and in the determination of the proportion, the base, the collection, and the duration of the tax.

15. The collectivity of women, joined for tax purposes to the aggregate of men, has the right to demand an accounting of his administration from any public agent.

16. No society has a constitution without the guarantee of rights and the separation of powers; the constitution is null if the majority of individuals comprising the nation have not cooperated in drafting it.

17. Property belongs to both sexes whether united or separate; for each it is an inviolable and sacred right; no one can be deprived of it, since it is the true patrimony of nature, unless the legally determined public need obviously dictates it, and then only with a just and prior indemnity.

Q *What "natural rights" does the first document proclaim? To what extent was this document influenced by the writings of the philosophes? What rights for women does the second document enunciate? Given the nature and scope of the arguments in favor of natural rights and women's rights in these two documents, what key effects on European society would you attribute to the French Revolution?*

Sources: Excerpt from Thomas Carlyle, *The French Revolution: A History*, Vol. I (George Bell and Sons, London, 1902), pp. 346–348. From Levy, D. G., Applewhite, H. B., & Johnson, M. D. (1979). *Women in Revolutionary Paris, 1789–1795*. Urbana: University of Illinois Press. Used with permission of the University of Illinois Press.

---

monarch, the new Legislative Assembly held its first session in October 1791. France's relations with the rest of Europe soon led to Louis's downfall.

On August 27, 1791, the monarchs of Austria and Prussia, fearing that revolution would spread to their countries, invited other European monarchs to use force to reestablish monarchical authority in France. The French fared badly in the initial fighting in the spring of 1792, and a frantic search for scapegoats began. As one observer noted, "Everywhere you hear the cry that the king is betraying us, the generals are betraying us, that nobody is to be trusted; . . . that Paris will be taken in six weeks by the Austrians. . . . We are on a volcano ready to spout flames."[4] Defeats in war coupled with economic shortages in the spring led to renewed political demonstrations, especially against the king. In August 1792, radical political groups in Paris attacked the royal palace, took the king captive, and forced the Legislative Assembly to suspend the monarchy and call for a national convention, chosen on the basis of universal male suffrage, to decide on the future form of government. The French Revolution was about to enter a more radical stage.

18–5d The Radical Revolution

In September 1792, the newly elected National Convention began its sessions. Dominated by lawyers and other professionals, two-thirds of its deputies were under the age of forty-five,

and almost all had gained political experience as a result of the Revolution. Almost all distrusted the king. As a result, the convention's first step on September 21 was to abolish the monarchy and establish a republic. On January 21, 1793, the king was executed, and the destruction of the old regime was complete. But the execution of the king created new enemies for the Revolution both at home and abroad.

In Paris, the local government, known as the Commune, whose leaders came from the working classes, favored radical change and put constant pressure on the convention, pushing it to ever more radical positions. Meanwhile, peasants in the west and inhabitants of the major provincial cities refused to accept the authority of the convention.

A foreign crisis also loomed large. By the beginning of 1793, after the king had been put to death, most of Europe—an informal coalition of Austria, Prussia, Spain, Portugal, Britain, the Dutch Republic, and even Russia—aligned militarily against France. Grossly overextended, the French armies began to experience reverses, and by late spring, France was threatened with invasion.

A Nation in Arms To meet these crises, the convention gave broad powers to an executive committee of twelve known as the Committee of Public Safety, which came to be dominated by Maximilien Robespierre (mak-see-meel-YENH ROHBZ-pyayr). For a twelve-month period, from 1793 to 1794, the Committee of Public Safety took control of France. To save the Republic from its foreign foes, the committee decreed a universal mobilization of the nation on August 23, 1793:

> Young men will fight, young men are called to conquer. Married men will forge arms, transport military baggage and guns and will prepare food supplies. Women, who at long last are to take their rightful place in the revolution and follow their true destiny, will forget their futile tasks: their delicate hands will work at making clothes for soldiers; they will make tents and they will extend their tender care to shelters where the defenders of the *Patrie* [nation] will receive the help that their wounds require. Children will make lint of old cloth. It is for them that we are fighting: children, those beings destined to gather all the fruits of the revolution, will raise their pure hands toward the skies. And old men, performing their missions again, as of yore, will be guided to the public squares of the cities where they will kindle the courage of young warriors and preach the doctrines of hate for kings and the unity of the Republic.[5]

In less than a year, the French revolutionary government had raised an army of 650,000 and by 1795 had pushed the allies back across the Rhine and even conquered the Austrian Netherlands.

The French revolutionary army was an important step in the creation of modern **nationalism**. Previously, wars had been fought between governments or ruling dynasties by relatively small armies of professional soldiers. The new French army was the creation of a "people's" government; its wars were now "people's" wars. The entire nation was to be involved in the war. But when dynastic wars became people's wars, warfare increased in ferocity and lack of restraint. The wars of the French revolutionary era opened the door to the total war of the modern world.

Reign of Terror To meet the domestic crisis, the National Convention and the Committee of Public Safety launched the "Reign of Terror." Revolutionary courts were instituted to protect the Republic from its internal enemies. Robespierre forced through the National Convention a law that denied suspects sent before the Revolutionary Tribunal all rights to defend themselves. This law increased the pace of executions. In the course of nine months, 16,000 people were officially killed under the blade of the guillotine—a revolutionary device designed for the quick and efficient separation of heads from bodies.

Revolutionary armies were set up to bring recalcitrant cities and districts back under the control of the National Convention. The Committee of Public Safety decided to make an example of Lyons (LYOHNH), which had defied the authority of the National Convention. By April 1794, some 1,880 citizens of Lyons had been executed. When the guillotine proved too slow, cannon fire was used to blow condemned men into open graves. A German observed:

> Whole ranges of houses, always the most handsome, burnt. The churches, convents, and all the dwellings of the former patricians were in ruins. When I came to the guillotine, the blood of those who had been executed a few hours beforehand was still running in the street. . . . I said to a group of [radicals] that it would be decent to clear away all this human blood. Why should it be cleared? one of them said to me. It's the blood of aristocrats and rebels. The dogs should lick it up.[6]

Equality and Slavery: Revolution in Haiti Early in the French Revolution, the desire for equality led to a discussion of what to do about slavery. A club called Friends of the Blacks advocated the abolition of slavery, which was achieved in France in September 1791. However, French planters in the West Indies, who profited greatly from the use of slaves on their sugar plantations, opposed the abolition of slavery in the French colonies. When the National Convention came to power, the issue was revisited, and on February 4, 1794, guided by ideals of equality, the government abolished slavery in the colonies.

In one French colony, slaves had already rebelled for their freedom. In 1791, black slaves in the French sugar colony of

Citizens in the New French Army. To save the Republic from its foreign enemies, the National Convention created a revolutionary army of unprecedented size. This illustration, from a book of paintings on the French Revolution by the Lesueur brothers, shows three citizens learning to drill, while a young volunteer is being armed and outfitted by his family.

DEA/G. DAGLI ORTI/Getty Images

Saint-Domingue (san doh-MAYNG) (the western third of the island of Hispaniola), inspired by the ideals of the revolution occurring in France, revolted against French plantation owners. Slaves attacked, killing plantation owners and their families and burning their buildings. White planters retaliated with equal brutality. One wealthy French settler reported, "How can we stay in a country where slaves have raised their hands against their masters?"

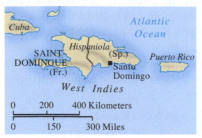

Revolt in Saint-Domingue

Eventually, leadership of the revolt was taken over by Toussaint L'Ouverture (too-SANH loo-vayr-TOOR) (1746–1803), a son of African slaves, who seized control of all of Hispaniola by 1801. Although Napoleon, the French leader, had accepted the revolutionary ideal of equality, he did not reject the reports of white planters that the massacres of white planters by slaves demonstrated the savage nature of blacks. In 1802, he reinstated slavery in the French West Indian colonies and sent an army that captured L'Ouverture, who died in a French dungeon within a year. But the French soldiers, weakened by disease, soon succumbed to the slave forces. On January 1, 1804, the western part of Hispaniola, now called Haiti, announced its freedom and became the first state in Latin America to win its independence. Despite Napoleon's efforts to the contrary, one of the French revolutionary ideals had triumphed abroad.

18–5e Reaction and the Directory

By the summer of 1794, the French had been successful on the battlefield against their foreign foes, making the Reign of Terror less necessary. But the Terror continued because Robespierre, who had become a figure of power and authority, became obsessed with purifying the body politic of all the corrupt. Many deputies in the National Convention were fearful, however, that they were not safe while Robespierre was free to act and gathered enough votes to condemn him. Robespierre was sent to the guillotine on July 28, 1794.

After the death of Robespierre, a reaction set in as more moderate middle-class leaders took control. The Reign of Terror came to a halt, and the National Convention reduced the power of the Committee of Public Safety. In addition, in August 1795 a new constitution was drafted that reflected the desire for a stability that did not sacrifice the ideals of 1789. Five directors—known as the Directory—acted as the executive authority.

Government under the Directory (1795–1799) was characterized by stagnation and corruption. The Directory faced political enemies on both the left and the right. On the right, royalists who wanted to restore the monarchy continued their agitation. On the left, radical hopes of power were revived by continuing economic problems. Battered from both sides, unable to solve the country's economic problems, and still carrying on the wars inherited from the Committee of Public Safety,

the Directory increasingly relied on the military to maintain its power. This led to a coup d'état in 1799 in which a popular military general, Napoleon Bonaparte (1769–1821), seized power.

18–6 THE AGE OF NAPOLEON

 Focus Question: Which aspects of the French Revolution did Napoleon preserve, and which did he destroy?

Napoleon dominated both French and European history from 1799 to 1815. The coup that brought him to power occurred exactly ten years after the outbreak of the French Revolution. In a sense, Napoleon brought the Revolution to an end, but he was also its child; he even called himself the Son of the Revolution. The French Revolution had made possible his rise first in the military and then to supreme power in France. Even beyond this, Napoleon had once said, "I am the Revolution," and he never ceased to remind the French that they owed to him the preservation of all that was beneficial in the revolutionary program.

18–6a The Rise of Napoleon

Napoleon was born in Corsica in 1769, only a few months after France had annexed the island. The son of an Italian lawyer whose family stemmed from the Florentine nobility, Napoleone Buonaparte (his birth name) grew up in the countryside of Corsica, a willful and demanding child who nevertheless developed discipline, thriftiness, and loyalty to his family. His father's connections in France enabled him to study first at a school in the French town of Autun, where he learned to speak French, and then to obtain a royal scholarship to study at a military school. At that time, he changed his first name to the more French-sounding Napoleon (he did not change his last name to Bonaparte until 1796).

NAPOLEON AND PSYCHOLOGICAL WARFARE

Politics & Government

IN 1796, AT THE AGE OF TWENTY-SEVEN, Napoleon Bonaparte was given command of the French army in Italy, where he won a series of stunning victories. His use of speed, deception, and surprise to overwhelm his opponents is well known. In this selection from a proclamation to his troops in Italy, Napoleon also appears as a master of psychological warfare.

Napoleon Bonaparte, Proclamation to French Troops in Italy (April 26, 1796)

Soldiers:

You have in a fortnight won six victories, taken twenty-one standards [flags of military units], fifty-five pieces of artillery, several strong places, and conquered the richest part of Piedmont [in northern Italy]; you have made fifteen thousand prisoners and killed or wounded more than ten thousand men. . . . You have won battles without cannon, crossed rivers without bridges, made forced marches without shoes, camped without brandy and often without bread. Only republican phalanxes, soldiers of liberty, would have been able to bear what you have borne. Thanks be to you, soldiers, for this. Your grateful country will owe its prosperity to you. . . .

The two armies which but recently attacked you with confidence are fleeing in consternation before you. Those misguided men who laughed at your misery and rejoiced in the thought of the triumphs of your enemies have been confounded.

But, soldiers, you have done nothing as yet compared with what there still remains to do. . . . The greatest obstacles undoubtedly have been overcome, but you still have battles to fight, cities to capture, rivers to cross. Is there any one among you whose courage is slackening? No. . . . All of you are burning to extend the glory of the French people. All long to humiliate those haughty kings who dare to contemplate placing us in fetters. All desire to dictate a glorious peace, one which will indemnify our country for the immense sacrifices which it has made; all would wish, as they return to their native villages, to be able to say proudly, "I was with the victorious army of Italy!"

 What themes did Napoleon use to play on the emotions of his troops and inspire them to greater efforts? Do you think Napoleon believed these words? Why or why not?

Source: From James Harvey Robinson, *Readings in European History* (Lexington, Mass.: Ginn and Co., 1906), p. 471.

Napoleon's military education led to his commission as a lieutenant in 1785, although he was not well liked by his fellow officers because he was short, spoke with an Italian accent, and had little money. For the next seven years, Napoleon spent much of his time reading the works of the philosophes, especially Rousseau, and educating himself in military matters by studying the campaigns of great military leaders from the past, including Alexander the Great, Charlemagne, and Frederick the Great. The French Revolution and the European war that followed broadened his sights and presented him with new opportunities.

Napoleon rose quickly through the ranks. In 1794, at the age of only twenty-five, he was made a brigadier general by the Committee of Public Safety. Two years later, he commanded the French armies in Italy, where he won a series of victories and returned to France as a conquering hero (see "Napoleon and Psychological Warfare"). After a disastrous expedition to Egypt, Napoleon returned to Paris, where he participated in the coup that gave him control of France. He was only thirty years old.

After the coup of 1799, a new form of the Republic, called the Consulate, was proclaimed in which Napoleon, as first consul, controlled the entire executive authority of government. He had overwhelming influence over the legislature, appointed members of the administrative bureaucracy, commanded the army, and conducted foreign affairs. In 1802, Napoleon was made consul for life, and in 1804, he returned France to monarchy when he crowned himself Emperor Napoleon I.

18–6b Domestic Policies

One of Napoleon's first domestic policies was to establish peace with the oldest and most implacable enemy of the Revolution, the Catholic Church. In 1801, Napoleon arranged a concordat with the pope that recognized Catholicism as the religion of a majority of the French people. In return, the pope agreed not to raise the question of the church lands confiscated in the Revolution. As a result of the concordat, the Catholic Church was no longer an enemy of the French government, and Frenchmen who had acquired church lands during the Revolution were assured that they would not be stripped of them, an assurance that made them supporters of the Napoleonic regime.

Napoleon's most enduring domestic achievement was his codification of the laws. Before the Revolution, France had some three hundred local legal systems. During the Revolution, efforts were made to prepare a single code of laws for the entire nation, but it remained for Napoleon to bring the work to completion in the famous Civil Code. This preserved most of the revolutionary gains by recognizing the principle of the equality of all citizens before the law, the abolition of serfdom and feudalism, and religious toleration. Property rights were also protected.

At the same time, the Civil Code strictly curtailed the rights of some people. During the radical phase of the French Revolution, new laws had made divorce an easy process for both husbands and wives and allowed sons and daughters to inherit

The Coronation of Napoleon. In 1804, Napoleon restored monarchy to France when he crowned himself emperor. In the coronation scene painted by Jacques-Louis David, Napoleon is shown crowning his wife, the empress Josephine, while the pope looks on. The painting shows Napoleon's mother seated in the box in the background, even though she was not at the ceremony.

property equally. Napoleon's Civil Code undid these laws. Divorce was still allowed but was made more difficult for women to obtain. Women were now "less equal than men" in other ways as well. When they married, their property came under the control of their husbands.

Napoleon also developed a powerful, centralized administrative machine and worked hard to develop a bureaucracy of capable officials. Early on, the regime showed that it cared little whether the expertise of officials had been acquired in royal or revolutionary bureaucracies. Promotion, whether in civil or military offices, was to be based not on rank or birth but on ability only. This principle of a government career open to talent was, of course, what many bourgeois had wanted before the Revolution.

In his domestic policies, then, Napoleon both destroyed and preserved aspects of the Revolution. Although equality and the opening of careers to talent were retained in the law code, the creation of a new aristocracy, the strong protection accorded to property rights, and the use of conscription for the military make it clear that much equality had been lost. Liberty had been replaced by an initially benevolent despotism that grew increasingly arbitrary. Napoleon shut down sixty of France's seventy-three newspapers and insisted that all manuscripts be subjected to government scrutiny before they were published. Even the mail was opened by government police.

18–6c Napoleon's Empire

When Napoleon became consul in 1799, France was at war with a second European coalition of Russia, Great Britain, and Austria. Napoleon realized the need for a pause and made a peace treaty in 1802. But war was renewed in 1803 with Britain, which was soon joined by Austria, Russia, and Prussia in the Third Coalition. In a series of battles from 1805 to 1807, Napoleon's Grand Army defeated the Austrian, Prussian, and Russian armies, giving Napoleon the opportunity to create a new European order.

The Grand Empire From 1807 to 1812, Napoleon was the master of Europe. His Grand Empire was composed of three major parts: the French Empire, dependent states, and allied states (see Map 18.4). Dependent states were kingdoms under the rule of Napoleon's relatives; these came to include Spain, the Netherlands, the kingdom of Italy, the Swiss Republic, the Grand Duchy of Warsaw, and the Confederation of the Rhine (a union of all German states except Austria and Prussia). Allied states were those defeated by Napoleon and forced to join his struggle against Britain; these included Prussia, Austria, Russia, and Sweden.

Within his empire, Napoleon sought acceptance of certain revolutionary principles, including legal equality, religious toleration, and economic freedom. In the inner core and dependent

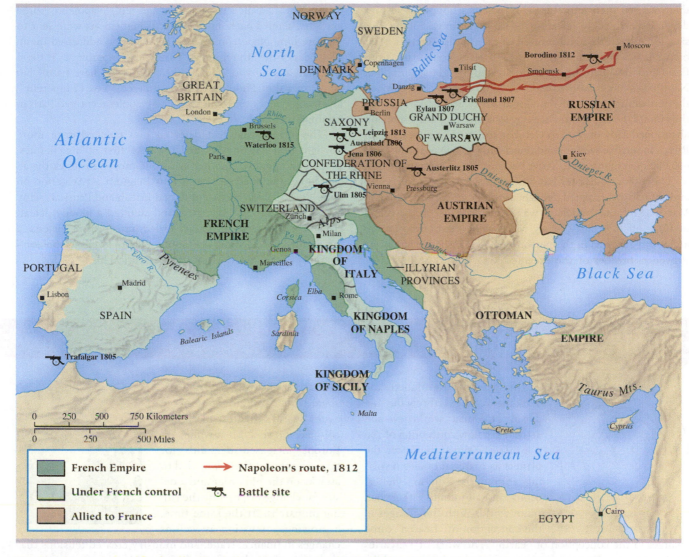

Map 18.4 Napoleon's Grand Empire. Napoleon's Grand Army won a series of victories against Austria, Prussia, and Russia that gave the French emperor full or partial control over much of Europe by 1807.

 On the European continent, what is the overall relationship between distance from France and degree of French control, and how can you account for this?

states of his Grand Empire, Napoleon tried to destroy the old order. Nobility and clergy everywhere in these states lost their special privileges. He decreed equality of opportunity with offices open to talent, equality before the law, and religious toleration. This spread of French revolutionary principles was an important factor in the development of liberal traditions in these countries.

Napoleon hoped that his Grand Empire would last for centuries; it collapsed almost as rapidly as it had been formed. As long as Britain ruled the waves, it was not subject to military attack. Napoleon hoped to invade Britain, but he could not overcome the British navy's decisive defeat of a combined French-Spanish fleet at Trafalgar in 1805. To defeat Britain, Napoleon turned to his **Continental system**. An alliance put into effect between 1806 and 1808, it attempted to prevent British goods from reaching the European continent in order to

weaken Britain economically and destroy its capacity to wage war. But the Continental system failed. Allied states resented it; some began to cheat and others to resist.

Napoleon also encountered new sources of opposition. His conquests made the French hated oppressors and aroused the patriotism of the conquered peoples. A Spanish uprising against Napoleon's rule, with British support, kept a French force of 200,000 pinned down for years.

The Fall of Napoleon The beginning of Napoleon's downfall came in 1812 with his invasion of Russia. The refusal of the Russians to remain in the Continental system left Napoleon with little choice. Although aware of the risks in invading such a huge country, he also knew that if the Russians were allowed to challenge the Continental system unopposed, others would soon follow suit. In June 1812, he led his Grand Army of more than 600,000 men into Russia. Napoleon's hopes for victory depended on quickly defeating the Russian armies, but the Russian forces retreated and refused to give battle, torching their own villages and countryside to keep Napoleon's army from finding food. When the Russians did stop to fight at Borodino, Napoleon's forces won an indecisive and costly victory. When the remaining troops of the Grand Army arrived in Moscow, they found the city ablaze. Lacking food and supplies, Napoleon abandoned Moscow late in October and made a retreat across Russia in terrible winter conditions. Only 40,000 of the original 600,000 men managed to arrive back in Poland in January 1813.

This military disaster led other European states to rise up and attack the crippled French army. Paris was captured in March 1814, and Napoleon was sent into exile on the island of Elba, off the coast of Italy. Meanwhile, the Bourbon monarchy was restored in the person of Louis XVIII, the count of Provence, brother of the executed king. (Louis XVII, son of Louis XVI, had died in prison at age ten.) Napoleon, bored on Elba, slipped back into France. When troops were sent to capture him, Napoleon opened his coat and addressed them: "Soldiers of the 5th regiment, I am your Emperor. . . . If there is a man among you would kill his Emperor, here I am!" No one fired a shot. Shouting "Vive l'Empereur! Vive l'Empereur!" the troops went over to his side, and Napoleon entered Paris in triumph on March 20, 1815.

The powers that had defeated him pledged once more to fight him. Having decided to strike first at his enemies, Napoleon raised yet another army and moved to attack the allied forces stationed in what is now Belgium. At Waterloo on June 18, Napoleon met a combined British and Prussian army under the duke of Wellington and suffered a bloody defeat. This time, the victorious allies exiled him to Saint Helena, a small, forsaken island in the South Atlantic. Only Napoleon's memory continued to haunt French political life.

CHAPTER SUMMARY

In the Scientific Revolution, the Western world overthrew the medieval, Ptolemaic worldview and arrived at a new conception of the universe: the sun at the center, the planets as material bodies revolving around the sun in elliptical orbits, and an infinite rather than finite world. With the changes in the conception of "heaven" came changes in the conception of "earth." The work of Descartes left Europeans with the separation of mind and matter and the belief that by using only reason they could, in fact, understand and dominate the world of nature.

Highly influenced by the new worldview created by the Scientific Revolution, the philosophes of the eighteenth century hoped that they could create a new society by using reason to discover the natural laws that governed it. They believed that education could create better human beings and a better human society. They attacked traditional religion as the enemy and created the new "sciences of man" in economics, politics, and education. Together, the Scientific Revolution of the seventeenth century and the Enlightenment of the eighteenth century constituted an intellectual revolution that laid the foundations for a modern worldview based on rationalism and secularism.

Everywhere in Europe at the beginning of the eighteenth century, the old order remained strong. Nobles, clerics, towns, and provinces all had privileges. Everywhere in the eighteenth century, monarchs sought to enlarge their bureaucracies to raise taxes to support large standing armies. The existence of these armies led to wars on a worldwide scale. Indeed, the Seven Years' War could be viewed as the first world war. Although the wars resulted in few changes in Europe, British victories en-

abled Great Britain to emerge as the world's greatest naval and colonial power. Meanwhile, in Europe increased demands for taxes to support these wars led to attacks on the old order and a desire for change not met by the ruling monarchs. At the same time, a growing population as well as changes in finance, trade, and industry created tensions that undermined the foundations of the old order. Its inability to deal with these changes led to a revolutionary outburst at the end of the eighteenth century that marked the beginning of the end for the old order. The revolutionary era of the late eighteenth century was a time of dramatic political transformations. Revolutionary upheavals, beginning in North America and continuing in France, spurred movements for political liberty and equality.

The documents promulgated by these revolutions, the Declaration of Independence and the Declaration of the Rights of Man and the Citizen, embodied the fundamental ideas of the Enlightenment and created a liberal political agenda based on a belief in popular sovereignty—the people as the source of political power— and the principles of liberty and equality. Liberty meant, in theory, freedom from arbitrary power as well as the freedom to think, write, and worship as one chose. Equality meant equality in rights, although it did not include equality between men and women.

CHAPTER TIMELINE

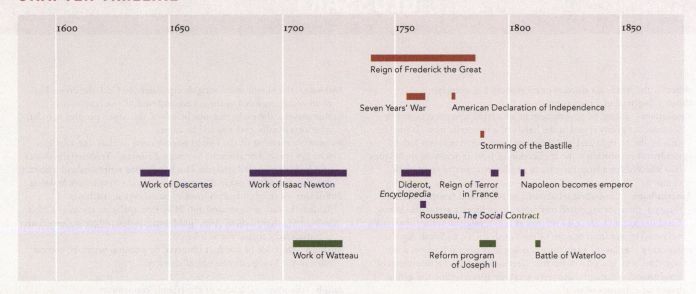

| | 1600 | 1650 | 1700 | 1750 | 1800 | 1850 |

Reign of Frederick the Great

Seven Years' War

American Declaration of Independence

Storming of the Bastille

Work of Descartes

Work of Isaac Newton

Diderot, *Encyclopedia*

Reign of Terror in France

Napoleon becomes emperor

Rousseau, *The Social Contract*

Work of Watteau

Reform program of Joseph II

Battle of Waterloo

CHAPTER REVIEW

Upon Reflection

Q What was the impact of the intellectual revolution of the seventeenth and eighteenth centuries on European society?

Q How was France changed by the revolutionary events between 1789 and 1799, and who benefited the most from these changes?

Q In what ways did Napoleon's policies reject the accomplishments of the French Revolution? In what ways did his policies strengthen those accomplishments?

Key Terms

Scientific Revolution (p. 509)
geocentric theory (p. 509)
heliocentric theory (p. 509)
world-machine (p. 511)
Cartesian dualism (p. 511)
rationalism (p. 511)
Enlightenment (p. 511)
scientific method (p. 511)
philosophes (p. 511)
separation of powers (p. 513)
deism (p. 514)
laissez-faire (p. 514)
feminism (p. 516)

Rococo (p. 516)
high culture (p. 518)
popular culture (p. 518)
cottage industry (p. 519)
agricultural revolution (p. 519)
patrician (p. 521)
rentiers (p. 521)
natural rights (p. 524)
enlightened absolutism (p. 524)
old order (p. 528)
old regime (p. 528)
nationalism (p. 533)
Continental system (p. 537)

Chapter Notes

1. R. Descartes, *Philosophical Writing*, ed. and trans. N. K. Smith (New York, 1958), pp. 118–119.
2. J. Locke, *An Essay Concerning Human Understanding* (New York, 1964), pp. 89–90.
3. Quoted in P. Burke, *Popular Culture in Early Modern Europe*, rev. ed. (New York, 1994), p. 186.
4. Quoted in W. Doyle, *The Oxford History of the French Revolution* (Oxford, 1989), p. 184.
5. Quoted in L. Gershoy, *The Era of the French Revolution* (Princeton, N.J., 1957), p. 157.
6. Quoted in Doyle, *Oxford History*, p. 254.

GLOSSARY

abbess   the head of a convent or monastery for women.

abbot   the head of a monastery.

absolutism   a form of government in which the sovereign power or ultimate authority rested in the hands of a monarch who claimed to rule by divine right and was therefore responsible only to God.

agricultural revolution   the application of new agricultural techniques that allowed for a large increase in productivity in the eighteenth century.

Amerindians   the earliest inhabitants of North and South America. Original theories suggested migration from Siberia across the Bering Land Bridge; more recent evidence suggests migration may also have occurred by sea from regions of the South Pacific to South America.

aristocracy   a class of hereditary nobility in medieval Europe; a warrior class who shared a distinctive lifestyle based on the institution of knighthood, although there were social divisions within the group based on extremes of wealth.

Atman   in Brahmanism, the individual soul.

bakufu   the centralized government set up in Japan in the twelfth century. *See also* shogunate system.

banners   originally established in 1639 by the Qing Dynasty, the eight banners were administrative divisions into which all Manchu families were placed. Banners quickly evolved into the basis of Manchu military organization, with each required to raise and support a prescribed number of troops.

Bao-jia **system**   the Chinese practice, reportedly originated by the Qin dynasty in the third century BCE, of organizing families into groups of five or ten to exercise mutual control and surveillance and reduce loyalty to the family.

bard   in Africa, a professional storyteller.

Baroque   a style that dominated Western painting, sculpture, architecture, and music from about 1580 to 1730, generally characterized by elaborate ornamentation and dramatic effects. Important practitioners included Bernini, Rubens, Handel, and Bach.

Bedouins   nomadic tribes originally from northern Arabia who became important traders after the domestication of the camel during the first millennium BCE. Early converts to Islam, their values and practices deeply affected Muhammad.

Berbers   an ethnic group indigenous to western North Africa.

bey   a Turkish provincial governor in the Ottoman Empire.

bhakti   in Hinduism, devotion as a means of religious observance open to all persons regardless of class.

Black Death   the outbreak of plague (mostly bubonic) in the mid-fourteenth century that killed from 25 to 50 percent of Europe's population.

bodhi   wisdom; sometimes described as complete awareness of the true nature of the universe.

bodhisattva   in some schools of Buddhism, an individual who has achieved enlightenment but, because of his great compassion, has chosen to renounce Nirvana and to remain on earth in spirit form to help all human beings achieve release from reincarnation.

Boers   the Afrikaans-speaking descendants of Dutch settlers in southern Africa who left the Cape Colony in the nineteenth century to settle in the Orange Free State and Transvaal; defeated by the British in the Boer War (1899–1902) and ultimately incorporated in the Union of South Africa.

bonsai   the cultivation of stunted trees and shrubs to create exquisite nature scenes in miniature; originated in China in the first millennium BCE and imported to Japan between 700 and 900 CE.

Brahman   the Hindu word roughly equivalent to God; the divine basis of all being; regarded as the source and sum of the cosmos.

Brahmanism   the early religious beliefs of the Aryan peoples in India, which eventually gave rise to Hinduism.

brahmin   a member of the Hindu priestly caste or class; literally "one who has realized or attempts to realize *Brahman*." Traditionally, duties of a *brahmin* included studying Hindu religious scriptures and transmitting them to others orally. The priests of Hindu temples are *brahmins*.

Buddhism   a religion and philosophy based on the teachings of Siddhartha Gautama around 500 BCE. Principally practiced in China, India, and other parts of Asia, Buddhism has 360 million followers and is considered a major world religion.

Bushido   the code of conduct observed by samurai warriors; comparable to the European concept of chivalry.

caliph   the temporal leader of the Islamic community.

calpulli   in Aztec society, a kinship group, often of a thousand or more, that served as an intermediary with the central government, providing taxes and conscript labor to the state.

capitalism   beginning in the Middle Ages, an economic system in which private owners invest in trade and goods in order to make profits.

caravels   mobile sailing ships with both lateen and square sails that began to be constructed in Europe in the sixteenth century.

Cartesian dualism   Descartes's principle of the separation of mind and matter (and mind and body) that enabled scientists to view matter as something separate from themselves that could be investigated by reason.

Catholic Reformation   a movement for the reform of the Catholic Church in the sixteenth century.

centuriate assembly   the chief popular assembly of the Roman Republic. It passed laws and elected the chief magistrates.

Chan   a Chinese Buddhist sect (Zen in Japanese) influenced by Daoist ideas, which called for mind training and a strict regimen as a means of seeking enlightenment.

chinampas   in Mesoamerica, swampy islands crisscrossed by canals that provided water for crops and easy transportation to local markets.

chivalry   the ideal of civilized behavior that emerged among the European nobility in the eleventh and twelfth centuries under the influence of the church; a code of ethics knights were expected to uphold.

chonmin   in Korea, the lowest class in society consisting of slaves and workers in certain undesirable occupations such as butchers; literally, "base people."

Christian humanism   an intellectual movement in northern Europe in the late fifteenth and early sixteenth centuries that combined interest in the classics of the Italian Renaissance with an interest in the sources of early Christianity, including the New Testament and the writings of the church fathers.

chu nom   an adaptation of Chinese written characters to provide a writing system for spoken Vietnamese; in use by the ninth century CE.

civilization   a complex culture in which large numbers of humans share a variety of common elements, including cities; religious, political, military, and social structures; writing; and significant artistic and intellectual activity.

civil service examination   an elaborate Chinese system of selecting bureaucrats on merit, first introduced in 165 CE, developed by the Tang Dynasty in the seventh century CE, and refined under the Song Dynasty; later adopted in Vietnam and with less success in Japan and

Korea. It contributed to efficient government, upward mobility, and cultural uniformity.

Columbian Exchange the exchange of animals, plants, and culture, but also communicable diseases and human populations including slaves, between the Western and Eastern Hemispheres that occurred after Columbus's voyages to the Americas.

common law law common to the entire kingdom of England; imposed by the king's courts beginning in the twelfth century to replace the customary law used in county and feudal courts that varied from place to place.

commune in medieval Europe, an association of townspeople bound together by a sworn oath for the purpose of obtaining basic liberties from the lord of the territory in which the town was located; also, the self-governing town after receiving its liberties.

conciliarism a movement in fourteenth- and fifteenth-century Europe that held that final authority in spiritual matters resided with a general church council, not the pope. It emerged in response to the Avignon papacy and the Great Schism and was used to justify the summoning of the Council of Constance (1414–1418).

Confucianism a system of thought based on the teachings of Confucius (551–479 BCE) that developed into the ruling ideology of the Chinese state. *See also* Neo-Confucianism.

conquistadors "conquerors." Leaders in the Spanish conquests in the Americas, especially Mexico and Peru, in the sixteenth century.

consuls the chief executive officers of the Roman Republic. Two were chosen annually to administer the government and lead the army in battle.

Continental system Napoleon's effort to bar British goods from the European continent in the hope of weakening Britain's economy and destroying its capacity to wage war.

Coptic a form of Christianity, originally Egyptian, that has thrived in Ethiopia since the fourth century CE.

cottage industry a system of textile manufacturing in which spinners and weavers worked at home in their cottages using raw materials supplied to them by capitalist entrepreneurs.

council of the plebs in the Roman Republic, a council only for the plebeians. After 287 BCE, however, its resolutions were binding on all Romans.

creoles in Latin America, American-born descendants of Europeans.

crusades in the Middle Ages, a series of military campaigns in defense of Christendom.

cuneiform "wedge-shaped." A system of writing developed by the Sumerians that consisted of wedge-shaped impressions made by a reed stylus on clay tablets.

daimyo prominent Japanese families who provided allegiance to the local shogun in exchange for protection; similar to vassals in Europe.

Dao a Chinese philosophical concept, literally "the Way," central to both Confucianism and Daoism, that describes the behavior proper to each member of society; somewhat similar to the Indian concept of *dharma*.

Daoism a Chinese philosophy traditionally ascribed to the perhaps legendary Lao Zi, which holds that acceptance and spontaneity are the keys to harmonious interaction with the universal order; an alternative to Confucianism.

deism belief in God as the creator of the universe who, after setting it in motion, ceased to have any direct involvement in it and allowed it to run according to its own natural laws.

demesne the part of a manor retained under the direct control of the lord and worked by the serfs as part of their labor services.

devshirme in the Ottoman Empire, a system (literally, "collection") of training talented children to be administrators or members of the sultan's harem; originally meritocratic, by the seventeenth century it had degenerated into a hereditary caste.

dharma a set of laws, dating to Vedic times, that set behavioral standards for all individuals and classes in Indian society.

dictator in the Roman Republic, an official granted unlimited power to run the state for a short period of time, usually six months, during an emergency.

diffusion hypothesis the hypothesis that the Yellow River valley was the ancient heartland of Chinese civilization and that technological and cultural achievements radiated from there to other parts of East Asia. Recent discoveries of other early agricultural communities in China have led to some modification of the hypothesis to allow for other centers of civilization.

diocese the area under the jurisdiction of a Christian bishop; based originally on Roman administrative districts.

divination the practice of seeking to foretell future events by interpreting divine signs, which could appear in various forms, such as in the entrails of animals, in patterns in smoke, or in dreams.

divine-right monarchy a monarchy based on the belief that monarchs receive their power directly from God and are responsible to no one except God.

dyarchy during the Qing Dynasty in China, a system in which all important national and provincial admininstrative positions were shared equally by Chinese and Manchus, which helped consolidate both the rule of the Manchus and their assimilation.

El Niño periodic changes in water temperature at the surface of the Pacific Ocean, which can lead to major environmental changes and may have led to the collapse of the Moche civilization in what is now Peru.

emir "commander" in Arabic, a title used by Muslim rulers in southern Spain and elsewhere.

encomienda a grant from the Spanish monarch to colonial conquistadors. *See also encomienda* system.

encomienda **system** the system by which Spain first governed its American colonies. Holders of an *encomienda* were supposed to protect the Indians as well as use them as laborers and collect tribute but in practice exploited them.

enlightened absolutism an absolute monarchy in which the ruler follows the principles of the Enlightenment by introducing reforms for the improvement of society, allowing freedom of speech and the press, permitting religious toleration, expanding education, and ruling in accordance with the laws.

Enlightenment an eighteenth-century intellectual movement, led by the philosophes, that stressed the application of reason and the scientific method to all aspects of life.

Epicureanism a philosophy founded by Epicurus in the fourth century BCE that taught that happiness (freedom from emotional turmoil) could be achieved through the pursuit of pleasure (intellectual rather than sensual pleasure).

eta in feudal Japan, a class of hereditary slaves who were responsible for what were considered degrading occupations, such as curing leather and burying the dead.

eunuchs men whose testicles have been removed. Eunuchs often played an important role at court in the Chinese imperial system, the Ottoman Empire, and the Mughal Dynasty, among others.

feminism the belief in the social, political, and economic equality of the sexes; also, organized activity to advance women's rights.

fief a landed estate granted to a vassal in exchange for military services.

filial piety in traditional China, in particular, a hierarchical system in which every family member has his or her place, subordinate to a patriarch who has certain reciprocal responsibilities.

Five Pillars of Islam the core requirements of the Muslim faith: belief in Allah and his prophet, Muhammad; prescribed prayers; observation of Ramadan; pilgrimage to Mecca; and giving alms to the poor.

five relationships in traditional China, the hierarchical interpersonal associations considered crucial to social order, within the family, between friends, and with the king.

foot binding an extremely painful process, common in China throughout the second millennium CE, that compressed girls' feet to half their natural size, representing submissiveness and self-discipline, which were considered necessary attributes of an ideal wife.

fudai daimyo during the Tokugawa Shogunate in Japan, less powerful lords who were directly subordinate to the shogunate; literally, "inside daimyo."

genin landless laborers in feudal Japan, who were effectively slaves.

geocentric theory the idea that the earth is at the center of the universe and that the sun and other celestial objects revolve around the earth.

global economy an interdependent economy in which the production, distribution, and sale of goods are accomplished on a worldwide scale.

good emperors the five emperors who ruled from 96 to 180 (Nerva, Trajan, Hadrian, Antoninus Pius, and Marcus Aurelius), a period of peace and prosperity for the Roman Empire.

Gothic a term used to describe the art and especially architecture of Europe in the twelfth, thirteenth, and fourteenth centuries.

Grand Council the top of the government hierarchy in the Song Dynasty in China.

grand vizier the chief minister in the Ottoman Empire, under the sultan.

guild an association of people with common interests and concerns, especially people working in the same craft. In medieval Europe, guilds came to control much of the production process and to restrict entry into various trades.

guru teacher, especially in the Hindu, Buddhist, and Sikh religious traditions, where the term is an important honorific.

Hadith a collection of the sayings of the Prophet Muhammad, used to supplement the revelations contained in the Qur'an.

harem the private living quarters of a ruler such as the sultan in the Ottoman Empire or the caliph of Baghdad; generally large and mostly inhabited by the extended family.

Hegira the flight of Muhammad from Mecca to Medina in 622, which marks the first date on the official calendar of Islam.

heliocentric theory the idea that the sun (not the earth) is at the center of the universe.

helots serfs in ancient Sparta who were permanently bound to the land that they worked for their Spartan masters.

heresy the holding of religious doctrines different from the official teachings of the church.

hieroglyphics a highly pictorial system of writing most often associated with ancient Egypt. Also used (with different "pictographs") by other ancient peoples such as the Maya.

high culture the literary and artistic culture of the educated and wealthy ruling classes.

Hinayana the scornful name for Theravada Buddhism ("lesser vehicle") used by devotees of Mahayana Buddhism.

Hinduism the main religion in India. It emphasizes reincarnation, based on the results of the previous life, and the desirability of escaping this cycle. Its various forms feature both asceticism and the pleasures of ordinary life and encompass a multitude of gods as different manifestations of one ultimate reality.

hominids the earliest humanlike creatures. They flourished in East and South Africa as long as 3 to 4 million years ago.

Hopewell culture a Native American society that flourished from about 200 BCE to 400 CE, noted for large burial mounds and extensive manufacturing. Largely based in Ohio, its traders ranged as far as the Gulf of Mexico.

hoplites heavily armed infantry soldiers used in ancient Greece in a phalanx formation.

iconoclasm an eighth-century Byzantine movement against the use of icons (pictures of sacred figures), which was condemned as idolatry.

iconoclast a member of an eighth-century Byzantine movement against the use of icons (pictures of sacred figures), which it condemned as idolatry.

imam an Islamic religious leader. Some traditions say there is only one per generation; others use the term more broadly.

indulgence the remission of part or all of the temporal punishment in purgatory due to sin; granted for charitable contributions and other good deeds. Indulgences became a regular practice of the Christian church in the High Middle Ages, and their abuse was instrumental in sparking Luther's reform movement in the sixteenth century.

interdict in the Catholic Church, a censure by which a region or country is deprived of receiving the sacraments.

ISIS radical terrorist group founded by Sunni dissidents after the fall of Saddam Hussein and the establishment of a Shi'ite-led government in Iraq. The group seeks to establish a caliphate for Muslims throughout the Middle East.

Jainism an Indian religion, founded in the fifth century BCE, that stresses extreme simplicity.

janissaries an elite core of eight thousand troops personally loyal to the sultan of the Ottoman Empire.

jati a kinship group, the basic social organization of traditional Indian society, to some extent specialized by occupation.

jihad in Islam, "striving in the way of the Lord." The term is ambiguous and has been subject to various interpretations, from the practice of conducting raids against local neighbors to the conduct of "holy war" against unbelievers.

joint-stock company a company or association that raises capital by selling shares to individuals who receive dividends on their investment while a board of directors runs the company.

justification by faith the primary doctrine of the Protestant Reformation; taught that humans are saved not through good works but by the grace of God, bestowed freely through the sacrifice of Jesus.

kami spirits worshiped in early Japan that resided in trees, rivers, and streams. *See also* Shinto.

karma a fundamental concept in Hindu (and later Buddhist, Jain, and Sikh) philosophy, that rebirth in a future life is determined by actions in this or other lives. The word refers to the entire process, to the individual's actions, and also to the cumulative result of those actions (for instance, a store of good or bad *karma*).

khanates Mongol kingdoms, in particular the subdivisions of Genghis Khan's empire ruled by his heirs.

kowtow the ritual of prostration and touching the forehead to the ground, demanded of all foreign ambassadors to the Chinese court as a symbol of submission.

kshatriya originally, the warrior class of Aryan society in India; ranked below (sometimes equal to) *brahmins*; in modern times often government workers or soldiers.

laissez-faire French for "leave it alone." An economic doctrine that holds that an economy is best served when the government does not interfere but allows the economy to self-regulate according to the forces of supply and demand.

latifundia large landed estates in the Roman Empire (singular: *latifundium*).

lay investiture the practice in which a layperson chose a bishop and invested him with the symbols of both his temporal office and his spiritual office; led to the Investiture Controversy, which was ended by compromise in the Concordat of Worms in 1122.

Legalism a Chinese philosophy that argued that human beings were by nature evil and would follow the correct path only if coerced by harsh laws and stiff punishments. Adopted as official ideology by the Qin dynasty, it was later rejected but remained influential.

liberal arts the seven areas of study that formed the basis of education in medieval and early modern Europe; consisted of grammar, rhetoric, and dialectic or logic (the *trivium*) and arithmetic, geometry, astronomy, and music (the *quadrivium*).

limited (constitutional) monarchy a system of government in which the monarch is limited by a representative assembly and by the duty to rule in accordance with the laws of the land.

lineage group   the descendants of a common ancestor; relatives, often as opposed to immediate family.

Longshan   a Neolithic society from near the Yellow River in China, sometimes identified by its black pottery.

madrasas   schools established by the Abbasid caliphs to popularize the teachings of Sunni religious orthodoxy.

maharaja   originally, a king in the Aryan society of early India (a great raja); later used more generally to denote an important ruler.

Mahayana   a school of Buddhism that promotes the idea of universal salvation through the intercession of bodhisattvas; originating in northwest Asia, it later spread along the Silk Road to China and Japan.

majlis   a council of elders among the Bedouins of the Roman era.

Malayo-Polynesian   a family of languages whose speakers originated on Taiwan or in southeastern China and spread from there to the Malay Peninsula, the Indonesian archipelago, and many islands of the South Pacific.

mandate of Heaven   the justification for the rule of the Zhou dynasty in China. The king was charged to maintain order as a representative of Heaven, which was viewed as an impersonal law of nature.

Manichaeanism   an offshoot of the ancient Zoroastrian religion that was later influenced by Christianity; became popular in central Asia in the eighth century CE.

manor   an agricultural estate operated by a lord and worked by peasants who performed labor services and paid various rents and fees to the lord in exchange for protection and sustenance.

mansa   in the West African state of Mali, a chieftain who served as both religious and administrative leader and was responsible for forwarding tax revenues from the village to higher levels of government.

maroons   camps for escaped slaves.

matrilinear   passing through the female line—for example, from a father to his sister's son rather than his own—as practiced in some African societies; not necessarily or even usually combined with matriarchy, in which women rule.

megaliths   large stones, widely used in Europe from around 4000 to 1500 BCE to create monuments, including sophisticated astronomical observatories.

mercantilism   an economic theory that held that a nation's prosperity depended on its supply of gold and silver and that the total volume of trade is unchangeable; therefore advocated that the government play an active role in the economy by encouraging exports and discouraging imports, especially through the use of tariffs.

Mesolithic Age   the period from 10,000 to 7000 BCE, characterized by a gradual transition from a food-gathering and hunting economy to a food-producing economy.

mestizos   the offspring of intermarriage between Europeans, originally Spaniards, and native American Indians.

Middle Passage   the journey of slaves from Africa to the Americas as the middle leg of the triangular trade.

Middle Path   a central concept of Buddhism, which advocates avoiding extremes of both materialism and asceticism; also known as the Eightfold Way.

mihrab   the niche in a mosque's wall that indicates the direction of Mecca, usually containing an ornately decorated panel representing Allah.

millet   an administrative unit in the Ottoman Empire used to organize religious groups.

monasticism   a movement that began in early Christianity whose purpose was to create communities of men and women who practiced a communal life dedicated to God as a moral example to the world around them.

monk   a man who chooses to live a communal life divorced from the world in order to dedicate himself totally to the will of God.

monotheism   having only one god; the doctrine or belief that there is only one god.

mulattoes   the offspring of Africans and Europeans, particularly in Latin America.

mystery religions   religions that involve initiation into secret rites that promise intense emotional involvement with spiritual forces and a greater chance of individual immortality.

nationalism   a sense of national consciousness based on awareness of being part of a community—a "nation"—that has common institutions, traditions, language, and customs and that becomes the focus of the individual's primary political loyalty.

nativist   the policy of protecting the interests of native-born or established inhabitants against those of immigrants.

natural law   a body of laws or specific principles held to be derived from nature and binding on all human society even in the absence of positive laws.

natural rights   certain inalienable rights to which all people are entitled. They include the right to life, liberty, and ownership of property; freedom of speech and religion; and equal treatment under the law.

Neo-Confucianism   the dominant ideology of China during the second millennium CE; combined the metaphysical speculations of Buddhism and Daoism with the pragmatic Confucian approach to society, maintaining that the world is real, not illusory, and that fulfillment comes from participation, not withdrawal. It encouraged an intellectual environment that valued continuity over change and tradition over innovation.

Neolithic Revolution   the development of agriculture, including the planting of food crops and the domestication of farm animals, around 10,000 BCE.

new monarchies   the governments of France, England, and Spain at the end of the fifteenth century, where the rulers were successful in reestablishing or extending centralized royal authority, suppressing the nobility, controlling the church, and insisting on the loyalty of all peoples living in their territories.

Nirvana   in Buddhist thought, enlightenment, the ultimate transcendence from the illusion of the material world; release from the "wheel of life."

Nok culture   in northern Nigeria, one of the most active early iron-working societies in Africa, artifacts from which date back as far as 500 BCE.

noncentralized societies   societies characterized by autonomous villages organized by clans and ruled by a local chieftain or clan head; typical of the southern half of the African continent before the eleventh century CE.

northern Renaissance humanism   see Christian humanism.

nun   a woman who withdraws from the world and joins a religious community; the female equivalent of a monk.

old order/old regime   the political and social system of France in the eighteenth century before the Revolution.

oligarchy   rule by a few.

Paleolithic Age   the period of human history when humans used simple stone tools (c. 2,500,000–10,000 BCE).

Panca Sila   the "five principles," a set of guiding objectives established by the 1945 Constitution in Indonesia.

pantheism   a doctrine that equates God with the universe and all that is in it.

pariahs   members of the lowest level of traditional Indian society, technically outside the class system itself; also known as untouchables.

paterfamilias   the dominant male in a Roman family whose powers over his wife and children were theoretically unlimited, though they were sometimes circumvented in practice.

patriarchy   a society in which the father is supreme in the clan or family; more generally, a society dominated by men.

patricians   great landowners who became the ruling class in the Roman Republic; in early modern Europe, a term used to identify the ruling elites of cities.

patrilinear   passing through the male line, from father to son; often combined with patriarchy.

Pax Romana "Roman peace"; the stability and prosperity that Roman rule brought to the Mediterranean world and much of western Europe during the first and second centuries CE.

phalanx a rectangular formation of tightly massed infantry soldiers.

pharaoh the most common title used for Egyptian kings. Pharaohs possessed absolute power and were seen as divine.

philosophes intellectuals of the eighteenth-century Enlightenment who believed in applying a spirit of rational criticism to all things, including religion and politics, and who focused on improving and enjoying this world rather than on the afterlife.

plebeians the class of Roman citizens who included nonpatrician landowners, craftspeople, merchants, and small farmers in the Roman Republic. Their struggle for equal rights with the patricians dominated much of the Republic's history.

pogroms organized massacres of Jews.

polis an ancient Greek city-state encompassing both an urban area and its surrounding countryside; a small but autonomous political unit where all major political and social activities were carried out in a central location (plural: *poleis*).

polygyny the practice of having more than one wife at a time.

polytheism having many gods; belief in or the worship of more than one god.

popular culture as opposed to high culture, the unofficial written and unwritten culture of the masses, much of which was passed down orally; centered on public and group activities such as festivals. In the twentieth century, the entertainment, recreation, and pleasures that people purchase as part of mass consumer society.

portolani charts of landmasses and coastlines made by navigators and mathematicians in the thirteenth and fourteenth centuries.

praetorian guard the military unit that served as the personal bodyguard of the Roman emperors.

praetors the two senior Roman judges, who had executive authority when the consuls were away from the city and could also lead armies.

Prakrit an ancient Indian language, a simplified form of Sanskrit.

predestination the belief, associated with Calvinism, that God, as a consequence of his foreknowledge of all events, has predetermined who will be saved (the elect) and who will be damned (the reprobate).

Protestant Reformation the western European religious reform movement in the sixteenth century that divided Christianity into Catholic and Protestant groups.

pueblo a three-story adobe communal house with a timbered roof. Pueblos were constructed by the Ancient Pueblo people in what is now the southwestern United States starting around the ninth century CE.

Pueblo Bonito a large settlement built in the ninth century CE by the Ancient Pueblo people in what is now New Mexico. It contained several hundred compounds housing several thousand residents.

purdah the Indian term for the practice among Muslims and some Hindus of isolating women and preventing them from associating with men outside the home.

Pure Land a Buddhist sect, originally Chinese but later popular in Japan, that taught that devotion alone could lead to enlightenment and release.

Puritans English Protestants inspired by Calvinist theology who wished to remove all traces of Catholicism from the Church of England.

quipu an Inka record-keeping system that used knotted strings rather than writing.

raja originally, a chieftain in the Aryan society of early India, a representative of the gods; later used more generally to denote a ruler.

Ramadan the holy month of Islam, during which believers fast from dawn to sunset. Because the Islamic calendar is lunar, Ramadan migrates through the seasons.

rationalism a system of thought based on the belief that human reason and experience are the chief sources of knowledge.

reincarnation the idea that the individual soul is reborn in a different form after death. In Hindu and Buddhist thought, release from this cycle is the objective of all living souls.

relics the bones of Christian saints or objects intimately associated with saints that were considered worthy of veneration.

Renaissance the "rebirth" of Classical culture that occurred in Italy between c. 1350 and c. 1550; also, the earlier revivals of Classical culture that occurred under Charlemagne and in the twelfth century.

Renaissance humanism an intellectual movement in Renaissance Italy based on the study of the Greek and Roman classics.

rentier a person who lives on income from property and is not personally involved in its operation.

rhetoric the art of persuasive oratory; in the Middle Ages, one of the seven liberal arts.

Rococo a style, especially of decoration and architecture, that developed from the Baroque and spread throughout Europe by the 1730s. Though still elaborate, it emphasized curves, lightness, and charm in the pursuit of pleasure, happiness, and love.

Romanesque a term used to describe the art and especially architecture of Europe in the eleventh and twelfth centuries.

ronin Japanese warriors made unemployed by developments in the early modern era, since samurai were forbidden by tradition to engage in commerce.

sacraments rites considered imperative for a Christian's salvation. By the thirteenth century, they consisted of the Eucharist or Lord's Supper, baptism, marriage, penance, extreme unction, holy orders, and confirmation of children; Protestant reformers of the sixteenth century generally recognized only two—baptism and communion (the Lord's Supper).

samurai literally, "retainers"; similar to European knights. Usually in service to a particular shogun, these Japanese warriors lived by a strict code of ethics and duty.

Sanskrit an early Indo-European language, in which the Vedas were composed, beginning in the second millennium BCE. It survived as the language of literature and the bureaucracy in India for centuries after its decline as a spoken tongue.

sati the Hindu ritual requiring a wife to throw herself on her deceased husband's funeral pyre.

satori enlightenment, in the Japanese (especially Zen) Buddhist tradition.

satrap a governor with both civil and military duties in the ancient Persian Empire, which was divided into satrapies, or provinces, each administered by a satrap.

satrapy one of the provinces of the ancient Persian Empire, each ruled by a satrap.

scholar-gentry in Song Dynasty China, candidates who passed the civil service examinations and whose families were nonaristocratic landowners; eventually, a majority of the bureaucracy.

scholasticism the philosophical and theological system of the medieval schools, which emphasized rigorous analysis of contradictory authorities; often used to try to reconcile faith and reason.

School of Mind a philosophy espoused by Wang Yangming during the mid-Ming era of China, which argued that mind and the universe were a single unit and knowledge was therefore obtained through internal self-searching rather than through investigation of the outside world; for a while, a significant but unofficial rival to Neo-Confucianism.

scientific method a method of seeking knowledge through inductive principles; uses experiments and observations to develop generalizations.

Scientific Revolution the transition from the medieval worldview to a largely secular, rational, and materialistic perspective; began in the seventeenth century and was popularized in the eighteenth.

senate the leading council of the Roman Republic; composed of about three hundred men (senators) who served for life and dominated much of the political life of the Republic.

separation of powers a doctrine enunciated by Montesquieu in the eighteenth century that separate executive, legislative, and judicial powers serve to limit and control each other.

serf a peasant who is bound to the land and obliged to provide labor services and pay various rents and fees to the lord; considered unfree but not a slave because serfs could not be bought and sold.

Shari'a a law code, originally drawn up by Muslim scholars shortly after the death of Muhammad, that provides believers with a set of prescriptions to regulate their daily lives.

sheikh originally, the ruler of a Bedouin tribe; later, also used as a more general honorific.

Shi'ite the second largest tradition of Islam, which split from the majority Sunni soon after the death of Muhammad in a disagreement over his succession; especially significant in Iran and Iraq.

Shinto a kind of state religion in Japan, derived from beliefs in nature spirits and until recently linked with belief in the divinity of the emperor and the sacredness of the Japanese nation.

shogun a powerful Japanese leader, originally military, who ruled under the titular authority of the emperor.

shogunate system the system of government in Japan in which the emperor exercised only titular authority while the shoguns (regional military dictators) exercised actual political power.

sipahis in the Ottoman Empire, local cavalry elites who held fiefdoms and collected taxes.

Socratic method a form of teaching that uses a question-and-answer technique to enable students to reach conclusions by using their own reasoning.

Sophists wandering scholars and professional teachers in ancient Greece who stressed the importance of rhetoric and tended toward skepticism and relativism.

State Confucianism the integration of Confucian doctrine with Legalist practice under the Han dynasty in China; became the basis of Chinese political thought until the modern era.

Stoicism a philosophy founded by Zeno in the fourth century BCE that taught that happiness could be obtained by accepting one's lot and living in harmony with the will of God, thereby achieving inner peace.

stupa originally, a stone tower holding relics of the Buddha; more generally, a place for devotion, often architecturally impressive and surmounted with a spire.

subinfeudation the practice in which a lord's greatest vassals subdivided their fiefs and had vassals of their own, and those vassals in turn subdivided their fiefs and so on down to simple knights, whose fiefs were too small to subdivide.

Sublime Porte the office of the grand vizier in the Ottoman Empire.

sudras the classes that represented the great bulk of the Indian population from ancient times, mostly peasants, artisans, or manual laborers; ranked below *brahmins, kshatriyas,* and *vaisyas* but above the pariahs.

Sufism a mystical school of Islam, noted for its music, dance, and poetry, which became prominent in about the thirteenth century.

sultan "holder of power"; a title commonly used by Muslim rulers in the Ottoman Empire, Egypt, and elsewhere; still in use in parts of Asia, sometimes for regional authorities.

Sunni the largest tradition of Islam, from which the Shi'ites split soon after the death of Muhammad in a disagreement over his succession.

Supreme Ultimate according to Neo-Confucianists, a transcendent world distinct from the material world in which humans live but to which humans may aspire; a set of abstract principles, roughly equivalent to the Dao.

Swahili a mixed African-Arabian culture that developed by the twelfth century along the east coast of Africa; also, the national language of Kenya and Tanzania.

Taika reforms the seventh-century "great change" reforms that established the centralized Japanese state.

taille a French tax on land or property, developed by King Louis XI in the fifteenth century as the financial basis of the monarchy. It was largely paid by the peasantry; the nobility and the clergy were exempt.

Tantrism a mystical Buddhist sect that emphasized the importance of magical symbols and ritual in seeking a path to enlightenment.

theocracy a government based on a divine authority.

Theravada a school of Buddhism that stresses personal behavior and the quest for understanding as a means of release from the wheel of life, rather than the intercession of bodhisattvas; predominant in Sri Lanka and Southeast Asia.

tozama daimyo during the Tokugawa Shogunate in Japan, the larger, more independent lords who were usually more distant from the center of shogunate power in Edo; literally, "outside daimyo."

Triangular Trade a term used to describe a form of international trade taking place between three countries or regions of the world.

tribunes of the plebs beginning in 494 BCE, Roman officials who were given the power to protect plebeians against arrest by patrician magistrates.

twice-born the males of the higher castes in traditional Indian society, who underwent an initiation ceremony at puberty.

tyranny rule by a tyrant.

tyrant in an ancient Greek *polis* (or an Italian city-state during the Renaissance), a ruler who came to power in an unconstitutional way and ruled without being subject to the law.

uji a clan in early Japanese tribal society.

ulama a convocation of leading Muslim scholars, the earliest of which shortly after the death of Muhammad drew up the *Shari'a*, a law code based largely on the Qur'an and the sayings of the Prophet, to provide believers with a set of prescriptions to regulate their daily lives.

umma the Muslim community as a whole.

vaisya the third-ranked class in traditional Indian society, usually merchants.

varna Indian classes or castes. *See also* caste system.

vassal a person granted a fief, or landed estate, in exchange for providing military services to the lord and fulfilling certain other obligations such as appearing at the lord's court when summoned and making a payment on the knighting of the lord's eldest son.

veneration of ancestors the extension of filial piety to include care for the deceased, for instance, by burning replicas of useful objects to accompany them on their journey to the next world.

vezir see vizier.

viceroy the administrative head of the provinces of New Spain and Peru in the Americas.

vizier the prime minister in the Abbasid caliphate and elsewhere, a chief minister.

well-field system the theoretical pattern of land ownership in early China, named for the appearance of the Chinese character for "well," in which farmland was divided into nine segments and a peasant family would cultivate one for its own use and cooperate with seven others to cultivate the ninth for the landlord.

wergeld "money for a man"; in early Germanic law, a person's value in monetary terms, which was paid by a wrongdoer to the family of the person who had been injured or killed.

White Lotus a Chinese Buddhist sect, founded in 1133 CE, that sought political reform; in 1796–1804, a Chinese peasant revolt.

world-machine Newton's conception of the universe as one huge, regulated, and uniform machine that operated according to natural laws in absolute time, space, and motion.

yangban the aristocratic class in Korea. During the Choson Dynasty, entry into the bureaucracy was limited to members of this class.

Yangshao a Neolithic society from near the Yellow River in China, sometimes identified by its painted pottery.

zamindars Indian tax collectors who were assigned land from which they kept part of the revenue. The British revived the system in a misguided attempt to create a landed gentry.

Zen (in Chinese, Chan or Ch'an) a school of Buddhism particularly important in Japan, some of whose adherents stress that enlightenment (*satori*) can be achieved suddenly, though others emphasize lengthy meditation.

ziggurat a massive stepped tower on which a temple dedicated to the chief god or goddess of a Sumerian city was built.

Zoroastrianism a religion founded by the Persian Zoroaster in the seventh century BCE, characterized by worship of a supreme god, Ahuramazda, who represents the good against the evil spirit, Ahriman.

DOCUMENTS

INDEX

João III (Portugal), 412
John (England), 342
John VI (Byzantine Empire), 373
Joint families, 490
Joint-stock company, 400, 436
Jomon people (Japan), 303
Jordan: statue from, 8
Joseph II (Austria), 525–526, 527
Josephine (France), 536
Judaea, 152
Judah: kingdom of, 28, 28–29, 152
Judaism. See Hebrews; Jews and Judaism
Julio-Claudian dynasty (Rome), 141
Julius II (Pope), 381, 423
Junkers (Prussia), 441
Junks (Chinese ships), 161
Jupiter Optimus Maximus (god), 152
Jurchen peoples, 275, 481
Juries: in Athens, 108
Justice. See Law(s); Punishment
Justification by faith alone, 423, 424, 426
Justinian (Byzantine Empire), 204, 357, 357–361, 359, 360, 459, 460

Ka (spiritual body, Egypt), 22
Ka'aba (Mecca), 188, *188*
Kabuki theater, 501
Kabul, 242, 244, 464
Kaempfer, Engelbert, *497*
Kaifeng, China, 275
Kailasa, Mount, 258
Kalidasa (Indian author), 258
Kamakura shogunate (Japan), 306–307, *307*, 309, 314
Kami (spirits), 311, 313
Kamikaze (divine wind, Japan), 307
Kampongs (villages), 263
Kanchipuram (Kanchi), 242, *246*
Kanem-Bornu, 228
"Kangnido" world map, 319
Kangxi (China): as divine-right ruler, *439*; on government, 478–479; portraits of, *439*, *478*; reign of, 482; Sacred Edict of, 482, 490, 500
Kanishka (Kushan monarch), 243
Kant, Immanuel, *513*
Karakoram mountains, 40
Karakorum, Mongol city at, 284, 395
Karli (Indian rock chamber), 61
Karma, 47, 52, 54, 55, 415
Kashgar, 281
Kautilya (India), 45
Kent, England: Germanic tribes in, 326
Kenya: European rule in, 216; Swahili in, 227, 414
Kepler, Johannes, 509–510
Khadija, 189
Khajuraho, India, 258
Khanates, Mongol, 284, 286, 345
Khanbaliq (Beijing), 271, 284, *285*, 318
Khayyam, Omar, 207
Khitan people, 275
Khmer people, *262*
Khoi people, 231–232
Khoisan language, 231
Khotan, 242, 281
Khubilai Khan (Mongols), 198, 271, 284, 285; Japan and, 306–307; Mongol Empire after, 286, 479
Khufu (Egypt), 22
Khurram (Mughal Empire), 467
Khusrau, Amir (poet), 250
Khyber Pass, 242, 252, 464
Kiev, 344, 345
Kilwa, 225–227, 397, 408; Great Mosque of, *227*
Kings and kingdoms: in Africa, 217–219, 220; in China, 71; of Dravidian-speaking peoples, 242; in Egypt, 19–20; European, 340–345, 346; Frankish, 326; Germanic, 326–331, *327*; in Ghana, 228, 229; in India, 44, 57, 245; in Israel, 28–29; in Korea, 317, *317*; in Napoleon's Grand Empire, 536; in Southeast Asia, 415; Sumerian, 13; vassals and, 331–333. See also Monarchs and monarchies; specific rulers and locations
Kinship groups: in Africa, 233; Aztec, 172; in China, 82, 490; in India, 48. See also Families

Kipchak: khanate of, 284
Kirghiz people, 275
Kisale, Lake, 231
Knights, 331–332
Knossus, 98
Koguryo kingdom (Korea), 316, 317
Kongo: kingdom of, 231, 397
Koran. See Qur'an
Korea: arts in, 318, *319*; Buddhism in, 317, 318; China and, 272, 286, 302, 316–317, 484, 494, 504; civil service examination in, 317, 504; economy in, 505; independence of, 302; Japan and, 303, *304*, 505; kingdoms of, 317, *317*; language in, 504; Mongols and, 318; religion in, 317, 318, 505
Koryo dynasty (Korea), 317–318. See also Korea
Kosovo: Battle of (1389), 371–372, 451
Kouros sculptures, 106, *106*, 113
Kowtow, 484, 485
Kozhikode. See Calicut
Kraak (Ming porcelain), *493*
Krishna (god), 59, 474
Kshatriya (Indian warrior class), 44, 46, 52, 53, 254
Kukulcan (Toltec), 170
Kush, 24, 216, 217–218, *218*
Kushan kingdom (India), 57, 242, *242*, 244
Kutub Minar, in India, *251*
Kuyuk Khan: Innocent IV correspondence with, 283
Kyongju, Korea, 317
Kyoto, Japan: Ashikaga shogunate at, 494; Golden Pavilion in, *314*, *315*; Ryoanji temple in, *316*, *316*
Kyushu, Japan, 302, 303, 494, 496

Labor: child, 88; in China, 89; in Egypt, 21; in Europe, 333; Inka, 181–182; plague and, 377; of slaves, 147–148; of women, 24, 49, 233. See also Forced labor; Industry; Peasants; Slavery; Slave trade; Workers
Laconians, 104
Lacquerware, 90, 492, 503
Lagash, Mesopotamia, 12
Lahore, 466
Laissez-faire, 514
Land: in Africa, 216; in Athens, 105; in China, 66, 86–87, 279, 487; in Egypt, 21; as fiefs, 331–333, 456; in High Middle Ages, 333–335; in India, 49; in Japan, 305, 498–499; in Latin America, 405; in Ottoman Empire, 456; in Rome, 138. See also Agriculture; Farming
Landed gentry. See Gentry
Landing of Marie de' Medici at Marseilles (Rubens), *443*
Landlords: plague and, 377. See also Land
Landscape painting: in China, 78; in Japan, 315, 503
Language(s): in Africa, 232, 235; Afrikaans, 408; Arabic, 204; Bantu family, 220; in China, 66, 91–92; Greek, 362; in India, 40, 59; Indo-European, 26; in Japan, 313; Korean, 504; Latin, 26, 131, 132, 143; Quechua, 182–183; Semitic, 13, *14*, 30; spoken, 43; Swahili, 227; in Vietnam, 322; Zapotec, 164. See also Writing
Laos: Buddhism in, 266
Lao Zi [Lao Tzu] (China), 77, *78*, Siddhartha Gautama and, 271
La Plata, 403
La Rochefoucauld-Liancourt (duc de), 509
Las Casas, Bartolomé de, 404, 405
Lascaux cave, 7
Last judgment: in Zoroastrianism, 36
Last Supper, The (Leonardo da Vinci), *381*
Late Empire (Rome), 151, 357, 358
Lateen sail, 395, 396
Later Han Dynasty (China), 86–87
Latifundia (estates), 138
Latin America: from c. 1500 to 1750, *403*; church and state in, 403; colonies in, 403; Haitian independence in, 534; marriages in, 428; Spanish conquest of, 403. See also Central America; South America; specific locations
Latin Christianity. See Roman Catholic Church

Latin Empire of Constantinople, 370
Latin language, 26, 131, 132, 143; Justinian's Code in, 359; literature in, 145–146; Renaissance and, 379
Latin peoples, 132
Latium, 131, 132, 145
Launay, marquis de, 509
Laureti, Tommaso, *130*
La Venta: Olmec site at, 164, 166
Law(s): in Byzantine Empire, 358–359; in England, 341; Germanic, 327, 328; in India, 45; Islamic, 473; Jewish, 29; in Mughal Empire, 465; ordeal in Germanic customary, 327, 328; in Ottoman Empire, 454; Roman, 133, 146–147; in university studies, 349. See also Law codes
Law codes: of Assura (Assyria), 33; of Hammurabi, 14–15; of Islam, 190, 465; in Japan, 304, 311; of Justinian, 358–359; in Rome, 146
Law of Manu, 47, 49, 50
Laws (scientific): of Kepler, 509–510; of motion (Newton), 510
Lay investiture, 345–346
League of Iroquois, 176
Leakey, Louis, 5, 163
Leakey, Mary, 5
Learning. See Education; Intellectual thought
Lechfeld, Battle of, 331
Legalism (China), 76, 81, 83, 88
Legates (Rome), 140
Legions and legionaries (Rome), 138
Legislative Assembly (France), 530, 532
Legislatures: in U.S., 524
Le Loi (Vietnam), 301–302
Leo III (Pope), 325, *325*, 364
Leo VI ("Leo the Wise," Byzantine Empire), 367
Leo IX (Pope), 369
Leo Africanus, 234, 393
Leonardo da Vinci, 380, *381*, 382–383
Leonidas (Sparta), 107
Lepanto, Battle of, 433, 453
Leptis Magna, *223*
Lesbians. See Homosexuality
Lesbos, 99
Le Tac (Vietnam), 321
"Letter from Catherine Zell to Ludwig Rabus of Memmingen," 430
"Letter from King Manuel of Portugal," 394
"Letter from Kuyuk Khan to Pope Innocent IV, A," 283
Letters of credit: Islamic, 201
"Letter to a King" (Huaman Poma), 183
"Letter to Fuscus Salinator" (Pliny the Younger), 145
"Letter to Genoa" (Malfante), 219
"Letter to King João, A" (Afonso I), 412
"Letter to the Viceroy of the Indies" (Toyotomi Hideyoshi), 496
Lever: Archimedean, *126*
Leyster, Judith, 445, *445*
Liberal arts curriculum, 349
Liberties. See Rights
Li Bo (Chinese poet), 296
Libraries: in Alexandria, 124; in Andalusia, 198
Libya, 23, 24, *223*
Libyan Desert, 220
Life expectancy: of Germanic women, 327. See also Mortality rates
Life of Caesar (Plutarch), 140
Life of Charlemagne (Einhard), 330
Life of Saint Godric, 337
Lifestyle: in Africa, 232–233; ancient, 2–3; in Athens, 116–117; in Bronze Age, 10; in China, 87–93, 275, 291–292, 481, 490–491; in Egypt, 24; in India, 48–49, 254–255; of Minoan Crete, 98; of Mongols, 283–284; in Rome, 145; of San people, 232; in Southeast Asia, 263, 417. See also Society
"Light, The" (Qur'an, Sura 24), 191
Lima, Peru, 179
Limited (constitutional) monarchy, 421, 442–443, 443, 444, 530
Limpopo River region, 231
Lineage groups: in Africa, 223, 233
Linguistics: in Europe, 59
"Linked verse" technique, 314, 501
Lion in Winter, The (film), 336, *336*